How to use your Connected Casebook

Step 1: Go to **www.CasebookConnect.com** and redeem your access code to get started.

Access Code:

Step 2: Go to your **BOOKSHELF** and select your Connected Casebook to start reading, highlighting, and taking notes in the margins of your e-book.

Step 3: Select the **STUDY** tab in your toolbar to access a variety of practice materials designed to help you master the course material. These materials may include explanations, videos, multiple-choice questions, flashcards, short answer, essays, and issue spotting.

Step 4: Select the **OUTLINE** tab in your toolbar to access chapter outlines that automatically incorporate your highlights and annotations from the e-book. Use the My Notes area for copying, pasting, and editing your book notes or creating new notes.

Step 5: If your professor has enrolled your class, you can select the **CLASS INSIGHTS** tab and compare your own study center results against the average of your classmates.

Is this a used casebook? Access code already scratched off?

You can purchase the Digital Version and still access all of the powerful tools listed above.
Please visit CasebookConnect.com and select Catalog to learn more.

PLEASE NOTE: Each access code can only be used once. This access code will expire one year after the discontinuation of the corresponding print title and must be redeemed before then. CCH reserves the right to discontinue this program at any time for any business reason. For further details, please see the Casebook Connect End User Agreement.

PIN: 9111149078 SitkWTE10

61701

WILLS, TRUSTS, AND ESTATES

ASPEN CASEBOOK SERIES

WILLS, TRUSTS, AND ESTATES

TENTH EDITION

ROBERT H. SITKOFF
John L. Gray Professor of Law
Harvard University

JESSE DUKEMINIER
Late Maxwell Professor of Law
University of California, Los Angeles

Published by Wolters Kluwer in New York.

Wolters Kluwer Legal & Regulatory U.S. serves customers worldwide with CCH, Aspen Publishers, and Kluwer Law International products. (www.WKLegaledu.com)

To contact Customer Service, e-mail customer.service@wolterskluwer.com, call 1-800-234-1660, fax 1-800-901-9075, or mail correspondence to:

Wolters Kluwer
Attn: Order Department
PO Box 990
Frederick, MD 21705

Design by Keithley & Associates, Inc.

Printed in the United States of America.

2 3 4 5 6 7 8 9 0

ISBN 978-1-4548-7642-7

Names: Sitkoff, Robert H., author. | Dukeminier, Jesse, author.
Title: Wills, trusts, and estates / Robert H. Sitkoff, John L. Gray Professor of Law; Jesse Dukeminier, Late Maxwell Professor of Law University of California, Los Angeles.
Description: Tenth edition. | New York: Wolters Kluwer Law & Business, [2017] | Series: Aspen casebook series | Includes index.
Identifiers: LCCN 2017019369 | ISBN 9781454876427
Subjects: LCSH: Wills—United States. | Estate planning—United States. | Future interests—United States. | Trusts and trustees—United States. | LCGFT: Casebooks.
Classification: LCC KF753.D85 2017 | DDC 346.7305—dc23 LC record available at https://lccn.loc.gov/2017019369

Certified Chain of Custody
Promoting Sustainable Forestry

www.sfiprogram.org
SFI-01681

SFI label applies to the text stock.

About Wolters Kluwer Legal & Regulatory U.S.

Wolters Kluwer Legal & Regulatory U.S. delivers expert content and solutions in the areas of law, corporate compliance, health compliance, reimbursement, and legal education. Its practical solutions help customers successfully navigate the demands of a changing environment to drive their daily activities, enhance decision quality and inspire confident outcomes.

Serving customers worldwide, its legal and regulatory portfolio includes products under the Aspen Publishers, CCH Incorporated, Kluwer Law International, ftwilliam.com and MediRegs names. They are regarded as exceptional and trusted resources for general legal and practice-specific knowledge, compliance and risk management, dynamic workflow solutions, and expert commentary.

JESSE DUKEMINIER, 1925–2003

For Tamara, my partner and heir apparent.
I will be forever grateful that you agreed to integrate our household
production functions and to sponsor joint franchisees.
—RHS

SUMMARY OF CONTENTS

CONTENTS

LIST OF ILLUSTRATIONS

PREFACE

As trusts and estates lawyers, we are in the business of succession. This simple truth was brought home to us in a deeply personal way with the unexpected passing of Jesse Dukeminier nearly fifteen years ago, three years after publication of the sixth edition, necessitating succession of authorship for this book. With this tenth edition, that process continues. Robert H. Sitkoff, a new coauthor in the seventh edition who assumed sole responsibility (trusteeship?) for this book in the ninth edition, becomes the lead author in this tenth edition. Jesse continues as a posthumous coauthor. James Lindgren and Stanley M. Johanson remain coauthors emeritus.

Wills, Trusts, and Estates is designed for use in a course on trusts and decedents' estates. Our basic aim in this tenth edition remains as before: to produce not merely competent practitioners, but lawyers who think critically about problems in family wealth transmission and are able to compare alternative solutions.

This tenth edition carries forward the redesign of the book that we undertook for the ninth edition. This edition thus has a two-color interior and a robust program of photos, documents, and other images. Case squibs and extraneous references have been resisted. Every chapter begins with a statement of its themes and how they tie into the broader themes of the book as a whole. As always, we have endeavored to preserve the essential character of the book, which of course traces back to Jesse's wit, erudition, and playfulness.

We begin in Chapter 1 by examining the organizing principle of freedom of disposition. Chapter 2, on intestacy, examines the disposition provided by law for those who do not make a will or use will substitutes. Chapters 3, 4, and 5, on wills, examine the problem of establishing the authenticity (Chapter 3, on formalities), the voluntariness (Chapter 4, on contests), and the meaning (Chapter 5, on construction) of a will. What makes this problem difficult and interesting is the "worst evidence" rule of probate procedure, whereby the best witness is dead by the time the court considers such matters. Chapter 6 introduces the trust, which can be used to effect a probate or a nonprobate transfer, and which is the centerpiece of contemporary estate planning. Chapter 7 examines the will substitutes and the system of private, nonprobate succession that has emerged as a competitor to public succession through probate. Chapter 8 examines what limits, if any, the law should impose on freedom of disposition by will or by will substitute for the protection of a surviving spouse or children. In Chapters 9 through 14 we return to the law of trusts to consider some more advanced issues: fiduciary administration (Chapter 9), alienation and modification (Chapter

10), charitable trusts (Chapter 11), powers of appointment (Chapter 12), construction of future interests (Chapter 13), and the Rule Against Perpetuities (Chapter 14). We close in Chapter 15 with a survey of the federal wealth transfer taxes.

Since the 1960s, the law of intestacy and of wills has undergone a thorough renovation. Initially, the change was brought on by a swelling public demand for cheaper and simpler ways of transferring property at death, avoiding expensive probate. Imaginative scholars then began to ventilate this ancient law of the dead hand, challenging assumptions and suggesting judicial and legislative innovation to simplify and rationalize it. Medical science complicated matters by creating varieties of parentage unheard of a generation earlier. Legal malpractice in drawing wills and trusts arrived with a bang. The nonprobate revolution, with its multitude of will substitutes, provided a system of private succession that began to compete with the court-supervised probate system. Scholars, science, malpractice liability, and market competition have been a potent combination for driving law reform, of which there has been much in the last generation — and more is yet to come, such as to address the rise of electronic or digital wills.

The use of trusts to transmit family wealth has become commonplace, not only for wealthy clients, but also for those of modest wealth. In expanding, trust law has annexed future interests and powers of appointment, reducing these two subjects largely to problems in drafting and construing trust instruments. The teachings of modern portfolio theory and the shifting nature of wealth from land to financial assets has put pressure on the law of trust investment and administration, which evolved in simpler times. In contemporary American trust practice, fiduciary obligation has replaced limitations on the trustee's powers as the principal mechanism for safeguarding the beneficiary from abuse by the trustee. Meanwhile, the burgeoning tort liability of modern times has spawned an asset protection industry and with it radical change in the rights of creditors to recourse against beneficial interests in trust.

Taxation of donative transfers has also changed dramatically. The unlimited marital deduction, which permits spouses to make unlimited tax-free transfers to each other, is now a central feature of estate planning. In 1986, Congress enacted the generation-skipping transfer tax, implementing a policy of wealth transfer taxation at each generation. This tax, like an invisible boomerang, has delivered a lethal blow to the Rule Against Perpetuities.

Throughout the book we emphasize the basic theoretical structure and the general philosophy and purposes that unify the field of donative transfers. We focus on function and purpose, not form. To this end, we have pruned away mechanical matters (such as a step-by-step discussion of how to probate a will and settle an estate, which is essentially local law, easily learned from a local practice book). At the same time, we have sought the historical roots of modern law. Understanding how the law became the way it is illuminates its continuing evolution and the sometimes exasperating peculiarities inherited from the past.

Although we organize the material in topical compartments, we have also sought a more penetrating view of the subject as a tapestry of humanity. Trusts and estates is a field concerned fundamentally with people and their most intimate relationships. Every illustration included, every behind-the-scenes peek, every quirk of the parties' behavior has its place as a piece of ornament fitting into the larger whole. Understanding the ambivalences of the human heart and the richness of human frailty, and realizing that even the best-constructed estate plans may, with the ever-whirling wheels of change, turn into sand castles, are essential to being a counselor at law, as opposed to being a mere lawyer. There is nothing like the death of a moneyed member of a family to show persons as they really are, virtuous or conniving, generous or grasping. Each case is a drama in human relationships and a cautionary tale. The lawyer, as counselor, drafter, or advocate, is an important figure in the dramatis personae.

For their sage advice on this revision, we thank Kevin Bennardo, Karen Boxx, Patricia Cain, Elizabeth Carter, Bridget Crawford, Barry Cushman, Judith Daar, Robert Danforth, Charles Donahue, Stephen Dycus, Steve Fast, David Feder, Todd Flubacher, Mark Glover, Iris Goodwin, Howard Helsinger, David Herzig, Steven Horowitz, David Horton, Elizabeth Kamali, Daniel Kelly, Diane Klein, Kristine Knaplund, Terry Kogan, John Langbein, Ray Madoff, Solangel Maldonado, F. Philip Manns, Goldburn Maynard, Ben McFarlane, Nancy McLaughlin, Ljubomir Nacev, Alan Newman, David Orentlicher, Benjamin Orzeske, Katherine Pearson, Jeff Pennell, John Plecnik, Andrzej Rapaczynski, Thomas Robinson, Amy Ronner, Randy Roth, Jeffrey Schoenblum, Paul Secunda, David Seipp, Thomas Simmons, Gary Spitko, Carla Spivak, Palma Strand, Max Straus, Eva Subotnik, Joshua Tate, Lee-ford Tritt, Suzanne Walsh, Judith Younger, Howard Zaritsky, and Diana Zeydel.

We owe a particularly large debt of gratitude to John Morley and Max Schanzenbach, who provided extensive comments on early drafts of every chapter; to the students in the Trusts and Estates course at Harvard in Fall 2016 for their role as beta testers of draft manuscript; and to Stephanie Willbanks, who assisted with tax matters throughout the book. Stephen Wiles and the Faculty Research and Information Delivery Assistance team at the Harvard Law Library provided crucial library and research support, and Jordan Browdy, Hannah Clark, Laura Cox, Renée Gagné, Katherine Hardiman, Victoria Hartmann, Jennifer Ho, Sandra Hough, Brook Jackling, Jeannette Leopold, Ben Sherwood, Samantha Thompson, Aaron Wiltse, and Ted Yale provided superb research assistance.

Three final expressions of gratitude are in order. First, Joe Terry (at Aspen) and Carol McGeehan (formerly of Aspen) brought rich intelligence and sound judgment to the project. Second, Molly Eskridge processed mounds of manuscript and proofs with astonishing efficiency and extraordinary good cheer. Finally, Troy Froebe and his colleagues at The Froebe Group executed the production process, which proved a greater challenge than any of us had expected, but they were more than equal to the task.

Robert H. Sitkoff
Jesse Dukeminier, 1925-2003

April 2017

Editors' note: All citations to state and federal statutes and regulations are to such authorities as they appeared on Lexis or Westlaw at year-end 2016 unless stated otherwise. The current edition of the legendary Scott treatise, Austin Wakeman Scott, William Franklin Fratcher & Mark L. Ascher, Scott and Ascher on Trusts (5th ed. 2006-2010), is cited throughout as Scott and Ascher on Trusts. Citations to Blackstone's Commentaries are to the facsimile of the first edition of 1765-1769 published in 1979 by the University of Chicago Press. Footnotes are numbered consecutively from the beginning of each chapter. Most footnotes in quoted materials have been omitted. Many citations in quoted materials have been omitted without indication or have been edited for readability. Editors' footnotes added to quoted materials are indicated by the abbreviation: — Eds.

Conflicts disclosure: In accordance with Harvard Law School's policy on conflicts of interest, Robert Sitkoff discloses certain outside activities, one or more of which may relate to the subject matter of this book, at https://helios.law.harvard.edu/Public/Faculty/ConflictOfInterestReport.aspx?id=10813.

ACKNOWLEDGMENTS

BOOKS AND ARTICLES

American Bar Association (ABA), excerpts from Model Rules of Professional Conduct. Copyright © 2017 by the ABA. Reprinted by permission. All rights reserved.

American College of Trust and Estate Counsel (ACTEC), Commentaries on the Model Rules of Professional Conduct (5th ed. 2016). Copyright © 2016 by the American College of Trust and Estate Counsel. Reprinted by permission. All rights reserved.

American Law Institute, Restatement (Third) of Property (1999, 2003, 2011); Restatement (Third) of Restitution and Unjust Enrichment (2011); Restatement (Second) of Trusts (1959); Restatement (Third) of Torts: Liability for Economic Harm (Council Draft No. 4, 2016); Restatement (Third) of Trusts (2003, 2007, 2012). Copyright © 1959, 1999, 2003, 2007, 2011, 2012, 2016 by the American Law Institute. Reprinted by permission. All rights reserved.

Ascher, Mark L., Austin Wakeman Scott & William Franklin Fratcher. Scott and Ascher on Trusts, Fifth Edition. Copyright © 2016 by Wolters Kluwer Legal & Regulatory. Reprinted by permission. All rights reserved.

Assessing Terri Schiavo: She Opened Pandora's Suitcase, Economist (Mar. 31, 2005). Copyright © 2005 by the Economist. Reprinted by permission. All rights reserved.

Bailey, Eric, Student Life Veers Into Armed Robbery Charges: Promising UC Santa Cruz Freshman and Her Boyfriend Are Accused as Collegiate Bonnie and Clyde, L.A. Times (Feb. 12, 1999). Copyright © 1999 by the Los Angeles Times. Reprinted by permission. All rights reserved.

Brooke, James, After Verdict, Trial Still Grips Denver, N.Y. Times, Mar. 21, 1997, at A26. Copyright © 1997 by the New York Times. Reprinted by permission. All rights reserved.

_____, A Web of Money, Drugs, and Death, N.Y. Times, Mar. 18, 1997, at A12. Copyright © 1997 by the New York Times. Reprinted by permission. All rights reserved.

Dukeminier, Jesse, & James E. Krier, The Rise of the Perpetual Trust, 50 UCLA L. Rev. 1303 (2003). Copyright © 2003 by Professor Krier and the UCLA Law Review. Reprinted by permission. All rights reserved.

Feder, David K., & Robert H. Sitkoff, Revocable Trusts and Incapacity Planning: More Than Just a Will Substitute, 24 Elder L.J. 1, 15 (2016). Copyright © 2016 by Professors Feder and Sitkoff. Adapted by permission. All rights reserved.

Frank, Robert, Shutting Out the Kids from the Family Fortune, Wall St. J. (May 10, 2011). Copyright © 2011 by Dow Jones, Inc. Reprinted by permission. All rights reserved.

Hirsch, Adam J., & William K.S. Wang, A Qualitative Theory of the Dead Hand, 68 Ind. L.J. 1 (1992). Copyright © 1992 by Indiana Law Journal. Reprinted by permission. All rights reserved.

Howard, John N., Profile in Optics: Leonard Thompson Troland, Optics & Photonics (June 2008). Copyright © 2008 by Optics and Photonics. Reprinted by permission. All rights reserved.

Jacobs, Deborah L., George Clooney Makes Estate Planning Sexy, Forbes (Feb. 23, 2012). Copyright © 2012 by Forbes. Reprinted by permission. All rights reserved.

Kelly, Daniel B., Restricting Testamentary Freedom: Ex Ante Versus Ex Post Justifications, 82 Fordham L. Rev. 1125 (2013). Copyright © 2013 by Professor Kelly. Reprinted by permission. All rights reserved.

Klick, Jonathan, & Robert H. Sitkoff, Agency Costs, Charitable Trusts, and Corporate Control: Evidence from Hershey's Kiss-Off, 108 Colum. L. Rev. 749 (2008). Copyright © 2008 by

Landers, Ann, Column (May 23, 2002). Copyright © 2002 by the Esther P. Lederer Trust. Reprinted by permission of Creators Syndicate, Inc. All rights reserved.

Langbein, John H., Major Reforms of the Property Restatement and the Uniform Probate Code: Reformation, Harmless Error, and Nonprobate Transfers, 38 ACTEC J. 1 (2012). Copyright © 2012 by Professor Langbein and ACTEC. Reprinted by permission. All rights reserved.

_____ , Rise of the Management Trust, Tr. & Est., Oct. 2004, at 52. Copyright © 2004 by Professor Langbein and Penton Media, Inc. Reprinted by permission. All rights reserved.

_____ , Substantial Compliance with the Wills Act, 88 Harv. L. Rev. 489 (1975). Copyright © 1975 by Professor Langbein and Harvard Law Review. Reprinted by permission. All rights reserved.

_____ , The Twentieth-Century Revolution in Family Wealth Transmission, 86 Mich. L. Rev. 722 (1988). Copyright © 1988 by Professor Langbein. Reprinted by permission. All rights reserved.

Lindgren, James, The Fall of Formalism, 55 Alb. L. Rev. 1009 (1992). Copyright © 1992 by Professor Lindgren. Reprinted by permission. All rights reserved.

Marsman, T. Frederik, Obituary, Boston Globe, Feb. 26, 1987, at 59. Copyright © 1987 by the Globe Newspaper Company, MA. Reprinted by permission. All rights reserved.

National Conference of Commissioners on Uniform State Laws (NCCUSL), excerpts from: the Uniform Premarital and Marital Agreement Act (2012); the Uniform Principal and Income Act (1994); the Uniform Probate Code (1969, 1990, 1993, 1997, 1998, 2008, 2010); the Uniform Prudent Investor Act (1994); the Uniform Transfers to Minors Act (1983, 1986); the Uniform Trust Code (2000, 2003, 2004, 2005, 2010). Copyright © 1969, 1983, 1986, 1990, 1993, 1994, 1997, 1998, 2008, 2010, 2012 by NCCUSL. Reprinted by permission. All rights reserved.

Newcomb, Alyssa, Gay Man Told to Marry Woman or Son Would Lose Inheritance, ABC News (Aug. 20, 2012). http://abcnews.go.com/US/gay-man-mary-woman-son-loseinheritance/story?id=17043550. Copyright © 2012 by ABC

News. Reprinted by permission. All rights reserved.

Posner, Richard A., Economic Analysis of Law (9th ed. 2014). Copyright © 2014 by Richard A. Posner. Reprinted by permission. All rights reserved.

Ross, Alice, Jedi Order Fails in Attempt to Register as Religious Group, Guardian (Dec. 19, 2016). Copyright © 2016 by Guardian News & Media Limited. Reprinted by permission. All rights reserved.

Saletan, William, Motherhood at 70, Slate (Dec. 9, 2008). Copyright © 2008 by the Slate Group. Reprinted by permission. All rights reserved.

Sitkoff, Robert H., The Lurking Rule Against Accumulations of Income, 100 Nw. U. L. Rev. 501 (2006). Copyright © 2006 by Professor Sitkoff. Adapted by permission. All rights reserved.

Sitkoff, Robert H., Trust Law as Fiduciary Governance Plus Asset Partitioning, in the Worlds of the Trust 428 (Lionel Smith ed. 2013). Copyright © 2013 by Professor Sitkoff. Reprinted by permission. All rights reserved.

Sitkoff, Robert H., & Max M. Schanzenbach, Jurisdictional Competition for Trust Funds: An Empirical Analysis of Perpetuities and Taxes, 115 Yale L.J. 356 (2005). Copyright © 2005 by Yale Law Journal and Professors Sitkoff and Schanzenbach. Reprinted by permission. All rights reserved.

_____ , The Prudent Investor Rule and Market Risk: An Empirical Analysis, 14 J. Emp. Legal Stud. 129 (2017). Copyright © 2017 by Professor Sitkoff and Schanzenbach. Reprinted by permission. All rights reserved.

Snow, Kate, & Rich McHugh, Mariecar Frias and Imaeyen Ibanga, Frozen Sperm Still Viable Decades Later, ABC News (Apr. 10, 2009). http://abcnews.go.com/GMA/OnCall/story?id=7303722&page=1#.UEdnIKRYtD4, Copyright © 2009 by ABC News. Reprinted by permission. All rights reserved.

Steele, Karen Dorn, Judge Divides Estate Among Kitty Oakes' Sons, The Spokesman Review (Dec. 10, 2008). http://www.spokesman.com/stories/2008/dec/10/judge-divides-estate-among-kitty-oakes-sons. Copyright © 2008 by the Spokesman-Review. Reprinted by permission. All rights reserved.

Waggoner, Lawrence W., From Here to Eternity: The Folly of Perpetual Trusts, Univ. Mich. L. Sch. Pub. L. & Legal Theory Research Paper No. 259

(2012). Copyright © 2012 by Professor Waggoner. Reprinted by permission. All rights reserved.

_____ , The UPC Authorizes Notarized Wills, 34 ACTEC J. 83 (2008). Copyright © 2008 by Professor Waggoner and ACTEC. Reprinted by permission. All rights reserved.

Yerak, Becky, Though There Was a Will, Fifth Third Found a Way to Save Boots, Chi. Trib. (Apr. 4, 2012). Copyright © 2012 by the Chicago Tribune. Reprinted by permission. All rights reserved.

PHOTOGRAPHS AND ILLUSTRATIONS

42 East 74th Street, New York, N.Y. (2012). Photograph. Courtesy of Bridget Crawford.

Bank window and parking space at issue in *Weber*. Photograph. Courtesy of Debra A. Buseman.

Barnes Foundation Gallery. Photographs. Copyright © 2017 by the Barnes Foundation. Reproduced by permission. All rights reserved.

Bentham, Jeremy (Auto-Icon). Photograph. Courtesy of Matt Brown / Flickr.

Biblis, Chris and Stella. Photograph. Copyright by Jeffery Salter. Reproduced by permission. All rights reserved.

Bishop, Princess Bernice Pauahi. Photograph by H.L. Chase. Copyright by the Bishop Museum. Reproduced by permission. All rights reserved.

Blattmachr, Jonathan, and king salmon. Photograph. Courtesy of Jonathan Blattmachr.

Block, Sophie, and Max. Photograph. Courtesy of Frank Dover and Brent Bernell.

Bogert, George Gleason. Photograph. Courtesy of the University of Chicago Library, Special Collections.

Bonds, Barry. Photograph. Copyright © 1992 by Craig Fuji / AP Photo. Reproduced by permission. All rights reserved.

Boots the cat. Photograph. Courtesy of Andrew Hayes, Vice President, Public Relations, Fifth Third Bank, Chicago, IL.

Buck, Beryl. Photograph. Courtesy of the Marin Community Foundation.

Buffet, Warren, and Bill and Melinda Gates. Photograph. Copyright © 2006 by Spencer Platt / Getty Images. Reproduced by permission. All rights reserved.

Cantil-Sakauye, Tani Gorre. Photograph. Copyright © 2010 by Robert Galbraith / Reuters / Alamy. Reproduced by permission. All rights reserved.

CartoonStock. Cartoons by Roy Delgado, Paul Kinsella, and Harley Schwadron. Copyright by CartoonStock. Reprinted by permission. All rights reserved.

Casner, A. James. Photograph. Courtesy of Art and Visual Materials, Historical and Special Collections, Harvard Law School Library.

Cristofani, Anthony, and Emma Freeman. Photograph. Copyright © 2000 by Bill Lovejoy / Santa Cruz Sentinel. Reproduced by permission of the YGS Group. All rights reserved.

Dacey, Norman, How to Avoid Probate! Book cover. Copyright © 1979 by MacMillan Publishers. Reproduced by permission. All rights reserved.

Decanting a bottle of wine. Photograph. Copyright by Andrew Safonov / Shutterstock. Reproduced by permission. All rights reserved.

Devi, Rajo, with daughter and husband, Bala Ram. Photograph. Copyright © 2008 by Devendra Uppal / AP Photo. Reproduced by permission. All rights reserved.

Divine, Father. Photograph. Copyright © 1954 by Bettmann Collection / Getty Images. Reproduced by permission. All rights reserved.

Duke, Doris. Photograph. Copyright © 2000 by Stringer / Hulton Archive / Getty Images. Reproduced by permission. All rights reserved.

Esposito, Nino, and Drew Bosee. Photograph. Copyright © 2015 by Jared Wickerham / Wick Photography. Reproduced by permission. All rights reserved.

Evander, Kerry I. Photograph. Courtesy of Judge Evander.

Fournier, George. Photograph. Courtesy of Richard D. Solman.

Goodson, Courtney Hudson. Photograph. Courtesy of Justice Goodson.

Gray, Horace. Photograph. Copyright by Kean Collection / Getty Images. Reproduced by permission. All rights reserved.

Gray, John Chipman. Photograph. Courtesy of Art and Visual Materials, Historical and Special Collections, Harvard Law School Library.

Gray, John Merrill "Jack," III, and his father John. Photograph. Courtesy of Jack Gray.

Harrison, New Jersey. Photographs of 304 Harrison Avenue and 317 Harrison Avenue (2012). Courtesy of Daniel Rayner.

Helmsley, Leona, and her dog, Trouble. Photograph. Copyright © 2008 by Splash News / Newscom. Reproduced by permission. All rights reserved.

Hershey, Milton S., and orphan boys. Photograph. Copyright by the Hershey Community Archives. Reproduced by permission. All rights reserved.

Jaworski, Leon. Photograph. Copyright © 1973 by AP Photo. Reproduced by permission. All rights reserved.

KenKut dispenser. Photograph. Copyright by KenKut Products, Inc. Reproduced by permission. All rights reserved.

Kennedy, Joseph P., Joseph P. Kennedy, Jr., and John F. Kennedy. Photograph. Copyright © 1938 by AP Photo. Reproduced by permission. All rights reserved.

Kenyon, Lord. Illustration. Courtesy of Art and Visual Materials, Historical and Special Collections, Harvard Law School Library.

Kuralt, Charles, and Elizabeth (Pat) Shannon. Photograph. Copyright © 1999 by AP Photo. Reproduced by permission. All rights reserved.

Landers, Ann. Photograph. Copyright by Esther P. Lederer Trust and Creators Syndicate, Inc. Reproduced by permission. All rights reserved.

Langbein, John H. Photograph. Courtesy of the Yale Law School Office of Public Affairs and Professor Langbein.

Langdale, Lord (Henry Bickersteth). Photograph. Courtesy of Art and Visual Materials, Historical and Special Collections, Harvard Law School Library.

Leach, W. Barton. Photograph. Courtesy of Art and Visual Materials, Historical and Special Collections, Harvard Law School Library.

Lee, Jason. Photograph. Courtesy of the Oregon State Archives.

Love, Susan. Photograph. Copyright © 1996 by Kevork Djansezian / AP Photo. Reproduced by permission. All rights reserved.

Manville, Tommy, and two female friends. Photograph. Copyright © 1938 by Bert

Morgan / Premium Archive / Getty Images. Reproduced by permission. All rights reserved.

Markowitz, Harry M. Photograph. Courtesy of Professor Markowitz.

Marshall, Margaret H. Photograph. Courtesy of Martha Stewart and Harvard Law School.

Marsman, Captain T. Frederik (Cappy). Photograph. Courtesy of the Webber Archives, Dana Hall School, Wellesley, MA.

Marx, Groucho. Photograph. Copyright © 1940 by A.F. Archive / Alamy. Reproduced by permission. All rights reserved.

Miller, Wiley. Cartoon. Copyright © 2007 by Wiley Ink / Andrew McMeel Publishing. Reproduced by permission. All rights reserved.

Monroe, Marilyn. Photograph. Copyright © 1953 by Frank Powolny / MPTV Images. Reproduced by permission. All rights reserved.

Mullarkey, Mary J. Photograph. Courtesy of Justice Mullarkey.

Musmanno, Justice. Photograph. Copyright © 1950 by Leonard McCombe / Time & Life Images / Getty Images. Reproduced by permission. All rights reserved.

The New Yorker Collection. Cartoons by Ed Arno © 1997; Peter Arno © 1940, 1942; Pat Byrnes © 2001, 2009; Roz Chast © 2007; Frank Cotham © 2010; Leo Cullum © 1995, 1999, 2004; Whitney Darrow, Jr. © 1960; Dana Fradon © 1986; William Hamilton © 2001, 2003; J.B. Handelsman © 1989; Edward Koren © 2011; Arnie Levin © 2000; Robert Mankoff © 1985; Warren Miller © 1981; Frank Modell © 1972; Paul Noth © 2013; Michael Shaw © 2005; Barbara Smaller © 2000, 2005, 2011; Bill Woodman © 1988. Reproduced by permission of the Cartoon Bank, a division of Condé Nast. All rights reserved.

Oakes, Kitty. Photograph. Copyright © 2008 by the Spokesman-Review. Reproduced by permission. All rights reserved.

Paternity test kit. Photograph. Courtesy of Identigene, LLC.

Posner, Richard A. Photograph. Reproduced by permission of Judge Posner.

Powell, Cleo Elaine. Photograph. Copyright © 2011 by Steve Helber / AP Photo. Reproduced by permission. All rights reserved.

Prince. Photograph. Courtesy of Scott Penner / Flickr.

WILLS, TRUSTS, AND ESTATES

CHAPTER 1

INTRODUCTION:
FREEDOM OF DISPOSITION

American law does not grant courts any general authority
to question the wisdom, fairness, or reasonableness of the donor's
decisions about how to allocate his or her property.

RESTATEMENT (THIRD) OF PROPERTY:
WILLS AND OTHER DONATIVE TRANSFERS
§ 10.1 cmt. c (Am. Law Inst. 2003)

THIS BOOK IS ABOUT the law of *gratuitous transfers*. Our focus is on the transfer of property at death, known as *succession*. We examine *probate* succession by *will* and *intestacy*, and *nonprobate* succession by inter vivos trust, pay-on-death contract, and other *will substitutes*. The American law of succession, both probate and nonprobate, is organized around the principle of *freedom of disposition*. We therefore begin in this chapter by considering the nature and scope of that principle.

American succession law embraces freedom of disposition, authorizing *dead hand* control, to an extent that is unique among modern legal systems. For example, American law allows a property owner to exclude her blood relations and to subject her dispositions to ongoing conditions. The right of a property owner to dispose of her property at death on terms that she prescribes has come to be recognized as a separate stick in the bundle of rights called property.

To be sure, freedom of disposition is not absolute, not even within the permissive American tradition. The law protects a donor's spouse and creditors, allows for the imposition of transfer taxes, and imposes a handful of anti–dead hand public policy constraints, the most venerable of which is the Rule Against Perpetuities. For the most part, however, the American law of succession facilitates rather than regulates the implementation of the decedent's intent. Most of the law of succession is concerned with enabling posthumous enforcement of the actual intent of the decedent or, failing this, giving effect to the decedent's probable intent.

We begin in Section A by considering the policy of freedom of disposition, its rationale, and the extent to which it is a constitutional imperative. In Section B, we consider the mechanics of succession, including the basic organization of probate administration and nonprobate modes of transfer. Finally, in Section C, we consider issues of professional responsibility in succession matters.

A. THE POWER TO TRANSMIT PROPERTY AT DEATH

Lawrence M. Friedman
Dead Hands: A Social History of Wills, Trusts, and Inheritance Law
3-4 (2009)

The whole edifice of the law of succession, legally and socially, rests on one brute fact: you can't take it with you. Death is inevitable, fundamental, and definitive. When people die, everything they think they own, everything struggled, scrimped, and saved for, every jewel and bauble, every bank account, all stocks and bonds, the cars and houses, corn futures or gold bullion, all books, CD's, pictures, and carpets—everything will pass on to somebody or something else. A certain amount can be spent on a funeral or a fancy coffin. A person can ask for, and get, an elaborate headstone and can buy a policy of "perpetual care" for the grave. People can, if they wish, be buried still wearing their favorite ring or a wedding band, or dressed in their favorite clothes. But these are incidentals.[1] . . . In the end, even the mightiest pharaoh probably took nothing at all to the other side.

This rite of passage, this transfer of goods at death, has tremendous social and legal importance. The transfer takes different forms in different societies, and in different times. There is no single name for the process. Here, . . . we call it *succession*—a shorthand way of summing up social processes and institutions and their legal echoes, which govern the way property moves from generation to generation and to the living from the dead. "Succession" includes the law of wills, the law of intestacy, the law of trusts (for the most part), the law of charitable foundations, the law concerning "death taxes," and even some aspects of an arcane field of law that lawyers call the law of future interests.

Obviously, when you die, you lose control in any literal sense. But human law can, and does, open the door to a certain amount of post-mortem control. The dead hand rules, if we let it, from beyond the grave, at least up to a point. The simplest way this is done is through a *will*, in which you have the right, if you follow certain

"Just so you know, I'm taking all this with me into the afterlife."

Frank Cotham/The New Yorker Collection/The Cartoon Bank

---

1. How about being buried while riding one's favorite motorcycle? *See* Nina Golgowski, Ohio Man Is Buried Riding His Harley-Davidson Motorcycle, N.Y. Daily News, Jan. 31, 2014.—Eds.

formalities, to specify who gets what when you die[;] . . . or, if there is no will, a body of rules of law, the law of *intestate succession*, gives you (by default) an estate plan. . . .

Succession . . . is a social process of enormous importance. In a rich country, the stock of wealth that turns over as people die, one by one, is staggeringly large. In the United States, according to one estimate, some $41 trillion will pass from the dead to the living in the first half of the twenty-first century. This figure has been disputed, and an argument rages among economists as to the exact amounts—all the way from "only" $10 trillion to the high estimate of $41 trillion.[2] But no matter who is right, clearly we are dealing with immense amounts of money.

1. Freedom of Disposition and the Dead Hand

The Restatement (Third) of Property aptly summarizes the central role of *freedom of disposition* in American law as follows:

> The organizing principle of the American law of donative transfers is freedom of disposition. Property owners have the nearly unrestricted right to dispose of their property as they please. . . .
>
> American law does not grant courts any general authority to question the wisdom, fairness, or reasonableness of the donor's decisions about how to allocate his or her property. The main function of the law in this field is to facilitate rather than regulate. The law serves this function by establishing rules under which sufficiently reliable determinations can be made regarding the content of the donor's intention.
>
> American law curtails freedom of disposition only to the extent that the donor attempts to make a disposition or achieve a purpose that is prohibited or restricted by an overriding rule of law. . . .
>
> Among the rules of law that prohibit or restrict freedom of disposition in certain instances are those relating to spousal rights; creditors' rights; unreasonable restraints on alienation or marriage; provisions promoting separation or divorce; impermissible racial or other categoric restrictions; provisions encouraging illegal activity; and the rules against perpetuities and accumulations.[3]

Sir Arthur Hobhouse

Freedom of disposition is not limited to lifetime transfers. Under American law, a person also has wide latitude to control the disposition of her property at death—what critics call "dead hand" control. More than 135 years ago, Sir Arthur Hobhouse argued famously against the "cold and numbing influence of the Dead Hand" thus:

---

2. *See* John J. Havens & Paul G. Schervish, Why the $41 Trillion Wealth Transfer Estimate Is Still Valid: A Review of Challenges and Comments, 7 J. Gift Plan. 11 (2003).—Eds.

3. Restatement (Third) of Property: Wills and Other Donative Transfers § 10.1 cmts. a, c (Am. Law Inst. 2003).

What could be more irrational than to maintain that each generation shall be considered more competent to foresee the needs of the coming one than that one, when arrived, is to see them? . . .

What I consider to be not conjectural, but proved by experience in all human affairs, is, that people are the best judges of their own concerns; or if they are not, that it is better for them, on moral grounds, that they should manage their own concerns for themselves, and that it cannot be wrong continually to claim this liberty for every Generation of mortal men.[4]

The idea that each generation has a moral right to the property of the prior generation has a distinguished pedigree in American thought. Thomas Jefferson put the point, which he considered "self evident," as follows: "[T]he earth belongs in usufruct to the living; . . . the dead have neither powers nor rights over it. The portion occupied by any individual ceases to be his when himself ceases to be, and reverts to the society."[5]

As a matter of positive law, however, history has settled the question differently. The American law of succession strongly embraces the principle of freedom of disposition.[6] The breadth of freedom of disposition in American law is unique among modern legal systems. Professor Ray Madoff explains:

Americans are largely free to impose whatever conditions they want, and their plans can often be imposed for as long as they want, even in perpetuity. . . . [M]ost countries limit the ability of people to direct their property after death by imposing systems of forced succession, which require that a large portion of their property (commonly up to 80 percent) be given to family members in designated shares. Even those countries that lack [forced succession] nonetheless grant courts the power to diverge from the instructions left in a person's will in order to effectuate a fairer distribution of a person's estate. This is unlike American law, where freedom of testation is paramount and the courts have no power to deviate from a person's will.[7]

In the American legal tradition, freedom of disposition at death is curbed only by wealth transfer taxation (see Chapter 15); the forced share for a surviving spouse (see Chapter 8); rules protecting creditors (see pages 47, 461); and a handful of venerable public policy constraints such as the Rule Against Perpetuities, the rule against trusts for capricious purposes, and the rule against restraints on alienation. In recent years, even these limits have been weakened, most strikingly by legislation in more than half the states that repeals the Rule Against Perpetuities to validate perpetual trusts (see Chapter 14 at page 906).

Crucially, no limit on freedom of disposition at death arises from the interest of an expectant beneficiary in receiving a future inheritance. To the contrary, the American law

4. Arthur Hobhouse, The Devolution and Transfer of Land, *in* The Dead Hand: Addresses on the Subject of Endowments and Settlements of Property 184-85 (1880).
5. Letter from Thomas Jefferson to James Madison (Sept. 6, 1789), *in* 6 The Works of Thomas Jefferson 3, 3-4 (Paul Leicester Ford ed., 1904).
6. *See* Robert H. Sitkoff, Trusts and Estates: Implementing Freedom of Disposition, 58 St. Louis U. L.J. 643 (2014).
7. Ray D. Madoff, Immortality and the Law: The Rising Power of the American Dead 6-7 (2010).

of succession is organized around the *donor's* freedom of disposition. A *donee's* interest in a future inheritance is a mere expectancy (see page 67), one that derives from the donor's freedom of disposition and that remains subject to the donor's change of mind.

Shapira v. Union National Bank
315 N.E.2d 825 (Ohio C.P. 1974)

HENDERSON, J. This is an action for a declaratory judgment and the construction of the will of David Shapira, M.D., who died April 13, 1973, a resident of this county. . . .

The portions of the will in controversy are as follows:

> *Item VIII.* All the rest, residue and remainder of my estate, real and personal, of every kind and description and wheresoever situated, which I may own or have the right to dispose of at the time of my decease, I give, devise and bequeath to my three (3) beloved children, to wit: Ruth Shapira Aharoni, of Tel Aviv, Israel, or wherever she may reside at the time of my death; to my son Daniel Jacob Shapira, and to my son Mark Benjamin Simon Shapira in equal shares, with the following qualifications: . . .
>
> (b) My son Daniel Jacob Shapira should receive his share of the bequest only, if he is married at the time of my death to a Jewish girl whose both parents were Jewish. In the event that at the time of my death he is not married to a Jewish girl whose both parents were Jewish, then his share of this bequest should be kept by my executor for a period of not longer than seven (7) years and if my said son Daniel Jacob gets married within the seven year period to a Jewish girl whose both parents were Jewish, my executor is hereby instructed to turn over his share of my bequest to him. In the event, however, that my said son Daniel Jacob is unmarried within the seven (7) years after my death to a Jewish girl whose both parents were Jewish, or if he is married to a non Jewish girl, then his share of my estate, as provided in item 8 above should go to The State of Israel, absolutely.

The provision for the testator's other son Mark, is conditioned substantially similarly. Daniel Jacob Shapira, the plaintiff, alleges that the condition upon his inheritance is unconstitutional, contrary to public policy and unenforceable because of its unreasonableness, and that he should be given his bequest free of the restriction. Daniel is 21 years of age, unmarried and a student at Youngstown State University. . . .

CONSTITUTIONALITY

Plaintiff's argument that the condition in question violates constitutional safeguards is based upon the premise that the right to marry is protected by the Fourteenth Amendment to the Constitution of the United States. . . . In Loving v. Virginia, 388 U.S. 1 (1967), the court held unconstitutional as violative of the Equal Protection and Due Process Clauses of the Fourteenth Amendment an antimiscegenation statute under which a black person and a white person were convicted for marrying. In its opinion the United States Supreme Court made the following statements, 388 U.S. at 12:

> There can be no doubt that restricting the freedom to marry solely because of racial classifications violates the central meaning of the Equal Protection Clause. . . .

The freedom to marry has long been recognized as one of the vital personal rights essential to the orderly pursuit of happiness by free men.

Marriage is one of the "basic civil rights of man," fundamental to our very existence and survival. . . . The Fourteenth Amendment requires that the freedom of choice to marry not be restricted by invidious racial discriminations. Under our Constitution, the freedom to marry, or not marry, a person of another race resides with the individual and cannot be infringed by the State.

From the foregoing, it appears clear, as plaintiff contends, that the right to marry is constitutionally protected from restrictive state legislative action. Plaintiff submits, then, that under the doctrine of Shelley v. Kraemer, 334 U.S. 1 (1948), the constitutional protection of the Fourteenth Amendment is extended from direct state legislative action to the enforcement by state judicial proceedings of private provisions restricting the right to marry. Plaintiff contends that a judgment of this court upholding the condition restricting marriage would, under Shelley v. Kraemer, constitute state action prohibited by the Fourteenth Amendment as much as a state statute.

In Shelley v. Kraemer the . . . Supreme Court held that the action of the states to which the Fourteenth Amendment has reference includes action of state courts and state judicial officials. Prior to this decision the court had invalidated city ordinances which denied blacks the right to live in white neighborhoods. In Shelley v. Kraemer owners of neighboring properties sought to enjoin blacks from occupying properties which they had bought, but which were subjected to privately executed restrictions against use or occupation by any persons except those of the Caucasian race. Chief Justice Vinson noted, in the course of his opinion at page 13: "These are cases in which the purposes of the agreements were secured only by judicial enforcement by state courts of the restrictive terms of the agreements."

In the case at bar, this court is not being asked to enforce any restriction upon Daniel Jacob Shapira's constitutional right to marry. Rather, this court is being asked to enforce the testator's restriction upon his son's inheritance. If the facts and circumstances of this case were such that the aid of this court were sought to enjoin Daniel's marrying a non-Jewish girl, then the doctrine of Shelley v. Kraemer would be applicable, but not, it is believed, upon the facts as they are. . . .

[T]he right to receive property by will is a creature of the law, and is not a natural right or one guaranteed or protected by either the Ohio or the United States constitution. . . . It is a fundamental rule of law in Ohio that a testator may legally entirely disinherit his children. . . . This would seem to demonstrate that, from a constitutional standpoint, a testator may restrict a child's inheritance. The court concludes, therefore, that the upholding and enforcement of the provisions of Dr. Shapira's will conditioning the bequests to his sons upon their marrying Jewish girls does not offend the Constitution of Ohio or of the United States.

PUBLIC POLICY

The condition that Daniel's share should be "turned over to him if he should marry a Jewish girl whose both parents were Jewish" constitutes a partial restraint upon marriage. If the condition were that the beneficiary not marry anyone, the restraint would be general or total, and, at least in the case of a first marriage, would be held to be contrary to public policy and void. A partial restraint of marriage which imposes only reasonable restrictions is valid, and not contrary to public policy; . . . The great weight of authority in the United States is that gifts conditioned upon the beneficiary's marrying within a particular religious class or faith are reasonable.

Plaintiff contends, however, that in Ohio a condition such as the one in this case is void as against the public policy of this state. In Ohio, as elsewhere, a testator may not attach a condition to a gift which is in violation of public policy. . . . Plaintiff's position that the free choice of religious practice cannot be circumscribed or controlled by contract is substantiated by Hackett v. Hackett, 150 N.E.2d 431 (Ohio App. 1958). This case held that a covenant in a separation agreement, incorporated in a divorce decree, that the mother would rear a daughter in the Roman Catholic faith was unenforceable. However, the controversial condition in the case at bar is a partial restraint upon marriage and not a covenant to restrain the freedom of religious practice; and, of course, this court is not being asked to hold the plaintiff in contempt for failing to marry a Jewish girl of Jewish parentage. . . .

It is noted, furthermore, in this connection, that the courts of Pennsylvania distinguish between testamentary gifts conditioned upon the religious faith of the beneficiary and those conditioned upon marriage to persons of a particular religious faith. In Clayton's Estate, 13 Pa. D. & C. 413 (Pa. Orphans' Ct. 1929), the court upheld a gift of a life estate conditioned upon the beneficiary's not marrying a woman of the Catholic faith. In its opinion the court distinguishes the earlier case of Drace v. Klinedinst, 118 A. 907 (Pa. 1922), in which a life estate willed to grandchildren, provided they remained faithful to a particular religion, was held to violate the public policy of Pennsylvania.[8] In Clayton's Estate, the court said that the condition concerning marriage did not affect the faith of the beneficiary, and that the condition, operating only on the choice of a wife, was too remote to be regarded as coercive of religious faith. . . .

The only cases cited by plaintiff's counsel in accord with [plaintiff's contention] are some English cases and one American decision. In England the courts have held that partial restrictions upon marriage to persons not of the Jewish faith, or of Jewish parentage, were not contrary to public policy or invalid. Hodgson v. Halford (1879 Eng.) L.R. 11 Ch. Div. 959. Other cases in England, however, have invalidated forfeitures of similarly conditioned provisions for children upon the basis of uncertainty or indefiniteness. . . . Since the foregoing decisions, a later English case has upheld a condition precedent that a granddaughter-beneficiary marry a person of Jewish faith and the child of Jewish parents. The court . . . found . . . no difficulty with indefiniteness where

---

8. In In re Estate of Laning, 339 A.2d 520 (Pa. 1975), the court stated that the Drace case was correctly decided on the grounds that the testator sought to require his grandchildren to "remain true" to the Catholic religion, and that enforcement of a condition that they remain faithful Catholics would require the court to determine the doctrines of the Catholic church. "Such questions are clearly improper for a civil court to determine." The court also upheld a provision in Laning's will that a gift be distributed to certain relatives who held "membership 'in good standing'" in the Presbyterian church. The court construed this provision to require only a formal affiliation with the specified church, avoiding improper inquiry into church doctrine. — Eds.

the legatee married unquestionably outside the Jewish faith. Re Wolffe, [1953] 2 All Eng. 697.[9]

The American case cited by plaintiff is that of Maddox v. Maddox, 52 Va. (11 Grattan's) 804 (1854). The testator in this case willed a remainder to his niece if she remain a member of the Society of Friends. When the niece arrived at a marriageable age there were but five or six unmarried men of the society in the neighborhood in which she lived. She married a non-member and thus lost her own membership. The court held the condition to be an unreasonable restraint upon marriage and void. . . . The court said that with the small number of eligible bachelors in the area the condition would have operated as a virtual prohibition of the niece's marrying, and that she could not be expected to "go abroad" in search of a helpmate or to be subjected to the chance of being sought after by a stranger. . . .

In arguing for the applicability of the Maddox v. Maddox test of reasonableness to the case at bar, counsel for the plaintiff asserts that the number of eligible Jewish females in this county would be an extremely small minority of the total population especially as compared with the comparatively much greater number in New York, whence have come many of the cases comprising the weight of authority upholding the validity of such clauses. There are no census figures in evidence. While this court could probably take judicial notice of the fact that the Jewish community is a minor, though important segment of our total local population, nevertheless the court is by no means justified in judicial knowledge that there is an insufficient number of eligible young ladies of Jewish parentage in this area from which Daniel would have a reasonable latitude of choice.[10] And of course, Daniel is not at all confined in his choice to residents of this county, which is a very different circumstance in this day of travel by plane and freeway and communication by telephone, from the horse and buggy days of the 1854 Maddox v. Maddox decision. Consequently, the decision does not appear to be an appropriate yardstick of reasonableness under modern living conditions.

Plaintiff's counsel contends that the Shapira will falls within the principle of Fineman v. Central National Bank, 175 N.E.2d 837 (Ohio App. 1961), holding that the public policy of Ohio does not countenance a bequest or device conditioned on

---

9. In In re Tuck's Settlement Trusts, [1978] 1 Ch. 49 (Eng.), a trust was set up by the first Baron Tuck, a Jew, for the benefit of his successors in the baronetcy. Anxious to ensure that his successors be Jewish, he provided for payment of income to the baronet on the condition that he be Jewish and married to a Jewish wife. The trust also provided that in the event of a dispute the decision of the Chief Rabbi of London would be conclusive. The court held that the conditions were not void for uncertainty. Lord Denning was of the view that if there was any uncertainty, it was cured by the Chief Rabbi arbitration clause. The other two judges declined to reach that issue. The question—who is a Jew—is not easy to answer, not even in Israel, where it has provoked continuing controversy. See Michael Stanislawski, A Jewish Monk? A Legal and Ideological Analysis of the Origins of the "Who Is a Jew" Controversy in Israel, in Text and Context: Essays in Modern Jewish History and Historiography (Eli Lederhendler & Jack Wertheimer eds., 2005).—Eds.

10. The American Jewish Yearbook of 1976 estimates the Jewish population of Youngstown, Ohio, to be 5,400 in 1974. Taking into consideration other U.S. census data about the male-to-female ratio and the ages of the population in Youngstown, we estimate that about 500 Jewish females were in the 15 to 24 age group. If this estimate is correct, do you think Daniel had "a reasonable latitude of choice"?—Eds.

the beneficiary's obtaining a separation or divorce from his wife. Counsel argues that the Shapira condition would encourage the beneficiary to marry a qualified girl just to receive the bequest, and then to divorce her afterward. This possibility seems too remote to be a pertinent application of the policy against bequests conditioned upon divorce. . . . Indeed, in measuring the reasonableness of the condition in question, both the father and the court should be able to assume that the son's motive would be proper. And surely the son should not gain the advantage of the avoidance of the condition by the possibility of his own impropriety.

Finally, counsel urges that the Shapira condition tends to pressure Daniel, by the reward of money, to marry within seven years without opportunity for mature reflection, and jeopardizes his college education. It seems to the court, on the contrary, that the seven year time limit would be a most reasonable grace period, and one which would give the son ample opportunity for exhaustive reflection and fulfillment of the condition without constraint or oppression. Daniel is no more being "blackmailed into a marriage by immediate financial gain," as suggested by counsel, than would be the beneficiary of a living gift or conveyance upon consideration of a future marriage—an arrangement which has long been sanctioned by the courts of this state.

In the opinion of this court, the provision made by the testator for the benefit of the State of Israel upon breach or failure of the condition is . . . significant . . . [because] it demonstrates the depth of the testator's conviction. His purpose was not merely a negative one designed to punish his son for not carrying out his wishes. His unmistakable testamentary plan was that his possessions be used to encourage the preservation of the Jewish faith and blood, hopefully through his sons, but, if not, then through the State of Israel. Whether this judgment was wise is not for this court to determine. But it is the duty of this court to honor the testator's intention within the limitations of law and of public policy. The prerogative granted to a testator by the laws of this state to dispose of his estate according to his conscience is entitled to as much judicial protection and enforcement as the prerogative of a beneficiary to receive an inheritance.

It is the conclusion of this court that public policy should not, and does not preclude the fulfillment of Dr. Shapira's purpose, and that in accordance with the weight of authority in this country, the conditions contained in his will are reasonable restrictions upon marriage, and valid.

NOTES

1. Incentive Trusts. In contemporary practice, conditional bequests such as in *Shapira* are more typically made in trust (see Chapter 6), sometimes called an *incentive trust*. Anecdotal evidence suggests that such trusts are more often focused on ensuring that a beneficiary does not adopt a frivolous lifestyle than encouraging religious observance or marriage to a preferred mate. As the investment guru and billionaire Warren Buffett put it, the "perfect" legacy for one's children is "enough money so that they would feel they could do anything, but not so much that they could do nothing."[11]

---

11. Richard I. Kirkland, Jr. & Carrie Gottlieb, Should You Leave It All to the Children?, Fortune, Sept. 29, 1986, at 18.

There is in fact some evidence that inherited wealth is associated with reduced work-force participation.[12] Enter the incentive trust. Professor Joshua Tate explains:

> The conditions that incentive trusts might impose can be divided into three broad categories. First are conditions that encourage the beneficiaries to pursue an education. Second are conditions that provide what might be termed moral incentives: incentives that reflect the settlor's moral or religious outlook or promote a particular way of living. Some of these conditions try to encourage the beneficiaries to contribute to charitable causes, while others discourage substance abuse or promote a traditional family lifestyle. Finally, there are conditions designed to encourage the beneficiaries to have a productive career.... Provided that these incentives do not violate public policy, courts generally will enforce them.[13]

Tate reports that some practitioners recommend "provisions that pay out a certain amount of money from the trust for every dollar that the beneficiary earns on her own." Other practitioners disagree, worrying that "hardwiring" a trust with inflexible provisions might frustrate the settlor's purpose.[14] For example, what if the beneficiary is injured or suffers a debilitating illness? What if the beneficiary stays at home with young children or to care for a grievously ill child? Should a court have the power to authorize deviation from the donor's instructions if doing so would further the purpose of the trust in light of unanticipated changes in circumstances? We take up trust modification in Chapter 10.

Sometimes a poorly drafted conditional bequest backfires, producing perverse results never intended by the donor. In *Shapira*, the court was unimpressed with the argument that the provision at issue would encourage Daniel "to marry a qualified girl just to receive the bequest, and then to divorce her afterward." But is the idea of marrying for money really so farfetched? Consider this report:

Serial husband Tommy Manville in his bathrobe with two female friends (c. 1938)
Bert Morgan/Premium Archives/Getty Images

> [T]he living can usually concoct schemes to outsmart the dead. Mr. Train recalled the saga of Tommy Manville, playboy heir to the Johns-Manville fortune. To prod him to settle down, according to Mr. Train, Mr. Manville's trust guaranteed him

---

12. *See* Jeffrey R. Brown, Courtney C. Coile & Scott J. Weisbenner, The Effect of Inheritance Receipt on Retirement, 92 Rev. Econ. & Stat. 425 (2010); Douglas Holtz-Eakin, David Joulfaian & Harvey S. Rosen, The Carnegie Conjecture: Some Empirical Evidence, 108 Q.J. Econ. 413 (1993).

13. Joshua C. Tate, Conditional Love: Incentive Trusts and the Inflexibility Problem, 41 Real Prop. Prob. & Tr. J. 445, 453 (2006).

14. David A. Handler & Alison E. Lothes, The Case for Principle Trusts and Against Incentive Trusts, Tr. & Est., Oct. 2008, at 31; *see also* Victoria J. Haneman, Incorporation of Outcome-Based Learning Approaches into the Design of (Incentive) Trusts, 61 S.D. L. Rev. 404 (2016).

$250,000 when he married. "So he married 13 times," Mr. Train says. "He'd pay the woman $50,000, pocket $200,000, get a quickie divorce and then, when he needed more money, he'd get married again."[15]

2. Lifetime Versus Testamentary Conditions. In 1994, we asked the lawyer who represented Daniel Shapira for information about the aftermath of the litigation. The lawyer contacted Mr. Shapira, who declined to give any information. It was a bitter experience, Mr. Shapira said, one that he wanted to forget. Was this what Dr. Shapira had intended as his posthumous legacy? Or was making a "ringing declaration of his core beliefs" so important to him that his son's embitterment was a foreseeable risk that he was willing to take?[16]

Judge Richard A. Posner

Judge Richard A. Posner suggests an intent-implementing rationale for giving courts leeway to modify a conditional gift made at death:

> Suppose a man leaves money to his son in trust, the trust to fail, however, if the son does not marry a woman of the Jewish faith by the time he is 25 years old. The judicial approach in such cases is to refuse to enforce the condition if it is "unreasonable." In the case just put, it might make a difference whether the son was 18 or 24 at the time of the bequest and how large the Jewish population was in the place where he lived.
>
> This approach may seem wholly devoid of an economic foundation, and admittedly the criterion of reasonableness is here an unilluminating one. Consider, however, the possibilities for modification that would exist if the gift were inter vivos rather than testamentary. As the deadline approached, the son might come to his father and persuade him that a diligent search had revealed no marriageable Jewish girl who would accept him. The father might be persuaded to grant an extension or otherwise relax the condition. If the father is dead, this kind of "recontracting" is impossible, and the presumption that the condition is a reasonable one fails.[17]

Senator Joseph Lieberman, the unsuccessful Democratic candidate for Vice President in 2000, declined to enforce a religious restriction as the executor of his uncle's estate. The restriction would have disinherited two of his cousins for marrying persons who were not born Jewish. Instead he brokered a deal whereby the spouses converted to Judaism and the cousins' shares were restored. Lieberman said that his uncle "knew who he was making the executor. . . . He knew that these were my cousins and that I love them, and that by my nature I'm not as hard as the will was. He knew what I would do."[18] Did Lieberman betray his uncle's trust or carry out his uncle's intent?

---

15. J. Peder Zane, The Rise of Incentive Trusts: Six Feet Under and Overbearing, N.Y. Times, Mar. 12, 1995, § 4, at 5.

16. David Horton, Testation and Speech, 101 Geo. L.J. 61, 66 (2012).

17. Richard A. Posner, Economic Analysis of Law § 19.6 (9th ed. 2014).

18. Phil Kuntz & Bob Davis, A Beloved Uncle's Will Tests Diplomatic Skills of Joseph Lieberman — Document Disinherits Children Who Failed Religious Test; Senator Tries to Mend Rift, Wall St. J., Aug. 25, 2000, at A1.

3. What Relief?   If the court in *Shapira* had found that the restraint on Daniel's marrying was unreasonable, it would have struck the condition, awarding him the bequest outright.[19] Is this relief consistent with the principle of freedom of disposition? Would not Dr. Shapira have preferred Daniel's share to go to Israel rather than to Daniel if the marriage provision could not be enforced? On the other hand, would not an order directing that the property pass to Israel be tantamount to giving effect to the condition? We shall see this issue again when we consider discriminatory charitable trusts in Chapter 11 at page 780.

4. Contrary to "Public Policy."   The rule against a will or trust provision that imposes an unreasonable restraint on marriage is a specific application of the more general rule against conditions that are *contrary to public policy*.[20] Some conditions are obviously impermissible on public policy grounds — for example, a condition requiring a beneficiary to commit a crime or a tort. In Thrupp v. Collett, (1858) 53 Eng. Rep. 844 (M.R.); 26 Beav. 125, the court declared void as against public policy a trust to pay certain regulatory fines. But what about other conditions? How much leeway should courts have to limit freedom of disposition in the name of "public policy"? How is a court to determine whether a condition violates public policy? Are courts competent to make such a judgment?

Charles Vance Millar, a prominent Canadian lawyer, died in 1926 with a will instructing that most of his estate be held for ten years and then be given to "the mother who has since my death given birth in Toronto to the greatest number of children." The Supreme Court of Canada upheld this provision as not against public policy.[21] Ten years later, four women, each of whom had given birth to nine children in those ten years, received the equivalent of $2 million each as the winners of what came to be known as the "Great Stork Derby."[22]

In 1993, the Associated Press reported on the will of a Romanian man who resented having been "nagged" by his wife to stop smoking. The man left everything to his wife on the condition that she smoke five cigarettes a day for the rest of her life.[23] Would this condition be upheld by an American court?

5. Restraints on Marriage.   The weight of authority holds that a *total* or *general restraint* on marriage or a provision encouraging divorce is void as contrary to public policy unless the donor's dominant purpose was to provide support until marriage or in the event of a divorce.[24] But how is a court to discern whether the donor's dominant

---

19. *See* Restatement (Third) of Trusts § 29 cmt. i(1) (Am. Law Inst. 2003); Restatement (Second) of Property: Donative Transfers § 6.1(1) (Am. Law Inst. 1983).

20. *See* Ruth Sarah Lee, Over My Dead Body: A New Approach to Testamentary Restraints on Marriage, 14 Marq. Elder's Advisor 55 (2012); Ronald J. Scalise, Jr., Public Policy and Antisocial Testators, 32 Cardozo L. Rev. 1315 (2011); Jeffrey G. Sherman, Posthumous Meddling: An Instrumentalist Theory of Testamentary Restraints on Conjugal and Religious Choices, 99 U. Ill. L. Rev. 1273 (1999); *see also* Adam J. Hirsch, Freedom of Testation/Freedom of Contract, 95 Minn. L. Rev. 2180 (2011).

21. In re Estate of Charles Millar, [1938] S.C.R. 1 (Can.).

22. *See* David Goldenberg, How a Dead Millionaire Convinced Dozens of Women to Have as Many Babies as Possible, FiveThirtyEight (Dec. 11, 2015), https://perma.cc/YH2R-L4YZ.

23. Reporter's Notes to Restatement (Third) of Trusts § 29 cmts. j-l (Am. Law Inst. 2003).

24. *See* Restatement (Second) of Property: Donative Transfers §§ 6.1, 7.1 (Am. Law Inst. 1983).

purpose was disruption or support? How hard would it be for a competent drafter to fit a conditional bequest within this exception?

An older line of cases recognizes an exception to the rule against a total restraint on marriage for a gift by a husband to his widow conditioned on her remaining unmarried. In Commonwealth v. Stauffer, 10 Pa. 350 (1849), for example, the court reasoned thus: "It would be extremely difficult to say, why a husband should not be at liberty to leave a homestead to his wife, without being compelled to let her share it with a successor in his bed, and to use it as a nest to hatch a brood of strangers to his blood. Such is not the policy of the . . . common law, which allows him to give his property on his own terms, or not at all; and, if he might not do the one, he would assuredly do the other." Would a court find this reasoning persuasive today?

The prevailing rule regarding a *partial restraint* on marriage, followed in *Shapira*, is that the restraint is invalid as unreasonable "if a marriage permitted by the restraint is not likely to occur. The likelihood of marriage is a factual question, to be answered from the circumstances of the particular case."[25] Suppose that Daniel Shapira were gay. Would the provision in Dr. Shapira's will requiring Daniel to marry a Jewish *woman* be enforceable? Would such a provision violate Daniel's right, recognized in Obergefell v. Hodges, 135 S. Ct. 2584 (2015), to marry a man?

Gay Man Told to Marry Woman or Son Would Lose Inheritance

By Alyssa Newcomb

The gay son of a deceased New York City businessman is fighting a stipulation in his late father's will that required him to marry the mother of his child or risk losing the child's inheritance.

Robert Mandelbaum, who is a Manhattan Criminal Court judge, said in court documents that his father, Frank Mandelbaum, knew he was gay and included his male partner in family activities. The elder Mandelbaum died in 2007 at the age of 73.

[The elder] Mandelbaum, who amassed a fortune after founding the ID-verification firm Intellicheck, died before his grandson, Cooper, now 16 months, was born.

Cooper's fathers, Robert Mandelbaum and Jonathan O'Donnell, married shortly after his birth via surrogate in 2011. It's unclear which of the men is Cooper's biological father.

The late businessman's will left behind a $180,000 trust for his grandchildren, including those who would be born after his death. The heirs will receive installments from ages 25 to 30, although the amounts will be contingent on the performance of the investment.

But Cooper will not be eligible for his inheritance because he has two dads, according to the terms of the will.

The words "child," "grandchild" and "descendant" include natural and adopted children and children born out of wedlock, according to the will, which was filed in Manhattan Surrogate's Court.

"However, such words shall specifically not include an adopted child of Robert, if adopted while Robert is a single person, or a biological child of Robert, if Robert shall not be married to the child's mother within six months of the child's birth," the will states.

Robert Mandelbaum is challenging the will on the basis that it would require him to enter into a "sham marriage" which would violate New York marriage-equality law.

Attorney Anne Bederka wrote that the stipulation Robert Mandelbaum marry a woman was "tantamount to expecting him either to live in celibacy, or to engage in extramarital activity with another man, and is therefore contrary to public policy."

Source: ABC News (Aug. 20, 2012).

_____

The parties settled in 2013 on terms that were not made public. *See* In re Mandelbaum, 2013 WL 3929822 (N.Y. Sur. 2013).

_____

25. Id. § 6.2 cmt. a.

In *Shapira*, the court distinguished the *Maddox* case of 1854 on the grounds that "in this day of travel by plane and freeway and communication by telephone," precedents on reasonableness from the "horse and buggy days" have little currency. Given the rise of JDate.com, Match.com, eHarmony, and the like, is geography still relevant in assessing reasonableness? Researchers report "that more than one-third of marriages in America now begin on-line. In addition, marriages that began on-line, when compared with those that began through traditional off-line venues, were slightly less likely to result in a marital break-up (separation or divorce) and were associated with slightly higher marital satisfaction among those respondents who remained married."[26]

The court in *Shapira* also reasoned that seven years was ample time to choose a mate. But Daniel was 21, so he would have had to marry by age 28. Was this reasonable in 1974? Would it be reasonable today? Census Bureau data show a median age at first marriage in 2015 of 29.2 for men and 27.1 for women, up from 23.1 and 21.1 respectively in 1974.[27]

6. The Restatement (Third) of Trusts.   In a break with prior Restatements and existing case law, the Restatement (Third) of Trusts takes the position that in reckoning what is contrary to public policy, courts should balance the donor's freedom of disposition "against other social values and the effects of deadhand control on the subsequent conduct or personal freedoms of others."[28] If "a provision is unnecessarily punitive or unreasonably intrusive into significant personal decisions or interests, . . . the provision may be invalid."[29] In the teeth of *Shapira* and similar cases, the Restatement includes as an illustration of an invalid condition a provision that would terminate a trust beneficiary's interest upon marriage to someone not of a particular religious faith.[30]

These Restatement provisions, which would authorize courts to curb freedom of disposition on the basis of subjective factors, are controversial.[31] In In re Estate of Feinberg, 919 N.E.2d 888 (Ill. 2009), the court declined to apply them. It upheld a testamentary trust in which a beneficiary who married outside of the Jewish faith would be treated as if the beneficiary had died on the day of the marriage:

> This case reveals a broader tension between the competing values of freedom of testation on one hand and resistance to "dead hand" control on the other. . . . When

---

26. John T. Cacioppo et al., Marital Satisfaction and Break-Ups Differ Across On-Line and Off-Line Meeting Venues, 110 Proc. Nat'l Acad. Sci. U.S. 10135 (2013); *see also* Michael J. Rosenfeld & Reuben J. Thomas, Searching for a Mate: The Rise of the Internet as a Social Intermediary, 77 Am. Soc. Rev. 523 (2012).

27. The raw data is available at https://perma.cc/U9FS-SEP8.

28. Restatement (Third) of Trusts § 29 cmt. i (Am. Law Inst. 2003).

29. Id. cmt. l.

30. Id. illus. 3. The reporter's notes criticize *Shapira* as an "unfortunate case[]," albeit "seemingly" consistent with prior law. Reporter's Note to id.

31. *See* Martin D. Begleiter, Taming the "Unruly Horse" of Public Policy in Wills and Trusts, 26 Quinnipiac Prob. L.J. 125, 135 (2012) (arguing that "the concept of public policy in the Restatement (Third) of Trusts appears inadequate on numerous grounds").

we determine that our answer to a question of law must be based on public policy, it is not our role to make such policy. Rather, we must discern the public policy of the state of Illinois as expressed in the constitution, statutes, and long-standing case law. . . . While the beneficiary restriction clause . . . has resulted in family strife, it is not "so capable of producing harm that its enforcement would be contrary to the public interest."

Restatements, of course, are persuasive rather than binding authority. It remains to be seen whether other courts will be persuaded by the more interventionist position urged by the Restatement (Third) of Trusts.

7. *Destruction of Property at Death.*   Should a testator be permitted to order the destruction of property at death? Suppose *T*'s will directs his executor to tear down *T*'s house because *T* does not want anyone else to live in it. Should a court order the house destroyed? *See* Eyerman v. Mercantile Trust Co., 524 S.W.2d 210 (Mo. App. 1975) ("a well-ordered society cannot tolerate" waste). If *T* had anticipated the result in *Eyerman*, might she have destroyed her house during life, earlier than would have given her the most pleasure? *See* Lior Jacob Strahilevitz, The Right to Destroy, 114 Yale L.J. 781 (2005).

Justice Hugo L. Black of the U.S. Supreme Court was of the view that private notes of the justices relating to Court conferences should not be published posthumously. Justice Black feared publication might inhibit free and vigorous discussion among

Though There Was a Will, Fifth Third Found a Way to Save Boots

By Becky Yerak

Boots, an 11-year-old cat from Berwyn, has narrowly avoided using up the last of her nine lives, thanks to trust officers at Fifth Third Bank who resisted carrying out a death sentence stipulated in the will of the cat's owner.

Georgia Lee Dvorak died recently at age 76. In a will she drew up more than 20 years ago, she stated that any cat or cats that she owned at the time of her death be euthanized "in a painless, peaceful manner" by a veterinarian's lethal injection.

But trust officers at Fifth Third Bank, which was appointed to manage Dvorak's estate, were squeamish about carrying out those terms on Boots. Dvorak was not survived by any relatives.

So on Monday, Fifth Third asked a Cook County probate court to set aside that provision of Dvorak's 1988 will as [the bank] had found a shelter to take Boots.

"It would violate public policy to euthanize a healthy housecat where an appropriate shelter has been identified," lawyers . . . plead to the court on behalf of Fifth Third.

Fifth Third's lawyers pointed out that  *Boots* Dvorak asked that most of her estate — estimated at nearly $1.4 million — go to animal-related causes. That was evidence of her commitment to the humane treatment of animals, they said. . . .

On Monday in a Cook County probate court, Judge Susan Coleman allowed Fifth Third to find more humane arrangements for Boots.

Source: Chi. Trib. (Apr. 4, 2012).

Justice Hugo L. Black

the justices. Black was struck ill, destroyed his conference notes, resigned from the Court, and died a few weeks later. Suppose that Justice Black had died suddenly while on the bench and that his will had directed his executor to destroy the notes. Could the executor do this without a court order? Should a court order destruction of the notes, which might have enormous value to Court historians? Who would have standing to object?

Franz Kafka bequeathed his diaries, manuscripts, and letters to his friend Max Brod, directing him to burn everything. Brod declined to do so on the grounds that Kafka's unpublished works were of great literary value. Should Brod have had a bonfire? Suppose that Franz Schubert and Giacomo Puccini had ordered their unfinished works destroyed at death, thus depriving the world of Schubert's unfinished Symphony in B Minor and Puccini's unfinished opera Turandot.[32] Should a court order destruction?

2. Justifying Freedom of Disposition

What is the policy basis for freedom of disposition? Why should property ownership include a right to control the disposition of that property after the owner's death? Can freedom of disposition be reconciled with the aspiration of equality of opportunity across and within generations?

a. The Donor's Prerogative

Adam J. Hirsch & William K.S. Wang
A Qualitative Theory of the Dead Hand
68 Ind. L.J. 1 (1992)

The traditional rationales for testamentary freedom are as varied as they are controversial. Perhaps oldest is the notion that testators have a natural right to bequeath. Having created wealth by the sweat of her brow, the testator is naturally free to do with it as she pleases — including passing it along to others. . . . Yet, from at least the seventeenth century, ideologists have disputed the natural theory of testation on various grounds. . . . William Blackstone . . . assert[ed] a natural right to dispose of property only during the testator's lifetime. At the moment of death, the testator lost her right to all species of property, self-made and inherited, on the theory that nature protects only the living. Jeremy Bentham, John Stuart Mill, and other utilitarian philosophers refused to concede even that much. For utilitarians, only the promotion of happiness could justify

---

32. Professor John Orth calls our attention to Virgil, who left instructions to destroy the Aeneid ("Of arms and the man I sing"), an unfinished work. The Emperor Augustus ordered the executors to disregard the order. Orth writes: "The course of Western literature would be unimaginable without 'arms and the man'! Who would have guided Dante in Hell?"

*"Researchers say I'm not happier for being richer, but
do you know how much researchers make?"*

Pat Byrnes/The New Yorker Collection/The Cartoon Bank

the granting of rights; the notion that persons, while living or dead, held rights of any sort flowing from nature was for Bentham "nonsense upon stilts." . . .

One argument, tracing back to the thirteenth century jurist Henry de Bracton, if not earlier, holds that freedom of testation creates an incentive to industry and saving. Bracton's assumption—shared by modern social scientists—was that persons derive satisfaction out of bequeathing property to others. To the extent that lawmakers deny persons the opportunity to bequeath freely, the subjective value of property will drop, for one of its potential uses will have disappeared. As a result, thwarted testators will choose to accumulate less property, and the total stock of wealth existing at any given time will shrink. . . .

Scholars have offered a number of objections and qualifications to this argument, however. As is often remarked, persons may strive to amass wealth over and above the needs of lifetime consumption for a variety of psychological and other reasons that have naught to do with the longing to bequeath. Persons accumulate to gratify their egos, to gain prestige, to gain power—and simply out of habit. . . . Furthermore, the productivity effect of testamentary freedom will be offset by the extent to which bequests dampen beneficiaries' incentives to produce their own wealth. . . .

Another argument for freedom of testation, also premised upon the goal of wealth enhancement, is that such freedom supports, as it were, a market for the provision of social services. Social life, like commercial life, is not a one-way street. Though classified by the law as "gratuitous" transfers, bequests within the family may in fact repay the beneficiary for "value" received (though of a sort not recognized as consideration under the common law). . . . The testator's power to bequeath encourages her beneficiaries to provide her with care and comfort. . . .

A secondary justification for the right of testation is that it would in practice be difficult to curtail. Were lawmakers to rescind the power of the will, testators would find other, less efficient ways to direct the distribution of their wealth. . . .

A final justification for freedom of testation . . . is simply that the power to bequeath comports with political preferences: "the desire to dispose of property by will is very general, and very strong. A compelling argument in favor of it is that it accords with human wishes."

Daniel B. Kelly
Restricting Testamentary Freedom:
Ex Ante Versus Ex Post Justifications
82 Fordham L. Rev. 1125 (2013)

Transferring property at death functions as another use of property; consequently, effectuating a donor's intent should maximize the donor's happiness. Testamentary freedom also aligns an individual's incentive to work, save, and invest with what is socially optimal, promoting capital accumulation and long-term productivity. In addition, a donor may have more information than either a legislature or court about the optimal distribution of property to family members or other donees. . . .

Yet the law does not privilege donative intent in all circumstances. . . . If so, under what circumstances should the courts intervene? . . . First, due to *imperfect information*, including unforeseen as well as unprovided-for contingencies, altering a will or trust may be desirable. Suppose a donor (D) leaves money for the cure of polio. Twenty years later, scientists discover a cure. Reallocating D's gift (e.g., to find the cure for another disease) is likely to be socially beneficial, and consistent with D's probable intent, even if D did not provide for this contingency in her will or trust.

Second, if a gift entails *negative externalities*, intervening may be desirable if the private incentive to give diverges from the socially optimal result. Suppose D has $10 million but D's spouse (S) and minor child (C) have $0. Assume S and C will receive public support if D disinherits them. Knowing this, D may reduce or eliminate a gift to S and C. As a result, the law may require that D provide some minimal level of support.

Third, legal intervention may be necessary due to considerations of *intergenerational equity*. Given its priority in time, the present generation may have an incentive, as well as the ability, to control property in ways that favor its own interests to the detriment of future generations. Assuming the measure of social welfare gives significant weight to the well-being of future generations, the private incentive of a donor living today may again diverge from the socially optimal result. . . .

NOTE

Freedom of Disposition and Its Alternatives. Wrangling among a decedent's survivors over succession to the decedent's property entails potentially significant private and social costs. Many families have been torn asunder by internecine litigation over succession. Society subsidizes this litigation by supplying the court system. But resolution of these disputes mainly settles the allocation of existing wealth rather than aiding in the creation of new wealth. The decedent's property may be consumed by litigation costs and relationships within the family may be irrevocably damaged. An orderly system of succession limits these costs.

In considering the possibilities for orderly succession, three options stand out as the most plausible:

a. Forced Succession.   The decedent's property could pass by mandatory or forced succession, such as a rule that provides for primogeniture or succession to a spouse, children, or other dependents or kin.

b. Freedom of Disposition.   The decedent's property could pass in accordance with the decedent's declared wishes if they are reliably preserved, or if not, then in accordance with a default system of succession that tracks the probable intent of a typical decedent.

c. Confiscation by the State.   The decedent's property could be confiscated by the state on the theory that the decedent's property rights terminate on death.

American law generally follows option (b), freedom of disposition, tempered by certain mandatory succession rights for spouses (see Chapter 8) and by wealth transfer taxation (see Chapter 15). Most other countries are closer to option (a), forced succession, honoring the decedent's wishes only with respect to property that remains after the forced shares are satisfied.[33]

History has shown option (c), confiscation by the state, to be problematic. In 1918, the Soviet Bolsheviks carried out the teachings of Marx and Engels and abolished inheritance. The law, translated into English, read: "Inheritance, testate and intestate, is abolished. Upon the death of the owner his property (movable and immovable) becomes the property of the [state]."[34] Within four years, however, inheritance was reestablished. The abolition of inheritance was unpopular and, on second thought, the Soviet rulers decided it was an institution that encouraged savings and provided an incentive to work. Inheritance was also viewed as a method of providing for dependents of the deceased, relieving the state of this burden, and of furthering family unity and stability. Before the dissolution of the Soviet Union, the Soviet law of inheritance did not much differ from the civil law of inheritance found in Western Europe.[35]

Karl Marx left a will directing the disposition of his property at death!

b. Concentrations of Wealth

A common argument against freedom of disposition is that it may be exercised in a manner that perpetuates inequalities in the distribution of wealth; concentrates economic power in the hands of

---

33. *See, e.g.,* Freedom of Testation (Reinhard Zimmermann ed., 2012).

34. [1918] 1 Sob. Uzak., RSFSR, No. 34, item 456, Apr. 26, 1918.

35. *See* Frances Foster, The Development of Inheritance Law in the Soviet Union and the People's Republic of China, 33 Am. J. Comp. L. 33 (1985).

With an estimated net worth of $3.7 billion, President Donald J. Trump was ranked 156 on the Forbes 400 in 2016. Forbes credits Trump's source of wealth as "television" and "real estate," but media reports indicate that he received millions of dollars from his father, whose connections smoothed Trump's entry into the real estate business.

a few, distorting politics and markets; and denies equal opportunity to the poor. "What is the most important for democracy," wrote Alexis de Tocqueville, "is not that there are no great fortunes; it is that great fortunes do not rest in the same hands. In this way, there are the rich, but they do not form a class."[36]

In 2016, the minimum wealth necessary to qualify for the Forbes 400 list of the Richest Americans was $1.7 billion. The top two slots went to Bill Gates (Microsoft) and Jeff Bezos (Amazon), with $81 billion and $67 billion, respectively. The combined wealth of the 400 Richest Americans was $2.4 trillion. Forbes does not include inheritance as a category for source of wealth, but many on the list obviously owe their positions to inherited wealth. Three of the top twenty slots are held by kin of Sam Walton, founder of Wal-Mart, and two are held by kin of Forrest Mars, inventor of M&M's chocolate candy and founder of the Mars candy company.

In thinking about financial inequality, it is important to distinguish between a person's stock of accumulated wealth and the person's income flow. Although *wealth* in the United States is quite concentrated, there is disagreement on the extent, if at all, that this concentration has increased in recent decades. By contrast, *income* inequality has clearly increased, with vast gains for those at the upper end of the income spectrum outpacing modest gains for those at the lower end. The widening inequality in income appears to stem from growing disparities in labor income rather than in capital income.[37] Let us consider what is known about wealth versus income inequality and their relationship to financial inheritance.[38]

Wojciech Kopczuk

*What Do We Know About the Evolution of
Top Wealth Shares in the United States?*

29 J. Econ. Persp. 47 (2015)

Given that the US economy has experienced rising inequality in its income and earning distributions, one would expect that the distribution of wealth would follow a similar path. However, available evidence on this topic is much more scant and conflicting than that on income and earnings. In fact, when Thomas Piketty reports direct estimates of wealth concentration for France, the United Kingdom, Sweden, and the United States in chapter 10 of [Capital in the Twenty-First Century (2014)], he finds as yet little evidence of dramatic increase in wealth concentration in any of these countries. . . .

---

36. 1 Alexis de Tocqueville, Democracy in America: Historical-Critical Edition of De la démocratie en Amérique 85 n.e (Eduardo Nolla ed., James T. Schleifer trans., Liberty Fund 2010) (1835).

37. *See* Steven N. Kaplan & Joshua Rauh, It's the Market: The Broad-Based Rise in the Return to Top Talent, 27 J. Econ. Persp. 35 (2013).

38. Of course, a person's labor income may trace to investment by an earlier generation in the human and cultural capital of the person, a subject we take up in the next section at page 22.

More broadly, as income inequality has grown in recent decades, the nature of wealth inequality has changed. Those in the top 1 percent of the US income and wealth distribution have less reliance on capital income and inherited wealth, and more reliance on income related to labor, than several decades ago. . . .

[W]ealth is . . . highly concentrated. The share of wealth [since the early 1900s] held by the top 10 percent has fluctuated between 65 and 85 percent of total wealth, the share of wealth held by the top 1 percent has ranged between 20 percent and as much as 45 percent of all wealth, and the share of wealth held by the top 0.1 percent ranged between less than 10 percent and as much as 25 percent. . . .

[T]he US distribution of income has not been stable in recent decades. There has been an increasing concentration of earnings over time, especially at the very top of the income distribution. . . . In addition, the nature of top incomes has changed since the 1920s—the last time when the share of income going to the top 1 percent was this high. In recent years, income at the top levels has been dominated by labor income; back in the 1920s, it was dominated by capital income. This change in the sources of income at the top suggests that the relationship between income inequality and wealth inequality has likely changed too.

The importance of inheritance[] as the source of wealth at [the] top of the wealth distribution peaked in the 1970s and has declined since then. . . . These observations suggest that the top of the wealth distribution is in flux. Individuals who are wealthy nowadays are less likely to come from wealth than in the past and more likely to have reached the top through earnings or entrepreneurial success.

Edward N. Wolff & Maury Gittleman
Inheritances and the Distribution of Wealth
or Whatever Happened to the Great Inheritance Boom?
12 J. Econ. Ineq. 439 (2014)

Previous estimates indicate that inheritances and gifts have accounted for about a quarter of total household wealth accumulation in the U.S. . . .

This paper will investigate two main questions. First, have inheritances and other wealth transfers become more important over time? Second, how much, if at all, do inheritances and other wealth transfers contribute to overall wealth inequality? . . .

The results indicate that, over the period from 1989 to 2007, the share of households reporting a wealth transfer fell by 2.5 percentage points. . . . However, the mean value of wealth transfers among recipients climbed over the period, by 23 percent. . . . The average value of inheritances received among *all* households did increase but at a slower pace, by 10 percent. . . . However, wealth transfers as a proportion of current net worth fell sharply over this period from 29 to 19 percent or by 10 percentage points. . . .

Thus, despite the fact that the baby boom generation was reaching "prime" inheritance age and the wealth of their parents was the highest in history for that age group, wealth transfers were less important in accounting for current net worth in 2007 than in 1989. There are several possible explanations. First, the period from 2001 to 2007 was a time of very high capital gains and consequently very rapid wealth growth, particularly because of the boom in housing prices and, to a lesser extent, stock prices. . . .

[T]he strength of capital gains over this period makes inheritances less important as a source of wealth accumulation. Second, life spans rose over this period. Since elderly people were living longer, the number of bequests per year declined. Indeed, richer people tend to live longer than poorer ones and the gap in life expectancies may also have risen over time. This trend would also lower the number of large bequests received per year. Third, as people live longer, their medical expenses might rise as they age and, as a result, less money is transferred to children at time of death. Fourth, the share of estates dedicated to charitable contributions might be rising over time.

With regard to the second major issue . . . , we found that wealth transfers tend to be equalizing in terms of the distribution of household wealth. Indeed, the addition of wealth transfers to other sources of household wealth had a sizeable effect on reducing the inequality of wealth. While it is true that richer households do receive greater wealth transfers than poorer ones, *as a proportion of their current wealth holdings*, wealth transfers are actually greater for poorer households than richer ones.[39]

c. Human and Cultural Capital

Uneven investment in the human capital of children by families and government, particularly in the form of education, is another possible source of inequality in wealth, income, and opportunity.

Stephen J. McNamee & Robert K. Miller, Jr.
The Meritocracy Myth
49, 57-60 (3d ed. 2014)

A common metaphor for the competition to get ahead in life is the foot race. The imagery is that the fastest runner—presumably the most meritorious—will be the one to break the tape at the finish line. But . . . economic competition . . . is more like a relay race in which we inherit a starting point from our parents. The baton is passed, and for a while, both parents and children run together. When the exchange is complete, the children are on their own as they position themselves for the next exchange to the next generation. Although each new runner may gain or lose ground in the competition, each new runner inherits an initial starting point in the race. . . .

Inheritance is more than bulk estates bequeathed to descendants; more broadly defined, it refers to the total impact of initial social-class placement at birth on future life outcomes.[40] Therefore, it is not just the superwealthy who are in a position to pass advantages on to children. Advantages are passed on, in varying degrees, to

---

39. The authors report that for households with a net wealth of $1 million, donative transfers comprised only 18 percent of that wealth. For households with a net wealth between $100,000 and $250,000, donative transfers comprised 26 percent of that wealth.—Eds.

40. For a study of the role of inheritance in "the perpetuation and likely even exacerbation of racial wealth disparities," see Palma Joy Strand, Inheriting Inequality: Wealth, Race, and the Laws of Succession, 89 Or. L. Rev. 453, 468 (2010).—Eds.

*"Meritocracy worked for my grandfather, it worked
for my father, and it's working for me."*

Barbara Smaller/The New Yorker Collection/The Cartoon Bank

all of those from relatively privileged backgrounds. Even minor initial advantages may accumulate during the life course. In this way, existing inequalities are reinforced and extended across generations. . . .

CHILDHOOD QUALITY OF LIFE

Children of the privileged enjoy a high standard of living and quality of life regardless of their individual merit or lack of it. For the privileged, this not only includes high-quality food, clothing, and shelter but also extends to luxuries such as travel, vacations, summer camps, private lessons, and a host of other enrichments and indulgences that wealthy parents and even middle-class parents bestow on their children. These advantages do not just reflect a higher standard during childhood but have important long-term consequences for future life chances. Children raised in privileged settings are much more likely to have better and more rapid physical, cognitive, emotional, and social development, better school readiness, and higher academic achievement. Conversely, children raised in poverty have higher risks for basically everything that is bad that can happen to them as adults later in life—dropping out of school, becoming victims of crime and violence, having more physical and mental health problems, having lower economic prospects, and having greater likelihood of familial disruption. . . .

Knowing with Which Fork to Eat

Cultural capital refers to what one needs to know to function as a member of the various groups to which one belongs. . . . All groups have norms, values, beliefs, ways of life, and codes of conduct that identify a group and define its boundaries. The culture of the group separates insiders from outsiders. Knowing and abiding by these cultural codes of conduct are required to maintain one's status as a member in good standing within the group. By growing up in privilege, children of the elite are socialized into elite ways of life. . . . [C]ultural capital includes, but is not limited to, interpersonal styles and demeanor, manners and etiquette, and vocabulary. Those from more humble backgrounds who aspire to become elites must acquire the cultural cachet to be accepted in elite circles, and this is no easy task. Those born to it, however, have the advantage of acquiring it "naturally" through inheritance, a kind of social osmosis that takes place through childhood socialization.

Having Friends in High Places

. . . Social capital refers to the "value" of whom you know. . . . For the most part, privileged people know other privileged people, and poor people know other poor people. Another nonmerit advantage inherited by children of the wealthy is a network of connections to people of power and influence. These are not connections that children of the rich shrewdly foster or cultivate on their own. The children of the wealthy travel in high-powered social circles; these connections provide access to power, information, and other resources. The difference between rich and poor is not in knowing people; it is in knowing people in positions of power and influence who can do things for you.

Early Withdrawals on the Family Estate

Children of the privileged do not have to wait until their parents die to inherit assets from them. Inter vivos transfers of funds and "gifts" from parents to children can be substantial, and in many cases represent a greater proportion of intergenerational transfers than lump-sum estates at death. Parents provide inter vivos transfers to children to advance their children's current and future economic interests, especially at critical junctures or milestones of the lifecycle. . . . These transfers continue beyond early childhood and include milestone events for adult children such as going to college, getting married, buying a house, and having their own children, or crisis events such as income shocks related to job loss, divorce, or medical crisis. . . .

One of the most common forms of inter vivos gifts is payment for children's education. . . . A few generations ago, children may have inherited the family farm or the family business. With the rise of the modern corporation and the decline of family firms and businesses, inheritance recently takes on more fungible or liquid forms, including cash transfers. Indeed, for many middle-class Americans, education has replaced tangible assets as the primary form by which advantage is passed on between generations.[41]

---

41. *See* John H. Langbein, The Twentieth-Century Revolution in Family Wealth Transmission, 86 Mich. L. Rev. 722 (1988). — Eds.

"How much is that in years of tuition?"
Pat Byrnes/The New Yorker Collection/The Cartoon Bank

NOTE

Investment in Human and Cultural Capital.   Would curtailing economic inheritances limit inequalities in human and cultural capital? Or might it exacerbate inequality by encouraging even more lifetime investment in children and grandchildren? Are there other public policies that might better alleviate inequalities in human and cultural capital? *See* Palma Joy Strand, Education-As-Inheritance Crowds Out Education-As-Opportunity, 59 St. Louis U. L.J. 283 (2015).

The federal tax code privileges investment in human capital by exempting from the gift tax any amount of tuition paid for the education of children, grandchildren, or anyone else (see page 934). Is this a sound tax policy? *See* Kerry A. Ryan, Human Capital and Transfer Taxation, 62 Okla. L. Rev. 223 (2010).

d. A Question of Tax Policy?

Perhaps the most important limit on freedom of disposition is the federal wealth transfer tax system: the *gift, estate,* and *generation-skipping transfer* taxes of the Internal Revenue Code. Although we defer our survey of the mechanics of those taxes until Chapter 15, let us now review briefly their history and current status.[42]

Death duties were known to the Greeks, Romans, and Egyptians, and existed in medieval England. In the early history of the United States, death taxes were levied only temporarily during times of urgent need for revenue. When relations with France

---

42. For a more thorough historical survey, see Louis Eisenstein, The Rise and Decline of the Estate Tax, 11 Tax L. Rev. 223 (1956), from which some of the ensuing discussion draws.

"It's a little less amusing when you hear your kids calling it 'the death tax.'"
William Hamilton/The New Yorker Collection/The Cartoon Bank

deteriorated in 1797, Congress imposed *stamp taxes* on transfers at death, but the taxes disappeared five years later when the revenue crisis passed. During the Civil War, Congress levied an *inheritance tax*—a tax levied on the beneficiary that varies with the beneficiary's closeness of relationship to the decedent—that was promptly repealed after the war. During the 1890s, seeking revenue to finance military encounters with Spain, Congress again imposed an inheritance tax, but then repealed it when the fighting ended.

The *estate tax* as we know it today (see page 943), a tax levied on the transferor's estate that is paid before any transfers are made, did not appear until World War I, again owing to an urgent need for revenue to finance a war. But this time Congress chose not to repeal the tax when the fighting stopped. The tax was retained in part in response to public hostility toward the enormous family fortunes that had been amassed during the "robber baron" era a generation earlier. During the Great Depression, President Franklin D. Roosevelt captured the mood of the country when he declared:

> The desire to provide security for one's self and one's family is natural and wholesome, but it is adequately served by a reasonable inheritance. Great accumulations of wealth cannot be justified on the basis of personal and family security. In the last analysis such accumulations amount to the perpetuation of great and undesirable concentration of control in a relatively few individuals over the employment and welfare of many, many others.
>
> Such inherited economic power is as inconsistent with the ideals of this generation as inherited political power was inconsistent with the ideals of the generation which established our Government.[43]

---

43. H.R. Rep. No. 74-1681, at 2 (1935).

In this way, debate over the proper scope of freedom of disposition, and its role in perpetuating inequality, has become a question of federal tax policy.[44]

In 1932, Congress added the *gift tax* (see page 930) to prevent avoidance of the estate tax (and the income tax) through inter vivos transfers to children and others.[45] During the 1930s and 1940s, Congress kept raising the rates until the maximum estate tax rate reached 77 percent. In 1976, the gift and estate tax systems were unified, so that one rate schedule applied to cumulative gratuitous transfers in excess of a threshold amount, whether the transfer was during life or at death. In 1986, to ensure a wealth transfer tax at each generation, Congress enacted the *generation-skipping transfer tax* (see page 975).

President Franklin D. Roosevelt
Mary Evans Picture Library/Alamy stock photo

The expansion of the federal wealth transfer tax system shifted into reverse in 2001, when Congress passed legislation that phased out the estate tax by raising the threshold for taxation and lowering the tax rate over the following nine years. In 2001, estates in excess of $1 million were taxed at a rate of 55 percent. By 2010, the estate tax disappeared entirely, making 2010 a tax-efficient year in which to die.[46] The 2001 legislation had a sunset clause, however, so that in 2011 the estate tax would return to its 2001 level. But late in 2010, before that clause took effect, Congress passed superseding legislation that imposed a tax in 2011 and 2012 on estates in excess of $5 million at a rate of 35 percent. On New Year's Day 2013, Congress made permanent an estate tax on estates in excess of $5 million (indexed for inflation) at a rate of 40 percent. In 2017, as this book went to press, the inflation-adjusted threshold for taxation was $5.49 million.[47]

In fiscal year 2015, the federal estate tax raised $17 billion, and the gift tax raised $2 billion, for a total of $19 billion—akin to a rounding error in the total $2.9 *trillion* in internal revenue collected by the federal government in that year.[48] Critics argue

---

44. *See* Paul L. Caron, The One-Hundredth Anniversary of the Federal Estate Tax: It's Time to Renew Our Vows, 57 B.C. L. Rev. 823 (2016).

45. *See* Jeffrey A. Cooper, Ghosts of 1932: The Lost History of Estate and Gift Taxation, 9 Fla. Tax Rev. 875 (2010).

46. There is some evidence that death is tax sensitive. Two different studies found changes in death rates around the time of changes in estate tax rules such that living longer or dying sooner would have a substantial tax consequence. As the authors of these studies concede, however, it is possible that some of the observed changes in death timing could reflect tax-motivated fraud in the reporting of the death date. *See* Joshua S. Gans & Andrew Leigh, Did the Death of Australian Inheritance Taxes Affect Deaths?, 6 Topics Econ. Analysis & Pol'y 1 (2006); Wojciech Kopczuk & Joel Slemrod, Dying to Save Taxes: Evidence from Estate-Tax Returns on the Death Elasticity, 85 Rev. Econ. & Stat. 256 (2003).

47. This exemption is worth more than its face value, as a variety of common estate planning techniques leverage the exemption to pass considerable wealth through it. *See, e.g.,* Edward J. McCaffery, Distracted from Distraction by Distraction: Reimagining Estate Tax Reform, 40 Pepp. L. Rev. 1235 (2013).

48. Internal Revenue Service Data Book 3 (2015).

that wealth transfer taxes are more trouble than they are worth, that in effect they are a lawyer tax on the wealthy that distorts lifetime savings and consumption while dulling useful incentives toward productivity. Supporters counter that, even if these taxes do not raise much revenue, they nonetheless add progressivity to the overall tax system, prevent plutocratic wealth concentration, encourage charitable giving, and make up for holes in the taxation of the very wealthy (in particular owing to the step up in basis for unrealized capital gains).[49]

NOTE

Alternatives to the Estate Tax.   Academic commentators tend to support the idea of a tax on inherited wealth, but not necessarily in the form of the current estate tax.[50] These reform proposals have not, however, gained political traction. Professor Madoff summarizes thus:

> We think of the estate tax as the only (or at least the most natural) way of imposing taxes on inheritances, but in fact there are several different systems that can be used. Although the estate and gift tax is imposed on the donor on the basis of the donor's accumulated lifetime and death time transfers, other possibilities exist that shift the focus to the recipient's finances. These include an "accessions tax," which imposes taxes on the recipient on the basis of the amount of gratuitous receipts received during the recipient's lifetime, or an inheritance tax which imposes taxes on the recipient on the amount of gratuitous transfers made, calculated on an annual basis. Still other alternatives involve modifications to the income tax system: either making the transfer of property a realization event for the donor (resulting in capital gains taxes on the gain), or treating gifts and bequests as taxable income to the recipient.
>
> The challenge in considering alternatives to our current tax system is that they need to succeed on many levels in order to be effective. For example, a successful tax system must be: fair (or appear to be fair) to the public at large; manageable for those taxpayers who are subject to it; enforceable by those charged with its enforcement; administrable by those charged with its administration; and consistent with the country's broader societal values.

---

49. *See, e.g.*, David Joulfaian, What Do We Know About the Behavioral Effects of the Estate Tax?, 57 B.C. L. Rev. 843 (2016); James R. Repetti, Democracy, Taxes, and Wealth, 76 N.Y.U. L. Rev. 825 (2001); Edward J. McCaffery, The Uneasy Case for Wealth Transfer Taxation, 104 Yale L.J. 283 (1994); Michael J. Graetz, To Praise the Estate Tax, Not to Bury It, 93 Yale L.J. 259 (1983).

50. *See, e.g.,* David G. Duff, Alternatives to the Gift and Estate Tax, 57 B.C. L. Rev. 893 (2016); Miranda Perry Fleischer, Divide and Conquer: Using an Accessions Tax to Combat Dynastic Wealth Transfers, 57 B.C L. Rev. 913 (2016); David J. Shakow, A Wealth Tax: Taxing the Estates of the Living, 57 B.C. L. Rev. 947 (2016); Goldburn P. Maynard Jr., Addressing Wealth Disparities: Reimagining Wealth Taxation as a Tool for Building Wealth, 92 Denv. U. L. Rev. 145 (2014); Lily L. Batchelder, What Should Society Expect from Heirs? A Proposal for a Comprehensive Inheritance Tax, 63 Tax L. Rev. 1 (2009); Joseph M. Dodge, Replacing the Estate Tax with a Reimagined Accessions Tax, 60 Hastings L.J. 997 (2009).

The tax systems that we currently have—the income tax system and the estate and gift tax system—may not meet all of these ideals, but their sheer familiarity often makes us more accepting of their limitations.[51]

3. From Feudalism to a Constitutional Right

Freedom of disposition has not been a constant across Anglo-American legal history. In the Middle Ages, the disposition of land at death was profoundly restricted by a political and social order that some historians call *feudalism*. In the feudal system, all English land ultimately belonged to the King, who gave various lords the right to use certain lands. In exchange, the lords promised to provide mounted knights and other military assistance (an obligation that was commuted for money payments over the course of the thirteenth century). The lords, in turn, granted these lands to others to use for farming and other purposes upon the tenants' rendering services to the lord.

Under the feudal system, most English land could not be devised. Upon the death of a landholder, the land descended by operation of law, with a one-third life interest, known as *dower*, going to the landowner's widow, and the rest of the fee simple interest going by *male primogeniture* to the landowner's eldest son, known as the *heir*. If the landowner had no sons, the land went to his daughters jointly.[52] Where applicable, this system prohibited a landowner from devising land to someone other than his heir, such as his daughters or younger sons. The main benefit of this system was that it kept ownership of land from becoming fragmented down the generations, which protected the King's ability to enforce the landowner's support obligations.

A second restriction imposed by feudalism was a set of obligations known as the *feudal incidents*, which applied if the land was held by military tenure. These required, among other things, that an heir make a payment to the King (or other feudal lord) when the heir received property by descent from his father, and gave the King the right to hold the land while the heir was a minor and to dictate whom an heiress would marry if she was unmarried.

At a time when most wealth consisted of inherited land, primogeniture and the feudal incidents imposed heavy burdens. As we shall see in Chapter 6 at page 386, English landowners eventually learned to avoid these burdens by way of the *use*, an early form of the *trust*. The use, which first appeared in the fourteenth century, allowed a landowner to transfer his property during his lifetime to third parties known as *feoffees to uses*, predecessors to our modern *trustees*, to hold the property for the

---

51. Ray D. Madoff, Considering Alternatives: Are There Methods Other Than the Estate and Gift Tax That Could Better Address Problems Associated with Wealth Concentration?, 57 B.C. L. Rev. 883, 886-87 (2016).

52. Male primogeniture is thus to be distinguished from the *fee tail male*, known to many by way of Jane Austen and Downton Abbey, under which a nephew or male cousin would succeed to land rather than a daughter. We take up the fee tail in connection with our treatment of the Rule Against Perpetuities in Chapter 14 at page 888.

landowner and his family during the landowner's life, and then upon the landowner's death to pass the property as the landowner had directed. Because primogeniture and the feudal incidents only applied when land descended from father to son by operation of law, transfer by way of feoffees to uses avoided these restrictions on testation.

In 1536, Parliament and King Henry VIII tried to prohibit the use through the Statute of Uses. Landowners fought back, however, and dissatisfaction with Henry's policies threatened the stability of the kingdom. Henry relented, allowing Parliament to pass the Statute of Wills in 1540. This statute gave a landowner the ability to dispose of two-thirds of his land by will free from the requirements of primogeniture and the feudal incidents. Over the next two centuries, primogeniture and the feudal incidents were eventually abolished by statute, with all land becoming freely devisable in the 1660s.[53]

England's history of restricted testation persuaded many thinkers in the eighteenth and nineteenth centuries that the disposition of property at death was not a right given by nature or the common law, and therefore that it could be restricted by statute. Blackstone, for example, took the view that inheritance was "certainly a wise and effectual, but clearly a political, establishment; since the permanent right of property, vested in the ancestor himself, was no *natural*, but merely a *civil* right."[54] In England and the United States, a married woman could not devise land without the consent of her husband until the Married Women's Property Acts of the mid- to late nineteenth century.

As late as the 1980s, the right to dispose property at death was generally thought not to be a natural right and certainly not one that was constitutionally protected. In Irving Trust Co. v. Day, 314 U.S. 556 (1942), the Supreme Court put the point thus:

> Rights of succession to the property of a deceased, whether by will or by intestacy, are of statutory creation, and the dead hand rules succession only by sufferance. Nothing in the Federal Constitution forbids the legislature of a state to limit, condition, or even abolish the power of testamentary disposition over property within its jurisdiction.

But in the 1980s, when the Court revived its interest in protecting private property through the Takings Clause of the Fifth Amendment,[55] the Court took a different view. In Hodel v. Irving, 481 U.S. 704 (1987), the Court invalidated § 207 of the Indian Land Consolidation Act, enacted in 1983, which prohibited the devise or inheritance of small fractional shares of land allotted to Native Americans. Over time, "as successive generations came to hold the allotted lands," what started as "40-, 80-, and 160-acre parcels became splintered into multiple undivided interests in land, with some parcels having hundreds and many parcels having dozens of owners."

---

53. For further reading, see J.H. Baker, An Introduction to English Legal History 223-80 (4th ed. 2002); J.M.W. Bean, The Decline of English Feudalism, 1215-1540, at 1-220 (1968); John H. Langbein et al., History of the Common Law 299-311 (2009); A.W.B. Simpson, A History of the Land Law 175-76 (2d ed. 1986).

54. 2 William Blackstone, Commentaries *11-13.

55. The Takings Clause reads as follows: "nor shall private property be taken for public use, without just compensation." U.S. Const. amend. V.

Section 207 provided that, instead of continued fractionation of these lands down the generations,[56] they
would escheat to the tribe whose land it was before the allot-
ment. In an opinion by Justice Sandra Day O'Connor, the
Court held that this provision worked a taking of property
for which the Fifth Amendment requires just compensation.
The Court reasoned that the owner's right to devise property
at death, like the right to exclude, is a significant aspect of
property ownership:

> [T]he character of the Government regulation here
> is extraordinary. . . . [T]he regulation here amounts to
> virtually the abrogation of the right to pass on a certain
> type of property—the small undivided interest—to
> one's heirs. In one form or another, the right to pass
> on property—to one's family in particular—has been
> part of the Anglo-American legal system since feudal
> times.[57] The fact that it may be possible for the owners

Justice Sandra Day O'Connor

of these interests to effectively control disposition upon death through complex
inter vivos transactions such as revocable trusts, is simply not an adequate substitute for the rights taken, given the nature of the property. Even the United States
concedes that total abrogation of the right to pass property is unprecedented and
likely unconstitutional. . . .

In holding that complete abolition of both the descent and devise of a particular class of property may be a taking, we reaffirm the continuing vitality of
the long line of cases recognizing the States', and where appropriate, the United
States', broad authority to adjust the rules governing the descent and devise of
property without implicating the guarantees of the Just Compensation Clause.
See, e.g., Irving Trust Co. v. Day, 314 U.S. 556, 562 (1942). The difference in this
case is the fact that both descent and devise are completely abolished; indeed they
are abolished even in circumstances when the governmental purpose sought to be
advanced, consolidation of ownership of Indian lands, does not conflict with the
further descent of the property.

There is little doubt that the extreme fractionation of Indian lands is a serious
public problem. It may well be appropriate for the United States to ameliorate fractionation by means of regulating the descent and devise of Indian lands. Surely it is
permissible for the United States to prevent the owners of such interests from further subdividing them among future heirs on pain of escheat. It may be appropriate
to minimize further compounding of the problem by abolishing the descent of such
interests by rules of intestacy, thereby forcing the owners to formally designate an
heir to prevent escheat to the Tribe. What is certainly not appropriate is to take the

---

56. In the contemporary property literature, commentators would call this an "anticommons"
problem. *See* Michael A. Heller, The Tragedy of the Anticommons: Property in the Transition from
Marx to Markets, 111 Harv. L. Rev. 621, 685-87 (1998).

57. Since *feudal times*, did you say? See page 29.—Eds.

extraordinary step of abolishing both descent and devise of these property interests even when the passing of the property to the heir might result in consolidation of property. Accordingly, we find that this regulation, in the words of Justice Holmes, "goes too far." Pennsylvania Coal Co. v. Mahon, 260 U.S. 393, 415 (1922).

NOTES

1. Nonprobate Transfers.   The Court's analysis in *Hodel* rests on the assumption that the right to transmit property at death is a separate, identifiable stick in the bundle of rights called property. If this right is taken away, compensation must be paid. But as the Court observed, the owners of the affected interests could direct the distribution of those interests at death "through complex inter vivos transactions such as revocable trusts," not unlike how feudal landowners avoided primogeniture and the feudal incidents by way of the use. The Court concluded, however, that these transfers are "not an adequate substitute for the rights taken." Was this conclusion well founded? Today more property passes at death by way of *will substitutes*, including revocable trusts, than in probate by will or intestacy. Nonprobate succession by will substitute is often simpler, cheaper, and more expeditious than probate succession by will or intestacy. We take notice of nonprobate succession later in this chapter at page 40 and give extended treatment to it in Chapter 7.

2. Forced Shares.   In most countries, such as those on the continent of Europe, a child is entitled to a minimum forced share in the estate of a parent. In the twentieth century, statutes were enacted across the United States giving a surviving spouse a *forced share*, typically one-third, of the decedent spouse's estate. Today all separate property states except Georgia provide a forced share to a surviving spouse (see Chapter 8). Are these statutes vulnerable to challenge as takings of property? Spousal forced shares were upheld in In re Estate of Magee, 988 So. 2d 1 (Fla. App. 2007), and Hamilton v. Hamilton, 879 S.W.2d 416 (Ark. 1994).

Although the statute at issue in *Hodel* spoke of "escheat" to the tribe, in effect the statute made the tribe the successor to the Native American owner of the affected fractioned land. Why is forced succession by a spouse permissible but forced succession by a tribe not permissible?

3. Transfer Taxes.   In New York Trust Co. v. Eisner, 256 U.S. 345 (1921), the Supreme Court upheld the constitutionality of the estate tax. In Bromley v. McCaughn, 280 U.S. 124 (1929), the Court upheld the gift tax. But neither case was litigated under the Takings Clause. After *Hodel*, would a confiscatory estate tax pass constitutional muster? *Compare* Kane v. United States, 942 F. Supp. 233 (E.D. Pa. 1996) (upholding retroactive increase in estate tax from 50 to 55 percent), *with* Richard A. Epstein, Takings: Private Property and the Power of Eminent Domain 303-05 (1985) (arguing that the estate tax is an unconstitutional taking).

4. The Antebellum South.   For a fascinating study of the legal minefield of devising property to slaves in the antebellum South, see Adrienne D. Davis, The Private Law

of Race and Sex: An Antebellum Perspective, 51 Stan. L. Rev. 221 (1999). The fundamental challenge was to uphold testamentary freedom without disrupting racial hier-
archies. Professor Davis examines the wills of white men who devised property to their
children borne by slave women, or to the slave women themselves, and the tensions and
contradictions in legal doctrine these devises caused.[58]

4. Posthumously Created Property Rights

In Hodel v. Irving, page 30, the Supreme Court held that the Fifth Amendment curtailed the power of the government to limit the right to pass property at death. But
what of a posthumous award of additional property rights? How is such property to
be distributed?

Shaw Family Archives Ltd. v. CMG Worldwide, Inc.
486 F. Supp. 2d 309 (S.D.N.Y. 2007)

McMAHON, J. . . . Marilyn Monroe, perhaps the most famous American sex symbol of
the twentieth century, died testate on August 5, 1962. Her will, which did not expressly
bequeath a right of publicity, contained the following residuary clause:

> SIXTH: All the rest, residue and remainder of my estate, both real and personal
> of whatsoever nature and whatsoever situate, of which I shall die seized or possessed
> or to which I shall be in any way entitled, or over which I shall possess any power of
> appointment by Will at the time of my death, including any lapsed legacies, I give,
> devise and bequeath as follows:
> (a) To MAY REIS the sum of $40,000 or 25% of the total remainder of my
> estate, whichever shall be the lesser.
> (b) To DR. MARIANNE KRIS 25% of the balance thereof, to be used by her
> [for the furtherance of the work of such psychiatric institutions or groups as she
> shall select]. . . .
> (c) To LEE STRASBERG the entire remaining balance.

The will also named Aaron Frosch, Ms. Monroe's New York-based attorney, as the
executor. It was subject to primary probate in New York County Surrogate's Court.

In 1968, six years after probate of the Monroe Estate had commenced, Lee Strasberg
married Anna Strasberg.[59] Lee Strasberg died in 1982, leaving his wife Anna Strasberg
as the sole beneficiary under his will. Upon the death of Mr. Frosch in 1989, the New
York Surrogate's Court appointed Anna Strasberg as Administratrix . . . of the Monroe
Estate. The Monroe Estate remained open until June 19, 2001, on which date the

---

58. For more on race and testation in the antebellum South, see Alfred L. Brophy & Douglas Thie,
Land, Slaves, and Bonds: Trust and Probate in the Pre-Civil War Shenandoah Valley, 119 W. Va. L. Rev.
345 (2016); Bernie D. Jones, Fathers of Conscience: Mixed-Race Inheritance in the Antebellum South
(2009); Kevin Noble Maillard, The Color of Testamentary Freedom, 62 SMU L. Rev. 1783 (2009).
59. For more on Lee Strasberg, see page 422.—Eds.

Surrogate's Court authorized the Administratrix to close the estate and transfer the residuary assets to MMLLC [Marilyn Monroe, LLC], a Delaware company formed by Ms. Strasberg to hold and manage the intellectual property assets of the residuary beneficiaries of Marilyn Monroe's will.

SFA [Shaw Family Archives, LLC] is a limited liability company organized under New York law with its primary place of business in New York. Its principals are the three children of the late photographer Sam Shaw. Among the photographs owned by SFA and comprising the Shaw Collection is a series of photographs of Marilyn Monroe, including many "canonical" Marilyn images. The copyrights to the Marilyn photographs are purportedly owned by Sam Shaw's daughters, Edith Marcus and Meta Stevens.

This dispute arises out of (1) the alleged sale of a T-shirt at a Target retail store in Indianapolis, Indiana on September 6, 2006, which bore a picture of Marilyn Monroe and the inscription of the "Shaw Family Archives" on the inside neck label and tag, and (2) the alleged maintenance of a website by SFA and Bradford [Licensing] through which customers could purchase licenses for the use of Ms. Monroe's picture, image and likeness on various commercial products. MMLLC asserts that it is the successor-in-interest to the postmortem right of publicity that was devised through the residuary clause of Ms. Monroe's will, and that the commercial use of Ms. Monroe's picture, image, and likeness by SFA and Bradford without MMLLC's consent violates its rights under Indiana's 1994 Right of Publicity Act. This statute, passed over three decades after Ms. Monroe's death, by a state with which she had (as far as the court is aware) absolutely no contact during her life, creates a descendible and freely transferable right of publicity that survives for 100 years after a personality's death. The statute purports to apply to an act or event that occurs within Indiana, regardless of a personality's domicile, residence, or citizenship. See Ind. Code §§ 32-36-1-1 to -20 (2007). . . .

Marilyn Monroe
Frank Powolny/MPTV

DISCUSSION

In their cross-motion for summary judgment, the SFA parties [SFA and Bradford] argue, *inter alia,* that even if a postmortem right of publicity in Marilyn Monroe's name, likeness and persona exists, MMLLC and CMG [Worldwide, Inc.] cannot demonstrate that they are the owners of that right because only property actually owned by a testator at the time of her death can be devised by will. Since neither New York nor California (the only possible domiciles of Ms. Monroe at the time of her death) — nor for that matter, Indiana — recognized descendible postmortem publicity rights at the time of Ms. Monroe's death in 1962, she could not transfer any such rights through her will, and MMLLC cannot be a successor-in-interest to them. Moreover, the SFA parties contend, neither the California nor the Indiana right of publicity statutes allow for the transfer of the publicity rights they recognize through the wills of personalities who were already deceased at the time of their enactment. The court agrees.

1. *Ms. Monroe did not have the testamentary capacity to devise property rights she did not own at the time of her death.*

MMLLC argues that its ownership interest in Ms. Monroe's postmortem right of publicity—assuming *arguendo* that such a right exists—stems from Ms. Monroe's valid devise of this right to Lee Strasberg through the residuary clause in her will. The court concludes—regardless of Ms. Monroe's domicile at the time of her death, and regardless of any rights purportedly conferred after her death by the Indiana Right of Publicity Act or by Cal. Civil Code § 3344.1 (2007)—Ms. Monroe could not devise by will a property right she did not own at the time of her death in 1962.

Descendible postmortem publicity rights were not recognized, in New York, California, or Indiana at the time of Ms. Monroe's death in 1962. To this day, New York law does not recognize any common law right of publicity and limits its statutory publicity rights to living persons. California recognized descendible publicity rights when it passed its postmortem right of publicity statute in 1984, 22 years after Ms. Monroe's death. Prior to that time, a common law right of publicity existed, but it was not freely transferable or descendible. Indiana first recognized a descendible, postmortem right of publicity in 1994, when it passed the Indiana Right of Publicity Act. See Ind. Code §§ 32-36-1-1 to -20. Prior to that time, rights of publicity were inalienable in Indiana, since they could only be vindicated through a personal tort action for invasion of privacy.

Thus, at the time of her death in 1962 Ms. Monroe did not have any postmortem right of publicity under the law of any relevant state. As a result, any publicity rights she enjoyed during her lifetime were extinguished at her death by operation of law.

Nevertheless, MMLLC argues that her will should be construed as devising postmortem publicity rights that were later conferred on Ms. Monroe by statute. Such a construction is untenable.

Indiana follows the majority rule that the law of the domicile of the testator at his or her death applies to all questions of a will's construction. There are disputed issues of fact concerning whether Ms. Monroe was domiciled in New York or California at the time of her death. (There is absolutely no doubt that she was not domiciled in Indiana.) However, it is not necessary to resolve the question of domicile because neither New York nor California—the only two states in which Ms. Monroe could conceivably have been domiciled—permitted a testator to dispose by will of property she does not own at the time of her death.

It is well-settled that, under New York law, "A disposition by the testator of all his property passes all of the property he was entitled to dispose of *at the time of his death.*" N.Y. Est. Powers & Trusts Law § 3-3.1 (2007) (emphasis added). The corollary principle recognized by the courts is that property not owned by the testator at the time of his death is not subject to disposition by will. . . .

California law does not differ from New York's. Section 21105 of the California Probate Code provides that, . . . "A will passes all property *the testator owns at death,* including property acquired after execution of the will." (emphasis added). . . .

Nor does § 2-602 of the Uniform Probate Code, which states that a will may pass "property acquired by the estate after the testator's death," have anything to do with the present case, because neither New York nor California is among the 18 states that have adopted the Uniform Probate Code in whole or even in part.[60] This court has not found, nor has MMLLC cited, any provision in either the New York or the California probate laws that codifies § 2-602. . . .

Even if, as MMLLC implies, there has been some recent shift away from the unequivocal rule that only property owned by the testator at the time of death can be passed by will (as evidenced by § 2-602 of the Uniform Probate Code), it does not help MMLLC's cause. "Testamentary disposition . . . is controlled by the law in effect *as of the date of death.*" Dep't of Health Services v. Fontes, 215 Cal. Rptr. 14, 15 (App. 1985) (emphasis added). There is no question — based on the case law recited above — that at the time of Ms. Monroe's death in 1962, neither New York nor California permitted a testator to dispose by will of property she did not own at the time of her death. Any argument that the residuary clause of Ms. Monroe's will could devise a postmortem right of publicity is thus doubly doomed because the law in effect at the time of Ms. Monroe's death did not recognize descendible postmortem publicity rights and did not allow for distribution under a will of property not owned by the testator at the time of her death.

2. Ms. Monroe did not "intend" to devise any rights she may have acquired under the Indiana or California right of publicity statute through the residuary clause of her will.

MMLLC argues that Marilyn Monroe intended to bequeath a postmortem right of publicity to her testamentary legatees. The argument is unpersuasive. . . . MMLLC makes much of Ms. Monroe's purported intent to include in her residuary estate all property "to which [she] shall be in any way entitled." In the absence of any other evidence concerning Ms. Monroe's intent, this boilerplate language is much too slender a reed on which to hang a devise of postmortem publicity rights that did not come into being until 22 years after her death. . . .

Even if the language Ms. Monroe employed clearly demonstrated her intent to devise property she had no capacity to devise, the effect would be to render the disposition invalid, because she had no legal right to dispose of property that did not exist at the time of her death. . . .

3. Neither the California nor the Indiana postmortem right of publicity statutes allows for testamentary disposition of the rights it recognizes by celebrities already deceased at the time of its enactment.

. . . MMLLC's case is doomed because both the California and Indiana postmortem right of publicity statutes recognize that an individual cannot pass by will a statutory property right that she did not possess at the time of her death. California's Civ. Code § 3344.1(b)-(d) provides that, if no transfer of a personality's postmortem right of

---

60. The comment to UPC § 2-602 (1990) explains: "This section is revised to assure that . . . a residuary clause in a will . . . passes property acquired by a testator's estate after his or her death." — Eds.

publicity has occurred before the personality's death, either "by contract or by means of a trust or testamentary documents," then the rights vest in certain statutorily specified heirs. Since a testamentary transfer has no effect until the testator's death, such a transfer could not be effectuated "before death" for purposes of the California statute. Thus, any rights bestowed by § 3344.1 on a personality already deceased at the time of its enactment could not be transferred by will (which is how the purported property right came to MMLLC from the Administratrix at the time the Monroe Estate wound up). It would vest instead in the persons provided for by statute.

The Indiana statute likewise provides that if a personality has not transferred her right of publicity by "contract," "license," "gift," "trust," or "testamentary document," the right will "vest" in those individuals entitled to her property through the "[o]peration of the laws of intestate succession applicable to the state administering the estate and property of the intestate deceased personality, regardless of whether the state recognizes the property rights set forth under this chapter." See Ind. Code §§ 32-36-1-16 to -18. Ms. Monroe's legatees under her will are not her statutory heirs for intestacy purposes.

Thus, even if a postmortem right of publicity in Marilyn Monroe's persona could have been created after her death, neither of the statutes that arguably bestowed that right allows for it to be transferred through the will of a "personality" who, like Ms. Monroe, was already deceased at the time of the statute's enactment. To the extent that other courts, including Joplin Enterprises v. Allen, 795 F. Supp. 349 (W.D. Wash. 1992) and Miller v. Glenn Miller Productions, 318 F. Supp. 2d 923 (C.D. Cal. 2004), assumed without explicitly deciding that California's right of publicity statute allows for the disposition of the rights it recognizes through wills of personalities already deceased at the time of its enactment, and that such disposition is permissible under the applicable probate principles, this court respectfully disagrees.

CONCLUSION

MMLLC's motion for summary judgment . . . is denied, and SFA's cross-motion for summary judgment . . . is granted.

NOTES

1. Posthumously Acquired Property. Suppose *T* dies owning Blackacre. *T* has one intestate heir, *X*, but before dying *T* executed a will giving all of *T*'s property to *Y*. Blackacre will pass under the will to *Y*. Two years later, *A* dies, leaving Whiteacre "to *T* if *T* survives me, but if *T* does not survive me, then to *T*'s estate." Who takes Whiteacre, *X* or *Y*? The issue is whether *T*'s will controls the disposition of property not owned by *T* at death but subsequently acquired by *T*'s estate. If *T*'s will controls, *Y* takes as the residuary beneficiary under the will. If not, *X* takes as *T*'s intestate heir. In In re Estate of Braman, 258 A.2d 492 (Pa. 1969), the court held that property subsequently acquired by *T*'s estate passed to *X*, the intestate heir, rather than to *Y*, the residuary devisee. The theory, as in *Shaw*, was that *T* lacked the power to control the disposition of property acquired after *T*'s death.

But would not both *T* and *A* prefer Whiteacre to pass under *T*'s will rather than by intestacy? Uniform Probate Code § 2-602 (Unif. Law Comm'n 1990), discussed in

Shaw, rejects *Braman*. It provides that all property owned at death as well as "all property acquired by the estate after the testator's death" pass under the testator's will. UPC § 3-1008 provides for subsequent administration if additional property of the estate is discovered after probate has closed.

2. Marilyn Monroe, California, and New York. Five months after the decision in *Shaw*, Arnold Schwarzenegger, then governor of California, signed legislation that amended the California publicity statute thus:

> (b) The rights recognized under this section are property rights, freely transferable or descendible, in whole or in part, by contract or by means of any trust or any other testamentary instrument, executed before or after January 1, 1985. The rights recognized under this section shall be deemed to have existed at the time of death of any deceased personality who died prior to January 1, 1985, and . . . shall vest in the persons entitled to these property rights under the testamentary instrument of the deceased personality effective as of the date of his or her death. In the absence of an express transfer in a testamentary instrument of the deceased personality's rights . . . , a provision in the testamentary instrument that provides for the disposition of the residue of the deceased personality's assets shall be effective to transfer the rights recognized under this section in accordance with the terms of that provision. The rights established by this section shall also be freely transferable or descendible by contract, trust, or any other testamentary instrument by any subsequent owner of the deceased personality's rights as recognized by this section. . . .

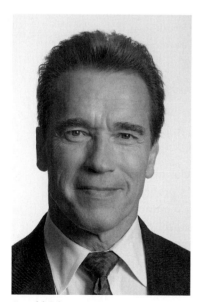

Arnold Schwarzenegger

> (p) The rights recognized by this section are expressly made retroactive, including to those deceased personalities who died before January 1, 1985.[61]

As amended, the California statute recognizes a posthumous right of publicity that is devisable at death, even by a general residuary clause in a will made before the statute was enacted. The session law explains the purpose of the amendment: "It is the intent of the Legislature to abrogate the summary judgment order[] entered in . . . Shaw Family Archives Ltd. v. CMG Worldwide."[62]

But for Marilyn Monroe, or rather for the successors to Lee Strasberg, her residuary devisee, the amendment was enacted by the wrong state. In Milton H. Greene Archives, Inc. v. Marilyn Monroe LLC, 692 F.3d 983 (9th Cir. 2012), the Ninth Circuit held that Monroe died a domiciliary of New York. Generally speaking, the law of the state where a decedent was domiciled at death governs the disposition of personal property, and the law of the state where the decedent's real property is located governs the disposition of real property. Consequently, New York rather than

---

61. Cal. Civ. Code § 3344.1 (2016).
62. 2007 Cal. Legis. Serv. Ch. 439 § 2 (S.B. 771).

California law governed Monroe's posthumous publicity rights, and New York does not recognize a descendible right of publicity.

3. A Descendible Right of Publicity and the Dead Hand. What is the policy basis for a descendible right of publicity? Is such a right needed to give celebrities an incentive to work hard and make useful contributions to society? Or is the right justified by a labor theory of property such that it would be unjust for someone other than the celebrity to profit from the celebrity's name or likeness? What are the social costs of dead hand control over one's likeness? Don't many celebrities owe aspects of their public personas to the celebrities of a prior generation? Don't Lady Gaga and Britney Spears owe a debt to Madonna, who in turn owes a debt to Marilyn Monroe?[63]

Who profits from the right of publicity? Monroe's successors have lobbied the New York legislature to adopt a posthumous right of publicity. Martin Sheen, Liza Minnelli, Al Pacino, and relatives of Babe Ruth, Jackie Robinson, and Mickey Mantle joined in the effort.[64]

Some celebrities support a descendible right of publicity so that they can prohibit use of their name and likeness after death. But wouldn't a descendible right of publicity be a valuable asset subject to estate taxation at death?[65] Would a tax on the value of a celebrity's name and likeness compel the celebrity's successors to exploit them commercially even if the celebrity's intention was to prevent just that? Robin Williams, the Academy Award winning actor and comedian who died in 2014, left his right of publicity to a charitable entity but also prohibited exploitation of that right for 25 years. Adam Yauch, one of the original Beastie Boys, died in 2012 with a will that, in a clause he added by hand, prohibited use of his "music or any artistic property" for advertising.

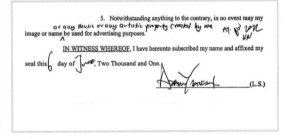

Provision of Robin Williams's trust concerning his right of publicity

Provision of Adam Yauch's will prohibiting use of his "music or any artistic property" for advertising

---

63. *See* Madoff, *supra* note 7, at 136-41; Joshua C. Tate, Immortal Fame: Publicity Rights, Taxation, and the Power of Testation, 44 Ga. L. Rev. 1 (2009); William A. Drennan, Wills, Trusts, Schadenfreude, and the Wild, Wacky Right of Publicity: Exploring the Enforceability of Dead-Hand Restrictions, 58 Ark. L. Rev. 43 (2005).

64. *See* James T. Madore, Celebrities Seek Shield After Death, Newsday, June 12, 2008, at A18.

65. *See* Bridget J. Crawford, Joshua C. Tate, Mitchell M. Gans & Jonathan G. Blattmachr, Celebrity, Death, and Taxes: Michael Jackson's Estate, 125 Tax Notes 345 (2009); Ray D. Madoff, Taxing Personhood: Estate Taxes and the Compelled Commodification of Identity, 17 Va. Tax Rev. 759 (1998).

B. THE MECHANICS OF SUCCESSION

1. Probate and Nonprobate Property

One court in each county has jurisdiction over the administration of a decedent's estate. The name of this court varies across jurisdictions. It may be called the surrogate's court, the orphan's court, the probate division of the district court or chancery court, or something else. But all of these courts are referred to collectively as *probate courts*. To go through *probate* is to have an estate administered in a probate court. For this reason, property that passes under a decedent's *will* (see Chapters 3 through 5) or by *intestacy* (see Chapter 2) is said to be *probate property*.

There was a time when probate was the only readily available way to transfer property with clear title at a person's death. However, because probate developed a reputation for being slow, cumbersome, and expensive, banks and other financial intermediaries developed nonprobate alternatives. Today much more property passes by nonprobate transfer via a *will substitute* than by probate transfer via a will or intestacy.[66] Property that passes by will substitute outside of probate is said to be *nonprobate property*.

     a. Inter Vivos Trust.   When property is put in trust, the trustee holds it for the benefit of one or more beneficiaries (see Chapters 6 and 9 through 14). The trustee distributes the property to the beneficiaries in accordance with the terms of the trust. Property held in a *testamentary trust* created under the decedent's will passes through probate, but property put in an *inter vivos* trust during the decedent's life passes in accordance with the terms of the trust, avoiding probate administration. Because the trustee holds legal title to the trust property, there is no need to change title by probate administration upon the death of the settlor. In contemporary practice, the inter vivos trust is generally preferred over the testamentary trust.

     b. Pay-on-Death (POD) and Transfer-on-Death (TOD) Contracts.   Today bank, brokerage, mutual fund, and pension and other retirement accounts commonly allow for a POD or TOD beneficiary designation under which the account custodian distributes the property at the decedent's death to the named beneficiary. To collect property held under a POD or TOD arrangement, all the beneficiary need do is file a death certificate with the custodian.

     c. Life Insurance.   The proceeds of a life insurance policy on the decedent's life are paid by the insurance company to the beneficiary named in the insurance

---

66. *See* Russell N. James III, The New Statistics of Estate Planning: Lifetime and Post-Mortem Wills, Trusts, and Charitable Planning, 8 Est. Plan. & Community Prop. L.J. 1, 27-28 (2015) (reporting extensive survey evidence showing predominance of nonprobate transfer); *see also* David Horton, In Partial Defense of Probate: Evidence from Alameda County, California 103 Geo. L.J. 605, 627 (2015) (estimating that only 7 percent of 2007 decedents in Alameda, California left probate estates, inferring that "desire for probate avoidance is more vociferous than ever").

contract. The company pays upon receipt of a death certificate of the insured. Life insurance is thus a form of POD contract that operates independently of probate administration.

d. Joint Tenancy.   Under the theory of joint tenancy, the decedent's interest vanishes at death. The survivor owns the whole property free of the decedent's interest. In order for the survivor to perfect title to jointly held real estate, the survivor need only file a death certificate with the local registrar of deeds. To perfect title over a joint bank or brokerage account, the survivor need only file a death certificate with the bank or broker.

The rise of nonprobate succession raises thorny questions of law and policy. Should the rules for the making of a valid will, which include a variety of execution formalities, be required of a will substitute? Should substantive limits on testation by will, such as rules protecting creditors and the spousal forced share, apply to a will substitute? Should the rules of construction developed in the law of wills apply to a will substitute? We give these and related questions extended treatment in our coverage of nonprobate transfers in Chapter 7.

Although nonprobate succession has become the norm, probate administration remains important. If a decedent did not arrange his affairs during life so that all of his property passes by nonprobate transfer and his family cannot divide up the property in private, probate administration fills the gap. If a dispute or other difficulty arises for a nonprobate transfer, the probate system will be called upon to resolve the matter. If cutting off the rights of creditors is important, probate may be desirable for its non-claim statutes, which bar claims not brought within a short period, typically one year after the decedent's death.

2. Probate Terminology

When a person dies and probate is necessary, the first step is the appointment of a *personal representative* to wind up the decedent's affairs. The personal representative is a *fiduciary* who collects and inventories the property of the decedent; manages and protects the property during the administration of the estate; processes the claims of creditors and files federal and state tax returns; and distributes the property to those entitled. The powers of a personal representative relate back to actions taken prior to the representative's formal appointment by the court, such as locating and securing the decedent's valuables immediately upon her demise.[67]

---

67. *See* UPC § 3-701 (1997). A particular difficulty involves securing the decedent's firearms without violating rules on firearm possession. *See* Lee-ford Tritt, Dispatches from the Trenches of America's Great Gun Trust Wars, 108 Nw. U. L. Rev. 743 (2014).

Probate in the Digital Age: What of Digital Assets?

There was a time when a personal representative could figure out how to wind up a decedent's financial affairs by reviewing the decedent's files and monitoring the decedent's mail for bills, bank statements, and the like. But today many people receive their bills and banking statements online and correspond with clients, customers, and others by email. Without access to the decedent's email accounts and digital records, which are typically password protected, how is the personal representative to wind up the decedent's affairs?

A related difficulty arises for a decedent's photos, music, writings, and other treasured possessions that increasingly exist only in digital form. Such possessions may be of tremendous value to the decedent's survivors, and sometimes they have substantial market value too. Authors, artists, and other makers of content are today increasingly inclined to keep their work in digital rather than physical form. Digital currencies, such as Bitcoin, likewise exist only in electronic rather than tangible physical form.

The problem of reconciling fiduciary administration for a deceased (or incapacitated) person with the rise of digital assets has caught the attention of law reformers. In 2014, the Uniform Law Commission promulgated a Uniform Fiduciary Access to Digital Assets Act (UFADAA). The premise of UFADAA as originally drafted was asset neutrality—the act treated digital assets like physical ones. Just as a personal representative can access a decedent's physical property and receive the decedent's physical mail, so too under UFADAA the representative could access the decedent's digital assets and email.

Privacy advocates and the tech industry objected on several grounds. First, they argued that digital assets are qualitatively different. For example, many email systems archive rather than delete old messages. UFADAA would therefore give a decedent's representative access to perhaps decades of old correspondence, in comparison to receiving paper mail on a going-forward basis. Second, critics argued that UFADAA would override any term in the decedent's service agreement with the digital service provider that provided for deletion of digital assets at the user's death, abridging the parties' freedom of contract. Third, critics argued that federal privacy laws, in particular the Electronic Communications Act of 1986, prohibit disclosure of the content of email and other digital assets without actual consent, in comparison to the default of implied consent under UFADAA.

In response to these criticisms, in 2015 the Uniform Law Commission promulgated a Revised

"User name and password?"
Arnie Levin/The New Yorker Collection/The Cartoon Bank

Uniform Fiduciary Access to Digital Assets Act (RUFADAA). Under RUFADAA, a personal representative may not access the *content* of a decedent's electronic communications without the decedent's consent as expressed in a will, trust, power of attorney, or other such writing, or via an online tool created by the service provider. However, the representative will have access to *records* of the decedent's electronic communications, such as the dates and times of messages and the addresses for the senders and recipients. In most cases, these records should be sufficient for the representative to gather information critical to winding up the decedent's affairs. The representative will also have access to the decedent's other digital assets that are otherwise accessible and not protected by federal privacy laws, such as digital currency and those stored on a hard drive or private server.

Under RUFADAA, a person retains autonomy to direct the posthumous disposition of her digital assets in accordance with the following hierarchy. First priority is given to a person's specific direction for a specific account as recorded by a specific online tool created by the service provider. A physical-world analogy is to a beneficiary designation in a pay-on-death or transfer-on-death bank or brokerage account. Second priority is given to the person's direction in a will, trust, power of attorney, or other such writing. Third priority is given to the terms-of-service agreement governing the account. If the agreement is silent with respect to fiduciary access and the user has provided no direction, RUFADAA's default rules apply. Accordingly, if the agreement prohibits third-party or fiduciary access, and the user has provided no direction, the fiduciary will have no access to the account.

As this book went to press in early 2017, already 21 states had adopted a version of RUFADAA.

If a decedent dies with a *will*, she is said to die *testate*. If a testate decedent in her will names the person who is to execute (i.e., to carry out the terms of) the will and administer the probate estate, such personal representative is usually called an *executor*.[68] If the will does not name an executor, the named executor is unable or unwilling to serve, or the decedent dies *intestate*, the court will name a personal representative who is generally called an *administrator*. The administrator is usually selected from a statutory list of persons who are given preference, typically in the following order: surviving spouse, children, parents, siblings, and creditors.

As far back as the records go, the words *will* and *testament* have been used interchangeably. Professor David Mellinkoff believes the phrase *last will and testament* is traceable to the law's habit of doubling English words with synonyms of French or Latin origin (e.g., *had and received, mind and memory, free and clear*), "helped along by a distinctive rhythm."[69]

A person dying testate was said to *devise* real property to *devisees* and to *bequeath* personal property (a legacy) to *legatees*. Using *devise* to refer to land and *bequest* to refer to personalty became a lawyerly custom little more than a hundred years ago.[70] But synonymous usage has returned, with the term devise, which is favored in the Restatement (Third) of Property,[71] probably more typical than bequeath.

For an intestate decedent, real property was said to *descend to heirs* and personal property was said to be *distributed to next-of-kin*. At common law, *heirs* and *next-of-kin* were not necessarily the same. When primogeniture, which applied only to land, was in effect, real property descended to the eldest son, but personal property was distributed equally among all the children (see page 29). Today a single *statute of descent and distribution* governs intestacy in almost all states, making the same persons intestate successors to both real and personal property. In modern usage, therefore, the word *heirs* usually means those persons designated by the applicable statute to take a decedent's intestate property (see page 67), both real and personal, and *next-of-kin* means the same thing.

In this book, we do not use the Latin suffix indicating feminine gender for women playing important roles in our cast: testator, executor, and administrator. Although *testatrix, executrix*, and *administratrix* are still sometimes used, other *-trix* forms either have disappeared from use (e.g., *donatrix, creditrix*) or would sound odd to the

---

68. In some states, a nonresident corporate fiduciary cannot be appointed as executor, and many states have restrictions on the appointment of a nonresident individual, such as requiring that the nonresident be a close relative or that a local co-executor or agent serve along with the nonresident. *See* Jeffrey A. Schoenblum, Multistate Guide to Estate Planning tbls. 3.01, 3.03 (2016).

69. David Mellinkoff, The Language of the Law 331-32 (1963).

70. *Cf.* William Shakespeare, King John, act 1, sc. 1, lines 109-10 (Henry Norman Hudson et al. eds., 1909) ("Upon his death-bed he by will bequeath'd/His lands to me.").

71. *See* Restatement (Third) of Property: Wills and Other Donative Transfers § 3.1 cmt. d (Am. Law Inst. 1999).

contemporary ear (e.g., *public administratrix*).[72] And, of course, it does not matter whether the person in the given role is a man or a woman. In Reed v. Reed, 404 U.S. 71 (1971), the Supreme Court held unconstitutional a statute that gave preference to a male to serve as executor or administrator.

3. Probate Administration

Probate serves three core functions: (1) it provides *evidence of transfer of title* to the new owners, making the property marketable again and allowing the new owner to fend off rival claimants; (2) it *protects creditors* by providing a procedure for payment of the decedent's debts; and (3) it *distributes the decedent's property* to those intended after the decedent's creditors are paid. In considering the sketch of probate administration that follows, think about how well probate serves these functions and whether other procedures would better serve these functions with greater speed and at lower cost. Competition from nonprobate modes of transfer has led to reforms such as unsupervised administration (discussed below), but probate still has a bad reputation for imposing needless costs and delays, even if no longer fair in many jurisdictions.

Although the general pattern of administering a probate estate is quite similar in all states, there is widespread variation in the details. The specific procedures in each state are governed by a collection of statutes and court rules that give meticulous instructions for each step in the process. Happily, this precludes our being concerned with specific rules and procedures. Instead, we shall present a generalized summary of probate administration.

a. Opening Probate and Choice of Law

Generally speaking, the law of the state where the decedent was domiciled at death governs the disposition of personal property, and the law of the state where the decedent's real property is located governs the disposition of real property. Consequently, the will should first be probated, or letters of administration should first be sought, in the jurisdiction where the decedent was domiciled at death. This is known as the *primary* or *domiciliary* jurisdiction. If the probate estate includes real property that is located in another jurisdiction, *ancillary probate* in that jurisdiction is required.

The main purpose of requiring an ancillary probate proceeding is to prove title to real property in the situs state's recording system and to protect local creditors. Ancillary administration may be costly, however, because the state may require that a resident be appointed personal representative and local counsel will likely be needed. Additional executor's commissions and attorney's fees may therefore be incurred. To avoid the costs and delay of an ancillary probate proceeding, lawyers commonly advise clients with real estate in another jurisdiction to put the property in an inter vivos trust

---

72. *See* Karen J. Sneddon, Not Your Mother's Will: Gender, Language, and Wills, 98 Marq. L. Rev. 1535, 1574-83 (2015) (arguing against continued use of the *-trix* suffix in the vocabulary of probate).

(see page 469). Because the trustee holds title to the trust property, there is no need to change title by probate administration upon the death of the settlor. The trust property is distributed or held in further trust in accordance with the terms of the trust.

Each state has a detailed statutory procedure for issuance of *letters testamentary* to an executor or *letters of administration* to an administrator authorizing the person to act on behalf of the estate. A person appointed as administrator must give *bond*, which insures against mismanagement or misappropriation. In most states, if the will names an individual rather than a bank or other corporate fiduciary as executor, the executor also must give bond unless the will waives the bond requirement. Although the security provided by a probate bond is beneficial in the event of a loss, this protection comes at a cost. Bond is usually obtained from an insurance company by paying a premium (such as $500 for a $100,000 bond), which will ultimately be paid out of the estate. Because the executor is typically a trusted family member, waiver of bond by will is common.

b. Common Form and Solemn Form Probate

Several states, mainly east of the Mississippi, follow the procedure formerly used by the English ecclesiastical courts in distinguishing between contentious and noncontentious probate proceedings. Under the English system, the executor had a choice of probating a will *in common form* or *in solemn form*.

Common form probate was an ex parte proceeding in which no notice or process was issued to any person. Due execution of the will was proved by the oath of the executor or such other witnesses as might be required. The will was admitted to probate at once, letters testamentary were granted, and the executor began administration of the estate. If no one raised any questions or objections, this procedure sufficed. However, within a period of years thereafter an interested party could file a *caveat*, compelling probate of the will in solemn form. Under probate in solemn form, notice to interested parties was given by citation, proper execution of the will was proved by the testimony of the attesting witnesses, and administration of the estate involved greater court participation. Ex parte or common form procedure is recognized in many states, sometimes preserving the common form/solemn form terminology, but more often not.

c. Formal and Informal Probate

The Uniform Probate Code (UPC) provides for both notice probate and ex parte probate. The former is called *formal probate* (rather than solemn form probate) and the latter *informal probate* (rather than common form probate). If the person asking for letters seeks informal probate, the validity of the will or determination of intestacy need not be litigated unless an interested party objects.[73]

---

73. Under UPC § 3-108, no proceeding, formal or informal, may be initiated more than three years from the date of death. If no will is probated within three years, the presumption of intestacy is conclusive. This three-year statute of limitations changes the common law, which permits a will to be probated at any time, perhaps many years after the testator's death. *See* Annot., 2 A.L.R.4th 1315 (1980, Supp. 2016).

UPC § 3-301 sets forth the requirements for informal probate. Without giving notice to anyone, the representative petitions for appointment. The petition must contain pertinent information about the decedent and the names and addresses of the spouse, the children or other heirs, and, if a will is involved, the devisees. If the petition is for probate of a will, the original will must accompany the petition (or an authenticated copy if the proceeding is ancillary). The executor swears that, to the best of her knowledge, the will was validly executed. Proof by the witnesses is not required. A will that appears to have the required signatures and that contains an attestation clause (see page 148) showing that requirements of execution have been met is probated without further proof (§ 3-303). Within 30 days, however, the personal representative must mail notice to every interested party, including heirs apparently disinherited by the will (§ 3-705). Any such party may file a petition for formal probate (§ 3-402).

Formal probate under UPC § 3-401 is a litigated judicial determination after notice to interested parties. A formal proceeding may be used to probate a will, to block an informal proceeding, or to secure a declaratory judgment of intestacy. Formal proceedings become final judgments if not appealed.

d. Supervised and Unsupervised Administration

In a *supervised administration*, as under UPC § 3-501, the personal representative is subject to the continuing authority of the probate court while administering the estate. This supervision can be time consuming and costly. Often the court must approve the inventory and appraisal of the estate; payment of debts; family allowance (see page 563); sale of real estate; borrowing of funds and mortgaging of property; leasing of property; proration of federal estate tax; personal representative's commissions; attorney's fees; preliminary and final distributions; and discharge of the personal representative. Under the supervised administration provisions of the UPC, the personal representative is empowered to act without interim court approvals, but she cannot make a distribution to the beneficiaries without approval from the court (§ 3-504).

The alternative is *unsupervised administration* in which, after appointment, the personal representative administers the estate without going back into court. Under UPC § 3-715, the representative has the broad powers of a trustee in dealing with the estate property and may collect assets, clear titles, sell property, invest in other assets, pay creditors, continue any business of the decedent, and distribute the estate — all without court approval.

Unsupervised administration is the default under the UPC, but an interested party can petition for supervised administration at any time (§ 3-502). The rationale is that the typical executor or administrator is a family member, as are the beneficiaries. In such circumstances, unless there is a dispute over the administration of the estate, intensive judicial supervision imposes needless costs on the estate and drains the judiciary's budget without an offsetting benefit. The benign experience with unsupervised nonprobate transfers, not to mention the typicality of informal divvying up of property in smaller estates, helped prove the viability of this reform.

e. Barring Creditors

Every state has a *nonclaim statute* that requires creditors to file claims within a specified time period. Claims filed thereafter are barred. Probate administration therefore may be advantageous if it is important to fix a date after which property can be distributed to the beneficiaries without concern about a subsequent claim by a creditor. This might be true for a deceased professional, such as a doctor or lawyer, as the statute of limitations on professional malpractice usually runs from discovery.

Nonclaim statutes come in two basic forms: (1) they bar claims not filed within a relatively short period after notice is given that probate proceedings have commenced, generally two to six months (four months under UPC § 3-801); or (2) they bar claims not filed within a longer period after the decedent's death, generally one to five years (one year under UPC § 3-803). Under the notice-based statutes in the first category, creditors are usually notified of the requirement to file claims only by publication in a newspaper. Under the statutes in the second category—called *self-executing* statutes—protection is provided after the time period has run whether or not probate proceedings are ever commenced.

The Supreme Court has held that the Due Process Clause requires that known or reasonably ascertainable creditors receive actual notice before they are barred by a notice-based statute running from the commencement of probate proceedings.[74] However, a one-year self-executing statute of limitations running from the decedent's death has been upheld by a state supreme court,[75] and most states have a similar self-executing statute. Another state supreme court has held that a reasonably ascertainable creditor that did not receive notice under the state's notice-based statute could still be barred by the state's self-executing statute.[76]

f. Closing the Estate

The personal representative of an estate is expected to complete the administration and distribute the assets as promptly as possible. But even if the administration is amicable, several required steps may prolong administration. Creditors must be identified and paid. Titles must be cleared. Taxes must be paid and tax returns accepted by the tax authorities (the personal representative is liable for failing to file these returns). Real estate or a business may have to be sold.

---

74. Tulsa Prof'l Collection Servs., Inc. v. Pope, 485 U.S. 478 (1988) (invalidating a statute barring known creditors two months after newspaper publication).

75. *See* State ex rel. Houska v. Dickhaner, 323 S.W.3d 29 (Mo. 2010).

76. *See* Jones v. Golden, 176 So. 3d 242 (Fla. 2015).

For a supervised administration, judicial approval is required to relieve the representative from liability, unless some statute of limitations runs upon a cause of action against the representative. The representative is not discharged from fiduciary responsibility until the court grants discharge. For an unsupervised administration, the estate may be closed by the personal representative, as under UPC § 3-1003, by filing a sworn statement that he has published notice to creditors, administered the estate, paid all claims, and sent a statement and accounting to all known distributees.

NOTE

The Cost and Delay of Probate.   Complaints about the cost and delay of probate are hardly new. Speaking of Jarndyce v. Jarndyce, a chancery proceeding involving an estate that is at the center of his novel Bleak House, Charles Dickens wrote:

> Jarndyce and Jarndyce drones on. This scarecrow of a suit has, in course of time, become so complicated, that no man alive knows what it means. The parties to it understand it least; but it has been observed that no two Chancery lawyers can talk about it for five minutes, without coming to a total disagreement as to all the premises. . . . Scores of persons have deliriously found themselves made parties in Jarndyce and Jarndyce, without knowing how or why; whole families have inherited legendary hatreds with the suit. The little plaintiff or defendant, who was promised a new rocking-horse when Jarndyce and Jarndyce should be settled, has grown up, possessed himself of a real horse, and trotted away into the other world.[77]

In the end, after the admission to probate of Jarndyce's true last will, "the whole estate is found to have been absorbed in costs."[78]

The administrative costs of contemporary probate are mainly probate court fees, the commission of the personal representative, the attorney's fee, and, sometimes, appraiser's and guardian ad litem's fees. If the personal representative is a family member, as is typical, she will usually serve without taking a commission, though attorney's fees may still be necessary.

In a study of probate matters in Alameda County, California, in 2008 and early 2009, Professor David Horton found that testate estates took an average of 16 months to close and intestate estates took an average of 18 months.[79] Regarding costs, Horton found that attorney's fees and personal representatives' commissions consumed 2.9 percent of the value of intestate estates and 2.3 percent of testate estates, with a range of 5.3 and 4.6 percent for the smallest intestate and testate estates respectively (those under $250,000) to 2.3 and 1.6 percent respectively for the largest (those over $749,000).[80]

---

77. Charles Dickens, Bleak House 16 (Penguin Classics ed. 1996) (1853).

78. Id. at 975.

79. *See* Horton, *supra* note 66, at 648-52.

80. Id. at 641 tbl. 1. In follow-up work, Horton found that fees in litigated cases averaged about 3.6 percent of estate value versus 2.9 percent otherwise. *See* David Horton, Wills Law on the Ground, 62 UCLA L. Rev. 1094, 1128 (2015).

"DADDY DOESN'T KNOW WHY BIRDS MIGRATE. ASK ME
ABOUT WAYS TO AVOID PROBATE."

Harley Schwadron/Cartoonstock

4. Can Probate Be Avoided?

Many clients want to know: *Can probate be avoided?* The answer is Yes, provided that during life the client arranges to transfer all of his property by way of will substitutes. For such a person, probate serves a backup function, catching overlooked property or property acquired after the inter vivos arrangements have been made.

Even for probate property, however, probate administration is not always necessary. As a practical matter, clearing title is not necessary for many items of personal property, such as furniture or personal effects, which are commonly divvied up by the survivors in private. A subsequent purchaser will assume that the possessor has title.

Statutes in almost every state, and UPC §§ 3-1201 to 3-1204, permit the decedent's successors to avoid probate if the amount of property involved is small, often requiring nothing more than an affidavit of the successor in a *summary administration*. In most states the figure defining a small estate eligible for summary administration ranges from $25,000 (as in UPC § 3-1201) to $100,000.[81] The limit in Oregon is $275,000!

Also common are statutory provisions permitting collection of small bank accounts or wage claims, or transfer of a motor vehicle certificate of title, upon affidavit by the decedent's successors.[82] By filling out the appropriate forms and presenting them to the

---

81. *See* Schoenblum, *supra* note 68, at tbl. 4; Joseph N. Blumberg, 51 Flavors: A Survey of Small Estate Procedures Across the Country, 28 Prob. & Prop. 31 (2014).

82. *See, e.g.*, Cal. Veh. Code § 5910 (2016) (vehicle transfer without probate).

bank, the employer, or the department of motor vehicles, the successor is able to collect the decedent's property or acquire a new certificate of title. Statutes in some states permit filing a will for probate as a title document (a "muniment of title"), with no formal administration to follow.[83]

With the rising popularity of nonprobate modes of transfer, the ready availability of summary administration by affidavit for small estates, and special provisions for transfer of motor vehicles and other items with formal title registration, probate administration is routinely avoided.[84] "What increasingly happens, therefore, when a modest or moderate wealth-holder dies is that [financial intermediaries] transfer the main assets, the DMV transfers the car, and anything that's left passes under an affidavit-based small-estate procedure, or by private agreement among the survivors."[85]

NOTES

1. A Probate Administration Problem.   Aaron Green died three weeks ago. His wife has come to your law firm with Green's will in hand. The will devises Green's entire estate "to my wife, Martha, if she survives me; otherwise to my children in equal shares." The will names Martha Green as executor. An interview with Mrs. Green reveals that the Green family consists of two adult sons and several grandchildren and that Green owned the following property: car ($15,000), furniture ($20,000), mutual fund ($10,000), joint checking account ($3,000), and life insurance policy naming Martha Green as beneficiary ($50,000). Mr. Green also had a pension plan naming Martha Green for survivor's benefits. Green owned no real property; he and his wife lived in a rented apartment. Green's debts consisted of last month's utility bills ($80) plus some consumer charge accounts: Visa card ($600 balance) and a local department store ($250). There is also a funeral bill ($8,000) and the cost of a cemetery lot ($600). Mrs. Green wants your advice.

   a. What should she do with the will? Must it be offered for probate? Must there be an administration of her husband's estate?

   b. Suppose instead that Green died intestate, and the state's statute of descent and distribution provides that if a decedent is survived by a spouse and children, one-half of his real and personal property shall descend to the spouse and the remaining one-half shall descend to the children.

   c. Suppose instead that Green also owned a house and lot worth $170,000 and another lot worth $16,000. The deeds to both tracts name Aaron Green as grantee. The residential property is subject to a mortgage with a current balance of $85,000;

---

83. *See, e.g.,* Tenn. Code Ann. § 32-2-111 (2016); Tex. Est. Code Ann. § 257.001 (2016).

84. *See* Horton, *supra* note 66, at 627 (noting that Alameda County reported 9,319 deaths in 2007, but finding only 668 corresponding probate cases).

85. John H. Langbein, Major Reforms of the Property Restatement and the Uniform Probate Code: Reformation, Harmless Error, and Nonprobate Transfers, 38 ACTEC L.J. 1, 16 (2012).

title to the other lot is free of encumbrances. Must (should?) Green's will be probated and his estate administered?

d. Suppose instead that Green comes to you and tells you that he does not have a will. He describes his family situation and the property owned by him, as described in the opening paragraph of this problem. His question: In view of his family situation and his modest estate, does he really need a will?

2. Universal Succession. The English system of court-supervised administration of estates, on which American law was modeled, was designed to protect creditors and beneficiaries from an untrustworthy executor or heir. On the continent of Europe and in Louisiana, there is an entirely different system, known as *universal succession*, which rarely involves a court at all. The heirs or the residuary devisees step into the shoes of the decedent at the decedent's death, taking the decedent's title and assuming all of the decedent's liabilities and the obligation of paying legacies according to the decedent's will. If, for example, *O* dies intestate, leaving *H* as *O*'s heir, *H* succeeds to ownership of *O*'s property and must pay all of *O*'s creditors and any taxes resulting from *O*'s death. If *O* has three heirs, they take *O*'s property as tenants in common at *O*'s death, with the ordinary rights of tenants in common. The payment of a commission to a fiduciary is not necessary, nor is a lawyer, unless the heirs decide they need legal advice.

UPC §§ 3-312 through 3-322 authorize universal succession as an alternative to probate administration. Under these provisions, the heirs or the residuary devisees may petition the court for universal succession. If the court ascertains that the necessary parties are included and that the estate is not subject to any current contest or difficulty, it issues a written statement of universal succession. The universal successors then have full power of ownership to deal with the assets of the estate. They assume the liabilities of the decedent to creditors, including tax liability. The successors are personally liable to other heirs omitted from the petition or, in the case of residuary devisees, to other devisees for the amount of property due them. No state has yet adopted these provisions of the UPC.[86]

C. PROFESSIONAL RESPONSIBILITY

Trusts and estates practice is mined with potential ethical pitfalls and malpractice traps. In a study by the American Bar Association, trusts and estates was ranked fourth in frequency of malpractice complaints among 25 categories of practice between 2008 and 2011.[87] Let us consider two recurring problems of professional responsibility in

---

86. *See* Karen J. Sneddon, Beyond the Personal Representative: The Potential of Succession Without Administration, 50 S. Tex. L. Rev. 449 (2009). In California, property that passes to the surviving spouse by intestacy or by will is not subject to administration unless the surviving spouse elects to have it administered. If the surviving spouse chooses not to have the property administered, the surviving spouse takes title to the property and assumes personal liability for the decedent's debts chargeable against the property. *See* Cal. Prob. Code §§ 13500-13660 (2016).

87. *See* Am. Bar Ass'n, Profile of Legal Malpractice Claims: 2008-2011, at 5 (2012).

trusts and estates practice: (1) a duty of competence owed to a client's intended beneficiaries in addition to the client, and (2) duties in joint representation of multiple persons in the same family.[88]

1. Duties to Intended Beneficiaries

Simpson v. Calivas
650 A.2d 318 (N.H. 1994)

HORTON, J. The plaintiff, Robert H. Simpson, Jr., appeals from a directed verdict, grant of summary judgment, and dismissal of his claims against the lawyer who drafted his father's will. The plaintiff's action, sounding in both negligence and breach of contract, alleged that the defendant, Christopher Calivas, failed to draft a will which incorporated the actual intent of Robert H. Simpson, Sr. to leave all his land to the plaintiff in fee simple. Sitting with a jury, the Superior Court (Dickson, J.) directed a verdict for the defendant based on the plaintiff's failure to introduce any evidence on . . . breach of duty. The trial court also granted summary judgment on collateral estoppel grounds based on findings of the Strafford County Probate Court and dismissed the action, ruling that under New Hampshire law an attorney who drafts a will owes no duty to intended beneficiaries. We reverse and remand.

In March 1984, Robert H. Simpson, Sr. (Robert Sr.) executed a will that had been drafted by the defendant. The will left all real estate to the plaintiff except for a life estate in "our homestead located at Piscataqua Road, Dover, New Hampshire," which was left to Robert Sr.'s second wife, Roberta C. Simpson (stepmother). After Robert Sr.'s death in September 1985, the plaintiff and his stepmother filed a joint petition in the Strafford County Probate Court seeking a determination, essentially, of whether the term "homestead" referred to all the decedent's real property on Piscataqua Road (including a house, over one hundred acres of land, and buildings used in the family business), or only to the house (and, perhaps, limited surrounding acreage). The probate court found the term "homestead" ambiguous, and in order to aid construction, admitted some extrinsic evidence of the testator's surrounding circumstances, including evidence showing a close relationship between Robert Sr. and plaintiff's stepmother. The probate court, however, did not admit notes taken by the defendant during consultations with Robert Sr. that read: "House to wife as a life estate remainder to son, Robert H. Simpson, Jr. . . . Remaining land . . . to son Robert A. [sic] Simpson, Jr." The probate court construed the will to provide Roberta with a life estate in all the real property. After losing the will construction action—then two years after his father's death—the plaintiff negotiated with his stepmother to buy out her life estate in all the real property for $400,000.

The plaintiff then brought this malpractice action, pleading a contract count, based on third-party beneficiary theory, and a negligence count. . . .

---

88. *See* Gerry W. Beyer, Avoid Being a Defendant: Estate Planning Malpractice and Ethical Concerns, 5 St. Mary's J. Leg. Mal. & Ethics 224 (2015).

The plaintiff raises . . . [these] issues on appeal: (1) whether the trial court erred in ruling that under New Hampshire law a drafting attorney owes no duty to an intended beneficiary; (2) whether the trial court erred in ruling that the findings of the probate court on testator intent collaterally estopped the plaintiff from bringing a malpractice action. . . .

We reverse and remand.

I. DUTY TO INTENDED BENEFICIARIES

. . . The critical issue, for purposes of this appeal, is whether an attorney who drafts a testator's will owes a duty of reasonable care to intended beneficiaries. We hold that there is such a duty.

As a general principle, "the concept of 'duty' . . . arises out of a relation between the parties and the protection against reasonably foreseeable harm." Morvay v. Hanover Insurance Co., 506 A.2d 333, 334 (N.H. 1986). The existence of a contract between parties may constitute a relation sufficient to impose a duty to exercise reasonable care, but in general, "the scope of such a duty is limited to those in privity of contract with each other." Robinson v. Colebrook Savings Bank, 254 A.2d 837, 839 (N.H. 1969). The privity rule is not ironclad, though, and we have been willing to recognize exceptions particularly where, as here, the risk to persons not in privity is apparent. In *Morvay*, for example, we held that investigators hired by an insurance company to investigate the cause of a fire owed a duty to the insureds to perform their investigation with due care despite the absence of privity. Accordingly, the insureds stated a cause of action by alleging that the investigators negligently concluded that the fire was set, thereby prompting the insurance company to deny coverage. *Morvay*, 506 A.2d at 335.

Because this issue is one of first impression, we look for guidance to other jurisdictions. The overwhelming majority of courts that have considered this issue have found that a duty runs from an attorney to an intended beneficiary of a will. Ronald E. Mallen & Jeffrey M. Smith, Legal Malpractice 3d ed. § 26.4, at 595 (1989 & Supp. 1992). A theme common to these cases, similar to a theme of cases in which we have recognized exceptions to the privity rule, is an emphasis on the foreseeability of injury to the intended beneficiary. As the California Supreme Court explained in reaffirming the duty owed by an attorney to an intended beneficiary:

> When an attorney undertakes to fulfill the testamentary instructions of his client, he realistically and in fact assumes a relationship not only with the client but also with the client's intended beneficiaries. The attorney's actions and omissions will affect the success of the client's testamentary scheme; and thus the possibility of thwarting the testator's wishes immediately becomes foreseeable. Equally foreseeable is the possibility of injury to an intended beneficiary. In some ways, the beneficiary's interests loom greater than those of the client. After the latter's death, a failure in his testamentary scheme works no practical effect except to deprive his intended beneficiaries of the intended bequests.

Heyer v. Flaig, 449 P.2d 161, 164-65 (Cal. 1969). We agree that although there is no privity between a drafting attorney and an intended beneficiary, the obvious foreseeability of injury to the beneficiary demands an exception to the privity rule.

The defendant in his brief, however, urges that if we are to recognize an exception to the privity rule, we should limit it to those cases where the testator's intent as expressed in the will—not as shown by extrinsic evidence—was frustrated by attorney error. . . . Under such a limited exception to the privity rule, a beneficiary whose interest violated the rule against perpetuities would have a cause of action against the drafting attorney, but a beneficiary whose interest was omitted by a drafting error would not. Similarly, application of such a rule to the facts of this case would require dismissal even if the allegations—that the defendant botched Robert Sr.'s instructions to leave all his land to his son—were true. We refuse to adopt a rule that would produce such inconsistent results for equally foreseeable harms, and hold that an intended beneficiary states a cause of action simply by pleading sufficient facts to establish that an attorney has negligently failed to effectuate the testator's intent as expressed to the attorney.

We are not the only court to reject the distinction urged by the defendant. In Ogle v. Fuiten, 466 N.E.2d 224, 225 (Ill. 1984), for example, nephews of the testator sued the testator's attorney for failing to provide in the will for the possibility that the testator's wife might not die in a common disaster, but might nonetheless fail to survive him by thirty days. The testator's wife died in the period not dealt with in the will, and without a provision in the will providing for this situation, the estate devolved by intestacy. On appeal after the dismissal of the nephews' claims, the court flatly rejected the argument that intended beneficiaries do not state a cause of action where the testator's alleged intent does not appear in the will.

The plaintiff also argues that the trial court erred in failing to recognize that the writ stated a cause of action in contract. We agree.

The general rule that a nonparty to a contract has no remedy for breach of contract is subject to an exception for third-party beneficiaries. Third-party beneficiary status necessary to trigger this exception exists where "the contract is so expressed as to give the promisor reason to know that a benefit to a third party is contemplated by the promisee as one of the motivating causes of his making the contract." Tamposi Associates, Inc. v. Star Market Co., 406 A.2d 132, 134 (N.H. 1979). We hold that where, as here, a client has contracted with an attorney to draft a will and the client has identified to whom he wishes his estate to pass, that identified beneficiary may enforce the terms of the contract as a third-party beneficiary.

Because we hold that a duty runs from a drafting attorney to an intended beneficiary, and that an identified beneficiary has third-party beneficiary status, the trial court erred by dismissing the plaintiff's writ.

II. COLLATERAL ESTOPPEL

The defendant insists, however, that even if a duty runs from a testator's attorney to an intended beneficiary, the superior court properly granted summary judgment on collateral estoppel grounds. We disagree. . . .

The primary question is whether the issues before the probate and superior courts were identical. We agree with defendant that comparison of the respective evidence which each court was competent to hear is one factor, but note that an identity of evidence is not dispositive of an identity of issues. Instead, determination of "identity" necessarily requires inquiry into each court's role and the nature of the respective findings.

The principal task of the probate court is to determine the testator's intent . . . limited by the requirement that it determine the "intention of the testator as shown by the language of the whole will." Dennett v. Osgood, 229 A.2d 689, 690 (N.H. 1967). In this effort, the probate court is always permitted to consider the "surrounding circumstances" of the testator, id., and where the terms of a will are ambiguous, as here, extrinsic evidence may be admitted to the extent that it does not contradict the express terms of the will. In re Estate of Sayewich, 413 A.2d 581, 584 (N.H. 1980). Direct declarations of a testator's intent, however, are generally inadmissible in all probate proceedings. The defendant argues that even though his notes of his meeting with the decedent recorded the decedent's direct declarations of intent, they could have been admissible as an exception to the general rule had there been a proper proffer. We need not reach the issue of whether the defendant's notes fall within an exception to the general rule because even assuming admissibility and therefore an identity of evidence, there remain distinct issues. Quite simply, the task of the probate court is a limited one: to determine the intent of the testator as expressed in the language of the will. Obviously, the hope is that the application of rules of construction and consideration of extrinsic evidence (where authorized) will produce a finding of expressed intent that corresponds to actual intent. Further, the likelihood of such convergence presumably increases as the probate court considers more extrinsic evidence; however, even with access to all extrinsic evidence, there is no requirement or guarantee that the testator's intent as construed will match the testator's actual intent.

The defendant, however, insists that whether or not required to do so, the probate court in this case did make an explicit finding of actual intent when it concluded: "There is nothing to suggest that [the testator] intended to grant a life estate in anything less than the whole." We need not reach the issue of whether this language constitutes a finding of actual intent because collateral estoppel will not lie anyway. Collateral estoppel is only applicable if the finding in the first proceeding was essential to the judgment of that court. Restatement (Second) of Judgments § 27. Inasmuch as the mandate of the probate court is simply to determine and give effect to the intent of the testator as expressed in the language of the will, a finding of actual intent is not necessary to that judgment. Accordingly, even an explicit finding of actual intent by a probate court cannot be the basis for collateral estoppel. . . .

Reversed and remanded.

NOTES

1. The Privity Defense.   In rejecting the privity defense, Vice-Chancellor Robert E. Megarry of England stated the argument against it succinctly:

> In broad terms, the question is whether solicitors who prepare a will are liable to a beneficiary under it if, through their negligence, the gift to the beneficiary is void. The solicitors are liable, of course, to the testator or his estate for a breach of the duty that they owed to him, though as he has suffered no financial loss it seems that his estate could recover no more than nominal damages. Yet it is said that however careless the solicitors were, they owed no duty to the beneficiary, and so they cannot be liable to her. If this is right, the result is striking. The only person who has a

valid claim has suffered no loss, and the only person who has suffered a loss has no valid claim.[89]

By our count, nine states still follow the old rule that a lack of privity between the drafter and an intended beneficiary bars a malpractice action by the beneficiary: Alabama, Arkansas, Colorado, Maine, Maryland, Nebraska, New York, Ohio, and Texas. In some of these states, such as New York and Texas, the drafter can be held liable in a suit by the testator's personal representative.

Figure 1.1

Privity Defense (2016)

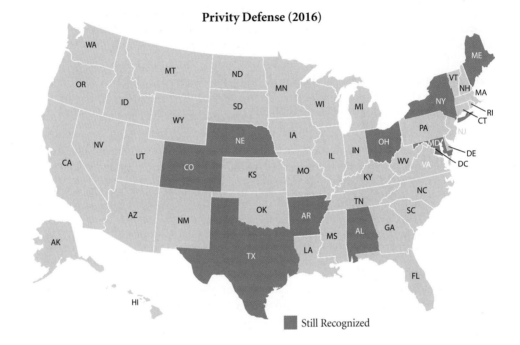

■ Still Recognized

2. Malpractice and Law Reform.   In *Simpson* the court held that in a malpractice action against the testator's lawyer, the testator's actual intent could be shown by extrinsic evidence. In Fabian v. Lindsay, 765 S.E.2d 132 (S.C. 2014), the court held likewise, reasoning that "extrinsic evidence is often 'vital' to proving an attorney's drafting error." But if extrinsic evidence of a testator's intent is a reliable enough basis to hold the testator's lawyer liable for malpractice, why not rely on it to reform the will to correct the drafting error and avoid the malpractice litigation altogether? What of the unjust enrichment of the unintended taker? We take up the admissibility of extrinsic evidence in construing wills and reforming wills for mistake in Chapter 5.

Nearly 35 years ago, Professor Jesse Dukeminier predicted that legal malpractice liability would prove to be a strong force for reform of property law.[90] Subsequent

---

89. Ross v. Caunters, [1980] 1 Ch. 297 at 302-303 (Eng.); *see also* Bradley E.S. Fogel, Attorney v. Client: Privity, Malpractice, and the Lack of Respect for the Primacy of the Attorney-Client Relationship in Estate Planning, 68 Tenn. L. Rev. 261 (2001).

90. *See* Jesse Dukeminier, Cleansing the Stables of Property: A River Found at Last, 65 Iowa L. Rev. 151 (1979).

developments have validated his prognostication. Today courts and legislatures are increasingly willing to discard old rules that had forbidden courts to excuse errors in will execution (see page 175); to correct mistakes by lawyers in drafting instruments to carry out the client's intent (see page 341); to cure or avoid perpetuities violations (see page 900); or to reform wills and trusts after the decedent's death to obtain tax advantages (see page 350).

3. Probate Court Jurisdiction.   In *Simpson*, the validity and construction of the will were matters for the probate court to decide. The negligence of the lawyer was a matter for a court of general jurisdiction, which entertains tort and contract suits. This is true in most states.

Historically, probate courts were inferior courts, with jurisdiction limited to determining the will's validity and supervising administration of the decedent's estate. In some states, probate judges may be laypersons, without legal training. Anyone can run for the office. The National Law Journal reported the election of an 18-year-old man, just six months out of high school, as probate judge for Valencia County, New Mexico.[91]

Today, most probate courts are better staffed and they are authorized to pass on more questions regarding wills, including the construction of wills. Nonetheless, most courts, like the New Hampshire Supreme Court, reject the claim that conclusions reached by the probate court about testator's intent in a construction suit are determinative in a malpractice suit. The issues and evidentiary rules for proving intent applied in the two proceedings are different. Meanwhile, probate courts continue to suffer from a poor reputation, in some cases well deserved.[92]

2. Joint Representation

A. v. B.
726 A.2d 924 (N.J. 1999)

POLLOCK, J. This appeal presents the issue whether a law firm may disclose confidential information of one co-client to another co-client. Specifically, in this paternity action, the mother's former law firm, which contemporaneously represented the father and his wife in planning their estates, seeks to disclose to the wife the existence of the father's illegitimate child. . . .

In the Family Part [i.e., the trial court], the husband . . . requested restraints . . . to prevent the firm from disclosing to his wife the existence of the child. The Family Part denied the requested restraints. The Appellate Division reversed and remanded "for the entry of an order imposing preliminary restraints and for further consideration."

[W]e reverse the judgment of the Appellate Division and remand the matter to the Family Part. . . .

---

91. Brian Noyd, A Judge Who's Thinking About Law School, Nat'l L.J., Dec. 24, 1984, at 39.

92. *See* Julia Belian, Hubris, 3 Est. Plan. & Community Prop. L.J. 1 (2010) (surveying corruption and scandal in various state probate courts); *see also* Bill Braun, Judge Facing Sex Charges Is Given New Assignment, Tulsa World, Apr. 29, 2008, at A13 (reporting that an Oklahoma judge accused of exposing himself to two women in a parking lot had been reassigned to the probate division pending resolution of the charges).

I

. . . In October 1997, the husband and wife retained Hill Wallack, a firm of approximately sixty lawyers, to assist them with planning their estates. On the commencement of the joint representation, the husband and wife each signed a letter captioned "Waiver of Conflict of Interest." In explaining the possible conflicts of interest, the letter recited that the effect of a testamentary transfer by one spouse to the other would permit the transferee to dispose of the property as he or she desired. The firm's letter also explained that information provided by one spouse could become available to the other. Although the letter did not contain an express waiver of the confidentiality of any such information, each spouse consented to and waived any conflicts arising from the firm's joint representation.

Unfortunately, the clerk who opened the firm's estate planning file misspelled the clients' surname. The misspelled name was entered in the computer program that the firm uses to discover possible conflicts of interest. The firm then prepared reciprocal wills and related documents with the names of the husband and wife correctly spelled.

In January 1998, before the husband and wife executed the estate planning documents, the mother coincidentally retained Hill Wallack to pursue a paternity claim against the husband. This time, when making its computer search for conflicts of interest, Hill Wallack spelled the husband's name correctly. Accordingly, the computer search did not reveal the existence of the firm's joint representation of the husband and wife. As a result, the estate planning department did not know that the family law department had instituted a paternity action for the mother. Similarly, the family law department did not know that the estate planning department was preparing estate plans for the husband and wife.

A lawyer from the firm's family law department wrote to the husband about the mother's paternity claim. The husband neither objected to the firm's representation of the mother nor alerted the firm to the conflict of interest. Instead, he retained Fox Rothschild to represent him in the paternity action. After initially denying paternity, he agreed to voluntary DNA testing, which revealed that he is the father. Negotiations over child support failed, and the mother instituted the present action.

After the mother filed the paternity action, the husband and wife executed their wills at the Hill Wallack office. The parties agree that in their wills, the husband and wife leave their respective residuary estates to each other. If the other spouse does not survive, the contingent beneficiaries are the testator's issue. The wife's will leaves her residuary estate to her husband, creating the possibility that her property ultimately may pass to his issue. Under N.J.S.A. 3B:1-2;:3-48, the term "issue" includes both legitimate and illegitimate children. When the wife executed her will, therefore, she did not know that the husband's illegitimate child ultimately may inherit her property.

The conflict of interest surfaced when Fox Rothschild, in response to Hill Wallack's request for disclosure of the husband's assets, informed the firm that it already possessed the requested information. Hill Wallack promptly informed the mother that it unknowingly was representing both the husband and the wife in an unrelated matter.

Hill Wallack immediately withdrew from representing the mother in the paternity action. It also instructed the estate planning department not to disclose any information about the husband's assets to the member of the firm who had been representing the mother. The firm then wrote to the husband stating that it believed it had an ethical obligation to disclose to the wife the existence, but not the identity, of his illegitimate child. Additionally, the firm stated that it was obligated to inform the wife "that her current estate plan may devise a portion of her assets through her spouse to that child." The firm suggested that the husband so inform his wife and stated that if he did not do so, it would. Because of the restraints imposed by the Appellate Division, however, the firm has not disclosed the information to the wife.

II

This appeal concerns the conflict between two fundamental obligations of lawyers: the duty of confidentiality, Rules of Professional Conduct (RPC) 1.6(a), and the duty to inform clients of material facts, RPC 1.4(b). The conflict arises from a law firm's joint representation of two clients whose interests initially were, but no longer are, compatible.

Crucial to the attorney-client relationship is the attorney's obligation not to reveal confidential information learned in the course of representation. Thus, RPC 1.6(a) states that "[a] lawyer shall not reveal information relating to representation of a client unless the client consents after consultation, except for disclosures that are impliedly authorized in order to carry out the representation." Generally, "the principle of attorney-client confidentiality imposes a sacred trust on the attorney not to disclose the client's confidential communication." State v. Land, 372 A.2d 297, 300 (N.J. 1977).

A lawyer's obligation to communicate to one client all information needed to make an informed decision qualifies the firm's duty to maintain the confidentiality of a co-client's information. RPC 1.4(b), which reflects a lawyer's duty to keep clients informed, requires that "[a] lawyer shall explain a matter to the extent reasonably necessary to permit the client to make informed decisions regarding the representation." In limited situations, moreover, an attorney is permitted or required to disclose confidential information. Hill Wallack argues that RPC 1.6 mandates, or at least permits, the firm to disclose to the wife the existence of the husband's illegitimate child. RPC 1.6(b) requires that a lawyer disclose "information relating to representation of a client" to the proper authorities if the lawyer "reasonably believes" that such disclosure is necessary to prevent the client "from committing a criminal, illegal or fraudulent act that the lawyer reasonably believes is likely to result in death or substantial bodily harm or substantial injury to the financial interest or property of another." RPC 1.6(b)(1). Despite Hill Wallack's claim that RPC 1.6(b) applies, the facts do not justify mandatory disclosure. The possible inheritance of the wife's estate by the husband's illegitimate child is too remote to constitute "substantial injury to the financial interest or property of another" within the meaning of RPC 1.6(b).

By comparison, in limited circumstances RPC 1.6(c) permits a lawyer to disclose a confidential communication. RPC 1.6(c) permits, but does not require, a lawyer to reveal confidential information to the extent the lawyer reasonably believes necessary "to rectify the consequences of a client's criminal, illegal or fraudulent act in furtherance of which the lawyer's services had been used." RPC 1.6(c)(1). Although RPC 1.6(c) does not define a "fraudulent act," the term takes on meaning from our construction of the word "fraud," found in the analogous "crime or fraud" exception to the attorney-client privilege. When construing the "crime or fraud" exception to the attorney-client privilege, "our courts have generally given the term 'fraud' an expansive reading." Fellerman v. Bradley, 493 A.2d 1239, 1245 (N.J. 1985).

We likewise construe broadly the term "fraudulent act" within the meaning of RPC 1.6(c). So construed, the husband's deliberate omission of the existence of his illegitimate child constitutes a fraud on his wife. When discussing their respective estates with the firm, the husband and wife reasonably could expect that each would disclose information material to the distribution of their estates, including the existence of children who are contingent residuary beneficiaries. The husband breached that duty. Under the reciprocal wills, the existence of the husband's illegitimate child could affect the distribution of the wife's estate, if she predeceased him. Additionally, the husband's child support payments and other financial responsibilities owed to the illegitimate child could deplete that part of his estate that otherwise would pass to his wife. . . .

The New Jersey RPCs are based substantially on the American Bar Association Model Rules of Professional Conduct ("the Model Rules"). RPC 1.6, however, exceeds the Model Rules in authorizing the disclosure of confidential information. . . . As adopted by the American Bar Association, Model Rule 1.6(b) permits a lawyer to reveal confidential information only "to the extent the lawyer reasonably believes necessary to prevent the client from committing a criminal act that the lawyer believes is likely to result in imminent death or substantial bodily harm." Unlike RPC 1.6, Model Rule 1.6 does not except information relating to the commission of a fraudulent act or that relating to a client's act that is likely to result in substantial financial injury. In no situation, moreover, does Model Rule 1.6 require disclosure. Thus, the Model Rules provide for narrower disclosure than that authorized by RPC 1.6.[93] . . .

Under RPC 1.6, the facts support disclosure to the wife. The law firm did not learn of the husband's illegitimate child in a confidential communication from him. Indeed, he concealed that information from both his wife and the firm. The law firm learned about the husband's child through its representation of the mother in her paternity action against the husband. Accordingly, the husband's expectation of nondisclosure of the information may be less than if he had communicated the information to the firm in confidence.

In addition, the husband and wife signed letters captioned "Waiver of Conflict of Interest." These letters acknowledge that information provided by one client could become available to the other. The letters, however, stop short of explicitly authorizing the firm to disclose one spouse's confidential information to the other. Even in the absence of any such explicit authorization, the spirit of the letters supports the firm's decision to disclose to the wife the existence of the husband's illegitimate child. . . .

---

93. As amended in 2002, Model Rule 1.6(b)(3) authorizes permissive disclosure "to prevent, mitigate or rectify substantial injury to the financial interests or property of another that is reasonably certain to result or has resulted from the client's commission of a crime or fraud in furtherance of which the client has used the lawyer's services."—Eds.

[A]n attorney, on commencing joint representation of co-clients, should agree explicitly with the clients on the sharing of confidential information. In such a "disclosure agreement," the co-clients can agree that any confidential information concerning one co-client, whether obtained from a co-client himself or herself or from another source, will be shared with the other co-client. Similarly, the co-clients can agree that unilateral confidences or other confidential information will be kept confidential by the attorney. Such a prior agreement will clarify the expectations of the clients and the lawyer and diminish the need for future litigation.

In the absence of an agreement to share confidential information with co-clients, the *Restatement* reposes the resolution of the lawyer's competing duties within the lawyer's discretion:

> [T]he lawyer, after consideration of all relevant circumstances, has the . . . discretion to inform the affected co-client of the specific communication if, in the lawyer's reasonable judgment, the immediacy and magnitude of the risk to the affected co-client outweigh the interest of the communicating client in continued secrecy.

[Restatement (Third) of the Law Governing Lawyers § 112 comment l (Proposed Final Draft No. 1, 1996) ("the Restatement").] . . .

[T]he American College of Trust and Estate Counsel (ACTEC) also favors a discretionary rule. It recommends that the "lawyer should have a reasonable degree of discretion in determining how to respond to any particular case." American College of Trust and Estate Counsel, ACTEC Commentaries on the Model Rules of Professional Conduct 68 (2d ed. 1995). . . .

Because Hill Wallack wishes to make the disclosure, we need not reach the issue whether the lawyer's obligation to disclose is discretionary or mandatory. In conclusion, Hill Wallack may inform the wife of the existence of the husband's illegitimate child. . . .

The law firm learned of the husband's paternity of the child through the mother's disclosure before the institution of the paternity suit. It does not seek to disclose the identity of the mother or the child. Given the wife's need for the information and the law firm's right to disclose it, the disclosure of the child's existence to the wife constitutes an exceptional case with "compelling reason clearly and convincingly shown."

The judgment of the Appellate Division is reversed and the matter is remanded to the Family Part.

NOTE

Engagement Letters in Joint Representation. Trusts and estates lawyers often represent multiple members of the same family—such as a husband and wife—in drafting wills, trusts, and powers of attorney, and in the administration of wills and trusts. In these situations, it is important at the outset for the lawyer to discuss with each client the issue of conflict of interests and the ground rules for sharing information. The lawyer should explain the advantages and disadvantages of joint representation, and then follow up with an *engagement letter* or other form of consent agreement.[94] In some states, an engagement letter or other written consent agreement is required.[95]

The American College of Trusts and Estates Counsel, the premier professional association for trusts and estates lawyers, suggests the following clause in an engagement letter for the joint representation of spouses:

> It is common for a husband and wife to employ the same lawyer to assist them in planning their estates. You have taken this approach by asking me to represent both of you in your planning. It is important that you understand that, because I will be representing both of you, you are considered my client, collectively. Ethical considerations prohibit me from agreeing with either of you to withhold information from the other. Accordingly, in agreeing to this form of representation, each of you is authorizing me to disclose to the other any matters related to the representation that one of you might discuss with me or that I might acquire from any other source. In this representation, I will not give legal advice to either of you or make any changes in any of your estate planning documents without your mutual knowledge and consent.[96]

What result in A. v. B. if the husband and wife had signed an engagement letter containing this clause?

---

94. *See* ACTEC Commentaries on the Model Rules of Professional Conduct 84-85 (5th ed. 2016).
95. *See* Anne-Marie Rhodes, Engagement Letters, 147 Tr. & Est. 25, 25 (2008).
96. ACTEC Engagement Letters: A Guide for Practitioners 11 (2d ed. 2007).

CHAPTER 2

INTESTACY: AN ESTATE PLAN BY DEFAULT

[I]t has been said that the abhorrence of courts to intestacy under a will
may be likened to the abhorrence of nature to a vacuum.

28 RULING CASE LAW § 189, AT 228 (1921)
(William M. McKinney & Burdett A. Rich eds., 1921)

A PERSON WHO DIES with a will is said to die *testate*. The probate property
of such a person is distributed in accordance with the terms of the person's
will. But at least half of the U.S. population dies without a will. Distribution of
the probate property of these people, who are said to die *intestate*, is governed by the
default rules of the law of *intestacy*. If a will disposes of only part of the probate estate,
the result is a *partial intestacy* in which the probate property not disposed of by the will
passes by intestacy. Intestacy is therefore the background law that supplies an estate
plan for intestate decedents.[1]

The law of intestacy has relevance beyond providing an estate plan by default for
persons who die intestate. Intestacy also influences testamentary dispositions, both by
expressing a legislative judgment about what is typical or normal and by giving default
meanings to terms such as "children" and "descendants." Moreover, by determining
who would take if a decedent died intestate, intestacy is often determinative of who has
standing to contest the decedent's purported will.

In accordance with the principle of freedom of disposition, the primary objective
in designing an intestacy statute is to carry out the probable intent of the typical intestate decedent — that is, to provide majoritarian default rules for property succession at
death. Unfortunately, this task often involves substantial guesswork, as people's preferences differ, and it is hard to know what most people who die intestate would want.
American law generally favors a decedent's spouse, then descendants, then parents, and
then collateral and more remote kindred.

---

1. Rules for intestate succession are common across legal systems. *See* Comparative Succession
Law II: Intestate Succession (Kenneth G.C. Reid, Marius J. de Waal & Reinhard Zimmermann eds.,
2015).

As social norms continue to evolve, however, and family and family-like relationships become ever more varied and complex, basing intestate succession on a model of a traditional family may no longer be apt. What of adoption, assisted reproductive technology, multiple marriages, blended families with stepchildren, and unmarried cohabiting partners? To track the probable intent of the typical intestate decedent, the law of intestacy must continually evolve.

We begin in Section A by considering why people fail to make a will and the purposes and sources of intestacy law. In Section B, we survey the structure of intestate succession. In Section C, we delve deeper into transfers to children, including the manner by which the law of intestacy has evolved to include adopted persons and persons born with the aid of assisted reproductive technology. Finally, in Section D, we examine bars to succession, including voluntary disclaimer and the rule that prohibits a slayer from inheriting from his victim.

A. AN ESTATE PLAN BY DEFAULT

1. Why Do So Many People Die Intestate?

Lawyers almost always advise their clients to make a will. In addition to identifying who will take the decedent's probate property, a will can designate guardians for minor children, name the fiduciary who will administer the estate, reduce probate costs by waiving a required bond (or surety on a bond), and achieve tax savings. Yet studies show that only about half of all adults — typically older, wealthier, and more educated persons — have a will.[2]

Some people put off making a will to avoid the unpleasantness of confronting mortality. That there are so many euphemisms for death — pass away, meet your maker, kick the bucket, buy the farm, and so on — reflects the urgent need of people to avoid the very word *death*.[3] Insurers call death insurance "life insurance," and agents are careful not to use the word death in their discussions with prospective clients ("If anything should happen to you." *If*, indeed!). As Freud wrote, "Our own death is indeed unimaginable, and whenever we make the attempt to imagine it we can perceive that we really survive as spectators. Hence . . . at bottom no one believes in his own death, or to put the same thing in another way, in the unconscious every one of us is convinced of his own immortality."[4]

Another reason people do not make a will is the time and cost involved. "Unlike other acts of legal significance, such as entering into a marriage or consumer contract, the will-making process is unfamiliar to most individuals and requires legal draftsmanship

---

2. *See, e.g.*, Russell N. James, The New Statistics of Estate Planning: Lifetime and Post-Mortem Wills, Trusts, and Charitable Planning, 8 Est. Plan. & Community Prop. L.J. 1, 15-26 (2015).

3. *See* Karen J. Sneddon, Memento Mori: Death and Wills, 14 Wyo. L. Rev. 211 (2014).

4. Sigmund Freud, Our Attitude Towards Death, *in* 4 Collected Papers 304-05 (Joan Riviere trans., 1925).

and compliance with testamentary formalities."[5] Increasingly, people make use of *will substitutes* that are often simpler and cheaper than a will, such as joint tenancy, payable-on-death designations on life insurance, pension plans, and bank, brokerage, and mutual fund accounts, or revocable trusts created during life. Today more property is transferred by these nonprobate modes of transfer than is transferred in probate by intestacy or by will. We examine nonprobate succession in Chapter 7.

Stu's Views

2. The Purpose of Intestacy Statutes

A person who does not make a will or use will substitutes, and whose family does not divide up his property in private,[6] is left with the law of intestacy as his estate plan by default. The distribution of the probate property of such a person is governed by the applicable *statute of descent and distribution*—that is, the intestacy statute.

In accordance with the principle of freedom of disposition, the primary objective in designing an intestacy statute is to carry out the probable intent of the typical intestate decedent. Empirical studies have been undertaken to determine popular preferences for intestate succession,[7] and a variety of intestacy law reforms reflect the findings of those studies. Nevertheless, "[a] plan that suits the majority is the most drafters of intestacy statutes can hope for; statutes cannot take into account the complex variety of preferences disclosed within these empirical studies."[8] On some questions, there is no clear majoritarian preference or preferences may be evolving. In such circumstances, should legislators favor the traditional view or the one that seems to be emerging? Should legislators look to how the issue is typically addressed in professionally drafted wills?

American intestacy law generally favors the decedent's spouse, then descendants, then parents, and then collaterals and more remote kindred. This structure reflects the findings of most empirical studies and also serves the secondary policy of protecting

---

5. Reid Kress Weisbord, Wills for Everyone: Helping Individuals Opt Out of Intestacy, 53 B.C. L. Rev. 877, 879 (2012).

6. *See* Naomi Cahn & Amy Ziettlow, "Making Things Fair": An Empirical Study of How People Approach the Wealth Transfer System, 22 Elder L.J. 325 (2015).

7. *See, e.g.*, Mary Louise Fellows, Rita J. Simon & William Rau, Public Attitudes About Property Distribution at Death and Intestate Succession Laws in the United States, 1978 Am. B. Found. Res. J. 319; Marvin B. Sussman, Judith N. Cates & David T. Smith, The Family and Inheritance (1970); Allison Dunham, The Method, Process and Frequency of Wealth Transmission at Death, 30 U. Chi. L. Rev. 241 (1963).

8. Alyssa A. DiRusso, Testacy and Intestacy: The Dynamics of Wills and Demographic Status, 23 Quinnipiac Prob. L.J. 36, 56 (2009).

Why the Settling of Prince's Estate Could Get Very, Very Messy

By Helaine Olen

Who will inherit Prince's fortune and take charge of his legacy—including the treasure trove of music the late pop icon is rumored to have recorded, but never released?

That's a good question.

On Tuesday, Prince's sister, Tyka Nelson, filed a request with a Minnesota court, claiming the renowned singer died without a will in place and asking that initial oversight of the estate go to a bank which, she said, her brother worked with during his lifetime....

According to Minnesota law, if a person dies intestate (that's lawyer-speak for without a will) and doesn't have a surviving spouse, children, parents, or grandchildren, the next in line to inherit would be his or her siblings. And, no, Minnesota law makes no legal distinction between full and half brothers and sisters.

Prince was divorced twice. His one child died shortly after birth. His parents are dead, too. This leaves not just his full sister, Nelson, but also seven half siblings as his equal inheritors. But not all of those siblings are still alive, so their rights transfer to their children. None of their personal relationships with their late brother or uncle is considered relevant....

Even further complicating the matters: It's almost certain the Internal Revenue Service is going to take an interest in Prince's wealth, as well. The IRS and the estate of Michael Jackson have battled for the better part of a decade.... Jackson's executors claimed it had a $7 million net worth when he died in 2009. The IRS begged to differ, claiming it was worth more than $1.1 billion. Among the matters under dispute: the value of Michael Jackson's image itself....

Prince

It's certainly not unheard of for a celebrity to die without a will. Amy Winehouse didn't have one. Neither did Sonny Bono. Moreover, wills and estate plans in and of themselves don't prevent disputes from breaking out. Multiple trusts and a prenuptial agreement did not stop Robin Williams' children from battling with their stepmother over the comedian's personal possessions....

But Prince was notorious for the control he exercised over his work—that's likely why there are so many unreleased recordings. And now a committee of heirs with possibly competing wants, needs, and interests will sort through it? Good luck with that.

Source: Slate (Apr. 27, 2016).

---

the economic health of the decedent's family. Although intestate succession is usually based on family relationships that are defined by marriage or blood, adopted persons and persons born with the assistance of reproductive technology are today generally treated as equivalent to their bloodline counterparts. In a majority of states, the law of intestacy does not provide for unmarried cohabiting partners, nor does it provide for step relations in a blended family, though in some states recent law reform has added persons in both categories to the list of intestate takers. If there are no surviving relations within the degree of kinship specified by the intestacy statute, the decedent's property *escheats*, meaning that it reverts to the state.

Debate over intestacy laws is fraught with questions of morality and the proper role of the state in establishing social norms. Some commentators have argued that shaping social norms and advancing other such policies are appropriate considerations in designing an intestacy statute. Thus, some have advocated for recognition of unmarried cohabiting partners, both same-sex and opposite-sex, as intestate takers on the grounds that recognition in intestacy would validate the propriety of such relationships. Other commentators have pushed back, arguing against the use of intestacy law to shape social norms.[9]

Even if you agree that the primary policy of intestacy law should be to carry out the probable intent of the typical intestate decedent, is there room for secondary policy considerations such as textual simplicity and ease of administration? What policies should inform the design of an intestacy statute when the probable intent of the typical intestate decedent is unknown or ambiguous?

You should compare the rules discussed below with your intuitions of the probable intent of the typical intestate decedent. Consider whether your intuitions are influenced by your personal values, and give thought to the proper roles of empiricism, intuition, and morality in designing an intestacy statute. The stakes extend beyond intestate succession. The law of intestacy supplies rules of construction applicable to wills, trusts, and other will substitutes, and it can be influential or even determinative of other questions, such as who qualifies for Social Security survivor benefits. The law of intestacy also influences the debate over the extent to which a person should be free to disinherit a spouse or children, a subject we take up in Chapter 8.

3. Heirship and the Expectancy of an Heir Apparent

No living person has *heirs*. To use the Latin phrase, *nemo est haeres viventis*. *A*'s heirs can be identified only by reference to the applicable intestacy statute at the moment of *A*'s death. The persons who would inherit the property of *A*, a living person, if *A* died within the next hour, are *A*'s *heirs apparent*. They have a mere *expectancy* that is both contingent on their surviving *A* and defeasible by *A*'s contrary disposition by will, will substitute, or lifetime gift. A person named in a will is a *devisee, legatee,* or *beneficiary*, not an heir. And like the interest of an heir apparent, the interest of a devisee is a mere expectancy until the death of the testator.

An expectancy of an inheritance is not a legal interest. It cannot be transferred at law. However, a purported transfer of an expectancy for an adequate consideration may be enforceable in equity if the court views it as fair under all the circumstances.[10]

---

9. *See, e.g.*, Susan Gary, The Probate Definition of Family: A Proposal for Guided Discretion in Intestacy, 45 U. Mich. J.L. Reform 787 (2012); Lee-ford Tritt, Technical Correction or Tectonic Shift: Competing Default Rule Theories Under the New Uniform Probate Code, 61 Ala. L. Rev. 273 (2010); Ronald J. Scalise, Jr., Honor Thy Father and Mother? How Intestacy Law Goes Too Far in Protecting Parents, 37 Seton Hall L. Rev. 171 (2006); Ralph C. Brashier, Inheritance Law and the Evolving Family (2004); Adam J. Hirsch, Default Rules in Inheritance Law: A Problem in Search of Its Context, 73 Fordham L. Rev. 1031 (2004); Frances H. Foster, The Family Paradigm of Inheritance Law, 80 N.C. L. Rev. 199 (2001); E. Gary Spitko, The Expressive Function of Succession Law and the Merits of Non-Marital Inclusion, 41 Ariz. L. Rev. 1063 (1999); *see also* Rebecca Friedman, Intestate Intent: Presumed Will Theory, Duty Theory, and the Flaw of Relying on Average Decedent Intent, 49 Real Prop. Tr. & Est. L.J. 565 (2015).

10. Undoubtedly, the most famous sale of an expectancy was the sale of Esau's birthright to Jacob for a bowl of pottage. Genesis 25:29-34. Would Esau's promise be enforceable under American law?

Should a release of an expectancy to the donor be subject to less judicial scrutiny than a transfer of an expectancy to a third party? *See* Katheleen R. Guzman, Releasing the Expectancy, 34 Ariz. St. L.J. 775 (2002).

"Bentley, I don't care if you <u>are</u> my heir apparent.
Stop peeking in here fifty times a day!"
Dana Fradon/The New Yorker Collection/The Cartoon Bank

4. Applicable Law and the Uniform Probate Code

Generally speaking, the law of the state where a decedent was domiciled at death governs the disposition of the decedent's personal property, and the law of the state where the decedent's real property is located governs the disposition of real property.

Because the law of intestacy can vary considerably from state to state, lawyers must be familiar with the intestacy statutes of the state in which they intend to practice.[11] We reproduce here the intestacy provisions of the Uniform Probate Code (UPC). In later chapters, we excerpt not only the UPC, but also the Uniform Trust Code (see page 389) and other uniform laws relevant to the topic under discussion. The Uniform Law Commission, which promulgates uniform laws for enactment by the states, has had a profound influence on the development of the law of wills, trusts, and estates.[12] So has the American Law Institute, through the Restatements of Property, of Trusts, and of Restitution and Unjust Enrichment.[13]

---

11. The intestate succession scheme of each state is summarized in Jeffrey A. Schoenblum, Multistate Guide to Estate Planning tbl. 7 (2016) (updated annually).

12. The Uniform Law Commission is

> comprised of state commissions on uniform laws from each state, the District of Columbia, . . . Puerto Rico, and the U.S. Virgin Islands. Each jurisdiction determines the method of appointment and the number of commissioners actually appointed. . . . While some commissioners serve as state legislators, most are practitioners, judges, and law professors. They serve for specific terms, and receive no salaries or fees for their work with the ULC. . . . The commissioners . . . draft[] and propos[e] specific statutes in areas of the law where uniformity between the states is desirable. It must be emphasized that the ULC can only propose — no uniform law is effective until a state legislature adopts it.

Uniform Law Commission, About the ULC, https://perma.cc/PA9C-D5ZT.

13. The American Law Institute holds itself out as "the leading independent organization in the United States producing scholarly work to clarify, modernize, and improve the law. ALI drafts, discusses, revises, and publishes Restatements of the Law, Model Codes, and Principles of law." American Law Institute, About ALI, https://perma.cc/Q4WT-MATC.

When the UPC was originally promulgated in 1969, the stated purpose of its intestacy provisions was "to reflect the normal desire of the owner of wealth as to disposition of his property at death."[14] About one-third of the states adopted laws substantially conforming to major parts of the 1969 UPC, and other states enacted particular sections. Article VI, dealing with nonprobate transfers, was substantially revised in 1989. Article II, dealing with intestacy and wills, was overhauled in 1990. Portions of the UPC have been revised further, most comprehensively in 2008. The 1990 and 2008 revisions were explained as follows: "The pre-1990 Code's basic pattern of intestate succession . . . was designed to provide suitable rules for the person of modest means who relies on the estate plan provided by law. The 1990 and 2008 revisions were intended to further that purpose, by fine tuning the various sections and bringing them into line with developing public policy and family relationships."[15] Is reform to align with "developing public policy" consistent with the principle of freedom of disposition?

You should compare the probate code of your state with the UPC and, to the extent they differ, consider whether the UPC approach is better or worse than the one adopted in your state. Figure 2.1, page 71, is a summary of the UPC intestacy provisions.

Uniform Probate Code (Unif. Law Comm'n 1990, as amended 2008)

§ 2-101. Intestate Estate

(a) Any part of a decedent's estate not effectively disposed of by will passes by intestate succession to the decedent's heirs as prescribed in this [code], except as modified by the decedent's will.

(b) A decedent by will may expressly exclude or limit the right of an individual or class to succeed to property of the decedent passing by intestate succession. If that individual or a member of that class survives the decedent, the share of the decedent's intestate estate to which that individual or class would have succeeded passes as if that individual or each member of that class had disclaimed his [or her] intestate share.

§ 2-102. Share of Spouse[16]

The intestate share of a decedent's surviving spouse is:

(1) the entire intestate estate if:

(A) no descendant or parent of the decedent survives the decedent; or

(B) all of the decedent's surviving descendants are also descendants of the surviving spouse and there is no other descendant of the surviving spouse who survives the decedent;

(2) the first [$300,000],[17] plus three-fourths of any balance of the intestate estate, if no descendant of the decedent survives the decedent, but a parent of the decedent survives the decedent;

---

14. UPC art. II, pt. 1, gen. cmt. (1969).

15. UPC art. II, pt. 1, gen. cmt. (2008).

16. The UPC's alternate section for community property states (§ 2-102A) provides for the same distribution of separate property as is in § 2-102 and further provides that community property passes to the surviving spouse whether or not the decedent is survived by descendants or parents. — Eds.

17. UPC § 1-109, added to the Code in 2008, provides for an annual adjustment, based on the Consumer Price Index, of the dollar amounts stated in the Code. — Eds.

(3) the first [$225,000], plus one-half of any balance of the intestate estate, if all of the decedent's surviving descendants are also descendants of the surviving spouse and the surviving spouse has one or more surviving descendants who are not descendants of the decedent;

(4) the first [$150,000], plus one-half of any balance of the intestate estate, if one or more of the decedent's surviving descendants are not descendants of the surviving spouse.

§ 2-103. Share of Heirs Other Than Surviving Spouse

(a) Any part of the intestate estate not passing to a decedent's surviving spouse under Section 2-102, or the entire intestate estate if there is no surviving spouse, passes in the following order to the individuals who survive the decedent:

(1) to the decedent's descendants by representation;

(2) if there is no surviving descendant, to the decedent's parents equally if both survive, or to the surviving parent if only one survives;

(3) if there is no surviving descendant or parent, to the descendants of the decedent's parents or either of them by representation;

(4) if there is no surviving descendant, parent, or descendant of a parent, but the decedent is survived on both the paternal and maternal sides by one or more grandparents or descendants of grandparents:

(A) half to the decedent's paternal grandparents equally if both survive, to the surviving paternal grandparent if only one survives, or to the descendants of the decedent's paternal grandparents or either of them if both are deceased, the descendants taking by representation; and

(B) half to the decedent's maternal grandparents equally if both survive, to the surviving maternal grandparent if only one survives, or to the descendants of the decedent's maternal grandparents or either of them if both are deceased, the descendants taking by representation;

(5) if there is no surviving descendant, parent, or descendant of a parent, but the decedent is survived by one or more grandparents or descendants of grandparents on the paternal but not the maternal side, or on the maternal but not the paternal side, to the decedent's relatives on the side with one or more surviving members in the manner described in paragraph (4).

(b) If there is no taker under subsection (a), but the decedent has:

(1) one deceased spouse who has one or more descendants who survive the decedent, the estate or part thereof passes to that spouse's descendants by representation; or

(2) more than one deceased spouse who has one or more descendants who survive the decedent, an equal share of the estate or part thereof passes to each set of descendants by representation.

§ 2-105. No Taker

If there is no taker under the provisions of this [article], the intestate estate passes to the state.

Summary of the UPC Intestacy Provisions   Figure 2.1

Facts	UPC Authority	Disposition
S; no D; no P	§ 2-102(1)(A)	all to S
S; D	§ 2-102(1)(B)	all to S if all D are also S's and S has no other surviving descendants
	§ 2-102(3)	$225,000 plus half of the rest to S if D are also S's and S has other descendants; other half to D
	§ 2-102(4)	$150,000 plus half of the rest to S if one or more D is not S's; other half to D
S; no D; P	§ 2-102(2)	$300,000 plus three-fourths of the rest to S; other one-fourth to P
no S; D	§ 2-103(a)(1)	all to D (per capita at each generation)
no S; no D; P	§ 2-103(a)(2)	all to P
no S; no D; no P; BorS	§ 2-103(a)(3)	all to BorS (per capita at each generation)
no S; no D; no P; no BorS; G or GD	§ 2-103(a)(4)	if both paternal and maternal G or GD, one-half to paternal G or GD and one-half to maternal G or GD (all to G or, if none, per capita at each GD generation); or
	§ 2-103(a)(5)	if survivors on one side only, all to G or GD on that side (all to G or, if none, per capita at each GD generation)
no S; no D; no P; no BorS; no G or GD	§ 2-103(b) § 2-105	stepchildren or, if none, then escheat to state; therefore, no "laughing heirs"

S = surviving spouse
D = surviving descendant(s) of decedent
P = surviving parent(s) of decedent

BorS = surviving sibling(s) of decedent; surviving descendant(s) of decedent's parents
G = surviving grandparent(s) of decedent
GD = surviving descendant(s) of grandparents

B. THE STRUCTURE OF INTESTATE SUCCESSION

We turn now to the structure of intestate succession. In accordance with the objective of carrying out the probable intent of the typical intestate decedent, the law of intestacy has evolved a set of elaborated default rules that provide for different outcomes depending on certain of a decedent's particular circumstances—for example, whether the decedent was married, had children, and so on.[18] Given the ever more varied and complex family and family-like relationships in contemporary society, however, a fair question is whether the circumstances considered by current law should be revised to account for these newer but increasingly common kinds of relationships.

---

18. *See* Adam J. Hirsch, Incomplete Wills, 111 Mich. L. Rev. 1423, 1424 (2013) (characterizing intestacy law as a "schedule of contingencies").

Across the states we find two areas of general agreement in current law. First, in all states, after the spouse's share, *descendants* take to the exclusion of *ancestors* and *collateral kindred*. Second, in most states, intestacy favors only *spouses* and *blood relations*, with the latter category today encompassing adopted persons and persons born of assisted reproductive technology. Other kinds of relationships are excluded, though reform in some states reflects the beginning of a trend toward recognizing *stepchildren* and *in-laws* as potential intestate takers.

Across the states we also find two areas of divergence. First, there is much variation in the size of the *surviving spouse's share*, ranging from one-fourth to the entirety of the decedent spouse's estate, and whether the survivor must share with the decedent's descendants or parents. Second, there are competing methods for implementing the principle of *representation* by which the descendants of a predeceased child take the child's share (the surviving descendants are said to "represent" the predeceased child).

1. Surviving Spouse

a. The Spouse's Share

Empirical studies show that, if there are no stepchildren, most persons want everything to go to the surviving spouse, thus excluding parents, siblings, and even children. This preference is particularly strong among persons with modest estates, who believe the surviving spouse may need the entire estate for support and will leave any remainder to the couple's children. The richer the person, the greater the desire that children or collaterals share with the spouse.

In most states, the surviving spouse receives at least a one-half share of the decedent's estate, which is a significant increase from the one-quarter or one-third that was typical earlier in the twentieth century. There are many variations in the specifics, however, such as giving the surviving spouse a lump sum plus one-half of the remainder, or giving the surviving spouse a one-half share if only one child survives and a one-third share if more than one child survives.

The current UPC provision for the surviving spouse is relatively generous. Under § 2-102(1), page 69, if all the decedent's descendants are also descendants of the surviving spouse, and the surviving spouse has no other descendants, so that there are no stepchildren, the surviving spouse takes the entire estate to the exclusion of the decedent's descendants. The theory of this provision is that the typical intestate decedent would want to provide financial security to the surviving spouse, and that the surviving spouse will pass any remainder to the couple's children.[19]

Giving everything to the spouse and nothing to the children was a novel statutory approach, but studies of estates with minor children show it to be the usual practice

---

19. *See* Lawrence W. Waggoner, The Multiple-Marriage Society and Spousal Rights Under the Revised Uniform Probate Code, 76 Iowa L. Rev. 223 (1991). The empirical studies on which the drafters relied are cited in the comment to UPC § 2-102.

of those leaving wills. It also has the virtue of avoiding a guardian for the property or a conservatorship for a minor child (see page 124). Thanks in large part to the influence of the UPC, intestacy statutes that in the absence of stepchildren give the surviving spouse the entirety of the decedent's estate are increasingly common.

The provisions in subsections (3) and (4), giving the surviving spouse less if either spouse has a child by someone other than the other spouse, were also unusual when originally proposed. But they follow from the surviving spouse's divided loyalties, reflecting a potential preference for his or her own children, in a blended family that includes stepchildren. These provisions are thus an adaptation of the law to the modern prevalence of multiple marriages and blended families.

If there is no descendant, about half of the states provide, as does UPC § 2-102(2), that the surviving spouse share the estate with the decedent's parents, if any. If no parent survives, the surviving spouse usually takes all to the exclusion of collateral relatives, as the UPC provides, but in a few states the spouse shares with the decedent's siblings.

NOTES

1. The Logic of UPC § 2-102(3)-(4).   Suppose Howard has two children by Wendy. Wendy has an additional child from a previous marriage. If Howard dies intestate, what will be Wendy's share under UPC § 2-102? If it is Wendy who dies intestate, what will be Howard's share? What is the basis for the different amounts provided under § 2-102(3) and (4)?

2. Length of Marriage.   Suppose *H* and *W* have been married for one year.[20] *H* dies, survived by *W* and a brother, but no parent. What is *W*'s share? The amount would not change even if *H* and *W* had been married for many years. Compare UPC § 2-203(b) (1990, rev. 2008), page 543, which takes into account the length of the marriage in determining the surviving spouse's *forced share*, that is, the mandatory share to which a spouse is entitled irrespective of the decedent spouse's will. Why is length of marriage relevant for the spouse's forced share but not the intestate share? In Arkansas, if the decedent has no descendants, a spouse of fewer than three years takes a one-half share, and a spouse of three or more years takes the entire estate.[21]

3. Invalid or Informal Marriage.   Suppose Henry dies intestate. Anne, with whom Henry had been living but to whom Henry was not married, would like to claim a spouse's share. Is Anne entitled to such a share if she thought she had married Henry, but the marriage was invalid? *See* Bedard v. Corliss, 973 N.E.2d 691 (Mass. App. 2012).

---

20. Or even just a few minutes, as in Estate of Neiderhiser, 2 Pa. D. & C.3d 302 (C.P. 1977), discussed in Chapter 8 at page 523, n.3.

21. *See* Ark. Code Ann. § 28-9-214 (2016); *see also* Jessica Feinberg, Gradual Marriage, 20 Lewis & Clark L. Rev. 1, 22-23 (2016).

b. Unmarried Cohabiting Partners

The policies that underpin the spousal intestate share—giving effect to the probable intent of the decedent and protecting those whom the decedent regarded as family—seem also to apply to unmarried cohabiting partners who are in a committed relationship. Studies show that a substantial majority of such partners want the surviving partner to take a share of the decedent partner's estate.[22] Should the law be revised to make a surviving unmarried cohabiting partner an heir? If so, should the surviving partner's succession rights mirror those of a formal spouse? Would such a reform in effect resurrect the notion of common law marriage?

Prior to the decision in Obergefell v. Hodges, 135 S. Ct. 2584 (2015), the question of whether to recognize intestacy rights for unmarried cohabiting partners was obscured by the more politically salient question of whether to permit marriage by same-sex couples. In lieu of recognizing same-sex marriage, some states enacted statutes that gave intestacy and other spousal rights to cohabiting partners in a registered "domestic partnership" or "civil union." After *Obergefell*, all couples—regardless of the sex of the partners—are permitted to marry. And in all states, a surviving spouse is an intestate heir of the decedent spouse.

But what of unmarried cohabiting partners, whether opposite sex or same sex, who choose not to marry, but for whom the nature of the relationship indicates that each partner would want the other to be an intestate heir? The demographic data show an unmistakable slowdown in marital families and increase in functional families through unmarried cohabitation. The 2010 census found that married couples accounted for 48.4 percent of households, down from 51.7 percent in the 2000 census, whereas in 2010 unmarried couples represented 6.6 percent of households, up from 5.2 percent in 2000.[23] Even more striking, between 2000 and 2010, a period in which the population grew by 9.71 percent, the number of married households increased by only 3.7 percent, whereas the number of unmarried couple households increased by 41.4 percent.[24]

The phenomenon of unmarried cohabitation is not an artifact of nonrecognition of same-sex marriage prior to *Obergefell*. To the contrary, the census data show that nearly 90 percent of unmarried cohabiting partners are opposite sex.[25] Unmarried couples are also increasingly having children. The 2010 census found that 39 percent of unmarried opposite-sex couple households, and 17 percent of unmarried same-sex

---

22. *See* Mary Louise Fellows, E. Gary Spitko & Charles Q. Strohm, An Empirical Assessment of the Potential for Will Substitutes to Improve State Intestacy Statutes, 85 Ind. L.J. 409 (2010); Mary Louise Fellows et al., Committed Partners and Inheritance: An Empirical Study, 16 Law & Ineq. 1 (1998).

23. Lawrence W. Waggoner, Marriage Is on the Decline and Cohabitation Is on the Rise: At What Point, If Ever, Should Unmarried Partners Acquire Marital Rights?, 50 Fam. L.Q. 215, 221 (2016).

24. Id. at 215.

25. Id. at 221-22.

couple households, included children.[26] We take up the inheritance rights of a non-marital child at page 108.

In thinking about how the law might be revised to make an unmarried cohabiting partner an heir, an obvious difficulty is crafting the trigger for status as a cohabiting partner.[27] One possible answer is a facts-and-circumstances test. But would such a test result in more litigation? Would it disserve couples who chose not to marry to avoid marriage-like property rules? What if the test were focused on objective factors such as living in a common household, intermingling finances, and sharing in parenting? Statutes recognizing marital rights for unmarried cohabiting partners based on the facts and circumstances have been enacted in Australia, Canada, and New Zealand, and one is pending in the United Kingdom.[28]

Another possible solution is a formal registry. But would a registry exclude unmarried committed partners who would want legal recognition but did not know to register? Lurking in the background are questions of class and race. "An unfortunate feature of some cohabiting couples is that they are at or below the poverty level: 'As compared with their married counterparts, unmarried parents are lower income, less educated, disproportionately nonwhite, and more likely to have children from multiple partners.' For many of them, they 'have not selected their situation, they have settled for it.'"[29]

In 1995, Professor Lawrence W. Waggoner proposed an amendment to the UPC—to become UPC § 2-102B—that would have provided a spousal-like intestate share for unmarried "committed partners." To be a committed partner a person had to "share a common household with the decedent in a marriage-like relationship." In 2002, the Joint Editorial Board for Uniform Trusts and Estates Acts (JEB-UTEA), the main oversight body for uniform law activity pertaining to trusts and estates, revisited Waggoner's proposal and asked Professor Thomas P. Gallanis to draft a model statute. Gallanis proposed spousal-like intestacy and elective share rights for

Professor Lawrence W. Waggoner was the reporter for the 1990 and 2008 revisions to UPC Article II and for the Restatement (Third) of Property: Wills and Other Donative Transfers, published in four volumes starting in 1999 and finishing in 2011.

---

26. Id. at 224.

27. *See* E. Gary Spitko, An Accrual/Multi-Factor Approach to Intestate Inheritance Rights for Unmarried Committed Partners, 81 Or. L. Rev. 255 (2002); *see also* Elizabeth S. Scott & Robert E. Scott, From Contract to Status: Collaboration and the Evolution of Novel Family Relationships, 115 Colum. L. Rev. 293 (2015).

28. *See* Waggoner, *supra* note 23, at 216, 233-34.

29. Waggoner, *supra* note 23, at 230 (quoting Clare Huntington, Postmarital Family Law: A Legal Structure for Nonmarital Families, 67 Stan. L. Rev. 167, 186-87 (2015), and Ira Mark Ellman, Marital Roles and Declining Marriage Rates, 41 Fam. L.Q. 455, 485 (2007)).

unmarried cohabiting partners established by registration or by proof of "sharing a common household."[30]

Both the Waggoner and the Gallanis proposals assumed that an intestate share for a surviving unmarried cohabiting partner should be the same as that for a surviving spouse. But must this be so? Professor E. Gary Spitko has argued for an accrual-type share that would increase over the length of the relationship.[31] Would this approach address the lack of certainty that follows from the lack of a formal marriage? Would it be consistent with the probable intent of the partners?

Although the UPC was revised extensively in 2008, none of the revisions addressed the rights of unmarried cohabiting partners, on which the UPC remains silent. Following *Obergefell*, however, in 2016 the JEB-UTEA again recommended that the Uniform Law Commission consider the question of intestacy and elective share rights for cohabiting partners.[32] That recommendation was being considered as this book went to press in early 2017.

c. The Problem of Simultaneous Death

A person succeeds to the property of a decedent only if the person survives the decedent for an instant of time. In the twentieth century, the development of travel by car and by airplane gave rise to an increase in simultaneous deaths of closely related persons — particularly spouses, who are apt to travel together. When a person dies simultaneously with his heir or devisee, does the heir or devisee succeed to the person's property? The problem of simultaneous death arises not only in intestacy, but also under wills, trusts, and other modes of nonprobate transfer in which the governing instrument does not avoid the problem by requiring a beneficiary to survive the donor by a stated period of time such as 30 or 60 days.

The original Uniform Simultaneous Death Act (USDA) (Unif. Law Comm'n 1940, rev. 1953), drafted to answer this question, provided that if "there is no sufficient evidence" of the order of deaths, each of two simultaneously dying persons was deemed to have predeceased the other, so neither inherited from the other. If an insured and the third-party beneficiary of a life insurance contract died simultaneously, the proceeds were distributed as if the insured survived the beneficiary. And if two joint tenants or community property owners, *A* and *B*, died simultaneously, one-half of the property was distributed as if *A* survived and one-half was distributed as if *B* survived.

At first, the USDA was thought to offer an elegant solution to the problem of simultaneous death. But courts were soon faced with the ghastly interpretive question of what constitutes "sufficient evidence" of the order of deaths. The tragic case of Janus v. Tarasewicz, 482 N.E.2d 418 (Ill. App. 1985), is illustrative. At issue in *Janus* was

---

30. T.P. Gallanis, Inheritance Rights for Domestic Partners, 79 Tul. L. Rev. 55, 87 (2004).

31. *See* Spitko, *supra* note 27.

32. The Board took notice in particular of a fresh "Draft Defacto Marriage Act" proposed by Professor Waggoner in 2016. See *supra* note 23, at 239-40.

the order of "death of a husband and wife, Stanley and Theresa Janus, who died after ingesting Tylenol capsules which had been laced with cyanide by an unknown perpetrator prior to its sale in stores." Having just returned from their honeymoon, Stanley and Theresa took the contaminated Tylenol at the home of Stanley's brother, Adam, who had died earlier that day, also from the contaminated Tylenol.

Not long after the two families were celebrating the wedding of their children, and then mourning the deaths of those children (and the death of Adam), they were fighting over the proceeds from Stanley's $100,000 life insurance policy. Stanley had named Theresa as the primary beneficiary and his mother as the contingent beneficiary. Under the USDA, if there was "sufficient evidence" that Theresa survived Stanley, the proceeds would be paid to her estate and then would pass by intestacy to her family. If not, the proceeds would be paid to Stanley's mother as the contingent beneficiary.

Applying the "sufficient evidence" test of the original USDA, the trial court took evidence on Stanley's and Theresa's responses to CPR at the scene; a paramedic's notes and recollections about their vital signs and the responsiveness of their pupils to light while en route to the hospital (neither "showed any signs of being able to breathe on their own while they were being transported"); their responsiveness to artificial respiration and other such interventions; the results of electrocardiograms and other tests administered in the hospital; and expert testimony about the meaning of all of this medical evidence.

The trial court ruled that "sufficient evidence" showed that Theresa had survived Stanley, if only for a day and half, and the appellate court affirmed:

> There is no dispute among the treating physicians and expert witnesses that Stanley Janus died in both a cardiopulmonary sense and a brain death sense when his vital signs disappeared en route to the hospital and were never reestablished.[33] . . . In contrast, . . . hospital personnel were able to reestablish a spontaneous blood pressure and pulse [for Theresa] which did not have to be artificially maintained by a pacemaker or medication. Once spontaneous circulation was restored in the emergency room, Theresa was put on a mechanical respirator and transferred to the intensive care unit. . . . Viewing the record in its entirety, we cannot say that the trial court's finding of sufficient evidence of Theresa's survivorship was against the manifest weight of the evidence.

Was this outcome, which awarded the proceeds from Stanley's insurance policy to Theresa's family, in accord with Stanley's likely intent? Was the court's close review of the medical evidence consistent with the purpose of the USDA to distribute property as if the donor (Stanley) had survived the beneficiary (Theresa) in the event of proximate

---

33. Under Uniform Determination of Death Act § 1 (Unif. Law Comm'n 1980), enacted in most states, "[a]n individual who has sustained either (1) irreversible cessation of circulatory and respiratory functions, or (2) irreversible cessation of all functions of the entire brain, including the brain stem, is dead."—Eds.

death from a common disaster? In light of this purpose, how much evidence of survivorship is enough to be "sufficient"?

Suppose H and W are killed in the crash of a private airplane. An autopsy reveals W's brain is intact and there is carbon monoxide in her bloodstream. H's brain, by contrast, is crushed, and there is no carbon monoxide in his bloodstream. In In re Bucci's Will, 293 N.Y.S.2d 994 (Sur. 1968), the court held this to be "sufficient evidence" of W's survival.

Taking notice of *Janus*, *Bucci*, and other cases "in which the representative of one of the individuals attempts, through the use of gruesome medical evidence, to prove that the one he or she represents survived the other by an instant or two,"[34] in 1993 the Uniform Law Commission amended the USDA to provide that an heir, devisee, or life insurance beneficiary who fails to survive by 120 hours (5 days) is deemed to have predeceased the decedent. A claimant must establish survivorship by 120 hours by clear and convincing evidence. UPC §§ 2-104 and 2-702 (1990, rev. 2008) provide likewise. The prefatory note to the revised USDA explains:

> Even in cases in which it is indisputable that one of the two survived the other, such as a case in which one is clearly dead at the scene of the accident and the other clearly dies in the ambulance on the way to the hospital, the policy of the original Act plainly should apply. . . . This version of the USDA, then, extends the application of the original Act to situations in which there is sufficient evidence that one of the individuals survived the other one, but the period of survival was insubstantial. . . . A clear and convincing evidence standard of proof of survival by 120 hours is imposed throughout in order to reduce litigation and to resolve close cases in favor of non-survival.

What result in *Janus* and *Bucci* under the newer 120-hour rule? Would those cases even have been litigated?

NOTES

1. A Common Disaster? The 120-hour rule of the amended USDA and UPC addresses roughly contemporaneous deaths even if they do not arise from a common disaster. Suppose H dies of a heart attack. The next day, while en route to the cemetery, W is killed by H's coffin, which was propelled into her when the hearse carrying them was hit from behind by another vehicle.[35] What result under the sufficient evidence test? What result under the 120-hour rule?

Suppose that, after W collapses, H calls 911 and then begins administering CPR. With the 911 operator still on the line, the call goes silent. When the paramedics arrive,

---

34. USDA pref. note (1993).
35. *See* Widow Is Killed by Husband's Coffin, Evening Stand. (London), Nov. 12, 2008; *see also* "Doubleheader" Funeral Service Held for NY Couple, Times Union, Feb. 22, 2013 (H died en route to W's funeral; impromptu double funeral).

they find *H* slumped over *W*, both dead.[36] What result under the sufficient evidence test? What result under the 120-hour rule?

2. Is 120 Hours Long Enough?   Suppose *W* is lacking in higher brain function, but her family insists that her heart and lungs be kept working on a ventilator for more than 120 hours, long enough to allow her to inherit from *H*, who died in the same disaster. Would the 30- or 60-day survivorship clauses common in well-drafted instruments be a better model for statutory reform? For example: "If my wife survives me by 30 days, I give to her. . . ."[37]

3. Severed Heads.   If you are interested in whether a severed head retains feeling and consciousness for a few moments after severance and therefore arguably remains alive for that period, the experiments carried out by French doctors after the invention of the guillotine are instructive. The doctors were trying to discover if death by guillotine was really instantaneous and painless, as Dr. Guillotin, the inventor, had claimed. They found that decapitated heads could wink in response to questions, as agreed in advance of decapitation.[38]

2. Descendants

In all states, after the spouse's share (if any) is set aside, children and descendants of deceased children take the remainder of the decedent's property to the exclusion of everyone else.[39]

a. Representation

When one of several children has died before a decedent, leaving descendants, all states provide that the child's descendants *represent* the dead child and divide the child's share among themselves.

Consider the family depicted in Figure 2.2, page 80. The intestate decedent, *A*, a widow, has three children. One of them, *C*, dies before *A*, survived by a husband and two children. *A* is survived by two children, *B* and *D*, and by five grandchildren, *E*, *F*, *G*, *H*, and *I*. *C*'s children take *C*'s share by representation, so *A*'s heirs are *B* (1/3), *D* (1/3), *F* (1/6), and *G* (1/6). *E*, *H*, and *I* take nothing. *C*'s spouse, the decedent's son-in-law, also takes nothing. In-laws are excluded as intestate successors in most states (see page 88).

---

36. *See* Washington Man Dies Trying to Revive Dead Wife, Seattle Times, Mar. 25, 2011.

37. Northern Trust, Will & Trust Forms 101-2 (2004).

38. *See* Alister Kershaw, A History of the Guillotine 80-89 (1958); *see also* Antonia Fraser, Mary Queen of Scots 539 (1969) (reporting that Mary's lips moved for a quarter of an hour after she was beheaded).

39. Parents of the decedent are therefore not heirs if the decedent leaves a child. Why should this be so (especially if the child is an adult)? Why isn't the decedent's property used to support aging parents rather than an able-bodied adult child?

Figure 2.2

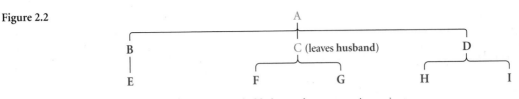

Survivors are in **bold**; deceased persons are in regular type.

In more complicated contexts, there are different views about what taking by representation means. The fundamental issue is whether the division into shares should begin at the generational level immediately below the decedent or at the closest generational level with a descendant of the decedent alive. "This primary-share generation is often described by the courts as the generation at which the 'stocks' or 'roots' are determined."[40] Consider the family depicted in Figure 2.3. *A* has two children, *B* and *C*. *B* predeceases *A*, leaving a child, *D*. *C* predeceases *A*, leaving two children, *E* and *F*. *A* dies intestate, leaving no surviving spouse, survived by *D*, *E*, and *F*. How is *A*'s estate distributed? There are three basic systems, with a twist in some states that might be considered a fourth system.[41]

Figure 2.3

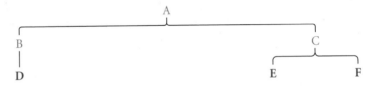

Survivors are in **bold**; deceased persons are in regular type.

(1) English Per Stirpes.   About one-third of the states follow the system of English distribution *per stirpes* ("by the stocks"). Sometimes called *strict per stirpes*, the English per stirpes system of representation treats each line of descent equally. The property is divided into as many shares as there are living children of the designated person and deceased children who have descendants living (thus the decedent's children are the root generation). The children of each deceased descendant represent their deceased parent and are moved into their parent's position beginning at the first generation below the designated person.

Returning to Figure 2.3, under English per stirpes *A*'s property is divided into two shares at the level of *A*'s children. So *D* takes *B*'s one-half by representation and *E* and *F* split *C*'s one-half by representation. Although this system produces unequal shares across the grandchildren (one-half for *D* versus one-fourth each for *E* and *F*), it produces equal shares across the decedent's lines of descent (each takes one-half). English per stirpes thus assures what is sometimes called *vertical equality*, with parity across

---

40. Restatement (Third) of Property: Wills and Other Donative Transfers § 2.3 cmt. d (Am. Law Inst. 1999).

41. *See* Schoenblum, *supra* note 11, at tbl. 7.

lines of descent, but at the expense of *horizontal equality* in the form of equal shares for each taker of equal degree of kinship to the donor.

(2) Modern Per Stirpes.   Nearly half of the states follow a modified version of English per stirpes that is called *modern per stirpes* or *per capita with representation.* Under this system, one looks first to see whether any children survived the decedent. If so, the distribution is identical to that under English per stirpes. If not, as in Figure 2.3, the estate is divided equally (per capita) at the first generation in which there are living takers, which is usually the generation of the decedent's grandchildren. Under modern per stirpes, in other words, the root generation at which the decedent's estate is divided into shares is the one nearest to the decedent in which one or more descendants of the decedent are alive. Any deceased descendant in that level is represented by her descendants using an English per stirpes distribution.[42]

Returning to Figure 2.3, because *B* and *C* are dead, and because *D*, *E*, and *F* are all grandchildren and so of equal degree of kinship to *A*, *A*'s estate is divided equally among *D*, *E*, and *F* in thirds. If *F* had predeceased *A*, leaving descendants, *F*'s descendants would represent *F* and take *F*'s one-third. Modern per stirpes thus treats equally each line of descent beginning at the closest living generation—a form of vertical equality with horizontal equality at the closest living generation. Two studies, albeit now more than 40 years old, found that an overwhelming majority of people prefer dividing the stocks at the closest generation in which someone is alive.[43]

(3) Per Capita at Each Generation (1990 UPC).   The remaining states, around a dozen, follow a newer, more complicated system of distribution known as *per capita at each generation*, which has been advocated by Professor Lawrence W. Waggoner since the early 1970s.[44] Section 2-106(b) of the 1990 UPC, for which Waggoner was the reporter, adopts this approach:

> (b) [Decedent's Descendants.] If, under Section 2-103(a)(1), a decedent's intestate estate or a part thereof passes "by representation" to the decedent's descendants, the estate or part thereof is divided into as many equal shares as there are (i) surviving descendants in the generation nearest to the decedent which contains one or more surviving descendants and (ii) deceased descendants in the same generation who left surviving descendants, if any. Each surviving descendant in the nearest

---

42. The twist that might be considered a fourth system, but that we treat as a variant on modern per stirpes, is in the representation of a deceased descendant below the closest generation with a living descendant. Modern per stirpes uses an English per stirpes distribution starting at the closest generation with a living descendant. Hence it could be called per capita with per stirpes representation. The 1969 UPC, by contrast, provides for representation as if the deceased descendant was the decedent—that is, it provides for distribution per capita with per capita representation. The distinction affects the actual distribution in only the rarest of cases. *See* Restatement (Third) of Property: Wills and Other Donative Transfers § 2.3 cmt. f (Am. Law Inst. 1999).

43. *See* Mary Louise Fellows et al., An Empirical Study of the Illinois Statutory Estate Plan, 1976 U. Ill. L.F. 717, 741 (95 percent of the persons interviewed); Comment, A Comparison of Iowans' Dispositive Preferences with Selected Provisions of the Iowa and Uniform Probate Codes, 63 Iowa L. Rev. 1041, 1111 (1978) (87 percent).

44. *See* Lawrence W. Waggoner, A Proposed Alternative to the Uniform Probate Code's System for Intestate Distribution Among Descendants, 66 Nw. U. L. Rev. 626 (1971).

generation is allocated one share. The remaining shares, if any, are combined and then divided in the same manner among the surviving descendants of the deceased descendants as if the surviving descendants who were allocated a share and their surviving descendants had predeceased the decedent.

Under UPC § 2-106(b), the initial division of shares is made at the closest generation in which one or more descendants are alive (the same root generation as under modern per stirpes), but the shares of deceased persons on that level are treated as one pot and are dropped down and divided equally among the representatives in the next generation. In the situation depicted in Figure 2.4, *D* takes a one-third share, and the two-thirds that would have passed to *B* and *C* had they been living is divided equally among all the children of *B* and *C*. Consequently, *E*, *F*, and *G* each take a two-ninths share.

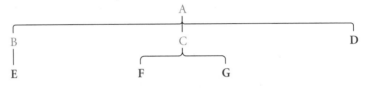

Survivors are in **bold**; deceased persons are in regular type.

The per capita at each generation system of representation achieves horizontal equality. It treats equally each taker of equal degree of kinship to the donor: "Equally near, equally dear." However, horizontal equality comes at the price of giving up vertical equality. In the situation depicted in Figure 2.4, *B*'s line takes two-ninths; *C*'s line takes four-ninths; and *D*'s line takes one-third (i.e., three-ninths).

NOTES

1. A Representation Problem.   Consider the circumstances depicted in Figure 2.5. *A* has two children, *B* and *C*. *B* predeceases *A*, leaving a child, *D*. *C* predeceases *A*, leaving two children, *E* and *F*. *E* predeceases *A*, leaving two children, *G* and *H*.

Figure 2.5

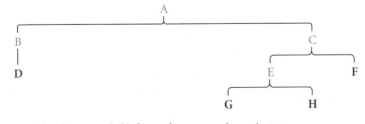

Survivors are in **bold**; deceased persons are in regular type.

Suppose *A* dies intestate, leaving no surviving spouse. How is *A*'s estate distributed under the English per stirpes system? Under the modern per stirpes system? Under the 1990 UPC? Under the intestacy statute of your state?

2. Another Representation Problem. Assume the same facts as in Note 1, except that, as depicted in Figure 2.6, *A* has another child, *Z*, and *F* has a child, *I*. *Z* predeceases *A*, leaving no descendants. *F* survives *A*, as does *F*'s child *I*.

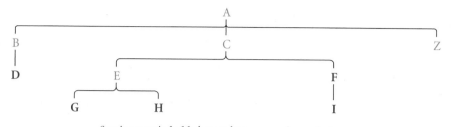

Figure 2.6

Survivors are in **bold**; deceased persons are in regular type.

Does the presence in the family tree of the surviving *I* and the deceased *Z* change the result under any of the intestacy systems? The answer is No. *I* does not take because her parent, *F*, is alive, and because no one in *Z*'s line remains, *Z*'s line is ignored.

3. Divergence Across All Three Systems. In each of the examples given thus far, at least two of the three representation systems produced the same result. In a more complicated context, all three systems could produce different results. Consider the (perhaps farfetched?) circumstances depicted in Figure 2.7.[45] *A* has three children, *B*, *C*, and *D*. *B* has two children, *E* and *F*, and one grandchild, *K*, the child of *E*. *C* has four children, *G*, *H*, *I*, and *J*, and four grandchildren, *L*, the child of *G*, *M* and *N*, the children of *H*, and *O*, the child of *J*. *D* has no children. If *A* dies intestate, survived by *F*, *I*, *J*, *K*, *L*, *M*, *N*, and *O*, then *A*'s estate will be distributed differently under English per stirpes, modern per stirpes, and the 1990 UPC. Do you see why?

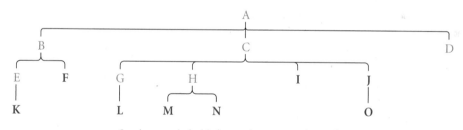

Figure 2.7

Survivors are in **bold**; deceased persons are in regular type.

4. Ascertaining Client Preferences. Which of the three systems do you prefer? Which would your parents prefer? Which would most decedents prefer? Are you sure? A questionnaire developed by one of the advisers to the UPC drafting committee revealed a divide between lawyers and their clients. Perhaps reflecting their training in traditional property law, 85 percent of the lawyers responding believed their clients wanted English per stirpes, but 71 percent of the clients themselves wanted distribution

---

45. We are indebted to Professor John Plecnik of Cleveland-Marshall College of Law for the suggestion.

per capita at each generation.[46] Although the sample was small (75 respondents) and the methodology problematic, the study suggests that lawyers' preferences may diverge from those of their clients.

b. Representation in Wills and Trusts

Suppose that a will or a trust makes a provision for "the descendants of *A*, per stirpes." Which of the representation systems will apply? The default rule of construction, applicable if the instrument does not define what is meant by "per stirpes," depends on the state. In some states, courts read "per stirpes" presumptively to call for the same representational system as provided by the state's intestacy laws. In other states, courts read "per stirpes" presumptively to reference English per stirpes (see Chapter 13 at page 875).

3. Ancestors, Collaterals, and Others

a. Parents

If an intestate decedent is survived by a descendant, the decedent's ancestors and collaterals do not take. In about half of the states, if there is no descendant, after deducting the spouse's share, the rest of the intestate's property is distributed to the decedent's parents, as under UPC § 2-102(2), page 69. In the remaining states the spouse takes to the exclusion of the decedent's parents.

b. Other Ancestors and Collaterals

If there is no spouse or parent, the decedent's heirs will be more remote ancestors or collateral kindred. All persons who are related by blood to the decedent but who are not descendants or ancestors are called *collateral kindred*. Descendants of the decedent's parents, other than the decedent and the decedent's descendants, are called *first-line collaterals*. Descendants of the decedent's grandparents, other than the decedent's parents and their descendants, are called *second-line collaterals*. The reason for this terminology is seen by glancing at the Table of Consanguinity depicted in Figure 2.8.

If the decedent is not survived by a spouse, descendant, or parent, in all jurisdictions intestate property passes to brothers and sisters and their descendants. The descendants of any deceased brothers and sisters (i.e., nephews and nieces) take by representation, usually in the same manner as the decedent's descendants. For example, UPC § 2-106(c), applicable to collaterals, is substantially similar to § 2-106(b), applicable to descendants; both provide for representation per capita at each generation.

---

46. Raymond H. Young, Meaning of "Issue" and "Descendants," 13 ACTEC Notes 225 (1988).

Figure 2.8

Table of Consanguinity

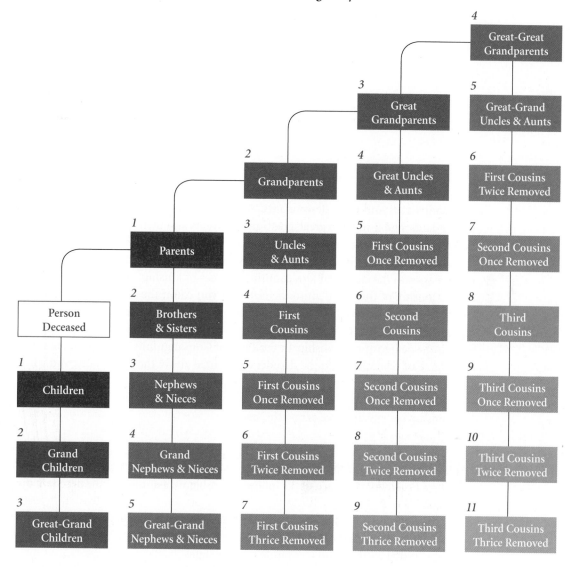

Figure 2.9, page 86, depicts circumstances involving an intestate distribution to collaterals with representation. Under the English per stirpes system, division into four shares is made at the root generation of *A*'s brothers and sisters. So, too, under the modern per stirpes system, because one sibling, *B*, is alive. Under both of these systems, *B* takes 1/4; *F* takes 1/4; *G* takes 1/12; *L*, *M*, and *N* take 1/36; *O* takes 1/12; *J* takes 1/8; and *P* takes 1/8. Under UPC § 2-106(c), *B* takes 1/4. The remaining 3/4 is divided into six shares of 1/8 each. *F*, *G*, and *J* take 1/8 each. The remaining 3/8 is divided into five shares of 3/40. *L*, *M*, *N*, *O*, and *P* take 3/40 each.

Figure 2.9

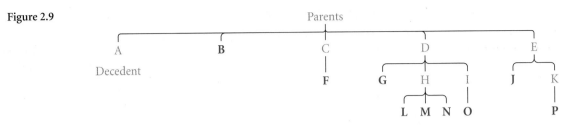

Survivors are in **bold**; deceased persons are in regular type.

If there are no first-line collaterals, the states differ on who is next in the line of succession. Most states use a *parentelic* system, under which the intestate estate passes to grandparents and their descendants, and if none to great-grandparents and their descendants, and if none to great-great-grandparents and their descendants, and so on down each line (*parentela*) descended from an ancestor until an heir is found.

Under a *degree-of-relationship* system, used in a minority of states, the intestate estate passes to the closest of kin, counting degrees of kinship. To ascertain the degree of relationship of the decedent to the claimant you count the steps (counting one for each generation) up from the decedent to the nearest common ancestor, and then you count the steps down from the common ancestor to the claimant. The total number of steps is the degree of relationship. In the Table of Consanguinity depicted in Figure 2.8, the degree of relationship to the decedent is printed above the upper left-hand corner of the box designating the relationship of the claimant.

There are numerous variations and mixtures of the parentelic and degree-of-relationship systems in force across the states.[47]

NOTE

Three Problems.   In each of the following problems, assume that the decedent died intestate:

    a. The decedent is survived by his mother, his sister, and two nephews (children of a deceased brother). How is the decedent's estate distributed under UPC § 2-103, page 70? Under the intestacy statute of your state?

    b. The decedent is survived by one first cousin on his mother's side and by two first cousins on his father's side. How is the decedent's estate distributed under UPC § 2-103? Under the intestacy statute of your state? Recall that UPC § 2-106, page 81, which defines representation, is based upon a goal of providing equal shares to those equally related to the decedent. Is the UPC treatment of the three first cousins consistent with that goal? Why are three grandchildren or three grandnephews treated alike but not three first cousins?

---

47. Massachusetts, for example, follows a degree-of-relationship system subject to a parentelic preference to break a tie between kin of equal degree. *See* Mass. Gen. Laws ch. 190B § 2-103(4) (2016).

c. The decedent is survived by *A*, the first cousin of the decedent's mother, and by *B*, the granddaughter of the decedent's first cousin on the decedent's maternal side. (You can locate these on the Table of Consanguinity in Figure 2.8.) How is the decedent's estate distributed under UPC § 2-103? Under the intestacy statute of your state?

c. Laughing Heirs

The number of possible collateral kindred is immense. Should the law permit intestate succession by distant relatives, known to lawyers as *laughing heirs*, who are so far removed from the decedent that they likely didn't know him and suffer no sense of bereavement upon learning of his death?

The Laughing Heirs of Ella Wendel, Ida Wood, and Henrietta Garrett

Ella Wendel, a recluse, died in 1931, leaving a will devising most of her $40 million estate to charity. The only persons who may contest a will are those who would take if the will is held invalid. Some 2,303 fortune hunters strove to establish they were her next of kin, so that they might contest her will as her intestate successors. Reams of evidence were fabricated, birth and death certificates altered, and tales spun of incest and children born out of wedlock. One man was sent to jail for fabricating evidence, and the Surrogate referred the activities of six lawyers to the Grievance Committee of the Bar. Ultimately nine persons were established to be her first cousins, and they settled out of court with the charities. In re Wendel, 257 N.Y.S. 87 (Sur. 1932); 262 N.Y.S. 41 (Sur. 1933); 287 N.Y.S. 893 (Sur. 1936). Justice John M. Harlan and Judge Henry J. Friendly played key roles in the litigation as young lawyers at the firm that represented the proponents. The story is told in Cloyd Laporte, John M. Harlan Saves the Ella Wendel Estate, 59 A.B.A. J. 868 (1973).

Ida Wood, the widow of a U.S. congressman from New York, died intestate in 1932. For more than 20 years, she and her two sisters (who predeceased her) had barricaded themselves in a New York hotel room, into which no one was permitted to enter. During her life Ida had spun a web of deceit to hide who she really was. The evidence finally accepted by the court showed she had been born Ellen Walsh in Ireland, had moved with her parents to Boston, and had been her husband's paramour for ten years before they married. Once married and propelled into

Ella Wendel

Ida Wood

Henrietta Garrett

high society, Ida drew a curtain across her past. She made up vague stories of having been born a Mayfield and brought up in New Orleans. Her mother, and some other members of her family, took the name Mayfield, and Ida carved "Mayfield" on their tombstones. Fearful of a depression, Ida kept $500,000 in cash tied around her waist. When she died, some 1,100 persons claimed to be her next of kin—including a great many persons named Mayfield from Louisiana. Ultimately, the court established as Ida's next of kin some first cousins once removed (none of whom Ida had seen since her marriage to Wood 65 years before). In re Wood, 299 N.Y.S. 195 (Sur. 1937). The whole fascinating story is recounted in Joseph A. Cox, The Recluse of Herald Square (1964).

Henrietta E. Garrett died intestate in Philadelphia in 1930, leaving an estate of over $17 million. Nearly 26,000 claims were filed by persons claiming to be her heirs. The testimony spanned more than 115,000 pages across 390 volumes. Finally, three persons were found to be first cousins of Henrietta. In 1953, after 23 years of litigation, the Supreme Court of Pennsylvania finally ordered the Garrett estate closed. Estate of Garrett, 94 A.2d 357 (Pa. 1953).

With the cases of Ella Wendel, Ida Wood, and Henrietta Garrett in mind, many years ago Professor David Cavers predicted that the rules of intestacy would be revised to abolish laughing heirs.[48] Many states have done so, typically by drawing the line at grandparents and their descendants, as under UPC § 2-103(a), page 70. In these jurisdictions there is no inheritance by relatives traced through great-grandparents or other more remote ancestors. If such a provision were applicable in the cases of Wendel, Wood, and Garrett, many of the claimants would have been excluded at the outset as being too remote.

d. Stepchildren and In-Laws

About a dozen states and the UPC as revised in 2008 recognize *stepchildren* as potential heirs. A recent development, these provisions reflect the increasing frequency of blended families and multiple marriages. Under UPC § 2-103(b), page 70, stepchildren take if there are no surviving grandparents or descendants of grandparents or more closely related kin. A few states, such as California, go even further and extend intestate succession not only to stepchildren but also to certain *in-laws*: mothers-in-law, fathers-in-law, brothers-in-law, and sisters-in-law—but not to sons-in-law or daughters-in-law![49]

The Brady Bunch, which originally aired from 1969 to 1974, involved a blended family.

NOTE

Succession in Blended Families.   Mike has three sons, all minors, from a prior marriage. Carol has three daughters, all minors, from a prior marriage. Mike and Carol marry, forming a blended family in which all six children live together in a common household. If Mike dies intestate, what will be the distribution of his probate property under the UPC? Does UPC § 2-103(b) match Mike's likely preferences? Would that provision more likely match his preferences if instead Mike and Carol had married later in life, when the six children were adults, and the blended family never lived together in a common household? As we shall see across this book, a disproportionate share of disputes over wills and trusts involve blended families.

e. Half-Bloods

In England, the common law courts excluded relatives of the half-blood (e.g., a half-sister) from inheriting

---

48. *See* David F. Cavers, Change in the American Family and the "Laughing Heir," 20 Iowa L. Rev. 203 (1935).

49. *See, e.g.,* Cal. Prob. Code § 6402(e), (g) (2016).

land through intestate succession. This rule has long been abolished in all American states. In a large majority of states, and under UPC § 2-107 (1990), a relative of the half-blood is treated the same as a relative of the whole-blood. But more limited rules abide in a minority of states.[50] For example, in a few states, including Florida and Texas, a half-blood is given a one-half share; this was the Scottish rule and was introduced in this country in Virginia.[51] In a few other states, a half-blood takes only when there are no whole-blood relatives of the same degree. In Oklahoma, half-bloods are excluded when there are whole-blood kindred in the same degree, the inheritance came to the decedent by an ancestor, and the half-blood is not a descendant of the ancestor.[52]

NOTE

A Half-Blood Intestacy Problem. F has one child, A, by his first marriage, and two children, B and C, by his second marriage. F is estranged from A and never tells his second wife or B and C of A's existence. F and his second wife die. Then C dies intestate, married but without descendants. How should C's property be distributed? *See* Estate of Griswold, 24 P.3d 1191 (Cal. 2001), discussed in Ralph C. Brashier, Half-Bloods, Inheritance, and Family, 37 U. Mem. L. Rev. 215 (2007). What if C died intestate, unmarried, and without descendants?

f. Escheat

If an intestate decedent leaves no survivors entitled to take under the intestacy statute, her probate property *escheats* to the state, as under UPC § 2-105 (1990).[53] An escheat of a substantial estate is rare. Relatives usually keep tabs on kinfolk of obvious wealth; the larger the estate, the more likely it is that someone will try to claim it. Moreover, heir-hunting firms seek out unknown or uninformed heirs, offering to disclose the name of an estate to which the person may be an heir in exchange for a share of the inheritance.

4. Disinheritance by Negative Will

An old rule of law holds that disinheritance is not possible by a declaration in a will that "my son John shall receive none of my property." To disinherit John—that is, to prevent John from taking an intestate share—John's father must devise his entire

---

50. *See* Ralph C. Brashier, Consanguinity, Sibling Relationships, and the Default Rules of Inheritance Law: Reshaping Half-Blood Statutes to Reflect the Evolving Family, 58 SMU L. Rev. 137, 161-86 (2005).

51. *See* Fla. Stat. Ann. § 732.105 (2016); Tex. Est. Code Ann. § 201.057 (2016); Va. Code Ann. § 64.1-2 (2016).

52. *See* Okla. Stat. tit. 84, § 222 (2016).

53. Why is the state the taker of last resort? Is this what the typical heirless intestate decedent would want? *See* John V. Orth, "The Laughing Heir": What's So Funny?, 48 Real Prop. Tr. & Est. L.J. 321 (2013).

estate to other persons. If there is a partial intestacy, because the will does not make a complete disposition of all of the decedent's property, John will take a share of the intestate property as an heir of the decedent notwithstanding the provision in the will disinheriting him.

UPC § 2-101(b), page 69, changes this rule and authorizes a *negative will* by way of an express disinheritance provision. The barred heir is treated as if he disclaimed his share, which means he is treated as having predeceased the decedent (see page 135).[54]

NOTE

Three Negative Will Problems.   *T* dies testate, survived by two siblings, *A* and *B*, and two nephews, *B*'s children, *X* and *Y*.

a. *T*'s will provides that "I hereby disinherit my brother, *B*," but makes no affirmative disposition. Who takes *T*'s probate property? *See* In re Estate of Samuelson, 757 N.W.2d 44 (N.D. 2008).

b. Suppose *T*'s will provides instead that "I do not want my brothers *A* or *B* or any of my other relatives to have one penny of my estate." What result? *See* In re Estate of Melton, 272 P.3d 668 (Nev. 2012).

c. Suppose *T*'s will provides instead that "I give my brothers *A* and *B* $1,000 each, and have intentionally omitted my brothers *C* and *D* from this will." *T* dies with an estate worth $10,000. What result? *See* In re Estate of Zeevering, 78 A.3d 1106 (Pa. Sup. 2013).

C. TRANSFERS TO CHILDREN

Contemporary family relations are increasingly diverse and complex. In view of the frequency of adoptions, multiple marriages, blended families, and single parenthood, plus the increasing prevalence of unmarried cohabiting partners and new reproductive technologies, it is increasingly difficult to discern what the typical intestate decedent would want in many of these situations. We now consider the treatment in contemporary intestacy law of (1) adopted children, (2) posthumously born children, (3) nonmarital children, and (4) children born with the aid of assisted reproductive technology. Although the present emphasis is on intestate succession, we will also give attention to the influence of intestacy on the interpretation of wills and trusts. We then consider two other topics relating to transfers to children: (5) the mechanics of an advancement on the inheritance of a child, and (6) the need for guardianships of the person and of the property for a minor child.

---

54. *But see* Adam J. Hirsch, Incomplete Wills, 111 Mich. L. Rev. 1423 (2013) (arguing that, in a partial intestacy, courts should be allowed to infer the testator's probable intent from her testate wishes).

1. Adopted Children

a. Formal Adoption

Hall v. Vallandingham
540 A.2d 1162 (Md. 1988)

GILBERT, C.J. . . . Since adoption was not a part of the common law, it owes its existence . . . to statutory enactments. . . . Maryland first enacted an Adoption Statute in Laws 1892, Ch. 244, and that law has continued in existence, in various forms, until the present time. The current statute, Maryland Code, Family Law Article Ann. § 5-308 provides, in pertinent part:

> (b) [A]fter a decree of adoption is entered:
>> (1) the individual adopted:
>>> (i) is the child of the petitioner for all intents and purposes; and
>>> (ii) is entitled to all the rights and privileges of and is subject to all the obligations of a child born to the petitioner in wedlock;
>> (2) each living natural parent of the individual adopted is:
>>> (i) relieved of all parental duties and obligations to the individual adopted; and
>>> (ii) divested of all parental rights as to the individual adopted; and
>> (3) *all rights of inheritance between the individual adopted and the natural relations shall be governed by the Estates and Trusts Article.* (Emphasis supplied.)

The applicable section of the Md. Estates and Trusts Code Ann. § 1-207(a), provides:

> An adopted child shall be treated as a natural child of his adopted parent or parents. On adoption, a child no longer shall be considered a child of either natural parent, except that upon adoption by the spouse of a natural parent, the child shall be considered the child of that natural parent. . . .

With . . . the [adoption] current statutes firmly in mind, we turn our attention to the matter sub judice.

Earl J. Vallandingham died in 1956, survived by his widow, Elizabeth, and their four children. Two years later, Elizabeth married Jim Walter Killgore, who adopted the children.

In 1983, twenty-five years after the adoption of Earl's children by Killgore, Earl's brother, William Jr., died childless, unmarried, and intestate. His sole heirs were his surviving brothers and sisters and the children of brothers and sisters who predeceased him.

Joseph W. Vallandingham, the decedent's twin brother, was appointed Personal Representative of the estate. After the Inventory and First Accounting were filed, the four natural children of Earl J. Vallandingham noted exceptions, alleging that they were entitled to the distributive share of their natural uncle's estate that their natural father would have received had he survived William. Est. & Trusts Art. § 3-104(b).

The Orphan's Court transmitted the issue to the Circuit Court for St. Mary's County. That tribunal determined that the four natural children of Earl, because of their adoption by their adoptive father, Jim Walter Killgore, were not entitled to inherit from William M. Vallandingham Jr.

Patently unwilling to accept that judgment which effectively disinherited them, the children have journeyed here where they posit to us:

> Did the trial court err in construing Maryland's current law regarding natural inheritance by adopted persons so as to deny the Appellants the right to inherit through their natural paternal uncle, when said Appellants were adopted as minors by their stepfather after the death of their natural father and the remarriage of their natural mother?

When the four natural children of Earl J. Vallandingham were adopted in 1958 by Jim Killgore, then Md. Ann. Code art. 16, § 78(b) clearly provided that adopted children retained the right to inherit from their natural parents and relatives.[55] That right of inheritance was removed by the Legislature in 1963 when it declared: "Upon entry of a decree of adoption, the adopted child shall lose all rights of inheritance from its parents and from their natural collateral or lineal relatives." Laws 1963, Ch. 174. Subsequently, the Legislature in 1969 enacted what is the current, above-quoted language of Est. & Trusts Art. § 1-207(a). Laws 1969, Ch. 3, § 4(c).

The appellants contend that since the explicit language of the 1963 Act proscribing dual inheritance by adoptees was not retained in the present law, Est. & Trusts Art. § 1-207(a) implicitly permits adoptees to inherit from natural relatives, as well as the adoptive parents.

The right to receive property by devise or descent is not a natural right but a privilege granted by the State. . . . Every State possesses the power to regulate the manner or term by which property within its dominion may be transmitted by will or inheritance and to prescribe who shall or shall not be capable of receiving that property. A State may deny the privilege altogether or may impose whatever restrictions or conditions upon the grant it deems appropriate. Mager v. Grima, 49 U.S. 490 (1850).

Family Law Art. § 5-308(b)(1)(ii) entitles an adopted person to all the rights and privileges of a natural child insofar as the adoptive parents are concerned, but adoption does not confer upon the adopted child *more* rights and privileges than those possessed by a natural child. To construe Est. & Trusts Art. § 1-207(a) so as to allow dual inheritance would bestow upon an adopted child a superior status. That status was removed in Laws 1963, Ch. 174 which, as we have said, expressly disallowed the dual inheritance capability of adopted children by providing that "the adopted child shall lose all rights of inheritance from its parents and from their natural collateral or lineal relatives." We think that the current statute, Est. & Trusts Art. § 1-207(a), did not alter the substance of the 1963 act which eliminated dual inheritance. Rather, § 1-207(a) merely "streamlined" the wording while retaining the meaning.

Family Law Art. § 5-308 plainly mandates that adoption be considered a "rebirth" into a completely different relationship. Once a child is adopted, the rights of both the natural parents and relatives are terminated. L.F.M. v. Department of Social Services,

---

55. "[N]othing in this subtitle shall be construed to prevent the person adopted from inheriting from his natural parents and relatives."

507 A.2d 1151 (Md. App. 1986). Est. & Trusts Art. § 1-207(a) and Family Law Art. § 5-308 emphasize the clean-cut severance from the natural bloodline. Because an adopted child has no right to inherit *from* the estate of a natural parent who dies intestate, it follows that the same child may not inherit *through* the natural parent by way of representation. What may not be done directly most assuredly may not be done indirectly. The elimination of dual inheritance in 1963 clearly established that policy, and the current language of § 1-207(a) simply reflects the continuation of that policy.

We hold that because § 1-207(a) eliminates the adopted child's right to inherit from the natural parent it concomitantly abrogated the right to inherit through the natural parent by way of representation.

"The Legislature giveth, and the Legislature taketh away."

Judgment affirmed.

NOTES

1. What Would William Jr. Have Wanted?   Would the decedent, William Jr., have wanted the children of his brother Earl to inherit from him in spite of their having been adopted by their stepfather? Why was this question not the focus of the court's analysis?

In a few states, as in *Hall*, an adopted child inherits only from adoptive parents and their relatives. In a few others, an adopted child inherits from both adoptive parents and genetic parents and their relatives. In a majority of states, an adopted child inherits from adoptive relatives and also from genetic relatives if the child is adopted by a stepparent.[56] UPC § 2-114(b) (1990) falls into the third category:

> An adopted individual is the child of his [or her] adopting parent or parents and not of his [or her] natural parents, but adoption of a child by the spouse of either natural parent has no effect on (i) the relationship between the child and that natural parent or (ii) the right of the child or a descendant of the child to inherit from or through the other natural parent.

2. The 2008 Amendments to the UPC.   The UPC provisions on inheritance between parents and children were extensively revised in 2008. Under the UPC as revised, the key determination is whether there is a *parent-child relationship*. If such a relationship exists, "the parent is a parent of the child and the child is a child of the parent for the purpose of intestate succession" by, from, or through the parent or the child (§ 2-116). Regarding adoption, a parent-child relationship exists between an adopted child and the adoptive parent (§ 2-118(a)), but not between an adopted child and the child's genetic parents (§ 2-119(a)), the latter subject to several exceptions (§ 2-119(b)-(d)):

> (b) [Stepchild Adopted by Stepparent.] A parent-child relationship exists between an individual who is adopted by the spouse of either genetic parent and:
>   (1) the genetic parent whose spouse adopted the individual; and

---

56. *See* James T.R. Jones, Intestate Inheritance and Stepparent Adoption: A Reappraisal, 48 Real Prop. Tr. & Est. L.J. 327 (2013).

(2) the other genetic parent, but only for the purpose of the right of the adoptee or a descendant of the adoptee to inherit from or through the other genetic parent.

(c) [Individual Adopted by Relative of a Genetic Parent.] A parent-child relationship exists between both genetic parents and an individual who is adopted by a relative of a genetic parent, or by the spouse or surviving spouse of a relative of a genetic parent, but only for the purpose of the right of the adoptee or a descendant of the adoptee to inherit from or through either genetic parent.

(d) [Individual Adopted after Death of Both Genetic Parents.] A parent-child relationship exists between both genetic parents and an individual who is adopted after the death of both genetic parents, but only for the purpose of the right of the adoptee or a descendant of the adoptee to inherit through either genetic parent.

If UPC § 2-119(b)(2) had been applicable in *Hall*, Earl's children, adopted by their stepfather, would have inherited from Earl's brother, William Jr. But William Jr. would not be able to inherit from Earl's children. In a stepparent adoption, the children can inherit from their genetic relatives, but the genetic relatives cannot inherit from the children. Is this consistent with the principle of freedom of disposition? Is it fair?

3. Double Inheritance?   Should a person who is related to an intestate decedent through two lines, one genetic and one adoptive, be entitled to two intestate shares? The issue arises, for example, if an aunt adopts her deceased sister's son, and then after the aunt dies one of the boy's maternal grandparents dies. *Compare* UPC § 2-113 (1990) (larger share only), *with* Jenkins v. Jenkins, 990 So. 2d 807 (Miss. App. 2008) (both shares).

b. Adult Adoption

What of an adoption of an adult rather than a minor?[57] Most intestacy statutes draw no distinction between the adoption of a minor and the adoption of an adult. In Tinney v. Tinney, 799 A.2d 235 (R.I. 2002), an 84-year-old woman adopted a 38-year-old man. The court held that the man was entitled to a child's share in the woman's intestate estate. "It is clear that the Legislature intended the term 'child' to mean son or daughter of a parent, regardless of age, and that there was no distinction intended between the inheritance rights of a 'child' adopted as a minor and 'persons' adopted as adults."[58]

In some states the adoption of one's lover is not permitted. In In re Adoption of Robert Paul P., 471 N.E.2d 424 (N.Y. 1984), the court held that a gay man, age 57, could not adopt his lover, age 50, despite New York statutes permitting adult adoption. The court reasoned that a sexual relationship was incompatible with a parent-child relationship. Other courts have disagreed. In Adoption of Swanson, 623 A.2d 1095 (Del.

---

57. *See* Richard C. Ausness, Planned Parenthood: Adult Adoption and the Right of Adoptees to Inherit, 41 ACTEC L.J. 241 (2016).

58. As with the adoption of a minor, adoption of an adult may sever the adoptee's relationship to her genetic family. In Kummer v. Donak, 715 S.E.2d 7 (Va. 2011), the decedent died intestate. Her heirs would have been her sister's children, but the sister had been adopted, at age 53, by her husband's aunt. The court held that the sister's descendants could not inherit from the decedent's estate.

Couple Seeks Right to Marry. The Hitch? They're Legally Father and Son

By Evan Perez & Ariane de Vogue

The legalization of same-sex marriage has given way to a new problem for a Pennsylvania couple, who technically are father and son.

Before states across the country began striking down bans on same-sex marriage and the Supreme Court ultimately decided the issue nationwide, some gay couples used adoption laws as a way to gain legal recognition as a family, and the related benefits such as inheritance and hospital visitation rights.

Nino Esposito, a retired teacher, adopted his partner Roland "Drew" Bosee, a former freelance and technical writer, in 2012, after more than 40 years of being a couple.

Now, they're trying to undo the adoption to get married and a state trial court judge has rejected their request, saying his ability to annul adoptions is generally limited to instances of fraud....

The adoption process Bosee and Esposito went through was not uncommon. Although it is difficult to gather hard numbers, the ACLU of Pennsylvania, a group supporting the couple, says it learned that many couples in states across the country lawfully took advantage of adoption laws in order to protect their relationships. Now these couples seek to marry, but first they must confront state adoption laws that provide no easy path to annulment.

In Pennsylvania, Esposito and Bosee knew other couples who successfully annulled their adoptions in order to marry.

Nino Esposito and Roland Bosee
Jared Wickerham/Wick Photography

They quickly made plans to do the same after Pennsylvania legalized marriage between same-sex couples in May 2014.

"We realized we could have a complete union, which is what we want," Esposito said....

But Judge Lawrence J. O'Toole, of the Court of Common Pleas of Allegheny County, ruled against the couple.... O'Toole said he was "sensitive to the situation" but noted that despite the fact Esposito and Bosee desire to marry, "they cannot do so because they are legally father and son."

"This Court welcomes direction from our appellate courts in handling parallel cases," O'Toole wrote.

Source: CNN (Nov. 3, 2015).

1993), a 66-year-old man was permitted to adopt a 51-year-old man, his longtime companion, to prevent claims against their estates by collateral relatives.[59] The Delaware court expressly rejected the New York holding.

The only persons who have standing to challenge the validity of a will are those who would take if the will were not valid. To gain standing to challenge the will, the decedent's collateral relatives must first overturn any adoption by the decedent. In Collamore v. Learned, 50 N.E. 518 (Mass. 1898), a 70-year-old man adopted three persons of ages 43, 39, and 25 respectively. The persons who would have been his heirs but for the adoptions were denied standing. Writing for the court, Justice Holmes remarked that adoption for the purpose of preventing a will contest was "perfectly proper."

c. Adoption and Wills and Trusts

Is a child adopted by *A* entitled to share in a gift in a will or trust by *A* to "my children," "my issue," "my descendants," or "my heirs"? Once adoption was recognized by statute, courts had little difficulty in answering this question in the affirmative. An adopted

---

59. Does adoption of one's lover give rise to criminal culpability for incest? *See* Terry L. Turnipseed, Scalia's Ship of Revulsion Has Sailed: Will Lawrence Protect Adults Who Adopt Lovers to Help Ensure Their Inheritance from Incest Prosecution?, 32 Hamline L. Rev. 95 (2009).

child is entitled to take under the will or trust of the adoptive parent just like a biological child. The probable intent of the donor, *A*, is evidenced by the fact of the adoption.

A more difficult problem is whether a child adopted by *A* is entitled to share in a gift in a will or trust by *T*, that is, by someone other than *A*. If *T* makes a gift to the "children," "issue," "descendants," or "heirs" of *A*, whether *T* would want to include persons adopted by *A* is less clear because *T* is not the adoptive parent. Courts have struggled with this issue. The early cases, influenced by the ancient reverence for blood relationships, held that the terms children, issue, and the like connoted a blood relationship, hence an adopted child could not take. These cases gave rise to the *stranger-to-the-adoption* rule: The adopted child is presumptively barred, whatever generic word is used, if the donor was not the adoptive parent. This was a rule of construction that could be overcome by evidence that the donor did intend to include persons adopted by others.

As adoption became more common and socially acceptable, courts carved exceptions to the stranger-to-the-adoption rule. An adopted child might be permitted to take if adopted before, but not after, the donor's death, on the theory that the donor knew of this child and must have contemplated the child's inclusion. Some courts also drew distinctions between a gift to "*A*'s children" and a gift to "*A*'s issue" or the "heirs of *A*'s body." Unlike the latter terms, which were thought to have a biological connotation, a gift to "*A*'s children" could be read to include *A*'s adopted children. Where judicial decisions were found unsatisfactory, legislatures started to create statutory exceptions. But this legislation was seldom retroactive and was sometimes ambiguous.

In most states today, a *minor* adopted by *A* is presumptively included in a gift by *T* to *A*'s children, issue, descendants, or heirs.[60] The theory is that *A* was likely in a true parent-child relationship with the adopted minor. By referencing the "children," "issue," "descendants," or "heirs" of *A*, *T* likely intended to include all persons with whom *A* had such a relationship. This presumption, a rule of construction, yields to a contrary expression of intent by the donor. But the law in many states has been changing slowly over time. Since these changes may not be retroactive, whether an adopted child is included may depend on what the law was at the testator's death in, say, 1951 or 1970.[61]

The following case adds yet another twist. Is an *adult* adopted by *A* included in a gift by *T* to the children, issue, descendants, or heirs of *A*? Should it matter if the adopted adult is *A*'s spouse?

Minary v. Citizens Fidelity Bank & Trust Co.
419 S.W.2d 340 (Ky. 1967)

OSBORNE, J. [Amelia S. Minary died in 1932, leaving a will devising her residuary estate in trust to pay the income to her husband and three sons, James, Thomas, and Alfred,

---

60. *See* Restatement (Third) of Property: Wills and Other Donative Transfers § 14.5(2) (Am. Law Inst. 2011).

61. As in Lowell v. Talcott, 14 N.E.3d 332 (Mass. App. 2014), and Elrod v. Cowart, 672 S.E.2d 616 (Ga. 2009), respectively.

for their respective lives. The trust was to terminate upon the death of the last surviving beneficiary, whereupon the corpus was to be distributed as follows:

> After the Trust terminates, the remaining portion of the Trust Fund shall be distributed to my then surviving heirs, according to the laws of descent and distribution then in force in Kentucky, and, if no such heirs, then to the First Christian Church, Louisville, Kentucky.

The husband died, then James died without descendants, then Thomas died leaving two children: Thomas Jr. and Amelia Minary Gant. In 1934, Alfred married Myra, and in 1959 he adopted her as his child. The trust terminated upon Alfred's death without biological descendants in 1963.]

The question herein presented is, "Did Alfred's adoption of his wife Myra make her eligible to inherit under the provisions of his mother's will?" More specifically, the question is, "Is Myra included in the term 'my then surviving heirs according to the laws of descent and distribution in force in Kentucky'?"

This has revived a lively question in the jurisprudence of this state and presents two rather difficult legal problems. The first being under what conditions, if any, should an adopted child inherit from or through its adoptive parent? We have encountered little difficulty with the problem of inheriting from an adoptive parent but the question of when will an adoptive child inherit through an adoptive parent has given us considerable trouble. As late as 1945 in Copeland v. State Bank and Trust Company, 188 S.W.2d 1017 (Ky.), we held without hesitation or equivocation that the words "heirs" and "issue" as well as "children" and all other words of similar import as used in a will referred only to the natural blood relations and did not include an adopted child.

In 1950, in Isaacs v. Manning, 227 S.W.2d 418 (Ky.), we adopted the contrary position and held that an adopted child was included in the phrase "heirs at law" wherein a will devised property to designated children and then upon their death to their heirs at law. In the course of the opinion, we said, "where no language [shows] a contrary intent . . . an adopted daughter clearly falls within the class designated." . . .

In 1953, in Major v. Kammer, 258 S.W.2d 506 (Ky.), we again held that an adopted child was included in the term "heirs at law," basing our decision upon the legislative changes made in the adoption laws and overruling Copeland v. State Bank and Trust Company, supra. In Edmands v. Tice, 324 S.W.2d 491 (Ky.), which was decided in 1959, we held that where testator used the word children, an adopted child could inherit through an adopted parent the same as if heirs at law or issue had been used. . . .

From the foregoing we conclude that when Amelia S. Minary used the phrase, "my then surviving heirs according to the laws of descent and distribution then in force in Kentucky," she included the adoptive children of her sons. This leaves us with the extremely bothersome question of: "Does the fact that Myra Minary was an adult and the wife of Alfred at the time she was adopted affect her status as an 'heir' under the will?" KRS 405.390 provides: "An adult person . . . may be adopted in the same manner as provided by law for the adoption of a child and with the same legal effect."

KRS 199.520 provides: "From and after the date of the judgment the child shall be deemed the child of petitioners and shall be considered for purposes of inheritance

Roz Chast/The New Yorker Collection/The Cartoon Bank

and succession and for all other legal considerations, the natural, legitimate child of the parents adopting it the same as if born of their bodies."

It would appear from examination of the authorities that the adoption of an adult for the purpose of making him an heir has been an accepted practice in our law for many years. However, here it should be pointed out that the practice in its ancient form made the person so adopted the legal heir of the adopting party only. This court has dealt with the problem of adopting adults for the purpose of making them heirs on several occasions. . . .

In 1957, in Bedinger v. Graybill's Executors, 302 S.W.2d 594 (Ky.), we had before us a case almost identical to the one here under consideration. In that case Mrs. Lulu Graybill, in 1914, set up a trust for her son Robert by will. She then provided after the death of the son that the trust "be paid over and distributed by the Trustee to the heirs at law of my said son according to the laws of descent and distribution in force in Kentucky at the time of his death." There was a devise over to others in the event that Robert died without heirs. Robert having no issue adopted his wife long after his mother's death. We held that the wife should inherit the same as an adopted child, there being no public policy against the adoption of a wife. However, it will be noted that in the course of the opinion it is carefully pointed out that the will directed the estate be paid to the "heirs at law of Robert" and did not provide that the estate should go to "my heirs," "his children" or to "his issue," indicating by this language that if the phrase had been one of the others set out the results might have been different. . . .

This case could properly be distinguished from Bedinger v. Graybill's Executors, supra, on the basis of the difference in language used in the two wills[;] however, no useful purpose could be served by so distinguishing them. The time has come to face again this problem which has persistently perplexed the court when an adult is adopted for the sole purpose of making him or her an heir and claimant to the estate of an ancestor under the terms of a testamentary instrument known and in existence at the time of the adoption. Even though the statute permits such adoption and even though it expressly provides that it shall be "with the same legal effect as the adoption of a child," we, nevertheless, are constrained to view this practice to be an act of subterfuge which in effect thwarts the intent of the ancestor whose property is being distributed and cheats the rightful heirs. We are faced with a situation wherein we must choose between carrying out the intent of deceased testators or giving a strict and rigid construction to a statute which thwarts that intent. In the *Bedinger* case there is no doubt but what the intent of the testatrix, as to the disposition of her property, was circumvented. It is our opinion that by giving a strict and literal construction to the adoption statutes, we thwarted the efforts of the deceased to dispose of her property as she saw fit.

When one rule of law does violence to another it becomes inevitable that one must then give way to the other. It is of paramount importance that a man be permitted to pass on his property at his death to those who represent the natural objects of his bounty. This is an ancient and precious right running from the dawn of civilization in an unbroken line down to the present day. Our adoption statutes are humanitarian in nature and of great importance to the welfare of the public. However, these statutes should not be given a construction that does violence to the above rule and to the extent that they violate the rule and prevent one from passing on his property in accord with his wishes, they must give way. Adoption of an adult for the purpose of bringing that person under the provisions of a preexisting testamentary instrument when he clearly was not intended to be so covered should not be permitted and we do not view this as doing any great violence to the intent and purpose of our adoption laws.

For the foregoing reasons the action of the trial court in declaring Myra Galvin Minary an heir of Amelia S. Minary is reversed.

The judgment is reversed.

NOTES

1. Laws Then in Force. In *Minary*, the trust property was to be distributed to the testator's "surviving heirs, according to the laws of descent and distribution *then in force in Kentucky* [emphasis added]." Why leave it to future legislatures to determine who will be the beneficiaries? See the discussion of UPC § 2-711 at page 880. In Fiduciary Trust Co. v. Wheeler, 132 A.3d 1178 (Me. 2016), the court held that the "intestate laws of Maine then in force" included adopted children at the termination of the trust even though in an earlier decision involving the same trust the court had held that a gift of income to the "issue" of the settlor's daughter did not include the daughter's adopted child.

2. Strategic Adult Adoption and Class Gifts. The cases are split on whether an adult adoptee is included in a class gift made by someone other than the adoptive parent. *Compare* In re Trust Created by Nixon, 763 N.W.2d 404 (Neb. 2009) (Yes: Donor's childless adult daughter adopted her adult cousin, avoiding a gift over to her adult brother's family, with whom she did not get along.), *with* Otto v. Gore, 45 A.3d 120 (Del. 2012) (No: Donor's adult daughter adopted her ex-husband, trying to increase the share allocated to her line of descent.).

To avoid this kind of litigation, wills and trusts today commonly provide expressly for the inclusion of adopted persons other than adopted adults. This drafting strategy uses age at the time of adoption as a proxy for the existence of a true parent-child relationship. For example: "In determining whether any person is a child or descendant for purposes of this will, children and descendants by both birth and adoption shall be included, except that . . . a person adopted when over the age of 18 years shall be excluded."[62] Section 2-705(c) of the 1990 UPC provides a default rule of construction to similar effect:

> [I]n construing a dispositive provision of a transferor who is not the adopting parent, an adopted individual is not considered the child of the adopting parent unless the adopted individual lived while a minor, either before or after the adoption, as a regular member of the household of the adopting parent.

As revised in 2008, the UPC states a more refined test. Section 2-705(f) of the UPC as revised presumptively excludes a person adopted after reaching the age of 18 from a gift to the adoptive parent's children, issue, descendants, or heirs by someone other than the adoptive parent unless the adoptive parent was the adoptee's stepparent or foster parent, or the adoptive parent "functioned as a parent of the adoptee before the adoptee" turned 18. The Restatement explains the underlying rationale thus:

> The purpose is to prevent someone other than the transferor from engaging in a manipulative adoption—such as adopting an adult (a spouse, for example, or a domestic partner) to make that person a beneficiary under a class gift created by someone else. The transferor has in effect given the donee authority, similar to the authority given an agent, to determine the donee's "children" or "issue." But the transferor's use of the term "children" or "issue" implies an intent to include only adoptees with whom the adopter had developed an actual parent-child relationship.[63]

3. Children "Adopted Out."   Does adoption remove the adoptee from a class gift to the adoptee's genetic parent's children, issue, descendants, or heirs? In In re Cecilia Kincaid Gift Trust for George, 278 P.3d 1026 (Mont. 2012), the court held that an adopted person was not included in a class gift to the descendants of the person's genetic parent.

But suppose *T* bequeaths a fund in trust "for my wife for life, then to my surviving descendants per stirpes." After *T*'s death, his son, *A*, dies survived by a wife and a minor child, *B*. *A*'s wife remarries, and her second husband adopts *B*. Then *T*'s wife dies. Is *B* entitled to share in *T*'s trust fund? *Compare* Newman v. Wells Fargo Bank, 926 P.2d 969

---

62. Northern Trust, Will & Trust Forms 101-25 (2004).
63. Restatement (Third) of Property: Wills and Other Donative Transfers § 14.5(2) cmt. c (Am. Law Inst. 2011).

Doris Duke and Adoptive Parent's Remorse

Doris Duke, the tobacco heiress, was the life beneficiary of two trusts created by her father, James Buchanan Duke, in 1917 and 1924. In 1924 James also created an endowment for Trinity College in North Carolina, funding it with $40 million, to which he added another $67 million when he died the following year. Doris was just shy of her thirteenth birthday. Trinity College changed its name to Duke University.

Late one evening in Rome in 1945, Miss Duke, who was then 33 years old, told a friend that her vast fortune was in some ways a barrier to happiness.

"All that money is a problem sometimes," Miss Duke told…a young American journalist…. "It happens every time. After I've gone out with a man a few times, he starts to tell me how much he loves me. But how can I know if he really means it? How can I ever be sure?"*

After Doris's death, the income from the two trusts created by her father was to be payable to Doris's children. Doris had no biological children. She did, however, have an adopted daughter. At the age of 75, Doris adopted Chandi Heffner, 35. Chandi had taken her name from the Hindu deity, Chandi, and was a Hare Krishna when Doris met her at a dance class. Subsequent to the adoption, Doris had a falling out with Chandi.

Doris Duke died in 1993, a billionaire, five years after adopting Chandi. She left her fortune to a charitable foundation over which she put her barely literate butler, Bernard Lafferty, in charge. After embarking on an extended spending spree, far exceeding the $500,000 a year Doris left him, the butler dropped dead some three years after Doris died. As for Chandi, Doris's will provided as follows:

TWENTY-ONE: As indicated in Article SEVEN, it is my intention that Chandi Heffner not be deemed to be my child for purposes of disposing of property under this my Will (or any Codicil thereto). Furthermore, it is not my intention, nor do I believe that it was ever my father's intention, that Chandi Heffner be deemed to be a child or lineal descendant of mine for purposes of disposing of the trust estate of the May 2, 1917 trust

Doris Duke
Getty Images Entertainment

which my father established for my benefit or the Doris Duke Trust, dated December 11, 1924, which my father established for the benefit of me, certain other members of the Duke family and ultimately for charity.

I am extremely troubled by the realization that Chandi Heffner may use my 1988 adoption of her (when she was 35 years old) to attempt to benefit financially under the terms of either of the trusts created by my father. After giving the matter prolonged and serious consideration, I am convinced that I should not have adopted Chandi Heffner. I have come to the realization that her primary motive was financial gain. I firmly believe that, like me, my father would not have wanted her to have benefitted under the trusts which he created, and similarly, I do not wish her to benefit from my estate.

Upon Doris Duke's death, Chandi Heffner sued the trustees of the Doris Duke Trust created by James Duke. She demanded that they pay her the income as the successive life beneficiary of the trust, worth $170 million at Doris's death. The trial court ruled against her. It held that an adult adoptee is not a child of the adoptive parent for purposes of a trust created by someone other than the adoptive parent. In re Trust of Duke, 702 A.2d 1008 (N.J. Ch. 1995). Chandi Heffner also sued the trustees of the other trust created by James Duke and the executors of Doris Duke, claiming that Doris had promised to support her. Eventually, the parties settled. Chandi Heffner received $60 million from the James Duke trusts in settlement of her claim to be a child of Doris and $5 million from the Doris Duke estate.

---

* Doris Duke, 80, Heiress Whose Great Wealth Couldn't Buy Happiness, Is Dead, N.Y. Times, Oct. 29, 1993, at B11.

(Cal. 1996) (looking at intestacy law as it existed at time of *T*'s death to determine *T*'s intent; *B* excluded), *with* Lockwood v. Adamson, 566 N.E.2d 96 (Mass. 1991) (*B* shares under *T*'s will even though *B* would not inherit from *T* under intestacy law). Under UPC § 2-705(b) (2008), *B* would share in *T*'s trust fund because the stepparent adoption rule of § 2-119(b)(2), page 93, would apply.

d. Equitable Adoption

Thus far we have considered formal adoptions. But the recognition of informal adoption by way of the *equitable adoption* doctrine, sometimes called *virtual adoption* or *adoption by estoppel,* can also affect the distribution of property at death.

O'Neal v. Wilkes
439 S.E.2d 490 (Ga. 1994)

FLETCHER, J. In this virtual adoption action, a jury found that appellant Hattie O'Neal had been virtually adopted by the decedent, Roswell Cook. On post-trial motions, the court granted a judgment notwithstanding the verdict to appellee Firmon Wilkes, as administrator of Cook's estate, on the ground that the paternal aunt who allegedly entered into the adoption contract with Cook had no legal authority to do so. We have reviewed the record and conclude that the court correctly determined that there was no valid contract to adopt.

O'Neal was born out of wedlock in 1949 and raised by her mother, Bessie Broughton, until her mother's death in 1957. At no time did O'Neal's biological father recognize O'Neal as his daughter, take any action to legitimize her, or provide support to her or her mother. O'Neal testified that she first met her biological father in 1970.

For four years after her mother's death, O'Neal lived in New York City with her maternal aunt, Ethel Campbell. In 1961, Ms. Campbell brought O'Neal to Savannah, Georgia, and surrendered physical custody of O'Neal to a woman identified only as Louise who was known to want a daughter. Shortly thereafter, Louise determined she could not care for O'Neal and took her to the Savannah home of Estelle Page, the sister of O'Neal's biological father. After a short time with Page, Roswell Cook and his wife came to Savannah from their Riceboro, Georgia home to pick up O'Neal. Page testified that she had heard that the Cooks wanted a daughter and after telling them about O'Neal, they came for her. [Mr. and Mrs. Cook were divorced in the 1970s.]

Although O'Neal was never statutorily adopted by Cook, he raised her and provided for her education and she resided with him until her marriage in 1975. While she never took the last name of Cook, he referred to her as his daughter and, later, identified her children as his grandchildren.

In November 1991, Cook died intestate. The appellee, Firmon Wilkes, was appointed as administrator of Cook's estate and refused to recognize O'Neal's asserted interest in the estate. In December 1991, O'Neal filed a petition in equity asking the court to declare a virtual adoption, thereby entitling her to the estate property she would have inherited if she were Cook's statutorily adopted child.

1. The first essential of a contract for adoption is that it be made between persons competent to contract for the disposition of the child. Winder v. Winder, 128 S.E.2d 56 (Ga. 1962); Rucker v. Moore, 199 S.E. 106 (Ga. 1938). A successful plaintiff must also prove:

> Some showing of an agreement between the natural and adoptive parents, performance by the natural parents of the child in giving up custody, performance by the child by living in the home of the adoptive parents, partial performance by the foster parents in taking the child into the home and treating [it] as their child, and . . . the intestacy of the foster parent.

Williams v. Murray, 236 S.E.2d 624 (Ga. 1977), quoting Habecker v. Young, 474 F.2d 1229, 1230 (5th Cir. 1973). The only issue on this appeal is whether the court correctly determined that Page was without authority to contract for O'Neal's adoption.

2. O'Neal argues that Page, a paternal aunt with physical custody of her, had authority to contract for her adoption and, even if she was without such authority, any person with the legal right to contract for the adoption, be they O'Neal's biological father or maternal aunts or uncles, ratified the adoption contract by failing to object.

As a preliminary matter, we agree with O'Neal that although her biological father was living at the time the adoption contract was allegedly entered into, his consent to the contract was not necessary as he never recognized or legitimized her or provided for her support in any manner. See Williams v. Murray, 236 S.E.2d 624 (Ga. 1977) (mother alone may contract for adoption where the father has lost parental control or abandoned the child); OCGA § 19-7-25, Code 1933, § 74-203 (only mother of child born out of wedlock may exercise parental power over the child unless legitimized by the father); see also OCGA § 19-8-10 (parent not entitled to notice of petition of adoption where parent has abandoned the child). What is less clear are the rights and obligations acquired by Page by virtue of her physical custody of O'Neal after her mother's death.

3. The Georgia Code defines a "legal custodian" as a person to whom legal custody has been given by court order and who has the right to physical custody of the child and to determine the nature of the care and treatment of the child and the duty to provide for the care, protection, training, and education and the physical, mental, and moral welfare of the child. OCGA § 15-11-43, Code 1933, § 24A-2901. A legal custodian does not have the right to consent to the adoption of a child, as this right is specifically retained by one with greater rights over the child, a child's parent or guardian. OCGA § 15-11-43, Code 1933, § 24A-2901 (rights of a legal custodian are subject to the remaining rights and duties of the child's parents or guardian); Skipper v. Smith, 238 S.E.2d 917 (Ga. 1977) (right to consent to adoption is a residual right retained by a parent notwithstanding the transfer of legal custody of the child to another person); Jackson v. Anglin, 19 S.E.2d 914 (Ga. 1942) (parent retains exclusive authority to consent to adoption although child is placed in temporary custody of another); Carey v. Phillips, 224 S.E.2d 870 (Ga. App. 1976) (parent's consent is required for adoption of child although child is in physical custody of another).

O'Neal concedes that, after her mother's death, no guardianship petition was filed by her relatives. Nor is there any evidence that any person petitioned to be appointed as her legal custodian. Accordingly, the obligation to care and provide for O'Neal, undertaken first by Campbell, and later by Page, was not a legal obligation but a familial obligation resulting in a custodial relationship properly characterized as something less than that of a legal custodian. Such a relationship carried with it no authority to contract for O'Neal's adoption. See *Skipper*, 238 S.E.2d at 919. While we sympathize with O'Neal's plight, we conclude that Page had no authority to enter into the adoption contract with Cook and the contract, therefore, was invalid.

4. Because O'Neal's relatives did not have the legal authority to enter into a contract for her adoption, their alleged ratification of the adoption contract was of no legal effect and the court did not err in granting a judgment notwithstanding the verdict in favor of the appellee. See Foster v. Cheek, 96 S.E.2d 545 (Ga. 1957) (adoption contract made between persons not competent to contract for child's adoption specifically enforceable where the parent with parental power over the child acquiesced in and ratified the adoption contract).

Judgment affirmed.

SEARS, J. dissenting. I disagree with the majority's holding that O'Neal's claim for equitable adoption is defeated by the fact that her paternal aunt was not a person designated by law as one having the authority to consent to O'Neal's adoption.

1. In Crawford v. Wilson, 78 S.E. 30 (Ga. 1913), the doctrine of equitable or virtual adoption was recognized for the first time in Georgia. Relying on the equitable principle that "equity considers that done which ought to have been done," id. at 32, we held that "an agreement to adopt a child, so as to constitute the child an heir at law on the death of the person adopting, performed on the part of the child, is enforceable upon the death of the person adopting the child as to property which is undisposed of by will," id. We held that although the death of the adopting parents precluded a literal enforcement of the contract, equity would "enforce the contract by decreeing that the child is entitled to the fruits of a legal adoption." Id. In *Crawford*, we noted that the full performance of the agreement by the child was sufficient to overcome an objection that the agreement was unenforceable because it violated the statute of frauds. Id. We further held that

> [w]here one takes an infant into his home upon a promise to adopt such as his own child, and the child performs all the duties growing out of the substituted relationship of parent and child, rendering years of service, companionship, and obedience to the foster parent, upon the faith that such foster parent stands in loco parentis, and that upon his death the child will sustain the legal relationship to his estate of a natural child, there is equitable reason that the child may appeal to a court of equity to consummate, so far as it may be possible, the foster parent's omission of duty in the matter of formal adoption. Id. at 33.

Justice Leah Sears was appointed to the Georgia Supreme Court in 1992 at age 36.

Although the majority correctly states the current rule in Georgia that a contract to adopt may not be specifically enforced unless the contract was entered by a person with the legal authority to consent to the adoption of the child, *Crawford* did not expressly establish such a requirement, and I think the cases cited by the majority that have established this requirement are in error.

Instead, I would hold that where a child has fully performed the alleged contract over the course of many years or a lifetime and can sufficiently establish the existence of the contract to adopt, equity should enforce the contract over the objection of the adopting parents' heirs that the contract is unenforceable because the person who consented to the adoption did not have the legal authority to do so. . . .

2. Moreover, basing the doctrine of equitable adoption in contract theory has come under heavy criticism, for numerous reasons. See Jan Ellen Rein, Relatives by Blood, Adoption, and Association: Who Should Get What and Why (The Impact of Adoptions, Adult Adoptions, and Equitable Adoptions on Intestate Succession and Class Gifts), 37 Vand. L. Rev. 711, 770-75, 784-86 (1984). For instance, as we acknowledged in *Crawford*, the contract to adopt is not being specifically enforced as the adopting parents are dead; for equitable reasons we are merely placing the child in a position that he or she would have been in if he or she had been adopted. See Rein at 774. Moreover, it is problematic whether these contracts are capable of being enforced in all respects during the child's infancy. See Rein at 773-74. Furthermore, because part of the consideration for these contracts is the child's performance thereunder, the child is not merely a third-party beneficiary of a contract between the adults involved but is a party thereto. Yet, a child is usually too young to know of or understand the contract, and it is thus difficult to find a meeting of the minds between the child and the adopting parents and the child's acceptance of the contract. Rein at 772-73, 775. I agree with these criticisms and would abandon the contract basis for equitable adoption in favor of the more flexible and equitable theory advanced by the foregoing authorities. That theory focuses not on the fiction of whether there has been a contract to adopt but on the relationship between the adopting parents and the child and in particular whether the adopting parents have led the child to believe that he or she is a legally adopted member of their family. Rein at 785-87.

3. Because the majority fails to honor the maxim that "[e]quity considers that done which ought to be done," and follows a rule that fails to protect a person with superior equities, I dissent. I am authorized to state that Justice Hunstein concurs in the result reached by this dissent.

NOTES

1. The Importance of Context.   Hattie O'Neal was African American. The town of Riceboro, Georgia, where she went to live, had a population of 767, of whom 751 were African Americans. There was no lawyer in Riceboro, but there were several in the county seat, Hinesville, 17 miles away.[64] Does this affect your view of the *O'Neal* case?

---

64. *See* Lynda Richardson, Adoptions That Lack Papers, Not Purpose, N.Y. Times, Nov. 25, 1993, at C1 (discussing the history and prevalence of informal adoptions in the African-American community, and noting that, "of the estimated one million black children in this country who do not live with a biological parent, nearly 800,000 have been informally adopted, usually by a grandparent").

Judge Divides Estate Among Kitty Oakes' Sons

By Karen Dorn Steele

Establishing a legal precedent, a Spokane County judge has ruled that the three illegally adopted sons of Kitty Oakes and Billy Tipton can inherit equal shares of her $300,000 estate....

Kathleen "Kitty" Tipton Oakes was a former stripper known as the "Irish Venus" who lived as bandleader Billy Tipton's wife in Spokane from 1962 until they separated in 1980. [When] Tipton died in 1989...paramedics discovered the prominent jazz musician who'd lived as a man was actually a woman.

The revelation triggered a media frenzy—and shock and anger for the three sons, who thought Tipton was their father. Two of the sons changed their names after learning of Tipton's secret....

In closing arguments, Lynn St. Louis, an attorney for the personal representative of Oakes' estate, told [Judge Michael] Price there are "compelling facts" to allow the three sons to inherit under the doctrine of "equitable adoption"—a legal theory not generally used in Washington state....

Oakes and Tipton "brought into their home three boys. The natural mothers apparently relinquished

custody, yet none are legally adopted. None of these boys were Kitty's biological child. Each testified they knew they had a biological mom who wasn't Kitty. But the Tiptons were a family.... Billy was dad; Kitty, mom," St. Louis said.

In his ruling, Price agreed.

Kitty Oakes
Photo Archives/The Spokesman-Review

"Until trial, the court didn't grasp the incredible life ramifications the Tipton children had dealt with.... They should know that they did nothing wrong here. They just tried as best they could to live with the hand they were dealt," Price said.

The three men will inherit equal shares of the estate, minus appropriate lawyers' fees....

If their claims had not held up, a scattered clan of paternal uncles and cousins in the Midwest and South stood to inherit Oakes' estate as "second tier" heirs.

Source: Spokesman Rev. (Dec. 10, 2008).

In *O'Neal*, the court was divided 5 to 2. Joining Justice Sears in her dissent was a white woman justice; the majority were all men, including one African American. Might women look at equitable adoption differently than men? See the views of Professor Rein, cited in Justice Sears's opinion, and Carol Gilligan, In a Different Voice: Psychological Theory and Women's Development (1982).

2. The Equitable Adoption Doctrine.   Under the equitable adoption doctrine, an oral agreement to adopt *A* between *H* and *W* and *A*'s genetic parents is inferred if *H* and *W* take baby *A* into their home and raise *A* as their child. As against *H* and *W*, equity treats *A* as if the contract to adopt had been performed by *H* and *W*. They are estopped to deny a formal adoption took place. Equitable adoption is recognized in a majority of states, but the details vary—and in some states the doctrine is rejected.[65]

In re Estate of Ford, 82 P.3d 747 (Cal. 2004), involved a foster child who was raised from the age of two by the decedent. The court rejected the foster child's claim to an intestate share of the decedent's estate, giving the property instead to a nephew and niece who had not seen the decedent for 15 years. The court held that, under California law, equitable adoption was based on contract, and the promise or intention to adopt must be proved by clear and convincing evidence. In Morgan v. Howard, 678 S.E.2d

---

65. *See, e.g.*, In re Estate of Scherer, 336 P.3d 129 (Wyo. 2014).

882 (Ga. 2009), the court likewise required clear and convincing evidence of the contract to adopt, as did the court in Dehart v. Dehart, 986 N.E.2d 85 (Ill. 2013).

Suppose that, before a formal adoption could be finalized, the adoptive parent dies. Does the fact of the in-process formal adoption provide sufficient proof of the deceased's intent to adopt to allow the child to inherit from the deceased under the doctrine of equitable adoption? *See* In re W.R. ex rel. S.W., 989 A.2d 873 (N.J. Super. 2009).

In Board of Education v. Browning, 635 A.2d 373 (Md. 1994), the court held that an equitably adopted child could not inherit through her adoptive parent to take from her adoptive parent's sister, even though the sister's estate would otherwise escheat. The court reasoned that the effect of equitable adoption should be limited to inheritance from the parent who is estopped. Many cases, such as Johnson v. Rogers, 774 S.E.2d 647 (Ga. 2015), hold that the doctrine does not apply to testate estates.

In Welch v. Wilson, 516 S.E.2d 35 (W. Va. 1999), a woman who was raised by her grandmother and stepgrandfather was treated as having been equitably adopted by the stepgrandfather, allowing her to inherit his entire estate. The court did not require a contract, nor did it mention estoppel, though it did note that the stepgrandparent was listed as the woman's parent on school records. The court focused primarily on the ample evidence of a close, loving parent-child relationship. Suppose the grandmother had died. Could the woman inherit as a daughter of her grandmother?[66] Is the equitable adoption doctrine robust enough to capture probable intent for persons who function as parents of children in nontraditional family arrangements?[67]

2. Posthumous Children

David Copperfield, the lead character in the book of the same name by Charles Dickens, explains at the outset:

> I was a posthumous child. My father's eyes had closed upon the light of this world six months when mine opened on it. There is something strange to me, even now, in the reflection that he never saw me; and something stranger yet in the shadowy remembrance that I have of my first childish associations with his white gravestone in the churchyard, and of the indefinable compassion I used to feel for it lying out alone there in the dark night, when our little parlour was warm and bright with fire and candle, and the doors of our house were—almost cruelly, it seemed to me sometimes—bolted and locked against it.[68]

The typical posthumous child, like David Copperfield, is conceived before, but born after, his father's death. For purposes of inheritance or of determining property

---

66. *See* Kristine S. Knaplund, Grandparents Raising Grandchildren and the Implications for Inheritance, 48 Ariz. L. Rev. 1 (2006).

67. *See* Irene D. Johnson, A Suggested Solution to the Problem of Intestate Succession in Nontraditional Family Arrangements: Taking the "Adoption" (and the Inequity) Out of the Doctrine of "Equitable Adoption," 54 St. Louis U. L.J. 271 (2009).

68. Charles Dickens, The Personal History of David Copperfield 4 (Vintage Classics ed. 2012) (1850).

rights, if it is to a child's advantage to be treated as in being from the time of conception rather than from the time of birth, then under longstanding principles of common law the child will be so treated if born alive.[69]

Courts have established a rebuttable presumption that the normal period of gestation is 280 days (10 lunar months). In Byerly v. Tolbert, 108 S.E.2d 29 (N.C. 1959), a child was born to the decedent's widow 322 days after his death. The child—through a guardian ad litem, of course—claimed an intestate share. The trial court held as a matter of law that the infant was not a child of the decedent. On appeal, the case was reversed. The child was entitled to have the issue submitted to a jury.

Uniform Parentage Act § 204 (Unif. Law Comm'n 2000, rev. 2002) establishes a rebuttable presumption that a child born to a woman within 300 days after the death of her husband is a child of that husband. But what if the mother's spouse is another woman? As this book went to press in early 2017, the Uniform Law Commission was in the process of revising the *marital presumption* of § 204 to reconcile it with the nationwide recognition of same-sex marriage after Obergefell v. Hodges, 135 S. Ct. 2584 (2015).[70]

3. Nonmarital Children

Although innocent of any sin or crime, children of unmarried parents—once called illegitimate or bastard children—were given harsh, pitiless treatment by the common law.[71] A nonmarital child was *filius nullius*, the child of no one, and could inherit from neither father nor mother. The child was the start of a new family tree; only the child's spouse and descendents could inherit from the child. If the child died intestate and left neither spouse nor descendants, the child's property escheated to the king or other overlord.

Both social norms and the law have since changed. In 2014, there were 1.6 million nonmarital children born in the United States, representing 40 percent of the nearly 4 million U.S. births that year.[72] In a 2015 Gallup poll of more than 1,000 people, 61 percent said that having a nonmarital child was "morally acceptable."[73] All states today permit inheritance by a nonmarital child from the child's mother. The rules respecting inheritance from the father, however, still vary.

In Trimble v. Gordon, 430 U.S. 762 (1977), the Supreme Court held unconstitutional as a denial of equal protection an Illinois statute denying a nonmarital child inheritance rights from the father. The Court held that state discrimination against

---

69. 1 William Blackstone, Commentaries *126.

70. See *infra* note 94 and text accompanying.

71. For Blackstone's description of the legal position at common law of such children, see 1 William Blackstone, Commentaries *442 ff.; 2 id. *247 ff. In the first book of Blackstone (1 id. *444) you may find out, if you wish, how a child could be "more than ordinarily legitimate."

72. Brady E. Hamilton et al., CDC, Nat'l Vital Statistics Reports, Births: Final Data for 2014, Nat'l Vital 2 (2015).

73. Jeff Jones & Lydia Saad, Gallup News Serv., Gallup Poll Social Series: Values and Beliefs (2015) (May 6-10, 2015 survey of 1,024 adults).

nonmarital children, though not a suspect classification subject to strict scrutiny, must have a substantial justification as serving an important state interest. The valid state interest recognized by the Court was obtaining reliable proof of paternity. The Court ruled that total statutory disinheritance from the father was not rationally related to this objective. The following year, in Lalli v. Lalli, 439 U.S. 259 (1978), the Court upheld a New York statute permitting inheritance by a nonmarital child from the child's father only if the father had married the mother or had been formally adjudicated the father by a court during the father's lifetime.

Most states permit paternity to be established by evidence of the subsequent marriage of the parents, acknowledgment by the father, an adjudication during the life of the father, or clear and convincing proof after his death.[74] Are these reforms adequate in light of the increasing number of unmarried cohabiting partners with children (see page 74)? What of parentage among same-sex couples (see page 120)?[75]

NOTES

1. The Rise of DNA Testing. Medical science has advanced considerably since the decisions in *Trimble* and *Lalli* were handed down in the late 1970s. DNA testing that can prove paternity to a virtual certainty is readily available.[76] In view of the reliability of such testing, is there still a justification that would pass constitutional muster for limiting inheritance by nonmarital children from their fathers?[77]

The trend is toward allowing posthumous proof of paternity by DNA evidence. In New York, for example, a nonmarital child may prove paternity by "evidence derived from a genetic marker test."[78] In In re Estate of Dicksion, 286 P.3d 283 (Okla. 2012), a nonmarital child proved that the decedent was his father by a comparison of the child's DNA with that of the decedent's brother. The court observed that recent decisions across the country "have embraced DNA testing to determine heirship." Courts have

DNA paternity test kits are now sold over the counter at drugstores across the country.

---

74. *See* Camille M. Davidson, Mother's Baby, Father's Maybe!—Intestate Succession: When Should a Child Born Out of Wedlock Have a Right to Inherit From or Through His or Her Biological Father?, 22 Colum. J. Gender & L. 531 (2011); Browne Lewis, Children of Men: Balancing the Inheritance Rights of Marital and Non-Marital Children, 39 U. Tol. L. Rev. 1 (2007); Linda Kelly Hill, Equal Protection Misapplied: The Politics of Gender and Legitimacy and the Denial of Inheritance, 13 Wm. & Mary J. Women & L. 129 (2006).

75. *See* Danaya C. Wright, Inheritance Equity: Reforming the Inheritance Penalties Facing Children in Nontraditional Families, 25 Cornell J.L. & Pub. Pol'y 1 (2015).

76. For a paternity case in which DNA testing was not enough, because the potential fathers were identical twin brothers, each of whom had slept with the mother, see State ex rel. Dep't of Soc. Servs. v. Miller, 218 S.W.3d 2 (Mo. App. 2007). From the case report you may find out, if you wish, how the court resolved which of the twins was the father.

77. *See* Paula A. Monopoli, Nonmarital Children and Post-Death Parentage: A Different Path for Inheritance Law?, 48 Santa Clara L. Rev. 857 (2008); *see also* Katharine K. Baker, Legitimate Families and Equal Protection, 56 B.C. L. Rev. 1647 (2015).

78. N.Y. Est. Powers & Trusts Law § 4-1.2(a)(2)(C) (2016).

even authorized disinterment of a decedent's body so that a claim of paternity might be assessed with DNA testing.[79]

Should a man who has acknowledged paternity and formed a relationship with the child later be allowed to repudiate the acknowledgment if subsequent DNA testing shows he is not the father? In Shondel J. v. Mark D., 853 N.E.2d 610 (N.Y. 2006), the court held in the negative. It reasoned that the best interests of the child who relied on the man's earlier acknowledgment estopped the man from later denying paternity.

2. Nonmarital Children and Wills and Trusts. Class gifts that use a biological term of relationship are commonly interpreted, as under UPC § 2-705(b) (2008), in accordance with the law of intestacy. The rules for proving the paternity of a non-marital child in intestacy therefore tend to apply also to wills and trusts by a purported parent of the child.

But what of a gift by *T* to the "children," "issue," "descendants," or "heirs" of *A*? Is a nonmarital child of *A* entitled to share in such a gift by *T*? Under UPC § 2-705(e) (2008), the answer is Yes—but only if *A* "functioned as a parent of the child before the child reached [18] years of age." Is this rule consistent with the probable intent of *T*? Is it fair to the child? Are either or both of these the proper criteria for evaluating the statute? UPC § 2-705(e) has been criticized by commentators on grounds of unfairness to nonmarital children.[80]

4. Reproductive Technology and New Forms of Parentage

Medical science now offers the making of a baby without coitus. Today the egg, sperm, and womb needed to make a baby can be provided by three separate persons, the first two even after the person has died, and the intention of all involved might be for still other persons to function as the parents of the baby.[81] In 2014, more than 70,000 children were born of reproductive technology in which the egg and the sperm were combined in a laboratory,[82] nearly 1.8 percent of all infants born in the United States.

Determining who should take from and through whom in intestacy or under a will or trust provision for a biological class such as "children," "descendants," or "issue" may be difficult in cases involving a new form of parentage. The probable intent of the decedent may not be obvious or may be in tension with the best interests of the child.[83] We shall consider posthumously conceived children first, and then we will turn to other forms of assisted reproduction, such as surrogacy and sperm and ova donation.

---

79. *See, e.g.,* In re Estate of Kingsbury, 946 A.2d 389 (Me. 2008).

80. *See* Paula A. Monopoli, Toward Equality: Nonmarital Children and the Uniform Probate Code, 45 U. Mich. J.L. Reform 995 (2012); Solangel Maldonado, Illegitimate Harm: Law, Stigma, and Discrimination Against Nonmarital Children, 63 Fla. L. Rev. 345 (2011).

81. It is possible today even to have a "three parent embryo." Judith Daar, Multi-Party Parenting in Genetics and Law: A View from Succession, 49 Fam. L.Q. 71 (2015).

82. This figure is drawn from data collected and published by the Centers for Disease Control and Prevention.

83. *See* Kristine S. Knaplund, Children of Assisted Reproduction, 45 U. Mich. J.L. Reform 899 (2012); Lee-ford Tritt, Sperms and Estates: An Unadulterated Functionally Based Approach to Parent-Child Property Succession, 62 SMU L. Rev. 367 (2009).

a. Posthumously Conceived Children

The decedent in Hecht v. Superior Court, 59 Cal. Rptr. 2d 222 (App. 1996), devised to his girlfriend 15 vials of his sperm that were on deposit in a sperm bank. His two adult children contested the devise and sought an order that the sperm be destroyed. The court, expressing exasperation at the children's unrelenting effort to frustrate their father's will, ordered all the vials to be distributed to the girlfriend.

Would a child conceived through the use of that sperm, a *posthumously conceived child*, be the decedent's child for purposes of intestate succession? Unlike a posthumous child, who is born after a parent's death but conceived while the parent is alive (see page 107), a posthumously conceived child is both born and conceived after the death of one or both of the child's genetic parents. Because marriage terminates at death, a posthumously conceived child is necessarily a nonmarital child.

The court in *Hecht* was not called upon to resolve the inheritance rights of a posthumously conceived child. But in the years since, posthumously conceived children have been born with increasing frequency, typically by use of the father's preserved sperm after the father's death from illness or in war, leaving courts and legislatures to struggle with the question of such children's rights in intestacy. The first decision on this question by an American court of last resort follows.

Woodward v. Commissioner of Social Security
760 N.E.2d 257 (Mass. 2002)

MARSHALL, C.J. The United States District Court for the District of Massachusetts has certified the following question to this court.

> If a married man and woman arrange for sperm to be withdrawn from the husband for the purpose of artificially impregnating the wife, and the woman is impregnated with that sperm after the man, her husband, has died, will children resulting from such pregnancy enjoy the inheritance rights of natural children under Massachusetts' law of intestate succession?

We answer the certified question as follows: In certain limited circumstances, a child resulting from posthumous reproduction may enjoy the inheritance rights of "issue" under the Massachusetts intestacy statute. . . .

Chief Justice Margaret H. Marshall, the first woman to be named Chief Justice of the Massachusetts Supreme Judicial Court, the oldest court in continuous existence in the Western Hemisphere

I

. . . In January, 1993, about three and one-half years after they were married, Lauren Woodward and Warren Woodward were informed that the husband had leukemia. At the time, the couple was childless. Advised that the husband's leukemia treatment might leave him sterile, the Woodwards arranged for a quantity of the husband's semen to be medically withdrawn and preserved, in a process commonly known as "sperm banking." The husband then underwent a bone marrow transplant. The treatment was not successful. The husband died in October, 1993, and the wife was appointed administratrix of his estate.

In October, 1995, the wife gave birth to twin girls. The children were conceived through artificial insemination using the husband's preserved semen. In January, 1996, the wife applied for two forms of Social Security survivor benefits: "child's" benefits . . . and "mother's" benefits.

The Social Security Administration (SSA) rejected the wife's claims on the ground that she had not established that the twins were the husband's "children" within the meaning of the Act . . . [because] they "are not entitled to inherit from [the husband] under the Massachusetts intestacy and paternity laws." . . .

The wife appealed to the United States District Court for the District of Massachusetts, seeking a declaratory judgment to reverse the commissioner's ruling.

The United States District Court judge certified the above question to this court because "[t]he parties agree that a determination of these children's rights under the law of Massachusetts is dispositive of the case and . . . no directly applicable Massachusetts precedent exists."

II

. . . [T]he parties have articulated extreme positions. The wife's principal argument is that, by virtue of their genetic connection with the decedent, posthumously conceived children must *always* be permitted to enjoy the inheritance rights of the deceased parent's children under our law of intestate succession. The government's principal argument is that, because posthumously conceived children are not "in being" as of the date of the parent's death, they are *always* barred from enjoying such inheritance rights.

Neither party's position is tenable. In this developing and relatively uncharted area of human relations, bright-line rules are not favored unless the applicable statute requires them. The Massachusetts intestacy statute does not. . . . On the other hand, with the act of procreation now separated from coitus, posthumous reproduction can occur under a variety of conditions that may conflict with the purposes of the intestacy law and implicate other firmly established State and individual interests. We look to our intestacy law to resolve these tensions. . . .

To answer the certified question . . . we must first determine whether the twins are the "issue" of the husband.

The intestacy statute does not define "issue." However, in the context of intestacy the term "issue" means all lineal (genetic) descendants, and now includes both marital and nonmarital descendants. The term "'[d]escendants' . . . has long been held to mean persons 'who by consanguinity trace their lineage to the designated ancestor.'" Lockwood v. Adamson, 566 N.E.2d 96, 98 (Mass. 1991). . . .

We must therefore determine whether, under our intestacy law, there is any reason that children conceived after the decedent's death who are the decedent's direct genetic descendants—that is, children who "by consanguinity trace their lineage to the designated ancestor"—may not enjoy the same succession rights as children conceived before the decedent's death who are the decedent's direct genetic descendants.

To answer that question we consider whether and to what extent such children may take as intestate heirs of the deceased genetic parent consistent with the purposes of the intestacy law, and not by any assumptions of the common law. In the absence of express legislative directives, we construe the Legislature's purposes from statutory indicia and judicial decisions in a manner that advances the purposes of the intestacy law.

The question whether posthumously conceived genetic children may enjoy inheritance rights under the intestacy statute implicates three powerful State interests: [1] the best interests of children, [2] the State's interest in the orderly administration of estates, and [3] the reproductive rights of the genetic parent. Our task is to

Michayla and Mackenzie Woodward, with their mother, Lauren Woodward
Amy Sweeney/The Salem News

balance and harmonize these interests to effect the Legislature's over-all purposes.

1. First and foremost we consider the overriding legislative concern to promote the best interests of children. "The protection of minor children, most especially those who may be stigmatized by their 'illegitimate' status . . . has been a hallmark of legislative action and of the jurisprudence of this court." Repeatedly, forcefully, and unequivocally, the Legislature has expressed its will that all children be "entitled to the same rights and protections of the law" regardless of the accidents of their birth. Among the many rights and protections vouchsafed to all children are rights to financial support from their parents and their parents' estates. See G.L. c. 119A, § 1 ("It is the public policy of this commonwealth that dependent children shall be maintained, as completely as possible, from the resources of their parents, thereby relieving or avoiding, at least in part, the burden borne by the citizens of the commonwealth"); G.L. c. 191, § 20 (establishing inheritance rights for pretermitted children); G.L. c. 196, §§ 1-3 (permitting allowances from estate to widows and minor children); G.L. c. 209C, § 14 (permitting paternity claims to be commenced prior to birth).

We also consider that some of the assistive reproductive technologies that make posthumous reproduction possible have been widely known and practiced for several decades. In that time, the Legislature has not acted to narrow the broad statutory class of posthumous children to restrict posthumously conceived children from taking in intestacy. Moreover, the Legislature has in great measure affirmatively supported the assistive reproductive technologies that are the only means by which these children can come into being. See G.L. c. 46, § 4B (artificial insemination of married woman). See also G.L. c. 175, § 47H; G.L. c. 176A, § 8K; G.L. c. 176B, § 4J; G.L. c. 176G, § 4 (insurance coverage for infertility treatments). We do not impute to the Legislature the inherently irrational conclusion that assistive reproductive technologies are to be encouraged while a class of children who are the fruit of that technology are to have fewer rights and protections than other children.

In short, we cannot, absent express legislative directive, accept the commissioner's position that . . . as a matter of law that all posthumously conceived children are automatically barred from taking under their deceased donor parent's intestate estate. We have consistently construed statutes to effectuate the Legislature's overriding purpose to promote the welfare of all children, notwithstanding restrictive common-law rules to the contrary. Posthumously conceived children may not come into the world the way the majority of children do. But they are children nonetheless. We may assume that the Legislature intended that such children be "entitled," in so far as possible, "to the same rights and protections of the law" as children conceived before death. See G.L. c. 209C, § 1.

2. However, in the context of our intestacy laws, the best interests of the posthumously conceived child, while of great importance, are not in themselves conclusive. They must be balanced against other important State interests, not the least of which is the protection of children who are alive or conceived before the intestate parent's death. In an era in which serial marriages, serial families, and blended families are not uncommon, according succession rights under our intestacy laws to posthumously conceived children may, in a given case, have the potential to pit child against child and family against family. Any inheritance rights of posthumously conceived children will reduce the intestate share available to children born prior to the decedent's death. Such considerations, among others, lead us to examine a second important legislative purpose: to provide certainty to heirs and creditors by effecting the orderly, prompt, and accurate administration of intestate estates.

The intestacy statute furthers the Legislature's administrative goals in two principal ways: (1) by requiring certainty of filiation between the decedent and his issue, and (2) by establishing limitations periods for the commencement of claims against the intestate estate. In answering the certified question, we must consider each of these requirements of the intestacy statute in turn.

First, . . . our intestacy law mandates that, absent the father's acknowledgment of paternity or marriage to the mother, a nonmarital child must obtain a judicial determination of paternity as a prerequisite to succeeding to a portion of the father's intestate estate. . . .

Because death ends a marriage, posthumously conceived children are always nonmarital children. And because the parentage of such children can be neither acknowledged nor adjudicated prior to the decedent's death, it follows that, under the intestacy statute, posthumously conceived children must obtain a judgment of paternity as a necessary prerequisite to enjoying inheritance rights in the estate of the deceased genetic father. Although modern reproductive technologies will increase the possibility of disputed paternity claims, sophisticated modern testing techniques now make the determination of genetic paternity accurate and reliable. . . .

We now turn to the second way in which the Legislature has met its administrative goals: the establishment of a limitations period for bringing paternity claims against the intestate estate. Our discussion of this important goal, however, is necessarily circumscribed by the procedural posture of this case and by the terms of the certified question. [The parties stipulated that, in this dispute over Social Security benefits, timeliness was not at issue.] . . .

Nevertheless, the limitations question is inextricably tied to consideration of the intestacy statute's administrative goals. In the case of posthumously conceived children, the application of the one-year limitations period of G.L. c. 190, § 7 is not clear; it may pose significant burdens on the surviving parent, and consequently on the child. It requires, in effect, that the survivor make a decision to bear children while in the freshness of grieving. It also requires that attempts at conception succeed quickly. Because the resolution of the time constraints question is not required here, it must await the appropriate case, should one arise.

3. Finally, the question certified to us implicates a third important State interest: to honor the reproductive choices of individuals. . . .

In A.Z. v. B.Z., 725 N.E.2d 1051 (Mass. 2000), we . . . recognized that individuals have a protected right to control the use of their gametes. Consonant with the principles identified in A.Z. v. B.Z., a decedent's silence, or his equivocal indications of a desire to parent posthumously, "ought not to be construed as consent." See Anne Reichman Schiff, Arising from the Dead: Challenges of Posthumous Procreation, 75 N.C. L. Rev. 901, 951 (1997). The prospective donor parent must clearly and unequivocally consent not only to posthumous reproduction but also to the support of any resulting child. After the donor-parent's death, the burden rests with the surviving parent, or the posthumously conceived child's other legal representative, to prove the deceased genetic parent's affirmative consent to both requirements for posthumous parentage: posthumous reproduction and the support of any resulting child.

This two-fold consent requirement arises from the nature of alternative reproduction itself. It will not always be the case that a person elects to have his or her gametes medically preserved to create "issue" posthumously. A man, for example, may preserve his semen for myriad reasons, including, among others: to reproduce after recovery from medical treatment, to reproduce after an event that leaves him sterile, or to reproduce when his spouse has a genetic disorder or otherwise cannot have or safely bear children. That a man has medically preserved his gametes for use by his spouse thus may indicate only that he wished to reproduce after some contingency while he was alive, and not that he consented to the different circumstance of creating a child after his death. Uncertainty as to consent may be compounded by the fact that medically preserved semen can remain viable for up to ten years after it was first extracted, long after the original decision to preserve the semen has passed and when such changed circumstances as divorce, remarriage, and a second family may have intervened.

Such circumstances demonstrate the inadequacy of a rule that would make the mere genetic tie of the decedent to any posthumously conceived child, or the decedent's mere election to preserve gametes, sufficient to bind his intestate estate for the benefit of any posthumously conceived child. Without evidence that the deceased intestate parent affirmatively consented (1) to the posthumous reproduction and (2) to support any resulting child, a court cannot be assured that the intestacy statute's goal of fraud prevention is satisfied. . . .

It is undisputed in this case that the husband is the genetic father of the wife's children. However, for the reasons stated above, that fact, in itself, cannot be sufficient to establish that the husband is the children's legal father for purposes of the devolution and distribution of his intestate property. In the United States District Court, the wife may come forward with other evidence as to her husband's consent to posthumously conceive children. She may come forward with evidence of his consent to support such children. We do not speculate as to the sufficiency of evidence she may submit at trial. . . .

III

. . . As these technologies advance, the number of children they produce will continue to multiply. So, too, will the complex moral, legal, social, and ethical questions that surround their birth. The questions present in this case cry out for lengthy, careful examination outside the adversary process, which can only address the specific circumstances of each controversy that presents itself. They demand a comprehensive response reflecting the considered will of the people.

In the absence of statutory directives, we have answered the certified question by identifying and harmonizing the important State interests implicated therein in a manner that advances the Legislature's over-all purposes. In so doing, we conclude that limited circumstances may exist, consistent with the mandates of our Legislature, in which posthumously conceived children may enjoy the inheritance rights of "issue" under our intestacy law. These limited circumstances exist where, as a threshold matter, the surviving parent or the child's other legal representative demonstrates a genetic relationship between the child and the decedent. The survivor or representative must then establish both that the decedent affirmatively consented to posthumous conception and to the support of any resulting child. Even where such circumstances exist, time limitations may preclude commencing a claim for succession rights on behalf of a posthumously conceived child. In any action brought to establish such inheritance rights, notice must be given to all interested parties.

[The clerk of the court was ordered to transmit an attested copy of this opinion to the district court.]

NOTES

1. Social Security Benefits and State Inheritance Law.   At issue in nearly all the reported cases involving the inheritance rights of a posthumously conceived child is eligibility for Social Security survivor's benefits. In Astrue v. Capato, 566 U.S. 541 (2012), the Supreme Court confirmed that a posthumously conceived child is eligible for Social Security survivor's benefits only if the child would be an intestate heir of the predeceased parent. But there is disagreement across the states on whether a posthumously conceived child can be an heir of the predeceased parent. Should Congress amend the Social Security Act to provide a national rule for survivor's benefits for posthumously conceived children? Are not the policies relevant to the Social Security program different from the policies, such as freedom of disposition and orderly succession of property, relevant to the design of intestate succession? Why doesn't the Social Security Act take into account whether a parent has disinherited a child by will?

2. Finality and Consent.   Suppose a man banks his sperm and records in writing his consent to posthumous conception with his widow. The widow then gives birth to the man's posthumously conceived child 22 years later. Should the child be entitled to inherit from her father? At what point does the need for finality in succession trump the interests of a posthumously conceived, later-born child? How much weight should be given to the probable intent of the predeceased parent? To the best interests of the child?

Frozen Sperm Still Viable Decades Later

By Kate Snow et al.

The birth of Stella Biblis on Feb. 25 was 22 years in the making.

Stella was conceived through in-vitro fertilization using frozen sperm her father, Chris Biblis, saved more than two decades ago.

Doctors believe 39-year-old Chris Biblis probably holds the world record for the amount of time sperm has been frozen before being used to create a baby.

Stella is living proof that sperm can survive frozen for decades.

And it was her father's decision as a teenager fighting leukemia that led to the medical marvel....

Doctors said teenage patients and their parents often don't think about the parenthood issue when they are dealing with cancer, whose treatment can often leave patients infertile. If patients are facing a life-threatening disease, the priority is surviving, not procreating.

"I was trying to get through high school and living one day at a time, hoping I was honestly going to make it," he said. "It was the furthest thing from my mind — being married or having a child."

And while it wasn't something he was considering, his mother, who now lives in Auburn, Ala., was planning ahead for a post-cancer life.

As Chris Biblis underwent chemotherapy, his mother persuaded the 16 year old to freeze some of his sperm. And he did on April 25, 1986, at Xytex International Ltd. in Atlanta.

Chris and Stella Biblis
Photo by Jeffery Salter

But in 1986 there were no guarantees that the technology would exist to take damaged sperm and successfully fertilize an egg....

Yet 22 years later — on June 12, 2008 — thanks in part to the advancement of infertility science, Chris Biblis' sperm was unfrozen and his wife, Melodie Biblis, was impregnated.

And now they have a daughter named Stella.

Source: ABC News (Apr. 10, 2009).

Suppose a man banks his sperm but, after he dies, there is a dispute about whether he consented to posthumous conception. What proof would show that the man "affirmatively consented" under *Woodward*? What about the extraction of sperm from dead or comatose men who do not consent, and the use of such sperm by someone other than a surviving spouse? The practice of harvesting sperm from deceased men raises difficult questions of law and ethics.[84]

3. Legislation and Law Reform. More than a dozen states have heeded the call in *Woodward* for legislative relief.[85] Under the California statute, "a child of the decedent conceived and born after the death of the decedent shall be deemed to have been born in the lifetime of the decedent" if there is clear and convincing evidence that (a) the decedent consented in a signed and dated writing; (b) within four months of the decedent's death, notice of the possibility of posthumous conception is served upon "a person who has the power to control the distribution" of the decedent's property; and (c) the child "was in utero within two years of the" decedent's death.[86]

Uniform Parentage Act § 707 (2000, rev. 2002), adopted in a handful of states, recognizes inheritance rights for a posthumously conceived child if the parent consented

---

84. *See, e.g.,* Restatement (Third) of Property: Wills and Other Donative Transfers § 14.8 cmt. k(1) (Am. Law Inst. 2011).

85. *See* Schoenblum, *supra* note 11, at tbl. 11.

86. Cal. Prob. Code § 249.5 (2016).

to posthumous conception in writing. UPC § 2-120, promulgated in 2008 and since adopted in a handful of states, provides that a posthumously conceived child inherits from the deceased parent if (1) during life the parent consented to posthumous conception in a signed writing or consent is otherwise proved by clear and convincing evidence, and (2) the child is in utero not later than 36 months or is born not later than 45 months after the parent's death.[87]

b. Posthumously Conceived Children and Wills and Trusts

Is a posthumously conceived child of *A* entitled to share in a gift by will or trust to a biological class such as to the "children," "issue," or "descendants" of *A*? An important wrinkle is that unlike an intestate succession to *A*'s estate, for which *A*'s death is the triggering event for distribution, for a gift by will or trust to *A*'s children, issue, or descendants, *A*'s death might not be the triggering event. For example, if a trust provides for quarterly distributions of income to *A*'s descendants, those distributions would be triggered by the passage of time without regard for whether *A* is alive or dead.

For a distribution to *A*'s descendants that is triggered other than by *A*'s death, such as the quarterly income example just given, the possibility of an afterborn child of *A*, whether conceived before or after *A*'s death, does not give rise to the same finality concerns. Under traditional law, membership in a class, such as "*A*'s descendants," is fixed with respect to a distribution whenever any member of the class becomes entitled to the distribution (see page 882). The possibility of an afterborn child of *A*, whether conceived before or after *A*'s death, does not undermine the finality of earlier distributions.

In re Martin B., 841 N.Y.S.2d 207 (Sur. 2008), is illustrative. James's father created a trust in 1969. The trust provided for periodic distributions of income to the father's descendants. Three years after James's death, a posthumously conceived child of James was born. Another posthumously conceived child of James was born two years after that. At issue was whether these children were eligible for subsequent distributions from the trust as descendants of James's father. Observing that "the concerns related to winding up a decedent's estate differ from those related to identifying whether a class disposition to a grantor's issue includes a child conceived after the [parent's] death but before the disposition became effective," the court ruled that, in the absence of evidence that James's father would have wanted the children to be excluded, they would be eligible for future distributions if alive at the time of those distributions. In effect, the court treated the children no differently than if James had been alive at their conception.

The Restatement (Third) of Property states the principle applied in *Martin B.* thus: "In cases in which the distribution date arises after the deceased parent's death, a child produced posthumously by assisted reproduction is in being on the date when the child

---

87. *See* Benjamin C. Carpenter, A Chip Off the Old Iceblock: How Cryopreservation Has Changed Estate Law, Why Attempts to Address the Issue Have Fallen Short, and How to Fix It, 21 Cornell J.L. & Pub. Pol'y 347 (2011); Kristine S. Knaplund, The New Uniform Probate Code's Surprising Gender Inequities, 18 Duke J. Gender L. & Pol'y 335 (2011); Browne Lewis, Graveside Birthday Parties: The Legal Consequences of Forming Families Posthumously, 60 Case W. Res. L. Rev. 1159 (2010).

is in utero for purposes of the class-closing rules, just as is any other child."[88] If the trigger for distribution is the deceased parent's death, however, then the same finality concerns arise as in intestacy. Statutes in an increasing number of states apply to such a case the same notice rules and time limits for a posthumously conceived child to be an heir.

Under the UPC as revised in 2008, whether a posthumously conceived child of A is included in a class gift in a will or trust by T to the "children," "issue," or "descendants" of A depends on whether the distribution is triggered by the predeceasing parent's death. If so, the child must have been living on that date or have been in utero not later than 36 months after or born not later than 45 months after (§ 2-705(g)(2)). If the distribution date is not the date of the predeceasing parent's death, the normal class closing rules apply, and the child is eligible to take if on that date the child is alive or is in utero and then born alive (§ 2-705(g)(1)). In either case, A must have consented to posthumous conception in a signed writing or A's consent must otherwise be proved by clear and convincing evidence (§§ 2-705(b) and 2-120(f)).

c. Surrogacy and Opposite-Sex Married Couples

An opposite-sex married couple can have a child through surrogacy in a variety of ways. The couple can combine the egg and sperm of either the couple or of third-party donors in such a way that a child born to a surrogate may have a genetic connection to both husband and wife, to only one of them, or to neither. The child may or may not have a genetic connection to the surrogate. Given the many possibilities, it is sometimes difficult to discern who is a parent of a child born to a surrogate.

The courts are by no means in agreement. Many states have neither statutory nor case law directly on point. Article 8 of the Uniform Parentage Act (2000, rev. 2002) provides comprehensive rules, but they have not been widely adopted. Professor Carla Spivack sums up the situation thus: "The law of surrogate motherhood in the United States is in a state of flux and confusion. States have widely differing laws, some enforcing surrogacy contracts, some banning them entirely, and some allowing them under certain circumstances. Many states have no laws regarding surrogacy contracts at all. No single statutory regime has won widespread acceptance."[89]

In Johnson v. Calvert, 851 P.2d 776 (Cal. 1993), a husband and wife signed a contract with a surrogate providing that an egg of the wife fertilized by the husband's sperm would be implanted in the surrogate and, after the child was born, it would be taken into the home of the husband and wife as their child. The surrogate agreed to relinquish all parental rights to the child. The surrogate later changed her mind, claiming parental rights. The court held that parenthood in surrogate mother cases should not be determined by who gave birth or who contributed genetic material, but should

---

88. Restatement (Third) of Property: Wills and Other Donative Transfers § 15.1 cmt. j (Am. Law Inst. 2011).

89. Carla Spivack, The Law of Surrogate Motherhood in the United States, 58 Am. J. Comp. L. 97, 97 (2010); *see also* Mary Patricia Byrn & Lisa Giddings, An Empirical Analysis of the Use of the Intent Test to Determine Parentage in Assisted Reproductive Technology Cases, 50 Hous. L. Rev. 1295 (2013).

turn on the intent of the parties as shown by the surrogacy contract. The court declared the husband and wife the sole parents.

In Michigan, by contrast, surrogacy for compensation is illegal. In a custody dispute over a child born to a surrogate, the dispositive consideration is the best interests of the child.[90] In New Jersey, an intended mother who has no genetic link to a child born to a surrogate must adopt the child to be recognized as the child's parent even if the child was produced with the sperm of the intended mother's husband.[91]

In some states, surrogacy agreements are prohibited or are enforceable only under certain conditions. In Hodas v. Morin, 814 N.E.2d 320 (Mass. 2004), the court upheld the choice of Massachusetts law in a surrogacy agreement between a New York surrogate and a Connecticut husband and wife. The contract called for the child, who was to be produced with an egg from the wife and sperm from the husband, to be born in Massachusetts. The court ruled that this provided a sufficient connection to justify application of Massachusetts law, which is favorable to surrogacy and allows for a pre-birth declaratory judgment on parentage, in spite of the strong New York public policy against commercial surrogacy. This rule invites what might be called "surrogacy tourism."[92]

Should the determination of who is a parent in custody and child support cases be conclusive of inheritance rights? Do the policies in the cases cited above, which are heavily influenced by the family law emphasis on the best interests of the child, apply to inheritance? What of the probable intent of the donor? Which should prevail if the best interests of the child are in tension with the donor's likely intent? These are difficult questions without easy answers.[93]

d. Assisted Reproduction and Same-Sex Couples

Parentage in a same-sex couple raises the question of whether a child can have two mothers or two fathers. In Adoption of Tammy, 619 N.E.2d 315 (Mass. 1993), noted in 107 Harv. L. Rev. 751 (1994), the court approved an adoption by the lesbian partner of Dr. Susan Love, the eminent breast cancer surgeon and best-selling author, of Love's child, who had been conceived by artificial insemination. The court held that both Love and the adoptive mother had post-adoptive rights and that the adopted child would inherit from and through both mothers as the child of each. Under V.L. v. E.L., 136 S. Ct. 1017 (2016), this judgment would be entitled to "full faith and credit" in other states.

The proposition that a child could have two mothers, accepted in *Tammy*, was also accepted in Elisa B. v. Superior Court, 117 P.3d 660 (Cal. 2005). In K.M. v. E.G., 117 P.3d 673 (Cal. 2005), the same court held that a woman who "supplie[s] her ova to impregnate her lesbian partner in order to produce children who would be raised in

---

90. Mich. Comp. Laws §§ 722.859, 722.861 (2016).

91. *See* In re T.J.S., 16 A.3d 386 (N.J. App. 2011), *aff'd,* 54 A.3d 263 (N.J. 2012) (per curiam).

92. I. Glenn Cohen, Circumvention Tourism, 97 Cornell L. Rev. 1309, 1324 (2012).

93. *See* Linda D. Elrod, A Child's Perspective of Defining a Parent: The Case for Intended Parenthood, 25 BYU J. Pub. L. 245 (2011); Browne C. Lewis, Three Lies and a Truth: Adjudicating Maternity in Surrogacy Disputes, 49 U. Louisville L. Rev. 371 (2011); Tritt, *supra* note 83.

their joint home" is a mother of the resulting children, as is the partner who gave birth to the children. The same circumstances were considered, with the same result, in D.M.T. v. T.M.H., 129 So. 3d 320 (Fla. 2013).

In Partanen v. Gallagher, 59 N.E.3d 1133 (Mass. 2016), the court held that a woman who was the nonmarital same-sex partner of the biological mother of a child was the presumptive second parent of the child under a statute that provides that "a man is presumed to be the father of a [nonmarital] child" if "he, jointly with the mother, received the child into their home and openly held out the child as their child." The court reasoned that the statute, although written "in gendered terms," should "be construed to apply to children born to same-sex couples."

In Raftopol v. Ramey, 12 A.3d 783 (Conn. 2011), the facts were similar to those in Johnson v. Calvert, discussed at page 119, except that the intended parents were two men in an unmarried partnership, one of whom provided the sperm to fertilize an egg from a third-party donor, and

Dr. Susan Love
Kevork Djansezian/AP photo

the gestational carrier was supportive of the men being named as co-parents. As in *Johnson*, the surrogacy contract provided that any resulting children would be taken into the home of the intended parents. After the surrogate became pregnant with twins, the men brought a declaratory judgment action to settle the question of parentage. The court held that parentage was controlled by the surrogacy contract, hence the two men — the sperm donor and his partner — would be the twins' parents without having to go through an adoption process.[94]

Following the nationwide recognition of same-sex marriage after Obergefell v. Hodges, 135 S. Ct. 2584 (2015), a new question has arisen. Should the *marital presumption*, under which a child born to a married woman is presumed to be the child of the woman's husband, be extended to same-sex marriages? In Gartner v. Iowa Department of Public Health, 830 N.W.2d 335 (Iowa 2013), the court held on constitutional grounds that the marital presumption must be applied also to a same-sex married couple — but not all courts agree.[95] As this book went to press in early 2017, the Uniform Law Commission was revising Uniform Parentage Act § 204 to extend its codification of the marital presumption to same-sex marriages.

e. The 2008 Amendments to the UPC

Under the 2008 amendments to the UPC, inheritance rights turn on whether a parent-child relationship exists (see page 93). With respect to a child born to a surrogate (a "gestational carrier"), UPC § 2-121 provides that in the absence of a court order to the

---

94. *See* Courtney G. Joslin, Leaving No (Nonmarital) Child Behind, 48 Fam. L.Q. 495 (2014).

95. *See* Paula A. Monopoli, Inheritance Law and the Marital Presumption After *Obergefell*, 8 Est. Plan. & Community Prop. L.J. 437 (2016); Douglas NeJaime, Marriage Equality and the New Parenthood, 129 Harv. L. Rev. 1185, 1240-49 (2016).

contrary, the surrogate does not have a parent-child relationship with the child unless no one else does. An intended parent of the child, meaning a person who entered into an agreement with the surrogate stating that the person would be the parent of the child, has a parent-child relationship with the child if the person functioned as a parent of the child within two years of the child's birth.

A child conceived by assisted reproduction other than posthumously or by gestational surrogacy is in a parent-child relationship and thus entitled to inherit by, from, or through the child's birth mother (§ 2-120(c)). There can also be a parent-child relationship with another person if the other person either consented in writing to assisted reproduction by the birth mother with the intent to be the other parent of the child or functioned as a parent of the child within two years of the child's birth (§ 2-120(f)).

5. Advancements and Hotchpot

If a child wishes to share in the intestate distribution of a deceased parent's estate, the child must permit the administrator to include in the determination of the distributive shares the value of any property that the decedent, while living, gave the child by way of an *advancement*.

a. Advancements at Common Law

At common law, any lifetime gift by the decedent to a child was presumed to be an advancement—in effect, a prepayment—of the child's intestate share. To avoid application of the doctrine, the child had the burden of establishing that the decedent did not intend the gift to be counted against the child's share of the estate. The doctrine is based on the assumption that a parent would want an equal distribution of assets among children and that true equality can be reached only if lifetime gifts by the parent are taken into account in determining the amount of the equal shares. When a parent makes an advancement to a child and the child predeceases the parent, the amount of the advancement is deducted from the shares of the child's descendants if other children of the parent survive.

b. Hotchpot

If a gift is treated as an advancement, it is accounted for in distributing the decedent's estate by bringing it into *hotchpot*. Here is how hotchpot works: Assume that the decedent, *O*, leaves no spouse, three children, *A*, *B*, and *C*, and an estate worth $50,000. One daughter, *A*, received an advancement of $10,000. To calculate the shares for *A*, *B*, and *C*, the $10,000 gift is added to the $50,000 estate, and the total $60,000 hotchpot is divided by three, resulting in a $20,000 share per child. But because *A* has already received a $10,000 advancement on her share, she receives only $10,000 from the estate. Her siblings each take $20,000. If instead *A* had been given property worth $40,000 as an advancement, *A* would not have to give back a portion of this amount (we know that *O* wanted *A* to have at least $40,000). *A* will stay out of hotchpot, and the decedent's $50,000 will be equally divided between the other two children.

NOTES

1. An Advancement Problem. Suppose that *O* has two children, *A* and *B*. *A* owns a successful business. *B* is a single parent who struggles to make ends meet. *O* makes regular gifts to *B*, but not to *A*, because *B* is in greater need. If *O*'s lifetime transfers to *B* are deemed to be advancements, then *A* will inherit more than *B* on the death of *O*. Is this result consistent with *O*'s probable intent? Why does the law regard favorable lifetime treatment of a child as a reason to disfavor that child at the parent's death? Is not favorable lifetime treatment good evidence that the decedent would have wanted the favored child to receive at least the same share of her estate as her other children? The common law of advancements answers this question in the negative.

2. Additional Advancement Problems. Consider the following situations:

a. *O* has three children. One daughter, *A*, lives with *O* on *O*'s farm until *O* dies. A few years before death, *O* deeds the farm to *A*. *O* dies intestate. *A* claims the gift is not an advancement but an extra gift for extraordinary services rendered to *O*. What result? *See* Thomas v. Thomas, 398 S.W.2d 231 (Ky. 1965).

b. Suppose that *O* gives his son, *B*, $20,000. *B* is ill and unable to work and support his family. Is this an advancement?

c. Suppose that *O*'s daughter, *C*, goes to Harvard Medical School and becomes a doctor. *O* pays the tuition. Is this an advancement?

c. Advancements in Modern Law

Largely because of the difficulty of proving the donor's intent, many states have reversed the common law presumption of advancement. In these states, a lifetime gift is presumed *not* to be an advancement unless it is shown to have been intended as such. Some states and UPC § 2-109(a) (1990), below, go even further, requiring that the intention to make an advancement be declared in a writing signed by the parent or child. The UPC also changes the common law rule if the child does not survive the parent. Under § 2-109(c), the advancement is not taken into account in determining the share of the child's descendants.

Requiring a writing to evidence an advancement all but eliminates the doctrine of advancements from the law of intestate succession. Although this avoids contentious litigation between family members about little-remembered lifetime gifts, it can lead to results that are contrary to a donor's clearly stated—but unwritten—intentions.

Uniform Probate Code (Unif. Law Comm'n 1990)

§ 2-109. Advancements

(a) If an individual dies intestate as to all or a portion of his [or her] estate, property the decedent gave during the decedent's lifetime to an individual who, at the decedent's death, is an heir[96] is treated as an advancement against the

---

96. UPC § 2-109 applies to advancements made to spouses and collaterals (such as nephews and nieces) as well as to lineal descendants. In most states, only gifts to lineal descendants are considered advancements.—Eds.

heir's intestate share only if (i) the decedent declared in a contemporaneous writing or the heir acknowledged in writing that the gift is an advancement or (ii) the decedent's contemporaneous writing or the heir's written acknowledgment otherwise indicates that the gift is to be taken into account in computing the division and distribution of the decedent's intestate estate.

(b) For purposes of subsection (a), property advanced is valued as of the time the heir came into possession or enjoyment of the property or as of the time of the decedent's death, whichever first occurs.

(c) If the recipient of the property fails to survive the decedent, the property is not taken into account in computing the division and distribution of the decedent's intestate estate, unless the decedent's contemporaneous writing provides otherwise.

NOTES

1. Setting Advancements Policy. Which of the following rules do you think is best?
   a. Gifts to children are presumptively advancements.
   b. Gifts to children are presumptively not advancements.
   c. Gifts to children are not advancements unless stated in writing to be advancements.
   d. Gifts to children are advancements unless stated in writing not to be advancements.

2. Advancement Provisions in Wills and Trusts.   Wills and trusts sometimes contain a provision instructing that certain lifetime gifts or distributions under the instrument are to be taken into account when making later distributions. Strictly speaking, such a provision does not involve an advancement, because there is no intestacy, but the concept is the same. For example: "Each payment to a child of mine under this paragraph shall be treated as an advancement and charged without interest against the share hereinafter provided for the child or his or her descendants."[97]

A related issue arises when after making a will the testator makes an inter vivos transfer to a devisee under the will. Should the transfer count at the testator's death against the devisee's gift under the will? The answer is provided by the doctrine of *satisfaction*, which we take up in Chapter 5 at page 383.

6. Guardianship and Conservatorship of Minors

Because a minor lacks legal capacity to manage property and to decide how and where to live, a client with a minor child should be advised to provide for the possibility of the child becoming orphaned, as we discuss below. In addition, all clients should be advised to provide for the possibility that, owing to old age or otherwise, the client might herself become incapacitated, as we discuss in Chapter 7 at page 498.

---

97. Northern Trust, Will & Trust Forms 101-10 (2004).

a. Guardian of the Person

A guardian of the person has responsibility for the minor's custody and care. As long as one parent of the child is living and competent, that parent is the natural guardian of the child's person. If only one of two parents dies, there is no need to appoint a guardian of the person. But if both parents die while a child is a minor, the court will appoint a guardian of the person, usually from among the nearest relatives. This person may not be whom the parents would want to have custody of the child.

For a parent with a minor child, therefore, an important reason to make a will is to designate a guardian of the person for the child. In most states, a parent's testamentary appointment of a guardian, although not formally binding, is nonetheless persuasive in the court's reckoning of the best interests of the child.[98] Testators commonly select a family member, often a sibling, or sometimes a friend. It is a good idea also to select an alternate. A guardianship of the person terminates when the minor reaches the age of majority or dies.

Guardianship of the person for a minor is covered by UPC §§ 5-201 to 5-210 (1998), which are based on the Uniform Guardianship and Protective Proceedings Act (Unif. Law Comm'n 1997).

b. Property Management Options

Another important reason for a parent with a minor child to have a will is to deal with the management of the child's property. A guardian of the person has no authority to deal with the child's property. Nor, obviously, does the child.

Several alternatives for surrogate fiduciary property management are available: (1) guardianship of the property, (2) conservatorship, (3) custodianship, and (4) trusteeship. Trusts are available only to persons who create them during life (an *inter vivos trust*) or who die testate and create one by will (a *testamentary trust*). If a parent dies intestate, leaving property to a minor child, a guardian of the property or a conservator must be appointed by a court, unless state law allows distribution of the minor's share to a custodian under the Uniform Transfers to Minors Act or to the person who has physical custody of the child.

(1) Guardianship of the Property.   In feudal times, the guardian of a minor ward, usually the overlord, took possession of the ward's lands. The guardian had the duty of supporting the ward, but all income from rents in excess of the amount necessary for support belonged to the guardian personally. Thus guardianships, then known as wardships, were very profitable for the guardian.

After the feudal incidents, including wardship, were abolished, a new kind of guardianship was recognized, giving the ward the rents from the property and the guardian only a management fee. But to protect the ward a guardian of the property was required to account annually to a court of chancery. To avoid a disagreeable contest later with

---

98. *See* Alyssa A. DiRusso & S. Kristen Peters, Parental Testamentary Appointment of Guardians for Children, 25 Quinnipiac Prob. L.J. 369 (2012).

the ward or chancellor, guardians sought approval for their actions in advance from the chancellor.

The product of this history, which emphasized guardianship's protective purpose, is a slow and expensive system of administration. For example, a guardian of the property may be unable to change investments without a court order. Third parties may be hesitant to deal with the guardian and the guardian ordinarily can use only the income from the property to support the ward; court approval is needed to go into principal.

(2) Conservatorship.   The expense and inflexibility of a guardianship for property has led to its replacement with a *conservator* system. Following the lead of UPC Article V (1998) and the Uniform Guardianship and Protective Proceeding Act (1997), in many states guardianship laws have been revised to allow a more trust-like arrangement. The guardian of the property has been renamed the *conservator* and given "title as trustee" to the protected person's property along with investment powers similar to those of a trustee. Appointment and supervision by a court is still required, but a conservator has far more flexible powers than a guardian, and only one trip to the courthouse annually for an accounting may be necessary. The conservatorship terminates when the minor reaches the age of majority or dies.

(3) Custodianship.   A *custodian* is a person who is given property to hold for the benefit of a minor under the Uniform Transfers to Minors Act (UTMA) (Unif. Law Comm'n 1983, rev. 1986) or its predecessor, the Uniform Gifts to Minors Act (UGMA) (Unif. Law Comm'n 1956, rev. 1966). Under these acts, some form of which has been enacted in every state, property may be transferred to a person, including the donor, as *custodian* for the benefit of the minor. A devise or gift may be made "to *X* as custodian for *A* under the [state] Uniform Transfers to Minors Act," thereby incorporating the provisions of the state's enactment and eliminating the necessity of drafting a trust instrument. Often the donor will choose herself as custodian for the minor, whether the donor is related to the minor or not.

The creation of a custodianship is simple. Most banks and other financial institutions have standard forms that can be filled out by a donor making a gift to a minor or by a fiduciary making a distribution to a minor. Well-drafted wills and trusts often include a *facility of payment clause* under which property to be distributed outright to a minor may be paid instead to a custodian or even to the parent or guardian of the minor. Even if there is no will or trust with express authorization to make a payment to the child's parents, many states have laws permitting a fiduciary to pay small sums to the custodial parent or to an account in the child's name alone. UPC § 5-104 (1998) authorizes distribution of sums not exceeding $5,000 per year.

If no power to transfer assets to a custodian is given in a will or trust, the UTMA, but not the earlier UGMA, allows the fiduciary to make payments to a custodian nonetheless. UTMA § 6. Payments to custodians in excess of $10,000 require court approval.

Under UTMA § 14(a), the custodian has discretionary power to expend

> for the minor's benefit so much of the custodial property as the custodian considers advisable for the use and benefit of the minor, without court order and without regard to (i) the duty or ability of the custodian personally or any other person to

support the minor, or (ii) any other income or property of the minor which may be applicable or available for that purpose.

To the extent that the custodial property is not so expended, the custodian is required to transfer the property to the minor on his attaining the age of 18 or 21, depending on the circumstances, or, if the minor dies before attaining the age of 18 or 21, to the estate of the minor.

A custodian has the power to manage the property and to reinvest it. However, the custodian is a fiduciary and is subject to "the standard of care that would be observed by a prudent person dealing with property of another." UTMA § 12(b). The custodian is not under the supervision of a court—as is a guardian or conservator—and no accounting to the court annually or at the end of the custodianship is necessary, but an interested party may require one if he wishes. UTMA §§ 12(e), 19. A custodianship is useful for modest gifts to a minor and is helpful in other cases to avoid a conservatorship or guardianship. But if a large amount of property is involved, a trust is usually preferable.

(4) Trusteeship. A trust is the most flexible of all property arrangements. Much of the latter part of this book is devoted to the law of trusts (see Chapters 6 and 9-14). The donor can tailor the trust specifically to family circumstances and the donor's particular desires. Under a guardianship or conservatorship, the child must receive the property at 18 and, under a custodianship, at 18 or 21, but a trust can postpone possession until the donor thinks the child is competent to manage the property—or can postpone possession entirely, requiring that some or even all of the property remain in trust for generations.

A sound estate plan will account for the possibility of a minor beneficiary. In almost all cases, the best way to do so is with a trust. Most well-designed estate plans provide for a trust over any property that is to pass to a minor beneficiary, such as if an adult beneficiary predeceases the donor, leaving a minor child as a substitute taker.

D. BARS TO SUCCESSION

We now turn to bars to succession, primarily (1) the rule that prohibits a slayer from inheriting from his victim, and (2) voluntary disclaimer. It bears emphasizing that these bars pertain not only to intestate succession, but also to gifts under wills, trusts, and other modes of nonprobate transfer.

1. The Slayer Rule

In re Estate of Mahoney
220 A.2d 475 (Vt. 1966)

SMITH, J. The decedent, Howard Mahoney, died intestate on May 6, 1961, of gunshot wounds. His wife, Charlotte Mahoney, the appellant here, was tried for the murder of Howard Mahoney in the Addison County Court and was convicted by jury of the crime of manslaughter in March, 1962. She is presently serving a sentence of not less than 12 nor more than 15 years at the Women's Reformatory in Rutland.

Howard Mahoney left no issue, and was survived by his wife and his father and mother. His father, Mark Mahoney, was appointed administrator of his estate which at the present time amounts to $3,885.89. After due notice and hearing, the Probate Court for the District of Franklin entered a judgment order decreeing the residue of the Estate of Howard Mahoney, in equal shares, to the father and mother of the decedent. An appeal from the judgment order and decree has been taken here by the appellant widow. The question submitted is whether a widow convicted of manslaughter in connection with the death of her husband may inherit from his estate.

The general rules of descent provide that if a decedent is married and leaves no issue, his surviving spouse shall be entitled to the whole of decedent's estate if it does not exceed $8,000. 14 Vt. Stat. Ann. (V.S.A.) § 551(2). Only if the decedent leaves no surviving spouse or issue does the estate descend in equal shares to the surviving father and mother. 14 V.S.A. § 551(3). There is no statutory provision in Vermont regulating the descent and distribution of property from the decedent to the slayer. The question presented is one of first impression in this jurisdiction.

Why Did Charlotte Mahoney Kill?

The court's statement of the facts in *Mahoney* is rather sparse. There is not even a hint of context for the killing. Why did Charlotte Mahoney kill her husband?

In Killers Shouldn't Inherit from Their Victims—Or Should They?, 48 Ga. L. Rev. 145 (2013), Professor Carla Spivack offers an answer. She says that the sociopathic killing of a relative in order to inherit is rare. A killing within a family is more typically "a product of that family's harmful, often violent, dynamics, from which, because of the failures of state and society, a family member sometimes can find no escape except murder." Regarding *Mahoney*, Spivack writes:

I suspected that Charlotte Mahoney's killing of her husband might have been related to spousal abuse. Considerable digging in the archives revealed support for my intuition. As it turns out, Charlotte Mahoney was the first woman to be tried for murder in Vermont in fifty years and her case generated considerable press: the archives of The Burlington Free Press and other local papers contain over twenty articles about her trial. They reveal signs that she suffered abuse at the hands of her husband, and that her killing of him was a result of that abuse. She testified that, on the day of the murder, they had been having an argument in front of the house: she had tried to get into a car that her husband was getting ready to drive and he slammed the window shut on her hand several times before rolling it down and punching her in the face. Getting out of the car, he chased her into the house, shouting that "he would kill her if he got her," and if she ever tried to leave him, he would kill her. She testified that he then slapped her face and pulled her by the arm. She locked herself in the bedroom, but he entered it through another door, carrying his rifle. She testified that, as she tried to escape the house through the front door, he "made a pass" at her with the butt of the gun, causing her to fall. Her dog jumped him, the gun went off, and he fell "in a sitting position on the floor." From this position, he cursed her and picked up the gun. She ran for help. When she returned, he was dead.

Some of the evidence in these accounts of abuse does not require a trained eye to detect: the physical assaults are explicit, as are the state doctor's finding of bruises on Charlotte Mahoney's neck and jaw. There are also more subtle signs, including the husband's reported threat to kill her if she ever tried to leave him, a threat typical of spousal-abuse situations. Other evidence adduced at trial gives rise to the same inference of abuse.... Of course, we will never know for sure what went on in the Mahoneys' marriage. But the evidence is sufficient to raise a serious question about the presence of abuse as a significant factor in this case.

Suppose Spivack is right about the context for *Mahoney*. Should such circumstances bear on the determination of whether an inheritance by a slayer is unjust enrichment (see page 131)?

In a number of jurisdictions, statutes have been enacted which in certain instances, at least, prevent a person who has killed another from taking by descent or distribution from the person he has killed. . . .

Courts in those states that have no statute preventing a slayer from taking by descent or distribution from the estate of his victim, have followed three separate and different lines of decision.

(1) The legal title passed to the slayer and may be retained by him in spite of his crime. The reasoning for so deciding is that devolution of the property of a decedent is controlled entirely by the statutes of descent and distribution; further, that denial of the inheritance to the slayer because of his crime would be imposing an additional punishment for his crime not provided by statute, and would violate the constitutional provision against corruption of blood. Carpenter's Estate, 32 A. 637 (Pa. 1895); Wall v. Pfanschmidt, 106 N.E. 785 (Ill. 1914); Bird v. Plunkett et al., 95 A.2d 71 (Conn. 1953).

(2) The legal title will not pass to the slayer because of the equitable principle that no one should be permitted to profit by his own fraud, or take advantage and profit as a result of his own wrong or crime. Riggs v. Palmer, 22 N.E. 188 (N.Y. 1889); Price v. Hitaffer, 165 A. 470 (Md. 1933); Slocum v. Metropolitan Life Ins., 139 N.E. 816 (Mass. 1923). Decisions so holding have been criticized as judicially engrafting an exception on the statute of descent and distribution and being "unwarranted judicial legislation." Wall v. Pfanschmidt, supra.

(3) The legal title passes to the slayer but equity holds him to be a constructive trustee for the heirs or next of kin of the decedent. This disposition of the question presented avoids a judicial engrafting on the statutory laws of descent and distribution, for title passes to the slayer. But because of the unconscionable mode by which the property is acquired by the slayer, equity treats him as a constructive trustee and compels him to convey the property to the heirs or next of kin of the deceased.

The reasoning behind the adoption of this doctrine was well expressed by Mr. Justice Cardozo in his lecture on "The Nature of the Judicial Process." "Consistency was preserved, logic received its tribute, by holding that the legal title passed, but it was subject to a constructive trust. A constructive trust is nothing but 'the formula through which the conscience of equity finds expression.' Property is acquired in such circumstances that the holder of legal title may not in good conscience retain the beneficial interest. Equity, to express its disapproval of his conduct, converts him into a trustee."

The New Hampshire court was confronted with the same problem of the rights to the benefits of an estate by one who had slain the decedent, in the absence of a statute on the subject. Kelley v. State, 196 A.2d 68 (N.H. 1963). Speaking for an unanimous court, Chief Justice Kenison said: "But, even in the absence of statute, a court applying common law techniques can reach a sensible solution by charging the spouse, heir or legatee as a constructive trustee of the property where equity and justice demand it." Kelley v. State, supra, at 69-70. We approve of the doctrine so expressed.

However, the principle that one should not profit by his own wrong must not be extended to every case where a killer acquires property from his victim as a result of the killing. One who has killed while insane is not chargeable as a constructive trustee, or if the slayer had a vested interest in the property, it is property to which he would have been entitled if no slaying had occurred. The principle to be applied is that the slayer should not be permitted to improve his position by the killing, but should not be compelled to surrender property to which he would have been entitled if there had been no killing. The doctrine of constructive trust is involved to prevent the slayer from profiting from his crime, but not as an added criminal penalty. Kelley v. State, supra, at 70; Restatement of Restitution, § 187(2), Comment a.

The appellant here was, as we have noted, convicted of manslaughter and not of murder. She calls to our attention that while the Restatement of Restitution approves the application of the constructive trust doctrine where a devisee or legatee murders the testator, that such rules are not applicable where the slayer was guilty of manslaughter. Restatement of Restitution, § 187, Comment e.

The cases generally have not followed this limitation of the rule but hold that the line should not be drawn between murder and manslaughter, but between voluntary and involuntary manslaughter. Kelley v. State, supra; Chase v. Jennifer, 150 A.2d 251, 254 (Md. 1959).

We think that this is the proper rule to follow. Voluntary manslaughter is an intentional and unlawful killing, with a real design and purpose to kill, even if such killing be the result of sudden passion or great provocation. Involuntary manslaughter is caused by an unlawful act, but not accompanied with any intention to take life. State v. McDonnell, 32 Vt. 491, 545 (1860). It is the intent to kill, which when accomplished, leads to the profit of the slayer that brings into play the constructive trust to prevent the unjust enrichment of the slayer by reason of his intentional killing. . . .

The cause now before us is here on a direct appeal from the probate court. Findings of fact were made below from which it appears that the judgment of the probate court decreeing the estate of Howard Mahoney to his parents, rather than to his widow, was based upon a finding of the felonious killing of her husband by Mrs. Mahoney. However, the appellees here have asked us to affirm the decree below by imposing a constructive trust on the estate in the hands of the widow.

But the Probate Court did not decree the estate to the widow, and then make her a constructive trustee of such estate for the benefit of the parents. The judgment below decreed the estate directly to the parents, which was in direct contravention of the statutes of descent and distribution. The Probate Court was bound to follow the statutes of descent and distribution and its decree was in error and must be reversed.

The Probate Court was without jurisdiction to impose a constructive trust on the estate in the hands of the appellant, even if it had attempted to do so. Probate courts are courts of special and limited jurisdiction given by statute and do not [have powers to establish] . . . purely equitable rights and claims. . . .

However, the jurisdiction of the court of chancery may be invoked in probate matters in aid of the probate court when the powers of that court are inadequate, and it appears that the probate court cannot reasonably and adequately handle the question. The jurisdiction of the chancery court in so acting on probate matters is special and limited only to aiding the probate court. The Probate Court, in making its decree, used the record of the conviction of the appellant for manslaughter for its determination that the appellant had feloniously killed her husband. If the jurisdiction of the court of chancery is invoked by the appellees here it will be for the determination of that court, upon proof, to determine whether the appellant wilfully killed her late husband, as it will upon all other equitable considerations that may be offered in evidence, upon charging the appellant with a constructive trust. "The fact that he is convicted of murder in a criminal case does not dispense with the necessity of proof of the murder in a proceedings in equity to charge him as a constructive trustee." Restatement of Restitution, § 187, Comment d.

The jurisdiction over charging the appellant with a constructive trust on the estate of Howard Mahoney lies in the court of chancery, and not in the probate court.

Decree reversed and cause remanded, with directions that the proceedings herein be stayed for sixty days to give the Administrator of the Estate of Howard Mahoney an opportunity to apply to the Franklin County Court of Chancery for relief. If application is so made, proceedings herein shall be stayed pending the final determination thereof. If application is not so made, the Probate Court for the District of Franklin shall assign to Charlotte Mahoney, surviving wife, the right and interest in and to the estate of her deceased husband which the Vermont Statutes confer.

NOTES

1. Slayers, Restitution and Unjust Enrichment, and Constructive Trust. The slayer rule applied in *Mahoney* is an application of the law of restitution and unjust enrichment. "Legal rules that give the property to the wrongdoer cannot simply be ignored, but they can be accommodated to the doctrine prohibiting unjust enrichment by a simple equitable device: a decree that the wrongdoer holds the property as constructive trustee for someone else."[99] A determination that enrichment is unjust is not a moral judgment but a legal one. "Enrichment is unjust, in legal contemplation, to the extent it is without adequate legal basis; and the law supplies a remedy for unjustified enrichment because such enrichment cannot conscientiously be retained."[100]

In *Mahoney*, the court authorized the imposition of a *constructive trust* on Charlotte Mahoney to prevent the *unjust enrichment* of her inheriting by reason of her wrongful killing. The Restatement (Third) of Restitution and Unjust Enrichment explains:

> On the traditional analysis, developed before the "slayer statutes" were adopted, the slayer was understood to take legal title to the property in question — by the Statute of Wills, by the law of inheritance, or under the insurance contract. Equity then intervened to alter the outcome, usually by declaring that the slayer held the assets in constructive trust for someone with a superior equitable claim.[101]

A constructive trust is a plastic remedy that courts of equity have long used to make restitution and prevent unjust enrichment. In Justice Cardozo's canonical formulation: "A constructive trust is the formula through which the conscience of equity finds expression. When property has been acquired in such circumstances that the holder of the legal title may not in good conscience retain the beneficial interest equity converts

---

99. Restatement (Third) of Restitution and Unjust Enrichment, ch. 5, topic 2, intro. note (Am. Law Inst. 2011).

100. Id. § 1 cmt. b.

101. Id. § 45 cmt. c.

him into a trustee."[102] A more direct expression of the concept is this: "If a defendant is unjustly enriched by the acquisition of title to identifiable property at the expense of the claimant or in violation of the claimant's rights, the defendant may be declared a constructive trustee, for the benefit of the claimant, of the property in question and its traceable product."[103] The sole duty of the constructive trustee is to convey the property to its rightful claimant.[104]

As we shall see throughout this book, the law of restitution and unjust enrichment, and the equitable remedy of constructive trust, play a major role in the field of wills, trusts, and estates.

2. Can a Donor Opt Out of the Slayer Rules?   Suppose *H*, aware of *W*'s psychological instability, provides in his will for the creation of a trust for the benefit of *W* even if *W* kills him. *W* then kills *H*. Does *W* take? In Wisconsin, the answer is Yes. Its slayer statute provides that the slayer rule does not apply if, under the circumstances, "the decedent's wishes would best be carried out" by not applying the rule, or if by specific reference to the rule the decedent said in his will that it should not apply.[105] In Louisiana, the answer is Maybe. Its slayer rule can be avoided if the slayer can prove "reconciliation with or forgiveness by the decedent,"[106] which perhaps can be shown by proof of the decedent's consent to the slaying, though elsewhere in Louisiana law those terms have been understood to reference subsequent rather than prior events. In all other states, the answer appears to be No.

3. Mercy Killing.   Suppose *H* suffers from a painful and terminal illness. At *H*'s request, *W* kills *H* or helps him commit suicide. Can *W* take from *H*'s estate? Does *W*'s "benign motive," and *H*'s "request and participation," remove the case from the scope of "the principle of preventing unjust enrichment that otherwise requires application of the slayer rule?"[107]

In In re Estate of Schunk, 760 N.W.2d 446 (Wis. App. 2008), *W* provided *H* with the loaded shotgun that *H* used to kill himself. The court held that *W*'s assisting *H* to commit suicide was not an unlawful and intentional killing within the meaning of the slayer statute. The court reasoned that the provision that allows a decedent to opt out of the rule's application reflects the "legislature's intent to allow a testator to dispose of his or her property as the testator wishes notwithstanding the fact that an intended beneficiary has unlawfully and intentionally deprived the testator of his or her life. . . . A testator might, for example, contemplate that an intended beneficiary might kill the testator in an act of euthanasia."

---

102. Beatty v. Guggenheim Exploration Co., 122 N.E. 378, 386 (N.Y. 1919).
103. Restatement (Third) of Restitution and Unjust Enrichment § 55(1) (Am. Law Inst. 2011).
104. If a constructive trustee refuses or is unable to convey the property, the court may order that the transfer be done by another or may enter a judgment transferring title. *See, e.g.,* Fed. R. Civ. P. 70(a)-(b).
105. Wis. Stat. § 854.14(6) (2016).
106. La. Civ. Code Ann. arts. 941, 943, 945 (2016).
107. Restatement (Third) of Property: Wills and Other Donative Transfers § 8.4 cmt. n (Am. Law Inst. 2003).

"Please read back that last remark in a more murdery voice."

Paul Noth/The New Yorker Collection/The Cartoon Bank

4. Variation Across the States.   Almost every state today, including Vermont,[108] has enacted a statute dealing with the rights of a slayer in the estate of a victim. But the details of these statutes vary considerably and often leave gaps to be resolved by the courts. Among the questions arising under these statutes, the following appear to give rise to the most litigation:

a. Does the statute apply to nonprobate transfers (joint tenancy, life insurance, pensions, and so on) as well as to wills and intestacy?   If the statute applies only to probate transfers, will a court apply to nonprobate transfers a common law slayer rule to prevent the unjust enrichment of a beneficiary profiting by killing? UPC § 2-803 (1990, rev. 1997) bars the slayer from succeeding to probate and nonprobate property.

b. If the slayer is barred from taking, who takes?   The prevailing view is that the slayer is treated as having predeceased the victim. UPC § 2-803 provides that the slayer is treated as having disclaimed the property. Under UPC § 2-1106, a disclaimant is treated as having "died immediately before" the victim. But what if there is a substitute gift in the slayer's descendants or other heirs?

In In re Estate of Covert, 761 N.E.2d 571 (N.Y. 2001), Edward fatally shot his wife, Kathleen, and then turned the gun on himself, completing the tragic murder-suicide. Applying the slayer rule of Riggs v. Palmer, 22 N.E. 188 (N.Y. 1889), cited in *Mahoney,* the court held that Edward could not take from Kathleen's estate.

---

108. Vt. Stat. Ann. tit. 14, § 322 (2016).

However, because Edward's devisees were innocent of Edward's crime, the court allowed them to take from Kathleen's estate. Applying a slayer statute, the court in Fiel v. Hoffman, 169 So. 3d 1274 (Fla. App. 2015), reached a similar result.

Some states extend the bar by statute to the slayer's descendants, as in Swain v. Estate of Tyre, 57 A.3d 283 (R.I. 2012). Other states limit the right of the slayer's descendants to take by case law. In In re Estate of Mueller, 655 N.E.2d 1040 (Ill. App. 1995), the decedent devised 60 percent of his estate to his second wife or, if she predeceased him, to her children by a prior marriage. He was later killed by a hit man who had been hired by his wife. The court held the devised property passed to the decedent's heirs rather than to his wife's children. The court suggested in dicta that the result would have been different if the devisees had been directly related to the decedent, rather than his stepchildren, connected to him only through his marriage to the slayer.[109]

c. Is a criminal conviction required?   UPC § 2-803(g) and most states provide that a final criminal conviction of a felonious and intentional killing is conclusive. Acquittal, however, is not dispositive of the acquitted individual's status as a slayer. In the absence of a conviction the court must determine whether, under the civil standard of preponderance of the evidence rather than the criminal standard of beyond a reasonable doubt, the individual would be found criminally accountable for the killing. If so, the individual is barred. The reason for using a civil standard of evidence is that the issue is preventing the unjust enrichment of the slayer profiting from her wrong, whereas at issue in a criminal proceeding is the accused slayer's liberty.

Suppose in a criminal proceeding the killer is found not to be culpable by reason of legal insanity. Does such a finding take the killing outside of the reach of the slayer rule? The common law rule, as observed in *Mahoney*, was that one "who has killed while insane is not chargeable as a constructive trustee." The cases are split on whether the same result obtains under the slayer statutes.[110]

The Unworthy Heir

In the United States, unworthy heirs—whose conduct bars inheritance—are usually limited to slayers. In nearly all other situations, intestate succession is fixed by status: bloodline kinship, marriage, or adoption. The broad freedom of disposition afforded by American law resolves the problem of an *unworthy heir* by enabling a person to make an alternate disposition by will or will substitute.

But aren't there some circumstances, beyond a slaying, that warrant statutory disinheritance of an heir even if the donor hasn't made an alternate disposition? Some states have begun to recognize further exceptions, in addition to the slayer rules, for

---

109. *See* Karen J. Sneddon, Should Cain's Children Inherit Abel's Property?: Wading Into the Extended Slayer Rule Quagmire, 76 UMKC L. Rev. 101 (2007).

110. *Compare* Osman v. Osman, 737 S.E.2d 876 (Va. 2013) (insane slayer barred), *with* Estate of Armstrong v. Armstrong, 170 So. 3d 510 (Miss. 2015) (insane slayer not automatically barred).

unworthy heirs.[111] In some states, a spouse who abandons the decedent is barred,[112] and in a few more parents are barred from taking from a child if the parent refused to support the child. UPC § 2-114 (2008) bars inheritance by a parent from a child if there is clear and convincing evidence that the parental rights of the parent could have been terminated for nonsupport, abandonment, abuse, or neglect. A handful of states — including California, Oregon, Pennsylvania, Illinois, and Washington — deny inheritance from elderly or other vulnerable relatives who were abused by the heir.[113]

The People's Republic of China provides an interesting contrast. In an illuminating article, Towards a Behavior-Based Model of Inheritance? The Chinese Experiment, 32 U.C. Davis L. Rev. 77 (1998), Professor Frances H. Foster examines the Chinese approach, which permits courts to rework the shares of a decedent's estate to punish misconduct or reward good behavior. Such a discretionary system is "highly time-and-labor intensive, requiring courts to evaluate on a case-by-case basis the conduct of all potential claimants and the most appropriate division of each estate. The flexibility that is the hallmark of the behavior-based model today may prove to be its greatest drawback in the future . . . [when] increased social mobility, accumulation of private property, and a rise in the popular use of courts will bring about an increase in the number and complexity of inheritance disputes."

Nonetheless, Foster concludes that the Chinese system has "significant advantages" over the American system, which does not penalize unworthy heirs. The Chinese system "recognizes the reality of support relationships today. It rewards contributions to the decedent's welfare by individuals outside the nuclear family, including blended and extended family members, nonmarital partners, and other unrelated parties." Foster suggests the Chinese system may provide guidance for reforming the American inheritance system to deal with problems of parental and child neglect and rewarding exemplary conduct, including, for instance, personally caring for a disabled person.[114]

2. Disclaimer

Sometimes an heir or a devisee will decline to take the property, a refusal that is called a *disclaimer*.[115] Disclaimers allow for post-mortem estate planning. The most common reasons for disclaiming are to reduce taxes or to keep property from creditors.

---

111. *See* Carla Spivack, Let's Get Serious: Spousal Abuse Should Bar Inheritance, 90 Or. L. Rev. 247 (2011); Anne-Marie Rhodes, Blood and Behavior, 36 ACTEC L.J. 143 (2010).

112. *See, e.g.,* In re Estate of Talerico, 137 A.3d 577 (Pa. Super. 2016). In Kentucky, a spouse who "voluntarily leaves the other and lives in adultery" is barred from taking from the estate of the other spouse. Ky. Rev. Stat. Ann. § 392.090(2) (2016). The state supreme court has interpreted the term "lives in adultery" to require "more than a single instance of adultery." Griffin v. Rice, 381 S.W.3d 198 (Ky. 2012).

113. *See, e.g.,* In re Estate of Evans, 326 P.3d 755 (Wash. App. 2014) (*T*'s son denied inheritance for financial abuse).

114. For a follow-up study, see Thomas E. Simmons, A Chinese Inheritance, 30 Quinnipiac Prob. L.J. 124 (2017).

115. By traditional usage, an heir *renounces*; a beneficiary under a will *disclaims*. Today, the two words are used interchangeably as synonyms. The term disclaimer is the one more commonly used to describe the formal refusal to take by an heir or a beneficiary.

a. From Common Law to Statutory Law

At common law, when a person died intestate, title to real and personal property passed to the decedent's heirs by operation of law. An intestate successor could not prevent title from passing to him. If the heir refused to accept (or, more precisely, to keep) the inheritance, the common law treated the heir's renunciation as if title had passed to the heir and then from the heir to the next intestate successor. The reason for this rule was that there always had to be someone seised of the land who was liable for the feudal obligations, a reason of no importance today. On the other hand, if a person died testate, the devisee could refuse to accept the devise, thereby preventing title from passing to the devisee. A gift, whether inter vivos or by will, requires acceptance by the donee.[116]

These different conceptions of how title passes produced different tax results. If an heir renounced his inheritance and the common law rule applied, the situation was treated as though the heir had received the intestate share and then made a taxable gift to the persons who took by reason of the renunciation. By contrast, if a devisee disclaimed a testamentary gift, there were no gift tax consequences.

To eliminate the difference between renouncing an intestate share and disclaiming a devise, the states enacted disclaimer legislation that treats the disclaimant as having died before the decedent or before the time of distribution, as under UPC §§ 2-1105 and 2-1106 (2002, rev. 2006).

NOTE

Disclaimer and Representation.   Consider the circumstances presented in Figure 2.10. *O* has two children, *A* and *B*. *A* has four children: *C*, *D*, *E*, and *F*. *B* dies, survived by one child, *G*. Then *O*, a widow, dies intestate. *O*'s heirs are *A* and *G*. Under all forms of representation, each takes one-half.

Figure 2.10

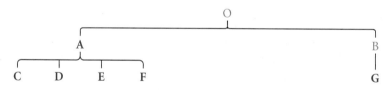

Survivors are in **bold**; deceased persons are in regular type.

But suppose *A* disclaims and the jurisdiction uses a per capita at each generation system of representation. Does *A*'s disclaimer entitle each of his children to one-fifth of *O*'s estate, increasing the share for his line of descent from one-half to four-fifths? Would this outcome be fair? Would it match the likely intent of *O*?

Under UPC § 2-1106(b)(3), such a strategic disclaimer is not possible, because only "the disclaimed interest," here one-half, passes to the descendants of a disclaimant who take by representation. So *C*, *D*, *E*, and *F* each take one-eighth, whereas *G*, who is of equal kinship to *O*, takes one-half. But what of the policy of "equally near, equally

---

116. *See* Mark Glover, Freedom of Inheritance, 2017 Utah L. Rev. (forthcoming).

dear" (see page 82)? If *A* had also predeceased *O*, then under both modern per stirpes and per capita at each generation (but not English per stirpes, which prioritizes vertical rather than horizontal equality), each grandchild would take one-fifth.

b. Avoiding Taxes

Suppose that *O* dies intestate, survived only by his sister, *A*, and *A*'s child, *B*. To pass the property to *B* without a gift or estate tax being levied on it when it leaves *A*'s hands, *A* may decide to disclaim the inheritance. If *A* disclaims, she is treated as having predeceased *O*, and *O*'s estate will pass under the intestacy law to *B*.

Older state disclaimer statutes tend to require that a disclaimer be made within nine months of the creation of the interest being disclaimed. The Uniform Disclaimer of Property Interests Act (UDPIA) (Unif. Law Comm'n 1999, rev. 2006), which in 2002 was absorbed into the UPC as §§ 2-1101 to 2-1117 and has been adopted in a little more than one-third of the states, does not specify a time limit.

The origin of the nine-month limit was not a state property law policy, but rather a reaction to the passage of Internal Revenue Code (I.R.C.) § 2518 in 1976. Under § 2518, only a "qualified disclaimer" will avoid the gift tax liability that would have resulted if a disclaimant inherited property and then gave it away. If a person disclaims under applicable state law but the disclaimer is not "qualified" under the federal tax code, gift tax liability results. To qualify under the federal tax code, the disclaimer must be made within nine months after the interest is created or after the donee reaches 21, whichever is later. So, in the example above, if *A* disclaims a year after *O*'s death, *A* is treated under the tax laws as having accepted the property and then having made a gift to *B*.

Given that disclaimers are often used for post-mortem tax planning, the decoupling of the time requirement under the UDPIA from I.R.C. § 2518 has become one of the main points of contention between the act's supporters and its critics.[117]

c. Avoiding Creditors

Most disclaimer statutes provide that a disclaimer *relates back for all purposes* to the date of the decedent's death. The UDPIA "continues the effect of the relation back doctrine, not by using the specific words, but by directly stating what the relation back doctrine has been interpreted to mean." UPC § 2-1106 cmt.

(1) Ordinary Creditors. Suppose *A* disclaims her interest in *O*'s estate. Most cases have held that *A*'s ordinary creditors cannot reach the disclaimed property. Because the disclaimer relates back to the date of *O*'s death, the property is treated as passing directly to others, bypassing the disclaimant. Moreover, so long as the disclaimer was made prior to the filing of a bankruptcy petition, the federal courts will respect the state law relation-back doctrine for claims against a bankrupt debtor.[118]

---

117. *Compare* Adam J. Hirsch, The Code Breakers: How States Are Modifying the Uniform Disclaimer of Property Interests Act, 46 Real Prop. Tr. & Est. L.J. 325 (2011), *with* William P. LaPiana, Some Property Law Issues in the Law of Disclaimers, 38 Real Prop. Prob. & Tr. J. 207 (2003).

118. *See* In re Laughlin, 602 F.3d 417 (5th Cir. 2010); In re Costas, 555 F.3d 790 (9th Cir. 2009).

If, however, a bankruptcy petition is filed before the debtor disclaims, courts almost invariably hold that the disclaimer is ineffective under federal bankruptcy law.[119] In a minority of states, an insolvent debtor who is not already in bankruptcy may not use a disclaimer to avoid his creditors.

(2) Federal Tax Lien.   Although in most states an ordinary creditor cannot reach property disclaimed by a debtor who is not already in bankruptcy, under Drye v. United States, 528 U.S. 49 (1999), the Internal Revenue Service is in a different position. In that case, Irma Deliah Drye died intestate, leaving her son, Rohn F. Drye, Jr., as the sole heir to her $233,000 estate. Prior to his mother's death, Drye ran up an unpaid $325,000 tax bill, prompting the IRS to file tax liens against all of Drye's "property and rights to property."

To keep his mother's estate away from the IRS and in the family, Drye disclaimed his interest. The estate therefore passed to Drye's daughter, Theresa, who was next in line under the applicable intestacy statute.

> Theresa Drye then used the estate's proceeds to fund [a] Trust, of which she and, during their lifetimes, her parents are the beneficiaries. Under the Trust's terms, distributions are at the discretion of the trustee, Drye's counsel Daniel M. Traylor, and may be made only for the health, maintenance, and support of the beneficiaries. The Trust is spendthrift,[120] and under state law, its assets are therefore shielded from creditors seeking to satisfy the debts of the Trust's beneficiaries.

The question before the Court was whether the disclaimer allowed the property to pass to Drye's daughter free of the federal tax lien. Under applicable state law, a disclaimer relates back to the date of the decedent's death, hence disclaimed property bypasses the disclaimant, who is treated as having predeceased the decedent. Drye argued "that state law is the proper guide to the critical determination whether his interest in his mother's estate constituted 'property' or 'rights to property.'" And under state law, the disclaimed interest passed directly to Drye's daughter, free of the tax lien because by operation of the relation-back principle the property was never his.

Speaking for a unanimous Court, Justice Ruth Bader Ginsburg rejected Drye's argument:

> The disclaiming heir . . . inevitably exercises dominion over the property. He determines who will receive the property—himself if he does not disclaim, a known other if he does. See Adam J. Hirsch, The Problem of the Insolvent Heir, 74 Cornell L. Rev. 587, 607-608 (1989). This power to channel the estate's assets warrants the conclusion that Drye held "property" or a "right to property" subject to the Government's liens. . . .
>
> Drye had the unqualified right to receive the entire value of his mother's estate (less administrative expenses), or to channel that value to his daughter. The control rein he held under state law, we hold, rendered the inheritance "property" or "rights

---

119. *See* David B. Young, The Intersection of Bankruptcy and Probate, 49 S. Tex. L. Rev. 351 (2007).

120. We take up spendthrift trusts, in which a beneficiary's interest is protected against claims by the beneficiary's creditors, in Chapter 10 at page 703.—Eds.

to property" belonging to him within the meaning of [the Internal Revenue Code], and hence subject to the federal tax liens that sparked this controversy.

NOTES

1. "Dominion" by the Disclaimant? Is it true, as suggested by Justice Ginsburg, that Drye had "dominion" over the property of his mother's estate by way of a "power to channel" the disposition of that property? Could Drye "channel" the property to his wife or a friend or a charity?

Justice Ruth Bader Ginsburg

The Court reasoned that Drye's knowledge of who would be the next taker, here his daughter, was enough to make his power to disclaim a "right to property" for the purpose of the application of federal tax liens. "The Internal Revenue Code's prescriptions are most sensibly read to look to state law for delineation of the taxpayer's rights or interests, but to leave to federal law the determination whether those rights or interests constitute 'property' or 'rights to property' within the meaning of" the federal tax laws.

In an earlier case, Morgan v. Commissioner, 309 U.S. 78 (1940), the Court elaborated on the relationship of federal tax law with state property law thus:

> State law creates legal interests and rights. The federal revenue acts designate what interests or rights, so created, shall be taxed. Our duty is to ascertain the meaning of the words used to specify the thing taxed. If it is found in a given case that an interest or right created by local law was the object intended to be taxed, the federal law must prevail no matter what name is given to the interest or right by state law.

2. Planning Options. Suppose that Irma Deliah Drye had executed a will that left her entire estate to her granddaughter, Theresa, thereby disinheriting her insolvent son, Rohn.[121] Would the IRS have had any recourse against the assets of Irma's estate? *See* Robert T. Danforth, The Role of Federalism in Administering a National System of Taxation, 57 Tax Law. 625 (2004). Suppose that Theresa promised Irma to make use of the bequest to support her father. Would the IRS be entitled to a constructive trust over the bequest to Theresa on an unjust enrichment theory? *See* Cabral v. Soares, 69 Cal. Rptr. 3d 242 (App. 2007).

d. Disclaimers to Qualify for Medicaid

Under the eighteenth- and nineteenth-century English Poor Laws, if a person could not pay for the person's care, the person's kin could be required to do so. Today, in the

---

121. At oral argument, Rohn's lawyer told the Court that a new will was in preparation at the time of Irma's death. Transcript of Oral Argument at 14, Drye v. United States, 528 U.S. 49 (1999) (No. 98-1101), 1999 WL 1050103.

United States, a person has a legal obligation to provide for the person's spouse and minor children, but not parents or siblings.

The federal and state governments offer a range of support programs for the poor and the elderly. Perhaps the most important, which provides medical assistance to needy people, is Medicaid, a cooperative state and federal program that enrolls almost one out of every five Americans. An applicant for Medicaid assistance must meet strict income and resource requirements, the details of which vary from state to state. Sometimes an applicant will impoverish himself to meet the applicable standards, often by making gifts to family members. However, giving away property may result in the disqualification of the applicant for a certain period of time depending on the nature of the transfer. Certain transfers are exempt, such as the transfer of a home to a spouse and a transfer in trust for certain disabled persons.[122]

Can a person who qualifies for Medicaid benefits that would be lost if the person were to inherit property preserve his eligibility by disclaiming that inheritance? The weight of authority says No.[123] For example, in Troy v. Hart, 697 A.2d 113 (Md. App. 1997), Paul Lettich, a Medicaid recipient, was entitled to a $100,000 inheritance from his sister's estate. He disclaimed, making each of his other two sisters $50,000 richer. After Lettich died, the administrator of his estate sought to rescind the disclaimer and reclaim the money. The court held that Lettich was required to report his inheritance to state Medicaid authorities, whether he disclaimed it or not. Although the court held the disclaimer valid, it suggested that the amounts passing to the sisters could be subject to a claim by the state for reimbursement of Lettich's Medicaid expenses.

The law in this area is complex and has been changing rapidly. Caution is advised.

---

122. *See* John A. Miller, Medicaid Spend Down, Estate Recovery and Divorce: Doctrine, Planning and Policy, 23 Elder L.J. 41 (2015); Sean R. Bleck, Barbara Isenhour & John A. Miller, Preserving Wealth and Inheritance Through Medicaid Planning for Long-Term Care, 17 Mich. St. U. J. Med. & L. 153 (2013).

123. *See* Adam J. Hirsch, Disclaimers and Federalism, 67 Vand. L. Rev. 1871, 1897 (2014).

CHAPTER 3

WILLS: FORMALITIES
AND FORMS

[N]o will shall be valid unless it shall be in writing
and executed in manner hereinafter mentioned.

WILLS ACT, 7 WM. 4 & 1 VICT. C. 26, § 9 (1837)

THE PROBATE CODE of every state includes a provision, known for historical reasons as the *Wills Act*, which prescribes rules for making a valid *will*. A person who dies with a valid will, known as a *testator*, is said to die *testate*. The probate property of a testate decedent is distributed in accordance with the decedent's — the testator's — will. By making a will in compliance with the Wills Act, a testator ensures that her probate property will be distributed in accordance with her actual intent rather than the presumed intent of intestacy. In this way, the Wills Act implements the principle of freedom of disposition.

A will is a peculiar legal instrument, however, in that it does not take effect until after the testator dies. In consequence, probate courts follow what has been called a "worst evidence" rule of procedure.[1] The witness who is best able to authenticate the will, to verify that it was voluntarily made, and to clarify the meaning of its terms is dead by the time the court considers such issues. This chapter and the next two respectively consider how the law of wills deals with the worst evidence problem in discerning the *authenticity*, the *voluntariness*, and the *meaning* of a will.

Our focus in this chapter is on *authenticity*, by which we mean the problem of discerning the bona fides of a purported act of testation. The Wills Act of every state requires compliance with particular *formalities* for making or revoking a will.[2] The main purpose of these formalities is to enable a court easily and reliably to assess the authenticity of a purported act of testation. The formalities also ensure a standardized

---

1. John H. Langbein, Will Contests, 103 Yale L.J. 2039, 2046 (1994) (book review).

2. Formalities for making a testamentary disposition are ubiquitous across legal systems. *See* Comparative Succession Law I: Testamentary Formalities (Kenneth G.C. Reid, Marius J. de Waal & Reinhard Zimmermann eds., 2011).

form for wills that simplifies judicial review of whether the testator intended an instrument to be her will, impresses upon the testator the significance of making a will, and protects the testator from manipulative imposition.

Accordingly, the challenge for legal institutional design is to prescribe a set of formalities, and a rule for the exactness with which those formalities must be complied, that balances the risk of probating an inauthentic will (a false positive) with the risk of denying probate to an authentic will (a false negative).[3] Both kinds of error dishonor a decedent's freedom of disposition. The former gives effect to a false expression of testamentary intent, overriding the decedent's prior will or the presumed intent of intestacy. The latter denies effect to a true expression of testamentary intent, leaving the decedent's property to be distributed under her prior will or intestacy.

We begin in Section A by considering the Wills Act formalities for making a will. In Section B, we consider the formalities for revoking a will. In Section C, we consider the question of what written materials, taken together, constitute a will. Finally, in Section D, we review how the law of wills and the law of contracts interact when a person contracts to make or not to revoke a will.

A. EXECUTION OF WILLS

Every state probate code includes a provision, known as the *Wills Act*, that prescribes rules for making a valid will. We now consider those rules as they pertain to: (1) *attested wills*, (2) *notarized wills*, and (3) *holographic wills*. You should compare the rules in the Wills Act of your state with those of the Uniform Probate Code (UPC), excerpted at page 144, and consider whether the UPC approach is better or worse than the one adopted in your state.

1. Attested Wills

a. The Core Formalities

There are three core formalities for the making of an attested will: (1) *writing*,[4] (2) *signature*, and (3) *attestation*.[5] But these three core formalities have been interpreted and augmented by additional formalities in ways that vary from state to state.[6] Some of this variation results from England having had multiple laws governing the execution

---

3. *See* Mark Glover, Probate Error Costs, 49 Conn. L. Rev. 613 (2016).

4. A minority of states permit nuncupative (oral) wills for persons in their last illness or for military personnel. These statutes can be used only in limited circumstances — for example, to devise personal property of small value. Typically a nuncupative will must be uttered before at least two persons, who must reduce the declaration to writing within a specified period. *See* Restatement (Third) of Property: Wills and Other Donative Transfers § 3.2 cmt. h (Am. Law Inst. 1999). Nuncupative wills admitted to probate are extremely rare.

5. Although some states once required three witnesses, today all but Louisiana require only two. Louisiana requires two witnesses plus a notary. *See* La. Civ. Code Ann. art. 1577 (2016).

6. *See* Jeffrey A. Schoenblum, 2016 Multistate Guide to Estate Planning tbl. 1 (2016).

Comparison of Statutory Formalities for Formal Wills   Figure 3.1

Statute of Frauds (Land) (1677)	Wills Act (1837)	Uniform Probate Code (1990)	Uniform Probate Code (1990, rev. 2008)
Writing	Writing	Writing	Writing
Signature	Subscription	Signature	Signature
Attestation via subscription by 3 witnesses	Attestation via subscription by 2 witnesses	Attestation via signature by 2 witnesses	Attestation via signature by 2 witnesses *or* notarization

of wills, primarily the Statute of Frauds (1677) and the Wills Act (1837), both of which served as models for American legislation.[7]

The Statute of Frauds, adopted in 1677, required a written will signed by the testator in the presence of three witnesses for a testamentary disposition of land. Less stringent formalities applied to testamentary dispositions of personal property. Having different rules for devising land and bequeathing personal property proved unsatisfactory. In 1837, England enacted a Wills Act requiring the same formalities for all wills regardless of the nature of the property disposed of under the will.

The formalities required by the Wills Act of 1837 were in some ways stricter than those required by the Statute of Frauds. Under the Statute of Frauds, the three witnesses did not have to be present at the same time and the testator did not have to sign at the end of the document. The Wills Act reduced the number of necessary witnesses to two, but it required that they both be *present* when the will was signed or acknowledged. It also required the will to be signed "at the foot or end thereof," which has come to be known as *subscription*. These two additional requirements have given rise to much litigation.

Some states copied the Statute of Frauds; others copied the Wills Act; and still others cobbled provisions from each. In a few states, such as New York, the legislature added a requirement that the testator must *publish* the will, declaring before the witnesses that the instrument is his will.

The Wills Act provision of the UPC is simpler. For each of the three core formalities — writing, signature, and attestation — UPC § 2-502, page 144, adopts the less strict requirement of the two English statutes. It includes none of the presence, subscription, or publication requirements that are found in some states. And, in a break from prior law, § 2-502 was amended in 2008 to allow notarization as an alternative to attestation by witnesses.[8]

---

7. In 1540, the Statute of Wills made some land devisable "by last will and testament in writing," but specified no signature or other formalities. Personal property was transferable at death by either a written or an oral will, perhaps entrusted to a priest as part of the last confession.

8. Both notarized wills, authorized by UPC § 2-502(a)(3)(B), and holographic wills, authorized by § 2-502(b), are treated later, at pages 197 and 198, respectively. We are concerned now only with attested wills, as under § 2-502(a)(1)-(3)(A).

Uniform Probate Code (Unif. Law Comm'n 1990, as amended 2008)

§ 2-502. Execution; Witnessed or Notarized Wills; Holographic Wills

(a) [Witnessed or Notarized Wills.] Except as otherwise provided in subsection (b) and in Sections 2-503, 2-506, and 2-513, a will must be:

(1) in writing;

(2) signed by the testator or in the testator's name by some other individual in the testator's conscious presence and by the testator's direction; and

(3) either:

(A) signed by at least two individuals, each of whom signed within a reasonable time after the individual witnessed either the signing of the will as described in paragraph (2) or the testator's acknowledgment of that signature or acknowledgment of the will; or

(B) acknowledged by the testator before a notary public or other individual authorized by law to take acknowledgments.

(b) [Holographic Wills.] A will that does not comply with subsection (a) is valid as a holographic will, whether or not witnessed, if the signature and material portions of the document are in the testator's handwriting.

(c) [Extrinsic Evidence.] Intent that a document constitute the testator's will can be established by extrinsic evidence, including, for holographic wills, portions of the document that are not in the testator's handwriting.

b. The Functions of Formalities

The main function of the Wills Act formalities is to enable a court to decide, without the benefit of live testimony from the testator, whether a purported will is authentic. The formalities are also said to serve several secondary functions: They standardize the form of wills; they impress upon the testator the significance of making a will; and they protect the testator from manipulative imposition. This main function and three secondary functions have come to be known as the *evidentiary*, the *channeling*, the *cautionary* or *ritual*, and the *protective* functions.[9] The formalities thus aid in resolving the question of whether the testator "indicate[d] finality of intention to transfer."[10] In more recent work, some have argued that testation also has an *expressive* function, giving the testator one last opportunity to make a statement, and that the exercise of this power can have psychological benefits in confronting mortality.[11]

---

9. The classic scholarly treatments are Lon L. Fuller, Consideration and Form, 41 Colum. L. Rev. 799 (1941), and Ashbel G. Gulliver & Catherine J. Tilson, Classification of Gratuitous Transfers, 51 Yale L.J. 1, 3 (1941); *see also* Lawrence M. Friedman, The Law of the Living, the Law of the Dead: Property, Succession, and Society, 1966 Wis. L. Rev. 340.

10. Gulliver & Tilson, *supra* note 9, at 3.

11. *See, e.g.*, Karen J. Sneddon, Memento Mori: Death and Wills, 14 Wyo. L. Rev. 211 (2014); Karen J. Sneddon, The Will as Personal Narrative, 20 Elder L.J. 355 (2013); Mark Glover, A Therapeutic Jurisprudential Framework of Estate Planning, 35 Seattle U. L. Rev. 427 (2012); David Horton, Testation and Speech, 101 Geo. L.J. 61 (2012); Diane J. Klein, How to Do Things with Wills, 32 Whittier L. Rev. 455 (2011).

John H. Langbein
Substantial Compliance with the Wills Act
88 Harv. L. Rev. 489 (1975)

1. The Evidentiary Function. — The primary purpose of the Wills Act has always been to provide the court with reliable evidence of testamentary intent and of the terms of the will; virtually all the formalities serve as "probative safeguards." The requirement of writing assures that "evidence of testamentary intent [will] be cast in reliable and permanent form." The requirement that the testator sign the will is meant to produce evidence of genuineness. The requirement that he sign at the end prevents subsequent interpolation. . . . The attestation requirement, the distinguishing feature of the so-called formal will, assures that the actual signing is witnessed and sworn to by disinterested bystanders. . . .

2. The Channeling Function. — . . . The channeling function has both social and individual aspects. . . . Compliance with the Wills Act formalities for executing witnessed wills results in considerable uniformity in the organization, language, and content of most wills. Courts are seldom left to puzzle whether the document was meant to be a will. . . .

The standardization of testation achieved under the Wills Act also benefits the testator. He does not have to devise for himself a mode of communicating his testamentary wishes to the court, and to worry whether it will be effective. Instead, he has every inducement to comply with the Wills Act formalities. The court can process his estate routinely, because his testament is conventionally and unmistakably expressed and evidenced. The lowered costs of routinized judicial administration benefit the estate and its ultimate distributees.

Holographic wills serve the channeling function less well, because the required formalities are less likely to resolve whether the document was meant as a will. . . .

3. The Cautionary Function. — A will is said to be revocable and ambulatory, meaning that it becomes operative only on death. Because the testator does not part with the least incident of ownership when he makes a will, and does not experience the "wrench of delivery" required for inter vivos gifts, the danger exists that he may make seeming testamentary dispositions inconsiderately, without adequate forethought and finality of intention. Not every expression that "I want you to have the house when I'm gone" is meant as a will. One purpose of many of the forms is to impress the testator with the seriousness of the testament, and thereby to assure the court "that the statements of the transferor were deliberately intended to effectuate a transfer." They caution the testator, and they show the court that he was cautioned.

The requirements of writing and signature, which have such major evidentiary significance, are also the primary cautionary formalities. Writing is somewhat less casual than plain chatter. As we say in a common figure of speech, "talk is cheap." More important than the requirement of written terms is that of written signature. "The signature tends to show that the instrument was finally adopted by the testator as his will and to militate against the inference that the writing was merely a preliminary draft, an incomplete disposition, or haphazard scribbling." . . .

4. The Protective Function. — Courts have traditionally attributed to the Wills Act the object "of protecting the testator against imposition at the time of execution." The requirement that attestation be made in the presence of the testator is meant "to prevent the substitution of a surreptitious will." Another common protective requirement is the rule that the witnesses should be disinterested, hence not motivated to coerce or deceive the testator.

NOTE

How Much Formality?   The evidentiary, channeling, cautionary or ritual, and protective functions could be served by countless alternative formalities. That a formality serves one or more of these functions does not, by itself, justify requiring the formality. Professor James Lindgren explains:

> In determining the proper level of formalities, we shouldn't ask whether this formality or that would serve the accepted purposes of formalities. Any formality would. If we required a secret handshake for willmaking that only lawyers knew, that would serve the cautionary or ritual function. In early Bavaria, to convey real property one had to box the ears of young boys.[12] Without that formality, conveyances were ineffective, even where possession occurred and the deal was never repudiated by the parties. This strange formality served all the main functions of formalities: ritual or cautionary, evidentiary, protective, and channeling. Yet it was a perverse and silly formality. Other formalities more reliably evidenced transfers.
>
> Instead of asking whether a formality serves a function of formalities, we should ask instead whether it promotes the intent of the testator at an acceptable administrative cost. We should not box the ears of little children just because it serves the ritual function; this is misplaced formalism.[13]

c. The Strict Compliance Rule

Under traditional law, a will must be executed in *strict compliance* with all the formal requirements of the applicable Wills Act.[14] The will must be in writing, signed by the testator, and attested by at least two witnesses. Any additional requirements mandated by the particular Wills Act must also be satisfied exactly.

The strict compliance rule guards against a spurious finding of authenticity—a *false positive*. A competent person not subject to undue influence, duress, or fraud is unlikely to execute an instrument in strict compliance with all of the Wills Act formalities unless the person intends the instrument to be his will. But by establishing a conclusive presumption of invalidity for an imperfectly executed instrument, the strict compliance rule denies probate even if the defect is innocuous and there is overwhelming evidence of authenticity—a *false negative*. In considering the materials that

---

12. Boxing the ears refers to striking someone hard on the side of the head. The idea was that, by creating a painful memory, the young boys would be good witnesses if a dispute later arose over the validity of the transfer. *See* Celia Wasserstein Fassberg, Form and Formalism: A Case Study, 31 Am. J. Comp. L. 627 (1983).—Eds.

13. James Lindgren, The Fall of Formalism, 55 Alb. L. Rev. 1009, 1033 (1992).

14. *See, e.g.,* In re Estate of Chastain, 401 S.W.3d 612 (Tenn. 2012) (requiring "strict compliance"); In re Estate of Henneghan, 45 A.3d 684 (D.C. 2012) (requiring "strict statutory compliance").

follow, keep in mind the question of whether relaxing the number of formalities, relaxing the exactness with which those formalities must be complied, or both might reduce the rate of false negatives without increasing the rate of false positives.[15]

Let us begin with an arresting but frustrating example. In In re Groffman, [1969] 1 W.L.R. 733 (PC), Charles Groffman, the testator, died three years after executing a will at the home of some friends. The will had been prepared by a solicitor (a lawyer), who had given it to Groffman to execute on his own. In intestacy, Groffman's widow, his second wife, would take the entire estate. Under the will, the widow would share the estate, including the marital home, with her daughter and stepchildren. The widow contested the will. "My Charlie wouldn't have done that to me," she is reported to have said.

The relevant facts as found by the court are follows: Mr. and Mrs. Groffman and Mr. and Mrs. Leigh were visiting Mr. and Mrs. Block. The three families were close. "They spent at least the summer holidays of 1964 together, and it was their custom to meet alternately at their respective houses, generally on a Tuesday night." On the night in question, the three families were all in the lounge of the Blocks' home. Mr. Groffman addressed Mr. Block and Mr. Leigh: "I should like you now to witness my will." Mr. Groffman gestured toward his coat. The folded will, which he had already signed, was in an inside pocket. Since the coffee table was "laden with coffee cups and cakes," Mr. Block and Mr. Groffman went into the adjacent dining room, where Mr. Block signed as witness. "Mr. Leigh, who seems to have been somewhat cumbrous in his movements, was left behind." Mr. Block returned to the lounge, and Mr. Leigh went to the dining room, where he signed as witness.

The litigation focused on the question of whether the witnesses were present together at the same time when Groffman acknowledged his signature on the will. The applicable statute—the English Wills Act of 1837—provided as follows, with the key language in italics:

> [N]o will shall be valid unless it shall be in writing and executed in manner hereinafter mentioned; . . . it shall be signed at the foot or end thereof by the testator, or by some other person in his presence and by his direction; *and such signature shall be made or acknowledged by the testator in the presence of two or more witnesses present at the same time*, and such witnesses shall attest and shall subscribe the will in the presence of the testator, but no form of attestation shall be necessary.

Although Mr. Groffman asked Mr. Leigh and Mr. Block together to witness his will, he had already signed it, and he did not acknowledge his signature to them both at the same time. Instead, he acknowledged his signature to them separately, one after the other, in the dining room. Thus, even though the court was "perfectly satisfied that the document was intended by the deceased to be executed as his will and that its contents represent his testamentary intentions," the court refused to admit the will to probate.

> As must appear from the fact that I have been satisfied that the document does represent the testamentary intentions of the deceased, I would gladly find in its

---

15. *See* Mark Glover, Minimizing Probate-Error Risk, 49 U. Mich. J.L. Reform 335 (2016).

favour; but I am bound to apply the statute. . . . [A]lthough I would gladly accede to the arguments for the plaintiffs if I could consistently with my judicial duty, in my view there was no acknowledgment or signature by the testator in the presence of two or more witnesses present at the same time; and I am bound to pronounce against this will.

NOTES

1. Present at the Same Time.   Given that the court in *Groffman* was "perfectly satisfied" that the will was authentic, why deny probate? What formalities were not satisfied exactly? Were not the evidentiary, channeling, cautionary or ritual, and protective functions satisfied by the manner in which Groffman executed his will? What would have been the result under UPC § 2-502(a), page 144?

2. Attestation Clauses.   Mr. Groffman's will contained an *attestation clause*. Such a clause recites that the will was duly executed in accordance with the particulars of the applicable Wills Act. Here is an example:

> We certify that the above instrument was on the date thereof signed and declared by JOHN DOE as his will in our presence and that we, at his request and in his presence and in the presence of each other, have signed our names as witnesses thereto, believing JOHN DOE to be of sound mind and memory at the time of signing.[16]

No state requires an attestation clause,[17] but such a clause gives rise to a rebuttable presumption of due execution. With an attestation clause, a will may be admitted to probate even if the witnesses predecease the testator or cannot recall the events of execution. If one of the witnesses testifies that the steps for due execution were not satisfied, as in *Groffman*, an attestation clause gives the proponent's lawyer ammunition for a vigorous cross-examination in which the witness may be impeached with the text of the clause. The will can be admitted to probate on the presumption of due execution despite a witness's contrary testimony, as under UPC § 3-406(3) (1990, rev. 2008).

In contemporary practice, the attestation clause is normally augmented with an affidavit in what has come to be known as a *self-proving will* (see page 161).

3. Lay Execution and Malpractice.   Mr. Groffman's will was prepared by a lawyer, but the lawyer did not supervise its execution. The lawyer "told [Groffman] very generally what was the right method of execution" and "relied in the main on the attestation clause to be a guide" in executing the will. The court remarked that the lawyer's conduct was "perfectly reasonable." Do you agree? Who do you suppose might have standing to

---

16. Northern Trust, Will & Trust Forms 101-35 (2004).
17. But Louisiana requires one for a notarial will. *See* La. Civ. Code Ann. art. 1577(2) (2016), applied in Succession of Smith, 146 So. 3d 917 (La. App. 2014).

sue the lawyer? The weight of authority holds that a lawyer does not have a duty to an intended beneficiary to ensure that the testator executes a new will in a timely fashion.[18]

Stevens v. Casdorph
508 S.E.2d 610 (W. Va. 1998)

PER CURIAM.... On May 28, 1996, [Paul and Patricia Casdorph] took Mr. Homer Haskell Miller to Shawnee Bank in Dunbar, West Virginia, so that he could execute his will.[19] Once at the bank, Mr. Miller asked Debra Pauley, a bank employee and public notary, to witness the execution of his will. After Mr. Miller signed the will, Ms. Pauley took the will to two other bank employees, Judith Waldron and Reba McGinn, for the purpose of having each of them sign the will as witnesses. Both Ms. Waldron and Ms. McGinn signed the will. However, Ms. Waldron and Ms. McGinn testified during their depositions that they did not actually see Mr. Miller place his signature on the will. Further, it is undisputed that Mr. Miller did not accompany Ms. Pauley to the separate work areas of Ms. Waldron and Ms. McGinn.

Mr. Miller died on July 28, 1996. The last will and testament of Mr. Miller, which named [his nephew] Mr. Paul Casdorph as executor, left the bulk of his estate to the Casdorphs.[20] The Stevenses, [who as] nieces of Mr. Miller [would share in his intestate estate], filed the instant action to set aside the will. The Stevenses asserted in their complaint that Mr. Miller's will was not executed according to the requirements set forth in W. Va. Code § 41-1-3 (1995). After some discovery, all parties moved for summary judgment. The circuit court denied the Stevenses' motion for summary judgment, but granted the Casdorphs' cross motion for summary judgment. From this ruling, the Stevenses appeal to this Court....

The Stevenses' contention is simple. They argue that all evidence indicates that Mr. Miller's will was not properly executed. Therefore, the will should be voided. The procedural requirements at issue are contained in W. Va. Code § 41-1-3 (1997). The statute reads:

> No will shall be valid unless it be in writing and signed by the testator, or by some other person in his presence and by his direction, in such manner as to make it manifest that the name is intended as a signature; and moreover, unless it be wholly in the handwriting of the testator, *the signature shall be made or the will acknowledged by him in the presence of at least two competent witnesses, present at the same time; and such witnesses shall subscribe the will in the presence of the testator, and of each other*, but no form of attestation shall be necessary. (Emphasis added.)

The relevant requirements of the above statute call[ ] for a testator to sign his/her will or acknowledge such will in the presence of at least two witnesses at the same

---

18. *See, e.g.*, Rydde v. Morris, 675 S.E.2d 431 (S.C. 2009); Parks v. Fink, 293 P.3d 1275 (Wash. App. 2013).

19. Mr. Miller was elderly and confined to a wheelchair.

20. Mr. Miller's probated estate exceeded $400,000.00. The will devised $80,000.00 to Frank Paul Smith, a nephew of Mr. Miller. The remainder of the estate was left to [Paul Casdorph and his wife, Patricia].

A photograph of the bank lobby, taken from Ms. Pauley's desk. Ms. Waldron's desk is at the far left and Ms. McGinn's teller station is at the far right. This photograph was before the court on appeal.

time, and such witnesses must sign the will in the presence of the testator and each other. In the instant proceeding the Stevenses assert, and the evidence supports, that Ms. McGinn and Ms. Waldron did not actually witness Mr. Miller signing his will. Mr. Miller made no acknowledgment of his signature on the will to either Ms. McGinn or Ms. Waldron. Likewise, Mr. Miller did not observe Ms. McGinn and Ms. Waldron sign his will as witnesses. Additionally, neither Ms. McGinn nor Ms. Waldron acknowledged to Mr. Miller that their signatures were on the will. It is also undisputed that Ms. McGinn and Ms. Waldron did not actually witness each other sign the will, nor did they acknowledge to each other that they had signed Mr. Miller's will. Despite the evidentiary lack of compliance with W. Va. Code § 41-1-3, the Casdorphs argue that there was substantial compliance with the statute's requirements, insofar as everyone involved with the will knew what was occurring. The trial court found that there was substantial compliance with the statute because everyone knew why Mr. Miller was at the bank. The trial court further concluded there was no evidence of fraud, coercion or undue influence. Based upon the foregoing, the trial court concluded that the will should not be voided even though the technical aspects of W. Va. Code § 41-1-3 were not followed.

Our analysis begins by noting that "[t]he law favors testacy over intestacy." In re Teubert's Estate, 298 S.E.2d 456, 458 (W. Va. 1982). However, we clearly held in Black v. Maxwell, 46 S.E.2d 804, 805 (W. Va. 1948), that "testamentary intent and a written instrument, executed in the manner provided by [W. Va. Code § 41-1-3], existing concurrently, are essential to the creation of a valid will." *Black* establishes that mere intent by a testator to execute a written will is insufficient. The actual execution of a written will must also comply with the dictates of W. Va. Code § 41-1-3. The Casdorphs seek to have this Court establish an exception to the technical requirements of the statute. In Wade v. Wade, 195 S.E. 339, 339 (W. Va. 1938), this Court permitted a narrow exception to the stringent requirements of the W. Va. Code § 41-1-3. This narrow exception is [as follows]:

> Where a testator acknowledges a will and his signature thereto in the presence of two competent witnesses, one of whom then subscribes his name, the other or first witness, having already subscribed the will in the presence of the testator but out of the presence of the second witness, may acknowledge his signature in the presence of the testator and the second witness, and such acknowledgment, if there be no indicia of fraud or misunderstanding in the proceeding, will be deemed a signing by the first witness within the requirement of Code, 41-1-3, that the witnesses must subscribe their names in the presence of the testator and of each other. . . .

Wade stands for the proposition that if a witness acknowledges his/her signature on a will in the physical presence of the other subscribing witness *and the testator*, then the will is properly witnessed within the terms of W. Va. Code § 41-1-3. In this case, none of the parties signed or acknowledged their signatures in the presence of each other. This case meets neither the narrow exception of *Wade* nor the specific provisions of W. Va. Code § 41-1-3. . . .

In view of the foregoing, we grant the relief sought in this appeal and reverse the circuit court's order granting the Casdorphs' cross-motion for summary judgment.

Reversed.

WORKMAN, J., dissenting. The majority once more takes a very technocratic approach to the law, slavishly worshiping form over substance. In so doing, they not only create a harsh and inequitable result wholly contrary to the indisputable intent of Mr. Homer Haskell Miller, but also a rule of law that is against the spirit and intent of our whole body of law relating to the making of wills.

There is absolutely no claim of incapacity or fraud or undue influence, nor any allegation by any party that Mr. Miller did not consciously, intentionally, and with full legal capacity convey his property as specified in his will. The challenge to the will is based solely upon the allegation that Mr. Miller did not comply with the requirement of West Virginia Code 41-1-3 that the signature shall be made or the will acknowledged by the testator in the presence of at least two competent witnesses, present at the same time. The lower court, in its very thorough findings of fact, indicated that Mr. Miller had been transported to the bank by his nephew Mr. Casdorph and the nephew's wife. Mr. Miller, disabled and confined to a wheelchair, was a shareholder in the [bank] with whom all those present were personally familiar. When Mr. Miller executed his will in the bank lobby, the typed will was placed on Ms. Pauley's desk, and Mr. Miller instructed Ms. Pauley that he wished to have his will signed, witnessed, and acknowledged. After Mr. Miller's signature had been placed upon the will with Ms. Pauley watching, Ms. Pauley walked the will over to the tellers' area in the same small lobby of the bank. Ms. Pauley

Justice Margaret L. Workman

explained that Mr. Miller wanted Ms. Waldron to sign the will as a witness. The same process was used to obtain the signature of Ms. McGinn. Sitting in his wheelchair, Mr. Miller did not move from Ms. Pauley's desk during the process of obtaining the witness signatures. The lower court concluded that the will was valid and that Ms. Waldron and Ms. McGinn signed and acknowledged the will "in the presence" of Mr. Miller. . . .

The majority's conclusion is precisely what was envisioned and forewarned in 1938 by the drafters of the *Wade* opinion: illiberal and inflexible construction, giving preeminence to the letter of the law and ignoring the spirit of the entire body of testamentary law, resulting in the thwarting of Mr. Miller's unequivocal wishes. . . .

The majority embraces the line of least resistance. The easy . . . answer is to say that the formal, technical requirements have not been met and that the will is therefore invalid. End of inquiry. Yet that result is patently absurd. That manner of statutory application is inconsistent with the underlying purposes of the statute. Where a statute is enacted to protect and sanctify the execution of a will to prevent substitution or fraud, this Court's application of that statute should further such underlying policy, not impede it. When, in our efforts to strictly apply legislative language, we abandon common sense and reason in favor of technicalities, we are the ones committing the injustice.

NOTE

In the Presence of Two Witnesses, Present at the Same Time.   Why was Mr. Miller's will denied probate? What formalities were not satisfied exactly? Were not the evidentiary, channeling, cautionary or ritual, and protective functions satisfied? What result under UPC § 2-502(a), page 144?

The Meaning of "Presence"

In *Casdorph*, the court found that the witnesses did not sign in the presence of the testator or each other, and that the testator did not sign in the presence of the witnesses. In *Groffman*, the court found that the testator did not make or acknowledge his signature in the presence of the witnesses at the same time. What does *presence* mean in will execution?

Line of Sight.   In England and in some American states, the requirement that the witnesses sign in the presence of the testator is satisfied only if the testator is capable of seeing the witnesses in the act of signing. Under this *line of sight* test, the testator does not actually have to see the witnesses sign but must be able to see them were the testator to look. An exception is made for a blind testator, for whom the test is whether the testator would have been able to see the witnesses sign from where the testator was standing or sitting if the testator had the power of sight.

Conscious Presence.   In other American states, the line of sight test has been rejected in favor of a *conscious presence* test.[21] Under this test, a witness is in the presence of the testator if the testator, through sight, hearing, or general consciousness of

---

21. For an example, see the Wills Act excerpted in In re Estate of Javier Castro, page 191.

events, comprehends that the witness is in the act of signing. The test is one of mental apprehension.

Uniform Probate Code. UPC § 2-502(a), page 144, dispenses altogether with the requirement that the witnesses sign in the testator's presence. For a testator who directs another person to sign on the testator's behalf (see page 154), the UPC requires conscious presence.

Three Examples. Consider the following problems on the meaning of presence:

a. Suppose two witnesses signed *T*'s will in *T*'s dining room while *T* was in her bedroom. *T* knew that the witnesses were signing and could have walked into the dining room to see them sign. Does this meet the line of sight test? Does this meet the conscious presence test? *See* Groat v. Sundberg, 73 A.3d 374 (Md. App. 2013); In re Estate of Fischer, 886 A.2d 996 (N.H. 2005).

b. Suppose *T*'s lawyer takes *T*'s will to *T*'s home, where *T* signs the will and the lawyer attests as a witness. The lawyer returns to her office with the will and has her secretary call *T* on the phone. By telephone, *T* requests the secretary to witness his will; the secretary then signs as an attesting witness. Can the will be probated? *See* In re McGurrin, 743 P.2d 994 (Idaho App. 1987); In re Jefferson, 349 So. 2d 1032 (Miss. 1977). Suppose instead *T* requests the secretary to witness and the secretary does so with *T* watching via computer or smartphone video call. Can the will be probated? *See* Whitacre v. Crowe, 972 N.E.2d 659 (Ohio App. 2012).

c. Suppose the president of a bank draws a will for a customer. The customer, seriously ill, drives to the bank and parks. The president takes the will to the cus-  tomer's car. The customer signs the will propped on his steering wheel. A bank teller, seated at a window overlooking the car, watches the customer sign. The president signs as a witness in the car and then takes the will to the teller inside the bank. The teller, sitting at the window, signs as witness and waves to the customer, who waves back. The president then takes the will outside to the customer, who asks the president to keep it. Has the teller signed as a witness in the presence of the testator? In In re Weber's Estate, 387 P.2d 165 (Kan. 1963), the court held, 4 to 3, No, because even though the testator could see the teller, the testator could not see the pen and will as the teller signed.[22] The

The window and parking space at issue in *Weber*

---

22. Debra A. Buseman, who supplied the photo above of the window and parking space at issue in *Weber*, writes to us as follows:

I started working at [the bank] in 1973. In my training, we were told never to witness a legal document from a distance, especially through a window. The story of this case was then told.

The only thing that has really changed from 1960 to the present is that handicap parking has been added. The photograph shows the approximate space in which Mr. Weber, pronounced with a long "e," was parked. On the inside, right below the window, was a small shelf that held the book court said that to apply the conscious presence test on these facts would permit it "to run wild."[23]

The "Signature" Requirement

The law in all states, as well as UPC § 2-502(a), page 144, requires the testator to sign the will. The purpose of the signature requirement is to provide evidence of finality, distinguishing the will from mere drafts or notes, and to provide evidence of genuineness. Handwritten text by the testator containing the testator's full name located at the end of the document will almost always satisfy the signature requirement. Problems arise when the testator's signature takes a different form.

Signature by Mark, with Assistance, or by Another.   Although a full name is preferable, a mark, cross, abbreviation, initials, or nickname can be sufficient. In In re

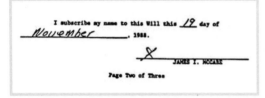

McCabe's signature by mark

Estate of McCabe, 274 Cal. Rptr. 43 (App. 1990), a lawyer prepared a will for James McCabe, who was very ill. Underneath the signature line was typed "James I. McCabe." While in the hospital, McCabe signed with an "X" because his hands were too shaky to write his name. The two attesting witnesses then signed. The court admitted the will to probate. The same result would have obtained if McCabe had written a shaky "Jim" rather than an "X." In In re Young, 397 N.E.2d 1223 (Ohio App. 1978), the court held that the letter *J* subscribed by Joseph Young, who was partially paralyzed, was a sufficient signature.

If McCabe had trouble holding the pen and a witness assisted McCabe in signing his name, the signature would be valid if McCabe intended to adopt the document as his will. So too, if someone else signed McCabe's name at his direction and in his presence, the will would be valid.[24]

An interesting variant was presented in Taylor v. Holt, 134 S.W.3d 830 (Tenn. App. 2003). A week before Steve Godfrey died, he composed his will using word processing software on his computer. In the presence of two witnesses, he typed a signature in a cursive font and then printed the document. The two witnesses signed the printed document by hand, and Godfrey also had the document notarized.

The will left Godfrey's entire estate to Doris Holt, a woman he was dating. After expressing Godfrey's enduring love and appreciation for Doris, the will concluded:

---

to record loan payments. I assume that this is where the document was signed. The shelf was used until approximately 1974, when the bank was remodeled.

Email from Debra A. Buseman to Robert H. Sitkoff (Oct. 11, 2012).

23. In Chester v. Smith, 677 S.E.2d 128 (Ga. 2009), a bank employee went to a customer's car in the bank's parking lot and watched the customer sign her will. The employee then brought the will to two tellers inside the bank to sign as witnesses. Applying a line of sight test, the court held the will invalid.

24. Could an infirm testator convey his consent to another signing his will on his behalf with only a smile? *See* Dying Man's Smile Validated His Will, N.Y. Times, Aug. 22, 1915, at 8.

Steve Godfrey's signature typed in a cursive font

The will in Taylor v. Holt

"Doris always remember that I do Love You and Muff."[25] The trial court held the will valid, and the appellate court affirmed:

> The definition of "signature" as used in the [Wills Act] is provided by Tenn. Code Ann. § 1-3-105(27), which states: "As used in this code, unless the context otherwise

---

25. James C. McSween, Jr., the winning counsel in *Taylor*, explains:

I inquired of Doris Holt, concerning the identity of "Muff" mentioned in the Will. It appears that this was a pet dog that Steve Godfrey had for several years. She told me that the dog anxiously awaited his return from work late each night, and would anticipate his arrival by furiously moving from window to door at the usual hour. Muff became very despondent after the death of Steve Godfrey and died within a few weeks.

Letter from James C. McSween, Jr., to Robert H. Sitkoff (Oct. 9, 2008).

requires: . . . 'Signature' . . . includes a mark, the name being written near the mark and witnessed, or any other symbol or methodology executed or adopted by a party with intention to authenticate a writing or record, regardless of being witnessed." . . .

In the case at hand, Deceased did make a mark that was intended to operate as his signature. Deceased made a mark by using his computer to affix his computer generated signature, and, as indicated by the affidavits of both witnesses, this was done in the presence of the witnesses. . . . Deceased simply used a computer rather than an ink pen as the tool to make his signature.

Suppose Godfrey had not printed the document, and instead the witnesses had "signed" their names below Godfrey's "signature" in the same cursive font. Could the digital word processing file be probated? *See* In re Estate of Javier Castro, page 191.

Order of Signing.   Another potential source of trouble is the order of signing. In general, the testator must sign or acknowledge the will before the witnesses attest. However, if they all sign "as part of a single (or continuous) transaction, the exact order of signing is not critical."[26] But what is a single or continuous transaction?

In the unfortunate case of In re Colling, [1972] 1 W.L.R. 1440 (Ch.), George Colling made a will in the hospital a few days before his death. He started to write his signature in the presence of two witnesses—Jackson, the patient in the bed next to his, and Sister Newman, a nurse. Although both witnesses were present when Colling started to sign, before he finished writing "Colling," Sister Newman had to attend to a patient in another part of the ward. In her absence Colling completed his signature, and Jackson witnessed the will in Colling's presence. Sister Newman then returned. Both Colling and Jackson acknowledged their signatures to her, and she signed as the second witness. The court held, "with great regret," that the will could not be probated because the testator did not complete his signature while both witnesses were present. The later acknowledgment did not suffice, because the testator must sign or acknowledge his signature before either of the witnesses attest.

Subscription and Addition After Signature.   Statutes in a handful of states, including New York,[27] have adopted the English Wills Act requirement that the testator sign the will "at the foot or end thereof," a requirement that is commonly called *subscription,* from the Latin *sub* ("under") and *scrib* ("to write").

Suppose that a typewritten will is found on which the following handwritten line appears just below the testator's signature: "I give Karen my diamond ring." Was the will signed "at the foot or end thereof"? Initially, the answer depends on when the handwritten line was added to the will. If done *after* the testator signed the will, the will would be admitted to probate, but the line would be ineffective as a subsequent unexecuted codicil (that is, a subsequent will that amends without replacing an earlier will, see page 218). But what if it was added *before* the testator signed her name? Arguably,

---

26. Restatement (Third) of Property: Wills and Other Donative Transfers § 3.1 cmt. m (Am. Law Inst. 1999).

27. *See* N.Y. Est. Powers & Tr. Law § 3-2.1(a)(1) (2016) ("at the end thereof").

in that circumstance the will would not satisfy the subscription requirement. Would it matter if the handwritten addition had not made a disposition of property but had said: "I appoint John executor"? *See* Bennett v. Ditto, 204 S.W.3d 145 (Ky. App. 2006).

Delayed Attestation.   Suppose a witness sees the testator make or acknowledge his signature, but the witness does not immediately sign the will. How long may the witness delay attestation without compromising the validity of the will? In New York, the witnesses must attest within 30 days.[28] Under UPC § 2-502(a)(3)(A), page 144, the witnesses must sign "within a reasonable time."

In a state that does not require the witnesses to sign the will in the presence of the testator, must the witnesses sign while the testator is still alive? The comment to UPC § 2-502(a)(3)(A) takes the position that a "reasonable time" could extend until after the testator's death. In In re Estate of Miller, 149 P.3d 840 (Idaho 2006), the court admitted to probate a will that had been signed by a witness after the testator's death and more than four years after the testator signed. California requires the witnesses to sign "during the testator's lifetime," but it also authorizes the application of the *harmless error rule* to defective attestation, including a witness's failure to sign before the testator dies (we take up the harmless error rule at page 176).[29]

d. Interested Witnesses and Purging Statutes

(1) From Disqualification to Purging

In early eighteenth-century England, an interested witness was not permitted to testify in court, hence a will attested by an interested witness could not be proved in probate. To alleviate this harsh outcome, in 1752 Parliament passed an act that came to be known as the *purging statute*.[30] This statute allowed a will attested by an interested witness to be admitted to probate, but it voided (purged) any bequest to the interested witness. A will attested by an interested witness would be valid, but the witness would not take his devise.

A slim majority of states in this country have purging statutes.[31] Most purge only the benefit that an interested witness would receive under a will that is in excess of what the witness would have received in intestacy (or, under some statutes, under an earlier will). The witness forfeits only the *excess benefit* afforded to the witness by the will. A few states still follow the English model and purge the witness of his entire devise. The purging statutes apply only to an interested witness who is necessary for a will's validity. If the will is witnessed by a sufficient number of disinterested witnesses, the interested witness is said to be *supernumerary* and may take his full devise.

An interesting variant, involving both an interested witness with no excess benefit and an interested witness who was possibly supernumerary, arose in In re Estate

---

28. *See id.* § 3-2.1(a)(4).
29. *See* Cal. Prob. Code § 6110(c) (2016).
30. 25 Geo. 2, c. 6, § I (1752).
31. *See* Schoenblum, *supra* note 6, at tbl. 1.

of Morea, 645 N.Y.S.2d 1022 (Sur. 1996). The will in that case had been attested by three witnesses, *A*, *B*, and *C*. *A* was disinterested. *B*, the testator's son, was a beneficiary under the will, but the devise to *B* was less than *B*'s intestate share, so *B* received no excess benefit to be purged. *C*, a friend of the testator, was also a beneficiary under the will. Because the applicable Wills Act required only two witnesses, and because the state followed the excess benefit rule, the will would have been valid, and both *B*'s and *C*'s devises enforceable, if only *A* and *B* had attested as witnesses. The court therefore held that *C* was supernumerary and did not need to be purged.

(2) The Trend Away from Purging

UPC § 2-505(b) (1990) and a substantial minority of states do not require that any of the witnesses be disinterested; an interested witness is not purged of his devise. Nonetheless, use of an interested witness may invite litigation and is not, to put it mildly, a sound practice. The comment to § 2-505 explains:

> Interest no longer disqualifies a person as a witness, nor does it invalidate or forfeit a gift under the will. Of course, the purpose of this change is not to foster use of interested witnesses, and attorneys will continue to use disinterested witnesses in execution of wills. But the rare and innocent use of a member of the testator's family on a home-drawn will is not penalized.
>
> This approach does not increase appreciably the opportunity for fraud or undue influence. A substantial devise by will to a person who is one of the witnesses to the execution of the will is itself a suspicious circumstance, and the devise might be challenged on grounds of undue influence. The requirement of disinterested witnesses has not succeeded in preventing fraud and undue influence; and in most cases of undue influence, the influencer is careful not to sign as a witness, but to procure disinterested witnesses.

A handful of states, such as California and Massachusetts, have adopted a middle ground in which a devise to a witness triggers a rebuttable presumption of undue influence, duress, or fraud.[32] The purging statutes, by contrast, in effect create a conclusive presumption of invalidity to the extent of the witness's excess benefit.

e. Model Execution Ceremony

In supervising a will execution, a lawyer should aspire to more than merely satisfying the formalities required by the Wills Act in the client's home state. The client may be domiciled elsewhere at death or may own real property in another state, or the will may exercise a power of appointment governed by the law of another state.

Under the usual choice of law rules, the law of the state where the decedent was domiciled at death governs the validity of a disposition by will of personal property, and the law of the state where real property is located governs the validity of a disposition by will of that property. Suppose a person executes a will while domiciled in Illinois,

---

32. *See* Cal. Prob. Code § 6112(c)-(d) (2016); Mass. Gen. Laws Ann. ch. 190B, § 2-505(b) (2016).

then moves permanently to New Jersey and dies there owning Florida real estate, some tangible personal property, and some stocks and bonds. New Jersey law will govern the validity of the disposition of the tangible and intangible personal property, and Florida law will govern the validity of the disposition of the real estate.[33]

Almost all states have a statute, such as UPC § 2-506 (1990), that recognizes as valid a will executed with the formalities required either by the state where the testator was domiciled at death, by the state where the will was executed, or by the state where the testator was domiciled when the will was executed.[34] But because these statutes are not uniform and not all states have such a statute, a careful lawyer in our highly mobile society will undertake to satisfy the formal requirements in all states.

If the procedure set forth below is followed,[35] the instrument will be valid in all states no matter where the testator is domiciled at the time of execution or at death or where the testator's property is located:[36]

(1) If the will consists of more than one page, the pages are fastened together securely. The will specifies the exact number of pages that it spans.
(2) Before calling in the witnesses and a notary, the lawyer confirms that the testator has read the will and understands its contents. The lawyer previews for the testator the rest of the execution ceremony.
(3) The lawyer, the testator, two (or three[37]) disinterested witnesses, and a notary are brought together in a room from which everyone else is excluded. (If the lawyer is a notary, an additional notary is unnecessary.) The door to the room is closed. No one enters or leaves the room until the ceremony is finished.
(4) The lawyer asks the testator the following three questions:

---

33. The Hague Convention of 1989 discards the situs rule for real property and the domicile rule for personal property, but it has not been ratified by the United States. Professor Schoenblum, this country's leading choice of law scholar in estate planning matters, is sharply critical of the Convention. *See* Jeffrey A. Schoenblum, Choice of Law and Succession to Wealth: A Critical Analysis of the Ramifications of the Hague Convention on Succession to Decedents' Estates, 32 Va. J. Int'l L. 83 (1991).

34. *See* Schoenblum, *supra* note 6, at tbl. 1.

35. This procedure is an up-to-date version of the ceremony recommended by Professor W. Barton Leach in his Cases on Wills 44 (2d ed. 1949) and subsequently refined by Professor A. James Casner in his work, Estate Planning § 3.1.1, now maintained by Professor Jeffrey N. Pennell.

36. If the client owns property in a foreign country or may die domiciled there, the law of the foreign country should be examined and the will executed in compliance with such law. *See, e.g.,* Jeffrey A. Schoenblum, Multistate and Multinational Estate Planning §§ 15.01-15.05 (2012 ed.); UPC §§ 2-1001 to 2-1010 (1990) (codifying the Uniform International Wills Act (1977)). Likewise, a client in a foreign country should not assume that a will valid there will be admitted to probate in a U.S. jurisdiction. *See, e.g.,* Malleiro v. Mori, 182 So. 3d 5 (Fla. App. 2015) (denying probate to a will that had been admitted to probate in Argentina).

37. Some lawyers use three witnesses to have a spare. Louisiana requires two witnesses plus a notary (see page 142, n.5), but a will executed elsewhere is entitled to probate if it is valid either in the state where executed or in the state of the testator's domicile. *See* La. Stat. Ann. § 9:2401 (2016). Pennsylvania is the only state that does not require witnesses (unless the testator signs by mark or by another). *See* 20 Pa. Cons. Stat. § 2502 (2016).

(a) "Is this your will?"[38]

(b) "Have you read it and do you understand it?"

(c) "Does it dispose of your property in accordance with your wishes?"

After each question the testator should answer "Yes" in a voice that can be heard by the witnesses and the notary. It is neither necessary nor customary for the witnesses to know the terms of the will. If the lawyer foresees a possible will contest, added precautions might be taken at this time (see page 305).

(5) The lawyer asks the testator the following question: "Do you request _____, _____, and _____ [the witnesses] to witness the signing of your will?" The testator should answer "Yes" in a voice audible to the witnesses.

(6) The witnesses should be standing or sitting so that all can see the testator sign. The testator signs (or initials) on the margin of each page of the will.[39] This is done for purposes of identification and to prevent subsequent substitution of pages. The testator then signs her name at the end of the will.

(7) One of the witnesses reads aloud the *attestation clause*, which attests that the foregoing things were done (see page 148).

(8) Each witness then signs and writes his or her address beside the signature. The testator and the other witnesses should be standing or sitting so that all can see each witness sign.

(9) Before the notary public the testator and the witnesses sign a *self-proving affidavit*, typed at the end of the will, swearing that the will was duly executed. The notary signs the affidavit and attaches the required seal.

(10) The lawyer reviews the documents to verify that all the signatures are in the correct places and that each page is initialed or signed in the margin.

(11) The lawyer writes a short memo to the file noting that the lawyer's usual execution protocols were followed.

(12) If the lawyer is retaining possession of the original (see page 161), the lawyer should place the original in the firm's vault or safe deposit box. The lawyer should also put copies, noted as such (perhaps with the word "copy" stamped on them), in the client's file — increasingly, these copies are electronic and preserved in the lawyer's digital archives. A common practice is to send a package to the client with a copy of the will, a copy of the client's other estate planning documents, and a cover letter stating where the originals are located.

---

38. The testator's declaration that the instrument is her will is called *publication*. The purpose of publication, which is required in some states, is to assure that the testator is under no misapprehension about the instrument that the testator is signing and to impress upon the witnesses the importance of the act and their consequent duty to vouch for the authenticity of the testator's signature. The testator may indicate to the witnesses that the instrument is a will by words, signs, or conduct. Even the words of another saying that the instrument is the testator's will may be sufficient. *See* Restatement (Third) of Property: Wills and Other Donative Transfers § 3.1 cmt. h (Am. Law Inst. 1999).

39. Louisiana requires the testator to sign "at the end of the testament and on each other separate page." La. Civ. Code Ann. art. 1577(1) (2016).

The Self-Proving Affidavit

Traditionally due execution of a will was proved after the testator's death by the witnesses testifying in court or by their submission of sworn affidavits. But the witnesses might be dead or unable to be found by the time of the testator's death. As we have seen, an *attestation clause* (see page 148), which recites that the will was duly executed in accordance with the particulars of the applicable Wills Act, helps to resolve this problem by giving rise to a rebuttable presumption of due execution.

A further innovation, encouraged by the Uniform Probate Code, is to have the witnesses make an affidavit swearing as to the will's due execution. Almost all states recognize such a *self-proving affidavit*. What differentiates a self-proving affidavit from an attestation clause is that the affidavit is a sworn declaration under oath.

UPC § 2-504 (1990, rev. 2008) authorizes two kinds of self-proving affidavits. Subsection (a) authorizes a *combined* attestation clause plus self-proving affidavit, so that the testator and the witnesses sign their names only once; this is called a *one-step* self-proving affidavit. Subsection (b) authorizes a *separate* self-proving affidavit to be affixed to a will already signed and attested. The affidavit must be signed by the testator and witnesses in front of a notary *after* the testator and witnesses have signed the will. Our model execution ceremony assumes the use of a *two-step* process, which is permitted in more states than is the one-step process.

UPC § 3-406(1) (1990, rev. 2008) provides that, if a will is self-proved, questions of due execution may not be contested "unless there is evidence of fraud or forgery affecting the acknowledgment or affidavit." Section 3-406 does not limit contests on other grounds, such as undue influence or lack of capacity. In states that have not adopted § 3-406 or a similar provision, a self-proved will may give rise to only a rebuttable presumption of due execution, as in Reeves v. Webb, 774 S.E.2d 641 (Ga. 2015).

Safeguarding a Will

The many reported cases involving notations, interlineations, or other markings on wills indicate that more than a few testators have attempted homemade revisions or partial revocations or, perhaps, have used their wills as memo pads on which to note contemplated modifications. Also, an occasional testator has taken too seriously the lawyer's advice on safeguarding the will, with the result that the will cannot be located after death.

These potential difficulties have prompted some lawyers to recommend that the client's original will be left in the lawyer's care. As suggested in our model execution ceremony, the client is typically given a copy of the will and a cover letter in which the location of the original will is noted. Keeping a client's will, however, may have the appearance of soliciting business, a potentially unethical practice. In State v. Gulbankian, 196 N.W.2d 733 (Wis. 1972), the Wisconsin Supreme Court discussed the ethics of this practice:

> Nor do we approve of attorneys' "safekeeping" wills. In the old days this may have been explained on the ground many people did not have a safe place to keep valuable papers, but there is little justification today because most people do have safe-keeping boxes, and if not, sec. 853.09, Stats., provides for the deposit of a will with

Safeguarding Oscar's Will

Consider the case of Oscar P.'s will, a true story told in a letter from Mr. A.J. Robinson, a lawyer in Amarillo, Texas. Mr. Robinson was counsel for one group of claimants under the will.

Two men walked into our office in late August and told us that they were Mr. P.'s nephews. They were completely covered with chigger bites from the top of their shoes to their belts. Their legs were swollen and red all over. They told us that their uncle had died in East Texas on a 40-acre farm. They said that he was found dead in his old house that did not have any doors or windows and that the floor was about to fall in, that he kept his eggs in a bucket hanging from a tree limb by wire to keep the snakes from stealing them, that he hung his milk from a tree limb, dangling in a creek, that there was no stove in the house and that he had a wheel barrow with the wheel running at about a 45 degree angle that he pushed to and from town to carry all his supplies. They had been informed that their uncle had left a will, and the entire family had descended on the place over the weekend to hunt for it. They had spent two days digging in every place that they could think of on the entire 40 acres, hunting for the will that they assumed was buried somewhere. When they were about to quit, someone decided to dig up the floor of the chicken house. Underneath the chicken house floor they found a gallon jar, and in the gallon jar was a half-gallon jar, and in the half-gallon was a quart, and in the quart was a pint, and in the pint was a half-pint, and in the half-pint was a key which appeared to fit some safe-deposit box. Upon checking all the banks in the neighboring towns, they finally found a bank that had a safe-deposit box that the key would fit. Upon opening the safe-deposit box they found P.'s holographic will. The first sentence recited that this was Oscar P.'s last will. The second sentence read: "You will find the key to my safety deposit box in a jar under the floor in the chicken house."

Oscar P. left a substantial estate.

the register in probate for safekeeping during the lifetime of the testator. The correct practice is that the original will should be delivered to the testator, and should only be kept by the attorney upon specific unsolicited request of the client.

The American College of Trust and Estate Counsel (ACTEC) takes the opposite view: "A lawyer who has drawn a will or other estate planning documents for a client may offer to retain the executed originals of the documents subject to the client's instructions."[40] The ACTEC view is more consistent with prevailing norms of practice than that of the Wisconsin court. A lawyer who safeguards wills for his clients should, however, have a succession plan for custody of the wills upon the lawyer's retirement or death.

Many states and UPC § 2-515 (1990) provide for the deposit of a will with the clerk of the probate court before death. Such depositories are seldom used. Few people know of their existence, and even if a testator knows of the option, there is no coordinated national death registry to connect the testator's family with the clerk of the probate court that has the will.

f. Ad Hoc Relief from Strict Compliance

The strict compliance rule creates a conclusive presumption of invalidity for an imperfectly executed will. Unless every last statutory formality is complied with exactly, the

---

40. ACTEC Commentaries on the Model Rules 170 (5th ed. 2016).

instrument is denied probate even if there is compelling evidence that the decedent intended the instrument to be his will. To avoid this harsh result, some courts have occasionally excused or corrected one or another innocuous defect in execution. Other courts have taken the position that there can be no relief from the rule of strict compliance. To get a feel for the ad hoc nature of relief from the strict compliance rule — and the need for a more principled way to avoid denying probate to an authentic but imperfectly executed will (a *false negative*) — consider the next two cases, which present nearly identical facts but reach opposite results.

In re Pavlinko's Estate
148 A.2d 528 (Pa. 1959)

BELL, J. Vasil Pavlinko died February 8, 1957; his wife, Hellen, died October 15, 1951. A testamentary writing dated March 9, 1949, which purported to be the will of Hellen Pavlinko, was signed by Vasil Pavlinko, her husband. The residuary legatee named therein, a brother of Hellen, offered the writing for probate as the will of Vasil Pavlinko, but probate was refused. The Orphans' Court, after hearing and argument, affirmed the decision of the Register of Wills.

The facts are unusual and the result very unfortunate. Vasil Pavlinko and Hellen, his wife, retained a lawyer to draw their wills and wished to leave their property to each other. By mistake Hellen signed the will which was prepared for her husband, and Vasil signed the will which was prepared for his wife, each instrument being signed at the end thereof. The lawyer who drew the will and his secretary, Dorothy Zinkham, both signed as witnesses. Miss Zinkham admitted that she was unable to speak the language of Vasil and Hellen, and that no conversation took place between them. The wills were kept by Vasil and Hellen. For some undisclosed reason, Hellen's will was never offered for probate at her death; in this case it was offered merely as an exhibit.

The instrument which was offered for probate was short. It stated: "I, *Hellen* Pavlinko, . . . do hereby make, publish and declare this to be *my* Last Will and Testament."

In the first paragraph she directed her executor to pay her debts and funeral expenses. In the second paragraph she gave her entire residuary estate to "my husband, Vasil Pavlinko . . . absolutely." She then provided:

> Third: If my aforesaid husband, Vasil Pavlinko, should predecease me, then and in that event, I give and bequeath:
>
> (a) To my brother-in-law, Mike Pavlinko, of McKees Rocks, Pennsylvania, the sum of Two Hundred ($200) Dollars.
>
> (b) To my sister-in-law, Maria Gerber, (nee Pavlinko), of Pittsburgh, Pennsylvania, the sum of Two Hundred ($200) Dollars.
>
> (c) The rest, residue and remainder of *my* estate, of whatsoever kind and nature and wheresoever situate, I give, devise and bequeath, absolutely, to *my brother*, Elias Martin, now residing at 520 Aidyl Avenue, Pittsburgh, Pennsylvania.
>
> I do hereby nominate, constitute and appoint my husband, Vasil Pavlinko, as Executor of this my Last Will and Testament.

It was then mistakenly signed "Vasil Pavlinko [Seal]."

While no attempt was made to probate, as Vasil's will, the writing which purported to be his will but was signed by Hellen, it could not have been probated as Vasil's will, because it was not signed by him at the end thereof.

The Wills Act of 1947 provides in clear, plain and unmistakable language in § 2: "Every will, . . . shall be in writing and shall be signed *by the testator* at the end thereof," 20 P.S. § 180.2, with certain exceptions not here relevant. The Court below correctly held that the paper which *recited* that it was the will of Hellen Pavlinko and intended and purported to give Hellen's estate to her husband, could not be probated as the will of Vasil and was a nullity.

In order to decide in favor of the residuary legatee, almost the entire will would have to be rewritten. The Court would have to substitute the words "Vasil Pavlinko" for "Hellen Pavlinko" and the words "my wife" wherever the words "my husband" appear in the will, and the relationship of the contingent residuary legatees would likewise have to be changed. To consider this paper—as written—as Vasil's will, it would give his entire residuary estate to "my husband, Vasil Pavlinko, absolutely" and "Third: If my husband, Vasil Pavlinko, should predecease me, then . . . I give and bequeath my residuary estate to my brother, Elias Martin." The language of this writing, which is signed at the end thereof by *Vasil* Pavlinko, is unambiguous, clear and unmistakable, and it is obvious that it is a meaningless nullity. . . .

Once a Court starts to ignore or alter or rewrite or make exceptions to clear, plain and unmistakable provisions of the Wills Act in order to accomplish equity and justice in that particular case, the Wills Act will become a meaningless, although well intentioned, scrap of paper, and the door will be opened wide to countless fraudulent claims which the Act successfully bars.

Decree affirmed. Each party shall pay their respective costs.

MUSMANNO, J., dissenting. Vasil Pavlinko and his wife, Hellen Pavlinko, being unlettered in English and unlearned in the ways of the law, wisely decided to have an attorney draw up their wills, since they were both approaching the age when reflecting persons must give thought to that voyage from which there is no return. They explained to the attorney . . . that he should draw two wills which would state that when either . . . had sailed away, the one remaining ashore would become the owner of the property of the departing voyager. Vasil Pavlinko knew but little English. However, his lawyer, fortunately, was well versed in his clients' native language, . . . Little Russian or Carpathian. The attorney thus discussed the whole matter with his two visitors in their language. He then dictated appropriate wills to his stenographer in English and then, after they had been transcribed, he translated the documents, paragraph by paragraph, to Mr. and Mrs. Pavlinko, who approved of all that he had written. The wills were laid before them and each signed the document purporting to be his or her will. The attorney gave Mrs. Pavlinko the paper she had signed and handed to her husband the paper he had signed. In accordance with customs they had brought with them from the old country, Mrs. Pavlinko turned her paper over to her husband. It did not matter, however, who held the papers since they were complementary of each other. Mrs. Pavlinko left her property to Mr. Pavlinko and Mr. Pavlinko left his property to Mrs. Pavlinko. They also agreed on a common residuary legatee, Elias Martin, the brother of Mrs. Pavlinko. . . .

Musmanno, J., Dissenting

A naval officer in World War II who served as a judge in the Nuremberg trials and led the investigation to confirm Hitler's death, Justice Musmanno was a striking individualist, sometimes injudicious, always colorful. In dissenting from a majority holding that Henry Miller's Rabelaisian *Tropic of Cancer*, a novel, was not obscene, *Commonwealth v. Robin*, 218 A.2d 546 (Pa. 1966), Musmanno wrote:

> "Cancer" is is not a book. It is a cesspool, an open sewer, a pit of putrefaction, a slimy gathering of all that is rotten in the debris of human depravity. And in the center of all this waste and stench, besmearing himself with its foulest defilement, splashes, leaps, cavorts and wallows a bifurcated specimen that responds to the name of Henry Miller. One wonders how the human species could have produced so lecherous, blasphemous, disgusting and amoral a human being as Henry Miller. One wonders why he is received in polite society.... From Pittsburgh to Philadelphia, from Dan to Beersheba, and from the ramparts of the Bible to Samuel Eliot Morison's Oxford History of the American People, I dissent.

In his first five years on the Pennsylvania Supreme Court, Musmanno filed more dissenting opinions than all the other members of that court had collectively filed in the preceding 50 years. One dissent got him into a lawsuit. In another case, Chief Justice Stern ordered that Musmanno's dissent not be published in the official state reports because he had not circulated it among the court. Musmanno sought mandamus to compel the state reporter to publish his dissent. The Supreme Court, with Musmanno not participating, denied the writ. *Musmanno v. Eldredge*, 114 A.2d 511 (Pa. 1955). Justice Musmanno then moved his case to the court of last resort, the law reviews. His side of the controversy can be found in Michael A. Musmanno, *Dissenting Opinions*, 60 Dick. L. Rev. 139 (1956). When asked whether he read Musmanno's dissents, Chief Justice Stern replied that he was not "interested in current fiction."

Musmanno was a leading force in establishing Columbus Day as a special day for Italian Americans. When Yale accepted the Vinland map as evidence that Norsemen and not an Italian, Christopher Columbus, were among the first Europeans to "discover" America, Musmanno immediately rose to the attack. He dropped all his duties and went to

Justice Musmanno, speaking volubly
Leonard McCombe/Time & Life/Getty Images

Yale to dispute the archeologists, embarked on a six-month speaking tour attacking the authenticity of the Vinland map, and wrote a book, *Columbus Was First!* (1966).

In 1974 the Yale Library pronounced the Vinland map a fake based on a report, later disputed, that the ink dated from the twentieth century. By 1996, Yale changed its mind again, allowing that the Vinland map may be authentic after all. The authenticity of the map continues to be debated today. Notwithstanding the map, scholars have reached a consensus that Musmanno's larger contention—that "Columbus Was First!"—is false. Excavations at L'Anse aux Meadows in present-day Newfoundland suggest that Vikings settled North America about five hundred years before Columbus.

Justice Musmanno's last opinion was a freewheeling dissent to a reversal of a rape conviction. The majority held that it was error for the judge to tell the jurors they would have to answer to God for their actions. *Commonwealth v. Holton*, 247 A.2d 228 (Pa. 1968). Wrote Musmanno:

> God is not dead, and judges who criticize the invocation of Divine Assistance had better begin preparing a brief to use when they stand themselves at the Eternal Bar of Justice on Judgment Day.... I am perfectly willing to take my chances with [the trial judge]... at the gates of Saint Peter and answer on our voir dire that we were always willing to invoke the name of the Lord in seeking counsel.... *Miserere nobis Omnipotens Deus!*

The next day, Columbus Day 1968, Justice Musmanno dropped dead and presumably this voir dire took place.

We have also said time[s] without number that the intent of the testator must be gathered from the four corners of his will. Whether it be from the four corners of the will signed by Vasil Pavlinko or whether from the eight corners of the wills signed by Vasil and Hellen Pavlinko, all set out before the court below, the net result is always the same, namely that the residue of the property of the last surviving member of the Pavlinko couple was to go to Elias Martin. . . .

Even if we accept the Majority's conclusion . . . that all provisions in the Pavlinko will, which refer to himself, must be regarded as nullities, . . . it does not follow that the residuary clause must perish. The fact that some of the provisions in the Pavlinko will cannot be executed does not strike down the residuary clause, which is meaningful and stands on its own two feet. We know that one of the very purposes of a residuary clause is to provide a catch-all for undisposed-of or ineffectually disposed-of property. . . . I see no insuperable obstacle to probating the will signed by Vasil Pavlinko. Even though it was originally prepared as the will of his wife, Hellen, he did adopt its testamentary provisions as his own. Some of its provisions are not effective but their ineffectuality in no way bars the legality and validity of the residuary clause which is complete in itself. I would, therefore, probate the paper signed by Vasil Pavlinko. Here, indeed, is a situation where we could, if we wished, consistent with authority and precedent, and without endangering the integrity of the Wills Act, put in to effect the time-honored proverb that "where there's a will, there's a way."

In re Snide
418 N.E.2d 656 (N.Y. 1981)

WACHTLER, J. This case involves the admissibility of a will to probate. The facts are simply stated and are not in dispute. Harvey Snide, the decedent, and his wife, Rose Snide, intending to execute mutual wills at a common execution ceremony, each executed by mistake the will intended for the other. There are no other issues concerning the required formalities of execution, nor is there any question of the decedent Harvey Snide's testamentary capacity, or his intention and belief that he was signing his last will and testament. Except for the obvious differences in the names of the donors and beneficiaries on the wills, they were in all other respects identical.

The proponent of the will, Rose Snide, offered the instrument Harvey actually signed for probate. The Surrogate decreed that it could be admitted, and further that it could be reformed to substitute the name "Harvey" wherever the name "Rose" appeared, and the name "Rose" wherever the name "Harvey" appeared. The Appellate Division reversed on the law, and held under a line of lower court cases dating back into the 1800's, that such an instrument may not be admitted to probate. We would reverse.

It is clear from the record, and the parties do not dispute the conclusion, that this is a case of a genuine mistake. It occurred through the presentment of the wills to Harvey and Rose in envelopes, with the envelope marked for each containing the will intended for the other. The attorney, the attesting witnesses, and Harvey and Rose, all proceed[ed] with the execution ceremony without anyone taking care to read the front pages, or even the attestation clauses of the wills, either of which would have indicated the error.

Crawling From the Wreckage: Sol Wachtler Uses His Experience Behind Bars to Help Mentally Ill

As chief judge on New York's highest court, Sol Wachtler was a nationally respected jurist on the fast track to become governor, maybe even a Supreme Court justice.

But all the accolades, admirers and aspirations vanished instantly when Wachtler was caught in a bizarre plot in 1992 to stalk and harass a former lover. His startling descent from being New York's top judge to federal prison inmate was recounted unflinchingly by Wachtler during a recent visit to Columbia Law School.

"The reason for that was my own fault. I don't blame anyone for what happened to me," he said. . . . Wachtler was invited to provide students with the perspective of a white-collar defendant caught in the criminal-justice system.

Wachtler suffers from bipolar disorder, which he said sparked the behavior that led to his imprisonment though [he] does not offer it as an excuse. He traces his illness to the late 1980s, when New York was embroiled in yet another fiscal crisis. The judiciary's budget was slashed 10 percent, and Wachtler, who also ran the state court system, was forced to lay off 500 workers. . . .

"It had an emotional impact on me that I just can't describe. It put me into a very deep depression," Wachtler told the students, most of whom were in elementary school when his fall from grace made him a scourge of the tabloids.

Around this time, Wachtler began a four-year affair that ended badly. His depression became more profound. It was compounded by a mix of prescribed amphetamines, tranquilizers, and anti-depressants.

"You have a dream, and a thought, and the next day you wake up and realize how stupid it is," Wachtler said. "Well, when you're in this state, you get up in the morning, it seems twice as brilliant as when you had it at night."

Wachtler was referring to the 13 months when he stalked his former girlfriend, socialite Joy Silverman, with hang-up calls, and anonymous, obscene letters that included a threat to kidnap her teenage daughter and extortion demands. He hoped Silverman would turn to him for help with the harassment.

Instead, she turned to the FBI, leading to Wachtler's arrest, a guilty plea to the kidnap threat and a 15-month prison term in 1993. His ornate chambers in the Court of Appeals in Albany were replaced by an 8 x 7 cell in solitary confinement, where he was placed for observation after arriving

Chief Judge Sol Wachtler

at a North Carolina prison where the mentally ill are housed.

"It's hard to describe what solitary confinement in a mental health unit is, screaming all night long," Wachtler said. "You can't sleep."

When he was released into the prison population, Wachtler was soon approached by an inmate who showed Wachtler an order he had signed denying the inmate a right to appeal. Three weeks later Wachtler was stabbed in his cell while dozing off, and suspects the inmate was his assailant.

The worst part of that encounter, Wachtler said, was being placed back in solitary for his protection. During that month he suffered delusions that included fears he was being attacked by a spider. "Had I been more mentally ill than I was," Wachtler said, "I would have become so terribly dysfunctional, and that is what is happening today" to other inmates who go untreated.

Wachtler's prison stay helped prompt him to lobby for a law in New York to keep the seriously mentally ill out of solitary confinement and provide them with treatment. . . .

Now 79, Wachtler was reinstated to the bar in 2007. He is now an adjunct professor at Touro Law Center on Long Island and also heads an alternative dispute resolution firm.

Source: Columbia Law School Press Release (Dec. 7, 2009).

Harvey Snide is survived by his widow and three children, two of whom have reached the age of majority. These elder children have executed waivers and have consented to the admission of the instrument to probate. The minor child, however, is represented by a guardian ad litem who refuses to make such a concession. The reason for the guardian's objection is apparent. Because the will of Harvey would pass the entire estate to Rose, the operation of the intestacy statute after a denial of probate is the only way in which the minor child will receive a present share of the estate.

The gist of the objectant's argument is that Harvey Snide lacked the required testamentary intent because he never intended to execute the document he actually signed. This argument is not novel, and in the few American cases on point it has been the basis for the denial of probate (see Nelson v. McDonald, 16 N.Y.S. 273 (Sup. 1891); Matter of Cutler, 58 N.Y.S.2d 604 (Sur. 1945); Matter of Bacon, 165 Misc. 259 (N.Y. Sur. 1937); see, also, Matter of Pavlinko, 148 A.2d 528 (Pa. 1959); Matter of Goettel, 184 Misc. 155 (N.Y. Sur. 1944)). However, cases from other common-law jurisdictions have taken a different view of the matter, and we think the view they espouse is more sound (Matter of Brander, 4 Dom. L. Rep. 688 [1952] [Canada]; Guardian, Trust & Ex'r's Co. of New Zealand v. Inwood, 65 N.Z. L. Rep. 614 [1946] [New Zealand]).

Of course, it is essential to the validity of a will that the testator was possessed of testamentary intent, however, we decline the formalistic view that this intent attaches irrevocably to the document prepared, rather than the testamentary scheme it reflects. Certainly, had a carbon copy been substituted for the ribbon copy the testator intended to sign, it could not be seriously contended that the testator's intent should be frustrated. Here the situation is similar. Although Harvey mistakenly signed the will prepared for his wife, it is significant that the dispositive provisions in both wills, except for the names, were identical.

Moreover, the significance of the only variance between the two instruments is fully explained by consideration of the documents together, as well as in the undisputed surrounding circumstances. Under such facts it would indeed be ironic—if not perverse—to state that because what has occurred is so obvious, and what was intended so clear, we must act to nullify rather than sustain this testamentary scheme. The instrument in question was undoubtedly genuine, and it was executed in the manner required by the statute. Under these circumstances it was properly admitted to probate.

In reaching this conclusion we do not disregard settled principles, nor are we unmindful of the evils which the formalities of will execution are designed to avoid; namely, fraud and mistake. To be sure, full illumination of the nature of Harvey's testamentary scheme is dependent in part on proof outside of the will itself. However, this is a very unusual case, and the nature of the additional proof should not be ignored. Not only did the two instruments constitute reciprocal elements of a unified testamentary plan, they both were executed with statutory formality, including the same attesting witnesses, at a contemporaneous execution ceremony. There is absolutely no danger of fraud, and the refusal to read these wills together would serve merely to unnecessarily expand formalism, without any corresponding benefit. On these narrow facts we decline this unjust course.

Nor can we share the fears of the dissent that our holding will be the first step in the exercise of judicial imagination relating to the reformation of wills. Again, we are dealing here solely with identical mutual wills both simultaneously executed with statutory formality.

For the reasons we have stated, the order of the Appellate Division should be reversed, and the matter remitted to that court for a review of the facts.

Jones, J., dissenting. . . . On the basis of commendably thorough world-wide research, counsel for appellant has uncovered a total of 17 available reported cases involving mutual wills mistakenly signed by the wrong testator. Six cases arise in New York, two in Pennsylvania, three in England, one in New Zealand and five in Canada. With the exception of the two recent Surrogate's decisions (*Snide* and Matter of Iovino, N.Y.L.J., April 16, 1980, at 14, col. 5) relief was denied in the cases from New York, Pennsylvania and England. The courts that have applied the traditional doctrines have not hesitated, however, to express regret at judicial inability to remedy the evident blunder. Relief was granted in the six cases from the British Commonwealth. In these cases it appears that the court has been moved by the transparency of the obvious error and the egregious frustration of undisputed intention which would ensue from failure to correct that error. . . .

I would adhere to the precedents, and affirm the order of the Appellate Division.

NOTES

1. Switched (or Crossed) Wills. Both *Pavlinko* and *Snide* involved switched or crossed wills, but they reached opposite results. Why?

2. Curing Defective Execution and Reformation. There are two distinct solutions for a switched wills error. One is to probate the instrument that the decedent *intended* to sign but did not. The difficulty with this solution is that the instrument was not signed by the decedent. Probating an unsigned instrument requires abandoning strict compliance for substantial compliance or the harmless error rule, doctrines for overcoming defective execution that we take up at pages 170 and 176 respectively.

The other solution for a switched wills error is to probate the will that the decedent *actually* signed but then to reform its terms to make sense. If reformation had been allowed in *Pavlinko*, the court would have substituted the name "Vasil" for "Hellen," just as in *Snide* the court substituted "Harvey" for "Rose."[41] We return to reformation of wills for mistake in Chapter 5.

3. Malpractice Liability. Did the lawyers who supervised the defective executions in *Pavlinko* and *Snide* commit malpractice by not verifying that each spouse signed the correct instrument? Under Simpson v. Calivas, page 52, would Vasil Pavlinko's intended beneficiaries have a malpractice claim against Vasil's lawyer? On what evidence would they rely to prove that Vasil intended to give them a devise? Is there a good reason why such evidence might be reliable enough to impose malpractice liability on the lawyer but not to overcome the defective execution?

4. Guardians ad Litem. When the interests of a minor or unborn person are at stake in a litigation, courts commonly appoint a *guardian ad litem* to represent those interests. In *Snide*, Harvey's two adult children waived any objections to the entire estate passing to Rose under the challenged will, but the guardian ad litem for Harvey's

---

41. In Marley v. Rawlings, [2014] UKSC 2, the United Kingdom Supreme Court allowed reformation, called *rectification* in English law, in a switched wills case.

Professor John H. Langbein

minor child objected. If Harvey's will were invalid, the estate would pass by intestacy, and the minor would receive a share. In opposing the will, therefore, the guardian prioritized the minor's financial interests without regard to Harvey's intent or the interests of the family as a whole. Doubtless the guardian was concerned about potential fiduciary liability to the minor if the guardian failed to pursue the minor's interests vigorously.

In Espinosa v. Sparber, Shevin, Shapo, Rosen & Heilbronner, 612 So. 2d 1378, 1379 n.1 (Fla. 1993), the court in dicta expressed the "hope" that a guardian "would not focus strictly on the financial consequences for the child, but would also consider such important factors as family harmony and stability."

g. The Substantial Compliance Doctrine

In 1975, Professor John H. Langbein of Yale Law School published a groundbreaking article, Substantial Compliance with the Wills Act, 88 Harv. L. Rev. 489 (1975), which sparked a movement away from the strict compliance rule. Writing with a fierce but arresting clarity, Langbein decried the "harsh and relentless formalism" of the strict compliance rule. "The most minute defect in formal compliance is held to void the will," he lamented, "no matter how abundant the evidence that the defect was inconsequential." To Langbein's way of thinking, "the insistent formalism of the law of wills" was "mistaken and needless," hence in urgent need of reform to allow for the possibility of "harmless error in the execution of wills. The . . . familiar concept of substantial compliance should now be applied to the Wills Act."

Under the substantial compliance doctrine as proposed by Langbein, the key question is whether the manner in which an instrument was executed satisfied the purposes of the Wills Act formalities. If so, the instrument should be *deemed* in *substantial compliance* with the Wills Act and admitted to probate:

> The finding of a formal defect should lead not to automatic invalidity, but to a further inquiry: [1] does the noncomplying document express the decedent's testamentary intent, and [2] does its form sufficiently approximate Wills Act formality to enable the court to conclude that it serves the purposes of the Wills Act?

Whereas the strict compliance rule imposes a conclusive presumption of invalidity for an imperfectly executed will, the substantial compliance doctrine would make the presumption of invalidity rebuttable.

The Unfulfilled Promise of Substantial Compliance

The high point of the substantial compliance doctrine was In re Will of Ranney, 589 A.2d 1339 (N.J. 1991). In that case, the testator's lawyer had meant to include at the end of the will a *one-step* self-proving affidavit, but he mistakenly used the language of a *two-step* affidavit instead. As we have seen (see page 161), a one-step affidavit combines the language of an attestation clause with that of a self-proving affidavit so that the testator and the witnesses sign the will just once, simultaneously executing it and swearing under oath as to its due execution. A two-step affidavit, which states that the will was already executed in compliance with the Wills Act, is meant to be signed after the testator and the witnesses first execute the will by signing it.

Accordingly, when the testator and the witnesses signed the affidavit before a notary, who notarized it, they made a false declaration. They had not first executed the will in strict compliance with the Wills Act, as the affidavit declared. The court therefore concluded that, "the signatures of the witnesses on the subject self-proving affidavit do not literally comply with the statutory requirements."

The court went on to say, however, that the absence of strict compliance "does not end the analysis." Instead, quoting Langbein's article—and specifically his two-part test for substantial compliance—the court held that a will may be probated with clear and convincing evidence that it substantially complies with the Wills Act:

> Compliance with statutory formalities is important not because of the inherent value that those formalities possess, but because of the purposes they serve. It would be ironic to insist on literal compliance with statutory formalities when that insistence would invalidate a will that is the deliberate and voluntary act of the testator. Such a result would frustrate rather than further the purpose of the formalities. . . .
>
> The execution of a last will and testament, however, remains a solemn event. A careful practitioner will still observe the formalities surrounding the execution of wills. When formal defects occur, proponents should prove by clear and convincing evidence that the will substantially complies with statutory requirements. Our adoption of the doctrine of substantial compliance should not be construed as an invitation either to carelessness or chicanery. The purpose of the doctrine is to remove procedural peccadillos as a bar to probate.

Ranney was the first decision by an American court of last resort to adopt the substantial compliance doctrine as Langbein had envisioned it. The court acknowledged the absence of strict compliance, but held that the conduct was close enough that probating the instrument would better serve the purposes of the Wills Act than denying probate.[42]

Most courts, however, have continued to require strict compliance. In In re Estate of Chastain, 401 S.W.3d 612 (Tenn. 2012), for example, a purported two-page will had been signed by three witnesses, but not *T*, because there was no space reserved at the end for *T*'s signature. *T* did sign an attached self-proving affidavit, as did the witnesses and a notary, and *T* and the witnesses initialed the first page of the will. The proponent argued that *T* "signed the Affidavit intending to sign the Will and believing he was signing the Will, so his signature on the Affidavit should be deemed

---

42. UPC § 2-504(c) codifies the specific result in *Ranney*: "A signature affixed to a self-proving affidavit attached to a will is considered a signature affixed to the will, if necessary to prove the will's due execution."

No space reserved for T's signature at the end of the will

T's signature on the self-proving affidavit

The second page of the two-page will in *Chastain*, with no space for *T*'s signature (left), and the notarized signatures on the self-proving affidavit (right).

sufficient." The court disagreed. It reasoned that only the legislature could authorize something less than strict compliance.[43]

Even in New Jersey, the doctrine evolved into something narrower than Langbein had intended. Perhaps the nadir of the doctrine was In re Will of Ferree, 848 A.2d 81 (N.J. Ch. 2003), aff'd, 848 A.2d 1 (N.J. App. 2004). In that case, the testator, Ronald Ferree, died in an apparent suicide. A "Last Will and Testament," dated 1999 and filled in by hand on a preprinted will form, was found near his body. The form was signed by Ferree and notarized, but it was not attested by two witnesses.

The court held that this manner of execution did not substantially comply with the Wills Act. Even if the notary were treated as a witness, there would still be only one rather than the required two.[44] The court reasoned that the substantial compliance doctrine adopted in *Ranney* "does not allow for the studied disregard of the formalities . . . still required by statute." But is this plausible? Did the testator deliberately botch the execution of his will? He obtained a preprinted will form, he filled it out, he signed

---

43. The court also took the view that *T*'s "signature on the separate Affidavit provides little, if any, insight about [*T*'s] beliefs and intentions concerning the unsigned two-page Will." Do you agree? Is there a plausible alternative explanation for the multiple authentications of the document by *T* and the witnesses? Did the manner of those authentications satisfy the evidentiary, channeling, cautionary or ritual, and protective functions?

44. The cases are split on whether a notary who signs in an act of notarization can be counted as an attesting witness. *Compare* In re Estate of Meyer, 367 P.3d 629, 643 (Wyo. 2016) (no), *with* In re Estate of Valcarce, 301 P.3d 1031 (Utah 2013) (yes).

#8 WILL (Unmarried Individual With No Children & Two or More Beneficiaries)

Last Will and Testament
of
RONALD D. FERREE

I, _RONALD FERREE_ presently residing at _40 WATERMAN AVE, RUMSON N.J. 07760_ being of full age and sound and disposing mind and memory, hereby make, publish and declare this to be my Last Will and Testament.

FIRST: I hereby revoke any and all Wills and Codicils by me anytime heretofore made. _THERE ARE NO OTHER_ (RF)

SECOND: I direct that all of my just debts and funeral expenses be paid out of my Estate as soon as practicable after my death. (RF)

THIRD: I am presently not married. (RF)

FOURTH: I hereby give, devise and bequeath all of my Estate, real, personal and mixed, of every kind and nature whatsoever and wheresoever situated, to the following named beneficiaries or their survivors in equal shares.

a. _MICHEAL FERREE (BROTHER) 2981 HEATHER_
Name and address of beneficiary

b. _COURT, JENSEN BEACH, FLA 34957_
Name and address of beneficiary

c. _BARBRA FERREE 2981 HEATHER Ct_
Name and address of beneficiary

d. _COURT, JENSEN BEACH, FLA 34957_
Name and address of beneficiary

e. _CHARLES CREEL (MY IRA-AT SMITH BARNEY_
Name and address of beneficiary _49 PARKER AVE, FAIRHAVEN N.J._

FIFTH: I nominate and appoint _MICHEAL FERREE_ as Executor/Executrix of this Will. In the event he/she shall predecease me or fails to serve as such Executor/Executrix, then in such event, I nominate and appoint _BARBRA FERREE_, Executor/Executrix of this my Last Will and Testament. I further direct that no appointee hereunder shall be required to give any bond for the faithful performance of his/her duties.

SIXTH: I give to my Executor/Executrix, authority to exercise all the powers, duties, rights and immunities conferred upon fiduciaries by law with full power to sell to mortgage and to lease, and to invest and re-invest all or any part of my Estate on such terms as he/she deems best.

IN WITNESS WHEREOF, I hereunto set my hand this _21ST_ day of _OCTOBER_, 19 _99_.

Jane F. Hartman
JANE F. HARTMAN
NOTARY PUBLIC OF NEW JERSEY
My Commission Expires July 15, 2003

Ronald D. Ferree
(SIGN HERE)
RONALD D. FERREE

Signed, sealed, published and declared by the above named testator, as and for his Last Will and Testament, in the presence of us, who at his request, in his presence, and in the presence of one another have hereunto subscribed our names as attesting witnesses, the day and year last written above.

_____ residing at _____

_____ residing at _____

_____ residing at _____

Disputed will of Ronald Ferree

it, and then he went to the trouble of having it notarized, which is perhaps even better evidence of finality of intent to transfer than attestation by two witnesses.[45]

Courts in other states have likewise given the doctrine a narrow application. In *Martina v. Elrod*, 748 S.E.2d 412 (Ga. 2013), the court held that a will was not self-proved because the affidavit signed by the witnesses and a notary did not include all of the language prescribed by the statute. The court did not consider, as Langbein had urged, whether the statutory purpose was satisfied. "The doctrine of substantial compliance, though tolerant of 'variations in the mode of expression' utilized to satisfy statutory requisites, nonetheless requires 'actual compliance as to all matters of substance.'" Is it coherent to say that "substantial compliance" requires "actual compliance"?

In *Smith v. Smith*, 348 S.W.3d 63 (Ky. App. 2011), the court held that a will signed by only one witness when two were required could never be in substantial compliance with the Wills Act. "Our view is that permitting the probate of a non-holographic document to which only one person has subscribed her name as witness is a violation of the express language of the statute, and the doctrine of substantial compliance is inapplicable in this situation." But Langbein had intended precisely the opposite. "Attestation by two witnesses where the statute calls for three, or by one where it asks for two, is a less serious defect," he wrote, "because the execution of the will was witnessed and the omission goes to the quantity rather than the quality of the evidence. Other evidence of finality of intention and deliberate execution might then suffice to show that the missing witness was harmless to the statutory purpose."

From Substantial Compliance to Harmless Error: Australia's Natural Experiment

In 1981, the Australian state of Queensland enacted a statute providing for probate of a will that substantially complies with the requisite formalities.[46] Six years earlier, in 1975, the same year in which Langbein published his substantial compliance article, South Australia enacted a harmless error or dispensing power statute. It provided for the probate of a document that was not properly executed if the court "is satisfied . . . that the deceased intended the document to constitute his will."[47] Whereas the *substantial compliance* doctrine allows a court to *deem* a noncompliant will to be in compliance with the Wills Act, a kind of "close enough" analysis, the *dispensing power* statute enacted in South Australia allows the court to *excuse* noncompliance if there is abundant evidence that the testator intended the document to be his will. This dispensing power to validate a will based on evidence of intent has come to be known in the United States as the *harmless error rule*.

In 1987, after observing the South Australian experience with harmless error and the Queensland experience with substantial compliance, Langbein concluded that the

---

45. Today, under UPC § 2-502(a)(3)(B), page 144, notarization is an alternative to attestation by two witnesses (see page 197).

46. Succession Act of 1981 (Qld.) s 9(a).

47. S. Austl. Wills Act Amendment Act (No. 2) 1975 (SA) s 9, amending Wills Act of 1936, 1936 (SA) s 12(2).

harmless error rule was preferable.[48] The reason was that "courts read into their substantial compliance doctrine a near-miss standard, ignoring the central issue of whether the testator's conduct evidenced testamentary intent." For example, Langbein had intended that the substantial compliance doctrine would forgive most defects in attestation. But the Queensland courts, presaging *Ferree* and *Smith*, had applied substantial compliance so narrowly that, because attestation generally served the purposes of formalities, they were unwilling to overlook innocuous attestation defects.

In South Australia, by contrast, the dispensing power fared better. After examining the first 41 South Australian cases after 1975, Langbein concluded:

> Implicitly, this case law has produced a ranking of the Wills Act formalities. Of the three main formalities—writing, signature, and attestation—writing turns out to be indispensable. Because section 12(2) requires a "document," nobody has tried to use the dispensing power to enforce an oral will. Failure to give permanence to the terms of your will is not harmless. Signature ranks next in importance. If you leave your will unsigned, you raise a grievous doubt about the finality and genuineness of the instrument. An unsigned will is presumptively only a draft, . . . but that presumption is rightly overcome in compelling circumstances such as in the switched-wills cases. By contrast, attestation makes a more modest contribution, primarily of a protective character, to the Wills Act policies. But the truth is that most people do not need protecting, and there is usually strong evidence that want of attestation did not result in imposition. The South Australian courts have been quick to find such evidence and to excuse attestation defects under the dispensing power.
>
> In devaluing attestation while insisting on signature and writing, the South Australian legislation and case law has brought the South Australian law of wills into a kind of alignment with the American law of will substitutes, that is, with our nonprobate system, where business practice has settled the forms for transfer. In life insurance beneficiary designations; in bank transfer arrangements such as pay-on-death accounts, joint accounts, and Totten trusts; in pension accounts; and in revocable inter vivos trusts, writing is the indispensable formality of modern practice, and signature is nearly as universal. Attestation, however, is increasingly uncommon. . . .
>
> Americans should . . . shudder that we still inflict upon our citizens the injustice of the traditional law, and we should join in this movement to rid private law of relics so embarrassing.[49]

In a 2007 study, Stephanie Lester reviewed 121 Australian cases decided since Langbein's study. She concluded that the dispensing power has continued to fare well—with one exception. In a few troubling cases, the court admitted a document to probate on the basis of its consistency with evidence of whom the decedent wanted to benefit rather than evidence that the decedent intended the document to be a will.

---

48. *See* John H. Langbein, Excusing Harmless Errors in the Execution of Wills: A Report on Australia's Tranquil Revolution in Probate Law, 87 Colum. L. Rev. 1 (1987).

49. Id. at 52-54.

Nonetheless, Lester, too, came away from her study of the more recent Australian cases persuaded that the harmless error rule better addressed the problem of innocuous execution defects than the substantial compliance doctrine.[50]

A dispensing power to excuse harmless errors has been enacted in the other Australian states, most Canadian states, New Zealand, South Africa, and in Israel, where it is accompanied by commentary that it is a *mitzvah*[51] to carry out the wishes of the decedent.[52]

NOTE

Abolish Attestation? In his 1987 study, Langbein found that in every South Australian case involving an attestation defect, the will was admitted to probate, a finding largely replicated by Lester in her 2007 study. If in almost every case attestation defects are going to be excused, why not categorically abolish the attestation requirement (a *rule*) rather than apply the harmless error rule on a case-by-case basis (a *standard*)?[53]

h. The Harmless Error Rule

A version of the harmless error rule, which is codified by UPC § 2-503 (1990, rev. 1997) and is endorsed by the Restatement (Third) of Property,[54] has been adopted by statute in eleven states: California, Colorado, Hawaii, Michigan, Montana, New Jersey,[55] Ohio, Oregon, South Dakota, Utah, and Virginia.[56]

---

50. *See* Stephanie Lester, Admitting Defective Wills to Probate, Twenty Years Later: New Evidence for the Adoption of the Harmless Error Rule, 42 Real Prop. Prob. & Tr. J. 577 (2007); *but see* John V. Orth, Wills Act Formalities: How Much Compliance Is Enough?, 43 Real Prop. Tr. & Est. L.J. 73 (2008) (taking issue with Lester's methods and opposing the harmless error rule).

51. The term *mitzvah* resists straightforward English translation, but the basic idea is a mix of commandment and good deed.

52. Succession Law, 5725-1965, § 25, 1964-65, (Isr.). In 2004, Section 25 was amended to allow probate of a defective will only if the will has "the basic elements" and the court "has no doubt that it reflects the testator's free and true wish[es]." Id. (as amended) (Aryeh Greenfield trans., 4th ed. 2005). The "basic elements" include a writing brought before two witnesses. Id. § 25(b)(2). The revised Israeli statute is thus "a Harmless Error Rule with threshold requirements." Samuel Flaks, Excusing Harmless Error in Will Execution: The Israeli Experience, 3 Est. Plan. & Community Prop. L.J. 27, 27 (2010).

53. *See* James Lindgren, Abolishing the Attestation Requirement for Wills, 68 N.C. L. Rev. 541 (1990); Daniel B. Kelly, Toward Economic Analysis of the Uniform Probate Code, 45 U. Mich. J.L. Reform 855 (2012).

54. *See* Restatement (Third) of Property: Wills and Other Donative Transfers § 3.3 (Am. Law Inst. 1999).

55. *New Jersey*, did you say? Adoption of the harmless error rule by New Jersey supersedes its case law on substantial compliance, including *Ranney* and *Ferree*.

56. In California and Ohio, the harmless error rule is limited to attestation errors. Cal. Prob. Code § 6110(c)(2) (2016); Ohio Rev. Code Ann. § 2107.24 (2016); *see also* Peter T. Wendel, California Probate Code Section 6110(c)(2): How Big Is the Hole in the Dike?, 41 Sw. L. Rev. 387 (2012). In Colorado and Virginia, the harmless error rule excludes signature errors other than switched will cases or, in Virginia, a signature on a self-proving affidavit instead of the will. Colo. Rev. Stat. § 15-11-503 (2016); Va. Code Ann. § 64.2-404 (2016).

Harmless Error Rule (2016)   Figure 3.2

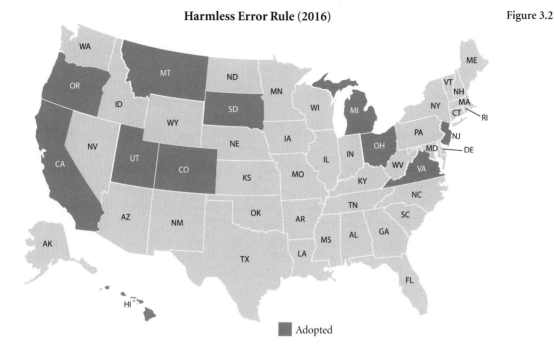

Adopted

Uniform Probate Code (Unif. Law Comm'n 1990, as amended 1997)

§ 2-503. Harmless Error

Although a document or writing added upon a document was not executed in compliance with Section 2-502, the document or writing is treated as if it had been executed in compliance with that section if the proponent of the document or writing establishes by clear and convincing evidence that the decedent intended the document or writing to constitute

(1) the decedent's will,

(2) a partial or complete revocation of the will,

(3) an addition to or an alteration of the will, or

(4) a partial or complete revival of his [or her] formerly revoked will or of a formerly revoked portion of the will.

Comment

By way of dispensing power, this new section allows the probate court to excuse a harmless error in complying with the formal requirements for executing or revoking a will. . . .

By placing the burden of proof upon the proponent of a defective instrument, and by requiring the proponent to discharge that burden by clear and convincing evidence (which courts at the trial and appellate levels are urged to police with rigor), Section 2-503 imposes procedural standards appropriate to the seriousness of the issue. . . .

The larger the departure from Section 2-502 formality, the harder it will be to satisfy the court that the instrument reflects the testator's intent. . . .

Section 2-503 means to retain the intent-serving benefits of Section 2-502 formality without inflicting intent-defeating outcomes in cases of harmless error.

NOTE

Litigation Incentives. How might the harmless error rule affect the frequency or scope of litigation over the validity of wills? On the one hand, the rule welcomes petitions to probate instruments that do not satisfy the Wills Act but for which there is strong evidence of testamentary intent. On the other hand, the rule might suppress or at least simplify some cases by softening the consequences of an innocuous execution defect. If the harmless error rule had been applicable in *Casdorph* (page 149), for example, would the will in that case have been challenged? If so, would not the resolution have been simpler given the abundant evidence of the testamentary intent?[57]

Even if the harmless error rule prompts litigation that might not otherwise have been brought, might the costs of those cases be worthwhile if they further the policy of freedom of disposition? If the rule eliminates some false negatives without appreciably increasing false positives, would not this reduction in error costs justify some increase in decision costs? The drafters of UPC § 2-503 exhorted courts to "police with rigor" the requirement of clear and convincing evidence. Will this heightened standard of proof limit decision costs by suppressing weak cases or at least allowing for expeditious dismissal of them?[58]

Let us consider a sampling of the emerging case law under the harmless error rule.

In re Estate of Hall
51 P.3d 1134 (Mont. 2002)

REGNIER, J. . . . James Mylen Hall ("Jim") died on October 23, 1998. At the time of his death, he was 75 years old and lived in Cascade County, Montana. His wife, Betty Lou Hall ("Betty"), and two daughters from a previous marriage, Sandra Kay Ault ("Sandra") and Charlotte Rae Hall ("Charlotte"), survived him.

---

57. *See* UPC § 2-503 cmt. (reporting suppression of litigation as the Israeli experience); *see also* In re Estate of Harless, 310 P.3d 550 (Mont. 2013) (avoiding dispute over validity of purported signature because clear and convincing evidence showed intent to make a will).

There is no before-and-after empirical study of probate filings in a jurisdiction that has adopted the harmless error rule. California adopted a modified version of the rule during the time period of Professor David Horton's study of probate filings in Alameda, California, for decedents dying in 2007. At the time of the rule's effectiveness, about half of the estates in his sample remained open, but in none did a party try to invoke the rule. *See* David Horton, Wills Law on the Ground, 62 UCLA L. Rev. 1094, 1139 (2015).

58. *Compare* Jane B. Baron, Irresolute Testators, Clear and Convincing Wills Law, 73 Wash. & Lee L. Rev. 3 (2016), *with* Mark Glover, In Defense of the Harmless Error Rule's Clear and Convincing Evidence Standard: A Response to Professor Baron, 73 Wash. & Lee L. Rev. Online 289 (2016); *see also* Katheleen R. Guzman, Intents and Purposes, 60 U. Kan. L. Rev. 305 (2011); Emily Sherwin, Clear and Convincing Evidence of Testamentary Intent: The Search for a Compromise Between Formality and Adjudicative Justice, 34 Conn. L. Rev. 453 (2002).

Jim first executed a will on April 18, 1984 (the "Original Will"). Approximately thirteen years later, Jim and Betty's attorney, Ross Cannon, transmitted to them a draft of a joint will (the "Joint Will").[59] On June 4, 1997, Jim and Betty met at Cannon's office to discuss the draft. After making several changes, Jim and Betty apparently agreed on the terms of the Joint Will. Jim and Betty were prepared to execute the Joint Will once Cannon sent them a final version.

At the conclusion of the meeting, however, Jim asked Cannon if the draft could stand as a will until Cannon sent them a final version. Cannon said that it would be valid if Jim and Betty executed the draft and he notarized it. Betty testified that no one else was in the office at the time to serve as an attesting witness. Jim and Betty, therefore, proceeded to sign the Joint Will and Cannon notarized it without anyone else present.

When they returned home from the meeting, Jim apparently told Betty to tear up the Original Will, which Betty did. After Jim's death, Betty applied to informally probate the Joint Will. Sandra objected to the informal probate and requested formal probate of the Original Will.

On August 9, 2001, Judge McKittrick heard the will contest. He issued the Order admitting the Joint Will to probate on August 27, 2001. Sandra appealed. . . .

In contested cases, the proponent of a will must establish that the testator duly executed the will. See Mont. Code Ann. (MCA) § 72-3-310. For a will to be valid, two people typically must witness the testator signing the will and then sign the will themselves. See MCA § 72-2-522(1)(c) [based on UPC § 2-502 (1990)[60]]. If two individuals do not properly witness the document, MCA § 72-2-523 [based on UPC § 2-503] provides that the document may still be treated as if it had been executed [properly] . . . if the proponent of the document establishes by clear and convincing evidence that the decedent intended the document to be the decedent's will.

Sandra urges this Court not to use MCA § 72-2-523 "to circumvent the statute requiring two witnesses to the execution of a will." Jim and Betty's failure to use witnesses, according to Sandra, was not an innocent omission on their part. . . . She primarily argues . . . that the Joint Will should be invalid as a matter of law because no one properly witnessed it.

Sandra's numerous arguments about why the will was improperly witnessed are irrelevant to this appeal. Neither party disputes that no witnesses were present at the execution of Jim and Betty's Joint Will as required by MCA § 72-2-522. In the absence of attesting witnesses, MCA § 72-2-523 affords a means of validating a will for which the Montana Legislature expressly provides. The only question before this Court, therefore, is whether the District Court erred in concluding that Jim intended the Joint Will to be his will under MCA § 72-2-523. We conclude that the court did not err.

The District Court made several findings of fact that supported its conclusion. In particular, it noted that the Joint Will specifically revoked all previous wills and codicils

---

59. A joint will is one instrument executed by two persons as the will of both — one will for two people (see page 257). — Eds.

60. That is, UPC § 2-502 before the addition in 2008 of the provision that validates notarization as an alternative to attestation (see page 197). — Eds.

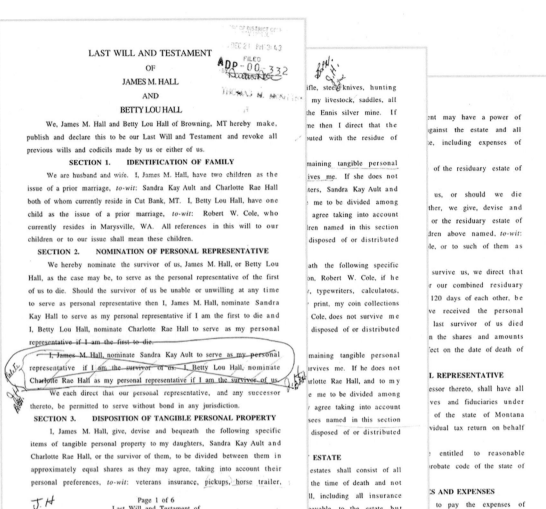

The first three pages of the
unattested joint will in *Hall*

made by either Jim or Betty. Furthermore, the court found that, after they had executed the Joint Will, Jim directed Betty to destroy the Original Will.

Sandra does not dispute any of the court's factual findings. She argues only that Betty testified that she and Jim had not executed the will even after they had signed it. In making this argument, she points to the following testimony:

Question: Do you know if [Jim] gave [Sandra and Charlotte] a copy of the new will?
Answer: I don't believe he did, no.
Question: Do you know why?

property is part of our probate estates and whether or not such taxes are payable by our estates or by the recipient of any such property. Such taxes and expenses should be paid out of the residuary estat~ ~~~~~~~ apportionment.

SECTION 7.   REVOCATION AND AMENDMENT

During our joint lifetimes each of us agree not to revoke this will, or any provision thereof, without the consent of the o~~~~ Upon the death of the first of us the survivor of us agrees to not revoke or amend this will.

IN WITNESS WHEREOF, we hereby subscribe our name instrument this _____ day of _____ , 1997 at County of Glacier, State of Montana.

James M. Hall   _Betty Lou Hall_
Testator   Testator

The foregoing instrument, consisting of _____ pages of wh the last, was on the _____ day of _____ , 199 and published by James M. Hall, and Betty Lou Hall, the test declared by the testators to be their Last Will and Testame presence of each of us, who, at the testators' req presence, and in the presence of each other now witnesses.

Signature of witness   Name and address of w

Signature of witness   Name and address of w

No witness signatures below the attestation clause

No witness signatures on notarized self-proving affidavit

Page 4 of 6
Last Will and Testament of
James M. Hall and Betty Lou Hall

STATE OF MONTANA   )
                   .ss
COUNTY OF GLACIER)

We, James M. Hall and Betty Lou Hall, _____ and _____, the testators and the witnesses, respectively, whose names are signed to the attached or foregoing instrument, being first duly sworn, do hereby declare to the undersigned authority that the testators signed and executed the instrument as their last will and that they had signed willingly, and that they executed it as their free and voluntary act for the purposes therein expressed; and that each of the witnesses, in the presence and hearing of the testators, signed the will as witness and that to the best of his or her knowledge each of the testators was at the time 18 or more years of age, of sound mind and ~~~~~ constraint or undue influence.

James M. Hall
Testator
Betty Lou Hall
Testator

_____
Witness

_____
Witness

Subscribed, sworn to and acknowledged before me by James M. Hall and Betty Lou Hall, the testators, and subscribed and sworn to before me by _____ and _____ witnesses, this 4 day of Jun , 1997.

(S E A L)
Notary Public for the State of Montana
Residing at: _____
My Commission expires: 12/5/9

Page 5 of 6
Last Will and Testament of
James M. Hall and Betty Lou Hall

The last two pages of the unattested joint will in *Hall*

Answer: Well, I guess because we didn't have the completed draft without all the scribbles on it.

Question: So he thought that will was not good yet?

Answer: No, he was sure it was good, but he didn't give it to the girls. And we didn't give it to my son. We didn't give it to anybody.

Question: Why?

Answer: Because it wasn't completely finished the way Ross was going to finish it.

This testimony may suggest that Betty believed that the Joint Will was not in a final form because of "all the scribbles on it." Nevertheless, she immediately goes on to state that she believed the will was good. When asked if it were Jim's and her intent for the Joint Will to stand as a will until they executed another one, she responded, "Yes, it was." The court could reasonably interpret this testimony to mean that Jim and Betty expected the Joint Will to stand as a will until Cannon provided one in a cleaner, more final form. Sandra points to no other evidence that suggests that Jim did not intend for the Joint Will to be his will.

For these reasons, we conclude that the District Court did not err in admitting the Joint Will into final probate. Because Jim directed Betty to destroy the Original Will, we also conclude that the District Court did not err in finding that these acts were acts of revocation of the Original Will under MCA § 72-2-527.

Affirmed.

NOTES

1. Clear and Convincing Evidence.   What was the clear and convincing evidence that Jim intended the "scribbled" document to be his will? Was Betty's testimony necessary to the outcome? Consider again the execution defects in *Groffman* (page 147), *Casdorph* (page 149), *Pavlinko* (page 163), and *Ferree* (page 172). Was there clear and convincing evidence of testamentary intent in those cases?

In In re Estate of Sky Dancer, 13 P.3d 1231 (Colo. App. 2000), *T* was found dead of gunshot wounds. The police discovered a four-page, typewritten instrument dated September 10, 1997, which was entitled "Last Will and Testament." However, the instrument "contained incomplete portions," and "the end of the testamentary text was followed by a large segment of blank page." There was no signature by *T* or any witnesses on the instrument. Instead, stapled to it were two additional pages, entitled "affidavit" and dated April 8, 1996, with *T*'s signature and the signatures of two witnesses. The court denied probate:

> Here, the "Will," or at least the dispositive portion of it, cannot be attributed to the decedent. It was not written by her in her own hand, it was not signed by her, and there is no evidence that she represented it to anyone, either orally or in writing, as her will. And, while there is no affirmative evidence to support the proposition here, the "Will" does not foreclose the possibility that some other person prepared or assembled the dispositive provisions of it.

2. Malpractice Not to Aim for Harmless Error in Exigent Circumstances?   Suppose you and a gravely ill client have marked up a draft will. You plan to meet again to execute a clean version at a later date. But you have doubts about whether the client will live until then. If there are no other witnesses available, but you are in a state that has adopted the harmless error rule, should you advise the client to sign the marked up draft, and should you sign it too, so that the draft perhaps could be admitted to probate under the harmless error rule if your client were to die before your next meeting? *See* Fischer v. Howe [2013] NSWLR 67 (Austl.).

3. Writing, Signature, and Attestation.   *Hall* is authority for the proposition that the harmless error rule may be invoked to excuse a defect in *attestation*. The Restatement (Third) of Property agrees: "Because attestation makes a more modest contribution to the purpose of the formalities, defects in compliance with attestation procedures are more easily excused."[61] But what about a defect in *signature*? Or what about a will that is not in *writing*? Let us take up each of these questions in turn.

In re Probate of Will and Codicil of Macool
3 A.3d 1258 (N.J. App. Div. 2010)

FUENTES, J. In his opening remarks before the trial court, plaintiff's counsel characterized this case as one that "challenges the chancellor." We agree. The facts underlying this case are so uniquely challenging that they have the feel of an academic exercise, designed by a law professor to test the limits of a student's understanding of probate law. But this case is not, of course, a mere didactic exercise. . . .

I

As correctly found by the trial court, the salient facts of this case are undisputed. Louise and Elmer Macool were married for forty years; this was, for both, their second marriage. Although they did not have biological children together, Louise raised Elmer's seven children from his prior marriage as if they were her own. These children are defendants Muriel Carolfi and Michael Macool, as well as James Macool, William Macool, Helen Wilson, Isabel Macool, and Mary Ann McCart. In addition to her seven step-children, Louise also had a very close relationship with her niece, plaintiff Mary Rescigno, whose mother died in childbirth.

Attorney Kenneth Calloway drafted wills for both Elmer and Louise Macool. On September 13, 1995, Louise executed a will naming her husband Elmer as the sole beneficiary of her entire estate, and also naming her seven step-children, step-granddaughter Theresa Stefanowicz, and step-great-grandson Alexander Stefanowicz as contingent beneficiaries. Elmer Macool was named as executor of her estate, and her stepsons James and Michael Macool were named as contingent co-executors.

On May 23, 2007, Louise executed a codicil to her will naming her stepchildren Muriel Carolfi and Michael Macool as contingent co-executors. Calloway drafted and witnessed both the September 13, 1995 will and the May 23, 2007 codicil.

Elmer Macool died on April 26, 2008. Less than a month later, on May 21, 2008, Louise went to Calloway's law office with the intent of changing her will. Toward that end, she gave Calloway a handwritten note that read as follows:

> get the same as the family *Macool gets*
> Niece
> Mary Rescigno [indicating address] If any thing happen[s] to Mary Rescigno[,] her share goes to he[r] daughter Angela Rescigno. If anything happen[s] to her it goes to her 2 children. 1. Nikos Stylon 2. Jade Stylon
> Niece + Godchild LeNora Distasio [indicating address] if anything happe[ns] to [her] it goes back in the pot

---

61. Restatement (Third) of Property: Wills and Other Donative Transfers § 3.3 cmt. b (Am. Law Inst. 1999).

I [would] like to have the house to be left in the family Macool.
I [would] like to have.
1. Mike Macool [indicating address]
2. Merle Caroffi [indicating address]
3. Bill Macool [indicating address]
Take

According to Calloway, after discussing the matter with Louise and using her hand-written notes as a guide, he "dictated the entire will while she was there." Either later that afternoon or the next morning, Calloway's secretary typed a draft version of Louise's will, with the word "Rough" handwritten on the top left corner of the document. When asked to explain what the word "rough" meant in this context, Calloway indicated:

> I mean [ ] it was the rough will. It had not been reviewed by me to make changes if I deemed any changes had to be made from what I believed I dictated. And I had reviewed it but I never got a chance to even tell my secretary to do it up and let's move.

Louise Macool's handwritten note

Bough

EXHIBIT NO. 7
(#).11.25-0
CSR ASSOCIATES

LAST WILL AND TESTAMENT

I, LOUISE R. MACOLL, of 123 E. Walnut Avenue, City of North Wildwood, County of Cape May and State of New Jersey, being of sound and disposing mind, memory and understanding, and fully aware of the natural objects of my bounty, do hereby make, publish and declare the following as and for my Last Will and Testament.

FIRST: I hereby revoke any and all former Wills and Codicils heretofore made by me at any time.

SECOND: I direct that my representative hereinafter named, pay out of my estate all of my just debts and funeral expenses as soon as may be convenient after my demise.

THIRD: All of the rest, residue and remainder of my estate of whatsoever the same may consist and wheresoever the same may be situate, I give, devise and bequeath in equal shares and share alike amongst the following individuals. My stepchildren, JAMES THOMAS MACOOL, MICHAEL MACOOL, MARY ANN McCART, WILLIAM MICHAEL MACOOL, MURIEL CAROFFI, HELEN WILSON, and ISABEL MACOOL, and to my step grandchildren, THERESA ANN DAILY and ALEXANDER SCHMIDT, and my niece, MARY RESCIGNO and my niece's godchild LENORA DISTASIO. Should MARY RESCIGNO predecease me or not be living ten (10) full days after my demise, then in that event, her share shall pass unto her daughter ANGELO RESCIGNO. If LENORA DISTASIO predeceases me then her respective shall lapse and be divided amongst the surviving heirs stated herein. If any other of the stepchildren or heirs predeceases me then their respective share shall lapse and be divided amongst the surviving heirs set forth herein. Should I still own my home located in North Wildwood, New Jersey at the time of my demise then I request that my three stepchildren, MICHAEL MACOOL, MERLE CAROFFI, and WILLIAM

[partial second page]

try to keep the home in the
rs wish to have their interest
to have the home appraised
te. I would hope that all the
opportunity to use the home

point MERLE CAROFFI and
my Last Will and Testament,
authority to dispose and sell
may die, seized or possessed
t public or private sale, and
em in the best interest of my
ces in the law therefore; and
of said Co- Executors for the
risdiction.

e taxes, assessed against my
ner, be paid out of my estate,
to seek recovery from any
iciary under policies of life
any estate or inheritance tax,
ities.

my name to this instrument
rn, do hereby declare to the
instrument as my Last Will;

that I sign it willingly; that I execute it as my free and voluntary act for the purposes therein expressed; and that I am 18 years of age or older, of sound mind, and under no constraint or undue influence.

_____
LOUISE R. MACOOL

Unsigned by the testator

[partial third page]

t and being duly sworn, do
t the Testatrix signed and
she signed it willingly; that
tatrix, hereby signs this Will
and that to the best of our
sound mind and under no

_____

WLEDGED before me by,
and sworn to before me by
_____, and _____ the witnesses, this _____ day of May, 2008.

_____

Unsigned "rough" draft of Louise Macool's new will

The draft will names as residuary beneficiaries Louise's nieces Mary Rescigno and Lenora Distasio, as well as all of her step-children, Theresa Stefanowicz, and Alexander Stefanowicz. Although the draft will substantially reflects Louise's handwritten notes, it does not provide a statement naming Angela Rescigno's two children as contingent beneficiaries of Rescigno's share of the estate. In addition, the draft makes only an oblique reference to the provision in the handwritten document to keep the house "in the family Macool," stating that "Michael Macool, Merle Caroffi, and William Macool be responsible to maintain . . . and to *try* to keep the home in the family *as long as possible.*" (Emphasis added.)

Louise left Calloway's office with the intention of having lunch nearby. Calloway expected her to make an appointment to review the draft will sometime after he had reviewed it. Sadly, Louise died approximately one hour after her meeting with Calloway. She thus never had the opportunity to see the draft will.

II

This matter came before the trial court as an action filed by plaintiff Mary Rescigno seeking to invalidate decedent's 1995 will and 2007 codicil, [and to] admit into probate the 2008 draft will that decedent neither read nor signed before her death. . . .

The trial court issued a comprehensive oral decision rejecting plaintiff's argument that the 2008 draft will met the requirements of N.J.S.A. 3B:3-3 [based on UPC § 2-503]. As a threshold issue, the court found that plaintiff had established, by clear and convincing evidence, "that as of the moment Ms. Macool met with Mr. Calloway it was her intention to have her testamentary plan altered to include Ms. Rescigno and Ms. Distasio." However, the court found insufficient evidence from which to conclude that decedent intended the particular draft document that Calloway prepared to be her will. Although this ruling conclusively disposed of plaintiff's claims, the court nevertheless construed N.J.S.A. 3B:3-3 "as requiring that any document which is going to be treated as a will based on the provisions of those statutes had to have been executed or signed in some fashion by the testator."

III

. . . [Plaintiff argues] that under N.J.S.A. 3B:3-3, the draft will should be admitted because there is clear and convincing evidence that decedent intended this document to constitute her will, or alternatively, a partial revocation of her prior will. In addressing this argument, we distinguish between evidence showing decedent's general disposition to alter her testamentary plans and evidence establishing, by clear and convincing evidence, that decedent intended the draft will prepared by Calloway to constitute her binding and final will.

In this respect, we agree with the trial court that the record clearly and convincingly shows that decedent intended to alter her testamentary plan to include Rescigno and Distasio when she met with Calloway in 2008. Decedent's handwritten notes, Calloway's testimony, and the draft will itself all support this finding. The court found, however, that plaintiff failed to establish, by clear and convincing evidence, that decedent intended the document denoted by Calloway as a "rough" draft to be her last and binding will. We agree.

Decedent's untimely demise prevented her from reading the draft will prepared by her attorney. She never had the opportunity to confer with counsel after reviewing the document to clear up any ambiguity, modify any provision, or express her final assent to this "rough" draft. Indeed, Calloway testified that although decedent's handwritten notes named Angela Rescigno's two children as contingent beneficiaries, he intentionally did not include them in the draft will because it was his practice to exclude "a third generation unless she told me that the first two were very old."

The trial court treated this omission as a minor discrepancy. We view it as evidence that this document was a work in progress, subject to reasonable revisions and fine tuning. Calloway's customary procedure or "practice" notwithstanding, decedent's notes clearly indicate that she wanted these two children specifically named as contingent beneficiaries. We have no way of knowing whether decedent would have approved of Calloway's approach or insisted that her wishes be strictly followed.

We reach a similar conclusion with respect to Calloway's attempt to include in the draft will two items specifically mentioned in decedent's notes: a provision keeping decedent's house "in the family Macool"; and a provision referencing Mike Macool, Muriel Carolfi (or "Merle Carofi," as written) and Bill Macool. We recognize that decedent's intentions with respect to these two items are unclear. It is precisely this lack of clarity that renders their inclusion in the draft will problematic. We do not know what practical arrangement or ownership concept decedent envisioned to keep the house "in the family Macool." Although the will drafted by Calloway reflects one possible interpretation of decedent's otherwise cryptic and ambiguous reference, we cannot conclude, with any degree of reasonable certainty, that this approach would have met with decedent's approval. Nor do we know whether she intended that the three named individuals receive a particular bequest. Her untimely death deprives us of any reasonably reliable means of determining decedent's testamentary intent as to these two items and whether she would have viewed their inclusion in the draft will as written as acceptable.

We hold that for a writing to be admitted into probate as a will under N.J.S.A. 3B:3-3, the proponent of the writing intended to constitute such a will must prove, by clear and convincing evidence, that: (1) the decedent actually reviewed the document in question; and (2) thereafter gave his or her final assent to it. Absent either one of these two elements, a trier of fact can only speculate as to whether the proposed writing accurately reflects the decedent's final testamentary wishes.

Although this holding effectively disposes of plaintiff's case, in the interest of completeness we will address the trial court's ruling requiring that a writing offered under N.J.S.A. 3B:3-3 be signed by the testator. Here . . . we are confronted with a dearth of case law authority. . . .

[W]e turn to the words chosen by the Legislature when it amended N.J.S.A. 3B:3-3:

> Although *a document* or writing added upon a document was *not executed in compliance with* N.J.S.A. 3B:3-2, the document or writing *is treated as if it had been executed in compliance with* N.J.S.A. 3B:3-2 *if the proponent of the document* or writing *establishes by clear and convincing evidence that the decedent intended the document or writing to constitute: (1) the decedent's will;* (2) a partial or complete revocation of the will; (3) an addition to or an alteration of the will; or (4) a partial or complete revival of his formerly revoked will or of a formerly revoked portion of the will. (Emphasis added.)

Applying the words and phrases emphasized to the facts of this case, we can reach the following result: plaintiff offered the draft will as a document "not executed in compliance with the N.J.S.A. 3B:3-2." . . . [That section, based on UPC § 2-502,] describes the requirements for two types of wills: the traditional [attested] will, N.J.S.A. 3B:3-2a [UPC § 2-502(a)], and that previously referred to as a holographic will, N.J.S.A. 3B:3-2b [UPC § 2-502(b)]. Both of these statutorily sanctioned forms of wills share one common requirement: the writing in question must be signed by the testator.

N.J.S.A. 3B:3-3 addresses a form of testamentary document that "was not *executed* in compliance with N.J.S.A. 3B:3-2." (Emphasis added.) In this context, the term "executed" is not synonymous with "signed." A will "executed" in compliance with the requirements of N.J.S.A. 3:3-2a means a will prepared in accordance with the dictates of the statute. . . .

N.J.S.A. 3B:3-2b has equally strict requirements for the admission to probate of a holographic will. In such a writing, all the material testamentary provisions must be in the testator's handwriting and the writing must be signed by the testator.

Against this backdrop, we are satisfied that a writing offered under N.J.S.A. 3B:3-3 need not be signed by the testator in order to be admitted to probate. To hold otherwise would render the relaxation available in N.J.S.A. 3B:3-3 inapplicable to N.J.S.A. 3B:3-2b. Stated differently, because the essence of a holographic will is that it must be in the testator's handwriting, the only conceivable relief offered by N.J.S.A. 3B:3-3 to this form of will must be that it need not be signed by the testator. . . .

A variation of the facts presented here offers a compelling case for construing N.J.S.A. 3B:3-3 as not requiring the testator's signature. Had decedent been able to read the draft will prepared by Calloway and thereafter express her assent to its content in the presence of witnesses or by any other reasonably reliable means, the trial court's misgivings concerning the absence of her signature would have been seen as needlessly formalistic and against the remedial purpose that animates N.J.S.A. 3B:3-3. . . .

IV

. . . By way of summary, we affirm the trial court's ruling denying plaintiff's application to probate a draft will that was never read by decedent Louise Macool. To be admitted into probate under N.J.S.A. 3B:3-3, the proponent of a writing intended to constitute the testator's will must prove, by clear and convincing evidence, that: (1) the decedent actually reviewed the document in question; and (2) thereafter expressed his or her final assent to it. We further affirm the trial court's decision to grant plaintiff's application for counsel fees but remand for the court to reconsider the amount of the award.

NOTES

1. Probating an Unsigned Instrument.   In suggesting that an unsigned instrument could be probated under the harmless error rule, *Macool* is in accord with the Restatement (Third) of Property:

> Among the defects in execution that can be excused, the lack of a signature is the hardest to excuse. An unsigned will raises a serious but not insuperable doubt about whether the testator adopted the document as his or her will. A particularly

attractive case for excusing the lack of the testator's signature is a crossed will case, in which, by mistake, a wife signs her husband's will and the husband signs his wife's will.[62]

Professor Theodore W. Dwight

Yet the court in *Macool* refused to probate the "rough" instrument before it. The court distinguished evidence of Mrs. Macool's intended dispositions from evidence that she intended the unsigned draft itself to be her will. Is this distinction meaningful in view of the language of UPC § 2-503, page 177? The court required the proponent to prove by clear and convincing evidence that the decedent in fact reviewed the instrument and thereafter assented to it. Is this a fair reading of the statute?

Suppose Mrs. Macool reviewed and approved the draft but then died just before or while in the process of signing it. Would the will be entitled to probate? Such circumstances are not entirely fanciful:

> Theodore W. Dwight, the founder of the modern Columbia Law School[,] . . . neglected to make a will until he was near death. After giving instructions for the preparation of his will, he had the draft brought to his bedside on the morning of June 18, 1892. Witnesses were present as the will execution began. Professor Dwight had written "Theodore W. Dwi" and a part of the letter "g" when he suddenly fell back and died. . . . The harmless-error doctrine was not recognized at this time, and Dwight's will was not enforced.[63]

In In re Anton Jr., 2015 WL 6085394 (N.J. Ch. Oct. 6, 2015), the court admitted to probate under the harmless error rule an unsigned instrument that *T* had intended to sign but did not because he died the day before his appointment with his lawyer to do so. *T* had said that the lawyer "did exactly what I asked him to do" and that "this Will is perfect as written." What result without the harmless error rule? In Litevich v. Probate Court, District of West Haven, 2013 WL 2945055 (Conn. Super. May 17, 2013), the court denied probate to an unsigned instrument prepared by the decedent using legalzoom.com. The decedent had paid to have the document printed and mailed to her but then she died before having a chance to execute it.

2. Notes and Correspondence. What of Mrs. Macool's handwritten but unsigned notes? Can a person's notes or correspondence be probated under the harmless error rule? Suppose *T* sends a letter to his lawyer. The letter expresses a desire to revoke *T*'s current will and replace it with a new will leaving *T*'s entire estate to *A*. While the lawyer is preparing the will, *T* dies. Is the letter entitled to probate under the harmless error rule? *Compare* Restatement (Third) of Property: Wills and Other Donative Transfers

---

62. Id.
63. Id. § 3.3 illus. 2 reporter's notes.

§ 3.3 illus. 1 (Am. Law Inst. 1999), *and* In re Beebee's Estate, 258 P.2d 1101 (Cal. App. 1953), *with* In re Estate of Kuralt, page 210.

Mr. Meeson's Will

In the curious 1888 novel, Mr. Meeson's Will, by H. Rider Haggard, a will that had been tattooed on the back and shoulders of a woman, Miss Augusta Smithers, was admitted to probate. The testator, the witnesses, and Miss Smithers had been marooned on an island after a shipwreck that, in Haggard's telling, proved to be eerily predictive of the later *Titanic* disaster. Knowing that the testator would not survive until their rescue, Miss Smithers allowed the testator to tattoo his will on her back with a long white fishbone and cuttlefish ink.

In subsequent litigation over the validity of the will, the issue arose whether Miss Smithers, who was herself put into evidence as the will, could also give testimony:

> She presents such a conceptual problem that characters constantly refer to sections of the Wills Act for guidance. Her solicitor worries whether skin may count as paper and concludes "if carefully removed and dried, [it] would make excellent parchment"; it is, therefore, merely "parchment in its green state" and satisfies section 1 of the Act. The Defense insists throughout that Augusta is not a person but a document, which they deny "is entitled to speak in its own explanation" because "there is no precedent for a document giving evidence." Even the judge's more philosophical question — "but is the skin the whole person?" — leads him to contemplate various acts of dismemberment: what if the Plaintiff "had persuaded the witness to be

"Augusta turned her back to the Judge, in order that he might examine what was written on it."

> partially skinned," or what if there were a case in which a will had been tattooed on a leg that was subsequently "cut off and produced before the court, either in a flesh or a mummified condition?" He concludes that Augusta's personality has not been "so totally lost and merged in — her documentary capacity" that she should lose her right to testify.

Cathrine O. Frank, Of Testaments and Tattoos: The Wills Act of 1837 and Rider Haggard's Mr. Meeson's Will, 18 Law & Lit. 323, 334 (2006).

Writings, Documents, and Electronic or Digital Wills

In the usual case, the requirement of a *writing* is easily satisfied because the will is written or typed on paper. But a will need not be on paper. All that is required is a reasonably permanent record of the markings that make up the will.[64] Today new technologies are putting pressure on this test. Could an electronic will in the form of a smartphone or tablet image or a computer file qualify as a writing under the Wills Act? If not, could the image or file be probated under the harmless error rule?

---

64. *See* id. § 3.1 cmt. i.

An interesting wrinkle is that, unlike most Wills Act provisions, such as UPC § 2-502, page 144, which speak of a "writing," the harmless error rule of UPC § 2-503, page 177, speaks of "a *document* or a writing added upon a *document*."[65] Do the terms "document" and "writing" have different meanings? Or are they synonyms?

The text of UPC § 2-502(c), which refers to "[i]ntent that a *document* constitute the testator's will,"[66] implies that the drafters regarded the terms as synonyms. So does the comment to UPC § 2-503, which in explaining the requirement of "a *document* or a writing added upon a *document*,"[67] references foreign decisions that "have never excused noncompliance with the requirement that a will be in *writing*."[68] The Restatement (Third) of Property likewise treats the terms as synonyms. It takes the position that "a *writing* is so fundamental to the purpose of the execution formalities that it cannot be excused as harmless. . . . Only a harmless error in executing a *document* can be excused."[69]

In the next case, the court treated a digital image created on a tablet as a "writing" under the Wills Act and as a "document" under the harmless error rule.

In re Estate of Javier Castro
No. 2013ES00140 (Ohio C.P. June 19, 2013)
27 Quinnipiac Prob. L.J. 412 (2014)

WALTHER, J. This matter came before the Court upon the Application to Probate Will and Application for Authority to Administer Estate filed by Miguel Castro. . . .

In late December 2012, Javier Castro presented at Mercy Regional Medical Center in Lorain, Ohio. He was told by medical personnel that he would need a blood transfusion. For religious reasons, he declined to consent to the blood transfusion. He understood that failure to receive the blood transfusion would ultimately result in his death.

On December 30, 2012, Javier had a discussion with two of his brothers, Miguel Castro and Albie Castro, about preparing a will. Because they did not have any paper or pencil, Albie suggested that the will be written on his Samsung Galaxy tablet. The Court is aware that a "tablet" is a one-piece mobile computer. Tablets typically have a touchscreen, with finger or stylus pen gestures replacing the conventional computer mouse. Albie had owned the tablet for a couple of months prior to the date in question. Albie's Samsung Galaxy tablet has a program or application called "S Note" that allows someone to "write" on the tablet with the stylus pen. The program then allows the writing to be preserved or saved exactly as the person has written it.

Miguel and Albie both testified that Javier would say what he wanted in the will and Miguel would handwrite what Javier had said using the stylus. Miguel and Albie both testified that each section would be read back to Javier and that the whole document was also read back to Javier. Testimony was had that Javier, Miguel, and Albie

---

65. Emphasis added.
66. Emphasis added.
67. Emphasis added.
68. Emphasis added.
69. Restatement (Third) of Property: Wills and Other Donative Transfers § 3.3 cmt. b (Am. Law Inst. 1999) (first emphasis added, second emphasis in original).

The electronic will in *Castro*: page one (left), page two (right), and page three (middle).

had discussions concerning each and every paragraph in the will. Before he could sign the will, Javier was transported to the Cleveland Clinic in Cleveland, Ohio.

Miguel testified that later that same date, at the Cleveland Clinic, Javier signed the will on the tablet in his presence. Albie also testified that Javier signed the will in his presence. Oscar DeLeon, nephew of Javier, arrived shortly thereafter and became the third witness to the will. Oscar testified that he did not see Javier sign the will; rather, Javier acknowledged in his presence that he had signed the will on the tablet.

After the will was executed, Albie retained possession of the tablet that contained the will. Albie testified that the tablet is password protected and has been in his continuous possession since December 30, 2012. Miguel and Albie testified that the will has not been altered in any way since it was signed by Javier on December 30, 2012. Both testified that the paper copy of the will presented to the Court . . . is an exact duplicate of the will in the tablet that was prepared and signed on December 30, 2012. . . .

Dina Cristin Cintron, niece of Javier, testified that Javier told her that he had signed the will on the Samsung Galaxy tablet. Similar testimony was also received from Marelisa Leverknight and Steve Leverknight, who testified that Javier told them he had signed the will on the tablet and that it contained his wishes.

Javier died on January 30, 2013.

On February 11, 2013, the Application to Probate Will and Application for Authority to Administer Estate were filed by Miguel Castro. On that same date, Miguel also presented a copy of a will purported to be signed by Javier. The will consists of three pages. The first two pages indicate that the will is the last will and testament of Javier Castro and has eleven numbered paragraphs. The eleven numbered paragraphs contain the naming of Miguel as Executor, dispositions of Javier's property, and instructions to the Executor. . . .

The third page contains the signature of Javier Castro along with the signatures of Miguel, Albie, and Oscar.

If the will were to be declared invalid, Javier's estate would pass by intestate succession. . . . Javier had no lineal descendants. In this case, Benjamin Castro, Sr. and Maria Castro, Javier's father and mother, respectively, would inherit his estate. Benjamin Castro, Sr. and Maria Castro did not . . . contest the admittance of the will. . . . [They also said that] if the will were to be declared invalid, [they] would still distribute the assets according to Javier's wishes as stated in the will. . . .

Ohio Rev. Code Ann. Section 2107.03 provides the method for making a will. It states in part:

> Except oral wills, every will shall be in *writing*, but may be handwritten or typewritten. The will shall be *signed* at the end by the testator or by some other person in the testator's conscious presence and at the testator's express direction. The will shall be attested and subscribed in the conscious presence of the testator, by two or more competent witnesses, who saw the testator subscribe, or heard the testator acknowledge the testator's signature. Id. (emphasis added).

The questions for the Court are as follows:

1) Is this a "writing" and was the will "signed," and

2) Has sufficient evidence been presented that this is the last will and testament of Javier Castro.

Section 2107.03 requires only that the will be in "writing." It does not require that the writing be on any particular medium. Nowhere else in Chapter 21 is "writing" defined. Although not necessarily controlling, section 2913.01(F) is instructive on the definition of a "writing."[70] It provides:

> "Writing" means any computer software, document, letter, memorandum, note, paper, plate, data, film, or other thing having in or upon it any written, typewritten,

---

70. Section 2913.01(F) is part of the definitions section in the state's criminal code pertaining to theft and fraud. — Eds.

or printed matter, and any token, stamp, seal, credit card, badge, trademark, label, or other symbol of value, right, privilege, license, or identification.

If the Court were to apply this definition of a writing to section 2107.03, the document on the Samsung Galaxy tablet would qualify as a "writing." The writing in this case includes the stylus marks made on the tablet and saved by the application software. I believe that the document prepared on December 30, 2012, on Albie's Samsung Galaxy tablet constitutes a "writing" under section 2107.03. To rule otherwise would put restrictions on the meaning of "writing" that the General Assembly never stated.

The tablet application also captured the signature of Javier. The signature is a graphical image of Javier's handwritten signature that was stored by electronic means on the tablet. Similarly, I believe that this qualifies as Javier's signature under section 2107.03. Thus, the writing was "signed" at the end by Javier.

Evidence was presented by six witnesses that Javier had stated that the document he signed on the tablet expressed his wishes and that it was his last will and testament. Testimony was elicited from all six witnesses that Javier never subsequently expressed any desire or intention to revoke, amend, or cancel the will.

As stated above, section 2107.03 provides in part: "The will shall be attested and subscribed in the conscious presence of the testator, by two or more competent witnesses, who saw the testator subscribe, or heard the testator acknowledge the testator's signature." This will contained no attestation clause. Rather, it merely contained the signature of the three men who testified that they witnessed the will.

Ohio Rev. Code Ann. Section 2107.24 provides:

(A) If a document that is executed that purports to be a will is not executed in compliance with the requirements of section 2107.03 of the Revised Code, that document shall be treated as if it had been executed as a will in compliance with the requirements of that section if a probate court, after holding a hearing, finds that the proponent of the document as a purported will has established, by clear and convincing evidence, all of the following:

(1) The decedent prepared the document or caused the document to be prepared.

(2) The decedent signed the document and intended the document to constitute the decedent's will.

(3) The decedent signed the document under division (A)(2) of this section in the conscious presence of two or more witnesses. As used in division (A)(3) of this section, "conscious presence" means within the range of any of the witnesses' senses, excluding the sense of sight or sound that is sensed by telephonic, electronic, or other distant communication.

The Court finds by clear and convincing evidence that Javier signed the will, that he intended the document to be his last will and testament, and that the will was signed in the presence of two or more witnesses. Therefore, all three subsections of section 2017.24 have been proven. . . .

The Court finds that the document signed on December 30, 2012, on the Samsung Galaxy tablet is the last will and testament of Javier Castro and should be admitted to probate. . . .

It is so ordered.

NOTES

1. Strict Compliance or Harmless Error? The court concluded that Castro's tablet will was in writing, that he had signed it, and that three witnesses had signed it. However, because the will lacked an attestation clause, the court concluded that it was not properly attested. This interpretation of the attestation requirement was almost certainly wrong. Attestation is normally understood to mean that the witnesses must sign the will, thereby attesting to the testator's signature, but not also to require an attestation clause (see page 148). Given the court's findings that the tablet image was a writing, that the testator had signed it, and that three witnesses had also signed it, the tablet will was in strict compliance with the Wills Act as normally interpreted.

Because the court doubted attestation under the Wills Act, however, it resolved the case under the state's harmless error rule statute. Finding clear and convincing evidence that Castro intended the tablet image to be his will, the court admitted the image to probate. Is *Castro* thus an example of the harmless error rule simplifying litigation? Might the court have been influenced by the unanimity among Castro's survivors that the tablet will was authentic — that is, the absence of a party opposing probate?

By admitting the will to probate under the harmless error rule, did not the court implicitly hold that the tablet image qualified as a "document" under the state's harmless error rule statute? What other digital emanations could be probated as a "document" under this reasoning? What of an email to a friend that "in the event of my death, I give you all of my property"? What of a tweet or a Facebook post that said the same thing? Does the lack of a tangible physical medium, and the ad hoc and often improvised nature of, say, a tweet, undercut the evidentiary, channeling, cautionary or ritual, and protective functions? Instead of applying the harmless error rule to these cases, would it be preferable to design a set of Wills Act formalities for electronic wills? Or would it be better to look in each case for clear and convincing evidence of testamentary intent?

2. Scant Authority on Electronic Wills. There is scant authority on the validity of an electronic will. In In re Yu, [2013] QSC 322, an Australian court admitted to probate a will that the decedent had typed on his iPhone. The text of the file opened with the words, "This is the last Will and Testament of *T*." The text made a complete disposition of *T*'s property, named an executor, and included *T*'s name typed again "at the end of the document in a place where on a paper document a signature would appear." The court held that the requirement of a "document" under the harmless error rule statute was satisfied by "the record on the iPhone of the document."

In Rioux v. Coulombe (1996), 19 E.T.R. 2d 201 (Can. Que. Sup.), Jaqueline Rioux left a suicide note directing the police

> to an envelope which contained a computer diskette marked "this is my will/ Jaqueline Rioux/february 1, 1996." The information on the diskette, when later printed out, contained unsigned directions of a testamentary nature. The testatrix had noted in her diary that she had written her will on a computer. The diskette

itself contained only one file which had been saved to memory on the same day that the deceased had noted in her diary that she had made a will on computer.

The court probated the will under a substantial compliance statute requiring that the "essential" formalities be met.

More recently, a handful of Australian decisions reached conflicting results on whether to probate a Microsoft Word file that the decedent purportedly intended to be a will. *Compare* Estate of Currie, [2015] NSWSC 1098 (allowing probate of "my_will. doc"), *and* Yazbek v. Yazbek, [2012] NSWSC 594 (allowing probate of "will.doc"), *with* Mahlo v. Hehir, [2011] QSC 243 (denying probate to "This is the last will and testament of T.docx").[71]

In 2001, Nevada enacted a statute authorizing electronic wills, subject to certain strict requirements, including a single original and some way of determining if the original has been altered.[72] In an omitted portion of the *Castro* opinion, the court took notice of the Nevada statute, stating that if Castro's "will had been created in Nevada, it would have complied with state law."

3. A Uniform Electronic Wills Act?   As this book went to press in early 2017, the Uniform Law Commission was in the process of forming a drafting committee for an act on electronic wills. The committee will be charged with "draft[ing] a uniform act or model law addressing the formation, validity and recognition of electronic wills. The committee may seek expansion of its charge to address end-of-life planning documents such as advance medical directives or powers of attorney."

4. Revocation of an Electronic Will.   As we shall see later in this chapter, one manner of revoking a will is by the testator's physical act of mutilating, obliterating, or destroying it (see page 217). Would a testator's act of dragging "my_will.doc" to the "trash" icon on her computer qualify as a revocation by physical act? What if the testator destroyed her computer or tablet or thumb drive with the intent to revoke a digital will stored on that device?

5. Video or Audio Wills.   Suppose that Robert Reed video records his spoken will. Then he puts a DVD with the recording in a sealed envelope, on which he signs his name and writes: "To be played in the event of my death only!" Does the DVD comply with the requirement that the will be a signed writing? In In re Estate of Reed, 672 P.2d 829 (Wyo. 1983), dealing with a videotape, the court held No. But could the DVD

---

71. *See* David Horton, Tomorrow's Inheritance: The Frontiers of Estate Planning Formalism, 58 B.C. L. Rev. (forthcoming 2017) (discussing several Australian cases on digital wills).

72. Nev. Rev. Stat. § 133.085 (2016); *see also* Joseph Karl Grant, Shattering and Moving Beyond the Gutenberg Paradigm: The Dawn of the Electronic Will, 42 U. Mich. J.L. Reform 105 (2008); Scott S. Boddery, Electronic Wills: Drawing a Line in the Sand Against Their Validity, 47 Real. Prop. Tr. & Est. L.J. 197 (2012); Gerry W. Beyer & Claire G. Hargrove, Digital Wills: Has the Time Come for Wills to Join the Digital Revolution?, 33 Ohio N.U. L. Rev. 865 (2007).

qualify as a "document" under the harmless error rule? In Estate of Wai Fun Chan, [2015] NSWSC 1107, and Mellino v. Wnuk & Ors, [2013] QSC 336, courts in Australia said Yes.

2. Notarized Wills

As amended in 2008, UPC § 2-502(a)(3), page 144, provides that a will is valid if it is signed by two witnesses *or* if it is *notarized*.[73] Thus far, this provision has been adopted only in Colorado and North Dakota.

Lawrence W. Waggoner
The UPC Authorizes Notarized Wills
34 ACTEC L.J. 83 (2008)

The will-execution formalities are thought to serve several functions—evidentiary, cautionary (ceremonial), channeling, and protective. A notarized will would seem to serve all of these functions. . . . A notarized will would almost always be upheld under the UPC's harmless-error rule. . . .

The American notary does not serve the same function as the notary in the European civil-law countries. The civil-law notary supervises the execution of an "authenticated will," in which the notary is a quasi-judicial officer who determines whether the testator has mental capacity and is free of duress and undue influence. Compliance with the American execution formalities does no such thing: A validly executed will is still subject to contest on grounds of lack of capacity, undue influence, duress, fraud, or forgery.

Allowing notarization as an optional method of execution can benefit practice. Cases have begun to emerge in which the supervising attorney, with the client and all witnesses present, circulates one or more estate-planning documents for signature, and fails to notice that the client or, in the case of the will, one of the witnesses has unintentionally neglected to sign one of the documents. Such an omission often, but not always, arises when the attorney prepares multiple estate-planning documents—a will, a durable power of attorney, a health-care power of attorney, and perhaps a revocable trust. It is common practice, and sometimes required by state law, that the documents other than the will be notarized. It would reduce confusion and chance for error if all of the documents could be executed with the same formality.

For a variety of reasons, some individuals avoid professional advice and attempt to execute wills on their own. As long as it is clear that the decedent adopted the document as his or her will, the law has no reason to deny validity on the ground of defective execution. The harmless-error rule is one curative measure for this problem. Allowing notarization as an optional method of execution is another. The public is accustomed to thinking that a document is made "legal" by getting it notarized. To some, this conception is mistakenly but understandably carried over to executing a will. A testator who goes to the trouble of going to a bank or even a . . . photocopy [or express delivery] store to get a home-drawn will notarized shows as much of a deliberate purpose

---

73. *See* Anne-Marie Rhodes, Notarized Wills, 27 Quinnipiac Prob. L.J. 419 (2014).

to make the will final and valid as asking a couple of individuals to sign as witnesses. In effect, the UPC as amended treats the notary as the equivalent of two attesting witnesses. The case law invalidating a notarized will after death arises from the decedent's ignorance of the statutory requirements, not in response to evidence raising doubt that the will truly represents the decedent's wishes.

NOTE

Notarization or Acknowledgment.   Although generally described as a notarized will provision, by its terms UPC § 2-502(a)(3)(B) is broader. It validates a will that has been "acknowledged by the testator before a notary public *or other individual authorized by law to take acknowledgments*" (emphasis added). In many states, a lawyer is permitted to take an acknowledgment by virtue of being an officer of the court. In such a state, would this provision validate a will signed by a lawyer but neither notarized nor signed by a second witness?

3. Holographic Wills

In a little more than half of the states, holographic wills are permitted. A *holographic will* is written by the testator's hand and is signed by the testator; it need not be attested by witnesses.[74] Holographic wills are of Roman origin and are a familiar feature of

Figure 3.3

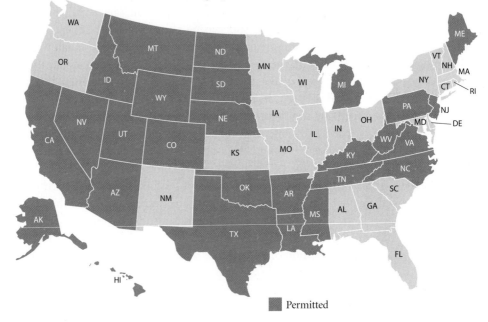

Holographic Wills (2016)

Permitted

---

74. Professor Elizabeth Carter of Louisiana State University calls to our attention that a holographic will is called an *olographic testament* in Louisiana. *See* La. Civ. Code Ann. art. 1575 (2016).

the civil law. They were introduced into this country by a 1751 Virginia statute and by the reception of the civil law into Louisiana. Holographs are authorized by UPC § 2-502(b), page 144.

a. Discerning Testamentary Intent

Ashbel G. Gulliver & Catherine J. Tilson
Classification of Gratuitous Transfers
51 Yale L.J. 1 (1941)

The exemption of holographic wills from the usual statutory requirements seems almost exclusively justifiable in terms of the evidentiary function. The requirement that a holographic will be entirely written in the handwriting of the testator furnishes more complete evidence for inspection by handwriting experts than would exist if only the signature were available, and consequently tends to preclude the probate of a forged document. . . . A holographic will is obtainable by compulsion as easily as a ransom note. While there is a certain ritual value in writing out the document, casual off-hand statements are frequently made in letters.[75]

In re Kimmel's Estate
123 A. 405 (Pa. 1924)

SIMPSON, J. One of decedent's heirs at law appeals from a decree of the orphans' court, directing the register of wills to probate the following letter:

> Johnstown, Dec. 12.
> The Kimmel Bro. and Famly
> We are all well as you can espec fore the time of the Year. I received you kind & welcome letter from Geo & Irvin all OK glad you poot your Pork down in Pickle it is the true way to keep meet every piece gets the same, now always poot it down that way & you will not miss it & you will have good pork fore smoking you can keep it from butchern to butchern the hole year round. Boys, I wont agree with you about the open winter I think we are gone to have one of the hardest. Plenty of snow & Verry cold verry cold! I dont want to see it this way but it will come see to the old sow & take her away when the time comes well I cant say if I will come over yet. I will wright in my next letter it may be to ruff we will see in the next letter if I come I have some very valuable papers I want you to keep fore me so if enny thing hapens all the scock money in the 3 Bank liberty lones Post office stamps and my home on Horner St goes to George Darl & Irvin Kepp this letter lock it up it may help you out. Earl sent after his Christmas Tree & Trimmings I sent them he is in the Post office in Phila working.
> Will clost your Truly,
> Father.

---

75. For a contemporary study of the phenomenon, see Deborah S. Gordon, Letters Non-Testamentary, 62 Kan. L. Rev. 586 (2014).—Eds.

"George[,] Darl & Irvin"?

Christie Phan, J.D. 2011, who came upon this case in Professor Joshua Tate's Fall 2010 trusts and estates course at SMU, was curious about the reference to "George Darl & Irvin." Should there have been a comma between George and Darl, representing two separate people? Earlier in the letter, the decedent addressed the recipients as his "Boys." But did he have other children, as implied by the appeal having been taken by one of his "heirs at law"?

To answer these questions, Phan reconstructed the family tree of the decedent, Harry A. Kimmel, from the relevant census records. She found that Harry, born in 1852 and evidently a "chair maker," was married to Sarah (b. 1854, d. 1912), and that in 1910 they had seven children: Oliver (b. 1879), Mary (b. 1879), Earl (b. 1885), Harry (b. 1887), George (b. 1889), Stephen Darl (b. 1894), and Irvin (b. 1896). So it appears that there should indeed have been a comma between George and Darl, and that George, Darl, and Irvin were the decedent's three youngest children—the only of his children who, as of 1920, a year before the decedent mailed the letter, were still living with the decedent. The appeal was taken by Oliver, the decedent's oldest child, who at the time was married with two children of his own (a later census shows Oliver with five children).

In 2009, the editors tried to obtain a copy of Kimmel's original letter from the probate court records. Alas, the original was lost soon after the trial court proceedings. All that we could find in the court records was a transcription of the letter and a pair of affidavits, one by the presiding judge and the other by the stenographer, stating that they could not find the original but that to the best of their knowledge they had accurately transcribed it.

This letter was mailed by decedent at Johnstown, Pa., on the morning of its date — Monday, December 12, 1921 — to two of his children, George and Irvin, who were named in it as beneficiaries; the envelope being addressed to them at their residence in Glencoe, Pa. He died suddenly on the afternoon of the same day.

Two questions are raised: First. Is the paper testamentary in character? Second. Is the signature to it a sufficient compliance with our Wills Act? Before answering them directly, there are a few principles, now well settled, which, perhaps, should be preliminarily stated.

While the informal character of a paper is an element in determining whether or not it was intended to be testamentary, this becomes a matter of no moment when it appears thereby that the decedent's purpose was to make a posthumous gift. On this point the court below well said: "Deeds, mortgages, letters, powers of attorney, agreements, checks, notes, etc., have all been held to be, in legal effect, wills. Hence, an assignment (Coulter v. Shelmadine, 53 A. 638 (Pa. 1902)), . . . a deed (Turner v. Scott, 51 Pa. 126 (1866)), a letter of instructions (Scott's Estate, 23 A. 212 (Pa. 1892)), a power of attorney (Rose v. Quick, 30 Pa. 225 (1858)), and an informal letter of requests (Knox's Estate, 18 A. 1021 (Pa. 1890)), were all held as wills."

It is equally clear that where, as here, the words "if enny thing hapens," condition the gift, they strongly support the idea of a testamentary intent; indeed they exactly state what is expressed in or must be implied from every will. True, if the particular contingency stated in a paper, as the condition upon which it shall become effective, has never in fact occurred, it will not be admitted to probate (Morrow's Appeal, 9 A. 660 (Pa. 1887); Forquer's Estate, 66 A. 92 (Pa. 1907)). In the present case, however, it is clear the contingency, "if enny thing hapens," was still existing when testator died suddenly on the same day he wrote and mailed the letter; hence, the facts not being disputed, the question of testamentary intent was one of law for the court (Davis' Estate, 118 A. 645 (Pa. 1922)).

As is often the case in holographic wills of an informal character, much of that which is written is not dispositive; and the difficulty, in ascertaining the writer's intent, arises largely from the fact that he had little, if any, knowledge of either law, punctuation, or grammar. In the present case this is apparent from the paper itself; and in this light the language now quoted must be construed:

> I think we are gone to have one of the hardest [winters]. Plenty of snow & Verry cold verry cold! I dont want to see it this way but it will come . . . well I cant say if I will come over yet. I will wright in my next letter it may be to ruff we will see in the next letter if I come I have some very valuable papers I want you to keep fore me so if enny thing hapens all . . . [the real and personal property specified] goes to George Darl and Irvin Kepp this letter lock it up it may help you out.

When resolved into plainer English, it is clear to us that all of the quotation, preceding the words "I have some very valuable papers," relate to the predicted bad weather, a doubt as to whether decedent will be able to go to Glencoe because of it, and a possible resolution of it in his next letter; the present one stating "we will see in the next letter if I come." This being so, the clause relating to the valuable papers begins a new subject of thought, and since the clearly dispositive gifts which follow are made dependent on no other contingency than "if enny thing hapens," and death did happen suddenly on the same day, the paper, so far as respects those gifts, must be treated as testamentary.

It is difficult to understand how the decedent, probably expecting an early demise—as appears by the letter itself, and the fact of his sickness and inability to work, during the last three days of the first or second week preceding—could have possibly meant anything else than a testamentary gift, when he said "so if enny thing hapens [the property specified] goes to George Darl and Irvin"; and why, if this was not intended to be effective in and of itself, he should have sent it to two of the distributees named in it, telling them to "Kepp this letter lock it up it may help you out."

The second question to be determined . . . [is whether] the word "Father," when taken in connection with the contents of the paper, show that it was "signed by him?" . . . If the word "Father" was intended as a completed signature to this particular character of paper, it answers all the purposes of the Wills Act. That it was so intended we have no doubt. It was the method employed by decedent in signing all such letters, and was mailed by him as a finished document. . . .

True, a formal will would not be so executed; but this is not a formal will. It is a letter, signed by him in the way he executed all such letters, and, from this circumstance, his "intent to execute is apparent" beyond all question.

Decree affirmed and appeal dismissed, the costs in this court to be paid by the estate of Harry A. Kimmel, deceased.

NOTES

1. Testamentary Intent? If you had asked Mr. Kimmel before he died whether his letter was a will, what would he have answered? Suppose instead you asked whether he meant for the letter to be evidence of his intended dispositions at death.[76] What would he have said? What of the instruction to the recipients to "Kepp this letter lock it up it may help you out"?[77]

Suppose *T* handwrites a letter to her friend, *A*, as follows: "*A*—If my assets are over \$750,000 at the time of my demise, I would like *B* to have \$50,000.00. It's not in the will but I trust you. That is my wish. Thanks, *T*. 12–7–12." Does this letter express testamentary intent? Is it entitled to probate as a holographic will? *See* In re Estate of McKagen, 90 Va. Cir. 118 (2015).

2. The Pros and Cons of Holographic Wills. Opponents of holographs argue that they are inartful and breed litigation, a conclusion based in part on appellate opinions.[78] But are the holographs described in appellate opinions fairly representative? Necessarily those are the holographs that spawned a contest and then an appeal.

In an intriguing study of the 145 holographic wills that were offered for probate during the years 1990 and 1995 in Allegheny County (Pittsburgh), Pennsylvania, Professor Stephen Clowney found that only 6 (4 percent) resulted in an objection or hearing of any kind.[79] On the other hand, in a more recent but much smaller sample of 32 holographs filed in Alameda County, California, for decedents who died in 2007, Professor David Horton found that 8 (25 percent) resulted in a litigated dispute (by contrast only 27 out of 300 attested wills resulted in litigation).[80] In both samples, many holographs lacked an executor or a residuary clause.[81] Nonetheless, Clowney concluded that

> holographs are an indispensable tool for testators who are either unwilling or unable to commission a traditional will. Homemade testaments provide a low-cost alternative to intestacy, improve the overall quantity of will-making, function as a safety-net for testators who fall suddenly ill, and rarely result in litigation. The triumph of holographic wills also suggests, strongly, that state legislatures should consider reducing the number of requirements necessary to create a formal, attorney-authored will. . . .
>
> The underlying truth is that scholars who base their opinion of holographs on a patchwork of humorous anecdotes and appellate level court decisions miss the rich diversity of testaments filed with the Register of Wills. The average person who chooses to execute a homemade will does not deserve to be lumped in with the occasional testator who is barely literate or takes the job less than seriously. The authors

---

76. *See* Mark Glover, A Taxonomy of Testamentary Intent, 23 Geo. Mason L. Rev. 569 (2016).

77. *See also* In re Morrison's Estate, 65 A.2d 384 (Pa. 1949) ("keep this it may be of use to you some day"); Blake's Estate v. Benza, 587 P.2d 271 (Ariz. App. 1978) ("SAVE THIS").

78. *See, e.g.*, Richard Lewis Brown, The Holograph Problem—The Case Against Holographic Wills, 74 Tenn. L. Rev. 93 (2006).

79. Stephen Clowney, In Their Own Hand: An Analysis of Holographic Wills and Homemade Willmaking, 43 Real Prop. Tr. & Est. L.J. 27, 59 (2008); *see also* Iris J. Goodwin, Access to Justice: What to Do About the Law of Wills, 2016 Wis. L. Rev. 947.

80. Horton, *supra* note 57, at 1134-35.

81. In Clowney's sample, 43 percent did not name an executor and 24 percent lacked a residuary clause. Clowney, *supra* note 79, at 47-49. In Horton's sample, 63 percent did not name an executor or did not include a residuary clause (Horton does not differentiate). Horton, *supra* note 57, at 1135.

of holographic wills are not foolish or feeble or unreliable. Whether through hard work or luck, the testators in this study generally managed to scrape together sizeable assets and then chose to distribute those assets with well-written documents of their own making. This instinct to convey property to loved ones arguably should be applauded, not the subject of derision.[82]

The Tractor Fender Will

Holographic wills are sometimes written *in extremis*, when the testator is close to death, with whatever materials are at hand. Holographs have been written on napkins, envelopes, address books, egg shells, walls, furniture — and a tractor fender.

Recently the Surrogate Court of the Judicial District of Kerrobert in Saskatchewan granted Letters of Administration with Will Annexed of a holograph writing scratched on a tractor fender (the Estate of Cecil George Harris). . . .

The facts of the Harris case were as follows. The deceased, a married man with two small children, was a wheat farmer. At noon on June 8th, 1948, he set out with a tractor and one-way disc to summer-fallow, telling his wife that he intended to work through the day and probably would not be back until almost ten in the evening. About an hour later he stopped the implements to do some oiling and make adjustments. After stepping down from the tractor seat, he put the tractor by mistake into reverse gear. As a result, it moved backwards pinning him between the two implements with his left leg caught under the left rear wheel of the tractor and the lower part of his body caught between the implements. Although he had the freedom of his arms, he was unable to reach the controls of the tractor. Eventually, the tractor engine died. He was still in this position some nine hours later when his wife, wondering at his absence, discovered him. She summoned help from the neighbors and at about 10:30 P.M. he was released and rushed to the hospital where he died, as a result of his injuries, within forty-eight hours.

When the deceased was discovered he was conscious and able to give instructions for releasing him. He remained conscious until given medical attention and stated that he had been

The will in Estate of Harris and the knife used to make the will

conscious during the whole of the time he was imprisoned.

On June 10th . . . [a neighbor] noticed the writing scratched on the fender. It read: "In case I die in this mess, I leave all to the wife. Cecil Geo. Harris."*

The knife used to scratch the will was discovered in Harris's clothes. The fender was taken to the solicitor's office and ultimately the piece containing the will was cut off, admitted to probate, and stored with the case files. The testator's handwriting was proved by affidavit.

---

* W.M. Elliott, Wills — Writing Scratched on Tractor Fender — Granting of Probate, 26 Can. B. Rev. 1242 (1948); *see also* Geoff Ellwand, An Analysis of Canada's Most Famous Holograph Will: How a Saskatchewan Farmer Scratched His Way into Legal History, 77 Sask. L. Rev. 1 (2014).

---

82. Clowney, *supra* note 79, at 28, 46-47.

3. Conditional Wills.   Suppose a will is written to become operative if death arises from a particular event, such as a surgery, or in a specified time frame, such as while on a journey. In *Kimmel*, the will was upon the condition, "if enny thing hapens," which the court read to mean "if I die."

In Eaton v. Brown, 193 U.S. 411 (1904), the testator wrote a holographic will saying: "I am going on a journey and may not ever return. If I do not, I leave everything to my adopted son." The testator returned from her journey but died some months later. The Supreme Court, per Justice Holmes, ordered the will probated: "Obviously the first sentence, 'I am going on a journey and may not ever return,' expresses the fact which was on her mind as the occasion and inducement for writing it. . . . She was thinking of the possibility of death or she would not have made a will. But that possibility at that moment took the specific shape of not returning from her journey, and so she wrote 'if I do not return,' before giving her last commands."

Most of the cases on conditional wills are in accord with Eaton v. Brown. They presume that the language of condition is not meant to be a condition but rather is a statement of the inducement for making the will.

b. Preprinted Will Forms

Suppose a person obtains a preprinted will form, completes the form by hand, and signs it, but does not have it attested by two witnesses. If strict compliance with the Wills Act is required, the form is not entitled to probate as a formal will. The form might, however, be entitled to probate as a holographic will if enough of its text was handwritten by the decedent.

In re Estate of Gonzalez
855 A.2d 1146 (Me. 2004)

ALEXANDER, J. . . . In August of 2001, Fermin Gonzalez visited his brother, Joseph, and Joseph's wife, Elizabeth. Gonzalez was planning to fly to Florida, and he wanted to prepare his will before he left. Gonzalez showed Elizabeth and Joseph two copies of a preprinted will form. On the first copy of the form, [reproduced below,] Gonzalez had handwritten his testamentary wishes. Elizabeth testified that he had already filled out the form by the time she saw it, but that she did see him sign the document. . . .

This document was signed by Gonzalez, but not by any witnesses. Additionally, several phone numbers and other notes appear to be written in the margins of the document.

Gonzalez also presented Elizabeth and Joseph with a blank copy of the form. Elizabeth testified that Gonzalez was planning to copy the information neatly onto the blank form, and that he asked Elizabeth, Joseph, and his mother to sign the blank form as witnesses. They signed the blank document.

Gonzalez became ill suddenly, and died on August 22, 2001. Three of Gonzalez's daughters, Kerry Gonzalez, Tara Gonzalez Grenon, and Kristin Gonzalez petitioned to probate the will. Todd and Alison Gurney, who are also Gonzalez's children, moved for a summary judgment, arguing that the will was not a valid holographic will.

LAST WILL AND TESTAMENT

A235-10
R235-04

BE IT KNOWN that I, FERMIN ARNALDO GONZALEZ , a resident of LOT 5 35 RUSSELL RD W NEWFIELD , County of YORK , in the State of MAINE , being of sound mind, do make and declare this to be my Last Will and Testament expressly revoking all my prior Wills and Codicils at any time made.

I. PERSONAL REPRESENTATIVE:

I appoint JOSEPH R. GONZALEZ & WALTER GONZALEZ JAMAICA PLAIN, MA. , as Personal Representative of this Will. Provide if this Personal Representative is unable or unwilling to serve then I appoint ELIZABETH GONZALEZ of 38 ROG... , as alternate Personal Representative. My Personal Representative shall carry out the provisions of this Will and pay my just debts, obligations and funeral expenses... Personal Representative shall not be required to post surety bond in this or any other... appraisal be made of my estate unless required by law.

II. GUARDIAN:

In the event I shall die as the sole parent of minor children, then I... as Guardian of said min... unable or unwilling to serve, then I appoint as alternate Guardian.

III. BEQUESTS:

I direct that after payment of all my just debts my property be beq... THAT THE PROPERTY ON LOT "5"/35 RUSSELL R... THE HOUSE, CABIN AND BARN. MY 18' FEATHER... PONTOON BOAT /w TRA... ALL OF THE CONTENTS OF MY PERSONAL INCLUDING MY 1953 MERCURY CAPRI ... MY 1971 FORD P.UP ALONG WI... GOLD I.D. BRACELET, STAINLESS STEEL R... ALL POWER TOOLS INCLUDING MY LAWN MOWER/TRACTOR. MY HORSE A ... MY 1990 CHRIS CRAFT CABIN CRUISER LOCATED ... BECOME THE PROPERTY OF MY THREE ... KERRY ANN GONZALEZ, TARA MAUREEN ... KRISTIN JULIA GONZALEZ. EACH HOU... AND SHOULD THEY DECIDE TO SELL ALL 10,000 (TEN THOUSAND) OF THE PROCEEDS ALL OF THE ABOVE BE GIVEN TO MY fa... GONZALEZ PHILIP AND 10,000 TEN THOUSA... MY MOTHER ...
SOL AMALIA GON...
Page 1 of 2
Execute and attest before a notary. Caution... consult an attorney before preparing a will.

ATAA

I ALSO WISH THAT SHOULD MY DAUGHTERS DECIDE TO SELL, LIQUIDATE ALL OF THE AFOREMENTIONED THAT MY BROTHERS JOSE, RAMON AND WALTER BE GIVEN THE FIRST RIGHTS TO PURCHASE ANY OR ALL PROPERTY, INCLUDING PERSONAL ITEMS. ALSO ORDER THAT MY DOG "MAGNOLIA" A JACK RUSSELL TERRIER SPANIC BE GIVEN TO MRS. ELIZABETH M. VAIL OF 7 WINFIELD COURT N.H. MY PONTOON BOAT & BOAT/TRAILER w/ MY MERCURY ENGINE COLOR GREEN & WHITE w/ TRAILER BECOME THE PROPERTY JOINTLY OF MY TWO BROTHERS JOSEPH AND WALTER GONZALEZ ALONG WITH $5,000 DOLLAR FOR THE CARE OF SAID ANIMAL. I ALSO WISH THAT THOMAS FRANCIS LYNCH JR. OF 69 PERRY ST E. WEYMOUTH MA. SEE TO MY PROPER DRESS AND GROOMING, IN MY MARINE CORPS DRESS BLUE UNIFORM w/ SABER UPON PREPARATION FOR M... WAKE & FUNERAL. IT IS ALSO MY WISH THAT THE FOLLOWING 3 PERSONS BE EXCLUDED FROM ANY AND ALL ACCESS TO MY FUNERAL ARRANGEMENTS THEY ARE: MAUREEN T. PHILP MY FORMER WIFE, COLLEEN T. CUNNINGHAM AND DAVIS E. MURPHY.

IN WITNESS WHEREOF, I have hereunto set my hand this ____ day of ____
Testator Signature

IV. WITNESSED: JANET FRANCIS HICKEY, AND JAMES F. FOLEY SR.

The testator has signed this will at the end and on each other separate page, and has declared or signified in our presence that it is his/her last will and testament, and in the presence of the testator and each other we have hereunto subscribed our names this ____ day of ____ (year).

X ____ Witness Signature ____ Address
X ____ Witness Signature ____ Address
X ____ Witness Signature ____ Address

ACKNOWLEDGMENT

State of MASS
County of SUFFOLK
We, ____

1-800-
355-8811

... the testator and the witnesses, respectively, whose names are signed to the attached and foregoing instrument, were sworn and declared to the undersigned that the testator signed the instrument as his/her Last Will and that each of the witnesses, in the presence of the testator and each other, signed the will as a witness.

Testator: Fermin A. Gonzalez   Witness X ____
Witness ____
Witness X ____

On ____ before me,
appeared ____
personally known to me (or proved to me on the basis of satisfactory evidence) to be the person(s) whose name(s) is/are subscribed to the within instrument and acknowledged to me that he/she/they executed the same in his/her/their authorized capacity(ies), and that by his/her/their signature(s) on the instrument the person(s), or the entity upon behalf of which the person(s) acted, executed the instrument.
WITNESS my hand and official seal.

Signature ____
Signature of Notary

Affiant ____ Known ____ Produced ID
Type of ID ____
(Seal)

Page ____ of ____   # 192   3.25
MIDDLETONS

The will in Estate of Gonzalez

After trial, the Probate Court denied the motion, and found that the will was a valid holographic will. . . .

The document that Gonzalez signed does not qualify as a will under 18-A Me. Rev. Stat. Ann. (M.R.S.A.) § 2-502 (1998), because it was not signed by any witnesses. Therefore, in order to be allowed or admitted to probate, the document must qualify as a holographic will under 18-A M.R.S.A. § 2-503 [based on the 1969 UPC]. A holographic will is one where "the signature and the material provisions are in the handwriting of the testator." 18-A M.R.S.A. § 2-503. The comment from the [1969] Uniform Probate Code helps to explain the meaning of the statutory language:

> By requiring only the "material provisions" to be in the testator's handwriting (rather than requiring, as some existing statutes do, that the will be "entirely" in the testator's handwriting) a holograph may be valid even though immaterial parts such as date or introductory wording be printed or stamped. A valid holograph might even be executed on some printed will forms if the printed portion could be eliminated and the handwritten portion could evidence the testator's will.

The Gurneys argue that Gonzalez did not execute a valid holographic will because a material provision of the will—evidence of testamentary intent—appears in the preprinted portion of the document, and was not handwritten. They maintain that the handwritten words are a list of what Gonzalez wanted to do with his property, but the handwritten words do not indicate that the conveyances were testamentary in nature.

We have not yet addressed the impact that preprinted will forms have on holographic wills. Most jurisdictions have dealt with this issue in one of two ways.

Some courts have looked to the preprinted language in order to determine the context of the handwritten words. In Estate of Muder, 765 P.2d 997, 1000 (Ariz. 1988), the Supreme Court of Arizona held that a person who handwrote his wishes on a preprinted will form had effectuated a valid holographic will because the person's testamentary intent was clear.[83] The court stated:

> We hold that a testator who uses a preprinted form, and in *his own handwriting* fills in the blanks by designating his beneficiaries and apportioning his estate among them and signs it, has created a valid holographic will. Such handwritten provisions may draw testamentary context from both the printed and the handwritten language on the form. We see no need to ignore the preprinted words when the testator clearly did not, and the statute does not require us to do so.

Other courts have ignored all of the preprinted words, and determined whether the handwritten words, taken alone, fulfill the requirements of a holographic will. See Estate of Black, 641 P.2d 754, 755 (Cal. 1982); Estate of Foxley, 575 N.W.2d 150, 154 (Neb. 1998).

We agree with the Supreme Court of Arizona and hold that printed portions of a will form can be incorporated into a holographic will where the trial court finds a testamentary intent, considering all of the evidence in the case. The Probate Court, after reviewing the document and hearing the evidence, explicitly found such an incorporation into the holographic will in this case: "[T]he hand-written material . . . implicitly adopted and incorporated the printed text on the form and converted the form into a more clear will."

---

83. At issue in *Muder* was a preprinted will form that was completed by hand, signed, and notarized, but attested by only one witness. The Arizona Supreme Court, 3 to 2, upheld the will as a valid holograph. The relevant handwritten language, inserted after a printed clause saying "I give to," read as follows: "My wife Retha F. Muder, our home and property in Shumway, Navajo County, car—pick up, travel trailer, and all other earthly possessions belonging to me, livestock, cattle, sheep, etc. Tools, savings accounts, checking accounts, retirement benefits, etc."—Eds.

The Uniform Probate Code comment [quoted earlier] states that "a holograph may be valid even though immaterial parts such as date or introductory wording be printed or stamped." The printed words in Gonzalez's will: "BE IT KNOWN that I _____, a resident of _____, County of _____, in the State of _____, being of sound mind, do make and declare this to be my Last Will and Testament expressly revoking all my prior Wills and Codicils at any time made" and "I direct that after payment of all my just debts my property be bequeathed in the manner following" are introductory phrases and may be preprinted. When filled in by the testator's handwriting, as here, they can become a valid statement of testamentary intent in a holographic will. . . .

Gonzalez's handwritten words may be read in the context of the preprinted words, and the Probate Court could properly find that the document is a valid holographic will.

The entry is: Judgment affirmed.

NOTES

1. Incorporation by Reference and Surplusage.   In *Gonzalez*, the court not only looked to the preprinted text to find testamentary intent, it also held that the handwritten text incorporated the preprinted text by reference (page 245), absorbing that text into the will. In many other states, the court would not look to the preprinted words, and the opposite result would obtain.

In In re Will of Ferree, 848 A.2d 81 (N.J. Ch. 2003), discussed at page 172, the court rejected the argument that a will form, reproduced at page 173, could be probated as a holographic will. The form had been completed by hand and signed by the testator and notarized. But the court applied the rule, rejected in *Gonzalez*, that the handwritten words "must be intelligible without resort to words not in the testator's handwriting. All other provisions, whether pre-printed, typed or written by others, are deemed surplusage and must be ignored." The handwritten text, by itself, read as follows:

> Ronald D. Ferree Ronald D. Ferree 40 Waterman Ave, Rumson N.J. 07760 There are no other rf rf rf Micheal Ferree (Brother) 2981 Heather Court, Jensen Beach, Fla 34957 Barbra Ferree 2981 Heather Ct Court, Jensen Beach, Fla 34957 Charles Creel (my IRA at Smith Barney) 49 Parker Ave, Fair Haven NJ Micheal Ferree Barbra Ferree 21st October 99 Ronald D. Ferree Ronald D. Ferree.

The court concluded that, because "the handwritten portions of this document—standing alone—mean nothing," the document could not be probated as a holographic will.

2. Harmless Error and Preprinted Forms.   Could the will in *Gonzalez* have been probated under the harmless error rule? What about the will in *Ferree*? Was there clear and convincing evidence in either that the decedent intended the preprinted form he filled in and signed to be his will? What of the testimony in *Gonzalez* that the testator intended to rewrite the will neatly on the blank form that he had asked the witnesses to sign?

Suppose *T* signs a donor card sent to her by a local charity. The card says in preprinted capital letters, "I am not taking action now, but my intention is," followed by three blank lines on which *T* writes, "my entire estate is to be left to [the charity]."

( ) My attorney has already been
    instructed to change my will.
( ) My attorney will be instructed
    by . . . . (date)

(c.) I AM NOT TAKING ACTION NOW, BUT
     MY INTENTION IS ~~~~~~~~~:

My entire estate . is to be left to North Shore Animal League

The total amount that the animal
shelter will someday receive is
$500,000.00 and I would like the
money used for:

(X) Food and shelter for the animals
( ) Adoption Fund to advertise for
    new owners
(X) Spaying and Neutering Program
'   Unrestricted use

                Sincerely,
Dorothy Southworth
                        4/19/89

The donor card in Estate of Southworth

T returns the card to the charity and then dies without taking further steps to devise her estate to the charity. Can the donor card be probated as a holographic will? Can it be probated under the harmless error rule? *See* Estate of Southworth, 59 Cal. Rptr. 2d 272 (App. 1996).

c. Signature and Handwriting

A holographic will must be written by the testator's hand and signed by the testator. Out of this simple formulation arise two problems: (1) where and how the testator must sign the holograph, and (2) how much of the holograph must be in the testator's handwriting.

(1) Signature

In almost all states that permit holographs, the testator may sign the will at the end, at the beginning, or anywhere else on the face of the document. But if the holograph is not signed at the end, there may be doubt whether the testator intended his name to be a signature. *Compare* Estate of Fegley, 589 P.2d 80 (Colo. App. 1978) (denying probate to a handwritten instrument reading, "I, Henrietta Fegley, being of sound mind and disposing memory, declare this instrument to be my last will," but not otherwise signed), *with* Estate of MacLeod, 254 Cal. Rptr. 156 (App. 1988) (reaching a contrary result on virtually identical facts).

In Williams v. Towle, 66 Cal. Rptr. 3d 34 (App. 2007), the testator did not sign his name at the end, but he did write his name, in block letters, on the top of the first page: "Last Will Etc. or What? of Homer Eugene Williams." The court admitted the will, reproduced on the next page, to probate.

(2) The Extent of the Testator's Handwriting

To what extent must a holographic will be in the testator's own handwriting? The statutes fall roughly into three generations.

(a) First Generation: "entirely written, signed, and dated." The first generation of holographic will statutes required that a holograph be "entirely written, signed, and dated" in the testator's handwriting. Under these statutes, holographs were sometimes struck down even if they included only one or two printed words. In In re Thorn's Estate, 192 P. 19 (Cal. 1920), the court struck down the testator's handwritten will because he had stamped the name of his home, Cragthorn, twice within its text.

In Estate of Dobson, 708 P.2d 422 (Wyo. 1985), the testator took her signed handwritten will to her local banker to discuss it with him. To make the will clearer, the banker penciled in certain numbers and parentheses and added to the devise of a tract of land, "including all mineral and oil rights," all with the consent of the testator. The court held the will could not be probated because it was not entirely in the decedent's handwriting.

The will in Williams v. Towle

Some courts interpreted the first generation statutes as requiring that the will be "entirely . . . dated," so that writing "May 1948" or "1965" was an insufficient dating of the instrument to allow probate, as in Estate of Carson, 344 P.2d 612 (Cal. App. 1959) ("May 1948"), and Estate of Hazelwood, 57 Cal. Rptr. 332 (App. 1967) ("1965").

A little more than a third of the states permitting holographs still require that a holograph be "entirely" in the handwriting of the testator.

(b) Second Generation (1969 UPC): "material provisions." The inconsistent and sometimes harsh results under the first generation statutes led the drafters of the 1969 UPC to require only "the signature and the material provisions" of the will to be in the testator's handwriting. The comment to this provision, quoted in *Gonzalez* at page 206, explains that a holographic will should be valid even if "immaterial parts such as date or introductory wording be printed or stamped. A valid holograph might even be executed on some printed will forms if the printed portion could be eliminated and the handwritten portion could evidence the testator's will."

The idea, which has come to be known as the *surplusage theory*, is that the handwritten portion of the instrument should be given effect as a holographic will if it makes sense without the text not written by the testator. As observed in *Gonzalez*, however, a split in the cases developed in dealing with wills for which part of a disposition (such as "I give") or the language necessary to establish testamentary intent (such as "last will and testament") was not handwritten. Are these "material provisions" that must be entirely handwritten? Some courts, as in *Gonzalez*, have been willing to look beyond the handwriting to make sense of a disposition or to find testamentary intent. Other courts, as in *Ferree*, have not.

About one-third of the states permitting holographs have a statute based on the 1969 UPC.

(c) Third Generation (1990 UPC): "material portions" and extrinsic evidence allowed. Unhappy with the refusal of some courts to look to the preprinted language of a form will to give context to the handwritten portions, the drafters of UPC § 2-502(b) (1990, rev. 2008), page 144, reworded the material provisions language of the 1969 UPC to require only that the "material portions" be handwritten. The Restatement explains:

> The purpose of changing from "material provisions" to "material portions" was to leave no doubt about the validity of a will in which immaterial parts of a dispositive provision—such as "I give, devise, and bequeath"—are not in the testator's handwriting. The material portion of a dispositive provision—which must be in the testator's handwriting under the [1990] UPC—are the words identifying the property and the devisee.[84]

The 1990 UPC also allows recourse to extrinsic evidence to establish testamentary intent. Section 2-502(c) provides: "Intent that a document constitute the testator's will can be established by extrinsic evidence, including, for holographic wills, portions of the document that are not in the testator's handwriting."

About one-third of the states permitting holographs have a statute based on the 1990 UPC.

d. Extrinsic Evidence

In re Estate of Kuralt
15 P.3d 931 (Mont. 2000)

[Charles Kuralt was born in North Carolina in 1934. From 1970 through 1994, Kuralt was the host of CBS News Sunday Morning. He became a homespun American icon known for his "On the Road" stories based on his travels around the country in a mobile home. Kuralt specialized in "big-hearted essays on topics others thought tiny," reporting "on horse-traders and a 93-year-old brickmaker, on the wonders of nature and the nature of other wonders, like the sharecropper in Mississippi who put nine children through college or the 103-year-old entertainer who performed at nursing homes."[85] Kuralt went through six motor homes across more than 500 On the Road stories. When in 1994 the beloved Kuralt retired from CBS News Sunday Morning, Saturday Night Live did a seemingly preposterous satire in which Norm MacDonald, as Kuralt, bid

---

84. Restatement (Third) of Property: Wills and Other Donative Transfers § 3.2 cmt. b (Am. Law Inst. 1999).
85. Joe Sexton, Charles Kuralt, 62, Is Dead, N.Y. Times, July 5, 1997, at 24.

farewell, saying that he would miss all the people he had met over the years — and had sex with.[86]

Sometimes life imitates art. In 1968, six years into his marriage to Suzanne Baird, who was known as Petie, Kuralt met a woman named Pat Baker, who was known as Patricia Elizabeth Shannon. Kuralt met Shannon while doing an On the Road story in Reno on her efforts to build a park for African-American children. Smitten, Kuralt asked Shannon to dinner, arriving to pick her up with a bouquet of roses in hand. Romance ensued. Kuralt visited with Shannon frequently. He provided financial support to her and her family. He bought her a vacation home in Ireland. According to Shannon, when she moved from Reno to the San Francisco Bay area in the early 1970s, she and Kuralt "went on picnics and we went sail[ing] and, you know, we acted like a family."[87] In 1985, she moved to a log cabin that Kuralt built for them in Montana.

Elizabeth (Pat) Shannon and Charles Kuralt, bundled against the chilly weather on Angel Island near San Francisco in the early 1970s, sharing a picnic of wine, cheese, and fruit
Independent Record/AP photo

Kuralt died on July 4, 1997, of either a heart attack or lupus (or both). Two weeks before he died, he wrote Shannon a letter assuring her that he would see to it that she would inherit his property in Montana. This opinion was the second decision by the Montana Supreme Court on whether that letter could be probated as a holographic will.]

TRIEWEILER, J. . . . Kuralt and Shannon desired to keep their relationship secret, and were so successful in doing so that even though Kuralt's wife, Petie, knew that Kuralt owned property in Montana, she was unaware, prior to Kuralt's untimely death, of his relationship with Shannon.

Over the nearly 30-year course of their relationship, Kuralt and Shannon saw each other regularly and maintained contact by phone and mail. Kuralt was the primary source of financial support for Shannon and established close, personal relationships with Shannon's three children. Kuralt provided financial support for a joint business venture managed by Shannon and transferred a home in Ireland to Shannon as a gift.

In 1985, Kuralt purchased a 20-acre parcel of property along the Big Hole River in Madison County, near Twin Bridges, Montana. Kuralt and Shannon constructed a cabin on this 20-acre parcel. In 1987, Kuralt purchased two additional parcels along the

---

86. The SNL sketch began with MacDonald as Kuralt talking in Kuralt's folksy manner about how much he would miss life "On the Road." After noting the beauty of the countryside, he confessed that it was the prospect of sex that had lured him on the road 37 years earlier and that this was what he would miss the most. He then recounted a string of sexual conquests, including the wife of Old Ned Harrigan, known for his ball of twine that was 67 feet around, and 75-year-old Thelma Ober, famous for her pumpkin pies. Saturday Night Live, Sunday Morning with Charles Kuralt (NBC television broadcast Apr. 9, 1994).

87. Larry King Live (CNN television broadcast Feb. 14, 2001).

Big Hole which adjoined the original 20-acre parcel. These two additional parcels, one upstream and one downstream of the cabin, created a parcel of approximately 90 acres and are the primary subject of this appeal.

On May 3, 1989, Kuralt executed a holographic will which stated as follows:

May 3, 1989

In the event of my death, I bequeath to Patricia Elizabeth Shannon all my interest in land, buildings, furnishings and personal belongings on Burma Road, Twin Bridges, Montana.

> Charles Kuralt
> 34 Bank St.
> New York, N.Y. 10014

Although Kuralt mailed a copy of this holographic will to Shannon, he subsequently executed a formal will on May 4, 1994, in New York City. This Last Will and Testament, prepared with the assistance of counsel, does not specifically mention any of the real property owned by Kuralt. The beneficiaries of Kuralt's Last Will and Testament were

"In the event of my death, I bequeath to Patricia Elizabeth Shannon..."

Kuralt's 1989 holograph

his wife, Petie, and the Kuralts' two children. Neither Shannon nor her children are named as beneficiaries in Kuralt's formal will. Shannon had no knowledge of the formal will until the commencement of these proceedings.

On April 9, 1997, Kuralt deeded his interest in the original 20-acre parcel with the cabin to Shannon. The transaction was disguised as a sale. However, Kuralt supplied the "purchase" price for the 20-acre parcel to Shannon prior to the transfer. After the deed to the 20-acre parcel was filed, Shannon sent Kuralt, at his request, a blank buy-sell real estate form so that the remaining 90 acres along the Big Hole could be conveyed to Shannon in a similar manner. Apparently, it was again Kuralt's intention to provide the purchase price. The second transaction was to take place in September 1997 when Shannon, her son, and Kuralt agreed to meet at the Montana cabin.

Kuralt, however, became suddenly ill and entered a New York hospital on June 18, 1997. On that same date, Kuralt wrote the letter to Shannon which is now at the center of the current dispute:

June 18, 1997

Dear Pat—

Something is terribly wrong with me and they can't figure out what. After cat-scans and a variety of cardiograms, they agree it's not lung cancer or heart trouble or blood clot. So they're putting me in the hospital today to concentrate on infectious diseases. I am getting worse, barely able to get out of bed, but still have high hopes for recovery . . . if only I can get a diagnosis! Curiouser and curiouser! I'll keep you informed. I'll have the lawyer visit the hospital to be sure you <u>inherit</u> the rest of the place in MT. if it comes to that.

I send love to you & [your youngest daughter,] Shannon. Hope things are better there!

Love,
C.

Enclosed with this letter were two checks made payable to Shannon, one for $8000 and the other for $9000. Kuralt did not seek the assistance of an attorney to devise the remaining 90 acres of Big Hole land to Shannon. Therefore, when Kuralt died unexpectedly, Shannon sought to probate the letter of June 18, 1997, as a valid holographic codicil to Kuralt's formal 1994 will.

The Estate opposed Shannon's Petition for Ancillary Probate based on its contention that the June 18, 1997 letter expressed only a future intent to make a will. The District Court granted partial summary judgment for the Estate on May 26, 1998. Shannon appealed from the District Court order which granted partial summary judgment to the Estate. This Court, in In re Estate of Kuralt (*Kuralt I*), 981 P.2d 771 (Mont. 1999), reversed the District Court and remanded the case for trial in order to resolve disputed issues of material fact. Following an abbreviated evidentiary hearing, the District Court issued its Findings and Order. The District Court held that the June 18, 1997 letter was a valid holographic codicil to Kuralt's formal will of May 4, 1994 and accordingly entered judgment in favor of Shannon. The Estate now appeals from that order and judgment. . . .

"*I'll have the lawyer visit the hospital to be sure you <u>inherit</u> the rest of the place in MT. if it comes to that.*"

Kuralt's 1997 letter to Shannon from the hospital

Did the District Court err when it found that the June 18, 1997 letter expressed a present testamentary intent to transfer property in Madison County?

The Estate contends that the District Court made legal errors which led to a mistaken conclusion about Kuralt's intent concerning the disposition of his Montana property. The Estate argues that the District Court failed to recognize the legal effect of the 1994 will and therefore erroneously found that Kuralt, after his May 3, 1989 holographic will, had an uninterrupted intent to transfer the Montana property to Shannon. The Estate further argues that Kuralt's 1994 formal will revoked all prior wills, both expressly and by inconsistency. This manifest change of intention, according to the Estate, should have led the District Court to the conclusion that Kuralt did not intend to transfer the Montana property to Shannon upon his death.

Montana courts are guided by the bedrock principle of honoring the intent of the testator. On remand, the District Court resolved the factual question of whether Kuralt intended the letter of June 18, 1997 to effect a testamentary disposition of the Montana property. As we stated in *Kuralt I*, the "question of whether that letter contains the necessary animus testandi becomes an issue suitable for resolution by the trier of fact." 981 P.2d at 778. The argument on appeal, while clothed as a legal argument, addresses factual findings made by the District Court. However, if the factual findings of the District Court are supported by substantial credible evidence and are not otherwise clearly erroneous, they will not be reversed by this Court.

The record supports the District Court's finding that the June 18, 1997 letter expressed Kuralt's intent to effect a posthumous transfer of his Montana property to Shannon. Kuralt and Shannon enjoyed a long, close personal relationship which continued up to the last letter Kuralt wrote Shannon on June 18, 1997, in which he enclosed checks to her in the amounts of $8000 and $9000. Likewise, Kuralt and Shannon's children had a long, family-like relationship which included significant financial support.

The District Court focused on the last few months of Kuralt's life to find that the letter demonstrated his testamentary intent. The conveyance of the 20-acre parcel for no real consideration and extrinsic evidence that Kuralt intended to convey the remainder of the Montana property to Shannon in a similar fashion provides substantial factual support for the District Court's determination that Kuralt intended that Shannon have the rest of the Montana property.

The June 18, 1997 letter expressed Kuralt's desire that Shannon inherit the remainder of the Montana property. That Kuralt wrote the letter *in extremis* is supported by the fact that he died two weeks later. Although Kuralt intended to transfer the remaining land to Shannon, he was reluctant to consult a lawyer to formalize his intent because he wanted to keep their relationship secret. Finally, the use of the term "inherit" underlined by Kuralt reflected his intention to make a posthumous disposition of the property. Therefore, the District Court's findings are supported by substantial evidence and are not clearly erroneous. Accordingly, we conclude that the District Court did not err when it found that the letter dated June 18, 1997 expressed a present testamentary intent to transfer property in Madison County to Patricia Shannon. . . .

[W]e agree with the District Court's conclusion that the June 18, 1997 holograph was a codicil to Kuralt's 1994 formal will. Admittedly, the June 18, 1997 letter met the threshold requirements for a valid holographic will. Moreover, the letter was a codicil as a matter of law because it made a specific bequest of the Montana property and did not purport to bequeath the entirety of the estate. See Official Comments to § 72-2-527, MCA ("when the second will does not make a complete disposition of the testator's estate, the second will is more in the nature of a codicil to the first will"). The District Court was therefore correct when it concluded that the June 18, 1997 letter was a codicil. . . .

Accordingly, we affirm the judgment of the District Court.

NOTES

1. Epilogue—Death and Taxes.   Kuralt's 1994 formal will, which remained operative to the extent not amended by his 1997 letter to Shannon, provided that all transfer taxes due by reason of his death were to be paid out of his residuary estate. Because Kuralt's wife and children were the beneficiaries of the residue, the taxes attributable to the Montana property had to be paid out of their share, even though that property passed to Shannon. *See* In re Estate of Kuralt, 68 P.3d 662 (Mont. 2003). Do you suppose Kuralt intended that his wife and children pay the taxes on Shannon's share of his estate?

2. Testamentary Intent or Intended Disposition?   Recall the distinction made in *Macool*, page 183, between evidence of the decedent's intended dispositions and evidence that the decedent intended a certain instrument itself to be her will. In *Kuralt*, there was much evidence that Kuralt intended to give Shannon his Montana property, but there was little evidence that he intended the 1997 letter itself to be a will. If you had asked Kuralt whether that letter was a will, what do you think he would have said? Suppose instead you asked him whether his earlier 1989 letter, page 212, was a will. What do you think that he would have said?

The dissent in *Kuralt I* argued that the use of the future tense in the 1997 letter negated the possibility that Kuralt intended the letter itself to be a will:

> The letter of June 18, 1997, and the record in this case does not meet the standard of clear and convincing evidence. . . . The June 18, 1997 letter . . . contains this—and only this—language relating to the question of a holographic will: "I'll have the lawyer visit the hospital to be sure you inherit the rest of the place in MT. if it comes to that." That language clearly indicates that decedent Kuralt did not intend the letter to operate as a holographic will but, rather, expressed his intent that at a future date he would have a lawyer visit him in the hospital to be sure that Patricia Shannon would, by a document thereafter to be executed, inherit "the rest of the place in MT." Such language is precatory and expresses only a desire or wish. It certainly does not constitute imperative, direct terms of bequest.[88]

Suppose that, instead of writing to Shannon, Kuralt had written a similar letter to his lawyer: "I'll need you to visit the hospital to be sure Pat Shannon <u>inherits</u> the rest of the place in Montana if it comes to that." Would this letter be entitled to probate as a holographic will? *See* In re Beebee's Estate, 258 P.2d 1101 (Cal. App. 1953).

In Minton v. Minton, 374 S.W.3d 818 (Ark. App. 2010), the testator duly executed a formal will in 1999. Four years later, in 2003, the testator wrote a two-page note to two of his friends. This handwritten note (depicted below), which the testator signed and dated, stated that "if anything happens to me before I get the will changed I want to give," followed by various dispositions that were inconsistent with the 1999 will. The testator died in 2007 without having executed a new formal will. The court held that the 2003 note was a valid codicil that amended the 1999 will. The court reasoned that the note "states [the testator's] intent to 'give' to certain beneficiaries items of property in a way that modifies the percentages stated in the formal will. The fact that the writing references a future intention to incorporate these changes into a new formal will" does not mean that the testator did not intend the 2003 note to have binding force in the interim.

---

88. In re Estate of Kuralt, 981 P.2d 771, 778 (Mont. 1999) (Turnage, C.J., dissenting).

The 2003 handwritten note in Minton v. Minton

B. REVOCATION OF WILLS

An important corollary to the principle of freedom of disposition is that a person remains free to rework her estate plan until the moment of death. A will is said to be *ambulatory*, meaning that it is subject to amendment or revocation by the testator at any time prior to death. Although "undoing" rules are common across private law, they are especially prominent in the law of wills, because wills are frequently revised in the ordinary course of lifetime estate planning.

1. Revocation by Writing or by Physical Act

All states permit revocation of a will (1) by a subsequent *writing* executed with Wills Act formalities, and (2) by a *physical act* such as destroying, obliterating, or burning the will. An oral declaration that a will is revoked, without more, is not enough to revoke the will. If a duly executed will is not revoked in accordance with the applicable revocation statute, the will must be admitted to probate. UPC § 2-507 (1990), excerpted below, is fairly representative of the state revocation statutes.

Uniform Probate Code (Unif. Law Comm'n 1990)

§ 2-507. Revocation by Writing or by Act
  (a) A will or any part thereof is revoked:
    (1) by executing a subsequent will that revokes the previous will or part expressly or by inconsistency; or
    (2) by performing a revocatory act on the will, if the testator performed the act with the intent and for the purpose of revoking the will or

part or if another individual performed the act in the testator's conscious presence and by the testator's direction. For purposes of this paragraph, "revocatory act on the will" includes burning, tearing, canceling, obliterating, or destroying the will or any part of it. A burning, tearing, or canceling is a "revocatory act on the will," whether or not the burn, tear, or cancellation touched any of the words on the will. . . .

a. Express and Implied Revocatory Writings

A writing executed with Wills Act formalities may revoke an earlier will in whole or in part by *express revocation*. Most well-drafted wills open with an express revocation clause. Here is an example: "I, John Doe, a resident of _____, _____, make this my will and revoke all prior wills and codicils."[89]

A writing executed with Wills Act formalities may also revoke a prior will in whole or in part by *inconsistency* (sometimes called *implied revocation*). The issue arises when a testator executes a subsequent will that does not include an express revocation clause. The question is whether the testator intended the subsequent will to replace a prior will in whole or in part, or if instead he intended the subsequent will to supplement the prior will without disturbing its provisions.

The modern view, adopted by UPC § 2-507(c), is to treat a subsequent will that does not expressly revoke a prior will, but makes a *complete disposition* of the testator's estate, as presumptively revoking the prior will by inconsistency.[90] If the subsequent will does not make a complete disposition of the testator's estate, it is instead viewed as a *codicil*, and any property not disposed of under the codicil is disposed of in accordance with the prior will, as under UPC § 2-507(d).

A codicil is a testamentary instrument (i.e., a will) that supplements, rather than replaces, an earlier will. The later codicil supersedes the earlier will to the extent of inconsistency between them.[91] Here is an example: "I revoke the entirety of Article II of my will dated _____, and insert in lieu thereof the following new Article II: . . . In all other respects, I confirm and republish my will dated _____."[92]

NOTE

Wills, Codicils, and Inconsistency. In 2011, *T* executes a will that gives all her property to *A*. In 2016, *T* executes a will that gives her diamond ring to *B* and her car to *C*.

---

89. Northern Trust, Will & Trust Forms 102-1 (2004).

90. The older view was that, in the absence of an express revocation clause, a residuary devise in a subsequent will was not enough to revoke a specific devise in a prior will because the subsequent devise of the residue was not literally inconsistent with the prior specific devise. *See* Thomas E. Atkinson, Law of Wills 450-52 (2d ed. 1953).

91. UPC § 1-201(57) (1990) defines a will to include a codicil and any testamentary instrument that appoints an executor or revokes or revises another will. In a state that recognizes holographic wills, a holograph can revoke or revise an attested will, as in In re Estate of Kuralt, page 210.

92. Adapted from Northern Trust, Will & Trust Forms 113-1 (2004).

a. Suppose that, in early 2017, *T* dies. What is the proper distribution of *T*'s estate? Even if the 2016 will makes no reference to the 2011 will, the 2016 will is ordinarily treated as a codicil, and both instruments are entitled to probate. *B* takes the diamond ring, *C* takes the car, and *A* takes the remainder.

b. Suppose that, in early 2017, *T* destroys the 2016 codicil with the intention of revoking it. *T* dies later in 2017. The 2011 will is offered for probate. Should it be admitted? *See* Restatement (Third) of Property: Wills and Other Donative Transfers § 4.1 cmt. m (Am. Law Inst. 1999).

c. Suppose instead that *T* destroys the 2011 will with the intention of revoking it. After *T*'s death, the codicil is offered for probate. Should it be admitted? *See* id. cmt. n.

b. Formality in Revocation by Writing or Physical Act

Thompson v. Royall
175 S.E. 748 (Va. 1934)

HUDGINS, J. The only question presented by this record is whether the will of Mrs. M. Lou Bowen Kroll had been revoked shortly before her death.

The uncontroverted facts are as follows: On the 4th day of September, 1932, Mrs. Kroll signed a will, typewritten on the five sheets of legal cap paper; the signature appeared on the last page duly attested by three subscribing witnesses. H.P. Brittain, the executor named in the will, was given possession of the instrument for safe-keeping. A codicil typed on the top third of one sheet of paper dated September 15, 1932, was signed by the testatrix in the presence of two subscribing witnesses. Possession of this instrument was given to Judge S.M.B. Coulling, the attorney who prepared both documents.

On September 19, 1932, at the request of Mrs. Kroll, Judge Coulling and Mr. Brittain took the will and the codicil to her home where she told her attorney, in the presence of Mr. Brittain and another, to destroy both. But, instead of destroying the papers, at the suggestion of Judge Coulling, she decided to retain them as memoranda, to be used as such in the event she decided to execute a new will. Upon the back of the manuscript cover, which was fastened to the five sheets by metal clasps, in the handwriting of Judge Coulling, signed by Mrs. Kroll, there is the following notation:

> This will null and void and to be only held by H.P. Brittain instead of being destroyed as a memorandum for another will if I desire to make same. This 19 Sept. 1932.

> *M. Lou Bowen Kroll*

The same notation was made upon the back of the sheet on which the codicil was written, except that the name S.M.B. Coulling was substituted for H.P. Brittain; this was likewise signed by Mrs. Kroll.

Mrs. Kroll died October 2, 1932, leaving numerous nephews and nieces, some of whom were not mentioned in her will, and an estate valued at approximately $200,000. On motion of some of the beneficiaries, the will and codicil were offered for probate.

All the interested parties including the heirs at law were convened, and on the issue [of whether the purported will is valid or not] the jury found that the instruments dated September 4 and 15, 1932, were the last will and testament of Mrs. M. Lou Bowen Kroll. From an order sustaining the verdict and probating the will this writ of error was allowed.

For more than one hundred years, the means by which a duly executed will may be revoked have been prescribed by statute. These requirements are found in section 5233 of the 1919 Code, the pertinent parts of which read thus:

> No will or codicil, or any part thereof, shall be revoked, unless . . . by a subsequent will or codicil, or by some writing declaring an intention to revoke the same, and executed in the manner in which a will is required to be executed, or by the testator, or some person in his presence and by his direction, cutting, tearing, burning, obliterating, canceling, or destroying the same, or the signature thereto, with the intent to revoke.

The notations, dated September 19, 1932, are not wholly in the handwriting of the testatrix, nor are her signatures thereto attached attested by subscribing witnesses; hence under the statute they are ineffectual as "some writing declaring an intention to revoke." The faces of the two instruments bear no physical evidence of any cutting, tearing, burning, obliterating, canceling, or destroying. The only contention made by appellants is that the notation written in the presence, and with the approval, of Mrs. Kroll, on the back of the manuscript cover in the one instance, and on the back of the sheet containing the codicil in the other, constitute "canceling" within the meaning of the statute.

Both parties concede that to effect revocation of a duly executed will, in any of the methods prescribed by statute, two things are necessary: (1) The doing of one of the acts specified, (2) accompanied by the intent to revoke—the animo revocandi. Proof of either, without proof of the other, is insufficient. Malone v. Hobbs, 1 Rob. (40 Va.) 346 (1842). The proof established the intention to revoke. The entire controversy is confined to the acts used in carrying out that purpose. The testatrix adopted the suggestion of her attorney to revoke her will by written memoranda, admittedly ineffectual as revocations by subsequent writings, but appellants contend the memoranda, in the handwriting of another, and testatrix's signatures, are sufficient to effect revocation by cancellation. To support this contention, appellants cite a number of authorities which hold that the modern definition of cancellation includes "any act which would destroy, revoke, recall, do away with, overrule, render null and void, the instrument."

Most of the authorities cited that approve the above or a similar meaning of the word were dealing with cancellation of simple contracts, or other instruments that require little or no formality in execution. However, there is one line of cases which apply this extended meaning of "canceling" to the revocation of wills. The leading case so holding is Warner v. Warner's Estate, 37 Vt. 356 (1864). In this case proof of the intent and the act were a notation on the same page with, and below the signature of, the testator, reading: "This will is hereby cancelled and annulled. In full this 15th day of March in the year 1859," and written lengthwise on the back of the fourth page of the foolscap paper, upon which no part of the written will appeared, were these words,

"Cancelled and is null and void. (Signed) I. Warner." It was held this was sufficient to revoke the will under a statute similar to the one here under consideration.

In Evans' Appeal, 58 Pa. 238 (1868), the Pennsylvania court approved the reasoning of the Vermont court in *Warner*, but the force of the opinion is weakened when the facts are considered. It seems that there were lines drawn through two of the three signatures of the testator appearing in the Evans will, and the paper on which material parts of the will were written was torn in four places. It therefore appeared on the face of the instrument, when offered for probate, that there was a sufficient defacement to bring it within the meaning of both obliteration and cancellation. The construction of the statute in *Warner* has been criticized by eminent text-writers on wills, and the courts in the majority of the states in construing similar statutes have refused to follow the reasoning in that case. Jarman on Wills (6th Ed.) 147, note 1; Schouler on Wills (5th Ed.) § 391; Redfield on the Law of Wills (4th Ed.) 323-25.

The above, and other authorities that might be cited, hold that revocation of a will by cancellation within the meaning of the statute contemplates marks or lines across the written parts of the instrument or a physical defacement, or some mutilation of the writing itself, with the intent to revoke. If written words are used for the purpose, they must be so placed as to physically affect the written portion of the will, not merely on blank parts of the paper on which the will is written. If the writing intended to be the act of canceling does not mutilate, or erase, or deface, or otherwise physically come in contact with, any part of written words of the will, it cannot be given any greater weight than a similar writing on a separate sheet of paper, which identifies the will referred to, just as definitely as does the writing on the back. If a will may be revoked by writing on the back, separable from the will, it may be done by a writing not on the will. This the statute forbids. . . .

The attempted revocation is ineffectual, because testatrix intended to revoke her will by subsequent writings not executed as required by statute, and because it does not in any wise physically obliterate, mutilate, deface, or cancel any written parts of the will.

For the reasons stated, the judgment of the trial court is affirmed.

NOTES

1. Intent to Revoke. Given the "uncontroverted" proof of Mrs. Kroll's intent to revoke her will and codicil, why did the court conclude that neither had been revoked? Under the applicable statute, a will could be revoked by a writing "executed in the manner in which a will is required to be executed." Why did the court not accept the writings on Mrs. Kroll's will and codicil as revocations by formal or holographic will? What policy is served by the court's decision? Were the evidentiary, channeling, cautionary or ritual, and protective functions satisfied?

The statute also authorized revocation by a physical act of defacement to the will, that is, by "cutting, tearing, burning, obliterating, canceling, or destroying" the will. Why were the writings, which were made on the backsides of the codicil and the manuscript cover to the will, not physical acts of defacement with the intent to revoke sufficient to constitute a "canceling" under the statute? Could a testator "cancel" a will by orally declaring it to be cancelled?

Suppose that Judge Coulling had written in the top margin of the will: "I hereby revoke this will. 19/9/32," and then Mrs. Kroll signed her name below this notation. Would that have been a valid revocation by a physical act of canceling? *See* Maxwell v. Dawkins, 974 So. 2d 282 (Ala. 2006).

2. Malpractice. Although no one sued for legal malpractice in the 1930s, we have been told by Judge Coulling's grandson that for the rest of his life Judge Coulling suffered greatly from shame and loss of reputation because of the botched revocation of Mrs. Kroll's will and codicil. If Mrs. Kroll's heirs had sued Judge Coulling, on what evidence would they have relied to prove malpractice? Why is such evidence reliable enough to support malpractice liability but not to revoke the will and codicil?

3. Cancellation and Harmless Error in a Revocatory Writing. The UPC would change the result in *Thompson*. The last sentence of § 2-507(a)(2), page 217, allows for revocation by a physical act of cancellation whether or not the cancellation touches any of the words on the will. So the codicil, for which the cancellation was written on the back, would have been revoked. The will would be a closer call, because the cancellation was written on the back of the manuscript cover, not on the back of the will itself.[93] But even if the writing on the manuscript cover would not qualify as an act of cancellation under § 2-507(a)(2), surely it would qualify as a revocation by subsequent writing under the harmless error rule of § 2-503, page 177.

c. Presumption of Physical Act Revocation

Harrison v. Bird
621 So. 2d 972 (Ala. 1993)

HOUSTON, J. The proponent of a will appeals from a judgment of the Circuit Court of Montgomery County holding that the estate of Daisy Virginia Speer, deceased, should be administered as an intestate estate and confirming the letters of administration granted by the probate court to Mae S. Bird.

The following pertinent facts are undisputed:

Daisy Virginia Speer executed a will in November 1989, in which she named Katherine Crapps Harrison as the main beneficiary of her estate. The original of the will was retained by Ms. Speer's attorney and a duplicate original was given to Ms. Harrison. On March 4, 1991, Ms. Speer telephoned her attorney and advised him that she wanted to revoke her will. Thereafter, Ms. Speer's attorney or his secretary, in the presence of each other, tore the will into four pieces. The attorney then wrote Ms. Speer a letter, informing her that he had "revoked" her will as she had instructed and that he was enclosing the pieces of the will so that she could verify that he had torn up the original. In the letter, the attorney specifically stated, "As it now stands, you are without a will."

---

93. We are indebted to Professor Robert Bartow of Temple University School of Law and Professor Melanie Jacobs of Michigan State University College of Law, and to Professor Jacobs's student Joseph Weiler, J.D. 2007, for calling to our attention the significance of this detail.

Ms. Speer died on September 3, 1991. Upon her death, the postmarked letter from her attorney was found among her personal effects, but the four pieces of the will were not found. Thereafter, on September 17, 1991, the Probate Court of Montgomery County granted letters of administration on the estate of Ms. Speer, to Mae S. Bird, a cousin of Ms. Speer. On October 11, 1991, Ms. Harrison filed for probate a document purporting to be the last will and testament of Ms. Speer and naming Ms. Harrison as executrix. . . .

Thereafter, the circuit court ruled (1) that Ms. Speer's will was not lawfully revoked when it was destroyed by her attorney at her direction and with her consent, but not in her presence, see Ala. Code 1975, § 43-8-136(b);[94] (2) that there could be no ratification of the destruction of Ms. Speer's will, which was not accomplished pursuant to the strict requirements of § 43-8-136(b); and (3) that, based on the fact that the pieces of the destroyed will were delivered to Ms. Speer's home but were not found after her death, there arose a presumption that Ms. Speer thereafter revoked the will herself. . . .

[F]inding that the presumption in favor of revocation of Ms. Speer's will had not been rebutted and therefore that the duplicate original will offered for probate by Ms. Harrison was not the last will and testament of Daisy Virginia Speer,[95] the circuit court held that the estate should be administered as an intestate estate and confirmed the letters of administration issued by the probate court to Ms. Bird.

If the evidence establishes that Ms. Speer had possession of the will before her death, but the will is not found among her personal effects after her death, a presumption arises that she destroyed the will. See Barksdale v. Pendergrass, 319 So. 2d 267 (Ala. 1975). Furthermore, if she destroys the [duplicate] of the will in her possession, a presumption arises that she has revoked her will and all duplicates, even though a duplicate exists that is not in her possession. See Stiles v. Brown, 380 So. 2d 792 (Ala. 1980). However, this presumption of revocation is rebuttable and the burden of rebutting the presumption is on the proponent of the will. See *Barksdale*, supra.

Based on the foregoing, we conclude that under the facts of this case there existed a presumption that Ms. Speer destroyed her will and thus revoked it. Therefore, the burden shifted to Ms. Harrison to present sufficient evidence to rebut that presumption—to present sufficient evidence to convince the trier of fact that the absence of the will from Ms. Speer's personal effects after her death was not due to Ms. Speer's destroying and thus revoking the will. See Stiles v. Brown, supra.

---

94. Ala. Code § 43-8-136 provides as follows:

A will is revoked by being burned, torn, canceled, obliterated, or destroyed, with the intent and for the purpose of revoking it by the testator or by another person in his presence by his consent and direction. If the physical act is by someone other than the testator, consent and direction of the testator must be proved by at least two witnesses.

—Eds.

95. A duplicate original is not a copy but rather a second original. "If the testator executed more than one copy of the same will, each duplicate is considered to be the testator's will. The will is revoked if the testator, with intent to revoke, performs a revocatory act on one of the duplicates. The testator need not perform a revocatory act on all the duplicates." Restatement (Third) of Property: Wills and Other Donative Transfers § 4.1 cmt. f (Am. Law Inst. 1999).—Eds.

From a careful review of the record, we conclude, as did the trial court, that the evidence presented by Ms. Harrison was not sufficient to rebut the presumption that Ms. Speer destroyed her will with the intent to revoke it. We, therefore, affirm the trial court's judgment.

We note Ms. Harrison's argument that under the particular facts of this case, because Ms. Speer's attorney destroyed the will outside of Ms. Speer's presence, "[t]he fact that Ms. Speer may have had possession of the pieces of her will and that such pieces were not found upon her death is not sufficient to invoke the presumption [of revocation] imposed by the trial court." We find that argument to be without merit.

Affirmed.

NOTES

1. Revocation and the Meaning of "Presence."   Ms. Speer's lawyer (or his secretary) tore up Ms. Speer's will at her direction, which she had given to the lawyer over the telephone. Why was this not a valid revocation by physical act? What if she had instructed the lawyer in person to destroy her will, but the lawyer did not do so until after she had left his office? Should an attempted revocation by physical act that is ineffective owing to a presence defect be subject to the harmless error rule? We return to this question below at page 229.

Suppose the torn pieces of the will and the postmarked letter from the lawyer stating that "you are without a will" were found among Ms. Speer's personal effects in a file labeled "Revoked Will." What result? *See* SouthTrust Bank of Ala. v. Winter, 689 So. 2d 69 (Ala. App. 1996) (*T* put her will in a paper sack in a closet that she called "trash alley," telling a caretaker that she had "thrown away" her will and needed a new one; court held the will was not revoked).

2. Malpractice.   Suppose the torn pieces of Ms. Speer's will had been found at her death and were probated. Would Ms. Speer's lawyer be liable for malpractice? On what evidence would Ms. Speer's heirs have relied to prove that she had intended the will to be revoked? Why is such evidence reliable enough to impose liability on the lawyer but not to overcome the defective revocation?

Lost Wills and the Presumption of Revocation

The basis for the decision in *Harrison* that Ms. Speer's will had been revoked was not the tearing up of the will. The court relied instead on the presumption of revocation that arises when a will *last known to be in the testator's possession* cannot be found (or is found in a mutilated condition). The law presumes that the will cannot be found because the testator destroyed or mutilated it with the intent to revoke it. The Restatement explains:

> If a will is traced to the testator's possession and cannot be found after death, there are three plausible explanations for its absence: The testator destroyed it with the intent to revoke; the will was accidentally destroyed or lost; or the will was wrongfully destroyed or suppressed by someone dissatisfied with its terms. Of these

plausible explanations, the law presumes that the testator destroyed the will with intent to revoke it.

If a will is traced to the testator's possession and it is found after death with a revocatory act performed on it, there are two plausible explanations for its condition: The testator performed the act with the intent to revoke or the act occurred accidentally. It seems less likely, though still possible, that someone dissatisfied with the terms of the will performed a revocatory act on it and left it where it could be found. Of the plausible explanations for the condition of the will, the law presumes that the testator performed the act on the will with intent to revoke it.[96]

There is a split of authority on how much evidence is needed to overcome the presumption of revocation. Many cases had required clear and convincing evidence, but some more recent cases, following the Restatement, require only a preponderance.[97] If the presumption of revocation is rebutted, the will is entitled to probate if its contents can be proved, unless the party opposing probate proves the will was actually revoked.[98]

In In re Estate of Turner, 265 S.W.3d 709 (Tex. App. 2008), the presumption was rebutted under a preponderance standard by the testimony of a disinterested witness who saw the will on the day of the testator's death and the fact that the testator's disinherited siblings had access to the testator's house immediately after testator's death.

In Edmonds v. Edmonds, 772 S.E.2d 898 (Va. 2015), the presumption was rebutted under a clear and convincing evidence standard. Numerous disinterested witnesses testified that the decedent was satisfied with his estate plan, which was a mirror image to that of his wife of 40 years, and a copy of the will was found neatly preserved among the decedent's file of "important papers."

If a lost or mutilated will was *last known to have been in the possession of someone other than the testator*, there is no presumption of revocation, and the will is entitled to probate unless, of course, there is proof that the testator in fact revoked the will. If a lawyer loses a will held by him for safekeeping, the will is lost but not revoked, and it may be probated if its contents can be proved, as in Smith v. DeParry, 86 So. 3d 1228 (Fla. App. 2012).

The contents of a lost but unrevoked will can be proved by a photocopy, a digital copy, the drafter's notes or recollections, or by other clear and convincing evidence. The testator's exact words need not be proved; only the substance need be shown. If the contents of a lost will cannot be proved in full, the will is entitled to probate to the extent its contents are proved. In some states, such as Florida and New York, the proof must include a copy of the will or the testimony of disinterested witnesses.[99]

---

96. Restatement (Third) of Property: Wills and Other Donative Transfers § 4.1 cmt. j (Am. Law Inst. 1999).

97. *Compare* In re Estate of Beauregard, 921 N.E.2d 954 (Mass. 2010) (preponderance per Restatement), *and* Britt v. Sands, 754 S.E.2d 58 (Ga. 2014) (preponderance per statute), *with* Dan v. Dan, 288 P.3d 480 (Alaska 2012) (clear and convincing per court's assessment of common law).

98. *See* In re Estate of Trikha, 162 Cal. Rptr. 3d 175 (App. 2013).

99. *See* Fla. Stat. § 733.207 (2016); N.Y. Sur. Ct. Proc. Act § 1407 (2016).

NOTE

Lost Wills and Harmless Error?   A few years ago a New Jersey court invoked the harmless error rule of UPC § 2-503, page 177, to probate an *unexecuted copy* of the decedent's lost will. In re Estate of Ehrlich, 47 A.3d 12 (N.J. App. 2012). The decision, which the state high court declined to review,[100] is controversial because it seems implausible that the decedent intended the copy (rather than the signed original) to be his will.[101] The decedent had written "Original mailed to [the named executor]" on the copy that the court probated. To be sure, a copy of a will may be admitted into evidence to prove the contents of the will if the original has been lost but was not revoked. But in *Ehrlich* the court probated the copy itself. The court treated the copy as the decedent's will rather than as proof of the contents of the lost will. Under § 2-503, this is proper only with clear and convincing evidence that the decedent intended the copy itself to be his will.

d. Harmless Error in Revocation

In re Estate of Stoker
122 Cal. Rptr. 3d 529 (App. 2011)

GILBERT, J. . . . Destiny Gularte, Donald Karotick and Robert Rodriguez (appellants) appeal a judgment that denied a petition to probate a 1997 will . . . of Steven Wayne Stoker (decedent), and granted the petition of Danine Pradia and Darrin Stoker (respondents) to probate decedent's 2005 will. We conclude . . . that . . . the trial court did not err by ruling that the 2005 will was valid, and . . . [that] substantial evidence supports the judgment . . . that decedent had revoked the 1997 will. . . . We affirm.

On May 22, 1997, decedent executed a will and nominated Gularte to be the executor of his estate. In Article Two of the will, he listed Karotick and Gularte as the beneficiaries of gifts of personal property. In Article Three, he stated, "I give the residue of my estate to the trustee of the 1997 Steven Wayne Stoker Revocable Trust, created under the declaration of trust executed on the same date as, but immediately before, the execution of this will."[102] Gularte was listed as the successor trustee of that trust. Decedent died on February 27, 2008.

On March 17, 2008, Gularte filed a petition to probate the will and requested that she be appointed the executor. . . .

On March 25, Pradia filed an objection to Gularte's petition to probate the 1997 will and claimed that her father had executed a more recent will. She objected to Gularte being appointed executor. She said, "Gularte is the former girlfriend of my father. My father and [Gularte's] relationship ended in an angry moment in 2001, about 7 years

---

100. *See* In re Estate of Ehrlich, 59 A.3d 602 (N.J. 2013) (Table).

101. *See, e.g.,* Baron, *supra* note 58, at 40-44, 66.

102. This is known as a pour-over devise, and the will is said to be a pour-over will, because it provides for the residue of the testator's probate estate to be poured over into an inter vivos trust and administered in accordance with the terms of the trust. We take up pour-over wills in Chapter 7. — Eds.

ago. My father told me in November 2007 that he was afraid of [Gularte] and thought she was coming into his home and taking things."

On April 28, respondents filed a petition to probate a handwritten will signed by their father on August 28, 2005. The will provides, "To Whom It May Concern: I, Steve Stoker revoke my 1997 trust as of August 28, 2005. Destiny Gularte and Judy Stoker to get nothing. Everything is to go to my kids Darin [*sic*] and Danene [*sic*] Stoker. Darin [*sic*] and Danene [*sic*] are to have power of attorney over everything I own." The will contained no witnesses' signatures.

The 2005 will of Wayne Stoker

At trial, Anne Marie Meier testified that she was a very close friend of decedent. One night in 2005, decedent was discussing "estate planning," and he asked Meier to "get a piece of paper and a pen." He then dictated the terms of the 2005 will. Meier wrote that document in her handwriting "word for word" from decedent's dictation. She handed it to him, "he looked at it and he signed it." Decedent told Meier that this was his last will and testament.

The trial court found that respondents "established that the 2005 document was created at Decedent Stoker's direction and that he signed it," and that there was clear and convincing evidence that the 2005 will "evinces Decedent Stoker's intent." The court ruled that "[s]ince the 2005 will has been accepted for probate by this Court, the 1997 will has been revoked by operation of law." . . .

Appellants claim that the will does not meet the requirements for a "[f]ormal [w]itnessed [w]ill," and therefore the trial court erred by admitting it to probate. A will must be signed by the testator and at least two witnesses. (Cal. Prob. Code § 6110, subds. (b)(1) & (c)(1).) Here the 2005 will is signed by decedent, but it contains no witnesses' signatures. Two witnesses, however, saw decedent sign it, and they testified in court to verify that this will was genuine.

Respondents note that the Probate Code contains a provision that allows wills that are defective in form to be admitted to probate if they are consistent with the testator's intent. Section 6110, subdivision (c)(2) provides, "If a will was not executed in compliance with paragraph (1), the will shall be treated as if it was executed in compliance with that paragraph if the proponent of the will establishes by clear and convincing evidence that, at the time the testator signed the will, the testator intended the will to constitute the testator's will." Here the trial court found that the 2005 document constituted decedent's last will.

The Estate Planning of Steven Wayne Stoker

Dennis J. Balsamo, the winning counsel in *Stoker*, describes Mr. Stoker and his estate planning thus:

Mr. Stoker was dyslexic, with elementary-level reading and writing skills, so he relied upon others to do his correspondence. He hid his dyslexia well, however, so that most of his friends and associates had no idea about it. And why should they? He was a successful business-man who was worth a few million dollars at death.

In 1997 or so, Mr. Stoker called his lawyer late on a Friday afternoon. He told her that he needed a will because he was going to be in an off-road automobile race over the weekend. The lawyer, who did not know of Mr. Stoker's dyslexia, told him that it was too late for her to prepare a formal will but that he could make a holographic will on his own. She told him that a holographic will was valid if it was handwritten and if it was signed by the testator. Anyway, Mr. Stoker survived the race, and the lawyer later drafted the 1997 will and trust that are discussed in the opinion. Mr. Stoker's girlfriend, Destiny Gularte, was the principal beneficiary of Mr. Stoker's 1997 estate plan.

Mr. Stoker and Ms. Gularte broke up in 2001 after she became pregnant by another man. Later that year, while entertaining an old friend and her adult daughter, Mr. Stoker lamented how Ms. Gularte had done him wrong. He said that he was going to make sure that she never inherited anything from him. He went to his safe and retrieved his photocopies of the 1997 will and trust. (The opinion implies that he had the originals, but this is wrong; his lawyer had the originals, he had photocopies.) After his friend read the will and trust to him, he said

Steven Wayne Stoker

that he'd make sure right then and there that Ms. Gularte would get nothing. He took the documents, turned his back on his friend and her daughter, and sprayed the documents with urine. He then threw the documents into the fire pit around which they had been sitting. By the time of the trial, Mr. Stoker's friend was dead, but her adult daughter testified that the documents were able to burn because they were not saturated with urine. Mr. Stoker's urinating on them, it seems, was more in the nature of a symbolic spraying.

In 2005, as Mr. Stoker's health declined, some friends, a husband and wife, asked him if he had his "affairs in order." He said that he did not. He asked the wife to get a pen and paper so that she could write something out for him. She had done this for him many times before. He dictated the 2005 will to her in the presence of the husband. She read it back to him and he read it himself. He said that it expressed his wishes exactly, and he signed it with the husband and the wife looking on. They asked if he wanted them to sign as witnesses, but he said no. Remembering back to the instructions he had received from his lawyer about holographic wills, he told them the will was legal because it was handwritten and he had signed it.

Email from Dennis J. Balsamo to Robert H. Sitkoff (Oct. 10, 2012).

Appellants argue that the Legislature never intended this provision to apply to cases involving handwritten documents. We disagree. . . .

This statute applies to wills that are "in writing" and signed by the testator. (§ 6110, subd. (a); id., subd. (b)(1).) The 2005 document is a written will signed by decedent. The statute contains no language to indicate that the wills covered by this section are limited to typewritten wills. Consequently, handwritten non-holographic wills are not excluded from the scope of this statute. . . .

Appellants [also] contend there is no evidence to show that the 2005 document was intended to be decedent's will. They claim it does not contain "testamentary language," does not use the word will or make reference to death.

The document is certainly not a model will. But "[n]o particular words are necessary to show a testamentary intent" as long as the record demonstrates that the decedent intended the document to be his or her last will and testament. (In re Wunderle's Estate, 181 P.2d 874, 878 (Cal. 1947).)

Here decedent's testamentary intent is evident. The document provides that all of decedent's property will go to his children—the respondents, that the 1997 trust is revoked, that Gularte will receive "nothing," and that his children will have power of attorney "over everything."

Moreover, even if the document is ambiguous, the trial court properly admitted extrinsic evidence. (In re Torregano's Estate, 352 P.2d 505, 512 (Cal. 1960).) That evidence confirmed decedent's testamentary intent. Meier testified that decedent told her the document was "my last will and testament," and "[t]hese are my wishes." Johns testified that decedent told him that the will represented "his final wishes."

Appellants suggest that the record does not support a finding that decedent had any intent to revoke or that he had ever executed any revocation of the 1997 will and trust. We disagree. A will may be revoked where the testator executes a subsequent inconsistent will or where he or she burns or destroys the will. (§ 6120.) The 2005 will expressly and unequivocally provides that the 1997 trust was revoked. The statement in the will that his children were to receive all his property was an express revocation of the earlier 1997 will which purported to give this property to others.[103] In addition, Gretchen Landry, a friend of decedent's, testified that in 2001 decedent took his original copy of the 1997 will, urinated on it and then burned it. We hesitate to speculate how he accomplished the second act after the first. In any event, decedent's actions lead to the compelling conclusion he intended to revoke the 1997 will. . . .

The judgment is affirmed. Costs on appeal are awarded in favor of respondents.

NOTES

1. *Harmless Error in Revocation by Writing.* What were the defects in the execution of the 2005 handwritten instrument that required the harmless error rule to probate it? What was the clear and convincing evidence that Mr. Stoker intended the 2005 instrument to be his will? What of that evidence was extrinsic to the 2005 instrument? In assessing whether Mr. Stoker intended the 2005 instrument to revoke his 1997 will, what is the relevance, if any, of the evidence that he had urinated on and then burned that will (or a copy of it)?

2. *Revocation by Physical Act.* Suppose that the harmless error rule had not been available to validate the 2005 instrument. Would Mr. Stoker's acts of urinating on and then burning the 1997 will constitute a revocation by physical act? Would his estate be distributed any differently in intestacy than it was under the 2005 instrument?

The 2005 instrument expressly revoked Mr. Stoker's "1997 trust as of August 28, 2005." As we shall see in Chapter 7, even if the 2005 instrument could not have been probated as a will, it probably revoked the 1997 trust nonetheless (see page 453). If

---

103. An *express* revocation? The court's theory of revocation is one of *implied* revocation by *inconsistency*. Do you see why?—Eds.

so, the residuary devise in the 1997 will would have failed, and the residue would have passed by intestacy.

3. Harmless Error in Revocation by Physical Act?   We are told that Mr. Stoker in fact urinated on and then burned a photocopy of the 1997 will, not the original (see page 227). Is urinating on and then burning a photocopy of a will, rather than the original, enough to work a physical act revocation of the will? The weight of authority, as in In re Estate of Sullivan, 868 N.W.2d 750 (Minn. App. 2015), and In re Estate of Brewer, 35 N.E.3d 149 (Ill. App. 2015), holds that a physical act of revocation must be done to the original. But if *T*'s revocatory intent is clear, should relief be available in restitution by way of constructive trust? Or should the harmless error rule be applied to a physical act revocation?

There is case law support for relief in restitution. In Gushwa v. Hunt, 197 P.3d 1 (N.M. 2008), the testator wrote "revoked" on each page of a photocopy of his will, allegedly because a third party had wrongfully prevented him from obtaining the original. The court held that if this allegation was proved on remand, a *constructive trust* should be imposed on the unjustly enriched will beneficiary in favor of the testator's heirs.

In In re Estate of Tolin, 622 So. 2d 988 (Fla. 1993), the testator showed a photocopy of his codicil (with a formal blue backing) to a friend, a retired lawyer, and told the friend that he wanted to revoke the codicil. The friend, mistaking the photocopy for the original, told him that he could revoke the codicil by tearing up the document, which the testator did. The testator died, and the original will and codicil were offered for probate. The court held that a physical act upon a photocopy is not enough to revoke the original, and it admitted the codicil to probate. However, the court imposed a constructive trust on the unjustly enriched codicil beneficiary in favor of the will beneficiary.

The applicability of the *harmless error rule* to a botched revocation by physical act is unclear. UPC § 2-503, page 177, applies only to a "document or writing added upon a document." Hence, although § 2-503 may be invoked to overcome harmless error in the execution of a revocatory writing, as in *Stoker*, nothing in the text of § 2-503 speaks to harmless error in a revocation by physical act. But the Restatement (Third) of Property goes further than the UPC. It endorses application of the harmless error rule to a botched revocation by physical act, such as performing a revocatory act on a photocopy, provided that the testator's intent to revoke is proved by clear and convincing evidence:

> The revocatory act must be performed on the will. Performing the act on another document or on an unexecuted copy of the will is insufficient. If, however, the act was performed on the wrong document due to wrongdoing or mistake, a constructive trust may be imposed on the devisees of the will in favor of the persons who would have taken had the will been revoked. Alternatively, if the intent to revoke is proved by clear and convincing evidence, the failure to perform the act on the will, accompanied by performance of the act on a copy that the testator mistakes for the will, may be excused as a harmless error.[104]

---

104. Restatement (Third) of Property: Wills and Other Donative Transfers § 4.1 cmt. f (Am. Law Inst. 1999).

Does urinating on and then burning a copy of a will provide clear and convincing evidence of intent to revoke?

e. Partial Revocation by Physical Act

UPC § 2-507, page 217, and the statutes of most states authorize *partial revocation by physical act*. In a few states, a will cannot be revoked in part by an act of revocation; it can be revoked in part only by a subsequent writing.

The reasoning for the minority view is as follows. A total revocation by physical act causes the decedent's estate to pass either under an earlier will executed in compliance with the Wills Act or by intestacy. Either way, no additional formalities are required. A partial revocation by physical act, by contrast, might rearrange the testator's dispositive plan without complying with the formal requirements for making a will. A few cases have held that the testator can revoke a complete devise ("my car to *A*"), but cannot rearrange the shares in a single devise to increase the other devisee's gift. Here is an example: "$10,000 to *A* and *B*, residue to *C*." *T* later crosses out *B*. Under these cases, *A*'s gift cannot be increased this way. The $5,000 given to *B* falls into the residuary and goes to *C*.

The Restatement (Third) of Property endorses the majority view. It disapproves of "any distinction between revocation of a complete devise and rearranging shares within a single devise or otherwise rewriting the terms of the will by deleting selected words."[105] The Restatement calls this "a classic example of a distinction without a difference."

NOTE

A Partial Revocation Problem.   Suppose *T* executes a will that devises the residue of her estate to four named relatives. After *T*'s death some years later, her will is found in a stack of papers on her desk. One of the four names in the residuary clause has been lined out with a pencil. There is no direct evidence that *T* marked out the name.

a. What result in a state having a statute similar to UPC § 2-507? *Compare* In re Byrne's Will, 271 N.W. 48 (Wis. 1937), *with* In re Estate of Funk, 654 N.E.2d 1174 (Ind. App. 1995).

b. What result in a state that does not permit partial revocation by physical act? *See* Horst v. Horst, 920 N.E.2d 441 (Ohio App. 2009); Estate of Tier, 772 N.Y.S.2d 500 (Sur. 2004); Hansel v. Head, 706 So. 2d 1142 (Ala. 1997).

c. Suppose that *T*'s will is a holograph in a jurisdiction permitting holographic wills. What result? *See* Estate of Schumacher, 253 P.3d 1280 (Colo. App. 2011); La Rue v. Lee, 60 S.E. 388 (W. Va. 1908).

2. Dependent Relative Revocation

If a testator undertakes to revoke her will upon a mistaken assumption of law or fact, under the doctrine of *dependent relative revocation* (DRR) the revocation is ineffective

---

105. Id. cmt. i.

if the testator would not have revoked the will but for the mistaken belief. The basis for disregarding the revocation is that the testator's mistake negates her revocatory intent. A typical DRR case involves a testator who revokes a prior will under a belief that a new will is valid but, in fact, for some reason unknown to the testator, the new will is invalid. If the court finds that the testator would not have revoked her old will had she known that the new will was ineffective, the court will disregard the revocation and probate the destroyed prior will.

LaCroix v. Senecal
99 A.2d 115 (Conn. 1953)

BROWN J. . . . The testatrix, Celestine L. Dupre, died in Putnam on April 19, 1951, leaving as her heir at law and next of kin her niece, the plaintiff. The testatrix left a will dated March 26, 1951, and a codicil thereto dated April 10, 1951. These instruments were admitted to probate on May 22, 1951. Item five of the will reads as follows:

> All the rest, residue and remainder of my property of whatsoever the same may consist and wheresoever the same may be situated, both real and personal, I give, devise and bequeath one-half to my nephew, Nelson Lamoth of Taftville, Connecticut, to be his absolutely; the other one-half to Aurea Senecal of 200 Providence Street, Putnam, Connecticut, to be hers absolutely.

The codicil reads as follows:

> 1. I hereby revoke Item Five of said will and substitute for said Item Five the following: Item Five: All the rest, residue and remainder of property of whatsoever the same may consist and wheresoever the same may be situated, both real and personal, I give, devise and bequeath one-half to my nephew Marcisse Lamoth of Taftville, Connecticut, also known as Nelson Lamoth, to be his absolutely; the other one-half to Aurea Senecal of 200 Providence Street, Putnam, Connecticut to be hers absolutely.
> 2. I hereby republish and confirm my said will in all respects except as altered by this Codicil.

Aurea Senecal is not related to the testatrix. One of the three subscribing witnesses to the codicil was Adolphe Senecal, who at the time he witnessed the codicil was, and still is, the husband of Aurea Senecal. Section 6952 of the General Statutes, so far as material, provides as follows: "Every devise or bequest given in any will or codicil to a subscribing witness, or to the husband or wife of such subscribing witness, shall be void unless such will or codicil shall be legally attested without the signature of such witness . . . ; but the competency of such witness shall not be affected by any such devise or bequest." As the court pointed out in its memorandum of decision, any bequest to Aurea Senecal in item five of the codicil was void because her husband was a subscribing witness.[106] The question left to be answered, therefore, was whether the devise or bequest to the defendant Aurea under item five of the original will stands. It is to be

---

106. On the purging of an interested witness, see page 157. — Eds.

noted that the only difference between item five of the will and item five of the codicil is the substitution for the words "my nephew, Nelson Lamoth of Taftville, Connecticut," in the former, of the words "my nephew Marcisse Lamoth of Taftville, Connecticut, also known as Nelson Lamoth," in the latter. It is also to be noted that by the second paragraph of the codicil the testatrix confirmed the will "in all respects except as altered by this Codicil."

The defendants' brief suggests that the issue on this appeal is whether the doctrine of dependent relative revocation may be invoked to sustain a gift by will, when such gift has been revoked in a codicil which substantially reaffirmed the gift but was void as to it under § 6952 by reason of the interest of a subscribing witness. The gist of the doctrine is that if a testator cancels or destroys a will with a present intention of making a new one immediately and as a substitute and the new will is not made or, if made, fails of effect for any reason, it will be presumed that the testator preferred the old will to intestacy, and the old one will be admitted to probate in the absence of evidence overcoming the presumption. The rule has been more simply stated in these words: "[W]here the intention to revoke is conditional and where the condition is not fulfilled, the revocation is not effective." Matter of Macomber's Will, 87 N.Y.S.2d 308, 310 (App. Div. 1949). As is stated in that opinion at page 312, the doctrine has had wide acceptance in both England and the United States. It is a rule of presumed intention rather than of substantive law; and is applicable in cases of partial as well as total revocation. That it can only apply when there is a clear intent of the testator that the revocation of the old is made conditional upon the validity of the new is well brought out in Sanderson v. Norcross, 136 N.E. 170 (Mass. 1922), and in Estate of Kaufman, 155 P.2d 831 (Cal. 1945), where many cases are cited.

The doctrine has long been accepted in Connecticut, notwithstanding the plaintiff's claim that we should adopt the contrary view. In 1898, Justice Simeon E. Baldwin stated in a case involving a question of this nature: "It being [the testator's] manifest intention to revoke the provision in the will only for this purpose, so far as the purpose fails of effect, the revocation must fall with it. . . . The revocation of his former provision . . . was indissolubly coupled with the creation of the substituted provision." . . .

So far as the factual situation is concerned, it would be difficult to conceive of a more deserving case for the application of the doctrine of dependent relative revocation than the one before us. There is no room for doubt that the sole purpose of the testatrix in executing the codicil was, by making the very minor change in referring to her nephew, to eliminate any uncertainty as to his identity. Obviously, it was furthest from her intention to make any change in the disposition of her residuary estate. When the will and codicil are considered together, as they must be, to determine the intent of the testatrix, it is clear that her intention to revoke the will was conditioned upon the execution of a codicil which would be effective to continue the same disposition of her residuary estate. Therefore, when it developed that the gift under the codicil to the defendant Aurea was void, the conditional intention of the testatrix to revoke the will was rendered inoperative, and the gift to Aurea under the will continued in effect. The situation is well summed up in this statement by the court in a case on all fours with the one at bar: "When a testator repeats the same dispositive plan in a new will, revocation

DRR, Perpetuities, and Body Heat

In Body Heat, a steamy 1981 film noir set in Florida, Matty Walker (Kathleen Turner), a blonde bent on doing away with her rich older husband, entraps a not-so-smart young lawyer, Ned Racine (William Hurt), to do the dirty work.

The husband's existing will leaves half his fortune to Matty and half to his 10-year-old niece, Heather. After the husband is done in by Ned, Matty — a sometime legal secretary — produces a second will, written by Matty on stationery stolen from Ned's office, on which she has forged the signatures of her husband and — to his astonishment — Ned as a witness. The second witness is, well, it takes too long to explain. You'll have to stream the movie or find the DVD.

The second will leaves half of the husband's fortune to Matty, but it puts Heather's half in a trust that violates the Rule Against Perpetuities. At a family conference, the husband's lawyer, oozing unction at every pore, pronounces the second will void. As a result, the lawyer says, the husband died intestate, and under Florida law Matty takes her husband's entire estate. Little Heather and her mother meekly acquiesce and disappear from the movie. Matty ends up on an island paradise with all her husband's money and a new lover. The dupe Ned is left languishing in jail.

Although critics loved the movie, which was boffo at the box office, trusts and estates lawyers might grouse about how the film handled some legal issues. Before the movie was made, Florida had adopted a wait-and-see approach for perpetuities violations (see page 903). So the husband's lawyer was too quick on the trigger; the trust for Heather might not turn out to be void.

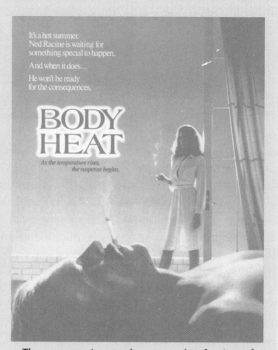

It's a hot summer.
Ned Racine is waiting for something special to happen.
And when it does...
He won't be ready for the consequences.

BODY HEAT

As the temperature rises, the suspense begins.

The screenwriter perhaps can be forgiven for this blunder. The movie was to be set in New Jersey, which at the time had not adopted wait-and-see. The movie was hastily moved to Florida at the last moment, and the script rewritten accordingly, owing to a Teamsters' strike that would have interfered with filming in New Jersey.

But even if the perpetuities mistake is understandable, what about the screenwriter's failure to reckon with DRR? Would not DRR have saved Heather's share?

---

of the old one by the new is deemed inseparably related to and dependent upon the legal effectiveness of the new." Estate of Kaufman, 155 P.2d 831, 834 (Cal. 1945). In short, in the words of the court in Matter of Macomber's Will, 87 N.Y.S.2d 308, 312 (App. Div. 1949), "the facts here fit well within the classic pattern of the rule in its most reliable aspect, and it ought to be applied to the facts of this case." . . .

There is no error.

NOTES

1. A DRR Problem. A clause of *T*'s typewritten will provides: "I bequeath the sum of $1,000 to my nephew, Charles Blake." *T* crosses out the "$1,000" and substitutes

"$1,500"—a larger bequest. *T* then writes her initials and the date in the right-hand margin opposite this entry. After *T*'s death some years later, her will is admitted to probate. Blake contends that he is entitled to $1,500 or, in the alternative, $1,000.

    a. What result in a state that recognizes holographic wills? *Compare* In re Estate of Foxley, 575 N.W.2d 150 (Neb. 1998), *with* Restatement (Third) of Property: Wills and Other Donative Transfers § 3.2 cmt. g illus. 9 (Am. Law Inst. 1999).

    b. What result if two witnesses observed the testator's modifications and then signed the will? *See* In re Will of Litwack, 827 N.Y.S.2d 582 (Sur. 2006).

    c. What result in a state that does not permit partial revocation by physical act?

    d. What result in a state that permits partial revocation by physical act? Should the court apply DRR? *See* Carpenter v. Wynn, 67 S.W.2d 688 (Ky. 1934).

    e. Suppose that *T* instead crosses out "$1,000" and substitutes "$500"—a smaller bequest. In a state that permits partial revocation by physical act, should the court apply DRR? *See* Ruel v. Hardy, 6 A.2d 753 (N.H. 1939).

2. Another DRR Problem. In his typewritten will, which contains a legacy of $5,000 to "John Boone," *T* crosses out "John" and writes in "Nancy." If strict compliance with the Wills Act is required, Nancy cannot take because the gift to her is not attested. In a state permitting partial revocation by physical act, should the legacy to John be given effect under DRR? *See* In re Houghten's Estate, 17 N.W.2d 774 (Mich. 1945); Estate of Lyles, 615 So. 2d 1186 (Miss. 1993). Suppose John was Nancy's father. How would this affect your analysis? *See* Carpenter v. Cosby, 34 So. 3d 1230 (Miss. App. 2010).

    In a state that recognizes holographic wills, the change from John to Nancy is probably not a valid holograph even if *T* signs his name on the margin. Standing alone, the handwritten words are insufficient to constitute a will. On the other hand, if *T*'s will were entirely handwritten and a valid holograph, the change from John to Nancy should be permitted. *See* Estate of Archer, 239 Cal. Rptr. 137 (App. 1987); Stanley v. Henderson, 162 S.W.2d 95 (Tex. 1942).

Restatement (Third) of Property:
Wills and Other Donative Transfers (Am. Law Inst. 1999)

§ 4.3. Ineffective Revocation (Dependent Relative Revocation)

    (a) A partial or complete revocation of a will is presumptively ineffective if the testator made the revocation:

        (1) in connection with an attempt to achieve a dispositive objective that fails under applicable law, or

        (2) because of a false assumption of law, or because of a false belief about an objective fact, that is either recited in the revoking instrument or established by clear and convincing evidence.

    (b) The presumption established in subsection (a) is rebutted if allowing the revocation to remain in effect would be more consistent with the testator's probable intention.

NOTES

1. Limitations on DRR.   With rare exceptions, courts have held that DRR applies only (1) if there is an alternative plan of disposition that fails, or (2) if the mistake is recited in the terms of the revoking instrument or, possibly, is established by clear and convincing evidence. The alternative plan of disposition is usually in the form of another will, either duly or defectively executed. By so limiting the doctrine, the kind of extrinsic evidence that can be considered is narrowed.[107]

2. An Alternative Disposition That Fails.   *T* writes "VOID" across her duly executed current will. Several days later she shows the defaced will to her lawyer and instructs the lawyer to prepare a new one.

a. Before the lawyer finishes preparing the new will, *T* dies. Does DRR apply so as to allow the court to disregard the revocation of the earlier will? In Mosley v. Lancaster, 770 S.E.2d 873 (Ga. 2015), the court refused to apply DRR, reasoning that *T* revoked the earlier will prior to her meeting with the lawyer.

b. The lawyer prepares a draft, but when he shows it to *T*, she tells the lawyer that it describes some property incorrectly and is wrong in some other ways that must be changed. Before the draft can be corrected and executed, *T* dies. The lawyer testifies who the beneficiaries were to be under the new will. Does DRR apply so as to allow the court to disregard the revocation of the earlier will? In Estate of Ausley, 818 P.2d 1226 (Okla. 1991), the court refused to apply DRR because the lawyer's testimony failed to prove a definite alternative plan of disposition.

3. Mistake Is Recited in the Revoking Instrument or Proved by Clear and Convincing Evidence.   *T*'s will bequeaths $5,000 to his old friend, Judy, and the residue of his estate to his brother, Mark.

a. *T* later executes a codicil as follows: "I revoke the legacy to Judy, since she is dead." In fact, Judy is still living and survives *T*. Does Judy take $5,000? In Campbell v. French (1797) 30 Eng. Rep. 1033; 3 Ves. Jun. 321, on similar facts, the court held that there was no revocation, "the cause being false."

b. Suppose the codicil had read: "I revoke the legacy to Judy, since I have already given her $5,000." In fact, the testator did not give Judy $5,000 during life. What result? *See* Witt v. Rosen, 765 S.W.2d 956 (Ark. 1989).

c. Suppose that the codicil had read: "I revoke the legacy to Judy." Evidence is offered that shows that three weeks prior to execution of the codicil, *T* was told by a friend that Judy had died, believing it to be true. In fact, Judy survives *T*. What result? *Compare* In re Salmonski's Estate, 238 P.2d 966 (Cal. 1951) (holding DRR not applicable because the mistake was not recited on the face of the will), *with* Estate of Anderson, 65 Cal. Rptr. 2d 307 (App. 1997) (holding DRR applicable

---

107. *See* Richard F. Storrow, Dependent Relative Revocation: Presumption or Probability?, 48 Real Prop. Tr. & Est. L.J. 497 (2014); Frank L. Schiavo, Dependent Relative Revocation Has Gone Astray: It Should Return to Its Roots, 13 Widener L. Rev. 73 (2006).

because the mistake was inferable from the dispositive instruments and supported by the drafter's testimony).

3. Revival of Revoked Wills

The doctrine of *revival* governs the reinstatement of a previously revoked will.[108] The question of revival typically arises under the following facts: *T* executes will 1. Subsequently, *T* executes will 2, which expressly revokes will 1 or does so by inconsistency. Later, *T* revokes will 2, commonly by physical act. If the doctrine of revival applies, the previously revoked will 1 is valid (is "revived") without having to be re-executed or republished by a later codicil (see page 244).

The states tend to fall within one of two groups on the question of whether will 1 is revived under the facts just posited. A majority of states hold that upon revocation of will 2, will 1 is revived if the testator so intends. Such intent may be shown from the circumstances surrounding the revocation of will 2 or from the testator's contemporaneous or subsequent oral declarations that will 1 is to take effect. UPC § 2-509 (1990), excerpted below, is fairly representative of statutes that follow the majority view.

A minority of states take the view that a revoked will cannot be revived unless re-executed with testamentary formalities or republished by being referred to in a later duly executed will. Application of the minority view, and its intersection with dependent relative revocation (DRR), is illustrated by In re Estate of Alburn, 118 N.W.2d 919 (Wis. 1963). In that case, *T* executed a will in 1955. In 1959, she executed a new will, which expressly revoked the 1955 will. In 1960, *T* tore up the 1959 will, intending to revive the 1955 will. *T* died a few years later.

At the time, Wisconsin followed the minority "no revival of revoked wills" rule: A revoked will may not be revived unless re-executed or republished by codicil. So the 1955 will was not revived when *T* destroyed the 1959 will. However, because the 1959 will more nearly approximated *T*'s intent than intestacy—that is, the 1959 will more nearly approximated the terms of the 1955 will than intestacy—the court applied DRR to disregard the revocation of the 1959 will. The (destroyed) 1959 will was admitted to probate, with its contents proved by a carbon copy.

The court's decision rested on the finding that the dispositions in the 1959 will more nearly approximated what *T* was trying to do—revive the 1955 will—than would an intestate distribution. But having made this finding, wouldn't the more sensible outcome be to probate the 1955 will, as *T* had intended? Under UPC § 2-509 and in a majority of states, including in Wisconsin today, *T*'s revocation of the 1959 will with the intent to revive the 1955 will would indeed revive the 1955 will, allowing it to be admitted to probate.

---

108. *See* Restatement (Third) of Property: Wills and Other Donative Transfers § 4.2 (Am. Law Inst. 1999).

Uniform Probate Code (Unif. Law Comm'n 1990)

§ 2-509. Revival of Revoked Will

(a) If a subsequent will that wholly revoked a previous will is thereafter revoked by a revocatory act under Section 2-507(a)(2), the previous will remains revoked unless it is revived. The previous will is revived if it is evident from the circumstances of the revocation of the subsequent will or from the testator's contemporary or subsequent declarations that the testator intended the previous will to take effect as executed.

(b) If a subsequent will that partly revoked a previous will is thereafter revoked by a revocatory act under Section 2-507(a)(2), a revoked part of the previous will is revived unless it is evident from the circumstances of the revocation of the subsequent will or from the testator's contemporary or subsequent declarations that the testator did not intend the revoked part to take effect as executed.

(c) If a subsequent will that revoked a previous will in whole or in part is thereafter revoked by another, later will, the previous will remains revoked in whole or in part, unless it or its revoked part is revived. The previous will or its revoked part is revived to the extent it appears from the terms of the later will that the testator intended the previous will to take effect.

NOTES

1. Revival Under the UPC.   Under UPC § 2-509(a), if a subsequent will that *wholly* revoked the previous will is itself revoked by physical act, the presumption is that the previous will remains revoked. Under § 2-509(b), if a subsequent will that *partly* revoked the previous will is itself revoked by physical act, the presumption is that the previous will is revived. Under § 2-509(c), if a subsequent will (will 2) that revoked a previous will (will 1) is itself revoked by another, later will (will 3), the previous will (will 1) is revived to the extent indicated by the later will (will 3).

2. A Revival Problem.   In 2017, *T* dies. *T*'s heir is *H*. *T*'s safe deposit box contains these three documents, all duly signed and witnessed:

(1) A will executed in 2007 devising all of *T*'s property to *A*.
(2) A will executed in 2014 devising all of *T*'s property to *B*.
(3) A document executed in 2015 reading: "I hereby revoke my 2014 will."

Under UPC § 2-509(c), who takes *T*'s property?

3. DRR After Revival and Harmless Error.   In a state that has enacted UPC § 2-509 on revival and § 2-503 on harmless error, is DRR still necessary? *See* UPC § 2-507 cmt. (1990).

4. Revocation by Operation of Law

In the time between execution of a will and the testator's death, which may span years or even decades, circumstances can change in ways that render the will stale or obsolete. The law of wills includes a variety of doctrines meant to address this problem, including several that presumptively revoke a will in whole or in part by operation of law in light of certain changed circumstances.[109] These rules of presumptive revocation, which rest on a legislative judgment about the typical testator's probable intent, can be overcome by evidence of contrary actual intent.

a. Divorce

Statutes in nearly all states provide that a divorce presumptively revokes any provision in a decedent's will for the decedent's divorced spouse. UPC § 2-804 prescribes a revocation-on-divorce rule not only for wills but also for nonprobate transfers.

Uniform Probate Code (Unif. Law Comm'n 1990, as amended 2017)

§ 2-804. Revocation of Probate and Nonprobate Transfers by Divorce; No Revocation by Other Changes of Circumstances

...(b) [Revocation Upon Divorce.] Except as provided by the express terms of a governing instrument,[110] a court order, or a contract relating to the division of the marital estate made between the divorced individuals before or after the marriage, divorce, or annulment, the divorce or annulment of a marriage:

(1) revokes any revocable

(A) disposition or appointment of property made by a divorced individual to his [or her] former spouse in a governing instrument and any disposition or appointment created by law or in a governing instrument to a relative of the divorced individual's former spouse,

(B) provision in a governing instrument conferring a general or nongeneral power of appointment on the divorced individual's former spouse or on a relative of the divorced individual's former spouse, and

(C) nomination in a governing instrument, nominating a divorced individual's former spouse or a relative of the divorced individual's former spouse to serve in any fiduciary or representative capacity, including a personal representative, executor, trustee, conservator, agent, or guardian; and

(2) severs the interests of the former spouses in property held by them at the time of the divorce or annulment as joint tenants with the right of survivorship [or as community property with the right of survivorship], transforming the interests of the former spouses into equal tenancies in common. . . .

(d) [Effect of Revocation.] Provisions of a governing instrument are given effect as if the former spouse and relatives of the former spouse disclaimed all provisions revoked by this section or, in the case of a revoked nomination in a fiduciary or representative capacity, as if the former spouse and relatives of the former spouse died immediately before the divorce or annulment. . . .

---

109. We take up other stale will doctrines in Chapter 5 at page 351 and in Chapter 8 at page 571.

110. The term "governing instrument" is defined in UPC § 1-201(18) to mean a deed, will, trust, insurance or annuity policy, account with a payable-on-death designation, pension plan, or other such nonprobate transfer. — Eds.

(f) [No Revocation for Other Change of Circumstances.] No change of circumstances other than as described in this section and in Section 2-803 effects a revocation. . . .

NOTE

Revocation on Divorce and Kin of an Ex-Spouse.   Suppose *T* executes a will devising his estate to his wife, and if his wife does not survive him, then to his wife's son (*T*'s stepson). *T* divorces his wife and then dies. *T*'s heirs are his children by a prior marriage. A state statute revokes all provisions in a will for a divorced spouse, treating the divorced spouse as having predeceased the testator. Does the stepson take *T*'s estate? *See* Friedman v. Hannan, 987 A.2d 60 (Md. 2010). Who takes under UPC § 2-804? *See* Estate of Marchwick, 234 P.3d 879 (Mont. 2010).

b. Marriage

Under old law, a premarital will is revoked upon marriage. Most states today have changed this rule by statute so that a premarital will remains valid in spite of a subsequent marriage, but a surviving *pretermitted spouse*—that is, a surviving spouse whom the decedent spouse married after executing his or her will—may take an intestate share of the deceased spouse's estate, unless the will indicates that the omission was intentional or the spouse is provided for in the will or by a will substitute. UPC § 2-301 (1990, rev. 1993), page 571, is representative. The effect of these statutes is to revoke a premarital will to the extent of a pretermitted spouse's intestate share. If one of the exceptions applies, in a separate property state the pretermitted spouse may be able to take an *elective* or *forced share* of the decedent spouse's estate. We take up the pretermitted spouse and elective share statutes in Chapter 8.

c. Birth of Children

A few states follow the old rule that marriage followed by birth of children revokes a will executed before marriage. This rule, which was not codified in the UPC, is rapidly disappearing. Instead, almost all states have *pretermitted child* statutes, which give a child born after the execution of a parent's will, and not mentioned in the will, a share in the parent's estate. UPC § 2-302 (1990, rev. 1993), page 575, is an example. Some pretermitted child statutes include children born before the execution of the will as well as children born thereafter. A pretermitted child statute, if applicable, results in a revocation of the parent's will to the extent of the share given to the child under the statute. We take up these statutes in Chapter 8.

C. COMPONENTS OF A WILL

In Section A of this chapter, we considered the formalities with which a will must be executed. We saw that if the applicable Wills Act is not complied with exactly in all its particulars, a testamentary instrument may not be entitled to probate even if there is no doubt that the testator intended the instrument to be her will. Yet it is possible for a writing that lacks the testator's signature or attestation by witnesses, or even for actions of the testator, to play a role in determining who will take what from the testator's estate. In this section, we are concerned with a handful of doctrines that can have this effect: (1) integration, (2) republication by codicil, (3) incorporation by reference, and (4) acts of independent significance.

1. Integration

Wills are often written on more than one sheet of paper. Under the doctrine of *integration*, all papers that are present at the time of execution and are intended to be part of the will are treated as part of the will.

In re Estate of Rigsby
843 P.2d 856 (Okla. App. 1992)

JONES, J. This appeal is taken by Betty Dorsey, sister of Decedent, Jessaline Pasquali Rigsby, from an order admitting a Holographic Will to probate as permitted under the provisions of 58 O.S. 1991 § 721(2). The document, as offered, consisted of two pages. The Will, as admitted to probate, consists of a single page.

The error, as urged on appeal, is the failure of the trial court to allow the second page to also be admitted. The purported Will was found by the surviving spouse, Don Rigsby, folded together in a ledger, but not otherwise fastened to each other. Both pages are written in the hand of the Decedent, and are initialled and dated at the top of each page with the same date. One page was signed at the bottom of the writing, leaving approximately two and one-half inches below it blank. This page, the parties agree, exhibits testamentary intent, beginning: "Inasmuch as I do not have a will, I would like to make the following arrangements in the event of my death." The second page, just as the other, is not numbered and does not refer to the first in any way. This page is a simple list of personal property, with each item followed by the name of an individual. Although this page is initialled at the top, it is not signed. . . .

Appellant raises . . . only one proposition to be discussed here, and that is do the two pages together constitute a valid holographic testamentary disposition of Decedent's property. . . .

Courts generally adhere strictly to statutory provisions regarding the execution, interpretation, and probate of wills. This rule is said to be especially true in the case of holographic wills. Thus, where the instrument offered consists of more than one sheet of paper, it must be made clearly apparent the testator intended that together they should constitute the last will and testament of the testator. In re Paull's Estate, 254 P.2d 357 (Okla. 1953).

The first page of the offered Will, admitted to probate, is dated and signed and appears to be complete as a single page. It makes no mention of a list such as the second offered page. There is no reference in either page to the existence of the other page. Additionally, the second page conflicts in part with the first page. An example of the conflict is the division of Decedent's jewelry. The first page divides the jewelry

"Inasmuch as I do not have a will, I would like to make the following arrangements in the event of my death."

The first of the two pages at issue in *Rigsby*

between her two boys and her sister. The second page gives the Indian jewelry lock box to Joe and Jay and Betty L., and the remainder of the whole estate is to be sold with the proceeds going to Don Rigsby. Additionally, the first page requests the money she has in the bank is to pay for horse breeding and boarding bills and futurity fees, while the second page gives the cash to Don. The second page could easily be interpreted as a work sheet listing Decedent's assets as a preliminary step before drafting the first page.

Accordingly, . . . the trial court did not err in concluding the first page alone constituted the complete Holographic Will of the Decedent, inasmuch as it does not clearly appear the second page was intended to be included with the first. . . .

Affirmed.

The second of the two pages at issue in *Rigsby*

NOTE

What Papers Constitute the Will?   The doctrine of integration addresses the question of which sheets of paper, present at the time of execution, were intended to be part of the will. The answer is usually obvious, as typically the pages are physically connected with a staple and are numbered, or, failing this, there is a sufficient connection of language carrying over from one page to another to show a coherent progression. The lawyer can avoid litigation by ensuring that the pages of the will are numbered and are fastened together before the testator signs, and by having the testator sign or initial each page of the will for identification (see page 160).

2. Republication by Codicil

Under the doctrine of *republication by codicil*, a validly executed will is treated as re-executed (i.e., *re*published) as of the date of the codicil. "A will is treated as if it were executed when its most recent codicil was executed, whether or not the codicil expressly republishes the prior will, unless the effect of so treating it would be inconsistent with the testator's intent."[111]

Updating the execution date of a will by republication can have significant consequences. Suppose that a testator revokes his first will by a second will and then executes a codicil to the first will. If the first will is republished, the second will is revoked by implication ("squeezed out"). The doctrine should be applied only if updating the will carries out the testator's intent. Thus:

> *Case 1.* The jurisdiction has a statute purging any gift to an attesting witness (see page 157). In 2015, *T* executes a will devising all his property to *A*. *A* and *B* are witnesses to the will. In 2016, *T* executes a codicil devising $5,000 to *C*. *C* and *D* are witnesses to the codicil. In 2017, *T* executes a second codicil devising a diamond ring to *C*. *D* and *E* are witnesses to the second codicil. Under the doctrine of republication by codicil, the will and first codicil are deemed to be re-executed in 2017 by the second codicil, which has two disinterested witnesses. *A* and *C* are not purged of their gifts.

In Estate of Nielson, 165 Cal. Rptr. 319 (App. 1980), the testator drew lines through the dispositive provisions of his typewritten will and wrote between the lines: "Bulk of Estate—1.—Shrine Hospital for Crippled Children—Los Angeles, $10,000—2. Society for Prevention of Cruelty to Animals." Near the margin of these cancellations and interlineations were the testator's initials and date. At the top and bottom of the will were the handwritten words, "Revised by Lloyd M. Nielson November 29, 1974." The court held the handwritten words constituted a holographic codicil that republished the typewritten will as modified.

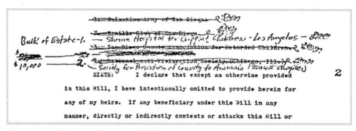

The revised dispositions in *Nielson*

---

111. Restatement (Third) of Property: Wills and Other Donative Transfers § 3.4 (Am. Law Inst. 1999).

3. Incorporation by Reference

a. Existing Writings

Incorporation by reference allows for a writing that was in existence but not present at the time of execution and that was not itself executed with testamentary formalities to be absorbed into the testator's will—a kind of constructive integration.

Uniform Probate Code (Unif. Law Comm'n 1990)

§ 2-510. Incorporation by Reference

A writing in existence when a will is executed may be incorporated by reference if the language of the will manifests this intent and describes the writing sufficiently to permit its identification.

Clark v. Greenhalge
582 N.E.2d 949 (Mass. 1991)

NOLAN, J. We consider in this case whether a probate judge correctly concluded that specific, written bequests of personal property contained in a notebook maintained by a testatrix were incorporated by reference into the terms of the testatrix's will.

We set forth the relevant facts as found by the probate judge. The testatrix, Helen Nesmith, duly executed a will in 1977, which named her cousin, Frederic T. Greenhalge, II, as executor of her estate. The will further identified Greenhalge as the principal beneficiary of the estate, entitling him to receive all of Helen Nesmith's tangible personal property upon her death except those items which she "designate[d] by a memorandum left by [her] and known to [Greenhalge], or in accordance with [her] known wishes," to be given to others living at the time of her death.[112] Among Helen Nesmith's possessions was a large oil painting of a farm scene signed by T.H. Hinckley and dated 1833. The value of the painting, as assessed for estate tax purposes, was $1,800.00.

In 1972, Greenhalge assisted Helen Nesmith in drafting a document entitled "MEMORANDUM" and identified as "a list of items of personal property prepared with Miss Helen Nesmith upon September 5, 1972, for the guidance of myself in the distribution of personal tangible property." This list consisted of forty-nine specific bequests of Ms. Nesmith's tangible personal property. In 1976, Helen Nesmith modified the 1972 list by interlineations, additions and deletions. Neither edition of the list involved a bequest of the farm scene painting.

Ms. Nesmith kept a plastic-covered notebook in the drawer of a desk in her study. She periodically made entries in this notebook, which bore the title "List to be given Helen Nesmith 1979." One such entry read: "Ginny Clark farm picture hanging over fireplace. Ma's room." Imogene Conway and Joan Dragoumanos, Ms. Nesmith's private home care nurses, knew of the existence of the notebook and had observed Helen Nesmith write in it. On several occasions, Helen Nesmith orally expressed to these

---

112. The value of Ms. Nesmith's estate at the time of her death exceeded $2,000,000.00, including both tangible and nontangible assets.

"If I could pick just one keepsake, I think it would be the mutual funds."
Barbara Smaller/The New Yorker Collection/The Cartoon Bank

nurses her intentions regarding the disposition of particular pieces of her property upon her death, including the farm scene painting. Helen Nesmith told Conway and Dragoumanos that the farm scene painting was to be given to Virginia Clark, upon Helen Nesmith's death.

Virginia Clark and Helen Nesmith first became acquainted in or about 1940. The women lived next door to each other for approximately ten years (1945 through 1955), during which time they enjoyed a close friendship. The Nesmith-Clark friendship remained constant through the years. In more recent years, Ms. Clark frequently spent time at Ms. Nesmith's home, often visiting Helen Nesmith while she rested in the room which originally was her mother's bedroom. The farm scene painting hung in this room above the fireplace. Virginia Clark openly admired the picture.

According to Ms. Clark, sometime during either January or February of 1980, Helen Nesmith told Ms. Clark that the farm scene painting would belong to Ms. Clark after Helen Nesmith's death. Helen Nesmith then mentioned to Virginia Clark that she would record this gift in a book she kept for the purpose of memorializing her wishes with respect to the disposition of certain of her belongings.[113] After that conversation, Helen Nesmith often alluded to the fact that Ms. Clark someday would own the farm scene painting.

---

113. According to Margaret Young, another nurse employed by Ms. Nesmith, Ms. Nesmith asked Ms. Young to "print[ ] in [the] notebook, beneath [her] own handwriting, 'Ginny Clark painting over fireplace in mother's bedroom.'" Ms. Young complied with this request. Ms. Young stated that Ms. Nesmith's express purpose in having Ms. Young record this statement in the notebook was "to insure that [Greenhalge] would know that she wanted Ginny Clark to have that particular painting."

Ms. Nesmith executed two codicils to her 1977 will: one on May 30, 1980, and a second on October 23, 1980. The codicils amended certain bequests and deleted others, while ratifying the will in all other respects.

Greenhalge received Helen Nesmith's notebook on or shortly after January 28, 1986, the date of Ms. Nesmith's death. Thereafter, Greenhalge, as executor, distributed Ms. Nesmith's property in accordance with the will as amended, the 1972 memorandum as amended in 1976, and certain of the provisions contained in the notebook. Greenhalge refused, however, to deliver the farm scene painting to Virginia Clark because the painting interested him and he wanted to keep it. Mr. Greenhalge claimed that he was not bound to give effect to the expressions of Helen Nesmith's wishes and intentions stated in the notebook, particularly as to the disposition of the farm scene painting. Notwithstanding this opinion, Greenhalge distributed to himself all of the property bequeathed to him in the notebook. Ms. Clark thereafter commenced an action against Mr. Greenhalge seeking to compel him to deliver the farm scene painting to her.

The probate judge found that Helen Nesmith wanted Ms. Clark to have the farm scene painting. The judge concluded that Helen Nesmith's notebook qualified as a "memorandum" of her known wishes with respect to the distribution of her tangible personal property, within the meaning of Article Fifth of Helen Nesmith's will.[114] The judge further found that the notebook was in existence at the time of the execution of the 1980 codicils, which ratified the language of Article Fifth in its entirety. Based on these findings, the judge ruled that the notebook was incorporated by reference into the terms of the will. Newton v. Seaman's Friend Soc'y, 130 Mass. 91, 93 (1881). The judge awarded the painting to Ms. Clark. . . . We . . . now hold that the probate judge correctly awarded the painting to Ms. Clark.

A properly executed will may incorporate by reference into its provisions any "document or paper not so executed and witnessed, whether the paper referred to be in the form of . . . a mere list or memorandum, . . . if it was in existence at the time of the execution of the will, and is identified by clear and satisfactory proof as the paper referred to therein." Id. at 93. The parties agree that the document entitled "memorandum," dated 1972 and amended in 1976, was in existence as of the date of the execution of Helen Nesmith's will. The parties further agree that this document is a memorandum regarding the distribution of certain items of Helen Nesmith's tangible personal property upon her death, as identified in Article Fifth of her will. There is no dispute, therefore, that the 1972 memorandum was incorporated by reference into the terms of the will.

The parties do not agree, however, as to whether the documentation contained in the notebook, dated 1979, similarly was incorporated into the will through the language of Article Fifth. Greenhalge advances several arguments to support his contention that the purported bequest of the farm scene painting written in the notebook was not incorporated into the will and thus fails as a testamentary devise. The points

114. Article Fifth of Helen Nesmith's will reads, in pertinent part, as follows: "that [Greenhalge] distribute such of the tangible property to and among such persons *as I may designate by a memorandum left by me and known to him, or in accordance with my known wishes*, provided that said persons are living at the time of my decease" (emphasis added).

raised by Greenhalge in this regard are not persuasive. First, Greenhalge contends that the judge wrongly concluded that the notebook could be considered a "memorandum" within the meaning of Article Fifth, because it is not specifically identified as a "memorandum." Such a literal interpretation of the language and meaning of Article Fifth is not appropriate.

"The 'cardinal rule in the interpretation of wills, to which all other rules must bend, is that the intention of the testator shall prevail, provided it is consistent with the rules of law.'" Boston Safe Deposit & Trust Co. v. Park, 29 N.E.2d 977, 979 (Mass. 1940), quoting McCurdy v. McCallum, 72 N.E. 75 (Mass. 1904). The intent of the testator is ascertained through consideration of "the language which [the testatrix] has used to express [her] testamentary designs," Taft v. Stearns, 125 N.E. 570, 571 (Mass. 1920), as well as the circumstances existing at the time of the execution of the will. The circumstances existing at the time of the execution of a codicil to a will are equally relevant, because the codicil serves to ratify the language in the will which has not been altered or affected by the terms of the codicil.

Applying these principles in the present case, it appears clear that Helen Nesmith intended by the language used in Article Fifth of her will to retain the right to alter and amend the bequests of tangible personal property in her will, without having to amend formally the will. The text of Article Fifth provides a mechanism by which Helen Nesmith could accomplish the result she desired; i.e., by expressing her wishes "in a memorandum." The statements in the notebook unquestionably reflect Helen Nesmith's exercise of her retained right to restructure the distribution of her tangible personal property upon her death. That the notebook is not entitled "memorandum" is of no consequence, since its apparent purpose is consistent with that of a memorandum under Article Fifth: It is a written instrument which is intended to guide Greenhalge in "distribut[ing] such of [Helen Nesmith's] tangible personal property to and among . . . persons [who] are living at the time of her decease." In this connection, the distinction between the notebook and "a memorandum" is illusory.

The appellant acknowledges that the subject documentation in the notebook establishes that Helen Nesmith wanted Virginia Clark to receive the farm scene painting upon Ms. Nesmith's death. The appellant argues, however, that the notebook cannot take effect as a testamentary instrument under Article Fifth, because the language of Article Fifth limits its application to "a" memorandum, or the 1972 memorandum. We reject this strict construction of Article Fifth. The language of Article Fifth does not preclude the existence of more than one memorandum which serves the intended purpose of that article. As previously suggested, the phrase "a memorandum" in Article Fifth appears as an expression of the manner in which Helen Nesmith could exercise her right to alter her will after its execution, but it does not denote a requirement that she do so within a particular format. To construe narrowly Article Fifth and to exclude the possibility that Helen Nesmith drafted the notebook contents as "a memorandum" under that Article, would undermine our long-standing policy of interpreting wills in a manner which best carries out the known wishes of the testatrix. See Boston Safe Deposit & Trust Co., 29 N.E.2d at 979. The evidence supports the conclusion that Helen Nesmith intended that the bequests in her notebook be accorded the same power and effect as those contained in the 1972 memorandum under Article Fifth.

We conclude, therefore, that the judge properly accepted the notebook as a memorandum of Helen Nesmith's known wishes as referenced in Article Fifth of her will. . . .

The judge further found that the notebook was in existence on the dates Helen Nesmith executed the codicils to her will [which republished her will], . . . and that it thereby was incorporated into the will pursuant to the language and spirit of Article Fifth. . . .

Lastly, the appellant complains that the notebook fails to meet the specific requirements of a memorandum under Article Fifth of the will, because it was not "known to him" until after Helen Nesmith's death. For this reason, Greenhalge states that the judge improperly ruled that the notebook was incorporated into the will. One of Helen Nesmith's nurses testified, however, that Greenhalge was aware of the notebook and its contents, and that he at no time made an effort to determine the validity of the bequest of the farm scene painting to Virginia Clark as stated therein. There is ample support in the record, therefore, to support the judge's conclusion that the notebook met the criteria set forth in Article Fifth regarding memoranda.

We note, as did the Appeals Court, that "one who seeks equity must do equity and that a court will not permit its equitable powers to be employed to accomplish an injustice." Pitts v. Halifax Country Club, Inc., 476 N.E.2d 222, 228 (Mass. App. 1985). To this point, we remark that Greenhalge's conduct in handling this controversy fell short of the standard imposed by common social norms, not to mention the standard of conduct attending his fiduciary responsibility as executor, particularly with respect to his selective distribution of Helen Nesmith's assets. We can discern no reason in the record as to why this matter had to proceed along the protracted and costly route that it did.[115]

Judgment affirmed.

NOTES

1. "A Writing in Existence When a Will Is Executed." Could the entry in the notebook, "Ginny Clark farm picture," have been incorporated by reference into Ms. Nesmith's will if it had not been made before the 1980 codicils? Was there any evidence that the entry was in fact made before the 1980 codicils?

The court said that Article Fifth of the will, which instructed the executor to distribute certain tangible personal property in accordance with a memorandum left by the testator, gave the testator "the right to alter and amend the bequests of tangible

---

115. And it had costly consequences for Greenhalge, the executor and residuary beneficiary of Helen Nesmith's will. A letter from Thomas D. Burns, counsel for Virginia Clark, to Jesse Dukeminier dated Sept. 27, 1993, reveals:

While the picture was later appraised at about $35,000, its stated value by the executor Greenhalge in the inventory was only $1500. I was awarded a fee of $80,000 by the Probate Court, which I settled for $70,000 to avoid an appeal. The executor, who was a very terrible guy, refused to give up the picture and I thought the case would be on a pro bono basis, but the Probate Judge who heard the case was so incensed by Greenhalge's conduct, he awarded me my full hourly rate upon application.

—Eds.

personal property in her will, without having to amend formally the will." Is this permissible under the incorporation by reference doctrine? In Cyfers v. Cyfers, 759 S.E.2d 475 (W. Va. 2014),[116] the court declined to incorporate an exhibit into a will because some of the text of the exhibit had been written after execution of the will:

> [T]here is no dispute that there was an Exhibit A attached to the Will at the time the Will was submitted to probate. There is, however, no evidence regarding what bequests were contained within Exhibit A at the time the Will was executed. Rather, . . . the Decedent's attorney . . . testified that at least some of the notations contained within Exhibit A were made after the Will was executed. . . . No additional evidence was offered by the parties to show what language was contained within Exhibit A on the date the Will was executed. . . . Given the uncertainty as to what bequests were contained in Exhibit A at the date of execution of the Decedent's Will, we are compelled to conclude that there was insufficient evidence to allow the incorporation of Exhibit A by reference into the Will.

If inconsistent with a traditional understanding of incorporation by reference, could *Clark* be understood as a precursor to the tangible personal property rule of UPC § 2-513, page 252? To the harmless error rule of UPC § 2-503, page 177?

2. Incorporating Printed Text into a Holographic Will. Suppose *T* writes the following in a signed and handwritten document: "When I die I want all of my property to be distributed in accordance with typed instructions that I have already put in a sealed envelope in my desk drawer." Is this a valid incorporation by reference? Can a holographic will incorporate a writing that is not in the testator's handwriting? The authorities are scarce and contradictory.

In Johnson v. Johnson, 279 P.2d 928 (Okla. 1955), *T*, a lawyer, prepared three typewritten paragraphs stating that the document was *T*'s will and making various bequests. The typewritten text was not signed by *T* or witnessed, and it appears to end mid-sentence. Beneath the typewritten text, at the bottom of the page, *T* wrote the following by hand: "To my brother James I give ten dollars only. This will shall be complete unless hereafter altered, changed or rewritten." *T* signed and dated the document below the handwritten portion.

The court held that "the valid holographic codicil incorporated the prior will by reference and republished and validated the prior will as of the date of the codicil, thus giving effect to the intention of the testator." Is this a proper application of the republication by codicil doctrine? Was the typewritten portion itself a validly executed will that could be republished, as in Estate of Nielson, page 244? Or is this a holding that the handwriting at the bottom of the page was a freestanding holographic will that incorporated the typewritten text by reference? Or should the court have denied probate on the grounds that the integration doctrine required treating the page as a single testamentary document? What result under the harmless error rule of UPC § 2-503, page 177?

---

116. In an opinion by Justice Margaret L. Workman (see page 151).

JOHNSON v. JOHNSON
Cite as, Okl., 279 P.2d 928

Okl.   933

31691

129067

~~~~ 564 PAGE ~~

FILED IN COUNTY COURT
OKLAHOMA COUNTY, OKLA.

JUL 2 1952

CLIFF MYERS, COURT CLERK

By _____ DEPUTY

I, D. G. Johnson also known as Dexter C. Johnson, of Oklahoma City, Oklahoma County, State of Oklahoma do hereby make, publish and declare this to be my last Will and Testamnt and revoke all former wills and codocils by me made.

FIRST: I direct my Executor to pay my just debts, last illness and burial expense.

SECOND: I give, devise and bequeath to my sister Beulah Johnson also known as Beulah J. Johnson and my brother V. C. Johnson also known as Victor C. Johnson all of the rest, residue and rrmainder of my estate, real, personal and mixed propertt, wherever situated and whatsoever kind and/or character, subject only to the following requests of my said brother and sister, namely and specifically that at a time when in the jydgment of my said sister and brother they shall deem the cpndition of the estate in a proper and suitable condition so to do without material injury~~~~~ damage to or otherwise detrimental to said estate and the properties reasonably disposed of to pay into a trust fund to be governed by my said sister and brother the sum of Fifty thousand dollars to be used for the erection of a new church in Montrose, Effingham County, State of Illinois on the site where the present church now stands being the church formerly attended by our family regularly and to build a parsonage of not less than six rooms, nor more than eight rooms on the lots owned by me across the street from said church site and said lots to be deeded to said church organization for the use of the minister to preside over the church aforesaid; also to use any sum remaining for a mauseloeum or suitable arrangement as my said sister and brother may determine proper and fitting for the graves of our family now buried there and any sum then remaining to generally improve said cemetery a ll as my said sister and brother may determine; if there be difference of opinions or desires in any matter, then the will and desire of my sister shall prevail. and further that a fund of Ten thousand dollars to be set up and invested in SAFE SECURITIES with reasonable rate of interest for the use and benefit of my great neice Joanna Johnson and a similiar sum for Joanna's sister with same conditions and to be paid to each of them in monthly payments of Seventy-five dollars each month beginning on their seventeenth birthday and thereafter until exhausted ans each shall have received the full sum together with it's accruals of ten thousand dollars or a total of twenty thousand dollars; I also request that a fund of ten thousand dollars be set up for the purpose of paying to my brother Joseph Evera d Johnson a monthoy stipend of fifty dollars each and every month during his life to begin ninety days after my death and to end with the death of my said brother or the exhaustion of the funds if they shall, exhaust prior to his death with any sum remaining to remune to the use and benefit of my brother Victor C. Johnson and sister Beulah J. Johnson, and yhe further sum of Five yhousand dollars to be paid within reasonable time to Alma L. Kloss friend of my sister Beulah J.Johnson in appreciation for her kindness and sincere friendship to and for my sister Beulah J. Johnson with the request tHat said Alma L. Kloss invest same in some good securities, government bonds or annuity, ~~~~~~~. I further suggest that my said sister and brother employ Claude Monnett, attorney and friend of mine be employed for a reasonable fee, to be agreed upon by ~~~~~~~~~~~ my sister, brother and Mr. Monnett for complete service but should they not agree then my said brother and sister shall employ whomsoever they may desire, being contious that nothing to be done without their consent and knowledge

The will in Johnson v. Johnson

In Berry v. Trible, 626 S.E.2d 440 (Va. 2006), after the lawyer sent *T* a draft will, *T* made handwritten changes to it, signing each page at the bottom. On one of the pages *T* wrote, "I Give and bequeath all," followed by an arrow pointing to her handwritten notation of the intended beneficiary.[117] The court held that the document could not be probated as a holograph, because the handwriting and the typed text were interwoven, "both physically and in sequence of thought."

The same issue arises in the context of a preprinted will form. In In re Estate of Gonzalez, page 204, the court held "that printed portions of a will form can be incorporated into a holographic will," but here, too, the cases are mixed (see page 209).

b. Subsequent Writings and Tangible Personal Property

In a break from traditional law, UPC § 2-513 (1990) allows a testator to dispose of tangible personal property by a separate writing, *even if prepared after the execution of the testator's will*, provided that the will makes reference to the separate writing. In effect, this provision authorizes what the court in Clark v. Greenhalge, page 245, said the testator had done in that case — namely, reserve the power to make and then continue to revise a list of bequests of tangible personal property without additional testamentary formalities. A slim majority of states has adopted a version of UPC § 2-513.

Uniform Probate Code (Unif. Law Comm'n 1990)

§ 2-513. Separate Writing Identifying Devise of Certain Types of Tangible Personal Property

Whether or not the provisions relating to holographic wills apply, a will may refer to a written statement or list to dispose of items of tangible personal property not otherwise specifically disposed of by the will, other than money. To be admissible under this section as evidence of the intended disposition, the writing must be signed by the testator and must describe the items and the devisees with reasonable certainty. The writing may be referred to as one to be in existence at the time of the testator's death; it may be prepared before or after the execution of the will; it may be altered by the testator after its preparation; and it may be a writing that has no significance apart from its effect on the dispositions made by the will.

NOTE

The Meaning of "Dispose Of" in UPC § 2-513.   *T* executes a will that references a separate writing for the disposition of tangible personal property. Sometime thereafter, *T* signs a typed memorandum, which she has notarized, that includes a schedule of gifts of certain items of tangible personal property. At the end of the memo, *T* instructs her executors to auction the remainder of her tangible personal property and to distribute the proceeds to five named persons. Is this instruction permissible under UPC § 2-513? In In re Last Will and Testament of Moor, 879 A.2d 648 (Del. Ch. 2005),

---

117. The case report includes an image of the marked up (draft?) will. *See* 626 S.E.2d at 448.

then-Vice Chancellor Leo E. Strine, Jr., upheld the instruction under § 2-513, reasoning that the statutory term "dispose of" did not mandate an in-kind distribution:

> The point of [the statute] is to provide testators with a more flexible means by which to devise their personal property. That legislative intention was accomplished, as are most public policy judgments, by a compromise between competing values. The more rigorous formalities required of the body of a will itself were relaxed, permitting a testator to dispose of personal property by a simple, unwitnessed writing that becomes an annex to the will. By that tradeoff, [the] legislature[ ] made the judgment

Leo E. Strine, Jr., was named Chief Justice of the Delaware Supreme Court in 2014.

Richard Drew/AP photo

This document is an add on to the current WILL of Betty R. Moor.

She wishes to have the following things distributed to the following people at the time of the reading of her current WILL. As of the 10th day of January, 2001 this document has become a part of the original document.

Item #1--Hutch table large (Grandmothers), to Marylin Moor

Item #2--1 box of Rose Medallion dishes & tea set (Grandmothers), to Marylin Moor

Item #3--Silverware with silver chest (Grandmothers), to Marylin Moor

Item #4--7 water color and pastel paintings by Emma H. Cooper (My Portrait), to Marylin Moor

Item #17--All Christmas ornaments to Mary Eveland

Item #18--Secretary desk in bedroom upstairs to Dede Pardee

Any items not listed in this WILL are to be auctioned, the capitol gain from the auction is to be dispersed to those stated in the aforesaid of this document.

I, Betty R. Moor, being in sound mind and body, do by placing my signature on this document affirm and attest that this document is to be added to my current registered WILL.

Witness
LISA K. BLANKENSHIP
NOTARY PUBLIC STATE OF MARYLAND
My Commission Expires September 17, 2003

Betty R. Moor   (SEAL) 3-9-01
                        Date

The memorandum in *Moor*

that the flexibility and convenience of this method were, on balance, worth the enhanced possibility that such a writing might not reflect the uncoerced, free will of the testator. . . .

The executors concede that a testator may convey an expensive painting directly in a separate writing, thereby giving the recipient ownership and the right to sell the painting for cash profit. As a result, it is difficult to conceive of what public policy offense occurs if the testator instead directs her executors to sell the painting and to convey the sale proceeds to certain persons. In either case, the economic incentives for designing persons, and the corresponding economic risk to the testator and other possible objects of her testamentary good wishes, remain the same. And, in either case, the crucial question should not turn on how many signatures were on the personal property memorandum, but on whether the personal property memorandum was the product of the testator's rational and uncoerced wishes.

Should there be an upper limit to the value of tangible personal property that can be disposed of by separate memorandum? An early draft of UPC § 2-513 imposed a $500 limit, but this limit was removed before promulgation of the final version.[118] In California, no single item passed in this way can have a value in excess of $5,000 and the total cannot exceed $25,000.[119]

4. Acts of Independent Significance

There is one more doctrine that sometimes permits extrinsic evidence to identify the beneficiaries or property passing under a will. If the beneficiary or property designations are identified by reference to acts or events that have a lifetime motive and significance apart from their effect on the will, the gift will be upheld under the doctrine of *acts of independent significance* (also called the doctrine of *nontestamentary acts*). This is true even if the terms of the will enable the testator to alter the beneficiaries or the property by a subsequent nontestamentary act. Case 2 illustrates some common applications of the acts of independent significance doctrine.

Case 2.   *T*'s will devises "the automobile that I own at my death" to her nephew, *N*, and gives $1,000 "to each person who shall be in my employ at my death." At the time the will is executed, *T* owns an old Toyota. Shortly before her death, *T* trades in the Toyota for a new BMW, with the result that *T* dies owning a $50,000 automobile rather than one worth $20,000. In the year before her death, *T* fires two long-time employees and hires three new ones.

Although *T*'s acquisition of the BMW significantly increased the value of her gift to *N*, it is unlikely that this motivated her purchase. It is more likely that she bought the car with her own use in mind. Likewise, *T*'s acts in hiring and firing employees were likely prompted by staffing needs rather than a desire to change the beneficiaries under her will.

---

118. *See* Adam J. Hirsch, Inheritance and Inconsistency, 57 Ohio St. L.J. 1057, 1106 n.142 (1996).
119. Cal. Prob. Code § 6132 (2016).

Uniform Probate Code (Unif. Law Comm'n 1990)

§ 2-512. Events of Independent Significance

A will may dispose of property by reference to acts and events that have significance apart from their effect upon the dispositions made by the will, whether they occur before or after the execution of the will or before or after the testator's death. The execution or revocation of another individual's will is such an event.

NOTES

The Contents Of.   Can a bequest of "the contents of" *T*'s home or *T*'s safe be enforced under the doctrine of acts of independent significance?

a. *T* bequeaths "the contents of my house" to *A.* In *T*'s house are a variety of belongings, including furniture, jewelry, artwork, and clothing, as well as a safe containing stock certificates and cash. Does *A* take these items? *See* In re Estate of Light, 895 N.E.2d 43 (Ill. App. 2008); In re Estate of Isenberg, 823 N.Y.S.2d 381 (App. Div. 2006).

b. *T* bequeaths "the contents of the right-hand drawer of my desk" to *A.* In the drawer at *T*'s death are a savings bank passbook in *T*'s name, a certificate for 100 shares of General Electric common stock, and a diamond ring. Does *A* take these items?

c. *T* bequeaths "the contents of my safe deposit box in Security Bank" to *B* and "the contents of my safe deposit box in First National Bank" to *C.* Do *B* and *C* take the items found in the respective boxes? *See* Annot., 5 A.L.R.3d 466 § 44 (1966, rev. 2016).

d. *T*'s will provides: "I have put in my safe deposit box in Continental Bank shares of stock in several envelopes. Each envelope has on it the name of the person I desire to receive the stock contained in the envelope." At *T*'s death, several envelopes are found in *T*'s safe deposit box, each with the name of a person written on the envelope. Inside each is a stock certificate. In one envelope is a certificate for 200 shares of Coca-Cola stock and on the envelope is written "For Ruth Moreno." Do Ruth Moreno and the other persons take the stock in the envelopes bearing their names? *See* Will of Le Collen, 72 N.Y.S.2d 467 (Sur. 1947); Smith v. Weitzel, 338 S.W.2d 628 (Tenn. App. 1960).

D. CONTRACTS RELATING TO WILLS

During life, a person may exercise her *freedom of contract* to bind herself to a particular exercise of her *freedom of disposition* at death by way of a *contract to make a will* or *not to revoke a will.* Contract law, not the law of wills, applies. To enforce the contract, the contract beneficiary must sue under the law of contracts and prove a valid contract.

If a party to a valid will contract dies leaving a will that does not comply with the terms of the contract, the will is probated in accordance with the Wills Act, but the contract beneficiary is entitled to a remedy for the breach. In some states, the remedy takes the form of damages. In others, courts impose a constructive trust in favor of the contract beneficiary to prevent the unjust enrichment of the will beneficiary. What makes the will beneficiary's enrichment unjust, warranting relief in restitution, is the testator's breach of contract. In still other states, courts speak of an award of specific performance, but the remedy in those cases more closely resembles a constructive trust than true specific performance, since the Wills Act requires probating the breaching will.

1. Contracts to Make a Will

A contract to make a will typically arises in the context of a premarital or divorce agreement or as part of an agreement to take care of a sick or older person.

Many states subject contracts to make a will to a Statute of Frauds provision, such as UPC § 2-514 (1990), which requires a signed writing for the contract to be enforced. In the absence of a signed writing, the contract beneficiary may be entitled to restitution of the value of services rendered to the decedent (*quantum meruit*). The difficulty

". . . and to my faithful valet, Sidney, whom I promised to remember in my will—'Hi there, Sidney'—!"

Marvin Tannenberg/Playboy Magazine

is that the beneficiary must still prove the existence of the agreement.[120] States that do not require a writing for a contract to make a will typically require clear and convincing evidence of the contract and its terms.

Uniform Probate Code (Unif. Law Comm'n 1990)

§ 2-514. Contracts Concerning Succession

A contract to make a will or devise, or not to revoke a will or devise, or to die intestate, if executed after the effective date of this [article], may be established only by (i) provisions of a will stating material provisions of the contract, (ii) an express reference in a will to a contract and extrinsic evidence proving the terms of the contract, or (iii) a writing signed by the decedent evidencing the contract. The execution of a joint will or mutual wills does not create a presumption of a contract not to revoke the will or wills.

NOTE

Caregiving and Contracts to Make a Will.   Suppose *T* agrees in a contract with *A* to leave everything to *A* at *T*'s death if *A* takes care of *T* for life. *T* executes a will leaving her estate to *A*. Subsequently, *A* changes her mind and decides not to care for *T*. *T* rescinds the contract. Upon *T*'s death, is *A* entitled to take under *T*'s will? In Trotter v. Trotter, 490 So. 2d 827 (Miss. 1986), the court held that *A* was entitled to take under the will. But was *A* unjustly enriched so that *A* would be liable to *T*'s heirs in restitution?

Suppose *W* promises her husband, *H*, that she will take care of him for his life in consideration of *H* devising Blackacre to her. Sometime thereafter, *H* dies, devising Blackacre to *A*. Is the contract enforceable by *W*? Has consideration been given by *W*? *See* Borelli v. Brusseau, 16 Cal. Rptr. 2d 16 (App. 1993) (unenforceable because no consideration; *W* had legal duty to care for *H*); In re Estate of Braaten, 96 P.3d 1125 (Mont. 2004) (applying presumption that services rendered to decedent by a relative are gratuitous; quantum meruit claim denied).[121]

2. Contracts Not to Revoke a Will

Cases involving a contract not to revoke a will typically involve a married couple that has executed a joint will or mutual wills. A *joint will* is one instrument executed by two persons as the will of both. When one of them dies, the instrument is probated as the decedent's will. Then, when the other dies, the instrument is again probated, this time as the will of the second decedent. Despite being relatively uncommon, joint wills have spawned a great deal of litigation. Well-counseled testators do not use them.

---

120. *See, e.g.,* Symons v. Heaton, 316 P.3d 1171 (Wyo. 2014) (rejecting contract claim by decedent's friend who had taken care of decedent in exchange for purported promise to inherit "everything").

121. Commentators have criticized the limited enforceability of a contract to make a will in favor of caregiving kin. *See* Thomas P. Gallanis & Josephine Gutler, Family Caregiving and the Law of Succession: A Proposal, 45 U. Mich. J.L. Reform 761 (2012); Joshua C. Tate, Caregiving and the Case for Testamentary Freedom, 42 U.C. Davis L. Rev. 129 (2008).

Mutual wills, also called *reciprocal* or *mirror-image wills,* are separate wills of two persons that contain mirror-image provisions. Mirror-image wills are common because spouses often want to favor the surviving spouse and then the same beneficiaries after the death of the survivor. The term *mutual wills* is also occasionally—and confusingly—used to describe a joint will or reciprocal or mirror-image wills that are accompanied by a contractual agreement not to revoke.

There are no legal consequences peculiar to joint or mirror-image wills unless they are subject to a contract. The difficulty is in proving the fact of such a contract and its terms.

Keith v. Lulofs
724 S.E.2d 695 (Va. 2012)

POWELL, J. The issue before this Court is whether the trial court erred in deciding that Walter Steven Keith ("Keith") failed to prove that the 1987 wills executed by Arvid L. Keith, Jr. ("Arvid") and Lucy F. Keith ("Lucy") were irrevocable, reciprocal wills. We hold that the trial court did not err and, therefore, will affirm the trial court's judgment. . . .

Arvid and Lucy were married in 1972. At the time of their marriage, each had a child from a previous marriage: Arvid had a son, Keith, and Lucy had a daughter, Venocia W. Lulofs ("Lulofs").

Arvid and Lucy executed wills on December 9, 1987, that were "mirror images" of each other. Each will left the estate first to the surviving spouse and then to Keith and Lulofs equally.

Arvid died on March 21, 1996, and his estate passed to Lucy pursuant to the 1987 will. Following Arvid's death, Lucy executed a new will on May 17, 1996, in which she left the entirety of her estate to Lulofs and made no provision for Keith. Lucy died in 2006. After Lucy's death, Lulofs attempted to probate Lucy's will, which Keith challenged.

The evidence also demonstrated that in 1994, Arvid and Lucy took out an insurance policy naming both Keith and Lulofs as the primary beneficiaries, each with a 50% share of the proceeds. Lucy changed the beneficiary percentages on the insurance policy on April 1, 1996, such that Keith would receive 22% and Lulofs would receive 78%. Lucy changed the insurance policy again on May 30, 1996, so that Lulofs received 100%.

Keith testified about several conversations that he had had about the wills and insurance policy. Specifically, he testified that in 1991, his father told him that he and Lucy made "reciprocal wills" leaving everything to Lulofs and him in equal shares. He testified that in 1994 Lucy mentioned the life insurance policy, saying that they did this so there "won't be any money to fight over once we die." He also testified that shortly before Arvid died, Arvid told him to "watch out for [Lucy]." Arvid told him that he was

Justice Cleo Elaine Powell, the first African-American woman to be appointed to the Virginia Supreme Court
Steve Helber/AP photo

going to ensure that everything was divided evenly. Keith testified that Lulofs told him in 2006 that their parents had reciprocal wills.

Lulofs testified that she recalled a discussion between Arvid, Lucy, Keith and herself about the life insurance policy, but did not remember the specifics of that conversation.

Keith argued that Arvid and Lucy executed reciprocal wills in 1987 that became an irrevocable contract upon the death of either party. He also alleged that the estate was to be funded with the proceeds of the life insurance policy and that the policy was evidence of the testators' intent to make the 1987 wills irrevocable.

Although the trial court concluded that the 1987 wills were "mutual and reciprocal," it found that the evidence was insufficient to prove that the wills reflected a contractual agreement to bind the survivor. . . .

On appeal, Keith makes two basic arguments. First, Keith contends that because the 1987 wills were "mirror image" wills, the testators intended them to be irrevocable. Second, he argues that even if the content of the wills does not clearly establish their contractual nature, he presented sufficient corroborative evidence of the testators' intent. Specifically, he asserts that 1) the testimony from Keith and Lulofs corroborated the 1987 wills; 2) the 1994 insurance policy indicates the intent that the 1987 wills were to be irrevocable upon the death of one testator; and 3) Keith's testimony about various out-of-court statements by Arvid corroborate the parties' intent. . . .

Where a party asserts that the wills are reciprocal and irrevocable, it is important to distinguish the law of wills and the law of contracts. A significant distinction between the two areas of law is that wills, unlike contracts, generally are unilaterally revocable and modifiable. A will does not become irrevocable or unalterable simply because it is drafted to "mirror" another testator's will. . . . "[T]he contractual nature of the instrument does not necessarily defeat its character as a will, but enables the party for whose benefit the contract was made to prevent, by resorting to a court of equity, a revocation which would destroy the compact or the trust created thereby." Williams v. Williams, 96 S.E. 749, 750 (Va. 1918) (citations omitted).

Thus, "when reciprocal testamentary provisions are made for the benefit of a third party, there is sufficient consideration for the contractual element of the will to entitle the beneficiary to enforce the agreement in equity, *provided* the contract itself is established." Salley v. Burns, 255 S.E.2d 512, 516 (Va. 1979). Proof of the contractual nature of this agreement between the testators must be "clear and satisfactory." Id. Such proof "may expressly appear in the language of the instrument, or it may be supplied by competent witnesses who testify to admissions of the testators, or it may result as an implication from the circumstances and relations of the parties and what they have actually provided for by the instrument." Id. at 516-17.

In Black v. Edwards, 445 S.E.2d 107, 109 (Va. 1994), this Court held that the mutual and reciprocal wills at issue were irrevocable contracts. We based that decision upon the unimpeached testimony of the drafting attorney who testified that the parties intended to draft reciprocal, irrevocable wills. Here, the attorney who drafted the wills for Arvid and Lucy in 1987 had no recollection of the wills or the circumstances under which they were prepared, nor did he remember the 1996 will that he drafted for Lucy after Arvid's death. . . .

The language at issue . . . in the 1987 wills [provides]:

> I give, devise and bequeath unto my beloved [spouse] if [spouse] survives me by thirty days, all of my property and estate, real, personal and mixed, wherever situate, whether now acquired or acquired hereafter, to be [spouse's] in fee simple and [spouse's] absolute property. . . .
>
> In the event that my [spouse] predeceases me or fails to survive me by thirty days, I give, devise and bequeath all of my property of every sort, kind and description, real, personal, and mixed, unto [Keith] and [Lulofs] in equal shares, share and share alike. . . .

The interpretation urged by Keith would create the very real risk that any testator who executes a will that "mirrors" another will and contains language similar to that contained in the wills at issue here, would be unintentionally hamstrung by the death of the purportedly reciprocal testator. In fact, the testator would be unable to provide for any future spouse or any child born or adopted during a later marriage. Such an interpretation is unreasonable.

The language of these "mirror image" wills is insufficient alone to form a contract and, therefore, Keith failed to meet his burden to show that the 1987 wills were irrevocable. . . .

Keith argued that even if the express language of the wills was not sufficient to establish a contract, he presented sufficient circumstantial evidence to establish that Arvid and Lucy intended for the wills to be contracts. We disagree.

In pertinent part the Dead Man's Statute, Code § 8.01-397, provides:

> In an action by or against a person who, from any cause, is incapable of testifying, or by or against the committee, trustee, executor, administrator, heir, or other representative of the person so incapable of testifying, no judgment or decree shall be rendered in favor of an adverse or interested party founded on his uncorroborated testimony.

This statute was enacted largely to provide relief from the harsh common law rule that would have prohibited testimony from the surviving witness and, therefore, the nature and quantity of the corroboration will vary depending on the facts of the case. Corroboration may, and often must, be shown through circumstantial evidence, but each point need not be corroborated nor must the corroboration rise to the level of confirmation as long as the corroboration strengthens the testimony provided by the surviving witness.

Here, Keith provided no independent evidence or testimony to corroborate his testimony regarding the contractual nature of the wills. Keith's argument that Lulofs' testimony corroborates his is without merit. Lulofs merely testified that she recalled a discussion about the insurance policy between herself, Keith, Arvid and Lucy, but Lulofs could not recall the specifics of that conversation. Further, the existence of the insurance policy itself does not provide corroboration. An insurance policy taken out seven years after the wills were executed cannot provide evidence as to the intent of the testators at the time the wills were drafted. Thus, no evidence in this record corroborates Keith's testimony as required by the Dead Man's statute. . . .

For the foregoing reasons, we will affirm the judgment of trial court.
Affirmed.

NOTES

1. Why a Contract Not to Revoke?   *Keith* involves a typical fact pattern in the cases involving a contract not to revoke a will. *H* and *W* want the surviving spouse to take everything, with anything left at the survivor's death to be divided equally among their children from prior marriages. Knowing that the survivor will have closer ties to his or her own children, they are uncomfortable leaving the disposition of their combined estates entirely in the control of the survivor. When we take up trusts later in this book, you will find that this dilemma almost always can be better solved with inter vivos and testamentary trusts than with a will contract.[122]

2. Clear and Convincing Evidence and the Statute of Frauds.   Some courts have been too quick to infer a contract from the use of a joint will or from a common dispositive scheme in mirror-image wills. The majority view, followed in *Keith*, is that the execution of a joint will or mirror-image wills does not, by itself, give rise to a presumption of contract. The contract must be proved by clear and convincing evidence (what the court in *Keith* called "clear and satisfactory").

In some cases, the court searched the language of a joint will for indications of agreement, sometimes finding that plural first-person pronouns such as *we* and *our* indicated a contract not to revoke, as in Glass v. Battista, 374 N.E.2d 116 (N.Y. 1978). Such litigation can be avoided by inserting in every joint will a provision declaring that the will is or is not subject to a contract not to revoke. But the lawyer who is astute enough to be aware of this problem probably also knows that joint wills are notorious litigation-breeders that should not be used at all.

Many states subject will contracts to a Statute of Frauds provision, such as UPC § 2-514, page 257. What result in *Keith* if § 2-514 were applicable? *See* Oravec v. Phillips, 785 S.E.2d 295 (Ga. 2016).

3. Reconciling Will Contracts with the Wills Act.   Why is it that a contract to make or not to revoke a will can be proved with clear and convincing evidence or with a signed writing, but (generally speaking) a will must be proved with a signed *and attested* writing? *See* Adam J. Hirsch, Formalizing Gratuitous and Contractual Transfers: A Situational Theory, 91 Wash. U. L. Rev. 797 (2014).

4. The Dead Man's Statutes.   The *dead man's statutes* bar an interested party from testifying about a decedent's oral statements in support of a claim against the decedent's estate. The purpose is to protect the estate from false claims. The theory is that, because the decedent cannot give rebuttal testimony, the survivor's lips should be sealed too.[123]

---

122. Or perhaps the law should allow for an irrevocable will? *See* Alex M. Johnson, Jr., Is It Time for Irrevocable Wills?, 53 U. Louisville L. Rev. 393 (2016).

123. *See, e.g.*, Taylor v. Taylor, 643 N.E.2d 893, 896 (Ind. 1994) ("The central purpose of the Dead Man's statute is to ensure that when one party to a transaction has had her lips sealed by death the other party's lips are sealed by law.").

The prevailing view among evidence scholars is that the dead man's statutes exclude evidence of a valid claim more often than they protect the estate from a false claim.[124] Most states have abrogated the rule, and it is not in the Federal Rules of Evidence. Some states have replaced the rule with a more permissive variant, such as giving the court discretion to admit the testimony if the court first determines that the decedent in fact made the statement, or, as in *Keith*, allowing the testimony if corroborated by other evidence.

5. Problems of Interpretation.   Tricky questions of interpretation arise under contracts between spouses not to revoke their wills:

a. Suppose in *Keith* that a contract had been proved. After Arvid's death, what rights in the property would Lucy have had during her lifetime? Would she be restricted in what she could do with her own property as well as the property she received from Arvid? *See* Estate of Draper v. Bank of America, 205 P.3d 698 (Kan. 2009); In re Estate of Erickson, 841 N.E.2d 1104 (Ill. App. 2006).

b. Suppose Lucy put the bulk of her property in a revocable trust to pay the remainder, on her death, to Lulofs, or that Lucy made Lulofs a joint tenant on all of Lucy's bank accounts. Would this be a breach of contract? *Compare* Self v. Slaughter, 16 So. 3d 781 (Ala. 2008) (breach), *with* Estate of Hedrick v. Lamach, 324 P.3d 1202 (Mont. 2014) (not a breach).

c. Suppose Lucy wanted to take a new boyfriend on a round-the-world cruise. Would that have been permitted? Suppose she wanted to buy him a diamond-studded Rolex watch?

d. Suppose Lucy had inherited property from her brother or won the lottery after Arvid died. Would the contract apply to the new property? Do you see the practical problem?

6. Forced Share; Pretermitted Share; Revocation on Divorce.   Suppose in *Keith* a contract not to revoke had been proved, and that Lucy married Bernie and then predeceased him without having changed her will. Can Bernie take his *forced share* of Lucy's estate? Could he take an intestate share as a *pretermitted spouse*, because Lucy executed her will prior to their marriage? Or should the contract beneficiaries have priority over a subsequent spouse? *Compare* Gregory v. Estate of Gregory, 866 S.W.2d 379 (Ark. 1993) (contract beneficiaries prevail), *with* Via v. Putnam, 656 So. 2d 460 (Fla. 1995) (subsequent spouse prevails).[125]

Suppose that Lucy and Arvid divorced and then Arvid died without having executed a new will. The state revocation-on-divorce statute would apply to the will, revoking the provisions for Lucy. But could she still take her share by enforcing the contract? *See* In re Estate of Pence, 327 S.W.3d 570 (Mo. App. 2010).

---

124. *See* Kenneth S. Broun, McCormick on Evidence § 65 (7th ed. 2014); *see also* State Farm Fire & Casualty Co. v. Prinz, 743 S.E.2d 907 (W. Va. 2013) (abrogating the "heavily antiquated" dead man's statute under the court's power to make rules of evidence).

125. *See also* Carolyn L. Dessin, The Troubled Relationship of Will Contracts and Spousal Protection: Time for an Amicable Separation, 45 Cath. U. L. Rev. 435 (1996).

CHAPTER 4

WILLS: CAPACITY
AND CONTESTS

It has been said . . . that a will is more apt to be the subject of litigation
than any other legal instrument. To say the least, it is an instrument
frequently made the subject of litigation. Usually it is the most important
document executed in a person's lifetime. This immediately suggests
that a will representing the true wishes of a testator of sound mind
should be so prepared and executed as to be invulnerable, if possible,
to an improper attack.

LEON JAWORSKI
10 Baylor L. Rev. 87, 88 (1958)

BY MAKING A WILL, a person can direct the distribution of his probate property at death, avoiding the default distribution of intestacy. But what if the
person's will, although properly executed, was not *voluntarily* made? It follows
from the principle of freedom of disposition that only a voluntary act of testation
should be enforced.

In this chapter, we consider the grounds for a *will contest* in which the contestant alleges that a will executed with proper formalities was nonetheless not voluntary because of the *incapacity* of the testator or the *undue influence, duress,* or *fraud* of
another. We also consider the parallel claim that the decedent would have made a new
will but for the undue influence, duress, or fraud of another. Although an unexecuted
will cannot be probated, the decedent's frustrated intent can be honored in *restitution,*
preventing *unjust enrichment,* by imposing a *constructive trust* in favor of the decedent's
intended beneficiary.

The complication in these matters, as in the prior chapter, is the *worst evidence*
problem inherent to probate procedure whereby the best witness is dead by the time
the issue is litigated. The line between indelicate but lawful persuasion on the one hand,
and undue influence and duress on the other, can be difficult to discern in posthumous
litigation. Distinguishing between the peculiarities of old age and true mental infirmity
can be equally vexing. Judges and juries may be tempted to find undue influence or
incapacity if the testator's dispositions seem unfair or unnatural.

The law governing will contests attempts to balance the risk of giving effect to an involuntary act of testation with the risk of denying effect to a voluntary one. If courts are too reluctant to set aside a will, the unscrupulous will find profit in manipulating vulnerable testators. But if courts are too willing to set aside a will, those with standing may bring a contest as a means to extract an unjustified settlement.

We begin in Section A by considering claims of mental incapacity and insane delusion. In Section B, we consider undue influence and the elaborate scheme of inferences, presumptions, and burden shifting that imposes structure on this unruly concept. We also examine precautionary measures to be considered if a contest is anticipated. In Section C, we consider duress and its relationship to undue influence. In Section D, we consider fraud and its overlap with undue influence. Finally, in Section E, we consider the tort of interference with inheritance, which has emerged as a rival to will contests and actions in restitution for cases involving undue influence, duress, or fraud.

A. CAPACITY TO MAKE A WILL

1. Mental Capacity

The mental capacity required to make a will is minimal.[1] Although the phrasing varies across jurisdictions, the basic substance is fairly captured by the Restatement thus:

> [T]he testator . . . must be capable of knowing and understanding in a general way [1] the nature and extent of his or her property, [2] the natural objects of his or her bounty, and [3] the disposition that he or she is making of that property, and must also be capable of [4] relating these elements to one another and forming an orderly desire regarding the disposition of the property.[2]

The test for *testamentary capacity* is one of capability, not actual knowledge. If the test were one of actual knowledge, a reasonable mistake about whether a child was alive or the value of a parcel of land would incapacitate the testator for not knowing the natural objects of his bounty or the nature and extent of his property.[3] Nor must the testator be of median intelligence, as this would incapacitate half the population. The low threshold for testamentary capacity is meant to respect the testator's personal autonomy while also assuring the testator that the disposition he desires will be carried out even after the onset of mental decay. In this way, the requirement of capacity implements the principle of freedom of disposition.[4]

---

1. In almost every state, and under Uniform Probate Code § 2-501 (Unif. Law Comm'n 1990), a person must be at least 18 years old to make a will. Should this age be reduced? *See* Mark Glover, Rethinking the Testamentary Capacity of Minors, 79 Mo. L. Rev. 69 (2014).

2. Restatement (Third) of Property: Wills and Other Donative Transfers § 8.1(b) (Am. Law Inst. 2003) (alterations added).

3. A testator need only have "enough knowledge about the nature and extent of his estate" to form a "rational desire as to the disposition of his property." Webb v. Reeves, 791 S.E.2d 35, 36 (Ga. 2016).

4. *See* Thomas E. Simmons, Testamentary Incapacity, Undue Influence, and Insane Delusions, 60 S.D. L. Rev. 175 (2015).

In re Wright's Estate
60 P.2d 434 (Cal. 1936)

SEAWELL, J. The petition for admission to probate of the will of Lorenzo B. Wright, deceased, having been denied on the ground of testamentary incapacity, the executrix named in said will herewith appeals to this court. The grounds urged for reversal are that the evidence is insufficient to sustain the judgment and order. . . .

The testator, Lorenzo B. Wright, died at Venice, California, May 2, 1933, at the age of sixty-nine years. Maud Wright Angell, the contestant, is his daughter and the nearest of kin. He left no other children. . . . Testator's wife died in 1921.

The decedent left an estate consisting of two improved parcels of land situated in Venice, California, and an interest in an estate situated in Salt Lake City, his former home, and some inconsequential personal property of unknown value. The petition for probate alleges that the total value of his estate does not exceed the sum of $10,000. His will was formally executed one year and four months prior to his death. By its terms he devised to Charlotte Josephine Hindmarch, fifty years of age and whom he describes as his friend, his house located at 722 Nowita Place and all his personal "belongings, monies, collateral, notes or anything of value"; he devised to his daughter, the contestant herein, the house located on lot nine, at 724 Nowita Place, and to his granddaughter, Marjorie Jean Angell, his interest in an estate in Salt Lake City. He gave to his grandson, his son-in-law and several other persons, relatives or friends, one dollar each.

We have in this proceeding the unusual spectacle of the drawer of the will, a notary public and realtor, and the two subscribing witnesses testifying that they were of the opinion that the testator was of unsound mind. The testimony of these three witnesses, like the testimony given by all the others, is far too weak and unsubstantial to support the judgment. To a great extent the grounds upon which the witnesses base their opinions are mere trivialities. If it could be said that the testimony of the three persons who participated in the creation of the will and who by their solemn acts gave the stamp of approval and verity to its due execution, and afterwards attempted to repudiate all they had done, had any convincing force or any substantial factual basis, their testimony would nevertheless be subject to the scrutiny and suspicion which courts rightfully exercise in considering the testimony of persons who out of their own mouths admit their guilt of self-stultification. It has been said that such testimony is "simply worthless." Courts, whenever called upon to express themselves on this subject, have not been sparing in the use of forceful language. In Werstler v. Custer, 46 Pa. 502, 503 (1864), the court said:

> The legal presumption is always in favor of sanity, especially after attestation by subscribing witnesses, for, as was said by Parsons, C.J., in Buckminster v. Perry, 4 Mass. 593, 594 (1808), it is the duty of the subscribing witnesses to be satisfied of the testator's sanity before they subscribe the instrument. No honest man will subscribe as a witness to a will, or any other instrument executed by an insane man, an imbecile, an idiot, or a person manifestly incompetent for any reason to perform, with legal effect, the act in question. A duty attaches to the witness to satisfy himself of the competency of the party before he lends his name to attest the act. Like a magistrate who takes an acknowledgment of a deed, he is to be reasonably assured

of the facts he undertakes to verify, else he makes himself instrumental in a fraud upon the public. . . .

It appears without contradiction that Lorenzo B. Wright, testator, met Mrs. Grace Thomas, a notary public and realtor with whom he had transacted business and whom he had known for many years, in the post office and asked her what her charge would be for drawing his will. He told her he was coming to her office to have her prepare his will. About three weeks thereafter he came alone to her office, bringing with him memoranda sheets upon which he had written the names of the persons whom he wished to enjoy his property and the specific shares thereof after his death. She prepared the will accordingly. She was not acquainted with any of the persons whose names appeared on the memoranda prepared by him. She testified that she believed at the time he executed the will that he was of unsound mind. Pressed for the grounds of her opinion she said it was the "funniest will she had ever seen" in that it gave $1 to each of a number of different persons she did not know; that she had thought him queer for a long time; that he did not have in mind the legal description of the property but that she had it listed for sale and rent. The above contains the entire substance of her testimony.

James Thomas, a witness to the will, was next called by the contestant. It does not appear what relation he bears, if any, to Mrs. Grace Thomas, the scrivener, or who solicited him to become a witness. He stated that he "believed" the testator was not of sound mind; that in his opinion testator had not been of sound mind for some years prior to the execution of the will. He seemed unable to give a single reason supporting his opinion.

G.W. Madden, the other subscribing witness, when pressed for the reason of his opinion that the testator "was not of sound mind" at the time he signed the will, was also unable to say more than that he considered him of unsound mind for some time prior to the making of the will.

Mrs. Brem had known testator for sixteen years and said it was her belief that he was of unsound mind on the day the will was executed. Pressed for the reasons of her opinion, she said he had had a serious operation some years prior; he once told her he had lost $50,000 in some bank failure and she was sure from the way he lived alone in his little shack, with all the dirt and junk he had, that he was not right; he once gave her a fish (he spent much time in fishing) which he said he had caught and she found it had been soaked in kerosene and when he asked her how she liked it he laughed and said he had put the kerosene on it before he brought it to her; once he came to her house and insisted on buying her household furniture and when told it was not for sale and that she had not offered it for sale he insisted on buying it anyway. Mr. Brem testified substantially as his wife had testified, but added the statement that "Mr. Wright often chased the children out of his yard and turned the hose on them and that children in the neighborhood were afraid of Mr. Wright." He did not explain why they often returned to his yard if they feared him.

Mrs. Daisy Smith, a cousin not named in the will, testified that she believed him to be unsound in mind. Her reasons were that he drank and was drunk much of the time since his wife died; that some years ago he suffered an injury to his head and several stitches were required to close the wound; that the injury seemed to change him; that he had a serious operation in 1921; on one or more occasions he ran out of the house only partly dressed and they had to follow him and had difficulty in getting him back to bed; that he picked up silverware and other articles from the garbage cans and hid these things around the house; that he picked up paper flowers from the garbage cans, and waste, and pinned them on rose bushes in his yard and took the witness to look at his roses; that he went away with a blanket wrapped around him and was gone several days and made no explanation as to where he went; that he took from his daughter's house a radio which the witness said he had given to his daughter and granddaughter without making any explanation as to why he did so. . . .

Marjorie Jean Angell, a granddaughter, placed her belief that testator was unsound of mind on the ground that he acted funny and queer; that he told a number of persons that he had sent Christmas presents and a turkey to them when he had not done so; . . . at times he would pass her on the street without speaking and at other times he would speak and seem friendly; one time he told her she had on too much rouge and powder or paint, when she did not have any amount on. . . .

Hariett E. McClelland said she had known testator for a number of years. She believed him to be of unsound mind. . . . The witness related an ailment which the testator had while living at her house during which he would be prone, hold his breath and appear to be dead; that when she returned from her quest for help she would find him up and walking about; that he said he did this to scare his neighbors and make them think he was dead. . . .

There is no evidence that testator suffered from settled insanity, hallucinations or delusions. Testamentary capacity cannot be destroyed by showing a few isolated acts, foibles, idiosyncrasies, moral or mental irregularities or departures from the normal unless they directly bear upon and have influenced the testamentary act. No medical testimony as to the extent of any injury the testator had received or its effect upon him either physically or mentally was introduced in the case. The burden was upon contestant throughout the case. Taking all the evidence adduced by contestant as true, it falls far below the requirements of the law as constituting satisfactory rebuttal of the inference of testamentary capacity. No proof whatever was offered tending to rebut the testator's ability to transact or conduct his business or to care for himself except in a few cases of illness brought about by natural causes or excesses or by accident. He went alone to the scrivener's with a list of beneficiaries prepared by himself, giving his daughter one piece of improved real property and Charlotte Josephine Hindmarch, whom he designated as his friend, the other. To his granddaughter he bequeathed his undivided interest in an estate known as the Brazier Estate, and he named seven others to whom he made nominal bequests. There is no evidence that he did not appreciate his relations and obligations to others, or that he was not mindful of the property which he possessed. The opinions or beliefs of those who testified that he was not of sound mind rest upon testimony of the most trivial character and do not establish testamentary incapacity at the time he executed his will. . . .

For the foregoing reasons the judgment and order are reversed.

NOTES

1. Professional Responsibility. Did Grace Thomas, the nonlawyer scrivener, engage in unauthorized practice of law? If the will had been denied probate, could she have been held liable for malpractice? *See* Biakanja v. Irving, 320 P.2d 16 (Cal. 1958).

"His will reads as follows: 'Being of sound mind and disposition, I blew it all.'"

Frank Modell/The New Yorker Collection/The Cartoon Bank

Did the scrivener act unethically in drafting a will for a man whom she considered incompetent? A lawyer may not draft a will for a person the lawyer believes to be incompetent, but the lawyer may rely on her own judgment of the client's capacity. The ACTEC Commentaries on the Model Rules of Professional Conduct explain:

> If the testamentary capacity of a client is uncertain, the lawyer should exercise particular caution in assisting the client to modify his or her estate plan. The lawyer generally should not prepare a will, trust agreement or other dispositive instrument for a client whom the lawyer reasonably believes lacks the requisite capacity. On the other hand, because of the importance of testamentary freedom, the lawyer may properly assist clients whose testamentary capacity appears to be borderline. In any such case the lawyer should take steps to preserve evidence regarding the client's testamentary capacity.[5]

2. Comparing Capacity Standards.   In most states, capacity to make a *will* requires less mental ability than to make a *contract* or to complete an irrevocable *lifetime gift*.[6] The reason is that a dead person does not need protection from economic loss and

---

5. ACTEC Commentaries on the Model Rules of Professional Conduct 162 (5th ed. 2016); *see also* Joseph Karl Grant, Running Past Landmines — The Estate Attorney's Dilemma: Ethically Counseling the Client with Alzheimer's Disease, 24 Elder L.J. 101 (2016).

6. *See* Lawrence A. Frolik & Mary F. Radford, "Sufficient" Capacity: The Contrasting Capacity Requirements for Different Documents, 2 NAELA J. 303 (2006); *see also* Robert Whitman, Capacity for Lifetime and Estate Planning, 117 Penn St. L. Rev. 1061 (2013).

is not at risk of impoverishment. To make an irrevocable lifetime gift, one must have capacity to make a will and "must also be capable of understanding the effect that the gift may have on the future financial security of the donor and of anyone who may be dependent on the donor."[7] The modern view is that the lower standard of capacity applicable to the making of a will also applies to the making of a revocable trust or other will substitute that is revocable until death.[8]

The law's disparate treatment of transfers during life and at death is nicely illustrated by Lee v. Lee, 337 So. 2d 713 (Miss. 1976). *T* was placed under a conservatorship in 1968 because of age and physical incapacity. Later, in 1970, *T* executed on the same day both a deed purporting to convey real property and also a will. The court held that the deed was void but the will was valid. The court reasoned that a person under a conservatorship is without the contractual power to execute a deed, but the person may nonetheless write a valid will during a lucid interval. The Restatement explains the concept of a *lucid interval* thus:

> A person who is mentally incapacitated part of the time but who has lucid intervals during which he or she meets the standard for mental capacity can, in the absence of an adjudication or statute that has contrary effect, make a valid will or a valid inter vivos donative transfer, provided such will or transfer is made during a lucid interval.[9]

In accordance with *Lee*, substantial authority holds that a person under a conservatorship may have testamentary capacity to make a will, as in Parish v. Parish, 704 S.E.2d 99 (Va. 2011). However, a lawyer should consult with the conservator before preparing a will for such a person. In In re Disciplinary Action Against Kuhn, 785 N.W.2d 195 (N.D. 2010), the court suspended a lawyer from practice for 90 days for failing to do so in violation of Model Rule of Professional Conduct 1.14 (2015) (client with diminished capacity).[10]

Interestingly, a greater mental ability is required to make a will than is required for *marriage*. Estate of Park, [1953] 3 W.L.R. 1012, is authority for the proposition that a person may have insufficient capacity to make a will but still have enough capacity to marry. Marriage alone will give the new spouse inheritance rights even if the other spouse lacks capacity to make a will. In Hoffman v. Kohns, 385 So. 2d 1064 (Fla. App. 1980), a housekeeper married her elderly employer. His will, made one day later, was set aside, but the marriage was held valid. The validity of a marriage may be challenged even after the death of one of the purported spouses, as in In re Estate of Laubenheimer, 833 N.W.2d 735 (Wis. 2013).

---

7. Restatement (Third) of Property: Wills and Other Donative Transfers § 8.1(c) (Am. Law Inst. 2003).

8. *See, e.g.*, id. § 8.1(b); Uniform Trust Code § 601 (Unif. Law Comm'n 2000).

9. Restatement (Third) of Property: Wills and Other Donative Transfers § 8.1(c) cmt. m (Am. Law Inst. 2003).

10. *See also* Nina A. Kohn & Catheryn Koss, Lawyers for Legal Ghosts: The Legality and Ethics of Representing Persons Subject to Guardianship, 91 Wash. L. Rev. 581 (2016).

Wilson v. Lane
614 S.E.2d 88 (Ga. 2005)

FLETCHER, C.J. After Executrix Katherine Lane offered Jewel Jones Greer's 1997 last will and testament for probate, Floyd Wilson filed a caveat, challenging Greer's testamentary capacity. A Jasper County Superior Court jury found that Greer lacked testamentary capacity at the time she executed her will, but the trial court granted Lane's motion for judgment notwithstanding the verdict. Wilson appeals. Because we agree that there was no evidence to show that Greer lacked testamentary capacity, we affirm.

A person is mentally capable to make a will if she "has sufficient intellect to enable [her] to have a decided and rational desire as to the disposition of [her] property." In this case, the propounders introduced evidence that the will in question distributed Greer's property equally to seventeen beneficiaries, sixteen of whom are blood-relatives to Greer. The only non-relative beneficiary is Katherine Lane, who spent much of her time caring for Greer before her death in 2000. The drafting attorney testified that in his opinion, at the time the 1997 will was signed, Greer was mentally competent, and that she emphatically selected every beneficiary named in the will. Numerous other friends and acquaintances also testified that Greer had a clear mind at the time the will was signed.

Thus, the propounders established a presumption that Greer possessed testamentary capacity. The caveators, however, never presented any evidence whatsoever showing that Greer was incapable of forming a decided and rational desire as to the disposition of her property, even when the evidence is examined in the light most favorable to their case.

The caveators challenged Greer's capacity by showing that she was eccentric, aged, and peculiar in the last years of her life. They presented testimony that she had an irrational fear of flooding in her house, that she had trouble dressing and bathing herself, and that she unnecessarily called the fire department to report a non-existent fire. But "[t]he law does not withhold from the aged, the feeble, the weak-minded, the capricious, the notionate, the right to make a will, provided such person has a decided and rational desire as to the disposition of his property." Hill v. Deal, 193 S.E. 858, 861 (Ga. 1937). Although perhaps persuasive to a jury, "eccentric habits and absurd beliefs do not establish testamentary incapacity." Sarajane Love, Wills and Administration in Georgia, § 45, at 82 (5th ed. 1988). All that is required to sustain the will is proof that Greer was capable of forming a certain rational desire with respect to the disposition of her assets.

In addition to Greer's eccentric habits, the caveators also introduced evidence of a guardianship petition filed for Greer a few months after the will was executed, the testimony of an expert witness, and a letter written by Greer's physician. None of that evidence, however, was sufficient to deprive Greer of her right to make a valid will, as none of it showed that she was incapable of forming a rational desire as to the disposition of her property.

The expert admitted that he had never examined Greer, and that his testimony was based solely on a cursory review of some of Greer's medical files. Further, he was equivocal in his testimony, stating only that "*it appears* that she was in some form of the early to middle stages of a dementia of the Alzheimer's type." Regardless of the stigma associated with the term "Alzheimer's," however, that testimony does not show how

Greer would have been unable to form a rational desire regarding the disposition of her assets. Indeed, the expert offered no explanation of how her supposed condition would affect her competency to make a valid will.

The testimony of Greer's physician also failed to show how she lacked testamentary capacity. In 1996, the physician wrote a letter stating that Greer "was legally blind and suffered from senile dementia." But the doctor testified that he was "not sure whether she had senile dementia at the time or not, even though I wrote that." He stated further that he only wrote the letter to try and assist Greer in obtaining help with her telephone bill because she had been having trouble with her eyes. In any event, a vague reference to "senile dementia" cannot eliminate testamentary capacity. If it could, it would undermine societal confidence in the validity and sanctity of our testamentary system.

Finally, as the dissent points out, Lane filed a guardianship petition in 1998, after the will was executed, proclaiming that Greer was no longer capable of managing her own affairs alone. According to the testimony, however, the petition was filed solely in order to satisfy the Department of Family and Children Services's concerns regarding Greer's ability to continue living on her own, and thus to allow Greer to remain in her home. Even if Greer's inability to live alone existed at the time the will was executed, which was not proven by any evidence, that fact bears no relation to her ability to form a rational desire regarding the disposition of her assets. . . .

[I]n this case, no testimony, expert or otherwise, was offered to establish that at the time the will was executed, Greer suffered from a form of dementia sufficient in form or extent to render her unable to form a decided and rational desire regarding the disposition of her assets. . . . At most, there was evidence that Greer was an eccentric woman whose mental health declined towards the end of her life. Accordingly, the evidence demanded a verdict upholding the validity of the will, and the trial court was correct to reverse the jury's contrary verdict. . . .

Judgment affirmed.

CARLEY, J., dissenting. I agree that the evidence in this case would have authorized a finding that Ms. Greer possessed the requisite testamentary capacity when she executed a will in September of 1997. However, the jury found that she lacked such capacity, and we must decide whether the evidence supports that finding. I submit that, when the evidence is construed most strongly in support of the jury's verdict in favor of the Caveators, it authorized the finding that Ms. Greer did not have sufficient intellect to enable her to make a decided and rational determination concerning the disposition of her estate. Therefore, I dissent to the affirmance of the trial court's grant of the Propounder's motion for judgment notwithstanding the verdict. . . .

Here, the Caveators presented expert medical opinion testimony showing that, at the time Ms. Greer executed the will, "she was in some form of the early to middle stages of a dementia of the Alzheimer's type." A year earlier, her own physician had expressed his belief that she exhibited "senile dementia." In January of 1998, a petition was filed which alleged that Ms. Greer was an "incapacitated" adult and sought the appointment of a guardian. This petition for guardianship was supported by the affidavit of her doctor, who stated his opinion that she had "dementia-Alzheimer's type," that she suffered from "poor memory, poor judgment, [was] difficult to reason with," and that she was "incapacitated on a permanent basis." The physician's affidavit also indicated that Ms. Greer was in present need of a guardian for both her person and her property. With regard to the guardianship of her person, the doctor noted that she "lacks sufficient understanding or capacity to make significant responsible decisions concerning . . . her person or is incapable of communicating such decisions." As for the guardianship of her property, the physician indicated that she was "incapable of managing . . . her estate, and [her] property . . . will be wasted or dissipated unless proper management is provided." The Caveator's expert testified that, if, as Ms. Greer's own doctor expressed in his affidavit, she was

> having profound problems in one month where [she] would be considered incapacitated or needing a guardian then you would be able to go backwards for a number of months, probably up to a year or two, at least, and say that [she] was having some sort of problem with [her] thinking.

It was only four months between the time she signed the instrument tendered for admission into probate and the petition alleging that she was "permanently incapacitated" due to "dementia" based upon Alzheimer's disease.

In addition to the expert medical opinion evidence showing that Ms. Greer suffered from dementia attributable to Alzheimer's disease shortly before, during and shortly after the time she executed the will, the Caveators introduced evidence which was indicative of the extent to which her mental acuity had been impaired. She had an irrational fear that her home was being flooded. She even refused to get into the bathtub, and insisted on sponge baths. Visitors to her home [were not allowed to flush the toilet]. . . .

There was additional evidence showing that in mid-December of 1997, only three months after executing the will, Ms. Greer was disoriented as to time and, believing that it was March, she was unaware that Christmas was imminent. She did not know her own social security number. She had a list of first names and telephone numbers, but could not provide last names for any of those on that list. As the majority notes, she called the fire department to report a non-existent fire. . . .

While no single element of the Caveators' proof, standing alone, might otherwise be a sufficient predicate for invalidating Ms. Greer's will, when the totality of the evidence as to her mental condition during the relevant time period is considered, a jury certainly would be authorized to find that she suffered from serious dementia. If the evidence supports such a finding, then the jury was authorized to return a verdict holding that she lacked the requisite testamentary capacity. Since the evidence supports the jury's verdict in favor of the Caveators, the trial court erred in granting the Propounder's motion for judgment n.o.v.

NOTE

The Burden of Persuasion and Age-Related Cognitive Decline. Proof of due execution ordinarily gives rise to a presumption of testamentary capacity. In a majority of states, as in *Wright* and *Wilson* and under Uniform Probate Code (UPC) § 3-407 (Unif. Law Comm'n 1990), once the proponent shows due execution, the contestant bears the ultimate burden of persuasion to show a lack of capacity. In a minority of states, including Massachusetts, New York, and Virginia, the proponent bears the ultimate burden of proving the testator had capacity if the contestant overcomes the presumption of capacity arising from due execution with some evidence of incapacity.[11]

Allocation of the ultimate burden of persuasion can affect the outcome in a close case, making it an important policy choice. There have been "remarkable improvements in life expectancy over the past century," resulting in a profound aging of the population.[12] Of the estimated 5.3 million Americans with Alzheimer's disease, 5.1 million are age 65 or older.[13] Yet "a mere diagnosis of Alzheimer's, dementia, or age-related memory deficits is not necessarily inconsistent with testamentary capacity because the relevant inquiry is whether the decedent was competent at the time the will was executed."[14]

2. Insane Delusion

A person may satisfy the test for testamentary capacity but nonetheless be suffering from an *insane delusion* that causes the entire will or a particular disposition to fail for lack of capacity. In Dougherty v. Rubenstein, 914 A.2d 184 (Md. 2007), the court explained the origins of the insane delusion doctrine:

> The "insane delusion rule" of testamentary capacity came into being almost 200 years ago, as the invention of British jurists in Dew v. Clark, 162 Eng. Rep. 410 (Prerog. 1826). The rule was devised to cover a gap in the existing law, which held that "idiots and persons of non-sane memory" could not make wills, but accepted as valid the will of a testator "who knew the natural objects of his or her bounty, the nature and extent of his or her property, and could make a 'rational' plan for disposition, but who nonetheless was as crazy as a March hare[.]" . . . Within a few years of the decision in Dew v. Clark, the insane delusion rule made its way into will contest cases in the United States.

Insane delusion is a legal rather than medical term of art.[15] A delusion is a false conception of reality. An insane delusion in the legal sense, which bears on testamentary capacity, is one to which the testator adheres against all evidence and reason to the contrary. In most states, if there is any evidence to support the testator's delusion, the delusion is not insane. The law thus draws a distinction between an insane delusion and a mistake. A mistake is susceptible to correction if the testator is told the truth. Under traditional law, courts do not reform or invalidate wills because of mistake (see Chapter 5), but they do invalidate wills or provisions thereof resulting from an insane delusion.

---

11. *See, e.g.*, In re Estate of Galatis, 36 N.E.3d 1247 (Mass. App. 2015); In re Estate of Alibrandi, 960 N.Y.S.2d 760 (App. Div. 2013); Kiddell v. Labowitz, 733 S.E.2d 622 (Va. 2012).
12. Nat'l Inst. on Aging et al., Global Health and Aging 2-3 (2011).
13. *See* Alzheimer's Association, 2015 Alzheimer's Disease Facts and Figures 16 (2015).
14. *Alibrandi*, 960 N.Y.S.2d at 763.
15. *See* Joshua C. Tate, Personal Reality: Delusion in Law and Science, 49 Conn. L. Rev. 891 (2017) (urging for reform toward a doctrine of "partial sanity").

To prevail in an insane delusion case, the contestant must show both that the testator labored under an insane delusion and that the will or some part thereof was a product of the insane delusion.[16] The typical delusion involves a false belief about a member of the testator's family. If an insane delusion does not affect the dispositions, then the will stands. Much of the litigation focuses on causation.

In re Strittmater's Estate
53 A.2d 205 (N.J. 1947)

On appeal from a decree of the Prerogative Court, advised by Vice-Ordinary Bigelow, who filed the following opinion:

"This is an appeal from a decree of the Essex County Orphans Court admitting to probate the will of Louisa F. Strittmater. Appellants challenge the decree on the ground that testatrix was insane.

"The only medical witness was Dr. Sarah D. Smalley, a general practitioner who was Miss Strittmater's physician all her adult life. In her opinion, decedent suffered from paranoia of the Bleuler type of split personality. The factual evidence justifies the conclusion. But I regret not having had the benefit of an analysis of the data by a specialist in diseases of the brain.

"The deceased never married. Born in 1896, she lived with her parents until their death [in] about 1928, and seems to have had a normal childhood. She was devoted to both her parents and they to her. Her admiration and love of her parents persisted after their death to 1934, at least. Yet four years later she wrote: 'My father was a corrupt, vicious, and unintelligent savage, a typical specimen of the majority of his sex. Blast his wormstinking carcass and his whole damn breed.' And in 1943, she inscribed on a photograph of her mother 'That Moronic she-devil that was my mother.'

"Numerous memoranda and comments written by decedent on the margins of books constitute the chief evidence of her mental condition. Most of them are dated in 1935, when she was 40 years old. But there are enough in later years to indicate no change in her condition. The Master who heard the case in the court below, found that the proofs demonstrated 'incontrovertably her morbid aversion to men' and 'feminism to a neurotic extreme.' This characterization seems to me not strong enough. She regarded men as a class with an insane hatred. She looked forward to the day when women would bear children

Eugen Bleuler (1857-1939), a Swiss psychiatrist, analyzed and named the condition schizophrenia, dividing it into several types, including paranoid. He believed that intense ambivalence, such as experiencing both love and hate toward an object, was a primary symptom of schizophrenia.

---

16. See Bradley E.S. Fogel, The Completely Insane Law of Partial Insanity: The Impact of Monomania on Testamentary Capacity, 42 Real Prop. Prob. & Tr. J. 67, 86-101 (2007); see also Alan J. Oxford, II, Salvaging Testamentary Intent by Applying Partial Invalidity to Insane Delusions, 12 Appalachian J.L. 83 (2012); Amy D. Ronner, Does Golyadkin Really Have a Double? Dostoevsky Debunks the Mental Capacity and Insane Delusion Doctrines, 40 Cap. U. L. Rev. 195 (2012).

without the aid of men, and all males would be put to death at birth. Decedent's inward life, disclosed by what she wrote, found an occasional outlet such as the incident of the smashing of the clock, the killing of the pet kitten,[17] vile language, etc. On the other hand,—and I suppose this is the split personality,—Miss Strittmater, in her dealings with her lawyer, Mr. Semel, over a period of several years, and with her bank, to cite only two examples, was entirely reasonable and normal.

"Decedent, in 1925, became a member of the New Jersey branch of the National Women's Party. From 1939 to 1941, and perhaps later, she worked as a volunteer one day a week in the New York office, filing papers, etc. During this period, she spoke of leaving her estate to the Party. On October 31, 1944, she executed her last will, carrying this intention into effect. A month later, December 6, she died. Her only relatives were some cousins of whom she saw very little during the last few years of her life.

"The question is whether Miss Strittmater's will is the product of her insanity. Her disease seems to have become well developed by 1936. In August of that year she wrote, 'It remains for feministic organizations like the National Women's Party, to make exposure of women's "protectors" and "lovers" for what their vicious and contemptible selves are.' She had been a member of the Women's Party for eleven years at that time, but the evidence does not show that she had taken great interest in it. I think it was her paranoic condition, especially her insane delusions about the male, that led her to leave her estate to the National Women's Party. The result is that the probate should be set aside."

PER CURIAM. The decree under review will be affirmed, for the reasons stated in the opinion of Vice-Ordinary Bigelow.

The National Woman's Party

Louisa Strittmater's intended beneficiary, the National Woman's Party (the court's reference to the National Women's Party was mistaken), was founded in 1916 by Alice Paul. It was among the most radical of the leading organizations that lobbied for the Nineteenth Amendment to the U.S. Constitution, which in 1920 granted women the right to vote. In 1917, after being convicted and imprisoned for nonviolent protests in front of the White House, Paul went on a hunger strike. She was then taken to a psychopathic ward and treated as mentally ill—an irony given the New Jersey Supreme Court's treatment of Strittmater 30 years later.

In 1921, Paul drafted an early version of the Equal Rights Amendment (ERA): "Men and women shall have equal rights throughout the United States and every place subject to its jurisdiction." Introduced in every Congress from 1923 through the early 1970s, the ERA finally passed in 1972 as revised thus: "Equality of rights under the law shall not be denied or abridged by the United States or any state on account of sex." The ERA then went to the states for ratification, but it failed because too few states ratified it before the 1982 deadline imposed by Congress.

Paul, who had a Ph.D. in economics and three law degrees (LL.B., LL.M., and D.C.L.), was a leader in lobbying Congress to add sex discrimination to the protections of Title VII in the 1964 Civil Rights Act. Until the sex amendment to Title VII passed the House of Representatives in 1964, the National Woman's Party was the only national women's organization that favored adding the prohibition of sex discrimination to that statute. Alice Paul died in 1977 at the age of 92.

Alice Paul

---

17. One wonders whether the clock was a "grandfather clock" or the kitten a "tomcat."—Eds.

NOTE

Insane Delusion and Social Context.   What was Louisa Strittmater's insane delusion? Did that delusion cause her bequest to the National Woman's Party? Might she have had another reason for favoring the Party over cousins with whom she had little contact?

Suppose that Strittmater had been devoutly religious and deeply involved in a conventional church. Would a substantial bequest to that church be vulnerable to contest on grounds of insane delusion? *See* Nalty's Adm'r v. Franzman's Ex'r, 299 S.W. 585 (Ky. App. 1927).

To what extent are findings of incapacity and insane delusion based on social constructions of what is normal? If *Strittmater* were to be decided today, would it come out the same way?

Breeden v. Stone
992 P.2d 1167 (Colo. 2000)

RICE, J. . . . This case involves a contested probate of a handwritten (holographic) will executed by Spicer Breeden, the decedent. Mr. Breeden died in his home on March 19, 1996, from a self-inflicted gunshot wound two days after he was involved in a highly publicized hit-and-run accident that killed the driver of the other vehicle.

Upon entering the decedent's home following his suicide, the Denver police discovered on his desk a handwritten document that read: "I want everything I have to go to Sydney Stone—'houses,' 'jewelwry,' [sic] stocks[,] bonds, cloths [sic]. P.S. I was *Not* Driving the Vehical—[sic]." At the bottom of the handwritten document, the decedent printed, "SPICER H. BREEDEN" and signed beneath his printed name.

Sydney Stone (Respondent) offered the handwritten document for probate as the holographic will of the decedent. The decedent had previously executed a formal will in 1991 and a holographic codicil leaving his estate to persons other than Respondent.[18] Several individuals filed objections to the holographic will, including Petitioners [Spicer Breeden's sister Holly Connell, brother Vic, and father Vic, Sr.], who alleged lack of testamentary capacity. . . .

On September 26, 1996, the probate court formally admitted the decedent's holographic will to probate. The court made several findings based on

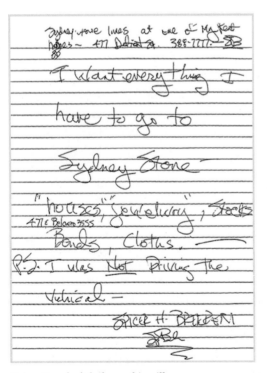

Spicer Breeden's holographic will

---

18. In the holographic codicil Breeden wrote: "I would very much like Caroline Johnson to have Gambo, my Pet Dog." Breeden also gave Johnson $15,000 in cash.—Eds.

the evidence presented. First, the court found that the decedent used cocaine and alcohol for several years prior to his death. . . . Relying on the autopsy report and testimony from the decedent's sister, the court found that the decedent used alcohol and cocaine on the evening of March 17 and between March 17 and 19, and that substantial alcohol was consumed proximate to the time of death. Based on the testimony of a number of the decedent's friends, the court found that the decedent's moods were alternately euphoric, fearful, and depressed, and that he was excessively worried about threats against himself and his dog from government agents, friends, and others.[19] . . .

After considering the evidence, the probate court found that Petitioners did not prove by a preponderance of the evidence that, because of the decedent's chronic use of alcohol and drugs or their use between March 17 and 19, he was not of sound mind when he executed the holographic will. In addition, the probate court held that the stress and anxiety that compelled the decedent to commit suicide did not deprive him of testamentary capacity. The court also found that the decedent's insane delusions regarding his friends, government agencies, and others, did not affect or influence the disposition of his property. . . .

TESTAMENTARY CAPACITY

. . . Until 1973, the proponents of a will assumed the burden of proving that the testator had testamentary capacity at the time he executed a will. However, in 1973, the legislature shifted this burden to the contestants of a will. Under Colo. Rev. Stat. § 15-12-407, [based on UPC § 3-407,] once a proponent of a will has offered prima facie proof that the will was duly executed, any contestant then assumes the burden of proving a lack of testamentary capacity, including a lack of sound mind, by a preponderance of the evidence. The issue of what constitutes sound mind has developed along two separate lines of inquiry, summarized below. . . .

THE *CUNNINGHAM* TEST

. . . [This court stated] the test for sound mind in 1953 in the landmark case Cunningham v. Stender, 255 P.2d 977, 981-82 (Colo. 1953), when we held that mental capacity to make a will requires that: (1) the testator understands the nature of her

---

19. According to the brief filed by Spicer Breeden's brother and sister, Spicer became increasingly irrational, paranoid, and delusional. He was convinced at one point that he was covered in bugs and would not calm down until a friend purchased Benadryl gel and rubbed it on his arms and legs. He thought that people were spying on him as undercover government agents. When he received a VCR rewinder as a gift, he stomped on it because he thought it had a listening device in it. He climbed onto his roof to destroy his antenna to prevent monitoring of him through his television. He cancelled his cable service and shredded his bills, cards, and letters. He had friends drive by his house to ensure that he was not being watched. He was convinced that the new sewer lines being installed in his neighborhood were a pretext for FBI surveillance. He thought that a close friend had planted a bomb in his house and that his father had planted drugs in his car. He changed his locks repeatedly. He spread corn flakes in the hall outside his bedroom so that a crunch would alert him to intruders. *See* Petitioners-Appellants' Opening Brief, Breeden v. Stone, Case No. 98 SC 570, at 5-9 (Apr. 19, 1999).

The Respondents argued that Breeden was not delusional about at least one thing: His friend Crow was indeed an FBI informer. Respondent's Answer Brief, Breeden v. Stone, Case No. 98 SC 570, at 22 n.8 (May 19, 1999). — Eds.

Spicer Breeden

Spicer Breeden was a member of one of Colorado's most prominent families, a descendant of patriarch Charles Boettcher.

Growing up in a mountaintop mansion, Spicer Breeden could survey a shining city stamped repeatedly with the name of his mother's family fortune: Boettcher.

A Boettcher gave Denver the downtown estate where the Governor resides. Boettcher Halls grace the city's botanical gardens, theater complex and natural history museum. On the far side of the Rockies, a Boettcher, Mr. Breeden's uncle, helped transform an old mining town into a glittering ski resort: Aspen. . . .

When Charles Boettcher died in 1948, he presided over a Rocky Mountain business empire: railroads, ranches, mines, meatpacking plants, cement factories, sugar mills, a life insurance company and the region's most powerful investment house.

As he neared his 96th birthday, the iron-willed entrepreneur told Time Magazine: "I like to work. I've worked hard all my life, and I suppose I'll keep working as long as I can raise a hand."

In contrast, his great-grandson, Spicer, never held a job. At age 13, Spicer Breeden inherited $2 million of the Boettcher fortune from his mother, who died of cancer. As an adult, he spent his time, court records show, using copious amounts of cocaine and racking up speeding tickets and two convictions for driving under the influence of alcohol or drugs.*

On March 17, 1996, while going about 110 miles an hour in his BMW, Breeden and his friend Peter Schmitz struck the car of Greg Lopez, a beloved columnist for the Rocky Mountain News, who was killed instantly. Lopez's widow gave birth to their child seven months after the accident.

The BMW stopped briefly, then sped off. After switching to an Audi sport wagon at Mr. Breeden's house, [Breeden and Schmitz] returned to bar-hopping in Denver's trendy Lower Downtown, according to testimony.

Two days later, on March 19, the police were knocking on Mr. Breeden's door, and the first television crew started broadcasting live from his front lawn. With furniture pushed against the doors and sleeping bags covering the windows, he drank rum, snorted cocaine and watched the television coverage.

Before turning his .357 Magnum revolver on his beloved chow, Gambo, wounding the dog, he scribbled a will that cut his entire family—father, brother and sister—out of his will. He left all his money, less than one-third of his mother's legacy, to [Sydney] Stone.†

Peter Schmitz was later acquitted of vehicular homicide. The jury foreman explained:

Very few witnesses agreed on anything; there was this jumble of information. But two witnesses for the prosecution testified that Breeden, in the year before his death, had said to them that if he ever killed someone in a crash, he would shoot himself and his dog. It's chilling how predictive that was.‡

_____

* James Brooke, A Web of Money, Drugs and Death, N.Y. Times, Mar. 18, 1997, at A12.

† Id.

‡ James Brooke, After Verdict, Trial Still Grips Denver, N.Y. Times, Mar. 21, 1997, at A26.

act; (2) she knows the extent of her property; (3) she understands the proposed testamentary disposition; (4) she knows the natural objects of her bounty; and (5) the will represents her wishes.

THE INSANE DELUSION TEST

This court has also held that a person who was suffering from an insane delusion at the time he executed the will may lack testamentary capacity. We first defined an insane delusion in 1924 as "a persistent belief in that which has no existence in fact, and which is adhered to against all evidence." In re Cole's Estate, 226 P. 143, 145 (Colo. 1924). We held that a party asserting that a testator was suffering from an insane delusion must meet the burden of showing that the testator suffered from such delusion.

We also have addressed the issue of the causal relationship necessary between an individual's insane delusion and his capacity to contract. In Hanks v. McNeil Coal Corp., 168 P.2d 256, 260 (Colo. 1946), . . . [we held] that

> [o]ne may have insane delusions regarding some matters and be insane on some subjects, yet [be] capable of transacting business concerning matters wherein such subjects are not concerned, and such insanity does not make one incompetent to contract unless the subject matter of the contract is so connected with an insane delusion as to render the afflicted party incapable of understanding the nature and effect of the agreement or of acting rationally in the transaction.

The *Hanks* case sets out a standard for the requisite causal connection between insane delusions and contractual capacity that is equally applicable to testamentary capacity. A number of other courts have applied a similar standard in the context of testamentary capacity by phrasing the inquiry as whether the delusion *materially* affects the contested disposition in the will. . . .

Based on Colorado precedent and . . . persuasive authority from other jurisdiction . . . , we hold that before a will can be invalidated because of a lack of testamentary capacity due to an insane delusion, the insane delusion must materially affect the disposition in the will.

CUNNINGHAM AND INSANE DELUSION TESTS ARE NOT MUTUALLY EXCLUSIVE

As the preceding case law indicates, the *Cunningham* and the insane delusion tests for sound mind have developed independently of each other.

The *Cunningham* test is most commonly applied in cases in which the objectors argue that the testator lacked general testamentary capacity due to a number of possible causes such as mental illness, physical infirmity, senile dementia, and general insanity.

The insane delusion test ordinarily involves situations in which the testator, although in possession of his general faculties, suffers from delusions that often take the form of monomania or paranoia.[20]

As such, the *Cunningham* and insane delusion tests, although discrete, are not mutually exclusive. In order to have testamentary capacity, a testator must have a sound mind. In Colorado, a sound mind includes the presence of the *Cunningham* factors *and* the absence of insane delusions that materially affect the will. As noted above, insane delusions are often material to the making of the will, and thus will defeat testamentary capacity. However, just as in the *Hanks* case, not all insane delusions materially affect

---

20. Monomania is defined as "insanity upon a particular subject only, and with a single delusion of the mind," while paranoia is defined as "chronic delusional insanity" that is marked by "a false premise, pursued by a logical process of reasoning to an insane conclusion." 1 William J. Bowe & Douglas H. Parker, Page on Wills § 12.31 (4th ed. 1960 & Supp. 1999).

the making of a will. Nonetheless, a testator suffering from an immaterial insane delusion must still meet the *Cunningham* sound mind test.

Accordingly, we hold that an objector may challenge a testator's soundness of mind based on both or either of the *Cunningham* and insane delusion tests. . . .

PROBATE COURT DECISION

. . . Petitioners argue that the trial court erred by: (1) applying both the *Cunningham* and the insane delusion tests in a case which involves only insane delusions; and (2) merging the *Cunningham* and the insane delusion tests.

Upon reviewing the decision of the probate court, we hold that the court correctly applied these two exclusive tests for testamentary capacity to find that the decedent was of sound mind at the time he executed his holographic will. The court found that the decedent had used alcohol and cocaine for several years prior to his death, had used alcohol and cocaine between March 17 and 19, suffered from mood swings, and worried excessively about threats against his and his dog's life. Despite these adverse findings, the court found that the decedent was of sound mind.

First, the court applied the *Cunningham* test and found that the decedent: (1) could index the major categories of the property comprising his estate; (2) knew his home and rental addresses; and (3) identified the devisee by name and provided her current address. The court noted that the will was "legible, logical in content, and reasonably set[ ] out [the decedent's] intent." In addition, the probate court considered the testimony of handwriting experts that indicated that at the time the decedent wrote the will, he was in command of his motor skills and his handwriting was unremarkable when compared to other exemplars. Based upon these factors, the trial court found that the decedent met the *Cunningham* test for sound mind.

Then, the probate court applied the insane delusion test to hold that although the decedent was suffering from insane delusions at the time he executed his will, "[his] insane delusions did not affect or influence the disposition of property made in the will." Cf. In re Haywood's Estate, 240 P.2d 1028, 1033 (Cal. App. 1952) (finding that a testator's hallucination of a headless wolf was not related to the making of the will). In so finding, the probate court considered the decedent's delusions regarding listening devices in his home and car and assassination plots against himself and his dog. In addition, the court weighed the testimony of numerous expert witnesses regarding the decedent's handwriting, his mental state near the time he executed the will, and the impact of his drug and alcohol use on his mental faculties. Further, the court considered testimony from several persons who stated that the decedent was not close to Petitioners, had infrequent contact with them, indicated to friends that he believed his father was irresponsible with money, disliked his sister's husband, and that his relationship with his brother was distant. In fact, the decedent had not made provisions for either Breeden Sr. or Connell in his earlier 1991 will. As such, the probate court concluded that the insane delusions from which the decedent suffered did not materially affect or influence the disposition made in the holographic will. . . .

In sum, the probate court order reflects that the court thoroughly considered all of the evidence presented by the parties and concluded that (1) the testator met the

Cunningham test for sound mind and (2) the insane delusions from which the decedent was suffering did not materially affect or influence his testamentary disposition. . . .

CONCLUSION

We hold that the probate court correctly applied the two exclusive tests for testamentary capacity to find that the testator, Spicer Breeden, was of sound mind at the time he executed the holographic will. . . . Accordingly, we affirm the decision of the court of appeals upholding the probate court's ruling that the decedent was of sound mind. . . .

NOTES

1. A Valid Holograph?   Breeden's handwritten note does not contain the word "will," does not mention death, and is not dated. Should it have been admitted to probate as a holographic will? We consider holographic wills in Chapter 3 at page 198.

2. Proving Causation.   The court concluded that Breeden's insane delusions did not "materially affect or influence" the will's provisions. In some older cases, including *Strittmater*, the court applied a lower standard for proving causation. The leading such case is In re Honigman's Will, 168 N.E.2d 676 (N.Y. 1960), in which the court, 4 to 3, denied probate to a will on the grounds that its dispositive provisions "might have been caused or affected" by the testator's insane delusion. In that case, after coming to believe that his wife was having an affair, the testator left her the minimum necessary to prevent her from taking a statutory forced share, leaving the rest to his brothers and sisters. The majority rejected the argument that there were good other reasons for the testator's disposition, such as his wife's independent fortune and his siblings' financial need. In effect, the court inferred causation, requiring the proponent to show that an arguably unnatural disposition within the testator's insane delusion was not in fact a product of that delusion.

B. UNDUE INFLUENCE

1. What Is Undue Influence?

Undue influence is one of the most bothersome concepts in all the law. The basic rule is simple enough: "A donative transfer is procured by undue influence if the wrongdoer exerted such influence over the donor that it overcame the donor's free will and caused the donor to make a donative transfer that the donor would not otherwise have made."[21]

---

21. Restatement (Third) of Property: Wills and Other Donative Transfers § 8.3(b) (Am. Law Inst. 2003). For a comparative survey, see Ronald J. Scalise, Jr., Undue Influence and the Law of Wills: A Comparative Analysis, 19 Duke J. Comp. & Int'l L. 41 (2008).

The problem is that shorthand formulations, such as the Restatement provision just quoted, do not answer the critical question of what influence is *undue*. How does one know if influence has "overcome the donor's free will"? Drawing a line between indelicate but permissible persuasion and influence that is undue can be frustratingly difficult. Moreover, because direct evidence of undue influence is rare, a contestant must typically rely on circumstantial evidence. The combination of murkiness in the meaning of undue influence and openness to circumstantial evidence invites strike suits by excluded family members and gives judges and juries leeway to rework the will of a decedent in accordance with their sense of fairness and morality.[22]

Yet most people agree that a vulnerable testator should be protected against imposition by cunning or domineering persons. The undue influence doctrine is meant to protect a testator's freedom of disposition from impositions that are less overtly coercive than fraud or threat of force but that overcome the will of the testator nonetheless. "The doctrine . . . protects against overreaching by a wrongdoer seeking to take unfair advantage of a donor who is susceptible to such wrongdoing on account of the donor's age, inexperience, dependence, physical or mental weakness, or other factor."[23] The paradigmatic case involves a caretaker who ingratiates himself with an elderly and infirm donor, isolating the donor from friends and family, after which the donor, at the suggestion of the caretaker, arranges to transfer property to the caretaker.

To impose structure on the unruly undue influence concept, courts have developed an elaborate scheme of inferences, presumptions, and burden shifting. The prevailing rule is that a contestant has the burden of proving that a will was procured by undue influence. However, the trier of fact may infer undue influence from circumstantial evidence that shows that "(1) the donor was *susceptible* to undue influence, (2) the alleged wrongdoer had an *opportunity* to exert undue influence, (3) the alleged wrongdoer had a *disposition* to exert undue influence, and (4) there was a *result* appearing to be the effect of the undue influence."[24] Circumstantial evidence is admissible "if it tends to prove or disprove" one of these elements.[25]

In most jurisdictions, a contestant is entitled to a presumption of undue influence if the contestant shows the existence of a *confidential relationship* between the alleged

---

22. *See, e.g.,* Irene D. Johnson, There's a Will, But No Way—Whatever Happened to the Doctrine of Testamentary Freedom and What Can (Should) We Do to Restore It?, 4 Est. Plan. & Community Prop. L.J. 105 (2011); Carla Spivack, Why the Testamentary Doctrine of Undue Influence Should Be Abolished, 58 U. Kan. L. Rev. 245 (2010); E. Gary Spitko, Gone But Not Conforming: Protecting the Abhorrent Testator from Majoritarian Cultural Norms Through Minority-Culture Arbitration, 49 Case W. Res. L. Rev. 275 (1999); Ray D. Madoff, Unmasking Undue Influence, 81 Minn. L. Rev. 571 (1997); Melanie B. Leslie, The Myth of Testamentary Freedom, 38 Ariz. L. Rev. 235 (1996).

23. Restatement (Third) of Property: Wills and Other Donative Transfers § 8.3(b) cmt. e (Am. Law Inst. 2003).

24. Id. (emphasis added).

25. In re Estate of Vestre, 799 N.W.2d 379, 385 (N.D. 2011).

influencer and the testator and one or more *suspicious circumstances* are present (see page 289). The concepts of confidential relationship and suspicious circumstances bring structure to the difficult task of reconstructing the nature of the decedent's relationship with the alleged wrongdoer. But the boundaries of these concepts can be elusive. Probably the best way to appreciate the challenge presented by undue influence, and to develop a lawyer's feel for the doctrine, is to immerse yourself in the cases.

2. Undue Influence in the Cases

In re Estate of Sharis
990 N.E.2d 98 (Mass. App. 2013)

SULLIVAN, J. Richard Spinelli appeals from a decision of a judge of the Probate and Family Court disallowing the will of his grandmother, Alice R. Sharis (Alice), on the grounds of lack of testamentary capacity and Spinelli's undue influence. We discern no error in the judge's conclusions that Spinelli was a fiduciary, and that the will was the product of undue influence. Accordingly, we affirm the judgment.[26]

1. *Background.* Born in 1916, Alice came to the United States from Turkey when she was twelve years old, and completed the seventh grade. She had three daughters, Virginia, Louise, and Florence, with her first husband, whom she divorced in 1959. She had sixteen surviving grandchildren and several great-grandchildren. The decedent married her second husband, Peter, in 1961. Peter, who predeceased Alice by thirteen months, suffered from Alzheimer's disease in the last years of his life and lived in a nursing home during the last six months of his life.

Spinelli is one of Alice's grandchildren. After separating from his wife in November, 2003, he asked Alice and Peter if he could move into their home. He remained there through Peter's illness and death and the death of Alice on February 13, 2010. He made no monetary contributions to the upkeep or running of the home, but he did drive Alice to medical appointments and other destinations.

The judge found that Spinelli gained nearly complete control of Alice and Peter's checking account between 2006 and 2008. Spinelli signed Peter's name to 119 checks between March 4, 2006, and February 4, 2008.[27]

Justice Mary T. Sullivan

---

26. Because of the result we reach on the claim of undue influence, we need not address whether the decedent possessed testamentary capacity at the time she executed her will.

27. He did not have the authority to sign Peter's name, nor did he have signature authority in his own name. Spinelli does not challenge these findings. . . .

Alice complained to one of her daughters and a granddaughter that she did not know where her money or checks were. On June 30, 2007, Alice signed a durable power of attorney, prepared by Spinelli, that took effect immediately and gave Spinelli broad powers.

Spinelli did not inform other family members of the power of attorney, or that he was signing checks on his grandparents' accounts. In February or March of 2008, Spinelli contacted an attorney, had an initial meeting, and inquired whether the attorney could draft a will for his grandmother. The attorney, a corporate lawyer who had been in practice approximately four years at that time, did not meet with Alice in person, and could not remember what she told him regarding the disposition of the assets of her estate. He called her at Spinelli's urging, had a short intake telephone conversation with her, and then assigned the actual drafting of the will to an associate in his office. The associate who actually drafted the will communicated by electronic mail (e-mail) only with Spinelli. There is no evidence that the associate communicated directly with Alice. Once the will was drafted and sent to Alice, the attorney conducted a brief, two-minute telephone conversation with her. No attorney reviewed the terms of the will in person with Alice, nor did an attorney attend the execution of the will. There is no evidence that either the attorney or the associate inquired, or that Alice explained, why she would favor Spinelli over her daughters and other grandchildren.

On July 23, 2008, Spinelli took Alice to the nursing home where her husband was a patient. She executed her will there, with nursing home staff as witnesses. Spinelli was nearby when the will was executed but was not in the room. The employees who witnessed the will did not observe any behavior that caused them to question whether Alice executed the will of her own free will.

The will provides that all of the Alice's assets be distributed to her husband, Peter, should he survive her. If not, the house and all of the assets and property contained therein were to go to Spinelli, along with all her stocks and securities. Her savings and checking accounts were distributed equally to her three daughters. The residuary was distributed equally among her three daughters and Spinelli.

Following the execution of the will, in September of 2008, Spinelli opened a checking account in his name in trust for Peter and Alice. Between September, 2008, and the date Alice died in February of 2010, the judge found, and Spinelli does not dispute, that he transferred $71,450 from the checking account to the trust account, and that substantial sums were then expended from the trust account. The judge found these transfers had the effect of disrupting Alice's bequest of her checking and savings accounts to her daughters. The judge found that Spinelli, who testified at trial, was not credible on key issues, including his control over bank accounts, his control over Alice's finances, and the circumstances under which he obtained the power of attorney.

2. *Discussion.* One of the decedent's daughters, Florence, brought this action contesting the will on grounds of lack of testamentary capacity and undue influence. Spinelli argues that the facts found by the judge do not support the inference that Spinelli unduly influenced his grandmother. We review the judge's findings for clear error, giving considerable respect to the judge's assessment of the testimony.

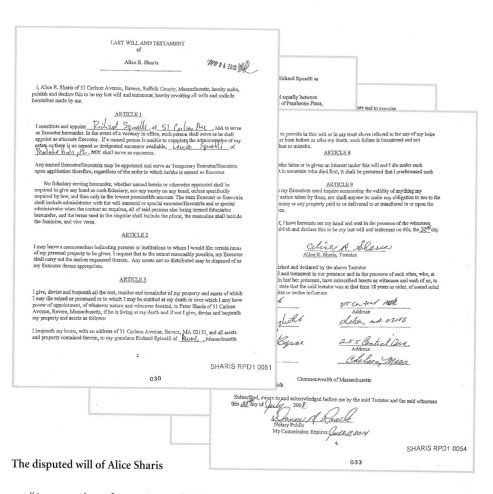

The disputed will of Alice Sharis

"Any species of coercion, whether physical, mental or moral, which subverts the sound judgment and genuine desire of the individual, is enough to constitute undue influence." Neill v. Brackett, 126 N.E. 93, 94 (Mass. 1920). A claim of undue influence is comprised of four elements: "(1) an unnatural disposition has been made (2) by a person susceptible to undue influence to the advantage of someone (3) with an opportunity to exercise undue influence and (4) who in fact has used that opportunity to procure the contested disposition through improper means." O'Rourke v. Hunter, 848 N.E.2d 382, 392-93 (Mass. 2006) (citations omitted).

While the burden of proof ordinarily rests with the party contesting the will, a "fiduciary who benefits in a transaction with the person for whom he is a fiduciary bears the burden of establishing that the transaction did not violate his obligations." Cleary v. Cleary, 692 N.E.2d 955, 961 (Mass. 1998). Spinelli does not contest the finding that he had a fiduciary relationship with Alice. Spinelli was the decedent's fiduciary under a broad durable power of attorney; he had near complete control of Alice's finances, and played an instrumental role in arranging for the will to be drafted and executed. It was therefore his burden to prove that the will was not the product of his undue influence.

a. *Independent counsel.* Spinelli contends that Alice had the advice of independent legal counsel and this fact alone militates against the undue influence as a matter of law. The rationale for shifting the burden to a fiduciary who benefits from a transaction with his principal is that "[t]he fiduciary can take precautions to ensure that proof exists that the transaction was fair and that his principal was fully informed, and he is in the best position after the transaction to explain and justify it." In re Estate of Moretti, 871 N.E.2d 493, 501 (Mass. App. 2007). "[T]he burden to prove the transaction was fair 'is generally met if the fiduciary shows that the principal made the request with full knowledge and intent . . . or with the advice of independent legal counsel.'" Rempelakis v. Russell, 842 N.E.2d 970, 979 (2006) (citation omitted). One of the functions of independent counsel is to provide documentation that the making and execution of a will is voluntary and knowing, thus lending transparency and credibility to the bequest.

The judge's finding that Alice lacked the advice of independent counsel is supported by the record. Spinelli selected the attorney, communicated with the drafting attorney by e-mail, filled in certain terms, and transported Alice to her husband's nursing home for the execution of her will. Strikingly, Alice never met the attorney in person and communicated with him briefly only twice by telephone. There is no evidence that the associate who drafted the will ever spoke with Alice; she communicated by e-mail with Spinelli. No attorney reviewed the terms of the will with Alice. Only Spinelli did so. Significantly, the decedent had no prior wills and there was no evidence that she was familiar with wills or their terminology. The attorney could not recall the specifics of his conversation with Alice or any specific advice he offered her with respect to the dispositions in her will. There was testimony at trial that Alice claimed to have no will. On this record, the judge's finding that the decedent lacked the benefit of independent advice of counsel was not clearly erroneous.

b. *Secrecy.* There was an aura of secrecy surrounding the estate planning, as no one in the family, other than Spinelli, was aware that Alice had executed a will before her death. The judge was not required to credit Spinelli's testimony that Alice requested that he keep the existence of the will confidential; in view of the judge's credibility findings it is clear that he did not do so. Although the judge found that the witnesses to the will did not observe any signs of duress or undue influence, the will was neither read in front of them nor was there any discussion of its terms during the execution. Spinelli alone was in a position to ensure that there was proof that Alice was fully informed and independently made the bequests at issue. There was no error in the judge's finding that he failed to do so.

c. *Susceptibility.* Although Spinelli suggests that Alice was not susceptible to undue influence, her advanced age, lack of familiarity with wills, and seventh grade education, coupled with Spinelli's nearly complete control of her finances, among other factors, permit the inference that she was susceptible to his influence. Spinelli clearly had the opportunity to exercise influence to his benefit. Notwithstanding that Spinelli lived with Alice during the last eight years of her life, the judge was not compelled to conclude that the dispositions made in Alice's will were natural. The judge did not credit evidence of a particularly close relationship between them. To the contrary, he found that Alice questioned why Spinelli needed to live with her and why he had stayed so long. Instead, the judge credited testimony of the relationship the decedent enjoyed with her children, grandchildren, and great-grandchildren, particularly her grand-daughter and her great-granddaughter.

d. *Sufficiency of the evidence.* . . . We find the facts enumerated above to be sufficient in and of themselves to support the conclusion that Spinelli did not meet his burden to prove that the will was executed without undue influence. "The conduct of a trusted advisor prior to the making of a will in which he is named as beneficiary may be such as to amount to undue influence voiding the will, without proof of specific acts of the advisor at the time the will was made." Doggett v. Morse, 12 N.E.2d 867, 389-90 (Mass. 1938).

In addition, the judge found that Spinelli's transfer of funds from the checking accounts into the trust account "disrupt[ed] Alice's bequest of her 'checking and savings accounts' to her daughters." Spinelli was unable adequately to explain where the money in the trust account went. Spinelli's failure to account fully for these funds was a proper matter of consideration for the judge, whose credibility findings we do not disturb.

It is true that there is no direct evidence that Spinelli unduly influenced the decedent. This is neither surprising nor telling. "In many instances a finding of undue influence rests largely on circumstantial evidence, since direct evidence of such influence is often difficult to establish." Maimonides Sch. v. Coles, 881 N.E.2d 778, 791 (Mass. App. 2008). Nor is there evidence that he emptied the trust account for his personal benefit. However, by depleting the checking account bequeathed to others, Spinelli preserved those assets bequeathed to him. "The nature of fraud and undue influence is such that they often work in veiled and secret ways. The power of a strong will over . . . one weakened by disease, over-indulgence or age may be manifest although not shown by gross or palpable instrumentalities. . . . When the donor is enfeebled by age or disease, although not reaching to unsoundness of mind, and the relation between the parties is fiduciary or intimate, the transaction ordinarily is subject to careful scrutiny." *Neill*, 126 N.E. at 94. Neither direct evidence nor evidence of appropriation of assets for personal use before death was required to support an inference of undue influence.

3. *Conclusion.* In sum, the judge's ruling that the decedent's will was the result of undue influence by Spinelli was not clear error. The judge permissibly found that Spinelli failed to meet his burden of proving that Alice, with full knowledge and intent, favored him over her children and other grandchildren without his undue influence.

Decree affirmed.

NOTES

1. Undue Influence and Testamentary Capacity. Testamentary capacity, a question of *status*, concerns the mental ability of the testator. Undue influence, a question of *conduct*, concerns the actions of a third party. Yet many cases involve allegations of both incapacity and undue influence, as in *Sharis.* The reason is that the mental status of the testator is relevant in assessing the testator's susceptibility to undue influence by another, and a will may be held invalid on both grounds, as in In re Estate of Lynch, 350 S.W.3d 130 (Tex. App. 2011).

2. Lifetime Transfers. The opinion in *Sharis* recites that Spinelli transferred $71,450 from the decedent's checking account to another account controlled by

Spinelli. A lifetime transfer procured by undue influence (or by duress or fraud) is voidable by the transferor. To prevent the *unjust enrichment* of the transferee, the property is recoverable in *restitution* by way of *constructive trust*.[28] At the death of the transferor, this claim passes to the fiduciary of the transferor's estate, who typically has the same standing to sue as did the decedent immediately prior to death, as under UPC § 3-703(c) (1990). The recovered property is included in the estate of the decedent and distributed accordingly, as in Monroe v. Marsden, 207 P.3d 320 (Mont. 2009).

A nonprobate transfer, such as a pay-on-death contract, can likewise be set aside for undue influence, with the recovered property returned to the estate of the decedent and distributed accordingly, as in Keul v. Hodges Blvd. Presbyterian Church, 180 So. 3d 1074 (Fla. App. 2015).

Presumptions and Burden Shifting in Undue Influence Cases

In *Sharis*, because Spinelli had been in a fiduciary relationship with Alice and suspicious circumstances were present, the court presumed undue influence and put the burden on him to prove that her will was voluntarily made.

Confidential Relationship.   Ordinarily a person is free to favor his own interests to the detriment of the interests of others. But in some situations involving a trusting relationship—what is called a *confidential relationship*—the law requires a person to be other-regarding because of the potential for abuse of that trust. In *Sharis*, Spinelli was in a per se confidential relationship with the decedent owing to his fiduciary status as the agent under her power of attorney (see page 502). The Restatement explains:

> [T]he term "confidential relationship" embraces three sometimes distinct relationships—fiduciary, reliant, or dominant-subservient. . . .
>
> A fiduciary relationship is one in which the confidential relationship arises from a settled category of fiduciary obligation. . . . For example, an attorney is in a fiduciary relationship with his or her client. . . . [A]n agent under a power of attorney is in a fiduciary relationship with his or her principal. . . .
>
> Whether a reliant relationship exists is a question of fact. The contestant must establish that there was a relationship based on special trust and confidence, for example, that the donor was accustomed to be guided by the judgment or advice of the alleged wrongdoer or was justified in placing confidence in the belief that the alleged wrongdoer would act in the interest of the donor. Examples might include the relationship between a financial adviser and customer or between a doctor and patient.
>
> Whether a dominant-subservient relationship exists is a question of fact. The contestant must establish that the donor was subservient to the alleged wrongdoer's dominant influence. Such a relationship might exist between a hired caregiver and an ill or feeble donor or between an adult child and an ill or feeble parent.[29]

---

28. *See* Restatement (Third) of Restitution and Unjust Enrichment §§ 15, 55 (Am. Law Inst. 2011).

29. Restatement (Third) of Property: Wills and Other Donative Transfers § 8.3 cmt. g (Am. Law Inst. 2003).

Suspicious Circumstances.   In addition to a confidential relationship, to trigger a presumption of undue influence a contestant must usually show the existence of *suspicious circumstances*. This requirement often can be satisfied by showing that the influencer procured the will. In *Sharis*, the court also emphasized the secrecy surrounding the new will, Alice's susceptibility to Spinelli's influence, and the absence of independent counsel. These are common examples of suspicious circumstances; the Restatement includes each among its more comprehensive list:

(1) the extent to which the donor was in a weakened condition, physically, mentally, or both, and therefore susceptible to undue influence;

(2) the extent to which the alleged wrongdoer participated in the preparation or procurement of the will or will substitute;

(3) whether the donor received independent advice from an attorney or from other competent and disinterested advisors in preparing the will or will substitute;

(4) whether the will or will substitute was prepared in secrecy or in haste;

(5) whether the donor's attitude toward others had changed by reason of his or her relationship with the alleged wrongdoer;

(6) whether there is a decided discrepancy between a new and previous wills or will substitutes of the donor;

(7) whether there was a continuity of purpose running through former wills or will substitutes indicating a settled intent in the disposition of his or her property; and

(8) whether the disposition of the property is such that a reasonable person would regard it as unnatural, unjust, or unfair, for example, whether the disposition abruptly and without apparent reason disinherited a faithful and deserving family member.[30]

Presumption and Burden Shifting.   In most states, if a presumption of undue influence is triggered, the burden shifts to the proponent to come forward with rebuttal evidence—for example, by showing that the presumed influencer "acted in good faith throughout the transaction and the grantor acted freely, intelligently, and voluntarily."[31] In the absence of such evidence, the contestant is entitled to judgment as a matter of law based on the inference of undue influence arising from the circumstances. The theory is that a person who benefits from a confidential relationship "can take precautions to ensure that proof exists that the transaction was fair and that his principal was fully informed, and he is in the best position after the transaction to explain and justify it."[32]

NOTE

Caregiver Statutes.   Statutes in a few states, including California, Illinois, and Maine, apply a presumption of undue influence to any gift to a caregiver above a

---

30. Id. cmt. h.
31. Jackson v. Schrader, 676 N.W.2d 599, 605 (Iowa 2003).
32. Cleary v. Cleary, 692 N.E.2d 955, 960 (Mass. 1998).

modest threshold.[33] A caregiver for these purposes is a person on whom the donor depends for health or other social services (but a spouse or other close family member is usually excluded). The statutory presumption of undue influence arises from the fact of the transfer to the caregiver; there is no need first to establish a confidential relationship or suspicious circumstances. The statutes are in disagreement on whether a preponderance of the evidence or clear and convincing evidence is necessary to rebut the presumption.[34] In some states, such as California, a "certificate of independent review" by an independent lawyer who counseled the donor provides a safe harbor if the certificate evidences compliance with certain procedural safeguards.[35]

In re Will of Moses
227 So. 2d 829 (Miss. 1969)

[Fannie Traylor Moses was thrice married; each of her husbands died. During the second marriage, she struck up a friendship with Clarence Holland, a lawyer 15 years her junior. After the death of her third husband, Holland became Mrs. Moses's lover as well as lawyer, and this relationship continued for several years until Mrs. Moses died at age 57. During the six or seven years preceding her death, Mrs. Moses suffered from serious heart trouble, had a breast removed because of cancer, and became an alcoholic. Three years before death she made a will devising almost all of her property to Holland. This will was drafted by a lawyer, Dan Shell, who had no connection with Holland, and who did not tell Holland of the will. Mrs. Moses's closest relative was an elder sister. The sister attacked the will on the ground of undue influence. The chancellor found undue influence and denied probate. Holland appealed.]

SMITH, J. . . . A number of grounds are assigned for reversal. However, appellant's chief argument is addressed to the proposition that even if Holland, as Mrs. Moses' attorney, occupied a continuing fiduciary relationship with respect to her on May 26, 1964, the date of the execution of the document under which he claimed her estate, the presumption of undue influence was overcome because, in making the will, Mrs. Moses had the independent advice and counsel of one entirely devoted to her interests. It is argued that, for this reason, a decree should be entered here reversing the chancellor and admitting the 1964 will to probate. . . .

The evidence supports the chancellor's finding that the confidential or fiduciary relationship which existed between Mrs. Moses and Holland, her attorney, was a subsisting and continuing relationship, having . . . ended only with Mrs. Moses' death. Moreover, its effect was enhanced by the fact that throughout this period, Holland was

---

33. *See* Cal. Prob. Code § 21380(a)(3) (2016); 755 Ill. Comp. Stat. 5/4a-10(a) (2016); Me. Rev. Stat., tit. 33 § 1022 (2016).

34. *Compare* 755 Ill. Comp. Stat. 5/4a-15(1) (2016) (preponderance), *with* Cal. Prob. Code § 21380(b) (2016) (clear and convincing).

35. *See* Cal. Prob. Code § 21384 (2016).

in almost daily attendance upon Mrs. Moses on terms of the utmost intimacy. There was strong evidence that this aging woman, seriously ill, disfigured by surgery, and hopelessly addicted to alcoholic excesses, was completely bemused by the constant and amorous attentions of Holland, a man 15 years her junior. There was testimony too indicating that she entertained the pathetic hope that he might marry her. Although the evidence was not without conflict and was, in some of its aspects, circumstantial, it was sufficient to support the finding that the relationship existed on May 26, 1964, the date of the will tendered for probate by Holland.

The chancellor's factual finding of the existence of this relationship on that date is supported by evidence and is not manifestly wrong. Moreover, he was correct in his conclusion of law that such relationship gave rise to a presumption of undue influence which could be overcome only by evidence that, in making the 1964 will, Mrs. Moses had acted upon the independent advice and counsel of one entirely devoted to her interest.

Appellant takes the position that there was undisputed evidence that Mrs. Moses, in making the 1964 will did, in fact, have such advice and counsel. He relies upon the testimony of the attorney in whose office that document was prepared to support his assertion.

This attorney was and is a reputable and respected member of the bar, who had no prior connection with Holland and no knowledge of Mrs. Moses' relationship with him. He had never seen nor represented Mrs. Moses previously and never represented her afterward. He was acquainted with Holland and was aware that Holland was a lawyer.

A brief summary of his testimony, with respect to the writing of the will, follows:

Mrs. Moses had telephoned him for an appointment and had come alone to his office on March 31, 1964. She was not intoxicated and in his opinion knew what she was doing. He asked her about her property and "marital background." He did this in order, he said, to advise her as to possible renunciation by a husband. She was also asked if she had children in order to determine whether she wished to "pretermit them." As she had neither husband nor children this subject was pursued no further. He asked as to the values of various items of property in order to consider possible tax problems. He told her it would be better if she had more accurate descriptions of the several items of real and personal property comprising her estate. No further "advice or counsel" was given her.

On some later date, Mrs. Moses sent in (the attorney did not think she came personally and in any event he did not see her), some tax receipts for purposes of supplying property descriptions. He prepared the will and mailed a draft to her. Upon receiving it, she telephoned that he had made a mistake in the devise of certain realty, in that he had provided that a relatively low valued property should go to Holland rather than a substantially more valuable property which she said she wanted Holland to have. He rewrote the will, making this change, and mailed it to her, as revised, on May 21, 1964. On the one occasion when he saw Mrs. Moses, there were no questions and no discussion of any kind as to Holland being preferred to the exclusion of her blood relatives. Nor was there any inquiry or discussion as to a possible client-attorney relationship with Holland. The attorney-draftsman wrote the will according to Mrs. Moses' instructions and said that he had "no interest in" how she disposed of her property. He testified "I try to draw the will to suit their purposes and if she (Mrs. Moses) wanted to leave him (Holland) everything she had, that was her business as far as I was concerned. I was trying to represent her in putting on paper in her will her desires, and it didn't matter to me to whom she left it . . . I couldn't have cared less."

When Mrs. Moses returned to the office to execute the will, the attorney was not there and it was witnessed by two secretaries. . . .

The attorney's testimony supports the chancellor's finding that nowhere in the conversations with Mrs. Moses was there touched upon in any way the proposed testamentary disposition whereby preference was to be given a nonrelative to the exclusion of her blood relatives. There was no discussion of her relationship with Holland, nor as to who her legal heirs might be, nor as to their relationship to her, after it was discovered that she had neither a husband nor children.

It is clear from his own testimony that, in writing the will, the attorney-draftsman, did no more than write down, according to the forms of law, what Mrs. Moses told him. There was no meaningful independent advice or counsel touching upon the area in question and it is manifest that the role of the attorney in writing the will, as it relates to the present issue, was little more than that of scrivener. The chancellor was justified in holding that this did not meet the burden nor overcome the presumption. . . .

Holland, of course, did not personally participate in the actual preparation or execution of the will. If he had, under the circumstances in evidence, unquestionably the will could not stand. It may be assumed that Holland, as a lawyer, knew this.

In Croft v. Alder, 115 So. 2d 683, 686 (Miss. 1959), this Court said that the presumption of undue influence in the production of a will may arise from "antecedent circumstances" about which its draftsman and the witnesses knew nothing. The rule, as stated in that case, is that undue influence will be presumed where the beneficiary "has been actively concerned in some way with the preparation or execution of the will, or where the *relationship* is coupled with some *suspicious circumstances*, such as mental infirmity of the testator." (emphasis added). . . .

The sexual morality of the personal relationship is not an issue. However, the intimate nature of this relationship is relevant to the present inquiry to the extent that its existence, under the circumstances, warranted an inference of undue influence, extending and augmenting that which flowed from the attorney-client relationship. Particularly is this true when viewed in the light of evidence indicating its employment for the personal aggrandizement of Holland. For that purpose, it was properly taken into consideration by the chancellor. . . .

[T]he decree of the chancery court will be affirmed.

ROBERTSON, J., dissenting. . . . Mrs. Fannie T. Moses was the active manager of commercial property in the heart of Jackson, four apartment buildings containing ten rental units, and a 480-acre farm until the day of her death. All of the witnesses conceded that she was a good businesswoman, maintaining and repairing her properties with promptness and dispatch, and paying her bills promptly so that she would get the cash discount. She was a strong personality and pursued her own course, even though her manner of living did at times embarrass her sisters and estranged her from them.

It was not contended in this case that Holland was in any way actively concerned with the preparation or execution of the will. Appellees rely solely upon the finding of the chancellor that there were suspicious circumstances. However, the suspicious circumstances listed by the chancellor in his opinion had nothing whatsoever to do with the preparation or execution of the will. These were remote antecedent circumstances having to do with the meretricious relationship of the parties, and the fact that at times Mrs. Moses drank to excess and could be termed an alcoholic, but there is no proof in this long record that her use of alcohol affected her will power or her ability to look after her extensive real estate holdings. . . .

The majority was indeed hard put to find fault with . . . [the actions of Dan Shell, the attorney who drew the will,] on behalf of his client. . . . He ascertained that Mrs. Moses was competent to make a will; he satisfied himself that she was acting of her own free will and accord, and that she was disposing of her property exactly as she wished and intended. No more is required.

There is not one iota of testimony in the voluminous record that Clarence Holland even knew of this will, much less that he participated in the preparation or execution of it. The evidence is all to the contrary. The evidence is undisputed that she executed her last will after the fullest deliberation, with full knowledge of what she was doing, and with the independent consent and advice of an experienced and competent attorney whose sole purpose was to advise with her and prepare her will exactly as she wanted it.

In January 1967, about one month before her death and some two years and eight months after she had made her will, she called W.R. Patterson, an experienced, reliable and honorable attorney who was a friend of hers, and asked him to come by her home for a few minutes. Patterson testified:

> She said, "Well, the reason I called you out here is that I've got an envelope here with all of my important papers in it, and *that includes my last will and testament,*" and says, "I would like to leave them with you if you've got a place to lock them up in your desk somewhere there in your office." . . .
>
> [A]nd she said, *"Now, Dan Shell drew my will for me two or three years ago,"* and she says, *"It's exactly like I want it,"* and says, *"I had to go to his office two or three times to get it the way I wanted it, but this is the way I want it,* and if anything happens to me I want you to take all these papers and give them to Dan," and she says, "He'll know what to do with them." (Emphasis added.)

What else could she have done? She met all the tests that this Court and other courts have carefully outlined and delineated. The majority opinion says that this still was not enough, that there were "suspicious circumstances" . . . , but even these were not connected in any shape, form or fashion with the preparation or execution of her will. They had to do with her love life and her drinking habits and propensities. . . .

If full knowledge, deliberate and voluntary action, and independent consent and advice have not been proved in this case, then they just cannot be proved. . . . I think that the judgment of the lower court should be reversed and the last will and testament of Fannie T. Moses executed on May 26, 1964, admitted to probate in solemn form.

NOTES

1. Gender Norms and Sexual Morality.   What role did the court's view of gender roles play in *Moses*? Why is a relationship between a younger man and an older woman suspect? If Fannie Moses had been a man named Frank, and Clarence Holland had been a woman named Clara, but otherwise the facts were the same, would the result have been the same?

What of the court's disclaimer that "[t]he sexual morality of the personal relationship is not an issue"? Should not a long-term sexual partner be regarded as a natural object of the decedent's bounty? Does not a sexual relationship spanning many years imply affection, perhaps even love? Why should sensual pleasures outside of marriage be evidence of *undue* influence?

In Kimbrough v. Estate of Kimbrough, 134 So. 3d 281 (Miss. 2014), the same court that 45 years earlier decided *Moses* said that if "a confidential relationship exists, an abuse of that relationship must be shown for the Contestants to raise a proper presumption of undue influence. The existence of a confidential relationship, standing alone, does not raise a presumption of undue influence." Was there evidence in *Moses* that Holland abused his relationship with Moses?

2. In re Kaufmann's Will.   In the infamous case of In re Kaufmann's Will, 205 N.E.2d 864 (N.Y. 1965), at issue was the will of Robert Kaufmann, a multimillionaire by inheritance, who beginning in 1951 made wills in successive years, each giving Walter Weiss a larger share of Robert's estate. In 1958, Robert executed a will, drafted by a prominent New York law firm, which left substantially all his property to Walter. Accompanying the will was a letter addressed to Robert's family, signed by Robert in 1951, and passed along with each subsequent will. The letter stated that when Robert met Walter, Robert was "terribly unhappy, highly emotional and filled to the brim with a grandly variegated group of fears, guilt and assorted complexes." It continued:

> Walter gave me the courage to start something which slowly but eventually permitted me to supply for myself everything my life had heretofore lacked: an outlet for my long-latent but strong creative ability in painting . . . , a balanced, healthy sex life which before had been spotty, furtive and destructive; an ability to reorientate myself to actual life and to face it calmly and realistically. All of this adds up to Peace of Mind. . . . I am eternally grateful to my dearest friend — best pal, Walter A. Weiss. What could be more wonderful than a fruitful, contented life and who more deserving of gratitude now, in the form of an inheritance, than the person who helped most in securing that life? I cannot believe my family could be anything else but glad and happy for my own comfortable self-determination and contentment and equally grateful to the friend who made it possible.

In 1951, Robert bought an expensive townhouse at 42 East 74th Street. He remodeled the top floor into an office for Walter. The rest of the house was lavishly furnished as a home for Robert and Walter. Walter ran the household, overseeing the cooking, cleaning, and entertaining; answering the mail and the telephone; paying bills from Robert's bank account; and recommending doctors for Robert's various complaints. A talented artist, Robert spent much of his time painting. He opened an art gallery where he exhibited his works and those of other artists.

In their social life, Robert and Walter appeared as a couple, entertaining on a grand scale and exhibiting love, affection, and mutual esteem. In business matters, Robert gave Walter, who had a law degree but did not practice, his confidence and trust. Walter took charge of Robert's bank accounts and investments as if they belonged to the both of them. The two men lived together until 1959, when Robert died unexpectedly.

Robert's family deeply resented Walter's presence and his interfering business advice about the family-owned Kay Jewelry Stores, in which Robert was a major shareholder. The 1951 letter appeared to confirm the family's suspicion Robert and Walter were gay. Upon Robert's death, his brother sued to have the 1958 will set aside for undue influence. In his pretrial deposition, Walter denied that a sexual relationship existed between the two men, but the appellate judges, and probably the jury as well, suspected that this was a lie. Walter did not take the stand at the trial and, therefore, was not subject to cross-examination.

After two jury trials, both finding undue influence, and an affirmance by the state intermediate appellate court, the state's high court affirmed:

The townhouse at 42 East 74th Street (2012)

> Where, as here, the record indicates that testator was pliable and easily taken advantage of, as proponent admitted, that there was a long and detailed history of dominance and subservience between them, that testator relied exclusively upon proponent's knowledge and judgment in the disposition of almost all of the material circumstances affecting the conduct of his life, and proponent is willed virtually the entire estate, we consider that a question of fact was presented concerning whether the instrument offered for probate was the free, untrammeled and intelligent expression of the wishes and intentions of testator or the product of the dominance of the beneficiary.

If Walter had been a woman named Wendy, but otherwise the facts were the same, would the result have been the same? Do you think this case would be decided the same way today? Are people less biased today than they were or have the biases simply changed?

3. Punitive Damages.   In a break from traditional law, in In re Estate of Stockdale, 953 A.2d 454 (N.J. 2008), the court authorized *punitive damages* in a will contest. The court held that punitive damages would be available on a showing, "by clear and convincing evidence, that the acts or omissions of the actor causing the harm [were motivated] by actual malice or accompanied by a wanton and willful disregard of persons who foreseeably might be harmed by those acts or omissions."

Would the standard for punitive damages under *Stockdale* have been met in *Sharis*? In *Moses*? Were not those cases decided on the basis of a presumption rather than actual evidence of wrongdoing? Might punitive damages aggravate the problem of strike suits or magnify the cost of error in policing the murky line between permissible persuasion and impermissible overpersuasion? Or should punitive damages be available in a will contest on grounds of deterrence or punishment?

Lipper v. Weslow
369 S.W.2d 698 (Tex. App. 1963)

McDONALD, C.J. This is a contest of the will of Mrs. Sophie Block, on the ground of undue influence. Plaintiffs, Julian Weslow, Jr.,[36] Julia Weslow Fortson and Alice Weslow Sale, are the 3 grandchildren of Mrs. Block by a deceased son; defendants are Mrs. Block's 2 surviving children, G. Frank Lipper and Irene Lipper Dover (half brother and half sister of plaintiffs' deceased father). (The will left the estate of testatrix to her 2 children, defendants herein; and left nothing to her grandchildren by the deceased son, plaintiffs herein.) Trial was to a jury, which found that Mrs. Block's will, signed by her on January 30, 1956, was procured by undue influence on the part of the proponent, Frank Lipper. The trial court entered judgment on the verdict, setting aside the will.

Defendants appeal, contending there is no evidence, or insufficient evidence, to support the finding that the will was procured by undue influence.

Testatrix was married 3 times. Of her first marriage she had one son, Julian Weslow (who died in 1949), who was father of plaintiffs herein. After the death of her first husband testatrix married a Mr. Lipper. Defendants are the 2 children of their marriage. After Mr. Lipper's death, testatrix married Max Block. There were no children born of this marriage. Max Block died several months after the death of testatrix.

On 30 January, 1956, Sophie Block executed the will in controversy. Such will was prepared by defendant, Frank Lipper, an attorney, one of the beneficiaries of the will, and Independent Executor of the will. The will was witnessed by 2 former business associates of Mr. Block. Pertinent provisions of the will are summarized as follows:

> "That I, Mrs. Sophie Block, . . . do make, publish and declare this my last will and testament, hereby revoking all other wills by me heretofore made."

> 1, 2, 3 and 4.

> (Provide for payment of debts; for burial in Beth Israel Cemetery; and for minor bequests to a servant, and to an old folks' home.)

> 5.

> (Devises the bulk of testatrix's estate to her 2 children, Mrs. Irene Lipper Dover and Frank Lipper (defendants herein), share and share alike.)

> 6.

> States that $7000. previously advanced to Mrs. Irene Lipper Dover, and $9300. previously advanced to Frank Lipper be taken into consideration in the final

---

36. Julian Weslow, Jr., became a professional dog trainer, famed throughout the Southwest for "snake proofing" hunting dogs. The dog is given a zap of electricity through an electric collar when the dog sniffs a defanged rattlesnake, which strikes at the dog simultaneously. Sometimes the dog leaps two feet straight up, but in any case the dog quickly learns to give snakes a wide berth thereafter. — Eds.

Sophie Block Was My Great-Great-Grandmother

Brent Bernell, J.D. 2011, who came upon this case while a law student at Harvard, writes to us as follows:

Sophie Block was my great-great-grandmother on my mother's side. My maternal grandfather, Frank Dover, is the son of Irene Lipper Dover, Sophie Block's daughter.

Sophie Block's son, G. Frank Lipper, went by the name George to those who knew him. George (Frank, to the court) was a lawyer, but practicing law was not his only occupation. He was also a homebuilder, a plumber, and an electrician. George was very close to his mother, but family lore is that Sophie asked him to write her will out of convenience. She didn't see any point in paying for a lawyer when George could draw the will for free.

Sophie was quite active until her death. Even on the day she died, Sophie had paid some bills and had gone out to lunch with friends. She was also strong willed. She had made known to my grandfather and others that she had no intention of leaving anything to Julian Weslow's widow or children. She never had a particularly good relationship with Bernice Weslow, and the relationship deteriorated after Julian died. In

Sophie and Max Block, fishing in Galveston, Texas, c. 1920

fact, my grandfather, who lived in Houston and visited Sophie often, had no recollection of even meeting the Weslows until the trial. My grandfather was in the courtroom for the entire trial and was surprised with the initial verdict, as most of the family knew of Sophie's wishes. However, after losing at the trial stage, George and Irene hired new lawyers and were very pleased to have the judgment reversed on appeal.

Email from Brent Bernell to Robert H. Sitkoff (June 16, 2011).

---

settlement of the estate; and cancels such amounts "that I gave or advanced to my deceased son, Julian."

7.

(Appoints G. Frank Lipper Independent Executor of the estate without bond.)

8.

(Provides that if any legatee contests testatrix's will or the will of her husband, Max Block, that they forfeit all benefits under the will.)

9.

"My son, Julian A. Weslow, died on August 6, 1949, and I want to explain why I have not provided anything under this will for my daughter-in-law, Bernice Weslow, widow of my deceased son, Julian, and her children, Julian A. Weslow, Jr., Alice Weslow Sale, and Julia Weslow Fortson, and I want to go into sufficient detail in explaining my relationship in past years with my said son's widow and his children, before mentioned, and it is my desire to record such relationship so that there will be no question as to my feelings in the matter or any thought or suggestion that my children, Irene Lipper Dover and G. Frank Lipper, or my husband, Max, may have influenced me in any manner in the execution of this will. During the time that my said son, Julian, was living, the attitude of his wife, Bernice, was at times, pleasant and friendly, but the majority of the years when my said son, Julian, was living, her attitude towards me and my husband, Max, was unfriendly and frequently months would pass when she was not in my home and I did not hear from her. When my said son, Julian, was living he was treated the same as I treated my other children; and, my husband, Max, and I gave to each of our children a home and various sums of money from time to time to help in taking care of medical expenses, other unusual expenses, as well as outright gifts. Since my said son Julian's death, his widow, Bernice, and all of her children have shown a most unfriendly and distant attitude towards me, my husband, Max, and my 2 children G. Frank Lipper and Irene Lipper Dover, which attitude I cannot reconcile as I have shown them many kindnesses since they have been members of my family, and their continued unfriendly attitude towards me, my husband, Max, and my said children has hurt me deeply in my declining years, for my life would have been much happier if they had shown a disposition to want to be a part of the family and enter into a normal family relationship that usually exists with a daughter-in-law and grandchildren and great grandchildren. I have not seen my grandson, Julian A. Weslow, Jr. in several years, neither have I heard from him. My granddaughter, Alice Weslow Sale, I have not seen in several years and I have not heard from her, but I heard a report some months ago that she was now living in California and has since married William G. Sale. My granddaughter, Julia Weslow Fortson, wife of Ben Fortson, I have not seen in several years and I was told that she had a child born to her sometime in December 1952, and I have not seen the child or heard from my said granddaughter, Julia, up to this writing, and was informed by a friend that Julia has had another child recently and is now living in Louisiana, having moved from Houston; and needless to say, my said daughter-in-law, Bernice, widow of my deceased son, Julian, I have not seen in several years as she has taken little or no interest in me or my husband, Max, since the death of my son, Julian, with the exception that Christmas a year ago, if I remember correctly, she sent some flowers, which I acknowledged, and I believe she had sent some greeting cards on some occasions prior to that time. My said daughter-in-law, Bernice Weslow, has expressed to me, on several occasions, an intense hatred for my son, G. Frank Lipper, and my daughter, Irene Lipper Dover, which I cannot understand, as my said children have always shown her and her children every consideration when possible, and have expressed a desire to be friendly with her, and them. My said children, G. Frank Lipper, and Irene Lipper Dover, have at all times been attentive to me and my husband, Max, especially during the past few years when we have not been well. I will be 82 years old in June of this year and my husband, Max, will be 80 years of age in October of this year, and we have both been in failing health for the past few years and rarely leave our home, and appreciate any attention that is given us, and my husband, Max, and I cannot understand the unfriendly and distant attitude of Bernice Weslow, widow of my said son, Julian, and his children, before mentioned."

10.

(Concerns personal belongings already disposed of.)
"In Testimony Whereof, I have hereunto signed my name. . . .
"(S) Sophie Block"
(Here follows attestation clause and signature of the 2 witnesses.)

The record reflects that the will in question was executed 22 days before testatrix died at the age of 81 years. By its terms, it disinherits the children of testatrix's son, who died in 1949. Defendant, Frank Lipper, gets a larger share than would have been the case if the plaintiffs were not disinherited. Defendant Lipper is a lawyer, and is admittedly the scrivener of the will. There is evidence that defendant Lipper bore malice against his dead half brother. He lived next door to testatrix, and had a key to her house. The will was not read to testatrix prior to the time she signed same, and she had no discussion with anyone at the time she executed it. There is evidence that the recitations in the will that Bernice Weslow and her children were unfriendly, and never came about testatrix, were untrue. There is also evidence that the Weslows sent testatrix greeting cards and flowers from 1946 through 1954, more times than stated in the will.

Plaintiffs offered no direct evidence pertaining to the making and execution of the will on January 30, 1956, and admittedly rely wholly upon circumstantial evidence of undue influence to support the verdict.

All of the evidence is that testatrix was of sound mind at the time of the execution of the will; that she was a person of strong will; that she was in good physical health for her age; and that she was in fact physically active to the day of her death.

Mrs. Weslow's husband died in 1949; and after 1952 the Weslows came about testatrix less often than before.

The witness Lyda Friberg, who worked at the home of testatrix from 1949 to 1952, testified that in *1952* she had a conversation with Bernice Weslow in which Mrs. Weslow told her if her children didn't get their inheritance she would "sue them through every court in the Union"; that she told testatrix about this conversation, and that testatrix told her "she would have those wills fixed up so there would be no court business," and that she wasn't going to "leave them (the Weslows) a dime." The foregoing was prior to the execution of the will on January 30, 1956.

Subsequent to the execution of the will, testatrix had a conversation with her sister, Mrs. Levy. Mrs. Levy testified:

Q. Who did she say she was leaving her property to?
A. She was leaving it to her son and her daughter.
Q. What else did she say about the rest of her kin, if anything?
A. Well she said that Julian's children had been very ugly to her; that they never showed her any attention whatever; they married and she didn't know they were married; they had children and they didn't let her know. After Julian passed away, she never saw any of the family at all. They never came to see her.
Q. Did she make any statement?
A. Yes she did. When she passed away, she didn't want to leave them anything; that they did nothing for her when she was living.

Shortly before she passed away, testatrix told Mrs. Augusta Roos that she was going to leave her property to her 2 children, and further:

Q. Did she give any reason for it?
A. Yes. She said that Bernice had never been very nice to her and the children never were over.

Again, subsequent to the making of her will, testatrix talked with Effie Landry, her maid. Mrs. Landry testified:

Q. Did Mrs. Block on any occasion ever tell you anything about what was contained in her will?

A. Yes.

Q. What did she tell you about that?

A. She said she wasn't leaving the Weslow children anything.

The only question presented is whether there is any evidence of undue influence. The test of undue influence is whether such control was exercised over the mind of the testatrix as to overcome her free agency and free will and to substitute the will of another so as to cause the testatrix to do what she would not otherwise have done but for such control.

The evidence here establishes that testatrix was 81 years of age at the time of the execution of her will; that her son, defendant Lipper, who is a lawyer, wrote the will for her upon her instruction; that defendant Lipper bore malice against his deceased half brother (father of plaintiffs); that defendant Lipper lived next door to his mother and had a key to her home; that the will as written gave defendant Lipper a larger share of testatrix's estate than he would otherwise have received; that while testatrix had no discussion with anyone at the time she executed the will, she told the witness Friberg, prior to executing the will, that she was not going to leave anything to the Weslows; and subsequent to the execution of the will she told the witnesses Mrs. Levy, Mrs. Roos, and Mrs. Landry that she had not left the Weslows anything, and the reason why. The will likewise states the reasons for testatrix's action. The testatrix, although 81 years of age, was of sound mind and strong will; and in excellent physical health. There is evidence that the recitation in testatrix's will about the number of times the Weslows sent cards and flowers were incorrect, to the extent that cards and flowers were in fact sent oftener than such will recites.

The contestants established a confidential relationship, the opportunity, and perhaps a motive for undue influence by defendant Lipper. Proof of this type simply sets the stage. Contestants must go forward and prove in some fashion that the will as written resulted from the defendant Lipper substituting his mind and will for that of the testatrix. Here the will and the circumstances might raise suspicion, but it does not supply proof of the vital facts of undue influence—the substitution of a plan of testamentary disposition by another as the will of the testatrix.

All of the evidence reflected that testatrix, although 81 years of age, was of sound mind; of strong will; and in excellent physical condition. Moreover, subsequent to the execution of the will she told 3 disinterested witnesses what she had done with her property in her will, and the reason therefor. A person of sound mind has the legal right to dispose of his property as he wishes, with the burden on those attacking the disposition to prove that it was the product of undue influence.

Testatrix's will did make an unnatural disposition of her property in the sense that it preferred her 2 children over the grandchildren by a deceased son. However, the record contains an explanation from testatrix herself as to why she chose to do such. She had a right to do as she did, whether we think she was justified or not.

Plaintiffs contend that the record supports an inference that testatrix failed to receive the cards and flowers sent to her, or in the alternative that she failed to know she received same, due to conduct of defendant Lipper. Here again, defendant Lipper had the opportunity to prevent testatrix from receiving cards or flowers from the Weslows, but we think there is no evidence of probative force to support the conclusion that he in fact did such. Moreover, the will itself reflected that *some* cards and flowers were in fact received by the testatrix, the dispute in this particular area, going to the number of times that such were sent, rather than to the fact that any were sent.

We conclude there is no evidence of probative force to support the verdict of the jury. The cause is reversed and rendered for defendants.

NOTES

1. Judges, Juries, and the Presumption of Undue Influence. The court in *Lipper* said that a confidential relationship and suspicious circumstances "simply sets the stage." The court required the contestants in addition to "prove in some fashion" the fact of undue influence. In most states, by contrast, a presumption of undue influence arises if, as in *Lipper*, there is a confidential relationship and suspicious circumstances. To overcome this presumption, the proponent must come forward with rebuttal evidence. Could a rational jury decide that Frank's evidence was not enough to rebut the presumption? Could a rational jury decide, as did the jury in this case, that the contestants proved "the vital facts of undue influence—the substitution of a plan of testamentary disposition by another as the will of the testatrix"? In most states, a contestant must prove undue influence by a preponderance of the evidence, but in a minority clear and convincing evidence is required.[37]

In a 1987 study of nine years of will contests in Davidson County (Nashville), Tennessee, Professor Jeffrey Schoenblum found that contestants won 38 percent of jury trials, but only 17 percent of bench trials.[38] In 1958, 15 years before being named Watergate special prosecutor, famed Texas lawyer Leon Jaworski expressed what is still the conventional wisdom on juries in will contests:

A fundamental truth to be borne in mind in writing a will is that the average jury, upon reviewing a will, is visited with a strong temptation to rewrite it in accordance with the jury's idea of what is fair and right rather than testing its validity according to the instructions of the court. The juror, although quite conscientious, has great difficulty refraining from substituting his own judgment for that of the testator and at times, especially in cases involving distributions considered prima facie unnatural, is inclined to show a marked sympathy for

Leon Jaworski

---

37. *See* Burkhalter v. Burkhalter, 841 N.W.2d 93, 101-02 (Iowa 2013) (collecting authorities).

38. *See* Jeffrey A. Schoenblum, Will Contests—An Empirical Study, 22 Real Prop. Prob. & Tr. J. 607 (1987).

the contestant. On the other hand, generally speaking, the tendency of the judge is to uphold the will, and the appellate courts will scrutinize the evidence closely to make certain that a finding of invalidity by the jury is warranted.[39]

2. Statement of Reasons. Mrs. Block's will included a statement (Article 9) setting forth her reasons for excluding Julian's children. Is this a sound practice? Or does it create litigable issues of fact? Is a recital in the will any less subject to influence than a disposition? Given the stilted legalese of "said" recital, who do you think probably wrote it? In a survey of reported undue influence cases, Professor Deborah Gordon found that "expressive, individualized language" stating reasons for what might appear to be an unnatural disposition is helpful in resisting a later claim of undue influence.[40]

When making a statement of reasons for disinheritance, the client should be cautioned against exposing the estate to a claim by a defamed survivor for testamentary libel.[41] A further problem, as Professor Judith McMullen observes, is that "some testators use explicit testamentary statements to vent their wrath at presumptive heirs. The statements may provoke disappointed heirs to challenge the will on principle."[42] Professor McMullen points to a few examples:

(a) Before anything else is done fifty cents be paid to my son-in-law to buy for himself a good stout rope with which to hang himself, and thus rid mankind of one of the most infamous scoundrels that ever roamed this broad land or dwelt outside of a penitentiary.

(b) Unto my two daughters, Frances Marie and Denise Victoria, by reason of their unfilial attitude toward a doting father, . . . I leave the sum of $1.00 to each and a father's curse. May their lives be fraught with misery, unhappiness, and poignant sorrow. May their deaths be soon and of a lingering malignant and torturous nature. May their souls rest in hell and suffer the torments of the condemned for eternity.[43]

Here is one more:

(c) To my wife I leave her lover, and the knowledge that I was not the fool she thought me; to my son I leave the pleasure of earning a living. For twenty years he thought the pleasure was mine.[44]

3. No-Contest Clauses. Article 8 of Mrs. Block's will in *Lipper* is an example of a *no-contest* or *in terrorem* clause. A no-contest clause deprives an unsuccessful contestant of her bequest under the challenged will. If enforceable and if accompanied by a substantial enough bequest, a no-content clause may deter a contest. A prospective

---

39. Leon Jaworski, The Will Contest, 10 Baylor L. Rev. 87, 88 (1958).

40. Deborah S. Gordon, Reflecting on the Language of Death, 34 Seattle U. L. Rev. 379, 418 (2011).

41. *See* Leona M. Hudak, The Sleeping Tort: Testamentary Libel, 27 Mercer L. Rev. 1147 (1976).

42. Judith G. McMullen, Keeping Peace in the Family While You Are Resting in Peace: Making Sense of and Preventing Will Contests, 8 Marq. Elder's Advisor 61, 85 (2006).

43. Id. at 85-86, drawing on Paul T. Whitcombe, Defamation by Will: Theories and Liabilities, 27 J. Marshall L. Rev. 749, 751-52 nn.13-14 (1994).

44. Hudak, *supra* note 41, at 1148.

contestant will be put to the choice of taking the smaller but certain provision in the will, or challenging the will for a chance at more if the will is set aside, but at the risk of taking nothing if the will is upheld.

Do you see the problem with the no-contest clause in Mrs. Block's will? Because she did not leave the plaintiffs anything, they had nothing to lose by bringing the contest.

In dealing with no-contest clauses, courts have been pulled in opposite directions by conflicting policies. Enforcement of such clauses could discourage unmeritorious litigation, family quarrels, and damage to the testator's reputation. But enforcement might also suppress objection to a flawed will. The most common rule, as under UPC §§ 2-517 and 3-905, is to enforce a no-contest clause only if the unsuccessful contestant lacked "probable cause" for bringing the contest. A handful of states do not enforce no-contest clauses at all. A little more than a dozen states enforce a no-contest clause even if there was probable cause for the contest or it was brought in good faith. Many states have extended their rules governing a no-contest clause in a will to apply also to such a clause in a trust.[45]

A lawyer with a client who wishes to contest a will (or a trust) that contains a no-contest clause is advised to investigate local law carefully. There are subtle differences from state to state not only on enforceability, but also on what steps may be taken prior to a formal contest without triggering the clause. Some states allow for limited discovery before commencing a formal contest.

Bequests to Lawyers and Fiduciary Appointments

Undue Influence. In *Lipper*, Mrs. Block's will named Frank, her son and lawyer, as a principal beneficiary. By statute or judicial decision, many states hold that a presumption of undue influence arises when a lawyer receives a bequest under a will that the lawyer drafted, unless the lawyer is closely related to the testator. In some states the presumption can be rebutted only by clear and convincing evidence, and in a few states the presumption is conclusive.[46]

The Los Angeles Times reported some years ago on a lawyer who opened an office adjacent to Leisure World, a retirement community, where he acquired 7,000 clients and prepared numerous wills and trusts leaving him millions of dollars. Responding to a public outcry, the legislature enacted a statute invalidating any donative transfer to a lawyer who drafts the dispositive instrument unless the lawyer is related by blood or marriage to the testator.[47] There is an exception permitting a gift to an unrelated lawyer who drafts the instrument if the client consults an independent lawyer who attaches a "Certificate of Independent Review." The reviewing lawyer must conclude that the gift is not a product of undue influence, duress, or fraud.[48]

---

45. *See* Deborah S. Gordon, Forfeiting Trust, 57 Wm. & Mary L. Rev. 455 (2015) (arguing that the policies relevant to no-contest clauses in wills are different from those relevant for trusts).

46. *See, e.g.,* Fla. Stat. Ann. § 732.806 (2016). In some states, a gift to a lawyer falls within the state's statute on a caregiver (see page 289).

47. *See* Cal. Prob. Code § 21380 (2016). The lawyer's story and resulting law reform is recounted in Paula A. Monopoli, American Probate: Protecting the Public, Improving the Process 39-56 (2003). The statute was since expanded to include a caregiver (see page 289).

48. Cal. Prob. Code § 21384 (2016).

"My goodness! Your dear old uncle seems to have left everything to <u>me</u>."
Peter Arno/The New Yorker Collection/The Cartoon Bank

Professional Responsibility. Should a lawyer who draws a will containing a bequest to the lawyer be subject to disciplinary action? John D. Randall, president of the American Bar Association from 1959 to 1960, was disbarred by the Iowa Supreme Court in 1979 for drafting a will that made him the beneficiary of a client's $4.5 million estate.[49]

Rule 1.8(c) of the Model Rules of Professional Conduct (2015) provides as follows:

> A lawyer shall not solicit any substantial gift from a client, including a testamentary gift, or prepare on behalf of a client an instrument giving the lawyer or a person related to the lawyer any substantial gift unless the lawyer or other recipient of the gift is related to the client. For purposes of this paragraph, related persons include a spouse, child, grandchild, parent, grandparent or other relative or individual with whom the lawyer or the client maintains a close, familial relationship.

The comment to Rule 1.8 further advises:

> If effectuation of a substantial gift requires preparing a legal instrument such as a will or conveyance the client should have the detached advice that another lawyer can provide. The sole exception to this Rule is where the client is a relative of the donee.

Even if the client is a relative of the lawyer, "the lawyer should exercise special care if the proposed gift to the lawyer or a related person is disproportionately large in relation to the gift the client proposes to make others who are equally related."[50] In Attorney Grievance Comm'n of Md. v. Brooke, 821 A.2d 414 (Md. 2003), although the court determined that there had been no undue influence, a lawyer was suspended from the practice of law for drafting a will for a longtime friend that gave the lawyer all of the friend's estate. The friend did not have the advice of independent counsel.

Fiduciary Appointments. May a lawyer draw a will or trust that names the lawyer as fiduciary? In *Lipper*, Mrs. Block's will named Frank as executor. A fiduciary appointment is not a gift, but the lawyer might be entitled to compensation for serving as fiduciary. The comment to Rule 1.8 addresses the issue:

> This Rule does not prohibit a lawyer from seeking to have the lawyer or a partner or associate of the lawyer named as executor of the client's estate or to another potentially lucrative fiduciary position. Nevertheless, such appointments will be subject to the general conflict of interest [rules] . . . when there is a significant risk that the lawyer's interest in obtaining the appointment will materially limit the

---

49. *See* Comm. on Prof'l Ethics v. Randall, 285 N.W.2d 161 (Iowa 1979).
50. ACTEC Commentaries on the Model Rules 128 (5th ed. 2016).

lawyer's independent professional judgment in advising the client concerning the choice of an executor or other fiduciary. In obtaining the client's informed consent to the conflict, the lawyer should advise the client concerning the nature and extent of the lawyer's financial interest in the appointment, as well as the availability of alternative candidates for the position.

The lawyer should explain "the role and duties of the fiduciary, the ability of a lay person to serve as fiduciary with legal and other professional assistance, and the comparative costs of appointing the lawyer or another person or institution as fiduciary."[51] In Lawyer Disciplinary Bd. v. Ball, 633 S.E.2d 241 (W. Va. 2006), the court disbarred a lawyer who, among other lapses, accepted $1.6 million in executor's commissions from the estates of two clients whose wills he drafted. The wills directed that he be paid an unusually large percentage of the estate as his executor's commission.

In In re Morrissey, 898 N.Y.S.2d 1 (App. Div. 2010), a prominent New York lawyer, Francis X. Morrissey, Jr., was disbarred after being convicted for participating in a scheme to defraud Brooke Astor, the doyenne of the New York social and philanthropic scene, and for forging a codicil to her will.

3. Planning for and Avoiding a Will Contest

a. Warning Signs

You should by now be able to recognize *warning signs* that a contest is more likely than usual. You should be concerned, for example, if an eccentric or older client's new testamentary scheme departs significantly from previous plans, if the testator has had multiple or blended families across multiple marriages, if the testator makes a substantial gift to a paramour, caretaker, or other non-family member who is not liked or trusted by the family, or if the testator criticizes a family member in the will or imposes the sort of conditions on a bequest that are likely to cause the beneficiary to bristle.

Perhaps the most common warning sign is an unnatural disposition, such as the unexpected omission of a close family member or an unexplainable distinction among family members of equal relation. This is particularly so if the testator disinherits, disfavors, or disparages a child. The child might view the will as a personal rejection by the parent,

"'And last but not least...'"

Whitney Darrow, Jr./The New Yorker Collection/The Cartoon Bank

---

51. Id. at 107.

prompting a contest to right the emotional injury. Professor McMullen relates an arresting example:

> In Nelson v. Daniels,[52] a disinherited son contested his mother's will alleging lack of testamentary capacity and undue influence. The will was executed sometime after the son and his mother had been embroiled in a legal dispute over some of the mother's property over which the son had had a power of appointment. The son allegedly transferred the property to himself. Despite the admitted conflict, the son apparently expected to inherit from his mother's estate, and he contested the will even though he had no material facts to support his claims. When asked if he knew of any other individual who could testify to his mother's lack of capacity, he responded: "Well, put it this way. You're not going to make me believe that my mother hated me the day she died." Thus, to the son, a portion of his mother's estate symbolized her love, and presumably her forgiveness for their past conflicts.[53]

b. Strategies

When warning signs are present, a prudent lawyer will consider whether additional precautionary measures should be undertaken to prevent a later contest or, failing that, to prevail in it.[54]

To begin with, the lawyer should take *extra precautions at the will execution*, such as using witnesses who will present well in court, perhaps friends of the testator or community leaders. The lawyer might also have more than the usual informal discussion with the client and the witnesses immediately before signing the will, such as asking the client to tell the witnesses about his dispositive plan and the reasoning behind it. Immediately after the will is executed, the lawyer might ask the witnesses to sign affidavits relating their impressions of the testator and what they saw, heard, and talked about at the time of the execution. Some lawyers also suggest making *multiple wills* across an extended period of time, each with the same disposition, so that a contestant would have to overcome each of those wills.

---

52. 1995 WL 535200 (Ohio App. 1995).

53. McMullen, *supra* note 42, at 81-82.

54. *See, e.g.*, Gerry W. Beyer, Will Contests — Prediction and Prevention, 4 Est. Plan. & Community Prop. L.J. 1 (2011); Elaine M. Bucher, Michael D. Simon & Alyse M. Reiser, The Best Defense Is a Good Offense, Tr. & Est., Mar. 2013, at 17. An unconventional and ultimately unsuccessful strategy to avoid a contest was employed by a Norwegian man who died in 2003:

> The man . . . left a will dividing his possessions among a long list of friends because he had no direct heirs. And, to be sure that no one challenged the document, he threatened to haunt any who tampered with the document.
>
> "I take a solemn and holy vow that, if at all possible, I will pursue you in the darkest hours of the night," he said in the will.
>
> His half sister, who wasn't one of the beneficiaries, took her chances and challenged the will in court. Apparently, the judge doesn't believe in ghosts, because he declared the will void since the two witnesses who signed it testified they didn't know what the document was. There have been no reports of mysterious late night occurrences from either the half sister or the judge.

You'll Be Sorry!, Wis. State J., Oct. 27, 2004, at C1.

Instead of a statement of reasons in the will, as in *Lipper*, the client might write, in the client's handwriting, a *letter to the lawyer* setting forth in detail the disposition the client wishes to make. Upon receiving the letter, the lawyer replies, detailing the consequences of the disposition for the client's family, and asks for a letter setting forth the reasons for the disposition. After receiving this letter, the will is drafted as the client wants. The letters are kept in the lawyer's files to show any prospective contestant or to enter into evidence at trial, if necessary.

Some lawyers recommend a *video recording* of a discussion between the testator and the lawyer during which the testator explains his dispositive plan. The discussion may include why the testator wants to disinherit an heir or otherwise deviate from the norm. But remember, any facts stated by the testator as justifying disinheritance may be contradicted by a contestant. In Patterson-Fowlkes v. Chancey, 732 S.E.2d 252 (Ga. 2012), the court held that certain "discrepancies" between the testator's videotaped statements and reality were insufficient to show that the testator lacked capacity. But the issue was litigated all the way to the state supreme court, delaying distribution and running up costs. Consider also that the elderly and infirm may look unwell in a video and many people do not perform as well as expected once a camera is pointed in their direction. An alternative is *dictation to a stenographer*.

A related idea, sometimes recommended when the testator wants to favor one child at the expense of another, is to hold a *family meeting* at which the testator explains his dispositive plan and rationale. Particularly if the favored child has special needs, such a meeting can go a long way in assuring that the psyche of the disfavored child is not bruised when the will is read.

A *professional examination* of the client's capacity immediately before executing a will or trust can make it much more difficult for a contestant to prove lack of capacity. If the client has no history of mental problems, it might be better to consult his family doctor, rather than a psychiatrist, so as not to raise suspicions of mental problems. But if the client already has a psychiatric history, then an expert might be warranted.

The lawyer might suggest a *no-contest clause*, though as in *Lipper*, the clause will have little potency unless the client is willing to make a significant bequest to the potential contestant (see page 302).

The lawyer might suggest that the client create and fund an *inter vivos trust* with an institutional trustee. Although trusts, too, can be contested (see page 465), as a practical matter it is harder to upset a trust if the settlor had a course of dealing with the trustee to evidence competence and the absence of influence. In most states, the existence of an inter vivos trust may be kept secret from an heir who is not a beneficiary of the trust (see page 682), as compared to a will, which is filed in the probate court for all to see. Still another potential advantage of an inter vivos trust is that it avoids a jury trial. The states are split on whether a will contest may be tried to a jury.[55] A trust dispute, by contrast, is tried before a judge in almost every state.

Outright *inter vivos gifts* can be attractive for similar reasons. Unlike a transfer at death, the donor is able to testify in defense of her sanity and the absence of undue

---

55. *See* Eunice L. Ross & Thomas J. Reed, Will Contests § 14:5 (2d ed. Supp. 2016). UPC § 1-306 (1990) provides for jury trial.

influence. Even if the donor's relations are aware that a gift has been made, they will often think twice or even three times before contesting an inter vivos gift for fear of angering the donor, who can write them out of her will.

It is sometimes suggested that the donor could *write a check* for, say, a thousand dollars or more as a gift to each potential contestant on the same day that the donor executes her will or trust. By cashing the check, the contestant invites a vigorous cross-examination in a subsequent contest on the question of why he accepted the gift if he thought that the donor lacked capacity or was being unduly influenced. The drawback to this strategy is that it might look like a lawyer's gimmick, and the contestant can argue that he did not know at the time of the donor's lack of capacity or the undue influence.

NOTES

1. Ante-Mortem or Living Probate. Statutes in eight states permit probate of a will during the testator's life, known as *ante-mortem* or *living probate*. The testator may institute an adversary proceeding to declare the validity of a will. The North Dakota statute expresses the concept crisply:

> Any person who executes a will disposing of the person's estate in accordance with this title may institute a proceeding . . . for a judgment declaring the validity of the will as to the signature on the will, the required number of witnesses to the signature and their signatures, and the testamentary capacity and freedom from undue influence of the person executing the will.[56]

Figure 4.1

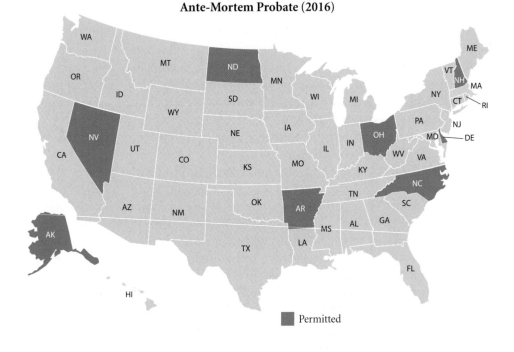

Ante-Mortem Probate (2016)

Permitted

---

56. N.D. Cent. Code § 30.1-08.1-01 (2016).

All beneficiaries named in the will and all of the testator's heirs apparent must be made parties to the action. When might this procedure be an attractive option? Do you see any difficulties with this procedure?

Ante-mortem probate was much debated as a solution to probate's worst evidence problem in the late 1970s and early 1980s, but then it faded from salience, and an effort to draft a uniform act on the subject was abandoned.[57] But lately the concept is again drawing attention, and in just the last few years several states—such as New Hampshire in 2014 and Delaware in 2015—have enacted statutes authorizing ante-mortem probate.[58] Anecdotal reports indicate an increase in ante-mortem probate proceedings by out-of-state testators looking to settle the matter by res judicata but who live in a state without an ante-mortem probate procedure.

George Washington's will included an arbitration clause.

2. Mediation and Arbitration. The nastiness and social costs of squabbles over estates has led some commentators to suggest mediation of contested probate matters or even mandatory arbitration clauses.[59] The argument is that alternative dispute resolution could reduce costs, avoid unwanted publicity, and perhaps salvage familial relations that might otherwise be torn asunder in a trial. Should mediation be required before trial, as in some divorce and other family law matters? If a will contest is anticipated, should the testator mandate mediation or arbitration? President George Washington concluded his 29-page will with an arbitration clause:

> My Will and direction expressly is, that all disputes (if unhappily any should arise) shall be decided by three impartial and intelligent men, known for their probity and good understanding; two to be chosen by the disputants—each having the choice of one—and the third by those two. Which three men thus chosen, shall, unfettered by Law, or legal constructions, declare their sense of the Testators intention; and such decision is, to all intents and purposes to be as binding on the Parties as if it had been given in the Supreme Court of the United States.

We take up arbitration provisions in trusts in Chapter 9 at page 622.

---

57. *See, e.g.,* John H. Langbein, Living Probate: The Conservatorship Model, 77 Mich. L. Rev. 63 (1978); Gregory S. Alexander & Albert M. Pearson, Alternative Models of Ante-Mortem Probate and Procedural Due Process Limitations on Succession, 78 Mich. L. Rev. 89 (1979).

58. *See* N.H. Rev. Stat. § 552:18 (2016); Del. Code tit. 12, § 1311 (2016).

59. *See, e.g.,* E. Gary Spitko, The Will as an Implied Unilateral Arbitration Contract, 68 Fla. L. Rev. 49 (2016); Victoria J. Haneman, The Inappropriate Imposition of Court-Ordered Mediation in Will Contests, 59 Clev. St. L. Rev. 513 (2011).

C. DURESS

When undue influence crosses the line into coercion, it becomes *duress*. "A donative transfer is procured by duress if the wrongdoer threatened to perform or did perform a wrongful act that coerced the donor into making a donative transfer that the donor would not otherwise have made."[60]

Latham v. Father Divine
85 N.E.2d 168 (N.Y. 1949)

DESMOND, J. The amended complaint herein has . . . been dismissed for insufficiency. Its principal allegations are these: plaintiffs are first cousins, but not distributes [heirs], of Mary Sheldon Lyon, who died in October, 1946, leaving a will, executed in 1943, which gave almost her whole estate to defendant Father Divine, leader of a religious cult, and to two corporate defendants in some way connected with that cult, and to an individual defendant (Patience Budd) said to be one of Father Divine's active followers; that said will has been, after a contest instituted by distributees, probated under a compromise agreement with the distributees, by the terms of which agreement, to which plaintiffs were not parties, the defendants just above referred to will receive a large sum from the estate; that after the making of said will, decedent on several occasions expressed "a desire and a determination to revoke the said will, and to execute a new will by which the plaintiffs would receive a substantial portion of the estate," "that shortly prior to the death of the deceased she had certain attorneys draft a new will in which the plaintiffs were named as legatees for a very substantial amount, totalling approximately $350,000"; that "by reason of the said false representations, the said undue influence and the said physical force" certain of the defendants "prevented the deceased from executing the said new Will"; that, shortly before decedent's death, decedent again expressed her determination to execute the proposed new will which favored plaintiffs, and that defendants "thereupon conspired to kill, and did kill, the deceased by means of a surgical operation performed by a doctor engaged by the defendants without the consent or knowledge of any of the relatives of the deceased."

Nothing is better settled than that, on such a motion as this, all the averments of the attacked pleading are taken as true. For present purposes, then, we have a case where one possessed of a large property and having already made a will leaving it to certain persons, expressed an intent to make a new testament to contain legacies to other persons, attempted to carry out that intention by having a new will drawn which contained a large legacy to those others, but was, by means of misrepresentations [fraud], undue influence, force [duress], and indeed, murder, prevented, by the beneficiaries named in the existing will, from signing the new one. Plaintiffs say that those facts, if proven, would entitle them to a judicial declaration, which their prayer for judgment demands, that defendants, taking under the already probated will, hold what they have

---

60. Restatement (Third) of Property: Wills and Other Donative Transfers § 8.3(c) (Am. Law Inst. 2003).

Father Divine

Father Divine, a charismatic religious leader during the Depression who proclaimed his own divinity, attracted thousands of believers, mostly African American, but some, like Mary Sheldon Lyon, were white. Whatever the merits of his claim, Father Divine was a master of theater. His inspirational sermons roused his followers to spirited expression. His exuberant and melodious services were standing room only. He preached racial equality and social action against segregation. He taught that there was only one race; people just had darker or lighter complexions.

The press of the time disparaged Father Divine as a con man of the cloth. But scholars searching for the roots of the African American churches' commitment to social action have come to reevaluate him. Many now view him as an influential and serious religious leader who gave his followers a feeling of goodness and worth, who crystallized the commitment of African American churches to the struggle for racial justice, and who stuck his thumb in the eye of the white establishment. He was chauffeured in a Rolls-Royce and a Duesenberg; inhabited the fanciest houses; hosted sumptuous feasts; and claimed for African Americans every perquisite of rich whites.*

The turn in Father Divine's fortunes, which transformed him from a minor religious figure into an adored incarnation of God, came as a result of a brush with the law in 1932. Father Divine had bought a large house in Sayville on the south shore of Long Island. On Sundays, flocks of the faithful from Harlem gathered there for joyous prayer sessions. The white neighbors objected. Father Divine was arrested for disturbing the peace and conducting a public nuisance. His arrest was picked up by the national press. Father Divine was pictured as a martyr to racial prejudice.

At trial, the jury found Father Divine guilty as charged. Some of Father Divine's partisans warned

Father Divine, calling the faithful to dinner
Bettmann/Getty Images

the judge that if he sent Father Divine to jail something terrible would happen to him. The judge, unheeding, gave Father Divine the maximum sentence of one year in jail. Three days later, the judge keeled over and died. "When the warden and the guards found out about it in the middle of the night," writes Professor Henry Louis Gates, Jr., "they raced to Father Divine's cell and woke him up. Father Divine, they said, your judge just dropped dead of a heart attack. Without missing a beat, Father Divine lifted his head and told them: 'I hated to do it.'"†

Although the story has been questioned, its repetition established Father Divine—among the believers—as an authentic voice of God. Father Divine left New York in the 1950s and retired to a 72-acre estate outside Philadelphia. His apparent powers of retribution faded. Judge Desmond, who wrote the opinion in *Latham*, died in 1987 at the age of 91.

* *See* Jill M. Watts, God, Harlem U.S.A.: The Father Divine Story (1992); Robert Weisbrot, Father Divine and the Struggle for Racial Equality (1983).

† Whose Canon Is It Anyway?, N.Y. Times, Feb. 20, 1989, § 7 (Book Review), at 1.

so taken as constructive trustees for plaintiffs, whom decedent wished to, tried to, and was kept from, benefiting.

We find in New York no decision directly answering the question as to whether or not the allegations above summarized state a case for relief in equity. But reliable texts, and cases elsewhere, see 98 A.L.R. 477 et seq., answer it in the affirmative. Leading writers, 3 Scott on Trusts, pp. 2371-2376; 3 Bogert on Trusts and Trustees, part 1, §§ 473-474, 498, 499; 1 Perry on Trusts and Trustees [7th ed.], pp. 265, 371, in one form or another, state the law of the subject to be about as it is expressed in comment i under § 184 of the Restatement of the Law of Restitution:

> *Preventing revocation of will and making new will.* Where a devisee or legatee under a will already executed prevents the testator by fraud, duress or undue influence from revoking the will and executing a new will in favor of another or from making a codicil, so that the testator dies leaving the original will in force, the devisee or legatee holds the property thus acquired upon a constructive trust for the intended devisee or legatee. . . .

While there is no New York case decreeing a constructive trust on the exact facts alleged here, there are several decisions in this court which, we think, suggest such a result and none which forbids it. Matter of O'Hara's Will, 95 N.Y. 403 (1884); Trustees of Amherst College v. Ritch, 45 N.E. 876 (N.Y. 1897); Edson v. Bartow, 48 N.E. 541 (N.Y. 1897), and Ahrens v. Jones, 62 N.E. 666 (N.Y. 1902), which need not be closely analyzed here as to their facts, all announce, in one form or another, the rule that, where a legatee has taken property under a will, after agreeing outside the will, to devote that property to a purpose intended and declared by the testator, equity will enforce a constructive trust to effectuate that purpose, lest there be a fraud on the testator.[61] . . . In each of those four cases first above cited in this paragraph, the particular fraud consisted of the legatee's failure or refusal to carry out the testator's designs, after tacitly or expressly promising so to do. But we do not think that a breach of such an engagement is the only kind of fraud which will impel equity to action. A constructive trust will be erected whenever necessary to satisfy the demands of justice. Since a constructive trust is merely "the formula through which the conscience of equity finds expression," Beatty v. Guggenheim Exploration Co., 122 N.E. 378, 380 (N.Y. 1919), its applicability is limited only by the inventiveness of men who find new ways to enrich themselves unjustly by grasping what should not belong to them. Nothing short of true and complete justice satisfies equity, and always assuming these allegations to be true, there seems no way of achieving total justice except by the procedure used here. . . .

This is not a proceeding to probate or establish the will which plaintiffs say testatrix was prevented from signing. . . . The will Mary Sheldon Lyon did sign has been probated and plaintiffs are not contesting, but proceeding on, that probate, trying to reach property which has effectively passed thereunder. . . .

This suit cannot be defeated by any argument that to give plaintiffs judgment would be to annul those provisions of the Statute of Wills requiring due execution by the testator. Such a contention, if valid, would have required the dismissal in a number of the suits herein cited. The answer is in Ahrens v. Jones, 62 N.E. at 668:

> The trust does not act directly upon the will by modifying the gift, for the law requires wills to be wholly in writing; but it acts upon the gift itself as it reaches the possession of the legatee, or as soon as he is entitled to receive it. The theory is that the will has full effect by passing an absolute legacy to the legatee, and that then equity, in order to defeat fraud, raises a trust in favor of those intended to be

---

61. These facts involve what is known as a "secret trust," a topic we take up in Chapter 6 at page 433. — Eds.

benefited by the testator, and compels the legatee, as a trustee ex maleficio, to turn over the gift to them.

The judgment of the Appellate Division, insofar as it dismissed the complaint herein, should be reversed, and the order of Special Term affirmed, with costs in this court and in the Appellate Division.

NOTE

A Dissenting Opinion. Another view of the litigation over Mary Sheldon Lyon's will is presented by Sara Harris, a biographer of Father Divine. Harris says that Mary Sheldon Lyon was a devotee of Father Divine from 1938 to 1946 and took the spiritual name of Peace Dove. "She was sweet goodness personified. That was why, when she attended banquets, she was always granted a holy seat at God's own table. That was why true followers made a fuss over her." Harris reports that, after Father Divine lost in the court of appeals and after subsequent lower court rulings adverse to him, a settlement was reached giving Father Divine a small fraction of the amount bequeathed him. Harris suggests that the court rulings were motivated, at least in part, by racial prejudice against Father Divine and a belief that his church (called a "cult" by the court) was not quite a legitimate religious group.[62]

Interference with Inheritance, Restitution and Unjust Enrichment, and Constructive Trust

A will contest is the traditional mode of remedying wrongful procurement of a will. But what if, as in *Latham*, a person wrongfully *prevents* the decedent from making a will or wrongfully interferes with a *nonprobate transfer*? Because a will can be probated only if it was executed in accordance with the Wills Act, and because a nonprobate transfer operates outside of the reach of probate, in such circumstances a will contest offers no relief. As in *Latham*, a disappointed expectant beneficiary must instead pursue the equitable remedy of *constructive trust* in an action in *restitution* to prevent *unjust enrichment*.

We have already seen the role of such actions in slayer cases (see page 131) and in the recovery of a wrongfully procured lifetime transfer (see page 287). Restitution by way of constructive trust also plays an important role as a complement to the will contest. The Restatement (Third) of Restitution and Unjust Enrichment explains:

> A claim in restitution with a remedy via constructive trust is the traditional response to wrongful interference that prevents a donative transfer, given the inability of probate to enforce an intended disposition that was never carried out. Wrongful interference may prevent either the making or the revocation of a will, codicil, or bequest; the alteration of prior dispositions, such as a substitution of insurance or trust beneficiaries; or the making of an intended inter vivos gift.[63]

---

62. Sara Harris, Father Divine 278-81 (1953).
63. Restatement (Third) of Restitution and Unjust Enrichment § 46 cmt. e (Am. Law Inst. 2011) (emphasis removed).

In In re Silva's Estate, 145 P. 1015 (Cal. 1915), *W* tricked *H*, who wanted to revoke his will, into thinking that she had destroyed it for him. After *H*'s death, *W* offered the will for probate, as she would take more under the will than in intestacy. *H*'s other heirs contested the will on the grounds of *W*'s fraud. The court upheld the probate of the will, because (owing to *W*'s fraud) it had not in fact been revoked in accordance with the Wills Act. But the court suggested an alternative cause of action: "If relief can be given at all for such a wrong, it must be sought by suit in equity to declare the wrong-doer a trustee for the heirs with respect to the property received by such wrongdoer in virtue of the will." The heirs then brought such an action against *W*. In Brazil v. Silva, 185 P. 174 (Cal. 1919), the court held that the heirs had stated a valid cause of action in restitution for constructive trust.

In Pope v. Garrett, 211 S.W.2d 559 (Tex. 1948), some but not all of the decedent's expectant heirs, "by physical force or by creating a disturbance," prevented the decedent from executing a will in favor of her friend. The decedent lapsed into a coma and died shortly thereafter. The court imposed a constructive trust in favor of the friend on all the heirs, not just those who had wrongfully prevented execution of the new will. The court reasoned that the innocent heirs, too, would be unjustly enriched if they were permitted to keep property acquired by reason of the wrongful acts of the other heirs. The Restatement explains: "Because liability in unjust enrichment does not depend on fault, the claim of an intended donee . . . may be asserted against a person who was guilty of no misconduct in obtaining the property in question."[64]

Relief in restitution is also available to rectify wrongdoing in connection with probate administration. In Caldwell v. Taylor, 23 P.2d 758 (Cal. 1933), a son petitioned for a constructive trust to be imposed upon property that his father bequeathed to the father's purported wife. The son alleged that the purported wife had procured the will by deceiving the father into believing that "she was a woman of fine character and good reputation and prior to her marriage to him was a single woman." During the six-month limitations period for contesting the will, she deceived the son "with the intent and purpose" of inducing him not to bring a contest. The son later discovered that the purported wife, a "grossly immoral woman of the streets," was in fact married to someone else at the time she purported to marry the father. The court held that the son had stated a valid claim in restitution owing to the wife's "extrinsic fraud," meaning fraud separate from the underlying ("intrinsic") fraud worked upon the father, in the misrepresentations that induced the son not to contest the will. The availability of relief in restitution to prevent unjust enrichment from fraud in the probate process, as in *Caldwell*, is codified by UPC § 1-106 (1990).

D. FRAUD

The test for *fraud* is easy to state: "A donative transfer is procured by fraud if the wrong-doer knowingly or recklessly made a false representation to the donor about a material fact that was intended to and did lead the donor to make a donative transfer that the

---

64. *See* id. cmt. h.

donor would not otherwise have made."[65] In practice, however, fraud can be difficult to detect and prove. Claims of fraud usually involve fraud in the *execution* or fraud in the *inducement*.

(1) Fraud in the Execution.   Fraud in the execution occurs when a person intentionally misrepresents the character or contents of the instrument signed by the testator, which does not in fact carry out the testator's intent. For example, if *T* asks her heir apparent to bring *T* the document prepared for *T* as a will so that *T* can sign it, and the heir apparent knowingly brings *T* a document other than the intended will, and then *T* signs it, believing it to be her will, this would be fraud in the execution. Although the unexecuted will in this example cannot be admitted to probate, in a *restitution* action *T*'s freedom of disposition can be honored, and *unjust enrichment* prevented, by imposing a *constructive trust* on the heir apparent (and any other heirs) in favor of *T*'s intended beneficiaries.

(2) Fraud in the Inducement.   Fraud in the inducement occurs when a misrepresentation causes the testator to execute or revoke a will, to refrain from executing or revoking a will, or to include particular provisions in the wrongdoer's favor.

A claim of fraud in the inducement is different from a claim of undue influence. In a case of fraud, the testator retains her free agency, and freely makes a new estate plan, but does so as a result of having been misled. In a case of undue influence, the testator makes a new estate plan because of influence that overcomes the testator's free will. In practice fraud and undue influence are often alleged together.

The potential for overlap between fraud and undue influence is well illustrated by McDaniel v. McDaniel, 707 S.E.2d 60 (Ga. 2011). In that case, a dispute between the two sons of the testator, the court upheld the denial of probate to the testator's will on the grounds of the propounding son's undue influence and fraud:

> (a) *Undue Influence*: . . . [T]he jury in this case was clearly authorized to find that the 2007 will was the result of undue influence. When the testator could no longer care for his sick wife of over 60 years, the caveator [one of their sons] moved in with them and provided the care his mother and father needed with little help from the propounder [the other son]. After [the testator's wife, the parties' mother] died, the propounder and his wife encouraged the caveator and his wife to [go to Florida] for a vacation and in their absence poisoned the testator's mind against the caveator, telling him falsely that the caveator had stolen all his money, that he was now broke, and that the caveator had abandoned him and would not return. . . .
>
> [A]cting under the influence of the propounder and his wife, the testator secured a restraining order that prevented the caveator from seeing him for six months after the caveator returned from Florida, and the propounder made sure that the caveator was never left alone with their father again. Although the jury found that the testator had sufficient testamentary capacity, he was elderly and showing signs of declining mental acuity before the 2007 will was executed, and his symptoms had increased after his wife passed just a few weeks earlier. . . .

---

65. Restatement (Third) of Property: Wills and Other Donative Transfers § 8.3(d) cmt. j (2003).

Wiley Miller/Non Sequitur/Wiley Ink, Inc./Andrews McMeel Syndication

[T]he 2007 will radically changed the distribution of the estate envisioned by the testator's 2002 will, which would have divided the estate equally between the testator's two grown sons, to a scheme awarding 89% of the estate to the propounder and nothing to the caveator. . . . We therefore conclude that evidence . . . authorized the jury's finding that the 2007 will was the product of undue influence. . . .

(b) *Fraud*: There was also sufficient evidence to support the jury's finding that the will was procured by fraud. The evidence showed that after the propounder and his wife encouraged the caveator and his wife to go on vacation in Florida, they embarked on a campaign to convince the testator that the caveator had stolen all his money, left him broke, and abandoned him by moving to Florida. These were misrepresentations, but they worked; the testator changed his will to disinherit the caveator completely. As a result of these misrepresentations, the [testator] went into the meeting with the attorney who drafted the 2007 will intending to leave his entire estate to the propounder, and he would have done so were it not for the attorney's suggestion that he leave something to the caveator's children, who were the testator's grandchildren. Accordingly, we conclude that the evidence supports the jury's finding that the 2007 will was procured through "misrepresentation" and "fraudulent practices upon the testator's fears, affections, or sympathies."

NOTE

Proving Causation.   A donative transfer is invalid for fraud only if the donor would not have made the transfer if the donor had known the true facts. But how can we know what the donor would have done if not misled? In re Carson's Estate, 194 P. 5 (Cal. 1920), is a dramatic illustration of the problem. In that case, J. Gamble Carson went through a marriage ceremony with Alpha O. Carson, who quite reasonably assumed that they were married. After living together happily for a year, Alpha died, devising most of her estate to "my husband J. Gamble Carson." It then came to light that Alpha had been "seduced by a marital adventurer into a marriage with him which was no marriage in the eyes of the law because of the fact, which he concealed from her, that he had already had at least one, if not more, spouses, legal and illegal, who were still living and undivorced." Was the devise the fruit of the fraud?

> Now a case can be imagined where, nothing more appearing, as in this case, than that the testatrix had been deceived into a void marriage and had never been undeceived, it might fairly be said that a conclusion that such deceit had affected a bequest to the supposed husband would not be warranted. If, for example, the parties had lived happily together for 20 years, it would be difficult to say that the wife's bequest to her supposed husband was founded on her supposed legal relation with him, and not primarily on their long and intimate association. It might well be that if undeceived at the end of that time her feeling would be, not one of resentment at the fraud upon her, but of thankfulness that she had been deceived into so many years of happiness. But, on the other hand, a case can easily be imagined where the reverse would be true. If in this case the will had been made immediately after marriage, and the testatrix had then died within a few days, the conclusion would be well-nigh irresistible, in the absence of some peculiar circumstance, that the will was founded on the supposed legal relation into which the testatrix had been deceived into believing she was entering. Between these two extreme cases come those wherein it cannot be said that either one conclusion or the other is wholly unreasonable, and in those cases the determination of the fact is for the jury. Of that sort is the present.

The 20-year happy marriage case posited in *Carson* came to pass in In re Estate of Richmond, 701 N.W.2d 897 (N.D. 2005), albeit the evidence showed only mistake and not fraud. In 1982, Donald and Lois thought that they had married. Unknown to both of them, Donald was still married to his first wife. In 2003, after 21 years of supposed marriage, Lois died, leaving a will devising the home in which they had lived "to my husband Donald." Lois's daughter from her first marriage challenged the will for fraud in the inducement. Citing *Carson,* the court rejected the daughter's claim for want of evidence "that Donald engaged in fraudulent conduct or that Lois would not have devised to Donald the home the couple shared together for more than 20 years" if she had known their marriage was invalid.

E. TORTIOUS INTERFERENCE WITH AN EXPECTANCY

Restatement (Second) of Torts § 774B (Am. Law Inst. 1979) recognizes intentional interference with an expected inheritance or gift as a valid cause of action. This theory extends to expected inheritances the protection some courts have accorded commercial expectancies, such as the prospect of obtaining employment or customers. Under this theory, the plaintiff must prove that the interference involved tortious conduct, which under the cases includes undue influence, duress, or fraud. The tort cannot be invoked if the challenge is based on the testator's mental incapacity. Although there was little support for § 774B in the cases at the time of its promulgation, in the years since courts in almost half the states have recognized this new tort.

Schilling v. Herrera
952 So. 2d 1231 (Fla. App. 2007)

ROTHENBERG, J. . . . Mr. [Edward] Schilling, the decedent's brother, sued Ms. [Maria] Herrera, the decedent's caretaker, for intentional interference with an expectancy of inheritance. . . . The amended complaint alleges that in December 1996, Mignonne Helen Schilling (the decedent) executed her Last Will and Testament, naming her brother and only heir-at-law, Mr. Schilling, as her personal representative and sole beneficiary, and in May 1997, she executed a Durable Power of Attorney, naming Mr. Schilling as her attorney-in-fact.

In December 1999, the decedent was diagnosed with renal disease, resulting in several hospitalizations. During this period, Mr. Schilling, who resides in New Jersey, traveled to Florida to assist the decedent. In January 2000, the decedent executed a Power of Attorney for Health Care, naming Mr. Schilling as her attorney-in-fact for health care decisions.

On January 12, 2001, when the decedent was once again hospitalized, Mr. Schilling traveled to Florida to make arrangements for the decedent's care. After being released from the hospital, the decedent was admitted to a rehabilitation hospital, then to a health care center, and then to the Clairidge House for rehabilitation. While at the Clairidge House, Ms. Herrera became involved in the decedent's care, and when the decedent was discharged from the Clairidge House on December 16, 2001, Ms. Herrera notified Mr. Schilling.

After being discharged from the Clairidge House, the decedent returned to her apartment, and Ms. Herrera began to care for her on an "occasional, as needed basis." In 2003, when the decedent's condition worsened and she was in need of additional care, Ms. Herrera converted her garage into a bedroom, and the decedent moved in. The decedent paid Ms. Herrera rent and for her services as caregiver.

When Mr. Schilling spoke to Ms. Herrera over the phone, Ms. Herrera complained that she was not getting paid enough to take care of the decedent, and on April 10, 2003, Mr. Schilling sent Ms. Herrera money. While living in the converted garage, the decedent became completely dependent on Ms. Herrera. In September 2003, without Mr. Schilling's knowledge, Ms. Herrera convinced the decedent to prepare and execute a new Power of Attorney, naming Ms. Herrera as attorney-in-fact, and to execute a new Last Will and Testament naming Ms. Herrera as personal representative and sole beneficiary of the decedent's estate.

Mr. Schilling visited the decedent in March of 2004. On August 6, 2004, the decedent died at Ms. Herrera's home.

On August 24, 2004, Ms. Herrera filed her Petition for Administration. On December 2, 2004, following the expiration of the creditor's period, Ms. Herrera petitioned for discharge of probate. On December 6, 2004, *after the expiration of the creditor's period and after Ms. Herrera had petitioned the probate court for discharge of probate, Ms. Herrera notified Mr. Schilling for the first time that the decedent, his sister, had passed away on August 6, 2004.* Shortly thereafter, in late December 2004, the Final Order of Discharge was entered by the probate court. Mr. Schilling alleges that prior to being notified of his sister's death on December 6, 2004, he attempted to contact the decedent through Ms. Herrera, but Ms. Herrera did not return his calls until the conclusion of probate proceedings and did not inform him of his sister's death, thereby depriving him of both the knowledge of the decedent's death and the opportunity of contesting the probate proceedings. Mr. Schilling further alleges that prior to the decedent's death, Ms. Herrera regularly did not immediately return his phone calls, and that Ms. Herrera's "intentional silence was part of a calculated scheme to prevent [Mr.] Schilling from contesting the Estate of Decedent, and was intended to induce [Mr.] Schilling to refrain from acting in his interests to contest the probate proceedings in a timely fashion, as [Mr.] Schilling was used to long delays in contact with [Ms.] Herrera, and did not suspect that the delay was intended to fraudulently induce [Mr.] Schilling to refrain from acting on his own behalf." Finally, Mr. Schilling alleges that he expected to inherit the decedent's estate because he was the decedent's only heir-at-law and because he was named as the sole beneficiary in the 1996 will; Ms. Herrera's fraudulent actions prevented him from receiving the decedent's estate, which he was entitled to; and but for Ms. Herrera's action of procuring the will naming her as sole beneficiary, he would have received the benefit of the estate.

After Mr. Schilling filed his amended complaint, Ms. Herrera filed a . . . motion to dismiss, arguing [that Mr. Schilling failed to state a cause of action and that he was barred from bringing his claim because he failed to exhaust his probate remedies]. The trial court granted the motion to dismiss with prejudice, finding that Ms. Herrera had no duty to notify Mr. Schilling of the decedent's death as Mr. Schilling did not hire Ms. Herrera to care for the decedent, and therefore, there was "no special relationship giving rise to a proactive responsibility to provide information." The trial court also found that Mr. Schilling was barred from filing a claim for intentional interference with an expectancy of inheritance because he failed to exhaust his probate remedies. . . .

To state a cause of action for intentional interference with an expectancy of inheritance, the complaint must allege the following elements: (1) the existence of an expectancy; (2) intentional interference with the expectancy through tortious conduct; (3) causation; and (4) damages. Claveloux v. Bacotti, 778 So. 2d 399, 400 (Fla. App. 2001), citing Whalen v. Prosser, 719 So. 2d 2, 5 (Fla. App. 1998). The court in *Whalen* clearly explained that the purpose behind this tort is to protect the testator, not the beneficiary:

> Interference with an expectancy is an unusual tort because the beneficiary is authorized to sue to recover damages primarily to protect the testator's interest rather than the disappointed beneficiary's expectations. The fraud, duress, undue influence, or other independent tortious conduct required for this tort is directed at the testator. The beneficiary is not directly defrauded or unduly influenced; the testator is. Thus, the common law court has created this cause of action not primarily to protect the beneficiary's inchoate rights, but to protect the deceased testator's former right to dispose of property freely and without improper interference. In a sense, the beneficiary's action is derivative of the testator's rights. *Whalen*, 719 So. 2d at 6.

In the instant case, the trial court's ruling was based on the fact that the amended complaint fails to allege that Ms. Herrera breached a legal duty owed to Mr. Schilling. However, as the *Claveloux* court noted, there are four elements for a cause of action for intentional interference with an expectancy of inheritance, and breach of a legal duty is not one of the elements. This is consistent with the *Whalen* court's explanation that the "fraud, duress, undue influence, or other independent tortious conduct required for this tort *is directed at the testator. The beneficiary is not directly defrauded or unduly influenced; the testator is.*" Id. (emphasis added). We, therefore, review the amended complaint to determine if it sufficiently pleads a cause of action for intentional interference with an expectancy of inheritance.

In essence, the amended complaint alleges that Mr. Schilling was named as the sole beneficiary in the decedent's last will and testament; that based on this last will and testament, he expected to inherit the decedent's estate upon her death; that Ms. Herrera intentionally interfered with his expectancy of inheritance by "convincing" the decedent, while she was ill and completely dependent on Ms. Herrera, to execute a new last will and testament naming Ms. Herrera as the sole beneficiary; and that Ms. Herrera's "fraudulent actions" and "undue influence" prevented Mr. Schilling from inheriting the decedent's estate. Based on these well-pled allegations, we conclude that the amended complaint states a cause of action for intentional interference with an expectancy of inheritance. Therefore, the trial court erred, as a matter of law, in dismissing the amended complaint on that basis.

Mr. Schilling also contends that the trial court erred in finding that he was barred from filing a claim for intentional interference with an expectancy of inheritance as he failed to exhaust his probate remedies. We agree.

In finding that Mr. Schilling was barred from filing his action for intentional interference with an expectancy of inheritance, the trial court relied on DeWitt v. Duce, 408 So. 2d 216 (Fla. 1981). In *DeWitt*, the testator's will was admitted to probate after his death. Thereafter, the plaintiffs filed a petition for revocation of probate of the testator's will, but voluntarily dismissed the petition, choosing to take under the will instead of challenging the will in probate court. More than two years later, the plaintiffs filed their claim for intentional interference with an inheritance, arguing that the defendants exercised undue influence over the testator at a time when he lacked testamentary capacity, causing the testator to execute the probated will, which was less favorable to the plaintiffs and more favorable to the defendants than the testator's previous will. . . .

In answering the . . . question [whether availability of probate remedies forecloses a suit for tortious interference], the Florida Supreme Court stated that "[t]he rule is that if adequate relief is available in a probate proceeding, then that remedy must be exhausted before a tortious interference claim may be pursued." Id. at 218. The Court, however, stated that an exception to this general rule is that "[i]f the defendant's fraud is not discovered until after probate, plaintiff is allowed to bring a later action for damages since relief in probate was impossible." Id. at 219. The Court also noted that "[c]ases which allow the action for tortious interference with a testamentary expectancy are predicated on the inadequacy of probate remedies." Id. In conclusion, the Florida Supreme Court held:

> In sum, we find that [plaintiffs] had an adequate remedy in probate *with a fair opportunity to pursue it.* Because they lacked assiduity in failing to avail themselves

of this remedy, we interpret Fla. Stat. Ann. § 733.103(2) as barring [plaintiffs] from a subsequent action in tort for wrongful interference with a testamentary expectancy, and accordingly answer the certified question in the affirmative. Id. at 221.

Therefore, the Court's holding that the plaintiffs were barred from pursuing their claim for intentional interference with an expectancy of inheritance, was based on the fact that the plaintiffs had an adequate remedy in probate; the plaintiffs had a fair opportunity to pursue their remedy; and the plaintiffs' failure to pursue their remedy was due to their lack of diligence.

We find that *DeWitt* is factually distinguishable, and therefore inapplicable. A review of the amended complaint reflects that Mr. Schilling has alleged two separate frauds. The first alleged fraud stems from Ms. Herrera's undue influence over the deceased in procuring the will, whereas the second alleged fraud stems from Ms. Herrera's actions in preventing Mr. Schilling from contesting the will in probate court. We acknowledge that pursuant to *DeWitt,* if only the first type of fraud was involved, Mr. Schilling's collateral attack of the will would be barred. However, language contained in *DeWitt* clearly indicates that a subsequent action for intentional interference with an expectancy of inheritance may be permitted where "the circumstances surrounding the tortious conduct effectively preclude adequate relief in the probate court." Id. at 219. . . .

In the instant case, we must accept the facts alleged by Mr. Schilling as true. He alleges in the amended complaint that when the decedent began to live in Ms. Herrera's home, pursuant to powers of attorney executed by the decedent, Mr. Schilling was the decedent's attorney-in-fact; throughout the decedent's numerous illnesses, Mr. Schilling made decisions regarding the decedent's care; Mr. Schilling traveled to Miami on numerous occasions to visit the decedent, whose condition progressively worsened; Mr. Schilling stayed in contact with Ms. Herrera while the decedent was living in her home; Mr. Schilling relied on Ms. Herrera to obtain information regarding the decedent; Mr. Schilling sent money to Ms. Herrera to pay for the decedent's care; after the decedent passed away, Mr. Schilling called Ms. Herrera numerous times, but she would not return his calls; and Ms. Herrera did not inform Mr. Schilling of his sister's death until after she petitioned for discharge of probate. As the facts in the amended complaint sufficiently allege that Mr. Schilling was prevented from contesting the will in the probate court due to Ms. Herrera's fraudulent conduct, we find that the trial court erred in finding that Mr. Schilling's claim for intentional interference with an expectancy of inheritance was barred.

Accordingly, we reverse the order dismissing Mr. Schilling's amended complaint, and remand for further proceedings.

NOTES

1. Tort Law as an Alternative to Inheritance Law. Since the promulgation of Restatement (Second) of Torts § 774B (Am. Law Inst. 1979), courts in roughly half the states have recognized the interference-with-inheritance tort, though several courts of last resort have rejected it,[66] and in some states the cases of the intermediate appellate courts are contradictory.[67]

An interference-with-inheritance tort claim is not a will contest. It does not challenge the probate of a will, but rather seeks to recover damages from the defendant for wrongful interference with the plaintiff's expectation of an inheritance. For a variety of strategic reasons, a disappointed expectant beneficiary might prefer to litigate in tort. For example, in In re Estate of Ellis, 923 N.E.2d 237 (Ill. 2009), the court held that the tort claim is not subject to the short statute of limitations on a will contest, but rather to the longer tort limitations period, which may not start until the plaintiff reasonably could have become aware of the claim. Punitive damages may be recovered in an interference-with-inheritance tort action, as in Huffey v. Lea, 491 N.W.2d 518 (Iowa 1992), but almost never in a will contest or restitution action (see page 295). Rules barring testimony by an interested witness in probate may not apply in a tort suit, as in In re Estate of Hatten, 880 So. 2d 1271 (Fla. App. 2004). In a few states, a plaintiff can bring an interference-with-inheritance action prior to the donor's death, as under Harmon v. Harmon, 404 A.2d 1020 (Me. 1979), even though the donor could thereafter change her will yet again.

As in *Schilling*, most courts that have recognized the interference-with-inheritance tort require the plaintiff to pursue probate remedies if they are available. A failure to do so usually results in barring a later suit in tort, as in Wilson v. Fritschy, 55 P.3d 997 (N.M. App. 2002). In some states, however, courts allow a tort suit even if relief is available in probate. In Theriault v. Burnham, 2 A.3d 324 (Me. 2010), the court held that the preponderance of the evidence standard applied in an interference-with-inheritance tort suit even though the plaintiff would have been required to adduce clear and convincing evidence on the same issue if he had litigated in probate. In an earlier decision, Plimpton v. Gerrard, 668 A.2d 882 (Me. 1995), the same court had acknowledged that a disappointed expectant beneficiary could avoid the rule requiring a bench trial in probate by suing in tort instead.

2. Scholarly Debate.   Most commentators have applauded the rise of the interference-with-inheritance tort, arguing that the tort is needed to fill a gap in which relief in probate is unavailable or insufficient.[68] Bucking the consensus, Professors John Goldberg and Robert Sitkoff are sharply critical of the tort.[69] They contend that recognizing the tort creates a pernicious rivalry with inheritance law, one that reflects a forgetting of restitution, and that the tort is incompatible with fundamental principles of the common law of torts:

---

66. *See* Manon v. Orr, 856 N.W.2d 106 (Neb. 2014); Stewart v. Sewell, 215 S.W.3d 815 (Tenn. 2007); Economopoulos v. Kolaitis, 528 S.E.2d 714 (Va. 2000); Vogt v. Witmeyer, 665 N.E.2d 189 (N.Y. 1996).

67. *See, e.g.,* Anderson v. Archer, 490 S.W.3d 175, 176 (Tex. App. 2016) (declining to recognize the tort in conflict with other Texas appellate courts that have recognized it).

68. *See, e.g.,* Diane J. Klein, "Go West, Disappointed Heir": Tortious Interference with Expectation of Inheritance—A Survey with Analysis of State Approaches in the Pacific States, 13 Lewis & Clark L. Rev. 209 (2009); Irene D. Johnson, Tortious Interference with Expectancy of Inheritance or Gift—Suggestions for Resort to the Tort, 39 U. Tol. L. Rev. 769 (2008).

69. *See* John C.P. Goldberg & Robert H. Sitkoff, Torts and Estates: Remedying Wrongful Interference with Inheritance, 65 Stan. L. Rev. 335 (2013).

E. Tortious Interference with an Expectancy

When a claim for wrongful interference with the donor's freedom of disposition is pursued in a will contest or an action in restitution, it is governed by specialized rules and procedures that reflect principled (if contestable) policy judgments about how best to address the "worst evidence" problem inherent in finding the true intent of a deceased person. By resolving inheritance disputes on different procedural and remedial terms, the tort allows a disappointed beneficiary to circumvent those rules and procedures. . . .

The emergence of a rival tort regime for resolving inheritance disputes is troubling because it has not been accompanied by any serious consideration of whether adjudication in tort is preferable on grounds of policy. Quite the opposite, courts have recognized the tort primarily out of ignorance and confusion. . . .

[T]he plaintiff [in *Schilling*] could have brought an action in restitution for constructive trust. Although the opinion does not hint at this possibility—it reads as if the tort were the plaintiff's only hope—relief in restitution for extrinsic fraud in a probate matter is well established. A comparison of *Schilling* with *Caldwell v. Taylor*, [page 314,] is instructive. . . .

The transformation of restitution into tort in *Schilling* created not just redundancy but also rivalry. It allowed the plaintiff to try a simple will contest before a jury, with access to punitive damages, and in circumvention of the proponent's presumptive right to pay costs out of the estate. If the plaintiff had been required instead to bring an action in restitution for constructive trust, there would have been no jury and almost certainly no punitive damages. . . .

To prevail on a tort claim, the plaintiff must establish that the defendant violated a right of the plaintiff not to be injured in the manner enjoined by the tort. As Justice Cardozo explained in the canonical *Palsgraf* case, a tort plaintiff "sues in her own right for a wrong personal to her, and not as the vicarious beneficiary of a breach of duty to another." . . .

Courts that [recognize] the interference-with-inheritance tort . . . have recognized, if only dimly, that they are departing from basic principles of tort law. The *Schilling* court . . . acknowledged that "[i]nterference with an expectancy is an *unusual* tort because the beneficiary is authorized to sue to recover damages primarily to protect the testator's interest rather than the disappointed beneficiary's expectations." The court continued, "*In a sense*, the beneficiary's action is *derivative* of the testator's rights." The court's concession that it is "unusual" for tort law to recognize a claim that is "in a sense . . . derivative" was its way of acknowledging, without resolving, the deep conflict between the tort and the *Palsgraf* principle. In the law of torts, derivative claims are not merely "unusual"; they are not recognized.[70]

3. The Restatement (Third) of Torts.   As this book went to press in early 2017, the American Law Institute was preparing to take up at its Annual Meeting later that year a revision to Restatement (Second) of Torts § 774B, for inclusion in the new Restatement (Third) of Torts: Liability for Economic Harm. Following the criticisms of Professors Goldberg and Sitkoff, the draft revision takes the position that the tort should not be allowed "to interfere with probate law or to provide a way for a plaintiff

---

70. Id. at 365, 371-72, 380-81 (Goldberg and Sitkoff's emphasis).

to avoid its limits and restrictions," and that the tort should be applied in a manner that "complement[s] restitutionary remedies, not displace[s] them."[71] Thus, the tort would not be allowed even if probate "offers less generous relief than would be attainable in tort," if "the [probate] limitations period has expired," or if "the defendant's fraud or other misconduct has prevented the plaintiff from making a timely claim in probate" so long as the probate court has "a procedure for reopening the case."[72] The draft also exhorts courts to "be mindful of restrictions that the law of restitution places on comparable claims," such as a heightened standard of proof, and it cautions against an award of punitive damages if the plaintiff prevailed on the basis of a presumption of undue influence rather than direct evidence of the kind of egregious conduct that would warrant such damages.[73]

4. The Probate Exception to Federal Jurisdiction. The most famous (and perhaps most salacious) interference-with-inheritance tort case involves Vickie Lynn Marshall, better known as Anna Nicole Smith, who alleged that her stepson tortiously interfered with her expected gift from her deceased husband, Texas oil magnate J. Howard Marshall. Although the Texas probate court with jurisdiction over Marshall's estate rejected Smith's inheritance law claims, her tort claim against her stepson was litigated in federal court incident to her bankruptcy proceeding.

Smith's tort litigation produced the most recent pronouncement by the Supreme Court on the *probate exception to federal jurisdiction*, which Judge Posner has called "one of the most mysterious and esoteric branches of the law of federal jurisdiction."[74] This exception, which appears to be based on a misunderstanding of English legal history,[75] prohibits federal courts from entertaining a suit that encroaches on the traditional jurisdiction of state probate courts. In Marshall v. Marshall, 547 U.S. 293 (2006), the Court held that Smith's claim fell outside of the exception because it was an action for damages that would not interfere with any probate proceedings or the probate court's control over Marshall's estate. Consequently, if the requirements for diversity jurisdiction are met, an interference-with-inheritance tort suit may be litigated in federal court.

---

71. Restatement (Third) of Torts: Liability for Economic Harm § 17 cmt. a (Am. Law Inst., Council Draft No. 4, 2016).

72. Id. cmt. c.

73. Id. cmt. f.

74. Dragan v. Miller, 679 F.2d 712, 713 (7th Cir. 1982) (Posner, J.); *see also* James E. Pfander & Michael J.T. Downey, In Search of the Probate Exception, 67 Vand. L. Rev. 1533 (2014) ("Among the enigmas of federal jurisdiction, the probate exception surely ranks with the most arcane.").

75. *See* John F. Winkler, The Probate Jurisdiction of the Federal Courts, 14 Prob. L.J. 77 (1997).

CHAPTER 5

WILLS: CONSTRUCTION

"When I use a word," Humpty Dumpty said in rather a scornful tone,
"it means just what I choose it to mean—neither more nor less."

LEWIS CARROLL
Through the Looking Glass, and What Alice Found There 123
(Henry Altemus Co. 1897) (1871)

IN THE PRIOR TWO CHAPTERS, we considered the validity of wills, in particular the difficulties in assessing the authenticity and voluntariness of a purported will in posthumous legislation. We now shift our attention in this chapter to the *construction of wills*, that is, the process of determining the *meaning* that should be attributed to a will. In accordance with the principle of freedom of disposition, "[t]he controlling consideration in determining the meaning of a donative document is the donor's intention."[1] But how should a testator's intention be determined? The words of a will may be ambiguous or may suggest an intent different from what other evidence indicates was the testator's actual or likely intent.

The complication in these matters, as in the prior two chapters, is the *worst evidence* problem inherent to probate procedure whereby the best witness is dead by the time the issue is litigated. Without live testimony from the testator, discerning the testator's actual intent can be difficult. Should a court consider only the *plain meaning* of a will, excluding *extrinsic evidence* of intent? What if the language of the will is ambiguous on its face? What if a seemingly clear provision is ambiguous as applied to the facts? What if there is clear and convincing evidence that the language of the will misrenders the testator's intent owing to an innocent mistake by the scrivener? Should courts have the power to *reform* a will to correct a mistaken term?

Another difficulty in construing wills stems from the gap in time that intervenes between the making of a will and the testator's death. During this gap, which may span years or even decades, circumstances can change in ways that render the will stale or obsolete. A named beneficiary might die or the nature and scope of the testator's

---

1. Restatement (Third) of Property: Wills and Other Donative Transfers § 10.1 (Am. Law Inst. 2003).

property might change. How is a *stale will* to be applied to unanticipated changes in circumstances?

We begin in Section A with mistaken and ambiguous language in wills. We consider the traditional plain meaning and no reformation rules as well as the modern trend toward allowing extrinsic evidence to clarify meaning and correct mistakes. In Section B, we consider the stale will problem in the context of a predeceasing beneficiary, which causes a gift to *lapse*. In Section C, we consider the stale will problem in the context of changes in the testator's property after execution of the will. In both of these situations, if the testator's actual intent is not evident, the court will apply rules of construction that are meant to implement the probable intent of the typical testator.

A. MISTAKEN OR AMBIGUOUS LANGUAGE IN WILLS

1. Plain Meaning and No Reformation

In construing wills, a majority of states follow—or purport to follow—two rules that, operating in tandem, bar the admission of extrinsic evidence to vary the terms of a will. The first is the *plain meaning* or *no extrinsic evidence* rule. Under this rule, extrinsic evidence may be admitted to resolve certain ambiguities, but the plain meaning of the words of a will cannot be disturbed by evidence that the testator intended another meaning. The closely related second rule is the *no reformation* rule. Under this rule, courts may not reform a will to correct a mistaken term to reflect what the testator intended the will to say. In Sanderson v. Norcross, 136 N.E. 170 (Mass. 1922), the court put the point thus:

> Courts have no power to reform wills. . . . [M]istakes of testators cannot be corrected. Omissions cannot be supplied. Language cannot be modified to meet unforeseen changes in conditions. The only means for ascertaining the intent of the testator are the words written and the acts done by him.

The usual justification for these rules is the worst evidence problem. Because a testator is unable to corroborate or refute extrinsic evidence of intent that is at odds with the words of her will, she is protected from fraud and error by categorically excluding such evidence. It is sometimes also said that admitting evidence of intent other than the language of the will would violate the requirement of the Wills Act that a testamentary disposition be in writing, signed by the testator, and attested by witnesses. On this view, compliance with the Wills Act establishes a conclusive validation of the written words of the will that may not be challenged on the basis of extrinsic evidence of a different intent.

Mahoney v. Grainger
186 N.E. 86 (Mass. 1933)

RUGG, C.J. This is an appeal from a decree of a probate court denying a petition for distribution of a legacy under the will of Helen A. Sullivan among her first cousins who are contended to be her heirs at law. The residuary clause was as follows: "All the rest and residue of my estate, both real and personal property, I give, devise and bequeath to my heirs at law living at the time of my decease, absolutely; to be divided among them equally, share and share alike."

The trial judge made a report of the material facts in substance as follows: The sole heir at law of the testatrix at the time of her death was her maternal aunt, Frances Hawkes Greene, who is still living and who was named in the petition for probate of her will. The will was duly proved and allowed on October 8, 1931, and letters testamentary issued accordingly. The testatrix was a single woman about sixty-four years of age, and had been a school teacher. She always maintained her own home but her relations with her aunt who was her sole heir and with several first cousins were cordial and friendly. In her will she gave general legacies in considerable sums to two of her first cousins. About ten days before her death the testatrix sent for an attorney who found her sick but intelligent about the subjects of their conversation. She told the attorney she wanted to make a will. She gave him instructions as to general pecuniary legacies. In response to the questions "Whom do you want to leave the rest of your property to? Who are your nearest relations?" she replied "I've got about twenty-five first cousins . . . let them share it equally." The attorney then drafted the will and read it to the testatrix and it was executed by her.

The trial judge ruled that statements of the testatrix "were admissible only in so far as they tended to give evidence of the material circumstances surrounding the testatrix at the time of the execution of the will; that the words heirs at law were words in common use, susceptible of application to one or many; that when applied to the special circumstances of this case that the testatrix had but one heir, notwithstanding the added words 'to be divided among them equally, share and share alike,' there was no latent ambiguity or equivocation in the will itself which would permit the introduction of the statements of the testatrix to prove her testamentary intention." Certain first cousins have appealed from the decree dismissing the petition for distribution to them.

There is no doubt as to the meaning of the words "heirs at law living at the time of my decease" as used in the will. Confessedly they refer alone to the aunt of the testatrix and do not include her cousins.

A will duly executed and allowed by the court must under the statute of wills (G.L. [Ter. Ed.] c. 191, § 1 et seq.) be accepted as the final expression of the intent of the person executing it. The fact that it was not in conformity to the instructions given to the draftsman who prepared it or that he made a mistake does not authorize a court to reform or alter it or remould it by amendments. The will must be construed as it came from the hands of the testatrix. Polsey v. Newton, 85 N.E. 574 (Mass. 1908). Mistakes in the drafting of the will may be of significance in some circumstances in a trial as to the due execution and allowance of the alleged testamentary instrument. Richardson v. Richards, 115 N.E. 307 (Mass. 1917). Proof that the legatee actually designated was not the particular person intended by the one executing the will cannot be received to aid in the interpretation of a will. Tucker v. Seaman's Aid Society, 7 Metc. 188, 210 (Mass. 1843). When the instrument has been proved and allowed as a will oral testimony as to the meaning and purpose of a testator in using language must be rigidly excluded. Saucier v. Fontaine, 152 N.E. 95 (Mass. 1926).

It is only where testamentary language is not clear in its application to facts that evidence may be introduced as to the circumstances under which the testator used that language in order to throw light upon its meaning. Where no doubt exists as to the property bequeathed or the identity of the beneficiary there is no room for extrinsic evidence; the will must stand as written. Barker v. Comins, 110 Mass. 477, 488 (1872); Best v. Berry, 75 N.E. 743, 744 (Mass. 1905).

In the case at bar there is no doubt as to the heirs at law of the testatrix. The aunt alone falls within that description. The cousins are excluded. The circumstance that the plural word "heirs" was used does not prevent one individual from taking the entire gift. Calder v. Bryant, 184 N.E. 440 (Mass. 1933).

Decree affirmed.

NOTES

1. No Reformation. Why did the court in *Mahoney* deny reformation? "The will," said the court, "must be construed as it came from the hands of the testatrix." Did the will come from the hands of Helen Sullivan or the hands of her lawyer?

2. Malpractice and Unjust Enrichment. Under Simpson v. Calivas, page 52, would Sullivan's lawyer be liable to Sullivan's cousins for malpractice? Should he have inquired further about Sullivan's family tree? On what evidence would the cousins rely to prove that the lawyer's negligence frustrated Sullivan's intent? Why is such evidence reliable enough to impose liability on the lawyer but not to reform the will? Was Sullivan's aunt unjustly enriched? Might she be liable to the cousins in an action for restitution by way of constructive trust?

3. No Ambiguity. Under the plain meaning rule, extrinsic evidence may be admitted to resolve an ambiguity. Why was this exception not applicable in *Mahoney*? The court said that there was "no doubt as to the meaning of the words 'heirs at law living at the time of my decease' as used in the will." Do you agree? Why wasn't the lawyer's testimony a reason to doubt the meaning of the term "heirs" as used in the will? Why use the plural "heirs" if Sullivan's intent was to refer to her aunt alone?

In Gustafson v. Svenson, 366 N.E.2d 761 (Mass. 1977), the testator devised property to Enoch Anderson or "his heirs per stirpes." Enoch predeceased the testator, leaving a wife but no descendants. Enoch's widow was his heir. The court held that testimony of the drafter that the testator did not intend Enoch's devise to go to his widow was inadmissible. The phrase "heirs per stirpes" was not ambiguous, despite the plural term ("heirs") and the reference to multigenerational representation ("per stirpes"). Enoch's widow took the devise.

In In re Estate of Smith, 555 N.E.2d 1111 (Ill. App. 1990), the testator left a bequest to "PERRY MANOR, INC., Pinckneyville, Illinois." At the time the will was executed, Perry Manor, Inc., a Nevada corporation, operated a nursing home called Perry Manor in Pinckneyville. Before the testator died, Perry Manor, Inc., sold the nursing home to Lifecare Center of Pinckneyville, Inc. Lifecare continued to operate the nursing home under the name Perry Manor. Which company should get the bequest? The court gave it to the Nevada corporation, which alone fit exactly the literal description of the legatee: "PERRY MANOR, INC." The words, "Pinckneyville, Illinois," which were not capitalized, merely described the location of the named legatee at the time of execution. Because there was no ambiguity, extrinsic evidence of the testator's intent was inadmissible. To consider such evidence "would have the same effect as rewriting the will." Suppose that the legatee had been described as "PERRY MANOR," without the "INC." What result?

In In re Estate of Scale, 830 N.Y.S.2d 618 (App. Div. 2007), the testator left 10 percent of his residuary estate to "The Audubon Society of New York State." Both the National Audubon Society, which was founded in 1905 and operated in New York as Audubon New York, and the Audubon Society of New York State, Inc., which was founded in 1987 and operated under the name Audubon International, claimed the bequest. The court held that "the testator's failure to include 'Inc.' in naming his beneficiary does not render the will ambiguous." The trial court should not have admitted testimony by the lawyer who drafted the will to clarify which organization the testator had intended. "[I]f courts should permit the substitution of the draft[er's] recollection of what the testator told him . . . for the language of the will itself, the instrument would cease to be the repository of the decedent's testamentary program. . . . In short, as the will unambiguously dictates, the legacy must be paid to the state organization expressly named therein." Was the will unambiguous?

The *Smith* and *Scale* cases are reminiscent of National Society for the Prevention of Cruelty to Children v. Scottish National Society for the Prevention of Cruelty to Children, [1915] A.C. 207 (H.L.). In that case, a Scotsman, who had always lived in Scotland and had left several bequests to Scottish charities by will, bequeathed £500 to "The National Society for the Prevention of Cruelty to Children." This was the charter name of a society in London with which the testator had no relationship. Near the testator's home was a branch office of the *Scottish* National Society for the Prevention of Cruelty to Children. The testator was familiar with the Scottish charity. Should the £500 go to the London or the Scottish charity? The House of Lords held that the charity in London should get the money because the testator "had by name designated" it.[2]

4. Testamentary Intent.   In *Mahoney*, the court said that if "no doubt exists as to the property bequeathed or the identity of the beneficiary there is no room for extrinsic evidence; the will must stand as written." Suppose an actor executes a will in a theatrical performance. Is not extrinsic evidence allowed to establish that the will was a prop and not intended to be real? If there is an allegation of incapacity or undue influence, is not extrinsic evidence admissible to resolve the allegation? Why is extrinsic evidence admissible to resolve questions of testamentary intent but not to discern the meaning of a will?

In the ugly case of Fleming v. Morrison, 72 N.E. 499 (Mass. 1904), Francis Butterfield had his lawyer, Sidney Goodrich, draft a will leaving Butterfield's entire estate to Mary Fleming. After Butterfield signed the will and Goodrich signed as the first witness, but before the other witnesses had signed, Butterfield told Goodrich "that this was a 'fake'

---

2. For criticism of this case in a classic article on the meaning of words, see Zechariah Chafee, Jr., The Disorderly Conduct of Words, 41 Colum. L. Rev. 381, 385 (1941).

will" meant to induce Fleming to sleep with Butterfield. The court denied probate to the will on the basis of Goodrich's testimony that Butterfield intended the instrument to be a sham.[3] "We are of [the] opinion that it is competent to contradict by parol the solemn statements contained in an instrument that it is a will; that it has been signed as such by the person named as the testator, and attested and subscribed by persons signing as witnesses."

If testimony of the drafting lawyer is admissible to show that a duly executed will, which recites that it is the testator's will, is not intended as such—thus contradicting the words of the instrument—why can't the lawyer testify that the plain meaning of the words of the will was not the meaning intended by the testator?

In re Estate of Cole
621 N.W.2d 816 (Minn. App. 2001)

CRIPPEN, J. The will of decedent Ruth N. Cole states a bequest to her friend, appellant Veta J. Vining, in "the sum of two hundred thousand dollars ($25,000)." Appellant disputes the trial court's determination to consider testimony of the will's scrivener that explains the contradictory language of the will. We affirm.

FACTS

Ruth N. Cole executed a will on July 1, 1999, and died testate on July 8, 1999. Respondent personal representative petitioned the court for a construction of the will to find that appellant's bequest was for $25,000. After appellant contested the construction, the personal representative moved for summary judgment, basing the motion principally upon the affidavit and file notes of the scrivener, attorney Robert C. Black, III. Black's affidavit explains that he used his computer to "copy and paste" another paragraph of the will bequeathing "two hundred thousand dollars ($200,000.00)" to another individual and changed the name to Veta Vining. Black then changed the numerals to $25,000, the amount chosen by his client, but failed to change the words indicating the amount to "twenty-five thousand dollars." Appellant offered no evidence to contradict Black's affidavit or file notes and did not request the opportunity to cross-examine Mr. Black.

The trial court classified the bequest as patently ambiguous because the inconsistency appears on the face of the instrument. Referring to historic precedents for admitting direct evidence of intention for latent but not patent ambiguities, the court concluded that the distinction serves no useful purpose. The court then undertook the task of assessing the credibility of the evidence and found that the scrivener's testimony was reliable, that no genuine issue of material fact remained for further litigation, and

---

3. What do you think of the ethics of the lawyer Sidney Goodrich? Should he have participated in making the sham will? *See* Model Rule of Prof'l Conduct 1.2(d) (2015) ("A lawyer shall not counsel a client to engage, or assist a client, in conduct that the lawyer knows is criminal or fraudulent."). Should he have warned Fleming about Butterfield's intentions? *See* Model Rule of Prof'l Conduct 1.6 (2015) (permitting disclosure of confidential information to prevent "substantial bodily harm" or "a crime or fraud").

> **5.4** To my friends Arlene and Richard Deick, jointly, or if one of them should predecease me, then to the survivor of them solely, the following:
>
>   a. The sum of fifty thousand dollars ($50,000); and
>
>   b. An amount equal to the unpaid obligation owing by Arlene and Richard Deick, as of the date of my death as identified by the terms and conditions of that certain Contract for Deed entered into between myself, as seller, and Arlene and Richard Deick, as purchasers, dated February 26, 1988, and filed for record in Hennepin County on July 1, 1988, as document No. 5426544, regarding real estate located at 6521 Tingdale, Edina, Hennepin County, Minnesota, and legally described as:
>
>   Lot 19 and South 10 feet of Lot 20, Block 17, Normandale Second Addition.
>
>   The gift is intended to forgive all amount outstanding to me under said Contract for Deed. In the event no monies are owed, this gift shall lapse and be of no effect.
>
> If both Arlene and Richard Deick should predecease me, these gifts shall lapse.
>
> **5.5** To my friend, James Rutherford, Edina, Minnesota, the sum of two hundred thousand dollars ($200,000). If James Rutherford should predecease me, this gift shall lapse.
>
> **5.6** To my friend, Lois Leick, the sum of fifty thousand dollars ($50,000).
>
> **5.7** To my friend, Kathleen Heidelberg, the sum of two hundred thousand dollars ($200,00.00). If Kathleen Heidelberg should predecease me, this gift shall lapse.
>
> **5.8** To my friend, Veta Vining, the sum of two hundred thousand dollars ($25,000).
>
>   _____
>   Ruth Cole
>
> page 3   P8 991367

The clause at issue: "To my friend, Veta Vining, the sum of two hundred thousand dollars ($25,000)."

Page 3 of the will of Ruth N. Cole

that the bequest to appellant Vining must be construed as "the sum of twenty-five thousand dollars ($25,000)." . . .

ANALYSIS

. . . The history of the construction of wills and other instruments has been shaped by two overriding rules. First, the court is to avoid doing any violence to the words employed in the instrument and to distrust the reliability of looking to sources outside the instrument for information about its meaning; second, the court is to effectuate the testator's intent. Thus, the common-law use of outside sources was suspect and only grudgingly permitted. . . .

To avoid declaring bequests void for uncertainty, courts began to consider evidence of the testator's intent with respect to so-called equivocations, often referred to as latent ambiguities, which involve instruments that describe a person or thing in terms equally applicable to more than one when the surrounding circumstances are taken into account. E.g., Wheaton v. Pope, 97 N.W. 1046, 1048 (Minn. 1904). Courts also created exceptions permitting direct evidence of the testator's intent in certain other circumstances. . . .

Notwithstanding the developments for admission of evidence showing the testator's intentions, some authorities continue to state that no direct evidence of intent should be considered when construing patent ambiguities, i.e., those contradictions appearing on the face of the instrument. See 4 William J. Bowe & Douglas H. Parker, Page on the Law of Wills § 32.9 (3d ed. 1961). This rule calls for closer examination because, as Bowe and Parker recognize, "it undoubtedly would be a step forward in the development of our law to discard the distinction [between patent and latent ambiguities] entirely." Id. § 32.7, at 258. As appellant observes, no Minnesota court has determined whether all ambiguities can be construed using direct evidence of the testator's intention, but the supreme court has cautiously noted that such evidence is available for some cases of ambiguity. In re Estate of Chase, 234 N.W. 294, 295 (Minn. 1931).

We are satisfied that the trial court correctly denigrated the usefulness of a distinction between patent and latent ambiguities for determining what type of extrinsic evidence should be considered when construing ambiguous or contradictory provisions. Because it is reasonable for the Minnesota judiciary to weigh evidence of the testator's declarations of intent, the basis for the patent/latent distinction appears outmoded. Moreover, we appreciate, in general, the frustration scriveners encounter in trying to express perfectly their client's wishes, which frequently creates ambiguities, such that justice requires consideration of extrinsic evidence to determine intent. . . .

In looking to authorities, we find the primary reflection of modern law enunciated by our colleagues in Wisconsin: "If, after examining the surrounding circumstances at the time of the will's execution an ambiguity or inconsistency persists, we may resort to extrinsic evidence and the rules of will construction." In re Estate of Lohr, 497 N.W.2d 730, 736 (Wis. App. 1993); see also Wilson v. Flowers, 277 A.2d 199, 206 (N.J. 1971) ("[D]irect statements of intention should be admitted no matter what the form of the ambiguity.").

Subject to [two] limitations, [neither] of which bears on the immediate case, the scrivener's testimony may be employed to resolve contradictory provisions in the will. In re Estate of Lohr suggests the first limitation: The surrounding circumstances should be examined first and direct evidence of the testator's intention should be considered only if the ambiguity or contradiction persists. 497 N.W.2d at 736. The Arizona Court of Appeals suggests the second limitation: Extrinsic evidence is to be used to determine what the testator meant by the words used, not to determine an intent that cannot be found in the words employed in the instrument. In re Estate of Smith, 580 P.2d 754, 757 (Ariz. App. 1978). In this case, the trial court construed what the testator meant by the words she used. . . .

Finally, we find little or no modern authority to contradict our determination of the law in this case. Appellant cites In re Gollhofer's Estate, 111 N.Y.S.2d 831, 833-34 (Surr. 1952), which indeed determines that direct evidence of a testator's intent cannot be employed to determine what the testator intended by a bequest of "Twenty five ($2500) Dollars." Id. at 833. The absence of any discussion of the basis for the rule excluding direct evidence of intent diminishes the weight of *Gollhofer* and other modern recitations of the rule.

Nothing in the history of Minnesota case law suggests cause for blinding the courts to evidence of the testator's intention in cases where the will contains contradictory language. . . .

Affirmed.

NOTES

1. Patent Ambiguity. A *patent ambiguity* is evident from the face of a will—in *Cole*, the inconsistency between "two hundred thousand dollars" and "$25,000." Under traditional law, extrinsic evidence is not admissible to clarify a patent ambiguity. The court is confined to the four corners of the will even if as a result the ambiguous devise fails and the property passes by intestacy. Increasingly, however, as in *Cole*, courts are inclined to admit extrinsic evidence to resolve a patent ambiguity.[4]

2. Latent Ambiguity. A *latent ambiguity* manifests itself only when the terms of a will are applied to the facts. Latent ambiguity usually takes one of two forms: a description for which two or more persons or things fit exactly, or a description for which no person or thing fits exactly but two or more persons or things fit partially. In most states, extrinsic evidence is admissible to resolve a latent ambiguity.

a. Equivocation. The first type of latent ambiguity, when two or more persons or things fit the description exactly (e.g., a devise "to my niece Alicia," when in fact the testator has two nieces named Alicia), is called *equivocation*. These are the cases in which admission of extrinsic evidence, including direct expressions of the testator's intent, first began. The courts reasoned that extrinsic evidence merely made the terms of the will more precise without adding to them, which would be forbidden. In Succession of Bacot, 502 So. 2d 1118 (La. App. 1987), *T* left "all to Danny." The court chose one of three lovers, all named Danny, based on extrinsic evidence showing who had the closest relationship to *T*.

b. Personal Usage. An amusing line of equivocation cases gave rise to the *personal usage* exception to the plain meaning rule. If extrinsic evidence shows that a testator habitually used a term in an idiosyncratic manner, the evidence is admissible to show that the testator used that term in accordance with his personal usage rather than its ordinary meaning. In Moseley v. Goodman, 195 S.W. 590 (Tenn. 1917), the testator left $20,000 to "Mrs. Moseley." Mrs. Lenore Moseley, the wife of the owner of the cigar store where the testator traded, but whom the testator had never met, claimed the bequest. So did Mrs. Lillian Trimble, whom the testator called "Mrs. Moseley." Trimble's husband was a salesman in Moseley's cigar store and was called "Moseley" by the testator. His wife—dubbed "Mrs. Moseley" by the testator—managed the apartment house where the testator lived and did kind things for him. The court held that the bequest went to Mrs. Trimble.

---

4. *See* Andrea W. Cornelison, Dead Man Talking: Are Courts Ready to Listen? The Erosion of the Plain Meaning Rule, 35 Real Prop. Prob. & Tr. J. 811, 819-20 (2001).

Why in *Moseley* was evidence that "Moseley" meant "Trimble" admissible but in *Mahoney* evidence that "heirs" meant "cousins" was not? Is there a limiting principle that distinguishes the ambiguity in *Moseley* from the mistake in *Mahoney*?

c. No Exact Fit.   The second type of latent ambiguity, in which a description in a will does not exactly fit any person or thing, is more common. In Estate of Ihl v. Oetting, 682 S.W.2d 865 (Mo. App. 1984), the testator devised his home to "Mr. and Mrs. Wendell Richard Hess, or the survivor of them, presently residing at # 17 Barbara Circle." When the will was executed in 1979, Wendell Hess and his wife Glenda resided at 17 Barbara Circle. Soon thereafter Wendell divorced Glenda, they sold 17 Barbara Circle, and Wendell married Verna.

At the testator's death in 1983, Verna, relying on the rule that a will speaks as of the testator's death, claimed the "Mrs. Hess" share of the devise. She argued that no extrinsic evidence should be admitted since there was no ambiguity—she alone met the description of "Mrs. Wendell Richard Hess." The court disagreed. It found that a latent ambiguity arose from the description of the beneficiaries as "residing at # 17 Barbara Circle." Verna Hess met the description of Mrs. Wendell Richard Hess, but she never resided at 17 Barbara Circle. Glenda met the description of the Mrs. Hess residing at 17 Barbara Circle when the will was executed, but she no longer met that description at the time of the testator's death. The court admitted extrinsic evidence that showed an intent that the devise go to the earlier Mrs. Hess, Glenda.

3. Collapsing the Distinction Between Patent and Latent Ambiguities.   Whether an ambiguity is patent or latent is often subjective. In In re Estate of Black, 27 Cal. Rptr. 418 (App. 1962), the testator, a resident of northern California, left her estate "to the University of Southern California known as The U.C.L.A." The trial court ruled there was no ambiguity and construed the gift to be "to the university in Southern California known as The U.C.L.A." The appellate court reversed, holding the devise to be ambiguous. However, the ambiguity was deemed latent, not patent, so extrinsic evidence could be admitted to resolve it:

> The provision in question is not, on its face, susceptible to one of two constructions. The language is clear, intelligible and suggests a single meaning. A reader unacquainted with the fact that there are two universities in Southern California, one known as the University of Southern California, and another commonly referred to by the initials U.C.L.A., would readily attribute to said provision the meaning that it refers to an institution named "University of Southern California," which is known by the initials U.C.L.A.

Suppose the devise had been "to the New York Law School known as N.Y.U." Patent or latent ambiguity?

Modern courts are increasingly inclined to admit extrinsic evidence to resolve both patent and latent ambiguities, as in *Cole*, a trend that is endorsed by the Restatement (Third) of Property.[5]

---

5. *See* Restatement (Third) of Property: Wills and Other Donative Transfers § 11.2 cmt. d (Am. Law Inst. 2003); Univ. of S. Ind. Found. v. Baker, 843 N.E.2d 528 (Ind. 2006); In re Lock Revocable Living Trust, 123 P.3d 1241 (Haw. 2005).

4. Malpractice Liability for Ambiguity. Should a lawyer who drafts an ambiguous will be liable in malpractice for the costs incurred in litigation to construe the will? *Compare* Ventura Cnty. Humane Soc'y v. Holloway, 115 Cal. Rptr. 464 (App. 1974) ("[T]he task of proving whether claimed ambiguity was the result of negligence of the drafting attorney or whether it was the deliberate choice of the testator, would impose an insurmountable burden on the parties. . . . The duty thus created would amount to a requirement to draft litigation-proof legal documents."), *with* Angela M. Vallario, Shape Up or Ship Out: Accountability to Third Parties for Patent Ambiguities in Testamentary Documents, 26 Whittier L. Rev. 59 (2004) (arguing that drafting a will with a patent ambiguity should be prima facie evidence of negligence).

2. Ad Hoc Relief for Mistaken Terms

By establishing a conclusive presumption of correctness for the words of a duly executed will, the no reformation rule guards against a spurious finding of mistake—a *false positive*. But this benefit comes at the cost of denying relief even if there is overwhelming evidence of mistake and the testator's actual intent—a *false negative*. To avoid this harsh result, courts have sometimes corrected a mistake under the guise of using extrinsic evidence to construe a supposedly ambiguous term.

To get a feel for the ad hoc nature of relief from the no reformation rule—and the need for a more principled way to deal with mistaken terms in wills—consider the next two cases. In each case, the court denied having the power to reform the will, yet the court nonetheless preferred extrinsic evidence of the testator's actual intent over the contrary but mistaken language in the will.

Arnheiter v. Arnheiter
125 A.2d 914 (N.J. Ch. 1956)

SULLIVAN, J. Burnette K. Guterl died on December 31, 1953, leaving a last will and testament which has been admitted to probate by the Surrogate of Essex County. By paragraph 2 of said will her executrix was directed "to sell my undivided one-half interest of premises known as No. 304 Harrison Avenue, Harrison, New Jersey," and use the proceeds of sale to establish trusts for each of decedent's two nieces.

This suit comes about because the decedent did not own or have any interest in 304 Harrison Avenue either at her death or at the time her will was executed. At the hearing it was established that the decedent, at the time her will was executed and also at the time of her death, owned an undivided one-half interest in 317 Harrison Avenue, Harrison, New Jersey, and that this was the only property on Harrison Avenue that she had any interest in.

Plaintiff-executrix has applied to this court to correct an obvious mistake and to change the street number in paragraph "2" of the will to read "No. 317 Harrison Avenue" instead of "No. 304 Harrison Avenue." Relief cannot be granted to the plaintiff in the precise manner sought. It matters not that an obvious mistake in the form of a misdescription is proved. A court has no power to correct or reform a will or

304 Harrison Avenue (2012)   317 Harrison Avenue (2012)

change any of the language therein by substituting or adding words. The will of a decedent executed pursuant to statute is what it is and no court can add to it.

Plaintiff, however, is not without recourse. In the construction of wills and other instruments there is a principle *"falsa demonstratio non nocet"* (mere erroneous description does not vitiate), which applies directly to the difficulty at hand.

> Where a description of a thing or person consists of several particulars and all of them do not fit any one person or thing, less essential particulars may be rejected provided the remainder of the description clearly fits. This is known as the doctrine of *falsa demonstratio non nocet.* Clapp, 5 N.J. Practice, § 114, at 274. . . .

Turning to the problem at hand and to the description of the property as set forth in paragraph 2 of the will, we find the street number "304" to be erroneous because decedent did not own that property. If we disregard or reject that item of description, the will then directs the executrix "to sell my undivided one-half interest of premises known as Harrison Avenue, Harrison, New Jersey." Since it has been established that the decedent, at the time of her death and also when she executed her will, had an interest in only one piece of property on Harrison Avenue, Harrison, New Jersey; that her interest was an undivided one-half interest; that the property in question is 317 Harrison Avenue; and that decedent made no other specific provision in her will relating to 317 Harrison Avenue, we are led inevitably to the conclusion that even without a street number, the rest of the description in paragraph 2 of the will is sufficient to identify the property passing thereunder as 317 Harrison Avenue.

Judgment will be entered construing decedent's will as aforesaid.

NOTES

1. Falsa Demonstratio Non Nocet. What is the difference between the principle that "mere erroneous description does not vitiate," recognized by the Supreme Court in Patch v. White, 117 U.S. 210 (1886), and reformation for mistake? Did not the court in *Arnheiter* give effect to extrinsic evidence of the testator's actual intent rather than the contrary but mistaken language in the will? Why go through this doctrinal contortion? Why not be candid about the power to reform wills but subject the exercise of that power to appropriate safeguards such as a heightened standard of proof?

2. Construction or Reformation?   In In re Will of Goldstein, 363 N.Y.S.2d 147 (App. Div. 1975), another misdescription case ("east" for "west" and "Third Street" for "Sixth Street"), the court said that it was a

> long held rule of construction that courts will strive, wherever possible, to give effect to every part of a will. When the testatrix' intention is manifest from the context of the will and surrounding circumstances but is endangered and obscured . . . by inept and inaccurate modes of expression, the court, to effectuate the intention, may change or mold the language.

If a court were to "change or mold the language" of a will, would this be *construction* or *reformation*?

In re Gibbs' Estate
111 N.W.2d 413 (Wis. 1961)

Petitions by respondent Robert W. Krause for the construction of a portion of the wills of George Gibbs and his wife Lena Adele Gibbs.

Mrs. Gibbs died April 11, 1960, and Mr. Gibbs died May 27, 1960. Mrs. Gibbs' will was executed October 21, 1958, and Mr. Gibbs executed his will May 5, 1960.

Mrs. Gibbs, by the Second Article of her will, bequeathed all her estate to her husband if he survived her by more than 60 days, but he did not. In all other respects the wills were closely similar, particularly the Third Article of hers and the Second Article of his. By paragraph 1 of each certain personal effects were bequeathed, and by paragraph 2 of each the remaining estate was disposed of by a series of subparagraphs, each (with one exception) bequeathing a specified percentage thereof. . . .

Subparagraph 2, (9) of Article Third of Mrs. Gibbs' will is identical with subparagraph 2, (i) of Article Second of Mr. Gibbs' will. Each reads as follows:

> To Robert J. Krause, now of 4708 North 46th Street, Milwaukee, Wisconsin, if he survives me, one per cent (1%).

Respondent Robert W. Krause of Milwaukee, who has never resided at 4708 North 46th street, alleged that he had been an employee of Mr. Gibbs for 30 years and was a friend of the family of both Mr. and Mrs. Gibbs for many years. He alleged that Robert J. Krause who lives at 4708 North 46th street was unknown to the Gibbs and that each of them intended to name respondent as legatee.

At the hearing, respondent offered evidence in support of his allegations. It was received over objection of Robert J. Krause. . . . The court found that the address given in the wills had been inadvertently stated and that both decedents intended to refer to respondent Robert W. Krause as legatee. Orders were accordingly entered in each estate on February 23, 1961. Robert J. Krause appealed. . . .

FAIRCHILD, J. . . . The evidence leads irresistibly to the conclusion that Mr. and Mrs. Gibbs intended legacies to respondent, and that the use of the middle initial "J." and the address of North 46th street resulted from some sort of mistake.

Respondent testified that he met Mr. Gibbs about 1928. From 1930 to 1949 he was employed as superintendent of a steel warehouse where Mr. Gibbs was his superior. They worked in close contact. Until 1945 the business belonged to the Gibbs Steel Company. In that year the business was sold, but Mr. Gibbs stayed on for four years in a supervisory capacity. Respondent remained with the new company until 1960. After 1949 Mr. Gibbs occasionally visited the plant and saw the respondent when there. From 1935 to 1955 respondent took men occasionally to the Gibbs home to do necessary work about the place. He also visited there socially several times a year and saw both Mr. and Mrs. Gibbs. Mrs. Gibbs had made a few visits at the plant before 1949 and respondent had seen her there. Mr. Gibbs did not visit respondent's home, although on a few occasions had telephoned him at home. Mr. Gibbs always called respondent "Bob."

Miss Krueger, who had been the Gibbs' housekeeper for 24 years up to 1958 and was a legatee under both wills, corroborated much of respondent's testimony. She also testified that Mr. Gibbs had told her he made a will remembering various people including "the boys at the shop," referring to them as "Mike, Ed and Bob.". . .

The attorney who drew several wills for Mr. and Mrs. Gibbs produced copies of most of them. They were similar in outline to the wills admitted to probate except that Mr. Gibbs' wills executed before Mrs. Gibb's death bequeathed his property to her, if she survived. The first ones were drawn in 1953 and each contained a bequest to "Robert Krause, of Milwaukee, Wisconsin, if he survives me, one per cent (1%)." There was testimony that Mrs. Gibbs' will, executed in August, 1955, contained the same language. In the 1957 wills the same bequest was made to "Robert Krause, now of 4708 North 46th Street, Milwaukee, Wisconsin." In several other instances street addresses of legatees were given for the first time in 1957. In the 1958 wills the same bequest was made to "Robert J. Krause, now of 4708 North 46th Street, Milwaukee, Wisconsin." The scrivener also produced a hand-written memorandum given to him by Mr. Gibbs for the purpose of preparing Mr. Gibbs' 1958 will, and the reference on that memorandum corresponding to the Krause bequest is "Bob, 1%." Four bequests (to Gruener, Krause, Preuschl and Owen) appear in the same order in each of the wills and are reflected in the memorandum referred to as "Fred Gruener, Bob, Mike, and Ed." Gruener, Preuschl and Owen were former employees of Gibbs Steel Company, as was respondent. . . .

Prior to 1950 respondent had lived at several different locations. From 1950 until April, 1960, he lived at 2325 North Sherman boulevard. We take judicial notice that this address and 4708 North 46th street are in the same general section of the city of Milwaukee, and that both are a number of miles distant from the Gibbs' home. We also take judicial notice that the telephone directory for Milwaukee and vicinity listed 14 subscribers by the name of Robert Krause with varying initials in October, 1958, and 15 in October of 1959. The listing for appellant gives his middle initial J. as well as his street address.

The only evidence which suggests even a possibility that Mr. or Mrs. Gibbs may have known of appellant may be summarized as follows:

For a time, appellant had a second job as a part time taxi driver, and he recalled an elderly lady who was his passenger on a lengthy taxi trip in June, 1955. He did not recall where he picked her up. He had driven her across the city, waiting for her while she visited in a hospital, and then driven her back across the city. The place where he let her out, however, was not her home. He did not recall that she had given him her name, but she had inquired as to his. They had conversed about the illness of appellant's wife and his working at an extra job in order to make ends meet. She had expressed sympathy and approval of his efforts. Presumably when he was notified that his name appeared in the Gibbs' wills as legatee, he endeavored to find an explanation of his good fortune and concluded that the lady in question must have been Mrs. Gibbs. The 1955 taxi ride, however, could not explain the gift to Robert Krause in the 1953 wills, and it is clear that the same legatee was intended in the Krause bequests in all the wills. Moreover, appellant's description of his taxi passenger differed in several particulars from the description of Mrs. Gibbs given by other witnesses. . . .

[T]he county court could reach no other conclusion upon consideration of the extrinsic evidence than that Mr. and Mrs. Gibbs intended to designate respondent as their legatee. The difficult question is whether the court could properly consider such evidence in determining testamentary intent.

Under rules as to construction of a will, unless there is ambiguity in the text of the will read in the light of surrounding circumstances, extrinsic evidence is inadmissible for the purpose of determining intent. Estate of Breese, 96 N.W.2d 712 (Wis. 1959). . . .

The terms of the bequest exactly fit appellant and no one else. There is no ambiguity. "An ambiguity is not that which may be made doubtful by extrinsic proof tending to show an intention different from that manifested in the will, but it must grow out of the difficulty of identifying the person whose name and description correspond with the terms of the will." Ward v. Epsy, 25 Tenn. (6 Hum.) 447 (1846).

Under the circumstances before us, can a court properly consider evidence showing that some of the words were used by mistake and should be stricken or disregarded? It is traditional doctrine that wills must not be reformed even in the case of demonstrable mistake. Estate of Grove, 95 N.W.2d 788 (Wis. 1959); Will of Hipsch, 62 N.W.2d 18 (Wis. 1953). This doctrine doubtless rests upon policy reasons. The courts deem it wise to avoid entertaining claims of disappointed persons who may be able to make very plausible claims of mistake after the testator is no longer able to refute them.

Although the courts subscribe to an inflexible rule against reformation of a will, it seems that they have often strained a point in matters of identification of property or beneficiaries in order to reach a desired result by way of construction. In Will of Stack, 251 N.W. 470 (Wis. 1933), where the will devised "Block 64," the court included part of block 175 in the provision to conform to the unexpressed intent of the testator. In Will of Boeck, 152 N.W. 155 (Wis. 1915), where the will devised the "northeast quarter of the northwest quarter" of a section, which was not owned by the testator, the court held such provision passed the southeast quarter of the northwest quarter, to conform to the misexpressed intent of the testator. . . .

In Miller's Estate, 26 Pa. Super. 443 (1904), testator left property to "William Wilson's children." Relying on evidence that testator frequently confused William Wilson with his brother Seth, the court held the gift should go to the children of Seth Wilson, who had been intended by the testator. In Groves v. Culp, 31 N.E. 569 (Ind. 1892), testator devised a remainder interest in part of lot 15 to his daughter. The court, to conform to testator's true intent, included part of lot 16 in this devise. . . .

We conclude that details of identification, particularly such matters as middle initials, street addresses, and the like, which are highly susceptible to mistake, particularly in metropolitan areas, should not be accorded such sanctity as to frustrate an otherwise clearly demonstrable intent. Where such details of identification are involved, courts should receive evidence tending to show that a mistake has been made and should disregard the details when the proof establishes to the highest degree of certainty that a mistake was, in fact, made.

We therefore consider that the county court properly disregarded the middle initial and street address, and determined that respondent was the Robert Krause whom testators had in mind.

Orders affirmed.

NOTE

A Detail of Identification.   Is the identity of a beneficiary under a will a mere "detail" of identification? What is the limiting principle that qualifies *Gibbs* as an exercise in construing an ambiguous term rather than the reformation of a mistaken term? Professors John Langbein and Lawrence Waggoner suggest that there is none:

> The court's reasoning is wholly persuasive, except when advanced in support of the point in issue, which is how to justify treating this case as an exception to the general rule against reformation for mistake. Nothing that the court says distinguishes this case from those covered by the no-reformation doctrine; the main factors that the court mentions apply in many alleged mistake cases. The label "detail" is conclusory and, especially in a case in which the detail is the designation of the beneficiary under a duly executed will, highly inappropriate. . . . The critical element that the court cites to justify its admitted "disregard" of the term in the will is the quality of the proof of mistake. The opinion does not suggest (and in truth could not have discovered) a limiting principle for thinking that "when the proof establishes to the highest degree of certainty that a mistake was, in fact, made," relief should lie only when the mistake is a "detail," whatever detail means. Proof of such quality regarding any aspect of the will, detail or not, would be equally cogent and should lead to relief for the same reason. If this were a court that took seriously the argument that the Wills Act forbids substituting unattested language for mistaken language, it could not have distinguished this case; an unattested term was proved by means of extrinsic evidence and preferred over the term contained in the testator's duly executed will.[6]

---

6. John H. Langbein & Lawrence W. Waggoner, Reformation of Wills on the Ground of Mistake: Change of Direction in American Law?, 130 U. Pa. L. Rev. 521, 534-35 (1982) (emphasis removed); *see also* Mary Louise Fellows, In Search of Donative Intent, 73 Iowa L. Rev. 611, 642-46 (1988).

3. Openly Reforming Wills for Mistake

Today a growing number of courts are willing to reform a mistaken term in a will, and to do so openly. We have already seen one such case: In re Snide, page 166. Rose and Harvey, a married couple, each signed the mirror-image will intended for the other. At Harvey's death, Rose offered the will that Harvey actually signed, which said that it was the will of Rose, for probate as Harvey's will. The court upheld the probate of the will and the lower court's order of reformation "to substitute the name 'Harvey' wherever the name 'Rose' appeared, and the name 'Rose' wherever the name 'Harvey' appeared." The court stressed, however, that it was addressing a "very unusual case" involving "narrow facts." It denied that its decision was "the first step" toward "reformation of wills" generally.

In Erickson v. Erickson, 716 A.2d 92 (Conn. 1998), the court took that step. It held that extrinsic evidence of mistake by a scrivener is admissible and, if proved by clear and convincing evidence, the court may reform the will to reflect the testator's actual intent. The court saw no principled difference between using extrinsic evidence to correct a mistaken term versus to clarify an ambiguity (as in *Cole*), to identify the property subject to a bequest (as in *Arnheiter*), or to identify the beneficiary (as in *Gibbs*). The court also reasoned that there was no discernable policy difference between mistake on the one hand, and undue influence, duress, fraud, or lack of mental capacity on the other. If the testator's lawyer had misrendered the testator's intent "deliberately and fraudulently, rather than innocently but mistakenly," relief would be available, typically by way of constructive trust (see page 313). The court held that relief for an innocent mistake should likewise be available by way of reformation.

Although still a minority position, reformation of a will to correct a mistake that is proved by clear and convincing evidence is no longer uncommon. In an influential provision published in 2003, the Restatement (Third) of Property endorsed reformation of wills.[7] In 2008, a similar provision was added to the Uniform Probate Code (UPC), excerpted below. In part owing to the influence of these authorities, the issue of reformation to correct a mistake in a will is increasingly being confronted openly, with courts and legislators deciding whether to adopt reformation with a heightened standard of proof, rather than obscuring the problem with a strained application of the rules of construction for ambiguities.

Uniform Probate Code (Unif. Law Comm'n 2008, as amended 2010)

§ 2-805. Reformation to Correct Mistakes

The court may reform the terms of a governing instrument, even if unambiguous, to conform the terms to the transferor's intention if it is proved by clear and convincing evidence what the transferor's intention was and that the terms of the governing instrument were affected by a mistake of fact or law, whether in expression or inducement.

---

7. Restatement (Third) of Property: Wills and Other Donative Transfers § 12.1 (Am. Law Inst. 2003).

In re Estate of Duke
352 P.3d 863 (Cal. 2015)

Chief Justice Tani Gorre Cantil-Sakauye, the second woman to serve as the Chief Justice of the California Supreme Court

Robert Galbraith/Reuters/Alamy

CANTIL-SAKAUYE, C.J. . . . In 1984, when Irving Duke was 72 years of age, he prepared a holographic will in which he left all of his property to "my beloved wife, Mrs. Beatrice Schecter Duke," who was then 58 years of age. He left to his brother, Harry Duke, "the sum of One dollar." He provided that "[s]hould my wife . . . and I die at the same moment, my estate is to be equally divided—[¶] One-half is to be donated to the City of Hope in the name and loving memory of my sister, Mrs. Rose Duke Radin. [¶] One-half is to be donated to the Jewish National Fund to plant trees in Israel in the names and loving memory of my mother and father—[¶] Bessie and Isaac Duke." . . .

The will appointed Beatrice the executrix of the estate. The only change Irving ever made to his will was the addition, in 1997, of the statement that "[w]e hereby agree that all of our assets are community property." Beatrice died in July 2002, but the will was not changed to select a new executor.

Irving died in November 2007, leaving no spouse or children. . . . In March 2008, two charities, the City of Hope (COH) and the Jewish National Fund (JNF), petitioned for probate and for letters of administration. In October 2008, Robert and Seymour Radin (the Radins) filed a petition for determination of entitlement to estate distribution. The Radins are the sons of Irving's sister, Rose Duke Radin, who predeceased Irving. Their petition alleged that they are entitled to the distribution of Irving's estate as Irving's sole intestate heirs.

The Radins moved for summary judgment. They did not challenge the validity of the will. Instead, they asserted that the estate must pass to Irving's closest surviving intestate heirs, the Radins, because Irving did not predecease Beatrice, nor did Irving and Beatrice "die at the same moment," and there is no provision in the will for disposition of the estate in the event Irving survived Beatrice. In opposition to the motion, COH and JNF offered extrinsic evidence to prove that Irving intended the will to provide that in the event Beatrice was not alive to inherit Irving's estate when Irving died, the estate would be distributed to COH and JNF. The probate court concluded that the will was not ambiguous, and on that ground, it declined to consider extrinsic evidence of Irving's intent, and granted summary judgment for the Radins. . . .

We granted review to consider whether the rule [against reformation of an unambiguous will for mistake] should be reconsidered. For the reasons set forth below, we hold that the categorical bar on reformation of unambiguous wills is not justified and that reformation is permissible if clear and convincing evidence establishes an error in the expression of the testator's intent and establishes the testator's actual specific intent at the time the will was drafted.

The clause at issue:
"Third—Should my wife Beatrice Schecter Duke and I die at the same moment, my estate is to be equally divided—"

The will at issue in *Duke*

DISCUSSION

California law allows the admission of extrinsic evidence to establish that a will is ambiguous and to clarify ambiguities in a will. Estate of Russell, 444 P.2d 353 (Cal. 1968). As COH and JNF acknowledge, however, California law does not currently authorize the admission of extrinsic evidence to correct a mistake in a will when the will is unambiguous. Estate of Dominici, 90 P. 448 (Cal. 1907). . . . [W]e . . . consider whether the common law rule categorically barring the reformation of wills is warranted . . . and we conclude that the categorical bar on reformation is not justified. . . .

No sound basis exists to forbid the reformation of unambiguous wills in appropriate circumstances

. . . In California, extrinsic evidence is generally admissible to correct errors in documents, including donative documents other than wills. [Citations to cases involving contracts, releases, irrevocable trusts, insurance policies, and deeds omitted.—Eds.] . . .

In addition, California courts have admitted extrinsic evidence to apply to the *construction* of a will to accomplish what is arguably or has the effect of reforming a will.

For example, admission of extrinsic evidence that the testator referred to her siblings as the "'Broude Trust'" allowed the court to correct the testator's error in leaving everything to the "'Broude Trust Fund'" instead of to her siblings. Estate of Glow, 25 Cal. Rptr. 416 (App. 1962). . . .

Principles allowing the admission of extrinsic evidence to identify and resolve ambiguities in wills have also been invoked to correct attorneys' drafting errors and thereby to reform wills. For example, . . . in Estate of Anderson, 65 Cal. Rptr. 2d 307 (App. 1997), a later will expressly revoked all prior wills, but due to attorney error, the later will failed to include a provision exercising a testamentary power of appointment over a portion of a trust. As a result, the later will failed to carry out the testatrix's intent that the half of the trust over which she had a power of appointment go to her daughter rather than to the issue of her late husband. The court held that extrinsic evidence was admissible to determine whether the testatrix intended to revoke the earlier will's provision exercising her power of appointment.

Extrinsic evidence is admissible not only to aid in the construction of a will, but also to determine whether a document was intended to be a will. Halldin v. Usher, 321 P.2d 746 (Cal. 1958). In addition, courts have long recognized that extrinsic evidence is admissible to prove that a will has been lost or destroyed, and to prove its contents. Prob. Code § 8223; Swift v. Superior Court, 247 P.2d 6 (Cal. 1952).

Thus, extrinsic evidence is admitted to correct donative documents other than wills after the donor's death. Moreover, myriad circumstances exist in which California courts appropriately admit evidence to establish a testator's intentions. Because extrinsic evidence is not inherently more reliable when admitted for these various purposes than when admitted to correct an error in a will, Professors John Langbein and Lawrence Waggoner, leading advocates of an extension of the doctrine of reformation to unambiguous wills, conclude that evidentiary concerns do not explain or justify the bar on reformation of wills. . . . John H. Langbein & Lawrence W. Waggoner, Reformation of Wills on the Ground of Mistake: Change of Direction in American Law?, 130 U. Pa. L. Rev. 521, 524-29 (1982). To overcome the objection that reformed language is unattested, they look to principles related to the statute of frauds.

Like the statute of wills, the statute of frauds requires certain documents to be evidenced by a writing subscribed by the party. If not evidenced by such a writing, a contract subject to the statute of frauds is invalid. Civ. Code § 1624. "'The primary purpose of the Statute [of Frauds] is evidentiary, to require reliable evidence of the existence and terms of the contract and to prevent enforcement through fraud or perjury of contracts never in fact made.'" Sterling v. Taylor, 152 P.3d 420, 425 (Cal. 2007). Once sufficient written evidence of an agreement is presented, the evidentiary purpose is served, and extrinsic evidence is admissible to clarify ambiguous terms and to reform the writing to correct a mistake, even when the writing is intended to be a complete and exclusive statement of the parties' agreement. Id.

In correcting a contract subject to the statute of frauds, a court is not enforcing an oral contract, but is instead enforcing a written contract in accordance with the parties' actual agreement. To overcome the presumption that the writing is accurate, we have required clear and convincing evidence of a mistake before allowing reformation of a contract. Nat. Auto. & Cas. Co. v. Indus. Accident Comm'n, 206 P.2d 841 (Cal. 1949).

In contrast to cases involving the statute of frauds, which may or may not involve a party who is deceased, cases arising under the statute of wills always involve a testator who is deceased and therefore cannot explain his or her intentions. We have already recognized, however, in the context of inheritance rights, that imposing a burden of proof by clear and convincing evidence is a means to address evidentiary concerns related to the circumstances that the principal witness is deceased and statutory formalities were not followed. Estate of Ford, 82 P.3d 747 (Cal. 2004). . . . Therefore, the fact that the testator will always be unavailable to testify does not warrant a categorical bar on the admission of extrinsic evidence to reform a will. . . .

In cases in which clear and convincing evidence establishes both a mistake in the drafting of the will and the testator's actual and specific intent at the time the will was drafted, it is plain that denying reformation would defeat the testator's intent and result in unjust enrichment of unintended beneficiaries. Given that the paramount concern in construing a will is to determine the subjective intent of the testator, Estate of Russell, supra, only significant countervailing considerations can justify a rule categorically denying reformation.

The Radins cite various factors in support of their contention that reformation of wills should never be allowed, some of which we have addressed above. First, they distinguish wills from other written instruments, noting that probate of a will always occurs after the testator's death, whereas contract litigation typically occurs when the parties to the contract are alive, and trust administration "frequently" begins before the testator's death. In addition, anyone may claim to be an intended beneficiary of a will, but the parties to a contract typically are few. We are not persuaded by these arguments in favor of a categorical bar on reformation. As we have noted, the death of a principal witness has not been viewed as a reason to deny reformation in other contexts. Also, although anyone may claim to be an intended beneficiary of a will, an appropriately tailored reformation remedy will alleviate concerns regarding unintended beneficiaries; it is unlikely that there will be many persons who have a connection to a testator and can produce clear and convincing evidence both of a mistake in the drafting of the will at the time the will was written and of the testator's specific intentions concerning the disposition of property. . . .

Second, the Radins express concern that reformation overrides the formalities required to execute a will. The fact that reformation is an available remedy does not relieve a testator of the requirements imposed by the Statute of Wills. Therefore, the formalities continue to serve various functions associated with the rituals of will execution, such as warning the testator of the seriousness of the act and clearly identifying the document as a will. To the extent reformation is inconsistent with the formalities' evidentiary purpose of establishing the testator's intent in a writing, the inconsistency is no different from the tension between reformation and the statute of frauds. . . .

Third, . . . the Radins assert that allowing reformation will result in a significant increase in probate litigation and expenses. Claimants have long been entitled, however, to present extrinsic evidence to establish that a will is ambiguous despite the fact that it appears to be unambiguous. Estate of Russell, supra. Therefore, probate courts already receive extrinsic evidence of testator intent from claimants attempting to reform a will through the doctrine of ambiguity. The task of deciding whether the evidence establishes by clear and convincing evidence that a mistake was made in the drafting of the will is a relatively small additional burden, because the court is already evaluating the evidence's probative value to determine the existence of an ambiguity.[8] To the extent additional claims are made that are based on a theory of mistake rather than a theory of ambiguity, the heightened evidentiary standard will help the probate court to filter out weak claims. . . .

Although allowing reformation of an unambiguous will in appropriate instances will overturn many decades of precedent, we conclude that principles of stare decisis do not compel continued adherence to the rule at issue. The interest in ensuring certainty, predictability, and stability has been undermined by the inconsistent application of the principles applicable to the construction of wills. As noted above, in the course of applying the doctrine that an ambiguous will may be clarified through the admission of extrinsic evidence, courts have essentially reformed wills. . . .

Rather than introducing uncertainty into estate planning, allowing reformation of a will upon a clear and convincing showing of a mistake in expression and the testator's actual and specific intent helps ensure that the testator's affairs are settled as intended. And . . . adoption of the doctrine will not diminish the principles of law that encourage the preparation of well-drafted, properly executed wills. "Precisely because the reformation doctrine is a rule of litigation, no draftsman would plan to rely on it when proper drafting can spare the expense and hazard of litigation." Langbein & Waggoner, supra, 130 U. Pa. L. Rev. at 587. . . .

Finally, allowing reformation in these circumstances is consistent with the Legislature's efforts to apply the same rules of construction to all donative documents, see Prob. Code §§ 21101 et seq., and will promote fairness in the treatment of estates, regardless of the tools used for estate planning. . . . [A]llowing reformation of trusts and other instruments, but never of wills, appears to favor those with the means to establish estate plans that avoid probate proceedings, and to deny a remedy with respect to the estates of individuals who effect their plans through traditional testamentary documents. Denying reformation in these circumstances seems particularly harsh with respect to individuals who write wills without the assistance of counsel, and are more likely to overlook flaws in the expression of their intent.

As the Radins note, to date only a few states allow reformation of wills. However, both the Restatement Third of Property and the Uniform Probate Code now support the remedy. The Restatement's reformation provision appeared in the tentative draft of March 1995, and in the final draft issued in 2003. The Uniform Probate Code's provision authorizing the reformation of wills was added in 2008, and five states have adopted that provision. In addition, Washington, which has not adopted the Uniform Probate Code, has provided by statute that an unambiguous will "may be reformed . . . to conform the terms to the intention of the testator" upon clear and convincing evidence of a mistake. Wash. Rev. Code § 11.96A.125 (2011). [In 2013, South Carolina adopted a similar statute. S.C. Code Ann. § 62-2-601.—Eds.] In Connecticut, extrinsic evidence is admissible to prove a scrivener's error in a will, and a correction will be

---

8. These issues are decided by the court; there generally is no right [in California] to a jury trial in a will contest. Prob. Code § 825.

made upon a clear and convincing showing of error. Erickson v. Erickson, 716 A.2d 92 (Conn. 1998). Courts in New York and New Jersey have also applied a more liberal approach to correcting flaws in wills. In re Herceg, 747 N.Y.S.2d 901 (Surr. 2002); Engle v. Siegel, 377 A.2d 892 (N.J. 1977). . . .

> ### The charities have articulated a valid theory that will support reformation if established by clear and convincing evidence

COH and JNF contend that Irving actually intended at the time he wrote his will to provide that his estate would pass to COH and JNF in the event Beatrice was not alive to inherit his estate when he died, but that his intent was inartfully expressed in his will and thus there is a mistake in the will that should be reformed to reflect his intent when the will was drafted. Their contention, if proved by clear and convincing evidence, would support reformation of the will to reflect Irving's actual intent. . . .

[T]he alleged mistake concerns Irving's actual intent at the time he wrote the will. . . . [R]eformation of a document that is subject to the statute of frauds or the statute of wills entails the enforcement of the written document in a manner that reflects what was intended when the document was prepared. If Irving's only intent at the time he wrote his will was to address the disposition of his estate in the circumstances in which he died before Beatrice or they died simultaneously, his will accurately reflects his intent. In that circumstance, his mistake, if any, would be in failing subsequently to modify the will after Beatrice died, and that mistake would not be related to the will he wrote and that COH and JNF seek to have reformed. . . .

CONCLUSION

We hold that an unambiguous will may be reformed to conform to the testator's intent if clear and convincing evidence establishes that the will contains a mistake in the testator's expression of intent at the time the will was drafted, and also establishes the testator's actual specific intent at the time the will was drafted. We reverse the judgment of the Court of Appeal and remand the matter to the Court of Appeal with directions to remand the case to the trial court for its consideration of extrinsic evidence as authorized by our opinion.

NOTES

1. Proving Mistake and Actual Intent.   Reformation of a will under *Duke*, UPC § 2-805, page 341, and the Restatement (Third) of Property requires clear and convincing evidence of a mistake in rendering the testator's actual intent at the time of the making of the will.[9] The court in *Duke* differentiated a mistake in rendering the testator's "actual intent at the time he wrote the will" from a "mistake . . . in failing subsequently to modify the will" to account for a subsequent change in that intent. Professors Langbein and Waggoner put the point thus: "The specter looms of the

---

9. *See* Restatement (Third) of Property: Wills and Other Donative Transfers § 12.1 (Am. Law Inst. 2003).

reformation doctrine leading the courts into just that quagmire that the Wills Act has been designed to fence off, claims based on putative intent ('if only my aunt had known how much I loved her, she'd have left me more')."[10] Is this a meaningful distinction that courts can police reliably?

Does the holographic nature of the will at issue in *Duke* complicate proving a mistaken rendering of the testator's actual intent at the time of the making of the will? Consider again *Gibbs*, *Arnheiter*, *Cole*, and *Mahoney*, each of which involved a will drafted by a lawyer. What result in each of those cases if reformation had been available?

2. Clear and Convincing Evidence. The Restatement (Third) of Property explains the rationale for requiring clear and convincing evidence thus:

> The higher standard of proof . . . imposes a greater risk of an erroneous factual determination on the party seeking reformation than on the party opposing reformation. Tilting the risk of an erroneous factual determination in this fashion is appropriate because the party seeking reformation is seeking to establish that a donative document does not reflect the donor's intention. This tilt also deters a potential plaintiff from bringing a reformation suit on the basis of insubstantial evidence.[11]

The Restatement distinguishes between using extrinsic evidence to resolve an ambiguity versus to reform a mistake, and justifies applying a different standard of proof to each, as follows:

> A document that is unambiguous is entitled to a strong (but not irrebuttable) presumption of correctness, that is, to a strong presumption that it accurately expresses the donor's intention. An unambiguous document may be reformed, but to do so takes a showing *by clear and convincing evidence* that the donor's intention differed from the terms of the document.
>
> An ambiguous document is not entitled to a presumption of correctness because the ambiguity establishes that the document does not adequately express the donor's intention. Consequently, in a construction suit to resolve ambiguities . . . , the donor's intention need only be established by a *preponderance of the evidence*.[12]

3. The Contrary View. In Flannery v. McNamara, 738 N.E.2d 739 (Mass. 2000), a majority of the Massachusetts Supreme Judicial Court declined to "join, what the Restatement terms, 'the minority but growing view,' under which mistaken wills can be reformed." The court continued:

> [T]he reformation of a will, which would dispose of estate property based on unattested testamentary language, would violate the Statute of Wills. Strong policy reasons also militate against the requested reformation. To allow for reformation in

---

10. Langbein & Waggoner, *supra* note 6, at 584.

11. Restatement (Third) of Property: Wills and Other Donative Transfers § 12.1 cmt. e (Am. Law Inst. 2003).

12. Id. § 10.2 cmt. i; *see also* Wayne M. Gazur, Coming to Terms with the Uniform Probate Code's Reformation of Wills, 64 S.C. L. Rev. 403, 414-17 (2012).

this case would open the floodgates of litigation and lead to untold confusion in the probate of wills. It would essentially invite disgruntled individuals excluded from a will to demonstrate extrinsic evidence of the decedent's "intent" to include them. The number of groundless will contests could soar. We disagree that employing "full, clear and decisive proof" as the standard for reformation of wills would suffice to remedy such problems. Judicial resources are simply too scarce to squander on such consequences.

Not all of the justices agreed with this analysis. In a concurring opinion, two of the justices said:

> The most common argument against reformation is the one adopted by the court that allowance of the remedy would open the floodgates to "invite disgruntled individuals excluded from a will to demonstrate extrinsic evidence of the decedent's 'intent' to include them." There is a short and complete answer that discloses the speciousness of this statement. That answer, given by the Restatement, is that reformation is not available, as matter of law, to an individual claiming that he is the true object of the testator's bounty, because the will states the testator's intent accurately, and the testator's mistake, if one occurred at all, was his own subsequent failure to execute a codicil or new will to carry out his new intent.

4. Inter Vivos Trusts and the Uniform Trust Code. As noted by the court in *Duke*, reformation has long been available to correct mistakes in inter vivos trusts, deeds of gift, and other nonprobate transfers. A peculiar consequence of the no reformation rule, therefore, is that a *testamentary* trust cannot be reformed but an identical *inter vivos* trust with the same mistake can be, and this is true even after the settlor is dead. Is this distinction sound? Is it required by the Wills Act?

Uniform Trust Code (UTC) § 415 (2000), adopted by a majority of states, authorizes reformation for mistake in a trust, including testamentary trusts.[13] In a state such as Massachusetts, in which the courts adhere to the no reformation rule for wills but the legislature has adopted UTC § 415 for trusts,[14] by statute a mistake in a testamentary trust may be reformed but by case law a mistake in an outright devise may not be. Is there a sound basis for this distinction?

5. Malpractice Liability for Mistake. The will in *Duke* was a holograph written by the testator. But the wills in *Gibbs*, *Arnheiter*, *Cole*, and *Mahoney* were drafted by lawyers. Under Simpson v. Calivas, page 52, could the testators' intended beneficiaries sue the lawyers for malpractice? Professor Langbein argues that malpractice liability is an inadequate substitute for reformation:

> Malpractice liability does nothing about the cases in which lawyers are not involved or not culpable. When there is a lawyer to sue, he or she may be wholly or partially judgment-proof — for example, when the lawyer is uninsured or underinsured. For devises of unique property, such as the family home or the family Bible, relief in

---

13. *See, e.g.*, Megiel-Rollo v. Megiel, 162 So. 3d 1088, 1090 (Fla. App. 2015) (inter vivos trust, after settlor's death); In re Trust of O'Donnell, 815 N.W.2d 640 (Neb. App. 2012) (testamentary trust).

14. Mass. Gen. Laws Ann. ch. 203E, § 415 (2016).

"What do you mean, 'Have your lawyer call my lawyer'?. . .
you are my lawyer!"
Robert Mankoff/The New Yorker Collection/The Cartoon Bank

damages cannot be adequate. Most importantly, what is wrong with the malpractice solution is that, by transforming the mistake claim into tort, it neglects the unjust enrichment intrinsic to mistake cases. . . . Because the mistaken devisee has no claim of entitlement, he or she is unjustly enriched. The malpractice solution leaves the unjust enrichment unremedied and instead creates a needless loss to be charged against the drafter. The mistake remedies (harmless error, reformation) respond to the simple truth that preventing loss is better than compensating loss.[15]

Should a lawyer who drafts a mistaken will be liable in malpractice for the costs incurred in litigation to reform the will?[16] In the absence of reformation, could the unjust enrichment of the mistaken takers be prevented in an action for restitution by way of constructive trust brought by the intended beneficiaries?[17]

6. Reformation (and Modification) for Tax Advantage. Many courts today are inclined to grant a petition to reform a will or other donative instrument to correct a mistake or oversight in drafting that would prevent a tax advantage sought by the donor. Courts also commonly modify an instrument to achieve a subsequent tax savings that is consistent with the donor's probable intent. This practice is codified by UPC § 2-806 (2008) and UTC § 416 (2000) and is endorsed by the Restatement (Third)

---

15. John H. Langbein, Curing Execution Errors and Mistaken Terms in Wills, 18 Prob. & Prop. 28, 31 (2004).

16. *See* Carlson v. Sweeney, Dabagia, Donoghue, Thorne, Janes & Pagos, 895 N.E.2d 1191 (Ind. 2008) (allowing claim against drafting lawyer for costs incurred in successful reformation action).

17. *See* Victoria J. Haneman, Changing the Estate Planning Malpractice Landscape: Applying the Constructive Trust to Cure Testamentary Mistake, 80 UMKC L. Rev. 91 (2011).

of Property.[18] We take further notice of reformation and modification of trusts for tax reasons in Chapter 10 at page 742.

B. DEATH OF BENEFICIARY BEFORE DEATH OF TESTATOR

Even if a will is unambiguous and its terms are unaffected by mistake, the gap in time between its execution and the testator's death may cause interpretive difficulties. During this gap, which may span years or even decades, circumstances can change in ways that render the will stale or obsolete.[19] We have already seen one *stale will* doctrine: the rule that revokes a bequest to a spouse on divorce (see page 239). In this section, we consider the rules that apply if a named beneficiary predeceases the testator. In the next section, we consider the rules that deal with changes in the testator's property. In both circumstances, if the testator's actual intent is not evident, the court will apply rules of construction that are meant to implement the probable intent of the typical testator.

1. Lapsed and Void Devises

If a devisee does not survive the testator, the devise fails and is said to have *lapsed*. The common law rule is that a gift made by will is subject to a condition that the devisee survive the testator, unless the testator specifies otherwise. Nearly all states, however, have enacted *antilapse statutes* that, under certain circumstances, substitute another beneficiary for the predeceased devisee.[20] Before examining those statutes, it is important to get a firm hold on the common law default rules for lapsed devises. These rules apply if the will does not provide otherwise and an antilapse statute is not applicable.

(a) Specific or General Devise. If a specific or general devise lapses, the devise falls into the residue. Thus:

> *Case 1.* T's will devises her watch (a specific devise) to A, $10,000 (a general devise) to B, and the rest of her estate (the residuary devise) to C. A and B predecease T. Under the common law, the watch and the $10,000 fall into the residue and go to C.

(b) Residuary Devise. If the residuary devise lapses, the heirs of the testator take by intestacy. Thus, in Case 1 above, if C had predeceased T, the residue would lapse and pass by intestacy. If only a share of the residue lapses, such as when one of two residuary

---

18. *See* Restatement (Third) of Property: Wills and Other Donative Transfers § 12.2 (Am. Law Inst. 2003).

19. *See* Adam J. Hirsch, Text and Time: A Theory of Testamentary Obsolescence, 86 Wash. U. L. Rev. 609 (2009); *see also* David Horton, Wills Law on the Ground, 62 UCLA L. Rev. 1094, 1129-30 (2015) (finding that two-thirds of wills probated in 2007 in Alameda County, California had been executed more than 1,000 days before the testator's death).

20. For critical surveys of lapse and antilapse, see Eloisa C. Rodriguez-Dod, "I'm Not Quite Dead Yet!": Rethinking the Anti-Lapse Redistribution of a Dead Beneficiary's Gift, 61 Clev. St. L. Rev. 1017 (2013); Richard F. Storrow, Wills and Survival, 34 Quinnipiac L. Rev. 447 (2016).

devisees predeceases the testator, at common law the lapsed share passes by intestacy to the testator's heirs rather than to the remaining residuary devisees. Thus:

> *Case 2.* After making several specific and general devises to various persons, *T* devises the residue of her estate one-half to *A* and one-half to *B*. *A* predeceases *T*. *A*'s one-half share goes to *T*'s heirs by intestacy, not to *B*.

The *no-residue-of-a-residue* rule, followed in In re Estate of Russell, excerpted below, was probably laid down by English courts to protect the interests of the primogenitary heir. Today only a small number of states still follow the rule.[21] The vast majority of states have rejected the rule, as does UPC § 2-604(b) (1990, rev. 2002). The reasoning of the majority is that, in the circumstances of Case 2, *T* would have probably preferred *B* to take *T*'s entire estate rather than for *B* to take half with the other half passing by intestacy to *T*'s heirs.[22] This assumption is consistent with the typical practice in professionally drafted wills of providing that the share of a predeceasing residuary beneficiary passes to the other residuary takers.[23]

(c) Class Gift. If a devise is to a class of persons, and one member of the class predeceases the testator, the surviving members of the class divide the gift. Thus:

> *Case 3.* *T* devises $10,000 to the children of *A* (a class gift). One child of *A*, *B*, predeceases *T*. At *T*'s death, *T* is survived by another child of *A*, *C*. Because this is a class gift, *C* takes the entire $10,000.

Much turns, therefore, on whether a gift to a group of persons is a class gift, a question we take up later in this section at page 368.

(d) Void Devise. If a devisee is already dead at the time the will is executed, or the devisee is a dog or cat or some other ineligible taker, the devise is *void*. The same rules that apply to a lapsed devise also apply to a void devise.

In re Estate of Russell
444 P.2d 353 (Cal. 1968)

SULLIVAN, J. Georgia Nan Russell Hembree appeals from a judgment (Prob. Code, § 1240[24]) entered in proceedings for the determination of heirship decreeing inter alia that under the terms of the will of Thelma L. Russell, deceased, all of the residue of her estate should be distributed to Chester H. Quinn.

Thelma L. Russell died testate on September 8, 1965, leaving a validly executed holographic will written on a small card. The front of the card reads:

---

21. *See, e.g.*, In re Estate of McFarland, 167 S.W.3d 299 (Tenn. 2005) (retaining the rule by 3 to 2 vote).

22. *See* Restatement (Third) of Property: Wills and Other Donative Transfers § 5.5 cmt. o (Am. Law Inst. 1999).

23. *See, e.g.,* Northern Trust, Will & Trust Forms 111-4 (2004) ("Any gift under this article which fails for lack of a beneficiary shall augment proportionately the remaining gifts under this article.").

24. Hereafter unless otherwise indicated all section references are to the Probate Code.

Turn
the card   March 18-1957
I leave everything
I own Real &
Personal to Chester
H. Quinn & Roxy Russell
Thelma L. Russell

The reverse side reads:

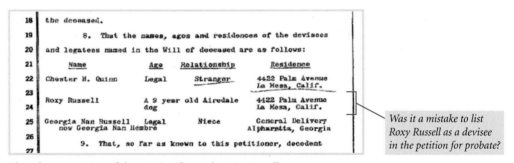

The front of Thelma L. Russell's holographic will

My ($10.) Ten dollar gold
Piece & diamonds I leave
to Georgia Nan Russell.
Alverata, Geogia [sic]

Chester H. Quinn was a close friend and companion of testatrix, who for over 25 years prior to her death had resided in one of the living units on her property and had stood in a relation of personal trust and confidence toward her. Roxy Russell was testatrix' pet dog which was alive on the date of the execution of testatrix' will but predeceased her.[25] Plaintiff is testatrix' niece and her only heir-at-law.

In her petition for determination of heirship plaintiff alleges, inter alia, that "Roxy Russell is an Airedale dog";[26] that section 27 enumerates those entitled to take by will; that "Dogs are not included among those listed in . . . Section 27. Not even Airedale dogs"; that the gift of one-half of the residue of testatrix' estate to Roxy

18	the deceased.
19	8. That the names, ages and residences of the devisees
20	and legatees named in the Will of deceased are as follows:
21	
22	Name	Age	Relationship	Residence
	Chester H. Quinn	Legal	Stranger	4422 Palm Avenue La Mesa, Calif.
23	
24	Roxy Russell	A 9 year old Airedale dog		4422 Palm Avenue La Mesa, Calif.
25	Georgia Nan Russell now Georgia Nan Hembre	Legal	Niece	General Delivery Alpharetta, Georgia
26	
27	9. That, so far as known to this petitioner, decedent

Was it a mistake to list Roxy Russell as a devisee in the petition for probate?

The relevant portion of the petition for probate in *Russell*

25. The record indicates the existence of two Roxy Russells. The original Roxy was an Airedale dog which testatrix owned at the time she made her will, but which, according to Quinn, died after having had a fox tail removed from its nose, and which, according to the testimony of one Arthur Turner, owner of a pet cemetery, was buried on June 9, 1958. Roxy was replaced with another dog (breed not indicated in the record before us) which, although it answered to the name Roxy, was according to the record, in fact registered with the American Kennel Club as "Russel's [sic] Royal Kick Roxy."

26. In his "Petition for Probate of Holographic Will and for Letters of Administration with the Will Annexed," [reproduced above,] Quinn included under the names, ages, and residences of the devisees and legatees of testatrix the following: "Roxy Russell, A 9 year old Airedale dog, [residing at] 4422 Palm Avenue, La Mesa, Calif." [Is this correct? Since the will was executed when the first Roxy was alive, isn't the second Roxy a pretermitted Airedale? — Eds.]

Russell is invalid and void; and that plaintiff was entitled to such one-half as testatrix' sole heir-at-law.

At the hearing on the petition, plaintiff introduced without objection extrinsic evidence establishing that Roxy Russell was testatrix' Airedale dog which died on June 9, 1958. To this end plaintiff, in addition to an independent witness, called defendant pursuant to former Code of Civil Procedure section 2055 (now Evid. Code, § 776). Upon redirect examination, counsel for Quinn then sought to introduce evidence of the latter's relationship with testatrix "in the event that your Honor feels that there is any necessity for further ascertainment of the intent above and beyond the document." Plaintiff's objections on the ground that it was inadmissible under the statute of wills and the parol evidence rule "because there is no ambiguity" and that it was inadmissible under section 105, were overruled. Over plaintiff's objection, counsel for Quinn also introduced certain documentary evidence consisting of testatrix' address book and a certain quitclaim deed "for the purpose of demonstrating the intention on the part of the deceased that she not die intestate." Of all this extrinsic evidence only the following infinitesimal portion of Quinn's testimony relates to care of the dog: "Q [Counsel for Quinn] Prior to the first Roxy's death did you ever discuss with Miss Russell taking care of Roxy if anything should ever happen to her? A Yes." Plaintiff carefully preserved an objection running to all of the above line of testimony and at the conclusion of the hearing moved to strike such evidence. Her motion was denied.

The trial court found, so far as is here material, that it was the intention of testatrix "that Chester H. Quinn was to receive her entire estate, excepting the gold coin and diamonds bequeathed to" plaintiff and that Quinn "was to care for the dog, Roxy Russell, in the event of Testatrix's death. The language contained in the Will, concerning the dog, Roxy Russell, was precatory in nature only, and merely indicative of the wish, desire and concern of Testatrix that Chester H. Quinn was to care for the dog, Roxy Russell, subsequent to Testatrix's death."[27] The court concluded that testatrix intended

---

27. The memorandum decision elaborates on this point, stating in part: "The obvious concern of the human who loves her pet is to see that it is properly cared for by someone who may be trusted to honor that concern and through resources the person may make available in the will to carry out this entreaty, desire, wish, recommendation or prayer. This, in other words, is a most logical example of a precatory provision. It is the only logical conclusion one can come to which would not do violence to the apparent intent of Mrs. Russell."

The trial court found further: "Testatrix intended that Georgia Nan Russell Hembree was not to have any other real or personal property belonging to Testatrix, other than the gold coin and diamonds." This finding also was elaborated on in the memorandum decision: "In making the will it is apparent she had Georgia on her mind. While there is other evidence in the case about Thelma Russell's frame of mind concerning her real property and her niece, which was admitted by the Court, over counsel's vigorous objection, because it concerned testatrix' frame of mind, a condition relevant to the material issue of intent, nevertheless this additional evidence was not necessary to this Court in reaching its conclusion." The additional evidence referred to included an address book of testatrix upon which she had written: "Chester, Don't let Augusta and Georgia have one penny of my place if it takes it all to fight it in Court. Thelma."

to and did make an absolute and outright gift to Mr. Quinn of all the residue of her estate, adding:

> There occurred no lapse as to any portion of the residuary gift to Chester H. Quinn by reason of the language contained in the Will concerning the dog, Roxy Russell, such language not having the effect of being an attempted outright gift or gift in trust to the dog. The effect of such language is merely to indicate the intention of Testatrix that Chester H. Quinn was to take the entire residuary estate and to use whatever portion thereof as might be necessary to care for and maintain the dog, Roxy Russell.[28]

Judgment was entered accordingly. This appeal followed.

Plaintiff's position before us may be summarized thusly: That the gift of one-half of the residue of the estate to testatrix' dog was clear and unambiguous; that such gift was void and the property subject thereof passed to plaintiff under the laws of intestate succession; and that the court erred in admitting the extrinsic evidence offered by Quinn but that in any event the uncontradicted evidence in the record did not cure the invalidity of the gift. . . .

[W]e think it is self-evident that in the interpretation of a will, a court cannot determine whether the terms of the will are clear and definite in the first place until it considers the circumstances under which the will was made so that the judge may be placed in the position of the testator whose language he is interpreting. . . . Failure to enter upon such an inquiry is failure to recognize that the "ordinary standard or 'plain meaning,' is simply the meaning of the people who did *not* write the document." (9 Wigmore on Evidence § 2462 (3d ed. 1940).) . . .

[E]xtrinsic evidence of the circumstances under which a will is made (except evidence expressly excluded by statute) may be considered by the court in ascertaining what the testator meant by the words used in the will. If in the light of such extrinsic evidence, the provisions of the will are reasonably susceptible of two or more meanings claimed to have been intended by the testator, "an uncertainty arises upon the face of a will" (§ 105) and extrinsic evidence relevant to prove any of such meanings is admissible. . . . If, on the other hand, in the light of such extrinsic evidence, the provisions of the will are not reasonably susceptible of two or more meanings, there is no uncertainty arising upon the face of the will . . . and any proffered evidence attempting to show an intention *different* from that expressed by the words therein, giving them the only meaning to which they are reasonably susceptible, is inadmissible. . . .

Examining testatrix' will in the light of the foregoing rules, we arrive at the following conclusions: Extrinsic evidence offered by plaintiff was admitted without objection and indeed would have been properly admitted over objection to raise and resolve the latent ambiguity as to Roxy Russell and ultimately to establish that Roxy Russell was a dog. Extrinsic evidence of the surrounding circumstances was properly considered in

---

28. The trial court also said: "To ascribe to her the belief that her dog could acquire real property with all the rights and obligations incident to ownership is to describe a person who would probably be incompetent to make a will at all. There is no other evidence of incompetency and certainly incompetency is not presumed." — Eds.

order to ascertain what testatrix meant by the words of the will, including the words: "I leave everything I own Real & Personal to Chester H. Quinn & Roxy Russell" or as those words can now be read "to Chester H. Quinn and my dog Roxy Russell."

However, viewing the will in the light of the surrounding circumstances as are disclosed by the record, we conclude that the will cannot reasonably be construed as urged by Quinn and determined by the trial court as providing that testatrix intended to make an absolute and outright gift of the entire residue of her estate to Quinn who was "to use whatever portion thereof as might be necessary to care for and maintain the dog." No words of the will give the entire residuum to Quinn, much less indicate that the provision for the dog is merely precatory in nature. Such an interpretation is not consistent with a disposition which by its language leaves the residuum in equal shares to Quinn and the dog.[29] A disposition in equal shares to two beneficiaries cannot be equated with a disposition of the whole to one of them who may use "whatever portion thereof as might be necessary" on behalf of the other. . . .

Accordingly, since in the light of the extrinsic evidence introduced below, the terms of the will are not reasonably susceptible of the meaning claimed by Quinn to have been intended by testatrix, the extrinsic evidence offered to show such an intention should have been excluded by the trial court. Upon an independent examination of the will we conclude that the trial court's interpretation of the terms thereof was erroneous. Interpreting the provisions relating to testatrix' residuary estate in accordance with the only meaning to which they are reasonably susceptible, we conclude that testatrix intended to make a disposition of all of the residue of the estate to Quinn and the dog in equal shares; therefore, as tenants in common. As a dog cannot be the beneficiary under a will the attempted gift to Roxy Russell is void.[30]

There remains only the necessity of determining the effect of the void gift to the dog upon the disposition of the residuary estate. That portion of any residuary estate that is the subject of a lapsed gift to one of the residuary beneficiaries remains undisposed of by the will and passes to the heirs-at-law (§§ 92, 220). The rule is equally applicable with respect to a void gift to one of the residuary beneficiaries (§ 220). Therefore, notwithstanding testatrix' expressed intention to limit the extent of her gift by will to plaintiff one-half of the residuary estate passes to plaintiff as testatrix' only heir-at-law (§ 225). We conclude that the residue of testatrix' estate should be distributed in equal shares to Chester H. Quinn and Georgia Nan Russell Hembree, testatrix' niece.

The judgment is reversed. . . .

NOTES

1. *The No-Residue-of-a-Residue Rule.*   The no-residue-of-a-residue rule (see page 352), which was not attacked by Chester's counsel or questioned by the court, necess-

---

29. Is this a fair paraphrasing of the will? Did Thelma Russell write "in equal shares"? —Eds.

30. As a consequence, the fact that Roxy Russell predeceased the testatrix is of no legal import. As appears, we have disposed of the issue raised by plaintiff's frontal attack on the eligibility of the dog to take a testamentary gift and therefore need not concern ourselves with the novel question as to whether the death of the dog during the lifetime of the testatrix resulted in a lapsed gift. (§ 92.)

itated the litigation to resolve whether Thelma meant a gift to Chester alone or to Chester and Roxy. If the rule had not been applicable, as in the vast majority of states and under UPC § 2-604(b), Chester would have taken the entire residuary estate.

2. Ambiguity and Extrinsic Evidence.   The decision in *Russell*, cited in In re Estate of Duke, page 342, is often cited for its abrogation of the no extrinsic evidence rule. The court held that extrinsic evidence should be admitted "so that the judge may be placed in the position of the testator whose language he is interpreting." Only then can the judge determine whether "the terms of the will are clear and definite." So the extrinsic evidence showing that Roxy Russell was a dog, an ineligible taker under a will, was properly admitted. (We consider trusts for pet animals in Chapter 6 at page 422.)

But after admitting this evidence, the court held that the only reasonable construction of the will was a gift of the residue "in equal shares to Quinn and the dog." Is it plausible that Thelma Russell envisioned Chester and Roxy as co-owners of her rental units? Why was the will not "reasonably susceptible" to a construction giving Quinn the entire residue and imposing on him a precatory request to take care of the dog? Isn't this more likely and more consistent with the evidence that Russell did not want to die intestate and did not want Georgia, her heir, to take anything other than her gold coin and diamonds? Should the court have read Russell's address book notation not to "let Augusta and Georgia have one penny of my place" as a negative will (see page 89)?

2. Antilapse Statutes

Now let us turn to the effect of an antilapse statute upon a lapsed gift. In a sense, antilapse statutes are misnamed. They do not prevent a lapse; rather, they substitute other beneficiaries, usually the dead beneficiary's descendants, if certain requirements are met. A typical antilapse statute, such as UPC § 2-605 (1969), excerpted below, provides that if a predeceased devisee is related to the testator in a prescribed way and is survived by one or more descendants who also survive the testator, those descendants are substituted for the predeceased devisee.

Uniform Probate Code (Unif. Law Comm'n 1969)

§ 2-605. Antilapse; Deceased Devisee; Class Gifts

If a devisee who is a grandparent or a lineal descendant of a grandparent of the testator is dead at the time of execution of the will, fails to survive the testator, or is treated as if he predeceased the testator, the issue of the deceased devisee who survive the testator by 120 hours take in place of the deceased devisee and if they are all of the same degree of kinship to the devisee they take equally, but if of unequal degree then those of more remote degree take by representation. One who would have been a devisee under a class gift if he had survived the testator is treated as a devisee for purposes of this section whether his death occurred before or after the execution of the will.

a. Presumed Intent

The theory behind the antilapse statutes is one of *presumed intent*. The idea is that, for certain predeceasing devisees, the testator would prefer a substitute gift to the devisee's descendants rather than for the gift to pass in accordance with the common law of lapse. Thus:

> *Case 4.* T devises her entire estate "one-half to my son *A* and one-half to my daughter *B*." *B* predeceases *T*, leaving a child, *C* (see Figure 5.1). At *T*'s death, what happens to *B*'s share? At common law, it would lapse and, being a residuary devise, would pass by intestacy, one-half to *A* and one-half to *C*. So *A* would take three-quarters of *T*'s estate and *C* would take one-quarter. If the no-residue-of-a-residue rule does not apply, *B*'s share would go to *A*, leaving *A* with the entire estate and *C* with nothing. If an antilapse statute applies, *B*'s share would pass to *C*, leaving *A* with one-half and *C* with one-half. Antilapse statutes rest on the assumption that *T* would prefer a substitute gift to *C* than for *B*'s share to pass by intestacy or to *A*.

Figure 5.1

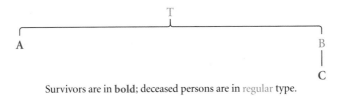

Survivors are in **bold**; deceased persons are in regular type.

b. Scope

An antilapse statute applies to a lapsed devise *only* if the devisee bears the particular relationship to the testator specified in the statute. Some statutes apply to descendants of the testator. Others are broader, applying to descendants of the testator's parents or grandparents, or to all kindred of the testator, and occasionally to kindred of the testator's spouse as well. In a few states, the statute applies to all devisees, whether a relative of the testator or not. The antilapse statute in the 1969 UPC, excerpted on page 357, applies to a devise to a grandparent or a lineal descendant of a grandparent. The 1990 UPC adds a devise to a stepchild. Thus:

> *Case 5.* T devises her home to her niece, *B*, and the residue of her estate to *A*. *B* predeceases *T*, leaving a child, *C*, who survives *T* (see Figure 5.2). Under the UPC antilapse statute, *C* takes *T*'s home because *B* is a descendant of *T*'s grandparent. If the antilapse statute applies only to *T*'s descendants, *C* does not take *T*'s home. The lapsed devise falls into the residue given to *A*.

Figure 5.2

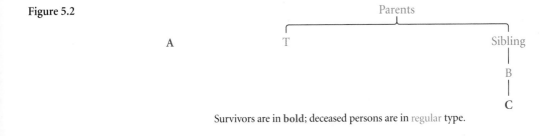

Survivors are in **bold**; deceased persons are in regular type.

Experience suggests that most antilapse statutes are too narrowly drawn.[31] What do you think? Would the typical testator want descendants to be substituted for a predeceasing devisee in every case? And why substitute *descendants* only? Why not substitute *heirs*, including a spouse?

c. Default Rules

Because the antilapse statutes are designed to implement presumed intent, they prescribe default rules that yield to an expression of the testator's actual intent that is contrary to the statute. Thus:

> *Case 6.* *T* devises her entire estate "one-half to my son *A* and one-half to my daughter *B*, but if *A* or *B* or both do not survive me, then I give such predeceasing child's share to my friend *F*." *B* predeceases *T*, leaving a child, *C* (see Figure 5.3). At *T*'s death, *T*'s estate will pass one-half to *A* and one-half to *F*. The antilapse statute does not apply to *B*'s share, because *T* has provided expressly for the possibility of *B* predeceasing *T*.

Figure 5.3

Survivors are in **bold**; deceased persons are in regular type.

In Case 6, the testator's intent contrary to the antilapse statute is stated expressly and is confirmed by the alternative devise to *F*. If a will is not as clear, courts may struggle with the question of whether it imposes a condition of survival that precludes application of the antilapse statute. Thus:

> *Case 7.* *T* devises her estate "to my living brothers and sisters, *A*, *B*, *C*, *D*, and *E*, to share and share alike." *A*, *B*, and *C* predecease *T*, each leaving descendants (per Figure 5.4 on page 360, *F*, *G*, and *H* respectively). *T* dies. Do the descendants of *A*, *B*, and *C* take the respective shares of each? The question is whether the terms "living" and "share and share alike" express a condition of survival contrary to the antilapse statute. In Allen v. Talley, 949 S.W.2d 59 (Tex. App. 1997), the court held that this language precluded application of the antilapse statute. The surviving siblings, *D* and *E*, take the entire estate. The court in In re Estate of Raymond, 764 N.W.2d 1 (Mich. 2009), likewise held that a devise "to my brothers and sisters that survive me" imposed a condition of survival precluding the antilapse statute.

---

31. *See* Susan F. French, Antilapse Statutes Are Blunt Instruments: A Blueprint for Reform, 37 Hastings L.J. 335 (1985).

Figure 5.4

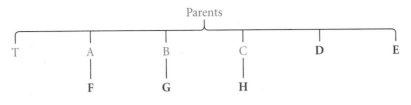

Survivors are in **bold**; deceased persons are in regular type.

Case 8. Same facts as in Case 7, except the will does not include the term "living." What result? The issue is whether the term "share and share alike," by itself, precludes application of the antilapse statute. In Belardo v. Belardo, 930 N.E.2d 862 (Ohio App. 2010), the court applied the antilapse statute, reasoning that "share and share alike" did not impose a requirement of survival. *D* and *E* each take one-fifth, and the three one-fifth shares of the estate that would have gone to the deceased siblings, *A*, *B*, and *C*, pass to their respective descendants (in Figure 5.4, *F*, *G*, and *H* respectively).

d. Words of Survivorship

UPC § 2-603(b)(3) (1990, rev. 2008) introduces an additional complexity. It provides that "words of survivorship, such as in a devise to an individual 'if he survives me,' or in a devise to 'my surviving children,' are not, in the absence of additional evidence, a sufficient indication of an intent contrary to the application of this section."[32] Thus:

Case 9. *T* devises Blackacre "to my son Sidney, if he survives me," and devises the residue of his estate to his wife, Wilma. Sidney dies in his father's lifetime, leaving a daughter, Debby. *T* is survived by Wilma and Debby. Who takes Blackacre, Wilma or Debby? The issue is whether the words "if he survives me" impose a condition of survivorship. The majority of cases have held that an express requirement of survivorship, such as "if he survives me," precludes the antilapse statute. Under UPC § 2-603(b)(3), however, the term "if he survives me" is not enough to impose a condition of survivorship, and the antilapse statute applies nonetheless, substituting Debby for her father.

The comment to UPC § 2-603 explains the rationale for reversing the majority rule that words of survivorship establish an intention contrary to the antilapse statute:

The argument [for the majority rule] is that attaching words of survivorship indicates that the testator thought about the matter and intentionally did not provide a substitute gift to the devisee's descendants. At best, this is an inference only, which may or may not accurately reflect the testator's actual intention. An equally plausible inference is that the words of survivorship are in the testator's will merely because the testator's lawyer used a will form with words of survivorship.

---

32. The UPC includes a similar provision in its antilapse rule for trusts, § 2-707, discussed in Chapter 13 at page 865.

The Restatement (Third) of Property amplifies on this reasoning as follows:

Because such a survival provision is often boiler-plate form-book language, the testator may not understand that such language could disinherit the line of descent headed by the deceased devisee. When the testator is older than the devisee and hence does not expect the devisee to die first, or if the devisee was childless when the will was executed, it seems especially unlikely that a provision requiring the devisee to survive the testator was intended to disinherit the devisee's descendants.... [C]ourts should be cautious in automatically concluding that survival language manifests a deliberate decision by the testator to disinherit the line of descent headed by a deceased devisee.... [T]he trier of fact should be especially reluctant to find that survival language manifests a contrary intent in cases in which the deceased devisee is one of the testator's children, or other direct descendant, and the effect of refusing to apply the antilapse statute would be to disinherit one or more grandchildren or great-grandchildren.[33]

UPC § 2-603(b)(3) has come under sharp criticism from commentators. Professor Mark Ascher writes:

Apparently, the revisers believe their own antilapse provisions are likely to reflect any particular testator's intent more faithfully than *the testator's own will*. This conclusion is not only pretentious, it disputes what should be obvious—that most testators expect *their wills* to dispose of their property *completely*—without interference from a statute of which they have never heard. Instead of allowing "if he survives me" to mean what almost everyone would expect it to mean, the revisers have translated it into, "if he survives me, and, if he does not survive me, to his issue who survive me." For those unfamiliar with estate planning esoterica, therefore, it has become yet more difficult to figure out what the words in a will actually mean. The uninitiated apparently have three options: hire a competent estate planner, go to law school, or curl up with *Alice in Wonderland*.[34]

The rule of UPC § 2-603(b)(3) has received a chilly reception in the state legislatures. It has been adopted in only seven states (Alaska, Colorado, Hawaii, Michigan, Montana, New Mexico, and North Dakota). At least five states (Arizona, Florida, Minnesota, Ohio,[35] and Utah) have modified their enactments of § 2-603 to preserve the majority rule. The Florida statute is illustrative: "Words of survivorship . . . , such as 'if he survives me,' or to 'my surviving children,' *are a sufficient indication* of an intent contrary to the application of" the antilapse statute.[36] And the two most populous states, California and Texas, have enacted statutes that codify the majority rule.[37]

---

33. Restatement (Third) of Property: Wills and Other Donative Transfers § 5.5 cmt. h (Am. Law Inst. 1999).

34. Mark L. Ascher, The 1990 Uniform Probate Code: Older and Better, or More Like the Internal Revenue Code?, 77 Minn. L. Rev. 639, 654-55 (1993).

35. The Ohio statute strikes an interesting balance. It says that "surviving" or "living" is not, by itself, enough to impose a condition of survivorship, but "to my child, if my child survives me," is enough. Ohio Rev. Code Ann. § 2107.52(C)(1)-(2) (2016).

36. Fla. Stat. Ann. § 732.603(3)(a) (2016) (emphasis added).

37. *See* Cal. Prob. Code § 21110(b) (2016); Tex. Est. Code Ann. § 255.151 (2016).

Other states that have adopted the 1990 UPC, such as Massachusetts, have dropped § 2-603 or have removed from it paragraph (b)(3).[38]

On the other hand, UPC § 2-603(b)(3), which is endorsed by the Restatement (Third) of Property, may nonetheless influence outcomes in states that have not adopted it.

Ruotolo v. Tietjen
890 A.2d 166 (Conn. App. 2006)

LAVERY, C.J. . . . [On March 1, 1990, John N. Swanson executed a will leaving one-half of the residue of his estate "to Hazel Brennan of Guilford, Connecticut, if she survives me." Hazel Brennan, the testator's stepdaughter, died on January 2, 2001, 17 days before the testator. The applicable antilapse statute, Conn. Gen. Stat. § 45a-441, provides as follows:

> When a devisee or legatee, being a child, stepchild, grandchild, brother or sister of the testator, dies before him, and no provision has been made in the will for such contingency, the issue of such devisee or legatee shall take the estate so devised or bequeathed.

Hazel Brennan's daughter, Kathleen Smaldone, sought to take Hazel's share under this statute. The lower court held that the testator's use of the term "if she survives me" provided for the contingency that Brennan might not survive the testator, precluding application of the antilapse statute.] We disagree and, accordingly, reverse the judgment of the Superior Court. . . .

HISTORY

At common law, when a named beneficiary under a will predeceased the testator, the share of the deceased beneficiary passed not to his descendants, but rather "lapsed." . . .

In 1783, the Massachusetts legislature enacted the first antilapse statute. . . . Today, antilapse statutes have been enacted in every state except Louisiana. . . .

Although varying in scope, all antilapse statutes provide that when a particular devisee predeceases the testator, the devise does not fall into the residue or pass to the testator's heirs by intestacy, but rather descends to the issue of the predeceased devisee. "Although . . . commonly called 'antilapse' statutes, the label is somewhat misleading. Contrary to what the label implies, antilapse statutes do not reverse the common-law rule of lapse because they do not abrogate the law-imposed condition of survivorship. . . . What the statutes actually do is modify the devolution of lapsed devises by providing a statutory substitute gift in the case of specified relatives." Edward C. Halbach, Jr. & Lawrence W. Waggoner, The UPC's New Survivorship and Antilapse Provisions, 55 Alb. L. Rev. 1091, 1101 (1992). . . .

---

38. *See* Mass. Gen. Laws Ann. ch. 190B, § 2-603 (2016).

OUR ANTILAPSE STATUTE

... The [Connecticut] antilapse statute today provides that "[w]hen a devisee or legatee, being a child, stepchild, grandchild, brother or sister of the testator, dies before him, and no provision has been made in the will for such contingency, the issue of such devisee or legatee shall take the estate so devised or bequeathed." § 45a-441. Other than adding siblings and stepchildren to the class of applicable devisees and legatees [in 1987], no substantive change has been made to our antilapse statute since [it was first enacted in] 1821....

Plainly, the purpose underlying our antilapse statute is the prevention of unintended disinheritance. Its passage reflects a legislative determination that, as a matter of public policy, when a testator fails to provide for the possibility that a particular beneficiary might predecease him, the lineal descendants of that beneficiary take the applicable share.[39] ...

Under Connecticut law, the antilapse statute applies unless a "provision has been made in the will for such contingency." A review of the antilapse statutes presently in effect in forty-eight other jurisdictions reveals that this language is unique to our statute. It is not disputed that the "contingency" referenced in § 45a-441 is the death of a devisee or legatee prior to that of the testator. What is contested is the proper construction of the "provision has been made in the will" language.

The appellees contend that inclusion of words of survivorship in a will constitutes a provision for such contingency, thereby rendering the antilapse statute inapplicable. Because the bequest in the present case contains the condition "if she survives me," they claim § 45a-441 is inoperative. That simple and seemingly persuasive argument fails, however, on closer examination....

[A]lthough the precise wording of the condition in our antilapse statute is unique, its existence is not. Like other states, Connecticut enacted its statute to counteract the harsh results of the common-law rule of lapse. Like other states, Connecticut conditioned operation of the antilapse statute on the intent of the testator as expressed in the will. Accordingly, the critical inquiry is whether an intent contrary to § 45a-441 is so manifested.

Our inquiry into whether words of survivorship evince a contrary intent sufficient to defeat the antilapse statute is guided by the following principles. Antilapse statutes "will apply unless testator's intention to exclude its operation is shown with reasonable certainty." 4 W. Bowe & D. Parker, Page on the Law of Wills (Rev. ed. 2005) § 50.11, at 96. Section 5.5 of the Restatement (Third) of Property, Wills and Other Donative Transfers (1999), addresses antilapse statutes. Comment (f) to that section provides in relevant part: "Antilapse statutes establish a strong rule of construction, designed to carry out presumed intention. They are based on the constructional preference against disinheriting a line of descent.... Consequently, these statutes should be given the widest possible sphere of operation and should be defeated only when the trier of fact

---

39. Is this "public policy" characterization of the antilapse statutes consistent with the principle of freedom of disposition? Is the basis for the antilapse statute a public policy preference for a substitute gift in the descendants of a predeceased devisee or a judgment about the probable intent of the typical testator in such circumstances? — Eds.

determines that the testator wanted to disinherit the line of descent headed by the deceased devisee." Hence, the burden is on those who seek to deny the statutory protection rather than on those who assert it.

Finally, we are mindful that our statute was enacted to *prevent* operation of the rule of lapse. Our statute is remedial in nature and must be liberally construed. Accordingly, we resolve any doubt in favor of the operation of § 45a-441.

The bequest at issue states, "one-half . . . of [the residue] property to Hazel Brennan of Guilford, Connecticut, *if she survives me*." (Emphasis added.) Our task is to determine the significance of those words of survivorship. While the present case is one of first impression in Connecticut, numerous other states have considered the question of whether words of survivorship, such as "if she survives me," demonstrate a contrary intent on the part of the testator sufficient to negate operation of the antilapse statute. . . .

OTHER AUTHORITY

Whether words of survivorship alone constitute sufficient evidence of a contrary intent on the part of the testator so as to prevent application of the antilapse statute is a question on which sibling authority is split. Some courts have concluded that words of survivorship demonstrate sufficient contrary intent. Illustrative of that line of cases is Bankers Trust Co. v. Allen, 135 N.W.2d 607 (Iowa 1965). In that case, the Supreme Court of Iowa stated: "The bequest to Mary in Item III is conditioned on her surviving the testator. We have held many times . . . that our antilapse statute . . . does not apply to a bequest so conditioned. . . . This is on the theory that a bequest to one 'if she survives me' manifests an intent that the bequest would lapse if the named beneficiary dies before the testator." Id. at 611.

Underlying that view is the presumption that the testator knowingly and deliberately included the words of survivorship. As one New York court explained: "[T]hese words were used by the testator in a will drawn by an experienced attorney. Some meaning must be attributed to them—and the meaning is clear—that survivorship was a condition precedent to the receipt of the residuary estate. If words were held to be devoid of meaning, then this court would be rewriting the testator's will." In re Robinson's Will, 236 N.Y.S.2d 293, 295 (Surr. 1963). That presumption has pitfalls of its own, however.

Inclusion of words of survivorship provides neither objective evidence that a conversation about § 45a-441 took place nor objective evidence that the testator considered seriously the possibility of nonsurvival or inquired about the meaning of expressions such as "lapsed bequest" and the protections of the antilapse statute. "Because such a survival provision is often boiler-plate form-book language, the testator may not understand that such language could disinherit the line of descent headed by the deceased devisee. When the testator is older than the devisee and hence does not expect the devisee to die first . . . it seems especially unlikely that a provision requiring the devisee to survive the testator was intended to disinherit the devisee's descendants." 1 Restatement (Third), supra, § 5.5, cmt. h, at 385. . . .

If [the testator] intended the bequest to lapse, the testator could have explicitly so provided. The testator also could have made an alternative devise, which "indicates a contrary intent, and hence overrides an antilapse statute." 1 Restatement (Third), supra, § 5.5, cmt. g, at 384. That the testator did neither in the present case informs our consideration of whether he intended disinheritance.

The argument is further weakened by the fact that, under the interpretation of § 45a-441 provided by the Probate Court and the Superior Court, the result is not merely that Brennan's share lapses; her share passes to the intestate estate. Thus, at its crux, the contention of the appellees asks us to presume that, although not explicitly provided for, the testator *intended* intestacy as to Brennan's share. That argument confounds Connecticut law, which presumes that a testator designed by his will to dispose of his entire estate and to avoid intestacy as to any part of it. In addition, the bequest to Brennan was residuary in nature. "Residuary language expresses an intention to . . . avoid intestacy." Indulging in the presumption that the testator intended to avoid intestacy militates against a finding that he intended for Brennan's share to lapse.

Another presumption bears consideration. In Clifford v. Cronin, 117 A. 489 (Conn. 1922), our Supreme Court . . . stated that "the testator is presumed to know the law and that his will is drawn accordingly.". . . If we must presume that the testator was aware of our antilapse statute, we must also equally presume that he was aware that it is remedial in nature and provided a liberal construction in Connecticut. In that event, the testator would have known that any ambiguity arising from the probate of his will, absent an express indication to the contrary, would be resolved in favor of operation of the statute.

Alternatively, another line of cases from various jurisdictions concludes that words of survivorship alone are insufficient to defeat an antilapse statute. . . .

In Detzel v. Nieberding, 219 N.E.2d 327 (Ohio Prob. 1966), the will provided in relevant part, "To my beloved sister, Mary Detzel, provided she be living at the time of my death." Mary Detzel predeceased the testator. In considering the operation of Ohio's antilapse statute, the court noted that "[a]ntilapse statutes are remedial and should receive a liberal construction[.]" Accordingly, "[a]ll doubts are to be resolved in favor of the operation of the antilapse statute. . . . [T]o render [the] statute inoperative contrary intent of testator must be plainly indicated." The court continued: "To prevent operation of the Ohio antilapse statute when a devise is made to a relative conditioned upon the survival of the testator by the relative, and the relative predeceases the testator leaving issue who survive the testator, it is necessary that the testator, in apt language, make an alternative provision in his will providing that in the event such relative predeceases or fails to survive the testator such devise shall be given to another specifically named or identifiable devisee or devisees." Although we do not agree that the only way to negate operation of an antilapse statute is by providing an alternate devise, *Detzel* is persuasive nevertheless. *Detzel* has never been reversed, although another Ohio court characterized it as "clearly and completely erroneous." Shalkhauser v. Beach, 233 N.E.2d 527, 530 (Ohio Prob. 1968). The Uniform Probate Code, however, seems to agree with the logic of *Detzel*.

In 1990, a revised Uniform Probate Code was promulgated, which contained a substantially altered antilapse statute. Notably, § 2-603(b)(3) provides that "words of survivorship, such as in a devise to an individual 'if he survives me,' or in a devise to 'my surviving children,' are not, in the absence of additional evidence, a sufficient indication of an intent contrary to the application of this section." Unif. Prob. Code § 2-603(b)(3). The comment to that section explains that this expansion of anti-lapse protection was necessary because "an antilapse statute is remedial in nature. . . . [T]he remedial character of the statute means that it should be given the widest possible latitude to operate" in considering whether in an individual case there is an indication of a contrary intent sufficiently convincing to defeat the statute. The Restatement Third of Property, supra, agrees; and that proposition is consonant with Connecticut law. In sum, we agree with those jurisdictions that have held that mere words of survivorship do not defeat antilapse statutes. . . .

CONCLUSION

Our antilapse statute was enacted to prevent operation of the rule of lapse and unintended disinheritance. The statute is remedial and receives a liberal construction. Any doubts are resolved in favor of its operation. We therefore conclude that words of survivorship, such as "if she survives me," alone do not constitute a "provision" in the will for the contingency of the death of a beneficiary, as the statute requires, and thus are insufficient to negate operation of § 45a-441. Our conclusion today effectuates the intent of the General Assembly in enacting this remedial statute. Should a testator desire to avoid application of the antilapse statute, the testator must either unequivocally express that intent or simply provide for an alternate bequest. Because the testator in the present case did neither, the protections of the antilapse statute apply. Accordingly, the bequest to Brennan does not lapse, but rather descends to her issue.

The judgment is reversed and the case is remanded for further proceedings consistent with this opinion.

NOTES

1. Affirmed. The decision in *Ruotolo* excerpted above was affirmed by the Connecticut Supreme Court: "The Appellate Court properly resolved [the] issue in its concise and well reasoned opinion. Because that opinion fully addresses all arguments raised in this appeal, we adopt it as a proper statement of the issue and the applicable law concerning that issue."[40]

2. A Dissenting Opinion. Professor Jeffrey Cooper gives a scathing review of *Ruotolo*. He argues, among other things, that the court misread the relative weight of authority on the question of whether words of survivorship preclude application of the antilapse statute. The "case law from other jurisdictions," Cooper writes,

> reveals not an even split of authority but rather a clear majority rule that a requirement of survival, without more, generally is sufficient to negate application of an anti-lapse statute. Others undertaking such comparative analyses similarly have concluded that the "overwhelming weight of authority" runs counter to the Appellate Court's approach. While Connecticut's courts obviously need not defer

---

40. *Ruotolo v. Tietjen*, 916 A.2d 1, 1 (Conn. 2007) (per curiam).

to precedents from other jurisdictions, the Appellate Court's comparative analysis of other states' anti-lapse statutes failed to properly frame the question before it and failed to make clear that the court was declining to follow a well-established majority rule.[41]

Ruotolo can be contrasted with McGowan v. Bogle, 331 S.W.3d 642 (Ky. App. 2011). In *McGowan*, the court was "not persuaded that the revisions to the [UPC] warrant a deviation from" the majority rule that words of survivorship—in that case "living brothers and sister who survive me"—preclude application of the antilapse statute.

3. The No-Residue-of-a-Residue Rule Revisited.   In concluding that the term "if he survives me" did not impose a condition of survival, the court was influenced by the constructional preference for avoiding intestacy. The court assumed that Hazel's share, being a residuary devise, would pass by intestacy if the antilapse statute did not apply. But must this be so? In an omitted footnote, the court observed that the Restatement (Third) of Property rejects the no-residue-of-a-residue rule, and that abrogating the rule would be "consistent with the presumption that a testator intends to avoid intestacy." Yet the court did not question whether to continue to abide by the rule. Nor did any of the parties on appeal. Should they have?

The appellate briefs reveal that the testator's heirs were cousins not mentioned in the will, and that the other half of the residue was left in equal shares to four named persons, including Hazel's daughter, Kathleen. The court's decision therefore gave Kathleen her mother's one-half share plus her own one-eighth share. Is it likely that the testator would have preferred this outcome to dividing Hazel's share among Kathleen and the other residuary beneficiaries?

4. The Importance of Good Lawyering.   A good lawyer does not rely upon presumptions. Instead, she makes the client's intent clear by providing what happens if the intended devisee does not survive the testator. If there is a gift over to another devisee, the lawyer should specify what happens if the second devisee predeceases the testator. Thus, for example, "to A if A survives me, but if A does not survive me, to B if B survives me, and if both A and B do not survive me, to be added to the residue of my estate."[42]

The drafters of UPC § 2-603(b)(3) meant to ensure that the dispositive provisions of a will reflect informed decisions by the testator rather than rote inclusion of survivorship boilerplate. But stamping out boilerplate by statute turns out to be a difficult undertaking. In some practices, UPC § 2-603(b)(3) has prompted the design of new boilerplate that entirely disclaims the antilapse statute. Here is an example: "No lapse or antilapse statute shall apply to any disposition of property under this will."

Suppose a will makes a series of specific and general devises without providing for the contingency of a devisee predeceasing the testator, but it includes a residuary

---

41. Jeffrey A. Cooper, A Lapse in Judgment: Ruotolo v. Tietjen and Interpretation of Connecticut's Anti-Lapse Statute, 20 Quinnipiac Prob. L.J. 204, 213 (2007).

42. *See* John L. Garvey, Drafting Wills and Trusts: Anticipating the Birth and Death of Possible Beneficiaries, 71 Or. L. Rev. 47, 49-54 (1992); *see also* Horton, *supra* note 19, at 1152-53 (finding 71 lapsed gifts in sample of 332 wills, 49 of which avoided antilapse because the testator named an alternative taker).

clause that references "the residue of my estate, including any lapsed devises."[43] Does the inclusion of "lapsed devises" in the residuary clause preclude application of the antilapse statute? *Compare* Lacis v. Lacis, 355 S.W.3d 727 (Tex. App. 2011) (Yes), *with* Blevins v. Moran, 12 S.W.3d 698 (Ky. App. 2000) (No).

5. *Reading UPC § 2-603.*   UPC § 2-603 includes a complex system of priorities for primary and secondary substitute gifts to determine when the descendants of the primary taker have priority over the secondary taker or the secondary taker's descendants. The curious student can find § 2-603 and its official comment, which together run over 7,000 words, through the Uniform Law Commission's Web page or on Westlaw.

3. Class Gifts

Under the lapse rules, a *class gift* is treated differently from a gift to individuals. If a class member predeceases the testator, the surviving members of the class divide the total gift, including the deceased member's share, unless an antilapse statute applies.

a. What Is a Class?

A class gift arises if the testator was *group minded*. A testator is said to be group minded if he uses a class label in describing the beneficiaries, such as "to *A*'s children" or "to my nephews and nieces." A gift to named beneficiaries who form a natural class may be construed as a class gift if the court decides that the testator would have wanted the survivors to divide the share of a predeceasing beneficiary rather than for it to lapse.

Restatement (Third) of Property: Wills and Other Donative Transfers
(Am. Law Inst. 2011)

§ 13.1 Class Gift Defined; How Created

(a) A class gift is a disposition to beneficiaries who take as members of a group. Taking as members of a group means that the identities and shares of the beneficiaries are subject to fluctuation.

(b) A disposition is presumed to create a class gift if the terms of the disposition identify the beneficiaries only by a term of relationship or other group label. The presumption is rebutted if the language or circumstances establish that the transferor intended the identities and shares of the beneficiaries to be fixed.

§ 13.2 Class Gift Distinguished From Disposition to Beneficiaries Whose Identities and Shares Are Fixed; How Created

(a) A disposition does not create a class gift if the identities and shares of the beneficiaries are fixed.

---

43. As in Northern Trust, Will & Trust Forms 101-3 (2004). Another problem is that some lawyers will continue to use traditional will forms that make use of language such as "if he survives me" because they are not aware of the new statutory rule. *See* Martin D. Begleiter, Article II of the Uniform Probate Code and the Malpractice Revolution, 59 Tenn. L. Rev. 101, 126-30 (1991).

(b) In determining whether a disposition is to beneficiaries whose identities and shares are fixed, the following rules apply:

(1) If the terms of a disposition expressly fix the identities and shares of the beneficiaries, the disposition is to beneficiaries whose identities and shares are fixed.

(2) If the terms of a disposition identify the beneficiaries (i) by their names or (ii) by a term of relationship or other group label and either by name or number or by name and number, the disposition is presumed to be to beneficiaries whose identities and shares are fixed. The presumption is rebutted if the language or circumstances establish that the transferor intended the beneficiaries to take as a class, i.e., as members of a group.

Dawson v. Yucus
239 N.E.2d 305 (Ill. App. 1968)

[Nelle G. Stewart died on May 29, 1965. The second clause of her will provided as follows:

> Through the Will of my late husband, Dr. Frank A. Stewart, I received an undivided one-fifth (1/5) interest in two hundred sixty-one and thirty-eight hundredths (261.38) acres of farm lands located in . . . Sangamon County, Illinois, and believing as I do that those farm lands should go back to my late husband's side of the house, I therefore give, devise and bequeath my one-fifth (1/5) interest in said farm lands as follows: One-half (1/2) of my interest therein to Stewart Wilson, a nephew, now living in Birmingham, Michigan and One-half (1/2) of my interest to Gene Burtle, a nephew, now living in Mission, Kansas.

Stewart devised the residue of her estate to Ina Mae Yucus and Hazel Degelow. Gene Burtle, one of the nephews to whom Stewart devised her interest in the farm, predeceased her. At issue was whether the gift to the nephews Wilson and Burtle was a class gift, so that the surviving nephew, Wilson, would take Burtle's share. If not, Burtle's lapsed share would pass to Yucus and Degelow as part of the residue. Prior to the litigation, Wilson conveyed his interest in Burtle's share to Burtle's surviving children, who were substituted as plaintiffs. The trial court held that a gift to individuals and not a class gift was intended.]

JONES, J. . . . At the trial the court found that the death of Gene Burtle prior to that of the testatrix created a latent ambiguity and admitted extrinsic evidence relating to testatrix' intentions. . . . [Of the] relatives of Dr. Stewart, only Gene Burtle and Stewart Wilson had a close personal relationship with the testatrix. Gene Burtle died on May 15, 1963, and the testatrix knew of his death but made no changes in her previously executed will. There was evidence from four witnesses that in conversations had with testatrix she stated she wanted the one-fifth interest in the farm to go either to her husband's side of the house, or to Gene Burtle and Stewart Wilson because she felt especially close to them and none other of Dr. Stewart's relatives had any contact with her.

The trial court held, we think correctly, that clause two of testatrix' will did not create a class gift and that the gift in that clause to Gene Burtle lapsed and, pursuant to the Illinois Lapse Statute, Chapt. 3, Sec. 49, I.R.S. 1965, passed into the residue of her estate.

The definition of class gifts and pertinent rules of construction as followed by Illinois courts are set forth in the case of Strohm v. McMullen, 89 N.E.2d 383 (Ill. 1949):

> The definition of a class gift adopted by this court, as laid down by Mr. Jarman in his work on Wills, Vol. I, p. 534, 5th Am. Ed., is:
>
> "A gift to a class is defined . . . as a gift of an aggregate sum to a body of persons uncertain in number at the time of the gift, to be ascertained at a future time, and who are all to take in equal or in some other definite proportions, the share of each being dependent for its amount upon the ultimate number of persons."
>
> "A class, in its ordinary acceptation, is a number or body of persons with common characteristics or in like circumstances, or having some common attribute, and, as applied to a devise, it is generally understood to mean a number of persons who stand in the same relation to each other or to the testator." Blackstone v. Althouse, 116 N.E. 154 (Ill. 1917). And it has been definitely decided in this State that in determining whether a devise is to a class or to individuals depends upon the language of the will. If from such language it appears that the amounts of their shares are uncertain until the devise or bequest takes effect, the beneficiaries will generally be held to take as a class; but where at the time of making the gifts the number of beneficiaries is certain, and the share each is to receive is also certain, and in no way dependent for its amount upon the number who shall survive, it is not a gift to a class, but to the individuals.
>
> There is an exception to the rule that naming the individual prevents the gift from becoming a class gift, stated in Strauss v. Strauss, 2 N.E.2d 699 (Ill. 1936), holding that the mere fact that the testator mentions by name the individuals who make up the class is not conclusive, and that if the intention to give a right of survivorship is collected from the remaining provisions of the will, as applied to the existing facts, such an intention must prevail.

Admittedly the gift in clause two is not made with the usual generic class description such as "children," "brothers," "nephews," "cousins," "issue," "descendants," or "family" but is in fact to two named individuals, conditions which militate against construction of the clause as a class gift. However, plaintiffs argue that because of the death of Gene Burtle prior to that of the testatrix a latent ambiguity exists and extrinsic evidence was properly received to show the true intention of the testatrix in clause two of her will, and that the phrase in clause two, "and believing as I do that these farm lands should go back to my husband's side of the house," together with the extrinsic evidence, clearly requires class gift construction. . . .

In this case the testatrix named the individuals, Stewart Wilson and Gene Burtle, and gave them each a one-half portion of her interest in the farm, thus making certain the number of beneficiaries and the share each is to receive. The shares in no way depend upon the number who shall survive the death of the testatrix. There is nothing in the language of the will that indicates the testatrix intended to create a class or survivorship gift. The only other provision of the will, also contained in clause two, that has any bearing on the question is the statement, "believing as I do that those farm lands should go back to my late husband's side of the house." While it is true that this language recites testatrix' desire that the one-fifth interest in the farm go back to her husband's side of the house, it does not indicate a survivorship gift was intended. Her intention to return the farm to her husband's side of the house was fulfilled when she named Stewart Wilson and Gene Burtle as the donees of the interest. . . .

Further emphasis for the result we have reached is supplied by other factors found in the will and extrinsic evidence. First, the testatrix created a survivorship gift of the residue of her estate in the ninth clause of her will, thus indicating she knew how to manifest an intent to create a class or survivorship gift; hence, the language of clause two, phrased differently, was intended to create a gift to individuals distributively. . . . Secondly, the common characteristic of the alleged class described by plaintiffs is that of relation to Dr. Stewart, or, in the words of clause two, the class is of "my late husband's side of the house." However, this characteristic is also shared by three other heirs of Dr. Stewart of the same degree of relationship to him as Stewart Wilson and Gene Burtle. It thus appears that Gene Burtle and Stewart Wilson do not constitute the alleged class but are individuals named from the class. . . .

The devise in clause two was not to persons who come within the designation of a class but was to individuals distributively. It was not so made or limited to prevent the operation of the Illinois Lapse Statute which must be given its intended effect. The court below correctly held that upon the death of Gene Burtle prior to that of the testatrix the devise to him lapsed and passed under the residuary clause of the will. The Decree will be affirmed.

Affirmed.

NOTES

1. Antilapse Statutes and Spouses.   Should the antilapse statutes apply to gifts to kin of the testator's spouse? What result in *Dawson* if the antilapse statute applied?

2. Discerning Group Mindedness.   The court in *Dawson* employed a rather formal analysis of whether the testator was group minded. It all but said that a group label, such as "my husband's nephews," plus dynamic shares that vary in accordance with the size of the group, are necessary to find a class gift. Because Nelle Stewart named two devisees and specified their shares, the court concluded that she did not intend a class gift.

But these factors are only proxies for whether the testator wanted the surviving members of the group to take the share of a predeceasing member. Under Restatement (Third) of Property: Wills and Other Donative Transfers § 13.2(b)(2), page 368, these factors establish a presumption against a class gift that may be rebutted by language or circumstances indicating that a class was intended. Treating these factors as conclusive "obscure[s] the fact that what is known as a gift to a class is simply a legal device by which they can make a kind of distribution not specifically required by the words of the will. They imply that a class or a gift to a class is something which exists in a will and can be detected by a trained eye. . . . [T]his is not the case."[44]

---

44. Thomas M. Cooley, II, What Constitutes a Gift to a Class, 49 Harv. L. Rev. 903, 931-32 (1936).

In Sullivan v. Sullivan, 529 N.E.2d 890 (Mass. App. 1988), the testator devised her property "to my nephews Marshall John McDonough, and David Condon McDonough, and to my niece Martha McDonough Sullivan, in equal shares, that is one-third each." She omitted two nieces from whom she was estranged. The named nephews and nieces were given fixed shares. One mentioned nephew, Marshall, predeceased the testator without descendants. To avoid lapse, the court held the devise was a class gift and divided Marshall's share equally between the survivors David and Martha.

The court in *Sullivan* relied on Old Colony Trust Co. v. Treadwell, 43 N.E.2d 777 (Mass. 1942), which explained:

> It is the general rule that where there is a gift by will of a fund or residue to several legatees who are named, to be divided among them in equal shares, the gift is to them as individuals, and this is true even though the named individuals do in fact constitute a class and are described as a class. But this rule is one of construction, not a positive rule of law, and hence must, when required, bow to the cardinal rule for the construction of wills, namely, that the intention of the testator is to be ascertained from the whole instrument, attributing due weight to all its language, considered in the light of the circumstances known to him at the time of its execution and, when so ascertained, that it be given effect unless some positive rule of law forbids.

b. Application of Antilapse Statutes to Class Gifts

Almost all states apply their antilapse statutes to a single-generation class gift such as to "children" or "siblings,"[45] and most statutes so provide, as does UPC § 2-605 (1969), page 357. In states where the statute is unclear, courts reason that the antilapse statutes are designed to carry out the typical testator's intent, and that the typical testator would prefer for a deceased class member's share to go to that member's descendants rather than to the surviving members of the class. In a few states, the antilapse statutes do not apply to dispositions to class members who died before execution of the will. These states assume that the testator did not have the dead class member in mind and did not want his descendants to take. Thus:

> *Case 10.* T, a widow, dies leaving a will devising Blackacre "to my sisters," and devising her residuary estate to her stepson, S. When T executed the will, T had two sisters living, A and B. One sister, C, died before the will was executed, leaving a child, F, who survived T. A died during T's lifetime leaving two children, D and E. T is survived by B, D, E, F, and S (see Figure 5.5). Who takes Blackacre? Assuming the antilapse statute applies to devises to sisters, in most states B takes a one-third share, D and E split a one-third share, and F takes a one-third share. In a minority of states, F does not share because C was dead when the will was executed, and Blackacre goes one-half to B and one-half split between D and E. If the antilapse statute did not apply to class gifts, B, as the sole surviving member of the class, would take Blackacre.

---

45. There is no need to apply an antilapse statute to a gift to a multigenerational class such as to "issue" or "descendants," because such a gift absorbs the concept of representation familiar from inheritance law (see page 79). Suppose T's will devises his estate "to my descendants." T has a son, B, and a daughter, C. B dies, leaving a daughter, D. Then T dies. D takes B's share by representation.

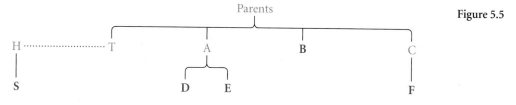

Figure 5.5

Survivors are in **bold**; deceased persons are in regular type.

4. Summary Diagram

Figure 5.6 summarizes the rules for a lapsed devise.

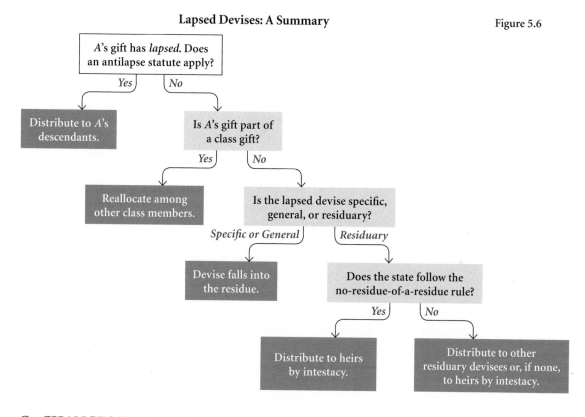

Lapsed Devises: A Summary

Figure 5.6

C. CHANGES IN PROPERTY AFTER EXECUTION OF WILL

We turn now to the problem of a will that has been made stale or obsolete by changes in circumstances since execution that affect the property that is subject to the will. As before, if the testator's actual intent is not evident, the court will apply rules of construction that are meant to implement the probable intent of the typical testator.

1. Ademption by Extinction

Suppose a will includes a specific devise of an item of property, but the testator sells or gives the item away before death. What happens to the devise? A specific devise of real or personal property is subject to the doctrine of *ademption by extinction*. Thus:

Case 11. T's will devises Blackacre to her son, John, and the residuary estate to her daughter, Mary. Some years later, the testator sells Blackacre and uses the sale proceeds to purchase Whiteacre, then dies without having changed her will. Under traditional law, the gift of Blackacre is adeemed (from the Latin *adimere*: to take away). Because the testator does not own Blackacre at her death, the devise fails. John has no claim to Whiteacre, as the will does not devise Whiteacre to him.

Ademption applies only to *specific* devises. Examples are gifts of "my property at 123 Main Street," "my car," or "my three-carat diamond ring given to me by my Aunt Jane." Ademption does not apply to *general, demonstrative,* or *residuary* devises.

A devise is *general* if the testator intends to confer a benefit out of the general property of the estate rather than to give a particular asset—for example, a devise of $100,000 to *A*. If there is not $100,000 in cash in the testator's estate at death, the legacy is not adeemed; other property must be sold to satisfy *A*'s general legacy.

A *demonstrative* devise is a hybrid: a general devise, yet payable from a specific source. If the specified source is insufficient, the devise is not adeemed, but rather is satisfied out of other of the testator's property. Suppose that the testator's will gives *B* "the sum of $100,000 to be paid from the proceeds of sale of my Apple stock." Most courts would hold this to be a demonstrative devise. In raising the $100,000, the executor must comply with the direction to sell the Apple stock. But if the testator does not own $100,000 worth of Apple stock, other property must be sold in order to raise the full $100,000.

A *residuary* devise conveys that portion of the testator's estate not otherwise effectively devised by other parts of the will, such as a devise to *A* of "all the rest, residue, and remainder of my property and estate."

Under the traditional *identity theory* of ademption, if a specifically devised item is not in the testator's estate, the gift is extinguished. Under the newer *intent theory*, if the specifically devised item is not in the testator's estate, the beneficiary may nonetheless be entitled to the replacement or cash value of the original item, if the beneficiary can show that this is what the testator would have wanted. In Case 11, under the intent theory John would be entitled to Whiteacre if he could show that *T* intended him to take Whiteacre as a replacement for Blackacre.

In re Estate of Anton
731 N.W.2d 19 (Iowa 2007)

APPEL, J. In this case, we consider whether the sale of certain property by an attorney-in-fact prior to the death of the testator resulted in ademption of a specific property bequest. . . .

FACTUAL BACKGROUND

In 1972, the testator, Hestor Mary Lewis Anton (Mary), married Herbert Anton, the father of Gretchen Coy. It was the second marriage for both Herbert and Mary. During this marriage, Gretchen, Mary's stepdaughter, deeded a piece of real property to her stepmother and father. Herbert and Mary built a duplex on the property. After the death of Herbert in 1976, Mary became the sole owner of the duplex property.

In 1981, Mary executed a will. In the will, she bequeathed half of her interest in the duplex to Gretchen. The remaining half interest was bequeathed to her biological son, Robert Lewis. Mary bequeathed the remainder of her estate to Robert and her daughter, Nancy Ezarski.

In 1986, Mary was involved in a serious automobile accident. After the accident, she lived in a series of nursing homes. For a short period of time, she lived in a nursing home called Riverside. Thereafter, she moved to Green Hills Health Center in Ames, where she had a private suite. Among other things, Mary suffered from Huntington's Chorea, a malady that impacts the nervous system.

Shortly after the accident, Mary executed a durable power of attorney authorizing her daughter Nancy to manage her financial affairs.[46] The power of attorney took effect immediately. The document was a "durable" power of attorney: it explicitly stated that it would remain in full force and effect until Mary's death and would be unaffected by any mental or physical disability that might occur after its execution.

From 1986 until Mary's death on December 2, 2003, Nancy handled her mother's financial affairs. There is no evidence in the record indicating that Nancy did anything improper in connection with Mary's assets.

On Memorial Day 1998, Nancy and her mother discussed selling the family residence to provide her mother with necessary support. After this conversation, staff at the nursing home advised Nancy that she should not discuss financial matters with her mother as it would exacerbate her condition and cause distress. As a result of this input from nursing home staff, Nancy and her mother had no further discussions regarding her financial affairs.

Nancy, acting as attorney-in-fact, began selling her mother's assets in order to pay her ongoing living expenses. Mary was generally aware her assets were being sold off to pay for her expenses. Her only concern was that she would have enough money to continue living at Green Hills. There was, however, no evidence that Mary was ever aware that the duplex was sold.

By 2003, the only asset remaining in Mary's estate was the duplex. The combined income from that asset and from her husband's trust was insufficient to meet her ongoing expenses. At this point, Nancy listed the duplex property for sale. Nancy then received a call from Gretchen's son, who informed Nancy of the terms of Mary's will and told her she could not sell the duplex.

In light of the phone call from Gretchen's son, Nancy took the duplex off the market and contacted an attorney, who issued an opinion stating that Nancy had the power and authority to sell the duplex. The attorney also advised, however, that the trustee of the Harold R. Lewis Trust had the discretion to distribute the principal of the trust to Mary for her health, well-being, and maintenance. Nancy then contacted the trust officer at First National Bank to inquire about obtaining a loan from the trust. She was informed that the bank preferred that all of Mary's assets be sold prior to invading the trust's principal. As a result, Nancy believed she had no other choice but to sell the property, which was accomplished on August 28, 2003.

---

46. We take up powers of attorney in Chapter 7 at page 502. —Eds.

The evidence in the record regarding Mary's capacity at the time of the sale is thin. Nurses' notes indicate that on April 16, 2003, Mary had "periods of confusion." A social service progress note dated October 9, 2003, six weeks after the sale, makes reference to "advanced dementia." Nancy herself appeared to have concerns regarding Mary's mental state. Nancy indicated in a phone conversation with Gretchen Coy in June 2003 that Mary "sleeps almost all the time." The letter to Nancy from the estate's attorney recalled Nancy's indication that Mary was not competent to handle her affairs at the time the sale of the duplex was being considered. At trial, however, Nancy testified that her mother was "not incompetent" at the time of the duplex's sale.

The net proceeds of the duplex's sale were $133,263. Nancy began to pay Mary's living expenses out of the proceeds. At the time of Mary's death, the remaining balance was $104,317.38. . . .

LEGAL BACKGROUND

A

. . . In the early twentieth century, this court adopted the identity theory of ademption. Under the identity rule, if specifically bequeathed property was not found in the estate at the time of death, the bequest was adeemed. . . . Beginning in the 1960s, however, this court began to depart from the rigid application of the identity theory in all settings.

For example, in In re Estate of Bierstedt, 119 N.W.2d 234 (Iowa 1963), this court considered whether the sale by a guardian of specifically bequeathed real estate without the knowledge and consent of an incompetent testator caused ademption by extinction under the identity rule. In this case, the court rejected application of a "rigid identity rule" and applied what it called a "modified intention" approach. The court noted that the order establishing the guardianship demonstrated that Bierstedt was incompetent at the time the land was sold, thereby creating a presumption of lack of testamentary capacity. As a result, because the testator did not have the testamentary capacity to, in effect, work a change in the will, the sale could not be considered to manifest an intention on the part of the testator to modify the will. Therefore, no ademption occurred.

Similarly, in In re Estate of Wolfe, 208 N.W.2d 923 (Iowa 1973), this court considered whether the destruction of property which was the subject of a specific bequest, contemporaneous with the death of the testator, worked an ademption. In this case, the testator had specifically bequeathed his automobile, a 1969 Buick Electra, to his brother. The testator was killed in an automobile accident in which his automobile was a total loss. Insurance proceeds that included the value of the auto were paid to the estate. The brother claimed he was entitled to the proceeds. In holding for the brother and against the estate, the court rejected the identity rule and emphasized that the intent of the testator is paramount in determining whether an ademption has occurred. As a result, the court reasoned that where property is missing from the estate because of some act or event involuntary as to the testator, there is no ademption.

In summary, our cases hold that the identity rule will not be rigidly applied in all cases. Under what the court has called the "modified intention theory," the identity rule will not be applied to cases where specifically devised property is removed from the estate through an act that is involuntary as to the testator. This includes cases where the property is sold by a guardian, or conservator, or is destroyed contemporaneously with the death of the testator. Until now, however, we have not had occasion to consider whether ademption occurs when specifically devised property is sold by an attorney-in-fact.

B

. . . While there are many cases in other states involving acts of court-appointed guardians where the testators are incompetent, there are only a few cases dealing with the question of whether acts of an agent pursuant to a durable power of attorney cause ademption of specific bequests. The cases have not reached uniform results.

The first case dealing with the question is Estate of Graham, 533 P.2d 1318 (Kan. 1975). In this case, a specific devise of real estate was sold by an agent pursuant to a power of attorney to support the testator's stay in a rest home. After the death of the testator, the beneficiary of the specific bequest sought the balance of the proceeds remaining in the estate.

The Kansas Supreme Court held that no ademption occurred. The court emphasized that the devise was not conveyed with the full knowledge and consent of the testator during his lifetime. The court noted that it seemed logical that the same legal principles should apply to a conveyance by an attorney-in-fact acting under a power of attorney as are applicable to the acts of a guardian. The court noted that were the rule otherwise, an attorney-in-fact hostile to one of the beneficiaries may adeem a gift through the sale of specifically devised property. The court emphasized, however, that the beneficiary was entitled only to the unexpended balance of the proceeds of specifically devised property.

The Ohio Supreme Court considered this question in Estate of Hegel, 668 N.E.2d 474 (Ohio 1996). In this case, Hegel sold the principal's house after she had become incompetent pursuant to a durable power of attorney. The principal's will devised the house to Hegel. Upon the principal's death, Hegel claimed entitlement to the cash proceeds of the sale that remained in the principal's estate. The probate court held that the devise had been adeemed by extinction. On appeal, the Court of Appeals of Ohio reversed in a 2-1 decision.

The Ohio Supreme Court reversed the court of appeals in a 4-3 decision and held that the specific devise was adeemed. The majority emphasized that while the Ohio legislature had passed a nonademption statute in regard to the actions of court-appointed guardians, it did not extend the rule to agents acting under durable powers of attorney.[47] The majority further noted that it did not regard those acting under powers of attorney as the same as guardians. The majority indicated that attorneys-in-fact have more freedom and can act without court approval as the principal's alter ego. . . .

---

47. Professor Ljubomir Nacev of Northern Kentucky University calls to our attention that the Ohio statute was since amended to apply also to an agent acting under a durable power of attorney. *See* Ohio Rev. Code § 2107.501(B) (2016). — Eds.

ANALYSIS

Although the identity rule has been subject to substantial criticism and has been abandoned or substantially altered in the Uniform Probate Code and the Restatement (Third) of Property, neither party questioned its continued vitality either in the district court or on appeal. See Unif. Probate Code § 2-606 (1997) (adopting "'intent' theory" of ademption); Restatement (Third) of Prop.: Wills and Other Donative Transfers § 5.2(c) (1999) (specific devise fails if property is not in estate "unless failure of devise would be inconsistent with testator's intent"). Instead, the parties have focused on whether Mary was competent at the time of sale and whether the rule in *Bierstedt* should be extended to cases involving attorneys-in-fact. In this posture, we do not examine the continued vitality of the identity rule, but simply apply the principles established in our case law to the facts of this case. For the reasons expressed below, we hold that the sale of the duplex by an attorney-in-fact under the circumstances presented did not result in ademption of the bequest.

A

. . . If Mary was incompetent at the time of sale of the duplex, the act would clearly be involuntary as to her. The question then arises whether the rule in *Bierstedt* should be extended to cases involving the sale of specifically devised property by an attorney-in-fact, or whether the extension should be rejected.

We follow the approach in In re Estate of Graham. It is true, however, that there are some differences between the appointment of a guardian by a court and the selection of an agent with durable power of attorney by a competent testator prior to the onset of any mental infirmity. For example, in the case of the execution of a durable power of attorney, the principal has the power to choose the agent and to approve the scope of the agent's powers.

The rationale of *Bierstedt*, however, is that ademption does not occur when specifically devised property is sold as a result of acts that are involuntary to the testator. The rationale of our cases is that ademption occurs where a testator had knowledge of a transaction involving a specific devise, realizes the effect of the transaction on his or her estate plan, and has an opportunity to revise the will. Where these elements are not present, no ademption occurs. The focus of analysis is on the testator and whether the testator has made a deliberate decision not to revise the will, and not on the nature of the agency causing the involuntary act.

The legal context[ ] of In re Estate of Hegel [is] distinguishable. In [that case], the legislature had stepped in to amend the probate code to specifically exclude acts of guardians from the rule of ademption. The legislative failure to exclude acts of agents pursuant to durable powers of attorney was found to be significant. The Iowa legislature, however, has not taken [similar action]. . . .

B

. . . In the alternative, assuming that Mary was competent at the time of the duplex's sale, the question arises as to whether an ademption should occur based, not upon the act of the attorney-in-fact in selling the property, but upon the intent of the testator expressed prior to the sale. Specifically, the estate claims that Mary on Memorial Day 1998 knew that her assets would need to be sold for her support and specifically approved of the sale of her residence by her attorney-in-fact. There appears to have been no specific discussion, however, of the sale of the duplex at any time. Further, it is conceded that Mary had no knowledge of the actual sale of the duplex over five years later. Nancy simply sold it without telling her mother in order to avoid aggravating her condition.

We do not question the wisdom of Nancy's decision to sell the property without consulting Mary. Our only concern is the legal consequences that flow from it. This case thus raises the question of what result should occur where the principal is competent, but the attorney-in-fact sells a specific devise without the knowledge of the testator.

If Mary was aware of the transaction, was aware of the impact the transaction had on her estate plan, and did not change her will, ademption would, of course, occur under the identity theory. Here, however, Mary only had a general knowledge that assets may need to be sold for her support at some time in the future. This is simply not the same as contemporaneous knowledge that an asset that is subject to a specific devise has, in fact, been removed from the estate. Most ordinary persons would not run down to the lawyer's office to change their will in light of a remote future contingency that has not been specifically discussed and which may or may not occur in the future. An expression of intent in the indefinite future to sell assets for support is not sufficient to cause ademption under our "modified intention theory" where the testator is not aware that the specific action has taken place.

It is true that Nancy did not sell the duplex until all other sources of revenue had been exhausted for her mother's support. It may well be that, under the circumstances, her mother would have assented to the sale of the duplex in 2003 had she been asked. But under our cases, the relevant issue is not whether Mary would have assented to the sale had she been asked, but rather whether Mary had the opportunity to change her will once she knew that the duplex was no longer part of her estate. Under the record here, she simply did not have that opportunity.

C

There remains a question of remedy. Gretchen seeks to recover $72,625, or half the proceeds realized upon the sale of the duplex. Some courts have held that where ademption does not occur, the devisee is entitled to the entire value notwithstanding the fact that the proceeds may have been used for the care of the testator. In re Estate of Mason, 397 P.2d 1005, 1007 (Cal. 1965). We have considered the issue, however, and have held that in cases where specific devises are removed from the estate as a result of an involuntary act, the devisee is entitled only to the proceeds which have not been expended on the support of the testator. Stake v. Cole, 133 N.W.2d 714, 717 (Iowa 1965). We see no reason to depart from Iowa precedent. As a result, Coy is entitled to $52,158.69....

CONCLUSION

For the reasons expressed above, we hold that under the facts and circumstances of this case, the sale of the duplex did not cause ademption to the extent that there were specifically identifiable proceeds in the estate at the time of death. The ... matter is remanded to the district court for proceedings not inconsistent with this opinion.

NOTES

1. The Identity Theory—A Rule Tempered by Exceptions.   In states following the identity theory, courts and legislatures have developed several exceptions to avoid ademption in cases in which, as in *Anton*, the property is not in the estate because of an accident or the action of someone other than the testator, or in which the facts otherwise indicate a high likelihood that the testator did not intend for ademption.

Many courts and UPC § 2-608(a) (1969, rev. 1987) give the devisee any unpaid amount of a condemnation award for the property or any unpaid casualty insurance proceeds after the property has been destroyed. In In re Estate of Sagel, 901 A.2d 538 (Pa. Super. 2006), *T* died in the crash of a small plane that he owned. *T*'s will left the plane and his Rolex watch to his son, *A*. The court held that *A* was entitled to the property insurance proceeds for the destruction of the plane and the watch.

To avoid ademption, courts will sometimes classify a devise as general or demonstrative rather than specific. If *T* devises "100 shares of Tigertail Corporation" to *A*, and *T* owns no shares of Tigertail at death, the court may declare this to be a general devise if Tigertail Corporation was a widely held stock traded on a major exchange. *A* is entitled to the value of 100 shares of Tigertail at *T*'s death. On the other hand, if *T* had said "*my* 100 shares of Tigertail," most courts would consider this a specific devise that would adeem to the extent the shares are missing at death.

Another route to avoiding ademption under the identity theory is to classify the inter vivos disposition as a change in form, not substance. Suppose that after *T* executes her will giving "my 100 shares of Tigertail Corporation" to *A*, Tigertail Corporation merges into Lion Corporation, which retires the Tigertail stock and issues in its place 85 shares of Lion stock for every 100 shares of Tigertail. Most courts hold that a corporate merger or reorganization is only a change in form, not substance, and *A* takes the 85 shares of Lion stock. In Stanford v. Paris, 703 S.E.2d 488 (N.C. App. 2011), *T* made a specific devise of stock in a family company that was dissolved and its assets transferred to a family partnership. The court held the devise was not adeemed. The devisee was entitled to *T*'s interest in the partnership.

Suppose *T* devises "my brokerage account in the First National Bank" to *A*. After executing her will, *T* closes the account at First National and transfers the funds to a new brokerage account at Second National Bank. Is the change one of form or substance? *Compare* Ruby v. Ruby, 973 N.E.2d 361 (Ill. App. 2012) (change in form only, not adeemed), *and* In re Estate of Geary, 275 S.W.3d 835 (Tenn. App. 2008) (same), *with* Church v. Morgan, 685 N.E.2d 809 (Ohio App. 1996) (change in substance, adeemed).

2. The Intent Theory—A Standard Tempered by Presumptions.   The 1990 UPC abandons the identity theory and adopts the intent theory. In addition to codifying the familiar exceptions from the identity theory jurisdictions (§ 2-606(a)(1)-(4) and (b)), the 1990 UPC provides additional exceptions for replacement property (§ 2-606(a)(5)), and for the pecuniary value of property disposed of during the testator's lifetime if the devisee can show that the testator did not intend ademption (§ 2-606(a)(6)).[48]

Uniform Probate Code (Unif. Law Comm'n 1990, as amended 1997)

§ 2-606. Nonademption of Specific Devises; Unpaid Proceeds of Sale, Condemnation, or Insurance; Sale by Conservator or Agent

(a) A specific devisee has a right to specifically devised property in the testator's estate at the testator's death and to:

(1) any balance of the purchase price, together with any security agreement, owed by a purchaser at the testator's death by reason of sale of the property;

(2) any amount of a condemnation award for the taking of the property unpaid at death;

(3) any proceeds unpaid at death on fire or casualty insurance or on other recovery for injury to the property;

(4) any property owned by the testator at death and acquired as a result of foreclosure, or obtained in lieu of foreclosure, of the security interest for a specifically devised obligation;

(5) any real property or tangible personal property owned by the testator at death which the testator acquired as a replacement for specifically devised real or tangible personal property; and

(6) if not covered by paragraphs (1) through (5), a pecuniary devise equal to the value as of its date of disposition of other specifically devised property disposed of during the testator's lifetime but only to the extent it is established that ademption would be inconsistent with the testator's manifested plan of distribution or that at the time the will was made, the date of disposition or otherwise, the testator did not intend ademption of the devise.

(b) If specifically devised property is sold or mortgaged by a conservator or by an agent acting within the authority of a durable power of attorney for an incapacitated principal, or a condemnation award, insurance proceeds, or recovery for injury to the property is paid to a conservator or to an agent acting within the authority of a durable power of attorney for an incapacitated principal, the specific devisee has the right to a general pecuniary devise equal to the net sale price, the amount of the unpaid loan, the condemnation award, the insurance proceeds, or the recovery.

(c) The right of a specific devisee under subsection (b) is reduced by any right the devisee has under subsection (a). . . .

NOTES

1. Replacement Property. Under UPC § 2-606(a)(5), if *T* executes a will bequeathing "my Ford car" to *A* and later sells the Ford and buys a Rolls-Royce, is *A* entitled to

---

48. *See* Daniel B. Kelly, Toward Economic Analysis of the Uniform Probate Code, 45 U. Mich. J.L. Reform 855, 882-85 (2012).

the Rolls? Suppose *T* sold the Ford and bought two cars, a Honda and a Rolls-Royce. What result? Suppose *T* sold the Ford and bought a motorcycle. What result? An example in the comment to § 2-606 implies that *A* would take the Rolls-Royce in the first case, but it gives no clear guidance on the outcome if *T* bought a Honda and a Rolls or if *T* bought a motorcycle.

If *T* devises Blackacre to *A*, but then sells it and keeps the proceeds, is the devise adeemed or does *A* take the proceeds? *Compare* Melican v. Parker, 711 S.E.2d 628 (Ga. 2011) (not adeemed, *A* takes the proceeds), *with* In re Estate of Donovan, 20 A.3d 989 (N.H. 2011) (adeemed). If *T* buys Whiteacre with the proceeds, is *A* entitled to Whiteacre? *See* Fletcher v. Ellenburg, 609 S.E.2d 337 (Ga. 2005) (Whiteacre not a substitute, gift of Blackacre adeemed).

2. Burden of Proof.   As originally drafted, UPC § 2-606(a)(6) put the burden on the party claiming ademption, in effect creating "a mild presumption against ademption."[49] This provision was criticized on the grounds that it would increase litigation and that it changed the meaning of a bequest of "my diamond ring" to "my diamond ring or its equivalent value," muddying up clear language and inserting an alternate devise that the testator did not make.[50] In 1997, § 2-606(a)(6) was amended to put the burden on the party opposing ademption — that is, the burden was put on the party seeking the pecuniary value of specifically devised property not in the estate. Does this amendment answer the muddying-the-waters criticism?

2. Stock Splits and the Problem of Increase

Suppose that *T* executes a will devising 100 shares of stock of Tigertail Corporation to *A*. Subsequently, Tigertail Corporation splits its stock three for one. At *T*'s death, *T* owns 300 shares of Tigertail stock. Does *A* take 100 shares or 300 shares? The old approach was to ask whether the bequest was specific or general. If the court found *T* intended to bequeath particular shares in *T*'s possession, the bequest was termed specific and *A* received the specified shares (100) as well as any accretions in a stock split (200). On the other hand, if the court found *T* did not have in mind particular property but instead desired to confer a general benefit, *A* received only 100 shares of stock.

This mechanical approach misconceives the basic nature of a stock split, which is a change in form, not substance. The market value of 300 shares of Tigertail after the split should be approximately the same as 100 shares before the split. The key insight is that the shares held after the split represent the same proportional ownership in the corporation as the number of shares held before the split. Most modern courts and the Restatement (Third) of Property have discarded the old approach in the case of stock splits and have held that, subject to a showing of contrary intent, a devisee of stock is entitled to additional shares received by the testator as a result of a stock split.[51]

---

49. In re Estate of Schreiber, 357 P.3d 920, 923-24 (Mont. 2015).
50. *See* Ascher, *supra* note 34, at 646-47.
51. *See* Restatement (Third) of Property: Wills and Other Donative Transfers § 5.3 (Am. Law Inst. 1999).

Some courts treat stock dividends differently from stock splits. They analogize a stock dividend to a cash dividend and conclude that the devisee cannot logically be awarded the former when he is denied the latter. But this analogy ignores the reality of corporate finance that after a stock dividend, as after a stock split, the testator's percentage of ownership remains the same. Under UPC § 2-605(a)(1) (1990) and the Restatement,[52] stock dividends are treated the same as stock splits: The beneficiary gets them along with the other shares.

3. Satisfaction of General Pecuniary Bequests

The doctrine of *satisfaction* (sometimes known as *ademption by satisfaction*) may be applicable if a testator makes an inter vivos transfer to a devisee after executing the will. If the testator is a parent of the beneficiary (or stands in loco parentis) and sometime after executing the will transfers to the beneficiary property of a similar nature to that devised by the will, there is a rebuttable presumption that the gift is in satisfaction of the devise made by the will. The doctrine is akin to that of advancements under intestacy law (see page 122). Thus:

> *Case 12.*   *T*'s will devises $50,000 to her son, *S*, and her residuary estate to her daughter, *D*. After executing the will, *T* gives *S* $30,000. There is a presumption that the gift was in partial satisfaction of the legacy, so that *S* will take only $20,000 at *T*'s death.

The doctrine of satisfaction usually applies to general pecuniary bequests but not to specific bequests. When specific property (such as a painting or the family Bible) is devised to a beneficiary, but then is given to that beneficiary during the testator's life, the gift is adeemed by extinction, not by satisfaction.

Because the intent of the testator is frequently difficult to ascertain, some states have enacted statutes requiring that the intention of a testator to adeem by satisfaction be shown in writing, as under UPC § 2-609 (1990) and the Restatement (Third) of Property,[53] paralleling the UPC rule on advancements (§ 2-109, page 123).

4. Exoneration of Liens

Suppose that *T*'s will devises Blackacre to her daughter, *A*. At *T*'s death, Blackacre is subject to a mortgage that secures a debt on which *T* was personally liable. Does *A* take Blackacre subject to the mortgage, or is she entitled to have the debt paid out of residuary assets so that the title will pass to *A* free of the lien?

In some states, *A* takes Blackacre free of the mortgage. These jurisdictions follow the common law doctrine of *exoneration of liens*. Under this doctrine, if a will makes a specific disposition of real or personal property that is subject to a mortgage to secure a debt on which the testator is personally liable, it is presumed that the testator wanted the debt, like other debts, to be paid out of the residuary estate.[54]

---

52. *See* id.
53. *See* id § 5.4.
54. *See, e.g.,* Estate of Fussell v. Fortney, 730 S.E.2d 405 (W. Va. 2012).

Does this presumption accord with the probable intent of the typical testator? Did *T* expect that *A* would take Blackacre free of the mortgage, possibly depleting the residue? Dissatisfaction with the exoneration doctrine has led to the enactment, in some states, of statutes reversing the common law rule, as under UPC § 2-607 (1990).

5. Abatement

The problem of *abatement* arises if an estate lacks sufficient assets to pay the decedent's debts as well as all devises. In such circumstances, some devises must be abated or reduced. By dividing up a limited pie among claimants of different priorities, abatement functions like bankruptcy.

In the absence of an indication in the will of how devises should abate, devises ordinarily abate in the following order: (1) residuary devises are reduced first, (2) general devises are reduced second, and (3) specific and demonstrative devises are the last to abate and are reduced pro rata. This plan is believed to follow the testator's intent that specific devises be given effect before general devises, and both be given effect before a residuary devise.

But the residuary devisee is often the most important. Consider this example:

> *Case 13.* *T* executes a will in which she devises $300,000 to charity *B*, $100,000 to charity *C*, and the residue of her estate to her son, *A*. At the time of the will's execution, *T* has $800,000 in assets. *T* then becomes ill and undergoes an experimental treatment costing $500,000. The treatment fails, and *T* dies with an estate of $300,000. Under traditional abatement rules, *A* takes nothing, *B* takes $225,000, and *C* takes $75,000.

Is it likely that *T* would have wanted the charities, *B* and *C*, to take to the exclusion of her son, *A*? UPC § 3-902 (1990) provides that "if the testamentary plan . . . would be defeated by" the usual order of abatement, "the shares of the distributees abate as may be necessary to give effect to the intention of the testator." What result in Case 13 under § 3-902? *See* In re Estate of Tateo, 768 A.2d 243 (N.J. App. 2001) (holding that a specific devise to *T*'s son would not be given priority over general devises to *T*'s daughter and grandchildren).

Good lawyers avoid abatement problems through sound drafting. In Case 13, if *T* had devised one-half of the residue of her estate (perhaps capped at $400,000) to the charities and the rest to her son *A*, then all three gifts would have adjusted automatically with the size of *T*'s estate. For this reason, it is often a sound practice to make substantial devises to multiple devisees in the form of shares of the residue, perhaps with a dollar cap.

CHAPTER 6

TRUSTS: CHARACTERISTICS AND CREATION

> Of all the exploits of Equity the largest and the most important
> is the invention and development of the Trust. . . .
> This perhaps forms the most distinctive achievement of
> English lawyers. It seems to us almost essential to civilization,
> and yet there is nothing quite like it in foreign law.
>
> **FREDERIC W. MAITLAND**
> Equity: A Course of Lectures 23
> (John Brunyate ed., 2d ed. 1936)

IN CONTEMPORARY PRACTICE, trusts have eclipsed wills as the preferred vehicle for implementing a donor's freedom of disposition. A *trust* is a legal arrangement in which a *settlor* conveys property to a *trustee* to hold as a *fiduciary* for one or more *beneficiaries*. The trustee takes *legal title* to the trust property, which allows the trustee to deal with third parties as owner of the property. The beneficiaries have *equitable title* to the trust property, which allows them to hold the trustee accountable for breach of the trustee's fiduciary duties. The beneficiaries are typically entitled to periodic distributions from the trust income and sometimes from the trust principal as well.

Trusts may be *testamentary*, created by will and arising in probate. Or they may be *inter vivos*, created during the settlor's lifetime by *declaration of trust* or by *deed of trust*, often as a *will substitute* to avoid probate. "The purposes for which we can create trusts," says the leading treatise, "are as unlimited as our imagination."[1] These uses range from providing financial support for a surviving spouse and children in accordance with their respective needs, to structuring commercial enterprises such as mutual funds and asset securitization. The key to the trust's versatility as an instrument for conveyance and management of property is that it "separate[s] the benefits of ownership from the burdens of ownership."[2]

We focus in this book on the use of the trust in donative transfers, including as a will substitute (see Chapter 7) and for fiduciary administration on behalf of others (see

---

1. Scott and Ascher on Trusts § 1.1.
2. Id.

Chapters 9 through 14). In both contexts, the trust implements the principle of freedom of disposition by projecting the donor's dispositive plan across time.

In this chapter, we introduce the basic functional elements of a trust. In Section A, we survey the history of the trust, the sources of modern trust law, the varied uses of the trust in contemporary practice, and the bifurcation of ownership that is the hallmark characteristic of a common law trust. In Section B, we consider the rules governing the creation of a trust, distinguishing the trust from other kinds of property arrangements.

A. THE TRUST IN AMERICAN LAW

1. Origins of the Trust

The ancestor of the modern trust is the medieval *use*. Legal historians have traced the use back to the middle of the thirteenth century, when the Franciscan friars came to England. Because the friars were forbidden to own property, benefactors conveyed land to friends of the friars, to hold to the use of the friars. *O*, owner of Blackacre, would *enfeoff A* and his heirs to hold Blackacre *to the use of* the friars. By this transfer, the legal fee simple passed from *O*, the *feoffor to uses*, to *A*, the *feoffee to uses*, who held it for the benefit of the *cestui que use*, the mendicant order. The cestui que use took possession of Blackacre, but legal title was held by *A*.

Figure 6.1

From the Use to the Trust[3]

Original Term	Modern Term
use, feoffment to uses	trust
feoffor to uses	settlor (also grantor, trustor)
feoffee to uses	trustee
cestui que use	beneficiary

Initially, uses were not enforceable in the civil courts.[4] Because no common law form of action existed for the cestui to bring an action against the feoffee, the law courts — paralyzed by the rigidity of their procedures — offered no relief. *A* could expel the cestui and use the property to benefit himself. Such disloyalty was unconscionable to the chancellor, the "keeper of the king's conscience," who as a matter of equity compelled feoffees to uses to perform as they had promised.

Once the chancellor enforced uses, removing the risk of faithless feoffees, the use became increasingly popular. Landowners soon found additional applications for the

---

3. This table is adapted from John H. Langbein, Renée Lettow Lerner & Bruce P. Smith, History of the Common Law: The Development of Anglo-American Legal Institutions 300 (2009).

4. There is some evidence that ecclesiastical courts enforced early uses. *See* R.H. Helmholz, The Early Enforcement of Uses, 79 Colum. L. Rev. 1503 (1979); *see also* David J. Seipp, Trust and Fiduciary Duty in the Early Common Law, 91 B.U. L. Rev. 1011 (2011) (describing other ways in which the common law took account of uses).

use, for example to avoid the rule of male primogeniture requiring land to descend to the eldest son (see page 29). *O* would enfeoff Blackacre to *A* and his heirs to the use of *O* during *O*'s lifetime and then to the use of such persons as *O* might appoint by will. The chancery courts enforced such arrangements, making the use a viable *will substitute* that avoided primogeniture. Landowners also employed uses, both before and after the chancellor began enforcing them, to avoid other feudal obligations, known as *feudal incidents* (see page 29), which resulted in a dramatic decline in tax collections.

King Henry VIII

Searching for a way to restore his feudal incidents and replenish his treasury, Henry VIII endeavored to abolish the use. Henry interested himself in a lawsuit, putting into doubt the legality of the use. Fearing that uses might become unenforceable, with drastic consequences for the cestuis, on Henry's urging Parliament reluctantly enacted the Statute of Uses in 1535. Legal title was taken away from the feoffee to uses and given to the cestui que use. In the words of the time, the use was "executed," that is, each equitable interest was converted into a legal interest. The former cestuis—now clothed with legal title—could breathe easy, but they had to pay the king his due upon death.

Although the purpose of the Statute of Uses was to abolish uses, imaginative lawyers found holes in the statute. For example, courts eventually held that the statute did not operate if the feoffee to uses was given *active duties* to perform—that is, if he had duties beyond simply holding title to the property. This interpretation of the statute permitted chancery to reassert its equitable jurisdiction over uses under the new name of *trust*. The feoffee to uses, now called the *trustee*, was again accountable to the cestuis, now called the *beneficiaries*. The English law of trusts, developed over the years by the chancellors, was brought to America by the colonists, and it became part of American law.

2. Sources of Law

Although nominally based on case law, American trust law has for many years been influenced significantly by the Restatements of Trusts and by a pair of multivolume scholarly treatises. More recently, American trust law has also become substantially codified by state-level legislation.

Max M. Schanzenbach & Robert H. Sitkoff
The Prudent Investor Rule and Trust Asset Allocation: An Empirical Analysis
35 ACTEC L.J. 314 (2010)

A quiet revolution in American trust law is upon us. Traditional rules, unchanged for decades, have been revised substantially or, in some cases, reversed. . . .

Some of the new trust law has been produced top-down by the American Law Institute and the Uniform Law Commission, through the Restatements and Uniform Acts. The top-down process is typified by academic reporters (drafters) and advisors working in concert with practitioner representatives from the American College of Trust and Estate Counsel and the Section on Real Property, Trusts, and Estates of the American Bar Association. In general, the top-down reforms are designed to update the law in view of the transformation of the irrevocable trust into a management device for financial assets, the increasingly common use of the revocable trust as a will substitute, and the rise of the statutory business trust.

Other major changes to the trust law canon have been bottom-up, driven by local lawyers and bankers in response to the increasingly national scope of the competition for trust business. These reforms are implemented through the lobbying efforts of state bar and bankers' associations, spurred on by a desire to attract or retain trust business. As a consequence, the bottom-up reforms tend to promote dead hand control, reflecting the commercial necessity of appealing to apparent donor preferences.

These dual modes of law reform, which operate either in tandem or in opposition depending on the issue, have produced a thoroughly revised and increasingly statutory trust law. Today the state legislatures, not the state courts, are the makers of American trust law. The new statutory trust law is clearer, an important development given the national character of modern trust practice and the lack of deep case law precedent in many states. But being statutory, the new law is also less supple and may prove harder to change.

NOTES

1. The Early Restatements and Great Treatises.   The codification of American trust law traces back to the enormously influential First and Second Restatements of Trusts, published by the American Law Institute respectively in 1935 and 1959. The reporter for both, Professor Austin Wakeman Scott of Harvard, published a multi-

Professor Austin Wakeman Scott

Professor George Gleason Bogert

volume treatise that tracked the organization of the Restatements and cited them constantly. Courts and commentators came to rely on the Restatements and Scott's closely
allied treatise, plus the competing multivolume treatise by Professor George Gleason
Bogert of the University of Chicago, as authoritative statements of the law. Today there
is a Third Restatement and a fresh edition of the Scott treatise, now renamed Scott and
Ascher on Trusts, and a new edition of the Bogert treatise is in progress.

2. Toward the Uniform Trust Code.   Several uniform laws, promulgated across the
twentieth century, have been influential in the development of the law of trusts.[5] The
Uniform Trustee Powers Act (Unif. Law Comm'n 1964) modernized the law of trustee
powers by codifying the expansion of trustee powers commonly found in well-drafted
trust instruments (see page 591). Article VII of the Uniform Probate Code (Unif. Law
Comm'n 1969) provided a modest codification of the law of trust administration.
The Uniform Statutory Rule Against Perpetuities (Unif. Law Comm'n 1986) reformed
the common law Rule Against Perpetuities (see page 904). The Uniform Prudent
Investor Act (Unif. Law Comm'n 1994), the core reforms of which have been adopted
by every state, updated the law of trust investment (see page 624). The widely enacted
Uniform Principal and Income Act (Unif. Law Comm'n 1931, rev. 1962 and 1997),
governs the allocation of investment returns between life and remainder beneficiaries
(see page 669).

   This process of codifying the law of trusts piecemeal culminated with the promulgation by the Uniform Law Commission in 2000 of the Uniform Trust Code (UTC).
The first systematic, national codification of American trust law, the UTC has been well
received. At year-end 2016, it had been enacted in 32 jurisdictions (see Figure 6.2, at
page 390).[6]

   In general, the drafters of the UTC codified the prevailing common law rules of
American trust law. On some issues, however, the drafters took the additional steps
of updating or reforming existing law—or even offering their own innovations.[7]
Throughout the remainder of this book, we often reproduce or describe the UTC provisions relevant to the topic under discussion. In areas in which the UTC diverges from
the common law, you should consider whether the UTC approach is better than traditional law and any alternative you can imagine. Enacting jurisdictions have sometimes
made changes to the UTC not only to account for local practice, but also, and more
interestingly, in response to disagreement with policy choices encoded in the UTC.

   A word about the architecture of the UTC: Most of its provisions state *default rules*
that may be overridden by the terms of the trust. The only exceptions are the *mandatory rules* scheduled in UTC § 105(b) (2000, rev. 2005), such as "the duty of a trustee to
act in good faith and in accordance with the terms and purposes of the trust and the

---

   5. *See* John H. Langbein, Why Did Trust Law Become Statute Law in the United States?, 58 Ala.
L. Rev. 1069 (2007).
   6. Alabama, Arizona, Arkansas, District of Columbia, Florida, Kansas, Kentucky, Maine,
Maryland, Massachusetts, Michigan, Minnesota, Mississippi, Missouri, Montana, Nebraska, New
Hampshire, New Jersey, New Mexico, North Carolina, North Dakota, Ohio, Oregon, Pennsylvania,
South Carolina, Tennessee, Utah, Vermont, Virginia, West Virginia, Wisconsin, and Wyoming.
   7. *See* David M. English, The Uniform Trust Code (2000): Significant Provisions and Policy
Issues, 67 Mo. L. Rev. 143 (2002).

Figure 6.2   **Uniform Trust Code (2016)**

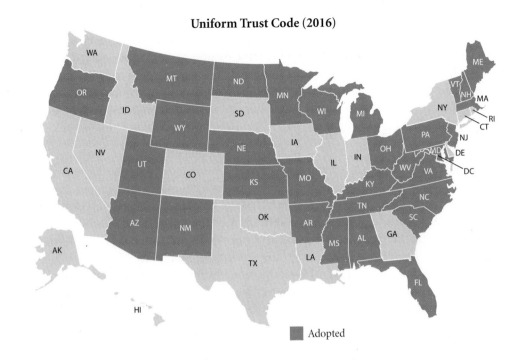

interests of the beneficiaries" (see page 676). This statutory design thus brings clarity to the scope of mandatory rules in trust law. Any provision of the UTC that is not
scheduled in UTC § 105(b) is a default that may be varied by the terms of the trust.[8]

3. The Restatement (Third) of Trusts.   The Restatement (Third) of Trusts, which
spans four volumes published between 2003 and 2012, likewise codifies prevailing common law trust rules, but not always. Especially with respect to the rights of a beneficiary's
creditors to trust assets (see page 701) and trust modification and termination (see
page 733), the Restatement takes positions that depart from both traditional law and
the more modest innovations of the UTC. For these provisions, you should consider
whether the Restatement's approach would lead to better outcomes than traditional law,
the UTC, or any alternative reform you can imagine. Consider also whether it is sensible
for a Restatement, which is persuasive authority only, to take a position that is at odds
with a popular uniform act, which is binding statutory law in a state that has enacted it.

4. The "Bottom-Up" Reforms.   Another important engine for reform in this field,
which has led to increased codification, is lobbying by local lawyers and bankers—
what Professors Schanzenbach and Sitkoff call "bottom-up" law reform. This category
includes legislation designed to fill gaps in the uniform acts or to make the state more
competitive in the jurisdictional competition for trust business.[9] In the chapters that

---

8. *See* John H. Langbein, Mandatory Rules in the Law of Trusts, 98 Nw. U. L. Rev. 1105 (2004).
9. *See, e.g.,* Robert H. Sitkoff & Max M. Schanzenbach, Jurisdictional Competition for Trust Funds:
An Empirical Analysis of Perpetuities and Taxes, 115 Yale L.J. 356 (2005); Daniel G. Worthington &
Mark Merric, Which Situs Is Best in 2016?, Tr. & Est., Jan. 2016, at 61.

follow, we will encounter numerous examples of bottom-up developments such as the validation of perpetual trusts (see page 906) and self-settled asset protection trusts (see page 712); the enactment of statutes authorizing unitrusts for dealing with the principal and income problem (see page 670); legislation allowing waiver of the duty to diversify (see page 653) and the duty to give information to a beneficiary (see page 680); protection of a directed trustee from liability in what has come to be known as a directed trust (see page 662); and the proliferation of statutes that authorize transfer of the property of an old trust into a new trust, known as trust decanting (see page 742). You should consider whether these bottom-up reforms are good or bad policy and, if the latter, why they have been adopted nonetheless.

3. Vocabulary, Typology, and Illustrative Uses

A person who creates a trust is the *settlor, grantor,* or *trustor.* The word settlor comes from our English legal ancestors, who spoke of making a settlement in trust. A trust may be created during the settlor's life: an *inter vivos trust.* Or it may be created by will: a *testamentary trust.* The settlor of a testamentary trust is the testator. Once established, a testamentary trust is necessarily *irrevocable.* An inter vivos trust, by contrast, may be *revocable* or *irrevocable,* depending on the intent of the settlor. An inter vivos trust may be created either by *declaration of trust,* whereby the settlor declares himself to be trustee of certain property, or by *deed of trust,* whereby the settlor transfers to the trustee the property to be held in trust. These various modes of trust creation — by will, by declaration, and by deed — are codified by UTC § 401 (2000) and are considered in the next section of this chapter (see page 401).

Trust Typology   Figure 6.3

	Inter Vivos	Testamentary
Creation	Declaration of Trust or Deed of Trust	Will
Type of Transfer	Nonprobate (Will Substitute)	Probate
Revocability	Revocable or Irrevocable	Irrevocable

Because a testamentary trust is created by will, it involves a probate transfer. An inter vivos trust, by contrast, can be used as a *will substitute* to avoid probate (see Chapter 7). At the death of the settlor, the trust property is distributed or held in further trust in accordance with the terms of the trust. In this use of the trust as a will substitute, we find a modern echo of the ancient use of the trust (then the *use*) to avoid primogeniture and the feudal incidents (see pages 29 and 387). Thus:

Case 1. Revocable Trust.   O declares herself trustee of certain property for the benefit of O for life, and then on O's death, to pay the principal to O's descendants. O retains the power to revoke the trust. Unless O revokes the trust, on O's death her descendants will be entitled to the remainder of the trust property independent of any probate administration of O's estate.

The modern trust is not merely a will substitute. It is also commonly used for managerial intermediation by imposing ongoing *fiduciary administration*. By making a transfer in trust rather than outright, a settlor ensures that the property will be managed and distributed by a trustee in accordance with the settlor's wishes as expressed in the terms of the trust. A trust also allows the settlor to postpone important decisions about the investment and distribution of the trust property, leaving those decisions to the trustee to be made in light of changing market conditions and the beneficiaries' evolving circumstances and capabilities. Here are two examples:

> *Case 2. Trust for Incompetent Person.*   *O*'s son *A* is mentally or physically impaired and is unable to manage property. *O* transfers property to *X* in trust to support *A* for life, remainder to *A*'s descendants, and if *A* dies without descendants, to *O*'s daughter *B*.

> *Case 3. Discretionary Trust.*   *O* transfers property to *X* in trust. The trust instrument gives *X* discretion to pay any amount of income or principal to *A* or for *A*'s benefit. Or, *X* might be given discretion to pay trust income to any one or more of a class of persons, such as *A* and her descendants, and to distribute the trust property to *A*'s descendants at *A*'s death.

In Case 2, the trust ensures fiduciary administration on behalf of *A*, the disabled beneficiary. In Case 3, the trust ensures fiduciary administration and also provides *protection from creditors*. We take up fiduciary administration in Chapter 9 and the asset protection features of trust law in Chapter 10. The trust in Case 3 may also lessen the *income tax* burden on the family by allowing the trustee to distribute income to the beneficiaries who are in the lowest tax brackets.

Here are two examples of the use of the trust in *estate and gift tax planning*, the latter also involving fiduciary administration necessitated by the incapacity of the beneficiary:

> *Case 4. Testamentary Marital Trusts.*   The federal estate tax law permits a deduction for property given to the surviving spouse (see Chapter 15 at page 967). The following structure qualifies for the marital deduction: *H* devises property to *X* in trust to pay the income to *W* for her life, and then on her death to pay the principal to *H*'s children. No estate taxes are payable at *H*'s death. Such a trust might be particularly useful if *W* needs professional money management or is the stepparent of *H*'s children and might not devise the property to them if it were left to her outright.

> *Case 5. Trust for Minor.*   The federal gift tax law allows a tax-free gift of $14,000 per year per donee (see page 934). An outright gift to a minor creates special problems, however, as the minor is legally unable to manage her property. To facilitate annual tax-free gifts of $14,000 to his minor daughter *A*, *O* creates a discretionary trust for the benefit of *A* before she reaches 21, with all principal and any accumulated income distributed to *A* when she reaches 21. Every year *O* can make a tax-free gift of $14,000 to the trustee for *A*.

These examples barely scratch the surface of the myriad uses to which trusts may be put!

NOTE

Statistics on Trust Usage.   Data on the use of trusts — especially inter vivos trusts, which arise by private agreement without a filing with the state — is patchy, but there is some.

Federal law requires banks and other trust institutions that are part of the Federal Reserve System to make annual reports of their trust holdings. These reports indicate roughly $918 billion held in about 710,000 private and charitable trust accounts as of year-end 2015, for an average account size of around $1.29 million. These eye-popping figures significantly understate the total number of trusts and the aggregate value of trust property. They exclude all trusts for which the trustee is an individual, a private trust company, or otherwise is not in the Federal Reserve System.[10] For example, trust companies in South Dakota that are subject to supervision by state banking authorities reported to those authorities more than $226 billion in assets at year-end 2015. Many of those assets would not be included in the Federal Reserve data.[11]

Another source of data on trust usage is tax returns. Many trustees must file a federal income tax return, Form 1041, if the trust earns income. Aggregating the figures reported on these returns for trusts that are clearly identifiable as irrevocable and not subject to the control of the donor yields some staggering sums. In filing-year 2014, the Internal Revenue Service received more than 2.1 million such returns reporting $121.5 billion in gross income, $4.3 billion in fiduciary fees, and $2.65 billion in attorney, accountant, and other professional services fees. Because these figures exclude all revocable trusts and some irrevocable trusts, they too understate total trust usage.[12]

4. Bifurcation of Ownership[13]

The hallmark characteristic of a common law trust is *bifurcation*: The trustee holds *legal title* to the trust property, but the beneficiaries have *equitable* or *beneficial* ownership. Two categories of issues arise from this splitting of legal and equitable ownership: (a) the effect on the rights of third parties with respect to the trust property and the property of the trustee personally (*asset partitioning*), and (b) the powers and duties of the trustee and the corresponding rights of the beneficiaries (*fiduciary administration*).

(a) Asset Partitioning and the Rights of Third Parties.   Asset partitioning rules, a familiar feature of organizational law, separate the personal property and obligations of an organization's insiders from the property and obligations of the organization.[14] For an organization that enjoys juridical entity status, such as a corporation, asset

---

10. The editors thank Professor Max M. Schanzenbach of Northwestern University School of Law for furnishing us with the Federal Reserve trust data.

11. The editors thank the South Dakota Banking Commission for the South Dakota trust data.

12. The figures reported in this paragraph are derived from estimates released by the Statistics of Income Division of the Internal Revenue Service.

13. Portions of this section are adapted from Robert H. Sitkoff, Trust Law as Fiduciary Governance Plus Asset Partitioning, *in* The Worlds of the Trust 428 (Lionel Smith ed., 2013); *see also* Daniel Clarry, Fiduciary Ownership and Trusts in a Comparative Perspective, 63 Int'l & Comp. L.Q. 901 (2014).

14. *See* Henry Hansmann & Reinier Kraakman, The Essential Role of Organizational Law, 110 Yale L.J. 387 (2000).

partitioning is easy. There was a clean and obvious line between the property and obligations of Steve Jobs, on the one hand, and the property and obligations of Apple, the corporation for which he was the chief executive officer, on the other. Jobs and Apple could each sue or be sued, or enter into transactions, with respect to the separate property of each.

For a common law trust, such straightforward asset partitioning is not possible. Strictly speaking, a trust is not a juridical entity but rather is a fiduciary relationship. A trust cannot sue, be sued, hold property, or transact in its own name. Instead, the trustee sues, is sued, holds property, and transacts with respect to trust property in the trustee's fiduciary capacity as such. Both substantive and semantic consequences ensue.

As a substantive matter, because legal title to the trust property belongs to the trustee, under traditional law the trustee was personally liable for the debts and obligations arising from ownership of the trust property. The trustee's personal liability was offset, however, by a right to indemnification out of the trust fund. A plumber who repaired a broken toilet in a rental building held in trust could recover his fee from the trustee personally, but after paying the plumber, the trustee would indemnify himself out of the trust fund. This clumsy and formalistic ritual, which is codified in authorities as late as the Restatement (Second) of Trusts,[15] served no functional purpose.

Prevailing American trust law has since been revised so that a creditor of a trustee in the trustee's fiduciary capacity recovers directly out of the trust fund without recourse against the property of the trustee personally.[16] And even though the trustee has legal title to the trust property, a personal creditor of the trustee has no recourse against the trust property.[17] Thus:

> *Case 6.* *O* devises Blackacre in trust to *X* to pay income to *A* for life and the remainder to *B* on *A*'s death. *X* contracts to sell Blackacre to *Y* for $100,000. *Y* may enforce the contract to buy Blackacre by suit against *X* in *X*'s capacity as trustee. *X* takes the proceeds from the sale of Blackacre as trustee, not personally. If *Z* has a judgment against *X* for an injury caused by *X*'s negligence unrelated to the trusteeship, *Z* has no recourse against Blackacre or the proceeds from the sale of Blackacre.

From the perspective of third parties, modern law in effect splits the trustee into "two distinct legal persons: a natural person contracting on behalf of himself, and an artificial person acting on behalf of the beneficiaries."[18]

As a semantic matter, Americans have come to reify the trust, referring to it as if it were an entity—e.g., "an agent owes a duty to the trust,"[19] or "to prevent unjust enrichment of the trust."[20] Such usages are a convenient shorthand for the technically accurate but more awkward locution of the trustee acting in his fiduciary capacity as

---

15. *See* Restatement (Second) of Trusts §§ 244, 261-265 (Am. Law Inst. 1959); *see also* Scott and Ascher on Trusts §§ 26.1-26.7.

16. *See* UTC § 1010 (2000); Restatement (Third) of Trusts §§ 105-106 (Am. Law Inst. 2012).

17. *See* UTC § 507 (2000); Restatement (Third) of Trusts § 42 cmt. c (Am. Law Inst. 2003).

18. Hansmann & Kraakman, *supra* note 14, at 416; *see also* Henry Hansmann & Ugo Mattei, The Functions of Trust Law: A Comparative Legal and Economic Analysis, 73 N.Y.U. L. Rev. 434 (1998); George L. Gretton, Trusts Without Equity, 49 Int'l & Comp. L.Q. 599 (2000).

19. Uniform Prudent Investor Act § 9 (Unif. Law Comm'n 1994).

20. UTC § 709 (2000).

"My only crime, Denise, was loving you too much.
That and embezzling your trust fund."

Leo Cullum/The New Yorker Collection/The Cartoon Bank

trustee. Reifying the trust in expression is also an embrace of substantive function over technical form. The contemporary American trust is in function (though not in juridical form) an entity.[21]

(b) Fiduciary Administration and the Rights of the Beneficiaries.   The trust's split of legal and equitable ownership puts responsibility for managing the trust property in the hands of the trustee. The trustee has "all of the *powers* over trust property that a legally competent, unmarried individual has with respect to individually owned property."[22] But the beneficiaries, not the trustee, bear the consequences of the trustee's exercise of these powers.[23] To protect the beneficiaries from abuse by the trustee, "in deciding whether and how to exercise the powers of the trusteeship," the trustee "is subject to and must act in accordance with the [trustee's] *fiduciary duties.*"[24]

In contrast to an arm's length relationship, in which each party is free to be self-serving, in a trust relationship the law requires the trustee, as a fiduciary, to subordinate her interests to those of the beneficiaries (see Chapter 9). Under the *duty of loyalty*, the trustee must administer the trust solely in the interest of the beneficiaries; self-dealing

---

21. *See* Restatement (Third) of Trusts ch. 21, intro. note (Am. Law Inst. 2012) (observing that "the trust is treated as an entity to such an extent that it is no longer inappropriate to refer to claims against or liabilities of a 'trust'").

22. Id. § 85(1)(a) (emphasis added).

23. *See* Robert H. Sitkoff, An Agency Costs Theory of Trust Law, 89 Cornell L. Rev. 621 (2004).

24. Restatement (Third) of Trusts § 86 (Am. Law Inst. 2007) (emphasis added); *see also* id. § 70 cmts. a, d.

is presumptively prohibited. Under the *duty of prudence*, the trustee is held to an objective standard of care and must administer the trust in a manner suited to the purpose of the trust and the needs of the beneficiaries. Important *subsidiary rules*, which reinforce and elaborate the loyalty and care norms, include the *duty of impartiality* to show due regard for the respective interests of the beneficiaries; the *duty not to commingle* the trust property with the trustee's own property; and the *duty to inform and account* to the beneficiaries.

In the event of a trustee's breach of duty, the beneficiary is entitled to remedies that include compensatory damages to restore the trust estate and trust distributions to what they would have been but for the breach and disgorgement by the trustee of any profit to the trustee owing to the breach.[25] The former is a standard measure of make-whole compensatory damages. The latter is a restitutionary remedy, typically in the form of a constructive trust, to prevent unjust enrichment of the trustee. A trustee who breaches her fiduciary duties may also be denied compensation and removed as trustee.

NOTE

The Four Functions of Trusteeship. Trusteeship involves four overlapping functions: custodial, administrative, investment, and distribution.[26] The *custodial* function involves taking custody of the trust property and properly safeguarding it. The *administrative* function includes accounting and recordkeeping as well as making tax and other required filings. The *investment* function involves reviewing the trust assets and making and implementing a prudent investment program as part of an overall strategy reasonably suited to the purpose of the trust and the circumstances of the beneficiaries. The *distribution* function involves making disbursements of income or principal to the beneficiaries in accordance with the terms of the trust. If a trust gives the trustee discretion over distributions, the trustee must exercise that discretion prudently, in good faith, and in accordance with the circumstances of the beneficiaries and the terms of the trust. In contemporary practice, naming a professional trustee and dividing the functions of trusteeship among different persons has become increasingly common (see Chapter 9 at page 661).

5. A Trust Compared with a Legal Life Estate

Private trusts commonly create successive beneficial interests. Trust income is often payable to a beneficiary or class of beneficiaries for life, perhaps to be followed by life interests in another class of beneficiaries, with the trustee to distribute the trust property to yet another class of beneficiaries upon termination of the trust. The creation of a trust therefore usually involves the creation of one or more equitable future interests as well as a present interest in the income.

---

25. *See* UTC § 1002(a) (2000); Restatement (Third) of Trusts § 100 (Am. Law Inst. 2012).
26. The four functions noted above are an extension of the three suggested in John H. Langbein, The Uniform Prudent Investor Act and the Future of Trust Investing, 81 Iowa L. Rev. 641, 665 (1996).

Case 7. *O* transfers securities worth $100,000 to *X* in trust, to pay the income to *A* for life and then to *B* for life. On the death of the survivor of *A* and *B*, the trustee is to distribute the trust principal to *B*'s descendants then living. *X* has legal title to the trust property and has a fiduciary duty to manage the property for the sole benefit of the named beneficiaries. *A* has an equitable life estate. *B* has an equitable remainder for life. *B*'s descendants have an equitable contingent remainder in fee simple. *O* has an equitable reversionary interest. If on the death of the survivor of *A* and *B* there are no descendants of *B* then living, the trust property will revert to *O* (or to *O*'s successors if *O* has died in the meantime).

Today, most life estates and future interests are equitable rather than legal interests; they are created in trusts (see Chapter 13). Legal life estates and future interests in personal property are rare and almost always unwise. Legal life estates and future interests in land are a bit less rare but are also almost always unwise. Let us compare a legal life estate ("to *A* for life, remainder to *A*'s descendants") with an equitable life estate ("to *X* in trust for *A* for life, remainder to *A*'s descendants").

a. Legal Life Estate

A legal life tenant has no power to sell a fee simple unless such a power is granted in the instrument creating the life estate. Otherwise, to sell a fee simple all the remainderpersons and reversioners must agree to the sale or the life tenant must obtain judicial approval. The same analysis pertains to obtaining a mortgage or leasing the property. Still another problem is waste. The life tenant may want to take oil out of the land, cut timber, or take down a still usable building. But each of these actions may constitute waste, entitling the remainderpersons to an injunction or damages.

If land is involved, someone must pay taxes and maintain the property. The general rule is that the life tenant has a duty to pay taxes and keep the property in repair. Life estates in personal property also pose problems. Personal property often requires expert management (think of stocks, bonds, and other financial assets). The application of the law of waste to life estates in personal property is uncertain.

If the life tenant gets into debt, the creditor can seize the life estate and sell it. Of course, very little may be realized upon sale. Often the creditor will buy it on judicial sale for a small amount, and if the life tenant lives a long time the creditor reaps a windfall. If the debtor is a remainderperson, the creditor may be able to seize the remainder and sell it. As with the life estate, the remainder may sell for very little, and the creditor usually will be the purchaser.

Many other problems may arise: trespassers may damage the property; the government may exercise eminent domain; a third party may be injured on the premises. If the respective rights of the life tenant and the remainderpersons are not addressed in the governing document, expensive court proceedings might be required to sort them out.[27]

---

27. *See, e.g.,* Hoskins v. Beatty, 343 S.W.3d 639 (Ky. App. 2011) (resolving whether a life tenant with a right to consume the property could transfer it to herself and then dispose of it at death (no), and whether she was entitled to keep the income from the property and dispose of it at death (yes)).

b. Equitable Life Estate — A Trust

All of the difficulties just described for a legal life estate are resolved or mitigated by a trust. If a house held in trust needs a new roof or if a plot of land should be sold for development, the trustee usually has broad enough powers to act promptly and to allocate the costs and benefits fairly between life and remainder beneficiaries. Even if the settlor creates a wide array of exotic beneficial interests such as a life tenant, multiple remainders, and a variety of executory interests, if those interests are in trust, third parties need deal only with the trustee.[28] The law of fiduciary administration, which we take up in Chapter 9, spells out the trustee's duties in managing trust property and in balancing the interests of life and remainder beneficiaries. And, unlike a legal estate, an equitable interest in trust can be put out of the reach of creditors, protecting an incautious beneficiary from himself (see Chapter 10).

NOTE

Abolish the Legal Life Estate?   Why not convert all legal life estates into trusts by statute? What purposes are served in having two bodies of law, one applicable to legal life estates and one applicable to life estates in trust? Pennsylvania has abolished life estates in personalty, converting the life tenant into a trustee.[29] Statutes in a handful of other states require the life tenant to account like a trustee, and courts in some states may require the life tenant to give security, but courts in other states reject the notion that a life tenant owes trustee-like duties.[30]

The English Law of Property Act of 1925 abolished the legal life estate in England. Today English law recognizes only two kinds of legal estates: the fee simple absolute in possession and the leasehold. Apart from leaseholds, all life estates and future interests of every kind — remainders, executory interests, reversions, possibilities of reverter, rights of entry — are equitable interests. The holder of the possessory interest holds the property in trust for the other interested parties. Should similar legislation be adopted in this country?[31]

6. Business Trusts

Although this book is focused primarily on the use of the trust in gratuitous transfers, it is worth mentioning the extraordinary role of the trust in commercial transactions. In the late 1800s and early 1900s, before the corporate form had matured, large-scale business enterprises regularly organized in trust form — the common law *business*

---

28. *See* Thomas W. Merrill & Henry E. Smith, The Property/Contract Interface, 101 Colum. L. Rev. 773, 847-49 (2001).

29. *See* Pa. Cons. Stat. Ann. tit. 20, § 6113 (2016).

30. *See, e.g.,* Alford v. Thibault, 990 N.E.2d 93 (Mass. App. 2013) (holding that life tenant did not owe fiduciary duty to remainderperson).

31. *See* C. Dent Bostick, Loosening the Grip of the Dead Hand: Shall We Abolish Legal Future Interests in Land?, 32 Vand. L. Rev. 1061 (1979); Ronald Maudsley, Escaping the Tyranny of Common Law Estates, 42 Mo. L. Rev. 355 (1977).

trust. The umbrella entity for John D. Rockefeller's Standard Oil Company was a trust, for example, not a corporation. The prevalence of the business trust in the United States explains why in this country we have anti*trust* law, not competition or monopoly law, as such bodies of law are known abroad.

In the late 1800s and early 1900s, entrepreneurs used the business trust to escape the heavy regulation of the corporate form. The business trust was so common in Massachusetts, where corporate ownership of real estate was prohibited, that the term *Massachusetts trust* became synonymous with business trust.[32]

Over the course of the twentieth century, the corporation became the preferred form for large enterprise organization. Yet the trust remains a vital cog in the modern economy.[33] The trust is still the preferred form of organization for mutual funds, which were known in the 1920s and 1930s as "investment trusts,"[34] and trusts are commonly used in asset securitization and for employee pension funds. Thus:

> *Case 8. Mutual Fund.* *T*, an investment professional, pools certain assets belonging to *A*, *B*, *C*, and others like them in a common fund to be managed by *T*. *A*, *B*, *C*, and the other investors each receive tradable shares in the fund. This pooling of assets achieves economies of scale, allows for professional portfolio management, and facilitates diversification. In managing the common fund, *T* is subject to a fiduciary obligation to *A*, *B*, *C*, and the other investors in the fund.[35]

> *Case 9. Asset Securitization.* *O*, a bank, makes loans to individuals secured by mortgages on the individuals' homes. *O* sells its rights to receive payments on the loans to *T* as trustee of an asset securitization trust. To pay for those rights, *T* sells the right to receive payments from the trust to *A*, *B*, and *C*. *T* manages the portfolio of individual loans, collecting payments on the loans from the borrowers, subject to a fiduciary obligation to *A*, *B*, and *C*.

> *Case 10. Pension Fund.* *X* hires *A* to work in *X*'s business. *X* agrees to pay a weekly wage to *A* and to contribute an amount representing 10 percent of *A*'s weekly wage to a pension trust for the benefit of *A*, payable to *A* upon her retirement. Until *A*'s retirement, the pension trust is managed by a professional trustee who is subject to a fiduciary obligation to *A*. We take up pension and retirement plans, which commonly allow for nonprobate transfer at death and are generally subject to federal law, in Chapter 7.

At mid-year 2016, pension and retirement accounts held $24.5 trillion and mutual funds held $16.35 trillion. The asset securitization industry is likewise worth in excess

---

32. *See* John Morley, The Common Law Corporation: The Power of the Trust in Anglo-American Business History, 116 Colum. L. Rev. 2145 (2016).

33. *See* John H. Langbein, The Secret Life of the Trust: The Trust as an Instrument of Commerce, 107 Yale L.J. 165 (1997); Steven L. Schwarcz, Commercial Trusts as Business Organizations: Unraveling the Mystery, 58 Bus. Law. 559 (2003).

34. *See* John Morley, Collective Branding and the Origins of Investment Fund Regulation, 6 Va. L. & Bus. Rev. 341, 347 n.9 (2012).

35. Mutual funds are subject to regulation under the Investment Company Act of 1940 and other federal securities laws. *See id.* at 362-66.

of $1 trillion. In terms of aggregate dollars, therefore, the commercial uses of the trust appear to exceed by a wide margin the use of the trust in gratuitous transfer.

Like the law governing donative trusts, the law of business trusts has been increasingly codified. A little more than half the states have enacted business trust statutes, giving rise to the *statutory business trust*.[36] Most mutual funds and asset securitization transactions that use the trust form employ a statutory trust rather than one arising under the common law. The leading business trust statute is the Delaware Statutory Trust Act of 1988.[37] A uniform act patterned on the Delaware statute, the Uniform Statutory Trust Entity Act, was promulgated by the Uniform Law Commission in 2009 and revised in 2011.

7. Foreign Trust Law

In the epigraph that opens this chapter, Frederic W. Maitland, the great scholar of the common law, asserts that "there is nothing quite like [the trust] in foreign law." This refrain is often repeated. But if the trust is "almost essential to civilization," skepticism about its uniqueness to the common law seems appropriate. In truth, foreign law has evolved a variety of legal arrangements that resemble the trust, albeit without the separation of legal and beneficial ownership that is characteristic of the common law trust.[38] A trust-like device—the *fideicommissum*—existed in Roman law. The English judges who developed the trust may have been influenced by the German *Treuhand*. In Hindu law, one finds a trust-like device called *benami*. In Islamic law, one finds the *waqf*.[39]

Today there is trust law in China and Japan, and trusts or trust-like devices are found in a host of other countries, including some that follow the civil law tradition.[40] In 1985, the Hague Convention on the Law Applicable to Trusts and on Their Recognition was established to provide guidance on the recognition of, and choice of law for, trusts in jurisdictions that lack a native trust law.[41]

A fairer claim is that the use of the trust for donative transfer is a distinctive feature of the Anglo-American legal tradition. Outside of Anglo-American practice, donative transfer by way of trust is rare, reflecting the typicality of forced shares and so more limited of freedom of disposition in those systems (see page 19). Interest abroad in the trust and trust-like devices, and the enactment of authorizing statutes in the

---

36. *See* Robert H. Sitkoff, Trust as "Uncorporation": A Research Agenda, 2005 U. Ill. L. Rev. 31.

37. Del. Code Ann. tit. 12, §§ 3801-3863 (2016).

38. *See* Clarry, *supra* note 13; Ruiqiao Zhang, A Comparative Study of the Introduction of Trusts into Civil Law and Its Ownership of Trust Property, 21 Tr. & Trustees 902 (2015).

39. *See* Scott and Ascher on Trusts § 1.10; Hamid Harasani, Toward the Reform of Private "Waqfs": A Comparative Study of Islamic "Waqfs" and English Trusts (2015).

40. *See, e.g.,* Trusts in Prime Jurisdictions (Alon Kaplan et al. eds., 4th ed. 2016); Frances H. Foster, American Trust Law in a Chinese Mirror, 94 Minn. L. Rev. 602 (2010).

41. *See* Emmanuel Gaillard & Donald T. Trautman, Trusts in Non-Trust Countries: Conflicts of Laws and the Hague Convention on Trusts, 35 Am. J. Comp. L. 307 (1987).

civil law countries in particular, has been focused instead on the commercial uses of the trust.[42]

B. CREATION OF A TRUST

The creation of a trust requires (1) *intent* by the settlor to create a trust; (2) *ascertainable beneficiaries* who can enforce the trust; and (3) specific *property*, the *res*, to be held in trust. In addition, if the trust is testamentary or is to hold land, (4) a *writing* may be required to satisfy the Wills Act or the Statute of Frauds.

1. Intent to Create a Trust

No particular form of words is necessary to manifest an intent to create a trust. Not even the word *trust* or *trustee* is required. The settlor need only manifest an intent to create the fiduciary relationship known by the law as a trust.[43] A person who is ignorant of trust law may therefore create a trust. A transfer of property to *X* "for the use and benefit" of *A*, for example, is typically held to create a trust.[44]

a. Testamentary Trust

A *testamentary trust* is created by will. Discerning whether a testator intended to create a trust involves construing the will (see Chapter 5). In a well-drafted will, the testator's intent to create a trust is stated clearly. Here is an example:

> All the residue of my estate, wherever situated, including lapsed devises, but excluding any property over which I may have a power of appointment, I give to XYZ Trust Company, of Chicago, Illinois, as trustee, to be held in trust and disposed of as follows:[45]

If a testator's intent to create a trust is not stated clearly, it may be inferred from the language and structure of the will in light of all the circumstances. Lux v. Lux, 288 A.2d 701 (R.I. 1972), is illustrative. Philomena Lux died testate in 1968. At issue was whether she devised certain real property to her grandchildren outright or in trust. The pertinent provisions of her will were as follows:

> 2. All the rest, residue and remainder of my estate, real and personal, of whatsoever kind and nature, and wherever situated, of which I shall die seized and possessed, or over which I may have power of appointment, or to which I may be in any manner entitled at my death, I give, devise and bequeath to my grandchildren, share and share alike.

---

42. *See* Madeleine Cantin Cumyn, Reflections Regarding the Diversity of Ways in Which the Trust Has Been Received or Adapted in Civil Law Countries, *in* Reimagining the Trust: Trusts in Civil Law 1, 14 (Lionel Smith ed., 2012).

43. *See* UTC § 402(a)(2) (2000); Restatement (Third) of Trusts § 13 (Am. Law Inst. 2003).

44. *See* Scott and Ascher on Trusts § 4.2.

45. Adapted from Northern Trust, Will & Trust Forms 101-3 (2004).

3. Any real estate included in said residue shall be maintained for the benefit of said grandchildren and shall not be sold until the youngest of said grandchildren has reached twenty-one years of age.

4. Should it become necessary to sell any of said real estate to pay my debts, costs of administration, or to make distribution of my estate or for any other lawful reason, then, in that event, it is my express desire that said real estate be sold to a member of my family.

The court construed this language as expressing an intent that the "real estate be held in trust for the benefit of [the testator's] grandchildren." The court explained:

[N]o particular words are required to create a testamentary trust. The absence of such words as "trust" or "trustee" is immaterial where the requisite intent of the testator can be found. . . . A trust never fails for lack of a trustee. . . .

When the residuary clause in the instant case is viewed in its entirety, it is clear that Philomena did not give her grandchildren a fee simple title to the realty. It appears that she, realizing the nature of this bequest and the age of the beneficiaries, intended that someone would hold and manage the property until they were of sufficient age to do so themselves. The property is income-producing and apparently she felt that the ultimate interest of her grandchildren would be protected if the realty was left intact until the designated time for distribution. The use of the terms "shall be maintained" and "shall not be sold" is a strong indication of Philomena's intent that the property was to be retained and managed by some person for some considerable time in the future for the benefit of her son's children. This is a duty usually associated with a trustee. We therefore hold that Philomena's will does create a trust on her real estate.

Having found the trust, the question of who shall serve as trustee is easily answered. The general rule is that, unless a contrary intention appears in the will or such an appointment is deemed improper or undesirable, the executor would be named to the position of trustee. . . . [T]he Superior Court . . . is authorized to appoint a trustee whenever an instrument creating a trust fails to name the residuary fiduciary.

NOTES

1. A Trust Will Not Fail for Want of a Trustee. A trust may have one trustee or several. A trustee may be an individual or a corporation. A trustee may be the settlor (if the trust is inter vivos), a beneficiary, or a third party. If a will names someone as trustee of a testamentary trust but the named person refuses the appointment or dies, and no successor trustee is named in the will, the court will appoint a successor. If the testator intends to create a trust but fails to name a trustee, the court will appoint one, usually the executor, as in *Lux*. The underlying principle, which is fundamental to the law of trusts, is commonly stated thus: *A trust will not fail for want of a trustee.*[46]

---

46. If the court finds that the trust powers were *personal to the named trustee*, then the trust will fail without that trustee. This exception is rarely invoked. In the usual case, the settlor intends for the trust to continue for its stated purposes and not only so long as a particular person serves as trustee. *See* Restatement (Third) of Trusts § 31 (Am. Law Inst. 2003).

2. Active Duties. Under traditional law, codified by UTC § 402(a)(4) (2000), the trustee must have some active duties to perform. If the trustee has no duties at all, the trust is said to be "passive" or "dry," and it fails. The beneficiaries take legal title to the trust property. Findings of a passive trust, as in In re Mannara, 785 N.Y.S.2d 274 (Sur. 2004), are rare but not unheard of in modern practice.

3. Precatory Language. In a surprisingly recurrent pattern, a testator expresses a "wish," "hope," or "recommendation" that property be used by the devisee in some particular manner. The problem is that this language does not clearly indicate whether the testator intended to create a trust, with fiduciary duties imposed on the devisee, or merely an unenforceable moral obligation. If the language indicates the latter, it is said to be *precatory*. Courts sometimes speak of *precatory trusts*, meaning unenforceable dispositions of this sort.[47]

In Colton v. Colton, 127 U.S. 300 (1888), the testator devised his entire estate to his wife and then continued, "I recommend to her the care and protection of my mother and sister, and request her to make such gift and provision for them as in her judgment will be best." Was this a bequest to the wife outright or in trust for the benefit of the testator's mother and sister? The Court framed the problem thus:

> On the one hand, the words may be merely those of suggestion, counsel, or advice, intended only to influence, and not to take away, the discretion of the legatee growing out of his right to use and dispose of the property given as his own. On the other hand, the language employed may be imperative in fact though not in form, conveying the intention of the testator in terms equivalent to a command, and leaving to the legatee no discretion to defeat his wishes, although there may be a discretion to accomplish them by a choice of methods, or even to define and limit the extent of the interest conferred upon his beneficiary.

After parsing the language of the will and the context in which it was drafted, the Court concluded that the testator intended to create a trust. But compare *Colton* with Estate of Brill v. Phillips, 76 So. 3d 695 (Miss. 2011). In *Brill*, the court held a devise to A "with the understanding that A will take care of my mother" to be precatory and not meant to create a trust.

The lesson is to be clear in your drafting. For example: "I wish, but do not legally require, that C permit D to live on the land."

b. Deed of Trust

Unlike a testamentary trust, which is created by will and so must satisfy the Wills Act, and an inter vivos trust of land, which must satisfy the Statute of Frauds (see page 436), no particular formalities are required to create an inter vivos trust of personal property. If the court determines that a transfer of property by O to T was intended to be in trust for the benefit of A, T is subject to fiduciary duties to A.

---

47. *See* Alyssa A. DiRusso, He Says, She Asks: Gender, Language, and the Law of Precatory Words in Wills, 22 Wis. Women's L.J. 1 (2007); Frank L. Schiavo, Does the Use of "Request," "Wish," or "Desire" Create a Precatory Trust or Not?, 40 Real Prop. Prob. & Tr. J. 647 (2006).

Jimenez v. Lee
547 P.2d 126 (Or. 1976)

O'CONNELL, C.J. This is a suit brought by plaintiff against her father to compel him to account for assets which she alleges were held by defendant as trustee for her. Plaintiff appeals from a decree dismissing her complaint.

Plaintiff's claim against her father is based upon the theory that a trust arose in her favor when two separate gifts were made for her benefit. The first of these gifts was made in 1945, shortly after plaintiff's birth, when her paternal grandmother purchased a $1,000 face value U.S. Savings Bond which was registered in the names of defendant "and/or" plaintiff "and/or" Dorothy Lee, plaintiff's mother. It is uncontradicted that the bond was purchased to provide funds to be used for plaintiff's educational needs. A second gift in the amount of $500 was made in 1956 by Mrs. Adolph Diercks, one of defendant's clients. At the same time Mrs. Diercks made identical gifts for the benefit of defendant's two other children. The $1,500 was deposited by the donor in a savings account in the names of defendant and his three children.

In 1960 defendant cashed the savings bond and invested the proceeds in common stock of the Commercial Bank of Salem, Oregon. Ownership of the shares was registered as "Jason Lee, Custodian under the Laws of Oregon for Betsy Lee [plaintiff]." At the same time, the joint savings account containing the client's gifts to defendant's children was closed and $1,000 of the proceeds invested in Commercial Bank stock.[48] Defendant also took title to this stock as "custodian" for his children.

The trial court found that defendant did not hold either the savings bond or the savings account in trust for the benefit of plaintiff and that defendant held the shares of the Commercial Bank stock as custodian for plaintiff under the Uniform Gift to Minors Act.[49] Plaintiff contends that the gifts for her educational needs created trusts in each instance and that the trusts survived defendant's investment of the trust assets in the Commercial Bank stock.

It is undisputed that the gifts were made for the educational needs of plaintiff. The respective donors did not expressly direct defendant to hold the subject matter of the gift "in trust" but this is not essential to create a trust relationship. It is enough if the transfer of the property is made with the intent to vest the beneficial ownership in a third person. That was clearly shown in the present case. Even defendant's own testimony establishes such intent. When he was asked whether there was a stated purpose for the gift, he replied:

> Mother said that she felt that the children should all be treated equally and that she was going to supply a bond to help with Elizabeth's educational needs and that she

---

48. The specific disposition of the balance of this account is not revealed in the record. Defendant testified that the portion of the gift not invested in the stock "was used for other unusual needs of the children." Defendant could not recall exactly how the money was used but thought some of it was spent for family vacations to Victoria, British Columbia, and to satisfy his children's expensive taste in clothing.

49. The Uniform Transfers to Minors Act, which is the successor to the Uniform Gifts to Minors Act, is examined in Chapter 2 at page 126.—Eds.

Judge Jason Lee

Jason Lee, the defendant in Jimenez v. Lee, was elected to the Oregon Court of Appeals in 1974, unseating an incumbent judge. As a result of the bitter campaign, a newspaper reporter sued the state bar under Oregon's open records law to reveal its disciplinary records on Lee. In 1975, Lee filed to run for the Oregon Supreme Court seat of Chief Justice O'Connell, who was retiring in 1976. The decision in Jimenez v. Lee, written by Chief Justice O'Connell, was handed down on March 18, 1976. The next day, March 19, Jason Lee withdrew from the Supreme Court race.

In June 1976, the Supreme Court decided the reporter's lawsuit and ordered the Jason Lee disciplinary records opened to the public.* Lee's files weighed 15 pounds and revealed many complaints. A public letter of reprimand, for ambulance chasing and for directing his secretary as a notary to execute false acknowledgments, had been issued to Lee in 1965. In an article published in 2002, a Justice of the Oregon Supreme Court pointed to the conduct of Lee in his campaigns for judicial office as a catalyst for reform of judicial elections in that state.†

Judge Lee remained on the Court of Appeals. In 1980, while still sitting on that court, Lee died of a heart attack. Lee's will left all his property to his second wife, Merie. If Merie predeceased him (she didn't), his will devised his property in trust for his grandchildren. "I leave nothing but my love to my children."

Judge Jason Lee

———————

* Sadler v. Or. State Bar, 550 P.2d 1218 (Or. 1976).
† Paul J. De Muniz, Politicizing State Judicial Elections: A Threat to Judicial Independence, 38 Willamette L. Rev. 367, 379-82 (2002).

The editors thank Professor Valerie Vollmar of Willamette University College of Law for providing the information in this note.

---

was naming me and Dorothy, the ex-wife and mother of Elizabeth, to use the funds as may be most conducive to the educational needs of Elizabeth.

Defendant also admitted that the gift from Mrs. Diercks was "for the educational needs of the children." There was nothing about either of the gifts which would suggest that the beneficial ownership of the subject matter of the gift was to vest in defendant to use as he pleased with an obligation only to pay out of his own funds a similar amount for plaintiff's educational needs.

Defendant himself demonstrated that he knew that the savings bond was held by him in trust. In a letter to his mother, the donor, he wrote: "Dave and Bitsie [plaintiff] & Dorothy are aware of the fact that I hold $1,000 each for Dave & Bitsie in trust for them on account of your E-Bond gifts." It is fair to indulge in the presumption that defendant, as a lawyer, used the word "trust" in the ordinary legal sense of that term. . . .

Having decided that a trust was created for the benefit of plaintiff, it follows that defendant's purchase of the Commercial Bank stock as "custodian" for plaintiff under the Uniform Gift to Minors Act was ineffectual to expand defendant's powers over the trust property from that of trustee to that of custodian.[50]

———————

50. If defendant were "custodian" of the gifts, he would have the power under the Uniform Gift to Minors Act, Or. Rev. Stat. (O.R.S.) § 126.820, to use the property "as he may deem advisable for the support, maintenance, education and general use and benefit of the minor, in such manner, at such time or times, and to such extent as the custodian in his absolute discretion may deem advisable and proper, without court order or without regard to the duty of any person to support the minor, and

Defendant's attempt to broaden his powers over the trust estate by investing the trust funds as custodian violated his duty to the beneficiary "to administer the trust solely in the interest of the beneficiary." Restatement (Second) of Trusts § 170 (1959).

The money from the savings bond and savings account are clearly traceable into the bank stock. Therefore, plaintiff was entitled to impose a constructive trust or an equitable lien upon the stock so acquired. Plaintiff is also entitled to be credited for any dividends or increment in the value of that part of the stock representing plaintiff's proportional interest. Whether or not the assets of plaintiff's trust are traceable into a product, defendant is personally liable for that amount which would have accrued to plaintiff had there been no breach of trust. Defendant is, of course, entitled to deduct the amount which he expended out of the trust estate for plaintiff's educational needs. However, before he is entitled to be credited for such expenditures, he has the duty as trustee to identify them specifically and prove that they were made for trust purposes. A trustee's duty to maintain and render accurate accounts is a strict one. . . .

Defendant did not keep separate records of trust income and trust expenditures. He introduced into evidence a summary of various expenditures which he claimed were made for the benefit of plaintiff. It appears that the summary was prepared for the most part from cancelled checks gathered together for the purpose of defending the present suit. This obviously did not meet the requirement that a trustee "maintain records of his transactions so complete and accurate that he can show by them his faithfulness to his trust." . . .

Defendant contends that even if a trust is found to exist and that the value of the trust assets is the amount claimed by plaintiff there is sufficient evidence to prove that the trust estate was exhausted by expenditures for legitimate trust purposes. Considering the character of the evidence presented by defendant, it is difficult to understand how such a result could be reached. As we noted above, the trust was for the educational needs of plaintiff. Some of the expenditures made by defendant would seem to fall clearly within the purposes of the trust. These would include the cost of ballet lessons, the cost of subscribing to a ballet magazine, and other items of expenditure related to plaintiff's education. But many of the items defendant lists as trust expenditures are either questionable or clearly outside the purpose of an educational trust. For instance, defendant seeks credit against the trust for tickets to ballet performances on three different occasions while plaintiff was in high school. The cost of plaintiff's ticket to a ballet performance might be regarded as a part of plaintiff's educational program in learning the art of ballet, but defendant claims credit for expenditures made to purchase ballet tickets for himself and other members of the family, disbursements clearly beyond the purposes of the trust. . . .

---

without regard to any other funds which may be applicable or available for the purpose." As custodian defendant would not be required to account for his stewardship of the funds unless a petition for accounting were filed in circuit court no later than two years after the end of plaintiff's minority. O.R.S. § 126.875. As the trustee of an educational trust, however, defendant has the power to use the trust funds for educational purposes only and has the duty to render clear and accurate accounts showing the funds have been used for trust purposes. *See* O.R.S. § 128.010; Restatement (Second) of Trusts § 172 (1959).

Ask Ann Landers

Dear Ann Landers: I am a 15-year-old girl. When my sister and I were born, my parents set up college accounts with our parents named as trustees. My parents divorced seven years ago, and my mother discovered that Dad had gone into those accounts and withdrawn half the balances. He opened new savings accounts for my sister and me, listing himself as the sole trustee.

My sister recently discovered that her account has no money in it. When I asked Dad to see my balance statement, he was evasive and said I was "too young to understand." He would not let me withdraw any money from the account. I'm pretty sure he has spent all of it. My mother cannot possibly afford to pay for all our college expenses. How can I approach Dad about what's going on without hurting his feelings? Is there any way I can get the money back?

—Loving Daughter in North Carolina

Dear Daughter: Don't be so worried about hurting Dad's feelings. He should be honest with you about the money so you can prepare for your future.

Ann Landers

If the funds are gone, there is no way you can get them back. Ask your father point-blank if there is money left in the account and how much. Tell him you need to know so you can start saving for college as soon as possible. Meanwhile, be prepared to check out student loans and scholarships at state universities. Lack of money is no reason to miss out on a college education.

—Ann Landers

_____

If Ann Landers had asked you what advice she should give Loving Daughter, what would you have said? This column ran on May 23, 2002. Ann Landers, whose real name was Ester Pauline Lederer, died a month later. Her twin sister, Pauline Ester Phillips, was the author of a competing advice column called Dear Abby. She died in early 2013.

The case must, therefore, be remanded for an accounting to be predicated upon a trustee's duty to account, and the trustee's burden to prove that the expenditures were made for trust purposes. . . . In determining whether defendant has met this strict burden of proof, the trial court must adhere to the rule that all doubts are resolved against a trustee who maintains an inadequate accounting system.

The decree of the trial court is reversed and the cause is remanded for further proceedings consistent with this opinion.

NOTES

1. What Was at Stake? In *Jimenez*, because the court determined that a trust was intended, the father was subject to fiduciary duties to the beneficiary, his daughter. If he wrongfully disposed of the trust property, his daughter could recover the property unless it was in the hands of a bona fide purchaser for value. If he sold trust property and acquired other property with the proceeds, she could enforce the trust upon the newly acquired property (see Chapter 9 at page 599). If he failed to maintain adequate records, the court could resolve the resulting uncertainty against him (see Chapter 9 at page 656).

2. Accepting Trusteeship. Because a trustee is subject to extensive fiduciary obligation and is therefore exposed to substantial potential liability, the law does not impose trusteeship upon a person unless the person accepts by words or con-duct.[51] Once a person accepts appointment as trustee, under traditional law she can be released from office only with the consent of the beneficiaries or by court order. UTC § 705 (2000, rev. 2001) modifies this rule to allow for resignation by a trustee with 30 days' notice to all interested parties. Professionally drafted trusts often contain a pro-vision to similar effect. For example: "Any trustee may resign at any time by written notice to each beneficiary then entitled to receive or eligible to have the benefit of the income from the trust."[52]

   3. Trust Distinguished from Equitable Charge.   The difference between a trust and an *equitable charge* deserves mention. If a testator devises property to a person, subject to the payment of a certain sum of money to a third person, the testator creates not a trust but an equitable charge, as in In re Estate of Stephano, 981 A.2d 138 (Pa. 2009). An equitable charge creates a security interest in the transferred property; there is no fiduciary relationship. The relationship between the holder of the charge and the beneficiary is more in the nature of a debtor and secured creditor.

c. Declaration of Trust

Under a *declaration of trust*, a settlor simply declares himself to be trustee of certain property. The settlor may also be a beneficiary of the trust. Thus:

> *Case 11.* O makes a written declaration of trust declaring herself trustee of $100,000 held at First National Bank, to pay the income to herself for life, and then on her death the funds are to pass to A. Even though O is the settlor, sole trustee, and sole income beneficiary, this is a valid trust.

   To have a valid trust, the trustee must owe fiduciary duties to someone other than herself. If O were the sole trustee and also the sole beneficiary, the equitable and legal titles would *merge*, leaving O with absolute legal title, as under UTC § 402(a)(5) (2000). Merger is quite rare, however, because most trusts have additional beneficiaries, as in Case 11.
   A declaration of trust of personal property requires no particular formalities. It does not require delivery or an instrument of transfer. The settlor need only mani-fest an intention to hold certain of the settlor's property in trust for an ascertainable beneficiary. In In re Smith's Estate, 22 A. 916 (Pa. 1891), the decedent had kept cer-tain bonds in an envelope in a bank safe-deposit box. On the envelope he had written that the bonds were "held for" his nephew. He recorded interest on the bonds to the nephew in a notebook. The court held that these facts showed an intent to create a trust by declaration.
   In Otto v. Gore, 45 A.3d 120 (Del. 2012), H and W each signed a written declaration of trust regarding certain stock in their business. The court held that the signed trust instrument, although strong evidence of an intent to create a trust, was not conclusive. H and W did not disclose the existence of the instrument to anyone and they continued

---

51. *See* UTC § 701 (2000); Restatement (Third) of Trusts § 35 (Am. Law Inst. 2003).
52. Adapted from Northern Trust, Will & Trust Forms 201-20 (2004).

to act as if they owned the shares outright. Other indicia of an intent to create a trust that had been present for other trusts created by *H* and *W* around the same time, such as initialing the attached schedule of property and obtaining a tax identification number, were lacking. The court held that no trust had arisen.

In contrast to a declaration of trust, an *outright gift* requires the donor to deliver the property to the donee. Delivery can be constructive or symbolic, rather than physical, but delivery of some kind is required.[53] Intention alone is not enough to perfect the gift. Consequently, if a donor manifests an intention to make a gift but fails to complete delivery, the question may arise whether the manifestation can be recharacterized as a declaration of trust.

Hebrew University Ass'n v. Nye
169 A.2d 641 (Conn. 1961)

KING, J. The plaintiff obtained a judgment declaring that it is the rightful owner of the library of Abraham S. Yahuda, a distinguished Hebrew scholar who died in 1951. The library included rare books and manuscripts, mostly relating to the Bible, which Professor Yahuda, with the assistance of his wife, Ethel S. Yahuda, had collected during his lifetime. Some of the library was inventoried in Professor Yahuda's estate and was purchased from the estate by his wife. There is no dispute that all of the library had become the property of Ethel before 1953 and was her property when she died on March 6, 1955, unless by her dealings with the plaintiff between January, 1953, and the time of her death she transferred ownership to the plaintiff. While the defendants in this action are the executors under the will of Ethel, the controversy as to ownership of the library is, in effect, a contest between two Hebrew charitable institutions, the plaintiff and a charitable trust or foundation to which Ethel bequeathed the bulk of her estate.

The pertinent facts recited in the finding may be summarized as follows: Before his death, Professor Yahuda forwarded certain of the books in his library to a warehouse in New Haven with instructions that they be packed for overseas shipment. The books remained in his name, no consignee was ever specified, and no shipment was made. Although it is not entirely clear, these books were apparently the ones which Ethel purchased from her husband's estate. Professor Yahuda and his wife had indicated to their friends their interest in creating a scholarship research center in Israel which would serve as a memorial to them. In January, 1953, Ethel went to Israel and had several talks with officers of the plaintiff, a university in Jerusalem. One of the departments of the plaintiff is an Institute of Oriental Studies, of outstanding reputation. The library would be very useful to the plaintiff, especially in connection with the work of this institute. On January 28, 1953, a large luncheon was given by the plaintiff in Ethel's

---

53. A *constructive delivery* gives the donee the means of obtaining the property, such as a key. A *symbolic delivery* gives the donee something symbolic of the object, for example a written instrument handed over when manual delivery is impractical. *See* Restatement (Third) of Property: Wills and Other Donative Transfers § 6.2 cmt. g (Am. Law Inst. 2003). For an example, see Mirvish v. Mott, 965 N.E.2d 906 (N.Y. 2012). For a comprehensive study of gifts under the common law and the civil law, see Richard Hyland, Gifts: A Study in Comparative Law (2009).

Professor Abraham S. Yahuda

Professor Yahuda was a child prodigy whose work as a linguist and scholar, as well as his private collection of rare books and manuscripts, were renowned across the globe.

Shalom Ezekiel Yahuda...published his first book, *Kadmoniyyot ha-Aravim* ("Arabs' Antiquities") at the age of fifteen.... An extraordinarily competent linguist[,] he published extensively on theological matters as well as on Jewish-Arab relations. During his life Yahuda travelled widely and acquired an extensive and valuable collection of books and manuscripts. He died in New Haven, Connecticut, in 1951, but such was the high regard in which he was held that a year after his death his body was moved to Israel where he was given a state burial in... Jerusalem.*

In addition to the religious texts remarked upon by the court, Yahuda's collection—appraised at the time of the litigation at $80,000—included original documents signed by Napoleon and many of the nonscientific papers of Sir Isaac Newton. Yahuda had

been in an intense competition with the British economist John Maynard Keynes for the Newton papers. The Keynes collection of Newton's papers is held today by King's College at the University of Cambridge.

Yahuda's collection, which included exten-

Professor Yahuda

sive writings by Newton on alchemy, theology, and the Bible, was characterized by Albert Einstein in a letter to "My Dear Yahuda" as "a most interesting look into the mental laboratory of this unique thinker." The Yahuda collection is held today by the Jewish National and University Library in Jerusalem.

---

* P.E. Spargo, Sotheby's, Keynes and Yahuda: The 1936 Sale of Newton's Manuscripts, *in* The Investigation of Difficult Things: Essays on Newton and the History of the Exact Sciences 115, 125 (P.M. Harman & Alan E. Shapiro eds., 1992).

honor and was attended by many notables, including officials of the plaintiff and the president of Israel. At this luncheon, Ethel described the library and announced its gift to the plaintiff. The next day, the plaintiff submitted to Ethel a proposed newspaper release which indicated that she had made a gift of the library to the plaintiff. Ethel signed the release as approved by her. From time to time thereafter she stated orally, and in letters to the plaintiff and friends, that she "had given" the library to the plaintiff. She refused offers of purchase and explained to others that she could not sell the library because it did not belong to her but to the plaintiff. On one occasion, when it was suggested that she give a certain item in the library to a friend, she stated that she could not, since it did not belong to her but to the plaintiff.

Early in 1954, Ethel began the task of arranging and cataloguing the material in the library for crating and shipment to Israel. These activities continued until about the time of her death. She sent some items, which she had finished cataloguing, to a warehouse for crating for overseas shipment. No consignee was named, and they remained in her name until her death. In October, 1954, when she was at the office of the American Friends of the Hebrew University, a fund-raising arm of the plaintiff in New York, she stated that she had crated most of the miscellaneous items, was continuously working on cataloguing the balance, and hoped to have the entire library in Israel before the end of the year. Until almost the time of her death, she corresponded with the plaintiff about making delivery to it of the library. In September, 1954, she wrote the president of the plaintiff that she had decided to ship the library and collection, but that it was not to be unpacked unless she was present, so that her husband's ex libris could be affixed to the books, and that she hoped "to adjust" the matter of her Beth Yahuda and her relations to the plaintiff. A "beth" is a building or portion of a building dedicated to a particular purpose.

The complaint alleged that the plaintiff was the rightful owner of the library and was entitled to possession. It contained no clue, however, to the theory on which ownership was claimed. The prayers for relief sought a declaratory judgment determining which one of the parties owned the library and an injunction restraining the defendants from disposing of it. The answer amounted to a general denial. The only real issues raised in the pleadings were the ownership and the right to possession of the library. As to these issues, the plaintiff had the burden of proof. The judgment found the "issues" for the plaintiff, and further recited that "a trust [in relation to the library] was created by a declaration of trust made by Ethel S. Yahuda, indicating her intention to create such a trust, made public by her." We construe this language, in the light of the finding, as a determination that, at the luncheon in Jerusalem, Ethel orally constituted herself a trustee of the library for future delivery to the plaintiff. The difficulty with the trust theory adopted in the judgment is that the finding contains no facts even intimating that Ethel ever regarded herself as trustee of any trust whatsoever, or as having assumed any enforceable duties with respect to the property. The facts in the finding, in so far as they tend to support the judgment for the plaintiff at all, indicate that Ethel intended to make, and perhaps attempted to make, not a mere promise to give, but an executed, present, legal gift inter vivos of the library to the plaintiff without any delivery whatsoever.

Obviously, if an intended or attempted legal gift inter vivos of personal property fails as such because there was neither actual nor constructive delivery, and the intent to give can nevertheless be carried into effect in equity under the fiction that the donor is presumed to have intended to constitute himself a trustee to make the necessary delivery, then as a practical matter the requirement of delivery is abrogated in any and all cases of intended inter-vivos gifts. Of course this is not the law. A gift which is imperfect for lack of a delivery will not be turned into a declaration of trust for no better reason than that it is imperfect for lack of a delivery. Courts do not supply conveyances where there are none. This is true, even though the intended donee is a charity. The rule is approved in 1 Scott, Trusts § 31.

It is true that one can orally constitute himself a trustee of personal property for the benefit of another and thereby create a trust enforceable in equity, even though without consideration and without delivery. 1 Scott, op. cit. § 28; § 32.2, p. 251. But he must in effect constitute himself a trustee. There must be an express trust, even though oral. It is not sufficient that he declare himself a donor. 1 Scott, op. cit. § 31, p. 239; 4 id. § 462.1. While he need not use the term "trustee," nor even manifest an understanding of its technical meaning or the technical meaning of the term "trust," he must manifest an intention to impose upon himself enforceable duties of a trust nature. Cullen v. Chappell, 116 F.2d 1017 (2d Cir. 1941); Restatement (Second), 1 Trusts §§ 23, 25; 1 Scott, op. cit., pp. 180, 181. There are no subordinate facts in the finding to indicate that Ethel ever intended to, or did, impose upon herself any enforceable duties of a trust nature with respect to this library. The most that could be said is that the subordinate facts in the finding might perhaps have supported a conclusion that at the luncheon she had the requisite donative intent so that, had she subsequently made a delivery of the property while that intent persisted, there would have been a valid, legal gift inter vivos. . . . The judgment, however, is not based on the theory of a legal gift inter vivos but on that of a declaration of trust. Since the subordinate facts give no support for a judgment on that basis, it cannot stand.

[The court remanded the case for a new trial at which the plaintiff could present its case on other theories than a declaration of trust.]

Hebrew University Ass'n v. Nye
223 A.2d 397 (Conn. Super. 1966)

PARSKEY, J. Most of the facts in this case are recited in Hebrew University Assn. v. Nye, 169 A.2d 641 (Conn. 1961). Additionally, it should be noted that at the time of the announcement of the gift of the "Yahuda Library" the decedent gave to the plaintiff a memorandum containing a list of most of the contents of the library and of all of the important books, documents and incunabula. . . .

The plaintiff claims a gift inter vivos based on a constructive or symbolic delivery. . . . For a constructive delivery, the donor must do that which, under the circumstances, will in reason be equivalent to an actual delivery. It must be as nearly perfect and complete as the nature of the property and the circumstances will permit. The gift may be perfected when the donor places in the hands of the donee the means of obtaining possession of the contemplated gift, accompanied with acts and declarations clearly showing an intention to give and to divest himself of all dominion over the property. It is not necessary that the method adopted be the only possible one. It is sufficient if manual delivery is impractical or inconvenient. Constructive delivery has been found to exist in a variety of factual situations: delivery of keys to safe deposit box; pointing out hiding places where money is hidden; informal memorandum.

Examining the present case in the light of the foregoing, the court finds that the delivery of the memorandum coupled with the decedent's acts and declarations, which clearly show an intention to give and to divest herself of any ownership of the library, was sufficient to complete the gift. If the itemized memorandum which the decedent transmitted had been incorporated in a formal document, no one would question the validity of the gift. But formalism is not an end in itself. "Whatever the value of the notion of forms, the only use of the forms is to present their contents." Holmes in Justice Oliver Wendell Holmes — His Book Notices and Uncollected Letters and Papers, p. 167 (Shriver Ed.). This is not to suggest that forms and formalities do not serve a useful and sometimes an essential purpose. But where the purpose of formalities is being served, an excessive regard for formalism should not be allowed to defeat the ends of justice. The circumstances under which this gift was made — a public announcement at a luncheon attended by a head of state, accompanied by a document which identified in itemized form what was being given — are a sufficient substitute for a formal instrument purporting to pass title. . . .

Rules of law must, in the last analysis, serve the ends of justice or they are worthless. For a court of equity to permit the decedent's wishes to be doubly frustrated for no better reason than that the rules so provide makes no sense whatsoever. "The plastic remedies of the chancery are moulded to the needs of justice." Foreman v. Foreman, 167 N.E. 428, 429 (N.Y. 1929). . . .

The court recognizes, in arriving at this result, that it is abrogating in some respects the requirement of delivery in a case involving an intended gift inter vivos. Obviously, it would be neither desirable nor wise to abrogate the requirement of delivery in any and all cases of intended inter-vivos gifts, for to do so, even under the guise of enforcing equitable rights, might open the door to fraudulent claims. But neither does it mean that the present delivery requirement must remain inviolate. "Equity is not crippled . . . by an inexorable formula." Marr v. Tumulty, 175 N.E. 356, 357 (N.Y. 1931). If it be argued that hard cases make bad law, the short response is, not while this court sits. . . .

Accordingly, judgment may enter declaring that the plaintiff is the legal and equitable owner of the "Yahuda Library" and has a right to the immediate possession of its contents.

NOTES

1. Professor Scott and Doctrinal Purity. The Scott treatise, favoring doctrinal purity, disapproves of cases in which the court recasts a gift as a declaration of trust because the intention to make a gift is plain but delivery is lacking.

> If the donor manifests the intention to make a gift but delivers neither the property, a deed of gift, nor any other instrument evidencing the gift, the gift is generally incomplete. . . . It frequently happens, therefore, that an intended gift fails for lack of delivery. In such a case, the donee may urge the court to recharacterize the imperfect gift as a complete and irrevocable declaration of trust by the donor. Especially when the intent to make a gift is clear, the temptation to uphold the transaction by finding that the donor intended a trust can be strong, since it is so easy to create a trust. It may be that the requirement of delivery is merely a relic from a time in which symbolism was more important than intention. But if we do away with the delivery requirement for a gift, there is no need to call a gift a declaration of trust. On the other hand, if sound policy underlies the delivery requirement, if it draws a helpful line between transactions that are inchoate and those that are final, it ought not be possible to evade the requirement by the simple device of calling a failed gift a declaration of trust, especially given the fact that the donor clearly never intended to create a trust. Thus, although courts have occasionally found that donors intended to create trusts on evidence that showed only an intention to make a gift, they have much more frequently refused to do so.[54]

2. The Modern Restatements. The Restatement (Third) of Trusts provides: "If a property owner intends to make an outright gift inter vivos but fails to make the transfer that is required in order to do so, the gift intention will not be given effect by

---

54. Scott and Ascher on Trusts § 5.1; *but see* Sarajane Love, Imperfect Gifts as Declarations of Trust: An Unapologetic Anomaly, 67 Ky. L.J. 309 (1979) (taking the opposite view).

treating it as a declaration of trust."[55] This would have pleased Professor Scott. But the commentary that accompanies this provision fuzzes up the picture:

> If the manifestations of intention provide reliable, objective evidence of a deceased property owner's intended purpose and there is no indication that this purpose has been abandoned, the conduct and words ordinarily are interpreted as intending a type of transaction that would be effective to accomplish this purpose under the circumstances. That is, the preferred interpretation in marginal cases of this type is not that the property owner was merely expressing an intention to make a gift in the future but rather that the owner intended a declaration of trust.[56]

If a client or a judge asked you to summarize the position of the Restatement (Third) of Trusts on this issue, how would you answer? What result in *Nye* if it had been decided under this Restatement?

The Restatement (Third) of Property is clearer. It provides that "a gift of personal property can be perfected on the basis of donative intent alone if the donor's intent to make a gift is established by clear and convincing evidence."[57] Under this Restatement, failure to satisfy the formality of delivery can be excused as harmless error if there is clear and convincing evidence of donative intent. The analogy is to excusing noncompliance with the formalities for executing a will (see page 176). What result in *Nye* if it had been decided under this Restatement?

2. Trust Property

Under traditional law, a trust cannot exist without *trust property*, often called the *res*.[58] The res need not, however, be land or a substantial sum of money. The res may be a penny or any other interest in any type of property.[59] Contingent remainders, leasehold interests, choses in action, royalties, life insurance policies—any interest that is transferrable—may be put in trust. What is necessary is a specifically identified interest in property.

Unthank v. Rippstein
386 S.W.2d 134 (Tex. 1964)

STEAKLEY, J. Three days before his death C.P. Craft penned a lengthy personal letter to Mrs. Iva Rippstein. The letter was not written in terms of his anticipated early death; in fact, Craft spoke in the letter of his plans to go to the Mayo Clinic at a later date. The portion of the letter at issue reads as follows:

---

55. Restatement (Third) of Trusts § 16(2) (Am. Law Inst. 2003).

56. Id. cmt. d.

57. Restatement (Third) of Property: Wills and Other Donative Transfers § 6.2 cmt. yy (Am. Law Inst. 2003); *see also* Adam J. Hirsch, Formalizing Gratuitous and Contractual Transfers: A Situational Theory, 91 Wash. U. L. Rev. 797 (2014).

58. As we shall see in Chapter 7 at page 467, the sole exception to this rule is under legislation such as the Uniform Testamentary Additions to Trusts Act for an inter vivos trust that is to be funded at the death of the settlor by a devise, known as a *pour over*, in the settlor's will.

59. *See* Restatement (Third) of Trusts § 40 cmt. b (Am. Law Inst. 2003).

Used most of yesterday and day before to "round up" my financial affairs, and to be sure I knew just where I stood before I made the statement that I would send you $200.00 cash the first week of each month for the next 5 years, provided I live that long, also to send you $200.00 cash for Sept. 1960 and thereafter send that amount in cash the first week of the following months of 1960, October, November and December. [opposite which in the margin there was written:]

I have stricken out the words "provided I live that long" and hereby and herewith bind my estate to make the $200.00 monthly payments provided for on this Page One of this letter of 9-17-60.

Mrs. Rippstein, Respondent here, first sought, unsuccessfully, to probate the writing as a [holographic] codicil to the will of Craft. The Court of Civil Appeals held that the writing was not a testamentary instrument which was subject to probate. In re Craft Estate, 358 S.W.2d 732 (Tex. App. 1962). We refused the application of Mrs. Rippstein for writ of error with the notation "no reversible error."

The present suit was filed by Mrs. Rippstein against the executors of the estate of Craft, Petitioners here, for judgment in the amount of the monthly installments which had matured, and for declaratory judgment adjudicating the liability of the executors to pay future installments as they mature. The trial court granted the motion of the executors for summary judgment. The Court of Civil Appeals reversed and rendered judgment for Mrs. Rippstein, holding that the writing in question established a voluntary trust under which Craft bound his property to the extent of the promised payments; and that upon his death his legal heirs held the legal title for the benefit of Mrs. Rippstein to that portion of the estate required to make the promised monthly payments.

In her reply to the application for writ of error Mrs. Rippstein states that the sole question before us is whether the marginal notation constitutes "a declaration of trust whereby [Craft] agrees to thenceforth hold his estate in trust for the explicit purpose of making the payments." She argues that Craft imposed the obligation for the payment of the monies upon all of his property as if he had said "I henceforth hold my estate in trust for [such] purpose." She recognizes that under her position Craft became subject to the Texas Trust Act in the management of his property. Collaterally, however, Mrs. Rippstein takes the position that it being determinable by mathematical computation that less than ten per cent of the property owned by Craft at the time he wrote the letter would be required to discharge the monthly payments, the "remaining ninety per cent remained in Mr. Craft to do with as he would." Her theory is that that portion of Craft's property not exhausted in meeting his declared purpose would revert to him by way of a resulting trust eo instante with the legal and equitable title to such surplus merging in him.

These arguments in behalf of Mrs. Rippstein are indeed ingenious and resourceful, but in our opinion there is not sufficient certainty in the language of the marginal notation upon the basis of which a court of equity can declare a trust to exist which is subject to enforcement in such manner. The uncertainties with respect to the intention of Craft and with respect to the subject of the trust are apparent. The language of the notation cannot be expanded to show an intention on the part of Craft to place his property in trust with the result that his exercise of further dominion thereover would be wrongful except in a fiduciary capacity as trustee, and under which Craft would be subject to suit for conversion at the hands of Mrs. Rippstein if he spent or disposed of his property in a manner which would defeat his statement in the notation that a monthly payment of $200.00 in cash would be sent her the first week of each month. It is manifest that Craft did not expressly declare that all of his property, or any specific portion of the assets which he owned at such time, would constitute the corpus or res of a trust for the benefit of Mrs. Rippstein; and inferences may not be drawn from the language used sufficient for a holding to such effect to rest in implication. The conclusion is compelled that the most that Craft did was to express an intention to make monthly gifts to Mrs. Rippstein accompanied by an ineffectual attempt to bind his estate in futuro; the writing was no more than a promise to make similar gifts in the future and as such is unenforceable. The promise to give cannot be tortured into a trust declaration under which Craft while living, and as trustee, and his estate after his death, were under a legally enforceable obligation to pay Mrs. Rippstein the sum of $200.00 monthly for the five-year period. . . .

The judgment of the Court of Civil Appeals is reversed and that of the trial court is affirmed.

NOTES

1. The Intent of C.P. Craft.   What policies are served by refusing to give effect to C.P. Craft's written instructions? If a gratuitous promise is made in a writing that shows unambiguously that the donor intended to be bound, should the court give effect to the writing as a declaration of trust? What would be the trust res? *See* Jane B. Baron, The Trust Res and Donative Intent, 61 Tul. L. Rev. 45 (1986) (arguing that the trust res requirement often defeats donative intent).

In the earlier decision cited by the court, Craft's letter was refused probate as a holographic will on the grounds that it did not evidence testamentary intent. What result under Uniform Probate Code (UPC) § 2-502(b)-(c) (Unif. Law Comm'n 1990, rev. 2008), page 144, as applied in In re Estate of Kuralt, page 210? What result under UPC § 2-503, page 177?

2. Is a Transfer of Property Necessary?   A trust may be created by *declaration of trust* without a transfer of property. All that is necessary is a manifestation of intent by the settlor to hold certain of his property, over which he already has legal title, in trust for one or more beneficiaries. In Taliaferro v. Taliaferro, 921 P.2d 803 (Kan. 1996), the court upheld as a valid declaration of trust a writing in which the settlor declared himself as trustee of certain property identified in a schedule attached to the written declaration. "No further document transferring title to the property was required."

How is this different than what transpired in *Unthank?* Why precisely was Craft's letter to Mrs. Rippstein not a valid declaration of trust? Hint: Does it express intent to declare a trust over *specific* property?

A trust created by *deed of trust*, by contrast, does require a transfer of property. In Trott v. Jones, 157 S.W.3d 592 (Ark. App. 2004), *O* attempted to create a trust of certain real property and the proceeds of a bank account with *A* and *B* as trustees. Although the trust instrument identified the intended trust corpus, *O* did not deliver to *A* and *B* a deed to the real property, nor did *O* retitle the bank account. The court held that, because *O* did not convey the property to the intended trustees, *O* had not created a valid trust. Relying on the Restatement, the court contrasted a trust with a third-party trustee from a declaration of trust thus:

> Restatement (Third) of Trusts § 10(c) . . . provides that a trust is created if the owner of property declares herself trustee of the property for the benefit of one or more others, or for the declarant and one or more others, even though there is no transfer of the title to the trust property. However, the same does not hold true when the settlor designates a third party to serve as trustee. In that situation, the Restatement provides that, if a property owner undertakes to make a donative inter vivos disposition in trust by transferring property to another as trustee, an express trust is not created if the property owner fails during life to complete the contemplated transfer of the property. Restatement (Third) of Trusts § 16(1). . . . [W]hen an owner of property intends to create an inter vivos trust other than by declaration, the owner must transfer the property to the intended trustee.

Should the requirement of a transfer of property to create a trust with a third-party trustee be relaxed — in effect, a harmless error rule for trust creation — if there is abundant evidence of the putative settlor's present intent to create a trust?[60]

3. Trust Distinguished from Debt.   A debt provides an interesting contrast to a trust. In a *debt*, the debtor agrees to pay a sum of money to a creditor — for example, a loan made by a bank (the creditor) to a borrower (the debtor). In spite of the debt, title to the debtor's property remains with the debtor. In a *trust*, by contrast, the trustee holds legal title to specific trust property — the trust res — for the benefit of the beneficiary. To protect the beneficiary from abuse by the trustee, the trustee is subject to fiduciary duties, including a duty not to commingle the trust property with the trustee's own property.

Money deposited in a bank ordinarily creates a debt. The depositor's money is not segregated from the bank's general funds. The depositor is entitled to be repaid a sum of money rather than to trace the particular funds deposited. The bank's debt to the depositor, however, can serve as a res if the depositor declares a trust over it (a declaration of trust) or transfers it to another to hold in trust (a deed of trust).

4. Resulting Trusts.   Iva Rippstein argued that C.P. Craft, after declaring a trust over all of his property, had a resulting trust in the amount of his property not required to meet the payments to her. A resulting trust is an *equitable reversionary interest* that arises by operation of law in two situations, the first of which was at issue in the case: (a) if an express trust fails or makes an incomplete disposition, or (b) if one person pays the purchase price for property and causes title to the property to be taken in the name of another person who is not a natural object of the purchaser's bounty.[61] Thus:

> *Case 12. Failure of Express Trust.*   O devises property to X in trust to pay the income to A for life, and on A's death to distribute the property to A's then living

---

60. *See* David Horton, Tomorrow's Inheritance: The Frontiers of Estate Planning Formalism, 58 B.C. L. Rev. (forthcoming 2017).

61. *See* Restatement (Third) of Trusts §§ 8-9 (Am. Law Inst. 2003).

descendants. *A* dies without descendants. Because the remainder to *A*'s descendants fails, *X* holds the remainder on resulting trust for *O*'s heirs or devisees.

Case 13. Purchase Money Resulting Trust.   *B* purchases Blackacre with money supplied by *A*. Unless *B* can show that *A* intended to make a gift to *B*, *B* holds title to Blackacre on resulting trust for *A*.

In both of these examples, the holder of the property is not entitled to the beneficial interest, which "is said 'to result' (that is, it reverts) to the transferor or to the transferor's estate or other successor(s) in interest."[62] Once a resulting trust is found, the trustee must convey the property to the beneficial owner upon demand.

5. Future Profits and Other Expectancies.   In *Brainard v. Commissioner*, 91 F.2d 880 (7th Cir. 1937), the settlor of a trust sought to obtain an income tax advantage by declaring a trust of his *future profits* from certain stock trading. The declaration did not encompass his existing portfolio, but rather the profits that might arise from subsequent trading. The settlor's purpose was to have those profits taxed at the lower brackets of the beneficiaries, who were his wife, mother, and children. This would have worked under the tax law at the time,[63] but only if he had created a trust. The court held that there was no trust because there were no profits at the time of the declaration. The Restatement (Third) of Trusts summarizes the applicable principle thus: "An expectation or hope of receiving property in the future, or an interest that has not come into existence or has ceased to exist, cannot be held in trust."[64]

3. Ascertainable Beneficiaries

a. The Beneficiary Principle

A private trust must have one or more *ascertainable beneficiaries* to whom the trustee owes fiduciary duties and who can call the trustee to account. This rule, which is codified by UTC § 402(a)(3) (2000), follows from the more fundamental principle that a private trust must be for the benefit of the beneficiaries.[65]

The beneficiaries need not, however, be ascertained when the trust is created—they need only be ascertainable within the period of the applicable Rule Against Perpetuities (see Chapter 14).[66] For example, a trust created by *O* for the benefit of her children would be valid even if *O* were childless. The courts would protect the interests of the unborn children, typically by appointing a guardian ad litem (see page 167), and those children would be born (or not) within *O*'s lifetime. On the other hand, if the beneficiaries are too indefinite to be ascertainable, the attempted trust will fail for want of an ascertainable beneficiary.

---

62. Id. § 7 cmt. a.
63. Under the current rules for taxing income in grantor trusts (see Chapter 15 at page 981), the tax avoidance strategy attempted in *Brainard* is no longer available.
64. Restatement (Third) of Trusts § 41 (Am. Law Inst. 2003).
65. *See* Langbein, *supra* note 8, at 1107-11.
66. *See* Restatement (Third) of Trusts § 44 cmt. c (Am. Law Inst. 2003).

Clark v. Campbell
133 A. 166 (N.H. 1926)

SNOW, J. The ninth clause of the will of deceased reads:

> My estate will comprise so many and such a variety of articles of personal prop-
> erty such as books, photographic albums, pictures, statuary, bronzes, bric-a-brac,
> hunting and fishing equipment, antiques, rugs, scrapbooks, canes and masonic jew-
> els, that probably I shall not distribute all, and perhaps no great part thereof, during
> my life by gift among my friends. Each of my trustees is competent by reason of
> familiarity with the property, my wishes and friendships, to wisely distribute some
> portion at least of said property. I therefore give and bequeath to my trustees all my
> property embraced within the classification aforesaid in trust to make disposal by
> the way of a memento from myself, of such articles to such of my friends as they, my
> trustees, shall select. All of said property, not so disposed of by them, my trustees are
> directed to sell and the proceeds of such sale or sales to become and be disposed of
> as a part of the residue of my estate.

The question here reserved is whether . . . the bequest for the benefit of the testator's
"friends" must fail for the want of certainty of the beneficiaries.

By the common law there cannot be a valid bequest to an indefinite person. There
must be a beneficiary or a class of beneficiaries indicated in the will capable of coming
into court and claiming the benefit of the bequest. This principle applies to private but
not to public trusts and charities. The basis assigned for this distinction is the difference
in the enforceability of the two classes of trusts. In the former there being no definite
cestui que trust to assert his right, there is no one who can compel performance, with
the consequent unjust enrichment of the trustee; while in the case of the latter, performance is considered to be sufficiently secured by the authority of the Attorney General
to invoke the power of the courts. . . .

That the foregoing is the established doctrine seems to be conceded, but it is contended in argument that it was not the intention of the testator by the ninth clause
to create a trust, at least as respects the selected articles, but to make an absolute gift
thereof to the trustees individually. . . . It is a sufficient answer to this contention that
the language of the ninth clause does not warrant the assumed construction. . . . When
the clause is elided of unnecessary verbiage the testator is made to say:

> I give to my trustee my property (of the described class) in trust to make disposal
> of to such of my friends as they shall select.

It is difficult to conceive of language more clearly disclosing an intention to create
a trust. . . . In the first clause of the will the testator nominates three trustees, and an
alternate in case of vacancy. Throughout the will these nominees are repeatedly and
invariably referred to as "my trustees," whenever the testator is dealing with their trust
duties. Whenever rights are conferred upon them individually, as happens in the fifth,
sixth, and eighth clauses, they are as invariably severally referred to solely by their individual names. . . .

It is further sought to sustain the bequest as a power. The distinction apparently
relied upon is that a power, unlike a trust, is not imperative and leaves the act to be

done at the will of the donee of the power. But the ninth clause by its terms imposes upon the trustees the imperative duty to dispose of the selected articles among the testator's friends. If, therefore, the authority bestowed by the testator by the use of a loose terminology may be called a power, it is not an optional power but a power coupled with a trust to which the principles incident to a trust so far as here involved clearly apply. . . .

We must, therefore, conclude that this clause presents the case of an attempt to create a private trust. . . .

The question presented, therefore, is whether or not the ninth clause provides for definite and ascertainable beneficiaries so that the bequest therein can be sustained as a private trust. . . .

Like the direct legatees in a will, the beneficiaries under a trust may be designated by class. But in such case the class must be capable of delimitation, as "brothers and sisters," "children," "issue," "nephews and nieces." A bequest giving the executor authority to distribute his property "among his relatives and for benevolent objects in such sums as in their judgment shall be for the best" was sustained upon evidence within the will that by "relatives" the testator intended such of his relatives within the statute of distributions as were needy, and thus brought the bequest within the line of charitable gifts and excluded all others as individuals. Goodale v. Mooney, 60 N.H. 528, 536 (1881). Where a testator bequeathed his stocks to be apportioned to his "relations" according to the discretion of the trustee, to be enjoyed by them after his decease, it was held to be a power to appoint amongst his relations who were next of kin under the statute of distribution. . . .

In the case now under consideration the cestuis que trust are designated as the "friends" of the testator. The word "friends" unlike "relations" has no accepted statutory or other controlling limitations, and in fact has no precise sense at all. Friendship is a word of broad and varied application. It is commonly used to describe the undefinable relationships which exist not only between those connected by ties of kinship or marriage, but as well between strangers in blood, and which vary in degree from the greatest intimacy to an acquaintance more or less casual. . . . There is no express evidence that the word is used in any restricted sense. The only implied limitation of the class is that fixed by the boundaries of the familiarity of the testator's trustees with his friendships. If such familiarity could be held to constitute such a line of demarcation as to define an ascertainable group, it is to be noted that the gift is not to such group as a class, the members of which are to take in some definite proportion (1 Jarman, Wills, 534; 2 Schouler, Wills, 1011) or according to their needs, but the disposition is to "such of my friends as they, my trustees, may select." No sufficient criterion is furnished to govern the selection of the individuals from the class. The assertion of the testator's confidence in the competency of his trustees "to wisely distribute some portion" of the enumerated articles "by reason of familiarity with the property, my wishes and friendships," does not furnish such a criterion. . . .

It was the evident purpose of the testator to invest his trustees with the power after his death to make disposition of the enumerated articles among an undefined class with practically the same freedom and irresponsibility that he himself would have exercised if living; that is, to substitute for the will of the testator the will and discretion of the trustees. Such a purpose is in contravention of the policy of the statute which provides that "no will shall be effectual to pass any real or personal estate . . . unless made by a person . . . in writing, signed by the testator or by some one in his presence and by his direction, and attested and subscribed in his presence by three or more credible witnesses." P.L. c. 297, § 2.

Where a gift is impressed with a trust ineffectively declared and incapable of taking effect because of the indefiniteness of the cestui que trust, the donee will hold the property in trust for the next taker under the will, or for the next of kin by way of a resulting trust. . . . The trustees therefore hold title to the property enumerated in the paragraph under consideration, to be disposed of as a part of the residue, and the trustees are so advised. . . .

Case discharged.

NOTES

1. Trust or Power of Appointment? Professor Scott argued that if there is a transfer in trust for members of an indefinite class of persons, such as to the testator's friends, no enforceable trust is created, but the transferee has a discretionary power to convey the property to such members of the class as he may select.[67] In other words, the transferee has a nonfiduciary *power of appointment.* If the class of beneficiaries is described such that some person might reasonably be said to answer the description, such a power is valid.

Beneficiaries are often given powers of appointment. *T* may devise his residuary estate, in trust, "for my wife, *W*, for life, and then to distribute the trust property to such of my descendants as *W* appoints by will." This power of appointment is discretionary; it is a nonfiduciary power that may be exercised "arbitrarily as long as the exercise is within the scope of the power."[68] If *W* fails to exercise the power, the trust property passes to the persons named in *T*'s will as the takers in default of appointment or to *T*'s heirs. We take up powers of appointment in Chapter 12.

In *Clark,* the court held that the testator did not create a power of appointment, because the power was given to *trustees* whose powers over the trust property necessarily are held in a fiduciary capacity. The testator created not an optional power but a "power coupled with a trust" to which the requirement of an ascertainable beneficiary applied. An ascertainable beneficiary who could enforce the trustees' duties was necessary for validity. If the power of selection had been given "to my sister Polly and my friend Herbert," by contrast, and not "to Polly and Herbert, *trustees* (or *executors*)," it would have been a valid nonfiduciary power of appointment. What is the drafting moral here?

2. The Uniform Trust Code. *Clark* reflects the orthodox view that a power in a trustee is not valid unless there is an ascertainable beneficiary. But why not follow

---

67. *See* Scott and Ascher on Trusts § 12.9.
68. Restatement (Third) of Property: Wills and Other Donative Transfers § 17.1 cmt. g (Am. Law Inst. 2011).

Professor Scott's suggestion and honor the donor's intent by interpreting a transfer in trust for an indefinite class of persons as a nonfiduciary power of appointment? UTC § 402(c) adopts Scott's suggestion:

> A power in a trustee to select a beneficiary from an indefinite class is valid. If the power is not exercised within a reasonable time, the power fails and the property subject to the power passes to the persons who would have taken the property had the power not been conferred.[69]

What result in *Clark* under the UTC?

3. Marilyn Monroe's Will Revisited.   The will of Marilyn Monroe (see page 33) contained the following clause: "I give and bequeath all of my personal effects and clothing to Lee Strasberg,[70] or if he should predecease me, then to my Executor here-inafter named, it being my desire that he distribute these, in his sole discretion, among my friends, colleagues and those to whom I am devoted." Does this language express an intent to create a trust? Does it specify an ascertainable beneficiary? Are you curious about what happened to the property? Professor Alyssa DiRusso reports:

Lee Strasberg
Larry Armstrong/L.A. Times

> Strasberg never distributed any of [Monroe's] personal effects to the friends or colleagues to whom Marilyn was devoted. In fact, Strasberg requested the return of several of Marilyn's possessions that she had given to a colleague. When Strasberg died, he left a will granting Marilyn's personal effects to his wife. Mrs. Strasberg, like her husband, chose not to submit to Marilyn's "desire." While Mrs. Strasberg has donated a few of Marilyn's items to be auctioned or displayed to benefit charity, she has not transferred any of Marilyn's property to any of Marilyn's friends or colleagues.[71]

b. Pet and Other Noncharitable Purpose Trusts

The beneficiary principle is not absolute. It is not applicable to a charitable trust, which instead must be for a *charitable purpose* (see Chapter 11). In addition, the trend in the cases, codified by the UTC and statutes in all states, has been toward allowing enforceable trusts for pet animals (§ 408) and certain other noncharitable purposes (§ 409), which under traditional law would be invalid for want of an ascertainable beneficiary.

---

69. Restatement (Third) of Trusts § 46 (Am. Law Inst. 2003) is to similar effect.

70. Lee Strasberg achieved considerable notoriety in his own right as an actor and acting coach in the method acting tradition. In 1952, he was named the artistic director of the prestigious Actor's Studio, a position that he held until his death in 1982. In addition to Monroe, Strasberg's students included James Dean, Robert De Niro, Jane Fonda, Dustin Hoffman, Paul Newman, and Al Pacino.—Eds.

71. DiRusso, *supra* note 47, at 3-4.

In re Searight's Estate
95 N.E.2d 779 (Ohio App. 1950)

HUNSICKER, J. George P. Searight, a resident of Wayne county, Ohio, died testate on November 27, 1948. Item "third" of his will provided:

> I give and bequeath my dog, Trixie, to Florence Hand of Wooster, Ohio, and I direct my executor to deposit in the Peoples Federal Savings and Loan Association, Wooster, Ohio, the sum of $1000.00 to be used by him to pay Florence Hand at the rate of 75 cents per day for the keep and care of my dog as long as it shall live. If my dog shall die before the said $1000.00 and the interest accruing therefrom shall have been used up, I give and bequeath whatever remains of said $1000.00 to be divided equally among those of the following persons who are living at that time, to wit: Bessie Immler, Florence Hand, Reed Searight, Fern Olson and Willis Horn.

At the time of his death, all of the persons, and his dog, Trixie, named in such item third, were living.

Florence Hand accepted the bequest of Trixie, and the executor paid to her from the $1000 fund, 75 cents a day for the keep and care of the dog. The value of Trixie was agreed to be $5.

The Probate Court [held item third valid]. . . .

The questions presented by this appeal on questions of law are:

1. Is the testamentary bequest for the care of Trixie (a dog) valid in Ohio —
   (a) as a proper subject of a so-called "honorary trust"?
   (b) as not being in violation of the rule against perpetuities? . . .

1(a). . . . We do not have, in the instant case, the question of a trust established for the care of dogs in general or of an indefinite number of dogs, but we are here considering the validity of a testamentary bequest for the benefit of a specific dog. This is not a charitable trust, nor is it a gift of money to the Ohio Humane Society or a county humane society, which societies are vested with broad statutory authority, Section 10062, General Code, for the care of animals.

Text writers on the subject of trusts and many law professors designate a bequest for the care of a specific animal as an "honorary trust"; that is, one binding the conscience of the trustee, since there is no beneficiary capable of enforcing the trust.

The rule in Ohio, that the absence of a beneficiary having a legal standing in court and capable of demanding an accounting of the trustee is fatal and the trust fails, was first announced in Mannix v. Purcell, 19 N.E. 572 (Ohio 1888). . . .

In 1 Scott on the Law of Trusts, Section 124, the author says:

> There are certain classes of cases similar to those discussed in the preceding section in that there is no one who as beneficiary can enforce the purpose of the testator, but different in one respect, namely, that the purpose is definite. Such, for example, are bequests for the erection or maintenance of tombstones or monuments or for the care of graves, and bequests for the support of specific animals. It has been held in a number of cases that such bequests as these do not necessarily fail. It is true that the legatee cannot be compelled to carry out the intended purpose, since there is no one to whom he owes a duty to carry out the purpose.

Even though the legatee cannot be compelled to apply the property to the designated purpose, the courts have very generally held that he can properly do so, and that no resulting trust arises so long as he is ready and willing to carry it out. The legatee will not, however, be permitted to retain the property for his own benefit; and if he refuses or neglects to carry out the purpose, a resulting trust will arise in favor of the testator's residuary legatee or next of kin. . . .

The object and purpose sought to be accomplished by the testator in the instant case is not capricious or illegal. He sought to effect a worthy purpose—the care of his pet dog.

Whether we designate the gift in this case as an "honorary trust" or a gift with a power which is valid when exercised is not important, for we do know that the one to whom the dog was given accepted the gift and indicated her willingness to care for such dog, and the executor proceeded to carry out the wishes of the testator.

> Where the owner of property transfers it upon an intended trust for a specific non-charitable purpose and there is no definite or definitely ascertainable beneficiary designated, no trust is created; but the transferee has power to apply the property to the designated purpose, unless he is authorized by the terms of the intended trust so to apply the property beyond the period of the rule against perpetuities, or the purpose is capricious.

I Restatement of the Law of Trusts, Section 124.

To call this bequest for the care of the dog, Trixie, a trust in the accepted sense in which that term is defined is, we know, an unjustified conclusion. The modern authorities, as shown by the cases cited earlier in this discussion, however, uphold the validity of a gift for the purpose designated in the instant case, where the person to whom the power is given is willing to carry out the testator's wishes. Whether called an "honorary trust" or whatever terminology is used, we conclude that the bequest for the care of the dog, Trixie, is not in and of itself unlawful.

1(b). In Ohio, by statute, Section 10512-8, General Code, the rule against perpetuities is specifically defined, and such statute further says:

> It is the intention by the adoption of this section to make effective in Ohio what is generally known as the common law rule against perpetuities.

It is to be noted, in every situation where the so-called "honorary trust" is established for specific animals, that, unless the instrument creating such trust limits the duration of the trust—that is, the time during which the power is to be exercised—to human lives, we will have "honorary trusts" established for animals of great longevity, such as crocodiles, elephants and sea turtles. . . .

If we then examine item third of testator's will, we discover that, although the bequest for his dog is for "as long as it shall live," the money given for this purpose is $1000 payable at the rate of 75¢ a day. By simple mathematical computation, this sum of money, expended at the rate determined by the testator, will be fully exhausted in three years and 238 1/3 days. If we assume that this $1000 is deposited in a bank so that interest at the high rate of 6% per annum were earned thereon, the time needed

A Tax on the Dog?

In *Searight's Estate*, the Department of Taxation of Ohio argued that an inheritance tax was levied on the amount used for the care of Trixie. The applicable statute levied a tax on all property passing to a "person, institution or corporation." In an omitted portion of the opinion, the court decided that a dog was none of these, and no inheritance tax was levied on the amount used for Trixie's care. A tax was levied, however, on the contingent amount passing to the five persons on the death of Trixie.

In the probate court proceedings, the Department also argued that a dog is personal property and, as such, Trixie was a thing of value that should have been taxed as an inheritance of Florence Hand. The executor of the estate of George P. Searight testified:

> If the Court please: I am an innocent bystander of this situation and am not personally interested one way or the other except to be right. Let me say this to the Court, — I wrote this provision in the Will, and frankly, the question as to whether the dog was taxable or not was never considered. I had no idea we would have such a problem. When the time came to make the Will George was concerned that when something happened to him that the dog was not to go to the dog pound. In fact he had as much affection for his dog as for his relatives. He lived with the dog and lived down there like a recluse.

> So far as the tax matter is concerned, let me take Mr. Annat's last contention, so far as taxing the dog as a thing of value. The dog may have a value of two, three or five dollars. It has no value other than that of a mongrel fox-terrier dog. Frankly I would say it could be argued that the fair market value of the dog was zero. If Florence tried to sell the dog I don't think she could give it away. On the contention of whether or not it is a thing of value I am not disposed to argue. Whether it can be sold, I don't know. I do know this, — George had it and I know there was some question about Florence taking it, and only because he made that instruction in the Will she took it.

The parties settled the matter by agreeing that the dog had a value of $5 and Florence Hand owed a tax on that. The executor's final accounting reported that $255.75 was distributed to Florence Hand for the care of Trixie, who died on October 30, 1949, after being struck by a car. The balance of the $1,000 was divided among the five legatees.

to consume both principal and interest thereon (based on semiannual computation of such interest on the average unused balance during such six month period) would be four years, 57 1/2 days.

It is thus very apparent that the testator provided a time limit for the exercise of the power given his executor, and that such time limit is much less than the maximum period allowed under the rule against perpetuities. . . .

We therefore conclude that the bequest in the instant case for the care of the dog, Trixie, does not, by the terms of the creating instrument, violate the rule against perpetuities. . . .

The judgment of the Probate Court is affirmed.

NOTES

1. Accommodating Trusts for Pets and Other Noncharitable Purposes. The problem in *Searight's Estate* is the trust law equivalent of the outright bequest in In re Estate of Russell, page 352. In *Russell*, the court construed the testator's will as making an outright devise to Roxy Russell, the testator's pet dog. But of course Roxy could not take ownership of any of the testator's property; Roxy was personal property of the testator.

The same reasoning applies within the law of trusts when looking for an ascertainable beneficiary. A pet animal, being property, cannot be the beneficiary of a trust (but it can be the res!). The animal can no sooner bring suit to enforce the trustee's fiduciary duties than could a lamp or a watch or a parcel of land. Nor can a trust for the care of a particular animal be salvaged as a charitable trust, as this is not a valid charitable purpose (see Chapter 11).

Yet many people want to establish trusts for the care of their pet animals, with which they have intense and loving relationships. They also want trusts for other non-charitable purposes such as the maintenance of graves and the saying of masses. Why not adapt the law to allow for such trusts so long as the purpose is not capricious or against public policy?[72] The question is perhaps most pressing in the case of trusts for pets. Nearly two-thirds of U.S. households (almost 80 million homes) include a pet—14.3 million birds, 85.8 million cats, 77.8 million dogs, 7.5 million equine, 105 million fish, 9.3 million reptiles, and 12.4 million "small animals."[73]

To accommodate the desire for trusts for noncharitable purposes and for pet animals in particular, two adaptations have evolved: (a) common law honorary trusts, and (b) statutory pet and other noncharitable purpose trusts.[74]

a. Common Law Honorary Trusts. Following the lead of the First and Second Restatements of Trusts,[75] many courts allowed what has come to be known as an *honorary trust*, as in *Searight's Estate*. In an honorary trust, the transferee is not under a legal obligation to carry out the settlor's stated purpose, hence the qualifier honorary, but if the transferee declines or neglects to do so, she holds the property upon a resulting trust and the property reverts to the settlor or the settlor's successors.[76]

In drafting an honorary trust, care must be taken not to offend the Rule Against Perpetuities (see Chapter 14).[77] Under the common law Rule, an honorary trust for a noncharitable purpose is void if it can last beyond all relevant lives in being at the creation of the trust plus 21 years. If the honorary trust is for a pet animal, the pet is *not* a validating life. Given that cockatoos can live to be 80, and tortoises have been known to live for over 150 years, avoiding a perpetuities violation can be challenging.

b. Uniform Acts and Other Statutes. Every state has enacted legislation that permits a trust for a pet animal, typically for the life of the animal, and often other noncharitable purposes such as perpetual maintenance of a grave or other burial

---

72. *See* Adam J. Hirsch, Bequests for Purposes: A Unified Theory, 56 Wash. & Lee L. Rev. 33 (1999).

73. Am. Pet Prods. Ass'n, Industry Statistics and Trends (2015-2016), available at https://perma.cc/KW2T-7XQ9.

74. *See* Richard C. Ausness, Non-Charitable Purpose Trusts: Past, Present, and Future, 51 Real Prop. Tr. & Est. L.J. 321 (2016); Frances H. Foster, Should Pets Inherit?, 63 Fla. L. Rev. 801 (2011).

75. *See* Restatement (First) of Trusts § 124 (Am. Law Inst. 1935); Restatement (Second) of Trusts § 124 (Am. Law Inst. 1959).

76. *See* Scott and Ascher on Trusts § 12.11.

77. *See* Adam J. Hirsch, Trusts for Purposes: Policy, Ambiguity, and Anomaly in the Uniform Laws, 26 Fla. St. U. L. Rev. 913, 930-50 (1999).

The "Trouble" with Leona Helmsley's Will

Perhaps the most famous trust for a pet animal arose under the will of Leona Helmsley, the luxury hotelier and New York real estate magnate who was dubbed the "Queen of Mean" by the tabloids for her harsh treatment of employees. Helmsley previously served an 18-month stint in federal prison for tax evasion. A witness testified that Helmsley had said: "We don't pay taxes. Only the little people pay taxes."

Helmsley died in 2007 with a will that left $12 million in trust for the benefit of her dog, Trouble, a Maltese poodle that Helmsley called Princess. Helmsley directed that upon Trouble's death, the dog should be interred next to her in the Helmsley Mausoleum, a direction that could not lawfully be followed, as New York law at the time prohibited burial of animals in human cemeteries.

Helmsley made a few modest bequests to people. She gave $100,000 to her chauffeur; $5 million outright plus a life interest in a $10 million trust to her brother; and $5 million outright plus a life interest in a $5 million trust to two of her four grandchildren (the other two she expressly disinherited). The favored grandchildren's respective rights to distributions from their trusts were conditioned, however, on their each visiting their father's grave at least once a year. Helmsley directed that "a register to be signed by each visitor" be "placed in the Helmsley Mausoleum," and that the trustees "shall rely on" the register exclusively "in determining whether" the grandchildren satisfied the visitation requirement. One wonders whether the grandchildren could satisfy the visitation condition for two years at a time by signing the register just before and after the clock strikes 12 on New Year's Eve.

Many were critical of Helmsley's will. The New York Times characterized Helmsley as a "posthumous control freak." But some were sympathetic. President Donald J. Trump, who had been Helmsley's rival in the New York real estate scene, is reported to have said, "The dog is the only thing that loved her and deserves every single penny of it."

The remainder of the Helmsley fortune, estimated to be worth in the neighborhood of $4 billion, was left to a charitable trust that she had created previously. To make her wishes for the charitable trust clear, in 2003 Helmsley signed a "Mission Statement" that said that the trustees should support (1) "the provision of care for dogs," and (2) "the provision of medical and health care services for indigent people, with emphasis on providing care to children." In 2004, Helmsley signed a superseding Mission Statement that dropped the

Leona Helmsley with her dog, Trouble
Splash News/Newscom

purpose of medical care for indigent children but kept the provision of care for dogs. Helmsley, it may be said, truly left her fortune to the dogs—or so she tried. In subsequent litigation, the New York courts ruled that the Mission Statements did not bind the trustees. In 2009, the trustees announced their first set of distributions, $136 million in all, of which only $1 million went to canine causes.

But what of the two disinherited grandchildren and Trouble's trust? The grandchildren contested Helmsley's will on the grounds of lack of capacity. A quick settlement was reached under which they shared a $6 million payout and the trust for Trouble was reduced to $2 million.

Like most states, New York has a statute that validates trusts for pet animals but authorizes the court to reduce the size of the trust if it "substantially exceeds the amount required for the intended use."[*] In limiting the trust to $2 million, the court relied on evidence of Trouble's yearly expenses, including $100,000 for security and $8,000 for grooming, and on the dog's life expectancy.

Proponents of pet trusts were delighted. One was quoted as saying: "One of the greatest moments in my life was when the judge awarded two million in the Helmsley case. It's not the reduction that's important; it's that the judge said two million was appropriate. It's a landmark case, for a judge to be able to say that we have a case for that amount of money."

Trouble died on December 13, 2010, at the age of 12, and was cremated. The funds remaining in Trouble's trust were added to the corpus of Helmsley's charitable trust, which in 2015 was worth $5.55 billion.[†] It is unknown whether Trouble's remains are in the Helmsley Mausoleum, which is private property.

---

[*] N.Y. Est. Powers & Trusts Law § 7-8.1(d) (2016).

[†] As reported on the trust's Form 990 filed with the IRS for the fiscal year ending on March 31, 2015. We discuss Form 990 in Chapter 11 at page 804.

Warren Miller/The New Yorker Collection/The Cartoon Bank

place. Many of these statutes are based on UTC §§ 408-409 (2000) or UPC § 2-907 (1990, rev. 1993). Under these provisions, a trust for a pet animal or certain other noncharitable purposes is valid, but the court is authorized to reduce the amount of the trust property if it is excessive. The UTC and UPC deal with the problem of enforcement, following the lead of trusts for minors and other incompetents, by authorizing a person named by the settlor or the court to enforce the trustee's fiduciary duties.

Perhaps the oddest pet trust statute is in Washington. It authorizes a trust for a pet animal, but only if the animal has vertebrae.[78] Wendy Goffe, a lawyer based in Seattle, tells us that the vertebrae limitation was inserted by a legislator who for obscure reasons was worried about the wasteful appointment of guardians ad litem for ant farms. The bar association's draft of the bill, says Goffe, did not discriminate against ants, slugs, or any other invertebrates, though now such animals will have to be provided for by an out-of-state trust.

The California pet trust statute is also noteworthy. A trust for the benefit of a pet animal alive at the settlor's death is valid for the life of the animal, as is typical, and the trust is enforceable by a person named by the settlor or by the court. But the statute also authorizes enforcement by "any person interested in the welfare of the animal or any nonprofit charitable organization that has as its principal activity the care of animals."[79] Is this a good idea?

2. The Rule Against Perpetuities.   The assumption of a 6 percent interest rate in *Searight's Estate* is inconsistent with the common law Rule Against Perpetuities, which considers what might happen rather than what is likely to happen. We take up the what-might-happen rule of the common law Rule in Chapter 14 at page 894.

---

78. Wash. Rev. Code § 11.118.010 (2016).
79. Cal. Prob. Code § 15212(c) (2016).

4. A Written Instrument?

The law of trusts, standing alone, does not require a writing to create a valid trust. An oral inter vivos trust of personal property, whether by declaration or by transfer to another as trustee, is enforceable.[80] However, a testamentary trust must be in writing to satisfy the Wills Act, and an inter vivos trust of land must be in writing to satisfy the Statute of Frauds.[81]

Let us consider (a) an oral inter vivos trust of personal property, (b) an attempted oral testamentary trust, and (c) an attempted oral inter vivos trust of land. As we shall see, an oral trust for the disposition of personal property at death, although permissible, is in tension with the policy values of the Wills Act. And the central policy of the law of restitution, preventing unjust enrichment, sometimes calls for relief by way of constructive trust if an oral trust fails for noncompliance with the Wills Act or the Statute of Frauds.

a. Oral Inter Vivos Trusts of Personal Property

Uniform Trust Code (Unif. Law Comm'n 2000)

§ 407. Evidence of Oral Trust

Except as required by a statute other than this [Code], a trust need not be evidenced by a trust instrument, but the creation of an oral trust and its terms may be established only by clear and convincing evidence.

In re Estate of Fournier
902 A.2d 852 (Me. 2006)

DANA, J. Faustina Fogarty appeals from a judgment entered in the Aroostook County Probate Court denying her petition for a declaratory judgment that she was the beneficiary of an oral trust created by her brother, the late George Fournier. . . .

I. BACKGROUND

In 1998 or 1999, Fournier asked a couple who were friends with him if they would "hold some money for him." They said they would, and Fournier delivered two boxes, each containing $200,000 cash, to their home. Fournier asked them to hold the $400,000 in secret until his death and then deliver it to his sister, Faustina Fogarty. Fournier explained that Fogarty "needed it more" than his other sister, Juanita Flanigan.[82] Although he requested secrecy from his friends, Fournier told both Flanigan and her daughter that his friend was holding money for him.

---

80. *See* Restatement (Third) of Trusts § 20 (Am. Law Inst. 2003).

81. Id. §§ 17, 22.

82. Apparently in recognition of Fogarty's financial need, Fournier gave her a gift of $100,000 in 2002.

George Fournier, Bachelor and Recluse

Richard D. Solman, the winning counsel in *Fournier*, describes Mr. Fournier and his relationship with Josephat and Yvette Madore, the trustees, as follows:

> George Fournier was a bachelor and a bit of a recluse. As it turns out, he regularly kept hundreds of thousands of dollars hidden in various places throughout his home. No one knows how, when, or where he accumulated his money, but he was a very frugal spender.
>
> He became friends with a Josephat Madore, who was employed in the transportation department at the local school. Later, Josephat and his wife, Yvette, took it upon themselves to check on George from time to time, to take him to medical appointments, etc.
>
> Although they were never social friends, George trusted the Madores and eventually asked them to hold $400,000 in cash until his death. He also appointed Josephat as his attorney-in-fact under a general power of attorney.
>
> It is unclear why George did not prepare a written trust agreement. Perhaps he did not want to spend the money. The evidence suggests that George didn't want the government to tax the money on his death. He told the Madores that he had already paid taxes on the money once.
>
> George did have a will, which was prepared by an attorney subsequent to the delivery of the cash to the Madores. However, there was no reference in the will to the cash held by the Madores or the trust.*

George Fournier

Fournier's will, dated January 10, 2000, provided for several cash bequests (including a gift of $5 to his sister Rose); gave his Maine residence to his sister Juanita Flanigan and his grandnephew Curtis King; gave a separate Maine property, "including the boats, buildings, garages and other outbuildings," to Faustina Fogarty; and gave the residue in equal shares to Flanigan, Fogarty, and King.

---

* Email from Richard D. Solman to Robert H. Sitkoff (Aug. 14, 2008).

Fournier died in 2005, survived by Fogarty and Flanigan. Under his will, Fogarty was appointed the personal representative of his estate. Upon learning of Fournier's death, Fogarty and her son met privately with the couple, and the husband gave Fogarty the money. Fogarty petitioned for a declaratory judgment to establish that during his lifetime Fournier had created an oral trust for her benefit. Following a hearing, the court denied her petition and she brought this appeal.

II. DISCUSSION

A. The Law

"A trust may be created by [t]ransfer of property to another person as trustee during the settlor's lifetime." 18-B Maine Revised Statutes (M.R.S.) § 401(1) (2005). Section 402(1) provides, in pertinent part:

A trust is created only if:
   A. The settlor has capacity to create a trust;
   B. The settlor indicates an intention to create the trust;
   C. The trust has a definite beneficiary . . . ;
   D. The trustee has duties to perform; and
   E. The same person is not the sole trustee and sole beneficiary.

Although a trust need not be in writing, the creation of an oral trust must be established by clear and convincing evidence. 18-B M.R.S. § 407. . . .

B. The Evidence Presented at the Hearing

At the hearing, the husband engaged in the following colloquy with Fogarty's attorney:

Q. [W]hat instructions did Mr. Fournier give you in regard to this money?

A. Hold that money until he's dead. Return the money to [Fogarty], and that's what I did.

Q. Did Mr. Fournier tell you who the money was for?

A. He just said [Fogarty]. Nobody else. . . .

Q. Did Mr. Fournier tell you why he wanted the money to go to his sister [Fogarty]? . . .

A. . . . He said [Fogarty] had a big family, that she's the one that would need more money, you know? And then he mentioned a couple of names, you know? He said [Flanigan] was a wealthy woman, [and h]e didn't want Curtis [King] to get the money.[83] . . .

Q. At any time did Mr. Fournier tell you that he wanted part of this 4 hundred thousand to go to [Flanigan], or anybody else?

A. The only thing he told me was money had to go to [Fogarty]. . . .

Q. . . . Was the only time he talked about the four hundred thousand the first time he brought it to you[?]

A. Never talked about the four hundred thousand beside that[.]

The wife testified as follows:

I asked [Fournier] what are we supposed to do with this money if something happens to you [and h]e says it would go to [Fogarty]. . . . And after a year or two I asked [Fournier] are you ready to take back your money, [and] he says, no, leave it where it is[, i]t's for [Fogarty]. I feel she needs it more. Because I knew he had another sister, and I asked about the other sister. He said the other sister, she's well off. She has plenty of money, and I feel [Fogarty] would need it more.

Flanigan's daughter testified that Fournier told her about the money, saying: "If anything should happen to me, I am giving [the husband] some money to hold for me." Additionally, Flanigan testified that Fournier told her that the husband was holding money for her and Fogarty.

C. The Court's Factual Findings and Legal Conclusions

The [probate] court found that Fournier instructed the couple that, upon his death, they should "deliver the money to Faustina Fogarty, the personal representative named

---

83. Richard D. Solman, the winning counsel in *Fournier,* writes as follows: "George reportedly felt that Curtis had wasted the inheritance he had received when his mother (George's sister) had died." Email from Richard D. Solman to Robert H. Sitkoff (Aug. 14, 2008). — Eds.

in his Will." The court reasoned that, in telling Flanigan's daughter about the money,[84] Fournier evinced an intent that the money pass through his estate. The court further reasoned, somewhat inconsistently, that, in giving Fogarty $100,000 in 2002, Fournier decreased her financial need, potentially obviating the need for a trust for her benefit.

Applying 18-B M.R.S. § 402(1), the court concluded that, despite Fournier's instructions to the couple, no trust had been created. The court ordered that the $400,000 was part of Fournier's estate.

D. Analysis

While we discern no error in the court's finding that Fournier instructed the couple to deliver the money to Fogarty, we discern clear error in its finding that Fogarty was to take the money as personal representative. Neither Fournier's discussion with Flanigan's daughter, nor his previous gift to Fogarty contradicts the overwhelming evidence (provided primarily by the couple) that Fournier intended Fogarty to take the money in her individual capacity.

Applying 18-B M.R.S. § 402(1) to the foregoing findings, we conclude that Fournier created an oral trust in which the couple was to hold the money during his lifetime and turn it over to Fogarty personally after his death.

The entry is: Judgment vacated and remanded to the Probate Court for entry of a judgment in favor of Faustina Fogarty.

NOTES

1. Epilogue.   Six weeks after the Maine Supreme Judicial Court rendered the decision in *Fournier* excerpted above, Juanita Flanigan petitioned the probate court for a new trial. The basis for her petition was a note found by a real estate agent in an unlocked metal box under a bureau in George Fournier's home. In a variety of ink and

Signature of Josephat Madore

Subsequently discovered note in *Fournier*

---

84. Although Flanigan testified that Fournier told her the husband was holding money "for the two of us," the court does not appear to have credited Flanigan's testimony. Indeed, the court found that Flanigan had "recently suffered a stroke and [was] still in the process of recovery" and that her "memory [was] not good."

pencil notations, the note, evidently written by Fournier, referenced $400,000 given to Josephat Madore that was to be used to "reimburse" Flanigan, Faustina Fogarty, and Curtis King. King's name was crossed out. The note, which was dated about a year after Fournier gave Madore and his wife the disputed $400,000 in cash, was not signed by Fournier. But it was signed by Madore!

The probate court granted Flanigan's petition and, after a new trial, concluded that the note showed that the oral trust was for the benefit of Flanigan, Fogarty, and King. It ordered the $400,000 to be divided among them in equal shares. On appeal, the Supreme Judicial Court affirmed in In re Estate of Fournier, 966 A.2d 885 (Me. 2009).

2. Clear and Convincing Evidence. As in *Fournier*, an oral trust that provides for the disposition of personal property at the death of the settlor may be proved by oral testimony. Does the requirement of clear and convincing evidence, as in most states and under UTC § 407, page 429, satisfy the evidentiary, channeling, ritual (or cautionary), and protective functions of the Wills Act? How can the outcome in *Fournier* be squared with cases such as In re Groffman, page 147, and Stevens v. Casdorph, page 149, in which a signed will for which authenticity was not in doubt was denied probate because of an innocuous defect in attestation? Does *Fournier* provide an argument in favor of relaxing the strict compliance rule for wills? Or is the subsequent litigation in *Fournier* a cautionary tale about allowing transfers at death without much in the way of formalities?

b. Secret Testamentary Trusts and the Wills Act

Olliffe v. Wells
130 Mass. 221 (1881)

[Ellen Donovan died in 1877, leaving a will devising her residuary estate to the Rev. Eleazer M.P. Wells "to distribute the same in such manner as in his discretion shall appear best calculated to carry out wishes which I have expressed to him or may express to him." Wells was named executor. Ellen's heirs brought suit, claiming the residue should be distributed to them. In his answer, Wells stated that Ellen Donovan, before and after the execution of the will, had orally expressed to him her wish that her estate be used for charitable purposes, and especially for the poor, aged, infirm, and needy under the care of St. Stephen's Mission of Boston. Wells further stated that he desired and intended to distribute the residue for these purposes. The parties agreed that the facts alleged in the answer should be taken as true.]

GRAY, C.J. Upon the face of this will the residuary bequest to the defendant gives him no beneficial interest. It

Chief Justice Horace Gray, appointed to the Massachusetts Supreme Judicial Court at age 36, the youngest justice in its history, later served as an Associate Justice of the U.S. Supreme Court. His half-brother, Professor John Chipman Gray of Harvard, came up with the formulation of the Rule Against Perpetuities still used today (see page 888).
Kean Collection/Getty Images

expressly requires him to distribute all the property bequeathed to him, giving him no discretion upon the question whether he shall or shall not distribute it, or shall or shall not carry out the intentions of the testatrix, but allowing him a discretionary authority as to the manner only in which the property shall be distributed pursuant to her intentions. The will declares a trust too indefinite to be carried out, and the next of kin of the testatrix must take by way of resulting trust, unless the facts agreed show such a trust for the benefit of others as the court can execute. Nichols v. Allen, 130 Mass. 211 (1881). . . .

It has been held in England and in other States, although the question has never arisen in this Commonwealth, that, if a person procures an absolute devise or bequest to himself by orally promising the testator that he will convey the property to or hold it for the benefit of third persons, and afterwards refused to perform his promise, a trust arises out of the confidence reposed in him by the testator and of his own fraud, which a court of equity, upon clear and satisfactory proof of the facts, will enforce against him at the suit of such third persons. . . .

Upon like grounds, it has been held in England that, if a testator devises or bequeaths property to his executors upon trusts not defined in the will, but which, as he states in the will, he has communicated to them before its execution, such trusts, if for lawful purposes, may be proved by the admission of the executors, or by oral evidence, and enforced against them. . . . And in two or three comparatively recent cases it has been held that such trusts may be enforced against the heirs or next of kin of the testator, as well as against the devisee. . . . But these cases appear to us to have overlooked or disregarded a fundamental distinction.

Where a trust not declared in the will is established by a court of chancery against the devisee, it is by reason of the obligation resting upon the conscience of the devisee, and not as a valid testamentary disposition by the deceased. Cullen v. Attorney General, L.R. 1 H.L. 190. Where the bequest is outright upon its face, the setting up of a trust, while it diminishes the right of the devisee, does not impair any right of the heirs or next of kin, in any aspect of the case; for if the trust were not set up, the whole property would go to the devisee by force of the devise; if the trust set up is a lawful one, it enures to the benefit of the cestuis que trust; and if the trust set up is unlawful, the heirs or next of kin take by way of resulting trust.

Where the bequest is declared upon its face to be upon such trusts as the testator has otherwise signified to the devisee, it is equally clear that the devisee takes no beneficial interest; and, as between him and the beneficiaries intended, there is as much ground for establishing the trust as if the bequest to him were absolute on its face. But as between the devisee and the heirs or next of kin, the case stands differently. They are not excluded by the will itself. The will upon its face showing that the devisee takes the legal title only and not the beneficial interest, and the trust not being sufficiently defined by the will to take effect, the equitable interest goes, by way of resulting trust, to the heirs or next of kin, as property of the deceased, not disposed of by his will. Sears v. Hardy, 120 Mass. 524, 541, 542 (1876). They cannot be deprived of that equitable interest, which accrues to them directly from the deceased, by any conduct of the

The Reverend Eleazer M.P. Wells

Eleazer Mather Porter Wells, born in 1783, entered Brown University at the age of 22 but was dismissed as a result of a practical joke played on a professor by his roommates. (O tempora! O mores!) Thereafter he was deeply affected by a profound religious experience, including voices in the night saying, "Go and do my work." At age 40, Wells entered the ministry, becoming an Episcopal priest.

In 1843, at age 60, Wells opened St. Stephen's Mission. From there he provided food, nursing care, clothing, and shelter for the poor of the West End of Boston. On one occasion he was able to keep the fire at the mission going by burning 100 old volumes of Voltaire's writings, which had been given to the mission. These proved good kindling. Wells is quoted as having said, "Well, even the worst of men are put to good uses for the benefit of others."

The great Boston fire of 1872 destroyed St. Stephen's Mission. For the remaining years of his life Wells worked to revitalize the mission to no avail. Wells died in 1878 at age 95. A resolution adopted by the clergy of the Episcopal Diocese of Massachusetts paid tribute to Wells as

The Rev. Wells

[a] clergyman of stainless reputation and incorruptible integrity; an enthusiast in his sacred calling, especially in his self-selected mission to the destitute and afflicted, the outcast and the erring.... The work of Dr. Wells, continued so long a period at St. Stephen's Mission in Boston, and as the trusted almoner of very many of his fellow citizens, and withal his pure and consistent life as a man of God and of unremitting prayer, furnish a splendid commendation of religion.

The editors thank Mark J. Duffy, Archivist of the Episcopal Diocese of Massachusetts, for providing the information in this note.

devisee; nor by any intention of the deceased, unless signified in those forms which the law makes essential to every testamentary disposition. A trust not sufficiently declared on the face of the will cannot therefore be set up by extrinsic evidence to defeat the rights of the heirs at law or next of kin. . . .

Decree for the plaintiffs.

NOTE

Secret and Semisecret Trusts. Olliffe v. Wells is the origin of the distinction between a secret and a semisecret trust, still followed in most states. The distinction is this: If Ellen Donovan had left a bequest to the Reverend Wells absolute on its face, without anything in the will indicating an intent to create a trust, a promise by the Reverend Wells to Ellen Donovan to use the bequest for St. Stephen's Mission would be enforceable in restitution by a constructive trust imposed upon Wells. This is called a *secret trust* because the will indicates no trust. Courts admit evidence of the promise for the purpose of preventing the Reverend Wells from unjustly enriching himself by keeping the bequest. Having admitted proof of the promise, courts prevent unjust enrichment by imposing a constructive trust on Wells for the benefit of St. Stephen's Mission.

On the other hand, if the will indicates that the Reverend Wells is to take the bequest as trustee but does not identify the beneficiary (as in Olliffe v. Wells), the bequest is said to be a *semisecret trust*, and it fails. Because the will shows on its face an intent for Wells to take as trustee, it is not necessary to admit evidence of Wells's promise in order to prevent his unjust enrichment. Such evidence is excluded, and the semisecret trust fails for want of an ascertainable beneficiary in the terms of the will.[85]

But what of the intestate heirs who receive the property subject to the failed gift to Wells? Are not they unjustly enriched owing to the frustration of Ellen Donovan's intent that the property pass to the unidentified beneficiary? Why is extrinsic evidence admissible to enforce a secret trust, for which there is no indication on the face of the will, but not for a semisecret trust, for which the will on its face gives some indication of the intent to make a trust?

The Restatement (Third) of Restitution and Unjust Enrichment takes the position, as in England and in a few states, that relief should be available in both secret and semisecret trust cases:

> If the problem is approached from the perspective of unjust enrichment, ... it is impossible to draw a persuasive distinction between the "secret trust" and the "semi-secret trust" whose intended beneficiary is known. In either case, failure to give effect to the intent of the donor will result in unjust enrichment at the expense of the intended donee. It is the secret trustee who would be unjustly enriched in the first case; the decedent's remaining legatees or legal heirs, in the second.[86]

The weight of authority in the United States, at least for now, still follows Olliffe v. Wells.[87]

c. Oral Inter Vivos Trusts of Land and the Statute of Frauds

Suppose *O* deeds land to *X* upon an oral trust to pay the income to *A* for life and upon *A*'s death to convey the land to *B*. The Statute of Frauds, which requires a writing to evidence a conveyance of land, prevents the enforcement of this arrangement as an express trust. Does this mean that *X* is permitted to keep the land?

The cases are split between permitting *X* to retain the land, on the grounds that the Statute of Frauds forbids proof of the oral trust, and allowing relief in restitution by way of constructive trust imposed on *X* to prevent his unjust enrichment.[88] A constructive trust in favor of *A* and *B* will be imposed if the transfer was wrongfully obtained by fraud or duress; if *X* was in a confidential relationship with *O*; or if the transfer was made in anticipation of *O*'s death. Most of the cases involve one of these situations.

More common than an oral trust for a third party is one for the benefit of the transferor. Judging by the cases, a surprising number of persons put title to land in another,

---

85. In Taylor v. Holt, 134 S.W.3d 830 (Tenn. App. 2003), page 154, at issue was the will of Steve Godfrey (depicted at page 155). Godfrey devised his estate to his friend Doris: "Doris you know how we have talked about how I want everything done and I know you will do it that way. So I am leaving everything I have to you, because I know you will take care of it like you always have." Is this a semisecret trust or mere precatory words?

86. Restatement (Third) of Restitution and Unjust Enrichment § 46 cmt. g (Am. Law Inst. 2011); *see also* Restatement (Third) of Trusts § 18 cmt. c (Am. Law Inst. 2003) (similar).

87. *See, e.g.,* Pickelner v. Adler, 229 S.W.3d 516 (Tex. App. 2007).

88. *See* Scott and Ascher on Trusts § 6.11.

relying upon the transferee's oral promise to reconvey upon request. Some of the transferors are attempting to avoid creditors or spouses or to achieve some tax benefit. Of course, any lawyer knows these transferors are asking for trouble, and human nature being what it is, usually they get it.

A comparison of Hieble v. Hieble, 316 A.2d 777 (Conn. 1972), with Pappas v. Pappas, 320 A.2d 809 (Conn. 1973), is instructive. In *Hieble,* a mother transferred title to certain real property from herself alone to herself in joint tenancy with her son and daughter. The mother was fearful of a return of cancer and wanted to avoid probate. The son and daughter agreed to reconvey the property to the mother if she remained healthy. Several years later, the son refused his mother's request to reconvey his interest in the property, so the mother brought suit. The court concluded that a constructive trust should be imposed on the basis of the oral agreement and the confidential relationship of the parties.

In *Pappas,* Andrew Pappas, age 67, married a 23-year-old woman while on a visit to Greece. On their return, marital difficulties arose. Just prior to the wife's suing for divorce, Andrew conveyed certain real estate to his son. The son agreed to transfer the property back to Andrew once his marital difficulties were over. In the divorce action, Andrew testified that he made the conveyance for consideration in satisfaction of certain financial and other obligations. After the divorce action was concluded, Andrew demanded a reconveyance, but the son refused. The court held that a constructive trust could not be imposed upon the son because Andrew, in misrepresenting the nature of the transfer in the divorce action, had perpetrated a fraud on the court and therefore had unclean hands.

CHAPTER 7

NONPROBATE TRANSFERS AND PLANNING FOR INCAPACITY

> [A] will substitute serves the function of a will. It shifts the right to
> possession or enjoyment to the donee at the donor's death.
> In this sense, a will substitute is in reality a nonprobate will.
>
> RESTATEMENT (THIRD) OF PROPERTY:
> WILLS AND OTHER DONATIVE TRANSFERS
> § 7.2 cmt. a (Am. Law Inst. 2003)

A DONOR MAY EXERCISE her freedom of disposition at death other than by will in probate. In this chapter, we examine revocable inter vivos trusts, life insurance and other pay-on-death and transfer-on-death contracts, pension plans and retirement accounts, and other legal arrangements that have the effect of passing property at death outside of probate. Taken together, these *will substitutes* constitute a nonprobate system of private succession that competes with the public probate system—and private succession is winning. More wealth passes by way of will substitutes than by probate.[1]

The rise of private succession raises two main legal questions. First, must a will substitute be executed with *Wills Act formalities* to be effective to pass property at death? Second, to what extent should the policy-based substantive limits on testation by will and the default rules of construction applicable to a will, collectively the *subsidiary law of wills*, apply to a will substitute? Courts and legislatures have struggled with these questions, in particular the second. An added complication is that federal law preempts state law as regards most pension accounts and life insurance policies that are obtained as a benefit of employment.

---

1. *See* Russell N. James III, The New Statistics of Estate Planning: Lifetime and Post-Mortem Wills, Trusts, and Charitable Planning, 8 Est. Plan. & Community Prop. L.J. 1, 27-28 (2015) (reporting extensive survey evidence showing predominance of nonprobate transfer); *see also* David Horton, In Partial Defense of Probate: Evidence from Alameda County, California, 103 Geo. L.J. 605, 627-28 (2015) (estimating that only 7 percent of 2007 decedents in Alameda, California left probate estates, inferring widespread probate avoidance).

As a practical matter, the use of multiple will substitutes can result in an estate plan that lacks coordination. To avoid this problem, many lawyers recommend creating a revocable trust and making it the beneficiary of the client's will and various will substitutes.[2] The revocable trust has thus emerged as the successor to the will as the centerpiece instrument in contemporary estate planning.

In this chapter, we also examine the challenge of planning for the possibility of a person's future incapacity. We focus on property management and health care decision making for an incapacitated person, examining the default rules and the ways in which revocable trusts, durable powers of attorney, and health care directives are used to opt out of those defaults. It is a sad fact of the human condition that a period of mental and physical decay may precede death. Planning for incapacity is therefore as much a part of trusts and estates practice as planning for death, one that is of growing importance owing to ever increasing human longevity.

We begin in Section A by considering the rise of the nonprobate system. In Section B, we consider the revocable trust, the most will-like of the will substitutes. In Section C, we consider the other main will substitutes: life insurance, pension and retirement accounts, and other pay-on-death and transfer-on-death arrangements. In Section D, we consider planning for incapacity.

A. THE RISE OF NONPROBATE SUCCESSION

John H. Langbein
Major Reforms of the Property Restatement and the Uniform Probate Code: Reformation, Harmless Error, and Nonprobate Transfers
38 ACTEC L.J. 1 (2012)

The deepest trend now affecting the day-to-day reality of gratuitous transfers in the United States is the nonprobate revolution, by which I mean the burgeoning use of will substitutes to transfer property on death. . . .

THE WILL SUBSTITUTES

Will substitutes are modes of transfer that operate outside the state-operated transfer system of probate administration, hence largely outside the law of wills and intestacy. In contemporary practice, there are five major types of will substitute: (1) the revocable inter vivos trust; (2) life insurance; (3) various types of pay-on-death (POD) bank accounts; (4) transfer-on-death (TOD) securities accounts; and (5) pension accounts, primarily of the individual-account variety. Each of these types is associated with and supported by its own industry—respectively, the trust industry,

---

2. As we have seen (see page 394), the vernacular of American trust practice reifies the trust, referring to it as if it were an entity (e.g., "to name the trust as the beneficiary"). Although technically incorrect, reifying the trust provides a convenient shorthand, "the trust," for the more awkward locution of "the trustee acting in the trustee's capacity as such."

which is composed of trust companies and trust and estate lawyers; the insurance industry; the commercial banking industry; the securities industry; and the various financial-service providers who have come to constitute the pension industry. . . .

How did the financial service entities such as banks and mutual fund companies come to be competitors of the probate system? Financial intermediation is intrinsically administrative. "Administrators intermediate between savers and borrowers, between passive owners and active users of capital. Pooling wealth and servicing the resulting liabilities involves recurrent transactions and communications. Once a bureaucracy appropriate to those tasks is in operation, only a [modest] adaptation is [needed] to extend [the] functions and procedures [of the intermediary] to include the transfer of account balances on death."

The association of the will substitutes with particular types of financial administration helps explain a distinctive and structurally troublesome feature of the nonprobate system: Apart from the revocable trust, the other main will substitutes—sometimes called mass will substitutes—are asset-specific. That is, each type is a transfer system that is limited to the particular type of asset that the particular type of financial intermediary happens to offer and to service: Insurance companies transfer insurance accounts arising under insurance policies, banks transfer bank account balances, and so forth.

The reason that this feature of the mass will substitutes is troublesome is that there is seldom any estate planning logic to asset-specific transfers. In the probate and trust world, we do not use a separate will or trust for each asset. We know how to make a specific devise when one is wanted, but our default norm is to consolidate assets of all types under the residuary clause of one instrument of transfer, the will or the trust. If there is to be good estate planning with respect to most nonprobate assets, the estate planner has to coordinate many separate transfers. It is not uncommon for a propertied person to have a dozen or more will-like beneficiary designations in effect on various banking, investment, insurance, and pension accounts. Dealing with this multiplicity of transfers—coordinating them into a sensible plan, and keeping beneficiary designations up to date in accord with changing circumstances—has become a central problem of modern estate planning. . . .

Most wealth transfer on death today occurs through the nonprobate system, for the simple reason that most personal wealth is now held in financially intermediated account forms that invite nonprobate transfer. The trend toward such forms of wealth has produced financial services industries of stupendous size. . . .

THE RELATIONS OF THE PROBATE AND NONPROBATE SYSTEMS

. . . I have spoken of the nonprobate modes of transfer as free-market competitors of the state-operated system of transfer on death. A prospective transferor can use the state system of probate, or the private systems operated by Vanguard, Metropolitan Life, Wells Fargo, and the like. We see similar choices in the spread of arbitration: Parties in dispute can use the state system of courts, judges, and procedures, or the parties can contract out of the state system in favor of private providers. Education provides comparable choices: You can send your child to a public school, or to a private one. In law-and-economics terms, your decision to use private transfer-on-death services is a Coasean determination to contract out of the state system of probate administration.

The image of Darwinian struggle between state and non-state transfer systems should not, however, be exaggerated. The state has been playing an important hand in encouraging the growth of the nonprobate system, both by allowing nonprobate transfers, and by devising varieties of state-operated transfer that work in tandem with the free-market providers to facilitate probate avoidance. Consider, for example, the procedures for transferring title to a decedent's motor vehicle. Typically, these state statutes allow the department of motor vehicles to transfer the title on receipt of an affidavit from a survivor, who attests that the decedent did not otherwise leave assets requiring probate. Moreover, in most states, there is a similar, affidavit-based procedure for small estates that allows a survivor to collect and distribute other assets belonging to a decedent when the total involved is below a statutorily set ceiling. These measures reinforce the nonprobate system by allowing expeditious transfer of assets that have traditionally been probate property.[3]

The probate system also supports the nonprobate system by serving a standby role for troubled transfers. Nonprobate beneficiary designations all but invariably name the transferor's probate estate as the final contingent distributee. Thus, if the beneficiaries designated on an account form "predecease the transferor or cannot be identified, the financial intermediary remits the fund to probate distribution. . . . Likewise, if the proper course of distribution is for some reason doubtful, or if contest threatens, financial intermediaries can force the probate (or other) courts to decide the matter," either by interpleading or by refusing suspect claims and forcing the claimants to contest. In consequence, the nonprobate system "execute[s] easy transfers and shunt[s] the hard ones over to probate. . . . In the nonprobate system, genuine disputes still reach the courts, but routine administration does not."

What increasingly happens, therefore, when a modest or moderate wealth-holder dies is that Vanguard, Met Life, and Wells Fargo transfer the main assets, the DMV transfers the car, and anything that's left passes under an affidavit-based small-estate procedure, or by private agreement among the survivors. Until lately, probate was still necessary to clear title when a decedent died owning real property, but nonprobate transfer forms have now been extended even there. . . . [I]n 2009 the Uniform Law Commission promulgated the Uniform Real Property Transfer on Death Act, which allows the owner of real property to execute and record a revocable beneficiary designation effective to transfer the property on the owner's death.

If you want to understand the contraction in demand for estate planning services among moderate wealth holders, combine the elimination across the last generation of federal estate tax exposure for such persons with the rise of the nonprobate system and you have much of the explanation. For better or worse, and in my view it is worse, nonprobate all too often means nonlawyer. The ease with which an account owner can fill out a financial institution's beneficiary designation form seems to imply that professional estate planning guidance is no longer needed. The focus on avoiding probate deflects attention from considerations that laypersons often do not apprehend, such as the desirability of planning for contingencies such as lapse or incapacity. . . .

---

3. On small estate and motor vehicle procedures, see page 49. — Eds.

GOALS OF THE LAW REVISION PROJECTS

... [T]he size of the nonprobate system [means] that there is no turning back, no possibility of restoring a probate-centered system of wealth transfer on death. Public suspicion of probate is too great, not to mention the power of the financial services industry.

When, therefore, in the law revision process, we came to deal with the rise of the nonprobate system, we concentrated on improving it rather than impeding it. . . . [I]n both the [Uniform Probate] Code and the Restatement [(Third) of Property], we took steps to clarify that the Wills Act does not govern nonprobate transfers, and accordingly, that Wills Act formal requirements do not apply. As a matter of ordinary business practice, the financial services firms that operate the mass will substitutes invariably require beneficiary designations to be in writing and to be signed by the transferor. In this way, the nonprobate system replicates by contract the two main Wills Act formal requirements, writing and signature, but dispenses with attestation. . . .

[I]n the UPC and the Restatement, we [also] undertook to unify the rules of construction across the two transfer systems. The most prominent example is the divorce revocation rule. In most states, either by statute or case law, it has long been settled that if John executes a will devising property to his spouse Mary, and John and Mary thereafter divorce, Mary will not take under the will. The law presumes that John's devise to Mary was impliedly conditioned on the persistence of the marriage, and should be treated as revoked on divorce. . . . In many states, the divorce revocation statute spoke only to wills, not having foreseen and addressed the identical problem in the will substitutes. When, therefore, John's life insurance policy or his TOD security account named Mary as the beneficiary, she would take. What we did in the UPC was expressly to extend the divorce revocation statute to the will substitutes. Our guiding principle was to treat functionally comparable transfers alike. We did the same with the UPC slayer statute, which denies any benefit, probate or nonprobate, to a designated beneficiary who feloniously and intentionally kills the transferor. Similarly, the UPC makes the 120 hour rule for survivorship applicable both to probate and to nonprobate transfers, and it extends the UPC's antilapse regime to both.

The Property Restatement recognizes these statutory developments and deduces from them a constructional principle for situations in which a state's statute law or case law still speaks by terms only to probate transfers, namely, that will substitutes should be "to the extent appropriate, subject . . . to rules of construction and other rules applicable to testamentary disposition."

NOTES

1. Legal Questions Raised by Nonprobate Succession. The rise of nonprobate succession raises two questions of law that have frustrated courts and legislatures to varying degrees. The first is whether *Wills Act formalities* should be required of will substitutes. Today this question has been resolved in the negative. In modern law, a will substitute is valid even without Wills Act formalities.[4]

---

4. *See* Restatement (Third) of Property: Wills and Other Donative Transfers § 7.1(b) (Am. Law Inst. 2003).

The second question is whether the *subsidiary law of wills*, meaning the policy-based substantive limits on testation by will and the rules of construction applicable to a will, should apply also to will substitutes. Law reform to answer this question "has been halting and incomplete, in part owing to debate over the extent to which courts can implement these reforms in the absence of statutory warrant and the lack of political salience for the issue. The preemptive force of federal law has stymied certain reforms in the context of life insurance and pension accounts offered as a benefit of employment."[5] Professor Langbein quotes the Restatement (Third) of Property for the proposition that the subsidiary law of wills is applicable to a will substitute "to the extent appropriate."[6] But what does appropriateness mean? And who decides?

2. Probate Procedure and Nonprobate Succession.   There was a time when probate was the only readily available way to transfer property with clear title at a person's death. However, because probate tended to be slow, cumbersome, and expensive, banks and other financial intermediaries developed nonprobate alternatives. With most personal wealth held today in financial assets, more property passes by nonprobate transfer than through probate.

The widespread use of nonprobate succession has led to significant reform of probate. The adoption of unsupervised probate administration (see page 46), for example, was prompted by the benign experience with unsupervised nonprobate transfers. Similarly, the movement to excuse defects in will execution and to correct mistaken terms in wills (see pages 176 and 341) has drawn on decades of benign experience with will substitutes that require fewer formalities, and on the long history of reformation to correct mistakes in contracts and inter vivos trusts.

The proliferation of will substitutes and the dominance of nonprobate succession also complicates making a coherent overall estate plan. As we shall see later in this chapter, the combined use of a *revocable inter vivos trust* and *pour-over will* has become the method of choice for solving this problem. But this solution is dependent on the lawyer's awareness of the client's nonprobate transfers and the client's continued coordination of subsequent will substitutes with the client's revocable trust.[7]

B. REVOCABLE TRUSTS[8]

Of all the will substitutes, the *revocable trust* most resembles a will in nature and function. Like a will, a revocable trust may be drafted precisely to the donor's liking. Like a will, a revocable trust is not inherently asset specific, but rather may be funded with any or even all of the donor's property. Like a will, a revocable trust is ambulatory, meaning that it is subject to amendment or revocation by the donor. And like a will,

---

5. David J. Feder & Robert H. Sitkoff, Revocable Trusts and Incapacity Planning: More Than Just a Will Substitute, 24 Elder L.J. 1, 15 (2016).

6. Restatement (Third) of Property: Wills and Other Donative Transfers § 7.2 (Am. Law Inst. 2003).

7. *See* Melanie B. Leslie & Stewart E. Sterk, Revisiting the Revolution: Reintegrating the Wealth Transmission System, 56 B.C. L. Rev. 61 (2015).

8. Portions of this section are adapted from Feder & Sitkoff, *supra* note 5.

under modern law a revocable trust gives the beneficiaries no rights until the death of the donor.

1. The Wills Act and a Present Transfer

A revocable trust may be created by a *deed of trust* whereby the settlor *transfers* to the trustee the property to be held in trust. On the settlor's death, the trust property is distributed or held in further trust in accordance with the terms of the trust. In the interim, the settlor is free to revoke the trust and take back the trust property.

A revocable trust may also be created by a *declaration of trust* whereby the settlor *declares* himself to be trustee of certain property for his own benefit during his life, with the remainder to pass at his death in accordance with the terms of his declaration. Because the settlor retains the power (as settlor) to revoke the trust and take back the trust property, and because the settlor (as trustee) has control over management of the property, there is little discernable change in the settlor's relation to the property during his lifetime. In function, then, there is little discernable difference between such a trust and a will, except that at death the trust operates outside of probate.

For a time, courts struggled with the question of whether a revocable trust should be effective to transfer property at the settlor's death without Wills Act formalities. Such a trust, explained Justice Holmes, has "a very testamentary look."[9] Some courts refused to enforce a revocable trust to the extent that it was "testamentary in character."[10]

Other courts took a different view. They upheld the validity of a revocable trust for deathtime transfer by conceptualizing the trust as making an inter vivos transfer. The theory was that upon creation of the trust, the settlor gave the remainder beneficiary a future interest—that is, a present property right—that would become possessory at the settlor's death. The Restatement (Third) of Property summarizes this inter vivos or present transfer theory thus:

> [T]he traditional explanation for why will substitutes are not wills is the present-transfer theory. A will substitute need not be executed in compliance with the statutory formalities required for a will because a will substitute effects a present transfer of a nonpossessory future interest or contract right, the time of possession or enjoyment being postponed until the donor's death.[11]

The leading case adopting the present transfer theory is Farkas v. Williams, 125 N.E.2d 600 (Ill. 1955). Albert Farkas declared a trust of certain mutual fund shares for the benefit of himself during life, with the remainder to be distributed to Richard Williams at Farkas's death. Farkas retained the right to all cash dividends; to sell or otherwise dispose of the stock and keep the proceeds; to change the remainder beneficiary; and to revoke the trust. Farkas died, survived by Williams, without having revoked or amended the trust.

---

9. Bromley v. Mitchell, 30 N.E. 83, 84 (Mass. 1892).

10. Betker v. Nalley, 140 F.2d 171, 173 (D.C. Cir. 1944).

11. Restatement (Third) of Property: Wills and Other Donative Transfers § 7.1 cmt. a (Am. Law Inst. 2003).

The question presented was whether Farkas had created a valid trust, so that Williams would take the remainder, or if instead the trust was an "attempted testamentary disposition[] and invalid for want of compliance with the statute on wills." Reasoning that Williams received a right in the trust property upon creation, the court upheld the trust as an inter vivos transfer. The interest that passed to Williams, technically "a contingent equitable interest in remainder,"[12] differentiated the trust from a will. Under a will, nothing passes to a devisee until the testator's death. While the testator is alive, the devisee has only an expectancy (see page 67). By contrast, upon creation of the trust Williams took a future interest that, subject to a variety of conditions, would become possessory at the death of Farkas.

The court supported its present transfer reasoning by pointing to trust fiduciary law. Unlike a testator, who retains full dominion and control over his property until death, the court said that Farkas owed fiduciary duties to Williams. True, Farkas had the power "to vote, sell, redeem, or otherwise deal in the stock." But Farkas held this power as trustee, and "as trustee he must so conduct himself in accordance with the standards applicable to trustees generally." Accordingly, "if, without having revoked the trust, Farkas as trustee had given the stock away without receiving any consideration therefor," or if Farkas "had pledged the stock improperly for his own personal debt," then "Williams would have had an enforceable claim against Farkas' estate for whatever damage had been suffered."

The court contrasted Farkas's fiduciary duties under the trust with the absence of any duties in a testator under a will. "[A] testator could waste the property or do anything with it he wished during his lifetime without incurring any liability to those designated by the will to inherit the property." Farkas, by contrast, was subject to fiduciary duties to Williams.

But does this reasoning come to grips with Farkas's retained power to revoke the trust and take back the trust property at any time and for any reason? In light of Farkas's unconditional power of revocation, what could he do that would give rise to a successful lawsuit by Williams for breach of duty? Even the court acknowledged that a suit by Williams might not be "feasible," because if Williams sued "Farkas could then revoke the trust." But more importantly, the "controlling consideration" in interpreting a donative instrument is the donor's intent.[13] If without first formally revoking the trust Farkas took an action that abridged Williams's (entirely defeasible) remainder interest, would not the more sensible interpretation—that is, the interpretation more

---

12. As a matter of traditional future interests law, a settlor's exercise of a power of revocation over a revocable trust is viewed as divesting the interest of a remainder beneficiary (see page 862). Thus, if *O* were to declare a revocable trust over certain property "for *O* for life, then to *A*," we would say that *A* has a vested remainder subject to complete divestment by *O*'s exercise of her power of revocation. In *Farkas*, however, the settlor also conditioned the remainder beneficiary's interest on the beneficiary surviving the settlor, making it a contingent remainder, as the court correctly identified. As these examples show, whether under traditional law a future interest is "vested" or "contingent" is not determined by the certainty or uncertainty of future possession.

13. Restatement (Third) of Property: Wills and Other Donative Transfers § 10.1 (Am. Law Inst. 2003).

in accord with Farkas's intent—be that the action constituted an implied revocation to that extent?[14]

2. Abandoning the Present Transfer Fiction

Legal formalisms aside, the policy question at issue in *Farkas* was whether a revocable trust should be effective to pass property at death without Wills Act formalities. After many years of benign experience with deathtime transfer by revocable trusts and other will substitutes lacking the formalities of a will, an alternative explanation for their validity emerged. The Restatement (Third) of Property explains:

> [W]ill substitutes need not be characterized as effecting a present transfer to escape characterization as a will. Rather, the donor is free to transfer wealth on death either in the probate system or in the nonprobate system or in both. When using the non-probate system, the donor uses its forms, which typically arise from the commercial practice of financial intermediaries. When using the state-operated transfer system of probate administration, the donor uses the forms appropriate to that system (for testation) or allows that system to operate by default (in the case of intestacy). The statute of wills does not require wealth transfers on death to occur by probate; the statute merely requires that probate transfers comply with the statute's formalities. Because the statute of wills does not govern nonprobate transfers, wealth hold-ers may use these alternative wealth-transfer systems on death by means of will substitutes.[15]

Under this reasoning, a revocable trust can be openly acknowledged as a will substitute—in effect, a nonprobate will. Even if a "settlor serves as sole trustee or co-trustee, or reserves the right to veto, direct, or otherwise control the acts of another trustee in the administration or distribution of the trust estate," the trust is valid and may transfer property to a remainder beneficiary at the death of the settlor without Wills Act formalities.[16]

Acknowledging that a revocable trust is a will substitute allows us to stop search-ing for a present transfer and instead to focus on the settlor's intent. In *Farkas*, given the settlor's unconditional power to revoke the trust and take back the trust property, the more sensible interpretation is that any action by Farkas that impaired Williams's interest in the trust was an implied revocation to that extent. On this view, Farkas owed no duties to Williams while the trust was revocable. Modern law, including Uniform Trust Code (UTC) § 603 (Unif. Law Comm'n 2000, rev. 2004), excerpted below, and the Restatement (Third) of Trusts, has embraced this view.[17]

---

14. *See* John H. Langbein, The Nonprobate Revolution and the Future of the Law of Succession, 97 Harv. L. Rev. 1108, 1127-28 (1984).

15. Restatement (Third) of Property: Wills and Other Donative Transfers § 7.1 cmt. a (Am. Law Inst. 2003).

16. Restatement (Third) of Trusts § 25 cmt. b (Am. Law Inst. 2003).

17. *See id.* § 74(1).

Uniform Trust Code (Unif. Law Comm'n 2000, as amended 2004)

§ 603. Settlor's Powers; Powers of Withdrawal

(a) While a trust is revocable [and the settlor has capacity to revoke the trust], rights of the beneficiaries are subject to the control of, and the duties of the trustee are owed exclusively to, the settlor.

(b) During the period the power may be exercised, the holder of a power of withdrawal[18] has the rights of a settlor of a revocable trust under this section to the extent of the property subject to the power.

Fulp v. Gilliland
998 N.E.2d 204 (Ind. 2013)

RUSH, J. Revocable trusts are popular substitutes for wills, intended to provide non-probate distribution of people's estates after their deaths, allowing them to retain control and use of their assets during their lifetimes. . . . We . . . address an issue of first impression in Indiana: while a revocable trust is revocable, whom does the trustee serve? . . .

FACTS

Soon after Ruth and Harold Fulp Sr. married, they moved to the family farm, where they raised their three children — Harold Jr., Nancy, and Terry. Harold Sr. farmed the land; Junior later joined him, then took over after Senior's death. A few years later, Ruth

placed the farm into the Ruth E. Fulp Revocable Trust. As the Trust's primary beneficiary, Ruth could use its assets; as trustee, she could sell them; and as settlor, she could "alter, amend or revoke" the Trust "in any respect." In addition, the Trust required the trustee — unless another term of the trust provided otherwise — to "administer the trust solely in the interest of the beneficiaries," "treat multiple beneficiaries impartially," and "preserve the trust property." Upon Ruth's death, the trust would become irrevocable, and the successor trustee would distribute any remaining assets to the children.

As Ruth got older, she moved to the Indiana Masonic Home and decided to sell the farm to pay for her living expenses there. But she wanted to keep the farm in the family, so she approached Harold Jr., who was interested in buying it. He offered her a discounted price per acre — the same price Nancy's daughter had previously paid Ruth for another portion of the farm. Ruth agreed and said "what I did for one I can do for the other." But Harold Jr. cautioned

Justice Loretta Rush, first appointed to the Indiana Supreme Court in 2012, became the first woman to be named Chief Justice of that court in 2014.

---

18. Under UTC § 103(11), a "power of withdrawal" is "a presently exercisable general power of appointment," which we take up in Chapter 12 at page 809. — Eds.

her that the farm was worth more than the $450,252 he was offering. Indeed, an appraisal later showed it was worth more than $1 million.

Harold Jr.'s lender, Farm Credit, drew up the purchase agreement, and Ruth signed it. When Nancy found out, she objected because she "wanted her share." . . .

After a bench trial, the trial court found that Ruth was competent to sell the farm, the price paid for the farm was adequate, and Harold Jr. exerted no undue influence. Still, the court . . . found that Ruth breached her fiduciary duty to the children by selling the farm at a low price. . . .

Harold Jr. appealed. The Court of Appeals agreed with the trial court that if Ruth had sold the farm as *trustee,* she would have breached a fiduciary duty to her children. But it also recognized that if Ruth had such a duty, her conflicting rights and duties as trustee would essentially render the Trust irrevocable. To avoid that untenable result, the court instead concluded that Ruth sold the farm as *settlor,* so that the purchase agreement "in effect" amended the Trust. . . .

Nancy [appealed] . . . , asking us to decide whether the trustee of a revocable trust owes a duty to the settlor alone or also to the remainder beneficiaries. We granted [the appeal] to address that issue, and we conclude that while a revocable trust is revocable, the trustee only owes a duty to the settlor. Therefore, Ruth was free to sell the farm as trustee, as the purchase agreement reflected, without breaching any fiduciary duty. . . .

REVOCABLE TRUSTS

Ruth held the farm in a revocable trust. Revocable trusts have become popular estate planning tools and substitutes for wills because they allow settlors to avoid probate and guardianship, to have greater privacy, and to manage their assets. . . . [U]nlike other trusts, settlors of revocable trusts continue using the trust property during their lives and retain the power to revoke or amend the trust at any time. . . . When Ruth agreed to sell the farm, her Trust was fully revocable, and she was its settlor, trustee, and primary beneficiary. . . .

INTERPRETING RUTH'S TRUST

We must interpret the terms of the Trust to determine the duties it imposed upon Ruth as trustee, and to determine whether the sale of the farm breached any of those duties. Our primary purpose "in construing a trust instrument is to ascertain and give effect to the settlor's intention." Univ. of S. Ind. Found. v. Baker, 843 N.E.2d 528, 532 (Ind. 2006). . . .

RUTH'S FIDUCIARY DUTIES

Nancy argues that Ruth as trustee breached a fiduciary duty to the remainder beneficiaries by selling the farm for below market value. . . . We disagree with Nancy's argument that the Trust imposed on Ruth an additional duty to her own children. . . .

Whether the trustee of a revocable trust owes a duty to remainder or contingent beneficiaries while the trust is revocable is an issue of first impression in Indiana, but other states have concluded that trustees owe no such duty while a trust is revocable.

We find Justice Guzman's concurrence in Moon v. Lesikar, 230 S.W.3d 800, 806 (Tex. App. 2007), persuasive. There, a contingent beneficiary of a revocable trust argued that her rights were violated when the settlor/trustee of a revocable trust sold trust property for well below fair market value. Justice Guzman concluded that if the settlor/trustee of a revocable trust owed the contingent beneficiaries a duty, the settlor/trustee's rights and duties would conflict because "the settlor, in his capacity as trustee, would have a duty to prevent *himself*, in his capacity as settlor, from revoking the trust." Id. at 809. Because this illogical conclusion would render the trust "no longer . . . freely revocable," Justice Guzman concluded that the trustee's duty was to the settlor not the contingent beneficiaries, while the trust was still revocable. Id. at 809-10. . . .

[T]he Uniform Trust Code takes a similar position: "While a trust is revocable . . . , rights of the beneficiaries are subject to the control of, and the duties of the trustee are owed exclusively to, the settlor." Unif. Trust Code § 603(a) (amended 2010). Courts in states that have enacted the Uniform Trust Code have easily concluded that trustees exclusively owe a duty to settlors—and indeed, we can find no jurisdiction that holds otherwise. E.g., In re Stephen M. Gunther Revocable Living Trust, 350 S.W.3d 44, 47 (Mo. App. 2011) (finding "[t]he trustee owed no duty to the beneficiaries prior to the settlor's death"). . . .

With those general trust law principles in mind, we turn to Ruth's duties under her Trust. Our primary purpose in interpreting the Trust is to implement her intent as settlor, *Univ. of S. Ind. Found.*, 843 N.E.2d at 532, and two provisions of Ruth's Trust show she intended to owe a duty only to herself. First, Article I provides that Ruth could revoke the Trust for any reason at any time, which shows that she intended to control the farm and treat it as her own property. Second, Article II provides that the Trust is for Ruth's "use and benefit"—including the right to use all Trust assets. The children's interest in the Trust is purely secondary and arises only if Ruth chooses not to divest them and if she chooses not to use all of the assets. So as trustee, Ruth's fiduciary duty was to herself, as settlor and primary beneficiary. Stated differently, Ruth was her own master.

But Nancy argues that Ruth's duty as trustee also extends to her remainder beneficiary children. To find that Ruth owed such a duty, however, would bring her rights and duties into conflict—she would have to serve two masters. . . . [S]uch conflicting duties would essentially make her Trust irrevocable, because complying as trustee with her own wishes to revoke the Trust would breach her purported duty to the remainder beneficiaries by placing her own interests above theirs. In sum, Nancy's argument fails because it would defeat, rather than implement, the settlor's intent.

Nancy nevertheless argues that the terms of Article V of the Trust compel the counterintuitive conclusion that Ruth's duty as trustee also extended to her children. That provision, titled Trustee's Duties, states: "*Unless the terms of the trust provide otherwise,* the Trustee also has a duty: 1. to administer the trust solely in the interest of the beneficiaries; 2. to treat multiple beneficiaries impartially; . . . [and] 4. to preserve the trust property" (emphasis added). Here, though, Article V would conflict with other rights and duties given to Ruth while the Trust is revocable and she is still primary beneficiary. For instance, Ruth cannot have a duty to administer the Trust solely in the interest of the beneficiaries, when Article I lets her remove any beneficiary anytime. And she cannot have any duty to preserve the Trust's assets, when Article II gives her the right to consume them. By contrast, no such conflict exists in applying Article V to a successor trustee once the Trust has become irrevocable and Ruth is no longer primary beneficiary—at that time, the successor trustee can readily administer the trust for the beneficiaries, treat them impartially, and preserve the Trust property. But until then, Article V by its terms must yield to Ruth's own powers as settlor, trustee, and primary beneficiary.

Accordingly, Ruth as trustee owed a duty only to herself. As primary beneficiary, she was entitled to use the Trust assets for her own benefit—and here, selling the farm

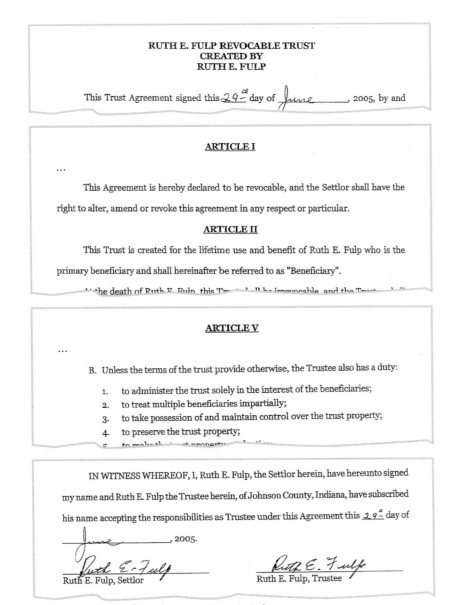

Relevant provisions from the trust at issue in *Fulp*

benefitted her by providing her with money for her care while keeping the farm in the family. The sale did not breach any duty to Ruth's remainder beneficiaries because she owed them no duty. Since Ruth complied with the terms of the Trust, we must next determine whether its terms comply with the Indiana Trust Code. . . .

In 2013, the Legislature amended the Trust Code to declare the same rule we announce today—that while a trust is revocable, the trustee's duty is only to the settlor: "While a trust is revocable and the settlor has the capacity to revoke the trust: . . . (2) the duties of the trustee are owed exclusively to . . . the settlor." I.C. § 30-4-3-1.3(a) (Supp. 2013). That provision is materially identical to Uniform Trust Code section 603, discussed above—and though this amendment took effect after Ruth executed the Trust, Trust Code amendments apply retroactively unless they would "adversely affect a right given to any beneficiary . . . [or] relieve any person from any duty or liability imposed by the terms of the trust or under prior law." I.C. § 30-4-1-4(b) (Supp. 2013). As detailed above, this statute captures Ruth's intent, and does not adversely affect the rights of any of the beneficiary children because their rights were subject to Ruth's right as settlor to revoke the Trust. Similarly, the law does not relieve any person of a duty because while the Trust was revocable, Ruth owed a duty only to herself. Therefore, under both the terms of the Trust and under Indiana law, Ruth owed no duty to her remainder beneficiary children. . . .

CONCLUSION

We conclude that under the terms of the Trust and the Trust Code Ruth owed her children no fiduciary duties and was free to sell her farm at less than fair market value. . . . The judgment of the trial court is therefore reversed and remanded, with instructions to grant specific performance of the purchase agreement.

NOTES

1. No Present Interest.   Consistent with the weight of modern authority and UTC § 603(a), page 448, the court in *Fulp* held that a beneficiary of a revocable trust has no legally enforceable interest while the trust is revocable. The trustee is subject to the control of the settlor, and only the settlor may enforce the trustee's fiduciary duties. In the words of the Restatement, the trustee "has a duty to comply with a direction of the settlor even though the direction is contrary to the terms of the trust or the trustee's normal fiduciary duties."[19]

If, as in *Fulp*, the settlor is also the trustee, then any action by the settlor-trustee that diminishes the interest of a beneficiary cannot be a breach of trust but rather is an implied revocation to that extent. The settlor-trustee of a revocable trust cannot be compelled by a beneficiary to account or to provide information and is not subject to liability for breach of trust.[20] In *Fulp*, Ruth's sale of the farm for less than fair market

---

19. Restatement (Third) of Trusts § 74 (Am. Law Inst. 2003).
20. Id. cmt. a(1).

value was in effect a revocation of the trust as to the difference, and Nancy lacked standing to complain.

Trust law has thus evolved to accommodate the widespread use of the revocable trust as a will substitute. Just as a beneficiary under a will has no rights until the testator's death (see page 67), a beneficiary of a revocable trust has no rights while the trust remains revocable by the settlor. In both situations, the beneficiary has a mere expectancy rather than a cognizable legal right. Yet in almost every state a revocable trust is valid to transfer property at the settlor's death without Wills Act formalities.[21]

2. Enforcement After the Settlor's Death.   Suppose in *Fulp* that Ruth had chosen a third-party trustee, that the trustee had looted the trust without Ruth's knowledge but while Ruth was alive and competent, and that Ruth died thereafter without discovering the looting. After Ruth's death, who has standing to demand an accounting for the period prior to Ruth's death and to seek redress for a breach of trust in that period? Would Nancy and the other beneficiaries have such standing? Would the fiduciary of Ruth's estate? There is a profound split of authority on these questions,[22] reflecting deep conceptual disagreement about whether a revocable trust is purely a will substitute, so that only the fiduciary of Ruth's estate would have standing, or if instead the settlor probably meant for the beneficiaries to be able to enforce the settlor's rights against the trustee after the settlor's death.

Suppose instead that a third-party trustee looted the trust while Ruth was alive but without capacity to sue. Upon Ruth's incapacity, would Nancy and the other beneficiaries have standing? Or would standing be limited to Ruth's agent under a power of attorney or court-appointed conservator? We take up these questions later in this chapter, at page 501, in connection with incapacity planning.

3. Revoking or Amending a Revocable Trust

Under traditional law, an inter vivos trust created by a written instrument was presumed to be *irrevocable* unless there was an express or implied reservation by the settlor of a power to revoke the trust. In recent years, however, the opposite presumption has taken hold. Following UTC § 602(a), excerpted below, the majority view today is that an inter vivos trust is *revocable* unless declared to be irrevocable. Professor English, the reporter for the UTC, explains:

> The provisions of the UTC on revocable trusts ... are ... among the Code's most important and innovative provisions. The biggest change is a reversal of the common law presumption that trusts are irrevocable. Reflecting the increasing, if not predominant, use of the revocable trust in the United States, the Code ... [provides] that a trust is revocable absent clarifying language in the terms of the trust.

---

21. Id. § 25 cmt. b.

22. *Compare* In re Estate of Giraldin, 290 P.3d 199 (Cal. 2012) (after settlor's death, beneficiaries may enforce trustee's duties in period prior to settlor's death), *and* Tseng v. Tseng, 352 P.3d 74 (Or. App. 2015) (same), *with* In re Trust No. T-1 of Trimble, 826 N.W.2d 474 (Iowa 2013) (beneficiary is not entitled to an accounting for period prior to settlor's death), *and* In re Stephen M. Gunther Revocable Living Trust, 350 S.W.3d 44 (Mo. App. 2011) (same).

Professional drafters routinely state whether a trust is revocable or irrevocable. Providing a presumption in the statute is, therefore, most relevant to self-drafted trusts or trusts prepared by less competent counsel. These trusts, when silent, are more often than not intended to be revocable.[23]

A corollary to the presumption of irrevocability was the rule that, to amend or revoke a trust, the settlor had to follow precisely the method for amendment or revocation specified by the terms of the trust. Courts reasoned that, because a beneficiary had a cognizable interest in the trust, that interest could be defeated only in accordance with the terms of the trust. A trust that specified a manner of amendment or revocation was interpreted as permitting amendment or revocation only in the manner specified.

The shift to a presumption of revocability has been accompanied by a change in the rules for how a revocable trust may be amended or revoked. Today the majority view, as under UTC § 602(c), excerpted below, is that a revocable trust can be amended or revoked in any manner that clearly manifests the settlor's intent to do so, unless the trust instrument specifies a particular method of amendment or revocation and makes that method exclusive. This reversal in the law reflects the acceptance of the idea that a revocable trust is a will substitute in which the beneficiary has no interest while the trust remains revocable.

Uniform Trust Code (Unif. Law Comm'n 2000, as amended 2003)

§ 602. Revocation or Amendment of Revocable Trust

(a) Unless the terms of a trust expressly provide that the trust is irrevocable, the settlor may revoke or amend the trust. This subsection does not apply to a trust created under an instrument executed before [the effective date of this [Code]]. . . .

(c) The settlor may revoke or amend a revocable trust:

(1) by substantial compliance with a method provided in the terms of the trust; or

(2) if the terms of the trust do not provide a method or the method provided in the terms is not expressly made exclusive, by:

(A) a later will or codicil that expressly refers to the trust or specifically devises property that would otherwise have passed according to the terms of the trust; or

(B) any other method manifesting clear and convincing evidence of the settlor's intent.

(d) Upon revocation of a revocable trust, the trustee shall deliver the trust property as the settlor directs. . . .

---

23. David M. English, The Uniform Trust Code (2000): Significant Provisions and Policy Issues, 67 Mo. L. Rev. 143, 186-87 (2002).

Patterson v. Patterson
266 P.3d 828 (Utah 2011)

PARRISH, J. . . . Shortly before she passed away in 2006, Darlene Patterson (Darlene) executed an amendment (the Amendment) to the Darlene Patterson Family Protection Trust (the Trust). The purpose of the Amendment was to remove Darlene's son Ronald Patterson (Ron) as a beneficiary. On summary judgment, the district court invalidated the Amendment based on its interpretation of our opinion in Banks v. Means, 52 P.3d 1190 (Utah 2002). The trustee, Randy Patterson (Randy), appeals. We reverse the district court's grant of summary judgment and hold that the Amendment is valid under a provision of the Utah Uniform Trust Code (the UUTC), Utah Code section 75-7-605, [based on UTC § 602,] which has statutorily overruled our holding in *Banks*.

BACKGROUND

Darlene Patterson created the Darlene Patterson Family Protection Trust in 1999. The Trust property was to be used for Darlene's benefit during her lifetime. Upon her death, Darlene's children were to each receive a portion of any remaining Trust property. The Trust was a "living" or "inter vivos" trust, in which Darlene "reserve[d] the right to amend, modify, or revoke the Trust in whole or in part, including the principal, and the present or past undisbursed income from such principal." The document states that "revocation or amendment . . . may be in whole or in part by written instrument." And the Trust provides that "[t]he interests of the beneficiaries are presently vested interests subject to divestment which shall continue until this Trust is revoked or terminated other than by death."

In 2006, Darlene executed the Amendment. The purpose of the Amendment was to remove Darlene's son Ron as a beneficiary of the Trust. The Amendment stated, "I have intentionally not provided anything for my son Ronald S. Patterson (or his descendants) since I have already properly provided for this son during his lifetime as I felt was appropriate." Eleven months after executing the Amendment, Darlene passed away.

> C. <u>Division of Trust Estate</u>. Subject to the inheritance advancement in paragraph B4 above, the remainder of the Trust Estate (including any remaining real estate) shall be divided by the Trustee among my following children on a per stirpes basis: Gary E. Patterson, Judy Ann Henry, Rex A. Patterson, Vicky D. Romero, Ricky A. Patterson, and Randy D. Patterson. I have intentionally not provided anything for my son Ronald S. Patterson (or his descendants) since I have already properly provided for this son during his lifetime as I felt was appropriate. Any share set aside for the descendants of a deceased child shall be divided among the descendants of that child by right of representation.

The provision explaining the exclusion of Ronald S. Patterson

Shortly after his mother passed away, Ron filed a lawsuit against the Trust and Darlene's estate in which he sought a declaration that the Amendment was void because it violated the terms of the Trust. Subsequently, Ron sought partial summary judgment. . . .

The district court granted Ron's motion for partial summary judgment. . . . Concluding that it was bound by *Banks* and its progeny, the district court ruled that the Amendment was invalid because it attempted to completely divest Ron of his interest in the Trust without revoking the Trust, as required by *Banks*. . . .

ANALYSIS

Randy argues that the district court erred in deciding the case under *Banks* and in concluding that the Amendment was void. He asks us to validate his mother's intent to terminate Ron's interest by overruling *Banks*. In the alternative, Randy asks us to apply a provision of the UUTC, which he contends has statutorily overruled *Banks*. Ron responds that *Banks* remains good law and should not be overruled by this court. . . .

We conclude that the UUTC has statutorily overruled *Banks*. The UUTC, which allows for liberal modification of revocable trusts, directly conflicts with our holding in *Banks* that a settlor must strictly comply with the terms of a trust in order to modify it. Applying the UUTC to the undisputed facts in this case, we hold that the Amendment effectively terminated Ron's interest in the Trust. . . .

In *Banks*, the settlor had executed a trust instrument in which her children were named as joint beneficiaries. In the trust instrument, the settlor reserved "the right to amend, modify or revoke th[e] Trust in whole or in part." The trust also stated that "[o]n the revocation of this instrument in its entirety, the Trustee shall deliver to the [settlor] . . . all of the Trust property." The *Banks* trust also provided that the interests of the beneficiaries were "vested interests subject to divestment which shall continue until this Trust is revoked or terminated other than by death."

Days before her death, the settlor executed an amendment to the trust. Under the terms of the amendment, the settlor's sister became the primary beneficiary and the settlor's children became alternate beneficiaries, who would take only if the settlor's sister predeceased her. The children challenged the amendment.

We began our analysis by reciting the general common law rule that "[a] trust is a form of ownership in which the legal title to property is vested in a trustee, who has equitable duties to hold and manage it for the benefit of the beneficiaries." We also stated that "[t]he creation of a trust involves the transfer of property interests" which "cannot be taken from [the beneficiaries] except in accordance with a provision of the trust instrument."

Applying this general framework, we concluded that although the settlor expressly reserved the right to amend, modify, or revoke the trust, she had also created vested interests in her children by specifically providing that those interests would continue until the trust was revoked or terminated. Thus, we concluded that a complete revocation was required to "divest" a beneficiary's interest. Because the settlor had only amended the trust rather than completely revoking it, we held that her attempt to terminate the interests of her children was invalid. . . .

In 2004, the Utah Legislature enacted the UUTC. . . . The UUTC contains an article dedicated solely to revocable trusts. Utah Code Ann. §§ 75-7-604 to -607 (Supp. 2011). The structure and content of the article reflects a legislative acknowledgment of the increasingly widespread use of revocable trusts as substitutes for wills. For example, the UUTC provides that the capacity standard for wills applies in determining whether a settlor had capacity to create a revocable trust. Id. § 75-7-604. And, like challenges to wills, challenges to revocable trusts must be brought within a limited amount of time after the settlor's death. . . .

Most importantly, the UUTC treats a living trust as the functional equivalent of a will. Indicative of this fact is the UUTC's treatment of revocation and amendment. It is black letter law that a testator has complete control to amend, modify, or revoke his will during his lifetime. Similarly, the UUTC recognizes that during the period in which a revocable trust is in effect, all of the rights held by beneficiaries are controlled exclusively by the settlor. Utah Code Ann. § 75-7-606(1) (Supp. 2011)[, based on UTC § 603(a), page 448]. Thus, just as a testator has flexibility over the manner in which he can revoke all or part of his will, the UUTC contains a provision[, id. § 75-7-605, based on UTC § 602, page 454,] giving a settlor wide latitude to effectuate his control over the disposition of trust assets. . . .

The UUTC directly conflicts with the holding of *Banks*. Under *Banks*, the settlor's intent at the time of creation of the trust was paramount because "[o]nce the settlor has created the trust he is no longer the owner of the trust property and has only such ability to deal with it as is expressly reserved to him in the trust instrument." *Banks*, 52 P.3d at 1192. Thus, in *Banks* we noted that "a settlor has the power to modify or revoke a trust only if and to the extent that such power is explicitly reserved by the terms of the trust." Id. Under this framework, a settlor may revoke or amend the trust only by strictly complying with its terms. In contrast, the UUTC does not require strict compliance with trust provisions governing revocation or amendment. And unless the trust document specifies a method of amendment that is expressly made exclusive, the UUTC provides a settlor of a revocable trust with wide latitude in the method of amendment, revocation, or modification. . . .

By enacting the UUTC, the legislature has demonstrated its intent to treat revocable living trusts as will equivalents. Like a will, over which the testator has absolute control until the testator's death, the UUTC provides the settlor of a revocable trust with complete control over the trust until the settlor's death. To achieve this end, the UUTC allows settlors multiple avenues to amend or revoke a revocable trust. When the UUTC is read together with the legislative directive to liberally construe it in a manner effectuating the intent of settlors, it directly conflicts with the strict compliance standard that we articulated in *Banks*. Therefore, our *Banks* holding must give way to the statute. . . .

Having determined that the UUTC, rather than *Banks*, controls this case, we now apply the statute to determine the validity of Darlene's Amendment. Randy argues that the Amendment is valid because the terms of the Trust do not provide an exclusive method of amendment or revocation and the Amendment qualifies as a clear expression of Darlene's intent to terminate Ron's interest as a beneficiary. We agree.

Under section 75-7-605, [based on UTC § 602, page 454], a "settlor may revoke or amend a revocable trust . . . by substantially complying with a method provided in the terms of the trust." Utah Code Ann. § 75-7-605(3)(a) (Supp. 2011). Alternatively, if the terms of a revocable trust do not provide a method for revocation or amendment that is "expressly made exclusive," the settlor may amend or revoke the trust by "any . . . method manifesting clear and convincing evidence of the settlor's intent." Id. § 75-7-605(3)(b)(ii).

Here, . . . Darlene "reserve[d] the right to amend, modify or revoke the Trust in whole or in part." And the Trust states that "revocation or amendment . . . may be in whole or in part by written instrument."

We conclude that the terms of the Trust do not provide a method for amendment or revocation that is expressly made exclusive. The Trust states that it "may" be amended or revoked by written instrument "delivered in writing to the then acting Trustee." But it does not expressly state that this is the *only* permissible method. Thus, under the provisions of the UUTC, Darlene could amend or revoke the trust by "any . . . method manifesting clear and convincing evidence of [her] intent." Utah Code Ann. § 75-7-605(3)(b)(ii). The Amendment satisfies this requirement. In it, Darlene specifically revised the distribution provisions of the Trust, stating, "I have intentionally not provided anything for my son Ronald S. Patterson (or his descendants) since I have already properly provided for this son during his lifetime as I felt was appropriate." In so doing, Darlene modified that part of the Trust instrument that named Ron as a beneficiary. And she did so in a manner that provides clear and convincing evidence of her intent to eliminate Ron's interest in the Trust. Thus, the Amendment is valid.

CONCLUSION

. . . The UUTC seeks to effectuate settlors' intent by allowing for liberal amendment or revocation of revocable trusts. Applying the UUTC to the facts of this case, we hold that Darlene's Amendment is valid. The terms of the Trust do not specify an exclusive method for amendment or revocation and the Amendment constitutes a clear expression of Darlene's intent to terminate Ron's interest.

NOTES

1. Revocation by Writing. Suppose that Darlene had executed a subsequent will that expressly revoked her inter vivos trust and that this will is found among her papers at death. Under UTC § 602(c)(2)(A), page 454, does it revoke the trust? *See* In re Schlicht, 329 P.3d 733 (N.M. App. 2014). Suppose that the will stated Darlene's intent "to dispose of all property that I have the right to dispose of by will" but did not expressly revoke the trust. What result? *See* Gardenhire v. Superior Court, 26 Cal. Rptr. 3d 143 (App. 2005).

What about the provision in the trust instrument providing for revocation by delivery to the trustee? Was the will delivered to the trustee? *See* In re Estate of Lowry,

418 N.E.2d 10 (Ill. App. 1981). Is delivery to the trustee necessary? Suppose that a third party were trustee. Would the revocation be valid? *See In re Estate of McCreath*, 240 P.3d 413 (Colo. App. 2009).

2. Revocation by Physical Act?   Suppose Darlene tore both her will and her trust into many pieces. Would this be a revocation of the will? A revocation of the trust? *See Salem United Methodist Church v. Bottorff*, 138 S.W.3d 788 (Mo. App. 2004).

In *In re Estate of Stoker*, page 226, after expressing disdain for the terms of his revocable trust, the settlor urinated on and then set fire to the trust instrument (or perhaps to a copy of it). Under UTC § 602(c)(2)(B), page 454, would this be a "method manifesting clear and convincing evidence of the settlor's intent" to revoke the trust? Does it matter if these acts were done to a copy instead of the original?

4. The Subsidiary Law of Wills

Should the policy limits on testation by will, primarily rules that protect creditors and spouses, apply also to a revocable trust? Should the rules of construction for wills, such as simultaneous death and revocation on divorce, apply to a revocable trust?[24] The Restatement (Third) of Property answers these questions thus:

> Although the validity of a will substitute does not depend on its being executed in compliance with the statutory formalities required for a will, a will substitute serves the function of a will. It shifts the right to possession or enjoyment to the donee at the donor's death. In this sense, a will substitute is in reality a nonprobate will. A will substitute is therefore, to the extent appropriate, subject to substantive restrictions on testation and to rules of construction and other rules applicable to testamentary dispositions. Substantive restrictions on testation constitute important policies restricting disposition of property after the owner's death that should not be avoidable simply by changing the form of the death-time transfer. By contrast, rules of construction and other interpretative devices aid in determining and giving effect to the donor's intention or probable intention and hence should apply generally to donative documents.[25]

State Street Bank and Trust Co. v. Reiser
389 N.E.2d 768 (Mass. App. 1979)

KASS, J. State Street Bank and Trust Company (the bank) seeks to reach the assets of an inter vivos trust in order to pay a debt to the bank owed by the estate of the settlor of the trust. We conclude that the bank can do so.

---

24. *See* Kent D. Schenkel, The Trust-as-Will Portmanteau: Trill or Spork?, 27 Quinnipiac Prob. L.J. 40 (2013).

25. Restatement (Third) of Property: Wills and Other Donative Transfers § 7.2 cmt. a (Am. Law Inst. 2003).

Wilfred A. Dunnebier created an inter vivos trust on September 30, 1971, with power to amend or revoke the trust and the right during his lifetime to direct the disposition of principal and income. He conveyed to the trust the capital stock of five closely held corporations. Immediately following execution of this trust, Dunnebier executed a will under which he left his residuary estate to the trust he had established.

About thirteen months later Dunnebier applied to the bank for a $75,000 working capital loan. A bank officer met with Dunnebier, examined a financial statement furnished by him and visited several single family home subdivisions which Dunnebier, or corporations he controlled, had built or were in the process of building. During their conversations, Dunnebier told the bank officer that he had controlling interests in the corporations which owned the most significant assets appearing on the financial statement. On the basis of what he saw of Dunnebier's work, recommendations from another bank, Dunnebier's borrowing history with the bank, and the general cut of Dunnebier's jib, the bank officer decided to make an unsecured loan to Dunnebier for the $75,000 he had asked for. To evidence this loan, Dunnebier, on November 1, 1972, signed a personal demand note to the order of the bank. The probate judge found that Dunnebier did not intend to defraud the bank or misrepresent his financial position by failing to call attention to the fact that he had placed the stock of his corporations in the trust.

Approximately four months after he borrowed this money Dunnebier died in an accident. His estate has insufficient assets to pay the entire indebtedness due the bank. . . .

During the lifetime of the settlor, . . . the bank would have had access to the assets of the trust. When a person creates for his own benefit a trust for support or a discretionary trust, his creditors can reach the maximum amount which the trustee, under the terms of the trust, could pay to him or apply for his benefit. Restatement (Second) of Trusts § 156(2) (1959). This is so even if the trust contains spendthrift provisions. Restatement (Second) of Trusts § 156(1) (1959). Under the terms of Dunnebier's trust, all the income and principal were at his disposal while he lived.

We then face the question whether Dunnebier's death broke the vital chain. His powers to amend or revoke the trust, or to direct payments from it, obviously died with him, and the remainder interests of the beneficiaries of the trust became vested. The contingencies which might defeat those remainder interests could no longer occur. . . .

As an estate planning vehicle, the inter vivos trust has become common currency. Frequently, as Dunnebier did in the instant case, the settlor retains all the substantial incidents of ownership because access to the trust property is necessary or desirable as a matter of sound financial planning. Psychologically, the settlor thinks of the trust property as "his," as Dunnebier did when he took the bank's officer to visit the real estate owned by the corporation whose stock he had put in trust. . . . In other circumstances, persons place property in trust in order to obtain expert management of their assets, while retaining the power to invade principal and to amend and revoke the trust. It is excessive obeisance to the form in which property is held to prevent creditors from reaching property placed in trust under such terms.

This view was adopted in *United States v. Ritter*, 558 F.2d 1165, 1167 (4th Cir. 1977). In a concurring opinion in that case Judge Widener observed that it violates public policy for an individual to have an estate to live on, but not an estate to pay his debts with. The Internal Revenue Code institutionalizes the concept that a settlor of a trust who retains administrative powers, power to revoke or power to control beneficial enjoyment "owns" that trust property and provides that it shall be included in the settlor's personal estate. I.R.C. §§ 2038 and 2041.

We hold, therefore, that where a person places property in trust and reserves the right to amend and revoke, or to direct disposition of principal and income, the settlor's creditors may, following the death of the settlor, reach in satisfaction of the settlor's debts to them, to the extent not satisfied by the settlor's estate, those assets owned by the trust over which the settlor had such control at the time of his death as would have enabled the settlor to use the trust assets for his own benefit. . . .

So ordered.

NOTES

1. Creditors and Revocable Trusts.   Under traditional law, a creditor of the settlor had no recourse against property in the settlor's revocable trust unless the settlor was also a beneficiary of the trust. The settlor's power to revoke and take back the property was not considered equivalent to ownership of the property. This rule was expressed in the Restatement (Second) of Trusts as follows: "[A] power of revocation reserved by the settlor cannot be reached by his creditors. If he revokes the trust and recovers the trust property, the creditors can reach the property; but they cannot compel him to revoke the trust for their benefit."[26]

Modern law rejects this reasoning. The settlor's power to revoke the trust and take back the trust property is regarded as equivalent to ownership and, hence, the trust property is subject to the claims of the settlor's creditors during life and at death.[27] This rule, which is codified by UTC § 505(a)(3) (2000) and the Restatement (Third) of Trusts,[28] aligns state trust law on creditor rights with the treatment of revocable trust property for federal income and estate tax purposes (see pages 981 and 960). A similar evolution is evident in the law governing the rights of creditors in property subject to a general power of appointment (see page 815).

2. Creditors and Other Nonprobate Transfers.   When it comes to satisfying the debts of a decedent, not all nonprobate assets are created equal. Although creditors may reach property in a revocable trust settled by the decedent, they cannot reach certain other nonprobate transfers. The creditors of a joint tenant cannot reach the jointly held property after the joint tenant's death (see page 497). Life insurance proceeds are usually exempt from the insured's creditors if payable to a spouse or child, and

---

26. Restatement (Second) of Trusts § 330 cmt. o (Am. Law Inst. 1959).
27. *See, e.g.*, Watterson v. Burnard, 986 N.E.2d 604 (Ohio App. 2013).
28. Restatement (Third) of Trusts § 25 cmt. e (Am. Law Inst. 2003).

retirement benefits are also usually exempt. U.S. savings bonds with a pay-on-death beneficiary may be exempt as well.[29]

UPC § 6-102 (1998) permits the decedent's creditors to reach nonprobate transfers (except joint tenancies in real estate), such as revocable inter vivos trusts and joint bank accounts, if the probate estate is insufficient to pay the debts.

3. Spousal Rights and Revocable Trusts. Suppose Dunnebier had been married when he settled his revocable trust. Would his widow's right to an *elective* or *forced share* of his estate apply to the trust property? *See* Sullivan v. Burkin, 460 N.E.2d 572 (Mass. 1984), page 528. Suppose that Dunnebier married after executing his pour-over will and settling the trust. Suppose further that after the wedding, Dunnebier amended the trust to make a provision for his new wife but left the will unchanged. After his death, would his widow be entitled to a *pretermitted share* of his estate on the grounds that she was not mentioned in Dunnebier's premarital will? *See* In re Estate of Prestie, 138 P.3d 520 (Nev. 2006), page 572. In answering these questions, what is the relevance that the elective share is a policy-based limit on freedom of disposition, whereas the pretermitted share is an intent-implementing rule of construction? *See* In re Estate of Jackson, 194 P.3d 1269 (Okla. 2008), page 583.

Clymer v. Mayo
473 N.E.2d 1084 (Mass. 1985)

Hennessey, C.J. [Clara Mayo, a professor of psychology at Boston University, executed a will in 1963 naming her husband, James, as the primary beneficiary. In 1964, she named James as the beneficiary of her B.U. group life insurance policy. In 1965, she made him the beneficiary of her B.U. retirement plans. On February 2, 1973, Clara executed a new will and a revocable trust. Under the new will, the bulk of her estate was to pour over into the trust. James was the life beneficiary under the trust, with remainder interests in Clara's nieces and nephews, B.U., and Clark University. Clara named the trustees of her revocable trust as the beneficiaries of her B.U. group life insurance policy. Later, she named the trustees as the beneficiaries of her B.U. retirement plans. In this way, Clara unified the disposition of all of her property through her revocable trust.

In 1978, Clara and James divorced. Clara changed the beneficiary designation of her life insurance to Marianne LaFrance, but she left the trustees as the beneficiaries of her pension plans and James as the life beneficiary of the trust. After Clara died in 1981, litigation ensued. Among the questions presented was whether James's interest in the trust was revoked as a result of the divorce. The Massachusetts revocation-on-divorce statute applied to devises under a will. Could this statute be applied to

---

29. *See* Elaine H. Gagliardi, Remembering the Creditor at Death: Aligning Probate and Nonprobate Transfers, 41 Real Prop. Prob. & Tr. J. 819 (2007).

Clara's revocable trust on the theory that it was a will substitute that was enmeshed with her will?]

[T]he trust had no practical significance until her death in 1981. The decedent executed both her will and indenture of trust on February 2, 1973. She transferred no property or funds to the trust at that time. The trust was to receive its funding at the decedent's death, in part through her life insurance policy and retirement benefits, and in part through a pour-over from the will's residuary clause....

During her lifetime, the decedent retained power to amend or revoke the trust. Since the trust was unfunded, her co-trustee was subject to no duties or obligations until her death. Similarly, it was only as a result of the decedent's death that [James] could claim any right to the trust assets. It is evident from the time and manner in which the trust was created and funded, that the decedent's will and trust were integrally related components of a single testamentary scheme. For all practical purposes the trust, like the will, "spoke" only at the decedent's death. For this reason [James]'s interest in the trust was revoked by operation of G.L. c. 191, § 9 [providing that divorce revokes an ex-spouse's interests under a will], at the same time his interest under the decedent's will was revoked.

It has reasonably been contended that in enacting G.L. c. 191, § 9, the Legislature "intended to bring the law into line with the expectations of most people.... Divorce usually represents a stormy parting, where the last thing one of the parties wishes is to have an earlier will carried out giving everything to the former spouse." Raymond Young, Probate Reform, 18 Boston B.J. 7, 11 (1974). To carry out the testator's implied intent, the law revokes "any disposition or appointment of property made by the will to the former spouse." It is indisputable that if the decedent's trust was either testamentary or incorporated by reference into her will, [James]'s beneficial interest in the trust would be revoked by operation of the statute. However, the judge stopped short of mandating the same result in this case.

Treating the components of the decedent's estate plan separately, and not as parts of an interrelated whole, brings about inconsistent results. Applying c. 191, § 9, the judge correctly revoked the will provisions benefiting [James]. As a result, the decedent's personal property—originally left to [James]—fell into the will's residuary clause and passed to the trust....

[We conclude] that the legislative intent under G.L. c. 191, § 9, is that a divorced spouse should not take under a [revocable] trust executed in these circumstances. In the absence of an expressed contrary intent, that statute implies an intent on the part of a testator to revoke will provisions favoring a former spouse. It is incongruous then to ignore that same intent with regard to a trust funded in part through her will's pour-over at the decedent's death. As one law review commentator has noted, "[t]ransferors use will substitutes to avoid probate, not to avoid the subsidiary law of wills. The subsidiary rules are the product of centuries of legal experience in attempting to discern transferors' wishes and suppress litigation. These rules should be treated as presumptively correct for will substitutes as well as for wills." John H. Langbein, The Nonprobate Revolution and the Future of the Law of Succession, 97 Harv. L. Rev. 1108, 1136-37 (1984).

Restricting our holding to the particular facts of this case—specifically the existence of a revocable pour-over trust funded entirely at the time of the decedent's death—we conclude that G.L. c. 191, § 9, revokes [James's] interest under [the trust]. . . .

So ordered.

NOTES

1. Revocation on Divorce and Revocable Trusts. Some revocation-on-divorce statutes, such as the one at issue in *Clymer*, refer to wills and are located in the state's probate code. Courts have struggled with the question of whether these statutes should be applied to will substitutes.[30] In *Clymer*, the court looked to substance rather than form. It stressed that the trust was coordinated with the will to fashion a unified estate plan that would not take effect until Clara's death. But suppose Clara had settled additional revocable trusts or had other nonprobate transfers that were not coordinated with her will. What result? Was the "interrelated whole" of the estate plan essential to the court's reasoning? Does not the theory of the revocation-on-divorce statutes pertain to all nonprobate transfers? The Restatement (Third) of Property explains:

> Historically, some of the rules of construction were formulated only for wills because wills then constituted the principal means of transmitting property at death. Some rules of construction were placed in the probate code, which led the legislature to draft them as rules applicable to wills. As will substitutes have proliferated and become alternative means of passing property at death, legislatures and courts have sometimes been slow to expand the scope of these rules to transactions to which they should be fully applicable in policy.[31]

UPC § 2-804 (1990, rev. 1997), page 239, applies to both wills and will substitutes. It revokes a disposition in favor of a former spouse in a "governing instrument," which is defined in UPC § 1-201(18) to mean a deed, will, trust, insurance or annuity policy, account with a pay-on-death or transfer-on-death designation, pension plan, or other such nonprobate transfer. Since the decision in *Clymer*, Massachusetts adopted § 2-804.[32]

Even in states that have adopted modern revocation-on-divorce statutes, such as UPC § 2-804, two difficulties persist. First, it is not entirely settled whether the Constitution permits the statute to be applied to a beneficiary designation made before the effective date of the statute. Most courts have upheld retroactive application, but a few have not.[33] Second, under Egelhoff v. Egelhoff, 532 U.S. 141 (2001), page 486, federal law preempts the application of state revocation-on-divorce statutes to most pension

---

30. *See* Susan N. Gary, Applying Revocation-on-Divorce Statutes to Will Substitutes, 18 Quinnipiac Prob. L.J. 83 (2004).

31. Restatement (Third) of Property: Wills and Other Donative Transfers § 7.2 cmt. a (Am. Law Inst. 2003).

32. *See* Mass. Gen. Laws Ann. ch. 190B, § 2-804 (2016).

33. *Compare* Buchholz v. Storsve, 740 N.W.2d 107 (S.D. 2007) (upholding retroactive application), *with* Whirlpool Corp. v. Ritter, 929 F.2d 1318 (8th Cir. 1991) (retroactive application of Oklahoma statute unconstitutional).

accounts and life insurance obtained as a benefit of employment. The obvious lesson is that a divorcing client must be advised to update the client's estate plan, including all death beneficiary designations, to remove the former spouse.

2. Abatement and Ademption. Perhaps because the revocable trust is the most will-like of all the will substitutes, courts have applied to revocable trusts most of the rules of construction from the law of wills. For example, in Handelsman v. Handelsman, 852 N.E.2d 862 (Ill. App. 2006), the court applied the state's *abatement* rules for wills (see page 384) to a revocable trust in which there was not enough property to make all of the cash payments called for by the trust instrument on the settlor's death. In Wasserman v. Cohen, 606 N.E.2d 901 (Mass. 1993), the court applied the state's *ademption* doctrine for wills (see page 373) to a revocable trust that called for a transfer of specific property to a particular beneficiary on the death of the settlor. The property was not in the trust at the settlor's death because the settlor had sold it to a third party.

3. The Antilapse Controversy. Suppose O creates a revocable trust providing that, on O's death, the trust property is to be divided between O's children, A and B. Then A dies, survived by two children, C and D. How should the trust property be distributed on O's death? If the trust were created under O's will, and A predeceased O, the anti-lapse statute would apply, and A's share would be redirected to C and D. Should the same result obtain for a revocable trust? Legislation in about a third of the states, and UPC § 2-707 (1990, rev. 2008), answers this question in the affirmative. However, § 2-707 is complex and controversial, in part because it includes the rule of UPC § 2-603(b)(3), that words such as "if he survives me," without more, do not impose a condition of survivorship (see page 360). We take up § 2-707 and the application of antilapse rules to trusts in Chapter 13 at page 865. Under traditional law, in the example above A would have had a remainder that would pass under A's will or by intestacy.

4. Capacity and Limitation Periods for Revocable Trusts. The capacity required to make a donative transfer is higher in most states for a lifetime transfer than for a deathtime transfer (see page 268). The rationale is that the state has an interest in protecting living donors, but not dead ones, from impoverishment. Is the making of a revocable trust more like a lifetime transfer or a transfer at death? The modern view, adopted by UTC § 601 (2000), is that the "capacity required to create, amend, revoke, or add property to a revocable trust, or to direct the actions of the trustee of a revocable trust, is the same as that required to make a will."

The UTC also unifies the limitations period for contesting wills and revocable trusts. Both UPC § 3-108(a) (1993), which applies to will contests, and UTC § 604(a)(1), which applies to revocable trusts, provide for a three-year limitations period in which to bring a challenge. The time starts to run at the death of the testator or settlor. However, because a revocable trust is often used for more expeditious administration and distribution than in probate, UTC § 604(a)(2) provides that the limitations period can be shortened to 120 days from notice if the trustee sends the prospective contestant "a copy of the trust instrument and a notice informing the person of the trust's existence, of the trustee's name and address, and of the time allowed for commencing a proceeding."

5. Revocable Trusts in Contemporary Practice

In contemporary practice, the revocable trust has replaced the will as the centerpiece instrument governing property transfer at death. A revocable trust avoids probate to the extent it is funded during the settlor's life, and it allows the settlor to consolidate the disposition of all her property, probate and nonprobate, under one instrument. Consolidation is accomplished by naming the trustee as the beneficiary of all the settlor's will substitutes and as the beneficiary under the settlor's will (a pour-over will). To change her estate plan later, the settlor need only amend her revocable trust. In this way, the revocable trust has come to function as the will did in the days before the proliferation of will substitutes.

Figure 7.1

Unified Estate Planning via Revocable Trust

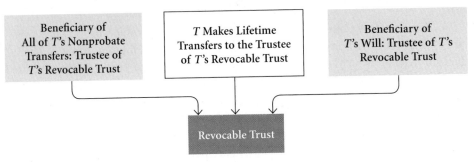

a. The Pour-Over Will

The concept of a *pour-over will* is simple. *O* sets up a revocable trust with himself or a third party as trustee. *O* then executes a will devising his probate estate to the trustee of that trust. Here is a sample pour-over provision:

> I give my residuary estate to the then acting trustee under the trust agreement executed by me on _____ __, 20__, and known as the *O* 20__ Revocable Trust, of which I am now trustee and *X* is named as successor trustee, to be added to the trust estate and held under that trust agreement as in effect at my death.[34]

A pour-over will only controls the disposition of the testator's probate property. If the testator makes a later will substitute, the will substitute rather than the will governs the disposition of the property subject to that will substitute.[35]

When the law in this area was first developing, two theories were useful in validating a pour over of probate property into the decedent's revocable trust. The first was *incorporation by reference* (see page 245). A will can incorporate by reference a document in existence at the time the will is executed, but not amendments to the document made after the will is executed. Hence, incorporation by reference cannot be used to validate a pour over into a trust that is amended after the will is executed. Moreover, a

---

34. Adapted from Northern Trust, Will & Trust Forms 110-15 (2004).
35. *See, e.g.,* Jimenez v. Corr, 764 S.E.2d 115 (Va. 2014).

trust instrument incorporated by reference into the will gives rise to a testamentary trust at the death of the settlor rather than a transfer to an already existing inter vivos trust.

The second theory was the doctrine of *acts of independent significance* (see page 254). Under this doctrine, a will may dispose of property by referring to some act or event that has significance apart from disposing of probate assets — in this context, by reference to a trust that disposes of property transferred to the trust during life. The trust instrument does not have to be in existence when the will is executed, but the trust must have some property in it prior to the testator's death. The assets poured over from the settlor's probate estate to the trust, like the assets the settlor earlier transferred to the trust, are subject to the terms of the trust.

Note the differences between incorporation by reference and acts of independent significance. Incorporation requires that the trust instrument be in existence at the time the will is executed. Independent significance requires that the trust have some property transferred to it during the settlor's life. Neither permits a pour over into an unfunded revocable trust drafted or amended after execution of the will. To do this required statutory authorization.

b. Statutory Validation of a Pour Over into an Unfunded Revocable Trust

Estate planners sought the enactment of legislation permitting a will to pour over into an unfunded revocable trust even if the trust was created or amended after the pour-over will was executed. The Uniform Testamentary Additions to Trusts Act (UTATA) (Unif. Law Comm'n 1960, rev. 1991), in its original 1960 form, validated a pour over of probate assets into a revocable trust only if the trust instrument was executed before or concurrently with the will. The 1990 UPC dropped the requirement of previous or concurrent execution. UPC § 2-511, and the conforming 1991 revision to UTATA, permits the trust instrument to be executed or amended after the will. Under these statutes, a will can pour over the testator's probate assets to "the then acting trustee of a trust that I will execute," if the testator thereafter executes the trust instrument before dying.

NOTE

Reconciling Revised UTATA and Incorporation by Reference. Given that UTATA now permits a pour over to a trust that is created *after* the will is executed, why does UPC § 2-510, page 245, codifying the doctrine of incorporation by reference, continue to require a writing to be in existence when the will is executed? And why is UPC § 2-513, page 252, which authorizes the use of a subsequent writing for disposition of personal property, limited to tangible personal property? Is there any reason why a signed later writing should be treated differently from a signed later trust instrument?

c. Deathtime Considerations

As we have just seen, a revocable trust is commonly used to consolidate for coordinated disposition at death all of the settlor's property, both probate and nonprobate. But a revocable trust is itself a will substitute that *avoids probate* to the extent that the settlor transfers property to the trust during life. Because the trustee holds legal title to

Norman Dacey and How to Avoid Probate!

Perhaps no single person has done more to advance the rise of the revocable trust than Norman F. Dacey, author of the runaway bestseller, How to Avoid Probate! The first edition, published in 1965, opened with a slashing attack on lawyers who benefit from the probate system:

> The probate system, conceived generations ago as a device for protecting heirs, has now become their greatest enemy. Almost universally corrupt, it is essentially a form of private taxation levied by the legal profession upon the rest of the population. All across the land, both large and small estates are being plundered by lawyers specializing in "probate practice."

After denouncing the "extortionate" legal fees and other disadvantages of probate, Dacey offered a way to avoid the problem completely: Declare yourself trustee of all your property, with the trust property to pass to named beneficiaries upon your death. In other words, do what Albert Farkas and Ruth Fulp did in Farkas v. Williams, page 445, and Fulp v. Gilliland, page 448. Dacey's book contains do-it-yourself trust and will forms designed for various kinds of assets and different family situations.

The legal profession was not amused by Dacey's book. The New York County Lawyers' Association sought an injunction to ban the sale of the book in New York on the grounds that Dacey, a nonlawyer, was giving legal advice. The New York Court of Appeals held that Dacey's readers were not his clients because the book was sold to the public at large and no relationship of personal trust and confidence arose. N.Y. Cty. Lawyers' Ass'n v. Dacey, 234 N.E.2d 459 (N.Y. 1967). Dacey then sued the New York County Lawyers' Association for $5 million in damages for interfering with his right to free speech. He lost. Dacey v. N.Y. Cty. Lawyers' Ass'n, 423 F.2d 188 (2d Cir. 1969). Dacey also sued the Florida Bar Association for publishing a book review that Dacey

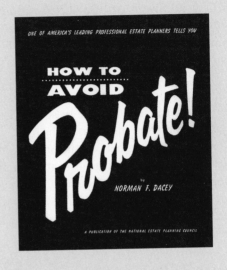

ONE OF AMERICA'S LEADING PROFESSIONAL ESTATE PLANNERS TELLS YOU

HOW TO AVOID Probate!

by NORMAN F. DACEY

A PUBLICATION OF THE NATIONAL ESTATE PLANNING COUNCIL

thought was libelous. Dacey v. Fla. Bar, Inc., 427 F.2d 1292 (5th Cir. 1970). He lost again. This litigation, of course, helped to promote the book. Eventually, Dacey sold two and a half million copies before the book finally went out of print after five editions in 1993.

Subsequently, to avoid income tax on the royalties, Dacey moved to Ireland, but lawyers had their revenge when the Commissioner of Internal Revenue (a lawyer!) pursued Dacey and forced him to pay back taxes and penalties. Dacey v. Commissioner, T.C. Memo 1992-187. In 1988, Dacey renounced his U.S. citizenship and became a citizen of Ireland. He died in London in 1994.

Since Dacey first published his book, there has been a groundswell of public demand for a simpler and less costly probate system. Reform has occurred in many states, often in the form of adoption of the Uniform Probate Code, particularly its informal probate, unsupervised probate, and small estate procedures (see page 45).

the trust property, there is no need to change title by probate administration upon the death of the settlor. Instead, at the death of the settlor the property is held in further trust or is distributed in accordance with the terms of the trust. Either way, because a revocable trust does not arise in probate, it is not subject to *ongoing supervision* by a probate court, as is a testamentary trust.

Another benefit of avoiding probate by way of a funded revocable trust is *privacy*. Unlike a will, which upon filing in the probate court becomes a court record open to the public, a revocable trust need not be filed with a court unless a dispute arises.[36] So there is a privacy advantage to a revocable trust relative to a will, one that persists even in a state that has reformed probate to make it cheaper and faster.

Still another advantage of a funded revocable trust is *continuity in property management* upon the settlor's death. Even if the settlor had been acting as the sole trustee, at the settlor's death a successor trustee can act immediately and without need for a court order. The trust property can be distributed to the beneficiaries right away if that is what the terms of the trust provide. In contrast, property held by a decedent outright must be marshaled by the personal representative, whose appointment must be confirmed by the probate court, and then distribution of the property may be delayed until the conclusion of the probate proceeding.

A revocable trust is often better suited to *multistate estate planning* than a will. Perhaps the most salient illustration is that a revocable trust can be used to avoid a second probate (an *ancillary probate*) for real property in another state. A settlor of a revocable trust also has broader freedom than a testator in *choice of law*, in particular if the trust is to be funded with financial assets that can be deposited with an out-of-state trustee.[37] The additional cost and inconvenience may be small compared to the possible advantages. There is abundant evidence, for example, of widespread use of out-of-state trusts to take advantage of those states' repeal of the *Rule Against Perpetuities* (see Chapter 14 at page 906).[38] In a few states, a married person may be able to use an out-of-state revocable trust to deny a *forced share* to a surviving spouse (see Chapter 8 at page 534).

A revocable trust can be *contested* for lack of capacity and undue influence. In practice, however, it is generally more difficult to set aside a funded revocable trust than a will. Unlike a will, heirs who are not beneficiaries of the trust are not usually entitled to see the trust instrument (see Chapter 9 at page 682). If a trust continues as an ongoing operation for years before the settlor dies, generating monthly or yearly statements and involving various property transfers by a third-party trustee, a court is likely to be reluctant to set the trust aside. In most states litigation over trusts is tried before a judge rather than a jury. All told, if a will contest is foreseen, a funded revocable trust with a third-party trustee may be advisable (see page 307).

---

36. *See* Frances H. Foster, Trust Privacy, 93 Cornell L. Rev. 555 (2008). In In re Estate of Hearst, 136 Cal. Rptr. 821 (App. 1977), William Randolph Hearst had created a testamentary trust to care for his descendants and relatives. After Patty Hearst was kidnapped by the Symbionese Liberation Army, the trustees asked the court to cut off public access to the probate files in Hearst's estate, fearing that radicals would find hitherto unnoticed members of the family and the location of their homes and properties. The court agreed to restrict public access while the Hearst family was in danger of attack. If Hearst had created a revocable inter vivos trust of his property, the family records would have been private without the need for a special ruling.

37. The law of a testator's domicile will generally apply to a testamentary trust, because it was created by a will probated in that state, regardless of the testator's intent that the law of another state apply. UPC § 2-703 (1990) provides that a testator may select the state law that will govern the meaning and effect of his will, including trusts created by the will, unless that law is contrary to the domiciliary state's law protecting the surviving spouse or other public policy. Where adopted, § 2-703 lessens the need to create an inter vivos trust to invoke the law of another state. It is not always obvious, however, if another state's law will be deemed contrary to the public policy of the domiciliary state.

38. *See, e.g.*, Robert H. Sitkoff & Max M. Schanzenbach, Jurisdictional Competition for Trust Funds: An Empirical Analysis of Perpetuities and Taxes, 115 Yale L.J. 356 (2005).

"Trust Mills" and Unauthorized Practice of Law

The public demand for revocable trusts has sparked a cottage industry that markets inter vivos trusts directly to the public. Lawyers have fought these purveyors of living trusts, derisively called trust mills, by alleging unauthorized practice of law, with some notable successes. *See* Angela M. Vallario, Living Trusts in the Unauthorized Practice of Law: A Good Thing Gone Bad, 59 Md. L. Rev. 595 (2000).

In 2009, the Ohio Supreme Court upheld a fine of $6.4 million against a group of nonlawyers who had been marketing revocable trusts. The fine was calculated by multiplying the number of plans sold, 3,202, by their cost, $1,995. Columbus Bar Ass'n v. Am. Family Prepaid Legal Corp., 916 N.E.2d 784 (Ohio 2009). In Illinois, the "assembly, drafting, execution, and funding of a living trust" by a nonlawyer or by a corporation not authorized to do trust business is a misdemeanor (or a felony if the offense is repeated). 815 Ill. Comp. Stat. Ann. 505/2BB (2016). In Landheer v. Landheer, 891 N.E.2d 975 (Ill. App. 2008), the court read this statute to void a trust amendment drafted for the settlor by a nonlawyer, though it said that the settlor, even if not a lawyer, could lawfully prepare her own trust documents.

What about a will-drafting computer program, such as Quicken WillMaker Plus, or an online Web site such as willing.com or LegalZoom.com, which generate will and trust forms according to the user's answers to a set of standard questions? State bar associations have a mixed record of success in challenging these kinds of digital document assistance services. *See* Deborah L. Rhode & Lucy Buford Ricca, Protecting the Profession or the Public? Rethinking Unauthorized-Practice Enforcement, 82 Fordham L. Rev. 2587 (2014).

A potential downside to the use of a revocable trust as a will substitute is the lack of certainty about the applicability of the constructional aids in the *subsidiary law of wills*. The rules for wills dealing with lapse, ademption, simultaneous death, revocation on divorce, apportionment of death taxes, and so on may not apply to a revocable trust, depending on the rule and the jurisdiction.[39] Most of these issues can be solved by appropriate drafting, but only if the drafter anticipates the problem.

In probate, a *nonclaim statute* is applicable to the decedent's creditors (see Chapter 1 at page 47). If a creditor does not file a claim within a relatively short period of time, the creditor is forever barred. In many states there is no similar short limitations period for revocable trusts. If it is important to cut off the rights of creditors—as might be true for a professional such as a doctor or lawyer who is subject to a statute of limitations on malpractice that runs from discovery of the malpractice—probate might be preferable.

d. Lifetime Considerations

Although the revocable trust is now widely regarded as a will substitute, it still has lifetime consequences that figure into contemporary estate planning.

A revocable trust can facilitate *property management by a fiduciary*. A settlor can select a third-party trustee to manage a funded revocable trust, with duties that as we have seen run only to the settlor (page 447). This arrangement may be desirable if the settlor wants to be relieved of the burdens of day-to-day management of the trust property. On the other hand, putting property in trust can create some inconveniences.

---

39. *See* Jeffrey A. Schoenblum, Multistate Guide to Trusts and Trust Administration tbl. 1 (2012).

A third party, such as a bank, may want to see a copy of the trust instrument or require a certification under UTC § 1013 (2000) to verify that the trustee has the power to engage in a proposed transaction.

A funded revocable trust can be used in *planning for incapacity*, a subject we take up later in this chapter at page 498. Even if the settlor names himself as the initial trustee, a successor trustee can take over and act expeditiously to protect the trust property in the event of the settlor's incapacity. By contrast, obtaining a judicial order of incapacity and establishing a *conservatorship* is cumbersome and expensive, and it may involve unwanted publicity (see page 499). Moreover, because the rules governing a trustee's powers tend to be more liberal than those applicable to the powers of a conservator, it is usually easier for a trustee to deal with partnership interests, exercise options, borrow money, participate in reorganizations, and the like.

A revocable trust may be useful in *keeping title clear*, such as when a newly married person wants to avoid commingling separate property with property acquired during the marriage. Spouses who move from a community property state to a separate property state sometimes create a revocable trust for their community property to preserve a stepped-up income tax basis on the property when one spouse dies (see page 555).

There are no federal *income, gift, or estate tax* benefits to the creation of a revocable trust. For federal tax purposes, property in a revocable trust is treated as though it were owned by the settlor during the settlor's lifetime and upon the settlor's death. We take up the federal gift and estate taxes in Chapter 15.

C. THE OTHER WILL SUBSTITUTES

1. Life Insurance

Life insurance is a euphemism for death insurance. It shifts the economic risk of premature death to an insurance company. By buying into a pool with other people worried about the same risk, those who do not die prematurely in effect compensate the beneficiaries of those who do. The domestic life insurance industry is massive. In 2014, benefit payments totaled $109.8 billion and the total value of all policies in force at year end was $20.1 trillion.[40]

Life insurance is commonly used to insure against lost income on the death of a wage earner. For a person with dependents, experts often recommend buying life insurance worth anywhere between 6 and 30 times the insured's annual income. The amount suitable depends on the age, wealth, and family circumstances of the insured. A younger person with small children and little savings needs more insurance than a person with more wealth and fewer dependents. The trick is to balance the cost of the premiums with the need to get enough insurance to protect the financial security of the insured's family in the event of the insured's death. A too common mistake is not insuring against the death of a partner who is not a wage earner but rather works inside the home. Replacing childcare and other household production can be quite expensive,

---

40. *See* Am. Council of Life Insurers, Life Insurers Fact Book 50 tbl. 5.2, 66 tbl. 7.1 (2015).

"No, but I can tell you the meaning of whole or term life insurance."
Michael Shaw/The New Yorker Collection/The Cartoon Bank

and the death of a partner may limit the ability of the survivor to earn money by working outside of the home.

Term life insurance is the simplest and most common type of life insurance. A term policy is a contract that obligates the insurance company to pay the named beneficiary if the insured dies within the policy's term—commonly 1, 5, 10, 20, or even 30 years. Because there is no saving feature or cash surrender value, term policies are less expensive than permanent insurance. Young parents who are healthy can usually obtain 20- or 30-year term policies, covering the period of acute vulnerability before their children are self-sufficient, at relatively low cost. For a premium of under $1,000 a year that remains fixed over the term of the policy (a "level" premium), a 30-year-old woman in excellent health can obtain a $2 million, 30-year term life insurance policy. Some term policies allow for conversion to permanent insurance at the expiration of the term irrespective of subsequent changes in the insured's health.

Whole life insurance, also called *ordinary* or *straight* life insurance, combines life insurance with a savings plan. The policy eventually becomes *paid up* or *endowed*, after which no further premiums are owed. Because whole life insurance is permanent, lasting until the insured's death, it is certain to result in a payment by the insurer and is thus the most expensive form of life insurance available. There are newer and less expensive variations on permanent life insurance, such as *universal* or *variable* life insurance.

The owner of a life insurance policy, or the beneficiary after the insured's death, is typically entitled to select from an array of *settlement options* for the receipt of death benefits. These options tend to include a lump sum, interest for years followed by payment of the principal, or periodic payments of interest and principal.

Life insurance contracts have long been valid to transfer property on death without Wills Act formalities. The long and benign experience with pay-on-death provisions in life insurance contracts was cited by reformers in support of validating similar provisions in bank and brokerage accounts and other contracts. More difficult has been the question of whether life insurance should be subject to the subsidiary law of wills.

Cook v. Equitable Life Assurance Society
428 N.E.2d 110 (Ind. App. 1981)

RATLIFF, J. Margaret A. Cook, Administratrix C.T.A. of the Estate of Douglas D. Cook (Douglas); Margaret A. Cook; and Daniel J. Cook (Margaret and Daniel) appeal from an entry of summary judgment granted by the trial court in favor of Doris J. Cook Combs (Doris) in an interpleader action brought by The Equitable Life Assurance Society of the United States (Equitable). We affirm.

FACTS

Douglas purchased a whole life insurance policy on March 13, 1953, from Equitable, naming his wife . . . , Doris, as the beneficiary. On March 5, 1965, Douglas and Doris were divorced. The divorce decree made no provision regarding the insurance policy, but did state the following: "It is further understood and agreed between the parties hereto that the provisions of this agreement shall be in full satisfaction of all claims by either of said parties against the other, including alimony, support and maintenance money."

After the divorce Douglas ceased paying the premiums on his life insurance policy, and Equitable notified him on July 2, 1965, that because the premium due on March 9, 1965, had not been paid, his whole life policy was automatically converted to a paid-up term policy with an expiration date of June 12, 1986. The policy contained the following provision with respect to beneficiaries:

BENEFICIARY. The Owner may change the beneficiary from time to time prior to the death of the Insured, by written notice to the Society, but any such change shall be effective only if it is endorsed on this policy by the Society. . . .

On December 24, 1965, Douglas married Margaret, and a son Daniel, was born to them. On June 7, 1976, Douglas made a holographic will in which he bequeathed his insurance policy with Equitable Life to his wife and son, Margaret and Daniel:

Last Will & Testimint (sic)

I Douglas D. Cook

Being of sound mind do Hereby leave all my Worldly posessions (sic) to my Wife and son, Margaret A. Cook & Daniel Joseph Cook. being my Bank Accounts at Irwin Union Bank & trust to their Welfair (sic) my Insurance policys (sic) with Common Welth of Ky. and Equitable Life. all my machinecal (sic) tools to be left to my son if He is Interested in Working with them If not to be sold and money used for their welfair (sic) all my Gun Collection Kept as long as they, my Wife & Son (sic) and then sold and money used for their welfair (sic)

I sighn (sic) this
June 7-1976
at Barth Conty
Hospital Room
1114 Bed 2
/s/ Douglas D. Cook
/s/ 6-7-76 Margaret A. Cook wife
/s/ Chas. W. Winkler
/s/ Mary A. Winkler

The will of Douglas Cook

This will was admitted to probate in Bartholomew Superior Court after Douglas's death on June 9, 1979. On August 24, 1979, Margaret filed a claim with Equitable for the proceeds of Douglas's policy, but Equitable deposited the proceeds, along with its complaint in interpleader, with the Bartholomew Circuit Court on March 14, 1980. Discovery was made; interrogatories and affidavits were filed; and all parties moved for summary judgment. The trial court found that there was no genuine issue as to any material fact respecting Doris's claim to the proceeds of the policy and entered judgment in her favor as to the amount of the proceeds plus interest, a total of $3,154.09. Margaret and Daniel appeal from this award. . . .

DISCUSSION AND DECISION

. . . Margaret and Daniel do not dispute the facts in this case, yet they contend that the court's entry of summary judgment was erroneous because Indiana law does not require strict compliance with the terms of an insurance policy relative to a change of beneficiary in all cases. They argue, therefore, that strict compliance with policy provisions is not required for the protection of either the insurer or the insured once the proceeds have been paid by the insurer into court in an action for interpleader and that the court should shape its relief in this case upon the equitable principle "that the insured's express and unambiguous intent should be given effect." . . .

Doris agrees that less than strict compliance with policy change requirements may be adequate to change a beneficiary where circumstances show the insured has done everything within his power to effect the change. Nevertheless, Doris asserts that Indiana adheres to the majority rule finding an attempt to change the beneficiary of a life insurance policy by will, without more, to be ineffectual. We agree with Doris. . . .

Almost one hundred years ago our supreme court in Holland v. Taylor, 12 N.E. 116 (Ind. 1887), enunciated the general rule still followed in Indiana: an attempt to change the beneficiary of a life insurance contract by will and in disregard of the methods prescribed under the contract will be unsuccessful. . . .

Indiana courts have recognized exceptions to the general rule that strict compliance with policy requirements is necessary to effect a change of beneficiary. Three exceptions were noted by this court . . . in Heinzman v. Whiteman, 139 N.E. 329, 331 (Ind. App. 1923):

> 1. If the society has waived a strict compliance with its own rules, and in pursuance of a request of the insured to change the beneficiary, has issued a new certificate to him, the original beneficiary will not be heard to complain that the course indicated by the regulations was not pursued.
> 2. If it be beyond the power of the insured to comply literally with the regulations, a court of equity will treat the change as having been legally made.
> 3. If the insured has pursued the course pointed out by the laws of the association, and has done all in his power to change the beneficiary; but before the new certificate is actually issued, he dies, a court of equity will decree that to be done which ought to be done, and act as though the certificate had been issued.

The public policy considerations undergirding this rule and its limited exceptions involve protection of the rights of all the parties concerned and should not be viewed, as appellants advocate, for the exclusive protection of the insurer. Indiana, in fact, has specifically rejected this position. In Stover v. Stover, 204 N.E.2d 374, 380 (Ind. App. 1965), the court recognized an insured's right to rely on the provisions of the policy in regard to change of beneficiary:

> We must reject appellant's contention that the provisions set forth in the certificate, as mentioned above, are for the exclusive benefit of the insurance company and may be waived at will. The deceased insured himself is entitled to rely upon such provisions that he may at all times know to whom the proceeds of the insurance shall be payable.

In *Holland* the court also recognized that the beneficiary had a right in the executed contract which was subject to defeat only by a change of beneficiary which had been executed in accord with the terms of the insurance contract: "In that contract Anna

Laura, the beneficiary, had such an interest as that she had, and has, the right to insist that in order to cut her out, the change of beneficiary should be made in the manner provided in the contract." 12 N.E. at 119. . . .

Clearly it is in the interest of insurance companies to require and to follow certain specified procedures in the change of beneficiaries of its policies so that they may pay over benefits to persons properly entitled to them without subjection to claims by others of whose rights they had no notice or knowledge. Certainly it is also in the interest of beneficiaries themselves to be entitled to prompt payment of benefits by insurance companies which do not withhold payment until the will has been pro-bated in the fear of later litigation which might result from having paid the wrong party. . . . Finally, society's interest in the conservation of judicial energy and expense will be served where the rule and its limited exceptions are clearly stated and rigor-ously applied. . . .

Under the law of Indiana, therefore, in order for appellants to have defeated the motion for summary judgment in this case they must have made some showing that the insured had done all within his powers or all that reasonably could have been expected of him to comply with the policy provisions respecting a change of benefi-ciary, but that through no fault of his own he was unable to achieve his goal. Here there is no such indication or implication. Douglas was divorced in March of 1965 and remarried in December 1965. He was notified in July 1965 of the change in his policy, but took no action. A son was born of his second marriage. Eleven years after his divorce Douglas attempted to change the beneficiary of his insurance policy by a holographic will, but did not notify Equitable. He then lived three years after making that will. There is no indication that Douglas took any action in the fourteen years between his divorce from Doris and his death, other than the making of the will, to change the beneficiary of his life insurance policy from Doris to Margaret and Daniel. Surely, if Douglas had wanted to change the beneficiary he had ample time and opportunity to comply with the policy requirements. Nothing in the record sug-gests otherwise. . . .

We may be sympathetic to the cause of the decedent's widow and son, and it might seem that a departure from the general rule in an attempt to do equity under these facts would be noble. Nevertheless, such a course is fraught with the dangers of eroding a solidly paved pathway of the law and leaving in its stead only a gaping hole of uncer-tainty. Public policy requires that the insurer, insured, and beneficiary alike should be able to rely on the certainty that policy provisions pertaining to the naming and chang-ing of beneficiaries will control except in extreme situations. We, therefore, invoke a maxim equally as venerable as the one upon which appellants rely in the determination of this cause: Equity aids the vigilant, not those who slumber on their rights.

Judgment affirmed.

NOTES

1. Slumbered on His Rights?   Look at Douglas Cook's will. Is it fair to say, as did the court, that he slumbered on his rights? Was it unreasonable for Cook, who it seems was only passably literate, to believe that his will would supersede his earlier beneficiary designation? Most states allow for a change in life insurance beneficiary designation by substantial compliance with the terms of the policy.[41] Did Cook substantially comply?

2. Revocation on Divorce—Again.   *Cook* is another example of the recurring problem, which we saw in Clymer v. Mayo, page 462, of what to do with a will substitute that names an ex-spouse as a beneficiary. In many states, the statute that revokes a will provision for an ex-spouse does not apply to life insurance contracts. UPC § 2-804 (1990, rev. 2002), page 239, is unusual in that it does apply to life insurance. If § 2-804 applied in *Cook*, the result would have been different,[42] because the policy was obtained privately. If the policy had been obtained as a benefit of employment, however, under Egelhoff v. Egelhoff, 532 U.S. 141 (2001), page 486, the state revocation-on-divorce statute would be preempted by federal law.

Why was the divorce decree not enough to sever Doris's interest in Cook's insurance policy? Should Cook have been advised by his divorce lawyer to update his estate plan and about the need separately to file paperwork with the insurance company to remove Doris as a beneficiary?

3. The Beneficiary's Interest?   The court reasoned that the insurance company, Cook, and the named beneficiary each had an interest in relying on the change-of-beneficiary terms of the policy. But would it have prejudiced the company to give effect to Cook's will? The company had deposited the proceeds with the court pending a decision on who was the rightful taker. Is it plausible that the beneficiary had a reliance interest in the specific manner by which a new beneficiary would be named? Until Cook died, he retained the right to change his beneficiary designation at any time and for any reason. Is there a sound policy reason for allowing revocation of a revocable trust by any method that clearly manifests the settlor's intent (see page 453), but requiring a change in insurance beneficiary to be made only in the manner specified by the terms of the policy?

4. A Superwill?   Would it be a good idea to permit a *superwill*, that is, to allow the testator's will to trump the beneficiary designations in all nonprobate transfers? Washington has adopted a superwill statute, though it excludes life insurance.[43] A superwill would resolve the problem of updating beneficiary designations across a testator's many and sometimes forgotten nonprobate instruments. But what would be the drawbacks? Would a superwill draw the otherwise expeditious nonprobate modes of transfer into probate, holding up payment until the will is held valid?

The Restatement (Third) of Property endorses the superwill concept, but in a manner that also protects financial intermediaries:

> Insurance contracts, multiple-party accounts, pension accounts, and other will substitutes commonly require the account owner to follow a particular procedure

---

41. *See, e.g.*, Minnesota Life Ins. Co. v. Kagan, 724 F.3d 843, 851-52 (7th Cir. 2013).

42. *See, e.g.*, Thrivent Fin. v. Andronescu, 300 P.3d 117 (Mont. 2013).

43. *See* Wash. Rev. Code §§ 11.11.003-11.11.901 (2016) (superwill statute); id. § 11.02.005(10) (excluding life insurance); *see also* In re Estate of Collister, 382 P.3d 37 (Wash. App. 2016) (applying the life insurance exception).

for altering or amending the beneficiary designation, such as completing a form supplied by the financial intermediary or other payor. Such a term governs as a matter of the contract between the account owner and the financial intermediary or payor. It sometimes happens that the account owner misunderstands this requirement and attempts to revoke the beneficiary designation by will. . . .

In such cases, when the financial intermediary or other payor has paid the beneficiary of record on the account in good faith before learning of the later inconsistent designation in the will, the account term is effective to protect the financial intermediary or payor from liability to the beneficiary designated in the will. In such circumstances, that intended beneficiary is remitted to an action in restitution against the account-designated beneficiary who received the payment.

When the financial intermediary or payor receives notice of the inconsistent beneficiary designation contained in the subsequent will before paying the beneficiary of record on the account, the financial intermediary or payor should pay the proceeds as directed under the will, notwithstanding the failure of the account owner to comply with the account term specifying account-specific procedures for revocation or alteration. If the financial intermediary or payor is uncertain about the priority or effectiveness of the attempted revocation or alteration by will, the financial intermediary or payor may discharge its responsibilities by interpleading and/or paying the proceeds into court.[44]

What result in *Cook* if the Restatement rule had applied?

2. Pension and Retirement Plans

In 2013, more than half of all American workers had access to an employer- or union-sponsored pension or retirement plan.[45] At mid-year 2016, pension and retirement accounts held the staggering sum of $24.5 trillion (up from $18.5 trillion in 2012), representing a little more than a third of U.S. household financial assets.[46]

The original purpose of pension and retirement plans was to secure the retirement of workers and their spouses. But beginning in the 1970s and with increasing frequency ever since, propertied persons have used pension and retirement accounts for tax-advantaged saving and investing during life, culminating in a nonprobate transfer at death. Such accounts are therefore a central concern in contemporary estate planning. In this section we consider: (a) the reasons for the dramatic growth in pension and retirement plans, (b) the principal types of pension and retirement accounts, and (c) the rules for succession of pension and retirement assets at the account holder's death.

---

44. Restatement (Third) of Property: Wills and Other Donative Transfers § 7.2 cmt. e (Am. Law Inst. 2003).

45. *See* Craig Copeland, Employment-Based Retirement Plan Participation: Geographic Differences and Trends, 2013, Emp. Benefit Res. Inst. Issue Brief 1 (Oct. 2014).

46. This and subsequent statistics on pension and retirement accounts are taken from Inv. Co. Inst., Release: Quarterly Retirement Market Data, Second Quarter 2016 (Sept. 26, 2016).

a. The Growth in Pension and Retirement Plans

John H. Langbein
The Twentieth-Century Revolution in Family Wealth Transmission
86 Mich. L. Rev. 722 (1988)

Neither on the prairie nor in the cities of Abraham Lincoln's day had anybody ever heard of a pension fund. Your life expectancy was such that you were unlikely to need much in the way of retirement income. If you did chance to outlive your period of productive labor, you were in general cared for within the family. . . .

The way to begin thinking about the pension revolution is to grasp the magnitude of the underlying demographic phenomena that brought it about. Life expectancy . . . [t]oday is seventy-five years and climbing.[47] . . .

Not only have the demographics altered so that the elders are routinely surviving for long intervals beyond their years of employment, but in consequence of the transformation in the nature of wealth, their property has taken on a radically altered character. That family farm or family firm that was the source of intrafamilial support in former times has become ever more exceptional. Most parental wealth (apart from the parents' own human capital) now takes the form of financial assets, which embody claims upon those large-scale enterprises that have replaced family enterprise. . . .

In propertied families, today's elderly no longer expect much financial support from their children. The shared patrimony in farm or firm that underlay that reverse transfer system in olden times has now largely vanished. Instead, people of means are expected to foresee the need for retirement income while they are still in the workforce, and to conduct a program of saving for their retirement. Typically, these people have already undertaken one great cycle of saving and dissaving in their lives—that program by which they effected the investment in human capital for their children. Just as that former program of saving was oriented toward a distinctively modern form of wealth, human capital, so this second program centers on the other characteristic form of twentieth-century wealth, financial assets.

A priori, we might expect that individuals would be left to save for retirement without government guidance, much as they are left alone to save and spend for other purposes, but that has not been the case. Instead, the federal government has intervened by creating irresistible tax incentives to encourage people to conduct much or most of their retirement saving in a special mode, the tax-qualified pension plan.

There are three crucial advantages to conducting retirement saving through a tax-qualified pension plan. First, most contributions to the plan are tax-deferred. When my employer contributes to a qualified pension or profit-sharing plan on my behalf, or when I contribute to a defined contribution plan such as a 401(k) or, in the case of

---

47. A baby born in the United States in 2013 had a life expectancy of 81.2 if a girl and 76.4 if a boy. A person who had reached age 65 in 2013 had a further life expectancy of 20.5 years if female (for 85.5 years in total) and 17.9 years if male (for 82.9 years in total). *See* Nat'l Ctr. for Health Statistics, Health, United States, 2015: With Special Feature on Racial and Ethnic Health Disparities, 93-94 tbl. 14 (May 2016).—Eds.

academic personnel, a 403(b), I am saving with pretax dollars. If I am in the 25-percent bracket, the Treasury is contributing to my pension savings plan 25 cents in foregone taxation for my 75 cents in foregone consumption. The second great tax advantage is that the earnings on qualified plan investments accrue and compound on a tax-deferred basis. It is not until the employee retires and begins to receive distributions of his pension savings that he pays income tax on the sums distributed. The third major advantage . . . is that, because most retirees have lower taxable income in their retirement years than in their peak earning years, they find that distributions from pension accounts are usually taxed at lower marginal rates. . . .

The . . . tax attractions of conducting retirement saving through the medium of a tax-qualified pension plan are simply overwhelming.

NOTE

Tax Savings May Continue Beyond Death.   Because retirement accounts allow for the accumulation of wealth without taxation, many well-to-do account holders seek to maximize their contributions and to minimize distributions. In this way, the account functions more like a tax-sheltered vehicle for saving and investing than a true retirement fund. To reorient these accounts toward retirement, federal law mandates minimum annual withdrawals after the account holder reaches the age of 70.5. But after the death of the account holder further distributions can be delayed, stretching the tax-deferred compounding feature of the account, by naming a much younger death beneficiary, which resets the clock on mandatory withdrawals and the tax obligation that they trigger.[48]

b. Types of Pension and Retirement Plans

Pensions and retirement accounts generally fall into one of three categories: (1) defined benefit plan, (2) defined contribution plan, or (3) individual retirement account.

(1) Defined Benefit Plan.   In a *defined benefit plan*, a retired employee typically receives a regular pension check for life (a life annuity) or the joint and several lives of the employee and the employee's spouse (a joint and survivor annuity). The size of the benefit depends on the number of years the employee participated in the plan and the employee's level of compensation around the time of retirement. With an annuitized pension, at the death of the employee (and the employee's spouse, if the annuity is joint and survivor), there is nothing left in the plan for the employee or the employee's spouse to pass on to others.

Defined benefit plans, which were once dominant, are today relatively rare among private employers. At mid-year 2016, private defined benefit plans held only $2.8 trillion, less than 12 percent of the total wealth in pension and retirement accounts at that time. Defined benefit plans remain common, however, for government employees. At mid-year 2016, federal, state, and local government pension plans held $5.2 trillion in assets, just over 20 percent of the total.

---

48. But note that capital gains within a retirement account will be taxed as ordinary income on distribution.

(2) Defined Contribution Plan. In a *defined contribution plan*, typified by a 401(k) account,[49] the employer or the employee, or both, make contributions to a specific account for the employee.[50] At mid-year 2016, Americans held $7 trillion in employment-related defined contribution plans (up from $4.7 trillion in 2012).

The employee usually makes the investment decisions for her account, typically by choosing from a menu of mutual funds and other such investment vehicles.[51] Target-date funds, in which the assets are reallocated more conservatively as the target retirement date approaches, are an increasingly popular investment option.

Once retired, the former employee controls the size and timing of distributions from the account, subject to spousal protection and certain distribution rules such as mandatory annual withdrawals beginning at age 70.5. At the employee's death, whatever is left in the account passes outside of probate in accordance with the employee's death beneficiary designation or, if there is no valid designation, in accordance with the rules specified in the plan documents. In consequence, the shift from typically annuitized pensions in defined benefit plans to tax-advantaged saving and investment accounts in defined contribution plans has created a massive and still growing category of nonprobate transfer.

(3) Individual Retirement Account. Structurally, an *individual retirement account* (IRA) has much in common with a defined contribution plan. The main difference is that an IRA is not established by an employer. Instead, the IRA is governed by the contract between the account holder and the custodial institution. But the tax benefits of an IRA are similar to tax benefits of a defined contribution plan.

An IRA is the main form of tax-advantaged retirement saving for many self-employed persons. Employees participating in their employer's pension plan may use an IRA for additional retirement saving. It is also common for a participant in a defined contribution plan to transfer his account balance to an IRA after retiring. If done properly, this transfer, known as a *rollover*, is tax free. At mid-year 2016, Americans held $7.5 trillion in IRAs (up from $5.1 trillion in 2012), most of which traces to rollovers.

An IRA owner controls the timing and amounts of withdrawals, subject to distribution rules similar to those for a defined contribution account. Any remainder at death passes outside of probate in accordance with the account holder's beneficiary designation or, if there is no valid designation, in accordance with the account agreement's default distribution rules. IRAs, too, are therefore a massive and still growing category of nonprobate transfer.

c. Succession Issues for Pension and Retirement Accounts

With so much wealth now held in pension and retirement accounts, these accounts should figure prominently in contemporary estate planning. Unfortunately, many

---

49. *See* Internal Revenue Code § 401(k) (2016).

50. *See* Edward A. Zelinsky, The Origins of the Ownership Society: How the Defined Contribution Paradigm Changed America (2007).

51. The plan sponsor is subject to a fiduciary duty of prudence in constructing and monitoring the menu of investment alternatives. *See* Tibble v. Edison Int'l, 135 S. Ct. 1823 (2015).

people do not appreciate the significance of their pension and retirement account death beneficiary designations. This problem is exacerbated by lawyers who continue to think of estate planning and retirement planning as separate areas of practice, and by clients who undo sound plans with new and uncoordinated beneficiary designations across their pension and retirement accounts. A further complication is that applicable state laws are inconsistent across states and sometimes in conflict with federal law. Although most IRAs are governed by state law, pension and retirement accounts obtained as a benefit of employment are generally governed by federal law.

Nunnenman v. Estate of Grubbs
374 S.W.3d 75 (Ark. App. 2010)

PITTMAN, J. In 2003, decedent Donald Grubbs transferred his individual retirement account (IRA) to Raymond James and Associates, Inc., naming appellant [Jeannie Christine Nunnenman] as the beneficiary to receive the residue in the event of his death. Decedent was hospitalized in May 2005 and died on June 9 of that year. On June 3, 2005, decedent summoned an attorney to the hospital, where decedent made and executed a last will and testament that did not mention the IRA account. This will left decedent's entire estate to his mother, Shervena Grubbs, who was also named as executrix. In that capacity, Shervena Grubbs filed this action for an injunction freezing the assets of the IRA account based on her assertion that a note that she found in decedent's Bible months after his death had the effect of changing the beneficiary designation in the IRA account to make her the beneficiary. The trial court agreed and awarded her the account. Appellant asserts that the trial court clearly erred in so doing. We agree, and we reverse.

This case requires construction of three documents: a will, an IRA, and a handwritten note, which was assertedly found by Shervena Grubbs in a Bible some time after decedent's death. . . .

An IRA constitutes a contract between the person who establishes the IRA for his or her retirement and the financial institution that acts as the custodian of the IRA. Like an insurance policy, an IRA includes designation of beneficiaries to receive the residue in the event of the retiree's death. . . .

There are no Arkansas cases dealing specifically with attempts to change IRA beneficiaries by will, but the cases involving insurance policy beneficiaries, cited by appellant, are analogous and instructive. It is generally held that, where a life insurance policy reserves to the insured the right to change the beneficiary but specifies the manner in which the change may be made, the change must be made in the manner and mode prescribed by the policy, and according to most courts any attempt to make such change by will is ineffectual. However, Arkansas law is contrary to the general rule: Arkansas holds that a change of beneficiary can in fact be accomplished in a will so long as the language of the will is sufficient to identify the insurance policy involved and an intent to change the beneficiary. Pedron v. Olds, 105 S.W.2d 70 (Ark. 1937). . . .

Decedent's IRA application and agreement with Raymond James and Associates, Inc., designated appellant as sole beneficiary of his IRA. Appellant was identified by

The will and IRA agreement provisions at issue in *Nunnenman*

name, social security number, and date of birth. The effect of this designation upon decedent's estate and the method of changing beneficiaries were specified as follows:

> I understand that if I designate "my will" or some variation thereof as my Beneficiary, that the Custodian shall interpret this term as my estate and that if I do not designate any Beneficiary, my Beneficiary shall also be deemed to be my estate. I understand that I may revoke this beneficiary designation at any time by completing and submitting a new beneficiary designation, which shall supercede all prior beneficiary designations. Such replacement designation shall be submitted on either a form provided by the Custodian for this purpose and/or in some other manner deemed acceptable to the Custodian.

Decedent's last will, made and executed [on June 3, 2005,] with the assistance of an attorney shortly before his death, expressly revoked any prior will and stated:

> I hereby give, devise, and bequeath all of my estate and property, of every kind and nature, and wherever situated, to my mother, Shervena T. Grubbs, should she survive me.

This testamentary provision is unambiguous. As appellant argues, it is also inadequate to effect a change of beneficiary because the language is insufficient to identify the IRA account involved and an intent to change the beneficiary. The trial court found, however, that decedent's IRA beneficiary was changed from appellant to appellee by virtue of a note that appellee assertedly found in a Bible in decedent's home after his death. This document, handwritten on a Nations Bank notepad, provided in its entirety as follows:

May 2005

My Will
I Donnie Grubbs want all of my estate All IRA and any SBC Telco and all other assets and worldly goods to go to my Mother Shervena Grubbs. Being of sound mind.

Donnie Grubbs

The handwritten note at issue in *Nunnenman*

The trial judge recognized in his letter opinion that this handwritten note appears dubious. He was right. It was found by appellee, who was the only person who could benefit from its discovery. The plausibility of appellee's account of this fortuitous discovery is not helped by the conflicts in the testimony at trial. Appellee testified that she found the note while at decedent's house in the company of decedent's former coworker, Mr. Tommy Moran, and that she immediately showed the note to Mr. Moran. However, Mr. Moran testified that appellee did not do so, and that he had never seen the document or known of its existence until the day of the trial.

Nevertheless, assuming that the note was authentic, and that it might properly be considered to contradict or vary the unambiguous terms of decedent's IRA beneficiary designation or his last will, the trial court clearly erred in finding that it was an effective change of decedent's IRA beneficiary. As appellant argues, if the note is regarded as a holographic will, it was revoked by the express terms of decedent's last will[52] and by operation of law pursuant to Ark. Code Ann. § 28-25-109(a)(1) (2004). If the note is not regarded as a will, then the rule permitting change of beneficiaries in a will has no application to it, and appellee had the burden of proving that decedent intended for the note to be a change of beneficiaries and did everything reasonably possible to effectuate a change of beneficiary. In light of the undisputed evidence that decedent could and did summon an attorney to his bedside mere days before his death and thereby execute a valid and unambiguous last will, the trial court could not reasonably find that decedent did everything reasonably possible to change beneficiaries given his failure to employ similar efforts to communicate his intent to do so to the custodian of the IRA.

Reversed and remanded.

NOTES

1. The Original Beneficiary Designation.   When Donald Grubbs first opened his IRA at Raymond James, he named Jeannie Christine Nunnenman, the appellant, as the death beneficiary. Were there formalities or other circumstances that would caution Donald about the significance of this designation? Do you think it likely that he read the fine print, which appears in small type above the designation box and states that a change in beneficiary must be made on a form provided by the company or in some other manner acceptable to the company?[53]

2. Changing a Beneficiary Designation.   Should courts insist on strict compliance with the terms of the contract to change a death beneficiary designation for an IRA? Should substantial compliance suffice? The cases are split.[54]

In *Nunnenman*, the court analogized an IRA to a life insurance policy, reasoning that the same rule for changing a beneficiary designation by will should apply to both. The majority rule, followed in Cook v. Equitable Life Assurance Society, page 473, is that a will is ineffective to change a life insurance beneficiary designation. In Arkansas, however, the opposite rule applies: If a will is specific enough, it can change a death beneficiary designation for a life insurance policy. Was Donald's 2005 holographic will, assuming it was authentic, specific enough to change his IRA beneficiary designation from Nunnenman to his mother?

Do you think it is reasonable for a person to believe that he could change the death beneficiary of an IRA by will? Look again at the will in In re Will of Ferree, reproduced at page 173. Was the reference to "my IRA at Smith Barney" specific enough to qualify under the Arkansas rule?

---

52. The formal June will provided that it revokes "all other Wills and Codicils at anytime heretofore made by me."—Eds.

53. *See* Stewart E. Sterk & Melanie B. Leslie, Accidental Inheritance: Retirement Accounts and the Hidden Law of Succession, 89 N.Y.U. L. Rev. 165 (2014).

54. *Compare* Smith v. Marez, 719 S.E.2d 226 (N.C. App. 2011) (requiring strict compliance), *with* In re Estate of Golas, 751 A.2d 229 (Pa. Super. 2000) (allowing substantial compliance).

3. The June 2005 Formal Will.   The court held that Donald's subsequent formal will revoked his holographic will. But did Donald intend for the formal will to revoke the change in IRA death beneficiary that he thought he had made with the holograph? If not, should the court have applied dependent relative revocation, page 231, to save the change in beneficiary designation?

The court faulted Donald for not doing "everything reasonably possible to change" the beneficiary designation. What more should he have done? Donald's formal will was drawn by a lawyer. Why didn't the lawyer inquire about Donald's nonprobate transfers and draft accordingly? Is it malpractice for a lawyer not to attend to a client's pension and retirement accounts when drawing a will for the client? *See* Powers v. Hayes, 776 A.2d 374 (Vt. 2001). Given the staggering sums now held in pension and retirement accounts, should not they be at the top of an estate planner's checklist of possible issues to discuss with the client?

Egelhoff v. Egelhoff
532 U.S. 141 (2001)

THOMAS, J. A Washington statute provides that the designation of a spouse as the beneficiary of a nonprobate asset is revoked automatically upon divorce. We are asked to decide whether the Employee Retirement Income Security Act of 1974 (ERISA), 29 U.S.C. § 1001 et seq., pre-empts that statute to the extent it applies to ERISA plans. We hold that it does.

I

Petitioner Donna Rae Egelhoff was married to David A. Egelhoff. Mr. Egelhoff was employed by the Boeing Company, which provided him with a life insurance policy and a pension plan. Both plans were governed by ERISA, and Mr. Egelhoff designated his wife as the beneficiary under both. In April 1994, the Egelhoffs divorced. Just over two months later, Mr. Egelhoff died intestate following an automobile accident. At that time, Mrs. Egelhoff remained the listed beneficiary under both the life insurance policy and the pension plan. The life insurance proceeds, totaling $46,000, were paid to her.

Respondents Samantha and David Egelhoff, Mr. Egelhoff's children by a previous marriage, are his statutory heirs under state law. They sued petitioner in Washington state court to recover the life insurance proceeds. Respondents relied on a Washington statute that provides:

Justice Clarence Thomas

> If a marriage is dissolved or invalidated, a provision made prior to that event that relates to the payment or transfer at death of the decedent's interest in a nonprobate asset in favor of or granting an interest or power to the decedent's former spouse is revoked. A provision affected by this section must be interpreted, and the

nonprobate asset affected passes, as if the former spouse failed to survive the decedent, having died at the time of entry of the decree of dissolution or declaration of invalidity.

Wash. Rev. Code § 11.07.010(2)(a) (1994).

That statute applies to "all nonprobate assets, wherever situated, held at the time of entry by a superior court of this state of a decree of dissolution of marriage or a declaration of invalidity." § 11.07.010(1). It defines "nonprobate asset" to include "a life insurance policy, employee benefit plan, annuity or similar contract, or individual retirement account." § 11.07.010(5)(a).

Respondents argued that they were entitled to the life insurance proceeds because the Washington statute disqualified Mrs. Egelhoff as a beneficiary, and in the absence of a qualified named beneficiary, the proceeds would pass to them as Mr. Egelhoff's heirs. In a separate action, respondents also sued to recover the pension plan benefits. Respondents again argued that the Washington statute disqualified Mrs. Egelhoff as a beneficiary and they were thus entitled to the benefits under the plan. . . .

Courts have disagreed about whether statutes like that of Washington are pre-empted by ERISA. To resolve the conflict, we granted certiorari.

II

. . . ERISA's pre-emption section, 29 U.S.C. § 1144(a), states that ERISA "shall supersede any and all State laws insofar as they may now or hereafter relate to any employee benefit plan" covered by ERISA. We have observed repeatedly that this broadly worded provision is "clearly expansive." N.Y. State Conference of Blue Cross & Blue Shield Plans v. Travelers Ins. Co., 514 U.S. 645, 655 (1995). But at the same time, we have recognized that the term "relate to" cannot be taken "to extend to the furthest stretch of its indeterminacy," or else "for all practical purposes pre-emption would never run its course." Id.

We have held that a state law relates to an ERISA plan "if it has a connection with or reference to such a plan." Shaw v. Delta Air Lines, Inc., 463 U.S. 85, 97 (1983). Petitioner focuses on the "connection with" part of this inquiry. Acknowledging that "connection with" is scarcely more restrictive than "relate to," we have cautioned against an "uncritical literalism" that would make preemption turn on "infinite connections." Travelers, supra, at 656. Instead, "to determine whether a state law has the forbidden connection, we look both to 'the objectives of the ERISA statute as a guide to the scope of the state law that Congress understood would survive,' as well as to the nature of the effect of the state law on ERISA plans." Cal. Div. of Labor Standards Enforcement v. Dillingham Constr., N.A., Inc., 519 U.S. 316, 325 (1997), quoting Travelers, supra, at 656.

Applying this framework, petitioner argues that the Washington statute has an impermissible connection with ERISA plans. We agree. The statute binds ERISA plan administrators to a particular choice of rules for determining beneficiary status. The administrators must pay benefits to the beneficiaries chosen by state law, rather than to those identified in the plan documents. The statute thus implicates an area of core ERISA concern. In particular, it runs counter to ERISA's commands that a plan shall "specify the basis on which payments are made to and from the plan," § 1102(b)(4), and that the fiduciary shall administer the plan "in accordance with the documents and instruments governing the plan," § 1104(a)(1)(D), making payments to a "beneficiary" who is "designated by a participant, or by the terms of [the] plan." § 1002(8). In other words, unlike generally applicable laws regulating "areas where ERISA has nothing to say," *Dillingham*, 519 U.S. at 330, which we have upheld notwithstanding their incidental effect on ERISA plans, this statute governs the payment of benefits, a central matter of plan administration.

The Washington statute also has a prohibited connection with ERISA plans because it interferes with nationally uniform plan administration. One of the principal goals of ERISA is to enable employers "to establish a uniform administrative scheme, which provides a set of standard procedures to guide processing of claims and disbursement of benefits." Fort Halifax Packing Co. v. Coyne, 482 U.S. 1, 9 (1987). Uniformity is impossible, however, if plans are subject to different legal obligations in different States.

The Washington statute at issue here poses precisely that threat. Plan administrators cannot make payments simply by identifying the beneficiary specified by the plan documents. Instead they must familiarize themselves with state statutes so that they can determine whether the named beneficiary's status has been "revoked" by operation of law. And in this context the burden is exacerbated by the choice-of-law problems that may confront an administrator when the employer is located in one State, the plan participant lives in another, and the participant's former spouse lives in a third. In such a situation, administrators might find that plan payments are subject to conflicting legal obligations.

To be sure, the Washington statute protects administrators from liability for making payments to the named beneficiary unless they have "actual knowledge of the dissolution or other invalidation of marriage," Wash. Rev. Code § 11.07.010(3)(a) (1994), and it permits administrators to refuse to make payments until any dispute among putative beneficiaries is resolved, § 11.07.010(3)(b). But if administrators do pay benefits, they will face the risk that a court might later find that they had "actual knowledge" of a divorce. If they instead decide to await the results of litigation before paying benefits, they will simply transfer to the beneficiaries the costs of delay and uncertainty. Requiring ERISA administrators to master the relevant laws of 50 States and to contend with litigation would undermine the congressional goal of "minimiz[ing] the administrative and financial burden[s]" on plan administrators—burdens ultimately borne by the beneficiaries. Ingersoll-Rand Co. v. McClendon, 498 U.S. 133, 142 (1990).

We recognize that all state laws create some potential for a lack of uniformity. But differing state regulations affecting an ERISA plan's "system for processing claims and paying benefits" impose "precisely the burden that ERISA pre-emption was intended to avoid." *Fort Halifax*, supra, at 10. And as we have noted, the statute at issue here directly conflicts with ERISA's requirements that plans be administered, and benefits be paid, in accordance with plan documents. We conclude that the Washington statute has a "connection with" ERISA plans and is therefore pre-empted.

III

Respondents suggest several reasons why ordinary ERISA pre-emption analysis should not apply here. . . .

[R]espondents emphasize that the Washington statute involves both family law and probate law, areas of traditional state regulation. There is indeed a presumption against pre-emption in areas of traditional state regulation such as family law. But that presumption can be overcome where, as here, Congress has made clear its desire for preemption. Accordingly, we have not hesitated to find state family law pre-empted when it conflicts with ERISA or relates to ERISA plans. See, e.g., Boggs v. Boggs, 520 U.S. 833 (1997) (holding that ERISA pre-empts a state community property law permitting the testamentary transfer of an interest in a spouse's pension plan benefits).

Finally, respondents argue that if ERISA pre-empts this statute, then it also must pre-empt the various state statutes providing that a murdering heir is not entitled to receive property as a result of the killing. In the ERISA context, these "slayer" statutes could revoke the beneficiary status of someone who murdered a plan participant. Those statutes are not before us, so we do not decide the issue. We note, however, that the principle underlying the statutes—which have been adopted by nearly every State—is well established in the law and has a long historical pedigree predating ERISA. See, e.g., Riggs v. Palmer, 22 N.E. 188 (N.Y. 1889). And because the statutes are more or less uniform nationwide, their interference with the aims of ERISA is at least debatable. . . .

The judgment of the Supreme Court of Washington is reversed, and the case is remanded for further proceedings not inconsistent with this opinion.

It is so ordered.

BREYER, J., dissenting. . . . The Court has previously made clear that the fact that state law "impose[s] some burde[n] on the administration of ERISA plans" does not necessarily require pre-emption. De Buono v. NYSA-ILA Med. and Clinical Servs. Fund, 520 U.S. 806, 815 (1997). Precisely, what is it about this statute's requirement that distinguishes it from the "myriad state laws" that impose some kind of burden on ERISA plans?

Indeed, if one looks beyond administrative burden, one finds that Washington's statute poses no obstacle, but furthers ERISA's ultimate objective—developing a fair system for protecting employee benefits. The Washington statute transfers an employee's pension assets at death to those individuals whom the worker would likely have wanted to receive them. As many jurisdictions have concluded, divorced workers more often prefer that a child, rather than a divorced spouse, receive those assets. Of course, an employee can secure this result by changing a beneficiary form; but doing so requires awareness, understanding, and time. That is why Washington and many other jurisdictions have created a statutory assumption that divorce works a revocation of a designation in favor of an ex-spouse. That assumption is embodied in the Uniform Probate Code; it is consistent with human experience; and those with expertise in the matter have concluded that it "more often" serves the

Justice Stephen Breyer

cause of "justice." John H. Langbein, The Nonprobate Revolution and the Future of the Law of Succession, 97 Harv. L. Rev. 1108, 1135 (1984).

In forbidding Washington to apply that assumption here, the Court permits a divorced wife, who *already* acquired, during the divorce proceeding, her fair share of the couple's community property, to receive in addition the benefits that the divorce court awarded to her former husband. To be more specific, Donna Egelhoff already received a business, an IRA account, and stock; David received, among other things, 100% of his pension benefits. David did not change the beneficiary designation in the pension plan or life insurance plan during the 6-month period between his divorce and his death. As a result, Donna will now receive a windfall of approximately $80,000 at the expense of David's children. The State of Washington enacted a statute to prevent precisely this kind of unfair result. But the Court, relying on an inconsequential administrative burden, concludes that Congress required it.

Finally, the logic of the Court's decision does not stop at divorce revocation laws. The Washington statute is virtually indistinguishable from other traditional state-law rules, for example, rules using presumptions to transfer assets in the case of simultaneous deaths, and rules that prohibit a husband who kills a wife from receiving benefits as a result of the wrongful death. It is particularly difficult to believe that Congress wanted to pre-empt the latter kind of statute. But how do these statutes differ from the one before us? Slayer statutes—like this statute—"govern the payment of benefits, a central matter of plan administration." And contrary to the Court's suggestion, slayer statutes vary from State to State in their details just like divorce revocation statutes. Indeed, the "slayer" conflict would seem more serious, not less serious, than the conflict before us, for few, if any, slayer statutes permit plans to opt out of the state property law rule. . . .

For these reasons, I disagree with the Court's conclusion. And, consequently, I dissent.

NOTES

1. *Revocation on Divorce and Slayers.*   In *Egelhoff*, the majority suggested that slayer rules differ from revocation-on-divorce rules in that the former have "a long historical pedigree" and "are more or less uniform nationwide." Is this a meaningful distinction? Is it a fair characterization of the law? See Chapter 2 at page 133.

2. *Preempting Post-Distribution Relief.*   The drafters of the UPC revocation-on-divorce rule anticipated the possibility of preemption. Under UPC § 2-804(h)(2), if the revocation-on-divorce rule "is preempted by federal law," then the recipient of a payment that would have been revoked by divorce "is obligated to return that payment . . . to the person who would have been entitled to it were this section . . . not preempted." Such post-distribution relief, which is in effect a statutory action for restitution to prevent unjust enrichment, does not touch plan administration governed by ERISA. For example, Samantha and David could have sued Donna, their ex-stepmother, to recover the payment made to her by the plan administrator. In Hillman v. Maretta, 133 S. Ct. 1943 (2013), however, the Court held unanimously that

such post-distribution relief is also preempted.[55] This holding has come under fierce criticism from commentators and the Uniform Law Commission.[56]

3. ERISA and the Subsidiary Law of Wills. After *Egelhoff* and *Hillman*, can any of the rules of construction applicable to probate transfers—revocation on divorce, slayer, simultaneous death, and the like—be applied to private employer-provided pension plans or life insurance policies? Is it likely that, in enacting ERISA, Congress intended to suppress these rules? If not, is it likely that Congress will amend ERISA to clarify that such rules should apply? How often do politicians even mention ERISA? Should plan administrators absorb these rules into their plan documents to make them applicable as a matter of contract?

ERISA also preempts state law on spousal share rights, replacing state law with a mandatory federal rule, a subject we take up in Chapter 8 at page 561.

Concurring in *Hillman*, Justice Samuel A. Alito, Jr., assumed that the holder of a life insurance policy could change her beneficiary designation by will. Is this assumption consistent with the law in most states?

4. Federal Common Law. Since *Egelhoff*, some courts have continued to apply various constructional rules familiar from the law of wills under the guise of federal common law. In Metro. Life Ins. Co. v. Johnson, 297 F.3d 558 (7th Cir. 2002), *H* tried to replace his ex-spouse as his death beneficiary under his pension plan, but on the beneficiary change form he checked the box for the wrong plan. The court held that ERISA preempted Illinois law, which would have validated the change as being in substantial compliance with the terms of the plan, but the court went on to hold that federal common law also recognizes substantial compliance.

In Ahmed v. Ahmed, 817 N.E.2d 424 (Ohio App. 2004), the court held that, even though ERISA preempted the Ohio slayer statute, as a matter of federal common law a slayer may not take under an ERISA plan. However, the court did not treat the slayer as having predeceased the victim, as under the Ohio statute, but instead directed that the insurance proceeds be paid to the victim's probate estate.

The majority in *Egelhoff* reasoned that preemption was necessary to ensure uniformity and ease of administration. In view of cases such as *Johnson* and *Ahmed*, has this goal been served? Is newly developing federal common law likely to be more uniform and easier to administer for plan officials than existing state law? Some revocation-on-divorce statutes, such as UPC § 2-804(g), protect a fiduciary from liability for making a payment if the fiduciary relied in good faith on the governing instrument and did not

---

55. Strictly speaking, at issue in *Hillman* was a preemption provision under another statute, but one that so closely resembles ERISA's preemption provision that the decision leaves no doubt about the result under ERISA.

56. *See* UPC § 2-804 cmt. (1990, rev. 2014); John H. Langbein, Destructive Federal Preemption of State Wealth Transfer Law in Beneficiary Designation Cases: Hillman Doubles Down on Egelhoff, 67 Vand. L. Rev. 1665 (2014); *see also* Lawrence W. Waggoner, The Creeping Federalization of Wealth-Transfer Law, 67 Vand. L. Rev. 1635 (2014).

have notice of a disqualifying divorce. If you were a pension plan official, would you rather be subject to UPC § 2-804 or developing federal common law?

3. Pay-on-Death and Transfer-on-Death Contracts

Of all the modes of nonprobate transfer, the pay-on-death (POD) contract was the most difficult for courts to countenance in the absence of authorizing legislation.[57] In re Atkinson's Estate, 175 N.E.2d 548 (Ohio Prob. 1961), is illustrative. *O* opened several bank accounts as "*O*, POD *A*." Reasoning that *A* did not have a present interest in the account during *O*'s life, the court held that the POD designation was a testamentary disposition that was invalid for want of Wills Act formalities. The court rejected *A*'s analogy of a POD account to a joint account with right of survivorship. In a joint tenancy bank account, both the depositor and the beneficiary have the power to withdraw the funds. In a POD account, the death beneficiary has no rights during the life of the depositor.

But is a present interest analysis the right way to think about the problem? In *Atkinson*, *O* executed a writing supplied by a neutral financial intermediary that named *A* as the death beneficiary. What policy is served by not enforcing this arrangement? Taking notice of the benign experience with POD provisions in life insurance contracts and for U.S. government bonds, modern law has come to accept the transparently testamentary POD contract as valid despite the lack of Wills Act formalities. The 1969 UPC authorized POD designations in all contracts, and almost every state has followed suit.[58]

Uniform Probate Code (Unif. Law Comm'n 1990, as amended 1998)

§ 6-101. Nonprobate Transfers on Death

A provision for a nonprobate transfer on death in an insurance policy, contract of employment, bond, mortgage, promissory note, certificated or uncertificated security, account agreement, custodial agreement, deposit agreement, compensation plan, pension plan, individual retirement plan, employee benefit plan, trust, conveyance, deed of gift, marital property agreement, or other written instrument of a similar nature is nontestamentary. This subsection includes a written provision that:

(1) money or other benefits due to, controlled by, or owned by a decedent before death must be paid after the decedent's death to a person whom the decedent designates either in the instrument or in a separate writing, including a will, executed either before or at the same time as the instrument, or later;

(2) money due or to become due under the instrument ceases to be payable in the event of death of the promisee or the promisor before payment or demand; or

(3) any property controlled by or owned by the decedent before death which is the subject of the instrument passes to a person the decedent designates either in the instrument or in a separate writing, including a will, executed either before or at the same time as the instrument, or later.

---

57. *See* Langbein, *supra* note 14, at 1128-29.
58. *See* Jeffrey A. Schoenblum, Multistate Guide to Estate Planning tbl. 5.01, Part 2 (2016).

NOTES

1. Transfer on Death (TOD) Security Accounts. In 1989, the Uniform Law Commission promulgated the Uniform Transfer on Death Security Registration Act, which permits securities to be registered in TOD form. As amended in 1998, the act has since been absorbed into the UPC as §§ 6-301 through 6-311. TOD registrations are now allowed in nearly all states. Most banks, brokerage houses, mutual funds, and other financial intermediaries allow POD and TOD designations on customers' accounts.

2. The Savings Account (Totten) Trust. In the landmark case of In re Totten, 71 N.E. 748 (N.Y. 1904), *O* made deposits in a savings account in the name of "*O*, as trustee for *A*." *O* retained the right to withdraw the funds. *A* was entitled to what remained in the account at *O*'s death. In this way, *O* undertook to create a POD savings account. The court upheld this arrangement as not testamentary, declaring that a "tentative" revocable trust had been created at the time of the deposit. Such savings account trusts have come to be known as *Totten trusts*. Under the UPC, the Totten trust is abolished as a formal category and is instead treated as a POD account.

Multiple-Party Bank and Brokerage Accounts

If a bank or brokerage account is joint and survivor, owned by "*A* and *B*, as joint tenants with right of survivorship," both *A* and *B* have the power to draw on the account, but if either of them dies, the survivor alone owns the balance, and it does not pass through probate. Sometimes, however, something other than a true joint tenancy is intended. *A*, a bank depositor, may open a joint account with *B*, intending only that *B* receive the balance upon *A*'s death — a POD account disguised as a joint account. Or *A* might intend that *B* have the power to draw on the account only for the convenience of *A*, but not for other purposes and not to receive the balance at *A*'s death — an agency or convenience account disguised as a joint account. Because banks and brokerage houses often give their customers a joint tenancy form without regard to the customer's particular intention, courts are sometimes left with the problem of discerning which type of account was intended.

Varela v. Bernachea
917 So. 2d 295 (Fla. App. 2005)

PER CURIAM. . . . [Cristina] Varela and [Carlos Alberto] Bernachea are both Argentinean citizens who met in Buenos Aires in late 2000. They developed a romantic relationship and traveled the world together. Bernachea was an attorney in Argentina for over 30 years, but has since retired and invested in American businesses and real estate. In late 2001, at Bernachea's behest, Varela stopped working and moved into his Sunny Isles Beach condominium where the two began living together. While they were a couple, Bernachea paid all of Varela's expenses and showered her with expensive gifts. Varela claimed that she never knew Bernachea was married. Moreover, she claimed Bernachea held her out as his wife. Bernachea disputed Varela's claims and asserted that Varela knew he had a wife, yet contented herself with being his mistress.

Whatever their true arrangement, on January 4, 2002, Bernachea added Varela as a joint tenant with a right of survivorship to his Merrill Lynch CMA account. Mr. Jorge Herrera, Bernachea's long-time banker, testified that he related the details of the transaction in Spanish and that Bernachea, a former practicing attorney, never stated that he did not understand the legal significance of a joint tenancy with a right of survivorship during the transaction. As a joint owner of the account, Varela received a Visa check card for the account, which she freely used. Herrera and his assistant Ms. Zoraida Rosa both testified below that they never received any instruction to restrict Varela's access to the account—be it via check or check card.

Bernachea took the position below that Varela's access to the Merrill Lynch account was restricted. Specifically, Bernachea testified that the parties maintained a separate joint account with Southtrust because Varela had check writing privileges for the Southtrust account, but lacked such privileges for the CMA account. Varela, on the other hand, testified that she and Bernachea maintained the separate Southtrust account because a Southtrust branch was conveniently located near their condominium, and they accessed the Southtrust account more frequently, largely to pay bills. Thus, the uncontested testimony established that Varela had the ability to access the CMA funds. Bernachea's testimony reflects his confusion, regarding whether Varela could only access the CMA account via her Visa check card, or could additionally access the account via conventional paper check. It was undisputed, however, that the CMA and Southtrust accounts were joint accounts and that the account funds were supplied by Bernachea.

On October 18, 2002, Bernachea suffered a heart attack in his Sunny Isles condominium. Varela called 911 and accompanied Bernachea to the hospital. While Bernachea was hospitalized, Varela stayed with him until Bernachea's daughters arrived from Argentina and barred Varela from both Bernachea's hospital room and his Sunny Isles condominium. Varela willingly vacated the apartment. On October 25, 2002, Varela visited the Merrill Lynch branch on Brickell Avenue. Once there, Varela wrote a $280,000.00 check on the CMA account and deposited it in her own name in a newly opened Merrill Lynch personal account.

A Brickell branch account executive, Mr. Daniel Diaz, called the Coral Gables Merrill Lynch branch to ensure that Varela was authorized to write such a check. Diaz spoke with Herrera, who confirmed that Varela was the joint CMA owner and had the ability to write a check up to the account balance. Nevertheless, two weeks after his release from the hospital Bernachea demanded that Merrill Lynch return the $280,000.00. Merrill Lynch complied and transferred the $280,000.00 into the CMA account. Varela contested this transfer, but Merrill Lynch would not return the funds.

Bernachea subsequently sued Varela and Merrill Lynch to settle the ownership status of the CMA account. . . . The [trial] court [found] that Bernachea was the sole CMA account owner because he lacked donative intent when he added Varela as a joint account owner. Varela appeals from the Final Judgment. We reverse. . . .

When a joint bank account is established with the funds of one person, a gift of the funds is presumed. This presumption may be rebutted only by clear and convincing evidence to the contrary. Spark v. Canny, 88 So. 2d 307 (Fla. 1956); De Soto v. Guardianship of De Soto, 664 So. 2d 66, 67 (Fla. App. 1995). In the instant case, the trial court erroneously found, in the absence of clear and convincing evidence, that Bernachea rebutted Varela's gift presumption.

The trial court premised its finding on Bernachea's claim that he lacked donative intent. The only evidence in support of this claim was Bernachea's own dubious testimony, claiming he misapprehended the significance of a joint tenancy, and only intended for Varela to possess "restricted" account access. However, Herrera, who the court found was a credible witness, testified that he specifically explained the details of a joint tenancy with a right of survivorship in Spanish without any questions from Bernachea, a former attorney. Thus, the court's finding that "[Bernachea] did not understand the significance of the 'joint tenancy with right of survivorship' . . . in the English form" is inconsistent with the facts and testimony that same court found credible. Moreover, Bernachea admitted that, per his wishes, Varela had the ability to make check card purchases and write checks on the CMA account to the account balance.

Clearly, Bernachea did not rebut Varela's gift presumption when he openly admitted that he gave Varela access to their joint account via check card. Contrary to Bernachea's attempt to define a distinction, there is no principled distinction between paper checks and check cards. In fact, the check card's raison d'être is its status as a convenient replacement for paper checks. This modern reality conflicts with the trial court's holding that unfettered account access via check card, represents "restricted status." Moreover, in direct contrast to the court's conclusion, Herrera and Rosa testified that Varela's account access was never restricted. Additionally, both Merrill Lynch branches approved Varela's $280,000.00 check because she was a joint account owner with the ability to write checks up to the account balance.

The Record does not support the trial court's finding, as a matter of law, that Bernachea demonstrated an absence of donative intent. Moreover, Bernachea failed to rebut the presumption that he intended to give Varela an equal interest in their joint bank account. Accordingly, we reverse the Final Judgment and remand with instructions to enter judgment for Varela, awarding her a one-half interest in the October 25, 2002, CMA account balance.

NOTES

1. *What Was at Stake?*   If a depositor intends a convenience or POD account, the other tenant is not entitled to treat the funds as her own while the depositor is still alive. This was the dispute in *Varela*. A similar issue can arise at the depositor's death. If a convenience account is intended, and not a POD account or joint tenancy, the survivor is not entitled to the balance on the death of the depositor. The obvious difficulty is in proving that the depositor did not intend a joint and survivor account if the depositor signed a joint and survivor form, as in Franklin v. Anna Nat'l Bank of Anna, 488 N.E.2d 1117 (Ill. App. 1986).

Many courts apply a presumption that a present gift is intended if a joint account is established and require clear and convincing evidence to rebut the presumption.[59] In

---

59. *See* Gregory Eddington, Survivorship Rights in Joint Bank Accounts: A Misbegotten Presumption of Intent, 15 Marq. Elder's Advisor 175 (2014).

Varela, the court held that Bernachea did not present clear and convincing evidence to rebut the presumption of a gift. But the court allowed Varela to keep only one-half of the balance. Since Bernachea could not overcome the presumption of a gift, why was it not within Varela's rights to take the entire balance?

In some states, the presumption of a gift is conclusive, and evidence to the contrary is not admissible. In Robinson v. Delfino, 710 A.2d 154 (R.I. 1998), the court reasoned that a conclusive presumption of a gift fits the "common understanding of the vast majority of people establishing joint bank accounts," and avoids the need "to have lawyers, trial judges, juries, and appellate judges perform post mortem cerebral autopsies and examinations in order to determine and second-guess what the subjective intent of the deceased joint owner of the account was at the time the account was created."

2. The Uniform Probate Code.   The UPC provisions for multiple-party bank accounts, which are based on the Uniform Multiple-Person Accounts Act (Unif. Law Comm'n 1989, rev. 1998) are found in §§ 6-201 through 6-227. The UPC authorizes a joint tenancy account with right of survivorship, an agency account, and a POD account. Forms for banks to use in establishing each type of account are provided.

Under the UPC, joint accounts belong to the named parties during their joint lifetimes "in proportion to the *net contribution* of each to the sums on deposit, unless there is clear and convincing evidence of a different intent" (§ 6-211(b) (emphasis added). Extrinsic evidence is admissible to show that a joint account was opened solely for the convenience of the depositor (§§ 6-203, 6-204, 6-212). What result in *Varela* if the net contribution rule of the UPC applied?

Even if the state had adopted the UPC provisions on multiple-party bank accounts, those provisions would not have applied in *Varela*. The account at issue was a brokerage account, even though it held only cash and allowed check writing and debit card access. Such accounts fall within the purview of UPC §§ 6-301 through 6-311, which govern security accounts (see page 493).

3. Antilapse Statutes.   Should the common law lapse rules and the antilapse statutes be applied to POD and TOD arrangements? The UPC imposes a requirement of survivorship on beneficiaries of POD bank accounts (§ 6-212) and TOD security accounts (§ 6-307). The UPC also includes an antilapse provision for nonprobate transfers (§ 2-706), which substitutes the surviving descendants of a predeceased named beneficiary.

4. Nonprobate Transfer of Real Property

The increasing use of will substitutes has moved succession of most financial assets and other personal property outside of the probate system. But real property, for which ownership is indicated in a recorded deed, is less suited to nonprobate transfer, as the deed must be changed by probate administration or otherwise. We have already seen how a revocable trust can be used to this end. Legal title to real property transferred during life to a revocable trust is held by the trustee, obviating the need for probate to change title to the property at the death of the settlor (page 467). Two other forms of nonprobate transfer are also used to transfer real property outside of probate: (1) joint tenancy, and (2) a TOD deed for real property.

(1) Joint Tenancy. Many family homes in this country are owned by husband and wife in a form of *joint tenancy*. Upon the death of one tenant, the surviving tenant owns the property absolutely. The common law theory is that each owned the entire property while they were both alive, and that the decedent's interest simply vanishes at death. No probate is necessary because nothing passes to the survivor.[60]

A joint tenancy in land is an imperfect will substitute. Upon creation, both tenants must agree to take most important actions. A person who transfers land into a joint tenancy cannot, during life, revoke the transfer or cancel the interest given to the other joint tenant. Because a joint tenant's interest in the property is extinguished at her death, she cannot devise her interest in the property by will. If a joint tenant wants someone other than the other joint tenant to take her share at death, she must sever the joint tenancy during life, converting it into a tenancy in common.

A creditor of a joint tenant ordinarily must seize the joint tenant's interest, if at all, during the joint tenant's life. Because the joint tenant's interest vanishes at death, there is nothing for the creditor to reach.

(2) A TOD Deed for Real Property. Suppose *T*, the owner of Blackacre, records a deed that purports to convey Blackacre "to *T*, transfer on death to *A*." *T* dies intestate, leaving *B* as her sole heir. Who takes Blackacre, *A* or *B*? The issue is whether real property can be passed at death outside of probate by a TOD deed.

A majority of states have enacted statutes, such as the Uniform Real Property Transfer on Death Act (Unif. Law Comm'n 2009), absorbed into the UPC as §§ 6-401

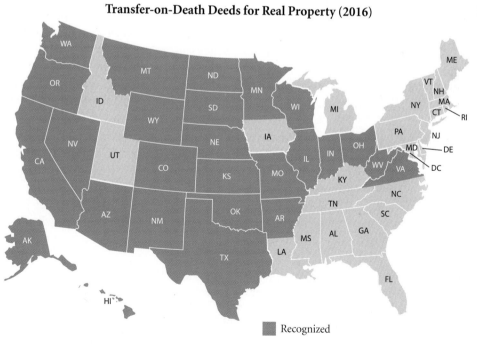

Transfer-on-Death Deeds for Real Property (2016)   Figure 7.2

▪ Recognized

---

60. *See* John V. Orth, The Paradoxes of Joint Tenancies, 46 Real Prop. Tr. & Est. L.J. 483 (2012).

through 6-407, which allow the transfer of real property by TOD deed. Under these statutes, *T* can identify the beneficiary who will succeed to Blackacre on *T*'s death by recording a TOD deed. During *T*'s life, the TOD beneficiary has no interest in Blackacre, and *T* retains the power to transfer it to others or to revoke the TOD designation. Does the recording of a deed satisfy the evidentiary, channeling, cautionary or ritual, and protective functions?

D. PLANNING FOR INCAPACITY[61]

Running in parallel with the nonprobate revolution has been what might be called a "gerontological revolution."[62] There have been "remarkable improvements in life expectancy over the past century," resulting in a profound aging of the population.[63] This increase in longevity has brought with it an increased chance that a person's last days, months, or even years will be spent in a state of mental or physical decay. Planning for this possibility is therefore as much a part of contemporary trusts and estates practice as is planning for property succession at death. Let us now consider the default rules and planning options for property management and health care decision making for an incapacitated person.

Britney Spears
James Atoa/Everett Collection/Alamy Live News

1. Property Management

a. Conservatorship

Much as intestacy is the default estate plan for a person who does not make a will or dispose of her property by will substitutes, in most states *conservatorship* is the default plan for managing the property of an incapacitated person who does not provide otherwise. Perhaps the most well known contemporary conservatorship is for the pop star Britney Spears.[64]

A conservator for an incapacitated person typically has broad powers to manage the person's property similar to those of a trustee, as under UPC § 5-425.[65] A conservator is also typically subject to fiduciary duties of loyalty and care comparable to those of a trustee, as under UPC §§ 5-418(1), 5-423. In states that use the older *guardianship*

---

61. Portions of this section are adapted from Feder & Sitkoff, *supra* note 5.

62. John H. Langbein, Major Reforms of the Property Restatement and the Uniform Probate Code: Reformation, Harmless Error, and Nonprobate Transfers, 38 ACTEC L.J. 1, 5 (2012).

63. Nat'l Inst. on Aging et al., Global Health and Aging 2-3 (2011).

64. *See* Serge F. Kovaleski & Joe Coscarelli, Is Britney Ready to Stand Alone?, N.Y. Times, May 8, 2016, at AR1.

65. The UPC provisions on conservatorship are based on the Uniform Guardianship and Protective Proceedings Act (Unif. Law Comm'n 1997-1998).

system, the powers of the guardian are more limited and judicial involvement is more substantial.

A conservatorship typically begins when an interested party files a petition with the appropriate court. Under UPC § 5-401, which is fairly representative, a court may appoint a conservator if it finds by clear and convincing evidence that the person for whose benefit the conservator is sought "is unable to manage property and business affairs because of an impairment in the ability to receive and evaluate information or make decisions" and by a preponderance of the evidence that the person "has property that will be wasted or dissipated unless management is provided or money is needed for the support, care, education, health, and welfare of the" person. A conservator can thus be appointed against the wishes of the person for whom the conservator acts. Priority for appointment as conservator is typically given, as under UPC § 5-413, to someone chosen in advance by the person, an agent under a durable power of attorney, or the person's spouse, adult child, or parent, in that order.

The main drawback to conservatorship is that it imposes substantial private and social costs. A conservatorship proceeding may be emotionally punishing, as it involves a formal allegation in court that a loved one is too mentally impaired to manage his property. Even if the petition is uncontested, it will be a public court document, which may invite unwanted publicity. In some cases, the alleged incompetent will resist the allegation. The ensuing litigation may make public unpleasant and embarrassing facts, and like any litigation, it is likely to be cumbersome and expensive.[66] When Groucho Marx was in his 80s, a court declared him incompetent against his wishes. He had been living with a woman, Erin Fleming, who said he preferred her as his guardian if he had to have one. After a messy court fight, with the newspapers titillating readers with intimate family details, a relative of Marx was appointed guardian.

Groucho Marx
A.F. Archive/Alamy

Because imposition of a conservatorship is a deprivation of liberty that requires due process, even modern conservatorship laws such as UPC § 5-406 provide for an elaborate court procedure to protect the alleged incompetent. Avoiding a conservatorship by advance planning, which is in effect a waiver of that process, is preferable and today is a normal and customary part of estate planning practice. Revocable trusts and durable powers of attorney, to which we turn next, are the principal solutions.

b. Revocable Trust

As we have seen, a funded *revocable trust* avoids probate and provides continuity in property management at the death of the settlor to the extent of the property held

---

66. *See* Bradley E.S. Fogel, Trust Me? Estate Planning with Revocable Trusts, 58 St. Louis U. L.J. 805, 818 (2014).

in the trust (page 467). A funded revocable trust may be used likewise to avoid a conservatorship and to provide continuity in the event of the settlor's incapacity. As in succession planning, even if the settlor had been the sole trustee, upon incapacity a successor trustee can take over without court involvement. In both situations, because the settlor can no longer manage her property, a surrogate fiduciary is necessary.

To be sure, the trustee can act only with respect to property put in the trust by the settlor before becoming incapacitated. For other property held by the settlor outright, only a conservator or an agent under a durable power of attorney will have the legal power to act. But a settlor who wants to avoid probate will need to transfer to the trust all her probate property anyway. And much as a pour-over will serves a backup role in property succession at death, a durable power of attorney can serve a similar backup role in the event of incapacity.

The main additional trust term needed to adapt a will substitute revocable trust to serve also as a conservatorship substitute is a mechanism for determining whether the settlor has become incapacitated. A familiar solution is to put the determination in the hands of the settlor's physician and one or more additional named persons, such as the settlor's spouse or children.[67] Here is a formbook example:

> For purposes of this agreement, I shall be considered to be unable to manage my affairs if I am under a legal disability or by reason of illness or mental or physical disability am unable to give prompt and intelligent consideration to financial matters. The determination as to my inability at any time shall be made by _____ and my physician, or the survivor of them, and the trustee may rely upon written notice of that determination.[68]

Because there will be no court involvement unless the settlor contests the private determination of incapacity, a provision such as this reduces the risk of litigation. Judicial oversight is not foreclosed, but it is not automatic. A conservatorship, by contrast, requires in every case a court petition that alleges incapacity.

A revocable trust meant to substitute for conservatorship typically will also include direction about use of the trust property during the settlor's incapacity. Here is a formbook example:

> If at any time or times I shall be unable to manage my affairs, the trustee may use such sums from the income and principal of the trust estate as the trustee deems necessary or advisable for the health and maintenance in reasonable comfort of myself and any person dependent upon me, or for any other purpose the trustee considers to be for my best interests.[69]

---

67. In Sterling v. Sterling, 194 Cal. Rptr. 3d 867 (App. 2015), which involved the alleged incapacity of Donald Sterling and the sale of the Los Angeles Clippers, the trust provided for a finding of incapacity as determined by two licensed physicians.

68. Northern Trust, Will & Trust Forms 201-1 (2004).

69. Id.

"Don't think for a minute that I've mellowed!"

Edward Koren/The New Yorker Collection/The Cartoon Bank

NOTE

Standing to Enforce a Revocable Trust Revisited. Part of what makes a funded revocable trust so attractive both as a will substitute and as a conservatorship substitute is that the settlor need not lose control over the trust property while she is alive and competent. In contrast to the era of Farkas v. Williams, page 445, in which courts posited a property right in the trust's remainder beneficiaries and corresponding fiduciary obligation in the trustee, today the trustee of a revocable trust is under a duty to comply with a direction from the settlor even if the direction is contrary to the terms of the trust, and the beneficiaries lack standing to enforce the trust (see page 452).

To the extent that a settlor intends a funded revocable trust to be a conservatorship substitute in addition to a will substitute, however, should not the beneficiaries have standing to enforce the trust during the settlor's incapacity? Although the authorities are split,[70] the trend is toward denying standing.[71] On this view, enforcement of a revocable trust with an incapacitated settlor will require court appointment of a conservator if the settlor does not have a suitable agent under durable power of attorney.

As originally drafted, UTC § 603(a), page 448, took the opposite view. Following the Restatement (Third) of Trusts,[72] the original version of UTC § 603(a) gave the

---

70. *Compare* Manon v. Orr, 856 N.W.2d 106 (Neb. 2014) (no standing), *with* Drake v. Pinkham, 158 Cal. Rptr. 3d 115 (App. 2013) (allowing standing).

71. *See* Feder & Sitkoff, *supra* note 5, at 34-38.

72. *See* Restatement (Third) of Trusts § 74(1) cmt. e (Am. Law Inst. 2003).

beneficiaries of a revocable trust standing upon the settlor's incapacity. In 2004, however, the Uniform Law Commission put the capacity qualification in brackets, signaling that enacting states are free to strike it. The comment explains that the brackets were added in response to the objection that the capacity qualification resulted in "a different rule for revocable trusts than for wills and that the rules for both should instead be the same."

What should be the default rule for beneficiary standing in a revocable trust when the settlor becomes incapacitated? Should a funded revocable trust be presumed to be a will substitute only? Or should the presumption be that it is also a conservatorship substitute?[73]

c. Durable Power of Attorney

A *power of attorney* creates an agency relationship in which an *agent* is given a written authorization to act on behalf of a *principal*. An agent under a power of attorney, traditionally called an *attorney-in-fact*,[74] can be granted the power to do almost anything for a principal. A written instrument setting forth the terms of the agent's authority provides evidence of that authority, which encourages third parties to deal with the agent as a representative of the principal.

Because at common law an agent's authority terminates on the principal's incapacity,[75] an ordinary power of attorney is of limited use in incapacity planning. Enter the *durable power of attorney*. Unlike an ordinary power of attorney, a durable power of attorney remains effective during the incapacity of the principal and until the principal dies. A durable power of attorney thus provides "a simple way to avoid guardianship [and conservatorship by] allowing an agent to manage a principal's assets when necessity or incapacity requires it."[76] A durable power of attorney can be drafted to be effective immediately upon signing or only upon the principal's incapacity (a *springing* durable power of attorney), as under UPC § 5B-109.[77]

In the absence of a statute, a power of attorney is governed by the common law of agency, which imposes *fiduciary duties of loyalty and care* on an agent and supplies default terms for the agency relationship. Every state has enacted a statute specifically authorizing a durable power of attorney and governing certain elements of the agency relationship.

---

73. *See* Feder & Sitkoff, *supra* note 5, at 42 (arguing that, in the "absence of evidence to the contrary, the presumption . . . should be that a person who arranges to avoid probate by funding a revocable trust likewise would want to avoid conservatorship as regards the trust property").

74. The term *attorney* means agent; an attorney-in-fact can be contrasted with an attorney-at-law, that is, a lawyer.

75. *See* Restatement (Third) of Agency § 3.08 cmt. b (Am. Law Inst. 2006).

76. Angela M. Vallario, The Uniform Power of Attorney Act: Not a One-Size-Fits-All Solution, 43 U. Balt. L. Rev. 85, 86 (2014); *see also* Linda S. Whitton, Durable Powers as an Alternative to Guardianship: Lessons We Have Learned, 37 Stetson L. Rev. 7 (2007).

77. *See* John C. Craft, Preventing Exploitation and Preserving Autonomy: Making Springing Powers of Attorney the Standard, 44 U. Balt. L. Rev. 407 (2015).

The Uniform Power of Attorney Act (Unif. Law Comm'n 2006),[78] absorbed into the UPC as §§ 5B-101 through 5B-302, authorizes a durable power of attorney, specifies the agent's fiduciary duties, and resolves which duties are mandatory and which may be overridden by the terms of the instrument (§ 5B-114).[79] The term *attorney-in-fact* is replaced with the more intuitive term *agent* (§ 5B-102(1)), and, in a reversal of prior law, all powers of attorney are presumed to be durable unless the instrument states otherwise (§ 5B-104).

Relative to a revocable trust, an important advantage of a durable power of attorney is that the agent can be authorized to act with respect to any of the principal's property, including property that was acquired after execution of the power. Unlike a revocable trust, which must be funded to be of use for incapacity planning, a durable power of attorney thus allows a person "to retain full legal and equitable ownership of his assets while delegating to the agent a defined scope of authority to act in the principal's stead."[80] In this respect, a durable power of attorney is the incapacity planning analogue to a will, which may direct the disposition at death of property acquired after execution of the will. But unlike a will, a durable power of attorney is private; there is no need for judicial involvement.

On the other hand, banks and other financial institutions are notoriously resistant to directions from an agent under a power of attorney.[81] An agent can compel the institution to accept his directions, but this may necessitate judicial involvement or at least the hassle of involving more senior officers within the institution. Part of the resistance by financial institutions to directions from an agent under a power of attorney stems from worry that the agent may be acting beyond the scope of his authority or in violation of his fiduciary duties.

The difficulty is that because an incapacitated principal cannot monitor the actions of an agent, making a power of attorney durable to survive incapacity gives rise to an increased risk of abuse by the agent. The very lack of oversight and ease of use that make powers of attorney so attractive in planning for incapacity also make them easy to abuse.[82] An incapacitated principal lacks the ability to sue the agent for breach of fiduciary duty, necessitating appointment of a conservator or an action by the fiduciary of the principal's estate after the principal's death. To ameliorate this problem, UPC § 5B-116 and statutes in some states give standing to sue an agent also to a spouse,

---

78. *See* Linda S. Whitton, The Uniform Power of Attorney Act: Striking a Balance Between Autonomy and Protection, 1 Phoenix L. Rev. 343 (2008).

79. *See* Linda S. Whitton, Understanding Duties and Conflicts of Interest—A Guide for the Honorable Agent, 117 Penn. St. L. Rev. 1037 (2013).

80. Whitton, *supra* note 78, at 345-46.

81. *See, e.g.,* id. at 352-53; Fogel, *supra* note 66, at 818; *see also* Paula Span, When Power of Attorney Becomes Power Struggle, N.Y. Times, May 10, 2016, at D5.

82. *See, e.g.,* Danica J. Brustkern, With Great Power Comes Great Culpability: Addressing Agency Costs in Durable Powers of Attorney, 50 Real Prop. Tr. & Est. L.J. 463 (2016); Karen E. Boxx, The Durable Power of Attorney's Place in the Family of Fiduciary Relationships, 36 Ga. L. Rev. 1 (2001); Nina A. Kohn, Elder Empowerment as a Strategy for Curbing the Hidden Abuses of Durable Powers of Attorney, 59 Rutgers L. Rev. 1 (2006); Carolyn L. Dessin, Acting as Agent Under a Financial Durable Power of Attorney: An Unscripted Role, 75 Neb. L. Rev. 574, 582 (1996).

parent, descendant, presumptive death beneficiary of the principal, and to other persons interested in the principal's welfare.

In spite of these shortcomings, the durable power of attorney remains "a staple of the modern estate plan."[83] Much as the will abides in property succession, if only to catch property not disposed of by revocable trust or otherwise, so too the durable power of attorney abides for "both the wealthy and non-wealthy for incapacity planning as well as convenience."[84]

In re Estate of Kurrelmeyer
895 A.2d 207 (Vt. 2006)

BURGESS, J. . . . In 1996, Louis Kurrelmeyer executed two durable general powers of attorney to appoint his wife, Martina Kurrelmeyer, and his daughter, Nancy Kurrelmeyer, as attorneys-in-fact. Louis Kurrelmeyer was competent at the time he executed the powers of attorney. In December of 2000, Martina, pursuant to her powers under the durable power of attorney, executed a document establishing the "Louis H. Kurrelmeyer Living Trust," with herself and Nancy as co-trustees. Days after she created the trust, Martina transferred certain real estate owned by her husband, the "Clearwater" property, to herself and Nancy as co-trustees of the trust. At the time of the creation of the living trust and the transfer of the Clearwater property, Louis Kurrelmeyer was no longer competent. Mr. Kurrelmeyer died testate a year later, and Martina was appointed executrix of his estate.

Louis Kurrelmeyer's last will and testament, executed in 1980, contained a specific provision for the Clearwater property. Under the will, Martina would take a life estate in the property, with responsibility for taxes and upkeep, and upon her death the property would pass to Mr. Kurrelmeyer's surviving children as joint tenants with rights of survivorship. In contrast, the terms of the trust provide Martina additional rights with regard to the property. Under the terms of the trust, Martina may occupy the home as long as she wishes and the trust is permitted to pay the expenses on the property should she fail to do so. The trustees would be required, however, on Martina's unilateral request, to sell the home, with the sale proceeds to be used either to purchase another home for Martina or, alternatively, to be added to the trust principal. Additionally, the trust provides that all income from the trust property would be paid to Martina, as well as so much of the principal as the trustees deem necessary and proper for her support. Upon Martina's death, the trust principal would be distributed to Louis's children, if they survived him, with any deceased child's share to be distributed to that child's descendants or held in trust until such descendants reached the age of twenty-five. The trust requires that there be at least one other trustee serving so long as Martina is serving as a co-trustee, and the co-trustees must act by mutual agreement.

During the probate administration of Louis Kurrelmeyer's estate, his son, Louis Kurrelmeyer Jr., objected to the exclusion of the Clearwater property from the inventory completed by Martina Kurrelmeyer. Claiming that Martina exceeded her authority

---

83. Vallario, *supra* note 76, at 86.
84. Whitton, *supra* note 76, at 9.

in creating the trust, Louis Jr. asked the probate court to set aside the trust and include the Clearwater property in the probate estate to be distributed in accordance with Mr. Kurrelmeyer's will.[85] The probate court upheld the trust, and the children appealed to the superior court. . . .

[In the superior court, the] children moved for a judgment in their favor, arguing that the power of attorney did not authorize creation of a revocable trust, that the transfer of the Clearwater property to the trust was a breach of Martina's fiduciary duty because it constituted self-dealing, and that the transfer violated the gift-giving proscription of the power of attorney. . . .

Granting summary judgment for the children, the superior court concluded that the power of attorney did not authorize Martina to create a trust. . . . Martina appealed. . . .

I

We first address Martina's claim that the trial court erred in concluding as a matter of law that the power of attorney did not authorize her to create a trust on Louis Kurrelmeyer's behalf. We . . . find that the express language of the power of attorney authorized the attorney-in-fact to create a trust. . . .

To determine whether the power of attorney authorized Martina to create a trust, we look to Mr. Kurrelmeyer's "written authorization," entitled "Durable General Power of Attorney." As its title suggests, this power of attorney is indeed "general" and quite broad. The power of attorney was to survive, and be unaffected by, the principal's subsequent disability or incompetence. It authorizes Martina, as attorney-in-fact, to act in the principal's name "in any way which I myself could do, if I were personally present, with respect to the following matters to the extent that I am permitted by law to act through an agent." Among the delineated powers, the first subsection authorizes the agent "[t]o add all of my assets deemed appropriate by my said attorney to any trust of which I am the Donor" by transferring in trust a variety of types of property, including stocks, bonds, bank accounts, real estate, and "other assets or property of any kind" owned by the principal. The subsection immediately following provides:

> In *addition*, I authorize my said attorney to: (i) execute *and deliver any assignments, stock powers, deeds or trust instruments*; (ii) sign my name to any instrument pertaining to or required in connection with the transfer of my property; . . . (viii) change life insurance beneficiaries . . . (x) convey any real estate, interest in real estate, any mortgages and notes or any beneficial interest in real estate which I may own or have any interest in; and (xi) record deeds of conveyance in the appropriate land records. (emphasis supplied).

---

85. At the time of his death, Louis Kurrelmeyer had three surviving children—Louis Jr., Nancy, and Ellen. Nancy subsequently passed away, and Ellen became executrix of Nancy's estate. Additionally, the trust designates Ellen as Nancy's successor co-trustee. . . . For the sake of simplicity, and because counsel for Louis Jr., Ellen, and Nancy's Estate have represented the children's interests as aligned in this appeal, as well as in the appeal to the superior court, we refer to appellees collectively as "the children."

DURABLE GENERAL POWER OF ATTORNEY

THIS DOCUMENT IS INTENDED TO CONFER A DURABLE POWER OF ATTORNEY. THIS POWER OF ATTORNEY SHALL NOT BE AFFECTED BY THE SUBSEQUENT DISABILITY OR INCOMPETENCE OF THE PRINCIPAL.

I, LOUIS H. KURRELMEYER, SR., of Shelburne, in the County of Chittenden and State of Vermont, have made, constituted and appointed, and by these presents do make, constitute and appoint MARTINA KURRELMEYER of Shelburne, in the County of Chittenden, and State of Vermont my true and lawful attorney (hereinafter referred to as my "Attorney"), for me and in my name, place and stead to act.

FIRST: In my name, place and stead in any way which I myself could do, if I were personally present, with respect to the following matters to the extent that I am permitted by law to act through an agent:

(a) To add all of my assets deemed appropriate by my said attorney to any trust of which I am the Donor by: assigning, transferring and delivering to said trust, its trustee or trustees, or a nominee for said trust, its trustee or trustees, any or all of my stocks, bonds, other securities, cash brokerage amounts, commodity accounts and accounts in commercial or savings banks, savings and loan associations, credit unions or other financial institutions (all hereafter called "bank"), life insurance (other than insurance policies owned by my said attorney upon my life) and annuity policies, qualified and other employee benefit plans, individual retirement accounts or plans, real estate, mortgages, partnership interests, investments in tangible personal property and other assets or property of any kind (real, personal or mixed) owned by me. I direct all banks, brokers, transfer agents, registrars, insurance companies, employee benefit plan and individual retirement account custodians, trustees and administrators to accept the directions of my said attorney to perform all acts necessary to make said transfers and beneficiary changed;

(b) In addition, I authorize m[...] execute and deliver any assignments,[...] trust instruments; (ii) sign my n[...] pertaining to or required in connect[...] my property; (iii) give full receipts[...] register the title to stock certifica[...] and other securities; (v) change the[...] standing in my name in any bank; (vii)[...] checks, drafts, certificates of de[...] instruments for the payment of money[...] me; (viii) change life insurance be[...] those of insurance policies owned by[...]

to sell any such mot[...]
convey title to the[...]

(i) To waive[...]
privilege I may pos[...]
access to medical a[...]
information which o[...]
be turned over to m[...]

hereof i[...]
to all[...]
without[...]
disposit[...]
have no[...]
attorney[...]

Any action taken by any bank or other financial institution, broker, issuer, obligor, safe deposit box company, warehouse, moving and storage company, retail or wholesale establishment, hotel, motel, apartment house, transfer agent, registrar, depositary, title insurance company or other person, custodian or any other agency or branch of the federal, state or local government or a foreign government or any other third-party in good faith reliance upon this Durable Power of Attorney shall be fully binding upon me, my heirs, personal representatives, conservator (or equivalent fiduciary) and assigns, and to that extent this Durable Power of Attorney shall not be deemed to have been revoked by my death.

THIRD: This Power of Attorney shall not be affected by my subsequent disability or incompetence.

IN WITNESS WHEREOF, I have hereunto signed my name and affixed my seal this 15th day of May, 1996.

IN PRESENCE OF:

Lisa L Baillargeon
Witness

Thomas N[...]
Witness

Lou Kurrelmeyer
Louis H. Kurrelmeyer, Sr.

STATE OF CHITTENDEN   )
) ss.
CHITTENDEN COUNTY   )

At _Burling_, in said County, on this _15_ day of _May_, 1996, personally appeared Louis H. Kurrelmeyer, Sr., signer and sealer of the foregoing instrument, and he acknowledged the same to be his free act and deed.

Before me _Thomas N[...]_
Notary Public

kurrl.poa

4

"This Power of Attorney shall not be affected by my subsequent disability or incompetence."

The power of attorney at issue in *Kurrelmeyer*

The text continues, authorizing the attorney-in-fact to examine and obtain copies of the principal's will. The attorney is authorized to "make gifts to members of my family (other than himself or herself) whom my said attorney has reason to believe I would have wished to benefit, but my said attorney shall not give any more than $10,000.00 per year to any one donee." Among other powers, the attorney-in-fact is also granted unrestricted access to, and an unrestricted right to remove, the contents from "any and all warehouses, safe deposit boxes, drawers, and vaults" owned in the principal's name alone and in common with others. The attorney-in-fact is authorized to disclaim interests in property on behalf of the principal, to convey title to his motor vehicles, to "convey any and all real estate owned by [the principal] to any person or entity," and, finally, the attorney-in-fact is authorized

[t]o do and perform all and every act and thing whatsoever necessary to be done in the premises, as fully to all intents and purposes as I might or could do if personally present, with full power of substitution and revocation, hereby ratifying and confirming all that my said attorney may do pursuant to this power.

We conclude that the express terms of the power of attorney unambiguously grant the attorney-in-fact the authority to create a trust and to add assets to a trust to accomplish estate planning objectives. The first subsection, empowering the attorney to add any and all assets to a trust of which he is the donor, does refer to a trust already in existence, but does not suggest lack of authority to create a new trust when considered together with the second subsection—granting the power "to execute and deliver . . . trust instruments" expressly in addition to adding assets to existing trusts. The phrase "trust instrument" is commonly understood to refer to the document that brings the trust into existence. Just as a subsequent provision authorizes the attorney-in-fact to "execute . . . deeds" and "easements," which we commonly read to include granting and conveying lands and creating rights of way, so too may the attorney-in-fact create a trust under the provision authorizing the attorney to "execute . . . trust instruments." Where a power is broadly drawn to include the authority to transact all business on behalf of the principal and delineates a variety of general acts, each particular task within the grant of authority need not be spelled out in exacting detail. Given the express language granting the authority to execute trust instruments, particularly in the context of the breadth of the attorney's other express powers, including, ultimately, her authority to fully substitute herself for the principal to do all things "whatsoever necessary . . . to all intents and purposes" as the principal "might or could do if personally present," we find that the agent's authority under this power of attorney includes the authority to create a trust on the principal's behalf.

II

Alternatively, the children argue that, even if the principal intended to authorize the attorney-in-fact to create a trust, the power to create a trust is personal to the settlor and non-delegable as a matter of law. We agree that certain acts may require personal performance as a matter of public policy, statutory law, or under the terms of an agreement. See Restatement (Second) of Agency § 17, cmt. b ("The making of affidavits as to knowledge and the execution of wills are illustrations of acts commonly required by statute to be done personally."). We do not agree, however, that delegation of authority to create a trust through a durable general power of attorney to serve the interests of the principal violates public policy as a matter of law, even when a trust's dispositive terms may serve a function similar to that of a will.

The use of a revocable living trust serves a number of legitimate purposes. Restatement (Third) of Trusts § 25, cmt. a (2003). For example, revocable trusts are widely used in estate planning and asset management as a means to avoid the costs and delays associated with probate administration, as a means to provide property management for settlors late in life by establishing trustees and successor trustees to assume continuing responsibility, and as a means to maintain privacy and flexibility in the management of assets beyond the life of the settlor. Revocable trusts allow the settlor to retain the ability to use the assets for support during lifetime, provide for ongoing asset management, and preserve the estate for the settlor's intended beneficiaries.

The fact that the trust here was created by an agent does not affect its legitimacy. See id. § 11(5) ("Under some circumstances, an agent under a durable power of attorney or the legal representative of a property owner who is under disability may create a trust on behalf of the property owner."); see also id., cmt. f (noting that despite restrictions against making a will for an incompetent person, it is proper for a principal to authorize an agent to create or modify a revocable inter vivos trust "to serve purposes that are financially advantageous to the estate, such as probate avoidance and managerial efficiency"). The children fail to demonstrate any sufficiently countervailing evil to compel this Court to declare such powers of attorney contrary to public policy and void as a matter of law. . . .

For the same reason that trusts can be beneficial to an estate, we are not persuaded on the current record that this trust is necessarily an invalid usurpation of the principal's last will and testament. The trial court was concerned that, by conveying Clearwater to the trust, Martina did "indirectly what she [could] not do directly," that is, alter the will by depriving the children of their expected inheritance of Clearwater's appreciation. When the principal expressly granted his attorney-in-fact the power to convey realty from his estate, he must have anticipated that the terms of his will might be so altered. It is not clear, then, why conveyance of Clearwater to a trust would be a per se impermissible alteration of the will, when the power of attorney expressly authorized Martina to convey any real estate outright to others. Therefore, these additional arguments do not persuade us that the trust must be rendered void as a matter of public policy.

III

The question of whether Martina's actions breached her fiduciary duties remains. Even though we conclude that Martina had authority from her principal to create a trust on his behalf, her authority to act under that power was not limitless. A fiduciary duty of loyalty is implied in every agency as a matter of law. The attorney-in-fact was prohibited from making gifts to herself by the express language of the power of attorney and was also prohibited from using the agency for her own benefit or the benefit of others except as authorized.

The children complained below that Martina's conveyance of the Clearwater property to the trust provided no benefit to Louis Kurrelmeyer, served no apparent tax or estate planning purpose, and was prohibited by the gifting provision of the power of attorney as well as by Martina's fiduciary duty of loyalty to her principal. Martina argued, in response, that the trust and conveyance were justified by generally recognized and prudent tax and estate planning objectives, that the conveyance of Clearwater to the trust could not, as a matter of law, constitute a gift prohibited by the power of attorney, and that the co-trustee approval requirement was a safeguard against any self-dealing.

Concluding, erroneously, that creating any new trust was void as beyond the authority of the attorney-in-fact, the superior court did not reach the additional question of whether the trust and conveyance were valid, as claimed by Martina, or a breach of fiduciary duty as claimed by the children. The court recognized general proscriptions against self-dealing by attorneys-in-fact and trustees, but did not address the parties' particular factual or legal claims on this topic. . . . [T]he parties do not appear to agree upon facts material either to Martina's contention that the dispositive terms of the trust and the conveyance of the Clearwater property were justified as prudent estate planning or to the children's contentions that the terms of the trust and the transfer of property were unauthorized self-dealing.

Therefore, we remand the case to the superior court for further proceedings to consider whether there was a breach of a fiduciary duty on the part of Martina Kurrelmeyer, as agent, in light of all the relevant circumstances at the time the trust was executed.

Reversed and remanded for further proceedings not inconsistent with this decision.

NOTES

1. Powers, Duties, and Findings on Remand. The court in *Kurrelmeyer* distinguished between powers and duties. The first question was whether Martina had the *power* to make and fund a revocable trust for Louis. The court held that such a power could be given to an agent, and it construed the language of the instrument at issue as having given Martina this power.

The second question was whether Martina's exercise of this power was consistent with her *fiduciary duties* of *loyalty* and *care*. An agent's exercise of a power, even one granted expressly by the principal, is subject to after-the-fact scrutiny for compliance with the agent's fiduciary duties. On remand, the trial court upheld the trust on the grounds that Martina's actions were in keeping with Louis's intent and best interests:

> We find that the wife's acts in creating the trusts and conveying the primary residence to them were fully in keeping with the principal's (decedent's) intent to give her full beneficial ownership of the house, including the right to sell it so as to purchase another house and live somewhere else. The wife's conveyance into the trusts carried out her husband's wishes and intentions, which had been discussed and formulated with [an] estate plan[ning] attorney, who credibly testified here. . . . Decedent's overarching goal was to provide for his surviving wife. Her acts

as his attorney-in-fact were in full accord therewith. . . . [Because] she did carry out the intention of her now deceased husband, . . . there was no breach of fiduciary duty—she remained loyal to her principal's intentions.[86]

2. Estate Planning by a Surrogate.   The court in *Kurrelmeyer* distinguished between a power to make a will and a power to make and fund a revocable trust. But is this a meaningful distinction? *See* Perosi v. LiGreci, 948 N.Y.S.2d 629 (App. Div. 2012). Why allow a principal to delegate the power to do one but not the other?[87]

The majority view, as under UTC § 602(e) and UPC § 5B-201(a)(1), is that although an agent cannot make a will for the principal, the agent can create, modify, or revoke a trust—but only if the power to do so is specifically granted by the power-of-attorney instrument. If this rule requiring specific authorization had applied in *Kurrelmeyer*, Martina would not have had the power to make the trust, as the Vermont court observed in In re Estate of Lovell, 25 A.3d 560 (Vt. 2011).

In some states and under UPC § 5-411(a), a court-appointed guardian or conservator has the power not only to make, amend, or revoke a trust for the protected person, but also to make, amend, or revoke the person's will. If the guardian or conservator's action is challenged, under UPC § 5-411(c), the court will review the action under a *substituted judgment* standard that, in accordance with the principle of freedom of disposition, considers whether the protected person would likely have undertaken the same action.[88]

3. Gifts and Enhanced Formalities.   Whether an agent may make *gifts* from the principal's property raises similar difficulties. In most states an agent cannot make a substantial gift without specific authorization. In many states and under UPC § 5B-217, the grant of such a power is subject to enhanced formality requirements. For example, the statutory form provided in UPC § 5B-301 requires the principal to write her initials next to the provision giving an agent the power to make gifts. The provision appears below the following warning:

> CAUTION: Granting any of the following will give your agent the authority to take actions that could significantly reduce your property or change how your property is distributed at your death. INITIAL ONLY the specific authority you WANT to give your agent.

Below this warning are also places for the principal to initial next to a power to create, amend, revoke, or terminate an inter vivos trust and to create or change death beneficiary designations and rights of survivorship. In In re Marriott, 927 N.Y.S.2d 269 (App. Div. 2011), the court required strict compliance with a similar form, holding that an "X" notation was insufficient unless intended as an initialing.

---

86. In re Estate of Kurrelmeyer, 2008 WL 7810419 (Vt. Super.), *aff'd*, 992 A.2d 316 (Vt. 2010).

87. *See* Ralph C. Brashier, The Ghostwritten Will, 93 B.U. L. Rev. 1803 (2013); *see also* Alexander A. Boni-Saenz, Personal Delegations, 78 Brook. L. Rev. 1231 (2013).

88. *See* Ralph C. Brashier, Conservatorships, Capacity, and Crystal Balls, 87 Temp. L. Rev. 1 (2014).

2. Health Care

a. Default Law

The Supreme Court has held that each person has a constitutional right to make health care decisions for herself, including the right to refuse medical treatment.[89] A person may exercise this right by an *advance directive* that states her wishes about refusing or terminating medical treatment or that appoints an agent to make such decisions for her.[90] In the absence of an advance directive, responsibility for an incompetent patient's health care decisions usually falls to the patient's spouse or next of kin.

To give a clear order of priority among potential decision makers, many states have enacted a statutory hierarchy. The Uniform Health-Care Decisions Act (Unif. Law Comm'n 1993) is representative. It provides that, in the absence of an advance directive, decisions are to be made by surrogates in the following order: (1) spouse, unless legally separated; (2) adult child; (3) parent; or (4) adult sibling (if there is more than one person in a class, the majority controls). As with intestate succession, which follows a similar order of priority, a fair question is whether these default rules should be revised to account for the increase in cohabiting unmarried partners (see page 74).

When making health care decisions for an incompetent patient, an agent is held to a *substituted judgment* standard of what the patient has chosen or would have chosen in that situation. Some commentators have suggested that, instead of or in addition to this standard, the agent should act in the *best interests* of the patient.[91] In end-of-life situations, however, it is often unclear what the patient would have wanted or even what is in the patient's best interests.[92]

b. Advance Directives

Every state has statutes providing for advance direction of health care, but these vary in their particulars and may require specific forms.[93] "In 2013, about 47 percent of adults over the age of 40 had an advance directive."[94]

Advance directives are of three basic types: (1) instructional directives, such as a *living will*, which specify either generally or by way of hypothetical examples how one

---

89. Cruzan v. Dir., Mo. Dep't of Health, 497 U.S. 261 (1990).

90. For an interesting suggestion toward a *sexual advance directive* that would allow for "advance planning to preserve the possibility of a sexual life" after incapacity, see Alexander A. Boni-Saenz, Sexual Advance Directives, 68 Ala. L. Rev. 1 (2016).

91. *See, e.g.,* Lawrence A. Frolik & Linda S. Whitton, The UPC Substituted Judgment/Best Interest Standard for Guardian Decisions: A Proposal for Reform, 45 U. Mich. J.L. Reform 739 (2012); Karen E. Boxx & Terry W. Hammond, A Call for Standards: An Overview of the Current Status and Need for Guardian Standards of Conduct and Codes of Ethics, 2012 Utah L. Rev. 1207.

92. *See, e.g.,* In re Estate of Border, 68 A.3d 946 (Pa. Super. 2013).

93. *See* Schoenblum, *supra* note 58, at tbl. 10. For commentary, see Nina A. Kohn, Matched Preferences and Values: A New Approach to Selecting Legal Surrogates, 52 San Diego L. Rev. 399 (2015); Lois Shepherd, The End of End-of-Life Law, 92 N.C. L. Rev. 1693 (2014); Joseph Karl Grant, The Advance Directive Registry or Lockbox: A Model Proposal and Call to Legislative Action, 37 J. Legis. 81 (2011); Dorothy D. Nachman, Living Wills: Is It Time to Pull the Plug?, 18 Elder L.J. 289 (2011).

94. U.S. Gov't Accountability Off., GAO-15-416, Advance Directives: Information on Federal Oversight, Provider Implementation, and Prevalence 21 (2015).

Assessing Terri Schiavo: She Opened Pandora's Suitcase

When they were children, Terri Schiavo's brother Bobby accidentally locked her in a suitcase. She tried so hard to get out that the suitcase jumped up and down and screamed. The scene predicted, horribly, how she would end, though by that stage she had neither walked nor talked for more than 15 years. By the time she finally died on March 31st, [2005,] her body had become a box out of which she could not escape.

More than that, it had become a box out of which the United States government, Congress, the president, the governor of Florida and an army of evangelical protestors and bloggers would not let her escape. Her life, whatever its quality, became the property not merely of her husband (who had the legal right to speak for her) and her parents (who had brought her up), but of the courts, the state, and thousands of self-appointed medical and psychological experts across the country....

All this outside interference could only exacerbate the real, cruel dilemmas of the case. After a heart attack in February 1990, when she was 26, Mrs Schiavo's brain was deprived of oxygen for five minutes and irreparably damaged. For a while, her family hoped she might be rehabilitated. Her husband Michael bought her new clothes and wheeled her round art galleries, in case her brain could respond. By 1993, he was sure it could not, and when she caught an infection he did not want her treated. Her parents disagreed, and claimed she could recover.

From that point the family split, and litigation started. Each side, backed by legions of supporters, accused the other of money-grubbing and bad faith. A Florida court twice ordered Mrs Schiavo's feeding tube to be removed and Jeb Bush, the governor of Florida, overruled it. The final removal of the tube, on March 18th, [2005,] was followed by an extraordinary scene, in the early hours of March 21st, when George Bush signed into law a bill allowing Mrs Schiavo's parents to appeal yet again to a federal court. But by then the courts, and two-thirds of Americans, thought that enough was enough. On March 24th the Supreme Court declined to hear the case.

Mrs Schiavo's own thoughts on the matter were fished out of the past and presented as each side wanted them to be. She never wanted to live on a machine, said her husband and her brother-in-law.... The chances are that she, like most young, active people, had barely thought about it, had never made a will, and probably never dreamed that her remarks at her grandmother's funeral lunch ("If I ever go like that, just let me go") would return to dominate decisions about her fate.

Terri Schiavo
AFP/Getty Images

Her life was so ordinary that accounts of her hardly ever mentioned what she had been. She was brought up in the leafy suburbs of northeastern Philadelphia, a quiet, plump girl who kept gerbils and a labrador and wanted to be a vet. At Archbishop Wood High School she was a moderate student, and dropped out of junior college to become a clerk for an insurance company. She worried constantly about her weight, sometimes dieting so hard that her bones showed, and it may have been bulimia that caused her heart attack. Michael Schiavo was the first boy she had dated; they got engaged after five months. She was allergic to salad and Benadryl, and adored "Starsky and Hutch".

Her "supporters" outside the Supreme Court last week, standing in silence with the word "Life" taped over their mouths, presumed to represent her views. She, dying slowly, had no views. To take the side of life, rather than death, is a fundamentally good philosophy; and an autopsy may yet show (though this seems doubtful) that her medical state was less appalling, and irreversible, than it seemed.

Nonetheless,...[a]n immense cloud of public interest came to conceal a dreadful, but private, dilemma that was for doctors and family members to solve with their consciences and their priests. As it was, in the current climate, there will probably be more Terri Schiavos.

Source: The Economist (Mar. 31, 2005).

On June 13, 2005, the medical examiner released his autopsy report on Terri Schiavo. Her brain was about half the size of normal, she was blind before death, and her condition was consistent with having been in a persistent vegetative state. The immediate cause of death was dehydration.

wants to be treated in end-of-life situations or in the event of incompetence; (2) *proxy directives*, such as a *health care proxy* or *durable power of attorney for health care*, which designate an agent to make health care decisions for the patient; and (3) *hybrid* or *combined directives* incorporating both of the first two approaches, directing treatment preferences and designating an agent to make substituted decisions.

The Uniform Health-Care Decisions Act takes a hybrid approach. It includes forms that create a durable power of attorney for health care and allow a person to indicate how aggressively the person would like to be treated. The agent must make decisions in accordance with the patient's wishes. A health care provider must follow the instructions unless they are contrary to the provider's conscience or to generally accepted medical practice.

NOTES

1. A Default Favoring Death?   Polls show overwhelmingly that most Americans would not want to be kept alive without hope of recovery. If a particular patient's wishes are not known, but under the circumstances most patients would choose to forgo continued treatment, should the default rule be no treatment?[95]

2. The Rise of Elder Law.   Elder law deals with a wide range of issues facing the elderly, including retirement, health care, Medicaid eligibility, competency and guardianship, discrimination, elder abuse, and housing and institutionalization. Practitioners in this area deal with many personal health issues, such as nursing home care and assisted living retirement communities. On the property side, lawyers can help with pension plans and Social Security, wills and will substitutes, durable powers of attorney, conservatorships, and trusts to preserve assets if the elderly person is admitted into a state institution.[96] Representing a client with diminishing capacity can be a special challenge, one that is governed by Rule 1.14 of the Model Rules of Professional Conduct (2015) (Client with Diminished Capacity).[97]

c. Physician Aid in Dying

In a 2016 Gallup poll of more than 1,000 adults, 69 percent said that a doctor "should be allowed by law to end the patient's life by some painless means" at the request of

---

95. *See* James Lindgren, Death by Default, 56 Law & Contemp. Probs. 185 (1993); *see also* Barbara A. Noah, In Denial: The Role of Law in Preparing for Death, 21 Elder L.J. 1 (2013).

96. *See* A. Kimberley Dayton & Molly M. Wood, Elder Law: Readings, Cases, and Materials (4th ed. 2015 rev.); Lawrence A. Frolik & Alison M. Barnes, Elder Law: Cases and Materials (6th ed. 2015); Lawrence A. Frolik & Richard L. Kaplan, Elder Law in a Nutshell (6th ed. 2014); *see also* Nina A. Kohn & Edward D. Spurgeon, A Call to Action on Elder Law Education: An Assessment and Recommendations Based on a National Survey, 21 Elder L.J. 345 (2014).

97. *See, e.g.,* ACTEC Commentaries on the Model Rules of Professional Conduct 159-70 (5th ed. 2016); Joseph Karl Grant, Running Past Landmines—The Estate Attorney's Dilemma: Ethically Counseling the Client with Alzheimer's Disease, 24 Elder L.J. 101 (2016).

"the patient and his or her family," and 53 percent said that physician aid in dying is "morally acceptable."[98]

By referendum in 1994, Oregon became the first U.S. state to authorize physician aid in dying. Under the Oregon Death with Dignity Act,[99] a physician is relieved of criminal and civil liability for prescribing a lethal dose of medicine to an adult if certain conditions are met. The adult must suffer from an incurable disease that is likely to produce death within six months, must make multiple separate requests (at least one in writing), must notify her next of kin, and must survive two waiting periods (one 15 days, the other 2 days). Since enactment through 2015, 1,545 people have had lethal prescriptions written and 991 patients have died from ingesting the prescribed medications.[100]

California, Colorado, Vermont, and Washington (by referendum) have since joined Oregon in authorizing physician aid in dying by legislation,[101] and Montana has done so by judicial decision.[102] In Gonzales v. Oregon, 546 U.S. 243 (2006), the Supreme Court upheld the Oregon law against a U.S. Justice Department interpretation of the federal Controlled Substances Act, which would have extended federal criminal liability to physicians acting under the state law.

3. Disposition of the Body

a. Post-Mortem Remains

Historically, a person other than a monarch has had little say about what is done to his body after death. The body was not considered to be property, so it was neither disposable by will nor owned by the decedent's estate or by his family. Until the twentieth century, burials were left to the jurisdiction of the church. With the rise of secularism, courts began to exercise discretion in carrying out the expressed wishes of the deceased person.

Mortal remains legislation in a majority of states codifies this power and gives a person something more than a hope, but not a complete assurance, that his wishes will be carried out at death.[103] In In re Estate of Whalen, 827 N.W.2d 184 (Iowa 2013), the court held that the decedent's directions in her will for the disposition of her mortal remains did not comply with the form required by the state's mortal remains statute. The court ordered that the decedent's estranged husband's directions, which were

---

98. Gallup News Serv., Euthanasia Still Acceptable to Solid Majority in U.S. (June 24, 2016) (May 4-8, 2016 survey of 1,025 adults), https://perma.cc/6ULN-VASX; *see also* David Orentlicher, Thaddeus Mason & Ben Rich, The Changing Legal Climate for Physician Aid in Dying, 311 JAMA 1961 (2014).

99. Or. Rev. Stat. §§ 127.800 *et seq.* (2016); *see also* Browne C. Lewis, A Graceful Exit: Redefining Terminal to Expand the Availability of Physician-Facilitated Suicide, 91 Or. L. Rev. 457 (2012).

100. *See* Or. Pub. Health Div., Oregon Death with Dignity Act: 2015 Data Summary 2 (2016).

101. *See* Cal. Health & Safety Code Ann. §§ 443 et seq. (2016); Vt. Stat. Ann. §§ 5281 et seq. (2016); Wash. Rev. Code §§ 70.245.901 et seq. (2016).

102. *See* Baxter v. State, 224 P.3d 1211 (Mont. 2009). So has Canada. *See* Carter v. Attorney Gen. of Canada, [2015] 1 S.C.R. 331.

103. *See* Tanya D. Marsh, The Law of Human Remains (2015).

Jeremy Bentham's Auto-Icon

When the moral philosopher Jeremy Bentham died in 1832, he left a will with specific instructions pertaining to the "disposal and preservation of the several parts of my bodily frame." His skeleton was to be "clad in one of the suits of black occasionally worn by me" and seated upright on a chair, under a placard reading "Auto-Icon."

Bentham suggested that his corpse might then be able to preside over regular meetings of his utilitarian followers. For ten years prior to his death, Bentham purportedly carried in his pocket a pair of glass eyes that were to be embedded into his embalmed head. Here, however, Bentham's plan went awry. His face was grossly disfigured in the process of preserving it, and a substitute wax replacement had to be created.

The real embalmed head was placed on the floor between Bentham's legs, where it resided until 1975, when it was kidnapped by a group of students demanding £100 for charity. The university paid £10, and the head of the great moral philosopher was returned.

Bentham's Auto-Icon

Since 2002, Bentham's real head has resided in a climate-controlled storeroom at the UCL Institute of Archeology. Those with appropriate reasons to pay a visit may still do so by appointment.

Source: Atlas Obscura, https://perma.cc/F33A-QMHG.

contrary to the decedent's wishes as expressed in her will, controlled the disposition of her remains.

If a person dies by violence or in suspicious circumstances, statutes in all states require an autopsy regardless of the wishes of the deceased person or next of kin.

b. Organ Donation

With the advent of dissection and cadaver organ transplantation, the first principle of law, medicine, and ethics—saving human life—became a relevant consideration in the disposition of the dead. To increase the quantity of cadaver organs for transplantation, all states have enacted some form of the Uniform Anatomical Gift Act (UAGA), first promulgated in 1968, revised in 1987, and again in 2006.

The UAGA permits a person to give her body to any hospital, physician, medical school, or body bank for research or transplantation. It also permits a gift of a body, or parts thereof, to any specified person for therapy or transplantation. Under the original UAGA of 1968, the gift can be made by a duly executed will or by a card carried on the person if "signed by the donor in the presence of two witnesses who must sign the document in his presence." Under the 1987 and 2006 revisions, the witnessing requirement was eliminated so that only the donor's signature is required. Many states have enacted additional legislation providing for an organ donation designation on the back of a driver's license, which the 1987 and 2006 revisions of UAGA also allow. The 2006 revision clarifies and expands the class of persons who can make a gift of a deceased person's body or parts to include agents under a power of attorney for health care.

The various anatomical gift statutes have not abated the shortage of organs. At year-end 2016, about 120,000 people were on the national waiting list to receive an organ

Professor Alvin E. Roth, winner of the 2012 Nobel Prize in Economics

donation.[104] In the arresting formulation of the Prefatory Note to the 2006 revision of the UAGA: "Every hour another person in the United States dies because of the lack of an organ to provide a life saving organ transplant."

There are many reasons for the shortage of organs: (a) difficulty imagining one's death and others' using one's organs; (b) fear that physicians might hasten death in order to obtain organs; (c) dread of being cut open after death, perhaps because of religious belief; and (d) simply not thinking about the matter.

Several commentators and entrepreneurs have suggested that a market in human organs be established. A market, after all, is the traditional way of allocating scarce resources.[105] In 1984, however, Congress forbade the sale of human organs.[106] The British Parliament outlawed the sale of human organs in 1989, after a public outcry over the sale of a kidney to a Londoner for £2,000 by a Turkish peasant flown to London for the operation. In 2012, a 17-year-old in China made headlines when it was revealed that he had sold a kidney for money to buy an iPad and an iPhone.[107] What about permitting a decedent's estate to sell the decedent's organs posthumously?[108]

Although an outright sale of an organ is prohibited, a swap by willing kidney donors whose intended donees are compatible only with the other donor is allowed. For example, *A* may give his kidney to *Y*, the daughter of *X*, who gives his kidney to *B*, the daughter of *A*. In 2012, the economist Alvin Roth was awarded a Nobel Prize in part for his work in developing an algorithm to organize such swaps. One chain of swaps involved 30 donated kidneys and thus 60 operations![109]

Most states have enacted *routine request* statutes, requiring hospitals to request from families of prospective donors at the time of death permission to remove organs

104. The U.S. Department of Health and Human Services provides current statistics at http://www.organdonor.gov/statistics-stories/statistics.html. Year-end 2016 statistics are archived at https://perma.cc/RL83-2VR4.

105. *See, e.g.,* Kristy Lynn Williams, Marisa Finley & J. James Rohack, Just Say No to NOTA: Why the Prohibition of Compensation for Human Transplant Organs in NOTA Should Be Repealed and a Regulated Market for Cadaver Organs Instituted, 40 Am. J.L. & Med. 275, 277 (2014).

106. National Organ Transplant Act, 42 U.S.C. § 274e (2016). The statute does not, however, prohibit compensation for donations of bone marrow for transplant. Flynn v. Holder, 684 F.3d 852 (9th Cir. 2012).

Suppose that the federal government gave a tax deduction to the estate of any cadaver organ donor. Should that be prohibited as a sale? *See* Lisa Milot, The Case Against Tax Incentives for Organ Transfers, 45 Willamette L. Rev. 67 (2008). Suppose that health insurance companies, as a result of collective bargaining or governmental requirement, offered lower premiums to persons who agreed to donate their organs at death. Would that be a sale?

107. *See* David Colker, Report: Chinese Teenager Sells Kidney to Buy iPhone, iPad, L.A. Times, Apr. 7, 2012.

108. *See* Reid Kress Weisbord, Anatomical Intent, 124 Yale L.J. F. 117 (2014).

109. *See* Kevin Sack, 60 Lives, 30 Kidneys, All Linked, N.Y. Times, Feb. 18, 2012, at A1.

for transplantation. A federal regulation also requires this as a condition of the hospital's Medicare eligibility.

Others have favored establishing a *mandated choice* in which every person would be required to answer, one way or the other, whether the person was willing to donate organs for transplantation after death. The question could be part of the application process for a driver's license. Another idea is to give priority to prior donor registrants in allocating organs among those on waiting lists for a transplant.[110] This has been called a *no give, no take* system.

Still another idea is to presume that a deceased person has consented to donation. Under such a *presumed consent* or *opt-out* system, usable organs would be routinely removed from cadavers unless an objection had previously been made, either by the deceased person during life or immediately after the decedent's death by a person acting on behalf of the decedent. In support of a presumption of donation, Professors Cass Sunstein and Richard Thaler argue that this would set the default rule closer to people's preferences:

> In many nations—Austria, Belgium, Denmark, Finland, France, Italy, Luxembourg, Norway, Singapore, Slovenia, and Spain—people are presumed to consent to allow their organs to be used, after death, for the benefit of others; but they are permitted to rebut the presumption, usually through an explicit notation to that effect on their drivers' licenses. In the United States, by contrast, those who want their organs to be available for others must affirmatively say so, also through an explicit notation on their drivers' licenses. The result is that in "presumed consent" nations over 90 percent of people consent to make their organs available for donation, whereas in the United States, where people have to take some action to make their organs available, only 28 percent elect to do so. We hypothesize that this dramatic difference is not a product of deep cultural differences, but of the massive effect of the default rule. Hence we would predict that a European-style opt-out rule in the United States would produce donation rates similar to those observed in the European countries that use this rule. Note in this regard that by one report, over 85 percent of Americans support organ donation—a statistic that suggests opt-outs would be relatively rare.[111]

The median opt-out rate in countries with organ donation as the default is a staggeringly low 1 percent. In Belgium, organ donation increased 119 percent in the first three years after the implementation of the law. Should an opt-out rule be adopted in the United States? The 2006 revision to UAGA adheres to the traditional opt-in approach.[112]

---

110. This policy was adopted in Israel, followed by a substantial increase in donor registrations. *See* Judy Siegel-Itzkovich, Privileges for Organ Donor Card Holders Extended, Jerusalem Post, Jan. 2, 2012; *see also* Judd B. Kessler & Alvin E. Roth, Organ Allocation Policy and the Decision to Donate, 102 Am. Econ. Rev. 2018 (2012).

111. Cass R. Sunstein & Richard H. Thaler, Libertarian Paternalism Is Not an Oxymoron, 70 U. Chi. L. Rev. 1159, 1191-92 (2003); *see also* Richard H. Thaler & Cass R. Sunstein, Nudge: Improving Decisions About Health, Wealth, and Happiness 176-82 (2008).

112. *See* David Orentlicher, Presumed Consent to Organ Donation: Its Rise and Fall in the United States, 61 Rutgers L. Rev. 295 (2009).

CHAPTER 8

LIMITS ON FREEDOM OF DISPOSITION: PROTECTION OF THE SPOUSE AND CHILDREN

> Commercial partnerships are voluntary contractual associations,
> and so, up to a point, are marriages. The "marriage market" is an apt
> metaphor for the elaborate process of search by which individuals seek
> marital partners with whom to form productive households.
>
> RICHARD A. POSNER
> Economic Analysis of Law § 5.2 (9th ed. 2014)

FOR THE MOST PART, the American law of succession is built on the principle of freedom of disposition. But this principle is not absolute. In this chapter, we consider limits on freedom of disposition for the protection of a surviving spouse and children.

In all but one of the separate property states, a surviving spouse is entitled to an *elective* or *forced share*, typically one-third, of the decedent spouse's estate. In the community property states, each spouse owns all earnings during the marriage in equal, undivided shares. There is no elective share because the surviving spouse already owns half of the couple's community property. Both separate property and community property states protect a *pretermitted* surviving spouse from accidental disinheritance by way of a premarital will that the decedent spouse neglected to update after the marriage.

Although there is general agreement across the states on the basic policy of protecting a surviving spouse, there is wide variation in the particulars. Many of the differences reflect a lack of consensus on whether spousal protection derives from a marital *support obligation* or rather is rooted in a *partnership theory* of marriage. Another source of divergence is differing views on the extent to which the elective share should apply to nonprobate property.

In contrast to a surviving spouse, in the American legal tradition a surviving child has no rights to a mandatory share of a decedent parent's estate. A property owner may disinherit her blood relations, including her children, if that is her desire. This rule stands in stark contrast with the other common law countries, where courts may override a testator's will for a child or other dependent of the testator. As with a pretermitted spouse, American law protects a child who is accidently omitted from a will—such as a child born after the execution of a will that does not contemplate subsequent children—but this is a default rule that may be overcome by express language in the will.

We begin in Section A by considering the rights of a surviving spouse by way of the separate property elective share and the community property sharing rules, and waiver of such rights by premarital or marital agreement. In Section B, we consider the intentional omission of a child, contrasting American law with that of the other common law countries. In Section C, we consider the pretermission statutes, which protect an omitted surviving spouse or child from unintentional disinheritance.

A. PROTECTION OF THE SURVIVING SPOUSE

1. The Elective Share of a Separate Property Surviving Spouse

In the United States, two basic marital property systems exist: the system of *separate property*, originating in the common law of England, and the system of *community property*, originating in Continental Europe and brought to this country by French and Spanish settlers. The two systems are quite different. Under separate property, spouses own separately all earnings and acquisitions from earnings during the marriage, unless they agree to a joint form of ownership. Under community property, spouses retain separate ownership of property brought to the marriage, but they own all earnings and acquisitions from earnings during the marriage in equal, undivided shares. The death of one spouse dissolves the community. The deceased spouse owns and has testamentary power over his or her half of the community. The surviving spouse owns the other half.

There are, to be sure, many variations among the states adhering to one or another of these systems, and community property ideas have made noticeable inroads into the common law separate property system. Nonetheless, separate property and community property are quite different ways of thinking about marital property ownership. Separate property stresses an individual's autonomy over her earnings. Community property views marriage as an economic partnership. Nine states have community property and three others offer a community property option.[1]

"Now read me the part again where I disinherit everybody."
Peter Arno/The New Yorker Collection/The Cartoon Bank

---

1. The nine community property states are Arizona, California, Idaho, Louisiana, Nevada, New Mexico, Texas, Washington, and Wisconsin. Alaska, South Dakota, and Tennessee offer a community property option (see page 555).

Community Property and Separate Property (2016)   Figure 8.1

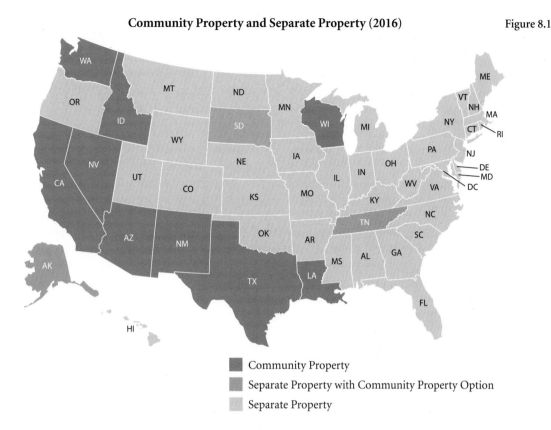

■ Community Property
■ Separate Property with Community Property Option
■ Separate Property

Under the separate property system, because whatever a spouse earns is his or hers, the question of what protection against disinheritance should be given to the other spouse arises. The answer in 40 out of the 41 separate property states (the exception is Georgia[2]) is to give the surviving spouse an *elective share*, sometimes called a *forced* or *statutory share*, of the decedent spouse's property. The term "elective share" arose because under the statutes, a surviving spouse can elect to take under the decedent's

---

2. Professor Verner Chaffin, a leading authority on Georgia wills law, approved on the grounds that the vast majority of spouses do support the surviving spouse after death and the elective share permits the surviving spouse to wreck a sound estate plan. *See* Verner F. Chaffin, A Reappraisal of the Wealth Transmission Process: The Surviving Spouse, Year's Support and Intestate Succession, 10 Ga. L. Rev. 447, 464-70 (1976). Professor Jeffrey Pennell examined probate court records of Georgia decedents in 1996 and 1997. He found infrequent disinheritance of spouses, and in most such cases a sound planning explanation. *See* Jeffrey N. Pennell, Minimizing the Surviving Spouse's Elective Share, 32 Heckerling Inst. on Est. Plan. ch. 9 (1998).

Not all of Professor Chaffin's students were convinced. In Note, Preventing Spousal Disinheritance in Georgia, 19 Ga. L. Rev. 427 (1985), the author argued for equitable distribution of a portion of the decedent's property to the surviving spouse. Observing that the Georgia Supreme Court adopted equitable distribution upon divorce on its own after the Georgia legislature failed to act, the author argued that the court should likewise extend equitable distribution to termination of marriage by death.

will or to renounce the will and take a fractional share of the decedent's estate. The typical elective share is one-third of all of the decedent's probate property plus certain nonprobate transfers. Spouses may waive their elective share rights by premarital or marital agreement (see page 544). In a community property state, there is no elective share, because each spouse owns one-half of the earnings of the other spouse during the marriage. Thus:

> *Case 1.* *H* works outside the home, earning $50,000 a year. *W* works in the home, earning no wages. Over the course of the marriage, *H* used his earnings to buy a house in his name, to open a bank account payable-on-death to his daughter, and to acquire $100,000 of stocks in his name. Under a separate property regime, *W* owns none of that property while *H* is alive. At *H*'s death, *W* has a right to an elective share over the house and the stocks but perhaps not the bank account because it is not in *H*'s probate estate. In a community property state, *W* owns half of *H*'s earnings during life, and thus at *H*'s death *W* already owns one-half of the acquisitions from those earnings (the house, the bank account, and the stocks). If *W* dies first, *W* can dispose of her half of the community property by will. In a separate property state, if *W* dies first, she has no property to convey (her elective share arises only if she outlives *H*).

a. Economic Partnership or Support Obligation?

The primary justification for the elective share is that the surviving spouse contributed to the decedent spouse's acquisition of wealth. This reflects a *partnership theory* of marriage. An older and narrower justification for the elective share is that marriage entails a *support obligation* that continues after death. Both theories justify the existence of *an* elective share. But they are often in tension when it comes to designing *the* elective share.

The partnership theory points toward giving a surviving spouse one-half of the decedent's property acquired during the marriage, mirroring the outcome in a community property state. The support theory would tend to justify a smaller percentage but would apply it to all of the decedent's property. It might also justify the survivor receiving all of the decedent's property up to a certain minimum amount or considering the survivor's other resources. Which of these theories will give a surviving spouse a larger amount depends on the aggregate value of the decedent's property and how much of it was acquired during the marriage.

The typical elective share, reflecting its roots in medieval dower (see page 563), is one-third of all of the decedent's probate property plus certain nonprobate transfers. It does not matter whether the marriage

"I married money, son, so that you might never have to."

William Hamilton/The New Yorker Collection/The Cartoon Bank

lasted one hour[3] or 83 years;[4] whether the surviving spouse has more or less property than the decedent spouse; whether the decedent spouse's property was acquired mainly before the marriage; or whether the property was obtained as a gift from a third party. In most separate property states, the elective share fraction, and the property to which it applies, is the same in all cases. Do these rules reflect the partnership theory? The support theory? A cobbling of the two?

Although we speak of a surviving *spouse's* elective share, in most cases it is a *widow's* share. As a matter of historical fact, men have tended to earn more than women, women have tended to outlive men, and marriage was restricted to a man and a woman. Accordingly, the prototypical situation across history to which the elective share has been applicable is a propertied dead husband and poorer widow. Viewed from this perspective, the real test of whether an elective-share system implements the partnership theory comes when a wife predeceases her husband—and all the elective-share systems fail this test. If a wife dies before her husband, she cannot dispose of any of the marital partnership property titled in her husband's name. Thus:

> *Case 2.* H owns $500,000 in acquisitions from his earnings and W owns $100,000 from her earnings. If W dies first, she can dispose of only her $100,000, and in most states H will have an elective share in that. If the couple had community property, W could dispose of her half of the $600,000 total by will.

Uniform Probate Code (1990, as amended 2008)

Article II, Part 2
Elective Share of Surviving Spouse
General Comment
The Partnership Theory of Marriage

The partnership theory of marriage, sometimes also called the marital-sharing theory, is stated in various ways. Sometimes it is thought of "as an expression of the presumed intent of husbands and wives to pool their fortunes on an equal basis, share and share alike." Mary Ann Glendon, The Transformation of Family Law 131 (1989). Under this approach, the economic rights of each spouse are seen as deriving from an unspoken marital bargain under which the partners agree that each is to enjoy a half interest in the fruits of the marriage, i.e., in the property nominally acquired by and titled in the sole name of either partner during the marriage (other than in property acquired by gift or inheritance). A decedent who disinherits his or her surviving spouse

---

3. Or less. In In re Neiderhiser's Estate, 2 Pa. D. & C.3d 302 (C.P. 1977), the groom dropped dead during the marriage ceremony, after he and the bride had each said "I will" (equal in other marriage ceremonies to "I do"). The court held that marriage is a contract that becomes binding upon the exchange of vows. On length of marriage and marital property rights, see J. Thomas Oldham, Should Separate Property Gradually Become Community Property as a Marriage Continues?, 72 La. L. Rev. 127 (2011).

4. *See* Mary Bowerman, Here's What a Couple Married for 83 Years Can Teach You About Lasting Love, USA Today, Feb. 11, 2016.

is seen as having reneged on the bargain.[5] Sometimes the theory is expressed in restitutionary terms, a return-of-contribution notion. Under this approach, the law grants each spouse an entitlement to compensation for non-monetary contributions to the marital enterprise, as "a recognition of the activity of one spouse in the home and to compensate not only for this activity but for opportunities lost." Id.

No matter how the rationale is expressed, the community-property system, including that version of community law promulgated in the Model Marital Property Act, recognizes the partnership theory, but it is sometimes thought that the common-law system denies it. In the ongoing marriage, it is true that the basic principle in the common-law (title-based) states is that marital status does not affect the ownership of property. The regime is one of separate property. Each spouse owns all that he or she earns. By contrast, in the community-property states, each spouse acquires an ownership interest in half the property the other earns during the marriage. By granting each spouse upon acquisition an immediate half interest in the earnings of the other, the community-property regimes directly recognize that the couple's enterprise is in essence collaborative.

The common-law states, however, also give effect or purport to give effect to the partnership theory when a marriage is dissolved by divorce.[6] If the marriage ends in divorce, a spouse who sacrificed his or her financial-earning opportunities to contribute so-called domestic services to the marital enterprise (such as child rearing and homemaking) stands to be recompensed. All states now follow the equitable-distribution system upon divorce, under which

> broad discretion [is given to] trial courts to assign to either spouse property acquired during the marriage, irrespective of title, taking into account the circumstances of the particular case and recognizing the value of the contributions of a nonworking spouse or homemaker to the acquisition of that property. Simply stated, the system of equitable distribution views marriage as essentially a shared enterprise or joint undertaking in the nature of a partnership to which both spouses contribute—directly and indirectly, financially and nonfinancially—the fruits of which are distributable at divorce.

John D. Gregory, The Law of Equitable Distribution ¶ 1.03, at p. 1-6 (1989).

The other situation in which spousal property rights figure prominently is disinheritance at death. . . . Elective-share law in the common-law states, however, has not

---

5. Somewhat anachronistically, Judge Posner puts the point thus:

> Another limitation on the power of a testator is the provision, found in the inheritance laws of all states, forbidding him to disinherit his widow completely. The limitation has an economic justification. The husband's wealth at death is likely, as we know, to be a product, in part, of the wife's work even if she never had any pecuniary income. Without statutory protection against disinheritance of her rightful share of her husband's estate, women could negotiate with their husbands for contractual protection (contracts to make bequests are enforceable). The statutory provision minimizes transaction costs.

Richard A. Posner, Economic Analysis of Law § 19.7, at 717-18 (9th ed. 2014).—Eds.

6. *See* Laura A. Rosenbury, Two Ways to End a Marriage: Divorce or Death, 2005 Utah L. Rev. 1227.—Eds.

caught up to the partnership theory of marriage. Under typical American elective-share law, including the elective share provided by the original [1969] Uniform Probate Code, a surviving spouse may claim a one-third share of the decedent's estate—not the 50 percent share of the couple's combined assets that the partnership theory would imply.

b. Unmarried Cohabiting Partners

Marriage brings many legal and economic consequences, mostly beneficial, to a surviving spouse, of which the elective share is just one. A surviving spouse is entitled to Social Security benefits based on the other spouse's earnings (see page 560), pension rights from the other spouse's job (see page 561), and to the federal estate tax marital deduction, which eliminates all estate taxes on property one married partner transfers to the other at death (see Chapter 15 at page 967). The policy justifications for these benefits, including the elective share, arguably apply to unmarried cohabiting partners who are in a committed relationship. Nevertheless, under traditional law a surviving cohabiting partner is not entitled to an elective share in the decedent partner's estate or to these other benefits unless they were married.

Prior to the decision in Obergefell v. Hodges, 135 S. Ct. 2584 (2015), the question of whether to extend elective share rights to unmarried cohabiting partners was obscured by the more politically salient question of whether to permit marriage by same-sex couples. In lieu of same-sex marriage, some states enacted statutes that gave elective share rights to cohabiting partners in a registered "domestic partnership" or "civil union." After *Obergefell*, all couples are permitted to marry regardless of the sex of the partners.

But what of unmarried cohabiting partners, whether opposite sex or same sex, who choose not to marry, but for whom the nature of the relationship indicates an economic partnership or an undertaking to provide support comparable to a marriage? Does the absence of a formal marriage indicate a rejection by the parties of the elective share? These questions are of growing policy significance, as the demographic data show an unmistakable slowdown in marital families and increase in functional families through unmarried cohabitation. For further discussion, including of the demographic data and the criteria for discerning a committed unmarried partnership, see Chapter 2 at page 74.

c. Variation Across the States

A word of caution is in order. Owing to the inability of legislators to decide definitively what is the purpose of the elective share—partnership or support—and to carry this purpose through to its logical ends, there is no subject in this book on which there is more statutory variation.[7] Even states adopting the 1969 or 1990 Uniform Probate Code (UPC), which had the purpose of bringing uniformity, made important substantive changes in the elective share provisions. Let us consider some areas of conceptual

---

7. *See* Jeffrey A. Schoenblum, Multistate Guide to Estate Planning tbl. 6.03 (2016); *see also* Christopher P. Cline, Jeffrey N. Pennell & Terry L. Turnipseed, Tax Management Portfolio, Spouse's Elective Share 841 (2012).

Paul Kinsella/Cartoonstock

difficulty, which bring into focus the differences between the partnership and support theories.

(1) Must the Surviving Spouse Accept a Life Estate?   Once the amount of the elective share has been determined, the surviving spouse is usually credited (*charged*, in the jargon) with the value of all other interests received under the will (and perhaps will substitutes too). If those amounts do not satisfy the elective share, the difference must be made up either by pro rata contributions from all the other beneficiaries, which is the majority and UPC rule, or from the residuary estate.

But suppose that the decedent has left the surviving spouse a life estate in a certain amount of property. Must the surviving spouse accept the life estate or its value in partial satisfaction of the elective share, as under medieval dower (see page 563)? Under the support theory, the answer should be Yes, because the surviving spouse requires support only during life. Under the partnership theory, the answer should be No, because the surviving spouse should have complete dominion over the survivor's share of the partnership property.

On this question the original 1969 UPC and the law of most states follow the partnership theory. If the surviving spouse renounces the life estate and elects to take her share in fee simple, she is *not* charged for the value of the life estate. In 1975, however, the 1969 UPC was amended to provide that a surviving spouse who rejects a life estate *is* charged an amount equal to one-half the total value of the property subject to the life estate. Charging the surviving spouse with the value of a life estate was carried over into the 1990 UPC. The practical effect is to force the surviving spouse to take the life estate given to her by the decedent's will. The intent of the UPC revisers was to cause as little distortion in the decedent's estate plan as possible.

Under heavy criticism from commentators, who tend to favor the partnership theory, in 1993 the Uniform Law Commission amended the UPC to provide that a life estate renounced by a surviving spouse is not charged against the spouse's elective share (§ 2-209). In almost all states today, a surviving spouse need not accept a life estate in satisfaction of the elective share.

(2) Subsequently Deceased Surviving Spouse.   Suppose *H* dies leaving a will that excludes *W*, and that *W* dies before exercising her right of election. Should *W*'s personal representative be allowed to renounce *H*'s will and take a forced share? If the answer is Yes, then *W*'s elective share of *H*'s property will pass to *W*'s heirs or devisees. If the answer is No, then all of *H*'s property will pass to *H*'s devisees. Under the support theory, the answer should be No, because after her death *W* has no need for support. Under the partnership theory, the answer should be Yes, because *W* is entitled to direct the disposition of her share of the property accumulated by the marital partnership.

In most states, and under UPC § 2-212 (1990, rev. 2008), the right of election may be exercised by the surviving spouse or a representative of the surviving spouse only during the surviving spouse's life. In Wilson v. Wilson, 197 P.3d 1141 (Or. App. 2008), the court held that a claim for an elective share filed by a representative on behalf of an incompetent surviving spouse was extinguished by the death of the surviving spouse. The court reasoned that the representative's authority to claim the surviving spouse's elective share was dependent on the surviving spouse's need for support, which ended with her death.

(3) Incompetent Surviving Spouse.   The *Wilson* case also raised the question of whether a guardian or other representative of an incompetent surviving spouse can elect against the decedent's will. A minority of states hold that a guardian can and should elect to take against the will if it is to the surviving spouse's economic benefit, calculated mathematically. A majority of states hold, as did the court in In re Estate of Cross, 664 N.E.2d 905 (Ohio 1996), that all the surrounding facts and circumstances should be taken into consideration. The majority view allows the representative to take into account the preservation of the decedent's estate plan and whether the surviving spouse would have wanted to abide by her deceased spouse's will.

The 1969 UPC took a different approach. Section 2-203 provided that a court, acting for an incompetent surviving spouse, could order election against the decedent spouse's will only "after finding that exercise is necessary to provide adequate support for the protected person during his probable life expectancy." This provision adopts the view that the elective share is for the support of the surviving spouse, not the protection of the surviving spouse's partnership share. But why should the elective share of a surviving spouse who happens to be incompetent at the decedent spouse's death be conditioned on the surviving spouse's need for support?

The 1990 UPC continued the view that the elective share is for support when the spouse is incompetent, but it implemented this view in a new way. UPC § 2-212 (1990, rev. 2008) provides that if a representative claims the elective share for an incompetent surviving spouse, the portion of the elective share that exceeds what the decedent spouse provided for the survivor must be placed in a *custodial trust* for the benefit of the surviving spouse. The trustee is given the power to expend income and principal for the surviving spouse's support, but upon the spouse's death the trustee must transfer the trust property to the residuary devisees under the will of the predeceased spouse or to the predeceased spouse's heirs. The theory is that, other than for support of the incompetent surviving spouse, the representative should not be able to upset the decedent's estate plan. The comment to § 2-212 says that the drafters wanted "to assure that that part of the elective share is devoted to the personal economic benefit and needs of the surviving spouse, but not to the economic benefit of the surviving spouse's heirs or devisees."

(4) Abandonment.   In a minority of states, the elective share is denied to a surviving spouse who abandoned or refused to support the deceased spouse.[8] As a practical

---

8. *See, e.g.,* N.Y. Est. Powers & Trusts Law § 5-1.2(a)(5) (2016); Va. Code Ann. § 64.2-308(A) (2016).

matter, proving abandonment can be tricky.[9] As a matter of policy, if the rationale for the elective share is sharing the economic fruits of marriage, why should one spouse lose that share upon leaving the other? Should the elective share apply only to property the abandoned spouse owned on the date of abandonment? In most community property states, if the couple separates, the earnings of both spouses continue to be community property until divorce. In California, earnings acquired after separation are not community property.

d. Nonprobate Property

The original elective share statutes gave the surviving spouse a fractional share, usually one-third, of the decedent's *estate*. In this context, the term estate was understood to mean the *probate estate*. With the increasing importance of nonprobate modes of transfer (see Chapter 7), the question arises whether the elective share should apply also to nonprobate transfers. Thus:

> *Case 3.* *W*, a successful lawyer, wishes to leave the bulk of her fortune to her daughter, *D*, rather than to her husband, *H*, even though she amassed this fortune during the marriage. Knowing of *H*'s right of election against her probate estate, *W* transfers $2.9 million to *X* in trust to pay income to *W* for life and the remainder to *D* on *W*'s death. *W* retains the right to revoke the trust. *W* then dies. *W*'s will leaves her entire probate estate, worth only $100,000, to *H*. Can *H* elect to take against the $2.9 million that, under the terms of the trust, will pass outside of probate to *D*?

In Case 3, unless *H*'s elective share is applied to *W*'s revocable trust, he will be effectively disinherited even though she left him all of her probate estate. The same issue would arise if *W* died intestate, having transferred all of her wealth outside of probate. Let us consider the judicial and legislative responses to the burgeoning use of nonprobate transfers and the potential for circumventing the elective share by avoiding probate.[10]

(1) Judicial Responses

Sullivan v. Burkin
460 N.E.2d 572 (Mass. 1984)

WILKINS, J. Mary A. Sullivan, the widow of Ernest G. Sullivan, has exercised her right, under G.L. c. 191, § 15, to take a share of her husband's estate. By this action, she seeks

---

9. *Compare* Purce v. Patterson, 654 S.E.2d 885 (Va. 2008) (finding that husband abandoned wife, even though they mutually agreed to separate, because of husband's lack of support for wife before and after the separation), *with* In re Estate of Riefberg, 446 N.E.2d 424 (N.Y. 1983) (finding that wife, who excluded husband from marital home and lived separately, did not abandon husband). Abandonment is especially tricky if rooted in an extramarital affair. *Compare* In re Estate of Peterson, 889 N.W.2d 753 (Mich. App. 2016) (finding no abandonment in spite of extramarital affair), *with* In re Estate of Talerico, 137 A.3d 577 (Pa. Super. 2016) (finding abandonment based on extramarital affair).

10. *See* Angela M. Vallario, The Elective Share Has No Friends: Creditors Trump Spouse in the Battle over the Revocable Trust, 45 Cap. U. L. Rev. 333 (2017).

a determination that assets held in an inter vivos trust created by her husband during the marriage should be considered as part of the estate in determining that share. A judge of the Probate Court for the county of Suffolk rejected the widow's claim and entered judgment dismissing the complaint. The widow appealed, and, on July 12, 1983, a panel of the Appeals Court reported the case to this court.

In September, 1973, Ernest G. Sullivan executed a deed of trust under which he transferred real estate to himself as sole trustee. The net income of the trust was payable to him during his life and the trustee was instructed to pay to him all or such part of the principal of the trust estate as he might request in writing from time to time. He retained the right to revoke the trust at any time. On his death, the successor trustee is directed to pay the principal and any undistributed income equally to the defendants, George F. Cronin, Sr., and Harold J. Cronin, if they should survive him, which they did. There were no witnesses to the execution of the deed of trust, but the husband acknowledged his signatures before a notary public, separately, as donor and as trustee.

Justice Herbert P. Wilkins, an intellectual leader of the Massachusetts court, made a specialty of trust cases. In addition to *Sullivan*, he wrote the opinions in Beals v. State Street Bank & Trust Co., page 821, and Dewire v. Haveles, page 869. From 1996 through 1999, Justice Wilkins was Chief Justice, a position once held by his father.

The husband died on April 27, 1981, while still trustee of the inter vivos trust. He left a will in which he stated that he "intentionally neglected to make any provision for my wife, Mary A. Sullivan and my grandson, Mark Sullivan." He directed that, after the payment of debts, expenses, and all estate taxes levied by reason of his death, the residue of his estate should be paid over to the trustee of the inter vivos trust. The defendants George F. Cronin, Sr., and Harold J. Cronin were named coexecutors of the will. The defendant Burkin is successor trustee of the inter vivos trust. On October 21, 1981, the wife filed a claim, pursuant to G.L. c. 191, § 15, for a portion of the estate.[11]

Although it does not appear in the record, the parties state in their briefs that Ernest G. Sullivan and Mary A. Sullivan had been separated for many years. We do know that in 1962 the wife obtained a court order providing for her temporary support. No final action was taken in that proceeding. The record provides no information about the

---

11. As relevant to this case, G.L. c. 191, § 15, provides:

The surviving husband or wife of a deceased person . . . within six months after the probate of the will of such deceased, may file in the registry of probate a writing signed by him or by her . . . claiming such portion of the estate of the deceased as he or she is given the right to claim under this section, and if the deceased left issue, he or she shall thereupon take one third of the personal and one third of the real property . . . except that . . . if he or she would thus take real and personal property to an amount exceeding twenty-five thousand dollars in value, he or she shall receive, in addition to that amount, only the income during his or her life of the excess of his or her share of such estate above that amount, the personal property to be held in trust and the real property vested in him or her for life, from the death of the deceased. . . .

value of any property owned by the husband at his death or about the value of any assets held in the inter vivos trust. At oral argument, we were advised that the husband owned personal property worth approximately $15,000 at his death and that the only asset in the trust was a house in Boston which was sold after the husband's death for approximately $85,000.

As presented in the complaint, and perhaps as presented to the motion judge, the wife's claim was simply that the inter vivos trust was an invalid testamentary disposition and that the trust assets "constitute assets of the estate" of Ernest G. Sullivan. There is no suggestion that the wife argued initially that, even if the trust were not testamentary, she had a special claim as a widow asserting her rights under G.L. c. 191, § 15. If the wife is correct that the trust was an ineffective testamentary disposition, the trust assets would be part of the husband's probate estate. In that event, we would not have to consider any special consequences of the wife's election under G.L. c. 191, § 15, or, in the words of the Appeals Court, "the present vitality" of Kerwin v. Donaghy, 59 N.E.2d 299, 306-07 (Mass. 1945).

We conclude, however, that the trust was not testamentary in character and that the husband effectively created a valid inter vivos trust. . . . A trust with remainder interests given to others on the settlor's death is not invalid as a testamentary disposition simply because the settlor retained a broad power to modify or revoke the trust, the right to receive income, and the right to invade principal during his life. . . . We believe that the law of the Commonwealth is correctly represented by the statement in Restatement (Second) of Trusts § 57, Comment h (1959), that a trust is "not testamentary and invalid for failure to comply with the requirements of the Statute of Wills merely because the settlor-trustee reserves a beneficial life interest and power to revoke and modify the trust. The fact that as trustee he controls the administration of the trust does not invalidate it."[12]

We come then to the question whether, even if the trust was not testamentary on general principles, the widow has special interests which should be recognized. Courts in this country have differed considerably in their reasoning and in their conclusions in passing on this question. . . .

The rule of Kerwin v. Donaghy, supra, 59 N.E.2d, at 306, is that

> [t]he right of a wife to waive her husband's will, and take, with certain limitations, "the same portion of the property of the deceased, real and personal, that . . . she would have taken if the deceased had died intestate" (G.L. [Ter. Ed.] c. 191, § 15), does not extend to personal property that has been conveyed by the husband in his lifetime and does not form part of his estate at his death. Fiske v. Fiske, 53 N.E. 916 (Mass. 1899). Shelton v. Sears, 73 N.E. 666 (Mass. 1905). In this Commonwealth a husband has an absolute right to dispose of any or all of his personal property in his lifetime, without the knowledge or consent of his wife, with the result that it will not form part of his estate for her to share under the statute of distributions (G.L. [Ter. Ed.] c. 190, §§ 1, 2), under his will, or by virtue of a waiver of his will. That is true even though his sole purpose was to disinherit her.

---

12. The Massachusetts court thus agreed with Farkas v. Williams, page 445, that a revocable inter vivos trust is valid to pass property at death without Wills Act formalities. — Eds.

In the *Kerwin* case, we applied the rule to deny a surviving spouse the right to reach assets the deceased spouse had placed in an inter vivos trust of which the settlor's daughter by a previous marriage was trustee and over whose assets he had a general power of appointment. The rule of Kerwin v. Donaghy has been adhered to in this Commonwealth for almost forty years and was adumbrated even earlier.[13] The bar has been entitled reasonably to rely on that rule in advising clients. In the area of property law, the retroactive invalidation of an established principle is to be undertaken with great caution. We conclude that, whether or not Ernest G. Sullivan established the inter vivos trust in order to defeat his wife's right to take her statutory share in the assets placed in the trust and even though he had a general power of appointment over the trust assets, Mary A. Sullivan obtained no right to share in the assets of that trust when she made her election under G.L. c. 191, § 15.

We announce for the future that, as to any inter vivos trust created or amended after the date of this opinion, we shall no longer follow the rule announced in Kerwin v. Donaghy. There have been significant changes since 1945 in public policy considerations bearing on the right of one spouse to treat his or her property as he or she wishes during marriage. The interests of one spouse in the property of the other have been substantially increased upon the dissolution of a marriage by divorce. We believe that, when a marriage is terminated by the death of one spouse, the rights of the surviving spouse should not be so restricted as they are by the rule in Kerwin v. Donaghy. It is neither equitable nor logical to extend to a divorced spouse greater rights in the assets of an inter vivos trust created and controlled by the other spouse than are extended to a spouse who remains married until the death of his or her spouse.

The rule we now favor would treat as part of "the estate of the deceased" for the purposes of G.L. c. 191, § 15, assets of an inter vivos trust created during the marriage by the deceased spouse over which he or she alone had a general power of appointment, exercisable by deed or by will. This objective test would involve no consideration of the motive or intention of the spouse in creating the trust. We would not need to engage in a determination of "whether the [spouse] has in good faith divested himself [or herself] of ownership of his [or her] property or has made an illusory transfer" (Newman v. Dore, 9 N.E.2d 966, 969 (N.Y. 1937)) or with the factual question whether the spouse "intended to surrender complete dominion over the property" (Staples v. King, 433 A.2d 407, 411 (Me. 1981)). Nor would we have to participate in the rather unsatisfactory process of determining whether the inter vivos trust was, on some standard, "colorable," "fraudulent," or "illusory."

What we have announced as a rule for the future hardly resolves all the problems that may arise. There may be a different rule if some or all of the trust assets were conveyed to such a trust by a third person. . . . If the surviving spouse assented to the

---

13. In early opinions, this court considered an intent to deny inheritance rights to be a ground for invalidating an inter vivos transfer, but in the first part of this century it abandoned that position. . . .

Opinions in this Commonwealth, and generally elsewhere, considering the rights of a surviving spouse to a share in assets transferred by the deceased spouse to an inter vivos trust have analyzed the question on grounds of public policy, as if establishing common law principles. These opinions have not relied in any degree on what the Legislature may have intended by granting a surviving spouse certain rights in the "estate" of a deceased spouse.

creation of the inter vivos trust, perhaps the rule we announce would not apply. We have not discussed which assets should be used to satisfy a surviving spouse's claim. We have not discussed the question whether a surviving spouse's interest in the intestate estate of a deceased spouse should reflect the value of assets held in an inter vivos trust created by the intestate spouse over which he or she had a general power of appointment. That situation and the one before us, however, do not seem readily distinguishable. . . . Nor have we dealt with other assets not passing by will, such as a trust created before the marriage or insurance policies over which a deceased spouse had control.

The question of the rights of a surviving spouse in the estate of a deceased spouse, using the word "estate" in its broad sense, is one that can best be handled by legislation. . . . But, until it is, the answers to these problems will "be determined in the usual way through the decisional process." Tucker v. Badoian, 384 N.E.2d 1195, 1202 (Mass. 1978) (Kaplan, J., concurring).

We affirm the judgment of the Probate Court dismissing the plaintiff's complaint. So ordered.

NOTES

1. Courts, Legislatures, and Making Elective Share Policy.   Why did the court apply its holding only prospectively to new trusts and existing trusts amended after the date of the opinion? Was there a reasonable reliance or other such interest that justified limiting the holding to prospective application?[14]

Did *Sullivan* fairly gloss the elective share statute in light of its purpose and the evolution of the revocable trust as a nonprobate will? In Bongaards v. Millen, 793 N.E.2d 335 (Mass. 2003), the Massachusetts court answered one of the several questions left open by *Sullivan*: Is trust property over which a decedent spouse had a general power of appointment, meaning a power to give to herself the trust property (see Chapter 12 at page 809), included in "the estate of the deceased" that is subject to the elective share if the trust was created by a third party? The court's answer was that "the trust property at issue here is . . . not subject to the plaintiff's elective share for the simple reason that the trust was created by a third party . . . and not by [the decedent spouse]." The court distinguished *Sullivan* as a limited gloss on the statute that "applies only to assets of a trust 'created during the marriage by the deceased spouse.'" The court continued:

> [T]here does not appear to be any ambiguity in the Legislature's use of the term "estate of the deceased" in G.L. c. 191, § 15. In context, "estate of the deceased" refers to the decedent's probate estate. . . .
>
> Regardless whether changing times and the modern array of possible will substitutes may make it advisable to expand the term beyond the mere probate estate, we are not at liberty to update statutes merely because, in our view, they no longer suffice to serve their intended purpose. . . . That the current version of the statute is woefully inadequate to satisfy modern notions of a decedent spouse's obligation to support the surviving spouse or modern notions of marital property does

---

14. *See* Gil J. Ghatan, The Incentive Problem with Prospective Overruling: A Critique of the Practice, 45 Real Prop. Tr. & Est. L.J. 179 (2010).

not authorize us to tinker with the statute's provisions in order to remedy those inadequacies. . . .

It could be argued that *Sullivan* already represents such a tinkering with the definition of "estate" for purposes of G.L. c. 191, § 15, and that ordinary principles of statutory construction should therefore not prevent us from continuing the process begun in *Sullivan*. However, that justification for a significant expansion of the term "estate" in G.L. c. 191, § 15, ignores the fact that *Sullivan* merely closed a loophole through which spouses had been able to evade § 15. As articulated in *Sullivan*, what was to remain part of the "estate" subject to the elective share was property that previously belonged to the deceased spouse. But for the spouse's artificially distancing the property from that "estate" by the creation of a trust while still, for all practical purposes, retaining absolute control over and use of the property, the property would have been part of the deceased spouse's probate, and hence the elective share, "estate." . . .

It is one thing for this court to plug loopholes to prevent a spouse's evasion of the elective share statute. It is quite another to expand the reach of the elective share statute itself and, by so doing, frustrate the intent of a third party who is a stranger to the marriage.

Is the *Bongaards* court's characterization of *Sullivan* fair? Did the *Sullivan* court, which referenced "significant changes since 1945 in public policy considerations," think it was merely closing a narrow loophole?

In *In re Estate of George*, 265 P.3d 222 (Wyo. 2011), the court held that a surviving spouse's elective share did not apply to property in a revocable trust created by the decedent spouse during the marriage. The court reasoned in a manner closer to *Bongaards* than to *Sullivan*: "Regardless of the many variations used in other states, until the Wyoming legislature adopts . . . the requirement that non-probate assets be added back to the probate estate for purposes of the elective share, the policy adopted by other states is largely irrelevant. . . . [T]his is a policy choice for the Wyoming legislature to consider, and either accept or reject."

2. Other Judicial Approaches. In *Sullivan*, the court rejected several tests applied in other states to determine which nonprobate transfers are subject to the surviving spouse's election.[15] The first, and most famous, is the *illusory transfer* test laid down by Newman v. Dore, 9 N.E.2d 966 (N.Y. 1937) (now superseded by statute, see page 535). In *Newman*, the court upheld a widow's claim that a revocable inter vivos trust established by her husband during their marriage was "illusory" and invalid.

Newman involved a second marriage, which is typical of the litigated cases (can you think of reasons why?).[16] The husband was 80 and his wife, his second, was in her 30s when they married. After four years of marriage, the wife sued for separation on the grounds that she could no longer abide her husband's perverted sexual habits. It is not clear what the octogenarian's alleged perversions were, though a newspaper story indicates that he had received monkey glands by surgical transplant. Indignant over

---

15. *See* Martin D. Begleiter, Grim Fairy Tales: Studies of Wicked Stepmothers, Poisoned Apples, and the Elective Share, 78 Alb. L. Rev. 521 (2015).

16. The classic study is William D. MacDonald, Fraud on the Widow's Share (1960).

his wife's allegations, the husband instructed his lawyer to disinherit her, and the lawyer came up with the idea of an inter vivos trust of all of the husband's property. The separation action was still pending at his death.[17]

After some years of confusion about the holding in *Newman*, courts held that an "illusory" revocable trust is a valid trust, but it counts as part of the decedent's assets subject to the elective share, so the trustee may have to contribute some of the trust property to make up the elective share. What kind of ownership rights retained by the decedent make a transfer illusory was left unclear in *Newman* and was little clarified in later cases. The key is said to be the amount of control retained by the decedent spouse. But how much is too much? Would it matter if these arrangements were made before rather than after marriage? Does the analysis depend on whether you adhere to the support theory or the partnership theory?

Some states adopted an *intent-to-defraud* test, as in In re Estate of Thompson, 434 S.W.3d 877 (Ark. 2014). In determining whether the decedent intended to defraud his surviving spouse of her elective share, some courts look for subjective intent. Others look for objective evidence of intent: the control retained by the transferor, the amount of time between the transfer and death, and the degree to which the surviving spouse is left without an interest in the decedent's property or other means of support.

Still other states consider whether the decedent had a *present donative intent* to transfer an interest in the property. This test focuses not on what the transferor retained, but on whether the transferor intended to make a present gift. Factors similar to those weighed in the intent-to-defraud test appear to be used in applying this test.

3. Elective Share, Revocable Trusts, and Choice of Law.   Either by statute or by judicial decision, in the majority of states a revocable trust created by the decedent spouse is included in determining the surviving spouse's elective share. But in some states, a revocable trust is not subject to the elective share.[18] Hence, if a married couple lives in a state that does not apply its own law to nondomiciliary sited property, it may be possible for one spouse to defeat the right of election of the other spouse by settling a revocable trust in one of the hold-out states.[19] Thus:

> *Case 4.* H and W, both 65 years of age, live in State Red. In State Red, a revocable trust created by the decedent is subject to the elective share. In State Blue, such a trust is not reachable by the surviving spouse. H sets up a revocable trust in State Blue, naming a State Blue bank as trustee. The trust instrument provides that the law of State Blue shall govern the trust. H transfers almost all his assets to the State Blue trustee of his revocable trust. H dies domiciled in State Red. Can W reach the assets in the trust in State Blue? *Compare* National Shawmut Bank of Boston v. Cumming, 91 N.E.2d 337 (Mass. 1950) (applying law of trustee's domicile to defeat elective share claim of spouse domiciled out of state), *with* In re Estate of Clark, 236

---

17. The details in this paragraph are drawn from Mark L. Ascher, Elias Clark, Grayson M.P. McCouch & Arthur W. Murphy, Cases and Materials on Gratuitous Transfers: Wills, Intestate Succession, Trusts, Gifts, Future Interests, and Estate and Gift Taxation 167 (6th ed. 2013).

18. *See* Jeffrey A. Schoenblum, Multistate Guide to Trusts and Trust Administration tbl. 1, q. 20 (2012).

19. *See* Cline, Pennell & Turnipseed, *supra* note 7, at A-32.

N.E.2d 152 (N.Y. 1968) (applying law of state where couple were domiciled, deeming it to have paramount interest).

UPC § 2-202(d) (1990, rev. 2008) provides that the law of the decedent's domicile governs the right to take an elective share of property located in another state.

(2) Statutory Reform

Dissatisfied with the vague tests laid down by courts, many states enacted statutes providing objective criteria for determining which nonprobate transfers are subject to the elective share. For the most part, these statutes include a list of nonprobate transfers that are added to the probate estate to constitute an *augmented estate* against which the surviving spouse's elective share is applied. The leading such statute, which was taken as a model for the 1969 UPC (see page 540), was adopted by New York in 1965. It replaced the illusory transfer test of Newman v. Dore, page 533, with a statutory scheme that subjects to the elective share the particular nonprobate transfers listed in the statute. Although an improvement on traditional statutes that are based on just the probate estate, such as the statute at issue in *Sullivan*, the question still arises whether a court should include in the elective share a type of nonprobate transfer not specifically mentioned in the statute.

In re Estate of Myers
825 N.W.2d 1 (Iowa 2012)

WATERMAN, J. This appeal presents a question of first impression: whether a surviving spouse's elective share, as defined in Iowa Code section 633.238 (Supp. 2009), includes pay-on-death (POD) assets. The probate court ruled that three of Karen Myers's assets, a checking account, certificate of deposit, and an annuity, all payable on her death to her daughters, should be included in the elective share of her surviving spouse, Howard Myers.

The assignees of Howard's elective share (assignees) argue the elective share should include POD assets under Sieh v. Sieh, 713 N.W.2d 194, 198 (Iowa 2006), which held the elective share includes assets in a revocable trust. The executor argues the general assembly, by amending section 633.238 in 2009, expressly limited the surviving spouse's elective share to the four categories of assets listed in the statute, none of which include POD assets. The probate court . . . ruled against the executor by comparing Karen's POD assets to the revocable trust at issue in *Sieh*. This interpretation would ensure the surviving spouse's elective share rights are not defeated through the use of nonprobate assets, such as POD accounts and annuities.

For the reasons explained below, we conclude the 2009 amendment . . . trumps *Sieh*. The controlling statutory language omits POD assets from the surviving spouse's elective share. Accordingly, we reverse the ruling of the probate court. . . .

BACKGROUND FACTS AND PROCEEDINGS

Karen died on November 2, 2009, survived by her spouse, Howard. Rex Picken, Karen's brother and the executor of her estate, [offered] Karen's will [for] probate on

Statement of the Iowa Attorney General on Surrender of Law License and Guilty Plea by Howard Myers

Howard Myers, a Webster City attorney, entered guilty pleas Tuesday to three counts of first-degree theft (class C felonies), and one count of second-degree theft (a class D felony). Myers, age 66, asked the court to be sentenced immediately.

District Court Judge Ronald Schechtman, Chief Judge of the 2nd Judicial District, sentenced Myers to three terms of up to ten years in prison for each of the three first-degree theft convictions, and up to five years in prison for the second-degree theft conviction. Schechtman ordered that the terms be served concurrently. It is expected that Myers will begin serving his sentence after a restitution hearing on November 5.

Schechtman ordered Myers to pay a fine of $24,050. Schechtman also ordered Myers to pay restitution to his victims. The final amount of restitution still is to be determined, but is expected to exceed $500,000.

Myers faced criminal charges made by the Attorney General's Office alleging theft from a 92-year-old client over whom Myers had power of attorney and who resides in a nursing home in Story City, and from the Ramona Russell and Helen Anderson trusts. The beneficiary of one of the trusts is Calvary Baptist Church of Webster City.

Myers also agreed to surrender his law license at the time he entered his plea. The plea and sentence were entered yesterday in Hamilton County District Court in Webster City.

The Attorney General's Office was asked by the Hamilton County Attorney to serve in the role of prosecutor to avoid a potential conflict of interest.

Source: Iowa Attorney Gen. (Oct. 23, 2002).

November 20. At the time of her death, Karen owned a number of assets, either jointly or individually, which were valued at $479,989.29. Howard became the sole owner of real estate and other property he and Karen owned as joint tenants with right of survivorship. Karen left no other property to Howard in her will, aside from some household furnishings. Karen bequeathed the rest of her property to her daughters and stepson.[20] The assets at issue in this appeal are a checking account and certificate of deposit at the First Federal Savings Bank valued at $91,085.71 and an annuity with River Resource Funds valued at $18,978.80. All three of these assets were accompanied by beneficiary designations that made them payable on death to Karen's daughters.

Howard filed for an elective share on June 30, 2010. . . . On February 9, 2011, Howard assigned his interest in Karen's estate, including his right to an elective share, to the heirs of DeLillian Peterson, the Ramona Russell Trust, and the Helen B. Anderson Trust. Howard, a former attorney who had surrendered his law license, assigned his interest in Karen's estate to satisfy a restitution judgment against him in a criminal action. Specifically, Howard had been convicted of second- and third-degree felony theft for stealing client funds.

On May 6, the assignees filed an application to set off the surviving spouse's share. The assignees requested that the probate court determine, as an initial matter, whether the checking account, certificate of deposit, and annuity should be included in Howard's elective share. The probate court relied on our 2006 decision in *Sieh*. There, we concluded that assets in a revocable trust were to be included in the surviving spouse's elective share, even though they were not explicitly mentioned in section 633.238 at

---

20. Notice the reference to a *step*son. This was a second marriage for both Howard and Karen. — Eds.

that time. 713 N.W.2d at 198. In reaching that conclusion, we emphasized the fact that "the decedent had complete control over the trust assets at all times prior to his death." Similarly, the probate court emphasized that Karen retained control over the POD assets before her death and, thus, concluded that these assets, like the assets of a revocable trust, should be included in Howard's elective share. This issue has divided the trial courts of our state. . . .

ANALYSIS

. . . In *Sieh*, Mary Jane Sieh, the surviving spouse of Edward Sieh, argued that she should receive, as part of her elective share, assets of a revocable *inter vivos* trust created by Edward several years before their marriage. The beneficiaries of this trust, Edward's children, argued that the revocable trust should not be included in Mary Jane's elective share, and the probate court agreed. We reversed, emphasizing that,

> because Edward had full control of the assets of the inter vivos trust at the time of his death, including the power to revoke the trust, the trust assets were property possessed by the decedent during the marriage and thus subject to the spouse's statutory share under section 633.238.

Id. at 195.

We reached this conclusion even though revocable trusts were not mentioned in section 633.238 at that time. Section 633.238 lists the assets that are to be included in the surviving spouse's elective share. . . . We reached this conclusion by relying on the Restatement (Third) of Property:

> Although property owned or owned in substance by the decedent immediately before death that passed outside of probate at the decedent's death is not part of the decedent's probate estate, such property is owned in substance by the decedent through various powers or rights, *such as the power to revoke, withdraw, invade, or sever,* or to appoint the decedent or the decedent's estate as beneficiary. Consequently, for purposes of calculating the amount of the [spouse's] elective share the value of property owned or owned in substance by the decedent immediately before death that passed outside of probate at the decedent's death to donees other than the surviving spouse is counted as part of the decedent's "estate." The decedent's motive in creating, exercising or not exercising any of these powers is irrelevant.

Id. at 197 (quoting Restatement (Third) of Property: Wills and Other Donative Transfers § 9.1 cmt. j (2003) (emphasis added)). Based on this Restatement provision, we concluded the fact Edward "had complete control over the trust assets at all times prior to his death . . . would allow the assets in the revocable trust to be included in the statutory share of Edward's spouse electing against the will." Id. at 198.

The assignees understandably argue *Sieh* should be read broadly to sweep into section 633.238 property within the decedent's control at the time of her death, such as the POD assets at issue here. The probate court agreed. We reach the opposite conclusion, based on the controlling statutory language as amended after *Sieh*. . . .

The general assembly amended section 633.238 in 2009. This amendment, effective July 1, 2009, "appl[ies] to estates of decedents and revocable trusts of settlors dying on or after" that date. 2009 Iowa Acts ch. 52, § 14(3). Karen died in November of 2009, so the statute applies as amended.

By this amendment, the legislature added "limited to" to section 633.238(1), with the result that section 633.238 now reads:

> 1. The elective share of the surviving spouse shall be *limited to* all of the following:
>
>   *a.* One-third in value of all the legal or equitable estates in real property possessed by the decedent at any time during the marriage which have not been sold on execution or other judicial sale, and to which the surviving spouse has made no express written relinquishment of right.
>
>   *b.* All personal property that, at the time of death, was in the hands of the decedent as the head of a family, exempt from execution.
>
>   *c.* One-third of all personal property of the decedent that is not necessary for the payment of debts and charges.
>
>   *d.* One-third in value of the property held in trust not necessary for the payment of debts and charges over which the decedent was a grantor and retained at the time of death the power to alter, amend, or revoke the trust, or over which the decedent waived or rescinded any such power within one year of the date of death, and to which the surviving spouse has not made any express written relinquishment.
>
> 2. The elective share described in this section shall be in lieu of any property the spouse would otherwise receive under the last will and testament of the decedent, through intestacy, or under the terms of a revocable trust.

Iowa Code § 633.238 (Supp. 2009) (emphasis added).

When interpreting a statute that has been amended, "we may consider the previous state of the law, circumstances surrounding the statute's enactment, and the text both before and after the amendment." Davis v. State, 682 N.W.2d 58, 61 (Iowa 2004). We presume that the law has been changed if the legislature added or deleted words from the statute, "unless the remaining language amounts to the same thing." Id. "When interpreting amendments, we will assume that the amendment sought to accomplish some purpose and was not a futile exercise." Id.

The postamendment version . . . states that "[t]he elective share of the surviving spouse *shall be limited to* all of the following." Iowa Code § 633.238 (emphasis added). It is clear that the legislature, by this language, intended to limit the property that would be included in the surviving spouse's elective share to the four categories of property specifically identified in the statute. This interpretation is consistent with the general assembly's explanation accompanying the House version of the bill. The explanation states, "The bill limits the elective share of the surviving spouse who elects to take against a decedent's will to the elective share portions contained in Code section 633.238 and does not include nonprobate or nontrust assets." H.F. 677, 83rd G.A., 1st Sess., explanation (Iowa 2009). We conclude the 2009 amendment legislatively abrogated *Sieh* in part. Under the controlling language of the amendment, the elective share is limited to those assets specifically enumerated . . . and cannot be judicially expanded.

The assignees did not assert in probate court or in their appellate brief that the POD assets fall into any of the four categories in section 633.238(1). The assignees, however, belatedly contended for the first time during oral argument to our court that these assets are included in the elective share under section 633.238(1)(c) as "personal property of the decedent." . . .

POD accounts, such as the checking and certificate of deposit accounts here, and annuities are nonprobate assets. Nonprobate assets are interests in property that pass outside of the decedent's probate estate to a designated beneficiary upon the decedent's death. Although these assets are the personal property of the grantor *before* death, they become the personal property of the designated beneficiaries upon the grantor's death pursuant to a contract between the grantor and the administrator of the account.

Section 633.238(1)(c) includes "[o]ne-third of all personal property of the decedent that is not necessary for the payment of debts and charges" in the surviving spouse's elective share. The legislative history accompanying the 2009 amendment confirms that this section is limited to personal property in the decedent's probate estate. Specifically, the explanation section accompanying that amendment states the surviving spouse's elective share is limited to those categories of property explicitly mentioned in section 633.238(1) and that it "does not include nonprobate . . . assets." H.F. 677, 83rd G.A., 1st Sess., explanation (Iowa 2009).

The assignees make a strong public policy argument that elective share rights may be defeated by the use of POD assets if we interpret section 633.238 to omit them. See Kurtz on Iowa Estates: Intestacy, Wills, and Estate Administration § 8.9 (3d ed. 1995) ("[T]he policies underlying elective share legislation could easily be defeated if the property owning spouse could transfer a substantial portion of her personal property during life, reduce the size of her personal estate and minimize or eliminate the value of property available to a spouse who elects against the will."). The assignees' policy argument is properly directed to the legislature. The Iowa legislature chose to include revocable trusts in the elective share under section 633.238(1)(d). We conclude further legislation would be required to include POD assets in the elective share.

Based on the plain meaning of the operative statutory language as amended in 2009, we hold that only the assets specifically enumerated in section 633.238 may be included in the surviving spouse's elective share. POD accounts and annuities are not included under section 633.238. We overrule *Sieh* to the extent it is inconsistent with this opinion. Because Karen's POD assets should not be included in Howard's elective share, we reverse the ruling of the probate court and remand the case for recalculation of payments owed to the assignees. . . .

CONCLUSION

For these reasons, the probate court erred by including Karen's POD assets in Howard's elective share. The probate court order is reversed and the case remanded for further proceedings consistent with this opinion.

Reversed and remanded.

NOTES

1. Excluding POD Contracts. The court in *Myers* took the view that it could not gloss the elective share statute to include POD contracts. Can this decision be reconciled with the decision of the Massachusetts court in *Sullivan*? Why would a leg-islature include revocable trusts but exclude POD contracts from the elective share? Is there a sound policy basis for this distinction? After *Myers*, what advice would you give a married client in Iowa who wanted to disinherit her spouse?

2. Creditors and Medicaid.   In *Myers*, the real parties in interest were creditors of Howard, to whom he had assigned his elective share rights, and Karen's daughters from her prior marriage, the POD beneficiaries of the nonprobate transfers at issue. In most states, an insolvent surviving spouse cannot be compelled by an ordinary creditor to take his elective share. However, the value of the elective share will be counted toward the surviving spouse's available resources in determining eligibility for Medicaid (see page 724). Hence, in most cases involving an election by a represen-tative for an incompetent surviving spouse (page 527), the need to preserve benefits eligibility is the dominant consideration.[21]

3. Delaware Absorbs the Federal Tax Law into the Elective Share.   Delaware takes an elegant approach to solving the problem of determining which nonprobate transfers are subject to the elective share. It defines the property subject to the elective share as all property includible in the decedent's gross estate under the federal estate tax, whether or not an estate tax return is filed. If a nonprobate transfer is taxable under federal law at death (as are revocable trusts, POD contracts, and joint tenancies), it is subject to the surviving spouse's elective share.[22] The Delaware statute has the advantage of incorporating into elective share law the inclusion principles of federal estate tax law, which focus on substance over form and evolved out of long experience with dec-edents trying to avoid the tax by lifetime and nonprobate transfers. We consider what property is includible in the gross estate in Chapter 15 at page 945.

e. The Uniform Probate Code

The drafters of the UPC embraced the concept of the New York statute of applying the elective share to an *augmented estate* that includes both the probate estate and certain nonprobate transfers (see page 535). However, the UPC also includes several innova-tions, including: (1) more broadly worded provisions that bring into the augmented estate any transfer in which the decedent spouse retains a right to possession or income (the federal tax code includes a similar rule for the estate tax); (2) attention to lifetime transfers made to the surviving spouse and the surviving spouse's own wealth, in order to achieve a fairer allocation between the spouses; and (3) with the 1990 version, atten-tion to the length of the marriage, increasing the share of a surviving spouse in a long marriage and decreasing the share in a short marriage.

(1) The 1969 Uniform Probate Code.   Under the 1969 UPC, the surviving spouse is entitled to an elective share of one-third of the augmented estate. Under UPC § 2-202 (1969), the augmented estate includes the probate estate plus the following

---

21. *See* Julia Belian, Medicaid, Elective Shares, and the Ghosts of Tenures Past, 38 Creighton L. Rev. 1111 (2005).

22. *See* Del. Code Ann. tit. 12, § 902 (2016).

nonprobate and inter vivos transfers made without consideration at any time *during the marriage*:

   a. a transfer in which the decedent retains the right to possession or income from the property;

   b. a transfer that the decedent can revoke or that permits the decedent to invade or dispose of the principal for his own benefit;

   c. a transfer in joint tenancy with someone other than the spouse;

   d. a transfer made within two years before death exceeding $3,000 per donee per year ($3,000 was, at the time, the maximum amount exempt from the federal gift tax under the annual exclusion; it is now $14,000 (see page 934)); and

   e. property given to the surviving spouse during life, including a life estate in a trust, and property received by the spouse at death derived from the decedent, such as life insurance and pensions.

The purpose of augmenting the probate estate with items (a) through (d) was, in the words of the comment, "to prevent the owner of wealth from making arrangements which transmit his property to others by means other than probate deliberately to defeat the right of the surviving spouse to a share." What result in *Sullivan*, *Bongaards*, and *Myers* under these provisions? Notice the limitation to transfers made during the marriage. A premarital transfer, including to a revocable trust created before the marriage, is not included in the augmented estate.[23]

The purpose of including in the augmented estate item (e), property given to the surviving spouse by the decedent during life, was to prevent a spouse who has been well provided for by lifetime or nonprobate transfers from electing against the will and claiming more than a fair share. The 1969 UPC also includes testamentary gifts to the spouse in the augmented estate, crediting them against the elective share to which the surviving spouse is entitled. Under UPC § 2-207 (1969), to the extent property in the augmented estate passes to the surviving spouse, that property is applied first in satisfaction of the elective share. If this is not enough, the remaining property of the augmented estate is applied, with liability apportioned pro rata among the other recipients.

The augmented estate system of the 1969 UPC was adopted and remains in effect in many states. In addition, the concept of augmenting the probate estate with transfers during marriage over which the decedent continued to have control influenced other states in revising their elective-share systems, even if they did not adopt the UPC.

(2) The 1990 Uniform Probate Code and 2008 Amendments.   The Uniform Law Commission further redesigned the UPC elective share in 1990. The purpose of the revisions was to achieve results even closer to those of a community property system.[24] As revised, the UPC tries to approximate the community property system by

---

23. *Compare* In re Estate of Chrisp, 759 N.W.2d 87 (Neb. 2009) (premarital revocable trust not included in augmented estate), *with* In re Estate of Fries, 782 N.W.2d 596 (Neb. 2010) (transfers of land during marriage to children of prior marriage, with retained right to possession or income, included in augmented estate).

24. *See, e.g.,* Stephanie J. Willbanks, Parting Is Such Sweet Sorrow, But Does It Have to Be So Complicated? Transmission of Property at Death in Vermont, 29 Vt. L. Rev. 895 (2005); Angela M.

increasing the percentage of the estate subject to the elective share based on the length of the marriage. The longer the marriage, the greater the percentage of the couple's property that is assumed to be marital.

The 1990 UPC also adds to the augmented estate many transfers made *before* marriage, as well as transfers during marriage, if the decedent retained substantial control over the property. It also includes property or powers received from others. In this respect, the 1990 UPC resembles the Internal Revenue Code, which subjects to estate taxation property transferred by the decedent during life over which the decedent retained substantial control as well as property subject to a general power of appointment given to the decedent by another.

The purpose of the augmented estate under the 1990 UPC is no longer, as under the 1969 UPC, to protect against "fraud on the widow's share," but rather "to bring elective-share law into line with the partnership theory of marriage," tempered by a minimum support obligation in the form of a $50,000 supplemental elective share amount:

> The general effect of implementing the partnership theory in elective-share law is to increase the entitlement of a surviving spouse in a long-term marriage in cases in which the marital assets were disproportionately titled in the decedent's name; and to decrease or even eliminate the entitlement of a surviving spouse in a long-term marriage in cases in which the marital assets were more or less equally titled or disproportionately titled in the surviving spouse's name. A further general effect is to decrease or even eliminate the entitlement of a surviving spouse in a short-term, later-in-life marriage (typically a post-widowhood remarriage) in which neither spouse contributed much, if anything, to the acquisition of the other's wealth, except that a special supplemental elective-share amount is provided in cases in which the surviving spouse would otherwise be left without sufficient funds for support.[25]

In 2008, the Uniform Law Commission made further revisions to the UPC elective share, mainly to the mechanics. As revised, the UPC provides for an equal split of marital property, but the proportion of each spouse's property that is deemed marital, includible in the augmented estate, is phased in based on the length of the marriage. The supplemental elective share amount was also increased to $75,000 and made subject to the inflation adjustment rules of UPC § 1-109 (2008).

UPC § 2-202 (1990, rev. 2008) provides that the elective share of a surviving spouse of a domiciliary decedent is "50 percent of the value of the marital-property portion of the augmented estate." The *augmented estate* is defined by § 2-203(a) to include the sum of the decedent's net probate estate (§ 2-204), plus the decedent's nonprobate transfers to others (§ 2-205), plus the decedent's nonprobate transfers to the surviving spouse (§ 2-206), plus the surviving spouse's property and nonprobate transfers to others (§ 2-207). The *marital-property portion* of the augmented estate is computed by

---

Vallario, Spousal Election: Suggested Equitable Reform for the Division of Property at Death, 52 Cath. U. L. Rev. 519 (2003); Alan Newman, Incorporating the Partnership Theory of Marriage into Elective-Share Law: The Approximation System of the Uniform Probate Code and the Deferred-Community-Property Alternative, 49 Emory L.J. 487 (2000).

25. UPC Art. II, Part 2, gen. cmt. (1990, rev. 2008).

multiplying the augmented estate by a percentage that is determined by the length of the marriage under § 2-203(b):

If the Decedent and the Spouse Were Married to Each Other	The Percentage Is
Less than 1 year	3%
1 year but less than 2 years	6%
2 years but less than 3 years	12%
3 years but less than 4 years	18%
4 years but less than 5 years	24%
5 years but less than 6 years	30%
6 years but less than 7 years	36%
7 years but less than 8 years	42%
8 years but less than 9 years	48%
9 years but less than 10 years	54%
10 years but less than 11 years	60%
11 years but less than 12 years	68%
12 years but less than 13 years	76%
13 years but less than 14 years	84%
14 years but less than 15 years	92%
15 years or more	100%

The elective share amount is half of the resulting marital-property portion of the augmented estate (§ 2-202). In funding the elective share, the UPC credits the surviving spouse with nonprobate transfers to the surviving spouse and marital assets that are already owned by the surviving spouse (§ 2-209). Thus:

Case 5. *H* and *W* have been married for 18 years. Under UPC §§ 2-202 and 2-203, 100 percent of the augmented estate is marital property subject to the surviving spouse's elective share of 50 percent. *H*'s augmented estate consists of:

$ 100,000	probate estate, devised to *A*
$ 150,000	nonprobate transfers to other beneficiaries
$ 25,000	life insurance payable to *W*[26]
$ 50,000	*H*'s half interest in joint tenancy held with *W*
$ 75,000	*W*'s property
$ 50,000	*W*'s half interest in the joint tenancy
$ 450,000	Total Augmented Estate

---

26. Should life insurance owned by the decedent be subject to the elective share? The 1969 UPC exempted it. The 1990 UPC includes it, a decision left undisturbed by the 2008 amendments. The life insurance industry has fought this, just as it has fought allowing the policy beneficiary to be changed by will (see page 477). What is the reason for the opposition?

W has an elective share of 50 percent of the whole, or $225,000. Since *W* already owns $75,000 in her own name, this amount is credited against her elective share, reducing it to $150,000. Also credited against the elective share are $25,000 in life insurance received by *W*, $50,000 for *H*'s half of the joint tenancy (which *W* takes by operation of law), and $50,000 for *W*'s half of the joint tenancy. Thus, the amount of *W*'s elective share payable to *W* out of *H*'s probate estate and nonprobate transfers is $25,000.

Although the drafters wanted the UPC elective share to produce results similar to that of a community property system, some differences remain. The 1990 UPC augmented estate, even as revised in 2008, includes all property of both spouses, and not only property acquired from earnings during the marriage. Community property, owned equally by the spouses, includes only earnings and acquisitions from earnings during the marriage. Community property does not include property brought to the marriage or acquired by gift or inheritance (so long as it is kept separate). The decedent spouse can dispose of his separate property any way he likes; the surviving spouse has no claim to it.

The drafters justified including all property of the spouses in the augmented estate on the grounds that it avoids problems of classifying property as community (earned) or separate, particularly if the couple has mixed their property. On the other hand, by including all property of the spouses in the elective share, the UPC requires the spouses to agree for property acquired before marriage or by inheritance to be separate at death.

f. Waiver by Premarital or Postnuptial Agreement

The right of election allows a surviving spouse to take a statutory share in spite of the will of the decedent spouse. As against the decedent spouse, the elective share is a policy-based substantive limit on freedom of disposition. But the surviving spouse need not make an election, and a spouse can waive her right to an elective share in advance. Typically, such a waiver occurs in a *premarital agreement*, also called a *prenuptial* or *antenuptial agreement*. Marriages that do not end by divorce will be brought to an end by death. Premarital agreements are therefore as much a part of trusts and estates practice as they are a part of matrimonial practice.

All separate property states enforce a waiver of the right of election by premarital agreement, and almost all also enforce a waiver agreed to during the marriage — a *postnuptial marital agreement*.[27] Yet there remains concern that a premarital or postnuptial agreement may not reflect an arm's-length bargain, or that even if the agreement was fully dickered, that its terms might be inequitable owing to the special nature of the relationship of the parties.

In just over half the states, the enforceability of a premarital agreement is governed by the Uniform Premarital Agreement Act (UPAA) (Unif. Law Comm'n 1983). The

---

27. *See* Schoenblum, *supra* note 7, at tbl. 6.04.

"In lieu of a pre-nup we decided just to label everything."

Barbara Smaller/The New Yorker Collection/The Cartoon Bank

UPAA overrides the presumption of fraud that some courts had attached to a pre-marital agreement if, in the court's view, the agreement made inadequate provision for a spouse in light of the other spouse's wealth. Under the UPAA, the party opposing enforcement must prove that the agreement either (1) was not voluntary, or (2) was unconscionable when executed and the party opposing enforcement did not have fair and reasonable disclosure of the other party's property and finances.[28] It is also a good practice for each spouse to have independent counsel, which is required in some states.

The Uniform Law Commission has since promulgated the Uniform Premarital and Marital Agreement Act (UPMAA) (Unif. Law Comm'n 2012), which supersedes the UPAA. The UPMAA expressly validates postnuptial marital agreements, called simply "marital agreements," and it applies the same rules for the enforceability of both premarital and marital agreements.[29]

---

28. *See* J. Thomas Oldham, With All My Worldly Goods I Thee Endow, or Maybe Not: A Reevaluation of the Uniform Premarital Agreement Act After Three Decades, 19 Duke J. Gender L. & Pol'y 83 (2011).

29. *See* Barbara A. Atwood & Brian H. Bix, A New Uniform Law for Premarital and Marital Agreements, 46 Fam. L.Q. 313 (2012); J. Thomas Oldham, Would Enactment of the Uniform Premarital and Marital Agreement Act in All Fifty States Change U.S. Law Regarding Premarital Agreements?, 46 Fam. L.Q. 367 (2012); *see also* Elizabeth R. Carter, Rethinking Premarital Agreements: A Collaborative Approach, 46 N.M. L. Rev. 354 (2016); Judith T. Younger, Lovers' Contracts in the Courts: Forsaking the Minimum Decencies, 13 Wm. & Mary J. Women & L. 349 (2007).

Uniform Premarital and Marital Agreement Act (Unif. Law Comm'n 2012)

§ 9. Enforcement

(a) A premarital agreement or marital agreement is unenforceable if a party against whom enforcement is sought proves:

(1) the party's consent to the agreement was involuntary or the result of duress;

(2) the party did not have access to independent legal representation under subsection (b);

(3) unless the party had independent legal representation at the time the agreement was signed, the agreement did not include a notice of waiver of rights under subsection (c) or an explanation in plain language of the marital rights or obligations being modified or waived by the agreement; or

(4) before signing the agreement, the party did not receive adequate financial disclosure under subsection (d).

(b) A party has access to independent legal representation if:

(1) before signing a premarital or marital agreement, the party has a reasonable time to:

(A) decide whether to retain a lawyer to provide independent legal representation; and

(B) locate a lawyer to provide independent legal representation, obtain the lawyer's advice, and consider the advice provided; and

(2) the other party is represented by a lawyer and the party has the financial ability to retain a lawyer or the other party agrees to pay the reasonable fees and expenses of independent legal representation.

(c) A notice of waiver of rights under this section requires language, conspicuously displayed, substantially similar to the following, as applicable to the premarital agreement or marital agreement:

"If you sign this agreement, you may be:

Giving up your right to be supported by the person you are marrying or to whom you are married.

Giving up your right to ownership or control of money and property.

Agreeing to pay bills and debts of the person you are marrying or to whom you are married.

Giving up your right to money and property if your marriage ends or the person to whom you are married dies.

Giving up your right to have your legal fees paid."

(d) A party has adequate financial disclosure under this section if the party:

(1) receives a reasonably accurate description and good-faith estimate of value of the property, liabilities, and income of the other party;

(2) expressly waives, in a separate signed record, the right to financial disclosure beyond the disclosure provided; or

(3) has adequate knowledge or a reasonable basis for having adequate knowledge of the information described in paragraph (1).

(e) If a premarital agreement or marital agreement modifies or eliminates spousal support and the modification or elimination causes a party to the agreement to be eligible for support under a program of public assistance at the time of separation or marital dissolution, a court, on request of that party, may require the other party to provide support to the extent necessary to avoid that eligibility.

(f) A court may refuse to enforce a term of a premarital agreement or marital agreement if, in the context of the agreement taken as a whole[:]

[(1)] the term was unconscionable at the time of signing[; or

(2) enforcement of the term would result in substantial hardship for a party because of a material change in circumstances arising after the agreement was signed].

(g) The court shall decide a question of unconscionability [or substantial hardship] under subsection (f) as a matter of law.

NOTES

1. Warnings and Independent Counsel. Some of the standards for enforcement stated in the UPMAA, such as the emphasis on independent counsel in § 9(a)(2)-(3) and the elaboration of what this means in § 9(b), reflect the evolution of practice norms and the law in some states since promulgation of the UPAA.[30] Others, such as the particular safe harbor disclosure in § 9(c), are more innovative. Do you think the safe harbor disclosure is useful? Do you think it is enough of a warning? Too much of a warning?

In In re Estate of Cassidy, 356 S.W.3d 339 (Mo. App. 2011), on the morning of their wedding day, *H* presented *W* with a premarital agreement prepared by his lawyer. The agreement recited, falsely, that both parties had consulted with independent counsel. In fact, *H* told *W* that she did not need a lawyer, and anyway there was no time for her to consult with one or even for her to study the agreement, which *H* told *W* was "just protocol." *W* signed the agreement, and then she and *H* were married. At *H*'s death, the court refused to enforce the waiver of *W*'s right of election on grounds of fraud and overreaching. There had not been full disclosure to *W* of the rights she was waiving and the nature and value of *H*'s property.

Barry Bonds
Craig Fuji/AP photo

How much protection is provided by access to independent counsel? In 1988, Barry Bonds, the current holder of Major League Baseball's single-season records for home runs, walks, on-base percentage, and slugging percentage, took his fiancée, Susann ("Sun") Margreth, to execute a premarital agreement just before they caught a plane to Las Vegas to be married. The agreement, which waived Sun's rights to Barry's current and future property, was explained to Sun by Barry's lawyers. Sun did not have independent counsel. She later claimed that her English skills were

---

30. *See, e.g.,* Owen v. Owen, 759 S.E.2d 468 (W. Va. 2014).

limited (she was born in Sweden). After having two children together, Barry and Sun separated in 1994. Sun contested the premarital agreement. In In re Marriage of Bonds, 5 P.3d 815 (Cal. 2000), the California Supreme Court held that the lack of independent counsel did not render Sun's waiver involuntary. The following year, the California legislature amended its enactment of the UPAA to require independent counsel or a written, knowing waiver, and seven days' advance notice.[31]

2. A Second Look?   The bracketed provision of UPMAA § 9(f)(2) authorizes a court to refuse enforcement of a term in a premarital or marital agreement that was executed in accordance with the rules of § 9(a) if the term would "result in substantial hardship . . . because of a material change in circumstances arising after the agreement was signed." This provision reflects current law in a substantial minority of states, albeit as applied to divorce.[32] We are aware of no reported appellate decision involving a second look at a waiver of the right of election. Instead, most of the litigation concerns the adequacy of financial disclosure, as in the next case.

Reece v. Elliott
208 S.W.3d 419 (Tenn. App. 2006)

FRANKS, J. Plaintiff's Declaratory Judgment suit to declare the antenuptial agreement invalid was dismissed by the Trial Court which held the agreement enforceable. On appeal, we affirm.

Plaintiff, widow of Eugene Reece, filed this declaratory judgment action against Linda Elliott and Diane Dempsey, Individually and as Co-Executrixes of the Estate of Eugene Reece.

Plaintiff stated that she was the surviving widow of Eugene Reece, that they had married on December 4, 1999, and Reece died intestate on July 5, 2003. Contemporaneously with the filing of this action, plaintiff applied for statutory benefits as surviving widow and attached a copy of the antenuptial agreement dated November 29, 1999. She sought a declaration regarding the rights and liabilities of the parties, and also sought rescission of the document based upon her late husband's failure to make a full disclosure regarding his assets and financial condition.

The Agreement attached states that Mr. Reece and petitioner had an interest in real and personal property identified in the attached lists, and that the property listed would be considered the separate property of each. The document further states that each party had children of prior marriages, and that each party desired to provide for his/her children from previous marriages by maintaining separate property and relinquishing marital property rights in the other's property. The document also states that each party recognized his/her right to dissent from the will of the other, and that each party waived that right as to said separate property. The parties affirmed in the

---

31. *See* Cal. Fam. Code § 1615(c) (2016). In In re Estate of Will, 88 Cal. Rptr. 3d 502 (App. 2009), the court held that the Family Code notice rules do not apply to waiver of spousal rights at death, which is instead governed by Cal. Prob. Code §§ 140-47 (2016) (requiring disclosure and in some circumstances independent counsel).

32. *See, e.g.,* Kelcourse v. Kelcourse, 23 N.E.3d 124 (Mass. App. 2015).

III.

WAIVER OF RIGHT TO DISSENT

Each party acknowledges by the signing of this AGREEMENT that they recognize their right of dissent from the Will of the other after their marriage pursuant to Tennessee Code Annotated §31-4-101, et seq., and particularly that the aforementioned statutes entitle them to a one-third (1/3) share of the other's estate. Each party agrees that he or she shall waive and claim no interest, either under the aforementioned statutes or otherwise, in any separate property of the other party other than that which may be left to him or her by that spouse's Will or by contract or by gift.

IV.

WAIVER OF RIGHT TO INTESTATE SUCCESSION

Each party acknowledges by the signing of this AGREEMENT that he or she shall waive and claim no interest, either under statute or otherwise, in any separate property, as defined

The waiver of the right of election at issue in *Reece*

document they had each consulted with and had the opportunity to consult with counsel, that they understood the full import of the document, and that a full disclosure of assets had been made.

Exhibit A to the document lists the separate property of Mr. Reece, and includes a residence in Ohio, its contents, and three vacant lots there. It also includes 230 acres in Morgan County, 1687 shares of JH Routh Packing Company stock, a promissory note due from Routh, various automobiles and equipment, a brokerage account at Fidelity, bank accounts at Citizens Bank in Tennessee and Ohio, and school bonds. Exhibit B is a list of separate property of petitioner, and it lists a residence in Knoxville and the contents thereof, a Grand Cherokee Laredo, a brokerage account at First Tennessee, an IRA, U.S. savings bonds, and a savings account and CD at First Tennessee. Values are not listed for every item.

In the defendants' Answer, they relied on the antenuptial agreement, and the defenses of estoppel, laches, release and waiver. During the trial, plaintiff testified that attorney James Brooks prepared the antenuptial agreement and she only met him when she picked it up. She testified that she consulted with an attorney, Debra Graham, who read over the document. She testified that the list of her property was prepared by her and then taken to Mr. Brooks to be typed up and attached to the agreement. She testified that Mr. Reece told her he had worked as a truck driver for Routh Packing Company, and he owned stock in the company. She testified the agreement set forth a number of shares of stock and that when she read the agreement, she saw his list of property, and saw that Routh Packing owed him $357,000.00. She testified that she fully understood those items would not belong to her in the event of his death, and that she would have no interest in his separate property. She went over the appropriate list

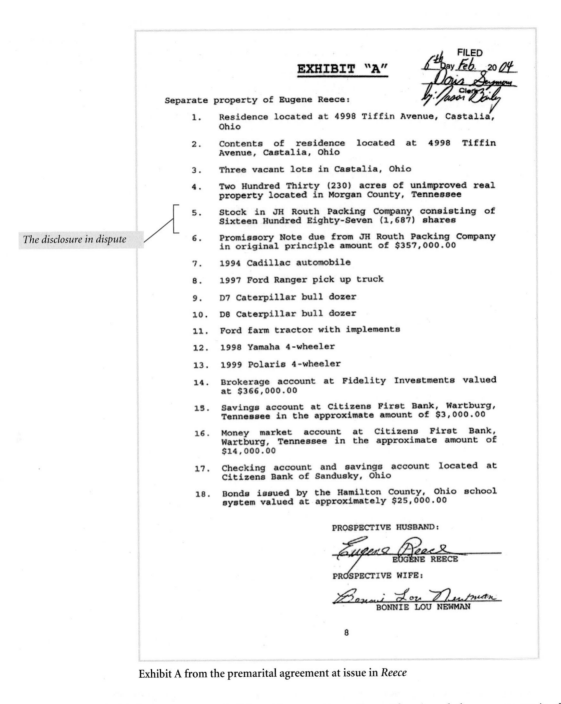

Exhibit A from the premarital agreement at issue in *Reece*

with her attorney and did not have any questions. She signed the agreement in the attorney's office, and the attorney's staff notarized her signature.

She further testified that she was not aware of any items of property that Reece failed to disclose, and that it did not matter if Reece owned 87 shares of stock or 1,687 shares, they were his. She said she did not know what she would have done if she had known the stock was worth a lot of money. She acknowledged that she did not discuss with her attorney the need to find out what the stock was worth, and that she did not know what the stock was worth in 1999. She elaborated that when she met with her attorney she did not consider having the attorney find out what the husband's value in Routh Packing was, because it was not a consideration, and that she did not disclose the values of her property on her list, but she told him what they were worth. She acknowledged that she did not ask Reece what the stock was worth because it was not important to her at the time because he was going to keep it anyway.

Following trial, the Trial Court stated that it was obvious from looking at Mr. Reece's list of property that he was a wealthy man, without taking into account the value of the stock, and that in the Court's opinion, the lack of value stated on the stock was not fatal to the agreement. The Court reiterated that the parties had entered into the agreement knowingly, they each had their own attorney, and that everything was revealed on the list and the wife could have investigated any items that she wanted to. He noted that nothing was hidden, and the wife herself did not put values on several of her assets, admitting that it was not important, because they both agreed the assets would go to their respective children. The Court found that the law required each party to have a clear idea of the nature and extent of the other's assets, which the Court found to be the case, and entered Judgment, finding the antenuptial agreement was valid and enforceable and dismissed plaintiff's action. . . .

[Plaintiff appealed, asking whether her husband's] failure to disclose the value of the stock would render the antenuptial agreement invalid and unenforceable[.]

Prenuptial/antenuptial agreements are favored by public policy in Tennessee, and will be upheld so long as the parties enter into the agreements voluntarily and knowledgeably. Tenn. Code Ann. § 36-3-501 deals with antenuptial or prenuptial agreements, and states:

> Notwithstanding any other provision of law to the contrary, . . . any antenuptial or prenuptial agreement entered into by spouses concerning property owned by either spouse before the marriage that is the subject of such agreement shall be binding upon any court having jurisdiction over such spouses and/or such agreement if such agreement is determined, in the discretion of such court, to have been entered into by such spouses freely, knowledgeably and in good faith and without exertion of duress or undue influence upon either spouse. The terms of such agreement shall be enforceable by all remedies available for enforcement of contract terms.

Plaintiff's sole argument is that she did not enter into the agreement with full knowledge of the value of the deceased's assets, because there was no value disclosed regarding the stock in Routh Packing Company.

In the case of Randolph v. Randolph, 937 S.W.2d 815 (Tenn. 1996), the Supreme Court interpreted the term "knowledgeably" as meaning that the proponent of the agreement had to prove that a full and fair disclosure of the nature, extent and value of the party's holdings was provided, or that such disclosure was unnecessary because the spouse had independent knowledge of the same. The Court said:

> The extent of what constitutes "full and fair" disclosure varies from case to case depending upon a number of factors, including the relative sophistication of the parties, the apparent fairness or unfairness of the substantive terms of the

agreement, and any other circumstance unique to the litigants and their specific situation. While disclosure need not reveal precisely every asset owned by an individual spouse, at a minimum, full and fair disclosure requires that each contracting party be given a clear idea of the nature, extent and value of the other party's property and resources. Though not required, a fairly simple and effective method of proving disclosure is to attach a net worth schedule of assets, liabilities and income to the agreement itself.

Id. at 821.

The Court also noted that while it was not required, representation by independent counsel was also a factor to take into account, and possibly the "best evidence that a party has entered into [an] antenuptial agreement voluntarily and knowledgeably." Id. at 822. . . .

In cases where antenuptial agreements have been enforced, we have made clear that the basic question which must be answered is whether the spouse was misled, where the proponent of the agreement makes a fair disclosure, even if it's not 100% exhaustive, and the spouse had the opportunity to ask questions and discover the extent of the other's holdings but failed to do so due to lack of interest, then the agreement has been held valid.

Here plaintiff had full knowledge that her husband was a man of wealth, as shown by the list of assets that was provided. The fact that there was no value listed for one particular asset, even though it was significant, would not invalidate the agreement that she entered freely. She consulted with independent counsel and admitted to clearly understanding what the agreement meant, and that she would have no claim to any of these assets. She had the opportunity to ask questions about the assets, and did not have her counsel investigate, stating that it "did not matter" because she knew the assets would not be hers. She admitted that her husband was never dishonest with her, and was very straightforward and open with her about his financial dealings and never misled her. The disclosure in the agreement demonstrates the husband's wealth, and the wife did not avail herself of the opportunity to ask him the value of the stock, nor make any independent investigation. We agree with the Trial Court that the wife was not misled, and under these circumstances, we agree with the Trial Court that the agreement entered is binding and enforceable on plaintiff. . . .

The Trial Court's Judgment is affirmed.

NOTE

Adequate Financial Disclosure.   To avoid a challenge to a premarital or marital agreement on the grounds of inadequate disclosure, it is advisable to prepare a schedule of each party's assets that includes a good faith valuation of each asset, and to attach the schedule to the agreement. A cautionary tale that reinforces the prudence of this practice is provided by In re Estate of Davis, 213 S.W.3d 288 (Tenn. App. 2006). In that case, the court held a premarital agreement invalid for insufficient disclosure:

> The question is whether Wife made a full and fair disclosure of the nature, extent, and value of her holdings. Assuming that Wife did make a list of her holdings, the

Agreement unequivocally states that such a list did "not purport to be all inclusive, the values set forth on which do not purport to be necessarily accurate but rather are estimates." Since Wife's list cannot be located, assuming there was a list, we are unable to determine if that missing list actually was sufficiently detailed such that there was a full and fair disclosure to Husband of Wife's holdings.

If this practice is not followed, the litigation may devolve into a question of whether the party challenging the agreement can be charged with constructive knowledge of the other party's property, as under UPMAA § 9(d)(3), page 546. In Lawrence v. Lawrence, 687 S.E.2d 421 (Ga. 2009), *W* was charged with constructive knowledge based on her awareness, rooted in more than two years of cohabitation, of *H*'s business dealings and wealth. In In re Estate of Martin, 938 A.2d 812 (Me. 2008), *W* was charged with constructive knowledge based on her access to *H*'s financial records.

2. Community Property[33]

a. The Spread of the Community Property System

Community property developed throughout the continent of Europe, purportedly spread by Germanic tribes after the fall of Rome. From these countries it was taken by European settlers to Central and South America, Mexico, and states along the southern and western borders of the United States. It is odd, then, that in England—separated from the European continent by only a 21-mile-wide channel of water—there arose the very different separate property system.

Why the English resisted so powerful an idea as the sharing principle of community property has intrigued scholars for generations. The most plausible explanations connect the separate property system with the English feudal system, dominated by a powerful king, which required succession of power (land) from father to son (see Chapter 1 at page 29). Women were supported by their husbands, but they were denied an ownership share of, or power over, their husbands' property. Whatever the reason for its existence, the English separate property system became well entrenched by the fourteenth century and was taken by the English settlers to the eastern seaboard of the United States, from where it spread westward.

A community property system has long existed in eight states (Arizona, California, Idaho, Louisiana, Nevada, New Mexico, Texas, and Washington), and Wisconsin adopted such a system in 1984 (see Figure 8.1 at page 521). These states contain nearly a third of the U.S. population. In the late twentieth century, many academics came to favor community property. In 1983, the Uniform Law Commission promulgated a Uniform Marital Property Act, since recast as a Model Act in recognition of its having been enacted in just one state—Wisconsin—in the almost 35 years since its promulgation. The act adopts community property principles, though it avoids the

---

33. The editors gratefully acknowledge Professor Karen Boxx of the University of Washington School of Law and Professor Joshua C. Tate of SMU Dedman School of Law for their assistance in updating the treatment of community property in this and the next section.

The Tax Code and the Almost Revolution in Marital Property

In the 1940s, with a steep increase in federal income tax rates to finance World War II, the income tax advantages of community property became very clear for a "traditional" married couple consisting of a "breadwinner" and a "homemaker." The earnings of the breadwinner were taxable one-half to the breadwinner and one-half to the homemaker (who owned one-half). Because of the graduated step-up in brackets, the total tax on earnings split between a husband and wife each reporting $50,000 could be considerably less than the one tax on the breadwinner's earnings of $100,000 in a separate property state. Similarly, federal estate taxes in community property states were lower because only the breadwinner's half of the community property was taxable at the breadwinner's death. In separate property states, all the breadwinner's earned property was taxable at death.

To reap these federal tax advantages, Michigan, Nebraska, Oklahoma, Oregon, and Pennsylvania adopted community property in the 1940s. Several more states had community property bills in the legislative hoppers. But this revolution in marital property was not to be. In 1948, Congress—a virtually all-male club*—intervened. Congress amended the Internal Revenue Code to eliminate the tax advantages of community property. The five states that had switched to community property switched back to separate property.†

To remove the income tax advantage, Congress permitted married couples to split their earned income equally between them by filing a joint return. Congress solved the estate tax problem by giving the first spouse to die an estate tax marital deduction, up to 50 percent of the value of his estate, for property left to the survivor in a form comparable to the outright ownership that a surviving spouse would have under community property. In 1982, the federal estate tax marital deduction was changed to incorporate a completely new principle: Transfers between spouses are no longer taxed at all, provided the donor spouse gives the donee spouse at least a life estate in the property (see Chapter 15 at page 970).

_____

*In the 80th Congress beginning in January 1948, there were 96 senators (all men) and 435 Representatives (6 women). Congress remains a mostly male club, but this is changing. The 115th Congress opened in January 2017 with 104 female members, including 21 female Senators.

† See Stephanie Hunter McMahon, To Save State Residents: States' Use of Community Property for Federal Tax Reduction, 1939-1947, 27 Law & Hist. Rev. 585 (2009); Carolyn C. Jones, Split Income and Separate Spheres: Tax Law and Gender Roles in the 1940s, 6 Law & Hist. Rev. 259 (1988).

term *community property* and uses *marital property* instead.[34] Alaska, South Dakota, and Tennessee have statutes that permit couples to opt into community property by way of a community property trust.

The fundamental principle of community property is that *during marriage* all earnings of the spouses (and property acquired from those earnings) are community property unless both spouses agree to separate ownership. Each spouse is the owner of an undivided one-half interest in the community property. The death of one spouse dissolves the community. The deceased spouse owns and has testamentary power over his or her half of the community; the surviving spouse already owns the other half.[35]

Property that is not community property is the separate property of one spouse or the other or, in the case of a tenancy in common or joint tenancy, of both. Separate property includes property acquired before marriage and property acquired during

_____

34. *See* Kathy T. Graham, The Uniform Marital Property Act: A Solution for Common Law Property Systems?, 48 S.D. L. Rev. 455 (2003).

35. *See* Terry L. Turnipseed, Community Property v. The Elective Share, 72 La. L. Rev. 161 (2011).

marriage by gift or inheritance. In Idaho, Louisiana, Texas, and Wisconsin,[36] income from separate property is community property. In the other community property states, income from separate property retains its separate character. In circumstances in which the characterization of property is doubtful, there is a strong presumption in favor of community property.

If property has been commingled, or acquired from both separate and community funds, tracing determines the portion of the property that is community. If there is insufficient evidence to establish the source of the funds, the presumption in favor of community property applies. Life insurance is especially tricky. If a husband uses his earnings after marriage to pay premiums on a whole life insurance policy acquired (see page 472) before marriage, some states, applying an inception-of-title rule, take the view that the policy remains the husband's separate property and the community is entitled only to a return of premiums paid with interest. Other states apply a pro rata rule, dividing the policy proceeds between separate and community property according to the proportion of payments paid. For a term life insurance policy (see page 472), the rule in many of the community property states is that the character of the funds used to pay the premium in the last term determines the character of the policy proceeds.[37] Community property states differ on characterization of other types of assets, such as personal injury recoveries and professional degrees.

To avoid tracing problems, a couple can make an agreement that will control the character of their property. They may change separate property into community property, or they may change community property into a joint tenancy, a tenancy in common, or sole ownership of one spouse. Couples sometimes agree that all their property is held as community property to achieve the favorable income tax treatment given community property. Upon the death of one spouse, under Internal Revenue Code (I.R.C.) § 1014 the entire value of community property receives a stepped-up basis for determining capital gains when the property is eventually sold. Any appreciation in value between acquisition and the date of the first spouse's death is never taxed as capital gain. If the property is not community property, only the decedent's one-half interest in the property receives a stepped-up basis.

NOTES

1. The Alaska, South Dakota, and Tennessee Community Property Trusts. Alaska, South Dakota, and Tennessee permit married couples to transfer personal property into a community property trust and provide in the trust agreement that the property is community property.[38] The settlors need not reside in Alaska, South Dakota, or Tennessee if they appoint a trustee in one of those states. A potential advantage of a community property trust is that it might enable residents of noncommunity property

---

36. In Wisconsin this is a default rule that can be varied by the spouse who owns the separate property. *See* Wis. Stat. §§ 766.31(4), 766.59 (2016).

37. *See, e.g.,* In re Marriage of Burwell, 164 Cal. Rptr. 3d 702 (App. 2013).

38. *See* Alaska Stat. §§ 34.77.100 to .160 (2016); S.D. Code Laws §§ 55-17-1 to -14 (2016); Tenn. Code Ann. §§ 35-17-101 to -108 (2016).

states to take advantage of I.R.C. § 1014, which provides a full stepped-up basis for community property upon the death of a spouse, as opposed to a step-up for only the decedent's half interest. There is, however, no case law or definitive ruling by the IRS on whether this plan will work.

2. Community Property with Right of Survivorship. Another innovation, adopted in Arizona, California, Idaho, Nevada, New Mexico, and Texas, is community property with a right of survivorship akin to a joint tenancy. Under this new form of community property, the decedent spouse cannot dispose of his share by will; instead it passes under a right of survivorship to the surviving spouse. The purpose is to avoid probate costs by passing the property to the surviving spouse outside of probate.

Because community property cannot be held in a common law joint tenancy, spouses in community property states previously had to convert community property to separate property before they could create a right of survivorship. Spouses who wish to create a right of survivorship in community property must be careful to comply with the requirements of the governing statute.[39] In Washington, community property can be held in joint tenancy,[40] hence the new form of community property with right of survivorship is not necessary.

b. Management and Disposition of Community Property

Either spouse in a community property state can dispose of his or her half of the couple's community property at death. The surviving spouse owns the other half, which is not, of course, subject to testamentary disposition by the deceased spouse. The one-half of the community property belonging to the deceased spouse may be devised to whomever the decedent pleases, the same as separate property. There is no elective share over the decedent spouse's half of the community property because the surviving spouse already owns the other half.

Because community property belongs to both spouses even if title appears on its face to be in the name of one spouse, problems arise over which spouse can manage the property and deal with third persons regarding the property. These problems may concern sale, leasing, mortgaging the property, or subjecting the property to creditors. Each community property state has different rules for these issues, but there are two general approaches. In most community property states, each spouse generally has the power to manage community property, but there are some exceptions for which both spouses are necessary, the most important being for a transaction involving real property. By contrast, Texas and Wisconsin give each spouse exclusive management over his or her earnings and property acquired with those earnings as long as they are held in the name of the earning spouse.

The recourse of a creditor of a spouse against the spouse's community property varies significantly across the community property states. Here, too, there are two general approaches: (a) the managerial system, and (b) the community debt system. In a

---

39. *See, e.g.,* Tex. Estates Code § 112.052(d) (2016) ("A survivorship agreement may not be inferred from the mere fact that an account is a joint account or that an account is designated as JT TEN, Joint Tenancy, or joint, or with other similar language.").

40. *See* Wash. Rev. Code Ann. § 64.28.040 (2016).

managerial state, the creditor has recourse against all community property subject to the debtor spouse's control. Under the community debt system, the creditor's claim is characterized as separate or community, and the creditor's rights follow accordingly.

To the extent that a spouse may act alone, that spouse may sell community property to a purchaser for valuable consideration. But neither spouse can make a gift of community property without the consent of the other spouse. Various remedies are available to a spouse who did not consent to a gift. Thus:

> *Case 6. H*, married to *W*, makes a gift of $100,000 in community property to their daughter. In most community property states, during *H*'s life *W* is entitled to set aside the entire gift and reclaim the property for the community. After *H* dies, in some community property states the gift is treated as if it were a devise by *H* of half, and *W* can reclaim the other half of the gift. In other community property states, *W* can reclaim the entire gift. Some community property states allow a unilateral gift if it is reasonable in light of the couple's circumstances. For example, in Texas the manager of community property (*H* in this instance) can make reasonable gifts to others, but excessive gifts are deemed in fraud of the other spouse's rights. If the court finds the gift to have been in fraud of *W*'s rights, *W* is entitled to reclaim all the funds if still married to *H,* or half if *H* is dead or they are divorced.

Most community property states follow an *item theory* under which the spouses own equal shares in each item of community property. Thus, if *H* and *W* own Blackacre (worth $50,000) and Whiteacre (worth $50,000), each owns a half share in each tract. *W*'s will cannot devise Blackacre to *H* and Whiteacre to *D*, her daughter by a previous marriage, even if *H* would end up receiving property equal to the value of his community share.[41] Some community property states, however, follow an *aggregate theory* that sometimes allows disposition of one asset, such as a life insurance policy, to someone other than the spouse if the spouse receives one-half of the total community property.[42]

Should a nonprobate transfer to a person other than a spouse be treated as an inter vivos gift or a death transfer when the donor spouse dies? If treated as a death transfer, the surviving spouse is entitled to one-half of it. If treated as an inter vivos gift, the surviving spouse may set aside the transfer to the extent state law allows for lifetime gifts, as in Case 6, above. Thus:

> *Case 7. W* opens a bank account, funding it with community property, naming her son from a prior marriage as a joint tenant with right of survivorship. Then *W* dies. If the account is treated as making a transfer at *W*'s death, *H* can claim only half of the funds. If the bank account is treated as a lifetime gift, then *H* is entitled to half and, depending on the state, the other half would pass to the son or to *W*'s estate. However, in a state that allows reasonable lifetime gifts by one spouse, *H* will have no rights to the account if the gift was reasonable under the circumstances.

---

41. Divorce is different. In most community property states, the divorce court may award specific items of community property to one spouse or the other, provided each spouse ends up with an equitable share of the aggregate value of community property. *See* James R. Ratner, Distribution of Marital Assets in Community Property Jurisdictions: Equitable Doesn't Equal Equal, 72 La. L. Rev. 21 (2011).

42. *See, e.g.,* In re Estate of Kirkes, 295 P.3d 432 (Ariz. 2013).

3. Migrating Couples and Multistate Property Holdings

The traditional conflict of laws rules used to determine which state law governs marital property are as follows:

(1) The law of the situs controls problems related to land.[43]
(2) The law of the marital domicile at the time that personal property is acquired controls the characterization of the property as separate or community.
(3) The law of the marital domicile at the death of one spouse controls the survivor's rights.

The application of these rules is examined briefly below.[44]

a. Moving from Separate Property to Community Property

If a married couple acquires property in a separate property state and moves to a community property state, serious problems of fairness to the surviving spouse may arise. Under traditional law, the law of the state where the couple is domiciled when movable property is acquired determines the ownership of that property. Thus, if the husband is the wage earner, in a separate property state all of the couple's property may be the husband's, and the wife is protected by the elective share. If the couple then moves to a community property state, the property remains the husband's separate property,[45] but as a result of the move the wife loses the protection of the elective share.

Several community property states, including California, give a remedy to the surviving spouse in this situation by way of *quasi-community property*. Quasi-community property is property owned by the husband or the wife acquired while domiciled elsewhere, which would have been characterized as community property if the couple had been domiciled in the community property state when the property was acquired. Real property situated outside the state is not treated as quasi-community property because the spouse retains in it any elective share or dower given by the law of the situs.[46]

---

43. Although the situs state has the power to control its land, it may choose to apply the law of the marital domicile. For example, UPC § 2-202(d) (1990, rev. 2008) provides that the rights of a spouse to an elective share in land located in the state shall be governed by the law of the decedent's domicile at death. Likewise, property located in a community property state that is acquired by a married person domiciled in a separate property state will not automatically be characterized as community property. If the purchase is financed by the person's own earnings, the situs community property state will generally consider those funds separate property of the purchasing spouse, and the real property purchased with that property will be characterized as separate property.

44. *See* Karen E. Boxx, Community Property Across State Lines: Square Pegs and Round Holes, 19 Prob. & Prop. 9 (2005).

45. If the husband moves unilaterally to a community property state, leaving the wife behind in the separate property state, community property jurisdictions differ in their treatment of the husband's subsequent earnings. *See* Jasmine B. Bertrand, Comment, What's Mine Is Mine Is Mine: The Inequitable Intersection of Louisiana's Choice-of-Law Provisions and the Movables of Migratory Spouses, 79 Tul. L. Rev. 493, 508-12 (2004).

46. The surviving spouse of a couple domiciled in a separate property state who buys land in a community property state may have the same elective share in the land as she would have in land in the domiciliary state. *See, e.g.*, Cal. Prob. Code § 120 (2016).

During the continuance of the marriage, quasi-community property is treated for most purposes as the separate property of the acquiring spouse. However, in a state that recognizes quasi-community property for probate purposes, one-half of the quasi-community property belongs to the surviving spouse at death, with the other half subject to testamentary disposition by the decedent.[47] A few community property states, such as Texas, use the concept of quasi-community property only in divorce actions and not in the division of decedents' estates.[48]

Quasi-community property, where recognized, is analogous to an elective share in the deceased spouse's property acquired from earnings while domiciled in another state.[49]

> *Case 8.* H and W are domiciled in Illinois. H saves $500,000 from his earnings, which he invests in stocks and bonds. In Illinois this is his separate property. H and W then retire to California. The stocks and bonds become quasi-community property in California. Upon H's death, W owns one-half of the stocks and bonds. If W dies first, she cannot dispose of any part of this wealth by will; H owns it all. By contrast, if H and W had moved to Texas, on H's death W would have no interest in the assets brought from Illinois.

To prevent a spouse from attempting to defeat the survivor's quasi-community property rights by inter vivos transfers, the surviving spouse may have the right to reach one-half of any nonprobate transfer of quasi-community property if the decedent retained possession or enjoyment, or the right to income, or the power to revoke or consume, or a right of survivorship.[50]

b. Moving from Community Property to Separate Property

Generally, a change in domicile from a community property state to a separate property state does not change the preexisting property rights of the spouses. Community property continues to be characterized as such if the couple and the property move to a separate property state. The Uniform Disposition of Community Property Rights at Death Act (Unif. Law Comm'n 1971), enacted in 16 separate property states, provides that community property brought into the state (and all property—including land in the state—traceable to community property) remains community property for purposes of testamentary disposition, unless the spouses have agreed to convert it into separate property. Under this act, community property brought into the state is not

---

47. If the nonacquiring spouse dies first, the quasi-community property belongs absolutely to the acquiring spouse; the nonacquiring spouse has no testamentary power over it.

48. Arizona, New Mexico, and Texas have adopted the quasi-community property concept for purposes of equitable division upon divorce. *See* Ariz. Rev. Stat. § 25-318 (2016); N.M. Stat. § 40-3-8 (2016); Tex. Fam. Code § 7.002 (2016). These states do not apply the quasi-community concept to marriages ending in death. *See* Kenneth W. Kingma, Property Division at Divorce or Death for Married Couples Migrating Between Common Law and Community Property States, 35 ACTEC L.J. 74, 93 (2009).

49. *See* Cal. Prob. Code §§ 66, 101 (2016); Idaho Code § 15-2-201 (2016); La. Civ. Code art. 3526 (2016); Wash. Rev. Code §§ 26.16.220 to .230 (2016); Wis. Stat. §§ 861.018 to .11 (2016).

50. *See* Cal. Prob. Code § 102 (2016); Idaho Code § 15-2-202 (2016).

subject to the elective share. On the other hand, in a state that has not adopted the act, a court might automatically convert any community property the spouses exchange in that state into a form of common law joint ownership.[51]

A couple moving community property into a separate property state should be careful to preserve its community nature, if doing so is desirable. If the community property is sold and the proceeds used to purchase other assets, title to the new property should be taken in the name of husband and wife as community property. If transfer agents, bankers, or title companies unfamiliar with community property resist, the spouses should take title in the name of both spouses, at the same time making a written agreement reciting their intent to retain the asset as community property. Or the spouses may preserve the community character of their property by creating a revocable trust of the community property and providing that all property of the trust is community property. If the inbound separate property state has not enacted the Uniform Disposition of Community Property Rights at Death Act, it may be advisable to select the law of a community property state to govern the trust.

Because lawyers in separate property states sometimes lack understanding of the community property system, they may recommend to couples who are bringing community property into a separate property state that they change the title to joint tenancy or some other separate property form. If this is done with the intent of changing community property into a common law concurrent interest, the step-up in tax basis is lost, and the lawyer could be liable for malpractice.[52]

4. Miscellaneous Additional Rights

a. Social Security

In the 1930s, Congress established the Social Security system, under which retirement benefits are paid to a worker *and the worker's spouse.* A spouse can generally draw his own earned benefits, if any, or one-half of the other spouse's benefits, whichever is greater. At the death of the other spouse, the surviving spouse is entitled to his own earned benefits, if any, or the full amount of the decedent spouse's benefits. Workers have no power to transfer their right to benefits to any other person or to divest the surviving spouse of his spousal right to benefits. A divorced former spouse of a worker may also have a right to benefits if the marriage lasted at least ten years.

Social Security benefits are computed by a formula that takes into account the amount of taxes paid into the system, the age of retirement, and the number of quarters worked (it takes 40 quarters — ten years — to be fully insured). In 2016, most people aged 65 or older were receiving Social Security benefits, with an average monthly benefit of $1,340 for retired workers and $2,210 for retired couples. The average monthly benefit for a surviving spouse was $1,285.[53]

---

51. *See* Jeremy T. Ware, Section 1014(B)(6) and the Boundaries of Community Property, 5 Nev. L.J. 704, 716-20 (2005).

52. *See* Paul L. Caron & Jay A. Soled, New Prominence of Tax Basis in Estate Planning, 150 Tax Notes 1569 (2016).

53. Soc. Sec. Admin., SSA Pub. No. 05-10024, Understanding the Benefits 23 (Mar. 2016).

That a surviving spouse of a worker may elect to take his own earned benefits or the full amount of the deceased spouse's benefits raises a question of horizontal equality across families in which one spouse was a wage earner as compared to families in which both spouses worked outside the home. Thus:

> *Case 9.* *H1* earns $80,000 a year. *W1* works in the home. *H1* retires and starts receiving Social Security benefits, but then dies in a boating accident with his neighbor, *H2*. Under the current system, *W1* receives *H1*'s full monthly retirement benefits, based on *H1*'s $80,000 salary, until she dies.

> *Case 10.* *H2* and *W2*, the neighbors of the couple in Case 9, each earn $40,000 a year. Both *H2* and *W2* retire and both receive Social Security benefits. Then *H2* dies in the boating accident with *H1*. *W2* is entitled to receive only her own Social Security benefits, based on her $40,000 salary, or her deceased husband's benefits based on his $40,000 salary—but not both.

W2's benefits in Case 10 will be smaller than *W1*'s in Case 9 even though both marriages paid equal amounts into the system based on equal overall wages.

b. Pension and Retirement Accounts

We already considered pension and retirement accounts, which at mid-year 2016 held the eye-popping sum of $24.5 trillion, in Chapter 7 at page 478. Most private pension plans provided as a benefit of employment are governed by the federal Employee Retirement Income Security Act of 1974 (ERISA), which per Egelhoff v. Egelhoff, page 486, preempts inconsistent state law.

As amended by the Retirement Equity Act in 1984, ERISA requires that the spouse of an employee have survivorship rights if the employee predeceases the spouse. The purpose is to ensure the retirement security of the surviving spouse. For a defined contribution plan (see page 481), the surviving spouse is entitled to the entire account balance. For a defined benefit plan that pays its primary benefits as an annuity rather than a lump sum (see page 480), generally those benefits must be paid as a joint and survivor annuity to the employee and his spouse. If the employee dies before retirement, the surviving spouse may be entitled to a preretirement survivor annuity.[54]

In Boggs v. Boggs, 520 U.S. 833 (1997), a first wife had a community property share in her husband's pension, which, under community property law, she could devise to whomever she pleased. She devised her share to her husband for life and then to her three sons. The husband married again after his first wife's death. Upon his death, the Supreme Court held that his pension benefits must be used to support his second wife, rather than be paid to the sons as named beneficiaries, in order to carry out ERISA's object to protect surviving spouses. ERISA preempted state community property law to the extent that it allowed the first wife to make a testamentary transfer of her interest in her husband's pension, making it unavailable to a second wife.[55]

---

54. *See* John H. Langbein, David A. Pratt, Susan J. Stabile & Andrew W. Stumpff, Pension and Employee Benefit Law 225-36 (6th ed. 2015).

55. *See* Cynthia A. Samuel & Katherine S. Spaht, Fixing What's Broke: Amending ERISA to Allow Community Property to Apply upon the Death of a Participant's Spouse, 35 Fam. L.Q. 425 (2001).

"It's just as easy to love a man with a pension
as to love a man without one."
Barbara Smaller/The New Yorker Collection/The Cartoon Bank

A spouse may waive her rights to benefits under the employee's pension plan, but ERISA complicates waivers with strict rules for validity. For example, waiver by a spouse under ERISA requires written consent that is notarized or witnessed by a plan representative. A premarital agreement cannot waive ERISA-covered pension rights because one who is not yet a "spouse" cannot waive spousal rights.[56]

c. Homestead

Most states have a homestead law that is designed to secure the family home to the surviving spouse and minor children, free of the claims of the decedent's creditors.[57] Such a homestead is frequently called a *probate homestead*. Although the details of these laws vary considerably, the surviving spouse will often have the right to occupy the family home (or maybe the family farm) for his lifetime. In some states, the homestead must be established by the decedent during life, usually by filing a declaration of homestead in some public office; in other states, the probate court has the power to set aside real

---

56. *See* Langbein et al., *supra* note 54, at 228-31. Another problematic requirement, which stymies long-term estate planning, is the rule that a waiver of certain benefits cannot be made more than 180 days before those benefits are eligible to be paid. *See* id. at 231.

57. *See* Schoenblum, *supra* note 7, at tbl. 6.01.

property as a homestead. The amount of the homestead exemption is absurdly small in some states and provides little protection to the surviving spouse. UPC § 2-402 (1990, rev. 2008) recommends $22,500, subject to the cost of living adjustment formula in § 1-109. But in several states the homestead exemption is rather substantial and may even exempt the family home from the claims of all creditors and devisees, regardless of its value. The right to occupy the homestead is usually given in addition to any other rights the surviving spouse has in the decedent's estate.

d. Personal Property Set-Aside

Related to homestead is the right of the surviving spouse (and sometimes of minor children) to receive tangible personal property of the decedent up to a certain value. UPC § 2-403 (1990, rev. 2008) sets the limit at $15,000, subject to the cost of living adjustment formula in § 1-109. These items, which are also exempt from creditors' claims, usually include household furniture and clothing, but may also include a car and farm animals. The set-aside is usually subject to several conditions and limitations, but, if these are met, the decedent usually has no power to deprive the surviving spouse of the exempt items.

e. Family Allowance

Every state has a statute authorizing the probate court to award an allowance for maintenance and support of the surviving spouse (and often of dependent children). The allowance may be limited to a fixed period (typically one year), or it may continue thereafter while the will is being contested or for the entire period of administration. As with the homestead and personal property set-aside, any family allowance is in addition to whatever other interests pass to the surviving spouse. Both the personal property set-aside and family allowance are personal to the surviving spouse and do not pass to the survivor's estate.

In some states, the maximum allowance that can be awarded is fixed by statute. In other states, a reasonable allowance tied to the spouse's standard of living is permitted. UPC § 2-404 (1990) provides for a reasonable allowance, which cannot continue beyond one year if the estate is inadequate to pay creditors. Maintenance of the decedent's spouse and dependent children is not allowed after the estate is closed. UPC § 2-405 authorizes the personal representative to determine the family allowance up to a stated limit without court order but subject to judicial review.

f. Dower and Curtesy

At common law, a widow had *dower* in all land of which her deceased husband had been seised during marriage and that was inheritable upon the husband's death. Dower entitles the widow to a life estate in one-third of her husband's qualifying land. Thus:

> *Case 11.* *H*, married to *W*, buys Blackacre, taking title in himself in fee simple. *H* subsequently dies. *W* is entitled to a life estate in one-third of Blackacre. If *W* had predeceased *H*, her dower interest would be extinguished.

The right of dower attaches the moment the husband acquires title to land or upon marriage, whichever is later. Dower remains inchoate until the husband's death, when it becomes possessory. Once inchoate dower has attached, the husband cannot sell the land free and clear of the wife's dower interest. In Case 11, if *H*, after buying Blackacre, had conveyed it to *A*, *A* would take title subject to *W*'s dower. If *W* survived *H*, *W* would be entitled to a life estate in one-third of Blackacre (now owned by *A*). No purchaser, bona fide or not, can cut off the wife's dower without her consent.

In feudal times, when land was the chief form of wealth, dower provided generous support to the widow of a propertied man. But today, when most wealth takes the form of liquid financial assets and human capital, dower may provide no protection at all. Dower has been abolished in all but a handful of states.[58] It functions today primarily to make the signatures of both spouses a practical requirement to the sale of one spouse's land.

At common law, a husband had a support interest in his wife's lands, called *curtesy*. It was comparable to dower except the husband did not acquire curtesy unless children were born of the marriage, and the husband was given a life estate in the entire parcel, not merely in one-third. Curtesy survives today in a handful of states, but in most of these it is only a label given to the support interest of the husband, which in fact has been made identical to the wife's support interest.

B. INTENTIONAL OMISSION OF A CHILD

1. American Law

In all states except Louisiana, a child or other descendant has no statutory protection against intentional disinheritance by a parent. Unlike that for a spouse, there is no requirement that a testator leave any property to a child, not even the proverbial one dollar.[59]

Even though a parent has the power to disinherit children, unless the parent does so in favor of a surviving spouse, the parent should think twice or, better, three times, before exercising the power. A will that disinherits a child is a risky affair that invites a will contest. Testamentary capacity, undue influence, and fraud are subtle and elastic doctrines that judges and juries sometimes use to rewrite the testator's distributive plan in an attempt to do justice (see Chapter 4). In contests by disinherited children, the trier of fact is sometimes influenced by its sympathies for the children and sense of fairness. This is well known to practicing lawyers, who will often advise a settlement with a disinherited child.[60]

---

58. *See* Schoenblum, *supra* note 7, at tbl. 6.01.

59. At common law, a child omitted from a parent's will had no remedy. It may have been thought necessary to leave an heir a shilling to disinherit him, but Blackstone says that this was wrong. "[T]he necessity of leaving the heir a shilling or some other express legacy, in order to disinherit him," is traceable to a Roman law notion that the testator had lost his memory or mind unless he gave some legacy to each child. 2 William Blackstone, Commentaries *503.

60. Professor Langbein suggests that "the American rule, by allowing liberal disinheritance of children, creates the type of plaintiff who is most prone to bring these actions." John H. Langbein, Book Review: Will Contests, 103 Yale L.J. 2039, 2042 (1994). Even so, he prefers "the American . . . testamentary freedom to disinherit children who turn out to be . . . disappointing and unsavory." Id.

"Everything I have, son, I have because your grandfather left it to me.
I see now that that was a bad thing."

Leo Cullum/The New Yorker Collection/The Cartoon Bank

The Louisiana forced share for children, which is derived from French law,[61] is called a *legitime*. Since 1995, it has protected against the disinheritance of children 23 and under, the mentally infirm, and the disabled (prior to 1995 it protected all children).[62] To address the problem of an unworthy child, disinheritance is allowed for "just cause," including:

(1) The child has raised his hand to strike a parent, or has actually struck a parent; but a mere threat is not sufficient.

(2) The child has been guilty, towards a parent, of cruel treatment, crime, or grievous injury. . . .

(6) The child, being a minor, has married without the consent of the parent. . . .

(8) The child, after attaining the age of majority and knowing how to contact the parent, has failed to communicate with the parent without just cause for a period of two years.[63]

The cause for disinheriting the child must have existed at the time of the will's execution.

---

61. *See* Ray D. Madoff, A Tale of Two Countries: Comparing the Law of Inheritance in Two Seemingly Opposite Systems, 37 B.C. Int'l & Comp. L. Rev. 333 (2014).

62. *See* La. Const. art. 12, § 5 (2016); La. Civ. Code Ann. art. 1493 (2016); Vincent D. Rougeau, No Bonds But Those Freely Chosen: An Obituary for the Principle of Forced Heirship in American Law, Civ. L. Commentaries 1, no. 3 (2008); Katherine Shaw Spaht, The Remnant of Forced Heirship: The Interrelationship of Undue Influence, What's Become of Disinherison, and the Unfinished Business of the Stepparent Usufruct, 60 La. L. Rev. 637 (2000).

63. La. Civ. Code Ann. art. 1621(A) (2016).

2. The Family Maintenance System of the Commonwealth

In 1900, New Zealand adopted a system of *family maintenance* under which a court has the power to override a decedent's will. The court can make distributions to a spouse, child, or other dependent of the decedent in accordance with the court's view of the dispositions that the testator ought to have made in light of all the circumstances. England, Australia, and most Canadian provinces have similar legislation.

Under the English statute, which is representative, the decedent's spouse or civil partner, former spouse or civil partner who has not remarried or formed a subsequent civil partnership, children, or any other person who was being maintained by the decedent, "may apply to the court for an order . . . that the disposition of the deceased's estate . . . is not such as to make reasonable financial provision for the applicant."[64] A spouse or civil partner is entitled to a financial provision that "would be reasonable in all the circumstances of the case" for a spouse or civil partner "to receive, whether or not that provision is required for his or her maintenance."[65] Other eligible survivors, such as children, are entitled to receive such financial provision "as it would be reasonable in all the circumstances of the case for the applicant to receive for his maintenance."[66]

Lambeff v. Farmers Co-operative Executors & Trustees Ltd.
56 SASR 323 (S. Austl. 1991)

MATHESON, J. The plaintiff is the only daughter of George Lambeff who died at Ceduna on 23 March 1989, aged 63. She claims provision from his estate pursuant to the provisions of the Inheritance (Family Provision) Act 1972.

The last will and testament of the deceased was made on 14 March 1988 and probate was granted to the defendants on 15 November 1989. They were the executors named in the will. The second and third defendants were the only sons of the deceased. The will directed that upon payment of debts and funeral expenses the whole estate should be held upon trust for the two sons in equal shares absolutely. As at the date of swearing of the first affidavit of the trust manager of the first defendant, namely, 28 February 1990, the estimated value of the assets in the estate was $220,058.87. As at 24 December 1990, he deposed that the value of the net estate was $209,522.76. The major assets were a home unit at 15/17 MacFarlane Street, Glenelg North, valued at approximately $50,000, in which the deceased's former de facto wife, Barbara Lambeff, the mother of his two sons, lived, and a leasehold property at Ceduna, upon which there was an old stable, 18 powered caravan sites and a sand mine, and valued at $144,500. In addition, the deceased was the joint owner of a property at 13 Park Terrace, Ceduna with Barbara Lambeff, the capital value of which, according to the Valuer-General, was $120,000. The deceased lived with Barbara Lambeff from about 1956 to 1980 with several separations. She is not a party to these proceedings.

---

64. *See* Inheritance (Provisions for Family and Dependants) Act 1975, c. 63, § 1 (U.K.), amended by Inheritance and Trustees' Powers Act 2014, c. 16, sch. 2 (U.K.).

65. Id. § 1(2)(a)-(aa).

66. Id. § 1(2)(b).

The deceased married the plaintiff's mother in Czechoslovakia on 28 June 1945 and the plaintiff was born there on 21 June 1946. The deceased, the plaintiff's mother and the plaintiff moved to Perth in the State of Western Australia in July 1950. The deceased and his wife separated in 1956, and in or about that year he commenced an association with Barbara Lambeff and moved to Ceduna where the deceased lived until his death. On 3 October 1957, the second defendant, Nicholas George Lambeff, was born and on 5 April 1961 the third defendant, Christopher Jordan Lambeff, was born. The deceased worked in Perth as a builder and continued so to work at Ceduna after setting up house there.

The plaintiff attended high school until the end of second year and then did a secretarial course at a technical college in Perth. Her mother married Leons Romanovskis in Perth on 29 December 1965. The plaintiff remained with her mother until October 1966, and then moved to Melbourne where she has lived and worked ever since. Her mother and her stepfather moved to Adelaide in about November 1974. At the time of her father's death, the plaintiff was employed by Scottish Amicable Life Assurance Society. Since the merger of that company with Colonial Mutual Life Assurance Society Ltd., the plaintiff has been working as a marketing officer. She proofreads marketing literature, assists with advertising and performs a variety of tasks within the marketing department. Her gross salary is $33,000. She has purchased a flat at 13 Hawkesburn Road, South Yarra. It cost $78,000 and the mortgage was $66,000. It will be repaid when she is 60. It was valued in January 1990 at $120,000. Her only other assets are clothes, furniture and jewellery. She is unmarried and has had no children.

It is convenient here to quote from the plaintiff's affidavit. . . .

> When I overcame my distress at being abandoned by my father in 1960, I wrote to him on three occasions, the first being in 1967, endeavouring to re-establish contact with him. I received no acknowledgment of the letters and interpreted this behaviour to be his total rejection of me. My letters were written at about five-yearly intervals. I believe the lack of response from my father at the time was due to the animosity he harboured towards my mother and/or the influence held over him by his de facto wife, Barbara. . . .

The defendant, Nicholas Lambeff, is 33 years of age. He has a wife and two children. They are expecting their third child. Nicholas Lambeff left school after attempting second year high school twice. He has four restricted building licences. He said that from about the age of 10 he worked for the deceased, helping him establish the caravan park, the largest asset of the estate. He said that any remuneration he received for his services was inadequate when compared with the number of hours he worked. He stated that he continued to help the deceased until his death because he had told him on many occasions that one day the caravan park would belong to him. He and his family have lived in the caravan park for about the last 15 years. He says that he and his wife have managed it since 1980, and for their livelihood they rely on the income earned from it and from some irregular contract work. His wife has no formal qualifications, but has assisted with the running of the caravan park and has worked as an assistant in a local chemist shop on a casual basis. They do not own any real estate. Their assets are worth approximately $27,500.

The defendant, Christopher Lambeff, is 30 years of age. He has a de facto wife and two children. He left school after failing fourth year high school, and has no qualifications. He also worked for his father from an early age in the caravan park. He has had various labouring jobs. His de facto wife has been a governess and a teacher's aide, but has not worked since the birth of their first child. They have no real estate. Their assets are worth approximately $30,350. They have been living at 13 Park Terrace, Ceduna, rent free, in the house now registered in the name of Barbara Lambeff. . . .

Section 7 of the Inheritance (Family Provision) Act states:

> (1) Where—
>> (a) a person has died domiciled in the State or owning real or personal property in the State; and
>> (b) by reason of his testamentary dispositions or the operation of the laws of intestacy or both, *a person entitled to claim the benefit of this Act is left without adequate provision for his proper maintenance, education or advancement in life,* the Court may in its discretion, upon application by or on behalf of a person so entitled,[67] order that such provision as the Court thinks fit be made out of the estate of the deceased person for the maintenance, education or advancement of the person so entitled. . . .
>
> (3) The Court may refuse to make an order in favour of any person on the ground that his character or conduct is such as, in the opinion of the Court, to disentitle him to the benefit of this Act, or for any other reason that the Court thinks sufficient. . . .

The plaintiff's case is that she was left without adequate provision for her proper advancement in life.

I was referred to the judgment of King, C.J., in Estate of Puckridge (1978) 20 S.A.S.R. 72. His Honour said (at 77):

> The words "advancement in life" have a wide meaning and application and there is nothing to confine the operation of the provision to an early period of life in the members of the family. In McCosker v. McCosker (1957), 97 C.L.R. 566, the expression was held to be wide enough to embrace the provision of capital for

---

67. Section 6 of the act currently defines "persons entitled" as follows:

(a) the spouse of the deceased person;
(b) a person who has been divorced from the deceased person;
(ba) the domestic partner of the deceased person;
(c) a child of the deceased person;
(g) a child of a spouse or domestic partner of the deceased person being a child who was maintained wholly or partly or who was legally entitled to be maintained wholly or partly by the deceased person immediately before his death;
(h) a child of the child of the deceased person;
(i) a parent of the deceased person who satisfies the court that he cared for, or contributed to the maintenance of, the deceased person during his lifetime;
(j) a brother or sister of the deceased person who satisfies the court that he cared for, or contributed to the maintenance of, the deceased person during his lifetime.

—Eds.

the poultry farming business of a claimant. The word "proper" is of considerable importance and means proper in all the circumstances of the case. The circumstances include the size of the estate, the needs of the applicants, the nearness or remoteness of the applicants' blood and personal relationship to the deceased, any special claims which the applicants may have on the bounty of the deceased, and competing claims of others.

In Bosch v. Perpetual Trustee Co. Ltd., [1938] A.C. 463 (P.C.) at 478-79, their Lordships said:

> that in every case the court must place itself in the position of the testator and consider what he ought to have done in all the circumstances of the case, treating the testator for that purpose as a wise and just, rather than a fond and foolish, husband or father.

As Dixon, C.J., said in Blore v. Lang (1960), 104 C.L.R. 124 at 128: "Some moral claim to which a wise and just testator might be expected to respond must exist, but it may rise out of relationship." . . .

I agree . . . that there are now two totally separate family units. I also agree that upon the evidence the plaintiff has a secure, well-paid job, that she has a substantial equity in her flat and that she has no dependants. She has good prospects of benefiting from the estates of her mother and stepfather, although the poor health of her stepfather raises a question mark over that. The deceased's sons, on the other hand, have little in the way of assets and they have families to support. The estate is by no means large. They are, however, both young and fit.

It may well be that the plaintiff has established that she has a special claim upon the estate within the meaning of some of the earlier cases. I do not need to find one, because I do not think it is necessary to show such a claim on a statute worded as is the South Australian statute. . . .

The plaintiff was abandoned by the deceased at the age of 10, and had no support from him thereafter. She later made efforts to befriend her father. She has done nothing to disentitle herself. It is true that she has acquitted herself reasonably well in life without her father's support, but I think she would have done better with proper support for her advancement in life. I think her claim succeeds, but in all the circumstances the provision should be modest. I order that the defendants pay her a legacy of $20,000 out of the estate.

NOTES

1. *Estate Planning in the Commonwealth.*   Suppose you are a lawyer in South Australia. *T*, a married man with $2 million in assets, asks you to draw a will for him that leaves half of his estate to charity, a quarter to his second wife, *W2*, and the remaining quarter split between his two children, *A* and *B*, from his first marriage. *T* explains that *W2* already has substantial assets and that his children both have good jobs and solid finances. Can you assure *T* that a court will give effect to his will as written? What advice would you give him?

2. Scholarly Debate.   Professor Frances Foster summarizes the debate over bringing the family maintenance system of the English Commonwealth to the United States:

> Proponents laud the model's flexibility, which they claim allows estate distribution to be "tailored to individual need" and "evolving lifestyles." They also cite the "strong ethical appeal" of the family maintenance model. They praise this approach for exalting the moral principle that familial responsibility does not terminate at death. They stress that the model addresses ethical issues on an individual level as well. The family maintenance model authorizes courts to evaluate on a case-by-case basis the morality of both the decedent's dispositive scheme and the claims of survivors. Proponents argue that by promoting private support of dependents the model not only provides moral guidance but also performs a vital social welfare function. They conclude that the family maintenance model offers the optimal mechanism to secure meaningful protection of family members with the least intrusion on freedom of testation. Unlike the alternative foreign and U.S. entitlement-based systems, they argue, the family maintenance scheme "does not apply automatically" but rather comes into play only upon petition by qualifying "aggrieved claimants."
>
> For critics of the family maintenance model, judicial discretion is a "terrible price" to pay for improved support of dependents. They view the model as fundamentally unsuited to the U.S. environment. They claim adoption of its discretionary scheme would be ill-advised, even "frightening" given the peculiarities of the U.S. probate system — a system, they argue, that is comprised of multiple, local probate courts, staffed often by lay judges chosen on the basis of politics rather than merit. For opponents, the costs of a discretionary redistribution scheme are also unacceptable. They contend it would "promote litigation," increase "information and administrative costs," and "deplete estates." Critics also argue that the family maintenance model would introduce such complexity and unpredictability into the U.S. probate process that it would undermine estate planning and obstruct simple, orderly transfer of property rights.[68]

Although the debate has consumed many pages in the law reviews,[69] there is no credible proposal currently pending in any state in this country to adopt a family maintenance system similar to that of the Commonwealth. It seems that American legislators agree with Professor Kristine Knaplund that "a family maintenance system violates our country's professed belief in freedom of testation."[70]

---

68. Frances H. Foster, Linking Support and Inheritance: A New Model from China, 1999 Wis. L. Rev. 1199, 1213-15.

69. *Compare* Deborah A. Batts, I Didn't Ask to Be Born: The American Law of Disinheritance and a Proposal for Change to a System of Protected Inheritance, 41 Hastings L.J. 1197 (1990) (recommending forced share legislation for children), *with* Ronald Chester, Disinheritance and the American Child: An Alternative from British Columbia, 1998 Utah L. Rev. 1 (recommending a Commonwealth family maintenance system).

70. Kristine S. Knaplund, Grandparents Raising Grandchildren and the Implications for Inheritance, 48 Ariz. L. Rev. 1, 16 (2006); *but see* Michelle Harris, Why a Limited Family Maintenance System Could Help American "Grandfamilies," 3 NAELA J. 239 (2007) (favoring family maintenance, responding to Professor Knaplund).

C. PROTECTION AGAINST UNINTENTIONAL OMISSION

Changes in circumstances in the gap in time between a will's execution and the testator's death may render the will stale. The rules dealing with revocation of a bequest to a spouse on divorce (see page 239), lapse and antilapse (see page 351), and ademption and abatement (see page 373), among others, mitigate the stale will problem. For cases in which the testator's actual intent is not evident, these rules are designed to implement the probable intent of the typical testator. We now consider the rules that in a similar vein protect the surviving spouse and children from unintentional disinheritance by a stale will.

1. Spouse Omitted from Premarital Will

At common law, a premarital will was revoked by the testator's marriage or marriage followed by the birth of issue. Although still in force in a few states, this rule has been overridden in most states by statutes that give a surviving spouse who is omitted from a premarital will an intestate share, otherwise leaving the premarital will intact. These statutes correct for the testator's assumed mistake in neglecting to update a premarital will by looking to intestacy for what a typical married person would want to pass to a surviving spouse. The statutes contain default rules that can be overcome by evidence that the testator deliberately omitted the surviving spouse and did not mistakenly fail to update the premarital will.

Uniform Probate Code (Unif. Law Comm'n 1990, as amended 1993)

§ 2-301. Entitlement of Spouse; Premarital Will

(a) If a testator's surviving spouse married the testator after the testator executed his [or her] will, the surviving spouse is entitled to receive, as an intestate share, no less than the value of the share of the estate he [or she] would have received if the testator had died intestate as to that portion of the testator's estate, if any, that neither is devised to a child of the testator who was born before the testator married the surviving spouse and who is not a child of the surviving spouse nor is devised to a descendant of such a child or passes under Sections 2-603 or 2-604 to such a child or to a descendant of such a child, unless:

(1) it appears from the will or other evidence that the will was made in contemplation of the testator's marriage to the surviving spouse;

(2) the will expresses the intention that it is to be effective notwithstanding any subsequent marriage; or

(3) the testator provided for the spouse by transfer outside the will and the intent that the transfer be in lieu of a testamentary provision is shown by the testator's statements or is reasonably inferred from the amount of the transfer or other evidence.

(b) In satisfying the share provided by this section, devises made by the will to the testator's surviving spouse, if any, are applied first, and other devises, other than a devise to a child of the testator who was born before the testator married the surviving spouse and who is not a child of the surviving spouse or a devise or substitute gift under Sections 2-603 or 2-604 to a descendant of such a child, abate as provided in Section 3-902.

In re Estate of Prestie
138 P.3d 520 (Nev. 2006)

HARDESTY, J. In this appeal, we consider whether an amendment to an inter vivos trust can rebut the presumption that a pour-over will is revoked as to an unintentionally omitted spouse. . . .

FACTS

In 1987, California residents Maria and W.R. Prestie were married in Las Vegas, Nevada. Maria and W.R. were divorced two years later yet maintained an amiable relationship. W.R. was later diagnosed with macular degeneration and moved to Las Vegas, where he purchased a condominium. Maria also moved to Las Vegas, although she initially resided in a separate residence.

In 1994, W.R. simultaneously executed in California a pour-over will and the W.R. Prestie Living Trust (the inter vivos trust). The pour-over will devised W.R.'s entire estate to the trust. W.R.'s son, appellant Scott Prestie, was named both the trustee and a beneficiary of the inter vivos trust. Neither the will nor the inter vivos trust provided for Maria.

As W.R.'s sight worsened, Maria provided care for W.R. by taking him to his doctor appointments, cooking, and cleaning his condominium. In 2000, Maria moved into W.R.'s condominium to better assist him with his needs. In 2001, W.R. amended the inter vivos trust to grant Maria a life estate in his condominium upon his death.[71] A few weeks later, Maria and W.R. were married for a second time. W.R. passed away approximately nine months later.

Maria eventually petitioned the district court for, among other things, a one-half intestate succession share of W.R.'s estate on the ground that W.R.'s will was revoked as to her under Nev. Rev. Stat. ("NRS") 133.110 (revocation of a will by marriage). Specifically, Maria argued that because she married W.R. without entering into a marriage contract and after he had executed his will, the will was revoked as to her because it did not contain a provision providing for her or a provision expressing an intention to not provide for her.

The probate commissioner found that W.R.'s will was executed before he remarried Maria in 2001 and that the amendment granting Maria a life estate in the condominium was to the inter vivos trust, not to W.R.'s will. The probate commissioner also concluded that, under NRS 133.110, W.R. and Maria did not have a marriage contract and W.R.'s will did not provide for Maria or express an intent to not provide for Maria. Therefore, the probate commissioner recommended that W.R.'s will be revoked as to

---

71. The amendment to the inter vivos trust was erroneously labeled a codicil. See NRS 132.070 (stating that a codicil is an addition to a will).

Maria. The district court subsequently entered an order adopting the probate commissioner's report and recommendations, and Scott Prestie appeals.

DISCUSSION

On appeal, . . . Scott argues that . . . W.R.'s amendment to the inter vivos trust rebutted the presumption of revocation of W.R.'s will as to Maria. . . .

NRS 133.110 provides for surviving spouses who are unintentionally omitted from their spouse's will:

> If a person marries after making a will and the spouse survives the maker, the will is revoked as to the spouse, unless provision has been made for the spouse by marriage contract, or unless the spouse is provided for in the will, or in such a way mentioned therein as to show an intention not to make such provision; and no other evidence to rebut the presumption of revocation shall be received.

Scott argues that W.R.'s amendment to the inter vivos trust, which gave Maria a life estate in W.R.'s condominium, means that Maria has been provided for under NRS 133.110. Moreover, Scott contends that W.R.'s amendment to the inter vivos trust rebuts the presumption of revocation under NRS 133.110. We disagree with both of these arguments. . . .

NRS 133.110 is unambiguous, and we have previously explained that it "provides for the presumptive revocation of a will if the testator marries after executing his will and his spouse survives him, unless he has provided for the surviving spouse by marriage contract, by provision in the will, or has mentioned her in such a way as to show an intention not to provide for her." Leggett v. Estate of Leggett, 494 P.2d 554, 556-57 (Nev. 1972). "The sole purpose of [NRS 133.110] is to guard against the unintentional disinheritance of the surviving spouse." Id. at 557. Thus, the *only evidence* admissible to rebut the presumption of revocation for the purposes of NRS 133.110 is a marriage contract, a provision providing for the spouse in the will, or a provision in the will expressing an intent to not provide for the spouse.

Accordingly, we reject the notion that an amendment to a trust, which provides for the spouse, is admissible to rebut the presumption of a will's revocation.[72] The plain language of NRS 133.110 dictates otherwise, and "we will not engraft, by judicial legislation, additional requirements upon the clear and unambiguous provisions of NRS 133.110." *Leggett*, 494 P.2d at 557.

W.R. executed his will before remarrying Maria; consequently, Maria could invoke the protections afforded to a spouse under NRS 133.110. Scott concedes that W.R.'s amendment to the inter vivos trust does not constitute a marriage contract and that no other marriage contract providing for Maria exists. Likewise, it is undisputed that

---

72. We are cognizant of the fact that modern estate planning regularly utilizes revocable inter vivos trusts with pour-over wills. This approach to estate planning usually results in amendments, if any, being made to the revocable trust and not the pour-over will. Given the clear and unambiguous language of NRS 133.110, we caution that a testator must modify his or her will in order to avoid the consequences resulting from the unintentional omission of a surviving spouse pursuant to NRS 133.110.

W.R.'s will did not contain a provision providing for Maria or a provision expressing an intent to not provide for her. Thus, the district court properly concluded that W.R.'s will is revoked as to Maria, as none of the three limited exceptions contained in NRS 133.110 is present. . . .

CONCLUSION

We conclude that an amendment to an inter vivos trust cannot serve to rebut the presumption that a will is revoked as to an unintentionally omitted spouse. NRS 133.110 unambiguously permits three exceptions to rebut the presumption of revocation, and an amendment to an inter vivos trust is clearly not one of them. . . . Accordingly, we affirm the district court's order.

NOTES

1. Nonprobate Transfers.   In *Prestie*, was Maria omitted from her husband's estate plan, or just from his will? In determining whether Maria was "provided for in the will," why did the court not look at the terms of the trust into which the will poured over? If the will had incorporated the trust by reference (see page 245), so that the terms of the trust had been absorbed into the will, would the result have been different? Is there a principled distinction between a pour-over will and incorporation by reference for discerning whether the surviving spouse was unintentionally omitted? Why not look beyond the face of the will to determine whether the omission of a spouse was intentional?

In 2009, the Nevada legislature amended the statute at issue in *Prestie* to except cases in which the surviving spouse "is provided for by a transfer of property outside of the will and it appears that the maker intended the transfer to be in lieu of a testamentary provision."[73] What result in *Prestie* under the revised statute? What if UPC § 2-301, page 571, had been applicable?[74]

2. UPC § 2-301 and Multiple Marriages.   If H marries W some years after making a will that devises everything to his daughter by a previous marriage, under UPC § 2-301 W is not entitled to an intestate share in H's estate. She must exercise her right to an elective share, which may give her less than an intestate share. On the other hand, if H had left his property by will to his alma mater, W would take an intestate share. What is the reason for this?

2. Unintentional Disinheritance of a Child

We turn now to the *pretermitted heir* statutes, designed to prevent the unintentional disinheritance of a child.[75] It was likely such a statute that induced Calvin Coolidge, noted for his economy of language, to add an opening phrase to his

---

73. Nev. Rev. Stat. § 133.110(1)(c) (2016).
74. *See* Ferguson v. Critopoulos, 163 So. 3d 330 (Ala. 2014).
75. *See* Adam J. Hirsch, Airbrushed Heirs: The Problem of Children Omitted from Wills, 50 Real Prop. Tr. & Est. L.J. 175 (2015).

The Will of Silent Cal

Calvin Coolidge's will read in its entirety:

"The White House"
Washington
Will of Calvin Coolidge of Northampton,
Hampshire County, Massachusetts

Not unmindful of my son John, I give all my estate both real and personal to my wife Grace Coolidge, in fee simple—Home at Washington, District of Columbia this twentieth day December, A.D. nineteen hundred and twenty six.

/s/ *Calvin Coolidge*

Signed by me on the date above in the presence of the testator and of each other as witnesses to said will and the signature thereof.

/s/ *Everett Sanders*
/s/ *Edward T. Clark*
/s/ *Erwin C. Geisser*

Many stories are told about Coolidge, who is said to have slept 11 hours a day, including a nap most afternoons of 2 to 4 hours. H.L. Mencken said that Coolidge's "chief feat" was "to sleep more and say less" than any other president.* Here are some of our favorite stories about "Silent Cal":

1. Once a society woman was seated next to Coolidge at a formal dinner. She playfully opened her conversation by saying, "You must talk to me, Mr. Coolidge. I made a bet today that I could get more than two words out of you." Coolidge replied, "You lose." And she did.

2. "When Coolidge was Vice-President, his successor as Governor of Massachusetts, Channing Cox, paid him a visit. Cox asked how Coolidge had been able to see so many visitors a day when he was Governor, but always leave the office at 5:00 P.M., while Cox himself found he often left as late as 9:00 P.M. 'Why the difference?' he asked. 'You talk back,' said Coolidge."

3. Coolidge once explained to his successor, Herbert Hoover, how to deal with "long-winded visitors": "If you keep dead still they will run down in three or four minutes."

4. In 1933, when Dorothy Parker, the writer and Algonquin Roundtable regular, heard the news that President Coolidge had died suddenly, she quipped, "How can they tell?"†

* Paul F. Boller, Jr., Presidential Anecdotes 234, 243-44 (rev. ed. 1996).

† Id. at 235, 239-41.

will—the shortest will of any president of the United States: "Not unmindful of my son John, ..." By this phrase, Coolidge demonstrated that his failure to provide for John was intentional and not a mistaken oversight, and therefore no pretermitted heir statute should apply. Many pretermitted heir statutes, such as UPC § 2-302 (1990, rev. 2003), excerpted below, apply only to children born after the execution of a will, but some protect children alive when the will was executed as well as after-born children.

Uniform Probate Code (Unif. Law Comm'n 1990, as amended 1993)

§ 2-302. Omitted Children

(a) Except as provided in subsection (b), if a testator fails to provide in his [or her] will for any of his [or her] children born or adopted after the execution of the will, the omitted after-born or after-adopted child receives a share in the estate as follows:

(1) If the testator had no child living when he [or she] executed the will, an omitted after-born or after-adopted child receives a share in the estate equal in value to that which the child would have received had the testator died intestate, unless the will devised all or substantially all of the estate to the other parent of the omitted child and that other parent survives the testator and is entitled to take under the will.

(2) If the testator had one or more children living when he [or she] executed the will, and the will devised property or an interest in property to one or more of the then-living children, an omitted after-born or after-adopted child is entitled to share in the testator's estate as follows:

(A) The portion of the testator's estate in which the omitted after-born or after-adopted child is entitled to share is limited to devises made to the testator's then-living children under the will.

(B) The omitted after-born or after-adopted child is entitled to receive the share of the testator's estate, as limited in subparagraph (A), that the child would have received had the testator included all omitted after-born and after-adopted children with the children to whom devises were made under the will and had given an equal share of the estate to each child.

(C) To the extent feasible, the interest granted an omitted after-born or after-adopted child under this section must be of the same character, whether equitable or legal, present or future, as that devised to the testator's then-living children under the will.

(D) In satisfying a share provided by this paragraph, devises to the testator's children who were living when the will was executed abate ratably. In abating the devises of the then-living children, the court shall preserve to the maximum extent possible the character of the testamentary plan adopted by the testator.

(b) Neither subsection (a)(1) nor subsection (a)(2) applies if:

(1) it appears from the will that the omission was intentional; or

(2) the testator provided for the omitted after-born or after-adopted child by transfer outside the will and the intent that the transfer be in lieu of a testamentary provision is shown by the testator's statements or is reasonably inferred from the amount of the transfer or other evidence.

(c) If at the time of execution of the will the testator fails to provide in his [or her] will for a living child solely because he [or she] believes the child to be dead, the child is entitled to share in the estate as if the child were an omitted after-born or after-adopted child.

(d) In satisfying a share provided by subsection (a)(1), devises made by the will abate under Section 3-902.

Gray v. Gray
947 So. 2d 1045 (Ala. 2006)

SEE, J. William Terry Gray, the executor of the estate of John Merrill Gray II ("John"), appeals the probate court's judgment finding that John Merrill Gray III ("Jack") is entitled to receive a share of John's estate under Ala. Code § 43-8-91 (1975). . . .

BACKGROUND

In 1981, John executed his will. At that time, John was married to Mary Rose Gray and had two children from a prior marriage, Robert B. Gray and Monica L. Muncher. John's will devised all of his estate to his wife Mary and did not include his two children.

My Dad Was John Merrill Gray II

Jack Gray, J.D. 2013, who came upon this case—*his* case—in Professor Alyssa A. DiRusso's Spring 2012 trusts and estates course at Cumberland School of Law, writes to us as follows:

> My dad, John Merrill Gray, II, was an attorney who had a small general practice in various cities throughout Alabama. While I am unsure if he ever did any wills, trusts, and estates work, I am certain that having his will contest make it all the way to the Alabama Supreme Court was not in his plan.

> My dad was 53 when he died suddenly in Birmingham, Alabama. His death was a surprise, though not wholly unexpected given the various demons he had battled throughout his life. I was 19 at the time, having just arrived home from my freshman year of college in Virginia.

> I had only learned of the existence of my half-siblings, Robert and Monica, a short time before my father's death. They were never a part of my life before my dad died. I first met Robert and Monica at my father's funeral, and have never seen or spoken with them since.

> The process of the will contest was trying on our family. I was never particularly close with anyone on my father's side of the family except for my father's brother, William Terry Gray, who was also the executor of my dad's will. I would spend time every summer with Uncle Terry and felt that we had a reasonably close and amicable relationship. My dad and Uncle Terry were estranged a short time after I was born in 1984. They had not spoken much in many years prior to my dad's death.

Jack Gray and his father John

> I was a sophomore in college when I learned that Uncle Terry, as executor, claimed the entirety of my father's estate without providing an inheritance for me. Uncle Terry was not amenable to a settlement providing for me, so we initiated the will contest on the ground that I was a pretermitted child. After Uncle Terry was awarded my father's estate, he intimated that he felt that all of my father's children, Robert, Monica, and me should have some share in my father's inheritance. To date, however, I have not received anything from my father's estate.

> Throughout the litigation I experienced first hand the emotions and strife these kinds of cases can bring to a family. The whole experience led me to enter law school, and, more importantly, made me keenly aware of the importance of planning to avoid a contest like mine.

Email from John Merrill "Jack" Gray III to Robert H. Sitkoff (June 14, 2012).

In 1984, John and Mary gave birth to John Merrill "Jack" Gray III. In 1989, John and Mary divorced. John and Mary's divorce judgment and property settlement included a provision creating a trust for Jack, which states that "[o]ne-half of all assets, inheritance or disbursements of any kind received by the Husband from his mother's estate shall be placed in trust for his son, Jack." Pursuant to Ala. Code § 43-8-137,[76] even though John's will devised all of his estate to Mary, Mary would not inherit under

---

76. Section 43-8-137 revokes "any disposition . . . made by the will to" a divorced former spouse "unless the will expressly provides otherwise. Property prevented from passing to a former spouse because of revocation by divorce . . . passes as if the former spouse failed to survive the decedent."—Eds.

John's will upon his death because John and Mary divorced. In 2004, John died without having changed his will.

William Terry Gray, the executor of John's estate, petitioned the Jefferson County Probate Court to probate John's will.[77] Jack petitioned the probate court for an order finding that he is entitled to a share of John's estate under Ala. Code § 43-8-91, which provides . . . :

> (a) If a testator fails to provide in his will for any of his children born or adopted after the execution of his will, the omitted child receives a share in the estate equal in value to that which he would have received if the testator had died intestate unless:
>> (1) It appears from the will that the omission was intentional;
>> (2) When the will was executed the testator had one or more children and devised substantially all his estate to the other parent of the omitted child; or
>> (3) The testator provided for the child by transfer outside the will and the intent that the transfer be in lieu of a testamentary provision be reasonably proven. . . .

The executor moved the probate court to dismiss Jack's petition. The executor argued that Ala. Code § 43-8-91(a)(2) applies because John had two children when he executed his will and devised substantially all of his estate to Jack's mother, Mary. Therefore, the executor argued, Jack was not entitled to his intestate share of John's estate. The executor also argued that Ala. Code § 43-8-91(a)(3) applies because, he argued, John provided for Jack in a nontestamentary transfer in lieu of a testamentary transfer when he established a trust in Jack's favor upon his divorce from Jack's mother. . . .

The probate court granted Jack's petition, holding that Jack is entitled to a distribution from John's estate equal in value to the share he would have received had John died intestate. The executor appeals. . . .

ANALYSIS

. . . We recognize the instruction of Ala. Code § 43-8-2, that the Probate Code be "liberally construed" to promote its underlying purposes, one of which is to "make effective the intent of a decedent in the distribution of his property." However, Ala. Code § 43-8-91(a)(2) does not place before the courts the issue of the decedent's intent, in contrast with § 43-8-91(a)(1) and (a)(3). Those provisions preclude the omitted child's inheritance under the will when "[i]t appears from the will that the omission was intentional" or "[t]he testator provided for the child by transfer outside the will and the intent that the transfer be in lieu of a testamentary provision be reasonably proven." In § 43-8-91(a)(2), the legislature has made assumptions regarding the testator's intent where the two stated factors are present. The courts are not invited to make further inquiry, as we are in § 43-8-91(a)(1) and (a)(3). . . .

Section 43-8-91 states that, if a child is born subsequent to the execution of a will and the will fails to provide for the child, the omitted child is entitled to a share of the

---

77. William Terry Gray, the executor, was the testator's brother and the contingent taker under the will. — Eds.

testator's estate, except in certain circumstances. One of those exceptions is that an omitted child is not entitled to a share of the estate if "[w]hen the will was executed the testator had one or more children and devised substantially all his estate to the other parent of the omitted child."[78]

In 1981, when John executed his will, he had two children by a prior marriage, and his will devised all of his estate to Jack's mother Mary. Therefore, § 43-8-91(a)(2) applies, and Jack may not receive a share of John's estate.

Jack argues that the exception in § 43-8-91(a)(2) should not apply to him because, he says, § 43-8-91(a)(2) "does not appear to contemplate a situation wherein the testator has children, divorces their mother, remarries, executes a will that makes no provision for any children whatsoever, than [sic] has a child with that second wife." Jack's brief, at 8-9. However, § 43-8-91(a)(2) states only two conditions for excluding an omitted child from an intestate share of the testator's estate: (1) the testator had one or more children at the time he executed his will, and (2) the testator's will devised substantially all of the testator's estate to the other parent of the omitted child. Because the statute is one of substance and is in derogation of the common law, we must construe it strictly and not extend its reach beyond its terms. Jack's argument, therefore, fails. The fact that John's other children were from a prior marriage is immaterial under § 43-8-91. Thus, Jack does not escape the exclusion found in § 43-8-91(a)(2). Accordingly, Jack is not entitled to receive a share of John's estate under § 43-8-91. . . .

Because, as § 43-8-91(a) makes clear, the entire provision is dealing only with omitted children who are "born or adopted after the execution of [the testator's] will," to adopt the construction [advanced in the dissent] that it is intended to apply only to a child "then in being" is to give to the statute a meaning opposite of what it says. We will leave such rewriting to the legislature, whose job it is to amend or repeal statutes. . . .

There is no ambiguity in this statute. . . . [E]ven if there were ambiguity, while the result provided by the legislature may or may not be the one that those of us on this Court would have provided, it certainly does not reach the level of absurdity required before this Court is compelled to conclude that the legislature meant something other than what its words convey.[79]

CONCLUSION

. . . Because we are reversing the probate court's order based on Ala. Code § 43-8-91(a)(2) and remanding the case to the probate court for further proceedings, we pretermit consideration of the executor's remaining arguments.

Reversed and remanded.

---

78. Ala. Code § 43-8-91(a)(2) does not distinguish an omitted child whose "other parent" is divorced from the testator after the testator executed his or her will from an omitted child whose "other parent" was divorced from the testator before the testator executed his or her will. The legislature could have limited § 43-8-91(a)(2) to only one of those categories by including language to that effect.

79. The legislature might well have assumed that in a case like this one it could anticipate that the child would be protected in the divorce proceeding, either directly or by a distribution of a share of the marital assets to the custodial parent. In this case, as we have previously noted, Jack was provided for in the divorce proceeding by the creation of a trust.

NOTES

1. Was Jack Mistakenly Omitted?   Why did the court in *Gray* not consider whether Jack was in fact mistakenly omitted from the will? Was he mistakenly omitted? In view of the trust created by the testator for the benefit of Jack, could the case have been resolved on the basis of Ala. Code § 43-8-91(a)(3)? *See* In re Estate of Hendler, 316 S.W.3d 703 (Tex. App. 2010). The statute at issue in *Gray* was based on the 1969 UPC. What result if UPC § 2-302 (1990, rev. 1993), page 575, had been applicable?

Pretermitted heir statutes can be classified as "Missouri" type or "Massachusetts" type. A Missouri-type statute is drawn to benefit children "not named or provided for" in the will. Extrinsic evidence of intent is not admissible. A Massachusetts-type statute allows the child to take "unless it appears that such omission was intentional and not occasioned by any mistake." Extrinsic evidence is admitted to show the presence or absence of an intent to disinherit.[80]

2. Two Pretermitted Child Problems.   Consider the following problems:

a. When *T* executes her will, she has two living children, *A* and *B*. Her will devises $7,500 to each child. *T* then has another child, *C,* and then *T* dies. To what amount is *C* entitled under UPC § 2-302, page 575? The official comment says *C* is entitled to $5,000, taken one-half from *A*'s devise (reducing it to $5,000) and one-half from *B*'s. Suppose that *T* had devised $10,000 to *A* and $5,000 to *B*. What would *C* take and where would it come from? How would the analysis change, if at all, under the 1969 UPC provision at issue in *Gray*?

b. In 1983, René executed a will providing for his three children, each by name. In 1984, René had a fourth child, a daughter Patricia. In 1986, René executed a codicil making minor changes to his will, but neglecting to add Patricia. Then René died. The state's pretermitted child statute, based on the 1969 UPC, applies to children born or adopted after the will was executed. Is Patricia entitled to a pretermitted child share? In Azcunce v. Estate of Azcunce, 586 So. 2d 1216 (Fla. App. 1991), the court held that the execution of the codicil republished the will as of the date of the codicil (see page 244), hence Patricia was not pretermitted. Is this a sound application of the doctrine of republication by codicil?[81]

3. Children or Descendants, After or Already Born.   Many pretermitted heir statutes, like UPC § 2-302, page 575, protect only children born or adopted *after* execution of the will. Applying such a statute, in In re Gilmore, 925 N.Y.S.2d 567 (App. Div. 2011), the court held that a child born before execution of the will was not pretermitted even if the testator had no knowledge of the child's existence. In Estate of Maher v. Iglikova, 138 So. 3d 484 (Fla. App. 2014), the court held that a nonmarital child born before execution of the will but legitimized after was not pretermitted.

---

80. *See* 83 A.L.R.4th 779 (1991, Supp. 2016); *see also* Shelly Kreiczer-Levy, Deliberative Accountability Rules in Inheritance Law: Promoting Accountable Estate Planning, 45 U. Mich. J.L. Reform 937, 954-57 (2012).

81. *See* Restatement (Third) of Property: Wills and Other Donative Transfers § 9.6 cmt. e (Am. Law Inst. 2003).

Other statutes, however, operate in favor of children *alive when the will was executed* as well as after-born children. Under the latter statutes, a testator's failure to name all living children invites a challenge. This problem is acute in the minority of states in which the statute applies not just to *children* but also to *descendants*.[82] In In re Estate of Laura, 690 A.2d 1011 (N.H. 1997), Edward executed a will expressly disinheriting his grandsons Richard and Neil. Neil died, leaving two children, Cecelia and Neil, III. Then Edward died. The applicable pretermitted heir statute provided as follows (emphasis added):

> Every child born after the decease of the testator, and every child or issue of a child of the deceased *not named or referred to in his will* [this is a Missouri-type provision], and who is not a devisee or legatee, shall be entitled to the same portion of the estate, real and personal, as he would be if the deceased were intestate.

The question was whether the great-grandchildren, Cecelia and Neil, III, were barred from taking as pretermitted heirs by Edward's express disinheritance of their father, Neil. The court held that a testator who names a descendant in an effort to disinherit him has referred to, and thus disinherited, the descendants of the named descendant.

Laura may be contrasted with Estate of Treloar, 859 A.2d 1162 (N.H. 2004). In *Treloar*, Josiah named "my son-in-law, Leon," the husband of Josiah's predeceased daughter, Evelyn, as executor of Josiah's will, but he did not mention Andrew and Peter, the children of Evelyn and Leon. The court held that the use of the term "son-in-law" in identifying Leon, only indirectly referring to Evelyn (and in a fiduciary appointment to boot), was insufficient to preclude application of the pretermitted heir statute to Andrew and Peter.

4. Overcoming the Pretermitted Heir Statutes. In most states, the pretermitted heir statute can be avoided by providing for descendants with representation. No descendant, whether born before or after the will's execution, will be pretermitted if *T* devises the residue of his estate "to my wife, *W*, if she survives me, or if she does not survive me, then to my descendants, per stirpes." However, all of *T*'s descendants are included in such a class, something *T* might want to avoid if, for example, he has been concealing the existence of a nonmarital child conceived in an adulterous relationship. In a jurisdiction in which the pretermission statute applies to children born before the execution of the will, can a testator exclude an existing child without mentioning the child by name?

Courts have been strict in requiring the testator to indicate clearly an intention to disinherit a child, either by express words or by necessary implication. In In re Estate of Robbins, 756 A.2d 602 (N.H. 2000), the will provided: "Except as otherwise expressly provided by this will . . . , I intentionally make no provisions for the benefit of any other heir of mine." The court held that this language did not disinherit a natural and an adopted child.

---

82. *See* id. cmt. d (noting that the statutes "vary widely").

Anna Nicole Smith and Blanket Disinheritance

In 2001, Vickie Lynn Marshall, better known as Anna Nicole Smith, executed a will in which she stated, "I have one child Daniel Wayne Smith." Smith left her entire estate "in trust for my child." The will also contained a blanket disinheritance clause: "Except as otherwise provided in this Will, I have intentionally omitted to provide for my spouse and other heirs, including future spouses and children and other descendants now living and those hereafter born or adopted, as well as existing future stepchildren and foster children."

On September 7, 2006, Smith gave birth to a daughter, Dannielynn Hope. Three days later, Daniel, then age 20, died. Five months later, on February 8, 2007, Anna died of what the coroner's report termed "combined drug toxicity." Could Dannielynn take from Smith's estate?

Under Cal. Prob. Code § 21620 (2016), "if a decedent fails to provide in a testamentary instrument for a child of [the] decedent born or adopted after the execution of all of the decedent's testamentary instruments, the omitted child shall receive a share in the decedent's estate equal in value to that which the child would have received if the decedent had died without having executed any testamentary instrument." However, this provision is qualified by Cal. Prob. Code § 21621 (2016), which provides that a "child shall not receive a share of the estate" if the "decedent's failure to provide for the child in the decedent's testamentary instruments was intentional and that intention appears from the testamentary instruments."

So Dannielynn's claim appeared to turn on whether the blanket disinheritance clause indicated that she was intentionally omitted from the will. But even if the disinheritance clause precluded application of the pretermitted child statute, Dannielynn's brother, Daniel, the sole named beneficiary, predeceased Smith without descendants. With no

```
1.                        ARTICLE I

          FAMILY DECLARATIONS AND STATUTORY DISINHERITANCES

     I am unmarried. I have one child DANIEL WAYNE SMITH. I have

no predeceased children nor predeceased children leaving issue.

     Except as otherwise provided in this Will, I have inten-

tionally omitted to provide for my spouse and other heirs,

including future spouses and children and other descendants now

living and those hereafter born or adopted, as well as existing

and future stepchildren and foster children.
```

The blanket disinheritance clause in Anna Nicole Smith's will

descendants of Daniel to be substituted for him by the antilapse statute (see page 357),* and no other residuary taker named in the will, could Dannielynn take the entire estate as Smith's sole heir in intestacy? Or would the express disinheritance clause count as a negative will (see page 89) that would prevent Dannielynn from taking by intestacy?

The court ruled that Dannielynn was the sole beneficiary of the trust under the will. Although Smith's will left her entire estate "in trust for my *child*," and it stated that her only child was Daniel, the trust provisions in the will also referred to "my *children*" and used other plural language such as "*their* accustomed manner of living" (emphasis added). In resolving this ambiguity in favor of including Dannielynn, the court relied on a declaration of the drafting lawyer, who said that even though Smith "did not expect to have any children in the future, if she did, she wanted them to share equally in the trust." The purpose of the disinheritance clause, said the lawyer, was to guard against claims against Smith's estate by Smith's estranged mother or others. "In retrospect," the lawyer acknowledged, "the language I used was too broad."

---

* Suppose Daniel did have a surviving descendant. Would the blanket disinheritance clause preclude application of the antilapse statute? *See* In re Estate of Tolman, 104 Cal. Rptr. 3d 924 (App. 2010).

The editors thank Bruce Ross, counsel for the executor of Smith's estate, for supplying us with the petition and the court's decision described in this note.

In re Estate of Jackson
194 P.3d 1269 (Okla. 2008)

TAYLOR, J. We are presented with this question of first impression: whether the assets of a revocable *inter vivos* trust are subject to the provisions of Oklahoma's pretermitted heir statute, 84 O.S. 2001, 132. . . . We answer . . . in the negative. . . .

FACTS

This appeal arises from a final decree in a probate proceeding of the estate of Walter Kinsley Jackson (Jackson). On August 18, 2003, Johnny C. Benjamin (Benjamin) filed a petition seeking to be named the personal representative of the estate of Jackson. In the petition, Benjamin alleged (1) Jackson died intestate, (2) Benjamin is Jackson's adult son, and (3) Benjamin is Jackson's sole surviving heir at law. . . .

On September 3, 2003, the trial court found Jackson died intestate, found Benjamin to be Jackson's son and entitled to Letters of Administration, and found Benjamin to be Jackson's sole heir at law.

Benjamin brought an intra-probate proceeding against Robena Butler and Harris Butler (together, the Butlers), the co-trustees of a revocable *inter vivos* trust established by Jackson and his wife, who had predeceased him. In the intra-probate proceeding, Benjamin sought the removal of the Butlers as co-trustees with him named as trustee in their place, sought the disgorgement of any trust assets which had been disbursed, and sought a determination that he was Jackson's pretermitted heir and entitled to all the trust's assets. Benjamin's position hinged on the September 3, 2003 order's findings that he was Jackson's son and that he was Jackson's heir at law. . . .

Benjamin then filed a motion for partial summary judgment in which . . . he argued that . . . the terms of title 84, section 132 applied to trusts, as well as wills; and that as Jackson's sole and pretermitted heir, he was entitled to all of the trust's assets. . . .

The trial court denied Benjamin's motion for partial summary judgment, finding that the terms of title 84, section 132 of the Oklahoma Statutes do not apply to a revocable *inter vivos* trust. . . .

The Court of Civil Appeals affirmed the trial court's judgment. . . . This Court granted Benjamin's petition for writ of certiorari. . . .

OKLAHOMA'S PRETERMITTED HEIR STATUTE

Disposing of property is an inalienable natural right throughout a person's lifetime. However, the right to control disposition of property after death and the right of inheritance are statutory. The Oklahoma Legislature has provided several means for disposing of one's property at death: one is by will and another is by trust. In Oklahoma's pretermitted heir statute, the Legislature has also provided a statutory method of inheritance for children whom a testator fails to provide for or to name in a will.

Here Benjamin invokes Oklahoma's pretermitted heir statute in his quest for a share of Jackson's assets and argues that it should be construed to extend to children omitted from revocable *inter vivos* trusts as well as wills. . . .

Oklahoma's pretermitted heir statute provides:

> When any testator *omits to provide in his will* for any of his children, or for the issue of any deceased child unless it appears that such omission was intentional, such child, or the issue of such child, must have the same share in the estate of the testator, as if he had died intestate, and succeeds thereto as provided in the preceding section.

84 O.S. 2001, 132 (emphasis added). This provision unambiguously pertains only to wills. It does not encompass a situation where a child is omitted from a trust, and we decline to extend its reach to revocable *inter vivos* trusts.

Benjamin relies on Thomas v. Bank of Oklahoma, N.A., 684 P.2d 553 (Okla. 1984). In *Thomas*, the spouse had placed her separate property in a revocable *inter vivos* trust but had retained the right of complete control and dominion over the trust assets. This Court ruled that a spouse could not defeat a surviving spouse's share of an estate under title 84, section 44 of the 1981 Oklahoma Statutes by placing the estate assets in a revocable *inter vivos* trust with the deceased spouse retaining control of the assets while living. This Court found that such a trust was illusory as to the surviving spouse. Benjamin argues here for an extension of *Thomas* to children. He submits that children should be treated the same as surviving spouses in that they are forced heirs under Oklahoma's pretermitted heir statute. We disagree. . . .

Title 84, section 44 of the 1981 statutes and its current counterpart, known as "forced heir" statutes, are limitations on a married person's power to dispose of his or her property. The forced heir statute limits a spouse's power to disinherit the surviving spouse; the statute secures to a surviving spouse the right to elect a minimum statutory share in the deceased spouse's estate which is superior to other legatees and devisees. A spouse may not disinherit a surviving spouse even with a clear expression of intent to do.

In contrast, Oklahoma's pretermitted heir statute found at title 84, section 132 is not a limitation on a testator's power to dispose of his or her property. Section 132 is an assurance that a child is not unintentionally omitted from a will. The pretermitted heir statute does not secure a child with a minimum statutory share of a parent's estate upon the death of a parent. Unlike a spouse, a testator can disinherit a child if the will shows a clear intent to do so. Unlike section 44's forced heir provisions, section 132 is ineffective against a testator's bequest of a pittance to a child. The limitation on a testator's power to disinherit a spouse, coupled with a testator's power to disinherit a child, prevents the extension of the *Thomas* decision to a child. . . .

CONCLUSION

The . . . trial court correctly found that the terms of Oklahoma's pretermitted heir statute do not extend to a revocable *inter vivos* trust. This decision left Benjamin with no claim to the trust assets. Because the trial court reached the correct result, we affirm. The Court of Civil Appeals' opinion is vacated, and the district court's judgment is affirmed.

NOTE

Pretermitted Heirs and Nonprobate Transfers.   Most pretermitted heir statutes refer only to wills and not to revocable trusts or other nonprobate modes of transfer. As in *Jackson,* courts have held that these statutes cannot be applied to a revocable trust used as a will substitute.

Should the pretermitted heir statutes be amended to apply to revocable trusts? Do not the same policies that underpin the statutory protection against mistaken omission from a will apply equally to mistaken omission from a revocable trust used as a will substitute? The Restatement (Third) of Trusts answers these questions in the affirmative:

> Sound policy suggests that a property owner's choice of form in using a revocable trust rather than a will as the central instrument of an estate plan should not deprive that property owner and the objects of his or her bounty of appropriate aids and safeguards intended to achieve likely intentions. Thus, although a particular statute of this general type fails to address trusts that are revocable but nontestamentary, the legislation should ordinarily be applied as if trust dispositive provisions that are to be carried out after the settlor's death had been made by will.[83]

The California pretermitted heir statute uses the term "testamentary instrument" instead of "will,"[84] and "testamentary instruments" is defined to include a decedent's will or revocable trust.[85] What result in *Jackson* under the California statute?

What about other nonprobate transfers such as joint bank accounts, POD contracts, and insurance contracts? Should these be subject to the pretermission statutes? Does the asset-specific nature of these transfers counsel a different policy? In Robbins v. Johnson, 780 A.2d 1282 (N.H. 2001), the court noted the difficulties presented by these questions:

> The plaintiffs urge us to extend the statute to the trust at issue as a matter of policy. We note that trusts are not the only type of so-called will substitutes by which individuals pass property at death. Other will substitutes include payable on death accounts, transfer on death accounts, life insurance proceeds to a named beneficiary, and pension funds. We believe that the legislature should decide whether, as a matter of policy, it wishes to extend the pretermitted heir statute to will substitutes, such as the trust at issue. Absent clear indication from the legislature that this is its intention, we decline to apply the statute to the trust.

---

83. Restatement (Third) of Trusts § 25 cmt. e(1) (Am. Law Inst. 2003).
84. Cal. Prob. Code §§ 21620-21621 (2016).
85. Id. § 21601.

CHAPTER 9

TRUSTS: FIDUCIARY ADMINISTRATION

[T]he normal private trust is essentially a gift, projected
on the plane of time and so subjected to a management regime.

BERNARD RUDDEN
44 Mod. L. Rev. 610, 610 (1981)

THE HALLMARK CHARACTERISTIC of a common law trust is bifurcation:
The trustee holds *legal title* to the trust property, and the beneficiaries have *equitable* or *beneficial* ownership. This separation of legal and beneficial ownership offers many advantages. For example, property transferred in trust during the settlor's life avoids probate. Because the trustee holds legal title to the property, there is no need to change title by probate administration upon the settlor's death (see Chapter 7). Another advantage, which we consider in this chapter, is managerial intermediation between the beneficiary and the trust property. The intermediary role of the trustee involves custody, administration, investment, and distribution of the trust property in accordance with the terms of the trust.

No one knows exactly what the future will bring. At best, a donor can make only an informed guess about the future needs and circumstances of a beneficiary. Moreover, a donor might not be ready to give full control over property to a competent and reliable beneficiary, much less one who has special needs, is very young or very old, or is feckless or profligate. Bifurcating ownership across time by making a gift in trust ameliorates all of these concerns. As we shall see, the trust is a powerful tool for implementing a donor's freedom of disposition across time.

By making a transfer in trust rather than outright, a settlor ensures that the property will be managed and distributed in accordance with his wishes as expressed in the terms of the trust. A trust allows the settlor to postpone important decisions about the investment and distribution of the trust property. Instead of imposing inflexible instructions in advance, the settlor may empower the trustee to decide how the property should be invested and distributed in light of changing market conditions and the beneficiaries' circumstances.

587

Use of a trust, however, puts the beneficiaries at the peril of mismanagement or even misappropriation by the trustee. Enter the law of *fiduciary administration*. Its purpose is to induce the trustee to adhere to the terms of the trust and to act prudently and in good faith in the best interests of the beneficiaries. Trustees are subject to primary fiduciary duties of *loyalty* and *prudence* and to a host of subsidiary duties such as keeping adequate records and disclosing information about the trust to the beneficiaries. A trustee who is found to be in breach may be removed from office, and the beneficiaries will be entitled to remedies that include disgorgement of any profit by the trustee and compensatory damages. These remedies are meant to deter breach, to make the beneficiaries whole, and to prevent unjust enrichment of the trustee.

We begin in Section A by considering the evolution from limited powers of trusteeship to expansive powers that are subject to strict fiduciary duties. In Section B, we consider the duty of loyalty, which requires a trustee to administer the trust in the sole interest of the beneficiaries. In Section C, we consider the duty of prudence, which imposes an objective standard of care in all functions of trusteeship. In Section D, we consider the duty of impartiality, which requires a trustee to act with due regard for the respective interests of the beneficiaries. In Section E, we consider the duty to provide information and to account to the beneficiaries.

A. FROM LIMITED POWERS TO FIDUCIARY ADMINISTRATION

In the days of yore, when the trust was used more for conveying land than for ongoing administration of property, trust law protected beneficiaries by giving the trustee only limited powers. In modern practice, in which trusts are commonly used to facilitate professional management of property on behalf of the beneficiaries, the trustee is given broad *powers* of administration, but the exercise of those powers is subject to the trustee's *fiduciary duties*. The Restatement (Third) of Trusts characterizes this as "a basic principle of trust administration," namely, that "a trustee presumptively has comprehensive powers to manage the trust estate and otherwise to carry out the terms and purpose of the trust, but that all powers held in the capacity of trustee must be exercised, or not exercised, in accordance with the trustee's fiduciary obligations."[1]

1. From Conveyance to Management

John H. Langbein
Rise of the Management Trust
143 Tr. & Est. 52 (2004)

The trust first developed for an age in which real estate was the principal form of wealth. We can trace the Lord Chancellor enforcing trusts (then called "uses") as far back as the 14th century. Until the later 17th century, the owner of freehold land was

---

1. Restatement (Third) of Trusts § 70 cmt. a (Am. Law Inst. 2007).

not allowed to pass the land by will and, thus, on the owner's death, the land had to descend by intestacy. The trust was a conveyancing device that defeated both the rigidities of intestacy (which still included primogeniture) and the burdensome taxes (called feudal incidents) that pertained when land passed on intestacy. The owner of land (the settlor) transferred the land to trustees to hold for the settlor for life and, on his death, to transfer the land to those survivors and in those shares specified in the terms of the trust. Then, as now, the trust served as a will substitute. . . .

Today's trust has ceased to be a conveyancing device for land and has become, instead, a management device for holding a portfolio of financial assets. The management trust is a response to the radical change away from family real estate as the dominant form of personal wealth. As the jurist Roscoe Pound observed in an arresting epigram, "Wealth in a commercial age is made up largely of promises." Most modern wealth takes the form of financial assets: equities, bonds, mutual fund shares, insurance contracts, pension and annuity interests, and bank accounts. Today's trust typically holds a portfolio of these complex financial assets, which are contract rights against the issuers. Such a portfolio requires skilled and active management. Investment decisions must be made and monitored, the portfolio rebalanced and proxies voted. Unusual assets, such as close corporation or partnership interests, commonly require even more active and specialized administration. By contrast, under the old conveyancing trust that held ancestral land, the beneficiaries commonly lived on the land and managed it. The trustees were, in truth, more stakeholders than managers; they were, in effect, nominees, with no serious powers or duties.

FROM AMATEUR TO PROFESSIONAL TRUSTEESHIP

The transformation in the nature of wealth that led to the management trust brought about a parallel transformation in trusteeship.

Trustees of old were unpaid amateurs, that is, family and community statesmen who lent their names and honor to a conveyancing dodge. Writing in the last years of the 19th century, the great legal scholar Frederic W. Maitland could still observe that "[a]lmost every well-to-do-man was a trustee."

Private trustees still abound, but the prototypical modern trustee is the fee-paid professional whose business is to enter into and carry out trust agreements. These entities thrive on their expertise in investment management, trust accounting, taxation, regulation and fiduciary administration. . . .

OVERCOMING TRUSTEE DISEMPOWERMENT

Another profound transformation that was essential to bring about the modern management trust was a reorientation in the way trust law went about the task of protecting trust beneficiaries. Because the trustee nominally owns the trust property, the trust relationship . . . puts the beneficiaries of a trust at the peril of trustee misbehavior; a trustee could, for example, misappropriate or mismanage the trust's assets.

Protecting the beneficiary against those dangers has always been the central concern of trust law. In the early centuries of the trust, when trustees were mostly stakeholders of ancestral land, it was relatively easy to keep them in check, simply by disabling them from doing much with the trust property. Thus, trust default law deliberately supplied no trustee powers. The trustee had only those powers that the trust instrument expressly granted, which were typically few, as the trustee's job was usually just to hold and convey to the remainderpersons. Stakeholder trustees did not need to transact. . . .

Trustee disempowerment was, therefore, the original system of beneficiary safeguard in the law of trusts, and it worked well enough as long as trustees had nothing much to do beyond standing as nominee owners of family land. But when the portfolio of financial assets displaced family land as the characteristic form of family wealth held in trust, disempowerment became quite counterproductive. The modern trustee conducts a program of investing and managing financial assets that requires extensive discretion to respond to changing market forces.

Two great steps were needed to adapt trust law to the rise of the management trust: Disempowerment had to be abandoned, and a new system of beneficiary safeguard had to be devised.

Broad empowerment legislation, such as the Uniform Trustees' Powers Act (1964), is now widespread. Such statutes authorize trustees to engage in every conceivable transaction that might enhance the value of trust assets (and professionally drafted instruments commonly contain such powers). The Uniform Trust Code (2000) completes this development, reversing the common law rule and providing the trustee [in § 815] with "all powers over the trust property which an unmarried competent owner has over individually owned property."

The Rise of Fiduciary Law

Equipping trustees with transactional power was only half the job of adapting the law to the needs of the management trust. The other half was the development of a substitute system of beneficiary safeguard. Trustees with transactional powers necessarily have the power to abuse as well as to advance the interests of beneficiaries. To prevent abuse, trustees were subject to duties, protective in nature, which were elaborated into a new body of law that we now recognize as trust fiduciary law.

All trust fiduciary law rests on two core principles, the care norm (the duty of prudent administration) and the loyalty norm (the duty to administer the trust for the benefit of the beneficiary). The many subrules—for example, the duties to keep and disclose records; to collect, segregate, earmark and protect trust property; to enforce and defend claims; to be impartial among multiple beneficiaries—are all applications of prudence and loyalty.

The modern law of trust administration is so centered on fiduciary law that we tend not to remember how recently that body of law has developed. . . . To be sure, principles of trust fiduciary law can be traced well back to the 18th century. . . . But these doctrinal impulses were not matters of great consequence until the last century or so. Only when financial assets came to displace ancestral land from the typical trust, and when empowerment triumphed over disempowerment, did trustees come routinely to exercise the levels of discretion over trust property that bring the fiduciary standards of care and loyalty into operation. As a practical matter, therefore, trust fiduciary law has been 20th-century and, now, 21st-century law.

NOTE

Three Kinds of Trusts in Practice.   American trust practice has fractured into three branches: (a) *business trusts* for commercial deals, (b) *revocable trusts* for nonprobate transfers, and (c) *irrevocable trusts* for ongoing fiduciary administration.[2]

   a. Business Trusts for Commercial Deals.   Business trusts are common law or statutory trusts created for a commercial purpose such as organizing a mutual fund or facilitating asset securitization. Because business trusts are not donative in purpose, but rather are integral to a commercial deal, they involve an exercise of freedom of contract, not freedom of disposition. We considered business trusts briefly in Chapter 6 at page 398.

   b. Revocable Trusts for Nonprobate Transfers.   The most common use of a revocable trust today is as a will substitute for conveying property at death outside of probate. Under traditional law, a trust is a fiduciary relationship in which a trustee holds legal title to certain property subject to fiduciary duties to administer the property for the benefit of one or more beneficiaries.[3] Yet in modern law a revocable trust need not have property, at least not initially, if it is to be funded by a pour-over will (see Chapter 7 at page 467). Moreover, the trustee of a revocable trust does not owe fiduciary duties to the beneficiaries, but rather is subject to the control of the settlor, to whom the trustee's duties run (see page 452). In modern practice, therefore, a revocable trust is a will substitute that avoids the burdens of probate in a manner reminiscent of how trusts were once used to defeat primogeniture and the feudal incidents (see Chapter 6 at page 387).[4]

   c. Irrevocable Trusts for Ongoing Fiduciary Administration.   An irrevocable trust involves ongoing fiduciary administration of property by a trustee in accordance with the settlor's intent. Increasingly, the trustee of such a trust is a fee-paid professional, and the trust property is a portfolio of liquid financial assets. What Professor Langbein aptly calls the rise of the management trust is the evolution of the trust from a device for conveying ancestral land into a vehicle for intergenerational, fiduciary management of financial wealth. The focus of this chapter is the ongoing fiduciary administration of irrevocable trusts.

2. Trustees' Powers

Under traditional law, a trustee's powers were limited to those granted expressly by the terms of the trust. As trusts came to be used for ongoing fiduciary administration, lawyers overcame the no-powers default rule of the common law by including an expansive schedule of trustees' powers in their trust instruments. Eventually, as broad powers provisions became a normal drafting practice and customary boilerplate, most

---

   2. In this taxonomy, we put to the side the *constructive trust*, which is a remedy commonly imposed to prevent unjust enrichment (see page 131), and the *resulting trust*, which is an equitable reversionary interest (see page 417).

   3. *See* Restatement (Third) of Trusts § 2 (Am. Law Inst. 2003).

   4. A funded revocable trust likewise avoids conservatorship (see Chapter 7 at 498).

states enacted statutes that presumptively gave trustees an expansive list of powers, such as under Uniform Trustees' Powers Act (UTPA) § 3(c) (Unif. Law Comm'n 1964).

Uniform Trust Code (UTC) § 815 (Unif. Law Comm'n 2000, rev. 2003) reflects the logical conclusion of this movement toward empowering trustees. Under § 815, in addition to the "powers conferred by the terms of the trust," by default a trustee has "all powers over the trust property which an unmarried competent owner has over individually owned property," plus "any other powers appropriate to achieve the proper investment, management, and distribution of the trust property." A trustee thus has the same default powers in dealing with trust property as would an outright owner. However, a trustee's "exercise of a power," whether granted by the terms of the trust or by statute, "is subject to the [trustee's] fiduciary duties."

NOTES

1. All Powers and Enumerated Powers.   UTC § 816 (2000) gives a trustee more than two dozen specific transactional powers, including the power to "acquire or sell property," to "deposit trust money in an account in a regulated financial-service institution," to "pay or contest any claim," and to "sign and deliver contracts." Given the sweeping "all powers" language of UTC § 815, what is the reason for the long list of specific powers in § 816? Is not the enumeration of specific powers in § 816 a redundancy? Professionally drafted trusts almost always include an expansive schedule of enumerated powers regardless of whether the state has adopted broad default powers legislation. Why is this practice advisable?

2. Duties of a Third Party Dealing with a Trustee.   Under traditional law, a third party dealing with a trustee was required to inquire whether the trustee had the power to undertake the proposed transaction. If the trustee did not have the power to do so, the third party could be held liable by the beneficiary for the trustee's breach. The purpose was to induce the third party to scrutinize the trustee's proposed course of action, protecting the beneficiary against overreaching. In practice, the effect was to deter third parties from dealing with trustees. Most states have abrogated this rule by statute, many following UTPA § 7 (1964) or UTC § 1012(a)-(b) (2000):

> (a) A person other than a beneficiary who in good faith assists a trustee, or who in good faith and for value deals with a trustee, without knowledge that the trustee is exceeding or improperly exercising the trustee's powers is protected from liability as if the trustee properly exercised the power.
>
> (b) A person other than a beneficiary who in good faith deals with a trustee is not required to inquire into the extent of the trustee's powers or the propriety of their exercise.

Moreover, UTC § 1013 (2000) authorizes a trustee to provide a third party with a "certification of trust" to verify that the trust is valid and that the trustee has the power to undertake a proposed transaction. The third party is entitled to "assume without inquiry the existence of the facts contained in the certification." The UTC drafters reasoned "that trust beneficiaries are helped more by the free flow of commerce than they were by the largely ineffective protective features of former law."[5]

3. Fiduciary Governance

With the broadening of trustees' powers, a new system of beneficiary safeguard was needed. Enter trust fiduciary law. In trust practice today, fiduciary governance has replaced limited powers as the primary means of protecting the beneficiary from abuse by the trustee. In the words of the Restatement, "even a power expressly conferred by the trust instrument, or by statute, is subject to the fundamental duties of prudence, loyalty, and impartiality, to a duty to adhere to the terms of the trust, and to the other fiduciary duties of trusteeship."[6]

Robert H. Sitkoff
Trust Law as Fiduciary Governance Plus Asset Partitioning
in The Worlds of the Trust 428 (Lionel Smith ed., 2013)

The underlying purpose of governance rules is to enable an organization's managers to act expeditiously on behalf of the organization and its beneficial owners while minimizing the agency costs arising from the separation of management and beneficial ownership. In the context of trust governance, the focus is safeguarding the beneficiary's interest from mismanagement or misappropriation by the trustee in circumstances in which the trustee must have discretionary powers of administration.

The traditional but now outmoded governance strategy for protecting the beneficiary's interests was to negate the agency problem by disempowering the trustee. Under traditional law, the trustee had no default powers to engage in market transactions over the trust property. The trustee's powers were limited to those granted expressly in the trust instrument. The problem with this disempowerment strategy is that in protecting the beneficiary from mis- or malfeasance by the trustee, the law also disabled the trustee from undertaking transactions useful for the beneficiary.

As trusts have come increasingly to be funded with liquid financial assets that require alert management in the face of swiftly changing financial markets, modern trust law has come to give the trustee broad *powers* to undertake any type of transaction, subject to the trustee's fiduciary *duties*. Modern law gives the trustee "all of the powers over trust property that a legally competent, unmarried individual has with respect to individually owned property."[7] However, "in deciding whether and how to exercise the powers of the trusteeship, [the trustee] is subject to and must act in accordance with the [trustee's] fiduciary duties."[8]

---

5. David M. English, The Uniform Trust Code (2000): Significant Provisions and Policy Issues, 67 Mo. L. Rev. 143, 209 (2002); *but see* Peter T. Wendel, The Evolution of the Law of Trustees' Powers and Third Party Liability for Participating in a Breach of Trust: An Economic Analysis, 35 Seton Hall L. Rev. 971 (2005) (criticizing abrogation of the traditional rules).

6. Restatement (Third) of Trusts § 70 cmt. a (Am. Law Inst. 2007).

7. Id. § 85(1)(a).—Eds.

8. Id. § 86.—Eds.

What has happened, in other words, is that modern trust law has come to substitute empowerment subject to fiduciary obligation for simple disempowerment as the preferred means for safeguarding the beneficiary's interests. The settlor need not spell out with specificity what the trustee should do in all possible future circumstances, an impossible task given transaction costs and the settlor's lack of clairvoyance. Instead, trust law provides the trustee with expansive default powers of administration, the trustee's exercise of which is subject to review ex post for compliance with the open-ended fiduciary duties of loyalty and prudence.

The fiduciary obligation thus minimizes transaction costs. Instead of trying in advance to reduce to writing provisions for every future contingency, the parties need only address expressly those contingencies that are important and likely enough to warrant the transaction costs of express provision. For all other contingencies, the fiduciary obligation fills the gap. A similar evolutionary pattern toward empowerment subject to fiduciary governance is apparent in the modern law of agency, partnerships, and corporations — all fields in which the agency problem arising from incomplete contracting in the separation of management and beneficial ownership is likewise prominent.

Viewed in this manner, the fiduciary governance strategy of modern law is intuitive. The functional core of fiduciary law is deterrence. The fiduciary is induced to act in the best interests of the beneficiary by the threat of after-the-fact liability for breach of the fiduciary standards of conduct. The core fiduciary duties are the duties of loyalty and prudence (or care). The duty of *loyalty* proscribes misappropriation and regulates conflicts of interest by requiring the fiduciary to act in the "best" or even "sole" interests of the principal. The duty of *prudence* or *care* prescribes the fiduciary's standard of care by establishing an objective "prudence" or "reasonableness" standard in which the meaning of prudence or reasonableness is informed by industry norms and practices.

Although the duties of loyalty and prudence are formulated in terms of open-ended standards, the normal accretive process of the common law has produced a rich body of interpretive authority on fiduciary matters. This mass of authority includes not only decades of case law, but also generations of treatises, restatements, and statutory codifications. Such authority improves predictability and reduces decision costs by providing instructive guidance on what the otherwise expansive duties of loyalty and prudence require of the trustee in particular circumstances. . . .

[T]he precise contours of the fiduciary obligation vary across fiduciary applications. . . . For example, the fiduciary obligation in . . . trust law is generally stricter than the fiduciary obligation in . . . corporate law. But those differences reflect the different contexts. The agency problem in a family trust in which the beneficiaries have no exit option and that is managed by a corporate fiduciary that cannot easily be replaced differs significantly from the agency problem in a large, publicly traded corporation from which a shareholder can separate easily by selling his shares in a thick securities market.

NOTES

1. What of Morality and Fairness?   Economics — the dismal science — is hardly the only mode of analysis for throwing light on the nature and function of fiduciary duties. Even a fleeting examination of the cases reveals that they are rife with the language of morality and fairness, not the cold balancing of costs and benefits. Probably the most famous example is this passage in Meinhard v. Salmon, 164 N.E. 545 (N.Y. 1928), written by Justice Cardozo when he was a judge on the New York Court of Appeals:

> Many forms of conduct permissible in a workaday world for those acting at arm's length, are forbidden to those bound by fiduciary ties. A trustee is held to something stricter than the morals of the market place. Not honesty alone, but the punctilio of an honor the most sensitive, is then the standard of behavior. As to this there has developed a tradition that is unbending and inveterate. Uncompromising rigidity has been the attitude of courts of equity when petitioned to undermine the rule of undivided loyalty by the "disintegrating erosion" of particular exceptions. Only thus has the level of conduct for fiduciaries been kept at a level higher than that trodden by the crowd. It will not consciously be lowered by any judgment of this court.

Justice Benjamin N. Cardozo

Is Cardozo's conception of the fiduciary obligation inconsistent with a functional account rooted in deterrence?

2. The Difference Between Power and Duty. Litigation over trust administration can involve one or both of two conceptually distinct allegations of breach of trust: (a) the trustee lacked the *power* to act as she did, or (b) the trustee's act, even if within her powers, was a breach of *duty*. Because in contemporary practice a trustee is typically given the same powers over the trust property as an outright owner, most of the litigation today involves a claim of breach of duty rather than an allegation that an action was beyond the scope of the trustee's powers.[9] The critical point is that "all powers held in the capacity of trustee must be exercised, or not exercised, in accordance with the trustee's fiduciary obligations."[10]

3. Who Is the Principal? Thus far we have been speaking of the trustee's fiduciary duties to the *beneficiaries*. This is consistent with traditional doctrine, under which a beneficiary or a co-trustee but not the settlor has standing to sue the trustee for breach of duty.[11] But the creation of a trust is an exercise of the settlor's freedom of disposition. Should not the *settlor* have the power to enforce the trust? And should not the settlor's intent prevail over any contrary wishes of the beneficiary? Professor Sitkoff has argued that

> the law should minimize the agency costs inherent in locating managerial authority with the trustee . . . and the residual claim with the beneficiaries . . . , but only to

---

9. *See* id. § 70 cmt. a(1).
10. Id. cmt. a.
11. *See* id. § 94(1).

the extent that doing so is consistent with the ex ante instructions of the settlor. . . . This qualification gives priority to the settlor over the beneficiaries as the trustee's primary principal. [My] positive claim is that, at least with respect to traditional doctrines, the law conforms to the suggested normative approach.[12]

In many respects, American trust law does indeed regard the settlor as the primary principal. A beneficiary cannot easily remove the trustee (see Chapter 10 at page 750), modify or terminate the trust without the settlor's consent (see page 727), or alienate her beneficial interest (see page 696). Moreover, the "controlling consideration" in trust construction is the settlor's intent (see Chapter 5 at page 325). The denial under traditional law of settlor standing to enforce a trust thus stands out as a discontinuity, one that has come under criticism from some commentators[13] and that has been eroded by recent law reform that grants the settlor standing to seek removal of a trustee (see Chapter 10 at page 751) and to enforce a charitable trust (see Chapter 11 at page 783).

B. THE DUTY OF LOYALTY

Perhaps the most fundamental principle of trust fiduciary law is the trustee's duty of undivided *loyalty* to the beneficiary. A trustee must administer the trust solely in the interests of the beneficiary. The same rule applies to personal representatives, executors, and administrators.[14]

Hartman v. Hartle
122 A. 615 (N.J. Ch. 1923)

FOSTER, V.C. Mrs. Dorothea Geick died testate on April 8, 1921, leaving five children, one of them being the complainant. She named her two sons-in-law executors, and they qualified. Among other matters the will expressly directed her executors to sell her real estate and to divide the proceeds equally among her children.

On February 9, 1922, the executors sold part of the real estate known as the Farm, at public auction, for $3,900 to one of testatrix' sons, Lewis Geick, who actually bought the property for his sister, Josephine Dieker, who is the wife of one of the executors.

On April 11, 1922, Mrs. Dieker sold the property to the defendant Mike Contra (and another, who is not a party to the action) for $5,500, part cash and part on mortgage.

---

12. Robert H. Sitkoff, An Agency Costs Theory of Trust Law, 89 Cornell L. Rev. 621, 624-25 (2004). For other analyses, some critical of Sitkoff, see M.W. Lau, The Economic Structure of Trusts (2011); Lee-ford Tritt, The Limitations of an Economic Agency Cost Theory of Trust Law, 32 Cardozo L. Rev. 2579 (2011); *see also* Deborah S. Gordon, Trusting Trust, 63 U. Kan. L. Rev. 497 (2015); Alan Newman, The Intention of the Settlor Under the Uniform Trust Code: Whose Property Is It, Anyway?, 38 Akron L. Rev. 649 (2005).

13. *See* Sitkoff, *supra* note 12, at 666-69; John H. Langbein, The Contractarian Basis of the Law of Trusts, 105 Yale L.J. 625, 664 (1995).

14. *See, e.g.*, Uniform Probate Code §§ 3-703, 3-711, 3-712 (Unif. Law Comm'n 1990).

The executors settled their final accounts on April 21, 1922, and at or about that time complainant expressed to the deputy surrogate her dissatisfaction with the price realized from the sale of the farm. About March 21, 1923, she filed her bill in this cause charging the sale of the farm to have been improperly and fraudulently made by the executors to Mrs. Dieker, and further charging that Mrs. Dieker and the other heirs of the testatrix had agreed at sale, because of slow bidding and inadequate price, to have the farm bid in for the benefit of all the heirs.

At the hearing each and every one of these allegations were shown to be untrue by the great weight of the testimony; and this proof was so conclusive that it left complainant with but one contention to sustain her case, viz. that under the law the sale of the property by the executors and trustee to Mrs. Dieker, the wife of one of them, without previous authority from the court, was illegal and void, and that it should be set aside and the farm resold, or, if that be found impossible because of the sale made by Mrs. Dieker to Contra, an innocent purchaser, then that complainant should have paid to her one-fifth of the $1,600 profits realized by Mrs. Dieker from the sale of the property.

It is the settled law of this state that a trustee cannot purchase from himself at his own sale, and that his wife is subject to the same disability, unless leave so to do has been previously obtained under an order of the court. Scott v. Gamble, 9 N.J. Eq. 218 (1852); Bassett v. Shoemaker, 20 A. 52 (N.J. App. 1890); Bechtold v. Read, 22 A. 1085 (N.J. Ch. 1891). And under the circumstances of the case complainant cannot be charged with laches under the view expressed in Bechtold v. Read, supra.

In view of the fact that the property is now owned by innocent purchasers, a resale cannot be ordered, but, as an alternative, Mrs. Dieker and the executors will be held to account for complainant's one-fifth share of the profits made on the resale of the property under the authority of Marshall v. Carson, 38 N.J. Eq. 250 (1884), and a decree will be advised to that effect.

In re Gleeson's Will
124 N.E.2d 624 (Ill. App. 1955)

CARROLL, J. Mary Gleeson, who died testate on February 14, 1952, owned among other properties, 160 acres of farm land in Christian County, Illinois. By her will admitted to Probate March 29, 1952, she nominated Con Colbrook, petitioner-appellee, (who will be referred to herein as petitioner) executor thereof. Petitioner was also appointed as trustee under the will and the residuary estate, including the aforesaid 160 acres of land, was devised to him in trust for the benefit of decedent's 3 children, Helen Black, Bernadine Gleeson, and Thomas Gleeson, an incompetent, who are respondents herein.

On March 1, 1950, the testatrix leased the 160 acres for the year ending March 1, 1951 to petitioner and William Curtin, a partnership. On March 1, 1951, she again leased the premises to said partnership for the year ending March 1, 1952. Upon the expiration of this latter lease the partnership held over as tenants under the provisions thereof and farmed the land until March 1, 1953, at which time petitioner leased the land to another tenant. While there is no written lease in evidence, the record indicates the terms thereof provided for payment to the lessor of $10 per acre cash rent and a share in the crops of 1/2 of the corn and 2/5 of the small grain.

The petitioner's appointment as trustee was confirmed by the Circuit Court of Christian County on April 29, 1953. On July 22, 1953, he filed his first semi-annual report. . . . The . . . respondents filed certain objections. . . .

The record indicates no dispute as to the fact that petitioner as trustee leased a portion of the real estate of the trust to himself as a partner of William Curtin and that petitioner received a share of the profits realized by him and Curtin from their farming operation of said real estate.

Upon a hearing the Court entered an order overruling the objection of the respondents to the report. From such order respondents have brought this appeal.

It is contended by respondents that the Circuit Court erred in overruling their objection for the reason that the law prohibits a trustee from dealing in his individual capacity with the trust and making a profit from such dealings.

The Courts of this state have consistently followed a general principle of equity that a trustee cannot deal in his individual capacity with the trust property. It was announced in the early case of Thorp v. McCullum, 1 Gilman 614 (Ill. 1844). It has since been followed in many cases involving the relationship between the trustee and the trust property. . . .

Petitioner recognizes the existence of this general rule, but argues that because of the existence of the peculiar circumstances under which the petitioner proceeded, the instant case must be taken to constitute one of the rare exceptions to such rule. The circumstances alluded to as peculiar are pointed out as being the facts that the death of Mrs. Gleeson occurred on February 14, 1952, only 15 days prior to the beginning of the 1952 farm year; that satisfactory farm tenants are not always available, especially on short notice; that the petitioner had in the preceding fall of 1951 sown part of the 160 acres in wheat to be harvested in 1952; that the holding over by the trustee and his partner was in the best interests of the trust; that the same was done in an open manner; that the petitioner was honest with the trust; and that it suffered no loss as a result of the transaction. . . .

Petitioner contends that since only 15 days intervened between the death of Mrs. Gleeson and the beginning of the farm year, and that good tenant farmers might not be available at such a time, it was in the interests of the trust that the petitioner continue to hold over for the year of 1952. No showing is made that petitioner tried to obtain a satisfactory tenant to replace Colbrook and Curtin on March 1, 1952. The record discloses that subsequent to the death of testatrix, petitioner discussed continuance of the farming operation with two of the beneficiaries under the trust and voluntarily raised the cash rent from $6 to $10 per acre. This evidence tending to show that petitioner was interested in continuing a tenancy under which he was leasing trust property to himself would seem to refute any contention that an effort to lease the property to anyone other than the partnership was made. The fact that the partners had sown wheat on the land in the fall of 1951 cannot be said to be a peculiar circumstance. It is not suggested that the trust would have suffered a loss if some one other than the petitioner had farmed the land in 1952 and harvested the wheat. It would appear that a satisfactory adjustment covering the matter of the wheat could have been made between the trust and the partnership without great difficulty.

The good faith and honesty of the petitioner or the fact that the trust sustained no loss on account of his dealings therewith are all matters which can avail petitioner nothing so far as a justification of the course he chose to take in dealing with trust property is concerned. . . .

We think . . . that the petitioner herein, upon the death of the testatrix, instead of conferring with her beneficiaries concerning continuance of his tenancy of the trust property, should have then decided whether he chose to continue as a tenant or to act as trustee. His election was to act as trustee and as such he could not deal with himself.

This Court, therefore, reaches the conclusion that the Circuit Court erred in over-ruling respondent's objection . . . to the trustee's . . . report. . . .

The judgment of the Circuit Court of Christian County is reversed and the cause remanded to that Court with directions to proceed in a manner consistent with the views herein expressed.

Reversed and remanded.

NOTES

1. The No-Further-Inquiry Rule. If a trustee undertakes a transaction that involves a conflict between the trustee's fiduciary capacity and personal interests, *no further inquiry* is made; the trustee's good faith and the fairness of the transaction are irrelevant. The only defenses that the trustee may raise are that: (a) the *settlor authorized* the particular conflict in the terms of the trust; (b) the *beneficiary consented* after full disclosure; or (c) the trustee obtained *judicial approval* in advance.[15]

In a case in which the no-further-inquiry rule does not apply, the beneficiary remains entitled to judicial review of whether the trustee acted fairly and in good faith, reflecting a mandatory core of fiduciary obligation that cannot be waived. The Restatement (Third) of Trusts explains:

> A trustee may be authorized by the terms of the trust, expressly or by implication, to engage in transactions that would otherwise be prohibited by the rules of undivided loyalty. . . . [H]owever, . . . no matter how broad the provisions of a trust may be in conferring power to engage in self-dealing or other transactions involving a conflict of fiduciary and personal interests, a trustee violates the duty of loyalty to the beneficiaries by acting in bad faith or unfairly.[16]

Under UTC § 105(b), excerpted below at page 676, the terms of a trust cannot vary "the duty of a trustee to act in good faith and in accordance with the terms and purposes of the trust and the interests of the beneficiaries."

2. Remedies for Breach.   In the event of a breach of duty by a trustee, a beneficiary is entitled to remedies that include *compensatory damages* to restore the trust estate and trust distributions to what they would have been but for the breach. The beneficiary

---

15. Restatement (Third) of Trusts § 78 cmts. c(1)-(3) (Am. Law Inst. 2007).
16. *See* id. cmt. c(2).

is also entitled to *disgorge* the trustee of any profit made on the breach.[17] Professor Sitkoff explains:

> The [beneficiary] is entitled . . . to be made whole for his losses incurred or gains foregone owing to the breach. But compensatory damages . . . [will not deter breach if the] gains to the breaching party . . . exceed the nonbreaching party's loss. . . . [T]he availability of a disgorgement remedy, which allows the [beneficiary] to take the [trustee's] gain even in excess of making the [trust] whole, reflects the additional deterrent and disclosure purposes of fiduciary law. Because the [trustee] is not entitled to keep the gains from breach, the [trustee] is deterred from unilateral breach, and is instead given an incentive to disclose the potential gains from breach and seek the [beneficiary's] consent.[18]

If the trustee has sold his own property to the trust, the beneficiary may compel the trustee to repay the purchase price and take back the property. If the trustee has bought trust property, the beneficiary may compel the trustee to restore the property to the trust. If in wrongfully disposing of trust property the trustee acquires other property, the beneficiary is entitled to enforce a *constructive trust* or *equitable lien* on the property so acquired, treating it as part of the trust.

In addition to these remedies against the trustee, the beneficiaries may also enforce a constructive trust or equitable lien against a third party who acquires trust property in consequence of the trustee's breach of trust, unless the third party is a good faith purchaser for value with no notice of the breach.[19]

3. Justifying the No-Further-Inquiry Rule. Some commentators have defended the no-further-inquiry rule on the grounds that it uses self-interest to induce the trustee to do what is best for the beneficiaries.[20] Because appropriating trust property is profitable for the trustee but often difficult for the beneficiaries to detect, the law infers disloyalty from the fact of self-dealing. The purpose is to deter conflicted transactions or to induce the trustee to seek advance judicial approval or to disclose the material facts to the beneficiaries and obtain their consent.

But surely some conflicted transactions might be in the best interests of the beneficiaries. If so, the absolute nature of the no-further-inquiry rule prevents some transactions that would be in the best interests of the beneficiaries. Yet the rule may be justifiable nonetheless if, on balance, "these deals are so frequently undesirable that the

---

17. *See, e.g.*, Miller v. Bank of America, N.A., 352 P.3d 1162 (N.M. 2015) (awarding compensatory damages and disgorging the trustee's profits).

18. Robert H. Sitkoff, The Economic Structure of Fiduciary Law, 91 B.U. L. Rev. 1039, 1048-49 (2011).

19. *See* Restatement (Third) of Restitution and Unjust Enrichment §§ 55-56, 66 (Am. Law Inst. 2011). The third party's lack of participation in the trustee's breach is not a defense. The beneficiary is entitled to restitution by way of a constructive trust or equitable lien to prevent the third party's unjust enrichment owing to the wrongdoing of the trustee. *See, e.g.*, Reinhardt Univ. v. Castleberry, 734 S.E.2d 117 (Ga. App. 2012).

20. *See* Robert Cooter & Bradley J. Freedman, The Fiduciary Relationship: Its Economic Character and Legal Consequences, 66 N.Y.U. L. Rev. 1045 (1991).

costs of extirpating the entire class of transaction (a *rule*) are less than the costs of case-by-case adjudication (the fairness *standard*)."[21] The Restatement puts the point thus:

> The rationale begins with a recognition that it may be difficult for a trustee to resist temptation when personal interests conflict with fiduciary duty. In such situations, for reasons peculiar to typical trust relationships, the policy of the trust law is to prefer (as a matter of default law) to remove altogether the occasions of tempta-tion rather than to monitor fiduciary behavior and attempt to uncover and punish abuses when a trustee has actually succumbed to temptation. . . . Viewed from the beneficiaries' perspective, . . . efforts to prevent or detect actual improprieties can be expected to be inefficient if not ineffective. Such efforts are likely to be wastefully expensive and to suffer from time lag and inadequacies of information, from a lack of relevant experience and understanding, and perhaps from want of resources to monitor trustee behavior and ultimately to litigate and expose actual instances of fiduciary misconduct.[22]

4. Exceptions and Structural Conflicts. The no-further-inquiry rule has been limited in recent years by recognition of a handful of *exceptions* for certain types or kinds of conflicted dealings that are likely to benefit the beneficiaries. Statutes in most states allow a corporate trustee to deposit trust assets with its own banking department and to invest the trust assets in a mutual fund operated by the trustee or an affiliate. Another exception allows the trustee to take reasonable compensation even though, strictly speaking, compensating herself with trust funds is self-dealing. These excep-tions are codified by UTC § 802(f), (h) (2000, rev. 2004).[23]

The no-further-inquiry rule is also inapplicable to a *structural conflict* created by the settlor. If *O* funds a trust with shares in Tigertail Corporation and then names as trustee *X*, a person who sits on the Tigertail board of directors, *X* will have a conflict of interest in voting the trust's shares in Tigertail—in particular, on the questions of his reelection as a director and approval of his director's fees. But this conflict is structural, created by the settlor rather than provoked by *X*. In such circumstances, *X* is not dis-abled by the conflict, and he may vote the trust's shares, but he must do so in the best interests of the beneficiaries.[24] A similar analysis applies to a trust in which the settlor names as trustee an income beneficiary, whose interests will sometimes be in conflict with those of the remainder beneficiary, or vice versa. We take up this issue in connec-tion with the duty of impartiality later in this chapter at page 667.

---

21. Robert H. Sitkoff, Trust Law, Corporate Law, and Capital Market Efficiency, 28 J. Corp. L. 565, 573-74 (2003).

22. Restatement (Third) of Trusts § 78 cmt. b (Am. Law Inst. 2007).

23. To similar effect, with additional commentary, see id. cmts. c(4), c(6), c(8).

24. *See* id. cmt. d(1); *see also* UTC § 802(g) (2000, rev. 2004) ("In voting shares of stock or in exercising powers of control over similar interests in other forms of enterprise, the trustee shall act in the best interests of the beneficiaries. If the trust is the sole owner of a corporation or other form of enterprise, the trustee shall elect or appoint directors or other managers who will manage the corpo-ration or enterprise in the best interests of the beneficiaries.").

In a structural or other authorized conflict-of-interest situation, "the conduct of the trustee in the administration of the trust will be subject to especially careful scrutiny."[25] As we have seen, "no matter how broad the provisions of a trust may be in conferring power to engage in self-dealing or other transactions involving a conflict of fiduciary and personal interests, a trustee violates the duty of loyalty to the beneficiaries by acting in bad faith or unfairly."[26] Accordingly a conflicted trustee who wants to satisfy her duties of prudence and loyalty should consider on an ongoing basis whether she needs independent legal or financial advice, should seek judicial instruction, or should petition for the appointment of a trustee ad litem to handle any conflict-sensitive matters.[27]

5. Scholarly Debate. Taking note of the proliferation of exceptions to the no-further-inquiry rule and the relaxation of the absolute standard of loyalty in corporate and other fiduciary settings, Professor Langbein suggests that the no-further-inquiry rule does more harm than good. He argues that a conflicted transaction should be sustained if the trustee can prove that the transaction was prudently undertaken in the best interests of the beneficiaries.[28] In reply, Professor Melanie Leslie argues that the no-further-inquiry rule helps offset the structural difficulties confronted by beneficiaries in monitoring the trustee.[29]

The underlying policy question is which governance strategy is better suited to addressing a trustee's conflicts of interest: a best-interests standard with the burden on the trustee (per Langbein), or a prohibition subject to a growing list of categorical exceptions (current law)?

In re Rothko
372 N.E.2d 291 (N.Y. 1977)

COOKE, J. Mark Rothko, an abstract expressionist painter whose works through the years gained for him an international reputation of greatness, died testate on February 25, 1970. The principal asset of his estate consisted of 798 paintings of tremendous value, and the dispute underlying this appeal involves the conduct of his three executors in their disposition of these works of art. In sum, that conduct as portrayed in the record and sketched in the opinions was manifestly wrongful and indeed shocking.

Rothko's will was admitted to probate on April 27, 1970 and letters testamentary were issued to Bernard J. Reis, Theodoros Stamos and Morton Levine. Hastily and within a period of only about three weeks and by virtue of two contracts each dated May 21, 1970, the executors dealt with all 798 paintings.

---

25. Restatement (Third) of Trusts § 37 cmt. f(1) (Am. Law Inst. 2007).
26. Id. § 78 cmt. c(2).
27. *See* id. § 37 cmt. g.
28. *See* John H. Langbein, Questioning the Trust Law Duty of Loyalty: Sole Interest or Best Interest?, 114 Yale L.J. 929 (2005).
29. *See* Melanie B. Leslie, In Defense of the No Further Inquiry Rule: A Response to Professor John Langbein, 47 Wm. & Mary L. Rev. 541 (2005).

Mark Rothko
Number 22 (1949)
Collection, The Museum of Modern Art, New York

By a contract of sale, the estate executors agreed to sell to Marlborough A.G., a Liechtenstein corporation (hereinafter MAG), 100 Rothko paintings as listed for $1,800,000, $200,000 to be paid on execution of the agreement and the balance of $1,600,000 in 12 equal interest-free installments over a 12-year period. Under the second agreement, the executors consigned to Marlborough Gallery, Inc., a domestic corporation (hereinafter MNY), "approximately 700 paintings listed on a Schedule to be prepared," the consignee to be responsible for costs covering items such as insurance, storage, restoration and promotion.[30] By its provisos, MNY could sell up to 35 paintings a year from each of two groups, pre-1947 and post-1947, for 12 years at the best price obtainable but not less than the appraised estate value, and that it would receive a 50% commission on each painting sold, except for a commission of 40% on those sold to or through other dealers.

Mark Rothko
Apic/Hulton Archive/Getty Images

Petitioner Kate Rothko, decedent's daughter and a person entitled to share in his estate by virtue of an election under EPTL § 5-3.3,[31] instituted this proceeding to remove the executors, to enjoin MNY and MAG from disposing of the paintings, to rescind the aforesaid agreements between the executors and said corporations, for a return of the paintings still in possession of those corporations, and for damages. She was joined by the guardian of her brother Christopher Rothko, likewise interested in the estate, who answered by adopting the allegations of his sister's petition and by demanding the same relief. The Attorney General of the State, as the representative of the ultimate beneficiaries of the Mark Rothko Foundation, Inc., a charitable corporation and the residuary legatee under decedent's will, joined in requesting relief substantially similar to that prayed for by petitioner. . . .

Following a nonjury trial covering 89 days and in a thorough opinion, the Surrogate found: that Reis was a director, secretary and treasurer of MNY, the consignee art gallery, in addition to being a coexecutor of the estate; that the testator had a 1969 inter vivos contract with MNY to sell Rothko's work at a commission of

---

30. A consignment is an agency relationship with possession (but not title) passing to the agent. *See, e.g.*, Restatement (Third) of Agency § 6.02 cmt. d (Am. Law Inst. 2006). — Eds.

31. Mark Rothko devised his residuary estate to the Mark Rothko Foundation, a charitable corporation, with Reis, Stamos, and Levine named as directors. N.Y. Est. Powers & Tr. Law § 5-3.3 (1967) provided that a child of a testator may set aside a testamentary disposition to charity to the extent it exceeds one-half of the testator's estate. Kate Rothko set aside the charitable gift in the amount permitted, with the result that one-half of the residuary gift passed to Rothko's heirs. So Kate Rothko, who was left nothing by Mark Rothko's will, had standing to attack the action of the executors. N.Y. Est. Powers & Tr. Law § 5-3.3 was repealed in 1981, and no state today still has such a statute (see Chapter 11 at page 767). — Eds.

only 10% and whether that agreement survived testator's death was a problem that a fiduciary in a dual position could not have impartially faced; that Reis was in a position of serious conflict of interest with respect to the contracts of May 21, 1970 and that his dual role and planned purpose benefited the Marlborough interests to the detriment of the estate; that it was to the advantage of coexecutor Stamos as a "not-too-successful artist, financially," to curry favor with Marlborough and that the contract made by him with MNY within months after signing the estate contracts placed him in a position where his personal interests conflicted with those of the estate, especially leading to lax contract enforcement efforts by Stamos; that Stamos acted negligently and improvidently in view of his own knowledge of the conflict of interest of Reis; that the third coexecutor, Levine, while not acting in self-interest or with bad faith, nonetheless failed to exercise ordinary prudence in the performance of his assumed fiduciary obligations since he was aware of Reis' divided loyalty, believed that Stamos was also seeking personal advantage, possessed personal opinions as to the value of the paintings and yet followed the leadership of his coexecutors without investigation of essential facts or consultation with competent and disinterested appraisers, and that the business transactions of the two Marlborough corporations were admittedly controlled and directed by Francis K. Lloyd. It was concluded that the acts and failures of the three executors were clearly improper to such a substantial extent as to mandate their removal . . . as estate fiduciaries. The Surrogate also found that MNY, MAG and Lloyd were guilty of contempt in shipping, disposing of and selling 57 paintings in violation of the temporary restraining order dated June 26, 1972 and of the injunction dated September 26, 1972; that the contracts for sale and consignment of paintings between the executors and MNY and MAG provided inadequate value to the estate, amounting to a lack of mutuality and fairness resulting from conflicts on the part of Reis and Stamos and improvidence on the part of all executors; that said contracts were voidable and were set aside by reason of violation of the duty of loyalty and improvidence of the executors, knowingly participated in and induced by MNY and MAG; that the fact that these agreements were voidable did not revive the 1969 inter vivos agreements since the parties by their conduct evinced an intent to abandon and abrogate these compacts. The Surrogate held that the present value at the time of trial of the paintings sold is the proper measure of damages as to MNY, MAG, Lloyd, Reis and Stamos. . . . It was held that Levine was liable for $6,464,880 in damages, as he was not in a dual position acting for his own interest and was thus liable only for the actual value of paintings sold MNY and MAG as of the dates of sale, and that Reis, Stamos, MNY and MAG, apart from being jointly and severally liable for the same damages as Levine for negligence, were liable for the greater sum of $9,252,000 "as appreciation damages less amounts previously paid to the estate with regard to sales of paintings." . . . The liabilities were held to be congruent so that payment of the highest sum would satisfy all lesser liabilities including the civil fines and the liabilities for damages were to be reduced by payment of the fine levied or by return of any of the

Reis, Stamos, and Levine

The executors were three of Rothko's intimate companions during his last years. Bernard J. Reis, a certified public accountant who had graduated from law school but had not been licensed to practice law, had acted for years as Rothko's business and professional advisor and confidant. Reis drafted Rothko's will.

Theodoros Stamos was a fellow artist in whose family plot Rothko was buried. Stamos entered into a personal contract with Marlborough Gallery, Inc., on January 1, 1971, whereby Marlborough became Stamos's exclusive art dealer agent for four years at a commission of 50 percent. The Surrogate found: "Executor Levine stated, and the court finds, that in a conversation in April, 1970, before the execution of the questioned agreements, executor Stamos related that Marlborough had evidenced interest in his paintings. The conversation led Levine to believe that Stamos was interested in entering into some contractual arrangement with Marlborough which indicated a conflict of interest on the part of Stamos. Levine testified that when he confronted Stamos with the impropriety of such motivation angry exchanges followed."*

Morton Levine, professor of anthropology at Fordham University, was chosen by Rothko to act as guardian of his two children. Kate Rothko came of age soon after her father's death and, at her insistence, Levine was removed as guardian of Christopher Rothko. The Surrogate said: "It

Theodoros Stamos
Eisenstaedt/Time & Life Pictures/
Getty Images

is recognized that Levine was neither an art expert nor an experienced fiduciary but he was an educated man who, despite his educational background and his position as a college professor, failed to exercise ordinary prudence in his performance of fiduciary obligations which he assumed. Levine's argument at best is a statement that he undertook a responsibility which he was unqualified to handle."†

---

* In re Rothko, 379 N.Y.S.2d 923, 940 (Sur. 1975).
† Id. at 942.

---

57 paintings disposed of, the new fiduciary to have the option in the first instance to specify which paintings the fiduciary would accept.

The Appellate Division . . . modified to the extent of deleting the option given the new fiduciary to specify which paintings he would accept. Except for this modification, the majority affirmed on the opinion of [the] Surrogate, with additional comments. Among others, it was stated that the entire court agreed that executors Reis and Stamos had a conflict of interest and divided loyalty in view of their nexus to MNY and that a majority were in agreement with the Surrogate's assessment of liability as to executor Levine and his findings of liability against MNY, MAG and Lloyd. The majority agreed with the Surrogate's analysis awarding "appreciation damages." . . . [Two dissenters] voted to modify and remit to determine the reasonable value of the paintings as of May, 1970, when estate contracts with MNY and MAG had their inception in writing.

Since the Surrogate's findings of fact as to the conduct of Reis, Stamos, Levine, MNY, MAG and Lloyd and the value of the paintings at different junctures were affirmed by the Appellate Division, if there was evidence to support these findings they are not subject to question in this Court and the review here is confined to the legal issues raised. . . .

In seeking a reversal, it is urged that an improper legal standard was applied in voiding the estate contracts of May, 1970, that the "no further inquiry" rule applies only to self-dealing and that in case of a conflict of interest, absent self-dealing, a challenged transaction must be shown to be unfair. The subject of fairness of the contracts is intertwined with the issue of whether Reis and Stamos were guilty of conflicts of interest. Scott is quoted to the effect that "[a] trustee does not necessarily incur liability merely because he has an individual interest in the transaction. . . . In Bullivant v. First National Bank, 246 Mass. 324, it was held that . . . the fact that the bank was also a creditor of the corporation did not make its assent invalid, *if it acted in good faith and the plan was fair* . . ." (emphasis added) (II Scott on Trusts, § 170.24, p.1384), and our attention has been called to the statement in Phelan v. Middle States Oil Corp., 220 F.2d 593, 603 that Judge Learned Hand found "no decisions that have applied [the no-further-inquiry rule] inflexibly to every occasion in which the fiduciary has been shown to have had a personal interest that might in fact have conflicted with his loyalty."

These contentions should be rejected. First, a review of the opinions of the Surrogate and the Appellate Division manifests that they did not rely solely on a "no further inquiry rule," and secondly, there is more than an adequate basis to conclude that the agreements between the Marlborough corporations and the estate were neither fair nor in the best interests of the estate. . . . The opinions under review demonstrate that neither the Surrogate nor the Appellate Division set aside the contracts by merely applying the no further inquiry rule without regard to fairness. Rather they determined, quite properly indeed, that these agreements were neither fair nor in the best interests of the estate.

To be sure, the assertions that there were no conflicts of interest on the part of Reis or Stamos indulge in sheer fantasy. Besides being a director and officer of MNY, for which there was financial remuneration, however slight, Reis, as noted by the Surrogate, had different inducements to favor the Marlborough interests, including his own aggrandizement of status and financial advantage through sales of almost one million dollars for items from his own and his family's extensive private art collection by the Marlborough interests. Similarly, Stamos benefited as an artist under contract with Marlborough and, interestingly, Marlborough purchased a Stamos painting from a third party for $4,000 during the week in May, 1970 when the estate contract negotiations were pending. The conflicts are manifest. Further, as noted in Bogert, Trusts and Trustees (2d ed.), "The duty of loyalty imposed on the fiduciary prevents him from accepting employment from a third party who is entering into a business transaction with the trust" (§ 543[S], p.573). "While he [a trustee] is administering the trust he must refrain from placing himself in a position where his personal interest or that of a third person does or may conflict with the interest of the beneficiaries" (Bogert, Law of Trusts [Hornbook Series, 5th ed.], p.343). Here, Reis was employed and Stamos benefited in a manner contemplated by Bogert (see also, Meinhard v. Salmon, 249 N.Y. 458, 464, 466-467). In short, one must strain the law rather than follow it to reach the result suggested on behalf of Reis and Stamos.

Levine contends that, having acted prudently and upon the advice of counsel, a complete defense was established.[32] Suffice it to say, an executor who knows that his coexecutor is committing breaches of trust and not only fails to exert efforts directed towards prevention but accedes to them is legally accountable even though he was acting on the advice of counsel (Matter of Westerfield, 32 App. Div. 324, 344; III Scott, Trusts [3d ed.], § 201, p.1657). When confronted with the question of whether to enter into the Marlborough contracts, Levine was acting in a business capacity, not a legal one, in which he was required as an executor primarily to employ such diligence and prudence to the care and management of the estate assets and affairs as would prudent persons of discretion and intelligence, accented by "[n]ot honesty alone, but the punctilio of an honor the most sensitive" (Meinhard v. Salmon, 249 N.Y. 458, 464, supra). Alleged good faith on the part of a fiduciary forgetful of his duty is not enough. He could not close his eyes, remain passive or move with unconcern in the face of the obvious loss to be visited upon the estate by participation in those business arrangements and then shelter himself behind the claimed counsel of an attorney. . . .

Further, there is no merit to the argument that MNY and MAG lacked notice of the breach of trust. The record amply supports the determination that they are chargeable with notice of the executors' breach of duty.

The measure of damages was the issue that divided the Appellate Division. The contention of Reis, Stamos, MNY and MAG, that the award of appreciation damages was legally erroneous and impermissible, is based on a principle that an executor authorized to sell is not liable for an increase in value if the breach consists only in selling for a figure less than that for which the executor should have sold. For example, Scott states:

> The beneficiaries are not entitled to the value of the property at the time of the decree if it was not the duty of the trustee to retain the property in the trust and the breach of trust consisted *merely* in selling the property for too low a price (emphasis added) (III Scott, Trusts (3d ed.), § 208.3, p.1687).

> If the trustee is guilty of a breach of trust in selling trust property for an inadequate price, he is liable for the difference between the amount he should have received and the amount which he did receive. He is not liable, however, for any subsequent rise in value of the property sold (Id., § 208.6, pp.1689-1690).

---

32. The three executors sought advice from their legal counsel about entering into the contracts with MAG and MNY. Counsel advised the executors that Reis had a conflict of interest.

By the same letter, this law firm advised the executors that a petition for advance approval of any contracts for liquidation of the estate through Marlborough Galleries would not be entertained by a surrogate. While it is true, as the law firm advised, that surrogates do not usually give advance approval concerning matters of business judgment which are within the province of executors, no indication was given that the opposite rule governs when a fiduciary faces a conflict of interest.

In re Rothko, 379 N.Y.S.2d 923, 936-37 (Sur. 1975). Did the law firm commit malpractice? — Eds.

A recitation of similar import appears in comment d under Restatement, Trusts, § 205:

> d. Sale for less than value. If the trustee is authorized to sell trust property, but in breach of trust he sells it for less than he should receive, he is liable for the value of the property at the time of the sale less the amount which he received. If the breach of trust consists *only* in selling it for too little, he is not chargeable with the amount of any subsequent increase in value of the property under the rule stated in Clause (c), as he would be if he were not authorized to sell the property (see §208) (emphasis added).

However, employment of "merely" and "only" as limiting words suggests that where the breach consists of some misfeasance, other than solely for selling "for too low a price" or "for too little," appreciation damages may be appropriate. Under Scott (§ 208.3, pp.1686-1687) and the Restatement (§ 208), the trustee may be held liable for appreciation damages if it was his or her duty to retain the property, the theory being that the beneficiaries are entitled to be placed in the same position they would have been in had the breach not consisted of a sale of property that should have been retained. The same rule should apply where the breach of trust consists of a serious conflict of interest which is more than merely selling for too little.

The reason for allowing appreciation damages, where there is a duty to retain, and only date of sale damages, where there is authorization to sell, is policy oriented. If a trustee authorized to sell were subjected to a greater measure of damages he might be reluctant to sell (in which event he might run a risk if depreciation ensued). On the other hand, if there is a duty to retain and the trustee sells there is no policy reason to protect the trustee; he has not simply acted imprudently, he has violated an integral condition of the trust.

"If a trustee in breach of trust transfers trust property to a person who takes with notice of the breach of trust, and the transferee has disposed of the property . . . [i]t seems proper to charge him with the value at the time of the decree, since if it had not been for the breach of trust the property would still have been a part of the trust estate" (IV Scott, Trusts [3d ed.], § 291.2). This rule of law which applies to the transferees MNY and MAG also supports the imposition of appreciation damages against Reis and Stamos, since if the Marlborough corporations are liable for such damages either as purchasers or consignees with notice, from one in breach of trust, it is only logical to hold that said executors, as sellers and consignors, are liable also pro tanto. . . .

[S]ince the paintings cannot be returned, the estate is therefore entitled to their value at the time of the decree, i.e., appreciation damages. These are not punitive damages in a true sense, rather they are damages intended to make the estate whole. Of course, as to Reis, Stamos, MNY and MAG, these damages might be considered by some to be exemplary in a sense, in that they serve as a warning to others, but their true character is ascertained when viewed in the light of overriding policy considerations and in the realization that the sale and consignment were not merely sales below value but inherently wrongful transfers which should allow the owner to be made whole. . . .

The decree of the Surrogate imposed appreciation damages against Reis, Stamos, MNY and MAG in the amount of $7,339,464.72 computed as $9,252,000 (86 works on canvas at $90,000 each and 54 works on paper at $28,000 each) less the aggregate amounts paid the estate under the two rescinded agreements and interest. Appellants chose not to offer evidence of "present value" and the only proof furnished on the subject was that of the expert Heller whose appraisal as of January 1974 (the month previous to that when trial commenced) on a painting-by-painting basis totaled $15,100,000. There was also testimony as to bona fide sales of other Rothkos between 1971 and 1974. Under the circumstances, it was impossible to appraise the value of the unreturned works of art with an absolute certainty and, so long as the figure arrived at had a reasonable basis of computation and was not merely speculative, possible or imaginary, the Surrogate had the right to resort to reasonable conjectures and probable estimates and to make the best approximation possible through the exercise of good judgment and common sense in arriving at that amount. . . . This is particularly so where the conduct of wrongdoers has rendered it difficult to ascertain the damages suffered with the precision otherwise possible. . . . Significantly, the Surrogate's factual finding as to the present value of these unreturned paintings was affirmed by the Appellate Division and, since that finding had support in the record and was not legally erroneous, it should not now be subjected to our disturbance. . . .

Accordingly, the order of the Appellate Division should be affirmed, with costs to the prevailing parties against appellants, and the question certified answered in the affirmative.

NOTES

1. Epilogue.   Reis, Stamos, and Levine were removed as executors of Rothko's will, and Kate was appointed sole administrator of her father's estate. Kate was not agreeable to the bill presented by her counsel in the amount of $7.5 million, so she hired another lawyer to resist its collection out of the estate. In view of the successful recovery of paintings then worth $40 million, the Surrogate allowed the lawyers a fee of $2.6 million, about twice their usual hourly rate.[33]

Marlborough Gallery paid most of the $9.2 million assessed as damages (on third-party liability for breach of trust, see page 600), but Reis, Stamos, and Levine were liable for the estate's legal fees and costs. Reis filed for bankruptcy in 1978. Stamos assigned his house to the Rothko estate, which permitted him to retain a life estate in it. In 1977, Marlborough Gallery owner Frank Lloyd was indicted on charges of evidence tampering by altering a gallery stock book containing the purchase and sale prices of Rothko works. A British subject, Lloyd was outside the country when the indictment was handed up. Upon his return in 1982, he was tried and convicted on the charges. He was required to set up a scholarship fund and art education programs at his gallery.

In 1983, a painting by Rothko sold for $1.8 million at a Sotheby's auction in New York. This price equaled the amount Marlborough A.G. was to pay for 100 paintings under its agreement with the executors. It was, at the time, the highest auction price ever paid for a modern work by an American artist. In 2007, one of Rothko's paintings—"White Center (Yellow, Pink and Lavender on Rose)," from 1950—sold

---

33. *See* In re Rothko, 414 N.Y.S.2d 444 (Sur. 1979).

for $72.8 million. In 2014, another Rothko—"No. 6 (Violet, Green and Red)," from 1951—sold for $186 million.

2. Damages and Structural Conflicts. The Scott treatise summarizes the rule of appreciation damages applied in *Rothko* thus: "[W]hen a trustee has engaged in improper self-dealing, the beneficiaries can set the sale aside and recover either the property itself or its value at the time of the decree, regardless of whether the trustee was authorized to sell the property to others, and regardless of whether the sale was for a fair price."[34]

This measure of damages is sharply criticized by Professor Richard Wellman. He argues that the recovery in *Rothko* against the two disloyal fiduciaries and the gallery should have been limited to restitution in the amount of the proceeds received by the gallery for sales and resales of the paintings, plus interest. Wellman's central point is that appreciation damages, a penalty, may be appropriate if a trustee sells an asset he has no authority to sell, but they are not appropriate if a trustee has authority to sell, but is guilty of disloyalty or self-dealing. Wellman writes:

> In such instances, it will usually be unclear whether the fiduciary has breached his duty of loyalty: liability is decided by hindsight and may arise in countless unforeseen ways. . . . Even in *Rothko*, the wrongfulness of the executors' conduct was not self-evident. For example, in 1969 Rothko sold a number of paintings to the gallery at prices comparable to those of the executors' 1970 sale and signed a long-term exclusive-consignment contract with the gallery. Further, Rothko knew that Reis and Stamos had personal ties to the gallery. These facts suggest that Rothko wanted his executors to deal with the gallery.[35]

Professor Langbein also directs attention to the possibility of a structural conflict: "Did the two executors provoke a disloyal conflict, or did they pursue a course of action that Rothko tacitly authorized when he selected fiduciaries who came with an embedded conflict? At this distance from the litigation, these questions that the court did not ventilate are hard to answer."[36]

3. Co-Trustees. Under traditional law, if there is more than one trustee of a private trust, they must act as a group and with unanimity, unless the trust instrument provides to the contrary. One co-trustee does not have the power alone to transfer or deal with the property. Since co-trustees must act jointly, a co-trustee is liable for the wrongful acts of a co-trustee to which she has consented or which, by her negligence, she failed to prevent.

Most states have abrogated the unanimity rule by statute, such as UTC § 703(a) (2000), so that a majority of trustees can act if there are three or more. This has long been the rule for a charitable trust. Each co-trustee remains, however, under a duty to take reasonable steps to prevent a breach of trust by her co-trustees, as under UTC

---

34. Scott and Ascher on Trusts § 24.10.

35. Richard V. Wellman, Punitive Surcharges Against Disloyal Fiduciaries—Is *Rothko* Right?, 77 Mich. L. Rev. 95, 113 (1978).

36. Langbein, *supra* note 13, at 666.

§ 703(g), if necessary by bringing an action for instructions or an injunction.[37] This rule applies even if the settlor limits the role or function of one of the co-trustees. "Even in matters for which a trustee is relieved of responsibility, ... if the trustee knows that a co-trustee is committing or attempting to commit a breach of trust, the trustee has a duty to take reasonable steps to prevent the fiduciary misconduct."[38]

What would you, as counsel for Levine, have advised him to do when the conflicts of interest of Reis and Stamos became apparent? Could Levine have escaped liability by resigning? *See* UTC § 705(c) (2000, rev. 2001); Restatement (Third) of Trusts § 36 cmt. d (2003). Should obtaining and following legal advice, as Levine did, provide a defense for breach of trust? *See* id. § 77 cmt. b(2) (2007).

C. THE DUTY OF PRUDENCE

After loyalty, the next great principle of trust fiduciary law is the duty of *prudence*, which imposes on a trustee an objective standard of care. UTC § 804 (2000) codifies the duty of prudence thus:

> A trustee shall administer the trust as a prudent person would, by considering the purposes, terms, distributional requirements, and other circumstances of the trust. In satisfying this standard, the trustee shall exercise reasonable care, skill, and caution.

The duty of prudence applies to all functions of trusteeship: custodial, administrative, investment, and distribution.

1. The Distribution Function

The distribution function involves making disbursements of income or principal to the beneficiaries in accordance with the terms of the trust, which may be mandatory or discretionary. In a *mandatory trust*, the trustee must make specified distributions. If O transfers property to X in trust to distribute all the income quarterly to A, X has no discretion over when, to whom, or in what amounts to make a distribution. It would be a breach of trust for X not to distribute all income quarterly to A.

In a *discretionary trust*, the trustee has discretion over when, to whom, or in what amounts to make a distribution. If O transfers property to X in trust to distribute all the income among A, A's spouse, and A's descendants in such amounts as the trustee determines, X must distribute all income currently, but has some discretion over to

---

37. As one Scots judge put the point:

> It is, of course, disagreeable to take a cotrustee by the throat, but if a man undertakes to act as trustee he must face the necessity of doing disagreeable things when they become necessary in order to keep the estate intact. A trustee is not entitled to purchase a quiet life at the expense of the estate, or to act as good-natured men sometimes do in their own affairs, in letting things slide and losing money rather than create ill feeling.

Miller's Trustees v. Polson, (1897) SC 1038, 1043 (Scot.).

38. Restatement (Third) of Trusts § 81 cmt. b (Am. Law Inst. 2007).

whom and in what amounts. This is a kind of discretionary trust known as a *spray trust*. Some discretionary trusts authorize the trustee to accumulate income and add it to principal. These are known as *sprinkle trusts*. In many discretionary trusts, the trustee's discretion over distributions is subject to a standard, such as "to provide for the beneficiary's support and maintenance." These are known as *support trusts*.

Discretionary trusts preserve flexibility in the distribution function across time.[39] In the example of a spray trust given in the prior paragraph, *X* may decide who among *A*, *A*'s spouse, and *A*'s descendants will receive the trust income. In this way, *O*, the settlor, postpones and delegates distribution decisions to *X*, the trustee, who may deal flexibly with changing circumstances in the years after the trust is created, which could span many decades. *X* can take into account births, deaths, marriages, and divorces; the evolving ability of *A*'s children and more remote descendants to manage property; changes in the economy and investment returns; changes in the law; and other circumstances that *O* could not have foreseen but that *X* will observe firsthand. As a fiduciary, *X* must exercise this discretion prudently, in good faith, and in accordance with the terms of the trust in light of the needs and circumstances of the beneficiaries.

a. Discretionary Distributions

Marsman v. Nasca
573 N.E.2d 1025 (Mass. App. 1991)

DREBEN, J. This appeal raises the following questions: Does a trustee, holding a discretionary power to pay principal for the "comfortable support and maintenance" of a beneficiary, have a duty to inquire into the financial resources of that beneficiary so as to recognize his needs? If so, what is the remedy for such failure? . . .

1. *Facts.* We take our facts from the findings of the Probate Court judge, supplemented on occasion by uncontroverted evidence. . . .

Sara Wirt Marsman died in September, 1971, survived by her second husband, T. Frederik Marsman (Cappy), and her daughter by her first marriage, Sally Marsman Marlette. Mr. James F. Farr, her lawyer for many years, drew her will and was the trustee thereunder.[40] . . .

Sara's will provided in relevant part:

> It is my desire that my husband, T. Fred Marsman, be provided with *reasonable maintenance, comfort and support* after my death. Accordingly, if my said husband is living at the time of my death, I give to my trustees, who shall set the same aside as a separate trust fund, one-third (1/3) of the rest, residue and remainder of my

---

39. Another advantage is protection against claims by a beneficiary's creditors (see Chapter 10 at page 696).

40. The will provided for two trustees; however, one resigned in April, 1972, and thereafter Farr acted as sole trustee. [James F. Farr, who died in 1993, was a prominent trusts and estates lawyer in Boston and the author of a leading practitioner's handbook, James F. Farr & Jackson W. Wright, Jr., An Estate Planner's Handbook (4th ed. 1979). He was also the author of the sixth edition of Augustus Peabody Loring's Trustee's Handbook, first published in 1898 and the bible of Boston trustees for several generations, referred to by the court in footnote 42, below. — Eds.]

T.F. Marsman, 85

T. Frederik Marsman, 85, of Wellesley, former director of horse riding at the Dana Hall School, died Tuesday at his home after a long illness.

A native of the Netherlands, Mr. Marsman received his equestrian training under several European masters. He was a captain when he came to this country in 1926 with the Netherlands Army Show Team.

Shortly after the trip, Mr. Marsman, who was called Cappy, returned to the United States as the manager of the Grayholm Stables in Rhode Island. During his 12 years there, he became a well-known figure in the ring shows of the East Coast.

One of the pioneers in developing dressage in this country, Mr. Marsman was the trainer and rider of Gygeo and Green Mountain, two champion dressage horses of the 1920s and 1930s. He held championships in dressage, jumping and four-in-hand driving.

For 30 years he was director of riding at Dana Hall School in Wellesley and at Teela-Wooket Camps in Vermont. He also was a judge in many national and Canadian horse shows.

Captain T. Frederik Marsman (Cappy)

Mr. Marsman leaves his wife, Margaret (Marsh); a daughter, Sasha Fernandes of Essex, Conn.; two grandchildren and a great-grandchild.

Source: Bos. Globe (Feb. 26, 1987).

estate . . . ; they shall pay the net income therefrom to my said husband at least quarterly during his life; and *after having considered the various available sources of support for him*, my trustees shall, if they deem it necessary or desirable from time to time, in their sole and uncontrolled discretion, pay over to him, or use, apply and/or expend for his direct or indirect benefit such amount or amounts of the principal thereof as they shall deem advisable for his *comfortable support and maintenance*. (Emphasis supplied). . . .

[The remainder interest was given to Sara's daughter Sally, who was Cappy's stepdaughter, and to Sally's family.]

The will also contained the following exculpatory clause:

No trustee hereunder shall ever be liable except for his own willful neglect or default.

During their marriage, Sara and Cappy lived well and entertained frequently. Cappy's main interest in life centered around horses. An expert horseman, he was riding director and instructor at the Dana Hall School in Wellesley until he was retired due to age in 1972. Sally, who was also a skilled rider, viewed Cappy as her mentor, and each had great affection for the other. Sara, wealthy from her prior marriage, managed the couple's financial affairs. She treated Cappy as "Lord of the Manor" and gave him money for his personal expenses, including an extensive wardrobe from one of the finest men's stores in Wellesley.

In 1956, Sara and Cappy purchased, as tenants by the entirety, the property in Wellesley which is the subject of this litigation. Although title to the property passed to

Cappy by operation of law on Sara's death, Sara's will also indicated an intent to convey her interest in the property to Cappy. In the will, Cappy was also given a life estate in the household furnishings with remainder to Sally.

After Sara's death in 1971, Farr met with Cappy and Sally and held what he termed his "usual family conference" going over the provisions of the will. At the time of Sara's death, the Wellesley property was appraised at $29,000, and the principal of Cappy's trust was about $65,600.

Cappy continued to live in the Wellesley house but was forced by Sara's death and his loss of employment in 1972 to reduce his standard of living substantially. He married Margaret in March, 1972, and, shortly before their marriage, asked her to read Sara's will, but they never discussed it. In 1972, Cappy took out a mortgage for $4,000, the proceeds of which were used to pay bills. Farr was aware of the transaction, as he replied to an inquiry of the mortgagee bank concerning the appraised value of the Wellesley property and the income Cappy expected to receive from Sara's trust.

In 1973, Cappy retained Farr in connection with a new will. The latter drew what he described as a simple will which left most of Cappy's property, including the house, to Margaret. The will was executed on November 7, 1973.

In February, 1974, Cappy informed [Farr] that business was at a standstill and that he really needed some funds, if possible. Farr replied in a letter in which he set forth the relevant portion of the will and wrote that he thought the language was "broad enough to permit a distribution of principal." Farr enclosed a check of $300. He asked Cappy to explain in writing the need for some support and why the need had arisen. The judge found that Farr, by his actions, discouraged Cappy from making any requests for principal.

Indeed, Cappy did not reduce his request to writing and never again requested principal. Farr made no investigation whatsoever of Cappy's needs or his "available sources of support" from the date of Sara's death until Cappy's admission to a nursing home in 1983 and, other than the $300 payment, made no additional distributions of principal until Cappy entered the nursing home.

By the fall of 1974, Cappy's difficulty in meeting expenses intensified.[41] Several of his checks were returned for insufficient funds, and in October, 1974, in order that he might remain in the house, Sally and he agreed that she would take over the mortgage payments, the real estate taxes, insurance, and major repairs. In return, she would get the house upon Cappy's death.

Cappy and Sally went to Farr to draw up a deed. Farr was the only lawyer involved, and he billed Sally for the work. He wrote to Sally, stating his understanding of the proposed transaction, and asking, among other things, whether Margaret would have a

---

41. After Sara's death, Cappy's income was limited, particularly considering the station he had enjoyed while married to Sara. In 1973, including the income from Sara's trust of $2,116, his income was $3,441; in 1974 it was $3,549, including trust income of $2,254; in 1975, $6,624, including trust income of $2,490 and social security income of $2,576. Margaret's income was also minimal; $499 in 1974, $4,084 in 1975, including social security income of $1,686. Cappy's income in 1976 was $8,464; in 1977, $8,955; in 1978, $9,681; in 1979, $10,851; in 1980, $11,261; in 1981, $12,651; in 1982, $13,870; in 1983, $12,711; in 1984, $12,500; in 1985, $12,567; in 1986, $12,558. The largest portion from 1975 on came from social security benefits.

right to live in the house if Cappy should predecease her. The answer was no. No copy of the letter to Sally was sent to Cappy. A deed was executed by Cappy on November 7, 1974, transferring the property to Sally and her husband Richard T. Marlette (Marlette) as tenants by the entirety, reserving a life estate to Cappy. No writing set forth Sally's obligations to Cappy.

The judge found that there was no indication that Cappy did not understand the transaction, although, in response to a request for certain papers by Farr, Cappy sent a collection of irrelevant documents. The judge also found that Cappy clearly understood that he was preserving no rights for Margaret, and that neither Sally nor Richard nor Farr ever made any representation to Margaret that she would be able to stay in the house after Cappy's death. . . .

Sally and Marlette complied with their obligations under the agreement. Sally died in 1983, and Marlette became the sole owner of the property subject to Cappy's life estate. Although Margaret knew before Cappy's death that she did not have any interest in the Wellesley property, she believed that Sally would have allowed her to live in the house because of their friendship. After Cappy's death in 1987, Marlette inquired as to Margaret's plans, and, subsequently, through Farr, sent Margaret a notice to vacate the premises. Margaret brought this action in the Probate Court.

After a two-day trial, the judge held that [Farr] was in breach of his duty to Cappy when he neglected to inquire as to the latter's finances. She concluded that, had Farr fulfilled his fiduciary duties, Cappy would not have conveyed the residence owned by him to Sally and Marlette. The judge ordered Marlette to convey the house to Margaret and also ordered Farr to reimburse Marlette from the remaining portion of Cappy's trust for the expenses paid by him and Sally for the upkeep of the property. If Cappy's trust proved insufficient to make such payments, Farr was to be personally liable for such expenses. Both Farr and Marlette appealed from the judgment, from the denial of their motions to amend the findings, and from their motions for a new trial. Margaret appealed from the denial of her motion for attorney's fees. . . . [W]e agree with the judge that Sara's will imposed a duty of inquiry on the trustee, but we disagree with the remedy and, therefore, remand for further proceedings.

2. Breach of trust by the trustee. Contrary to Farr's contention that it was not incumbent upon him to become familiar with Cappy's finances, . . . Sara's will clearly placed such a duty upon him. In his brief, Farr claims that the will gave Cappy the right to request principal "in extraordinary circumstances" and that the trustee, "was charged by Sara to be wary should Cappy request money beyond that which he quarterly received." Nothing in the will or the record supports this narrow construction. To the contrary, the direction to the trustees was to pay Cappy such amounts "as they shall deem advisable for his comfortable support and maintenance." This language has been interpreted to set an ascertainable standard, namely to maintain the life beneficiary "in accordance with the standard of living which was normal for him before he became a beneficiary of the trust." Woodberry v. Bunker, 268 N.E.2d 841, 844 (Mass. 1971).

Even where the only direction to the trustee is that he shall "in his discretion" pay such portion of the principal as he shall "deem advisable," the discretion is not absolute. "Prudence and reasonableness, not caprice or careless good nature, much less a desire on the part of the trustee to be relieved from trouble . . . furnish the standard of conduct." Boyden v. Stevens, 188 N.E. 741, 743 (Mass. 1934).

That there is a duty of inquiry into the needs of the beneficiary follows from the requirement that the trustee's power "be exercised with that soundness of judgment which follows from a due appreciation of trust responsibility." Id. In Old Colony Trust Co. v. Rodd, 254 N.E.2d 886 (Mass. 1970), the trustee sent a questionnaire to each potential beneficiary to determine which of them required assistance but failed to make further inquiry in cases where the answers were incomplete. The court agreed with the trial judge that the method employed by the trustee in determining the amount of assistance required in each case to attain "comfortable support and maintenance" was inadequate. There, as here, the trustee attempted to argue that it was appropriate to save for the beneficiaries' future medical needs. The court held that the "prospect of illness in old age does not warrant a persistent policy of niggardliness toward individuals for whose comfortable support in life the trust has been established. The payments made to the respondent and several other beneficiaries, viewed in light of their assets and needs, when measured against the assets of the trust show that little consideration has been given to the 'comfortable support' of the beneficiaries."

Farr, in our view, did not meet his responsibilities either of inquiry or of distribution under the trust. The conclusion of the trial judge that, had he exercised "sound judgment," he would have made such payments to Cappy "as to allow him to continue to live in the home he had occupied for many years with the settlor" was warranted.

3. *Remedy against Marlette.* [The trial court ordered Marlette to convey the house to Margaret on the theory that, had Farr not been in breach of trust, Cappy would have died owning the house and thus would have been able to devise it to Margaret. The appellate court vacated that order because Sally and Marlette were bona fide purchasers for value without notice of Farr's breach.]

4. *Remainder of Cappy's trust.* The amounts that should have been expended for Cappy's benefit are, however, in a different category. More than $80,000 remained in the trust for Cappy at the time of his death. As we have indicated, the trial judge properly concluded that payments of principal should have been made to Cappy from that fund in sufficient amount to enable him to keep the Wellesley property. . . . The remedy in such circumstances is to impress a constructive trust on the amounts which should have been distributed to Cappy but were not because of the error of the trustee. Even in cases where beneficiaries have already been paid funds by mistake, the amounts may be collected from them unless the recipients were bona fide purchasers or unless they, without notice of the improper payments, had so changed their position that it would be inequitable to make them repay. Here, the remainder of Cappy's trust has not yet been distributed, and there is no reason to depart from the usual rule of impressing a constructive trust in favor of Cappy's estate on the amounts wrongfully withheld. . . .

That Cappy assented to the accounts is also no bar to recovery by his estate. The judge found that he was in the dark as to his rights to receive principal for the upkeep of the home. An assent may be withdrawn by a judge "if it is deemed improvident or not conducive to justice." Swift v. Hiscock, 183 N.E.2d 875, 877 (Mass. 1962). [In addition, the accounts had not been approved by the court.][42] . . .

The amounts to be paid to Cappy's estate have not been determined. On remand, the Probate Court judge is to hold such hearings as are necessary to determine the amounts which should have been paid to Cappy to enable him to retain possession of the house.

5. *Personal liability of the trustee.* . . . [The] difficult question is the effect of the exculpatory clause. . . . In view of the judge's finding that, but for the trustee's breach, Cappy would have retained ownership of the house, the liability of the trustee could be considerable.

Although exculpatory clauses are not looked upon with favor and are strictly construed, such "provisions inserted in the trust instrument without any overreaching or abuse by the trustee of any fiduciary or confidential relationship to the settlor are generally held effective except as to breaches of trust 'committed in bad faith or intentionally or with reckless indifference to the interest of the beneficiary.'" New England Trust Co. v. Paine, 59 N.E.2d 263 (Mass. 1945). The actions of Farr were not of this ilk and also do not fall within the meaning of the term used in the will, "willful neglect or default."

Farr testified that he discussed the exculpatory clause with Sara and that she wanted it included. Nevertheless, the judge, without finding that there was an overreaching or abuse of Farr's fiduciary relation with Sara, held the clause ineffective. Relying on the fact that Farr was Sara's attorney, she stated: "One cannot know at this point in time whether or not Farr specifically called this provision to Sara's attention. Given the total failure of Farr to use his judgment as to [C]appy's needs, it would be unjust and unreasonable to hold him harmless by reason of the exculpatory provisions he himself drafted and inserted in this instrument."

Assuming that the judge disbelieved Farr's testimony that he and Sara discussed the clause, although such disbelief on her part is by no means clear, the conclusion that it "would be unjust and unreasonable to hold [Farr] harmless" is not sufficient to find the overreaching or abuse of a fiduciary relation which is required to hold the provision ineffective. See Restatement (Second) of Trusts § 222, Comment d (1959). We note that the judge found that Sara managed all the finances of the couple, and from all that appears, was competent in financial matters.

There was no evidence about the preparation and execution of Sara's will except for the questions concerning the exculpatory clause addressed to Farr by his own counsel. No claim was made that the clause was the result of an abuse of confidence.

The fact that the trustee drew the instrument and suggested the insertion of the exculpatory clause does not necessarily make the provision ineffective. Restatement (Second) of Trusts § 222, Comment d. No rule of law requires that an exculpatory

---

42. . . . In Loring, A Trustee's Handbook § 62 (Farr rev. 1962) the author states: "[P]reparing annual accounts, signed by the adult beneficiaries and allowing them to continue without adjudication is an unsafe procedure for the trustee." [On informal accountings, see page 691.—Eds.]

clause drawn by a prospective trustee be held ineffective unless the client is advised independently.

The judge used an incorrect legal standard in invalidating the clause. While recognizing the sensitivity of such clauses, we hold that, since there was no evidence that the insertion of the clause was an abuse of Farr's fiduciary relationship with Sara at the time of the drawing of her will, the clause is effective. . . .

The judgment is vacated, and the matter is remanded to the Probate Court for further proceedings to determine the amounts which, if paid, would have enabled Cappy to retain ownership of the residence. Such amounts shall be paid to Cappy's estate from the trust for his benefit prior to distributing the balance thereof to the [remainder beneficiaries].

So ordered.

NOTES

1. Duty to Inquire.   Because the trust instrument entitled Cappy not just to income but also to so much of the principal as the trustee deemed advisable for Cappy's "comfortable support and maintenance," the court held that the duty of prudence required Farr to inquire into Cappy's needs and circumstances. Why did Farr's request that Cappy explain his need for funds in writing not satisfy this obligation? Shouldn't Cappy's sale of his home to Sally have put Farr on notice of Cappy's financial distress? Why might Farr have been hesitant to make a discretionary distribution of principal?

2. The Beneficiary's Other Resources.   A troublesome source of litigation is whether a trustee, in exercising a discretionary power to use income or principal for a beneficiary's support, should consider the other resources available to the beneficiary. In *Marsman*, this question was answered expressly by the terms of the trust, which directed the trustees to consider "the various available sources of support" for Cappy. The default rule of construction applicable if the trust instrument does not address the issue is in flux. The Restatement (Second) of Trusts takes the position that a beneficiary's other resources presumptively should not be considered, but the Restatement (Third) of Trusts takes the opposite view that other resources presumptively should be considered.[43]

In In re Trusts for McDonald, 953 N.Y.S.2d 751 (App. Div. 2012), the court upheld a trustee's decision not to make a discretionary distribution to help pay for a beneficiary's college tuition because the beneficiary had other resources available for that purpose. The trustee, a parent of the beneficiary, had established a college savings account for the beneficiary, which was "more than adequate to provide for [the beneficiary's] college expenses." Following the Restatement (Third) of Trusts, the court held that "the exercise of the trustee's judgment in making discretionary distributions

---

43. *Compare* Restatement (Second) of Trusts § 128 cmt. e (Am. Law Inst. 1959), *with* Restatement (Third) of Trusts § 50 cmt. e (Am. Law Inst. 2003); *see also* Jeffrey A. Schoenblum, Multistate Guide to Trusts and Trust Administration tbl. 3 (2012) (surveying the states).

should be evaluated in light of the availability of other resources, including . . . the parental duty of support."

3. Professional Responsibility. James F. Farr rendered legal services for Sara, Cappy, Sally, and Marlette, all more or less at the same time. Whether one lawyer may represent multiple members of the same family concurrently depends on the circumstances.

Under Model Rule of Professional Conduct 1.7(b) (2015), a lawyer may represent multiple clients with adverse interests in a transaction (but not in litigation) if each client provides "informed consent, confirmed in writing," and the lawyer "reasonably believes" that he "will be able to provide competent and diligent representation to each affected client." The test is objective: The question is what an independent, competent lawyer would reasonably believe.

Did Farr have a waivable conflict that became nonwaivable when Cappy and Sally were on opposite sides of the house sale? "What was a tolerable conflict at the outset may develop into one that precludes the lawyer from continuing to represent one or more of the clients."[44]

b. Sole, Absolute, or Uncontrolled Discretion

A court will not interfere with a discretionary judgment of a trustee so long as the trustee acts reasonably and in good faith.[45] But suppose a settlor purports to free the trustee from fiduciary accountability by use of adjectives such as *sole, absolute,* or *uncontrolled* in describing the trustee's discretion. In *Marsman,* the trust instrument said that the decision to invade principal for Cappy's support was to be made by the trustee in his "sole and uncontrolled discretion." Yet the court found Farr's parsimony to be in breach of his fiduciary duties. In Stix v. Commissioner, 152 F.2d 562 (2d Cir. 1945), Judge Learned Hand described the underlying principle thus:

> [N]o language, however strong, will entirely remove any power held in trust from the reach of a court of equity. After allowance has been made for every possible factor which could rationally enter into the trustee's decision, if it appears that he has utterly disregarded the interests of the beneficiary, the court will intervene. Indeed, were that not true, the power would not be held in trust at all; the language would be no more than a precatory admonition.

What, then, are the limits on a trustee's sole, absolute, or uncontrolled discretion? Professor Scott argued for a subjective standard, emphasizing the trustee's "good faith"

Judge Learned Hand

---

44. ACTEC Commentaries on the Model Rules of Professional Conduct 103 (5th ed. 2016) (Rule 1.7).

45. *See* Restatement (Third) of Trusts § 87 cmt. c (Am. Law Inst. 2007).

and proper motives, and dispensing with the requirement of reasonableness. He wrote into the Restatement (Second) of Trusts a standard of whether the trustee acted "in a state of mind in which it was contemplated by the settlor that he would act. . . . [T]he trustee will not be permitted to act dishonestly, or from some motive other than the accomplishment of the purposes of the trust, or ordinarily to act arbitrarily without an exercise of his judgment."[46] Some courts, in applying this good faith standard, have held that a trustee must not act arbitrarily or capriciously, seemingly bringing in a reasonableness test under the guise of other words.

UTC § 814(a) (2000, rev. 2004) codifies the principle of judicial review of extended discretion thus:

> Notwithstanding the breadth of discretion granted to a trustee in the terms of the trust, including the use of such terms as "absolute," "sole," or "uncontrolled," the trustee shall exercise a discretionary power in good faith and in accordance with the terms and purposes of the trust and the interests of the beneficiaries.

The Restatement (Third) of Trusts provides similarly that "words such as 'absolute' or 'unlimited' or 'sole and uncontrolled' are not interpreted literally. Even under the broadest grant of fiduciary discretion, a trustee must act honestly and in a state of mind contemplated by the settlor. Thus, the court will not permit the trustee to act in bad faith or for some purpose or motive other than to accomplish the purposes of the discretionary power."[47]

In the final analysis, it appears that the difference between ordinary and extended discretion is one of degree. A trustee's exercise or nonexercise of a discretionary power must not only be in good faith but also reasonable with more elasticity in the concept of reasonableness if the trust instrument grants the trustee expanded discretion. In In re Trusts for McDonald, 953 N.Y.S.2d 751 (App. Div. 2012), the court put the point thus:

> The judicial deference afforded trustees . . . is particularly broad where the testator has manifested an intention to grant the trustee greater than ordinary latitude in exercising discretionary judgment. Here, the testator manifested a clear intention to grant the trustee the greatest latitude permitted by law in exercising discretionary judgment. While the phrase used by the testator, "as the Trustee deems advisable in [the Trustee's] sole discretion not subject to judicial review," does not relieve the trustee of all accountability, it manifests the testator's clear intent to grant the trustee the broadest extended discretion.

c. Exculpation Clauses

In *Marsman*, the trust Farr drafted for Sara included an *exculpatory* or *exoneration* clause, which excused the trustees—and so Farr himself!—from liability except for "willful neglect or default." The court upheld the clause because there was no evidence

---

46. Restatement (Second) of Trusts § 187 cmt. j (Am. Law Inst. 1959).
47. Restatement (Third) of Trusts § 50 cmt. c (Am. Law Inst. 2003); *see also* id. § 87 cmt. d (Am. Law Inst. 2007).

that Farr had inserted it in an abuse of confidence reposed by Sara. The court put the burden of proving such abuse on Margaret, which she could not satisfy.

Do you think it is ethical for a lawyer to include an exculpatory clause in a trust that names the lawyer as trustee? Should not the law presume abuse and put the burden on the trustee-drafter to prove fair disclosure and consent by the settlor? In Rutanen v. Ballard, 678 N.E.2d 133 (Mass. 1997), decided after *Marsman*, the Massachusetts Supreme Judicial Court refused to enforce an exculpatory clause inserted by the trustee-drafter. The court reasoned that "the failure of [trustee-drafter] to bring the clause to the settlor's attention and explain the implications of the clause was improper and rendered the clause ineffective to protect him."

UTC § 1008(b) (2000) follows *Rutanen* in rejecting *Marsman*:

> An exculpatory term drafted or caused to be drafted by the trustee is invalid as an abuse of a fiduciary or confidential relationship unless the trustee proves that the exculpatory term is fair under the circumstances and that its existence and contents were adequately communicated to the settlor.[48]

The Restatement (Third) of Trusts provides similarly that an exculpatory provision inserted by a trustee "is presumptively unenforceable. The presumption is rebuttable, and the clause will be given effect if the trustee proves that the exculpatory provision is fair ... and that the existence, contents, and effect of the clause were adequately communicated to or otherwise understood by the settlor."[49]

Thus far we have been supposing that the settlor's lawyer drafted the trust instrument and is named as trustee. Suppose instead that the trustee is a bank and the settlor uses a form supplied by the bank that includes an exculpatory provision. The same presumption of abuse applies so that the "provision relieving the trustee of liability for breach of trust is ineffective unless the settlor fully understood the nature of the provision and freely agreed to it."[50] But what if the settlor was represented by independent counsel? The comment to UTC § 1008 answers: "If the settlor was represented by independent counsel, the settlor's attorney is considered the drafter of the instrument even if the attorney used the trustee's form. Because the settlor's attorney is an agent of the settlor, disclosure of an exculpatory term to the settlor's attorney is disclosure to the settlor."

Even if a fully informed settlor knowingly includes an exculpation clause, the clause cannot exculpate *bad faith*, *reckless indifference*, or *intentional or willful neglect* by the trustee. The Restatement (Third) of Trusts explains:

> Notwithstanding the breadth of language in a trust provision relieving a trustee from liability for breach of trust, for reasons of policy trust fiduciary law imposes limitations on the types and degree of misconduct for which the trustee can be excused from liability. Hence, an exculpatory clause cannot excuse a trustee for a breach of trust committed in bad faith. Nor can the trustee be excused for a breach committed with indifference to the interests of the beneficiaries or to the terms and

---

48. For an application of this provision, see, e.g., Rafert v. Meyer, 859 N.W.2d 332 (Neb. 2015).
49. Restatement (Third) of Trusts § 96 cmt. d (Am. Law Inst. 2012).
50. Scott and Ascher on Trusts § 24.27.4.

purposes of the trust — that is, committed without reasonable effort to understand and conform to applicable fiduciary duties.[51]

This mandatory core of trust fiduciary law that may not be waived is codified by UTC § 1008(a) thus: "A term of a trust relieving a trustee of liability for breach of trust is unenforceable to the extent that it . . . relieves the trustee of liability for breach of trust committed in bad faith or with reckless indifference to the purposes of the trust or the interests of the beneficiaries." In New York, a testamentary trustee cannot be exonerated for failure to exercise reasonable care.[52]

In McNeil v. McNeil, 798 A.2d 503 (Del. 2002), at issue was a clause stating that the trustees' decisions were "not subject to review by any court." Observing that courts "flatly refuse to enforce provisions relieving a trustee of all liability," the court reviewed the trustees' actions nonetheless. The reason: "A trust in which there is no legally binding obligation on a trustee is a trust in name only and more in the nature of an absolute estate or fee simple grant of property." A few years earlier, in Armitage v. Nurse, [1998] Ch. 241 at 253 (Eng.), Lord Justice Millet applied the same principle to an English trust: "[T]here is an irreducible core of obligations owed by the trustees to the beneficiaries and enforceable by them which is fundamental to the concept of a trust. If the beneficiaries have no rights enforceable against the trustees there are no trusts." Professor Sitkoff summarizes thus:

> [T]he mandatory core of fiduciary law polices the line that differentiates a fiduciary relationship on the one hand from a fee simple or other such arrangement on the other. A person may give property to another person and authorize the other person to act whimsically with respect to the property. But this mode of transfer is an absolute gift, and this mode of holding property is fee simple.[53]

d. Mandatory Arbitration

Suppose a settlor, wanting to avoid the expense and publicity of fiduciary litigation, directs in the trust instrument that all disputes between a beneficiary and the trustee must be resolved by arbitration.[54] The authorities on whether such a provision

---

51. Restatement (Third) of Trusts § 96 cmt. c (Am. Law Inst. 2012).
52. N.Y. Est. Powers & Tr. Law § 11-1.7(a)(1) (2016).
53. Sitkoff, *supra* note 18, at 1047.
54. Recall the arbitration clause in George Washington's will (see page 309). Here is a modern formbook example:

> In order to save the cost of court proceedings and promote the prompt and final resolution of any dispute regarding the interpretation of my will (or my trust) or the administration of my estate or any trust under my will (or my trust), I direct that any such dispute shall be settled by arbitration administered by the American Arbitration Association under its AAA Wills and Trusts Arbitration Rules and Mediation Procedures then in effect. . . . The arbitrator(s) shall apply the substantive law (and the law of remedies, if applicable) of the state whose laws govern my will (or my trust). The arbitrator's decision shall not be appealable to any court, but shall be final and binding on any and all persons who have or may have an interest in my estate or any

is enforceable are scarce and contradictory,[55] and commentators are by no means in agreement on the policy analysis.[56]

The position of the UTC is unclear. The drafters said that "[s]ettlors wishing to encourage use of alternate dispute resolution may draft to provide it." But this remark is buried in the comment to § 816, on trustees' powers, and it does not make clear whether a mandatory arbitration provision is enforceable, as compared to one that merely encourages arbitration.[57]

In Schoneberger v. Oelze, 96 P.3d 1078 (Ariz. App. 2004), the court refused to enforce a mandatory arbitration provision. A settlor, said the court, "may not unilaterally strip trust beneficiaries of their right to access the courts absent their agreement." The court reasoned that participation in arbitration must be voluntary, and the beneficiaries did not consent, although the settlor had. In McArthur v. McArthur, 168 Cal. Rptr. 3d 785 (App. 2014), the court reached the same result on similar reasoning.

A weakness in the *Schoneberger* reasoning, however, is that a beneficiary's interest is derivative of the settlor's freedom of disposition. A trust is a conditional gift in which the beneficiary takes his interest subject to the conditions imposed by the settlor. On this view, the relevant question is not whether the *beneficiary* consented, but rather whether the *settlor* consented—and if so, whether requiring fiduciary disputes to be resolved by arbitration is within the settlor's freedom of disposition.

In 2008, the Arizona legislature enacted a statute that reversed *Schoneberger* by authorizing a settlor to mandate arbitration "to resolve issues between the trustee and [a beneficiary] with regard to the administration or distribution of the trust."[58] A handful of other states have enacted similar statutes.[59] In Rachal v. Reitz, 403 S.W.3d 840 (Tex. 2013), the court enforced a mandatory arbitration provision against the beneficiaries. The court reasoned that their claim was to enforce their interests as defined by the settlor in the terms of the trust, including the arbitration clause.

Against these statutes and *Rachal*, however, it could be argued that fiduciary enforcement in court should be part of the mandatory core of trust fiduciary law. A

---

trust under my will (or my trust), including unborn or incapacitated persons, such as minors or incompetents.

American Arbitration Ass'n, Wills and Trusts Arbitration Rules, Model Clause (June 1, 2012); *but see* E. Gary Spitko, A Critique of the American Arbitration Association's Efforts to Facilitate Arbitration of Internal Trust Disputes, *in* Arbitration of Trust Disputes 49 (S.I. Strong ed., 2016).

55. *See* Mary F. Radford, Trust Arbitration in United States Courts, *in* Arbitration of Trust Disputes 175 (S.I. Strong ed., 2016).

56. *See, e.g.,* Jessica Beess und Chrostin, Mandatory Arbitration Clauses in Donative Instruments: A Taxonomy of Disputes and Type-Differentiated Analysis, 49 Real Prop. Tr. & Est. L.J. 397 (2014); Erin Katzen, Arbitration Clauses in Wills and Trusts: Defining the Parameters for Mandatory Arbitration of Wills and Trusts, 24 Quinnipiac Prob. L.J. 118 (2011); Stephen Wills Murphy, Enforceable Arbitration Clauses in Wills and Trusts: A Critique, 26 Ohio St. J. Disp. Resol. 627 (2011).

57. *See* David M. English, Arbitration and the US Uniform Trust Code, *in* Arbitration of Trust Disputes 143 (S.I. Strong ed., 2016).

58. Ariz. Rev. Stat. § 14-10205 (2016).

59. *See, e.g.,* Fla. Stat. § 731.401 (2016); Mo. Rev. Stat. § 456.2-205 (2016); N.H. Rev. Stat. § 564-B:1-111A (2016); S.D. Codified Laws § 55-1-54 (2016); *see also* Lee-ford Tritt, Legislative Approaches to Trust Arbitration in the United States, *in* Arbitration of Trust Disputes 150 (S.I. Strong ed., 2016).

settlor may impose an exculpation clause, for example, but not if it exculpates bad faith or willful neglect, because accountability is essential to the nature of the trust relationship. The hard policy question raised by mandatory trust arbitration provisions is whether accountability in court, before a judge, is part of that essential core.

2. The Investment Function

The investment function involves reviewing the trust assets and then implementing an investment program that fits the purpose of the trust and the circumstances of the beneficiaries. In the materials that follow, we consider: (a) the evolution of the law of trust investment, culminating in the *prudent investor rule*; and (b) recurring problems in applying the rule, in particular the duty to diversify, the duty within a reasonable time to bring the initial trust portfolio into compliance with the rule, and the relevance of an instruction by the settlor not to diversify.

a. From Legal Lists to the Prudent Investor Rule

The shift from limited powers to fiduciary governance is perhaps most profound in trust investment. The law first prescribed *legal lists* of permitted investments, typically government bonds and first mortgages on real property. The legal lists were replaced by the *prudent man rule*, which was nominally more flexible, but as applied came to favor government bonds and disfavor stocks. Today all states have replaced the prudent man rule with the *prudent investor rule*, most following the Uniform Prudent Investor Act (UPIA) (Unif. Law Comm'n 1994). UPIA § 2(e) permits a trustee to "invest in any kind of property or type of investment" subject to the risk management rules prescribed by § 2(b) for "overall . . . risk and return objectives" and § 3 for "diversify[ing] the investments of the trust."

Uniform Prudent Investor Act (Unif. Law Comm'n 1994)

§ 1. Prudent Investor Rule

(a) Except as otherwise provided in subsection (b), a trustee who invests and manages trust assets owes a duty to the beneficiaries of the trust to comply with the prudent investor rule set forth in this [Act].

(b) The prudent investor rule, a default rule, may be expanded, restricted, eliminated, or otherwise altered by the provisions of a trust. A trustee is not liable to a beneficiary to the extent that the trustee acted in reasonable reliance on the provisions of the trust.

§ 2. Standard of Care; Portfolio Strategy; Risk and Return Objectives

(a) A trustee shall invest and manage trust assets as a prudent investor would, by considering the purposes, terms, distribution requirements, and other circumstances of the trust. In satisfying this standard, the trustee shall exercise reasonable care, skill, and caution.

(b) A trustee's investment and management decisions respecting individual assets must be evaluated not in isolation but in the context of the trust portfolio as a whole and as a part of an overall investment strategy having risk and return objectives reasonably suited to the trust.

(c) Among circumstances that the trustee shall consider in investing and managing trust assets are such of the following as are relevant to the trust or its beneficiaries:

(1) general economic conditions;

(2) the possible effect of inflation or deflation;

(3) the expected tax consequences of investment decisions or strategies;

(4) the role that each investment or course of action plays within the overall trust portfolio, which may include financial assets, interests in closely held enterprises, tangible and intangible personal property, and real property;

(5) the expected total return from income and the appreciation of capital;

(6) other resources of the beneficiaries;

(7) needs for liquidity, regularity of income, and preservation or appreciation of capital; and

(8) an asset's special relationship or special value, if any, to the purposes of the trust or to one or more of the beneficiaries.

(d) A trustee shall make a reasonable effort to verify facts relevant to the investment and management of trust assets.

(e) A trustee may invest in any kind of property or type of investment consistent with the standards of this [Act].

(f) A trustee who has special skills or expertise, or is named trustee in reliance upon the trustee's representation that the trustee has special skills or expertise, has a duty to use those special skills or expertise.

§ 3. Diversification

A trustee shall diversify the investments of the trust unless the trustee reasonably determines that, because of special circumstances, the purposes of the trust are better served without diversifying.

§ 4. Duties at Inception of Trusteeship

Within a reasonable time after accepting a trusteeship or receiving trust assets, a trustee shall review the trust assets and make and implement decisions concerning the retention and disposition of assets, in order to bring the trust portfolio into compliance with the purposes, terms, distribution requirements, and other circumstances of the trust, and with the requirements of this [Act].

NOTES

1. *The Restatement (Third) of Trusts.* The provisions of the UPIA excerpted above have counterparts in the Restatement (Third) of Trusts and were based on an earlier interim version of those Restatement provisions.[60]

---

60. *See* Restatement (Third) of Trusts §§ 90-92 (Am. Law Inst. 2007); Restatement (Third) of Trusts: Prudent Investor Rule § 227 (Am. Law Inst. 1992).

2. *Application to Charitable Endowments and Pension Funds.*   Uniform Prudent Management of Institutional Funds Act § 3 (Unif. Law Comm'n 2006), adopted in nearly every state, applies the prudent investor rule to charitable organizations in the management and investment of their endowment funds.

The Employee Retirement Income Security Act of 1974 (ERISA) governs the investment of most pension funds by the trustees managing the funds. The statutory standard governing investments is an early form of the prudent investor rule.[61] ERISA also provides that an ERISA trustee shall discharge his duties "solely in the interest of the participants and beneficiaries."[62]

Because the prudent investor rule applies to common law trusts, pension trusts, and charitable endowments, and because the rule has also been adopted across the British Commonwealth, the rule governs the investment management of many trillions of dollars.

Max M. Schanzenbach & Robert H. Sitkoff
The Prudent Investor Rule and Market Risk:
An Empirical Analysis
14 J. Emp. Legal Stud. 129 (2017)

The long tradition of equating stock investment with speculation deeply influenced the law of trust investment, which until recently discouraged investment in stock as "speculative" and favored investment in government bonds. . . .

In The Tragedy of Pudd'nhead Wilson, Mark Twain wrote: "October. This is one of the peculiarly dangerous months to speculate in stocks in. The others are July, January, September, April, November, May, March, June, December, August, and February."

THE LEGAL LISTS AND PRUDENT MAN RULE

Trust investment law "got off to a bad start." After the South Sea Bubble burst in 1720 [see Figure 9.1], the English Court of Chancery settled upon a list of presumptively proper investments. The list was later codified, albeit in a somewhat broader form, by statutes in England and across the United States. Reflecting the salience of default risk after the South Sea Bubble, these *legal lists* required risk avoidance. They tended to favor government bonds and first mortgages and to exclude investments in equity. Structurally, the legal lists were in keeping with the legal technology of the era, in which agency problems, such as between a trustee and a beneficiary, were resolved by limiting the agent's powers. . . .

In the seminal case of Harvard College v. Amory, 26 Mass. 446, 461 (1830), the Massachusetts Supreme Judicial Court rejected the legal list and adopted the *prudent man rule.* The court held that a trustee must "observe how men of prudence, discretion and intelligence manage their own

---

61. *See* 29 U.S.C. § 1104(a) (2012), as interpreted in 29 C.F.R. § 2550.404a-1(b) (2012).
62. 29 U.S.C. § 1104(a)(1) (2012).

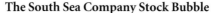

The South Sea Company Stock Bubble

Figure 9.1

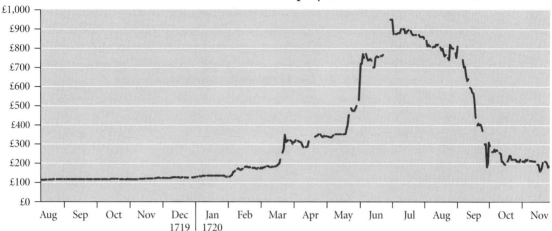

Source: Rik G.P. Frehen, William N. Goetzmann & K. Geert Rouwenhorst, New Evidence on the First Financial Bubble, 108 J. Fin. Econ. 585 (2013).

affairs, not in regard to speculation, but in regard to the permanent disposition of their funds, considering the probable income, as well as the probable safety of the capital to be invested." In the mid 1900s, after the American Bankers Association sponsored a model statute codifying *Amory*, most states abrogated their legal lists in favor of the prudent man rule.

The prudent man rule was phrased as a standard that called for case-by-case adjudication in light of all the circumstances. In application, however, courts generalized rules from the specific facts of prior cases, giving rise to "specific subrules prescribing the types and characteristics of permissible investments for trustees."[63] In this way, the risk-avoidance emphasis of the legal lists persisted. "Based on some degree of risk that was abstractly perceived as excessive, broad categories of investments and techniques often came to be classified as 'speculative' and thus as imprudent per se."[64] In the Restatement (Second) of Trusts, which was published in 1959, the American Law Institute took the position that investing in "speculative" stock, defined as a company without "regular earnings and paying regular dividends which may reasonably be expected to continue," buying securities on margin, or buying discounted bonds was presumptively improper.[65] By contrast, "[o]rdinarily it is proper for a trustee to invest in . . . bonds of the United States or of the State or of municipalities, in first mortgages on land, or in corporate bonds."[66]

The preoccupation under the prudent man rule with avoiding default risk encouraged investment in government bonds, exposing trusts to inflation risk, and invited hindsight bias in adjudication in the form of "post hoc searches for evidence that

---

63. Restatement (Third) of Trusts, ch. 17, intro. note (Am. Law Inst. 2007).—Eds.
64. Id.—Eds.
65. Restatement (Second) of Trusts § 227 cmt. m (1959).—Eds.
66. Id. cmt. f.—Eds.

investments were too risky."[67] The problem of hindsight bias was aggravated by the practice of reviewing each investment in isolation. If a risky investment failed to pay off, the trustee faced liability exposure even if the investment was sound in the context of the portfolio as a whole. The rule thus worked perversely against diversification.

THE PRUDENT INVESTOR RULE

1. Codifying Portfolio Theory

In the late 1970s, scholars and sophisticated practitioners began calling for reform of the prudent man rule. Drawing on modern portfolio theory and consensus views of financial economics prevailing at the time, the critics argued that the law should differentiate between market risk, which is inherent to participating in the market, and idiosyncratic risk, which is particular to a given investment. Generally speaking, to obtain a greater expected return, an investor must assume greater market risk. Market risk is thus compensated in that more exposure to market risk yields more expected return. Idiosyncratic risk, the critics argued, is different because it is generally uncompensated. Such risk can be reduced or even eliminated by diversifying. It follows, therefore, that the prudence of a given investment must be considered in light of its contribution to the overall portfolio's expected risk and return. Under the prudent man rule, however, courts evaluated the prudence of each investment in isolation, without regard to its place within the portfolio as a whole.

These criticisms led to a movement in the mid to late 1980s to revise the prudent man rule, refashioning it as a *prudent investor rule* that would reorient the law of trust investment from investment-level risk avoidance to portfolio-level risk management consistent with modern portfolio theory. The aspiration of the reform movement was "to free trustees from the old preoccupation with avoiding speculation." The rule implements two key reforms.[68] First, [under UPIA § 2(b), page 624,] "[a] trustee's investment and management decisions respecting individual assets must be evaluated not in isolation but in the context of the trust portfolio as a whole and as a part of an overall investment strategy having risk and return objectives reasonably suited to the trust." Second, [under UPIA § 3, page 625,] a trustee must "diversify the investments of the trust unless the trustee reasonably determines that, because of special circumstances, the purposes of the trust are better served without diversifying."

---

67. An infamous example is In re Chamberlain's Estate, 156 A. 42, 43 (N.J. Prerog. 1931):

It was common knowledge, not only amongst bankers and trust companies, but the general public as well, that the stock market condition at the time of testator's death [in August 1929] was an unhealthy one, that values were very much inflated, and that a crash was almost sure to occur. In view of this fact, I think it was the duty of the executors to dispose of these stocks immediately upon their qualification as executors, and that the loss to the estate resulting from their failure to act should be taken into consideration now in awarding them compensation for their services.

68. The reform also reversed the nondelegation rule of prior law, which we take up at page 658.—Eds.

Accordingly, the prudent investor rule requires a trustee not to avoid risk altogether but rather to evaluate the purpose and circumstances of the trust, to choose a commensurate level of overall market risk and expected return, and to avoid wasteful idiosyncratic risk. Upon assuming office, [under UPIA § 4, page 625,] a trustee has a "reasonable time" to "make and implement" a compliant investment program. What constitutes a reasonable time is context specific, depending for example on the liquidity of the trust assets and the tax and other transaction costs of reallocation.

A trustee is also under an "ongoing duty to monitor investments and to make portfolio adjustments if and as appropriate,"[69] for example, by rebalancing the portfolio in light of actual investment performance and changes in circumstances. In the words of the Supreme Court, "a trustee has a continuing duty to monitor trust investments and remove imprudent ones. This continuing duty exists separate and apart from the trustee's duty to exercise prudence in selecting investments at the outset."[70] The prudent inves-

Professor Harry M. Markowitz was awarded the 1990 Nobel Prize in Economics for his work on Modern Portfolio Theory.

tor rule thus governs the trustee's "continuing responsibility for oversight of the suitability of investments already made as well as the trustee's decisions respecting new investments."[71]

Widespread enactment of the prudent investor rule came after the American Law Institute endorsed it in a 1992 revision to the Restatement of Trusts and the Uniform Law Commission promulgated the UPIA in 1994. . . . By 2006, every state had adopted the UPIA or a nonuniform statute to similar effect.

2. Matching Market Risk with Trust Risk Tolerance

Structurally, the prudent investor rule is a facts-and-circumstances standard. By requiring "an overall investment strategy having risk and return objectives reasonably suited to the trust," the rule calls for "subjective judgments that are essentially unavoidable in the process of asset management, addressing the appropriate degree of risk to be undertaken in pursuit of a higher or lower level of expected return from the trust portfolio."[72] Part of what makes this judgment subjective is that "tolerance for risk varies greatly with the financial and other circumstances of the investor, or in the case of a trust, with the purposes of the trust and the relevant circumstances of the beneficiaries. A trust whose main purpose is to support an elderly widow of modest means will have a lower risk tolerance than a trust to accumulate for a young scion of great wealth."[73] . . .

---

69. Restatement (Third) of Trusts § 90 cmt. e(1) (Am. Law Inst. 2007). — Eds.
70. Tibble v. Edison Int'l, 135 S. Ct. 1823, 1828 (2015). — Eds.
71. UPIA § 2 cmt. — Eds.
72. Restatement (Third) of Trusts § 90 cmt. e(1) (2007). — Eds.
73. UPIA § 2 cmt. — Eds.

In "applying the fiduciary duty of prudent investing, it is essential to recognize that compensated risk is not inherently bad.". . . . The law has come to recognize that "[b]eneficiaries can be disserved by undue conservatism as well as by excessive risk-taking."[74]

3. . . . The Effect of the Rule in Practice

. . . [S]ince the reform, stockholdings in personal trusts have increased substantially. . . . Figure [9.2] traces the percentage of trust assets [held by trustees in the Federal Reserve System] in stock versus in "safe" assets, meaning government bonds, insured deposits, and money market funds, from 1986 to 2008. There are clear, mirror-image trends, with stockholdings increasing and "safe" holdings decreasing in the years after promulgation of the prudent investor rule in the Restatement . . . in 1992 and UPIA in 1994. Apart from the market crashes in 2002 and 2008, stockholdings have averaged between 60 and 70 percent of yearly trust assets, while "safe" holdings have averaged between 22 and 28 percent. Most of the remainder comprises corporate bonds and real estate.

Figure 9.2

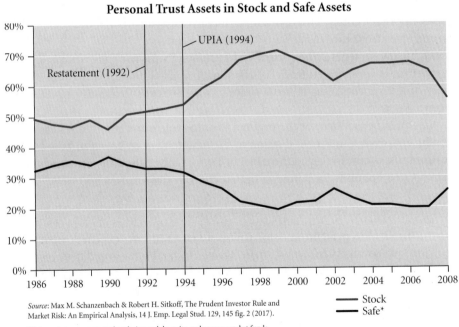

Personal Trust Assets in Stock and Safe Assets

Source: Max M. Schanzenbach & Robert H. Sitkoff, The Prudent Investor Rule and Market Risk: An Empirical Analysis, 14 J. Emp. Legal Stud. 129, 145 fig. 2 (2017).

*Safe assets are government bonds, insured deposits, and money market funds.

NOTES

1. Default Risk, Inflation Risk, and the Equity Premium.   Under the legal lists and then the prudent man rule, trustees invested heavily in government bonds, which have little *default risk*, but expose the trust estate to *inflation risk*. In a period in which the

---

74. Restatement (Third) of Trusts § 90 cmt. e(1) (2007).—Eds.

rate of inflation exceeds the interest rate on the bonds, the real value of the trust estate will shrink. A portfolio that includes stocks will have less inflation risk, because it is more likely to experience a return that exceeds the rate of inflation, but this comes at the cost of taking on more default risk. The obsession under prior law with guarding against default risk obscured the tradeoff with inflation risk.

Figure 9.3 presents summary statistics on average annual total return across asset classes between 1926 and 2014. In the same timeframe, the average annual rate of inflation was 3.0 percent. The persistence of higher average returns for stocks than bonds is known as the *equity premium*.[75] The underlying point is that there is a tradeoff between risk and return. To obtain a greater expectation of return, an investor must take on greater exposure to default risk.

Average Annual Total Returns by Asset Class (1926-2014)   Figure 9.3

Asset Class	Average Annual Return
Small Company Stocks	16.7%
Large Company Stocks	12.1%
Long-Term Corporate Bonds	6.4%
Long-Term Government Bonds	6.1%
Intermediate-Term Government Bonds	5.4%
U.S. Treasury Bills	3.5%

Source: Ibbotson SBBI Classic Yearbook: Market Results for Stocks, Bonds, Bills, and Inflation tbl. 2-1 (2015).

2. Prudent Risk Management.   Risk management is central to prudence in the investment function under the prudent investor rule. The Restatement (Third) of Trusts explains:

> The requirement of caution ordinarily imposes a duty to use reasonable care and skill in an effort to minimize or at least reduce diversifiable risks. . . . [T]hese are risks that can be reduced through proper diversification of a portfolio. Because market pricing cannot be expected to recognize and reward a particular investor's failure to diversify, a trustee's acceptance of this type of risk cannot, without more, be justified on grounds of enhancing expected return. . . .
>
> Another aspect of risk management deals with market risk, . . . or more descriptively for present purposes, simply nondiversifiable or compensated risk. The trustee's duties and objectives with respect to this second category of risk are not as distinct as those with respect to diversifiable risk. They involve quite subjective

---

75. *See, e.g.*, J. Bradford DeLong & Konstantin Magin, The U.S. Equity Return Premium: Past, Present, and Future, 23 J. Econ. Persp. 193 (2009).

judgments that are essentially unavoidable in the process of asset management, addressing the appropriate degree of risk to be undertaken in pursuit of a higher or lower level of expected return from the trust portfolio.[76]

The amount of *market risk* that is suitable for a given trust depends on its risk tolerance in light of the purpose of the trust and the circumstances of the beneficiaries. By contrast, the prudent practice with respect to *idiosyncratic risk*—that is, *diversifiable risk*—is quite specific. To the extent feasible, such risk should be avoided. By definition, such risk increases exposure to loss without any offsetting improvement in expected return. If ten companies have the same expected risk and return profile, then a portfolio of all ten stocks would have the same expected return as a portfolio of just one. But there will be less variance in the actual return of the ten-stock portfolio than in the portfolio of one, because in the larger portfolio losers will often be offset by winners. The single-stock portfolio presents more risk, as measured by variation in returns, without an offsetting increase in expected return.

b. Recurring Problems in Applying the Prudent Investor Rule

Most of the litigation under the prudent investor rule concerns diversification problems, often involving an allegation that a trustee failed within a reasonable time to diversify a portfolio that was concentrated at the time the trustee took office. In a fair number of these cases, the trustee has defended retention of the concentration on the basis of language in the trust instrument authorizing or perhaps even mandating retention. Let us consider representative examples of both of these kinds of cases.

(1) The Duty to Diversify and Inception Assets

In re Estate of Janes
681 N.E.2d 332 (N.Y. 1997)

LEVINE, J. Former State Senator and businessman Rodney B. Janes (testator) died on May 26, 1973, survived solely by his wife, Cynthia W. Janes, who was then 72 years of age. Testator's $3,500,000 estate consisted of a $2,500,000 stock portfolio, approximately 71% of which consisted of 13,232 shares of common stock of the Eastman Kodak Company.[77] The Kodak stock had a date-of-death value of $1,786,733, or approximately $135 per share.

Rodney B. Janes

Testator's 1963 will and a 1969 codicil bequeathed most of his estate to three trusts. First, the testator created a marital deduction trust consisting of approximately 50% of the estate's assets, the income of which was to be paid to Mrs. Janes for her life. In addition, it contained a generous provision for invasion of the principal for Mrs. Janes's benefit and gave her testamentary

---

76. Restatement (Third) of Trusts § 90 cmt. e(1) (Am. Law Inst. 2007).
77. Rodney B. Janes, born in 1892 in Rochester, New York, served in the New York State Senate from 1939 until 1946, representing the Rochester area. Kodak is headquartered in Rochester. —Eds.

power of appointment over the remaining principal. The testator also established a charitable trust of approximately 25% of the estate's assets which directed annual distributions to selected charities. A third trust comprised the balance of the estate's assets and directed that the income therefrom be paid to Mrs. Janes for her life, with the remainder pouring over into the charitable trust upon her death.

On June 6, 1973, the testator's will and codicil were admitted to probate. Letters testamentary issued to petitioner's predecessor, Lincoln Rochester Trust Company, and Mrs. Janes, as coexecutors, on July 3, 1973. Letters of trusteeship issued to petitioner alone. By early August 1973, petitioner's trust and estate officers, Ellison Patterson and Richard Young had ascertained the estate's assets and the amount of cash needed for taxes, commissions, attorneys' fees, and specific bequests.

In an August 9, 1973 memorandum, Patterson recommended raising the necessary cash for the foregoing administrative expenses by selling certain assets, including 800 shares of Kodak stock, and holding "the remaining issues ... until the [t]rusts [were] funded." The memorandum did not otherwise address investment strategy in light of the evident primary objective of the testator to provide for his widow during her lifetime. In a September 5, 1973 meeting with Patterson and Young, Mrs. Janes, who had a high school education, no business training or experience, and who had never been employed, consented to the sale of some 1,200 additional shares of Kodak stock. Although Mrs. Janes was informed at the meeting that petitioner intended to retain the balance of the Kodak shares, none of the factors that would lead to an informed investment decision was discussed. At that time, the Kodak stock traded for about $139 per share; thus, the estate's 13,232 shares of the stock were worth almost $1,840,000. The September 5 meeting was the only occasion where retention of the Kodak stock or any other investment issues were taken up with Mrs. Janes.

By the end of 1973, the price of Kodak stock had fallen to about $109 per share. One year later, it had fallen to about $63 per share and, by the end of 1977, to about $51 per share. In March 1978, the price had dropped even further, to about $40 per share. When petitioner filed its initial accounting in February 1980, the remaining 11,320 shares were worth approximately $530,000, or about $47 per share. Most of the shares were used to fund the trusts in 1986 and 1987.

In addition to its initial accounting in 1980, petitioner filed a series of supplemental accountings that together covered the period from July 1973 through June 1994. In August 1981, petitioner sought judicial settlement of its account. Objections to the accounts were ... filed by Mrs. Janes in 1982, and subsequently by the Attorney-General on behalf of the charitable beneficiaries (collectively, "objectants"). In seeking to surcharge petitioner for losses incurred by the estate due to petitioner's imprudent retention of a high concentration of Kodak stock in the estate from July 1973 to February 1980, during which time the value of the stock had dropped to about one third of its date-of-death value, objectants asserted that petitioner's conduct violated EPTL 11-2.2(a)(1), the so-called "prudent person rule" of investment. When Mrs. Janes died in 1986, the personal representative of her estate was substituted as an objectant.

Following a trial on the objections, the Surrogate found that petitioner, under the circumstances, had acted imprudently and should have divested the estate of the high concentration of Kodak stock by August 9, 1973. The court imposed a $6,080,269

Lies, Damned Lies, and Statistics

The opinion in *Janes* recites the price of Kodak stock on seven different dates between the testator's death in May of 1973 and the trustee's filing of its initial accounting in February of 1980. Those dates, prices, and amount of time (in months) between dates are summarized in the table below.

Date	Price	Interval
May 1973	$135	—
September 1973	$139	4 months
Year-End 1973	$109	3 months
Year-End 1974	$63	12 months
Year-End 1977	$51	36 months
March 1978	$40	3 months
February 1980	$47	23 months

As a reality check, we obtained monthly Kodak stock price data for every month between January of 1973 and February of 1980. The following graph plots our monthly data, which is an evenly spaced time series with 86 observations, and the court's uneven time series of 7 observations.

So much for the "seven-year period of steady decline in the value of the stock"! The general trend between 1973 and 1980 was indeed as the court described. But during the three-year gap in the court's data the price of Kodak stock rebounded to as high as $120 per share. The lesson: Beware of time-series data with uneven intervals!

The graph also demonstrates the critical importance of the court's choice of the date by which the concentration should have been divested (Part II of the opinion). Do you see why?

Later in the opinion, the court references "a seven-year period of steady decline in the value of the stock." Are you skeptical? Focus on the third column and the uneven intervals between the data points. Usually, financial time-series data such as the price of a stock over time is presented at regular intervals. Yet the seven data points recited by the court are at wildly variable intervals. Might the court's data be cherry-picked to suggest a spurious trend?

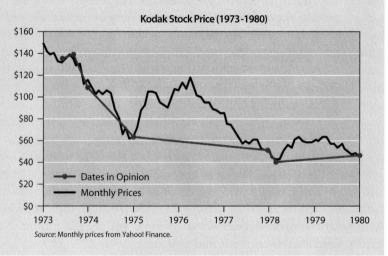

Kodak Stock Price (1973-1980)

Source: Monthly prices from Yahoo! Finance.

surcharge against petitioner and ordered petitioner to forfeit its commissions and attorneys' fees. In calculating the amount of the surcharge, the court adopted a "lost profits" or "market index" measure of damages espoused by objectants' expert—what the proceeds of the Kodak stock would have yielded, up to the time of trial, had they been invested in petitioner's own diversified equity fund on August 9, 1973.

The Appellate Division modified solely as to damages, holding that "the Surrogate properly found [petitioner] liable for its negligent failure to diversify and for its inattentiveness, inaction, and lack of disclosure, but that the Surrogate adopted an improper measure of damages." . . . [T]he Court held that the Surrogate's finding of imprudence, as well as its selection of August 9, 1973 as the date by which petitioner should have divested the estate of its concentration of Kodak stock, were "well supported" by the record. The Court rejected the Surrogate's "lost profits" or "market index" measure of damages, however, holding that the proper measure of damages was "the value of the capital that was lost"—the difference between the value of the stock at the time it should have been sold and its value when ultimately sold. Applying this measure, the Court reduced the surcharge to $4,065,029. We granted petitioner and objectants leave to appeal, and now affirm.

I. Petitioner's Liability

Petitioner argues that New York law does not permit a fiduciary to be surcharged for imprudent management of a trust for failure to diversify in the absence of additional elements of hazard, and that it relied upon, and complied with, this rule in administering the estate. Relying on Matter of Balfe, 274 N.Y.S. 284, mod. 280 N.Y.S. 128 (App. Div. 1935), petitioner claims that elements of hazard can be capsulized into deficiencies in the following investment quality factors: "(i) the capital structure of the company; (ii) the competency of its management; (iii) whether the company is a seasoned issuer of stock with a history of profitability; (iv) whether the company has a history of paying dividends; (v) whether the company is an industry leader; (vi) the expected future direction of the company's business; and (vii) the opinion of investment bankers and analysts who follow the company's stock." Evaluated under these criteria, petitioner asserts, the concentration of Kodak stock at issue in this case, that is, of an acknowledged "blue chip" security popular with investment advisors and many mutual funds, cannot be found an imprudent investment on August 9, 1973 as a matter of law. In our view, a fiduciary's duty of investment prudence in holding a concentration of one security may not be so rigidly limited.

New York followed the prudent person rule of investment during the period of petitioner's administration of the instant estate. This rule provides that "[a] fiduciary holding funds for investment may invest the same in such securities as would be acquired by prudent [persons] of discretion and intelligence in such matters who are seeking a reasonable income and the preservation of their capital" (EPTL 11-2.2[a][1]).[78] . . .

No precise formula exists for determining whether the prudent person standard has been violated in a particular situation; rather, the determination depends on an examination of the facts and circumstances of each case. In undertaking this inquiry, the court should engage in "a balanced and perceptive analysis of [the fiduciary's] consideration and action in light of the history of each individual investment, viewed at the time of its action or its omission to act" (Matter of Donner, 626 N.E.2d 922 (N.Y. 1993)). And, while a court should not view each act or omission aided or enlightened by hindsight, a court may, nevertheless, examine the fiduciary's conduct over *the entire course of the investment* in determining whether it has acted prudently. Generally, whether a fiduciary has acted prudently is a factual determination to be made by the trial court.

---

78. The recently enacted Prudent Investor Act [based on the UPIA (1994)] requires a trustee "to diversify assets unless the trustee reasonably determines that it is in the interests of the beneficiaries not to diversify, taking into account the purposes and terms and provisions of the governing instrument" (EPTL 11-2.3[b][3][C]). The act applies to investments "made or held" by a trustee on or after January 1, 1995 and, thus, does not apply to the matter before us (EPTL 11-2.3[a]).

As the foregoing demonstrates, the very nature of the prudent person standard dictates against any absolute rule that a fiduciary's failure to diversify, in and of itself, constitutes imprudence, as well as against a rule invariably immunizing a fiduciary from its failure to diversify in the absence of some selective list of elements of hazard, such as those identified by petitioner. Indeed, in various cases, courts have determined that a fiduciary's retention of a high concentration of one asset in a trust or estate was imprudent without reference to those elements of hazard (see, Matter of Donner, supra). The inquiry is simply whether, under all the facts and circumstances of the particular case, the fiduciary violated the prudent person standard in maintaining a concentration of a particular stock in the estate's portfolio of investments. . . .

Petitioner's restrictive list of hazards omits such additional factors to be considered under the prudent person rule by a trustee in weighing the propriety of any investment decision, as: "the amount of the trust estate, the situation of the beneficiaries, the trend of prices and of the cost of living, the prospect of inflation and of deflation" (Restatement [Second] of Trusts § 227, comment e). Other pertinent factors are the marketability of the investment and possible tax consequences (id., comment o). The trustee must weigh all of these investment factors as they affect the principal objects of the testator's or settlor's bounty, as between income beneficiaries and remainder persons, including decisions regarding "whether to apportion the investments between high-yield or high-growth securities" (Turano and Radigan, New York Estate Administration ch. 14, § P, at 409 [1986]).

Moreover, and especially relevant to the instant case, the various factors affecting the prudence of any particular investment must be considered in the light of the "circumstances of the trust itself rather than [merely] the integrity of the particular investment." . . .

Thus, the elements of hazard petitioner relies upon as demonstrating that, as a matter of law, it had no duty to diversify, suffer from two major deficiencies under the prudent person rule. First, petitioner's risk elements too narrowly and strictly define the scope of a fiduciary's responsibility in making any individual investment decision, and the factors a fiduciary must consider in determining the propriety of a given investment.

A second deficiency in petitioner's elements of hazard list is that all of the factors relied upon by petitioner go to the propriety of an individual investment "exclusively . . . as though it were in its own water-tight compartment," which would encourage a fiduciary to treat each investment as an isolated transaction rather than "in its relation to the whole of the trust estate." Thus, petitioner's criteria for elements of hazard would apply irrespective of the *concentration* of the investment security under consideration in the portfolio. That is, the existence of any of the elements of risk specified by petitioner in a given corporate security would militate against the investment even in a *diversified* portfolio, obviating any need to consider concentration as a reason to divest or refrain from investing. This ignores the market reality that, with respect to some investment vehicles, concentration itself may create or add to risk, and essentially takes lack of diversification out of the prudent person equation altogether. . . .

[I]n maintaining an investment portfolio in which Kodak represented 71% of the estate's stock holdings, and the balance was largely in other growth stocks, petitioner paid insufficient attention to the needs and interests of the testator's

In 2012, Kodak filed for bankruptcy, after which its stock traded for pennies a share.

72-year-old widow, the life beneficiary of three quarters of his estate, for whose comfort, support and anticipated increased medical expenses the testamentary trusts were evidently created. Testimony by petitioner's investment manager, and by the objectants' experts, disclosed that the annual yield on Kodak stock in 1973 was approximately 1.06%, and that the aggregate annual income from all estate stockholdings was $43,961, a scant 1.7% of the $2.5 million estate securities portfolio. Thus, retention of a high concentration of Kodak jeopardized the interests of the primary income beneficiary of the estate and led to the eventual need to substantially invade the principal of the marital testamentary trust.

Lastly, there was evidence in the record to support the findings below that, in managing the estate's investments, petitioner failed to exercise due care and the skill it held itself out as possessing as a corporate fiduciary. Notably, there was proof that petitioner (1) failed initially to undertake a formal analysis of the estate and establish an investment plan consistent with the testator's primary objectives; (2) failed to follow petitioner's own internal trustee review protocol during the administration of the estate, which advised special caution and attention in cases of portfolio concentration of as little as 20%; and (3) failed to conduct more than routine reviews of the Kodak holdings in this estate, without considering alternative investment choices, over a seven-year period of steady decline in the value of the stock.

Since, thus, there was evidence in the record to support the foregoing affirmed findings of imprudence on the part of petitioner, the determination of liability must be affirmed.

II. DATE OF DIVESTITURE

As we have noted, in determining whether a fiduciary has acted prudently, a court may examine a fiduciary's conduct throughout the entire period during which the investment at issue was held (see, Matter of Donner, supra). The court may then determine, within that period, the "reasonable time" within which divestiture of the

"Thank you, Bentley. We get the picture."

imprudently held investment should have occurred. What constitutes a reasonable time will vary from case to case and is not fixed or arbitrary. The test remains "the diligence and prudence of prudent and intelligent [persons] in the management of their own affairs." Thus, in *Donner*, we upheld both the Surrogate's examination of the fiduciary's conduct throughout the entire period during which the investment at issue was retained in finding liability, and the Surrogate's selection of the date of the testator's death as the time when the trustee should have divested the estate of its substantial holdings in high-risk securities.

Again, there is evidentiary support in the record for the trial court's finding, affirmed by the Appellate Division, that a prudent fiduciary would have divested the estate's stock portfolio of its high concentration of Kodak stock by August 9, 1973, thereby exhausting our review powers on this issue. Petitioner's own internal documents and correspondence, as well as the testimony of Patterson, Young, and objectants' experts, establish that by that date, petitioner had all the information a prudent investor would have needed to conclude that the percentage of Kodak stock in the estate's stock portfolio was excessive and should have been reduced significantly, particularly in light of the estate's over-all investment portfolio and the financial requirements of Mrs. Janes and the charitable beneficiaries.

III. DAMAGES

Finally, as to the calculation of the surcharge, we conclude that the Appellate Division correctly rejected the Surrogate's "lost profits" or "market index" measure of damages. Where, as here, a fiduciary's imprudence consists solely of negligent retention of assets it should have sold, the measure of damages is the value of the lost capital. Thus, the Surrogate's reliance on Matter of Rothko in imposing a "lost profit" measure of damages is inapposite, since in that case the fiduciary's misconduct consisted of deliberate self-dealing and faithless transfers of trust property.

In imposing liability upon a fiduciary on the basis of the capital lost, the court should determine the value of the stock on the date it should have been sold, and subtract from that figure the proceeds from the sale of the stock or, if the stock is still retained by the estate, the value of the stock at the time of the accounting. Whether interest is awarded, and at what rate, is a matter within the discretion of the trial court. Dividends and other income attributable to the retained assets should offset any interest awarded.

Here, uncontradicted expert testimony established that application of this measure of damages resulted in a figure of $4,065,029, which includes prejudgment interest at the legal rate, compounded from August 9, 1973 to October 1, 1994. The Appellate Division did not abuse its discretion in adding to that figure prejudgment interest from October 1, 1994 through August 17, 1995, $326,302.66 previously received by petitioner for commissions and attorneys' fees, plus postjudgment interest, costs, and disbursements.

Accordingly, the order of the Appellate Division should be affirmed, without costs.

NOTES

1. Prudent Man or Prudent Investor?   The court in *Janes* said that it applied the prudent man rule, progressively called the prudent person rule in New York, because the conduct at issue predated the effective date of the state's prudent investor statute, based on the UPIA, including its robust duty to diversify. But would the opinion read any differently if the case had been decided under the prudent investor rule? Are not the teachings of Modern Portfolio Theory evident in the court's reasoning? The court emphasized "the market reality that, with respect to some investment vehicles, concentration itself may create or add to risk."

Although a duty to diversify is detectable in the case law under the prudent man rule as far back as Appeal of Dickinson, 25 N.E. 99 (Mass. 1890), prior to *Janes* it was said that New York law did not include such a duty.[79] What could the trustee have done to protect itself against after-the-fact judicial review informed by evolving understandings of finance and prudent trust investment practices?

2. Inception Assets and Reasonable Time.   Under UPIA § 4, page 625, a trustee must diversify a concentration and otherwise reallocate the trust portfolio within a "reasonable time" of taking office as necessary to bring the trust into compliance with the prudent investor rule. What constitutes a reasonable time is a highly fact-intensive question that will vary from case to case. "[T]he reasonableness of . . . delay in making a

---

79. *See* Note, Trust Fund Investment in New York: The Prudent Man Rule and Diversification of Investments, 47 N.Y.U. L. Rev. 527, 533-35 (1972).

disposition depends on such factors as: the nature of the property involved; the reason the trustee is required to sell it; whether appraisals are necessary; whether there is a ready market for the property; and the relative degree of price efficiency in that market."[80]

In *Janes*, the court upheld the Surrogate's finding that the trustee should have divested the estate's concentration in Kodak two and a half months after the settlor's death. The court reasoned that by then the trustee "had all the information a prudent investor would have needed to conclude that the percentage of Kodak stock in the estate's stock portfolio was excessive and should have been reduced significantly." The court contrasted its earlier decision in Matter of Donner, 626 N.E.2d 922 (N.Y. 1993). In *Donner*, the court affirmed the Surrogate's surcharge of two co-executors for their failure to act immediately upon the death of the decedent to protect the estate against investment losses associated with certain of the initial assets of the estate. The court reasoned that, owing to the co-executor's prior relationship with the decedent, the relevant circumstances indicating immediate sale were already known to the co-executors, hence they should have acted right away upon the decedent's death.

3. How Much Diversification Is Enough?   How many different investments are needed to be well diversified?

> Empirical studies have shown that a small amount of diversification goes a long way. For example, it has been shown that a portfolio of ten stocks provides 88.5 percent of the possible advantages of diversification. A portfolio of 20 stocks provides 94.2 percent of the advantages of diversification. . . . Consequently, investors need a very good excuse for not holding a diversified portfolio, because investors who do not hold such portfolios are assuming risks that they could easily avoid through diversification.[81]

In light of the studies showing that diversifying into 20 to 30 unrelated large capitalization stocks removes most of the diversifiable risk from a stock portfolio, a good rule of thumb is that a concentration in a single security of more than 5 percent requires explanation. In In re HSBC Bank USA, N.A., 947 N.Y.S.2d 292 (App. Div. 2012), the court upheld several "overweight concentrations of certain securities" for which the trustee had explanations in a trust that was otherwise well diversified.

Bank trust departments usually have internal risk management protocols that require supervisory review of any portfolio with a concentration in excess of a stated threshold, commonly 10 or 20 percent, and documentation of the reasons for the concentration.

4. Professional Trustees and the Investment Policy Statement.   In all applications of the duty of prudence, if a "trustee possesses, or procured appointment by purporting to possess, special facilities or greater skill than that of a person of ordinary prudence,

---

80. Restatement (Third) of Trusts § 92 cmt. b (Am. Law Inst. 2007).
81. Jonathan R. Macey, An Introduction to Modern Financial Theory 24-26 (2d ed. 1998); *see also* Richard A. Brealey, Stewart C. Myers & Franklin Allen, Principles of Corporate Finance 175 (12th ed. 2016) (remarking that "you can get most of" the benefits of diversification with "20 or 30" stocks).

the trustee has a duty to use such facilities or skill."[82] UPIA § 2(f), page 625, absorbs this principle into the prudent investor rule.

As an internal process safeguard, the normal and customary practice among banks and other professional trustees is to prepare a written *investment policy statement* for each new trust account, reciting investment guidelines that reflect the purpose of the trust and the circumstances of the beneficiaries. Professors Schanzenbach and Sitkoff explain:

> An investment policy statement should specify "the account's risk tolerance," its "investment goals and return requirements," and "asset allocation guidelines." The usual practice, in accordance with the prudent investor rule, is to apply portfolio theory in "deciding how to allocate portfolio assets among the major asset categories."
>
> Consistent with the higher standard of care required of a professional trustee, courts have rebuked bank trustees for failing in a timely manner to "establish an investment plan." . . . "The lack of an investment policy statement, or the existence of a poorly developed one, is a weakness in portfolio management risk control. . . . Failure to create such a formal statement invites a presumption of imprudent conduct."
>
> After initial account review, an investment policy statement facilitates "[r]ebalancing . . . to maintain proper diversification," ensuring that the "portfolio avoids 'allocation drift' by not straying far from its targeted levels of risk and return." . . . Another benefit of an investment policy statement is having a "'paper trail' in the event of an audit, litigation, or a dispute."[83]

In *Janes*, the court chastised the trustee for (a) failing "initially to undertake a formal analysis of the estate and establish an investment plan consistent with the testator's primary objectives," and (b) failing to follow its protocol that "advised special caution and attention" to concentrations above 20 percent. In In re Hunter, 955 N.Y.S.2d 163 (App. Div. 2012), also involving a concentration in Kodak, the court likewise rebuked the trustee, a bank, for its failure to make a suitable investment plan within a reasonable time of the inception of the trusteeship and its failure to follow its internal protocols for dealing with a concentrated investment.

We take up a trustee's duty to keep records of the administration of the trust, including documentation of the reasoning for important investment decisions, later in this chapter at page 656. The higher standard of care applicable to a professional trustee, such as the banks in *Janes* and *Hunter*, intensifies this duty.

5. Excuses for Not Diversifying.   The duty to diversify under UPIA § 3, page 625, is not absolute. A trustee need not diversify if, "because of special circumstances, the purposes of the trust are better served without diversifying." A straightforward example is a trust that holds a family vacation home. Such a trust is not diversified because it is concentrated in a single asset. But the trustee could reasonably conclude

---

82. Restatement (Third) of Trusts § 77(3) (Am. Law Inst. 2007); *see also* UTC § 806 (2000) (similar).

83. Max M. Schanzenbach & Robert H. Sitkoff, The Prudent Investor Rule and Market Risk: An Empirical Analysis, 14 J. Emp. Legal Stud. 129, 138 (2017).

that the purpose of the trust, coordinating use and management of the vacation home, is best served by retaining the home. A trust that holds a surviving spouse's residence or a family farm, the latter as in In re Trust Created by Inman, 693 N.W.2d 514 (Neb. 2005), may likewise be better served without diversifying.

Another possible reason for not diversifying or for delaying diversification, recognized in the comment to UPIA § 3, is if the tax or other transaction costs of reorganizing the portfolio are likely to outweigh the benefits of diversification. A trustee invoking this rationale should be able to point to a documented analysis of the relevant costs and benefits to establish the trustee's prudence in not diversifying. A decision not to diversify a trust that holds a family business should likewise be supported by a documented analysis showing the prudence of the retention. Particularly if the business is closely held and not readily marketable, a prudent trustee weighing the relevant costs and benefits might conclude, as in In re Hyde, 845 N.Y.S.2d 833 (App. Div. 2007), that retention is in the best interests of the beneficiaries.

Diversification might not be necessary if the trust is but one piece of a larger program of wealth management such that the beneficiary's financial interests are diversified overall. UPIA § 2(c)(6), page 625, lists "other resources of the beneficiaries" as a relevant circumstance to be considered "in investing and managing trust assets."

Compensatory Damages for Imprudent Investment

The objective of compensatory damages for breach of trust is to make the beneficiary whole. The trustee must restore the trust estate and trust distributions to what they would have been but for the breach (on other remedies for breach, see page 599).

In *Janes*, the New York Court of Appeals awarded $4,065,029 in compensatory damages on a theory of *capital lost plus interest*. This amount represents the value of the trust's Kodak stock on August 9, 1973, the date by which the Surrogate had found the trustee should have divested, plus compound interest through October 1, 1994, minus the actual value of the trust on that date. The court said that in computing capital lost plus interest, the interest rate should be chosen within the discretion of the Surrogate, but it said nothing about how the Surrogate had made this choice. Our review of the record indicates that the interest rate varied from year to year between 6 and 9 percent,[84] tracking the state's legal rate of interest applicable to a delayed payment on a money judgment.

There can be wide variance in computing interest depending on the rate of interest used and whether it is compounded. Figure 9.4 shows the value of the trust's Kodak stock on August 9, 1973, which was $1,687,647.30, plus yearly compound interest for 21 years, roughly the period at issue in *Janes*, at three different plausible rates: (1) the historic average annual rate of inflation (3.0 percent); (2) the historic average annual rate of return on long-term government bonds (6.1 percent); and (3) the current New

---

84. We thank Professor Kenneth Joyce of the University of Buffalo Law School, State University of New York, for supplying us with the briefs and record on appeal. Professor Joyce was co-counsel on behalf of Mrs. Janes's estate before the New York Court of Appeals.

York legal rate of interest, a whopping 9 percent, well above prevailing market interest rates.[85] Is the legal rate a good proxy for the rate of return that the trust portfolio would have experienced?

Figure 9.4

Variance in Capital Lost Plus Interest

Interest Rate	Value in 21 Years
3.0%	$3,139,521.11
6.1%	$5,852,005.84
9.0%	$10,309,512.88

The primary alternative to capital lost plus interest is a *total return* measure. It requires the finder of fact, usually with the assistance of expert testimony, to compare the actual performance of the imprudent portfolio against the performance of a hypothetical prudent portfolio, and to award damages in the amount of the difference, perhaps adjusting for taxes and other expenses and for distributions. The Scott treatise explains:

> It has often been thought that the appropriate remedy . . . was to hold the trustee liable for the initial amount of the loss, plus statutory interest. . . . Yet such a remedy nearly always misses the mark, and often badly, when the interval between the breach and the remedy is substantial. If the applicable interest rate is lower than the total return (including both income and capital appreciation) that the trust would have earned in the absence of the breach, such a remedy plainly undercompensates the loss. By the same token, if the relevant interest rate is higher than what the trust's total return would have been, such a remedy may yield overcompensation. . . .
>
> These days, courts seem increasingly willing to calculate the trust estate's total loss not by reference to an initial loss, increased by statutory interest, but by reference to the more general concept of what it would take to make the trust estate whole. . . . In most cases, . . . determining what it would take to make the trust estate whole requires inquiry into what the trust *likely would have earned*, in the absence of the breach of trust.[86]

The Surrogate in *Janes* awarded total return damages of $6,080,269.[87] The Surrogate reasoned that this figure represented the amount "of the difference between what the estate actually received from the Kodak stock and what the estate would have received if the stock had been sold in August of 1973 and reinvested" in a prudent portfolio. For the model of a prudent portfolio, the Surrogate looked to the performance of "the bank's own diversified equity fund," of which less than 3 percent was invested in Kodak.

---

85. We discuss the average annual rate of inflation, and average annual total return across asset classes, at page 631. The legal rate of interest in New York is prescribed by N.Y. C.P.L.R. § 5004 (2016).

86. Scott and Ascher on Trusts § 24.9.

87. *See* In re Judicial Settlement of the Account of Lincoln First Bank, 630 N.Y.S.2d 472, 480-81 (Sur. 1995).

Like the choice of interest rate in a capital lost plus interest calculation, the choice of model portfolio is the key variable in a total return computation. In *Janes*, the record shows that other models produced measures of damages ranging between $4,065,029 and $7,530,547.

Which damages methodology better suits the prudent investor rule? Are there other relevant considerations, such as simplicity or transparency?

(2) The Terms of the Trust

The problem in *Janes* arose because Kodak stock comprised over 70 percent of the testator's $2.5 million stock portfolio at the time of his death. Does the fact of Janes's lifetime concentration tell us that he thought it a sensible investment strategy for the trustee? Suppose in his will Janes had expressly authorized retention of the Kodak stock, or, more difficult, that he had directed the trustee to retain the stock. Would such a provision save the trustee from liability for failing to diversify?

Wood v. U.S. Bank, N.A.
828 N.E.2d 1072 (Ohio App. 2005)

PAINTER, J. This case turns on a question of law that has received little judicial attention in Ohio. Does a trustee have a duty to diversify the assets of a trust when the language of the trust authorizes retention of a specific asset, namely stock in the corporate trustee?

We hold that even if the trust document allows the trustee to "retain" assets that would not normally be suitable, the trustee's duty to diversify remains unless there are special circumstances. Of course, a trustee's duty to diversify may be expanded, restricted, eliminated, or otherwise altered by the terms of the trust. But this statement is true only if the instrument creating the trust clearly indicates an intention to abrogate the common-law, now statutory, duty to diversify. . . .

I. THE TRUST

[The] husband [of plaintiff-appellant, Dana Barth Wood ("Wood")], John Wood II (we will use his first name because there are other Woods in the case), was a prominent Cincinnati attorney with estate-planning experience.[88] John created a trust worth over $8 million. Wood was a beneficiary of the trust. John served as trustee during his lifetime and named Star Bank the successor trustee. Star Bank, formerly First National Bank of Cincinnati, later became Firstar Bank. U.S. Bank is the successor-in-interest to First National, Star, and Firstar. At this writing at least, it is still U.S. Bank. Because it was the language used through most of the trial, we refer to the trustee as "Firstar" and

---

88. John Wood II was also known in Cincinnati for his prowess in golf — and for playing in shirt and tie. He qualified three times for the U.S. Open, and he is reported to have won the Cincinnati Country Club championship about 25 times. In his legal career, he was a partner for many years at Wood & Lamping, where he still kept an office at the time of his death at age 81. *See* Allen Howard, John Wood, Lawyer, Golf Legend, Cincinnati Enquirer, Oct. 6, 1998. — Eds.

the disputed stock as "Firstar stock." Nearly 80 percent of the trust assets were in Firstar stock. The rest was mostly Cincinnati Financial Corporation stock. . . .

The trust specifically gave Firstar the power "[t]o retain any securities in the same form as when received, including shares of a corporate Trustee . . . , even though all of such securities are not of the class of investments a trustee may be permitted by law to make and to hold cash uninvested as they deem advisable or proper." The unfortunate wording of this sentence makes it unclear whether the "advisable or proper"—a redundant couplet—applied to the cash only, not the other assets. Grammatically, that is the meaning. Luckily, our holding makes it unnecessary to construe this language; but we caution that this type of fuzzy drafting can create problems.

The trust did not last long—John had directed the trustee to distribute almost all the trust assets to the beneficiaries after paying the debts and expenses of the estate. Beginning in early 1998, Firstar had custody of the trust assets.

II. REVERSE DIVERSIFICATION

Shortly after John's death, Firstar's trust officers and the beneficiaries (including Wood) met to discuss the estate. . . .

At the meeting, Firstar recommended selling some stock to pay the debts and expenses of the estate and retaining the remainder pending the eventual distribution to the beneficiaries free of trust. The debts and expenses were nearly $4 million; the trust itself contained approximately $8 million, of which roughly $6 million was in Firstar stock. This plan did not call for selling any Firstar stock other than what was necessary to cover the taxes and other debts. Firstar trust officers premised the plan on Firstar stock's strong earnings momentum at the time, so it called for a sale of two-thirds of Cincinnati Financial stock and only about ten percent of the Firstar stock.

Since the original composition of the trust was 82 percent Firstar stock and 18 percent Cincinnati Financial stock, selling more of the Cincinnati Financial stock meant that the final trust was approximately 86 percent Firstar stock and only 14 percent Cincinnati Financial stock. The trust officers and Sean Wood (one of the other beneficiaries) testified that the parties agreed to the distribution plan. Firstar estimated that it would take 18 to 20 months to finalize the estate. At trial, Wood agreed that she had seen the distribution plan and did not object to it at the meeting. But she emphasized that she had asked Firstar to diversify once the stock started increasing in value.

Firstar held the assets during this time and did not diversify. . . . Firstar focused primarily on liquidating non-Firstar stock to raise estate-tax funds. Though approximately half of the Cincinnati Financial stock was sold (for around $1 million), only about ten percent of the Firstar stock was sold. Thus, Firstar stock made up an even higher percentage of the trust assets after the liquidation because there was so much of it to begin with.

Because of a Firstar merger, Firstar's stock increased from about $21 per share in October 1998 to almost $35 per share in early 1999. In April 1999, Wood asked Firstar to sell some of the stock. Harvey Knowles, Wood's advisor, also requested diversification. Neither Wood nor her attorneys and financial advisors made any written

*"I was spreading some risk around, and apparently
it all wound up in your portfolio."*

Leo Cullum/The New Yorker Collection/The Cartoon Bank

request that Firstar diversify the trust assets. Firstar did not sell any stock as a result of these requests.

Firstar's stock price plunged beginning in mid-1999. And by mid-2000, it was worth only $16 per share. It was around this time that Firstar made the final distribution to the beneficiaries. According to expert testimony based on calculations using an average mutual fund as the basis for estimating value, Firstar's failure to diversify cost Wood $771,099.[89]

III. A LAWSUIT, A JURY TRIAL, AND AN APPEAL

Wood sued Firstar, asserting that Firstar had violated Ohio law by failing to diversify the assets of the trust. . . . Wood claimed that, under [the Ohio UPIA], Firstar had a mandatory duty to diversify absent special circumstances. She also argued that Firstar had made no attempt to show special circumstances that would have relaxed its mandatory duty to diversify and that no such circumstances existed. . . .

Wood proposed jury instructions based on the UPIA. The trial court rejected the statute-based instructions, and over Wood's objections, the trial court adopted Firstar's abuse-of-discretion and estoppel instructions.

The jury returned a verdict against Wood. . . .

---

89. Is this capital lost plus interest, as in *Janes*, or a total return measure of damages (see page 642)? — Eds.

IV. To Diversify or Not to Diversify?

Because the issue of a trustee's duty to diversify is dispositive, we first address [this issue]. Wood argues that the trial court erred by providing the jury with an abuse-of-discretion standard and by refusing to instruct the jury in accordance with [the Ohio UPIA]. . . .

We must therefore first determine whether Firstar had a duty to diversify. Duties owed by a trustee to the beneficiaries are well established. "A trustee shall diversify the investments of a trust unless the trustee reasonably determines that, because of special circumstances, the purposes of the trust are better served without diversifying." R.C. 1339.54(B)[, based on UPIA § 3, page 625]. This duty may be expanded, restricted, eliminated, or otherwise altered by the trust instrument. R.C. 1339.52(C)[, based on UPIA § 1, page 624]. This duty, imposed by the UPIA, is the same one recognized by the common law; the common law is now codified.

V. It Means What It Says—and Nothing More

The language of John's last trust was unambiguous. It granted Firstar the power to retain its own stock in the trust even though Firstar would ordinarily not have been permitted to hold its own stock. Specifically, Firstar had the power "[t]o retain any securities in the same form as when received, including shares of a corporate Trustee . . . , even though all of such securities are not of the class of investments a trustee may be permitted by law to make and to hold cash uninvested as they deem advisable or proper."

Wood now presents "The Rule of Undivided Loyalty" to support her claim that the retention language in the trust did not lessen Firstar's duty to diversify. This rule states that "[t]he foremost duty which a fiduciary owes to its beneficiary is undivided loyalty." Ledbetter v. First State Bank & Trust Co., 85 F.3d 1537, 1540 (11th Cir. 1996). This rule prohibits the trustee's ownership of its own stock. Id. But it does not apply to prohibit ownership when the trustor gives the trustee the "authority to retain stock received from the trustor." Id. at 1544; see also Restatement (Third) of Trusts §§ 227(b) and 229, cmt. d (1992). The only restriction to the exception is that the trustee "must not act in bad faith or abuse its discretion." Id. But because the trustee still has the duty to act prudently, and diversification is normally called for, the retention language in this case did not affect the duty to diversify.

The retention clause merely served to circumvent the rule of undivided loyalty. The trust did not say anything about diversification. And the retention language smacked of the standard boilerplate that was intended merely to circumvent the rule of undivided loyalty—no more, no less. There were significant tax consequences that precluded John from diversifying by selling the Firstar stock during his lifetime, but that hurdle was removed upon his death. Had John wanted to eliminate Firstar's duty to diversify, he could simply have said so. He could have mentioned that duty in the retention clause. Or he could have included another clause specifically lessening the duty to diversify. But he did not. We hold that the language of a trust does not alter a trustee's duty to diversify unless the instrument creating the trust clearly indicates an intention to do so.

Wood also cites [Ohio UPIA §§ 3 and 4]. As we have already said, these provisions codified the common law, imposing mandatory investment standards upon the trustee, including the duty to diversify. Under [Ohio UPIA § 3], there is a single exception for the duty to diversify. This duty arises when the trustee "reasonably" determines that that there are "special circumstances." In this case, the question of special circumstances was never presented to the jury, even though identifying special circumstances was the only way that Firstar could possibly have been relieved of its duty to diversify.

In response, Firstar cites [Ohio UPIA § 1, which states that the prudent investor rule] "may be expanded, restricted, eliminated, or otherwise altered, without express reference to these sections by the instrument creating a trust." [It also] states, "A trustee is not liable to a beneficiary of a trust to the extent the trustee acted in reasonable reliance on the provisions of the trust."

The Third Restatement of Trusts states, "In making and implementing investing decisions, the trustee has a duty to diversify the investments unless, under the circumstances, it is not prudent to do so." Restatement (Third) of Trusts: Prudent Investor Rule § 227(b) (1992). And with regard to a trustee's duty regarding original investments, the comments to the Restatement indicate that a broad generalization is not enough to relieve a trustee of its duty to diversify:

> A general authorization in an applicable statute or in the terms of the trust to retain investments received as a part of a trust estate does not ordinarily abrogate the trustee's duty with respect to diversification or the trustee's general duty to act with prudence in investment matters.

Id. § 229 cmt. d.

This is precisely what the retention language here was—a general authorization. The Restatement continues,

> The terms of the trust, however, may permit the trustee to retain all the investments made by the settlor, or a larger proportion of them than would otherwise be permitted. Thus, a trust may be created by a will that directs or authorizes the trustee to retain all of the securities bequeathed to the trustee; or the will may provide that any or all such securities or some specific securities may be retained, as the trustee deems proper, without regard to the ordinary requirement of diversification.

Id. But the retention language here did not give the necessary authorization or direction.

We hold that to abrogate the duty to diversify, the trust must contain specific language authorizing or directing the trustee to retain in a specific investment a larger percentage of the trust assets than would normally be prudent. The authorization to "retain" here was not sufficient—it only authorized the trustee to retain its own stock—something it could not otherwise do. . . .

The instructions here stated, "The normal rule is that a trustee shall diversify the investments of a trust. If by the terms of the trust the trustee is permitted but not directed to retain investments originally transferred to the trust, the trustee is not liable for retaining them where there is no abuse of discretion in doing so. The trustee is not liable for the exercise of its discretion so long as the trustee acts in good faith and does not abuse its discretion. An abuse of discretion occurs if the trustee acts dishonestly or with an improper motive or fails to use his judgment or acts beyond the bounds of a reasonable judgment."

Under the facts of this case, we reject this instruction — it virtually assured a verdict for Firstar, as there were no allegations of dishonesty or fraud. . . .

VI. Timing and Special Circumstances . . .

A trustee who is authorized to retain assets but sells them is not liable merely because the securities later rise in value, or vice versa. Trustees should not be judged on hindsight.[90] Few would become trustees if they were liable every time they did not sell stock at the most propitious chance. But the problem here is that the trust would have benefited even more if Firstar had simply performed its duty to diversify. Wood's argument is not based on hindsight — it is simply based on Firstar's duty to diversify, absent special circumstances.

The "special circumstances" language generally refers to holdings that are important to a family or a trust. For example, in In re Trust Created by Inman, 693 N.W.2d 514 (Neb. 2005) the Nebraska Supreme Court recently held that there was no duty to diversify when the asset in question was a piece of farmland that had a special meaning to the family. We realize that Firstar stock is not farmland. But perhaps it had a special relationship to the family or to the trust. Or perhaps it did not. Further, this was not the case of a controlling interest in a family business — which might normally be an example of special circumstances. Either way, this question was for the jury. But the trial court's instructions improperly removed that question from the jury's consideration.

Because of the trial court's erroneous instruction here, the jury was not given the proper legal standard. The proper jury instruction would have simply quoted the appropriate statutory language, changing the ambiguous (to laypeople) *shall* to the proper *must:* "A trustee must diversify the investments of a trust unless the trustee reasonably determines that, because of special circumstances, the purposes of the trust are better served without diversifying." . . .

Given the improper law to apply, the jury could have come only to the conclusion that it did — namely, that Firstar had not "abused its discretion" in retaining the Firstar stock. But with the proper instructions, the jury may have gone the other way. Thus, we must order a new trial. . . .

Judgment reversed and cause remanded.

NOTES

1. Epilogue — The Jury Verdict on Remand.   A peculiar feature of the litigation in *Wood* is that it involved a jury. In most states, trust litigation is tried before a judge.

---

90. UPIA § 8 (1994) says: "Compliance with the prudent investor rule is determined in light of the facts and circumstances existing at the time of a trustee's decision or action and not by hindsight." — Eds.

Trust law, which was developed in the English chancery courts (see page 386), falls on the equity side of the division between law and equity. Ohio is among the small minority of states that allows jury trial for certain trust matters. On remand, the bank won—but of course there is no explanatory opinion. The trial judge entered a judgment for the bank in accordance with the jury verdict.

The entry of judgment in *Wood* on remand

2. Corporate Trustee's Own Shares.   The duty of loyalty generally disables a corporate trustee from purchasing or retaining its own stock. A settlor may override this default rule expressly or by implication in the terms of the trust. However, such an override "does not relieve the trustee of its duties to act with prudence and solely in the interest of the trust beneficiaries."[91] In *Wood*, although the trustee had the *power* to retain the settlor's Firstar stock, at issue was whether doing so was consistent with the trustee's fiduciary *duty* under the prudent investor rule.

3. Permissive Retention.   It is important to distinguish between a trust provision that *authorizes* a trustee to retain inception assets irrespective of diversification and one that *directs* the trustee to do so. A permissive power to retain property is common boilerplate in professionally drafted trusts. Here is an example:

> To retain any property (including stock of any corporate trustee hereunder or a parent or affiliate company) originally constituting the trust or subsequently added

---

91. Restatement (Third) of Trusts § 78 cmt. e(2) (Am. Law Inst. 2007).

thereto . . . ; the trustee may retain or make any investment without liability, even though it is not of a type, quality, marketability or diversification considered proper for trust investments.[92]

The prevailing view is that a permissive authorization to retain an undiversified portfolio does not excuse the trustee from liability if not diversifying was imprudent. In the words of the Scott treatise: "[T]he trustee ordinarily remains subject to the duty of prudence, notwithstanding the fact that the terms of the trust purport to waive the duty to diversify. Pursuant to this continuing duty of prudence, the trustee may continue to be subject to a duty to consider the need for diversification."[93]

In First Ala. Bank of Huntsville, N.A. v. Spragins, 475 So. 2d 512 (Ala. 1985), the court held that the trustee acted imprudently by maintaining a "portfolio [that] contained an inordinate amount of the Bank's holding company stock, in violation of sound management practices," despite authorization in the trust instrument for the trustee to manage the trust portfolio "regardless of any lack of diversification." Said the court: "We do not perceive, from the language of this trust, that the donor intended by his 'lack of diversification' provision to authorize acts of imprudence in the management of the trust to the point of disregarding the interests of the beneficiaries, the sole purpose of the trust arrangement in the first instance."

Once again we see the importance of not confusing *power* and *duty*. Even if a trustee has a power to retain assets irrespective of diversification, the exercise of that power must be prudent and in the best interests of the beneficiaries. The Restatement (Third) of Trusts explains:

> [T]he fact that an investment is permitted does not relieve the trustee of the fundamental duty to act with prudence. The fiduciary must still exercise care, skill, and caution in making decisions to acquire or retain the investment. . . .
>
> Whether and to what extent a specific investment authorization may affect the normal duty to diversify the trust portfolio can be a difficult question of interpretation. Because permissive provisions do not abrogate the trustee's duty to act prudently and because diversification is fundamental to prudent risk management, trust provisions are strictly construed against dispensing with that requirement altogether. Nevertheless, a relaxation in the degree of diversification may be justified under such an authorization by special opportunities for the trust or by special objectives of the settlor. . . .
>
> For this added risk, despite the presence of a permissive provision of this type, some reasonable justification must be found in the settlor's intentions or purposes or in some special opportunity (based, for example, on special skills) available to the trust.[94]

---

92. Northern Trust, Will and Trust Forms 201-31 (2004).
93. Scott and Ascher on Trusts § 19.2.
94. Restatement (Third) of Trusts § 91 cmt. f (Am. Law Inst. 2007).

4. Directed Retention and Deviation.   What about a direction to retain a trust's inception assets? In *Wood*, the court assumed that the settlor could have opted out of the duty to diversify, but held that he had not done so. In a survey of the case law, Professor Jeffrey Cooper found that courts are reluctant to find an effective negation of the duty to diversify.[95] If a settlor clearly directs the trustee to retain certain assets, however, the trustee must do so, "and the trustee may be subject to liability for disposing of them if they subsequently increase in value."[96]

But this is not the end of the story. A trustee's duty to conform to the terms of the trust is qualified by a duty to "petition the court for appropriate modification of or deviation from the terms of the trust" if conforming will "cause substantial harm to the trust or its beneficiaries."[97] A trustee must never act in a manner that is inimical to the interests of the beneficiaries or that will work harm upon them. If the terms of the trust require retention of specific assets, but retention would be imprudent, the trustee is under a "duty to apply to the court for permission to sell."[98] We take up modification and deviation in Chapter 10 at page 727.

Should courts allow deviation from a mandated investment strategy that is shown to be unsound or that will work harm upon the beneficiaries? At issue is the extent of the settlor's freedom of disposition to exert dead hand control over the investment function.

a. Suppose that a settlor directs that the stock of a company he had founded must be retained and never sold. If many years later the trust estate is at peril because the company has become unprofitable, should a court authorize the trustee to sell the stock? *See* Matter of Pulitzer, 249 N.Y.S. 87 (Sur. 1931), aff'd mem., 260 N.Y.S. 975 (App. Div. 1932), discussed at page 735.

b. Suppose that a settlor directs the trustee to invest only in insured bank accounts and government securities and forbids investment in corporate stock. If the trustee can show that the "investment restrictions have for many consecutive years reduced the income from [the] trust to essentially negligible amounts," and thus have frustrated the "trust's purpose of generating funds" for the beneficiary, should a court authorize the trustee to invest in stock? *See* In re Estate of Chamberlin, 23 N.Y.S.3d 658 (App. Div. 2016).

5. Scholarly Debate and Legislative Change.   Professor Langbein argues that courts should be receptive to petitions for deviation for the purpose of investment efficiency:

> When . . . trust assets are held for investment, and are easily diversifiable at no cost or at acceptable cost, I believe that the courts will come to view the advantages

---

95. *See* Jeffrey A. Cooper, Speak Clearly and Listen Well: Negating the Duty to Diversify Trust Investments, 33 Ohio N.U. L. Rev. 903 (2007); *see also* Trent S. Kiziah, J. Clay Singleton & Stewart A. Marshall, The Persistent Preference for Inception Assets, 40 ACTEC L.J. 151 (2014).

96. Scott and Ascher on Trusts § 19.3.3.

97. *See* Restatement (Third) of Trusts § 66(2) (Am. Law Inst. 2003).

98. Scott and Ascher on Trusts § 19.3.3; *see also* The Woodward School v. City of Quincy, 13 N.E.3d 579, 593 n.26 (Mass. 2014).

of diversification as so overwhelming that the settlor's interference with effective diversification will be treated as inconsistent with the requirement that the trust terms must be for the benefit of the beneficiaries. Settlor-directed underdiversification is an avoidable harm, akin to the harm that the courts have prevented by intervening against settlors' directions to waste or destroy trust property.[99]

The principle that a private trust must be for the benefit of the beneficiaries is codified by UTC §§ 105(b)(3) and 404 and is recognized in the Restatement (Third) of Trusts.[100] It is rooted in the venerable common law rule against trusts for capricious purposes. In Langbein's view, a trust cannot have the dominant purpose of retaining certain assets. For the trust to be valid, this purpose must be subordinate to the purpose of benefitting the beneficiaries.

Professor Cooper is not convinced. He argues that Langbein's application of the benefit-the-beneficiary principle to mandated investment strategies is misguided:

> Many investment restrictions are not the undesirable remnants of irrational dead hands, but are carefully-designed provisions intended to further a living settlor's unique estate planning goals. Applying an objective, dispassionate test of "benefit" would cut too deeply, setting aside these important restrictions as freely as it would set aside those imposed by less thoughtful trust settlors. . . . The interpersonal aspects of wealth transmission would be frustrated, as personal visions of trust settlors become subjugated to the dispassionate dictates of modern investment theory.[101]

Can these conflicting views be reconciled? Is the argument for respecting the "interpersonal aspects" of a gift in trust weaker as applied to an administrative direction than to a dispositive provision? Langbein and Cooper have continued their debate in the pages of the law reviews.[102]

A small but growing number of states, including Delaware, Georgia, New Hampshire, South Dakota, and Tennessee, have enacted legislation that validates the enforceability of a settlor's instruction not to diversify.[103] Delaware, for example, authorizes a settlor to specify "the circumstances, if any, in which the fiduciary must diversify investments."[104] A direction to retain certain property "shall be deemed to waive any duty of diversification . . . with respect to such property and shall exonerate the fiduciary from liability

---

99. John H. Langbein, Mandatory Rules in the Law of Trusts, 98 Nw. U. L. Rev. 1105, 1115 (2004).

100. Restatement (Third) of Trusts § 27(2) (Am. Law Inst. 2003).

101. Jeffrey A. Cooper, Empty Promises: Settlor's Intent, the Uniform Trust Code, and the Future of Trust Investment Law, 88 B.U. L. Rev. 1165, 1169-70 (2008).

102. *Compare* John H. Langbein, Burn the Rembrandt? Trust Law's Limits on the Settlor's Power to Direct Investments, 90 B.U. L. Rev. 375 (2010), *with* Jeffrey A. Cooper, Shades of Gray: Applying the Benefit-the-Beneficiaries Rule to Trust Investment Directives, 90 B.U. L. Rev. 2383 (2010); Jeffrey A. Cooper, Dead Hand Investing: The Enforceability of Trust Investment Directives, 37 ACTEC L.J. 365 (2011).

103. *See* Del. Code tit. 12, § 3303(a)(3) (2016); N.H. Rev. Stat. Ann. § 564-B:9-901(b) (2016); S.D. Codified Laws § 55-5-8 (2016); Tenn. Code Ann. § 35-14-105 (2016); Ga. Code Ann. § 53-12-341 (2016).

104. Del. Code tit. 12, §§ 3303(a)(3), 3304 (2016).

for retaining the property except in the case of wilful misconduct proven by clear and convincing evidence."[105] The term "wilful misconduct" is defined to mean "intentional wrongdoing, not mere negligence, gross negligence or recklessness," and "wrongdoing" means "malicious conduct or conduct designed to defraud or seek an unconscionable advantage."[106] What result in *Wood* under Delaware law?

6. Revocable Trusts.   In 1990, *T* conveys 1,500 shares of Enron stock in trust to *X*. The trust instrument provides that the trust may be revoked or amended by written instrument delivered to *X*. *T* then instructs *X* in writing to retain the Enron stock, and *X* does so. In 2001, Enron files for bankruptcy in the wake of public disclosure of accounting frauds at the company, and the stock price drops to zero. In 2002, *T* sues *X* for breach of the duty of prudence, arguing that *X* should have diversified the portfolio or at least warned *T* of the inherent danger in failing to diversify. What result? *See* McGinley v. Bank of America, 109 P.3d 1146 (Kan. 2005); Puhl v. U.S. Bank, N.A., 34 N.E.3d 530 (Ohio App. 2015).

7. Beneficiary Authorization.   Suppose the beneficiaries consent, in writing, to an undiversified portfolio and agree not to seek to surcharge the trustee for any losses from a lack of diversification. Should this agreement be enforced? Must the trustee first advise the beneficiaries about the perils of failing to diversify? *See* In re Saxton, 712 N.Y.S.2d 225 (App. Div. 2000). Because a trustee stands in a fiduciary relationship with the beneficiaries, a release from liability given by a beneficiary to a trustee is enforceable only if the beneficiary knew of her rights and of the material facts, as under UTC § 1009 (2000, rev. 2001) and the Restatement (Third) of Trusts.[107]

3. The Custodial and Administrative Functions

The *custodial function* involves taking title and custody of the trust property and properly safeguarding it. The *administrative function* includes recordkeeping, bringing and defending claims held in trust, accounting and giving information to the beneficiaries, and making tax and other required filings. In this section, we consider several subsidiary rules of trust fiduciary law that relate to the custodial and administrative functions. These rules flesh out the primary duties of loyalty and prudence as applied to recurring facts and circumstances for which customary practice has hardened into rules of trust fiduciary law.[108]

a. Duty to Collect and Protect Trust Property

A standard application of prudence in the custodial function is the duty to *collect* and *protect* the trust property without unreasonable delay. UTC § 809 (2000) codifies this

---

105. Id. § 3304. Curiously, the Delaware statutes use the British spelling of "wilful." In contemporary American usage, "willful" is more typical.
106. Id. § 3301(g).
107. *See* Restatement (Third) of Trusts § 97 (Am. Law Inst. 2012).
108. *See* Sitkoff, *supra* note 12, at 682-83.

duty thus: "A trustee shall take reasonable steps to take control of and protect the trust property." What is unreasonable delay, and what steps are reasonably necessary, depend on the circumstances.[109] Precious jewelry or a priceless work of art, for example, should be secured against theft and insured against loss.

In the case of a testamentary trust, the trustee should collect the assets from the executor as promptly as circumstances permit. The trustee must also examine the property tendered by the executor to verify it is what the trustee ought to receive. The trustee must pursue the executor to redress any breach of duty that diminished the assets intended for the trust. The same rules apply to a successor trustee in regard to the trust property tendered by a prior trustee. UTC § 812 (2000) codifies these duties at the inception of a trusteeship thus: "A trustee shall take reasonable steps to compel a former trustee or other person to deliver trust property to the trustee, and to redress a breach of trust known to the trustee to have been committed by a former trustee."

b. Duty to Earmark Trust Property

Another application of the duty of prudence in the custodial function is the duty to *earmark* trust property, that is, to designate it as trust property distinct from the trustee's own property. UTC § 810(c) (2000) codifies this duty thus: "[A] trustee shall cause the trust property to be designated so that the interest of the trust, to the extent feasible, appears in records maintained by a party other than a trustee or beneficiary." What this means is that "deposits of trust money in a bank should be made in a separate account in the name of the trustee as trustee," and "title to land acquired by a trustee should be taken and recorded in the name of the trustee as trustee."[110] The particular trust should also be identified. For example, title to land might be taken and recorded in the name of "*T* as trustee of the 2017 *O* Family Trust."

If trust property is not earmarked as such, a trustee might later claim that investments that proved profitable were the trustee's own and investments that lost value were made for the trust. A creditor of the trustee personally might try to attach trust property that is not earmarked, claiming that it belongs to the trustee personally rather than as trustee. That the personal creditors of a trustee cannot reach assets held by the trustee as trustee is a critical feature of trust law (see page 393), one that is reinforced by the earmarking rule.

Assets not subject to registration, such as bearer bonds or tangible personal property, fall within an exception to the earmarking requirement. Legislation in most states, such as UTC § 816(7)(B) (2000), empowers a trustee to "hold a security in the name of a nominee or in other form without disclosure of the trust so that title may pass by delivery." In such circumstances, the trustee must keep records indicating that the property belongs to the trust and the property must still be kept separate from the trustee's own property.[111]

Although normally a trustee should not mingle the property of two or more trusts, a trustee may make a joint investment from separate trusts if the trustee maintains clear

---

109. *See* Restatement (Third) of Trusts § 76 cmt. d (Am. Law Inst. 2007).
110. Id. § 84 cmt. d.
111. *See* id. cmt. d(2).

records of the respective interests. Pooling the assets of multiple trusts for a program of coordinated investment might make available additional investment opportunities while also allowing for economies of scale and improved diversification. UTC § 810(d) (2000) codifies pooled trust investment thus: "If the trustee maintains records clearly indicating the respective interests, a trustee may invest as a whole the property of two or more separate trusts."

Under older authority, if a trustee commits a breach of trust by failing to earmark a trust investment, the trustee is strictly liable for any loss, even if the loss was not caused by the failure to earmark. More recent authority takes the position that the trustee is liable only if the loss results from the failure to earmark and is not liable if the loss results from general economic conditions.[112]

c. Duty Not to Mingle Trust Funds with the Trustee's Own

An egregious breach of the earmarking rules, raising both loyalty and prudence concerns, involves the *commingling* of trust property with the trustee's own property. As under UTC § 810(b) (2000), a trustee must "keep trust property separate from the trustee's own property." A trustee who commingles trust property with his own is in breach of trust even if the trustee does not use the trust funds for his own purposes.

As with a breach of the duty to earmark, there is a divergence of views on the extent of a trustee's liability for commingling. The older view is that a trustee is strictly liable, even if the loss would have occurred had there been no commingling. More recent authority holds the trustee liable only to the extent the commingling caused the loss.[113]

d. Duty to Keep Adequate Records of Administration

A trustee must maintain *adequate records* of the trust property and the administration of the trust, as under UTC § 810(a) (2000), including documentation of important decisions and actions and the trustee's reasoning for those decisions and actions. Such recordkeeping (1) promotes prudent and loyal administration by imposing discipline on the trustee; (2) enables the beneficiaries to undertake a meaningful review of the trustee's administration of the trust; and (3) protects the trustee against hindsight review by memorializing the trustee's analysis of the relevant circumstances as they existed at the time of the decision or action. A summary in capsule form is this: Feed the file, the file is your friend.

The higher standard of care applicable to a professional trustee (see page 640), such as under UTC § 806 (2000), intensifies this duty to document the administration of the trust. Because a professional trustee understands the importance of record-keeping to sound fiduciary practice,[114] and because a professional trustee knows that a

---

112. *See* Scott and Ascher on Trusts § 17.11.3.

113. *See id.* § 17.11.1.

114. Federal law requires national banks "adequately [to] document the establishment and termination of each fiduciary account and [to] maintain adequate records for all fiduciary accounts." 12 C.F.R. § 9.8(a) (2016).

failure to maintain adequate records might cause a reviewing court "to resolve doubts against the trustee,"[115] such trustees tend to establish and follow recordkeeping protocols to ensure ongoing documentation of the administration of the trust. For a trustee that is a corporate entity rather than an individual, adequate documentation is also necessary for effective coordination within the entity over time.

We take up the rights of a beneficiary to request information about the administration of the trust, to affirmative disclosure of significant developments, and to periodic accountings later in this chapter at page 675.

e. Duty to Bring and Defend Claims

A trustee is under a duty, as under UTC § 811 (2000) (emphasis added), to "take reasonable steps to *enforce claims* of the trust and to *defend claims* against the trust." This duty, which is a routine application of the duty of prudence, is informed by the duty of cost sensitivity (see page 660). As the comment to § 811 explains, a prudent trustee will consider "the likelihood of recovery and the cost of suit and enforcement," litigating cost-effective claims and compromising or dropping claims that are not cost effective.

If a trustee improperly refuses or neglects to bring a claim held in trust against a third party—for example, against a lawyer whose malpractice in advising the trustee as trustee causes damage to the trust estate—the beneficiary may bring the action against the third party, combining it with an action against the trustee for unreasonably failing to do so. Quoting an earlier decision, the court in In re Blumenkrantz, 824 N.Y.S.2d 884 (Sur. 2006), described this form of derivative litigation thus:

> It is fundamental to the law of trusts that [beneficiaries] have the right . . . to sue for the benefit of the trust on a cause of action which belongs to the trust if the trustees refuse to perform their duty in that respect. The derivative suit is, in effect, a combination of two causes of action[,] one against the trustees for wrongfully refusing to sue and the other against the party who is liable to the trust.

The rationale for allowing the beneficiary to act on behalf of the trust in this instance is one of judicial economy. "In order to settle the controversy in a single suit and avoid multiplicity of suits, the beneficiary can join the third person with the trustee as co-defendants, and the matter will be disposed of in a single suit."[116]

4. Trustee Selection and Divided Trusteeship

Having considered the application of the duty of prudence to the distribution, investment, custodial, and administrative functions of trusteeship, we are now in a position to consider the settlor's choice of trustee and the increasing prevalence of divided trusteeship, including *delegation, co-trustees, powers of appointment,* and *directed trusts.*

---

115. Restatement (Third) of Trusts § 83 cmt. a(1) (Am. Law Inst. 2007).
116. Restatement (Second) of Trusts § 282 cmt. e (Am. Law Inst. 1959).

a. Choosing a Trustee

Trustee selection usually follows one of two patterns. In the first, the settlor asks a trusted friend or relative to serve. This person, an *individual trustee*, typically agrees to serve out of a sense of friendship or moral obligation, and may choose to forgo trustee's fees. A trustee who was a confidant of the settlor may have a strong sense of the settlor's wishes and values, which is conducive to effective discharge of the distribution function. But the individual may be inexperienced in investment or unfamiliar with the administrative duties of a trustee, in particular the need to keep records, file tax returns, and make periodic accountings, and the individual may become incompetent or die before the end of the trust's term.

To solve these and related problems, many settlors select a *corporate trustee*, such as a bank or trust company, that is experienced in the investment, custodial, and administrative functions. As compared to an individual, a corporate trustee is also more likely to remain solvent in the event of an award of damages for breach of trust. Institutional bureaucracy provides additional safeguards against disloyalty or imprudence, as do federal and state banking regulations. But the cost of expertise, deep pockets, and institutional safeguards can be substantial. In addition to the significant fees,[117] trust companies are sometimes perceived as inflexible and unresponsive, a perception that has influenced reform of the law governing trustee removal (see Chapter 10 at page 750).

In light of the evolution of trusteeship from mere title holder to manager with broad powers across varied functions, an increasingly common practice is to divide the functions of trusteeship among more than one individual or company. Division can be made by a trustee by *delegating* a function of trusteeship to one or more agents. Division can also be made by a settlor in the terms of the trust by naming *co-trustees* or by giving persons other than the trustee powers over specified functions in what has come to be known as a *directed trust*.

b. Delegation by a Trustee

Once a settlor has selected the trustee, the trustee may choose to delegate some of its powers to others. Under traditional law, a trustee was not permitted to delegate

---

117. The prevailing rule, codified by UTC § 708 (2000), allows the trustee to take reasonable compensation. The older rule, still followed in some states, is to set the trustee's commission by a statutory formula, usually a percentage of the trust corpus, a percentage of trust income, or some combination of the two. These default rules may be displaced by contrary agreement, and corporate trustees typically insist upon agreement to their published or other negotiated fee schedule before agreeing to serve.

For example, the current fee schedule (revised in 2014) for the Wilmington Trust Company in Delaware is as follows: For trusts with less than $3 million in principal value, 1.75 percent for the first $1 million, 1.55 percent for the next $1 million, plus 1.35 percent for the next $1 million. For trusts with more than $3 million in principal, 1.55 percent for the first $3 million, 1.05 percent for the next $2 million, 0.85 percent for the next $5 million, 0.75 percent for the next $10 million, 0.65 for the next $30 million, and 0.60 percent for the balance. Under this schedule, the annual fee for a $1 million trust would be $17,500; for a $5 million trust would be $67,500; and for a $10 million trust would be $110,000.

Roy Delgado/Cartoonstock

matters that the trustee could reasonably be expected to perform personally. Because this rule was understood to bar a trustee from delegating the investment function, two recurring patterns of cases emerged. In the first, a trustee who was ignorant of investment matters would obtain expert advice and then go through a charade of exercising independent judgment, concluding that—surprise!—the expert's advice was sound and should be followed. Although a de facto delegation, the trustee's conduct would be upheld. In the second type of case, an ignorant trustee would obtain expert advice but not go through the charade of exercising independent judgment. This trustee might be held in breach of trust.[118]

Prudent people seek help in dealing with matters beyond their ken. No one would fault a trustee who delegates to a plumber responsibility to fix a leaky pipe in one of the trust's properties or who delegates to an accountant responsibility for preparing trust income tax returns. Likewise, a trustee who knows little about investing best serves the beneficiaries by delegating the investment function to a professional.

The drafters of the prudent investor rule took the occasion of updating trust investment law also to reverse the old nondelegation rule. The theory was that satisfying the new prudent investor rule would require amateur trustees and others unfamiliar with

---

118. *See* John H. Langbein, Reversing the Nondelegation Rule of Trust-Investment Law, 59 Mo. L. Rev. 105 (1994).

investment management to delegate the investment function. Under UPIA § 9 (1994), a trustee may delegate the investment function, but in doing so the trustee must exercise reasonable care, skill, and caution in *selecting*, *instructing*, and *monitoring* the agent. The official comment explains:

> If the trustee delegates effectively, the beneficiaries obtain the advantage of the agent's specialized investment skills or whatever other attributes induced the trustee to delegate. But if the trustee delegates to a knave or an incompetent, the delegation can work harm upon the beneficiaries. . . . Section 9 of the Uniform Prudent Investor Act is designed to strike the appropriate balance between the advantages and the hazards of delegation.

UTC § 807 (2000), excerpted below, extends the delegation rule of UPIA § 9 to all functions of trusteeship, as does the Restatement (Third) of Trusts.[119]

Uniform Trust Code (Unif. Law Comm'n 2000)

§ 807. Delegation By Trustee

(a) A trustee may delegate duties and powers that a prudent trustee of comparable skills could properly delegate under the circumstances. The trustee shall exercise reasonable care, skill, and caution in:

(1) selecting an agent;

(2) establishing the scope and terms of the delegation, consistent with the purposes and terms of the trust; and

(3) periodically reviewing the agent's actions in order to monitor the agent's performance and compliance with the terms of the delegation.

(b) In performing a delegated function, an agent owes a duty to the trust to exercise reasonable care to comply with the terms of the delegation.

(c) A trustee who complies with subsection (a) is not liable to the beneficiaries or to the trust for an action of the agent to whom the function was delegated.

(d) By accepting a delegation of powers or duties from the trustee of a trust that is subject to the law of this State, an agent submits to the jurisdiction of the courts of this State.

NOTES

1. A Duty to Delegate?   Suppose a trustee lacks particular skills such that under the circumstances a prudent person would normally delegate to an expert. Does the duty of prudence require delegation in these circumstances? *See* Restatement (Third) of Trusts § 80 cmt. d(1) (2007).

2. Duty of Cost Sensitivity.   A routine application of the duty of prudence is a duty to control costs in the administration of the trust. Minimizing costs and expenses

---

119. *See* Restatement (Third) of Trusts § 80 (Am. Law Inst. 2007).

preserves trust assets for the beneficiaries. The comment to UTC § 805 (2000), which codifies a trustee's duty to "incur only costs that are reasonable," explains the application of this duty to delegation:

> In deciding whether and how to delegate, the trustee must be alert to balancing projected benefits against the likely costs. To protect the beneficiary against excessive costs, the trustee should also be alert to adjusting compensation for functions which the trustee has delegated to others.

3. Liability of Trustee and Agent.   Under UTC § 807(c), a trustee who exercises due care, skill, and caution in selecting, instructing, and monitoring an agent is not liable for any negligence or misconduct of the agent. Instead, under § 807(b), the agent owes a duty of reasonable care to the trust. In effect, the agent is substituted for the trustee with respect to the delegated function. "In accepting the delegation of a trust function from a trustee, an agent assumes a fiduciary role with fiduciary responsibilities."[120] Accordingly, the trustee's duty to enforce claims held in trust (see page 657) may require the trustee to bring an action against a negligent or disloyal agent to make the trust whole.

In Roberts v. Roberts, 536 S.E.2d 714 (Va. 2000), an individual executor hired a bank to assist him in administering a complicated decedent's estate. The executor tasked the bank with preparing the required federal estate tax return. The bank made an error in the return, which cost the estate about $40,000. The beneficiaries sought to surcharge the executor for the loss. The court held that the executor was not liable because he had exercised reasonable care in delegating to the bank the task of preparing the return. The court also held that the executor could not be held in breach for failing to sue the bank, as the beneficiaries had failed to show that such a suit would have been cost effective.

c. Division by a Settlor

A common dilemma for a settlor is that no one individual or company will be well suited to carry out all of the functions of trusteeship. A trusted friend or relative might be well suited for the distribution function, but not investment or administration. A corporate trustee will usually be experienced in custody, administration, and investment, but its staff might be unfamiliar with the beneficiaries' circumstances and the settlor's values, and the settlor might prefer the investment function to be conducted by an investment advisor with whom he has had a long relationship. In contemporary practice, such a settlor is increasingly likely to divide trusteeship from the outset in the terms of the trust.

(1) Co-Trustees

We have already seen one form of divided trusteeship by the settlor — the naming of *co-trustees,* as in In re Rothko, page 602. A settlor can name two or more co-trustees,

---

120. Id. cmt. g.

sometimes an individual and a corporate trustee, with complementary strengths and weaknesses.

Suppose, for example, that *H* names *W* and a local bank as co-trustees. *H* might intend for *W* to be in charge of distributions and for the bank to be responsible for custody and administration, and perhaps the investment function as well. Unless the terms of the trust provide otherwise, however, "each co-trustee has a duty . . . of active, prudent participation in the performance of all aspects of the trust's administration."[121] Moreover, even if the trust instrument explicitly divides the functions of trusteeship among the co-trustees, each trustee remains under a continuing duty to take reasonable steps to prevent a breach of trust by a co-trustee (page 610). Imaginative lawyers have therefore looked for other ways to divide trusteeship.

(2) Power of Appointment

In the example above of *H* naming *W* and a bank as co-trustees, *H* might instead be advised to give *W* a *power of appointment* over the trust property. *H* can name the bank as trustee but give *W* a power to appoint income or principal or both to herself or to others. Giving *W* this power, which she holds in a nonfiduciary capacity, gives *W* control over the distribution function. But *W* is not subject to fiduciary obligation in the exercise of the power, which is problematic if *H* wants to impose controls on distribution, such as if *H* or *W* or both have children from a prior marriage. We give extended consideration to powers of appointment, which are central in contemporary estate planning, in Chapter 12.

(3) Directed Trusts

In a *directed trust*, the trustee, sometimes called an *administrative trustee*, has legal title to the trust property but must follow the directions of a third party, commonly called a *trust director*, *trust protector*, or *trust adviser*, with respect to the investment, distribution, or administrative functions of trusteeship.[122] A directed trust thus differs from a co-trusteeship in that the third party powerholder in a directed trust is not a trustee with legal title to the trust property.

Examples of Directed Trusts.   Let us consider some stylized examples of directed trusts:

> *Case 1. Direction by Distribution Committee. O* conveys a fund in trust to *X*, a trust company, for the benefit of *O*'s surviving spouse and descendants. The trust instrument provides that *X* is responsible for custody, administration, and investment of the trust property, but may only make distributions as directed by a

---

121. Id. § 81 cmt. c.

122. Consider again the current fee schedule for the Wilmington Trust Company (see *supra* note 117). For a trust in which Wilmington has no investment responsibility other than taking direction, for the first $3 million its fee is 0.55 percent; for the next $2 million is 0.45 percent; for the next $5 million is 0.30 percent; for the next $10 million is 0.25 percent; and is 0.20 percent for the balance. Under this schedule, the annual fee for a $1 million directed trust would be $5,500; for a $5 million directed trust would be $25,500; and for a $10 million directed trust would be $40,500.

distribution committee consisting of *O*'s surviving spouse, *O*'s lawyer, and *O*'s business partner.

Case 2. Direction by Outside Investment Advisor.   *O* conveys a fund in trust to *X*, a trust company, for the benefit of *O*'s surviving spouse and descendants. The trust instrument provides that *X* is responsible for custody, administration, and distribution, but that *X* must invest the trust assets as directed by *Y*, an investment advisor who has had a long and successful relationship with *O*.[123]

Case 3. Power of Direction over Other Matters.   *T* devises property to *X*, a bank, in trust to pay the income to *A* for life and on *A*'s death to distribute the property to *A*'s descendants. *T* also names her trusted friend *P*, who lacks the skills to serve as trustee herself, as the trust protector. *T* empowers *P* as protector: (1) to modify the trust's terms;[124] (2) to change the situs of the trust; (3) to terminate the trust; and (4) to select a successor trust protector.

In Case 1, *O* is able to take advantage of *X*'s expertise in trust administration while leaving distribution decisions in the hands of people who are familiar with the family and *O*'s values. In Case 2, *O* is able to continue *Y*'s control over investment of the trust property, while giving the other functions of trusteeship, for which *Y* has no particular expertise, to a trust company. In Case 3, *T* ensures that the trust's terms can be adapted by someone familiar with *T*'s values in light of the family's evolving circumstances.

Fiduciary Duty in a Directed Trust.   The application of trust fiduciary law to a directed trust is uncertain. The case law is thin and the statutes are in disarray.[125] The main questions are two. First, to what extent is a trust director subject to fiduciary duty to the beneficiaries? Second, to what extent does a directed trustee have fiduciary responsibility for the actions of a trust director? Thus:

Case 1 Revisited.   Suppose in Case 1 that *O*'s surviving spouse tries to persuade *O*'s lawyer to give the spouse an increased distribution by promising to kick back some of the increase to the lawyer. Do *O*'s descendants have a claim against the lawyer for breach of duty? Does *X*, as trustee, have a duty enforceable by *O*'s descendants to verify the good faith of the distribution committee's instructions?

Case 2 Revisited.   Suppose in Case 2 that *Y* instructs *X* to invest in lottery tickets or some other obviously imprudent investment. Do the beneficiaries have a claim against *Y* for breach of duty? Does *X*, as trustee, have a duty enforceable by the beneficiaries to refuse to follow such a direction?

Case 3 Revisited.   Suppose in Case 3 that *P* directs a modification of the trust that would replace *A* and *A*'s descendants with *P*'s spouse as the primary beneficiary of the trust. Do the original beneficiaries have a claim against *P* for breach of duty?

---

123. *See, e.g.*, Shelton v. Tamposi, 62 A.3d 741 (N.H. 2013) (involving "investment directors").

124. *See, e.g.*, Minassian v. Rachins, 152 So. 3d 719 (Fla. App. 2014) (involving a "trust protector" with a power to modify the terms of the trust).

125. *See, e.g.*, Richard W. Nenno, Good Directions Needed When Using Directed Trusts, 42 Est. Plan. 12 (Dec. 2015).

Does *X*, as trustee, have an obligation enforceable by the remainder beneficiaries to verify the good faith of *P*'s instructions?

The Uniform Trust Code.   Under UTC § 808(b) (2000), if the terms of a trust give a person a power to direct a trustee, the trustee must follow the person's direction unless it is "manifestly contrary to the terms of the trust" or "would constitute a serious breach of a fiduciary duty" owed by "the person holding the power."[126] Under § 808(d), a person "who holds a power to direct a trustee is presumptively a fiduciary." But what is the difference between a direction that is contrary to the terms of the trust and one that is *manifestly* so? What is the difference between an ordinary breach of fiduciary duty and one that is *serious*?

Suppose a settlor gives a person a power to direct but indicates in the terms of the trust that the presumption of UTC § 808(d) does not apply so that the holder of the power is not a fiduciary. Must the trustee follow a direction from such a person that is in bad faith or that will work harm upon the beneficiaries? Under UTC § 105(b)(2) (2000, rev. 2005), page 676, a trustee is under an unwaivable duty "to act in good faith and in accordance with the terms and purposes of the trust and the interests of the beneficiaries." How does that provision apply when the trustee acts subject to someone else's direction?

Specialized State Legislation.[127]   A majority of states have specialized legislation on directed trusts. Almost all of the specialized legislation provides that a trust director is a fiduciary. However, what fiduciary duties apply and the extent to which those duties are default or mandatory is generally not spelled out.

The specialized legislation's treatment of a directed trustee is clearer. Every state with specialized legislation — including many that have adopted the UTC — rejects the rules prescribed by UTC § 808. Instead, the specialized legislation tends to follow one of two alternate approaches. In one group are the states, such as Alaska, New Hampshire, Nevada, and South Dakota, that fully relieve a directed trustee from liability for complying with an action of a trust director.[128] In these states, a beneficiary's only recourse for a bad direction by a trust director is an action against the director for breach of the director's fiduciary duty to the beneficiary.

The policy rationale underpinning this first approach is that duty should follow power. If a trust director is the exclusive holder of a power, the director should also be the exclusive bearer of fiduciary duty for that power. This approach does not necessarily reduce a beneficiary's rights, because the settlor of a directed trust could have made the trust director the sole trustee. On greater-includes-the-lesser reasoning, the settlor

---

126. Restatement (Third) of Trusts § 75 (Am. Law Inst. 2007) is similar to UTC § 808 but without the qualifier "manifestly."

127. With the permission of the Uniform Law Commission, portions of this and the next section are adapted from the comments to the year-end 2016 draft of the Uniform Directed Trust Act. One of the editors of this book, Professor Sitkoff, is the Chair of the drafting committee for that act.

128. *See* Alaska Stat. § 13.36.375 (2016); N.H. Rev. Stat. § 564-B:7-711 (2016); Nev. Rev. Stat. § 163.5549 (2016); S.D. Codified Laws § 55-1B-2 (2016).

should also be able to eliminate a directed trustee's duty and liability for complying with an action of a trust director.

In the other group, which includes Delaware, Illinois, Texas, and Virginia, are the states that provide that a directed trustee is not liable for complying with a direction of a trust director unless by doing so the trustee personally would engage in *willful misconduct* (or conduct rising to the level of some similar standard).[129] The policy rationale for these statutes is that, because a trustee stands at the center of a trust, the trustee must bear at least some duty even if the trustee is directed. Although the settlor could have made the trust director the sole trustee, the settlor did not do so. And under traditional understandings of trust law, a trustee must always be accountable to a beneficiary in some way (see page 621). However, to facilitate the settlor's intent that the trust director rather than the directed trustee be the primary or even sole decision maker, it is appropriate to reduce the trustee's duty below the usual level with respect to a matter subject to a power of direction.

Under this second group of statutes a beneficiary's main recourse for misconduct by a trust director is an action against the director for breach of the director's fiduciary duty to the beneficiary. But the beneficiary also has recourse against the trustee if the trustee's compliance with the trust director's action amounted to "willful misconduct" by the trustee. But what exactly is meant by "willful misconduct"?[130] Does it require more than gross negligence? Does it encompass recklessness? Can following a direction ever constitute willful misconduct?

The Uniform Directed Trust Act. The year-end 2016 draft of the Uniform Directed Trust Act (UDTA), which is slated to be approved by the Uniform Law Commission in final form in July 2017, follows the model of the second group. Under the draft UDTA, a third party with a *power of direction* over a trust is called a *trust director*. A trustee subject to such a power is called a *directed trustee*. A trust director is subject to the same fiduciary duty and liability as a trustee, which may be varied by the terms of a trust to the same extent that the terms of the trust could vary the duty and liability of a trustee. A directed trustee is not liable for taking "reasonable action" to comply with a trust director's power of direction unless by doing so "the trustee would engage in willful misconduct." Relative to a non-directed trust, the draft UDTA has the effect of increasing the total fiduciary duties owed to a beneficiary. The fiduciary duties of trusteeship are preserved in the trust director, and in addition the directed trustee also has a duty to avoid willful misconduct.

The draft UDTA also contains a raft of provisions that provide default rules for mechanical matters that a drafter might overlook in structuring a directed trust. For example, the draft UDTA provides default rules for acceptance, compensation, resignation, and removal of a trust director, and for limitations periods and other rules governing litigation against a trust director for breach of trust.

---

129. *See* 12 Del. Code § 3313 (2016); 760 Ill. Comp. Stat. 5/16.3 (2016); Tex. Prop. Code Ann. § 114.0031 (2016); Va. Code Ann. § 64.2-770 (2016).

130. Recall the Delaware definition at *supra* note 106 and text accompanying.

Perhaps more important, the draft UDTA clarifies that a power of direction over distributions, which is held in a fiduciary capacity, is different from a *power of appointment*, which is held in a nonfiduciary capacity (see Chapter 12 at page 812). The UDTA governs a power to direct distributions but not a power of appointment. To distinguish a fiduciary power to direct a distribution from a nonfiduciary power of appointment, the UDTA provides a rule of construction under which a power in person other than a trustee to designate a recipient of an ownership interest in trust property is presumptively a nonfiduciary power of appointment unless the terms of the trust indicate otherwise.

An innovative further provision of the draft UDTA provides that "[t]he terms of a trust may relieve a cotrustee from duty and liability with respect to a power of another cotrustee to the same extent that the terms of a trust may relieve a directed trustee from duty and liability with respect to a trust director's power of direction." Thus, under the draft UDTA a settlor may create a *co-trusteeship* with the same fiduciary structure as a directed trust. A settlor may reduce the duty and liability of one trustee regarding the powers held by another trustee (see page 610). The draft commentary explains that this provision "allows a settlor to choose either fiduciary regime for a cotrusteeship — the traditional rules of cotrusteeship or the more permissive rules of a directed trusteeship. There seems little reason to prevent the settlor from applying the fiduciary rules of this act to an arrangement that uses the labeling of cotrusteeship given that a settlor could choose the more permissive rules for a directed trusteeship by labeling one of the cotrustees as a trust director and another as a directed trustee."

d. Private Trust Company

New state laws have facilitated the formation of lightly regulated *private trust companies* meant to serve as trustee of one or more trusts within a single family. Of the $226 billion in trust assets reported at year-end 2015 by trust companies in South Dakota to state banking authorities (see Chapter 6 at page 393), $61 billion — more than 25 percent — was held by private trust companies.[131]

Professor Iris Goodwin explains the concept thus:

> [I]t is now . . . possible to create an unregulated or a "lightly regulated" trust company if the entity is limited in its purpose to serving as trustee of trusts benefiting a group of related people. . . . [T]he family must put in place a governance structure so that the family can, through the various administrative arms of the trust company, effectively control the investment of trust funds, among other things. The ownership interest is usually vested in individual family members. Family members also serve on the board of directors. The board can also include outside advisors of long standing.[132]

A private trust company allows for consolidation of functions of trusteeship that might otherwise be parceled out by way of a directed trust or by delegation. This might

---

131. The editors thank the South Dakota Banking Commission for these data.

132. Iris J. Goodwin, How the Rich Stay Rich: Using a Family Trust Company to Secure a Family Fortune, 40 Seton Hall L. Rev. 467, 472-77 (2010); *see also* Alan V. Ytterberg & James P. Weller, Managing Family Wealth Through a Private Trust Company, 36 ACTEC L.J. 623 (2010).

be desirable if the family wants to retain control over a family business or to ensure coordinated distributions from, and investment of, the family fortune across multiple family trusts. Professor Goodwin suggests that a private trust company also allows for the combination of "aggressive planning techniques (tax-driven and otherwise) . . . to secure and grow a fortune for untold generations to come."[133]

D. THE DUTY OF IMPARTIALITY

1. Due Regard and the Terms of the Trust

As we have seen, the duty of loyalty requires a trustee to act solely in the interests of the beneficiaries (see page 596). But what if there are two or more beneficiaries whose interests are not in perfect alignment? How is a trustee to sort between the conflicting interests of multiple beneficiaries? Enter the duty of *impartiality*, which is codified by UTC § 803 (2000) thus:

> If a trust has two or more beneficiaries, the trustee shall act impartially in investing, managing, and distributing the trust property, giving due regard to the beneficiaries' respective interests.

The duty of impartiality is, therefore, unfortunately named. It does not require impartiality in the sense of equality. Instead, it requires a trustee to give *due regard* to the beneficiaries' respective interests as defined by the settlor in the terms of the trust. A trustee must construe the trust instrument to determine the respective interests of the beneficiaries. In some circumstances, the terms of the trust will permit or even require the trustee to favor the interests of one beneficiary over another.[134]

In Howard v. Howard, 156 P.3d 89 (Or. App. 2007), *H* created a trust for the benefit of his wife, *W*, for life, with the remainder to be paid to his son, *S*. The trust instrument, which named *W* and *S* as co-trustees, provided that "my spouse's support, comfort, companionship, enjoyment and desires shall be preferred over the rights of the remaindermen." The lawyer who drafted the instrument testified that *H* "had a central desire to make sure that [*W*] was adequately provided for," and that the provision expressing a preference for *W*'s enjoyment was meant to "slant[] . . . questionable decisions in favor of [*W*]."

As co-trustee, *S* took the position that he and the other co-trustee, *W*, should consider *W*'s other sources of support, which were ample, and therefore that the co-trustees should follow "an investment strategy focused on preserving assets for distribution to the remainder beneficiaries." *W* took the opposite view. To resolve the dispute, *W* petitioned the court for instructions.[135] In light of the lawyer's testimony,

---

133. Goodwin, *supra* note 132, at 468.

134. *See* SunTrust Bank v. Merritt, 612 S.E.2d 818, 822 (Ga. App. 2005) ("In determining what is fair, we look to the trust instrument.").

135. One of the distinctive features of trust law is the ready availability of anticipatory relief, coming out of the petition for instructions in equity. "A trustee or beneficiary may apply to an appropriate court for instructions regarding the administration or distribution of the trust if there is reasonable

the negative inference arising from other beneficial interests being subject to consideration of the beneficiary's other resources, and the expression of preference for *W*'s "enjoyment and desires . . . over the rights of the remainderman," the court held that giving due regard to the respective interests of the beneficiaries required the co-trustees to favor *W*'s interests without regard to her other sources of support.

NOTES

1. Blended Families, Choice of Trustee, and Structural Conflicts.   It is common for a married settlor to want to assure the surviving spouse comfortable support during life, and then to pass whatever is left at the survivor's death to the settlor's descendants. In *Howard*, the complication was the blended family. Both the settlor and the surviving spouse had children from prior marriages. What language would you have recommended to assure comfortable support for the surviving spouse while protecting the remainder for the settlor's descendants? What if the surviving spouse is close in age to the decedent's children? Do these circumstances argue for a neutral corporate trustee?

The question of whether a trustee may or should consider a beneficiary's other resources in administering a trust is a matter of construction (see page 618). In *Howard*, the court put much emphasis on the reference to other resources in relation to distributions to other beneficiaries, and the absence of such a reference for distributions to *W*. In Harootian v. Douvadjian, 954 N.E.2d 560 (Mass. App. 2011), involving a surviving spouse life beneficiary who was also the trustee, a remainder beneficiary complained that the spouse

> abused her discretion as trustee by invading the trust principal for her support because she had assets of her own with which to pay her bills. . . . The trust provided that upon [the settlor's] death, the trustee had the power to invade the trust principal "for the support in reasonable comfort and maintenance of" [the spouse]. The Supreme Judicial Court has interpreted similar trust language as reflecting "the unequivocal intention that [the widow's] living expenses are to be borne exclusively by the trust income and principal." By contrast, "where there is language manifesting a contrary intention, the usual case being where a trustee's discretion to pay is qualified by such words as 'when in need' or 'if necessary,' we have reached the opposite result." . . . Without the requisite qualifying language in [this] trust, [the spouse] was not required to use her own assets before invading the trust principal to pay for her support.

---

doubt about the powers or duties of the trusteeship or about the proper interpretation of the trust provisions." Restatement (Third) of Trusts § 71 (Am. Law Inst. 2007). For example, a trustee or a beneficiary may apply for instructions "concerning the identity of the trust beneficiaries, the nature and extent of their interests, the proper allocation or apportionment of receipts or expenditures between income and principal, and the propriety of a trustee's plan of distribution on trust termination." Id. cmt. c. By contrast, "[i]f a matter rests within the sound discretion of the trustee, or is a matter of business judgment, the court ordinarily will not instruct the trustee how to exercise that discretion or judgment." Id. cmt. d.

The trustees in *Howard* and *Harootian* were conflicted. But their conflicts were structural, created by the settlor rather than provoked by the trustee (see page 601). As such, the no-further-inquiry rule did not apply. The conflicts were resolved under the rubric of impartiality rather than the rule of undivided loyalty.

2. Impartiality in a Construction Proceeding.   Suppose that there is an ambiguity in the trust instrument that can be resolved in a manner favorable to either the income beneficiary or the remainder beneficiary, but not both. In petitioning for a judicial construction, can the trustee argue in favor of one interpretation or the other? *See* Northern Trust Co. v. Heuer, 560 N.E.2d 961 (Ill. App. 1990).

2. The Principal and Income Problem

Although conflicts can arise among concurrent beneficiaries, impartiality problems are more common, as in *Howard*, among current and successive beneficiaries. Suppose *T* devises a fund in trust to *X* "to pay the income to *A* for life and then the principal to *B* on *A*'s death." Although the overall interests of *A* and *B* are aligned on matters such as self-dealing or embezzlement by *X*, their interests in the investment of the trust fund may be at odds. The problem is that under traditional fiduciary rules respecting allocation to *income* and *principal*, the particular *form* of an investment return determines its classification as income or principal. The income beneficiary, *A*, will prefer investments that produce returns that are classified as income while *B*, the principal beneficiary, will prefer investments that produce returns that are classified as principal.

Under traditional law, codified by the widely adopted Uniform Principal and Income Act (Unif. Law Comm'n 1931, rev. 1962), rents, cash dividends on common stock, and interest on bonds are classified as income, but increases in asset value, such as stock or land appreciation, are classified as principal.[136] If *X* invests in a stock that does not pay a dividend, so that the stock price appreciates faster as profits are accumulated within the company, *B* is advantaged at the expense of *A*. If *X* invests in a bond that pays interest but does not appreciate in value, *A* is advantaged at the expense of *B*. "A trustee who has investment discretion effectively chooses the income level by choosing the investments. The duty of impartiality constrains the trustee by requiring 'due regard' to the interests of principal and income, but within the sphere of discretion that the duty of impartiality permits, trustees commonly make investment decisions with a view to achieving the desired income level."[137]

---

136. To income the 1962 Act allocates: (1) rent; (2) interest on loans and bonds; (3) cash dividends on stock; (4) net profits from a business or farming operation; (5) royalties from natural resources (except 27 1/2 percent allocated to principal); and (6) royalties from patents and copyrights (but not in excess of 5 percent per year of inventory value).

To principal, increasing the corpus of the trust, the 1962 Act allocates: (1) proceeds from sale of property; (2) proceeds of insurance on property; (3) stock splits and stock dividends; (4) corporate distributions from a merger or acquisition; (5) payment of bond principal; (6) royalties from natural resources (27 1/2 percent); and (7) royalties from patents and copyrights in excess of 5 percent of inventory value.

137. John H. Langbein, The Uniform Prudent Investor Act and the Future of Trust Investing, 81 Iowa L. Rev. 641, 667 (1996).

The embrace of modern portfolio theory by the prudent investor rule brought into sharp relief the skewing effect in the investment function of allocating income and principal in the distribution function based solely on the form of the trust's investment returns. Professor Langbein explains:

> By distorting investment choices in order to maximize a particular form of return (whether dividends and interest or capital appreciation), conventional trust investment practices that are designed to satisfy principal-and-income concerns come into tension with Modern Portfolio Theory. Thus, for example, the trustee who is administering a trust that needs to achieve a high level of current income may feel obliged to invest heavily in bonds, even though it is known that equities outperform bonds across the long term on a total-return basis [see page 631 — Eds.]. The conventional principal-and-income rules drive that trustee to accept a lower total return in order to obtain a particular form of return — interest rather than capital appreciation.[138]

In the words of the Restatement, "only when beneficial rights do not turn on a distinction between income and principal is the trustee allowed to focus on total return . . . without regard to the income component of that return."[139]

To free the trustee's hand in crafting a portfolio for total return without regard for the formal characterization of that return as principal or income, the Uniform Principal and Income Act was revised in 1997. The revised act continues the traditional rule of allocation to income or principal on the basis of form, but § 104 of the revised act gives the trustee a *power to adjust* between income and principal:

> A trustee may adjust between principal and income to the extent the trustee considers necessary if the trustee invests and manages trust assets as a prudent investor, the terms of the trust describe the amount that may or must be distributed to a beneficiary by referring to the trust's income, and the trustee determines, after applying the rules [of formal allocation], that the trustee is unable to comply with [the duty of impartiality].

This adjustment power, a default rule, applies unless the settlor provides otherwise.

Another solution is a *unitrust*. The basic concept, which derives from the charitable remainder unitrust (see Chapter 15 at page 974), is that the settlor may set a percentage of the value of the trust corpus that must be paid to the income beneficiary each year. The corpus is then revalued each year. If an income beneficiary is entitled to 5 percent of the yearly value of the trust, and the trust holds $1 million, the income beneficiary is entitled to a distribution of $50,000. If the value of the trust increases in the next year to $1,200,000, the income beneficiary will be entitled to $60,000.

A unitrust frees the trustee to focus on risk and return without regard for the form in which that return comes. The percentage to be distributed need not be fixed; the

---

138. Id. at 667-68.
139. Restatement (Third) of Trusts § 90 cmt. i (Am. Law Inst. 2007).

settlor might key the percentage to the rate of inflation or prevailing interest rates. Many lawyers advise the smoothing of payments across time by requiring that the percentage be multiplied by the three-year rolling average value of the trust. In states that permit the conversion of a traditional principal and income trust into a unitrust, the percentage is usually set by statute, typically between 3 to 5 percent, and it is applied to a rolling average value over the prior three years.[140]

By year-end 2016, every state except North Dakota had enacted legislation validating a trustee's power to adjust between income and principal, a unitrust, or both.

In re Heller
849 N.E.2d 262 (N.Y. 2006)

ROSENBLATT, J. In September 2001, New York enacted legislation that transformed the definition and treatment of trust accounting income. The Uniform Principal and Income Act (EPTL art. 11-A) and related statutes, including the optional unitrust provision (EPTL 11-2.4), are designed to facilitate investment for total return on a portfolio. The appeal before us centers on the optional unitrust provision, which permits trustees to elect a regime in which income is calculated according to a fixed formula and based on the net fair market value of the trust assets. We hold that a trustee's status as a remainder beneficiary does not in itself invalidate a unitrust election made by that trustee. . . .

I

In his will, after making certain other gifts of personal property and money, Jacob Heller created a trust to benefit his wife Bertha Heller (should she survive him) and his children.[141] Heller provided that his entire residuary estate be held in trust during Bertha's life. He appointed his brother Frank Heller as trustee and designated his sons Herbert and Alan Heller as trustees on Frank's death. Every year Bertha was to receive the greater of $40,000 or the total income of the trust. Heller named his daughters (Suzanne Heller and Faith Willinger, each with a 30% share) and his sons and prospective trustees (Herbert and Alan Heller, each with a 20% share) as remainder beneficiaries.

Jacob Heller died in 1986, and his wife Bertha survives him. When Heller's brother Frank died in 1997, Herbert and Alan Heller became trustees. From that year until

Judge Albert M. Rosenblatt

---

140. *See* id. § 111 cmt. c.

141. Notice the reference to *his* children. Bertha was a second spouse. Gary B. Friedman, counsel for the appellant, explained to the editors as follows: "The marriage was long — 26 years — and Jacob died 22 years before Bertha. Before the unitrust conversion it was a fairly close family. The trustees and the other 2 remainderpersons were children from the first marriage." — Eds.

2001, Bertha Heller received an average annual income from the trust of approximately $190,000. In March 2003, the trustees elected to have the unitrust provision apply, pursuant to EPTL 11-2.4(e)(1)(B)(I). As required by EPTL 11-2.4(e)(1)(B)(III), they notified trust beneficiaries Bertha Heller, Suzanne Heller and Faith Willinger. The trustees sought to have unitrust treatment applied retroactively to January 1, 2002, the effective date of EPTL 11-2.4. As a result of that election, Bertha Heller's annual income was reduced to approximately $70,000.

Appellant Sandra Davis commenced this proceeding, as attorney-in-fact for her mother Bertha Heller, and on August 1, 2003 moved for summary judgment, seeking, among other things, an order annulling the unitrust election and revoking the letters of trusteeship issued to Herbert and Alan Heller. . . . Surrogate's Court . . . denied . . . her motion seeking annulment of the unitrust election itself and other relief.

Davis appealed Surrogate's Court's order, and Herbert and Alan Heller cross-appealed. The Appellate Division affirmed the order to the extent that it denied Davis's summary judgment motion. . . . It also granted leave to appeal and certified the following question to us: "Was the opinion and order of [the Appellate Division] dated August 15, 2005, properly made?" We conclude that it was and now affirm.

II

The 2001 legislation that forms the subject of this appeal was designed to make it easier for trustees to comply with the demands of the Prudent Investor Act of 1994. In addition to enacting EPTL article 11-A (Uniform Principal and Income Act), the Legislature both added EPTL 11-2.3(b)(5) to the Prudent Investor Act and included the optional unitrust provision, EPTL 11-2.4.

Under the former Principal and Income Act, a trustee was required to balance the interests of the income beneficiary against those of the remainder beneficiary, and was constrained in making investments by the act's narrow definitions of income and principal. A trustee who invested in nonappreciating assets would ensure reasonable income for any income beneficiary, but would sacrifice growth opportunities for the trust funds, as inflation eroded their value; if the trustee invested for growth, remainder beneficiaries would enjoy an increase in the value of the trust at the expense of income beneficiaries. Moreover, the need to invest so as to produce what the former Principal and Income Act defined as income led to investment returns that failed to represent the benefits envisaged as appropriate by settlors.

The Prudent Investor Act encourages investing for total return on a portfolio. Unless the governing instrument expressly provides otherwise, the act requires that trustees "pursue an *overall* investment strategy to enable the trustee to make appropriate present and future distributions to or for the benefit of the beneficiaries under the governing instrument, in accordance with risk and return objectives reasonably suited to the *entire* portfolio" (EPTL 11-2.3[b][3][A] [emphasis added]).

The 2001 legislation allows trustees to pursue this strategy uninhibited by a constrained concept of trust accounting income. First, the Prudent Investor Act now authorizes trustees

> to adjust between principal and income to the extent the trustee considers advisable to enable the trustee to make appropriate present and future distributions in

accordance with clause (b)(3)(A) if the trustee determines, after applying the rules in article 11-A, that such an adjustment would be fair and reasonable to all of the beneficiaries, so that current beneficiaries may be given such use of the trust property as is consistent with preservation of its value (EPTL 11-2.3[b][5][A]).

A trustee investing for a portfolio's total return under the Prudent Investor Act may now adjust principal and income to compensate for the effects of the investment decisions on distribution to income beneficiaries. Alternatively, the optional unitrust provision lets trustees elect unitrust status for a trust (EPTL 11-2.4), by which income is calculated according to a fixed formula.

In a unitrust pursuant to EPTL 11-2.4, an income beneficiary receives an annual income distribution of "four percent of the net fair market values of the assets held in the trust on the first business day of the current valuation year," for the first three years of unitrust treatment. This is true regardless of the actual income earned by the trust. Starting in the fourth year, the value of the trust assets is determined by calculating the average of three figures: the net fair market value on the first business day of the current valuation year and the net fair market values on the first business days of the prior two valuation years. Income generated in excess of this amount is applied to principal.

Under the 2001 legislation, then, a trustee may invest in assets, such as equities, that outperform other types of investment in the long term but produce relatively low dividend yields for an income beneficiary, and still achieve impartial treatment of income and remainder beneficiaries. The trustee may accomplish this either by adjusting as between principal and income or by electing unitrust status with the result that the income increases in proportion to the value of the principal. If a trust's assets are primarily interests in nonappreciating investments producing high yields for income beneficiaries, a unitrust election may initially result in a substantial decrease in the distribution to any income beneficiary, at least until the portfolio is diversified. This case presents such a scenario.

III

Davis argues that the trustees are barred as a matter of law from electing unitrust status because they are themselves remainder beneficiaries, and that, in any case, they may not elect unitrust status retroactively to January 1, 2002. The Appellate Division held that the legislation does not impede unitrust election by an interested trustee, that such an election is not inconsistent, per se, with common-law limitations on the conduct of fiduciaries and that the statute permits trustees to select retroactive application. We agree.

EPTL 11-2.3(b)(5), the 2001 statute that gives trustees the power to adjust between principal and income, expressly prohibits a trustee from exercising this power if "the trustee is a current beneficiary or a presumptive remainderman of the trust" or if "the adjustment would benefit the trustee directly or indirectly." Tellingly, the Legislature included no such prohibition in the simultaneously enacted optional unitrust provision, EPTL 11-2.4. Moreover, in giving a list of factors to be considered by the courts in determining whether unitrust treatment should apply to a trust, the Legislature mentioned no absolute prohibitions, and created a presumption in favor of unitrust application. We conclude that the Legislature did not mean to prohibit trustees who have a beneficial interest from electing unitrust treatment.

It is certainly true that the common law in New York contains an absolute prohibition against self-dealing, in that "a fiduciary owes a duty of undivided and undiluted loyalty to those whose interests the fiduciary is to protect" (Birnbaum v. Birnbaum, 539 N.E.2d 574 (N.Y. 1989)). "The trustee is under a duty to the beneficiary to administer the trust solely in the interest of the beneficiary" (Restatement (Second) of Trusts § 170(1) (1959)). In this case, however, the trustees owe fiduciary obligations not only to the trust's income beneficiary, Bertha Heller, but also to the other remainder beneficiaries, Suzanne Heller and Faith Willinger. That these beneficiaries' interests happen to align with the trustees' does not relieve the trustees of their duties to them. Here, we cannot conclude that the trustees are prohibited from electing unitrust treatment as a matter of common-law principle.

That the trustees are remainder beneficiaries does not, by itself, invalidate a unitrust election. Nevertheless, a unitrust election from which a trustee benefits will be scrutinized by the courts with special care. In determining whether application of the optional unitrust provision is appropriate, it remains for the Surrogate to review the process and assure the fairness of the trustees' election, by applying relevant factors including those enumerated in EPTL 11-2.4(e)(5)(A). Application of these factors here presents questions of fact precluding summary judgment. . . .

Accordingly, the order of the Appellate Division should be affirmed, with costs, and the certified question answered in the affirmative.

NOTES

1. Structural Conflicts and a Trustee-Beneficiary. The statutory adjustment power is usually denied to a trustee who is also a beneficiary, as under Uniform Principal and Income Act § 104(c)(7). In *Heller*, the court held that a trustee-beneficiary may, however, convert to a unitrust, subject to judicial review to "assure the fairness of the trustees' election." In reaching this result, the court emphasized the duty owed by the trustees to the other remainder beneficiaries. But was this fact critical? Would the outcome be different if the trustees were the only remainder beneficiaries? A trust in which the settlor names as trustee an income beneficiary or a remainder beneficiary presents a structural conflict of interest (see page 601). Is a unitrust preferable to the adjustment power as a matter of policy for dealing with this kind of conflict?

2. Federal Tax Law. A host of federal income, gift, and estate tax laws are keyed to the definitions of income and principal under state trust fiduciary law. Treasury regulations provide that what is deemed income by the exercise of an adjustment power or application of a unitrust percentage will generally be treated as income for federal tax purposes, provided that the adjustment or the unitrust is sanctioned by state statute and the amount deemed income is within 3 to 5 percent of the total value of the trust.[142]

---

142. *See* Treas. Reg. § 1.643(b)-1 (2016).

E. THE DUTY TO INFORM AND ACCOUNT

A trustee is under an ongoing duty, codified by UTC § 813 (2000, rev. 2004), excerpted below, to keep the beneficiaries informed about the administration of the trust, in particular by providing information needed by the beneficiaries to protect their interests in the trust. In this section, we consider: (1) the obligation of a trustee to respond promptly to a beneficiary's request for information; (2) a trustee's duty to make affirmative disclosure to the beneficiaries of significant developments or intended transactions; and (3) the rules governing repose for a trustee who makes an accounting or other report to the beneficiaries.

Uniform Trust Code (Unif. Law Comm'n 2000, as amended 2004)

§ 813. Duty to Inform and Report

(a) A trustee shall keep the qualified beneficiaries of the trust reasonably informed about the administration of the trust and of the material facts necessary for them to protect their interests. Unless unreasonable under the circumstances, a trustee shall promptly respond to a beneficiary's request for information related to the administration of the trust.

(b) A trustee:

(1) upon request of a beneficiary, shall promptly furnish to the beneficiary a copy of the trust instrument;

(2) within 60 days after accepting a trusteeship, shall notify the qualified beneficiaries of the acceptance and of the trustee's name, address, and telephone number;

(3) within 60 days after the date the trustee acquires knowledge of the creation of an irrevocable trust, or the date the trustee acquires knowledge that a formerly revocable trust has become irrevocable, whether by the death of the settlor or otherwise, shall notify the qualified beneficiaries of the trust's existence, of the identity of the settlor or settlors, of the right to request a copy of the trust instrument, and of the right to a trustee's report as provided in subsection (c); and

(4) shall notify the qualified beneficiaries in advance of any change in the method or rate of the trustee's compensation.

(c) A trustee shall send to the distributees or permissible distributees of trust income or principal, and to other qualified or nonqualified beneficiaries who request it, at least annually and at the termination of the trust, a report of the trust property, liabilities, receipts, and disbursements, including the source and amount of the trustee's compensation, a listing of the trust assets and, if feasible, their respective market values. Upon a vacancy in a trusteeship, unless a cotrustee remains in office, a report must be sent to the qualified beneficiaries by the former trustee. A personal representative, [conservator], or [guardian] may send the qualified beneficiaries a report on behalf of a deceased or incapacitated trustee.

(d) A beneficiary may waive the right to a trustee's report or other information otherwise required to be furnished under this section. A beneficiary, with respect to future reports and other information, may withdraw a waiver previously given. . . .

1. Responding to a Request for Information

A trustee is under a duty, as under UTC § 813(a), page 675, to respond promptly "to a beneficiary's request for information related to the administration of the trust." The theory is that, for a beneficiary to be able to protect her interest in the trust, the beneficiary must have access to information reasonably related to that interest.

Uniform Trust Code (Unif. Law Comm'n 2000, as amended 2005)

§ 105. Default and Mandatory Rules

(a) Except as otherwise provided in the terms of the trust, this [Code] governs the duties and powers of a trustee, relations among trustees, and the rights and interests of a beneficiary.

(b) The terms of a trust prevail over any provision of this [Code] except: . . .

(2) the duty of a trustee to act in good faith and in accordance with the terms and purposes of the trust and the interests of the beneficiaries;

(3) the requirement that a trust and its terms be for the benefit of its beneficiaries, and that the trust have a purpose that is lawful, not contrary to public policy, and possible to achieve; . . .

[(8) the duty under Section 813(b)(2) and (3) to notify qualified beneficiaries of an irrevocable trust who have attained 25 years of age of the existence of the trust, of the identity of the trustee, and of their right to request trustee's reports;]

[(9) the duty under Section 813(a) to respond to the request of a [qualified] beneficiary of an irrevocable trust for trustee's reports and other information reasonably related to the administration of a trust;] . . .

(13) the power of the court to take such action and exercise such jurisdiction as may be necessary in the interests of justice. . . .

Wilson v. Wilson
690 S.E.2d 710 (N.C. App. 2010)

WYNN, J. "[T]he beneficiary is always entitled to such information as is reasonably necessary to enable him to enforce his rights under the trust or to prevent or redress a breach of trust."[143] In the present case, the trial court held that Defendant-settlor Lawrence A. Wilson, Jr. could, by a provision in the trust instrument, deny Plaintiffs-

---

143. Taylor v. Nationsbank Corp., 481 S.E.2d 358, 362 (N.C. App. 1997) (quoting Restatement (Second) of Trusts § 173 cmt. c (1959)).

beneficiaries information necessary to prevent or redress a breach of trust. Because this result is contrary to law, we reverse the trial court's grant of a protective order and summary judgment to Defendants.

Defendant Lawrence A. Wilson, Jr. in 1992 created two irrevocable trusts, one for each of his two children. He made Defendant Lawrence A. Wilson, Sr. the trustee for both of the trusts, and included in both instruments the provision at issue in this case:

> The Trustee shall not be required by any law, rule or regulation to prepare or file for approval any inventory, appraisal or regular or periodic accounts or reports with any court or beneficiary, but he may from time to time present his accounts to an adult beneficiary or a parent or guardian of a minor or incompetent beneficiary.

> 2.10: ACCOUNTS. The Trustee shall not be required by any law, rule or regulation to prepare or file for approval any inventory, appraisal or regular or periodic accounts or reports with any court or beneficiary, but he may from time to time present his accounts to an adult beneficiary or a parent or guardian of a minor or incompetent beneficiary. If a parent or

The provision at issue in *Wilson*

On 28 September 2007, the beneficiaries ("Plaintiffs") filed suit, alleging a breach of fiduciary duty. Plaintiffs requested, among other things, that the trustee be required "to provide a full, complete, and accurate accounting of the Trusts from December 31, 1992 through the date on which the Order is entered." In support of their claims, Plaintiffs alleged that Defendant Trustee Wilson, Sr. had allowed Defendant Settlor Wilson, Jr. to take control of the assets of the Trusts, and that Defendant Settlor Wilson, Jr. subsequently invested the assets in his personal business ventures which were highly speculative and resulted in a substantial depreciation of assets. Plaintiffs further alleged that Defendant Trustee breached his statutory duty by failing to distribute income to Plaintiffs as required by the terms of the Trust Instruments.

Defendants filed an answer on 30 October 2007 pointing to the provision of the trust instruments that purportedly excused the trustee from providing an accounting. . . . Defendants filed a motion for a protective order . . . "on the grounds that by reason of the provisions of the Trust Instrument, the discovery sought herein may not be had." The motion requested a ruling on Defendants' prior motion for declaratory judgment to determine the beneficiaries' right to demand an accounting. . . . Defendants [then] filed a motion for summary judgment. . . . The trial court granted Defendants' motion[s]. . . .

Plaintiffs now appeal the trial court's orders on Defendants' motion for a protective order and partial declaratory judgment, and summary judgment and the award of costs to Defendants. . . .

The basic issue here is whether the trial court erred in its interpretation of the North Carolina Uniform Trust Code ("N.C. Trust Code"). The N.C. Trust Code "applies to any express trust, private or charitable, with additions to the trust, wherever and however created." N.C. Gen. Stat. § 36C-1-102 (2009). Section 36C-1-105[, based on UTC § 105, page 676,] provides:

> (b) The terms of a trust prevail over any provision of this Chapter except: . . .
>   (2) The duty of a trustee to act in good faith and in accordance with the terms and purposes of the trust and the interests of the beneficiaries. . . .
>   (9) The power of the court to take any action and exercise any jurisdiction as may be necessary in the interests of justice.

N.C. Gen. Stat. § 36C-1-105 (2009).

The N.C. Trust Code thus recognizes that a trustee has a mandatory duty to act in good faith and that the terms of the trust cannot prevail over the power of the court to act in the interests of justice. The N.C. Trust Code also recognizes that a trustee generally has a duty to account for the trust property to the beneficiaries. Section 36C-8-813[, based on UTC § 813, page 675,] provides:

> (a) The trustee is under a duty to do all of the following:
>   (1) Provide reasonably complete and accurate information as to the nature and amount of the trust property, at reasonable intervals, to any qualified beneficiary who is a distributee or permissible distributee of trust income or principal.
>   (2) In response to a reasonable request of any qualified beneficiary:
>   a. Provide a copy of the trust instrument.
>   b. Provide reasonably complete and accurate information as to the nature and amount of the trust property.
>   c. Allow reasonable inspections of the subject matter of the trust and the accounts and other documents relating to the trust.

N.C. Gen. Stat. § 36C-8-813 (2009).[144]

The North Carolina Commentary on this statute explains that "[t]his section departs significantly from the Uniform Trust Code." N.C. Gen. Stat. § 36C-8-813 North Carolina Commentary (2009). The commentary goes on to state that the drafters omitted those portions of the Uniform Trust Code that would require the trustee to keep qualified beneficiaries reasonably informed about the trust administration. The drafters instead inserted the rule from section 173 of the Restatement (Second) of Trusts (1959) requiring the trustees to give beneficiaries certain information upon request

---

144. "Qualified beneficiary" is defined at N.C. Gen. Stat. § 36C-1-103(15). Defendants do not argue on appeal that Plaintiffs are not qualified beneficiaries. [Based on UTC § 103(13), N.C. Gen. Stat. § 36C-1-103(15) defines a "qualified beneficiary" to mean a "living beneficiary" who, "on the date the beneficiary's qualification is determined," (a) is "a distributee or permissible distributee of trust income or principal"; (b) would be "a distributee or permissible distributee of trust income or principal if the interests of the [current] distributees . . . terminated on that date without causing the trust to terminate"; or (c) would be "a distributee or permissible distributee of trust income or principal if the trust terminated on that date." — Eds.]

and to permit the beneficiaries to inspect trust documents. This is not, however, listed as a mandatory rule that prevails over the terms of the trust instrument. *See* N.C. Gen. Stat. § 36C-1-105. The commentary concludes from this that:

> The settlor is free to override the provisions of subsections (a) and (b) regarding the information to be furnished to the beneficiaries by directing the trustee not to provide a beneficiary with any of the information otherwise required. . . . The mandatory rules in Section 105(b)(8) and (9) of the Uniform Trust Code would have prevented a settlor from overriding the provisions of Section 813(a) and (b)(2) and (3). . . . The drafters omitted these mandatory rules and decided not to apply any such rule to the provisions of subsections (a) and (b) of this section.

N.C. Gen. Stat. § 36C-8-813 North Carolina Commentary (2009).

The North Carolina Comment to section 36-1-105 elaborates on the drafter's decision:

> Whether and to what extent the settlor by the terms of the trust could prevent a beneficiary from receiving trust information was one of the more debatable issues of the Uniform Trust Code. The drafters concluded that in North Carolina the settlor should have the right to override any duty to furnish information imposed by G.S. 36C-8-813(a) and (b). Accordingly, the drafters decided not to impose a mandatory rule with respect to these provisions. This is consistent with the statement in Taylor v. Nationsbank, 481 S.E.2d 358, 362 (1997) where the court said that "trust beneficiaries are entitled to view the trust instrument from which their interest is derived" so long as that right is not waived by the settlor through "an explicit provision in the trust to the contrary."

N.C. Gen. Stat. § 36C-1-105 North Carolina Commentary (2009). . . .

The trial court found that "[t]he legislative commentary to N.C. Gen. Stat. § 36C-8-813 supports the conclusion that a settlor . . . may override, or negate, the requirement of disclosure to the Beneficiary . . . by drafting a provision in the Trust Instrument providing that such disclosures are not required." . . . The validity of this conclusion with regard to Plaintiffs' request for discovery is now at issue.

The N.C. Trust Code commentary cites Taylor v. Nationsbank as supporting the assertion that the settlor is free to override the provisions of § 36C-8-813 regarding a trustee's duty to provide trust information to the beneficiary. It is true that *Taylor* held "that absent an explicit provision in the trust to the contrary, plaintiffs as trust beneficiaries are entitled to view the trust instrument from which their interest is derived." *Taylor*, 481 S.E.2d at 362. But this holding by its terms applies only to the beneficiaries' entitlement to view *the trust instrument.*

Taylor reached this result by applying the rule in comment c of section 173 of the Restatement (Second) of Trusts: "the beneficiary is always entitled to such information as is reasonably necessary to enable him to enforce his rights under the trust or to prevent or redress a breach of trust." The *Taylor* Court held that the information plaintiffs sought, namely documents relating to the trust instrument including prior revoked drafts of the trust, was not reasonably necessary to enforce the plaintiffs' rights. Such is not the case here.

Applying the same rule to the present circumstances, we conclude that the information sought by Plaintiffs is reasonably necessary to enable them to enforce their rights under the trust. N.C. Gen. Stat. § 36C-8-813 does not override the duty of the trustee to act in good faith, nor can it obstruct the power of the court to take such action as may be necessary in the interests of justice. N.C. Gen. Stat. § 36C-1-105(b)(2), (9) (2009). Such action would clearly encompass the power of the court to . . . prevent or redress a breach of trust, any contrary provision in the trust instrument notwithstanding. *See* Wachovia Bank v. Willis, 454 S.E.2d 293, 295 (N.C. App. 1995) ("It is a fundamental rule that, when interpreting wills and trust instruments, courts must give effect to the intent of the testator or settlor, *so long as such intent does not conflict with the demands of law and public policy.*") (emphasis added).

This result, required by the rule in *Taylor,* is consistent with how other jurisdictions have approached this question. "Any notion of a trust without accountability is a contradiction in terms." Guardianship and Conservatorship of Sim, 403 N.W.2d 721, 736 (Neb. 1987). As the Oregon Supreme Court stated:

> If a fiduciary can be rendered free from the duty of informing the beneficiary concerning matters of which he is entitled to know, and if he can also be made immune from liability resulting from his breach of the trust, equity has been rendered impotent. The present instance would be a humiliating example of the helplessness into which courts could be cast if a provision, placed in a trust instrument through a settlor's mistaken confidence in a trustee, could relieve the latter of a duty to account. Such a provision would be virtually a license to the trustee to convert the fund to his own use and thereby terminate the trust. . . .

> We are, however, prepared to adopt the point of view of the Restatement that a trust instrument may lawfully relieve a trustee from the necessity of keeping formal accounts. When such a provision is found in a trust instrument, a beneficiary can not expect to receive reports concerning the trust estate. *But even when such a provision is made a part of the trust instrument, the trustee will, nevertheless, be required in a suit for an accounting to show that he faithfully performed his duty and will be liable to whatever remedies may be appropriate if he was unfaithful to his trust.*

Wood v. Honeyman, 169 P.2d 131, 164-66 (Or. 1946) (emphasis added).

In this case, we hold that the trial court erred by relying on the commentary to our statutes, which is not binding. *See* State v. Rupe, 428 S.E.2d 480, 488 (N.C. App. 1993). Applying the rule in *Taylor,* we hold that the information sought by Plaintiffs was reasonably necessary to enforce their rights under the trust, and therefore could not legally be withheld, notwithstanding the terms of the trust instrument. Any other conclusion renders the trust unenforceable by those it was meant to benefit. We therefore reverse the trial court's grant of summary judgment and award of costs to Defendants. . . .

Reversed.

NOTES

1. Negating a Beneficiary's Information Rights?   Should a settlor be able to negate a beneficiary's right to information about a trust in which the beneficiary has an interest? Without awareness of the trust and basic information about its administration, can the beneficiary effectively protect her interest in the trust? On the other hand, if knowing about the trust would encourage the beneficiary to adopt a slothful or profligate lifestyle, might the beneficiary's interests be best served by concealing the existence of the trust?

Under traditional law, a settlor may limit a beneficiary's right to information, not eliminate it completely. As we have seen, as a fiduciary a trustee must always act in good faith in the interests of the beneficiaries. A beneficiary to whom the trustee owes fiduciary duty is always entitled to call the trustee to account in court (see page 621). Under traditional law, therefore, a settlor cannot override a beneficiary's right to information reasonably necessary for the protection of the beneficiary's interest in the trust.[145] The Restatement (Third) of Trusts is in accord:

> By the terms of the trust . . . the settlor can limit the trustee's duty to disclose trust provisions or information on a reasonable basis, in order, for example, to lessen the risk of unnecessary or unwarranted loss of privacy, or the risk of adverse effects upon youthful or troubled beneficiaries about whose motivation or responsibility the settlor has concerns. Even limitations of these types, however, cannot properly prevent beneficiaries . . . from requesting and receiving information to the extent currently necessary for the protection of their interests.[146]

2. The Uniform Trust Code.   Under UTC § 105(b)(8)-(9) as originally drafted, a settlor could prevent a beneficiary from learning of a trust's existence, but only until the beneficiary reached age 25. This rule came under intense criticism from practicing lawyers. Many states that enacted the UTC omitted these provisions, providing instead that a beneficiary could be kept in the dark until a later age or, in some states, indefinitely if there is a third party to whom information must be given and who has standing to bring suit against the trustee for breach of trust.[147] Why did so many practicing lawyers object to § 105(b)(8)-(9)? Is the naming of a trust director (see page 662) with rights to information and to enforce the trust an adequate alternative safeguard against abuse by the trustee?

In 2004, the Uniform Law Commission put UTC § 105(b)(8)-(9) in brackets (see page 676), signaling that uniformity is not expected. The version of the UTC at issue in *Wilson* did not include the bracketed language. The state commentary explained that those provisions were omitted with the intention of permitting a settlor to override the disclosure duties prescribed by § 813. Why, then, did the court not enforce the provision in the trust that purported to release the trustee from any obligation to account to a beneficiary or a court? Did the court's holding depend on the provisions of § 105, which the state legislature had enacted, that make mandatory "the duty of a trustee to act in good faith and in accordance with the terms and purposes of the trust and the interests of the beneficiaries" and "the power of the court to take such action and exercise such jurisdiction as may be necessary in the interests of justice"?

---

145. *See, e.g.,* Restatement (Second) of Trusts § 173 cmt. c (Am. Law Inst. 1959).

146. Restatement (Third) of Trusts § 82 cmt. e (Am. Law Inst. 2007).

147. *See, e.g.,* Jay A. Soled et al., Quiet Trusts: When Mum's the Word to Trust Beneficiaries, 40 Est. Plan. 13 (July 2013).

Is striking a part of the UTC's codification of the common law enough to reverse that law? Suppose a state enacted the UTC but omitted § 802, which codifies the duty of loyalty. Would not the common law duty of loyalty abide in such a state? UTC § 106 provides that "[t]he common law of trusts and principles of equity supplement this [Code], except to the extent modified by this [Code] or another statute of this State."

The duty of a trustee under UTC § 813(b)(1), page 675, to furnish a copy of the trust instrument to a beneficiary upon request is not mandatory under § 105. A settlor can therefore direct that a beneficiary be shown only those portions of the trust instrument that are relevant to the beneficiary's interest.[148] The Restatement provision quoted above is in accord.

3. Revocable Trust as Secret Will.   Once a will is offered for probate, it becomes part of the public record. The testator's heirs are normally entitled to notice of the will's filing and have standing to contest its validity. Journalists may examine the will, and the court file is open to the public. A revocable trust, by contrast, is not normally filed in court or otherwise made public before or after the settlor's death. Only a person with an interest in the trust is entitled to information about it — and only to the extent necessary to protect the person's interest.

Should a donor be able to make what is in effect a secret will by using a revocable trust? Under traditional law, if a person's heirs are not beneficiaries of the trust, they would have no right to information about it. A California statute takes the opposite view. It provides that when a revocable trust becomes irrevocable because of the death of the settlor, the trustee shall provide a complete copy of the trust to any beneficiary *or heir* of the settlor who requests it.[149] This statute unifies the notice rules for a revocable trust, which is in effect a nonprobate will, with the notice rules for a will.

2. Affirmative Disclosure

Statutes in many states, and UTC § 813(c), page 675, impose on a trustee a duty of periodic accounting to the beneficiaries regarding the administration of the trust. Even in the absence of such a statute, a beneficiary may compel a trustee to render an accounting.[150] In addition to these accounting obligations, the common law has come to recognize a duty to make affirmative disclosure to the beneficiaries of significant developments or intended transactions.

Allard v. Pacific National Bank
663 P.2d 104 (Wash. 1983)

DOLLIVER, J. Plaintiffs Freeman Allard and Evelyn Orkney are beneficiaries of trusts established by their parents, J.T. and Georgiana Stone. Defendant Pacific National

---

148. *See, e.g.,* Schrage v. Seberger Living Trust, 52 N.E.3d 45 (Ind. App. 2016).

149. *See* Cal. Prob. Code § 16061.5 (2016); *see also* Frances H. Foster, Trust Privacy, 93 Cornell L. Rev. 555 (2008).

150. *See* Restatement (Third) of Trusts § 83 cmt. b (Am. Law Inst. 2007).

Bank (Pacific Bank) is the trustee of the Stone trusts. Plaintiffs appeal a King County Superior Court decision dismissing their action against Pacific Bank for breach of its fiduciary duties as trustee of the Stone trusts. . . .

We conclude . . . that Pacific Bank breached its fiduciary duties regarding management of the Stone trusts. . . .

J.T. and Georgiana Stone, both deceased, established trusts in their wills conveying their property upon their deaths to Pacific Bank to be held for their children and the issue of their children. The Stones' children, Evelyn Orkney and Freeman Allard, are life income beneficiaries of the Stone trusts. Upon the death of either life income beneficiary, the trustee is to pay the income from the trust to the issue of the deceased beneficiary. When all the children of the deceased beneficiary reach the age of 21 years, the trusts direct the trustee to distribute the trust corpus equally among the issue of that beneficiary.

In 1978 the sole asset of the Stone trusts was a fee interest in a quarter block located on the northwest corner of Third Avenue and Columbia Street in downtown Seattle. The trust provisions of the wills gave Pacific Bank "full power to . . . manage, improve, sell, lease, mortgage, pledge, encumber, and exchange the whole or any part of the assets of [the] trust estate." . . .

The Third and Columbia property was subject to a 99-year lease, entered into by the Stones in 1952 with Seattle-First National Bank (Seafirst Bank). The lease contained no rental escalation provision and the rental rate was to remain the same for the entire 99-year term of the lease. The right of first refusal to purchase the lessor's interest in the property was given to the lessee. The lease also contained several restrictive provisions. One paragraph required any repair, reconstruction,

The northwest corner of Third Avenue and Columbia Street (2013)

or replacement of buildings on the property by the lessee to be completed within 8 months from the date the original building was damaged or destroyed "from any cause whatsoever." Another paragraph provided that, upon termination of lease, the lessee had the option either to surrender possession of all improvements or to remove the improvements. The lease prohibited, without the lessor's consent, any encumbrance which would have priority over the lessor in case of the lessee's insolvency.

In June 1977 Seafirst Bank assigned its leasehold interest in the Third and Columbia property to the City Credit Union of Seattle (Credit Union). Eight months later, on February 14, 1978, Credit Union offered to purchase the property from Pacific Bank for $139,900. On April 25, 1978, Pacific Bank informed Credit Union it was interested in selling the property, but demanded at least $200,000. In early June 1978, Credit Union offered $200,000 for the Third and Columbia property. Pacific Bank accepted Credit Union's offer, and deeded the property to Credit Union on August 17, 1978. On September 26, 1978, Pacific Bank informed Freeman Allard and Evelyn Orkney of the sale to Credit Union.

On May 1, 1979, plaintiffs commenced the present action against Pacific Bank for breach of its fiduciary duties regarding management of the Stone trusts, against Credit Union and Seafirst Bank for participation in the alleged breach, and against Credit Union for conversion. Plaintiffs' complaint requested money damages from Pacific Bank, Credit Union, and Seafirst Bank. The complaint also requested the imposition of a constructive trust on the Third and Columbia property and the removal of Pacific Bank as trustee. . . .

Defendant contends it had full authority under the trust instrument to exercise its own judgment and impartial discretion in deciding how to invest the trust assets and a duty to use reasonable care and skill to make the trust property productive. It further contends the sale of the property was conducted in good faith and with honest judgment. Plaintiffs assert this discretion was limited by its fiduciary duties and that defendant in its management of the trusts breached its fiduciary duty.

Plaintiffs' argument regarding Pacific Bank's alleged breach of its fiduciary duties is twofold. First, Pacific Bank had a duty to inform them of the sale of the Third and Columbia property. Second, Pacific Bank breached its fiduciary duties by failing either to obtain an independent appraisal of the Third and Columbia property or to place the property on the open market prior to selling it to Seattle Credit Union. We agree with plaintiffs' position in both instances and hold defendant breached its fiduciary duty in its management of the trusts. . . .

The Stone trusts gave Pacific Bank "full power to . . . manage, improve, sell, lease, mortgage, pledge, encumber, and exchange the whole or any part of the assets of [the] trust estate." Under such an agreement, the trustee is not required to secure the consent of trust beneficiaries before selling trust assets. 3 A. Scott, Trusts § 190.5 (3d ed. 1967). The trustee owes to the beneficiaries, however, the highest degree of good faith, care, loyalty, and integrity. Esmieu v. Schrag, 563 P.2d 203, 207 (Wash. 1977).

Pacific Bank claims it was obligated to sell the property to Credit Union since Credit Union, as assignee of the lease agreement with Seafirst Bank, had a right of first refusal to purchase the property. Since it did not need to obtain the consent of the beneficiaries before selling trust assets, Pacific Bank argues it also was not required to inform the beneficiaries of the sale. We disagree. The beneficiaries could have offered to purchase the property at a higher price than the offer by Credit Union, thereby forcing Credit Union to pay a higher price to exercise its right of first refusal as assignee of the lease agreement. Furthermore, letters from the beneficiaries to Pacific Bank indicated their desire to retain the Third and Columbia property. While the beneficiaries could not have prevented Pacific Bank from selling the property, they presumably could have outbid Credit Union for the property. This opportunity should have been afforded to them.

On a previous occasion, we ruled the trustee's fiduciary duty includes the responsibility to inform the beneficiaries fully of all facts which would aid them in protecting their interests. Esmieu v. Schrag, supra. We adhere to the view expressed in *Esmieu*. That the settlor has created a trust and thus required the beneficiaries to enjoy their property interests indirectly does not imply the beneficiaries are to be kept in ignorance of the trust, the nature of the trust property, and the details of its administration. If the beneficiaries are able to hold the trustee to proper standards of care and honesty and procure the benefits to which they are entitled, they must know of what the trust property consists and how it is being managed.

The duty to provide information is often performed by corporate trustees by rendering periodic statements to the beneficiaries, usually in the form of copies of the ledger sheets concerning the trust. For example, such condensed explanations of recent transactions may be mailed to the beneficiaries annually, semiannually, or quarterly. Ordinarily, periodic statements are sufficient to satisfy a trustee's duty to beneficiaries of transactions affecting the trust property. . . .

The trustee must inform beneficiaries, however, of all material facts in connection with a nonroutine transaction which significantly affects the trust estate and the interests of the beneficiaries prior to the transaction taking place. The duty to inform is particularly required in this case where the only asset of the trusts was the property on the corner of Third and Columbia. Under the circumstances found in this case failure to inform was an egregious breach of fiduciary duty and defies the course of conduct any reasonable person would take, much less a prudent investor.

We also conclude Pacific Bank breached its fiduciary duties regarding management of the Stone trusts by failing to obtain the best possible price for the Third and Columbia property. Pacific Bank made no attempt to obtain a more favorable price for the property from Credit Union by, for example, negotiating to cancel the restrictive provisions in the lease originally negotiated with Seafirst Bank. The bank neither offered the property for sale on the open market, nor did it obtain an independent, outside appraisal of the Third and Columbia property to determine its fair market value. . . .

We agree with the Oregon Court of Appeals in Hatcher v. United States Nat'l Bank, 643 P.2d 359 (Or. App. 1982), that a trustee may determine the best possible price for trust property either by obtaining an independent appraisal of the property or by "testing the market" to determine what a willing buyer would pay. The record discloses none of these actions were taken by the defendant. By its failure to obtain the best possible price for the Third and Columbia property, defendant breached its fiduciary duty as the prudent manager of the trusts. . . .

We hold defendant breached its fiduciary duty and reverse the trial court on this issue. . . . The case is remanded for a determination of the damages caused to plaintiffs by defendant's breach of its fiduciary duties as trustee of the Stone trusts and a determination of the amount of attorney fees to be awarded plaintiffs from the trustee individually.

NOTE

A Nonroutine Transaction.   In *Allard*, the court held that the trustee was under a duty to make an affirmative disclosure to the beneficiaries of its intention to undertake a "nonroutine" transaction. *Allard* is the leading case on this duty. But what makes a transaction not routine? How is a trustee to know if an intended transaction or other development is significant enough to require affirmative disclosure? The Restatement

(Third) of Trusts offers "some generalizations" by way of examples of significant matters warranting affirmative disclosure:

> significant changes in trustee circumstances, including changes in the identities, number, or roles of trustees or in methods of determining trustee compensation; decisions regarding delegation of important fiduciary responsibilities or significant changes in arrangements for delegation; important adjustments being considered in investment or other management strategies; significant actions under consideration involving hard-to-value assets or special sensitivity to beneficiaries (such as liquidating or selling shares of a closely held business or a sale or long-term lease of a major real-estate holding); [and] plans being made for distribution on termination or partial termination (or perhaps subdivision) of the trust.[151]

Affirmative disclosure of such matters puts the beneficiaries on notice, giving them an opportunity to object or otherwise protect their interests, for example by seeking a court order enjoining the trustee from the proposed course of action or other relief to protect their interests.

3. Accountings and Repose

a. Judicial Accountings

A trustee is not liable to a beneficiary for a breach of trust if the facts of the breach are fairly disclosed in a formal accounting of the administration of the trust filed with the court, notice of the accounting is properly served on the beneficiary, and the beneficiary does not timely object. In effect, a judicial accounting by a trustee is an inverted suit for breach of trust. A beneficiary who does not object is barred by res judicata from later bringing a claim against the trustee that could have been brought in the accounting proceeding. This rule, which offers the trustee repose, provides a carrot to encourage the trustee to make regular and substantial accountings to the beneficiary. Res judicata will not protect a trustee, however, if the facts underlying a subsequent claim by the beneficiary were not adequately disclosed in the accounting.

National Academy of Sciences v. Cambridge Trust Co.
346 N.E.2d 879 (Mass. 1976)

REARDON, J. This matter is before us for further appellate review, the Appeals Court having promulgated an opinion.

The facts which give rise to the case are essentially as follows. Leonard T. Troland died a resident of Cambridge in 1932 survived by his widow, Florence R. Troland. By his will executed in April, 1931, he left all of his real and personal property to be held in trust by the Cambridge Trust Company (bank) with the net income of the trust, after expenses, "to be paid to, or deposited to the account of [his wife], Florence R. Troland" during her lifetime so long as she remained unmarried. He further provided that

---

151. Id. § 82 cmt. d.

[k]nowing my wife, Florence's, generosity and unselfishness as I do, I wish to record it as my intention that she should not devote any major portion of her income under the provisions of this will, to the support or for the benefit of people other than herself. It is particularly contrary to my will that any part of the principal or income of my estate should revert to members of my wife's family, other than herself, and I instruct the trustees to bear this point definitely in mind in making decisions under any of the options of this will.

The testator went on to provide in part that on his wife's death or second marriage the bank would transfer the trusteeship to The National Research Council of Washington, D.C., which the petition alleged to be an agency of the National Academy of Sciences (academy), to constitute a trust to be known as the Troland Foundation for Research in Psychophysics. . . .

The will was allowed, the trust was established as provided by the testator, and the bank paid the income thereof to the widow until her death in 1967. During the period from 1932 to 1945 the widow provided eighteen different mailing addresses for income checks to be transmitted to her by the bank. On February 13, 1945, she married Edward D. Flynn in West Palm Beach, Florida, and failed to advise the bank of her remarriage. Following her remarriage she lived in Perth Amboy, New Jersey. Commencing on April 14, 1944, she directed the bank to forward all her monthly checks to her in care of Kenneth D. Custance, her brother-in-law through marriage to her sister. Over the years these checks were forwarded to two Boston addresses and were made payable to "Florence R. Troland." Custance in turn forwarded the checks to Florence R. Flynn who indorsed them in blank "Florence R. Troland" and returned them to Custance who also indorsed them prior to depositing them in bank accounts in his name maintained at the State Street Bank and Trust Company in Boston and the National Bank of Wareham, Massachusetts. After Florence R. Flynn's death on December 25, 1967, the bank for the first time learned of her remarriage.[152] Throughout her second marriage Florence R. Flynn lived with her husband who was able to provide

---

152. A letter from Thomas Quarles, Jr., a lawyer in Manchester, New Hampshire, who came upon this case while a law student, discloses some interesting further information:

My father, Thomas Quarles, Sr., was the trust officer at the Cambridge Trust Company in charge of the Troland trust at the time of Florence Troland's death in 1967. . . .

Florence Troland was aware of the limitation in the trust that cut off her interest if she remarried. So was her brother-in-law, Kenneth Custance. Nevertheless, after her remarriage in 1945, he convinced her to keep quiet and to endorse her trust income check over to him. He told her that the money was needed to support a succession of spiritualist churches that he headed in the Onset, Massachusetts area. When Florence died in 1967, Kenneth apparently felt guilty about the years of fraud. At her funeral, he gave Florence's latest trust check to her surviving husband, who contacted the Cambridge Trust Company asking what he should do with it. It was only at that point that the Bank realized that through Mrs. Troland and Mr. Custance's fraud it had paid the wrong beneficiary for 22 years. Fortunately, my father kept his job. He had only been with the Bank for a few years and had only recently taken over the Troland trust.

Letter from Thomas Quarles, Jr., to Jesse Dukeminier, dated Dec. 1, 1986.—Eds.

Profile in Optics: Leonard Thompson Troland

By John N. Howard

Leonard Thompson Troland was…born April 26, 1889, in Norwalk, Conn., U.S.A. He graduated in 1912 from the Massachusetts Institute of Technology with a degree in biochemistry. He then studied psychology at Harvard, where he obtained a Ph.D. in 1915.…

When he returned to Harvard in 1916, one of his first efforts in the psychology laboratory was to investigate mental telepathy. (And he found no evidence that such a phenomenon existed.) In 1917, in collaboration with D.F. Comstock of MIT, he wrote a book on the nature of matter and electricity.…

During World War I, Troland worked for the Navy on the development of acoustical apparatus for detecting submarines. His scientific interests were numerous and varied, ranging from physiology to photography to psychology. He even attempted to develop an analytical framework for psychical research. As a biochemist, he put forward in 1914 one of the earliest theories describing the chemical origin of life on Earth. He suggested that autocatalytic enzymes (enzymes capable of stimulating the production of more of the same enzymes) produced in the Earth's primordial seas might be considered the earliest "primitive living bodies."…

Troland was a member of committees of the National Research Council on vision and aviation psychology, and, in 1922, he published a monograph, On the Present Status of Visual Science. At Harvard, he gave advanced courses in psychology, and he is said to have been one of the earliest to use the term "motivation" as a psychological mechanism. He followed up his 1926 book The Mystery of Mind with Fundamentals in Human Motivation in 1928.

By the late 1920s, he had published about 40 articles in scientific journals, mostly in vision and psychology, in addition to writing long chapters in several handbooks of psychology. Troland was also active in several learned societies.

With his many scientific papers and books, as well as his advanced lectures on psychology at Harvard, Troland was a busy man. And so far I've only described half of his interests and activities: From 1918 until 1925, he was also active in the Boston engineering firm of Kalmus, Comstock and Westcott, where he worked in color photography.

Troland not only developed and improved the old two-color process of color photography, but he invented and perfected the modern multicolor process in all its details. At the same time, he was chief engineer of the Technicolor Motion Picture Corporation of California, which maintained a Boston office chiefly to use Troland's services without compelling him to sever his connection with Harvard. In 1925, he was made director of research of Technicolor.

Leonard T. Troland

He devised and patented nearly all the photographic and mechanical apparatus for color motion pictures. Toward the end of 1929, the Boston office of the Technicolor Corporation was closed, and Troland decided, with reluctance, to resign his chair at Harvard so he could move to California and be nearer to this organization.

At this time (1930), he must have been very overworked. He had just published two large volumes of his work, The Principles of Psychophysiology—volume one on perception and problems of psychology (1929) and volume two on sensation (1930). By 1932, he was finishing the third volume, on cerebration and action. He was also hard at work on the fourth and final volume of this series, on the theory of mind and matter, which was not published until the mid-1930s.…

But under the strain of his incessant labors, his once-robust health gave way. He suffered from dizzy spells and occasional fainting, and his doctor advised him to take a break and rest a while. So he took a vacation to Hollywood with his wife.

On a nice day in late May 1932, he went with a friend on a hiking trip along the crest of Mount Wilson. Near the summit, he posed for a picture at the edge of a cliff, possibly with the observatory visible in the background. His friend looked through the viewfinder of his Kodak as he adjusted the focus, when, suddenly, Troland disappeared. Perhaps he had had another dizzy spell. His friend looked on in horror as Troland slipped over the edge and fell 250 feet to his death at the bottom of the rocky ravine below. He was just 43 years old.

Source: Optics & Photonics (June 2008).

support for her and who, although aware that she was receiving payments from the trust, was ignorant of the limitation on her rights to receive such payments. . . . The total of all checks collected by Florence R. Flynn following her marriage in 1945 up to the date of her death is $106,013.41. The twelfth through thirty-third accounts of the bank covering that period between her remarriage and October 8, 1966, were presented to the Probate Court for Middlesex County in separate proceedings and allowed. The academy had formal notice prior to the presentation of the twelfth through fourteenth accounts and the eighteenth through thirty-third accounts, and with respect to the fifteenth through seventeenth accounts assented in writing to their allowance. The academy, unaware of the widow's remarriage, did not challenge any of the accounts and they were duly allowed.

The petition brought in the Probate Court by the academy seeks revocation of the seven decrees allowing the twelfth through thirty-third accounts of the bank, the excision from those accounts of "all entries purporting to evidence distributions to or for the benefit of 'Florence R. Troland' . . . subsequent to February 13, 1945," the restoration by the bank to the trust of the amounts of those distributions with interest at the rate of six percent, a final account reflecting the repayments and adjustments, [and] appointment of the academy as trustee. . . .

Following hearing a judge of the Probate Court revoked the seven decrees allowing the twelfth through thirty-third accounts, ordered restoration to the trust of $114,314.18, representing amounts erroneously distributed to Florence R. Flynn plus Massachusetts income taxes paid on those amounts from trust funds, together with interest thereon in the sum of $104,847.17 through March 31, 1973, and interest thereafter at the rate of six percent per annum to the date of restoration in full. . . .

The issues before us have to do with the power of the Probate Court judge to order the revocation of the decrees allowing the twelfth through thirty-third accounts, and the propriety of charging the bank for the amounts erroneously disbursed. . . .

The bank recited in the heading of each of the challenged accounts that the trust was "for the benefit of Florence R. Troland," and stated in schedule E of each account (in the first four accounts specifically as "Distributions to Beneficiary") that monthly payments of $225 or more were made to "Florence R. Troland." The Appeals Court held that these recitals and statements "constituted a continuing representation by the bank to the academy and to the court that the widow remained 'Florence R. Troland' despite her (then unknown) remarriage to Flynn, and that she remained the sole income beneficiary of the trust." . . . The court further held that those representations were technically fraudulent in that "[t]hey were made as of the bank's own knowledge when the bank had no such knowledge and had made absolutely no effort to obtain it." . . . With these views we find ourselves substantially in accord.

The doctrine of constructive or technical fraud in this Commonwealth is of venerable origin. As we pointed out in Powell v. Rasmussen, 243 N.E.2d 167 (Mass. 1969), the doctrine here was developed in two opinions by Chief Justice Shaw. In Hazard v. Irwin, 18 Pick. 95, 109 (1836), it was defined in the following terms: "[W]here the subject matter is one of fact, in respect to which a person can have precise and accurate knowledge, and . . . he speaks as of his own knowledge, and has no such knowledge, his affirmation is essentially false." This rule was reiterated by Chief Justice Shaw in Page

v. Bent, 2 Met. 371, 374 (1841): "The principle is well settled, that if a person make[s] a representation of a fact, as of his own knowledge, in relation to a subject matter susceptible of knowledge, and such representation is not true; if the party to whom it is made relies and acts upon it, as true, and sustains damage by it, it is fraud and deceit, for which the party making it is responsible." In this case the marital status of Mrs. Troland/Flynn was a fact susceptible of precise knowledge, the bank made representations concerning this fact of its own knowledge when it had no such knowledge, and the academy to whom the representations were made relied on them to its detriment. While this standard of fraud in law has been developed primarily in the context of actions seeking rescission of contracts and of tort actions for deceit, we have indicated in past decisions that an analogous standard might be applicable to misrepresentations in the accounts of fiduciaries. See Greene v. Springfield Safe Deposit & Trust Co., 3 N.E.2d 254 (Mass. 1936); Welch v. Flory, 200 N.E. 900 (Mass. 1936); Brigham v. Morgan, 69 N.E. 418 (Mass. 1904).

We hold today that "fraud" as used in G.L. c. 206, § 24, contemplates this standard of constructive fraud at least to the extent that the fiduciary has made no reasonable efforts to ascertain the true state of the facts it has misrepresented in the accounts. This rule is not a strict liability standard, nor does it make a trustee an insurer against the active fraud of all parties dealing with the trust. Entries in the accounts honestly made, after reasonable efforts to determine the truth or falsity of the representations therein have failed through no fault of the trustee, will not be deemed fraudulent or provide grounds for reopening otherwise properly allowed accounts. However, in the instant case the probate judge found that the bank, through the twenty-two years covered by the disputed accounts, exerted "no effort at all . . . to ascertain if Florence R. Troland had remarried even to the extent of annually requesting a statement or certificate from her to that effect" and that "in administering the trust acted primarily in a ministerial manner and in disregard of its duties as a trustee to protect the terms of the trust." In these circumstances we have little trouble in concluding that the bank's representations as to the marital status of the testator's widow fully justified the reopening of the accounts.

Cases relied on by the bank in which this court refused to allow previously allowed accounts to be reopened are distinguishable in that either they did not involve representations of fact susceptible of precise knowledge but rather questions of judgment and discretion as to matters fully and frankly disclosed in the accounts . . . or that the alleged wrongful acts or mistakes of the trustee were discernible from an examination of the accounts, the trust documents and the law. . . . We adhere to our decisions that it is the duty of beneficiaries "to study the account presented to the Probate Court by the trustee, and to make their objections at the hearing." Greene v. Springfield Safe Deposit & Trust Co., supra, 3 N.E.2d at 257. However, in this case the fact of the widow's remarriage was not discernible from the most scrupulous examination of the accounts, the trust documents and the relevant law, and the bank cannot avoid responsibility here for its misrepresentations by alleging a breach of duty on the part of the academy.

As to the propriety of surcharging the bank for the amounts erroneously disbursed, when a trustee makes payment to a person other than the beneficiary entitled to receive the money, he is liable to the proper beneficiary to make restitution unless the payment was authorized by a proper court. . . . Since, as we have held the decrees allowing the twelfth through thirty-third accounts were revoked properly, the bank thus became liable to the academy to restore to the trust corpus the payments it made to Mrs. Troland/Flynn when she was not entitled to receive them. In addition to the amounts erroneously disbursed, the bank was also properly charged by the Probate Court judge with simple interest on those payments at the legal rate of six percent per annum. . . .

[T]he decree is affirmed.

NOTE

Liability for Distribution to Ineligible Person.   Under traditional law, a trustee was liable for a mistaken delivery of trust property to an ineligible person even if "[t]he trustee . . . reasonably believe[d] that the person" was a proper recipient.[153] Prudence was not a defense. More recent authority has softened this rule, giving the trustee a defense of "diligent, good-faith efforts or . . . reasonable reliance" on the terms of the trust.[154] In line with this trend, and to encourage trustees to make distributions expeditiously, UTC § 1007 (2000) provides:

> If the happening of an event, including marriage, divorce, performance of educational requirements, or death, affects the administration or distribution of a trust, a trustee who has exercised reasonable care to ascertain the happening of the event is not liable for a loss resulting from the trustee's lack of knowledge.

In *National Academy of Sciences*, the trustee was not protected against liability for the mistaken distributions because the accountings implicitly represented that the trustee had undertaken reasonable care in ascertaining whether Mrs. Troland had remarried. As under UPIA § 2(d), page 625, a trustee is under a duty to "make a reasonable effort to verify facts relevant to the . . . management of trust assets." What steps should the trustee have taken before making a distribution to Mrs. Troland? What would be a "reasonable effort to verify" her marital status?

b. Informal Accountings and Release

A formal judicial accounting, which is a court proceeding, is expensive. Typically the trustee will need to hire a lawyer and to prepare detailed accounting statements in the form that the local court requires. To hold down these costs, a settlor will sometimes provide that an *informal* (or *nonjudicial*) *accounting* to a beneficiary shall have the same effect as a judicial accounting if the beneficiary does not object to the informal accounting within a certain period of time. Here is a formbook example:

> A trustee . . . shall render an account of trust receipts and disbursements and a statement of assets at least annually to each beneficiary then entitled to receive or receiving the income from the trust and, in addition, to any other beneficiaries who are entitled to receive accounts under applicable state law. An account is

---

153. Restatement (Second) of Trusts § 226 cmt. b (Am. Law Inst. 1959).
154. Restatement (Third) of Trusts § 76 cmt. f (Am. Law Inst. 2007).

binding on each beneficiary who receives it and on all persons claiming by or through the beneficiary, and the trustee is released, as to all matters stated in the account or shown by it, unless the beneficiary commences a judicial proceeding to assert a claim within one year after the mailing or other delivery of the account.[155]

Under traditional law, the enforceability of an informal accounting provision was uncertain. Recall, for example, that in Marsman v. Nasca, page 612, the court included a footnote quoting a treatise edited by James F. Farr, the trustee, for the proposition that a nonjudicial accounting "is an unsafe procedure for the trustee." In that case the court declined to bind the beneficiary to his failure to object to the trustee's informal accountings. Modern courts, by contrast, are more receptive to an informal accounting provision, and many states permit an informal accounting by default even without an authorizing provision in the terms of the trust.

Under UTC § 813(c), page 675, a trustee is required to send the beneficiaries an annual "report" of the administration of the trust. The comment explains that § 813 uses "the term 'report' instead of 'accounting' . . . to negate any inference that the report must be prepared in any particular format or with a high degree of formality." For many trusts, this duty may be satisfied by giving "the beneficiaries . . . copies of the trust's income tax returns and monthly brokerage account statements." All that is essential is that "the report provides the beneficiaries with the information necessary to protect their interests."[156] Under UTC § 1005(a) (2000), a beneficiary who receives such a report has one year to object, otherwise the trustee obtains repose as to all matters fairly disclosed in the report.

A more difficult question is presented by a trust provision that purports to bind one beneficiary to an informal accounting assented to by another beneficiary. In Vena v. Vena, 899 N.E.2d 522 (Ill. App. 2008), the court held that a provision authorizing release of the trustee by a majority of the income beneficiaries was unenforceable as to the beneficiaries who did not give assent. In Jacob v. Davis, 738 A.2d 904 (Md. App. 1999), a remainder beneficiary petitioned for an accounting. The beneficiary wanted to examine whether the trustees had impermissibly favored the income beneficiaries. The trust instrument excused the trustee from judicial accountings and provided that an informal account rendered to the adult income beneficiaries, if approved in writing by those beneficiaries, "shall be a complete discharge to my Trustee with respect to all matters set forth in the account as fully and to the same extent as though the account had been judicially settled." The court granted the remainder beneficiary's petition in spite of this provision.

The reasoning of cases such as in Vena and Jacob is sharply criticized by Professor David Westfall. He argues that if an income beneficiary can be given a power of appointment that diminishes or destroys the remainder, there is no reason not to give effect to a clause permitting the income beneficiary to absolve the trustee from further accountability.[157] Do you find Westfall's argument compelling? Is there a meaningful

---

155. Northern Trust, Will and Trust Forms 201-19 (2004).

156. *Compare* Wells Fargo Bank, N.A. v. Cook, 775 S.E.2d 199 (Ga. App. 2015) (adequate report), *with* In re Rolf H. Brennemann Testamentary Trust, 849 N.W.2d 458 (Neb. 2014) (inadequate report).

157. *See* David Westfall, Nonjudicial Settlement of Trustees' Accounts, 71 Harv. L. Rev. 40 (1957).

difference between giving an income beneficiary a power of appointment over the remainder and a power to release the trustee from liability in administering the trust?

The Restatement (Third) of Trusts takes the position that a provision "that the trustee need only account or submit reports to a designated person . . . and that the approval of the trustee's account or report by that person shall discharge the trustee from liability" is effective if "(i) the other person in giving approval acts neither in bad faith nor in casual disregard of the interests or rights of the nonassenting beneficiaries and (ii) the accounting appropriately discloses material issues about the trustee's conduct."[158] The designated person's approval of an informal accounting is subject to judicial review for abuse.

The draft Uniform Directed Trust Act (UDTA) at year-end 2016, page 665, would enforce a provision authorizing a person to approve a trustee's report or accounting. But the person holding this power would be a trust director subject to fiduciary duty to the beneficiaries in the exercise of that power. Moreover, a beneficiary is a trust director under the draft UDTA to the extent that the beneficiary has a power of direction that affects the interest of another beneficiary. Thus, under the draft UDTA, one of several beneficiaries may be empowered to approve an informal accounting by a trustee, releasing the trustee from liability to the other beneficiaries. However, the beneficiary who approves the account is subject to fiduciary duties of loyalty and prudence to the other beneficiaries in approving (or refusing to approve) that accounting.

A similar set of issues pertains to a *release* from a beneficiary. As we have seen, because a trustee stands in a fiduciary relationship with the beneficiaries, a release from liability given by a beneficiary to a trustee is enforceable only if the beneficiary knew of her rights and of the material facts (see page 654). Suppose *O* transfers property to *X* in trust to pay the income to *A* for life, remainder to *A*'s children. *A* is now 42 years old, is not married, and has no descendants. To hold down expenses, *A* seeks to have the trustee account nonjudicially to her, agreeing to indemnify the trustee against any objections to its administration that might subsequently be made by a remainderperson. Should the trustee agree to this?

---

158. Restatement (Third) of Trusts § 83 cmt. d (Am. Law Inst. 2007).

CHAPTER 10

TRUSTS: ALIENATION
AND MODIFICATION

> The law, in its majestic equality, forbids the rich as well as the poor
> to sleep under bridges, to beg in the streets, and to steal bread.
>
> ANATOLE FRANCE
> Le Lys Rouge ch. 7 (1894)

B Y MAKING A GIFT IN TRUST rather than outright, a settlor ensures that the property will be managed and distributed in accordance with his wishes as expressed in the terms of the trust in spite of any contrary wishes of the beneficiaries. But are there limits on a settlor's freedom of disposition by way of a trust? In this chapter, we consider three limits within the law of trusts on freedom of disposition and therefore the reach of the dead hand.

The first limit concerns the extent to which a settlor may impose a *restraint on alienation* of a beneficial interest. In nearly all common law jurisdictions, a beneficiary of a *discretionary trust* cannot alienate his beneficial interest. And while a creditor of the beneficiary can attach future distributions, the creditor cannot compel the trustee to make a distribution. But American law goes further. Under American law, a creditor of a *spendthrift trust* beneficiary cannot attach any distributions to the beneficiary, and this is true even if the beneficiary has a current right to a mandatory distribution. With the spendthrift trust now permitted in all states, the policy debate has shifted to the question of whether to make exceptions for certain kinds of creditors, such as spouses and children or tort victims. Another question, put into issue by novel legislation in a growing number of domestic and offshore jurisdictions, is whether to allow creditors of the settlor recourse against a *self-settled asset protection trust* in which the settlor retains a beneficial interest.

The second limit concerns the power of a court to *modify* or *terminate* a trust without the consent of the settlor. American law has traditionally recognized only two grounds for modifying or terminating a trust without the settlor's consent: (1) by consent of all the beneficiaries if the modification or termination is not contrary to a *material purpose* of the settlor (the *Claflin* doctrine), and (2) *changed circumstances* not anticipated by the settlor that would defeat or substantially impair the accomplishment of the purposes of the trust (the *equitable deviation* doctrine). Recent law reform has somewhat liberalized these rules, though in most states they remain tied to the probable intent of the settlor. By contrast, more than half the states have come to recognize *trust decanting*, which is less obviously limited by the settlor's actual or probable intent. In a decanting, a trustee who has a discretionary power to distribute the trust property uses that power to distribute the property to a new trust with revised terms.

The third limit concerns *trustee removal*. Under traditional law, a court could remove a trustee only for cause as a remedy for breach of trust. Under modern law, trustee removal is more readily available. The Uniform Trust Code, for example, authorizes removal of a trustee by consent of all the beneficiaries if removal would be in the best interests of the beneficiaries and not contrary to a material purpose of the settlor. The hard policy question is how to give the trustee enough leeway to carry out the settlor's wishes without protecting lackadaisical or ineffective administration.

We begin in Section A by considering the rules governing alienation of a beneficial interest and the extent to which a creditor of a beneficiary may attach the beneficiary's interest in the trust. In Section B, we consider modification and termination of trusts, comparing traditional American law to that in the British Commonwealth. We also consider more recent developments such as trust decanting. Finally, in Section C, we consider trustee removal and the trend toward permitting removal without cause.

A. ALIENATION OF THE BENEFICIAL INTEREST

The rich have—at least in Anglo-American history—continually sought ways to secure their wealth to their children and grandchildren against the accidents of fortune, bad management, and irresponsible spending. The fee tail and, later, the strict settlement were the devices used in medieval and early modern England to keep land in the family. Discretionary and spendthrift trusts are their ideological descendants. Both make property available to a beneficiary but not to the beneficiary's creditors. In this section, we explore the use of trusts in asset protection, focusing on the rights of a beneficiary's creditors to obtain recourse against the beneficiary's interest in (1) a *discretionary trust*, (2) a *spendthrift trust*, and (3) a *self-settled asset protection trust*.

1. Discretionary Trusts

A common reason for creating a *discretionary trust* is to preserve flexibility in distributions over time. A trustee may be given discretion over when, to whom, or in what amount to make a distribution. The trustee must exercise this discretion in accordance with the trustee's fiduciary duties (see Chapter 9 at page 611).

Another common reason for creating a discretionary trust is asset protection. Generally speaking, a creditor of a discretionary trust beneficiary has little recourse against the beneficiary's interest in the trust, and the beneficiary cannot voluntarily alienate his interest. In Marsman v. Nasca, page 612, an ordinary creditor of Cappy, the life beneficiary with a discretionary interest in the trust principal, would not have been able to compel Farr, the trustee, to make a distribution of principal to Cappy or a payment from principal to the creditor. The creditor would have had no such recourse even if under the circumstances it would have been an abuse of discretion for Farr not to make a distribution to Cappy.

Traditional law recognizes two kinds of discretionary trusts: a *pure discretionary trust*, in which the trustee has absolute discretion over distributions to the beneficiary, and a *support trust*, in which the trustee is required to make distributions as necessary for the beneficiary's education or support. A third possibility, not formally recognized as a separate category by traditional law but nonetheless commonly used in practice, is a trust in which absolute discretion is combined with a distribution standard. Such a trust, an example of which was at issue in *Marsman*, has been aptly dubbed a *discretionary support trust*.[1]

a. Pure Discretionary Trust

Under traditional law, a creditor of a beneficiary of a *pure discretionary trust* has no recourse against the beneficiary's interest in the trust. Nor can the beneficiary voluntarily alienate her beneficial interest. A creditor or transferee cannot, by judicial order, compel the trustee to pay him. The theory was that the beneficiary does not have a property interest to transfer or for a creditor to attach. The Restatement (Second) of Trusts explains:

> In a discretionary trust it is the nature of the beneficiary's interest . . . which prevents the transfer of the beneficiary's interest. The . . . transferee or creditor cannot compel the trustee to pay anything to him because the beneficiary could not compel payment to himself or application for his own benefit.[2]

The difficulty with this theory is that it is not true. A discretionary beneficiary who is eligible for a distribution, even if not presently entitled to one, has standing to sue the trustee for redress of a breach of trust that affects trust property that could be distributed to the beneficiary.[3] Even if a trustee has sole, absolute, or uncontrolled discretion over distributions, a beneficiary may be entitled to an order directing the trustee to make a distribution that has been unreasonably or abusively withheld (see Chapter 9 at page 619).

In truth, the rule that a creditor of a discretionary trust beneficiary cannot compel a distribution, even if the beneficiary could, is a policy choice. In Scanlan v. Eisenberg, 669 F.3d 838 (7th Cir. 2012), the court put the point thus:

> It is true that . . . , in some cases, creditors are prevented from attaching the assets of a discretionary trust and have no remedy against the trustee until the trustee distributes the property. . . . These rules, however, are the result of underlying principles and policy considerations involving restraints on involuntary alienation. Those concerns . . . are distinct from the . . . beneficiary's right to hold trustees accountable

---

1. *See* Evelyn Ginsberg Abravanel, Discretionary Support Trusts, 68 Iowa L. Rev. 273 (1983).
2. Restatement (Second) of Trusts § 155 cmt. b (Am. Law Inst. 1959).
3. *See* Restatement (Third) of Trusts § 94 cmt. b (Am. Law Inst. 2012).

and ensure that they properly discharge their fiduciary duties when administering trust property. That in some contexts [the beneficiary's] interest in the Trusts' assets may not rise to the level of a "property interest" does not negate the fact that she and the Trustee stand in a fiduciary relationship.

Although a creditor cannot compel a trustee to make a distribution from a discretionary trust to satisfy a debt of a beneficiary, the creditor may be entitled to an order requiring that if the trustee chooses to make a distribution, he must pay it to the creditor before paying the beneficiary or anyone else. The order may stand until the creditor has been satisfied. This attachment procedure was approved in Hamilton v. Drogo, 150 N.E. 496 (N.Y. 1926), which involved a discretionary trust established by the will of the dowager Duchess of Manchester to protect her spendthrift son, the ninth duke, from the travails of penury. The court explained how the rule works thus:

> We may not interfere with the discretion which the testatrix has vested in the trustee any more than her son may do so. Its judgment is final. But at least annually this judgment must be exercised. And if it is exercised in favor of the duke [the beneficiary], then there is due him the whole or such part of the income as the trustee may allot to him. After such allotment, he may compel its payment. At least for some appreciable time, however brief, the award must precede the delivery of the income he is to receive, and during that time the lien of the execution attaches.

Uniform Trust Code (UTC) § 501 (Unif. Law Comm'n 2000, rev. 2005) is in accord with *Hamilton*: "To the extent a beneficiary's interest is not subject to a spendthrift provision, the court may authorize a creditor or assignee of the beneficiary to reach the beneficiary's interest by attachment of present or future distributions to or for the

---

The Ninth Duke of Manchester

William Angus Drogo Montague, ninth Duke of Manchester,

had been kept so short of cash as a boy, with pocket money of one penny a day, that he grew up with no real sense of its value. On an allowance of £400 a year at Cambridge, he ran up debts totalling £2,000. He spent much time in America, Africa, and India, avoiding creditors, looking for a rich wife, and sponging off his friends.... He was, on his own admission, "unrepentantly addicted" to gambling; he never kept accounts or made money successfully; and he was constantly the victim of gossip columnists and confidence tricksters.... In his artless autobiography, he candidly admitted that "sport has appealed to me more strongly than brain work, which may be one of the reasons why I have not succeeded in making money."*

After the ninth duke's death, the Manchester family fortunes continued in an irreversible decline set in motion by three spendthrift dukes in a row (the seventh, eighth, and ninth). All the family land was sold off to support high living. The tenth duke moved to Kenya seeking a new fortune, but Kenyan independence sank that venture. The eleventh duke became an alligator hunter in Australia, but after a while he moved back to England and became a business consultant in Bedford.

William Angus Drogo Montague, the ninth Duke of Manchester

* David Cannadine, The Decline and Fall of the British Aristocracy 403 (1999).

benefit of the beneficiary." In a few states, however, a *Hamilton* order is prohibited by statute.[4]

To summarize: Under *Hamilton* and UTC § 501, a creditor cannot compel a trustee to make a discretionary distribution. But the creditor can obtain an order requiring that, if any distributions are to be made to or for the benefit of the beneficiary, the creditor shall be paid first. Crediting the beneficiary's account on the trustee's books or making an oral or written declaration to the beneficiary may be a sufficient act to enable the creditor to seize that portion of the trust property while it is still in the hands of the trustee.

NOTES

1. A Hamilton Order.   Why is the procedure for cutting off distributions sanctioned in Hamilton v. Drogo helpful to a creditor given that the trustee can stop making distributions? Hint: Think of a game of chicken. Until the creditor is paid, the beneficiary cannot be paid either.

2. Circumventing a Hamilton Order?   *T* devises a fund in trust to *X* "to pay or to apply for the benefit of *A* so much of the income as *X* determines in *X*'s uncontrolled discretion." *C*, a creditor of *A*, obtains an order directing *X* to pay *C* before paying *A*. May *X* circumvent the order by paying directly for goods and services rendered to *A*? *See* Wilcox v. Gentry, 867 P.2d 281 (Kan. 1994) (holding in the negative).[5]

3. Equitable Division and Alimony on Divorce.   In many states, upon divorce a court makes an *equitable division* of a couple's "property." Should a present interest in a discretionary trust be subject to division? The trend in the cases, as in Pfannenstiehl v. Pfannenstiehl, 55 N.E.3d 933 (Mass. 2016), and Paulson v. Paulson, 783 N.W.2d 262 (N.D. 2010), is to exclude a present interest in a discretionary trust on the grounds that the interest, said to be "an expectancy," is too speculative for inclusion in the marital estate.[6]

b. Support Trust

Under traditional law, a beneficiary of a *support trust* cannot alienate her interest in the trust. Nor can an ordinary creditor of the beneficiary compel a distribution.[7] Young v. McCoy, 54 Cal. Rptr. 3d 847 (App. 2007), is illustrative. The plaintiff, Richard, sought an order against the trustee of a trust settled by his mother for his brother, Steven, to

---

4. *See, e.g.*, Alaska Stat. § 34.40.113 (2016); Mo. Stat. Ann. § 456.5-504(1) (2016); Mich. Comp. Laws § 700.7505 (2016); N.C. Gen. Stat. § 36C-5-504(b) (2016); Wyo. Stat. § 4-10-504(b) (2016).

5. *See also* Restatement (Third) of Trusts § 60 cmt. c (Am. Law Inst. 2003); Restatement (Second) of Trusts § 155 cmt. i (Am. Law Inst. 1959).

6. We take up application of equitable division to future interests in Chapter 13 at page 856.

7. *See* Restatement (Second) of Trusts § 154 (Am. Law Inst. 1959).

make good on a restitution judgment obtained by Richard "against Steven arising from Steven's attempted murder of Richard."[8] The court denied Richard's petition:

> Although the trust allows [the trustee] to make payments of interest and principal as she deems necessary for Steven's health, support, maintenance, and education, it also allows her to refuse to make such payments if, in her discretion, she determines that Steven does not need them. In this case, according to her uncontested declaration, [the trustee] believes, and Richard agrees, that such needs are being met by the state because Steven is serving a life prison term for attempting to kill Richard. As [the controlling statute] only permits the court to compel a trustee to pay income or principal to the creditor of a beneficiary if the trustee has, in the exercise of her discretion, determined to make payments to the beneficiary, and as [the trustee's] exercise of her discretion not to make such payments is not an abuse of her discretion, the court lacked the authority to compel [the trustee] to make any payment to Richard and properly denied his request.

A support trust insulates the trust property from some but not all of the beneficiary's creditors. Under traditional law, a child or spouse enforcing a claim for support or alimony and a supplier of necessities, such as a physician or grocer, has recourse against the trust property through the beneficiary's right to support.[9]

c. Discretionary Support Trust

In practice, absolute discretion is often combined with a distribution standard. For example: "to provide for the comfort and support of my daughter in the trustee's sole and absolute discretion." Traditional law does not treat such hybrid *discretionary support trusts* as their own category. Instead, courts have tended to treat them as pure discretionary trusts, foreclosing claims by all of the beneficiary's creditors.[10]

d. Collapsing the Categories

The UTC and the Restatement (Third) of Trusts collapse the distinction between discretionary trusts and support trusts, unifying the rules governing alienation and the rights of creditors for all trusts in which the trustee has any kind of discretion over distributions. The Restatement explains:

> Not only is the supposed distinction between support and discretionary trusts arbitrary and artificial, but the lines are also difficult — and costly — to attempt to draw. Attempting to do so tends to produce dubious categorizations . . . . The fact of the matter is that there is a continuum of discretionary trusts, with the terms of distributive powers ranging from the most objective (or "ascertainable," I.R.C. § 2041) of standards (pure "support") to the most open ended (e.g., "happiness") or vague ("benefit") of standards, or even with no standards manifested at all (for

---

8. "'It's a family dispute that escalated into a verbal dispute that escalated into a shooting,' said Sgt. Daniel Carnahan of the Los Angeles Police Department's West Valley Division." Theresa Moreau, Man Shoots Brother, Mom in Sibling Feud, Daily News, July 17, 1997, at N8.

9. *See* Restatement (Second) of Trusts § 157 (Am. Law Inst. 1959).

10. *See* Abravanel, *supra* note 1, at 281.

which a court will probably apply "a general standard of reasonableness").... All of these possibilities are subject to the same general principle that courts will interfere only to prevent abuse.[11]

Although the UTC and Restatement both collapse the various kinds of discretionary trusts into a single category, each states a different substantive rule. The Restatement takes the highly controversial position that, "if the terms of a trust provide for a beneficiary to receive distributions in the trustee's discretion, a transferee or creditor of the beneficiary is entitled to receive or attach any distributions the trustee makes or is required to make in the exercise of that discretion."[12] This is a significant break with prior law, under which only suppliers of necessities and spouses or children had such recourse and only if the trust was for support and not fully discretionary. A few state legislatures have taken the unusual step of enacting statutes that specifically reject this provision of the Restatement.[13]

The potential influence of the Restatement is also curtailed by the UTC, which is binding statutory authority in an enacting jurisdiction. UTC § 504 (2000, rev. 2004) provides that, subject to an exception for claims by a child or spouse for support or alimony, a creditor of a discretionary trust beneficiary cannot compel a distribution even if the beneficiary could do so.

Uniform Trust Code (Unif. Law Comm'n 2000, as amended 2004)

§ 504. Discretionary Trusts; Effect of Standard

(a) In this section, "child" includes any person for whom an order or judgment for child support has been entered in this or another State.

(b) Except as otherwise provided in subsection (c), whether or not a trust contains a spendthrift provision, a creditor of a beneficiary may not compel a distribution that is subject to the trustee's discretion, even if:

(1) the discretion is expressed in the form of a standard of distribution; or

(2) the trustee has abused the discretion.

(c) To the extent a trustee has not complied with a standard of distribution or has abused a discretion:

(1) a distribution may be ordered by the court to satisfy a judgment or court order against the beneficiary for support or maintenance of the beneficiary's child, spouse, or former spouse; and

(2) the court shall direct the trustee to pay to the child, spouse, or former spouse such amount as is equitable under the circumstances but not more than the amount the trustee would have been required to distribute to or for the benefit of the beneficiary had the trustee complied with the standard or not abused the discretion.

---

11. Reporter's Note to Restatement (Third) of Trusts § 60 cmt. a (Am. Law Inst. 2003).

12. Id. § 60.

13. *See, e.g.,* Ariz. Rev. Stat. § 14-10106(B) (2016); Del. Code Ann. tit. 12, § 3315(a) (2016); S.D. Codified Laws § 55-1-25 (2016).

(d) This section does not limit the right of a beneficiary to maintain a judicial proceeding against a trustee for an abuse of discretion or failure to comply with a standard for distribution. . . .

NOTE

A Creditor of an Insolvent Beneficiary.　*T* devises property to *X* in trust to pay so much of the income and principal to *A* as *X* determines is necessary for *A*'s comfortable support and maintenance. *A* is insolvent. *X* refuses to make a distribution to *A*. *B*, an ordinary creditor of *A*, sues *X* on the theory that, because *A* is insolvent, it is an abuse of discretion for *X* not to make a distribution to *A*, and thus *B* is entitled to stand in *A*'s shoes and compel that distribution. What result under traditional law? What result under UTC § 504? What result under the Restatement (Third) of Trusts? Although the Restatement says that "a transferee or creditor of the beneficiary is entitled to receive or attach any distributions the trustee makes or is required to make in the exercise of that discretion," the Restatement qualifies that language thus:

> [A] trustee's refusal to make distributions might not constitute an abuse as against an assignee or creditor even when, under the standards applicable to the power, a decision to refuse distributions to the beneficiary might have constituted an abuse in the absence of the assignment or attachment. This is because the extent to which the designated beneficiary might actually benefit from a distribution is relevant to the justification and reasonableness of the trustee's decision in relation to the settlor's purposes and the effects on other beneficiaries. Thus, the balancing process typical of discretionary issues becomes, in this context, significantly weighted against creditors, and sometimes against a beneficiary's voluntary assignees.[14]

What does this mean? In practice, will the Restatement lead to different results than the UTC or traditional law? Will it lead to more litigation?

e. Protective Trusts

Suppose a settlor wants a beneficiary to have a mandatory right to regular distributions but also wants the asset protection of a discretionary trust. Particularly in a jurisdiction that does not enforce spendthrift provisions (we take up spendthrift trusts next), this settlor should consider a mandatory trust subject to a protective provision. In a *protective trust*, the trustee is directed to pay income to *A*, but if *A*'s creditors attach *A*'s interest, it is automatically changed to a discretionary interest. Once *A*'s interest is discretionary, the creditors of *A* cannot demand any part of it.[15]

In England, which does not enforce spendthrift provisions, under the Trustee Act of 1925 a court will read a protective provision into any trust for which the settlor manifested an intent to create a protective trust.[16] In the words of a leading text on

---

14. Restatement (Third) of Trusts § 60 cmt. e (Am. Law Inst. 2003).
15. *See* id. § 57.
16. 15 & 16 Geo. 5, c. 19, § 33 (Eng.).

English trust law: "Protective trusts are created so as to protect the protected beneficiary against lack of experience in dealing with financial matters and the imprudence and folly to which that might lead. They are also created so as to afford protection to a beneficiary against the risk of insolvency."[17]

2. Spendthrift Trusts

A beneficiary of a *spendthrift trust* cannot voluntarily alienate her interest in the trust. Nor can her creditors attach her interest. This is true even if the beneficiary is entitled to mandatory distributions from the trust. Unlike a creditor of a discretionary trust beneficiary, a creditor of a spendthrift trust beneficiary cannot obtain an order attaching a future distribution to or for the benefit of a beneficiary.[18]

A spendthrift trust is created by imposing a restraint on a beneficiary's ability to transfer or otherwise alienate the beneficial interest. Thus:

Case 1. O conveys property to X in trust to pay the income to or for the benefit of A for life and on A's death to distribute the property to A's then-surviving descendants per stirpes. The trust instrument provides:

> The interests of beneficiaries in principal or income shall not be subject to the claims of any creditor, or to legal process, and may not be voluntarily or involuntarily alienated or encumbered.[19]

A cannot alienate and her creditors cannot attach her interest in the trust. X is free to make distributions to or for the benefit of A irrespective of any claims by a creditor of A.

Under traditional law, a trust is not spendthrift unless the settlor includes a spendthrift clause in the trust instrument. But spendthrift provisions are routinely included in professionally drafted trusts, if only by rote inclusion of formbook boilerplate, and a growing number of jurisdictions no longer require an express spendthrift provision.[20] In Delaware, for example, all trusts are presumptively spendthrift, and in New York all trusts are presumptively spendthrift with respect to income.[21]

The two decisions largely responsible for the recognition of spendthrift trusts in American law are Nichols v. Eaton, 91 U.S. 716 (1875), and Broadway National Bank v.

---

17. Lynton Tucker et al., Lewin on Trusts 230-31 (19th ed., 2015).

18. The comment to UTC § 502 (2000) explains: "[A] creditor of the beneficiary is prohibited from attaching a protected interest and may only attempt to collect directly from the beneficiary after a payment is made." However, under UTC § 506(b), a creditor can attach a mandatory distribution that the trustee has not made within a "reasonable time." The comment explains: "Following this reasonable period, payments mandated by the express terms of the trust are in effect being held by the trustee as agent for the beneficiary and should be treated as part of the beneficiary's personal assets."

19. Adapted from Northern Trust, Will & Trust Forms 201-15 (2004).

20. *See* Jeffrey A. Schoenblum, Multistate Guide to Trusts and Trust Administration tbl. 5, pt. 1 (2012).

21. Del. Code Ann. tit. 12, § 3536(a) (2016); N.Y. Est. Powers & Trusts Law § 7-1.5 (2016).

Justice Samuel F. Miller

Adams, 133 Mass. 170 (1882). In Nichols v. Eaton, Justice Samuel F. Miller inserted an elaborate dictum upholding spendthrift trusts:

> Why a parent, or one who loves another, and wishes to use his own property in securing the object of his affection, as far as property can do it, from the ills of life, the vicissitudes of fortune, and even his own improvidence, or incapacity for self-protection, should not be permitted to do so, is not readily perceived.

A few years later, in *Adams*, the Massachusetts court upheld the spendthrift trust, turning Justice Miller's dictum into a holding:

> The founder of this trust was the absolute owner of his property. He had the entire right to dispose of it, either by an absolute gift to his brother, or by a gift with such restrictions or limitations, not repugnant to law, as he saw fit to impose. His clear intention, as shown in his will, was not to give his brother an absolute right to the income which might hereafter accrue upon the trust fund, with the power of alienating it in advance, but only the right to receive semiannually the income of the fund, which upon its payment to him, and not before, was to become his absolute property. His intentions ought to be carried out, unless they are against public policy. . . .
>
> The rule of public policy which subjects a debtor's property to the payment of his debts, does not subject the property of a donor to the debts of his beneficiary, and does not give the creditor a right to complain that, in the exercise of his absolute right of disposition, the donor has not seen fit to give the property to the creditor, but has left it out of his reach.

The court in *Adams* thus conceived of the spendthrift trust as an exercise of the settlor's freedom of disposition. In In re Morgan's Estate, 72 A. 498 (Pa. 1909), the court reasoned similarly:

> When a trust of this kind has been created, the law holds that the donor has an individual right of property in the execution of the trust; and to deprive him of it would be a fraud on his generosity. For the law to appropriate a gift to a person not intended would be an invasion of the donor's private dominion. It is always to be remembered that consideration for the beneficiary does not even in the remotest way enter into the policy of the law. It has regard solely to the rights of the donor. Spendthrift trusts can have no other justification than is to be found in considerations affecting the donor alone. They allow the donor to so control his bounty, through the creation of the trust, that it may be exempt from liability for the donee's debts, not because the law is concerned to keep the donee from wasting it, but because it is concerned to protect the donor's right of property.

The deep policy question, on which American law diverges from that in England and the other common law countries, is whether to allow the dead hand to restrain alienation of a beneficial interest.[22] Under the leading case of Brandon v. Robinson, (1811) 34 Eng. Rep. 379 (Ch.); 18 Ves. Jun. 429, such a restraint is not enforceable in English law. In England and the other common law countries, courts conceptualize the trust property as belonging to the beneficiaries. In the American tradition, by contrast, the trust is regarded as a conditional gift, and a beneficiary takes his interest in the trust subject to any restrictions imposed by the settlor. Within American law, freedom of disposition includes the right to impose conditions on the beneficiary's enjoyment of the trust property, including a restraint on voluntary and involuntary alienation of the beneficial interest.

Recognition of the spendthrift trust has been sharply criticized. Professor John Chipman Gray, the great property teacher at Harvard (see Chapter 14 at page 888), was so outraged at the introduction of spendthrift trusts that he was moved to write his Restraints on the Alienation of Property, first published in 1883, in refutation of Nichols v. Eaton:

> The general introduction of spendthrift trusts would be to form a privileged class, who could indulge in every speculation, could practice every fraud, and, provided they kept on the safe side of the criminal law, could yet roll in wealth. They would be an aristocracy, though certainly the most contemptible aristocracy with which a country was ever cursed.[23]

In spite of Gray's strictures, by the time the second edition of his book was published 12 years later, the battle was lost. "State after State has given in its adhesion to the new doctrine," he acknowledged, "[a]nd yet I cannot recant."[24]

Today the spendthrift trust is recognized throughout the United States. The policy debate has shifted to the question of whether to make exceptions for certain kinds of creditors, such as spouses and children or tort victims.

Uniform Trust Code (Unif. Law Comm'n 2000, as amended 2005)

§ 502. Spendthrift Provision

(a) A spendthrift provision is valid only if it restrains both voluntary and involuntary transfer of a beneficiary's interest.

(b) A term of a trust providing that the interest of a beneficiary is held subject to a "spendthrift trust," or words of similar import, is sufficient to restrain both voluntary and involuntary transfer of the beneficiary's interest.

(c) A beneficiary may not transfer an interest in a trust in violation of a valid spendthrift provision and, except as otherwise provided in this [article],

---

22. *See* Joshua Getzler, Transplantation and Mutation in Anglo-American Law, 10 Theoretical Inquiries L. 355 (2009).

23. John Chipman Gray, Restraints on the Alienation of Property § 262, at 174 (1883).

24. Id. at iv-v (2d ed. 1895). For more recent commentary, see Kent D. Schenkel, Exposing the Hocus Pocus of Trusts, 45 Akron L. Rev. 63 (2012); Adam Hirsch, Spendthrift Trusts and Public Policy: Economic and Cognitive Perspectives, 73 Wash. U. L.Q. 1 (1995); Anne S. Emanuel, Spendthrift Trusts: It's Time to Codify the Compromise, 72 Neb. L. Rev. 179 (1993).

a creditor or assignee of the beneficiary may not reach the interest or a distribution by the trustee before its receipt by the beneficiary.

§ 503. Exceptions to Spendthrift Provision

(a) In this section, "child" includes any person for whom an order or judgment for child support has been entered in this or another State.

(b) A spendthrift provision is unenforceable against:

(1) a beneficiary's child, spouse, or former spouse who has a judgment or court order against the beneficiary for support or maintenance;

(2) a judgment creditor who has provided services for the protection of a beneficiary's interest in the trust; and

(3) a claim of this State or the United States to the extent a statute of this State or federal law so provides.

(c) A claimant against which a spendthrift provision cannot be enforced may obtain from a court an order attaching present or future distributions to or for the benefit of the beneficiary. The court may limit the award to such relief as is appropriate under the circumstances.

Scheffel v. Krueger
782 A.2d 410 (N.H. 2001)

DUGGAN, J. . . . In 1998, the [plaintiff, Lorie Scheffel, individually and as mother of Cory C.,] filed suit in superior court asserting tort claims against the defendant, Kyle Krueger. In her suit, the plaintiff alleged that the defendant sexually assaulted her minor child, videotaped the act and later broadcasted the videotape over the Internet. The same conduct that the plaintiff alleged in the tort claims also formed the basis for criminal charges against the defendant.[25] The court entered a default judgment against the defendant and ordered him to pay $551,286.25 in damages. To satisfy the judgment against the defendant, the plaintiff sought an attachment of the defendant's beneficial interest in the Kyle Krueger Irrevocable Trust (trust).

The defendant's grandmother established the trust in 1985 for the defendant's benefit. Its terms direct the trustee to pay all of the net income from the trust to the beneficiary, at least quarterly, or more frequently if the beneficiary in writing so requests. The trustee is further authorized to pay any of the principal to the beneficiary if in the trustee's sole discretion the funds are necessary for the maintenance, support and education of the beneficiary. The beneficiary may not invade the principal until he reaches the age of fifty, which will not occur until April 6, 2016.[26]

---

25. Having been turned in by his wife, who found the incriminating videotape among Krueger's belongings in their bedroom, Krueger was convicted of "eighty counts of aggravated felonious sexual assault, seven counts of attempted aggravated felonious sexual assault, two counts of felonious sexual assault, and one count of simple assault." State v. Krueger, 776 A.2d 720 (N.H. 2001).—Eds.

26. Krueger became eligible for parole in late 2015 or early 2016 and, so far as we can tell, has in fact been paroled.—Eds.

The beneficiary is prohibited from making any voluntary or involuntary transfers of his interest in the trust. Article VII of the trust instrument specifically provides:

> No principal or income payable or to become payable under any of the trusts created by this instrument shall be subject to anticipation or assignment by any beneficiary thereof, or to the interference or control of any creditors of such beneficiary or to be taken or reached by any legal or equitable process in satisfaction of any debt or liability of such beneficiary prior to its receipt by the beneficiary.

Asserting that this so-called spendthrift provision barred the plaintiff's claim against the trust, the trustee defendant moved to [dismiss the plaintiff's claim]. The trial court ruled that under N.H. Rev. Stat. ("RSA") 564:23 (1997), this spendthrift provision is enforceable against the plaintiff's claim and dismissed [the plaintiff's claim]. . . .

We first address the plaintiff's argument that the legislature did not intend RSA 564:23 to shield the trust assets from tort creditors, especially when the beneficiary's conduct constituted a criminal act. . . . "We interpret legislative intent from the statute as written, and therefore, we will not consider what the legislature might have said or add words that the legislature did not include." Rye Beach Country Club v. Town of Rye, 719 A.2d 623 (N.H. 1998).

We begin by examining the language found in the statute. RSA 564:23, I, provides:

> In the event the governing instrument so provides, a beneficiary of a trust shall not be able to transfer his or her right to future payments of income and principal, and a creditor of a beneficiary shall not be able to subject the beneficiary's interest to the payment of its claim.

The statute provides two exceptions to the enforceability of spendthrift provisions. The provisions "shall not apply to a beneficiary's interest in a trust to the extent that the beneficiary is the settlor and the trust is not a special needs trust established for a person with disabilities," RSA 564:23, II, and "shall not be construed to prevent the application of RSA 545-A or a similar law of another state [regarding fraudulent transfers]," RSA 564:23, III. Thus, under the plain language of the statute, a spendthrift provision is enforceable unless the beneficiary is also the settlor or the assets were fraudulently transferred to the trust. The plaintiff does not argue that either exception applies.

Faced with this language, the plaintiff argues that the legislature did not intend for the statute to shield the trust assets from tort creditors. The statute, however, plainly states that "a creditor of a beneficiary shall not be able to subject the beneficiary's interest to the payment of its claim." RSA 564:23, I. Nothing in this language suggests that the legislature intended that a tort creditor should be exempted from a spendthrift provision. Two exemptions are enumerated in sections II and III. Where the legislature has made specific exemptions, we must presume no others were intended. "If this is an omission, the courts cannot supply it. That is for the Legislature to do." Brahmey v. Rollins, 179 A. 186 (N.H. 1935).

The plaintiff argues public policy requires us to create a tort creditor exception to the statute. The cases the plaintiff relies upon, however, both involve judicially created spendthrift law. See Sligh v. First Nat'l Bank of Holmes County, 704 So. 2d 1020, 1024 (Miss. 1997). In this State, the legislature has enacted a statute repudiating the public policy exception sought by the plaintiff. This statutory enactment cannot be overruled, because "[i]t is axiomatic that courts do not question the wisdom or expediency of a statute." *Brahmey*, 179 A. 186, 192-93. Therefore, "[n]o rule of public policy is available to overcome [this] statutory rule." Id. . . .

Finally, the plaintiff asserts that the trial court erred in denying her request that the trust be terminated because the purpose of the trust can no longer be satisfied. The plaintiff argues that the trust's purpose to provide for the defendant's support, maintenance and education can no longer be fulfilled because the defendant will likely remain incarcerated for a period of years. The trial court, however, found that the trust's purpose "may still be fulfilled while the defendant is incarcerated and after he is released." The record before us supports this finding.

Affirmed.

NOTES

1. Tort Victims.   For a time, it was thought that an exception to spendthrift protection would develop for tort victims because they are involuntary creditors. In the words of the Scott treatise:

> In many of the cases that have held that the terms of the trust can put the interest of a beneficiary beyond the reach of creditors, the courts have laid some stress on the fact that the creditors had only themselves to blame for extending credit to such a person. The courts have said that before extending credit the creditors could have ascertained the extent and character of the debtor's resources. In this respect, however, the situation of a tort creditor is quite different from that of a contract creditor. The pedestrian who is about to be hit by an automobile has no opportunity to investigate the credit of the driver or to avoid being injured, no matter what the driver's resources are.[27]

Most states that have considered the question, however, have rejected an exception for tort victims.[28] In Sligh v. First National Bank of Holmes County, 704 So. 2d 1020 (Miss. 1997), the court held that a tort victim could recover against the tortfeasor's interest in a spendthrift trust. But the very next year the state legislature reversed *Sligh* and exempted spendthrift trusts from tort creditors.[29] UTC § 503, page 706, does not recognize an exception for tort creditors, and the comment makes clear that this was a deliberate choice by the drafting committee.[30] The only state with a clear exception for tort victims is Georgia.[31]

---

27. Scott and Ascher on Trusts § 15.5.5.
28. *See* Schoenblum, *supra* note 20, at tbl. 5, pt. 1.
29. Miss. Code Ann. § 91-9-503 (2016).
30. On the UTC creditor rights provisions, see Robert T. Danforth, Article Five of the UTC and the Future of Creditors' Rights in Trusts, 27 Cardozo L. Rev. 2551 (2006); Alan Newman, Spendthrift and Discretionary Trusts: Alive and Well Under the Uniform Trust Code, 40 Real Prop. Prob. & Tr. J. 567 (2005).
31. *See* Ga. Code Ann. § 53-12-80(d)(3) (2016).

The Restatement (Third) of Trusts does not recognize a general exception for tort creditors. But it does suggest that "evolving policy" might "justify recognition of other exceptions. . . . The nature or a pattern of tortious conduct by a beneficiary . . . may on policy grounds justify a court's refusal to allow spendthrift immunity to protect the trust interest and the lifestyle of that beneficiary, especially one whose willful or fraudulent conduct or persistently reckless behavior causes serious harm to others."[32] What does this mean? What result in *Scheffel* under the Restatement?

Suppose the trustee of a spendthrift trust is also a beneficiary. If the trustee-beneficiary is surcharged for breach of trust, may the other beneficiaries enforce the surcharge against the trustee-beneficiary's interest in the trust? *See* Chatard v. Oveross, 101 Cal. Rptr. 3d 883 (App. 2009). What do you suppose is the probable intent of the settlor in such a case?[33]

2. Children and Spouses. Judgments for child or spousal support, or both, can be enforced against the debtor's interest in a spendthrift trust in a majority of states and under UTC § 503(b)(1), page 706.[34] In such a state, a child or spouse can attach future distributions to the beneficiary, as in Berlinger v. Casselberry, 133 So. 3d 961 (Fla. App. 2013).

The reasoning of the majority is that the settlor's freedom of disposition is constrained by a public policy preference for making good on support orders obtained by a child or a spouse against the beneficiary. Shelley v. Shelley, 354 P.2d 282 (Or. 1960), is illustrative. In that case, the trustee argued that an exception from spendthrift protection for claims by children and spouses would be inconsistent with "the testator's privilege to dispose of his property as he pleases." The court disagreed:

> The privilege of disposing of property is not absolute; it is hedged with various restrictions where there are policy considerations warranting the limitation. Not all of these restrictions are imposed by statute. The rule against perpetuities, the rule against restraints on alienation, the refusal to recognize trusts for capricious purposes or for illegal purposes, or for any purpose contrary to public policy, are all instances of judge-made rules limiting the privilege of alienation. Many others could be recited. It is within the court's power to impose upon the privilege of disposing of property such restrictions as are consistent with its view of sound public policy, unless, of course, the legislature has expressed a contrary view. Our own statutes do not purport to deal with the specific question before us, that is as to whether there should be limitations on the owner's privilege to create a spendthrift trust. . . .
>
> We have no hesitation in declaring that public policy requires that the interest of the beneficiary of a trust should be subject to the claims for support of his children. . . . If we give effect to the spendthrift provision to bar the claims for support, we have the spectacle of a man enjoying the benefits of a trust immune from claims

---

32. Restatement (Third) of Trusts § 59 cmt. a(2) (Am. Law Inst. 2003).

33. *See* Restatement (Second) of Trusts § 257 cmt. f (Am. Law Inst. 1959).

34. *See* Timothy J. Vitollo, Uniform Trust Code Section 503: Applying Hamilton Orders to Spendthrift Interests, 43 Real Prop. Tr. & Est. L.J. 169, 185-92 (2008); *see also* Carolyn L. Dessin, Feed a Trust and Starve a Child: The Effectiveness of Trust Protective Techniques Against Claims for Support and Alimony, 10 Ga. St. U. L. Rev. 691 (1994).

which are justly due, while the community pays for the support of his children. We do not believe that it is sound policy to use the welfare funds of this state in support of the beneficiary's children, while he stands behind the shield of immunity created by a spendthrift trust provision. . . .

The duty of the husband to support his former wife should [likewise] override the restriction called for by the spendthrift provision. The same reason advanced above for requiring the support of the beneficiary's children will, in many cases, be applicable to the claim of a divorced wife; if the beneficiary's interest cannot be reached, the state may be called upon to support her.

3. Necessary Support and Other Exceptions.   A venerable exception to spendthrift protection, codified by UTC § 503(b)(2), page 706, allows a claimant who provided services necessary to protect a beneficiary's interest in a trust to recover against the beneficiary's interest. The theory, as explained in the comment to § 503, is that this exception ensures that a beneficiary can obtain "services essential to the protection or enforcement of the beneficiary's rights under the trust," such as legal representation.

Another longstanding exception is for a claimant who provided a beneficiary with necessities, such as medical care or food. The Restatement explains: "Failure to give enforcement to appropriate claims of this type would tend to undermine the beneficiary's ability to obtain necessary goods and assistance; and a refusal to enforce such claims is not essential to a settlor's purpose of protecting the beneficiary."[35] This exception was not codified in UTC § 503. The comment explains: "Most of these cases involve claims by governmental entities, which the drafters concluded are better handled by the enactment of special legislation as authorized by subsection (b)(3)."

In a few states, a creditor is permitted to reach a certain percentage (say, between 10 and 30 percent) of the trust income in a garnishment proceeding ordinarily applicable to wage earners.[36] Several other states provide a dollar cap on the amount of income or principal that can be shielded by a spendthrift provision.[37]

4. The Station-in-Life Rule.   In New York and a few other states, a beneficiary's creditors can reach spendthrift trust income in excess of the amount needed for the support of the beneficiary.[38] In determining what is necessary for the support of the beneficiary, courts developed a *station-in-life rule*. Creditors can reach only the amount in excess of what is needed to maintain the beneficiary in his station in life. This rule rendered these excess-income statutes useless to creditors of beneficiaries who are accustomed to luxury. John Chipman Gray was even more scornful of this exception than of spendthrift trusts generally:

The Statutes of New York, as interpreted by the Courts, provide that the surplus of income given in trust beyond what is necessary for the education and support of the beneficiary shall be liable for his debts. . . . The Court takes into account that the

---

35. Restatement (Third) of Trusts § 59 cmt. c (Am. Law Inst. 2003).

36. *See, e.g.,* Cal. Prob. Code § 15306.5 (2016) (25 percent).

37. *See, e.g.,* Okla. Stat. Ann. tit. 60, § 175.25(B)(2) (2016) (providing that trust income due to the beneficiary in excess of $25,000 per year is subject to garnishment by creditors).

38. N.Y. Est. Powers & Trusts Law § 7-3.4 (2016).

*"Typical trust-fund red from
a vanity vintner."*

William Hamilton/The New Yorker Collection/The Cartoon Bank

debtor is "a gentleman of high social standing, whose associations are chiefly with men of leisure, and who is connected with a number of clubs," and that his income is not more than sufficient to maintain his position according to his education, habits, and associations.

To say that whatever money is given to a man cannot be taken by his creditors is bad enough; at any rate, however, it is law for rich and poor alike; but to say that from a sum which creditors can reach one man, who has lived simply and plainly, can deduct but a small sum, while a large sum may be deducted by another man because he is "of high social standing," . . . is to descend to a depth of as shameless snobbishness as any into which the justice of a country was ever plunged.[39]

5. Federal Bankruptcy Law. The asset protection features of state trust law abide only at the sufferance of Congress, which thus far has chosen to allow them.[40] The federal Bankruptcy Code excludes from a debtor's bankruptcy estate any beneficial interest in trust that is not alienable "under applicable nonbankruptcy law," which includes state trust law.[41] Should the Bankruptcy Code be amended to allow tort judgments or claims for alimony or child support to be enforced against a bankrupt beneficiary's interest in a spendthrift or a discretionary trust? Is this a question on which there should be a national policy set at the federal level?

6. Pension Trusts. The federal Employee Retirement Income Security Act of 1974 (ERISA) provides: "Each pension plan [covered by the act] shall provide that benefits provided under the plan may not be assigned or alienated."[42] ERISA also provides, however, that these benefits may be reached for child support, alimony, or marital

39. Gray, *supra* note 23, at x-xi (2d ed. 1895).

40. *See* John K. Eason, Developing the Asset Protection Dynamic: A Legacy of Federal Concern, 31 Hofstra L. Rev. 23 (2002).

41. 11 U.S.C. § 541(c)(2) (2016).

42. 29 U.S.C. § 1056(d)(1) (2016).

property rights.[43] The principle underlying these provisions is that an employee's future retirement security should be protected against claims by non-family creditors.[44] Individual Retirement Accounts are likewise protected while held for the benefit of the worker.[45]

3. Self-Settled Asset Protection Trusts

Under traditional law, codified by UTC § 505 (2000), a person cannot shield assets from creditors by placing them in a trust for her own benefit. Even if a trust is discretionary, spendthrift, or both, the creditors of the settlor can reach the maximum amount that the trustee could pay to the settlor or apply for the settlor's benefit. Thus:

> *Case 2.* *O*, a surgeon, transfers property to *X* in trust to pay so much of the income and principal to *O* as *X* determines in *X*'s sole and absolute discretion. The trust includes a spendthrift clause. Five years later, *O* botches a routine surgery, causing grievous injury to the patient, *A*. *A* may enforce a malpractice judgment against the entire corpus of the trust because *X* could, in *X*'s discretion, pay the entire corpus to *O*.

Why is protection from creditors available only to recipients of *gifts* and not also to persons who *earn* wealth and then create a self-settled trust? The usual answer is that the principle of freedom of disposition that allows a donor to impose a restraint on alienation collapses if the donor and the donee are one and the same. "It is against public policy," reasoned the court in Vanderbilt Credit Corp. v. Chase Manhattan Bank, 473 N.Y.S.2d 242 (App. Div. 1984), "to permit the settlor-beneficiary to tie up her own property in such a way that she can still enjoy it but can prevent her creditors from reaching it." In Phillips v. Moore, 690 S.E.2d 620 (Ga. 2010), the court put the point thus:

> The invalidity of self-settled spendthrift trusts stems from the idea that no settlor . . . should be permitted to put his own assets in a trust, of which he is [a] beneficiary, and shield those assets with a spendthrift clause, because to do so is merely shifting the settlor's assets from one pocket to another, in an attempt to avoid creditors.

But suppose a state were to enact a statute authorizing a trust in which the settlor could have a beneficial interest that his creditors could not attach. Would this statute, reversing the common law, attract trust business to that state? Believing that the answer is Yes, a growing number of offshore and domestic jurisdictions have enacted such a statute, giving rise to what has come to be known as the *self-settled asset protection trust* (APT). If an APT statute were applicable in Case 1, *A* would have no recourse against the trust property.

The story of the recognition of APTs begins in the sunny Caribbean, South Pacific, and other exotic offshore locales. In the 1980s, a host of offshore jurisdictions — including the Bahamas, Barbados, Belize, Bermuda, Cayman Islands, Cook Islands, Cyprus, Gibraltar, Grenada, Liechtenstein, Mauritius, Nevis, Samoa, St. Lucia,

---

43. Id. § 1056(d)(3).
44. *See* John H. Langbein et al., Pension and Employee Benefit Law 221-25 (6th ed. 2015).
45. *See* Clark v. Rameker, 134 S. Ct. 2242 (2014).

and Turks and Caicos—amended their trust laws to allow a self-settled trust against which the settlor's creditors have no recourse.

The Cook Islands International Trusts Act of 1984, last amended in 2013, is representative. It authorizes a self-settled trust in which the settlor may have a beneficial interest that the settlor's creditors cannot attach, provided that the settlor is not a resident of the Cook Islands. The act therefore makes APTs available to everyone in the world except for those who reside in the Cook Islands, "a sure sign that the purpose of the statute was to attract foreign capital."[46] The act provides that no judgment rendered by a foreign court against an interest in a Cook Islands trust, or against the settlor, trustee, or beneficiary of such a trust, will be enforced by a Cook Islands court.

Jonathan Blattmachr and a king salmon on the Kasilof River in Alaska, c. late 1990s

In 1997, the Alaska legislature domesticated the APT concept. It enacted an APT statute that was drafted by Jonathan Blattmachr (a prominent New York trusts and estates lawyer), his brother (the head of a trust company based in Alaska), and an Alaska lawyer. The three had the idea while on a fishing trip. A few months later, Delaware enacted an APT statute. The official synopsis says that it "is similar to legislation recently enacted in Alaska. It is intended to maintain Delaware's role as the most favored domestic jurisdiction for the establishment of trusts."[47] In the years since, 15 other states have enacted APT statutes, bringing the total to 17 (see Figure 10.1, page 714).[48]

The politics underlying the validation of APTs is similar to that for the validation of perpetual trusts (see Chapter 14 at page 906). Local bankers and lawyers, who stand to benefit from an influx of trust assets, have lobbied for such legislation. However, the motivation for an APT is quite different from the motivation for a perpetual trust. Whereas interest in perpetual trusts was sparked by tax avoidance, interest in APTs is rooted in avoiding personal liability exposure.

The extent to which APTs are actually used in practice is unclear. Anecdotes abound of doctors and corporate executives who, in the face of rising insurance premiums, have dropped their coverage in favor of moving assets into an APT.[49] On this

---

46. Stewart E. Sterk, Asset Protection Trusts: Trust Law's Race to the Bottom?, 85 Cornell L. Rev. 1035, 1048 (2000).

47. H.R. 356, 139th Gen. Assemb., 71 Del. Laws 159 (1997).

48. Arkansas, Delaware, Hawaii, Michigan (effective 2017), Mississippi, Missouri, Nevada, New Hampshire, Ohio, Oklahoma, Rhode Island, South Dakota, Tennessee, Utah, Virginia, West Virginia, and Wyoming. Some commentators have read an older statute in Colorado as authorizing APTs against future creditors, see Colo. Rev. Stat. Ann. § 38-10-111 (2012), but in dicta the Colorado Supreme Court rejected that interpretation. *See* In re Cohen, 8 P.3d 429, 432-34 (Colo. 1999).

49. *See, e.g.,* Patricia Cohen, States in a Lucrative Fight to Be a Haven for the Wealth of the 1 Percent, N.Y. Times, Aug. 9, 2016, at B1; Arden Dale, Creditor-Proof Trusts Replacing Offshore

Figure 10.1

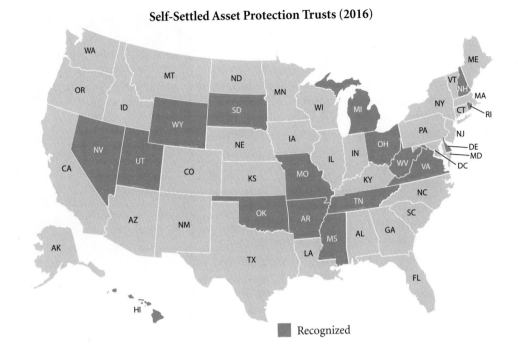

Self-Settled Asset Protection Trusts (2016)

account, the APT might be reckoned as a kind of self-help tort reform, a defensive strategy by trust lawyers against plaintiffs' lawyers. Practitioner-oriented journals are replete with articles that examine in great detail the pros and cons of the different APT statutes and evaluate their relative popularity.[50] On the other hand, an empirical study of trust fund location based on federal banking data from 1985 through 2003 found only "tentative evidence that validating APTs increases a state's trust business," though the data in that study is now more than a decade old, and most of the domestic APT statutes were enacted in the years since.[51]

Federal Trade Commission v. Affordable Media, LLC
179 F.3d 1228 (9th Cir. 1999)

WIGGINS, J. A husband and wife, Denyse and Michael Anderson, were involved in a telemarketing venture that offered investors the chance to participate in a project that sold such modern marvels as talking pet tags and water-filled barbells by means of late-night television. Although the promoters promised that an investment in the project would return 50 per cent in a mere 60 to 90 days, the venture in fact was a Ponzi

---

Accounts, Wall St. J., Aug. 8, 2013, at 8; Leslie Wayne, Paradise of Untouchable Assets, N.Y. Times, Dec. 15, 2013, at BU1.

50. *See, e.g.,* Mark Merric & Daniel G. Worthington, Find the Best Situs for Domestic Asset Protection Trusts, Tr. & Est., Jan. 2015, at 45; Richard W. Nenno, A Practitioner-Friendly Guide to the Delaware Asset-Protection Trust, 30 Prob. & Prop. 53 (2016).

51. Robert H. Sitkoff & Max M. Schanzenbach, Jurisdictional Competition for Trust Funds: An Empirical Analysis of Perpetuities and Taxes, 115 Yale L.J. 356, 411-12 (2005).

scheme, which eventually unraveled and left thousands of investors with tremendous losses. . . .

While the investors' money was lost in the fraudulent scheme, the Andersons' profits from their commissions remained safely tucked away across the sea in a Cook Islands trust. When the [Federal Trade] Commission brought a civil action to recover as much money as possible for the defrauded investors, the Andersons . . . claimed that they were unable to repatriate the assets in the Cook Islands trust because they had willingly relinquished all control over the millions of dollars of commissions in order to place this money overseas in the benevolent hands of unaccountable overseers, just on the off chance that a law suit might result from their business activities. The learned district court was skeptical . . . and [chose] to grant the Commission its requested preliminary relief.

An old adage warns that a fool and his money are easily parted. This case shows that the same is not true of a district court judge and his common sense. After the Andersons refused to comply with the preliminary injunction by refusing to return their illicit proceeds, the district court found the Andersons in civil contempt of court. The Andersons appealed. . . .

I

Sometime after April 1997, Denyse and Michael Anderson became involved with The Sterling Group ("Sterling"). Sterling sold such imaginative products as the "Aquabell," a water-filled dumbbell, the "Talking Pet Tag," and a plastic wrap dispenser known as "KenKut" by means of late-night television commercials broadcast between the hours of 11:00 P.M. and 4:00 A.M. The Andersons formed Financial Growth Consultants, LLC ("Financial") to serve as the primary telemarketer of media units, an investment that afforded purchasers the opportunity to receive a portion of the profits generated from the sales of Sterling's outlandish products. Financial's telemarketers thereupon set about locating prospective investors in the media unit scheme.

The media units sold for $5,000. Each media unit entitled the investor to participate in the sale of Sterling's products from 201 of the late-night commercials. Each product sold for $20.00. The investor would receive $7.50 for each product sold during his 201 commercials, up to a maximum of five products per commercial. According to Financial's telemarketers, the investors would likely receive $37.50 per commercial (from five products sold during each commercial) for a total of $7,537.50—an astronomical fifty percent return in sixty to ninety days. Financial, for its part, would receive forty-five percent of the investor's $5,000.00 investment, an amount that the Andersons assert is the industry standard.

It appears that Financial's telemarketers were especially skilled at marketing the media units. Financial may have raised at least $13,000,000 from investors in the media-unit scheme, retaining an estimated

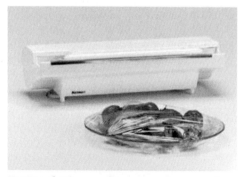

KenKut plastic wrap dispenser and a wrapped plate of strawberries

$6,300,000 in commissions for itself. Perhaps unsurprisingly to those not involved in the media-unit project, it turned out that Sterling could not sell enough Talking Pet Tags and Aquabells to return the promised yields to the media-unit investors. Instead, it appears that Sterling used later investors' investments to pay the promised yields to earlier investors — a classic Ponzi scheme.

On April 23, 1998, the Federal Trade Commission (the "Commission") filed a complaint in the United States District Court for the District of Nevada, charging the Andersons, Financial, and others with violations of the Federal Trade Commission Act (the "Act") and the Telemarketing Sales Rule for their participation in a scheme to tele-market fraudulent investments to consumers. Upon motion by the Commission, the district court issued an ex parte temporary restraining order against the defendants. After hearings on April 30 and May 8, 1998, the district court entered a preliminary injunction against the defendants, which incorporated the provisions of the temporary restraining order. Both the temporary restraining order and the preliminary injunction required the Andersons to repatriate any assets held for their benefit outside of the United States.

In July, 1995, the Andersons had created an irrevocable trust under the law of the Cook Islands. The Andersons were named as co-trustees of the trust, together with AsiaCiti Trust Limited ("AsiaCiti"), a company licensed to conduct trustee services under Cook Islands law. Apparently, the Andersons created the trust in an effort to protect their assets from business risks and liabilities by placing the assets beyond the jurisdiction of the United States courts. . . .

In response to the preliminary injunction, the Andersons faxed a letter to AsiaCiti on May 12, 1998, instructing AsiaCiti to provide an accounting of the assets held in the trust and to repatriate the assets to the United States to be held under the control of the

Charles Ponzi's Scheme

The term *Ponzi scheme* comes from Charles Ponzi's infamous swindle in the early 1920s. Ponzi discovered that, under the Universal Postal Convention then in effect, it was possible to buy a stamp in Europe that was worth a few cents more in the United States than it cost in Europe. Claiming that he could exploit this opportunity for postal arbitrage, Ponzi solicited investors with promises of returns on the order of 50 percent in just a few months. Investors were given tradable notes on which, for a time, Ponzi made good. But he did so by paying off earlier investors with proceeds raised from later investors. Ponzi did not actually undertake substantial postal arbitrage, and in view of the transaction costs, no wonder. Having taken in a reported $15 million from investors, it would have required exchanges of billions of stamps to achieve his promised returns.

Ultimately, as in the case of all Ponzi schemes, Ponzi's scheme collapsed. Investors recovered only 12 cents on the dollar, and Ponzi wound up serving a stint in prison — neither his first nor his last. Today the term Ponzi scheme is used to describe any scam in which subsequent receipts are used to make good on promises to earlier investors. Doing so gives the scam the appearance of genuine returns and the con artist a measure of credibility.

Charles Ponzi

district court. AsiaCiti thereupon notified the Andersons that the temporary restraining order was an event of duress under the trust, removed the Andersons as co-trustees under the trust because of the event of duress, and refused to provide an accounting or repatriation of the assets.[52] . . .

On May 7, 1998, the Commission moved the district court to find the Andersons in civil contempt for their failure to comply with the temporary restraining order's requirements that they submit an accounting of their foreign assets to the Commission and to repatriate all assets located abroad. At a hearing on June 4, 1998, the district court found the Andersons in civil contempt of court for failing to repatriate the trust assets to the United States and failing to provide an accounting of the trust's assets. The district court, however, continued the hearing until June 9, then until June 11, and finally until June 17, in an effort to allow the Andersons to purge themselves of their contempt. In attempting to purge themselves of their contempt, the Andersons attempted to appoint their children as trustees of the trust, but AsiaCiti removed them from acting as trustees because the event of duress was continuing. At the June 17 hearing, the district court indicated that it believed that the Andersons remained in control of the trust and rejected their assertion that compliance with the repatriation provisions of the trust was impossible. At the close of the June 17 hearing, the district judge ordered the Andersons taken into custody because they had not purged themselves of their contempt. The Andersons timely appealed the district court's issuance of the preliminary injunction and finding them in contempt. We affirm the district court.

II

[The court upheld the preliminary injunction.]

III

The next issue on appeal is the district court's finding the Andersons in contempt for refusing to repatriate the assets in their Cook Islands trust. . . . Based on the record before us, we find that the district court did not abuse its discretion in holding the Andersons in contempt. . . .

The temporary restraining order required the Andersons, in relevant part, to "transfer to the territory of the United States all funds, documents and assets in foreign countries held either: (1) by them; (2) for their benefit; or (3) under their direct or indirect control, jointly or singly." These provisions were continued in the preliminary

---

52. The Andersons' trust created the circumstances in which a foreign trustee would refuse to repatriate assets to the United States by means of so-called duress provisions. Under the trust agreement, an event of duress includes "[t]he issuance of any order, decree or judgment of any court or tribunal in any part of the world which in the opinion of the protector will or may directly or indirectly, expropriate, sequester, levy, lien or in any way control, restrict or prevent the free disposal by a trustee of any monies, investments or property which may from time to time be included in or form part of this trust and any distributions therefrom." Upon the happening of an event of duress, the trust agreement provides that the Andersons would be terminated as co-trustees, so that control over the trust assets would appear to be exclusively in the hands of a foreign trustee, beyond the jurisdiction of a United States court. . . . [Footnote relocated. — Eds.]

injunction. It is undisputed that the Andersons are beneficiaries of an irrevocable trust established under the laws of the Cook Islands. The Andersons do not dispute that the trust assets have not been repatriated to the United States. Instead, the Andersons claim that compliance with the temporary restraining order is impossible because the trustee, in accordance with the terms of the trust, will not repatriate the trust assets to the United States.

A party's inability to comply with a judicial order constitutes a defense to a charge of civil contempt. See United States v. Rylander, 460 U.S. 752, 757 (1983). The Andersons claim that the refusal of the foreign trustee to repatriate the trust assets to the United States, which apparently was the goal of the trust, makes their compliance with the preliminary injunction impossible.

Although the Andersons assert that their "inability to comply with a judicial decree is a complete defense to a charge of civil contempt, *regardless of whether the inability to comply is self-induced*" (emphasis added), we are not certain that the Andersons' inability to comply in this case would be a defense to a finding of contempt. It is readily apparent that the Andersons' inability to comply with the district court's repatriation order is the intended result of their own conduct—their inability to comply and the foreign trustee's refusal to comply appears to be the precise goal of the Andersons' trust. The Andersons claim that they created their trust as part of an "asset protection plan." . . . The "asset protection" aspect of these foreign trusts arises from the ability of people, such as the Andersons, to frustrate and impede the United States courts by moving their assets beyond those courts' jurisdictions. . . .

Because these asset protection trusts move the trust assets beyond the jurisdiction of domestic courts, oftentimes all that remains within the jurisdiction is the physical person of the defendant. Because the physical person of the defendant remains subject to domestic courts' jurisdictions, courts could normally utilize their contempt powers to force a defendant to return the assets to their jurisdictions. Recognizing this risk, asset protection trusts typically are designed so that a defendant can assert that compliance with a court's order to repatriate the trust assets is impossible:

> Another common issue is whether the client may someday be in the awkward position of either having to repatriate assets or else be held in contempt of court. A well-drafted [asset protection trust] would, under such a circumstance, make it impossible for the client to repatriate assets held by the trust. Impossibility of performance is a complete defense to a civil contempt charge.

Barry S. Engel, Using Foreign Situs Trusts for Asset Protection Planning, 20 Est. Plan. 212, 218 (1993).

Given that these offshore trusts operate by means of frustrating domestic courts' jurisdiction, we are unsure that we would find that the Andersons' inability to comply with the district court's order is a defense to a civil contempt charge. We leave for another day the resolution of this more difficult question because we find that the Andersons have not satisfied their burden of proving that compliance with the district court's repatriation order was impossible. It is well established that a party petitioning for an adjudication that another party is in civil contempt does not have the burden of showing that the other party has the capacity to comply with the court's order. Instead, the party asserting the impossibility defense must show "categorically and in detail" why he is unable to comply.

In the asset protection trust context, moreover, the burden on the party asserting an impossibility defense will be particularly high because of the likelihood that any attempted compliance with the court's orders will be merely a charade rather than a good faith effort to comply. Foreign trusts are often designed to assist the settlor in avoiding being held in contempt of a domestic court while only feigning compliance with the court's orders. . . .

With foreign laws designed to frustrate the operation of domestic courts and foreign trustees acting in concert with domestic persons to thwart the United States courts, the domestic courts will have to be especially chary of accepting a defendant's assertions that repatriation or other compliance with a court's order concerning a foreign trust is impossible. Consequently, the burden on the defendant of proving impossibility as a defense to a contempt charge will be especially high. . . .

The Andersons claim that they have "demonstrated to the district court 'categorically and in detail' that they cannot comply with the repatriation section of the preliminary injunction." The district court was not convinced and neither are we. While it is possible that a rational person would send millions of dollars overseas and retain absolutely no control over the assets, we share the district court's skepticism. The district court found, notwithstanding the Andersons' protestations, that

> As I look at the totality of the scheme of what I see before me at this time, I have no doubt that the Andersons can if they wish to correct this problem and provide the means of putting these funds in a position that they can be accountable if the final determination of the Court is that the funds should be returned to those who made these payments.

We cannot say that this finding was clearly erroneous. The Andersons had previously been able to obtain in excess of $1 million from the trust in order to pay their taxes. Given their ability to obtain, with ease, such large sums from the trust, we share the district court's skepticism regarding the Andersons' claim that they cannot make the trust assets subject to the court's jurisdiction.

Moreover, beyond this general skepticism concerning the Andersons' lack of control over their trust, the specifics of the Andersons' trust indicate that they retained control over the trust assets. These offshore trusts allow settlors, such as the Andersons, significant control over the trust assets by allowing the settlor to act as a cotrustee or "protector" of the trust. When the settlors retain this type of control, however, they can jeopardize the asset protection scheme because they will be subject to a U.S. court's personal jurisdiction and be forced to exercise their control to repatriate the assets.

The district court's finding that the Andersons were in control of their trust is well supported by the record given that the Andersons were the protectors of their trust. A protector has significant powers to control an offshore trust. A protector can be compelled to exercise control over a trust to repatriate assets if the protector's powers are not drafted solely as the negative powers to veto trustee decisions or if the protector's powers are not subject to the anti-duress provisions of the trust.[53] The Andersons' trust gives them affirmative powers to appoint new trustees and makes the anti-duress provisions subject to the protectors' powers, therefore, they can force the foreign trustee to repatriate the trust assets to the United States.

Perhaps the most telling evidence of the Andersons' control over the trust was their conduct after the district court issued its temporary restraining order ordering the repatriation of the trust funds. . . . After the Andersons claimed that compliance with the repatriation provisions of the temporary restraining order was impossible, the Commission revealed to the court that the Andersons were the protectors of the trust. The Andersons immediately attempted to resign as protectors of the trust. This attempted resignation indicates that the Andersons knew that, as the protectors of the trust, they remained in control of the trust and could force the foreign trustee to repatriate the assets.

Because we see no clear error in the district court's finding that the Andersons remain in control of their trust and could repatriate the trust assets, the district court did not abuse its discretion in holding them in contempt. We, therefore, affirm the district court's finding the Andersons in contempt. Given the nature of the Andersons' so-called "asset protection" trust, which was designed to frustrate the power of United States' courts to enforce judgments, there may be little else that a district court judge can do besides exercise its contempt powers to coerce people like the Andersons into removing the obstacles they placed in the way of a court. Given that the Andersons' trust is operating precisely as they intended, we are not overly sympathetic to their claims and would be hesitant to overly-restrict the district court's discretion, and thus legitimize what the Andersons have done.

Affirmed.

NOTES

1. Epilogue. Over the Christmas holiday in 1998, less than a month before the Ninth Circuit heard oral argument in *Affordable Media*, the district court purged the Andersons of their contempt, freeing them after six months in jail. In September 1999, two months after the Ninth Circuit rendered its decision and almost a year after the Andersons were freed, the FTC brought suit in the Cook Islands against AsiaCiti

---

53. . . . In provisions of the trust agreement that the Andersons conveniently fail to reference, the trust agreement makes clear that the Andersons, as protectors, have the power to determine whether or not an event of duress has occurred: "For the purpose of determining whether an Event of Duress has occurred pursuant to paragraph (c) and paragraph (d) of this clause (1)(a)(vi) of this Deed, *the written certificate of the Protector to that effect shall be conclusive.*" Trust Agreement (emphasis added). Moreover, the very definition of an event of duress that the Andersons assert has occurred makes clear that whether or not an event of duress has occurred depends upon the opinion of the protector: "The issuance of any order, decree or judgement of any court or tribunal in any part of the world *which in the opinion of the Protector* will or may directly or indirectly, expropriate." Trust Agreement (emphasis added). Therefore, notwithstanding the provisions of the trust agreement that the Andersons point to, it is clear that the Andersons could have ordered the trust assets repatriated simply by certifying to the foreign trustee that in their opinion, as protectors, no event of duress had occurred. . . . [Footnote relocated.—Eds.]

Limited, the trustee of the Andersons' offshore trust. The parties settled in 2002 for $1.2 million, the equivalent of six cents on the dollar; the FTC had sought $20 million. The settlement proceeds went to a fund for defrauded customers. The Andersons, meanwhile, served five-year (Michael) and three-year (Denyse) probation sentences coming out of a related state criminal prosecution.

2. Contempt and Offshore APTs. Professor Robert Danforth summarizes the typical features of an offshore APT:

> First, if the APT is properly established in a foreign country, in most cases a court in the United States will lack personal jurisdiction over the trustee. . . . Second, many offshore jurisdictions recognize the role of a trust "protector," a person granted special non-fiduciary powers to control the administration of the trust, with respect to such matters as removal and replacement of trustees, control over discretionary actions of the trustees, etc. By use of the trust protector mechanism, a settlor is able to vest in some trusted person substantial control over trust administration, while at the same [time] being able to resist the claim that the settlor himself or herself (whose actions will be subject to the authority of a United States court) retains such control. . . . Third, many offshore APTs include a so-called duress clause, under which the trustee is directed to ignore any directions received from a settlor or trust protector who is under duress[, which is defined to include] . . . a United States court's order. Finally, most offshore APTs also include a "flight" clause, under which the trustee is authorized to change the situs of the trust, change the applicable law, and move the trust assets to a new jurisdiction, if a claim against the trust threatens to be successful.[54]

Among lawyers who specialize in asset protection, *Affordable Media* is viewed as a cautionary tale on how not to draft an offshore APT. The blunder was giving the settlors, over whom a domestic court would have jurisdiction, affirmative powers to override or to replace the offshore trustee. "The Ninth Circuit seized upon these powers, which settlors typically do not include in offshore trusts, as evidence that the Andersons had power to arrange repatriation of trust assets."[55]

In practice, even a poorly structured APT may give the settlor leverage in negotiating with creditors. The lawyer who represented the plaintiff in In re Brooks, 217 B.R. 98 (Bankr. D. Conn. 1998), explains: "In *Brooks* we got a judgment essentially voiding this offshore trust. We then settled for approximately fifty cents on the dollar, because the enforcement problems were so significant."[56]

3. Conflict of Laws and the "Public Policy" Exception. Prevailing conflict of laws doctrine permits a court to refuse to apply the law of another jurisdiction if that law violates a strong public policy of the forum state. In Dahl v. Dahl, ___ P.3d ___, 2015 UT 79, at issue was a trust with a choice of law provision that pointed to Nevada. Under Nevada law, the trust would be construed as irrevocable, and the divorcing

---

54. Robert T. Danforth, Rethinking the Law of Creditors' Rights in Trusts, 53 Hastings L.J. 287, 309-10 (2002).

55. Sterk, *supra* note 46, at 1103.

56. Roundtable Discussion, 32 Vand. J. Transnat'l L. 779, 786 (1999).

spouse of the settlor would have no right to equitable division of the trust property. Under Utah law, by contrast, the trust would be construed as revocable, and the trust property would be subject to division. Concluding that Nevada law was contrary to Utah's "strong public policy interest in the equitable division of marital assets," the Utah court refused to enforce the "choice-of-law provision contained in the Trust," and instead "construe[d] the Trust according to Utah law."

Might a court in a state that does not recognize APTs refuse to enforce an out-of-state APT on the grounds that it violates the public policy of the forum state? In In re Huber v. Huber, 493 B.R. 798 (Bankr. W.D. Wash. 2013), the court applied the law of Washington, the forum state, rather than the law of Alaska, the state designated by the terms of the trust, to a purported APT. The court reasoned that Washington, not Alaska, had the most substantial relationship to the trust, and that "Washington has a strong public policy against self-settled asset protection trusts." The court included the trust property in the settlor's bankruptcy estate.[57]

4. Exception Creditors.   Most of the APT states recognize *exception creditors* who can recover against the settlor's interest in an APT. Many APT states allow claims by a spouse or a child, and some allow claims by a tort victim. The specifics vary across the states, and not all recognize one or another exception.[58] Nevada recognizes no exceptions.

5. Fraudulent Transfers and Voidable Transactions.   Should there be a distinction between an APT established (a) before a claim against the settlor is pending, threatened, or expected, and that leaves the settlor with enough funds to pay anticipated debts, versus (b) one established after a claim is pending, threatened, or expected, and that is funded with virtually all of the settlor's assets? Under the law of *fraudulent transfers*, codified by the widely adopted Uniform Fraudulent Transfer Act (UFTA) (Unif. Law Comm'n 1984), it is *actual fraud* to make a transfer with the intent to hinder, delay, or defraud creditors, and *constructive fraud* to make a transfer without receiving equivalent value if the transfer leaves the debtor with insufficient assets to pay anticipated debts. Several APT states have modified their fraudulent transfer laws, however, weakening them relative to the UFTA.[59]

In 2014, the Uniform Law Commission amended the UFTA, recasting it as the Uniform Voidable Transactions Act (UVTA) (Unif. Law Comm'n 2014). Among other things, the UVTA clarifies choice of law for reckoning whether a transfer with multi-state contacts is voidable. For a transfer by an individual, § 10 provides that the law of the debtor's principal residence controls. The UVTA has proved controversial, however, because the comment to § 4 says that a transfer to an APT is under historical understandings a voidable transfer "without regard to whether the transaction is directed

---

57. *See* Jonathan D. Blattmachr et al., Avoiding the Adverse Effects of Huber, Tr. & Est., July 2013, at 20; Ronald J. Mann, A Fresh Look at State Asset Protection Trust Statutes, 67 Vand. L. Rev. 1741, 1755-67 (2014) (surveying lower court decisions hostile to out-of-state APTs).

58. *See* David G. Shaftel, Tenth Annual ACTEC Comparison of the Domestic Asset Protection Trust Statutes (2016).

59. Id.

at an existing or identified creditor." On this reasoning, which is elaborated in the comment to § 10, a transfer to an out-of-state APT by a person whose principal residence is in a state that does not recognize APTs would be voidable even if the person had no pending, threatened, or expected claims against him. This analysis has been vigorously disputed by supporters of APTs and is subject to lively debate within the estate planning community. At year-end 2016, UVTA had been adopted in nine states.

6. *Professional Responsibility.* A lawyer involved in an effort to delay, hinder, or defraud a client's existing or foreseeable creditors is asking for trouble.[60] Consider first Model Rule of Professional Conduct 1.2(d) (2015): "A lawyer shall not counsel a client to engage, or assist a client, in conduct that the lawyer knows is criminal or fraudulent." Some states have recognized new theories of liability such as conspiracy to convey property fraudulently and intentional interference with contract, actions that may enable a creditor to assert a claim against the debtor's lawyer. There is also potential for a malpractice claim by the client if the strategy proves to be ineffective. On the other hand, as argued by a lawyer who works for the Wilmington Trust Company in Delaware, "attorneys might face exposure if they do not advise the client to [engage in asset-protection planning] and creditors later reach the client's assets."[61] Some asset protection lawyers require their clients to sign an affidavit swearing under oath as to the client's solvency, a practice that is required by the APT statutes in several states.

7. *Federal Bankruptcy Law Revisited.* As we have seen (see page 711), the Bankruptcy Code excludes from a debtor's bankruptcy estate any beneficial interest in trust that is not alienable "under applicable nonbankruptcy law."[62] Read literally, this provision protects a bankrupt settlor's beneficial interest in an APT, just as it protects a bankrupt beneficiary's interest in a third-party settled spendthrift or discretionary trust.

In 2005, during debate over the Bankruptcy Abuse Prevention and Consumer Protection Act, the Senate considered but ultimately rejected an amendment to the Code that would have included in the bankruptcy estate a beneficial interest in a self-settled trust in excess of $125,000 established within ten years of the bankruptcy filing. The failure of this amendment appears to have "had as much to do with a desire to get the Act through the Senate without complicating amendments as it did with any particular endorsement of [APTs]."[63] Congress did enact a claw back amendment that permits recovery against a debtor's interest in property transferred to a self-settled trust within ten years of bankruptcy if the transfer was made with actual intent to hinder,

---

60. *See, e.g.,* Iowa Supreme Court Attorney Disciplinary Bd. v. Ouderkirk, 845 N.W.2d 31 (Iowa 2014) (concluding, in an opinion spanning 21 pages(!) in the official reporter, that the disciplinary board had not met its burden of showing that a lawyer violated the ethical rules in assisting a client with a trust asset protection plan).

61. Richard W. Nenno, Planning with Domestic Asset-Protection Trusts, Part I, 40 Real Prop. Prob. & Tr. J. 263, 286 (2005).

62. 11 U.S.C. § 541(c)(2) (2016).

63. John K. Eason, Policy, Logic, and Persuasion in the Evolving Realm of Trust Asset Protection, 27 Cardozo L. Rev. 2621, 2674-75 (2006).

delay, or defraud a creditor.[64] In effect, this amendment establishes a longer federal limitations period for bringing a fraudulent transfer claim against a transfer to a self-settled trust.

4. Trusts for the State Supported

A person qualifies for Medicaid and public support benefits only if the person has few financial resources. The asset and income thresholds that will disqualify an applicant vary from state to state. In determining whether an applicant is under the disqualifying threshold, the question sometimes arises whether a trust in which the applicant has a beneficial interest should be counted as a resource available for the support of the applicant.[65] Federal law draws a distinction between (a) *self-settled trusts* (generally included when assessing financial need) and (b) *trusts created by third parties* (generally not included).

a. Self-Settled Trusts

For Medicaid purposes, a trust is self-settled, and therefore considered in the qualification decision, "if assets of the individual were used to form all or part of the corpus of the trust" and the trust was established by the individual, by the individual's spouse, or by a person or court with legal authority to act on behalf of, or on request of, the individual or the individual's spouse.[66] If the trust is revocable by the individual, the principal and all income of the trust are considered resources available to the individual. If the trust is irrevocable, any income or principal that under any circumstances could be paid to or applied for the benefit of the individual are considered resources of the individual. Hence, in the case of a discretionary trust, the Medicaid applicant is deemed to have resources in the maximum amount that could be distributed to him, assuming full exercise of discretion by the trustee in his favor.[67]

There are two important exceptions. First, a discretionary trust created by the will of one spouse for the benefit of the other spouse is not deemed a resource available to the other spouse.[68] This makes it possible for a spouse to create a wholly discretionary trust for the benefit of the surviving spouse, who may qualify for Medicaid if the survivor's other resources are below the eligibility amount.[69]

Second, a trust will not be considered a resource available to the Medicaid applicant if it is established for a disabled individual from the individual's property by a parent, grandparent, guardian of the individual, or by a court, and the trust provides that the state will receive upon the individual's death all amounts remaining in the trust up to

---

64. 11 U.S.C. § 548(e)(1) (2016).
65. *See* Bradley E.S. Fogel, *Scylla and Charybdis Attack: Using Trusts for Medicaid Planning and Non-Medicaid Asset Protection,* 35 ACTEC L.J. 45 (2009).
66. 42 U.S.C. § 1396p(d) (2016).
67. *See* Roskes v. Cnty. of Carver, 783 N.W.2d 220 (Minn. App. 2010).
68. *See* 42 U.S.C. § 1396p(d)(2)(A) (2016).
69. *See* Pohlmann v. Nebraska Dep't of Health and Human Servs., 710 N.W.2d 639 (Neb. 2006).

the total amount of medical assistance paid by the state.[70] This makes it possible, after an accident in which an individual is disabled, to settle the proceeds of a tort recovery in a trust to provide supplemental care for the individual above what the state provides, if the state is reimbursed out of the trust assets at the individual's death.

Because self-settled trusts generally prevent qualification for Medicaid, people who want to preserve their life savings for their descendants will sometimes impoverish themselves by giving the bulk of their property to their descendants, outright or in trust, usually retaining only enough property to cover the anticipated cost of their own care until they qualify for Medicaid. In such cases there is a period of ineligibility that may last for 60 months.[71]

b. Trusts Created by Third Parties

With respect to a trust established by a third person for the benefit of the applicant, Medicaid regulations provide that trust income or principal is "considered available both when actually available and when the applicant or recipient has a legal interest in a liquidated sum and has the legal ability to make such sum available for support and maintenance."[72] Under this provision, if a mandatory or support trust is created in which the beneficiary has a right to compel a distribution of income, the income is treated as a resource available to the beneficiary. But if a discretionary trust is created, the trust is not considered a resource available to the beneficiary unless it was intended to be used for the applicant's support.[73]

For a trust that has been set up by a third party for an institutionalized beneficiary, courts have generally followed the common law rules applicable to creditors of beneficiaries of mandatory, support, and discretionary trusts. If the beneficiary has a right to trust income or principal, the state can reach it. A spendthrift clause does not bar recovery because the state is furnishing necessaries to the beneficiary. Although UTC § 503 (2000, rev. 2005), page 706, does not include an exception for providers of necessary support, the exception under subsection (b)(3) for claims by the state covers cases in which the state provides such support.

Most of the litigation concerns discretionary trusts. Generally, the state cannot reach discretionary trusts nor consider them when determining eligibility for public benefits. Many discretionary trusts are hybrids, however, combining the purpose of support with discretion in the trustee (see page 700). If a beneficiary of a discretionary trust can, under some conceivable circumstances, obtain a court order requiring payment to the beneficiary, it is possible that the trust assets may be reached by the state.[74]

---

70. *See* 42 U.S.C. § 1396p(d)(4)(A) (2016).

71. *See* Schell v. Dep't of Pub. Welfare, 80 A.3d 844, 846 (Pa. Commw. 2013); *see also* Sean R. Bleck, Barbara Isenhour & John A. Miller, Preserving Wealth and Inheritance Through Medicaid Planning for Long-Term Care, 17 Mich. St. J. Med. & L. 153 (2013).

72. 45 C.F.R. § 233.20(a)(3)(ii)(D) (2016).

73. *See* Corcoran v. Dep't of Soc. Servs., 859 A.2d 533 (Conn. 2004).

74. *See* In re Estate of Gist, 763 N.W.2d 561 (Iowa 2009).

the last child has received his or her education and the Trustee, in its discretion, has determined that the purpose hereof has been accomplished.

At such time as this purpose has been accomplished and the Trustee has so determined, the *income from said trust and such part of the principal as may be necessary shall be used by said Trustee for the care, maintenance and welfare of my nephew, Woolson S. Brown and his wife, Rosemary Brown, so that they may live in the style and manner to which they are accustomed, for and during the remainder of their natural lives.* Upon their demise, any remainder of said trust, together with any accumulation thereon, shall be paid to their then living children in equal shares, share and share alike. (Emphasis added.)

The trustee complied with the terms of the trust by using the proceeds to pay for the education of the children of Woolson and Rosemary Brown. After he determined that the education of these children was completed, the trustee began distribution of trust income to the lifetime beneficiaries, Woolson and Rosemary.

On June 17, 1983, the lifetime beneficiaries petitioned the probate court for termination of the trust, arguing that the sole remaining purpose of the trust was to maintain their lifestyle and that distribution of the remaining assets was necessary to accomplish this purpose. The remaindermen, the children of the lifetime beneficiaries, filed consents to the proposed termination. The probate court denied the petition to terminate, and the petitioners appealed to the . . . Superior Court. The superior court reversed, concluding that continuation of the trust was no longer necessary because the only material purpose, the education of the children, had been accomplished. This appeal by the trustee followed. . . .

An active trust may not be terminated, even with the consent of all the beneficiaries, if a material purpose of the settlor remains to be accomplished. Restatement (Second) of Trusts § 337 (1959). This Court has invoked a corollary of this rule in a case where partial termination of a trust was at issue. In re Bayley Trust, 250 A.2d 516, 519 (Vt. 1969).

As a threshold matter, we reject the trustee's argument that the trust cannot be terminated because it is both a support trust and a spendthrift trust. It is true that, were either of these forms of trust involved, termination could not be compelled by the beneficiaries because a material purpose of the settlor would remain unsatisfied. See Restatement (Second) of Trusts § 337.

The trust at issue does not qualify as a support trust. A support trust is created where the trustee is directed to use trust income or principal for the benefit of an individual, but only to the extent necessary to support the individual. 2 A. Scott, Scott on Trusts § 154, at 1176; G. Bogert, Trusts and Trustees § 229, at 519 (2d ed. Rev. 1979). Here, the terms of the trust provide that, when the educational purpose of the trust has been accomplished and the trustee, in his discretion, has so determined, "the income . . . and such part of the principal as may be necessary shall be used by said Trustee for the care, maintenance and welfare of . . . [Rosemary and Woolson Brown] so that they may live in the style and manner to which they are accustomed." The trustee has, in fact, made the determination that the educational purpose has been accomplished and has begun to transfer the income of the trust to the lifetime beneficiaries. Because the trustee must, at the very least, pay all of the trust income to beneficiaries Rosemary and Woolson Brown, the trust cannot be characterized as a support trust.

Nor is this a spendthrift trust. "A trust in which by the terms of the trust or by statute a *valid restraint on the voluntary and involuntary transfer of the interest* of the beneficiary is imposed is a spendthrift trust." Restatement (Second) of Trusts § 152(2). (Emphasis added.) While no specific language is needed to create a spendthrift trust, id. at Comment c, here the terms of the trust instrument do not manifest Andrew J. Brown's intention to create such a trust. . . .

Although the issue as to whether a material purpose of the trust remains cannot be answered through resort to the foregoing formal categories traditionally imposed upon trust instruments, we hold that termination cannot be compelled here because a material purpose of the settlor remains unaccomplished. In the interpretation of trusts, the intent of the settlor, as revealed by the language of the instrument, is determinative. In re Jones, 415 A.2d 202, 205 (Vt. 1980).

We find that the trust instrument at hand has two purposes. First, the trust provides for the education of the children of Woolson and Rosemary Brown. The . . . Superior Court found that Rosemary Brown was incapable of having more children and that the chance of Woolson Brown fathering more children was remote; on this basis, the court concluded that the educational purpose of the trust had been achieved.

The settlor also intended a second purpose, however: the assurance of a life-long income for the beneficiaries through the management and discretion of the trustee. We recognize that, had the trust merely provided for successive beneficiaries, no inference could be drawn that the settlor intended to deprive the beneficiaries of the right to manage the trust property during the period of the trust. Estate of Weeks, 402 A.2d 657, 658 (Pa. 1979). Here, however, the language of the instrument does more than create successive gifts. The settlor provided that the trustee must provide for the "care, maintenance and welfare" of the lifetime beneficiaries "so that they may live in the style and manner to which they are accustomed, *for and during the remainder of their natural lives.*" (Emphasis added.) The trustee must use all of the income and such part of the principal as is necessary for this purpose. We believe that the settlor's intention to assure a life-long income to Woolson and Rosemary Brown would be defeated if termination of the trust were allowed.

Because of our holding regarding the second and continuing material purpose of the trust, we do not reach the question of whether the trial court erred in holding that the educational purpose of the trust has been accomplished.

Reversed; judgment for petitioners vacated and judgment for appellant entered.

NOTE

The Material Purpose in Brown.   Because all trusts interpose a trustee between the beneficiary and the trust property, would not the early termination of any trust offend the settlor's material purpose under the reasoning in *Brown*? If not, what precisely was the material purpose of the settlor that would have been offended by early termination?

Was it that the settlor did not want Woolson and Rosemary to have managerial control over the trust property? The Scott treatise summarizes the case law thus:

> The cases indicate that if the settlor's only purpose in creating the trust was to preserve the trust principal during the life of an income beneficiary, for eventual enjoyment by a remainder beneficiary, early termination ordinarily does not defeat a material trust purpose. In contrast, the cases also indicate that, if the settlor intended to protect the life beneficiary against his or her own mismanagement, termination before the life beneficiary's death would defeat a material trust purpose. Whether this, or any other material purpose, was among the settlor's purposes in creating the trust is, of course, a question of interpretation of the trust instrument, in light of all the circumstances.[82]

Because the trust in *Brown* did not contain a spendthrift clause, Woolson and Rosemary could have sold their interests in the trust for a lump sum. They also could have transferred their interests to their children. If they had done so, could the children have terminated the trust?

c. The UTC and the Restatement (Third) of Trusts

Statutes in several states have relaxed the conditions under which a trust may be modified by consent of the beneficiaries. Some of these statutes, and UTC § 411, excerpted below, preserve the traditional material purpose rule but permit modification or termination by consent of only some of the beneficiaries. A few statutes, and the Restatement (Third) of Trusts, weaken the material purpose rule, permitting modification or termination if the beneficiaries can persuade the court that "the reason(s) for termination or modification outweigh the material purpose."[83]

Uniform Trust Code (Unif. Law Comm'n 2000, as amended 2004)

§ 411. Modification or Termination of Noncharitable Irrevocable Trust by Consent

[(a) ... A noncharitable irrevocable trust may be modified or terminated upon consent of the settlor and all beneficiaries, even if the modification or termination is inconsistent with a material purpose of the trust.] ...

(b) A noncharitable irrevocable trust may be terminated upon consent of all of the beneficiaries if the court concludes that continuance of the trust is not necessary to achieve any material purpose of the trust. A noncharitable irrevocable trust may be modified upon consent of all of the beneficiaries if the court concludes that modification is not inconsistent with a material purpose of the trust.

[(c) A spendthrift provision in the terms of the trust is not presumed to constitute a material purpose of the trust.]

---

82. Scott and Ascher on Trusts § 34.1.
83. Restatement (Third) of Trusts § 65 (Am. Law Inst. 2003).

(d) Upon termination of a trust under subsection . . . (b), the trustee shall distribute the trust property as agreed by the beneficiaries.

(e) If not all of the beneficiaries consent to a proposed modification or termination of the trust under subsection . . . (b), the modification or termination may be approved by the court if the court is satisfied that:

(1) if all of the beneficiaries had consented, the trust could have been modified or terminated under this section; and

(2) the interests of a beneficiary who does not consent will be adequately protected.

NOTE

Claflin Under the UTC and the Restatement. The UTC carries forward the heart of the *Claflin* doctrine. Under § 411(b), a trust may not be modified or terminated if continuance of the trust is necessary to achieve a material purpose of the settlor. The comment says that a material purpose is one that is "of some significance." It quotes approvingly from the Restatement (Third) of Trusts thus:

> Material purposes are not readily to be inferred. A finding of such a purpose generally requires some showing of a particular concern or objective on the part of the settlor, such as concern with regard to a beneficiary's management skills, judgment, or level of maturity. Thus, a court may look for some circumstantial or other evidence indicating that the trust arrangement represented to the settlor more than a method of allocating the benefits of property among multiple intended beneficiaries, or a means of offering to the beneficiaries (but not imposing on them) a particular advantage. Sometimes, of course, the very nature or design of a trust suggests its protective nature or some other material purpose.[84]

Unlike the UTC, however, the Restatement significantly alters the material purpose rule. The Restatement provides:

> If termination or modification of the trust . . . would be inconsistent with a material purpose of the trust, the beneficiaries cannot compel its termination or modification except with the consent of the settlor or, after the settlor's death, *with authorization of the court if it determines that the reason(s) for termination or modification outweigh the material purpose.*[85]

This balancing test is based on Cal. Prob. Code § 15403(b) (2016), which the Restatement says "has apparently proved useful and noncontroversial in California since enactment in 1990."[86] But the California statute excludes spendthrift trusts, which largely defeats the reform, as spendthrift clauses are typical in professionally drafted instruments. Under the Restatement, by contrast, "spendthrift restrictions are not sufficient in and of themselves to establish, or to create a presumption of, a material

---

84. Id. cmt. d.
85. Id. § 65(2) (emphasis added).
86. Reporter's Notes to id. cmt. d.

purpose that would prevent termination by consent of all of the beneficiaries."[87] Do you see a parallel between the Restatement's minority position on creditor rights in discretionary and spendthrift trusts (pages 700 and 709) and its minority position on material purpose for modification and termination?

As originally drafted, UTC § 411(c) followed the Restatement in rejecting the prevailing rule in the cases that a spendthrift provision is a material purpose of the settlor prohibiting modification or termination. The drafters took the view that a spendthrift provision is common boilerplate, hence not enough without more to indicate a material purpose. In 2004, in response to this provision's chilly reception by state legislatures, the Uniform Law Commission put it in brackets, making it optional. Several enacting jurisdictions had deleted the provision or rewrote it so that a spendthrift clause would be assumed to state a material purpose.[88]

The UTC and the Restatement also differ on the question of whether unanimity of the beneficiaries is necessary for modification or termination by consent. UTC § 411(e) provides for modification or termination by consent of only some of the beneficiaries if the "interests of a beneficiary who does not consent will be adequately protected." The Restatement follows the traditional rule that consent must be obtained from or on behalf of all the beneficiaries.[89]

2. Deviation and Changed Circumstances

a. Traditional Law

Under the *equitable deviation* doctrine, a court will permit a trustee to deviate from the administrative terms of a trust if compliance would defeat or substantially impair the accomplishment of the purposes of the trust in light of changed circumstances not anticipated by the settlor. It is not enough to show that deviation would be advantageous or better for the beneficiaries. The proposed deviation must be necessary to accomplish a purpose of the trust.

In re Trust of Stuchell, 801 P.2d 852 (Or. App. 1990), is illustrative. By will executed in 1947, the testator established a testamentary trust for his family. The petitioner, Edna, was one of the two surviving life beneficiaries. Upon the death of the last life beneficiary, the principal of the trust was to be distributed to Edna's children or their surviving descendants per stirpes. At the time of the litigation, Edna had four children. One of them, John, age 25, was mentally disabled and unable to live independently. To preserve John's eligibility for public assistance, Edna petitioned the court to modify the trust so that John would not take his share outright on Edna's death.

---

87. Id. § 65 cmt. e.
88. *Compare* In re Pike Family Trusts, 38 A.3d 329 (Me. 2012) (noting that § 411(c), enacted in Maine as originally drafted, reverses the common law presumption that a spendthrift clause is a material purpose), *with* In re Trust D Under Last Will of Darby, 234 P.3d 793 (Kan. 2010) (noting that the version of § 411(c) enacted in Kansas provides that a spendthrift provision is presumed to be a material purpose).
89. Restatement (Third) of Trusts § 65 cmt. b (Am. Law Inst. 2003).

In December, 1989, petitioner requested the court to approve, on behalf of [John], an agreement, which had been approved by the other income beneficiary and remaindermen, to modify the trust. If the trust is not modified, [John's] remainder will be distributed directly to him if he survives the two life-income beneficiaries. If and when that happens, his ability to qualify for public assistance will be severely limited. The proposed modification provides for the continuation of the trust, if [John] survives the two life-income beneficiaries, and contains elaborate provisions that are designed to avoid his becoming disqualified, in whole or in part, for any public assistance programs. The stated purpose is to ensure that the trust funds be used only as a secondary source of funds to supplement, rather than to replace, his current income and benefits from public assistance.

Invoking the deviation doctrine (do you see why she could not invoke *Claflin*?), Edna argued that John's disability was an unanticipated circumstance that would defeat or substantially impair the purpose of the trust. The court denied Edna's petition. Quoting the Restatement (Second) of Trusts, the court held that deviation is not permitted "merely because such deviation would be more advantageous to the beneficiaries." The court reasoned that "the only purpose" of the proposed modification "is to make the trust more advantageous to the beneficiaries. The most obvious advantage would be to the three remaindermen who have consented to the amendment."

Do you think that the testator, who did not anticipate John's special needs, would have objected to the proposed modification once those needs became apparent? Why did the court not regard this as the relevant question? Courts have been much more liberal in permitting trustees to deviate from *administrative* terms owing to an unanticipated change of circumstances than they have been in permitting modification of *dispositive* provisions.

Perhaps the most celebrated case of deviation from an administrative term is In re Pulitzer, 249 N.Y.S. 87 (Sur. 1931), aff'd mem., 260 N.Y.S. 975 (App. Div. 1932). In 1911, Joseph Pulitzer's will created a trust for the benefit of his descendants. Pulitzer bequeathed to the trustees shares of stock in a corporation publishing the World newspapers (including one of the major papers of the day, the New York World), and his will provided that the sale of these shares was not authorized under any circumstances. After several years of large and increasing losses from the publication of the World, in 1931 the trustees petitioned the court to approve a sale of the shares. The court held that, even though a sale was prohibited by Pulitzer, it had the power to authorize a sale because the trust estate was in jeopardy, and it approved the sale. The court reasoned that the settlor's dominant purpose was to benefit the beneficiaries, and that a person of such "sagacity and business ability"

Joseph Pulitzer

could not have intended to keep the newspaper operating out of "mere vanity" if it put the trust in peril.

b. Extension to Dispositive Provisions

If an unanticipated change in circumstances can justify deviation from an administrative term, why not likewise permit deviation from a dispositive provision to adapt the trust's distribution scheme to changed circumstances? Is not the settlor's purpose in a dispositive provision also vulnerable to frustration owing to an unanticipated change in circumstances? Increasingly courts and legislatures are inclined to authorize deviation from dispositive provisions. Cal. Prob. Code § 15409 (2016), enacted in 1990, is illustrative. It authorizes a court to "modify the administrative *or dispositive* provisions of the trust or terminate the trust if, owing to circumstances not known to the settlor and not anticipated by the settlor, the continuation of the trust under its terms would defeat or substantially impair the accomplishment of the purposes of the trust [emphasis added]."

UTC § 412 (2000), excerpted below, adopts the modern view of equitable deviation as applicable to both administrative and dispositive terms. It also liberalizes the standard for deviation from a showing that failure to deviate will substantially impair the purposes of the trust to a showing that deviation will further the purposes of the trust. The Restatement (Third) of Trusts is similar.[90]

Uniform Trust Code (Unif. Law Comm'n 2000)

§ 412. Modification or Termination Because of Unanticipated Circumstances or Inability to Administer Trust Effectively

(a) The court may modify the administrative or dispositive terms of a trust or terminate the trust if, because of circumstances not anticipated by the settlor, modification or termination will further the purposes of the trust. To the extent practicable, the modification must be made in accordance with the settlor's probable intention.

(b) The court may modify the administrative terms of a trust if continuation of the trust on its existing terms would be impracticable or wasteful or impair the trust's administration.

(c) Upon termination of a trust under this section, the trustee shall distribute the trust property in a manner consistent with the purposes of the trust.

In re Riddell
157 P.3d 888 (Wash. App. 2007)

PENOYAR, J. The Trustee of a consolidated trust, Ralph A. Riddell, appeals the trial court's denial of his motion to modify the trust and create a special needs trust on

---

90. Id. § 66(1) ("The court may modify an administrative or distributive provision of a trust, or direct or permit the trustee to deviate from an administrative or distributive provision, if because of circumstances not anticipated by the settlor the modification or deviation will further the purposes of the trust.").

behalf of a trust beneficiary, his daughter, Nancy I. Dexter, who suffers from schizophrenia affective disorder and bipolar disorder.[91] . . .

FACTS

George X. Riddell and Irene A. Riddell were husband and wife with one child, Ralph. George's Last Will and Testament left the residue of his estate in trust for the benefit of his wife, his son, his daughter-in-law, and his grandchildren. George also created an additional trust (the Life Insurance Trust) for their benefit. Irene's Last Will and Testament left the residue of her estate in trust for the benefit of her son; her son's wife, Beverly Riddell; and her grandchildren.

The trusts contained a provision in which, upon the death of Ralph and Beverly, George and Irene's grandchildren would receive the trust's benefits until the age of thirty-five when the trusts would terminate and the trustee would distribute the principal to the grandchildren. Ralph is currently the Trustee. George and Irene are both deceased.

Ralph and Beverly have two children, Donald H. Riddell and Nancy. Both Donald and Nancy are more than thirty-five years old. Donald is a practicing attorney and able to handle his own financial affairs. Nancy suffers from schizophrenia affective disorder and bipolar disorder; by 1991 she received extensive outpatient care; and by 1997 she moved to Western State Hospital. She is not expected to live independently for the remainder of her life.

Both Ralph and Beverly are still living. Upon their death, the trusts will terminate because Nancy and Donald are both over the age of thirty-five; Nancy will receive her portion of her grandparents' trust principal, which is approximately one half of $1,335,000.

The Trustee, Ralph, . . . filed a petition in superior court, asking the trial court to consolidate the trusts and to modify the trust to create a "special needs" trust on Nancy's behalf, instead of distributing the trust principal to her. He explained that, under the current trust, when her parents die, Nancy's portion of the principal will be distributed to her and the trust will terminate. He argued that a special needs trust is necessary because, upon distribution, Nancy's trust funds would either be seized by the State of Washington to pay her extraordinary medical bills or Nancy would manage the funds poorly due to her mental illness and lack of judgment. He argued that the modification would preserve and properly manage Nancy's funds for her benefit.

The trial court granted the motion to consolidate the trusts but denied the motion to modify. It stated that it did not have the power to modify the trust unless unanticipated events existed that were unknown to the trust creator that would result in defeating the trust's purpose. The trial court found that the trust's purpose was "to provide for the education, support, maintenance, and medical care of the beneficiaries" and that a modification would only "permit[ ] the family to immunize itself financially from

---

91. For an explanation of *special* or *supplemental needs trusts*, see page 726. — Eds.

reimbursing the State for costs of [Nancy's medical] care." Relying on the Restatement (Second) of Trusts, it stated that it would not allow a modification "merely because a change would be more advantageous to the beneficiaries." . . .

Ralph moved for reconsideration, arguing that . . . the Restatement (Third) of Trusts gave the trial court . . . the authority to modify the consolidated trust into a special needs trust. Ralph argued that, because the grandparents directed the trust proceeds to be distributed to their grandchildren when they reach the age of thirty-five, the settlors intended that their grandchildren attain a level of responsibility, stability, and maturity to handle the funds before receiving the distribution. He also argued that due to Nancy's mental illness, allowing a distribution to her would defeat the settlors' intent and the trust's purpose.

The trial court denied the motion for reconsideration. It . . . agreed that the Restatement (Third) of Trusts . . . allowed the court to modify an administrative or distributive protection of a trust if, because of circumstances the settlor did not anticipate, the modification or deviation would further the trust's purpose. It then stated:

> I believe that there is a showing here that there is a circumstance that was, perhaps, not anticipated by the original settler [sic]; however, the purpose of the trust is to provide for the general support and medical needs of the beneficiaries. I think that modifying the trust in a fashion that makes some of those assets less available for that purpose than they would be under the express language of the trust presently is not consistent with the purpose of the trust.

The trial court reasoned that because the trust was written to provide for "medical care" and because creating a special needs trust would make some money unavailable for medical care expenses, the modification was inconsistent with the trust's purpose. Ralph now appeals.

ANALYSIS

. . . Ralph contends that the trial court erred in declining to modify the trust. He explains that a modification would further the trust's purpose because, if George and Irene had anticipated that Nancy would suffer debilitating mental illness requiring extraordinary levels of medical costs and make her incapable of managing her money independently, they would not have structured the trust to leave a substantial outright distribution of the trust principal to her. He contends that the settlors instead would have established a special needs trust to protect the funds because Nancy's medical bills would be extraordinary and covered by state funding. . . .

In Niemann v. Vaughn Community Church, 113 P.3d 463 (Wash. 2005), our Supreme Court held that trial courts may use "equitable deviation" to make changes in the manner in which a trust is carried out. The court outlined the two prong approach of "equitable deviation" used to determine if modification is appropriate. The court "may modify an administrative or distributive provision of a trust, or direct or permit the trustee to deviate from an administrative or distributive provision, if [1] because of circumstances not anticipated by the settlor [2] the modification or deviation will further the purposes of the trust." Niemann, 113 P.3d at 470. In Niemann, the court adopted the Restatement (Third) of Trusts and noted that [it] requires a lower threshold finding than the older Restatement and gives courts broader discretion in permitting deviation of a trust.

The first prong of the equitable deviation test is satisfied if circumstances have changed since the trust's creation or if the settlor was unaware of circumstances when the trust was established. Upon a finding of unanticipated circumstances, the trial court must determine if a modification would tend to advance the trust purposes; this inquiry is likely to involve a subjective process of attempting to infer the relevant purpose of a trust from the general tenor of its provisions.

The reason to modify is to give effect to the settlor's intent had the circumstances in question been anticipated. Courts will not ordinarily deviate from the provisions outlined by the trust creator but they undoubtedly have the power to do so, if it is reasonably necessary to effectuate the trust's *primary* purpose. *Niemann*, 113 P.3d at 471....

In this case, the trial court did not issue formal factual findings, but it stated in the oral ruling that there was a showing of a changed circumstance in this case. This meets the first prong. The settlor's intent is also a factual question. The trial court found in its oral ruling that the "stated" purpose of the trust is to provide for the beneficiaries' education, support, maintenance, and medical care. Thus, it found that this trust's primary purpose was to provide for Nancy during her lifetime. Because the trust was to terminate at age thirty-five, it was also the settlors' intent that Nancy have the money to dispose of as she saw fit, which would include any estate planning that she might choose to do.

There is no question that changed circumstances have intervened to frustrate the settlors' intent. Nancy's grandparents intended that she have the funds to use as she saw fit. Not only is Nancy unable to manage the funds or to pass them to her son, but there is a great likelihood that the funds will be lost to the State for her medical care. It is clear that the settlors would have wanted a different result.

In 1993, as part of the Omnibus Budget Reconciliation Act, Congress set forth a requirement for creating special needs trusts (or supplemental trusts), intended to care for the needs of persons with disabilities and preserve government benefits eligibility while allowing families to provide for the supplemental needs of a disabled person that government assistance does not provide. The Act exempted certain assets from those assets and resources counted for the purposes of determining an individual's eligibility for government assistance. Pub. L. 103-66, § 13611(b), codified at 42 U.S.C. § 1396p(d)(4)(A). A supplemental needs trust is a trust that is established for the disabled person's benefit and that is intended to supplement public benefits without increasing countable assets and resources so as to disqualify the individual from public benefits.

In this case, the trial court was concerned with fashioning a trust for Nancy that would allow the family to shield itself for "reimbursing the State" for the costs of her medical care due to her disability. But in 1993, Congress permitted the creation of special needs trusts in order to allow disabled persons to continue to receive governmental assistance for their medical care. Special needs trusts were created in order to allow disabled persons to continue receiving governmental assistance for their medical care, while allowing extra funds for assistance the government did not provide. Given this legal backdrop, the trial court should not have considered any loss to the State in determining whether an equitable deviation is allowed. The law invites, rather than discourages, the creation of special needs trusts in just this sort of situation. The proper focus is on the settlors' intent, the changed circumstances, and what is equitable for these beneficiaries.

George and Irene both died without creating a special needs trust but did not know of Nancy's mental health issues or how they might best be addressed. They clearly intended to establish a trust to provide for their grandchildren's general support, not solely for extraordinary and unanticipated medical bills.

A special needs trust may be established by a third party or by the disabled person that would be benefited by the trust. Trusts established or funded by the disabled person are subject to 42 U.S.C. § 1396p(d)(4)(A), which entitles the State to receive all remaining trust amounts upon trust termination for medical assistance paid on behalf of the disabled beneficiary. However, the State is not entitled to receive payback upon termination of a third party special needs trust for medical assistance provided for the disabled beneficiary. Here, the trust was established and funded by George and Irene Riddell for the beneficiary Nancy Dexter. It is a third party special needs trust. The trust is not subject to State assistance payback and is not required to have a payback provision.

We remand to the trial court to reconsider this matter and to order such equitable deviation as is consistent with the settlors' intent in light of changed circumstances.

NOTES

1. The Probable Intent of the Settlor. Why did the courts in *Riddell* and *Stuchell* reach opposite results on the same basic facts? Which outcome is more consistent with the probable intent of the respective settlors? Which is more consistent with the principle of freedom of disposition? "The objective [of deviation] is to give effect to what the settlor's intent probably would have been had the circumstances in question been anticipated."[92]

Although deviation under UTC § 412(a) must accord with the settlor's probable intent, deviation under subsection (b) from an administrative term that has become "wasteful" is not so limited. Compare waste as a basis for *cy pres* under UTC § 413, discussed in Chapter 11 at page 772.

2. A Duty to Seek Deviation? If the trustee in *Riddell* had not sought deviation, would he have been in breach of duty? Should a trustee who is aware of circumstances justifying deviation have a duty to petition the court? *See* Restatement (Third) of Trusts § 66 cmt. e (Am. Law Inst. 2003).

3. An Unanticipated Change in Circumstances. In 1950, *T* devised a fund worth $120,000 in trust to *X* to pay *A* and *B* each $100 per month for their lives and then to pay the remainder to a charity, *C*. In 2001, observing that the trust corpus had grown to $3.5 million and arguing that this growth was an unanticipated change in circumstances, the beneficiaries petition for an order terminating the trust and directing the

---

92. Restatement (Third) of Trusts § 66 cmt. a (Am. Law Inst. 2003).

trustee to pay $150,000 each to *A* and *B* and the $3.2 million balance to *C*. What result? *See* In re Estate of Somers, 89 P.3d 898 (Kan. 2004).

In 1997, *T* declared an irrevocable trust over $1 million for the benefit of her son, *S*, to pay the income to *S* and then to distribute the principal to him when he turned 55. At the time of the declaration, *S* was engaged to *D*; they married the following year. In 2009, when *S* was 54, *D* filed for divorce. Arguing that the dissolution of *S* and *D*'s marriage was an unanticipated change in circumstances, *T* petitioned the court for an order postponing *S*'s principal distribution until after the divorce proceedings. What result? *See* In re Stephen L. Chapman Irrevocable Trust Agreement, 953 N.E.2d 573 (Ind. App. 2011).

4. Combination, Division, and Uneconomic Trusts.   The court in *Riddell* combined similar trusts in order to eliminate redundant costs and achieve efficiencies in administration. Circumstances may also call for division of a trust into one or more separate trusts, for example if the beneficiaries have different tax or investment considerations or the number of beneficiaries makes administration of the trust unwieldy. Professionally drafted trusts commonly include provisions authorizing the trustee to combine or divide without court approval. Combination and division of trusts is authorized by UTC § 417 (2000) and the Restatement (Third) of Trusts.[93]

A related problem concerns a trust that has so declined in value that continuing it no longer makes economic sense. UTC § 414 (2000) authorizes modification or termination of uneconomic trusts, a practice endorsed by the Restatement.[94]

5. Mandatory Law?   Changing the facts in In re Pulitzer, page 735, Professor John Langbein asks what if the settlor had directed that deviation not be allowed even if the newspaper was likely to fail:

> Suppose . . . that the settlor in *Pulitzer* had foreseen and recited in the trust instrument the danger that the newspaper might become unprofitable, and he directed the trustees to continue operating it anyhow. In the actual case, the court refused to consider the possibility that a settlor of such "sagacity and business ability" could have intended "from mere vanity" to keep the newspaper operating at the expense of the trust. But suppose he had. Suppose the settlor spelled out that he foresaw the possibility that the paper would cease to be economically viable, but he wanted it maintained regardless of the impairment of the interests of the beneficiaries.[95]

In the circumstances posited by Langbein, should a court authorize sale of the newspaper stock nonetheless? UTC § 105(b)(4) (2000, rev. 2005) provides that a settlor cannot vary "the power of the court to modify or terminate a trust," such as under UTC §§ 411 and 412. The comment to § 412 explains: "Although the settlor is granted considerable latitude in defining the purposes of the trust, the principle that a trust

---

93. *See* id. § 68.

94. *See* id. § 66 cmt. d. Should it matter whether an uneconomic trust contains a spendthrift provision? *See* Philip J. Ruce, The Trustee and the Spendthrift: The Argument Against Small Trust Termination, 48 Gonz. L. Rev. 163 (2012).

95. John H. Langbein, Mandatory Rules in the Law of Trusts, 98 Nw. U. L. Rev. 1105, 1118 (2004).

have a purpose which is for the benefit of its beneficiaries precludes unreasonable restrictions on the use of trust property. An owner's freedom to be capricious about the use of the owner's own property ends when the property is impressed with a trust for the benefit of others."

c. Tax Objectives

Courts tend to be receptive to petitions seeking to modify or reform a trust to obtain an income or estate tax advantage. In some cases, courts have corrected a drafting error that, if left uncorrected, would result in a tax inefficiency, as in O'Connell v. Houser, 18 N.E.3d 344 (Mass. 2014). This is an application of *reformation*, an equitable remedy that conforms the trust instrument to what the settlor actually intended it to say.[96]

In other cases, courts have modified a trust because an unanticipated change in circumstance has frustrated the settlor's tax objectives. This is an application of *equitable deviation*. Permitting deviation to achieve the settlor's probable tax objectives is specifically authorized by UTC § 416 (2000), Uniform Probate Code (UPC) § 2-806 (Unif. Law Comm'n 2008), and the Restatement (Third) of Property.[97]

3. Trust Decanting

In common usage, to "decant" is to pour a liquid from one vessel into another, typically to separate the liquid from any sediment. An older red wine, for example, might be decanted to separate it from sediment that formed while the wine was cellared (decanting also aerates the wine, making it apt for a full-bodied younger wine too). In a *trust decanting*, a trustee who under the terms of the original trust (the *first trust*) has a discretionary power over distribution uses that power to distribute the trust property to a new trust (the *second trust*) with updated provisions, leaving behind the sediment of the first trust's stale provisions. Thus:

> *Case 3.* T devises a fund in trust to X to pay or apply so much of the income and principal to A or B as X determines from time to time in X's sole discretion. The terms of the first trust lack a provision for trustee succession and have been rendered tax inefficient by subsequent changes in the tax laws. X declares a new trust for the benefit of A and B with terms otherwise identical to the first trust, except the second trust includes a provision for trustee succession and other changes to achieve the settlor's intended tax objectives in light of current tax law. X funds the second trust with a distribution — a decanting — of the entire corpus of the first trust.

Most commentators point to Phipps v. Palm Beach Trust Company, 196 So. 299 (Fla. 1940), as the first trust decanting case. In *Phipps*, the court held that a trustee who has a discretionary power to distribute property to a beneficiary outright may

---

96. The IRS has recognized the retroactive effect of reformation. *See* I.R.S. Priv. Ltr. Rul. 201544005 (Oct. 30, 2015).

97. *See* Restatement (Third) of Property: Wills and Other Donative Transfers § 12.2 (Am. Law Inst. 2003).

also distribute the property to the beneficiary in further trust. Applying the prevailing rule applicable to a power of appointment (see Chapter 12 at page 837), the court concluded that a "power vested in a trustee to create an estate in fee includes the power to create or appoint any estate less than a fee unless the donor clearly indicates a contrary intent."[98] Is this consistent with the settlor's probable intent? The theory in favor of decanting is that, by giving a trustee a power to make an outright distribution, the settlor implicitly gave the trustee a power to make a conditional distribution in further trust.

Unlike a modification under the *Claflin* or deviation doctrines, however, which require a judicial determination that the modification would not interfere with a material purpose of the settlor (*Claflin*) or is necessary given unanticipated changed circumstances to further the purposes of the trust (deviation), a trust decanting does not require court involvement, and it may even permit the creation of a second trust that varies from a material purpose of the first trust. A decant-ing is subject to judicial review only if an interested party petitions the court and only for the trustee's compliance with the trustee's fiduciary duties under the first trust. Thus, the onus is on a beneficiary who objects to the decant-ing to bring an action for judicial review—and the nature of that review is somewhat unclear.[99]

Decanting a bottle of wine
Andrew Safonov/Shutterstock

For example, if in Case 3 above the second trust named only *A* as a beneficiary and *B* objected, *B* would need to bring an action against *X* for breach of fiduciary duty. Of course, the same would be true if *X* exercised her discretion under the terms of the trust to distribute the entire corpus outright to *A*. Does the settlor's grant to *X* of the greater power to distribute the entire corpus to *A*, excluding *B*, include the lesser power to decant the corpus into a new trust for *A* only?

Suppose in Case 3 that under the first trust *X* was required to distribute quarterly all income to *B*. Could *B*'s mandatory income interest be destroyed by a decanting into a second trust for *A* only or for *A* and *B* but without the mandatory income interest? Does the settlor's grant to *X* of the greater power to distribute the entire corpus to *A*, excluding *B*, include the lesser power to decant the corpus into a second trust without *B*'s right to mandatory income distributions?

In Morse v. Kraft, 992 N.E.2d 1021 (Mass. 2013), the trustee had "discretion to dis-tribute property directly to, or appl[y] for the benefit of, the trust beneficiaries." The court read "this broad grant of almost unlimited discretion as evidence of the settlor's

---

98. *See also* Restatement (Third) of Property: Wills and Other Donative Transfers § 19.14 cmt. f (Am. Law Inst. 2011) ("Subject to fiduciary standards and the terms of the power, a trustee or other fiduciary can exercise a fiduciary distributive power such as a power of invasion to create another trust.").

99. *See* Stewart E. Sterk, Trust Decanting: A Critical Perspective, 38 Cardozo L. Rev. (forthcoming 2017).

intent that the . . . trustee have the authority to distribute assets in further trust for the beneficiaries' benefit. Such interpretation is in keeping with the reading of similar trust language in *Phipps.*" However, the court declined to "recognize an inherent power of trustees of irrevocable trusts to exercise their distribution authority by distributing trust property in further trust, irrespective of the language of the trust." Under *Morse,* therefore, discerning the extent to which a trustee may decant at common law requires a construction of the terms of the trust.

Given the uncertainties surrounding common law decanting, the growing number of older trusts with stale terms, and the increasingly intense jurisdictional competition for trust funds, lawyers have successfully sought enactment of decanting statutes. New York adopted the first decanting statute in 1992. Alaska and Delaware followed respectively in 1998 and 2003. Since then, other states have adopted decanting statutes at an increasingly rapid pace. By year-end 2016, at least 25 states had enacted a decanting statute.[100] The statutes expand decanting by validating it in states that had not yet recognized it at common law. But many of the statutes also constrain decanting by imposing procedural and substantive safeguards.

Figure 10.2

Decanting Statutes (2016)

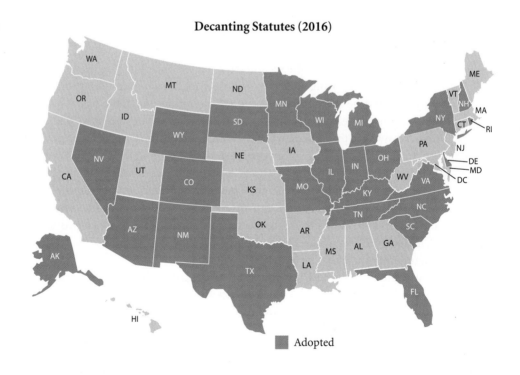

■ Adopted

---

100. Alaska, Arizona, Colorado, Delaware, Florida, Illinois, Indiana, Kentucky, Michigan, Minnesota, Missouri, Nevada, New Hampshire, New Mexico, New York, North Carolina, Ohio, Rhode Island, South Carolina, South Dakota, Tennessee, Texas, Virginia, Wisconsin, and Wyoming.

Harrell v. Badger
171 So. 3d 764 (Fla. App. 2015)

WALLIS, J. . . . Appellants, Joann Harrell ("Harrell") and Barbara Dake ("Dake"), appeal from a final judgment discharging Appellee, Charles Badger ("Badger"), as trustee of the Trust created by Appellants' mother, Rita Wilson ("Rita"). . . . We reverse the final judgment as a result of Badger's failure to comply with [the Florida decanting statute] and, noting Badger's numerous breaches of his fiduciary duty to the Trust, remand for an evidentiary hearing. . . .

In her will, Rita devised the remainder of her estate to the Trust for the specified purpose of benefitting Appellants' adopted brother, David Wilson ("Wilson"), as follows:

A. My Trustees shall pay over and distribute, free from any trust, the entire net income of the trust on a monthly basis for the benefit of my son, DAVID A. WILSON.

B. My Trustees shall have the full power and authority, exercisable in their sole and uncontrolled discretion, to pay to or for the benefit of my said son, for his support, maintenance and education or to meet emergencies such as illness, such amount or amounts of the principal of the Trust as my Trustees shall determine to be proper and necessary, and any such payment shall be free from trust and the judgment of my Trustees as to the propriety and amount of any such payment shall be conclusive and binding upon all persons.

THIRD: I devise all of the rest, residue and remainder of my estate, of whatsoever it shall consist and wherever situate, to my Trustees, hereinafter named, IN TRUST NEVERTHELESS, for the following uses and purposes:

A.   My Trustees shall pay over and distribute, free from any trust, the entire net income of the trust on a monthly basis for the benefit of my son, DAVID A. WILSON.

B.   My Trustees shall have the full power and authority, exercisable in their sole and uncontrolled discretion, to pay to or for the benefit of my said son, for his support, maintenance and education or to meet emergencies such as illness, such amount or amounts of the principal of the Trust as my Trustees shall determine to be proper and necessary, and any such payment shall be free from trust and the judgment of my Trustees as to the propriety and amount of any such payment shall be conclusive and binding upon all persons.

C.   In the event my said son should predecease me or upon the death

The will provisions in *Harrell* prescribing David Wilson's beneficial interest

The will provided that if Wilson predeceased Appellants, the remaining Trust principal would be distributed to them. The will appointed Rita's sisters as co-trustees; however, they resigned after Rita's death, and Wilson consented to Harrell's substitution as trustee. Following alleged disputes with Appellants, Wilson petitioned the trial court to remove Harrell and to appoint Wilson's neighbor, Badger, as trustee. Harrell thereafter voluntarily resigned as trustee.

On August 16, 2006, the trial court entered an order appointing Badger as trustee. The order required Badger to obtain a $300,000 trustee bond and to file semi-annual accountings. Badger failed to obtain the bond until September 12, 2007, and filed only one accounting in August 2007. Before obtaining the bond, Badger allegedly incurred $34,021 in personal expenses for Wilson's support. On February 16, 2007, Badger filed a motion seeking reimbursement of the personal expenses and approval from the trial court to employ his wife as the realtor for the sale of Rita's house—the sole remaining asset of the Trust. Despite holding a hearing on the motion, the trial court never entered an order approving Badger's requests.

Prior to posting bond, Badger approached Ross and Linda Littlefield (collectively "the Littlefields") with the intention of transferring the Trust's assets into a "special needs" trust designed to qualify Wilson for various government benefits. Badger retained Linda Littlefield as counsel for the Trust. In October 2007, Wilson signed a "joinder agreement" to create a sub-account of the Florida Foundation for Special Needs Trust ("FFSNT"), a "pooled trust" administered by the Littlefields. The joinder agreement designated Ross Littlefield as trustee and Wilson as the beneficiary of the sub-account. The agreement provided for the dissolution of the sub-account after Wilson's death, stating that any funds remaining in the sub-account would be subsumed into the FFSNT and used to provide for other beneficiaries of the pooled trust. The joinder agreement did not list Appellants as remainder beneficiaries or otherwise consider their interest in the original Trust.

Badger, his wife, and Wilson entered into an October 2007 "care agreement." The care agreement confused the contracting parties, to wit: requiring Badger's wife to care for Badger, not Wilson, and designating Wilson as a trustee without referencing any trust. Badger testified before the lower court that he did not read the terms of either the joinder or care agreement, and that he was unaware of any requirements to care for Wilson on the part of himself or his wife, despite later submitting "accountings" in which Badger purportedly received thousands of dollars from the various trusts for caregiving expenses.

In January 2008, Badger sold the house—employing his wife as realtor, without court-approval, for a five-percent sale commission—and immediately wired the net proceeds to the FFSNT. Badger did not provide notice to Appellants of the agreements, the sale of the house, or the transfer of all remaining Trust assets to the FFSNT.

The Littlefields subsequently transferred all funds from the FFSNT into another trust—the JNN Trust—apparently without consent from Wilson, Badger, or any other person associated with Wilson's sub-account. In 2010, the Littlefields were arrested, convicted, and sentenced to prison for the misappropriation of funds in the JNN Trust.

TRIAL [AND] FINAL JUDGMENT . . .

On September 21, 2011, Badger filed a motion to terminate the Trust, wherein he first notified Appellants of the agreements, the sale of the house, and the transfer of all funds into the FFSNT. He also filed a series of uncorroborated accountings, ostensibly listing all income and disbursements from the original Trust over the period of December 2007 through November 2012, including payments to and from the FFSNT and the JNN Trust. Appellants filed a counterpetition seeking damages for, among other alleged breaches, Badger's: (a) failure to obtain court approval prior to employing

Kissimmee Couple Plead Guilty to Defrauding Elderly Clients

By Susan Jacobson

A Kissimmee couple who stole nearly $2.9 million from elderly clients pleaded guilty in federal court Tuesday and could be sentenced to 10 years in prison each.

Linda Littlefield, a disbarred attorney also known as Linda Vasquez, and her former husband, Ross Littlefield, stole nearly $2.9 million from elderly clients and used the money to buy real estate and cars and prop up their other businesses.

Between 2007 and 2010, the Littlefields took more than $4.7 million from 26 clients, then began transferring money to accounts for their personal use. Their business, with an office in downtown Kissimmee, was called JNN Foundation.

Ross Littlefield, 48, sent falsified quarterly statements to clients making it appear as if their balances were greater than they actually were. In many cases, people lost most of their life savings.

The money was supposed to become part of a pooled trust designed to shelter assets while maintaining the beneficiaries' Medicaid eligibility.

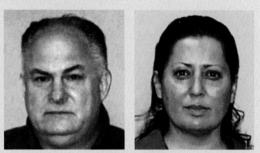

Ross Littlefield   *Linda Littlefield*

The Littlefields pleaded guilty to one count each of conducting a prohibited money transaction.

Linda Littlefield, 41, is serving a two-year state prison sentence after being convicted in Osceola Circuit Court of bilking an elderly couple who were her clients. Ross Littlefield received five years of probation in that case....

Several civil lawsuits are pending against the former couple.

Source: Orlando Sentinel (June 11, 2013).

his wife as the realtor for the Trust; (b) failure to notify Appellants of the sale of the house or the decantation of the Trust's assets into the FFSNT; and (c) cancellation of Appellants' remainder interest in the Trust. . . .

In the final judgment, the trial court concluded that the terms of Rita's will allowed Badger to invade the principal of the Trust "to any extent that [he] felt was in the best interests of [Wilson]." . . . In addressing the counterclaims, the trial court found that Appellants presented "absolutely no evidence" in support of their claims, and concluded that Appellants suffered no damages because the original Trust "would have been exhausted at some point in time." Accordingly, the trial court terminated the Trust, retroactively approved the employment of Badger's wife, and dismissed Appellants' claims for damages. . . .

THE DECANTATION WAS INVALID AS A RESULT OF BADGER'S FAILURE TO COMPLY WITH [THE FLORIDA DECANTING STATUTE]

. . . [The Florida decanting statute,] Fla. Stat. § 36.04117 (2008), provides, in relevant part:

(1)(a) Unless the trust instrument expressly provides otherwise, a trustee who has absolute power under the terms of a trust to invade the principal of the trust, referred to in this section as the "first trust," to make distributions to or for the benefit of one or more persons may instead exercise the power by appointing all or part of the principal of the trust subject to the power in favor of a trustee of another trust, referred to in this section as the "second trust," for the current benefit of one or more of such persons under the same trust instrument or under a different trust instrument; provided:

> 1. *The beneficiaries of the second trust may include only beneficiaries of the first trust;* [and
>
> 2. The second trust may not reduce any fixed income, annuity, or unitrust interest in the assets of the first trust.] . . .

> (4) *The trustee shall notify all qualified beneficiaries of the first trust, in writing, at least 60 days prior to the effective date of the trustee's exercise of the trustee's power to invade principal* pursuant to subsection (1), of the manner in which the trustee intends to exercise the power. A copy of the proposed instrument exercising the power shall satisfy the trustee's notice obligation under this subsection. If all qualified beneficiaries waive the notice period by signed written instrument delivered to the trustee, the trustee's power to invade principal shall be exercisable immediately. *The trustee's notice under this subsection shall not limit the right of any beneficiary to object to the exercise of the trustee's power to invade principal* except as provided in other applicable provisions of this code (emphasis added).

The instant application of section 736.04117, enacted in 2007, is a case of first impression. . . .

Here, section 736.04117(4) plainly and unambiguously requires a trustee to provide notice to "all qualified beneficiaries" of his intent to invade the principal of a trust at least 60 days prior to the invasion. Appellants are qualified beneficiaries, as defined in Fla. Stat. § 736.0103(16), of the Trust because of their interest in the distribution of any principal remaining after Wilson's death.[101] Badger improperly exercised his power to invade the principal of the Trust by failing to provide any notice to Appellants prior to transferring the entire contents of the Trust to the FFSNT.

Additionally, under section 736.04117(1)(a) (1)., the decantation of trust principal is limited to situations where the beneficiaries of the second trust "include only beneficiaries of the first trust." Here, the first trust defined Wilson as the primary beneficiary and Appellants as the contingent remainder beneficiaries. The second trust — the FFSNT sub-account — also defined Wilson as the primary beneficiary but provided a contingent remainder interest to beneficiaries of the other FFSNT sub-accounts. The second trust clearly included beneficiaries not contemplated by the original Trust, rendering Badger's decantation of all assets from the original Trust invalid.[102]

Accordingly, we reverse and remand for the trial court to conduct an evidentiary hearing to determine the value of the Trust at the time of the decanting, reduced by the

---

101. Based on UTC § 103(13), Fla. Stat. § 736.0103(16) defines a "qualified beneficiary" to be "a living beneficiary who, on the date the beneficiary's qualification is determined" (a) is "a distributee or permissible distributee of trust income or principal; (b) [w]ould be a distributee or permissible distributee of trust income or principal if the interests of the distributees described in paragraph (a) terminated on that date without causing the trust to terminate; or (c) [w]ould be a distributee or permissible distributee of trust income or principal if the trust terminated in accordance with its terms on that date." — Eds.

102. Because Badger's inclusion of the other FFSNT sub-accounts as remainder beneficiaries clearly violated section 736.04117(1)(a)1., we need not address whether that statute requires the inclusion of all beneficiaries of a first trust as beneficiaries of a successor trust.

money disbursed for Wilson's actual benefit, and enter an order requiring the return of the net value to the Trust. Additionally, we reverse the trial court's retroactive approval of Badger's employment of his wife and remand for entry of an order requiring the return of Trust funds paid in commission to Badger's wife. *See* Shriner v. Dyer, 462 So. 2d 1122, 1124 (Fla. 4th DCA 1984). Despite Badger's awareness that the employment of his wife created a conflict of interest, he proceeded to pay her commission from Trust funds without prior approval from the lower court. To the extent that any assets are restored to the Trust, we order Badger removed as its trustee. . . .

Reversed and remanded with instructions.

NOTES

1. Limits — Power and Duty Revisited. The decanting in *Harrell* was contrary to the Florida decanting statute in two respects: (a) the trustee failed to give advance notice, as required by the statute, and (b) the second trust included a new remainder beneficiary that was not a beneficiary of the first trust. The structure of the statute implies that the second of these violations, adding a beneficiary, renders the decanting invalid because the trustee does not have power to undertake such a decanting. But what about the trustee's failure to give notice? Does the trustee lack power to decant without first giving notice? Or is the decanting valid but the trustee liable for breach of the statutory duty to give notice?

The statute at issue in *Harrell* also prohibits the reduction of "any fixed income, annuity, or unitrust interest." Under this provision, the substance of which appears in many decanting statutes, a beneficiary's right under the first trust to a quarterly income distribution or a yearly unitrust payout must be carried forward into the second trust — and this is true even if the trustee could have distributed the entire corpus outright to another beneficiary.

The Uniform Trust Decanting Act (UTDA) (Unif. Law Comm'n 2015) follows a similar pattern. It recognizes a decanting power in a trustee of a discretionary trust subject to a handful of categorical limits and to the trustee's fiduciary duties.

2. A Decanting Problem. T devises a fund in trust to X "to pay H so much of the income and principal as X determines in X's sole discretion until H attains the age of 35, whereupon H shall distribute the entire trust estate to H." H, now age 34, is in an acrimonious divorce proceeding with W. To prevent W from having a claim on H's distribution at age 35, X decants the entire trust corpus into a new trust "to pay H so much of the income and principal as X determines in X's uncontrolled discretion," dropping the age 35 clause. Has X acted properly? Does W have standing to challenge X's actions? *See* Ferri v. Powell-Ferri, 116 A.3d 297 (Conn. 2015).

3. Variation Across the States. There is quite a bit of variation across the decanting statutes. Some of the more important points of cleavage are:

a. Should a trustee's power to decant depend on the breadth of the trustee's discretionary power to distribute? Following the decanting statutes in some states, UTDA § 12 provides that a trustee whose power to distribute is limited by an "ascertainable" or "reasonably definite" standard "must grant each beneficiary of the first trust beneficial interests [in the second trust] which are substantially similar to the beneficial interests of the beneficiary in the first trust." By contrast, if a trustee has broad discretion that is not limited by such a standard, then under UTDA § 11 the trustee may decant other than (i) adding a beneficiary who was not a beneficiary of the first trust, or (ii) reducing a beneficiary's fixed right to a distribution.

b. Is there an exception for creating a special needs trust?   In a few states and under UTDA § 13, a trustee may decant to create a special needs trust for a disabled beneficiary (see page 726) even if the trustee's discretion is otherwise limited by an ascertainable or reasonably definite standard. Statutory recognition of this power is in effect a per se private power of deviation of the type the court approved in In re Riddell, page 736. In In re Kroll, 971 N.Y.S.2d 863 (Sur. 2013), the court upheld a decanting to create a special needs trust against a challenge by the state attorney general.

c. Must a trustee give notice to the beneficiaries and other interested persons of an intended decanting?   In most but not all states, and under UTDA § 7, a trustee must give notice of an intended decanting to interested parties (60 days under the UTDA). In a few states, such as Delaware, Nevada, and South Dakota, the decanting statute does not require advance notice. But is not a decanting the kind of significant or nonroutine transaction that, under Allard v. Pacific National Bank, page 682, requires advance disclosure as a matter of common law?

d. May a trustee modify the first trust directly, without distributing to a second trust?   Under the UTDA and in some states, a trustee who has a decanting power can exercise that power by modifying the first trust directly, instead of distributing the property to a second trust. Does a settlor who gives a trustee a broad power to distribute principal intend for that trustee to have a broad power to modify the terms of the trust? On the other hand, is there a substantive difference between direct modification by the trustee and decanting into a second trust with different terms? Can you think of reasons why a direct modification might be preferable to decanting to a new trust?

C. TRUSTEE REMOVAL

Trustee removal has traditionally been understood as a remedy for breach of trust. In modern law, however, trustee removal is more freely granted, effectively as a modification of the trust, sometimes in circumstances that reveal a tension between the intent of the settlor and the wishes of the beneficiary. The difficulty is in giving the trustee enough leeway to carry out the settlor's wishes without protecting lackadaisical or ineffective administration.[103]

The balance struck by traditional law was to permit removal only for cause. A court would remove a trustee who was dishonest or who had committed a serious breach of

---

103. *See* Robert H. Sitkoff, An Agency Costs Theory of Trust Law, 89 Cornell L. Rev. 621, 663-64 (2004).

trust, but not one whose breach was minor or who had a simple disagreement with the beneficiary. A trustee who was chosen by the settlor, as compared to one named by a court, was even less readily removed.

Some have argued that the inability of beneficiaries to change trustees lessens competition among trust companies, contributes to higher trustees' fees, and leads to a cautious, even indifferent, style of trust management. Proponents of freer trustee removal also point to the proliferation of bank mergers and acquisitions, which often results in a new trust officer, one unknown to the settlor and unfamiliar with the beneficiaries, being assigned to the trust.[104]

Professionally drafted trusts commonly include a provision that overrides the default law of trustee removal by authorizing the beneficiaries or a third party to remove the trustee and appoint a successor (perhaps limited to an independent corporate trustee).[105] Should the default law of trustee removal be reformed accordingly?

UTC § 706(b) (2000) liberalizes trustee removal by authorizing removal for ineffective administration by the trustee, a change in circumstances, or by consent of all the beneficiaries if removal is in the best interests of the beneficiaries and not contrary to a material purpose of the settlor. Subsection (a) also changes the common law by giving the settlor of an irrevocable trust standing to petition for trustee removal.

Uniform Trust Code (Unif. Law Comm'n 2000)

§ 706. Removal of Trustee

(a) The settlor, a cotrustee, or a beneficiary may request the court to remove a trustee, or a trustee may be removed by the court on its own initiative.

(b) The court may remove a trustee if:

(1) the trustee has committed a serious breach of trust;

(2) lack of cooperation among cotrustees substantially impairs the administration of the trust;

(3) because of unfitness, unwillingness, or persistent failure of the trustee to administer the trust effectively, the court determines that removal of the trustee best serves the interests of the beneficiaries; or

(4) there has been a substantial change of circumstances or removal is requested by all of the qualified beneficiaries, the court finds that removal of the trustee best serves the interests of all of the beneficiaries and is not inconsistent with a material purpose of the trust, and a suitable cotrustee or successor trustee is available.

---

104. *See, e.g.,* Ronald Chester & Sarah Reid Ziomek, Removal of Corporate Trustees Under the Uniform Trust Code and Other Current Law: Does a Contractual Lens Help Clarify the Rights of Beneficiaries?, 67 Mo. L. Rev. 241 (2002).

105. Under prevailing law, the only limit on the exercise of such a power is that it "must conform to any valid requirements or limitations imposed by the trust terms." Restatement (Third) of Trusts § 37 cmt. c (Am. Law Inst. 2003). If the terms of the trust do not impose any requirements or limitations on the power to remove, then it may be exercised without cause. *See* Scott and Ascher on Trusts § 11.10.2.

(c) Pending a final decision on a request to remove a trustee, or in lieu of or in addition to removing a trustee, the court may order such appropriate relief under Section 1001(b) as may be necessary to protect the trust property or the interests of the beneficiaries.

Davis v. U.S. Bank National Association
243 S.W.3d 425 (Mo. App. 2007)

SULLIVAN, J. U.S. Bank National Association (Appellant) appeals from the trial court's summary judgment in favor of Harold A. Davis (Respondent). We affirm.

FACTUAL AND PROCEDURAL BACKGROUND

On May 3, 1967, Respondent's grandfather, Lorenz K. Ayers (Ayers), now deceased, executed a Living Trust Agreement (the Trust), pursuant to which Ayers appointed himself and Mercantile Trust Company, National Association (Mercantile), as Co-Trustees. On December 26, 1972, Ayers executed a Trust Indenture, pursuant to which Ayers appointed Mercantile as the Trustee[106] and Respondent as the income beneficiary of the Trust, entitled to receive the entire net income of the Trust for life. Upon Respondent's death, the principal of the Trust is to be divided among Respondent's then living children in equal shares and distributed to each child (in trust if under the age of 21 and "outright" if 21). Respondent currently has two children, Dillon A. Davis (Son) and Marguerite S. Davis (Daughter). The Trust provides that if Respondent has no surviving children upon his death, Respondent's share of the Trust "shall pass to his or her heirs at law who are direct descendants of [Ayers]." In the event that there are no heirs at law who are direct descendants of Ayers at the time of Respondent's death, the principal passes free of trust to Lafayette College, Easton, Pennsylvania.

On May 15, 2006, Respondent filed a petition (the Petition) . . . seeking the removal of Appellant as Trustee, the appointment of U.S. Trust Company of Delaware (UST) as successor Trustee, and an order transferring the Trust assets to UST.[107] . . .

After hearing arguments . . . the circuit court [granted Respondent's Motion for Summary Judgment and] . . . ordered the removal of Appellant as Trustee and appointed UST as successor Trustee of the Trust. This appeal follows. . . .

Judge Sherri B. Sullivan

---

106. Appellant is the successor by merger to Mercantile, and has been the sole current Trustee of the 1967 Trust and the 1972 Trust since 2001.

107. In 2007, the year in which this decision was handed down, Bank of America acquired U.S. Trust. — Eds.

Discussion

In 2004, the General Assembly enacted [the Missouri Uniform Trust Code], effective January 1, 2005. . . . Relevant to our discussion is Section 456.7-706.2(4) [based on UTC § 706(b)(4)], which provides for the removal of a trustee without any showing of wrongdoing by the trustee: . . .

> The court may remove a trustee if: . . .
>> (4) . . . removal is requested by all of the qualified beneficiaries and in either such case the party seeking removal establishes to the court that:
>>> (a) removal of the trustee best serves the interests of all of the beneficiaries;
>>> (b) removal of the trustee is not inconsistent with a material purpose of the trust; and
>>> (c) a suitable cotrustee or successor trustee is available and willing to serve.

In the instant case, Respondent's petition and motion for summary judgment alleged that all four elements of Section 456.7-706.2(4) were satisfied: the "qualified beneficiaries" of the Trust, as defined by Section 456.1-103(20) are Respondent, Son and Daughter; UST is available and willing to serve as successor corporate Trustee; removal of Appellant as Trustee was not inconsistent with a material purpose of the Trust; UST will charge lower fees and allow an independent investment adviser which is in the best interests of the beneficiaries; Respondent is a resident of Pennsylvania, and lives within a thirty-minute drive to UST and the investment advisor; Appellant is located in Missouri; [and] the proposed investment advisor has a complete understanding of Respondent and his family's unique personal financial situation and how the Trust co-ordinates with his family's financial objectives. . . .

In its Memorandum in Opposition to Respondent's Motion for Summary Judgment, Appellant maintained that a conflict of interest existed between Respondent and Son and Daughter . . . and therefore, Respondent could not represent the interests of Son and Daughter pursuant to Section 456.3-303; Respondent had failed to name necessary and indispensable parties to the lawsuit; Respondent had failed to show removal of the Trustee would best serve the interests of the beneficiaries; removal of the Trustee would be inconsistent with a material purpose of the Trust; and Respondent's Motion for Summary Judgment was premature as discovery was needed. . . .

Point I

In its first point [on appeal], Appellant asserts that Respondent's failure to join all of the remainder beneficiaries of the Trust as parties to his lawsuit deprived the court of subject matter jurisdiction. This assertion is incorrect. Section 456.7-706.2(4) only requires that "qualified beneficiaries" be joined in an action to remove a trustee. . . . A qualified beneficiary . . .

> means a beneficiary who, on the date the beneficiary's qualification is determined:
>> (a) is a permissible distributee;

(b) would be a permissible distributee if the interests of the permissible distributees described in paragraph (a) of this subdivision terminated on that date; or

(c) would be a permissible distributee if the trust terminated on that date.

Section 456.1-103(2) [based on UTC § 103(13)]. Based on the language of this section, Respondent and Son and Daughter are the permissible distributees if Respondent's interest or the Trust terminated at the time of the filing of this suit. As such, Respondent and Son and Daughter are all of the qualified beneficiaries of the Trust. The remote remainder beneficiaries of the Trust are not qualified beneficiaries. All of the qualified beneficiaries were before the Court and therefore, all of the necessary parties were before the court. . . .

Point II

In its second point, Appellant alleges that Respondent could not virtually represent Son and Daughter under Section 456.3-303(4).[108] We disagree. . . .

Respondent and Son and Daughter have substantially identical interests which are not in conflict with regard to removing Appellant as Trustee and implementing UST as Trustee. UST is within a thirty-minute drive of Respondent and Son and Daughter's house; changing the domicile of the Trust to Delaware would avoid out of state income tax being paid on Trust income; UST has a complete understanding of Respondent and his family's unique personal financial situation; and UST will charge lower fees than Appellant. . . .

Appellant maintains that there is an inherent conflict of interest between income beneficiaries and residual beneficiaries. However, this assertion has no basis in Missouri law. Further, Section 456.3-303(4) requires any conflict of interest to be "with respect to a particular question or dispute." As such, the determination as to the existence of a conflict of interest is undertaken on a case by case basis. In this case, we have found none, and Appellant has not shown us otherwise.

Accordingly, we find that Respondent demonstrated that there is no conflict of interest between himself and Son and Daughter with regard to changing the Trustee, and thus he could virtually represent them in doing so. Appellant presented no facts putting this issue into dispute. . . .

Point III

In its third point, Appellant maintains that there remain issues of fact as to whether or not removing the Trustee is in the best interests of all of the beneficiaries. Appellant claims that it presented facts in opposition to Respondent's summary judgment motion

---

108. Section 456.3-303(4), which is based on UTC § 303(6), provides: "To the extent there is no conflict of interest between the representative and the person represented or among those being represented with respect to a particular question or dispute . . . a parent may represent and bind the parent's minor or unborn child if a conservator, conservator ad litem, or guardian for the child has not been appointed." — Eds.

which called into question the validity of the reduced trustee fee which Respondent claimed would be achieved by Appellant's removal and replacement with UST.

In conjunction with his motion for summary judgment, Respondent submitted the affidavit of investment advisor Daniel M. McDermott, President of McDermott Advisory Group, LLC (McDermott). McDermott's affidavit includes the numbers he used to calculate all of Appellant's fees and the numbers used to calculate UST's fees and the investment management fees. His affidavit demonstrates how he calculated the annual savings of $10,259.55 by switching from Appellant to UST, resulting from a fee that is 23.94% lower than that being charged by Appellant, and the information on which such calculations were based. The documents reflecting the numbers he used in his calculation are attached to his affidavit. [A bank officer] testified by affidavit that he had reviewed McDermott's calculations and that McDermott's calculations accurately reflect the published fee schedule of UST and that the fees were properly applied in the calculation. Appellant did not dispute the numbers presented by McDermott, but rather merely criticized them as hearsay and speculative. However, Respondent presented documentary evidence in the form of published rates of the fees as currently charged. Under the statute, Respondent merely has to show that the change in Trustee somehow inured to his and the other beneficiaries' benefit. . . .

Appellant claims that the change in trustee is inconsistent with the material purpose of the Trust as the Trust clearly did not contemplate the change, but does contemplate keeping the same Trustee in the same state. Not only does this argument speculate as to what the Trust "contemplates" without any evidentiary support, but it is also irrelevant, because the statutory scheme provides for the change of Trustee as long as the terms of the Trust do not prohibit it, and the terms of the Trust in this case do not. See Section 456.7-706.2(4)(b). . . .

Respondent presented factually supported reasons why it would be beneficial to him and Son and Daughter to remove the present Trustee in lieu of UST and Appellant does not put any of those reasons into dispute. Nor does Appellant present us with any additional fact issues. Therefore, there are no remaining disputed factual matters into which Appellant is entitled to conduct more discovery. Additionally, Appellant presents no evidentiary support for its argument that its removal as Trustee is inconsistent with a material purpose of the trust. . . .

CONCLUSION

The trial court's judgment is affirmed.

NOTES

1. Removal Without Cause. In *Davis,* the court removed the trustee on the basis of UTC § 706(b)(4), page 751. That provision requires the court to determine whether removal "best serves the interests of all of the beneficiaries." In In re McKinney, 67 A.3d 824 (Pa. Super. 2013), the court elaborated on the meaning of this provision:

We conclude that courts should consider the following factors when determining whether a current trustee or a proposed successor trustee best serves the interests of the beneficiaries: personalization of service; cost of administration; convenience to the beneficiaries; efficiency of service; personal knowledge of trusts' and beneficiaries' financial situations; location of trustee as it affects trust income tax; experience; qualifications; personal relationship with beneficiaries; settlor's intent as expressed in the trust document; and any other material circumstances. No one factor in this nonexhaustive list will outweigh the others. Rather, the trial court is to consider these factors if the parties present evidence thereof, on a case-by-case basis.

In authorizing removal without a showing of wrongdoing or even mediocre performance, does the UTC tip the balance too far in favor of the beneficiaries? Is the requirement that removal not be "inconsistent with a material purpose of the settlor" enough to protect the settlor's intent? UTC § 706(b)(4) also authorizes removal on the basis of "a substantial change of circumstances." Might removal have been available in *Davis* on the grounds that the trustee was the successor entity after a merger with the original trustee named by the settlor? Because § 706 is not included in the schedule of mandatory rules in UTC § 105(b), it may be varied by the terms of the trust.

UTC § 706(b)(3) authorizes removal for "persistent failure of the trustee to administer the trust effectively." The comment says that "a long-term pattern of mediocre performance, such as consistently poor investment results when compared to comparable trusts," might warrant removal under this provision. The drafters meant to address "the concern that under traditional law beneficiaries have had little recourse when trustee performance has been indifferent, but not so egregious as to be in breach of trust."[109]

2. Duties of a Successor Trustee. A successor trustee is not liable for a breach of trust by a prior trustee. However, a successor might be held liable if she unreasonably fails to rectify a prior breach (see page 655) or if she continues the breaching practice. In such circumstances, the successor's liability arises from her own blunder in failing to remedy or in continuing the prior trustee's breach.[110]

3. Virtual Representation. Trusts and estates litigation often involves the interests of minor, unborn, or unascertained beneficiaries. In some circumstances, the court will appoint a *guardian ad litem* to protect the interests of such beneficiaries (see page 169). Another option is *virtual representation* by a party with similar interests.[111] UTC § 304 (2000) codifies the practice of virtual representation, which traces back to eighteenth-century England, thus:

> Unless otherwise represented, a minor, incapacitated, or unborn individual, or a person whose identity or location is unknown and not reasonably ascertainable, may be represented by and bound by another having a substantially identical interest

---

109. John H. Langbein, The Uniform Trust Code: Codification of the Law of Trusts in the United States, 15 Tr. L. Int'l 66, 76 (2001).

110. *See* Scott and Ascher on Trusts § 24.28.

111. *See* Susan T. Bart & Lyman W. Welch, State Statutes on Virtual Representation—A New State Survey, 35 ACTEC L.J. 368 (2010); Martin D. Begleiter, Serve the Cheerleader—Serve the World: An Analysis of Representation in Estate and Trust Proceedings and Under the Uniform Trust Code and Other Modern Trust Codes, 43 Real Prop. Tr. & Est. L.J. 311 (2008).

with respect to the particular question or dispute, but only to the extent there is no conflict of interest between the representative and the person represented.

The UTC expands virtual representation in two ways. First, it authorizes representation not only in litigation but also in transactions requiring consent of the beneficiaries. Second, under UTC § 303, which was at issue in *Davis*, a parent may represent a minor or unborn child, even if the parent does not have a similar personal interest, if there is no conflict of interest between the parent and the child "with respect to [the] particular question or dispute."

CHAPTER 11

TRUSTS: CHARITABLE PURPOSES, CY PRES, AND SUPERVISION

> In the case of an entity having no owners and established for the benefit
> of indefinite beneficiaries, who is the principal on whom the law can
> rely to monitor the agents and enforce the charitable purposes?
>
> EVELYN BRODY
> 57 Md. L. Rev. 1400, 1429 (1998)

THROUGH A CHARITABLE TRUST, a person can make a gift in support of a charitable purpose across time. In general, the same rules that apply to a private trust also apply to a charitable trust. This chapter examines three significant exceptions that differentiate a charitable trust from a private trust. First, a charitable trust must be for a *charitable purpose* rather than for one or more ascertainable beneficiaries. Second, because a charitable trust is exempt from the Rule Against Perpetuities (see Chapter 14) and so may endure forever, it is more freely modified under the *cy pres* doctrine. Third, because a charitable trust does not require an ascertainable beneficiary, it is subject to a different scheme of *enforcement*. Modern law relies on a combination of the state attorneys general, donors, and federal tax authorities, rather than beneficiaries, to enforce a charitable trust.

Most charities today are structured as nonprofit corporations or unincorporated associations rather than as charitable trusts. However, much of the basic law of charitable gifts, nonprofit corporations, and charitable foundations derives from the law of charitable trusts. Accordingly, the questions of law and policy considered in this chapter apply generally across the entire charity and nonprofit sector, which is massive. In 2013, public charitable organizations reported total assets of $3.22 trillion and revenue of $1.73 trillion.[1] The nonprofit sector is estimated to have contributed $905.9 billion to the U.S. economy that year, representing 5.4 percent of the country's gross domestic product.

---

1. The data reported in this paragraph are from Brice S. McKeever, The Nonprofit Sector in Brief 2015: Public Charities, Giving, and Volunteering 1 (Urban Inst. 2015).

We begin in Section A by considering what purposes qualify as charitable. In Section B, we consider modification of charitable trusts under the *cy pres* doctrine, which is unique to charitable trusts, and the deviation doctrine, which applies also to private trusts. In Section C, we consider enforcement of charitable trusts by state attorneys general, donors, and the Internal Revenue Service.

A. CHARITABLE PURPOSES

Unlike a private trust, which must be for the benefit of one or more ascertainable beneficiaries (see page 418), a charitable trust must be for one or more *charitable purposes*. The necessity of a charitable purpose, as compared to an ascertainable beneficiary, is the fundamental distinction between a private and a charitable trust.

Shenandoah Valley National Bank v. Taylor
63 S.E.2d 786 (Va. 1951)

MILLER, J. Charles B. Henry, a resident of Winchester, Virginia, died testate on the 23rd day of April, 1949. His will dated April 21, 1949, was duly admitted to probate and the Shenandoah Valley National Bank of Winchester, the designated executor and trustee, qualified thereunder.

Subject to two inconsequential provisions not material to this litigation, the testator's entire estate valued at $86,000, was left as follows:

> Second: All the rest, residue and remainder of my estate, real, personal, intangible and mixed, of whatsoever kind and wherever situate, . . . I give, bequeath and devise to the Shenandoah Valley National Bank of Winchester, Virginia, in trust, to be known as the "Charles B. Henry and Fannie Belle Henry Fund," for the following uses and purposes:
>
> (a) My Trustee shall invest and reinvest my trust estate, shall collect the income therefrom and shall pay the net income as follows:
>
> (1) On the last school day of each calendar year before Easter my Trustee shall divide the net income into as many equal parts as there are children in the first, second and third grades of the John Kerr School of the City of Winchester, and shall pay one of such equal parts to each child in such grades, to be used by such child in the furtherance of his or her obtainment of an education.
>
> (2) On the last school day of each calendar year before Christmas my trustee shall divide the net income into as many equal parts as there are children in the first, second and third grades of the John Kerr School of the City of Winchester, and shall pay one of such equal parts to each child in such grades, to be used by such child in the furtherance of his or her obtainment of an education.

By paragraphs (3) and (4) it is provided that the names of the children in the three grades shall be determined each year from the school records, and payment of the income to them "shall be as nearly equal in amounts as it is practicable" to arrange.

Paragraph (5) provides that if the John Kerr School is ever discontinued for any reason the payments shall be made to the children of the same grades of the school or schools that take its place, and the School Board of Winchester is to determine what school or schools are substituted for it.

Under clause "Third" the trustee is given authority, power, and discretion to retain or from time to time sell and invest and reinvest the estate, or any part thereof, as it shall deem to be the best interest of the trust.

The John Kerr School is a public school used by the local school board for primary grades and had an enrollment of 458 boys and girls so there will be that number of pupils or thereabouts who would share in the distribution of the income.

The testator left no children or near relatives. Those who would be his heirs and distributees in case of intestacy were first cousins and others more remotely related. One of these next of kin filed a suit against the executor and trustee, and others challenging the validity of the provisions of the will which undertook to create a charitable trust.

Paragraph No. 10 of the bill alleges: "That the aforesaid trust does not constitute a charitable trust and hence is invalid in that it violates the rule against the creation of perpetuities." . . .

The sole question presented is: does the will create a valid charitable trust?

Construction of the challenged provisions is required and in this undertaking the testator's intent as disclosed by the words used in the will must be ascertained. If his dominant intent as expressed was charitable, the trust should be accorded efficacy and sustained.

Charles B. Henry

The testator, Charles B. Henry, operated a fruit and vegetable stand until shortly before his death. In earlier years, he sold fruits and vegetables through the town from a horse-drawn wagon. Judge Robert K. Woltz, winning counsel in *Taylor* and later a judge in Virginia, explains:

> A number of years before his death he lost his only child, a very pretty little daughter. This, so I am told, profoundly affected him, causing him to become more and more a recluse and this became even more pronounced after the death of his wife, who predeceased him by some years. Along with this increasing withdrawal from general social intercourse, there seems to have developed an increasing tendency to become miserly. This was indicated by such things as avoidance of use of electric lights except when absolutely necessary and making the produce which was no longer salable a substantial part of his diet.
>
> Nonetheless, perhaps because of memory of his own deceased child, he seems to have maintained a strong affection for children generally.

As a fruit vendor, he was widely known among the older generation of local citizens.

> He saved and hoarded his money and made some investments, and I recollected being told by someone, possibly an official of the Shenandoah Valley Bank that when the Great Depression struck, he was frantic to the point of unnatural frenzy at the depreciation of his investments.
>
> My firm received the case as a result of the complainant being the babysitter for my partner's sister and brother-in-law and was the second or third cousin to Charlie Henry. For some time she had been helping to look after him and bringing him food, undoubtedly with that expectation so often disappointed that he would remember her in his will; in fact, I recollect that she claimed that he had flatly promised to do so or by artful insinuation had convinced her that he would. Her disappointment and resulting ire prompted her to seek counsel.

Letter to the editors, dated July 7, 1975, from the Hon. Robert K. Woltz.

But on the other hand, if the testator's intent as expressed is merely benevolent, though the disposition of his property be meritorious and evince traits of generosity, the trust must nevertheless be declared invalid because it violates the rule against perpetuities. . . .

Restatement of the Law of Trusts, sec. 368 . . . gives a comprehensive classification definition . . . :

Charitable purposes include:
  (a) the relief of poverty;
  (b) the advancement of education;
  (c) the advancement of religion;
  (d) the promotion of health;
  (e) governmental or municipal purposes; and
  (f) other purposes the accomplishment of which is beneficial to the community. . . .

In the law of trusts there is a real and fundamental distinction between a charitable trust and one that is devoted to mere benevolence. The former is public in nature and valid; the latter is private and if it offends the rule against perpetuities, it is void. . . .

We are, however, reminded that charitable trusts are favored creatures of the law enjoying the especial solicitude of courts of equity and a liberal interpretation is employed to uphold them. Zollman on Charities, sec. 570, p. 391; 2 Bogert on Trusts, sec. 369, p. 1129. . . .

Appellant contends that the gift . . . not only meets the requirements of a charitable trust as defined in Restatement of the Law of Trusts, supra, but specifically fits two of those classifications, viz.:

  (b) trusts for the advancement of education;
  (f) other purposes the accomplishment of which is beneficial to the community.

We now turn to the language of the will for from its context the testator's intent is to be derived. . . .

In paragraphs (1) and (2), respectively, of clause "Second" in clear and definite language the discretion, power and authority of the trustee in its disposition and application of the income are specified and limited. Yearly on the last school day before Easter and Christmas each youthful beneficiary of the testator's generosity is to be paid an equal share of the income. In mandatory language the duty and the duty alone to make cash payments to each individual child just before Easter and Christmas is enjoined upon the trustee by the certain and explicit words that it "shall divide the net income . . . and shall pay one of such equal shares to each child in such grades."

Without more, that language, and the occasions specified for payment of the funds to the children being when their minds and interests would be far removed from studies or other school activities definitely indicate that no educational purpose was in the testator's mind. It is manifest that there was no intent or belief that the funds would be put to any use other than such as youthful impulse and desire might dictate. But in each instance immediately following the above-quoted language the sentence concludes with the words or phrase "to be used by such child in the furtherance of his or her obtainment of an education." It is significant that by this latter phrase the trustee is given no power, control or discretion over the funds so received by the child. Full and complete execution of the mandate and trust imposed upon the trustee accomplishes no educational purpose. Nothing toward the advancement of education is attained by the ultimate performance by the trustee of its full duty. It merely places the income irretrievably and forever beyond the range of the trust.

Appellant says that the latter phrase, "to be used by such child in furtherance of his or her obtainment of an education," evinces the testator's dominant purpose and intent. Yet it is not denied that the preceding provision "shall divide the net income into as many equal parts . . . and shall pay one of each equal parts to such child" is at odds with the phrase it relies upon. The appended qualification, it says, however, discloses a controlling intent that the 450 or more shares are to be used in the furtherance of education, and it was not really intended that a share be paid to each child so that he or she could during the Christmas and Easter holidays, or at any other time, use it "without let or hindrance, encumbrance or care." With that construction we cannot agree. In our opinion, the words of the will import an intent to have the trustee pay to each child his allotted share. If that be true,—and it is directed to be done in no uncertain language—we know that the admonition to the children would be wholly impotent and of no avail.

In construing wills, we may not forget or disregard the experiences of life and the realities of the occasion. Nor may we assume or indulge in the belief that the testator by his injunction to the donees intended or thought that he could change childhood nature and set at naught childhood impulses and desires.

Appellant asserts that literal performance of the duty imposed upon it—pay to each child his share—would be impracticable and should not be done. Its position in that respect is stated thus: "We do not understand that under the law of Virginia a court would pay money for education into the hands of children who are incapable of handling it." It then says that the funds could be administered by a guardian or under sec. 8-751, Code, 1950 (where the amounts are under $500), a court could direct payment to be made to the recipient's parents.[2]

With these statements, we agree. But because the funds could be administered under applicable statutes has no bearing upon nor may that device be resorted to as an aid to prove or establish the testator's intent. We are of opinion that the testator's dominant intent appears from and is expressed in his unequivocal direction to the trustee to divide the income into as many equal parts as there are children beneficiaries and pay one share to each. This expressed purpose and intent is inconsistent with the appended direction to each child as to the use of his respective share and the latter phrase is thus ineffectual to create an educational trust. The testator's purpose and intent were, we think, to bestow upon the children gifts that would bring to them happiness on the two holidays, but that falls short of an educational trust.

If it be determined that the will fails to create a charitable trust for *educational purposes* (and our conclusion is that it is inoperative to create such a trust), it is earnestly

2. Compare the discussion of facility of payment provisions at page 126.—Eds.

insisted that the trust provided for is nevertheless charitable and valid. In this respect it is claimed that the two yearly payments to be made to the children just before Christmas and Easter produce "a desirable social effect" and are "promotive of public convenience and needs, and happiness and contentment" and thus the fund set up in the will constitutes a charitable trust. 2 Bogert on Trusts, sec. 361, p. 1090, and 3 Scott on Trusts, sec. 368, p. 1972. . . .

A trust from which the income is to be paid at stated intervals to each member of a designated segment of the public, without regard to whether or not the recipients are poor or in need, is not for the relief of poverty, nor is it a social benefit to the community. It is a mere benevolence—a private trust—and may not be upheld as a charitable trust. Restatement of the Law of Trusts, sec. 374, p. 1156:

> [I]f a large sum of money is given in trust to apply the income each year in paying a certain sum to every inhabitant of a city, whether rich or poor, the trust is not charitable, since although each inhabitant may receive a benefit, the social interest of the community as such is not thereby promoted.

In 2 Bogert on Trusts, sec. 380, we find:

> As previously stated, gifts which are mere exhibitions of liberality and generosity, without regard to their effect upon the donees, are not charitable. There must be an amelioration of the condition of the donees as a result of the gift, and this improvement must be of a mental, physical, or spiritual nature and not merely financial. Thus, trusts to provide gifts to children, regardless of their need, or to make Christmas gifts to members of a certain class, without consideration of need or effect, are not charitable. . . . (p. 1218.)
>
> Gifts which are made out of mere sentiment, and will have no practical result except the satisfying of a whim of the donor, are obviously lacking in the widespread social effect necessary to a charity. (p. 1219.) . . .

Payment to the children of their cash bequests on the two occasions specified would bring to them pleasure and happiness and no doubt cause them to remember or think of their benefactor with gratitude and thanksgiving. That was, we think, Charles B. Henry's intent. Laudable, generous and praiseworthy though it may be, it is not for the relief of the poor or needy, nor does it otherwise so benefit or advance the social interest of the community as to justify its continuance in perpetuity as a charitable trust. . . .

No error is found in the decrees appealed from and they are affirmed.

NOTES

1. The Rule Against Perpetuities. A charitable trust is exempt from the Rule Against Perpetuities (we take up the Rule in Chapter 14). In *Taylor*, Mr. Henry's "candy trust" was void under the Rule because the beneficial interest in the children in the first, second, and third grades of the John Kerr School was perpetual and the trust was not charitable. In Marsh v. Frost Nat'l Bank, 129 S.W.3d 174 (Tex. App. 2004), the testator had wanted to provide "a million dollar trust fund for every American 18 years or older" by accumulating income for 346 years. As in *Taylor*, this trust lacked a charitable purpose and so violated the Rule Against Perpetuities.

2. Charitable Purposes.   A trust is charitable if the settlor intended a recognized charitable purpose and the trust can reasonably be expected to further that purpose. The list of recognized *charitable purposes*, which traces back to a statute enacted by Parliament more than 400 years ago,[3] is codified by Uniform Trust Code (UTC) § 405(a) (Unif. Law Comm'n 2000) thus:

> A charitable trust may be created for the relief of poverty, the advancement of education or religion, the promotion of health, governmental or municipal purposes, or other purposes the achievement of which is beneficial to the community.[4]

It is sometimes said that a trust is charitable if it has many beneficiaries, or that to be charitable a trust must have many beneficiaries, but these statements are misleading. Having many beneficiaries is neither necessary nor sufficient for a valid charitable trust. For example, a trust established by *O*, who has 5,000 employees, to benefit such of his employees who are sick or needy may be charitable as promoting health and perhaps relieving poverty. But a trust by *O* for the general benefit of his numerous employees is not charitable because it does not advance a recognized charitable purpose. A trust to pay the salary of a single law professor may be charitable as furthering an educational purpose, but a trust for the benefit of lawyers generally is not charitable. A trust to provide scholarships or prizes for educational achievement may be charitable as furthering an educational purpose even if only one student will benefit. But a trust to educate a particular person or the descendants of the settlor is not charitable.[5]

A trust to promote a particular political party is not charitable. However, a trust for the improvement of the structure and methods of government in a manner advocated by a particular political party is charitable. In In re Estate of Breeden, 256 Cal. Rptr. 813 (App. 1989), the court upheld as charitable a trust to advance "the principles of socialism and those causes related to socialism," including supporting candidates for public office espousing socialistic views. A trust with the purpose of bringing about a change in the law may also be charitable. In Register of Wills for Baltimore City v. Cook, 216 A.2d 542 (Md. 1966), the court upheld as charitable a trust to support the passage of the Equal Rights Amendment.

Trusts for *benevolent* or *philanthropic* purposes should be avoided. Some older cases held that these words are broader in meaning than the word charitable, hence a trust for such a purpose may not qualify as charitable because the income could be used for a noncharitable purpose. Modern cases tend to construe these words as synonymous with charitable, but out of caution they should be avoided nonetheless.

---

3. The Statute of Charitable Uses Act 1601, 43 Eliz. I, c. 4 (Eng.). On the reception of this statute into American law, see Vidal v. Girard's Executors, 43 U.S. 127 (1844), and Steven P. Brown, The Girard Will and Twin Landmarks of Supreme Court History, 41 J. S. Ct. Hist. 7 (2016).

4. Both Restatement (Third) of Trusts § 28 (Am. Law Inst. 2003), and Restatement of Charitable Nonprofit Organizations § 1.01(b) (Am. Law Inst., Tentative Draft No. 1, 2016), are to similar effect.

5. *See* Restatement (Third) of Trusts § 28 cmt. a(1) (Am. Law Inst. 2003).

Jedi Order Fails in Attempt to Register as Religious Group

The Temple of the Jedi Order, members of which follow the tenets of the faith central to the Star Wars films, sought charitable status this year, but the Charity Commission [see page 805] has ruled that it does not meet the criteria for a religion under UK charity law.

The commission wrote that Jediism "lacks the necessary spiritual or non-secular element" it was looking for in a religion. . . .

It said the doctrine promoted by the group borrowed widely from other world religions and philosophies, but "the commission does not consider that the aggregate amounts to a sufficiently cogent and distinct religion." . . .

The Temple of the Jedi Order, based in Beaumont, Texas, is recognised as a charitable or non-profit group by the US Internal Revenue Service. Last year the charity regulator in New Zealand rejected an application by another group for Jediism to be considered a religion for charitable purposes. . . .

Brenna Cavell, 32, a psychologist and spokeswoman for the Temple, said the group was disappointed by the charity commission's decision. "We put a lot of work into the application and really did our best to illustrate why we do consider ourselves a religion and

why we believe we do offer benefits not just to our members but also to the public at large," she said.

The group had made the application to ensure that people who donated money towards the Temple's upkeep "have a sense of the legitimacy, that we do take it seriously and that any money that they do give to us is properly stewarded," she added. . . .

Yoda, Grand Master of the Jedi Order
Lucasfilm/Atlaspix/Alamy Stock Photo

In the UK, Jedi has been the most popular alternative religion in two consecutive editions of the census, after a national campaign led to more than 390,000 people (0.7% of the population) describing themselves as Jedi Knights on the 2001 census. Numbers fell sharply a decade later, but there were still 176,632 people who told the government they were Jedi Knights.

Source: The Guardian, Dec. 19, 2016.

3. Three Charitable Purpose Problems. Do any of the following involve the creation of a valid charitable trust?

a. O establishes a trust to provide scholarships based on academic achievement but with a preference for members of O's family. *See* United Bank, Inc. v. Blosser, 624 S.E.2d 815 (W. Va. 2005).

b. O establishes a trust to send a person through medical school upon her promise to practice in O's hometown. *See* In re Carlson's Estate, 358 P.2d 669 (Kan. 1961).

c. O conveys a fund to X, in trust, for such charitable purposes as X shall select. *See* Restatement (Third) of Trusts § 28 cmt. a (2003).

4. Tax Deduction. A client who establishes a charitable trust or makes a gift to a charity usually wants to qualify for the *tax deduction* allowed in calculating the client's income, estate, or gift tax liability.[6] The lawyer should verify whether the trust's purpose or the charity qualifies as charitable under federal tax law. Although there is much overlap, a purpose that is charitable under state law may not qualify as charitable under federal tax law. In Free Fertility Foundation v. Commissioner, 135 T.C. 21 (2010), the court held that a California nonprofit corporation with the purpose of

---

6. *See* Internal Revenue Code §§ 170 (income tax), 2055 (estate tax), 2522 (gift tax). We take up the estate tax charitable deduction in Chapter 15 at page 974.

providing sperm donated by the corporation's founder to women seeking to become pregnant (if approved by the founder) was not charitable for federal tax purposes.

5. Mortmain Statutes. Most states once had statutes permitting spouses and children to set aside deathbed wills making gifts to charity (such a statute was the basis for Kate Rothko's standing in In re Rothko, page 602). These statutes originated in the medieval fear of overreaching by priests taking the last confession and will. But the statutes restricted the share of an estate that could be left to charity even if the will was executed years before death. These statutes have all been repealed or declared unconstitutional as a denial of equal protection of the law or on substantive due process grounds.[7] Today claims of overreaching by a charity, religious or otherwise, are litigated under the ordinary contest grounds of undue influence, duress, or fraud.[8]

6. Trusts for Noncharitable Purposes. Under traditional law, a trust had to be for one or more ascertainable beneficiaries (a private trust) or be for a recognized charitable purpose (a charitable trust). Today, however, most states allow a trust for a *noncharitable purpose* that is not capricious (see Chapter 6 at page 426). First, many courts recognize an *honorary trust,* in which the trustee is not under a legal obligation to carry out the settlor's stated purpose, but if the transferee declines or neglects to do so, she holds the property upon a resulting trust and the property reverts to the settlor or the settlor's successors. Second, every state has enacted legislation, such as UTC §§ 408-409 (2000) or Uniform Probate Code (UPC) § 2-907 (Unif. Law Comm'n 1990, rev. 1993), that permits a trust for the benefit of a pet animal for the life of the animal or for certain other noncharitable purposes, such as perpetual maintenance of a grave.

B. CY PRES AND DEVIATION

1. Cy Pres

Cy pres is shorthand for the Norman French phrase *cy pres comme possible*, meaning "as nearly as possible." Under traditional *cy pres* doctrine, if a charitable trust's specific purpose becomes *illegal, impossible,* or *impracticable,* a court may direct application of the property to another purpose that is within the settlor's general charitable intent.[9] The doctrine addresses the risk that, because a charitable trust may have a perpetual existence, changed circumstances will render the trust's original purpose obsolete. In modern law, cy pres is also available if the trust becomes *wasteful.*

In England there was a royal prerogative power of cy pres as well as a judicial doctrine of cy pres. Under the prerogative power, charitable gifts were expected to comply

---

7. *See* Restatement (Third) of Property: Wills and Other Donative Transfers § 9.7 (Am. Law Inst. 2003).

8. *See* Jeffrey G. Sherman, Can Religious Influence Ever Be "Undue" Influence?, 73 Brook. L. Rev. 579 (2008).

9. Cy pres is applicable to all charitable dispositions, including charitable corporations, not just charitable trusts. *See* Restatement of Charitable Nonprofit Organizations § 3.02 cmt. f (Am. Law Inst., Tentative Draft No. 1, 2016).

with public policy as established by the king. Any deviations were corrected by the crown, regardless of the testator's intent. In Da Costa v. De Pas, (1754) 27 Eng. Rep. 150; 1 Amb. 228, a Jewish testator left money in trust to form an assembly for the purpose of teaching Jewish law and religion. Because the trust encouraged a religion other than the state religion, the chancellor referred it to the king for instructions. Applying prerogative cy pres, the king allotted the money to instruct foundlings in the Christian religion.

Largely as a reaction to the abuse of prerogative cy pres by the crown, disregarding the wishes of the donor, American courts were reluctant to adopt judicial cy pres. Over time, however, changes in circumstances made it difficult or impractical to administer charitable trusts as specifically intended by the donors. A nineteenth-century trust to care for old horses retired from pulling fire wagons and streetcars could not be administered for those purposes in the twentieth century. In consequence, American courts finally came to accept a judicial doctrine of cy pres.[10]

a. Illegal, Impossible, or Impracticable

In re Neher's Will
18 N.E.2d 625 (N.Y. 1939)

LOUGHRAN, J. The will of Ella Neher was admitted to probate by the Surrogate's Court of Dutchess County December 22, 1930. Paragraph 7 thereof made these provisions:

> I give, devise and bequeath my home in Red Hook Village, on the east side of South Broadway, consisting of house, barn and lot of ground . . . to the incorporated Village of Red Hook, as a memorial to the memory of my beloved husband, Herbert Neher, with the direction to said Village that said property be used as a hospital to be known as "Herbert Neher Memorial Hospital." The trustees of the Village of Red Hook, consisting of the President and the Trustees, shall constitute the managing board with full power to manage and operate said hospital as they deem wise for the benefit of the people of Red Hook, and each succeeding Board of Trustees shall constitute the Board of Trustees for said hospital, so that any person duly elected and qualified or duly appointed and qualified as a President or Trustee of the said Village of Red Hook shall be a trustee of said hospital during such person's lawful term of office, and shall be succeeded as a trustee on the hospital board by his successor on the Village Board.

All her other estate Mrs. Neher gave to relatives and friends.

On September 1, 1931, the trustees of Red Hook (hereinafter called the village) resolved to "accept the real property devised and bequeathed by the Will of Ella Neher, deceased, according to the terms of the Will of said Ella Neher."

In March, 1937, the village presented to the Surrogate's Court its petition asserting that it was without the resources necessary to establish and maintain a hospital on the property devised to it by the testatrix and that a modern hospital theretofore recently established in the neighboring village of Rhinebeck adequately served the

---

10. *See* Allison Anna Tait, The Secret Economy of Charitable Giving, 95 B.U. L. Rev. 1663 (2015).

needs of both communities. The prayer of this petition was for a decree "construing and reforming paragraph Seven of the last Will and Testament of said decedent directing and permitting your petitioner to receive said property and to erect and maintain thereon a building for the administration purposes of said Village to be known and designated as the Herbert Neher Memorial Hall, with a suitable tablet placed thereon expressing such memorial."

This petition the Surrogate denied on the single ground "that to read into the will a general intention to devote the property to charitable purposes instead of an intention to limit the use of the property to the operation of a hospital, would do violence to the expressed testamentary design of Mrs. Neher." The Appellate Division has affirmed the Surrogate. The village brings the case here by our leave. This gift was not a gift to a particular institution. There was to be no singular object of the bounty. This gift was one to a whole community—"to the incorporated Village of Red Hook." The idea initially expressed by the testatrix was that her home should be dedicated to the village in the name of her husband. The only question is whether this first stated design of beneficence at large is necessarily to be denied prime import, because of the words that immediately follow—"with the direction to said Village that said property be used as a hospital to be known as 'Herbert Neher Memorial Hospital.'" This last phrase, it is to be noticed, gave no hint in respect of a predilection for any certain type of the manifold varieties of medical or surgical care. Nor did the will make any suggestion as to management or control, save that the village trustees (as such) were designated as a governing board. So great an absence of particularity is a strong circumstance against the view that the instruction of the testatrix was of the substance of the gift.

When paragraph 7 of the will is taken as a whole, the true construction, we think, is that the paramount intention was "to give the property in the first instance for a general charitable purpose rather than a particular charitable purpose, and to graft on to the general gift a direction as to the desires or intentions of the testator as to the manner in which the general gift is to be carried into effect." Parker, J., in Matter of Wilson, [1913] 1 Ch. 314, 321. Such a grafted direction may be ignored when compliance is altogether impracticable and the gift may be executed cy pres through a scheme to be framed by the court for carrying out the general charitable purpose.

The order of the Appellate Division and the decree of the Surrogate's Court should be reversed and the matter remitted to the Surrogate's Court for further proceedings in accordance with this opinion, without costs.

NOTES

1. *Cy Pres and General Charitable Intent.* *Neher* involved an application of cy pres on grounds of impossibility or impracticability. The Restatement (Third) of Trusts explains:

[I]f a testator devises property in trust to establish and maintain an institution of a particular type but a similar institution already exists and is sufficiently effective that the testator's plan would serve no useful purpose, the intended purpose will not be enforced. . . . If property is given in trust for a particular charitable purpose and the amount given is insufficient to accomplish the intended purpose in a socially useful manner, the specified purpose fails and may be modified cy pres.[11]

At issue in *Neher* was not the failure of the designated purpose, but rather whether the testator had a *general charitable intent*. Under traditional law, a precondition to applying cy pres is a finding that the donor had a general rather than a specific charitable intent. The court, by a 4 to 3 vote, found a general charitable intent to benefit the village in the first clause of the testator's bequest, "to the incorporated Village of Red Hook, as a memorial to the memory of my beloved husband, Herbert Neher." The court reasoned that the specific direction that followed, to "be used as a hospital," was secondary to this general purpose.

UTC § 413(a) (2000) modifies the doctrine of cy pres by establishing a presumption that the donor had a general charitable intent.[12] The comment to § 413 explains:

> Traditional doctrine did not supply that presumption, leaving it to the courts to determine whether the settlor had a general charitable intent. If such an intent is found, the trust property is applied to other charitable purposes. If not, the charitable trust fails. . . . In the great majority of cases the settlor would prefer that the property be used for other charitable purposes. Courts are usually able to find a general charitable purpose to which to apply the property, no matter how vaguely such purpose may have been expressed by the settlor.

What result in *Neher* if it had been decided under the UTC?

By creating a presumption in favor of general charitable intent, the UTC also resolves a question that sometimes crops up in a charitable trust with a gift over — for example, a trust "for ABC Law School so long as Trusts and Estates is taught there, and if not, then for XYZ Hospital for the care of cancer patients." Some courts took the view that, in such a case, the settlor had a primary specific charitable intent and a secondary specific charitable intent. This interpretation precludes application of cy pres to the primary gift. The alternative view, which follows from a presumption of general charitable intent, is that a gift over is only one factor to be weighed in ascertaining whether the settlor had a general charitable intent that would allow application of cy pres to the primary gift.[13]

2. Approximating the Donor's Intent.   Following the literal meaning of the phrase *cy pres comme possible*, some authorities have said that the new purpose to which the property is applied must approximate as nearly as possible the donor's original stated

---

11. Restatement (Third) of Trusts § 67 cmt. c (Am. Law Inst. 2003).

12. The Restatements are in accord. *See id.* cmt. b; Restatement of Charitable Nonprofit Organizations § 3.02 cmt. b (Am. Law Inst., Tentative Draft No. 1, 2016). *Compare* Alberto B. Lopez, A Revaluation of Cy Pres Redux, 78 U. Cin. L. Rev. 1307 (2010) (criticizing the UTC), *with* C. Ronald Chester, Cy Pres: A Promise Unfulfilled, 54 Ind. L.J. 407 (1979) (criticizing traditional law).

13. *Compare* First Nat'l Bank of Chicago v. Canton Council of Campfire Girls, Inc., 426 N.E.2d 1198 (Ill. 1981) (refusing *cy pres* for primary gift), *with* In re Elizabeth J.K.L. Lucas Charitable Gift, 261 P.3d 800 (Haw. 2011) (allowing *cy pres* for primary gift); *see also* Restatement of Charitable Nonprofit Organizations § 3.02 cmt. e (Am. Law Inst., Tentative Draft No. 1, 2016).

purpose.[14] Increasingly, however, courts and legislatures have been satisfied with an alternative purpose that, in the words of the Restatement, "reasonably approximates the designated purpose."[15] The Restatement explains:

> In applying the cy pres doctrine, it is sometimes stated that the property must be applied to a purpose as near as possible to that designated by the terms of the intended trust. Increasingly, however, courts have recognized ... that the substitute or supplementary purpose need not be the *nearest possible* but one reasonably similar or close to the settlor's designated purpose, or "falling within the general charitable purpose" of the settlor. This is especially so when the particular purpose becomes impossible or impracticable of accomplishment long after the creation of the trust or when, among purposes reasonably close to the original, one has a distinctly greater usefulness than the others that have been identified. This more liberal application of cy pres is appropriate both because settlors' probable preferences are almost inevitably a matter of speculation in any event and because it is reasonable to suppose that *among relatively similar purposes* charitably inclined settlors would tend to prefer those most beneficial to their communities.[16]

UTC § 413(a)(3) provides likewise that in applying cy pres the court may "modify or terminate the trust by directing that the trust property be applied or distributed, in whole or in part, in a manner consistent with the settlor's charitable purposes."

3. Two Cy Pres Problems.   Consider the following:

a. T devises a fund in trust to the city of X to maintain a flower garden in a designated location in a city park. Thirty years later, X removes the garden to make room for a vacation resort and petitions the court to apply cy pres to allow X to recreate the flower garden elsewhere in the park. What result? Does it matter that X caused the impossibility that is the basis for its petition? *See* Kolb v. City of Storm Lake, 736 N.W.2d 546 (Iowa 2007) (allowing cy pres).

b. T devises property to X as trustee to pay the income to his niece A and, on A's death, to pay the principal to the dental school that T had graduated from 50 years earlier. T dies. Two years later, while A is still alive, the dental school is closed and its resources absorbed by the medical school of the same university. Eight years later, A dies, survived by a daughter, B. B argues that, because the dental school no longer exists, the gift fails and the trust property should revert to her on resulting trust as T's successor. The university asks the court to apply cy pres on the grounds that, though it no longer offers the basic degree in dental medicine, it continues to offer dental treatment for patients and post-graduate education in dentistry through its medical school and hospital. What result? *See* Obermeyer v. Bank of America, 140 S.W.3d 18 (Mo. 2004) (allowing cy pres).

---

14. *See, e.g.,* Estate of Elkins, 888 A.2d 815, 826 (Pa. Super. 2005) ("[U]nder the *cy pres* doctrine, a court is required to award the funds to a charity that most resembles the one that was to be the recipient of the trust.").

15. Restatement (Third) of Trusts § 67 (Am. Law Inst. 2003).

16. Id. cmt. d; *see also* Restatement of Charitable Nonprofit Organizations § 3.02 cmt. b (Am. Law Inst., Tentative Draft No. 1, 2016) (similar).

4. Justifying Cy Pres.   Because cy pres ultimately seeks to further the settlor's general intent, it has been justified as intent-implementing. In Judge Posner's words, "since no one can foresee the future, a rational donor knows that his intentions might eventually be thwarted by unpredictable circumstances and may therefore be presumed to accept implicitly a rule permitting modification of the terms of the bequest in the event that an unforeseen change frustrates his original intention."[17]

In Peter Luxton, Cy-Pres and the Ghost of Things That Might Have Been, 47 Conv. & Prop. Law 107 (1983), the author suggests that courts give greater importance to the settlor's intention in the early years of the trust but, at the end of the perpetuities period, treat the property as dedicated to charity. Should cy pres be applied more liberally after the period governed by the Rule Against Perpetuities has expired?

b. Wasteful

Under traditional law, a court may apply cy pres only if a designated charitable purpose becomes illegal, impossible, or impracticable. Today, however, many states and UTC § 413(a) (2000) also permit application of cy pres if the particular charitable purpose becomes *wasteful*. The Restatement explains what is meant by the term wasteful in this context:

> Another type of case appropriate to the application of cy pres, when not pre-cluded by the terms of the trust, is a situation in which the amount of property held in the trust exceeds what is needed for the particular charitable purpose to such an extent that the continued expenditure of all of the funds for that purpose, although possible to do, would be wasteful. . . .
>
> Faced with circumstances of the type required for cy pres intervention in a sur-plus-funds case, a court might broaden the purposes of the trust, direct application of the surplus funds to a like purpose in a different community, or otherwise direct the use of funds not reasonably needed for the original purpose to a different but reasonably similar charitable purpose.[18]

The impetus for this reform came from litigation involving the Buck Trust in San Francisco.

San Francisco Chronicle:
The Buck Trust

Beryl Buck, a childless widow, died in 1975. She was a resident of affluent Marin County, California, in the San Francisco Bay Area. Known as the hot-tub capital of the world, Marin is one of the nation's wealthiest counties. Mrs. Buck's will left the residue of her estate to the San Francisco Foundation, a community trust administering chari-table funds in Marin and four other counties in the San Francisco Bay Area (Alameda,

---

17. Richard A. Posner, Economic Analysis of Law § 19.3, at 712 (9th ed. 2014).
18. Restatement (Third) of Trusts § 67 cmt. c(1) (Am. Law Inst. 2003).

Contra Costa, San Francisco, and San Mateo).[19] The will directed that these funds, to be known and administered as the Leonard and Beryl Buck Foundation,

Beryl Buck

> shall always be held and used for exclusively non-profit charitable, religious or educational purposes in providing care for the needy in Marin County, California, and for other non-profit charitable, religious, or educational purposes in that county.

At the time of Mrs. Buck's death, the largest asset in her estate consisted of stock in Beldridge Oil Company, a privately held company with rich oil reserves in Southern California, founded by her father-in-law. In 1975, this stock was worth about $9 million, but soon thereafter, in 1979, Shell Oil won a bidding war and bought the stock in the Buck Trust for $260 million. By 1984, the corpus increased to well over $300 million, all of which was directed by Mrs. Buck's will to be spent on 7 percent of the Bay Area's residents in wealthy Marin County. This sudden embarrassment of riches threatened the integrity of the San Francisco Foundation in administering charitable dollars equitably in the Bay Area. In 1984, the Foundation sought judicial authorization to spend some portion of Buck Trust income in the other four counties.

The Foundation's petition for cy pres rested upon the following theory: The enormous increase in the value of principal was a posthumous surprise, a change in circumstances raising doubt whether Mrs. Buck, if she had anticipated such an event, would have limited her beneficence to Marin County. The Foundation argued that she would not have limited her beneficence to Marin County because: (a) she selected as trustee a community trust administering funds for the benefit of five counties; (b) other philanthropists, as shown by the 50 largest American charitable foundations (with the sole exception of the Buck Trust), reach out beyond their parochial origins as their resources grow and they seek to serve a more populous and diverse slice of humanity, following a principle of proportionality; and (c) in the face of such an increase in wealth, the donor would be less interested in a small geographical area and more interested in the efficiency of the charitable dollar.

The Foundation's action proved to be throwing fat into a fire. Marin County officials were outraged. One called the Foundation "grave-robbing bastards" and characterized

---

19. A bequest to a community trust qualifies as charitable. Scott and Ascher on Trusts § 37.2.4 explains the concept:

> These trusts are ordinarily created by the execution of an elaborate trust instrument under which named trustees undertake to hold property in trust for charitable purposes. The terms of the trust usually provide that its purposes are to be determined from time to time by a selected group of citizens who are to act as a distribution committee. Indeed, one of the purposes of these trusts is to provide flexibility in selecting charitable purposes. Instead of determining at the outset a single charitable purpose, the committee is to determine from time to time what the community's greatest needs are, and to provide for them. A community trust ordinarily begins with small contributions; thereafter, members of the community are invited to make further contributions by will or otherwise.

the cy pres petition as a "criminal attack upon the sanctity of wills." Marin officials were joined by the Marin Council of Agencies (a consortium of Marin County nonprofit agencies) in opposing the petition. Forty-six individuals and charitable organizations in the other four counties were allowed to intervene to object to the Marin-only limitation. The attorney general of California, as enforcer of charitable trusts, also intervened, arguing against cy pres and asking whether the Foundation was in violation of its fiduciary duties for bringing the suit and ought to be removed as trustee.

The case caused an uproar in San Francisco. At first, media commentators were incensed at all that money being spent in rich Marin, but then — on second thought — public opinion began to coalesce behind the idea that Mrs. Buck had the right to do with her property as she wished, and the San Francisco Foundation became an object of calumny.

Near the close of the respondent's case, after nearly six months of trial, the Foundation resigned as trustee, and the court dismissed the Foundation's cy pres petition. In the course of its opinion refusing to apply cy pres, not officially reported but reprinted in 21 U.S.F. L. Rev. 691 (1987), the trial court said:

> Ineffective philanthropy, inefficiency and relative inefficiency, that is, inefficiency of trust expenditures in one location given greater relative needs or benefits elsewhere, do not constitute impracticability. . . . Such situation is not the equivalent of impossibility; nor is there any threat that the operation of the trust will fail to fulfill the general charitable intention of the settlor.
>
> To the extent that concepts of effective philanthropy or efficiency relate to achieving the greatest benefit for the cost incurred they should not form the basis for modifying a donor's wishes. No law requires a testator to make a gift which the trustees deem efficient or to constitute effective philanthropy. Moreover, calculating "benefit" involves inherently subjective determinations; thus, what is "effective" or "efficient" will vary, depending on the interests and concerns of the person or persons making the determination. *Cy pres* does not authorize a court to vary the terms of the bequest merely because the variation will accommodate the desire of the trustee.
>
> To the extent that the term efficiency embraces the concept of relative need, it is not an appropriate basis for modifying the terms of a testamentary trust. . . . If it were otherwise, all charitable gifts, and the fundamental basis of philanthropy would be threatened, as there may always be more compelling "needs" to fill than the gift chosen by the testator. Gifts to Harvard or Stanford University, for example, could fail simply because institutions elsewhere are more needy. Similarly, needs in the Bay Area cannot be equated with the grueling poverty of India or the soul-wrenching famine in Ethiopia. Moreover, a standard of relative need would interpose governmental regulation on philanthropy because courts would be required to consider questions of comparative equity, social utility, or benefit, perhaps even wisdom, and ultimately substitute their judgments or those of the trustees for those of the donors. . . .
>
> The *cy pres* doctrine should not be so distorted by the adoption of subjective, relative, and nebulous standards such as "inefficiency" or "ineffective philanthropy" to the extent that it becomes a facile vehicle for charitable trustees to vary the terms of a trust simply because they believe that they can spend the trust income better

or more wisely elsewhere, or as in this case, prefer to do so. There is no basis in law for the application of standards such as "efficiency" or "effectiveness" to modify a trust, nor is there any authority that would elevate these standards to the level of impracticability.

No appeal was taken from the trial court decision in *Buck*. The court ordered the creation of the Marin Community Foundation, which would replace the San Francisco Foundation in administering the Buck Trust. The new foundation is governed by seven trustees, two appointed by the Marin County Board of Supervisors, one by the Marin Council of (Nonprofit) Agencies, one by the president of the University of California, one by the Interfaith Council of Marin, one by relatives of Mrs. Buck's husband, and one by the Marin Community Foundation board. The trial judge chose three Marin-based research institutes to divide a substantial portion of the income from the trust: The Buck Center on Aging, The Institute on Alcohol and Other Drug Problems, and The Marin Educational Institute.

Professor John Simon is highly critical of the supervisory role assumed by the trial court over the Buck Trust:

> The extraordinary command role the court reserved for itself over the decision-making process . . . violates the basic concept of private philanthropy and disregards the role assigned to charitable trustees in the nonprofit sector. . . .
>
> [I]t is not obvious that these programs would have been preferred by the donor over distributions to neighboring Bay Area counties served by the [San Francisco] Foundation. . . . [T]he fact that she picked a community foundation focused on the Bay Area as the instrument of her charity cannot be ignored when shaping a cy pres solution.[20]

The Foundation Directory reports that (as of June 30, 2016) the Marin Community Foundation, created by the trial court, had $1.6 billion in assets and made $75.9 million in grants over the course of the prior year. The San Francisco Foundation, without the Buck monies, had assets (also as of June 30, 2016) of $1.34 billion and made $132.9 million in grants.

NOTES

1. Wasteful: Efficiency or Surplus Funds? The drafters of UTC § 413(a) (2000) and the Restatement (Third) of Trusts had in mind that *wasteful* would not mean efficiency in the sense of relative need that was derided by the trial court in *Buck*, but rather in the sense of *surplus funds*. If a charitable trust holds property well in excess of what is needed for its particular charitable purpose, the UTC and Restatement now permit the application of cy pres to direct the use of the surplus funds to a reasonably similar purpose.[21]

---

20. John G. Simon, American Philanthropy and the Buck Trust, 21 U.S.F. L. Rev. 641, 666-68 (1987).

21. *See also* Restatement of Charitable Nonprofit Organizations § 3.02 cmt. c (Am. Law Inst., Tentative Draft No. 1, 2016).

2. Was the Buck Trust Wasteful?   Suppose that UTC § 413(a) had been applicable to the San Francisco Foundation's petition for cy pres. What result?

3. Another "Wasteful" Problem.   Suppose *T* devises a fund in trust to the city of *X* for the beautification of three cemeteries and the upkeep of certain plots. Thirty-five years later, *X* petitions the court for cy pres to allow *X* to redirect $50,000 of the trust's $75,000 corpus to capital improvements for the three cemeteries. *X* argues that $25,000 is plenty for beautification and plot upkeep, hence retention of the additional $50,000 would be wasteful. What result? *See* In re Trust of Lowry, 885 N.E.2d 296 (Ohio App. 2008) (denying cy pres).

2. Deviation

Cy pres, which is applicable to a charitable trust, may be contrasted with *equitable deviation* (see Chapter 10 at page 734), which is applicable to both private and charitable trusts. A court will permit a trustee to deviate from the administrative terms of a trust, such as those governing the investment management of the trust property, if compliance would defeat or substantially impair the accomplishment of the purposes of the trust in light of changed circumstances not anticipated by the settlor.[22] It is sometimes said that cy pres allows for modification of the donor's stated purpose, whereas deviation authorizes departure from administrative terms.[23] What is an administrative term and what is a purpose of the settlor, however, is not always clear. Courts have been known to interpret "administrative" broadly on sympathetic facts.

UTC § 412(a)-(b) (2000) blurs the line between cy pres and deviation:

> (a) The court may modify the administrative *or dispositive terms* of a trust . . . if, because of circumstances not anticipated by the settlor, modification or termination will further the purposes of the trust. To the extent practicable, the modification must be made in accordance with the settlor's probable intention.
>
> (b) The court may modify the administrative terms of a trust if continuation of the trust on its existing terms would be *impracticable* or *wasteful* or impair the trust's administration. [Emphasis added.]

Professor Ronald Chester suggests that the extension of deviation to dispositive terms might make cy pres redundant. He argues that a change in circumstances that makes a charitable trust illegal, impossible, impracticable, or wasteful would probably bring the deviation doctrine of UTC § 412(a) into play.[24] Further overlap is apparent in § 412(b), which authorizes deviation from an administrative term that has become "impracticable or wasteful." In City of Augusta v. Attorney General, 943 A.2d 582 (Me. 2008), decided under § 412, the court permitted the trustee of a charitable trust to sell certain land on which a school had been located. The school could no longer be

---

22. *See, e.g.,* In re Estate of Chamberlin, 23 N.Y.S.3d 658 (App. Div. 2016).

23. *See* Restatement of Charitable Nonprofit Organizations § 3.02 cmt. d (Am. Law Inst., Tentative Draft No. 1, 2016).

24. *See* Ronald Chester, Modification and Termination of Trusts in the 21st Century: The Uniform Trust Code Leads a Quiet Revolution, 35 Real Prop. Prob. & Tr. J. 697, 708-09 (2001).

maintained on that land because of subsequent dangerous conditions that could not be abated. The court required the trustee to apply the proceeds to a new school located elsewhere.

Perhaps the most talked about series of deviations involves the Barnes Foundation in Philadelphia.

Philadelphia Story: The Barnes Foundation

The Barnes Foundation, established in 1922 and originally based in the Philadelphia suburb of Merion, was created by Dr. Albert Barnes. Dr. Barnes was a chemist who invented Argyrol, which became a popular antiseptic that was also prescribed as eye drops for newborn babies to prevent blindness. Argyrol earned Dr. Barnes a great fortune, which he spent buying art in the early years of the twentieth century. Dr. Barnes descended on Paris, checkbook in hand, and, haunting the garrets and artists' studios in Montparnasse, bought dozens of paintings directly from artists. He amassed a collection of over 180 Renoirs, 60 Cézannes, 50 Matisses, 40 Picassos, and works by dozens of other artists including Manet, Monet, Seurat, and Van Gogh. Dr. Barnes hung these works five or six atop each other in a gallery he built in Merion. "At first glance, the display . . . looks almost haphazard. Paintings are lined up next to and above one another, sometimes inches apart, and they are labelled with only a single word on their frames."[25]

Son of a butcher in South Philadelphia, Dr. Barnes was high-hatted by Philadelphia Main Line society and by art critics and scholars who panned his art. But Barnes had his revenge. After his collection became celebrated, he would not let them see it. He barred entry to all except "plain people, that is, men and women who gain their livelihood by daily toil in shops, factories, schools, and stores." Dr. Barnes admitted some scholars and literati on a selective basis. A few others were able to sneak in disguised as chauffeurs, miners, or workmen.[26]

Dr. Barnes had unconventional theories about art education, developed with John Dewey. To further these theories, the Barnes Foundation was set up as an educational institution, not as an art gallery. The curriculum consisted solely of instruction in Barnes's aesthetic theories. Classes in Barnesian aesthetics were open to students for two hours in the afternoon.

When Dr. Barnes died in 1951, he left behind bylaws for the Barnes Foundation providing that no painting was ever to be moved from where he had hung it. No painting was to be sold or loaned. No painting could be added to the collection. Paintings from other galleries could not be exhibited at the Barnes gallery. The gallery was to be open to the general public only on Saturdays from September through June. Entrance fees were prohibited. Also

Dr. Albert Barnes

25. Jeffrey Toobin, Battle for the Barnes, The New Yorker, Jan. 21, 2002, at 34.
26. For a portrait of the irascible Dr. Barnes, see Howard Greenfeld, The Devil and Dr. Barnes (1987).

prohibited were "any society functions commonly designated receptions, teas, dinners, or banquets." The trustees were permitted to invest only in government bonds. Barnes mandated that these rules were "unamendable."

In 1961, the Pennsylvania attorney general brought a lawsuit, forcing the Barnes Gallery to open its doors to the general public two and one-half days a week in order to keep its charitable tax-exempt status. This suit was instigated by pressure from the Philadelphia Inquirer, which was then owned by Walter Annenberg, a noted art collector himself.

In 1988, upon the death of the last trustee appointed by Dr. Barnes, control of the Barnes Foundation passed to Lincoln University, a small, historically black college in Chester County, Pennsylvania. (Justice Thurgood Marshall was a graduate.) During his life, Barnes had always admired and enjoyed African American culture and art. The new trustees found the gallery, built in 1925, in a sad state of disrepair and the Foundation in financial distress. With an endowment of only $10 million (excluding the art, worth billions!), the Foundation did not even have enough income to secure the entire gallery. Half the gallery was open for two hours, the public was then shooed out, and after the guards moved to the other half, the public was readmitted to the other half for two hours.

The new trustees searched for ways to restore the facility and generate income. In the 1990s, they brought a series of lawsuits asking the court to authorize deviation from Barnes's rigid rules. The court authorized the trustees to open the gallery to the public three and one-half days a week during the whole year and to charge a $5 admission fee. The trustees were given greater discretion in investing the endowment to produce a higher yield. The trustees were permitted to hold fundraising events in the gallery. The trustees also sought permission to sell some of the collection, but this brought a great outcry. The trustees then proposed, and the court approved, a world tour of 50 priceless masterworks from the collection. The tour netted the Foundation about $17 million, of which $12 million was used to modernize the gallery. For those who could not see the paintings on the tour, the trustees produced a CD-ROM with photographs in color.

The world tour drew record crowds, more in Paris than had ever before lined up to see an art show. But the tour also brought protests from some Philadelphians, who were outraged that Dr. Barnes's intent had been violated in so many ways. The protestors—particularly the neighbors in Merion—were angry that the Foundation had been transformed from an educational institution serving a few into a museum drawing thousands of people in cars. Still, at the end of the tour, the paintings were rehung in the gallery exactly as the eccentric Dr. Barnes had hung them. Some of the greatest works were placed near the ceiling, difficult to see but hung according to his aesthetic theories.

The latest round in the "Battle for the Barnes" began in 2002. Explaining that the Foundation's dire financial condition threatened its survival, the trustees again asked the court to authorize deviation from Barnes's rules, this time to permit moving the collection from the recently renovated Merion building to a new gallery to be built in Philadelphia, close to the Philadelphia Museum of Art. The relocation plan was part of a deal between the trustees on the one hand, and the Pew Charitable Trusts and the

A wall ensemble at the old Barnes Foundation Gallery in Merion (left) and its counterpart at the new Barnes Foundation Gallery in Philadelphia (right). Clockwise from top: Seurat, *Models*; Corot, *Mme de Larochenoire, Wife of the Painter*; Cézanne, *Leda and the Swan*; Cézanne, *The Card Players*; Cézanne, *Bottle and Fruits*; Cézanne, *The Drinker*.
© 2017 The Barnes Foundation

Lenfest Foundation, both mainstays of Philadelphia philanthropy, on the other. The plan called for Pew and Lenfest to help the trustees raise money for the new facility and to replenish the Foundation's depleted endowment.

In January 2004, the court ruled that "the present location of the gallery is not sacrosanct, and relocation may be permitted *if necessary*." But the evidence before it did not make out a case of necessity. The court chided the trustees for their unwillingness to consider selling some of the paintings that were not part of the public display.[27] The court also had harsh words for the attorney general's office, which did little more than support the Foundation, "cheering on its witnesses. . . . The course of action chosen by the Office of the Attorney General prevented the court from seeing a balanced, objective presentation of the situation, and constituted an abdication of that office's responsibility."

The trustees tried again. After six days of further hearings, producing more than 1,200 pages of testimony, on December 13, 2004, the judge granted the trustees' petition, authorizing a move of the gallery to Philadelphia. On November 13, 2009, the Foundation held a groundbreaking ceremony for the new facility. By 2011, the Foundation had raised more than $200 million, of which $150 million was earmarked for construction costs and $50 million was to replenish the Foundation's endowment. On May 15, 2012, the new gallery opened. Today it houses the Barnes collection with public displays that closely resemble those of the prior Merion gallery.

---

27. On the complexities of selling paintings from a museum collection, known as deaccessioning, see Allison Anna Tait, Publicity Rules for Public Trusts, 33 Cardozo Arts & Ent. L.J. 421 (2015).

The new gallery, which is open six days a week and charges $25 for an adult ticket, celebrated its one millionth visitor in late 2015. The Foundation sells reproductions of some of the works in the collection. Color images are posted on the Foundation's Web site. The gallery is available for rent for private events. Critics say that Dr. Barnes must be spinning in his grave. But, maybe not. Reviewers suggest that the new gallery is indeed faithful to Dr. Barnes's aesthetic vision:

> Against all odds, the museum that opens to the public on Saturday is still very much the old Barnes, only better. . . . Barnes's exuberant vision of art as a relatively egalitarian aggregate of the fine, the decorative and the functional comes across more clearly, justifying its perpetuation with a new force. . . .
>
> The Merion building and its 24 galleries, and Barnes's arrangements within them, have been recreated with amazing fidelity in terms of proportions, window placement and finishings, albeit in a slightly more modern style. The structure is oriented to the south, exactly as in Merion; the same mustard-colored burlap covers the walls; the same plain wood molding outlines doors and baseboards.
>
> As for Barnes's arrangements, almost nothing is out of place: not one of the hundreds of great French paintings, none of the pieces of Americana, nor any of the Greek or African sculptures, the small New Mexican wood-panel santos or the scores of wrought-iron hinges, locks, door handles and whatnot that dot the interstices like unusually tangible bits of wallpaper pattern, often subtly reiterating the compositions of the paintings.[28]

NOTE

What Would You Have Done?   Would you have approved the trustees' deviations from Dr. Barnes's bylaws? Given the record before the court, and the evidence of unsustainability in Merion, did the judge have any viable alternatives?[29]

3. Discriminatory Trusts

Charitable trusts that furnish benefits to members of a particular race, gender, or religion, such as to "whites" or to "men," have been the subject of much litigation since the 1960s.[30] The issue is that the social consensus against such forms of discrimination informs the public benefit principle that is at the core of the charitable purpose doctrine. Howard Sav. Inst. v. Peep, 170 A.2d 39 (N.J. 1961), is illustrative. After Amherst

---

28. Roberta Smith, A Museum, Reborn, Remains True to Its Old Self, Only Better, N.Y. Times, May 18, 2012, at A1; *see also* Ada Louise Huxtable, The New Barnes Shouldn't Work — But Does, Wall St. J., May 25, 2012, at D4 ("The 'new' Barnes that contains the 'old' Barnes shouldn't work, but it does. It should be inauthentic, but it's not. It has changed, but it is unchanged. The architects have succeeded in retaining its identity and integrity without resorting to a slavishly literal reproduction.").

29. For analysis of restricted gifts and the complexity of ascertaining and honoring the wishes of the donor over time, see John K. Eason, Motive, Duty, and the Management of Restricted Charitable Gifts, 45 Wake Forest L. Rev. 123 (2010).

30. *See* Scott and Ascher on Trusts § 39.5.5.

College refused a bequest to be used for scholarships for Protestant boys on account of the religious restriction, the court removed the clause. The court reasoned that the testator's primary charitable purpose was to benefit the college.

If the trustee of a racially restrictive trust is a governmental body, such as a public school granting scholarships to whites, courts have held that administration of the trust would be discriminatory state action forbidden by the Equal Protection Clause of the Constitution, making the racial restriction unenforceable. The question then becomes: Would the settlor prefer the trust to continue without the racial restriction or to terminate? Applying cy pres or the deviation doctrine, most courts have held that the settlor would prefer the charitable trust to continue without the racial restriction, as in Trammell v. Elliott, 199 S.E.2d 194 (Ga. 1973) (bequest to a public institution for the benefit of "poor white boys and girls" given effect minus the racial limitation).

A contrary example is provided by the infamous cases of Evans v. Newton, 382 U.S. 296 (1966), and Evans v. Abney, 396 U.S. 435 (1970). In the 1966 decision, the Supreme Court held that Senator Augustus O. Bacon's bequest of land to the City of Macon in trust for a park for "white people" was unconstitutional, even if administered by private trustees, because the park was a public institution. In the 1970 decision, the Court upheld the determination of the Georgia courts that the trust could not be modified, and the property passed on resulting trust to Bacon's heirs, because Bacon would have preferred the trust to fail rather than operate free of the racial limitation.

If the trustee is a private individual and not a public body, enforcing the racial restriction is usually not unconstitutional as discriminatory state action. But a racially restrictive trust may nonetheless run afoul of some federal or state law forbidding racial discrimination. If so, the

Senator Augustus O. Bacon

question arises whether the court should apply cy pres or deviation to strike the racial restriction. Most courts have done so.

In Home for Incurables of Baltimore City v. University of Maryland, 797 A.2d 746 (Md. 2002), the court removed a racial restriction, illegal under state law, in a charitable bequest to the Home for Incurables of Baltimore City for the benefit of "white patients who need physical rehabilitation." The will also contained an alternative bequest to the University of Maryland in the event that the Home found the racial limitation "not acceptable." The alternative bequest was not subject to a racial limitation. The court held that the Home should take the bequest free from the racial limitation. The court reasoned that, by ordering the proceeds be paid to the University, the court would be giving effect to the illegal racial discrimination.

Restricting the benefits of a private charitable trust to one sex does not violate the Constitution, but it may violate other federal or state laws prohibiting sex discrimination. In such cases, courts have removed the sex restriction under the power of cy pres or deviation, as in In re Certain Scholarship Funds, 575 A.2d 1325 (N.H. 1990).

and for a scholarship program for Smithers Center patients in need of financial assistance. From 1992 to March 1995, she and, until his death in January 1994, [Mr.] Smithers successfully solicited millions of dollars' worth of donated goods and services for a total restoration of the building and organized the fundraiser, scheduled for April 1995. Then, in March 1995, just over a year after Smithers's death, the Hospital announced that it planned to move the Smithers Center into a hospital ward and sell the East 93rd Street building. The Hospital directed Mrs. Smithers, a month and a half before the fundraiser was scheduled to be held, to cancel the event. The Hospital's announced intentions aroused Mrs. Smithers's suspicions. . . . Mrs. Smithers notified the Hospital of her objections to the proposed relocation of the program and demanded an accounting of the Smithers Center's finances. . . .

[I]n May 1995 the Hospital disclosed that it had been misappropriating monies from the Endowment Fund since before Smithers's death, transferring such monies to its general fund where they were used for purposes unrelated to the Smithers Center. Mrs. Smithers notified the Attorney General, who investigated the Hospital's plan to sell the building and discovered that the Hospital had transferred restricted assets from the Smithers Endowment Fund to its general fund in what it called "loans." The Attorney General demanded the return of these assets and in August 1995 the Hospital returned nearly $5 million to the Smithers Endowment Fund, although it did not restore the income lost on those funds during the intervening years. . . .

In July 1998, the Attorney General entered into an [agreement] with the Hospital. Under the terms of this [agreement] the Hospital agreed to make no more transfers or loans from Gift funds for any purpose other than the benefit of the Smithers Center and to return to the Gift fund $1 million from the proceeds of any sale of the building.[36] The Attorney General did not require the Hospital to return the entire proceeds of such a sale, because he found that, contrary to Mrs. Smithers's contention, the terms of the Gift did not preclude the Hospital from selling the building.

Two months later, Mrs. Smithers commenced this suit to enforce the conditions of the Gift and to obtain an accounting by the Hospital of its handling of the Endowment Fund and property dedicated to the Smithers Center. The Hospital and the Attorney General were named . . . as defendants. Mrs. Smithers had obtained Special Letters of Administration from the Nassau County Surrogate's Court appointing her the Special Administratrix of Smithers's estate for the purpose of pursuing claims by the estate against the Hospital in connection with its administration of the Smithers Center. . . .

The Hospital [and the Attorney General] . . . moved to dismiss the complaint for lack of standing. [The Supreme Court, which in New York is a trial court, dismissed Mrs. Smithers's complaint.]

On appeal, the Attorney General's office, having reevaluated the matter "under the direction of the newly elected Attorney General," reversed its position and urged this Court to remand for a hearing on the merits to determine whether or not the building was subject to gift restrictions. If it were, then all proceeds of the sale would be subject to the same restrictions and could not be used for the Hospital's general

---

36. The hospital sold the 56 East 93rd Street mansion to the Spence School for $15 million, considerably more than the $1 million sum that the attorney general required the hospital to return. *See* Cerisse Anderson, Donor's Widow Wins Right to Sue Over Gift, N.Y.L.J., Apr. 6, 2001, at 1. — Eds.

purposes. . . . [T]he Attorney General urged that the issue of Mrs. Smithers's standing to bring the suit need not, and should not, be reached in this action, since he certainly had standing and had joined with her in seeking reversal and remand. . . .

While this appeal was pending, the Attorney General and the Hospital reached another agreement. This agreement raised some issues for the first time, but it brought the position of the Attorney General and the Hospital on other issues into accord with Mrs. Smithers's position. For example, the Hospital agreed to allocate the entire net proceeds of the sale of the building to the restricted purposes of the Gift and to restore the income lost as a result of the transfer of Gift funds to its general fund. Reversing his position again, the Attorney General returned to his predecessor's contention that Mrs. Smithers has no standing to bring this suit, and asked this Court to [affirm] the decision dismissing the complaint for lack of standing. . . .

The "newly elected Attorney General" was Eliot Spitzer. Son of a wealthy New York real estate magnate and a graduate of Harvard Law School, Spitzer gained notoriety for his aggressive pursuit of alleged wrongdoing in the securities industry. He was later elected governor, but resigned after admitting to be the person identified as "Client 9" in an FBI affidavit about a prostitution ring known as the Emperor's Club.

The sole issue before us is whether Mrs. Smithers, on behalf of Smithers's estate, has standing to bring this action. The Attorney General maintains that, with a few exceptions inapplicable here, standing to enforce the terms of a charitable gift is limited to the Attorney General. . . .

The question of whether the donor who is living and can maintain his or her own action need rely on the protection of the Attorney General to enforce the terms of his gift . . . was addressed in Associate Alumni of the General Theological Seminary of the Protestant Episcopal Church in the United States of America v. The General Theological Seminary of the Protestant Episcopal Church in the United States, 57 N.E. 626 (N.Y. 1900) . . . [:]

> The general rule is "If the trustees of a charity abuse the trust, misemploy the charity fund, or commit a breach of the trust, the property does not revert to the heir or legal representative of the donor unless there is an express condition of the gift that it shall revert to the donor or his heirs, in case the trust is abused, but the redress is by bill or information by the attorney-general *or other person having the right to sue.*" . . .

In dismissing Mrs. Smithers's complaint, Supreme Court replied on *Associate Alumni, supra,* . . . to hold that, since the Gift instruments do not provide Mrs. Smithers with the right of oversight, that right is vested exclusively in the Attorney General and Mrs. Smithers has no standing to sue. However, . . . [t]he holding of [*Associate Alumni*] explicitly forecloses the conclusion that the Attorney General's standing in these actions is exclusive. . . .

Supreme Court incorrectly characterized Mrs. Smithers as one who "positions herself as the champion and representative of the possible beneficiaries of the Gift," with no tangible stake because she has no position or property to lose if the Hospital alters its administration of the Gift. Mrs. Smithers did not bring this action on her own behalf or on behalf of beneficiaries of the Smithers Center. She brought it as the court-appointed special administratrix of the estate of her late husband to enforce his rights under his agreement with the Hospital through specific performance of that agreement. Therefore, the general rule barring beneficiaries from suing charitable corporations has no application to Mrs. Smithers. Moreover, the desire to prevent vexatious litigation by "irresponsible parties who do not have a tangible stake in the matter and have not conducted appropriate investigations" has no application to Mrs. Smithers either. Without possibility of pecuniary gain for himself or herself, only a plaintiff with a genuine interest in enforcing the terms of a gift will trouble to investigate and bring this type of action. Indeed, it was Mrs. Smithers's accountants who discovered and informed the Attorney General of the Hospital's misdirection of Gift funds, and it was only after Mrs. Smithers brought her suit that the Attorney General acted to prevent the Hospital from diverting the entire proceeds of the sale of the building away from the Gift fund and into its general fund. The Attorney General, following his initial investigation of the Hospital's administration of the Gift, acquiesced in the Hospital's sale of the building, its diversion of the appreciation realized on the sale, and its relocation of the rehabilitation unit, even as he ostensibly was demanding that the Hospital continue to act "in accordance with the donor's gift." Absent Mrs. Smithers's vigilance, the Attorney General would have resolved the matter between himself and the Hospital in that manner and without seeking permission of any court.

The donor of a charitable gift is in a better position than the Attorney General to be vigilant and, if he or she is so inclined, to enforce his or her own intent. Smithers was the founding donor of the Smithers Center, which he established to carry out his vision of "first class alcoholism treatment and training." In his agreement with the Hospital he reserved to himself the right to veto the Hospital's project plans and staff appointments for the Smithers Center. He and Mrs. Smithers remained actively involved in the affairs of the Smithers Center until his death, and she thereafter. During his lifetime, when Smithers found that, as he wrote on July 31, 1978, "[c]ertain things that were definitely understood were not carried out" by the Hospital, he decided not to donate the balance of the Gift. It was only when the Hospital expressly agreed to the various restrictions imposed by Smithers that he completed the Gift. The Hospital's subsequent unauthorized deviation from the terms of the completed Gift commenced during Smithers's lifetime and was discovered shortly after he died. To hold that, in her capacity as her late husband's representative, Mrs. Smithers has no standing to institute an action to enforce the terms of the Gift is to contravene the well settled principle that a donor's expressed intent is entitled to protection and the longstanding recognition under New York law of standing for a donor such as Smithers. We have seen no New York case in which a donor attempting to enforce the terms of his charitable gift was denied standing to do so. Neither the donor nor his estate was before the court in any of the cases urged on us in opposition to donor standing. The courts in these cases were not addressing the situation in which the donor was still living or his estate still existed. Cf. *Herzog Foundation v. University of Bridgeport*, 699 A.2d 995 (Conn. 1997).[37]

Moreover, the circumstances of this case demonstrate the need for co-existent standing for the Attorney General and the donor. The Attorney General's office was notified

---

37. *Herzog*, which denied(!) donor standing, is discussed at page 782.—Eds.

of the Hospital's misappropriation of funds by Mrs. Smithers, whose accountants performed the preliminary review of the Hospital's financial records, and it learned of the Hospital's closing of the detox unit—a breach, according to the Attorney General, of a specific representation—from Mrs. Smithers's papers in this action. Indeed, there is no substitute for a donor, who has a "special, personal interest in the enforcement of the gift restriction." Mrs. Smithers herself, who the Supreme Court found had no position to lose if the Hospital altered its administration of the Gift, has her own special, personal interest in the enforcement of the Gift restrictions imposed by her husband, as is manifest from her own fundraising work on behalf of the Smithers Center and the fact that the gala that she organized and that the Hospital ultimately cancelled was to be in her honor as well as her husband's. In any event, the Attorney General's interest in enforcing gift terms is not necessarily congruent with that of the donor. The donor seeks to have his or her intent faithfully executed, which by definition will benefit the beneficiaries, and perhaps also to erect a tangible memorial to himself or herself. In the June 16, 1971 letter to the Hospital in which Smithers created the Gift, he wrote that it "is to be used to set up the Smithers Alcoholism Treatment and Training Center." . . . We conclude that the distinct but related interests of the donor and the Attorney General are best served by continuing to accord standing to donors to enforce the terms of their own gifts concurrent with the Attorney General's standing to enforce such gifts on behalf of the beneficiaries thereof.

Mrs. Smithers, appointed the Special Administratrix of Smithers's estate for the purpose of pursuing claims by the estate against the Hospital in connection with its administration of the Smithers Center, therefore has standing to sue the Hospital for enforcement of the Gift terms. . . .

Order, Supreme Court, New York County, modified, on the law, to grant plaintiff's motion for a preliminary injunction to the extent of staying disbursement of the proceeds of the sale of the East 93rd Street building, to deny defendants' motion to dismiss the complaint and to reinstate the complaint, and otherwise affirmed, without costs.

FRIEDMAN, J., dissenting. . . . [The issue on appeal] is whether Adele Smithers, as the representative of her husband's estate, has standing to bring this action seeking to enforce the terms of a charitable gift given by her husband, the funding of which was completed approximately 12 years before this action was commenced. Because I believe that plaintiff does not have standing, I respectfully dissent.

In considering the subject of standing, I begin with the observation that, when a charitable gift is made, without any provision for a reversion of the gift to the donor or his heirs, the interest of the donor and his heirs is permanently excluded. Accordingly, in the absence of a right of reverter, the right to seek enforcement of the terms of a charitable gift is restricted to the Attorney General. . . .

The New York general rule on standing is not only consistent with the common-law approach (see Herzog Foundation v. University of Bridgeport, 699 A.2d 995 (Conn. 1997)), but also with the approach taken by the Restatement (Second) of Trusts (see §§ 391[e] & [f]). . . .

In holding that standing is generally restricted to the Attorney General, our courts have pointed out that a limited standing rule is necessary to protect charitable institutions from "vexatious litigation" by parties who do not have a tangible stake in the outcome of the litigation. While the majority believes that this concern does not apply to Mrs. Smithers because her motives are altruistic (and I agree that they are), the limited standing rule enunciated by our Court of Appeals is a prophylactic one that does not permit a case-by-case inquiry into the subjective motivations of the party commencing the action. . . .

[I]t is uncontroverted that the estate was not the donor of the gift. Thus, even if pure donor standing were recognized (as the majority concludes), this could not be a basis for granting standing to Mr. Smithers's estate. Next, to the extent that Mr. Smithers may have had standing based upon his right to exercise discretionary control over the gift, i.e., via the right to appoint key staffing positions, that right was personal to him, abated upon his death, and did not devolve to his estate. Hence, as plaintiff concedes that the estate has no right to exercise control over the gift, this may not be a basis of standing. Finally, since it is uncontroverted that the estate does not have a right of reverter in the gift or, in fact, any right to control the gift by way of appointment to staff positions or otherwise, it follows that there is no retained interest that could support a claim of standing. In view of this, I fail to perceive the legal basis for the majority's grant of standing to plaintiff. . . .

Accordingly, I vote to affirm the order dismissing the complaint.

NOTES

1. Epilogue. The parties in *Smithers* later reached a settlement. The hospital surrendered the right to use the Smithers name and its alcoholism center was renamed the Addiction Institute of New York. The hospital promised to use any remaining proceeds from the sale of the 56 East 93rd Street building for the treatment of alcoholism. It also agreed to return $6 million to the Smithers Foundation for a new substance abuse treatment center. In 2008, the Smithers Alcoholism Treatment and Training Center was opened at a St. John's Riverside Hospital facility in Yonkers, New York.

Adele C. Smithers and Derek Jeter, of the New York Yankees, at an event in 2006
G. Gershoff/Getty Images

In 2003, the probate court administering Mr. Smithers's estate ruled that Mrs. Smithers was entitled to be reimbursed for her costs in the litigation against the hospital. Although the "decedent's probate estate had no direct economic stake in the hospital proceedings," the court was satisfied that Mrs. Smithers "undertook this litigation with the best of motives, desiring nothing more than to vindicate her late husband's life's work that was allegedly being ignored by St. Luke's-Roosevelt Hospital." In re Estate of Smithers, 760 N.Y.S.2d 304 (Sur. 2003).

2. The Rise of Settlor Standing. Twenty years before *Smithers*, Professor Henry Hansmann argued in favor of donor standing to enforce charitable gifts thus:

[P]atrons will commonly feel a strong interest in seeing that the managers of non-profits adhere to their fiduciary duties. Thus, it makes sense to deny standing to [donors] only if the consequence would be large numbers of spite suits, strike suits, or suits filed through sheer idiocy—which are presumably what the courts and commentators have in mind when they raise the specter of "harassing" litigation—or of suits that, though based on a real grievance, are feebly litigated and thus do more harm than good. Yet it appears extraordinarily unlikely that suits of this nature would ever become a sufficiently significant problem to outweigh the benefits of enlisting [donors] into the enforcement effort.[38]

In just the last 15 years or so, many have come to agree. Today a majority of states allows the settlor of a charitable trust to enforce the trust. A few states, such as New York in *Smithers*, have done so by judicial decision. Most have recognized settlor standing by statute such as UTC § 405(c) (2000), which provides that "[t]he settlor of a charitable trust . . . may maintain a proceeding to enforce the trust." The Restatement (Third) of Trusts, in a provision that supersedes the contrary position taken by the Restatement (Second) of Trusts (see page 782), is in accord:

A suit for the enforcement of a charitable trust may be maintained only by the Attorney General or other appropriate public officer or by a co-trustee or successor trustee, *by a settlor*, or by another person who has a special interest in the enforcement of the trust.[39]

On the other hand, courts have resisted extension of this right to donors of other kinds of charitable gifts.[40]

3. A Settlor Standing Problem. *T* gives a fund in trust to *X* University to support a public policy school that emphasizes training for government service. After *T*'s death, the school uses the fund to support other departments in addition to the public policy school.[41] Does the executor of *T*'s estate have standing to sue *X* under UTC § 403(c)? Under *Smithers*? If so, does the standing right pass to *T*'s heirs or residuary takers? Suppose that *T* left his entire estate in equal shares to his children, *A* and *B*. What

38. Henry B. Hansmann, Reforming Nonprofit Corporation Law, 129 U. Pa. L. Rev. 497, 609 (1981). For additional commentary, see, e.g., Reid Kress Weisbord & Peter DeScioli, The Effects of Donor Standing on Philanthropy: Insights from the Psychology of Gift-Giving, 45 Gonz. L. Rev. 225 (2010); Evelyn Brody, From the Dead Hand to the Living Dead: The Conundrum of Charitable-Donor Standing, 41 Ga. L. Rev. 1183 (2007); Iris J. Goodwin, Donor Standing to Enforce Charitable Gifts: Civil Society vs. Donor Empowerment, 58 Vand. L. Rev. 1093 (2005); Ronald Chester, Grantor Standing to Enforce Charitable Transfers Under Section 405(c) of the Uniform Trust Code and Related Law: How Important Is It and How Extensive Should It Be?, 37 Real Prop. Prob. & Tr. J. 611 (2003).
39. Restatement (Third) of Trusts § 94(2) (Am. Law Inst. 2012) (emphasis added).
40. *See, e.g.*, Dodge v. Trustees of Randolph-Macon Woman's College, 661 S.E.2d 805 (Va. 2008) (refusing to apply UTC § 405(c) to a charity organized as a corporation rather than a trust); Courtenay C. and Lucy Patten Davis Foundation v. Colorado State University, 320 P.3d 1115 (Wyo. 2014) (refusing standing to donors of a charitable gift).
41. This problem is based on Robertson v. Princeton Univ., No. C-99-02 (N.J. Super. July 17, 2002). For discussion, see Iris J. Goodwin, Ask Not What Your Charity Can Do for You: Robertson v. Princeton Provides Liberal-Democratic Insights into the Dilemma of Cy Pres Reform, 51 Ariz. L. Rev. 75 (2009).

result if *A* wants to bring suit against *X* but *B* does not? Should it matter whether *A* seeks return of the fund or an injunction compelling *X* to comply with the terms of the gift? Will the right pass from *A* and *B* to their respective successors? Suppose the donor was not a natural person but rather an institution, as in *Herzog*. Does such a donor retain standing rights in perpetuity?

3. Local Politics

The emphasis thus far has been on the potential for settlor enforcement of charitable trusts to compensate for lackadaisical enforcement by the state attorneys general. Another worry is that when the attorney general does intervene in the operation of a charity, she will be tempted to curry favor with local voters by imposing local preferences at the expense of the trust's charitable purpose. Professor Evelyn Brody summarizes in capsule form thus: "Political cynics believe that 'A.G.' stands not for 'attorney general' but for 'aspiring governor.'"[42]

The Sweetest Place on Earth: Hershey's Kiss-Off[43]

The Hershey Company makes such familiar goodies as Reese's Pieces, Milk Duds, and of course, Hershey's Chocolate Bars, Kisses, and Syrup. The Company is based in Hershey, Pennsylvania, a town that fancies itself "The Sweetest Place On Earth." In Hershey, Cocoa Avenue intersects with Chocolate Avenue and the streetlights are shaped like Hershey's Kisses. Also based in Hershey is the Milton Hershey School, a boarding school that enrolls, feeds, and clothes 2,000 needy children. The School's operations are funded by the Milton Hershey School Trust, a Pennsylvania charitable trust that as of 2015 was worth roughly $12.1 billion,[44] more than all but the six largest U.S. university endowments.[45]

The Company, the School, and the Trust were all founded by Milton S. Hershey. For Hershey, a gifted confectioner, the lure of chocolate—the rich, sensual, and satisfying food derived from the cocoa bean—was irresistible. Chocolate had long been a pleasure of the upper class. But because it was so difficult to mass produce and ship in an edible and economically viable form, few others had ready access to it. Milk chocolate, a solid form of chocolate with a pleasing taste that could be mass produced and widely distributed at bearable cost, was the holy grail of chocolate making. The trick was to induce the water-based milk to combine with the oil-based cocoa.

Hershey's solution was to boil the milk to the brink of souring, which explains the bitter, harsh taste of Hershey's milk chocolate. Although panned by chocolate connoisseurs—who preferred the more subtle flavors of European chocolates such as Cadbury, Lindt, and Nestlé—for many Americans, Hershey's grittier chocolate was

---

42. Evelyn Brody, Whose Public? Parochialism and Paternalism in State Charity Law Enforcement, 79 Ind. L.J. 937, 946 (2004).

43. Adapted from Klick & Sitkoff, *supra* note 35.

44. As reported on the Trust's Form 990 filed with the IRS for the fiscal year ending on July 31, 2015. We discuss Form 990 at page 804.

45. Only Harvard ($36.4 billion), Yale ($25.6 billion), Texas ($24.1 billion), Princeton ($22.7 billion), Stanford ($22.2 billion), and MIT ($13.5 billion) have larger endowments. *See* 2015 NACUBO-Commonfund Study of Endowments (Fiscal Year 2015).

Milton S. Hershey and the Orphan Boys
Hershey Community Archives

their first encounter with the substance, and it was memorable. Hershey's chocolate became America's chocolate. And the town of Hershey became a model company town.

Hershey then turned his attention to the School, which he founded with his wife Catherine in 1909. Because they never had children of their own, the students enrolled in the School became their surrogate children. Milton later explained: "Well, I have no heirs; so I decided to make the orphan boys of the United States my heirs."[46]

In 1918, three years after Catherine died, Milton Hershey transferred substantially all of his assets—including his stock in the Company, then worth $60 million—to the Trust. Today, the Trust provides the School with an endowment that is remarkable not only for its size but even more so for its breathtaking lack of diversification. Of the Trust's $12.1 billion corpus, roughly $6.6 billion (more than 50 percent) is invested in the stock of the Hershey Company.[47] These holdings amount to nearly one-third of the Company's outstanding shares and, thanks to a dual-class stock structure, give the trustees approximately 80 percent of the Company's shareholder votes.

Increasingly aware of the perils of an undiversified portfolio, and after getting a nudge from the Pennsylvania attorney general's office, the trustees decided to sell the Trust's interest in the Company. In July 2002, when the Wall Street Journal broke the news of the trustees' plan, investors bid up the Company's stock price by 25 percent from $62.50 to $78.30.

---

46. Was this a correct usage of the technical term *heirs*? See page 67.

47. The $6.6 billion figure was computed by multiplying the stock price at year-end 2015, obtained from Google Finance, by the number of shares controlled by the Trust and the Hershey Trust Company, as reported in The Hershey Company's Form 10-K filed with the Securities and Exchange Commission for 2015. The figures in the next sentence are based on information reported in the same 10-K.

The thought of cashing out at a premium pleased the trustees, but Hershey residents and workers took a different view. They organized a "Derail the Sale" campaign. They put out yard signs with slogans such as "The Hershey Trust—An Oxymoron" and "Don't Shut Down Chocolate Town." They asked D. Michael Fisher, the Pennsylvania attorney general and the Republican candidate for governor in the looming November gubernatorial election, to remove the trustees and to block the sale.

Fisher petitioned the local court with jurisdiction over the Trust to enjoin the sale. At the hearing, the star witness was former Hershey CEO Richard Zimmerman. He predicted that an acquiring company would try to cut costs by shutting down less efficient operations. "And I suspect," said Zimmerman, "that one would start with the [main Hershey] plant that's nearly a hundred years old." In Zimmerman's view, although these actions might improve the profitability of the combined company, "there are very many more things in life more important than money." Calling Zimmerman's testimony "persuasive" and noting the "symbiotic relationship among the School, the community, and the Company," the judge enjoined the sale.

On appeal, the trustees argued that nothing in the Deed of Trust indicated that Milton and Catherine Hershey wanted the Trust to maintain its ownership of the Company, to undertake responsibility for the economic health of the local community, or to provide continuing employment for the Company's workers. On the contrary, the only beneficial interest named in the Deed of Trust was the School. And the Deed of Trust gave the trustees "full power and authority to invest" the trust assets to that end.

In reply, Fisher conceded that the Trust was "imprudently" undiversified "and that it would be 'desirable' for the Trust to diversify its holdings." But he also argued that "there was no testimony that it needs to do so immediately, within the next few days or weeks." By contrast, "the current employees of Hershey Foods would be worse off under an acquisition than they are now," and the sale of the Company "would seriously impair, if not destroy, the symbiotic relationship which has existed for many decades among the company, the School and its Trust, and the other institutions which together carry on Milton Hershey's unique vision."

While waiting for the appellate court to render a decision, the trustees gathered in a hotel in Valley Forge, Pennsylvania, to discuss their options. They had set a deadline of a few days earlier for bids for the Company. The top bid was from the Wm. Wrigley Jr. Company: $12.5 billion in cash and stock, or about $89 per share. The trustees' Valley Forge session was said to be "emotional," "rancorous," and "sometimes teary." The trustees were "embittered" by what they perceived to be pressure from the attorney general's office to diversify followed by Fisher's heated opposition. The trustees felt "overwhelmed by the outcry of protest from the community." The chairman of the board of trustees, who had received death threats, had been assigned an armed guard. The trustees deliberated for ten hours. William Wrigley delivered a "moving" speech in which he promised a commitment to the Hershey community and to keep the Hershey factories open. But the trustees voted 10 to 7 to reject Wrigley's bid and all the others too.

Investors took a dim view of the sale's cancellation. The Company's stock tumbled to $65 per share the next day, down 12 percent from the prior day's closing price of

$73.81. Hershey residents and workers, by contrast, received the news with a mix of relief and joy. "All I can say is hooray," one resident told the Associated Press. "I still want this company to be around for my grandchildren, so they can work here when they're old enough," said another. A former town supervisor who helped spearhead the "Derail the Sale" movement offered a more blunt assessment to the New York Times: "Our cash cow is safe; we're feeling really great." In something of an anticlimax, later that day the appellate court upheld the trial judge's injunction by a 4 to 1 vote.

After the trustees abandoned the sale, the trial judge dissolved the injunction but ordered the trustees to give the attorney general's office prompt written notice of any future intention to sell the Trust's controlling interest in the Company. The judge also criticized the trust board as being too large and too "distant and disconnected from the charitable interests they serve." Fisher later announced that the seven trustees who had voted in favor of continuing the sale, as well as three others who had opposed the sale, would be stepping down in favor of four new board members, all hailing from central Pennsylvania. Yet he still lost the gubernatorial election by a margin of almost 10 percent, and this in spite of running television ads in which he claimed to have saved over 6,000 Hershey jobs. The following year, President George W. Bush nominated Fisher to be a circuit judge for the United States Court of Appeals for the Third Circuit, and the Senate confirmed his appointment on December 9, 2003.

In 2002 and then again in 2004 the Pennsylvania legislature amended the state's prudent investor statute. As amended, the statute provides that "in making investment and management decisions," a trustee of a charitable trust must consider "the special relationship of [a trust asset] and its economic impact as a principal business enterprise on the community."[48] If the trust has "voting control of a publicly traded business corporation received as an asset from the settlor," the trustee may not sell that interest without first notifying the attorney general and the Pennsylvania employees of the business.[49] If the attorney general challenges the sale, the trustee may not go forward pending court review in which the attorney general must "prove by a preponderance of the evidence" that the sale "is unnecessary for the future economic viability of the corporation and must be prevented in order to avoid noncompliance with the [special relationship and economic impact provision] or an impairment of the charitable purpose of the trust."[50] These amendments were obviously fashioned for the Hershey Trust. "We have to be active and protect our economic assets," explained the state Senate majority leader.

Since 2002, the Company has explored several merger possibilities, but these efforts have been blocked by the Trust. In early 2007, after continued erosion of market share to competitors such as Mars, the maker of M&M's, Snickers, and Twix, the Company announced that it would lay off 1,500 workers, representing 12 percent of its workforce, and that it would open a new factory in Mexico. Shortly thereafter, Mars merged with Wrigley, a cruel irony given that Wrigley had pledged to preserve the Hershey factories if it had been allowed to buy the Company.

---

48. 20 Pa. Stat. Ann. § 7203(c)(6) (2016).
49. Id. § 7203(d)(1).
50. Id. § 7203(d)(3).

In 2016, Mondelez International, the food conglomerate that owns the Cadbury, Oreo, and Nabisco brands, offered to buy the Company. But two months later, after finding "no actionable path forward" in light of opposition from Pennsylvania politicians and the Trust, Mondelez gave up.[51] The Company's stock price, which jumped 17 percent on news of Mondelez's bid, dropped 12 percent on news of Mondelez's withdrawal.

The Trust, meanwhile, has been subject to a series of investigations by the state attorney general.[52] In 2013, the Trust and the attorney general reached an agreement that limited trustee compensation and imposed stricter conflict-of-interest rules in resolution of an investigation prompted by the Trust's purchase of a golf course that had been losing money but in which at least one of the trustees was an investor.[53] In 2016, in settlement of an investigation into the Trust's compliance with the 2013 agreement, five trustees agreed to retire (four others resigned during the investigation) and the Trust agreed to stricter appointment, compensation, and reimbursement rules.[54]

The School has also been touched by scandal. In 2011, it paid $3 million to five victims of sexual abuse committed by the son of one of the School's house parents.[55] More recently, the School has been investigated at least twice by the Justice Department for discriminating against disabled students, one of whom suffered from severe depression and committed suicide after being told that she could not return to the School.[56]

NOTES

1. Cy Pres, "Wasteful," and Charitable Trust Governance.   Professors Jonathan Klick and Robert Sitkoff undertook an econometric analysis of the Hershey Company's stock price movements during the 2002 sale window. They estimate that the attorney general's intervention to block the sale wiped out $2.7 billion in shareholder wealth, of which the Trust's share was $850 million — about $67,000 per resident of Hershey.[57] They argue that the town and the Trust would have been better off if the Trust had been permitted to diversify and then share some of the gains with the town "in cash or through a program of community enrichment." They also argue that the expansion of

---

51. *See* Annie Gasparro & Dana Cimilluca, Mondelez Drops Offer for Hershey, Wall St. J., Aug. 30, 2016, at A1.

52. For an overview, see Bob Fernandez, The Chocolate Trust: Deception, Indenture and Secrets at the $12 Billion Milton Hershey School (2015).

53. *See id.* at 187-92; *see also* Bob Fernandez, Hershey School's Purchase of Golf Course Helped Investors, Phila. Inq., Oct. 3, 2010, at A01; Bob Fernandez, AG Wants to Remove 3 Leaders of Hershey Trust, Phil. Inq., May 3, 2016, at A01.

54. *See* Maria Armental, Five Hershey Trust Directors to Retire in Settlement with Pennsylvania Attorney General, Wall St. J. (July 29, 2016); *see also* David Segal, Chocolate-Covered Conflict, N.Y. Times, July 31, 2016, at BU1 ("In the past 12 months the trust has spent more than $4 million on lawyers to investigate charges of misconduct that board members have lodged against one another.").

55. *See* Bob Fernandez, Sex-Abuse Case Shatters Hershey School, Phila. Inq., May 20, 2010, at A01.

56. *See* Bob Fernandez, Federal Probe Said to Target Hershey School Over Disabled Students, Phila. Inq. (May 19, 2016).

57. *See* Klick & Sitkoff, *supra* note 35, at 814-16.

cy pres to address surplus funds under the new heading of "wasteful" could improve the governance of charitable trusts:

> Whatever the other merits of broadening the grounds for cy pres, our findings suggest that cy pres in the case of an excess endowment may have the salutary effect of minimizing agency costs. Given the Trust's excess endowment, another $850 million would not affect the Trust's ability to fund the day-to-day operation of the School. As a result, there was little pressure on the trustees to maximize value and little risk for the Attorney General that blocking the sale would immediately imperil the School. Indeed, opponents of the trustees' diversification plan argued that the Trust had more money than it needed for its specific purpose and hence the Trust did not need to sell its interest in the Company.
>
> By contrast, if the trustees were under pressure to use the Trust's excess endowment to fund similar schools in other communities, the social welfare loss from failing to maximize the value of the Trust would have been more apparent. Consider that the trust instrument gives preference to local orphans but also allows for admission of orphans from across the country. Yet even though the Trust's corpus has grown dramatically, the School "served no more children at the start of 2005 than it did in 1963." What is more, the Trust's current plans for expansion of the School are both modest and limited to the single existing campus.[58]

In early 2010, citing a decline in income from the Trust's undiversified endowment, the School announced that it had put on hold its plan to expand from 1,850 to 2,000 students by 2013.[59] In 2012, the School announced that it was resuming movement "toward a goal of serving 2,000 students in the next several years."[60] In 2015, the School announced that "we accelerated our timeline and enrolled our 2,000th student ahead of schedule."[61] The School plans to expand to 2,300 students by 2020.[62] Critics argue nonetheless that, in light of the Trust's size, this expansion plan is too meager.[63]

2. Assessing the Politics. Professor Brody is sharply critical of how all three branches of the Pennsylvania government reacted to the trustees' plan in 2002 to sell the Company:

> The Hershey case shows each of the three branches of Pennsylvania government acting illegitimately. The attorney general practically treated the Hershey assets as his election campaign funds. The Orphans' Court's long experience with the Hershey Trust only served to continue a history of usurping the board's

---

58. Id. at 820-21.

59. *See* Bob Fernandez, Wealthy Hershey School Curbs Expansion Plan, Phila. Inq., Apr. 4, 2010, at D1.

60. Milton Hershey School, News Releases: Milton Hershey School Continues to Expand, Jan. 10, 2012.

61. Milton Hershey School, 2020 Vision, https://perma.cc/688Z-JBZA.

62. Id.

63. *See* Bob Fernandez, No Candy-Coating Lack of Charity at Hershey School, Phila. Inq. (Nov. 6, 2016); Will Yet Another Overhaul Rid the Hershey Trust Board of Its Crony Culture?, Phila. Inq., Dec. 22, 2016, at A14.

discretion—and this time it was even less justifiable, relating as it did to making prudent investments rather than to programs. Moreover, the particular local nature of the supervising court can compound the risk of parochialism, as one journalist observed: "That the directors should live anyplace beside Hershey seemed an affront to Morgan, a 71-year-old judge on retired status who has spent 30 years on Common Pleas Court of Dauphin County, of which the Orphans' Court is a division, and who attended college and law school at Dickinson, just a few miles from Hershey in Carlisle." Finally, the legislature singled out the Trust and effectively appropriated to the local community locked-in control of a publicly traded corporation—without, of course, rising to the level of a "taking" requiring payment of compensation.[64]

Although agreeing with Brody about the demerits of the "inflexible legislative" response to the aborted sale, Professor Mark Sidel is more sympathetic to the actions of the attorney general:

While [the] process occurred during, and appears to have been influenced by, a political and electoral process, that political process served as a transmission belt for public attitudes to be conveyed, for more information to be ascertained, and ultimately for a result to be achieved that directly addressed the questions of fiduciary duty and trustee responsibility with which the Hershey Trust Board wrestled. Here the changing nature of public interest under *parens patriae*, and the influence of political dialogue, was not an unfortunate concomitant or product of the process—it was integral to it, and, I would argue resulted in a better and more informed solution.[65]

4. Persons with a Special Interest in the Trust

Even under traditional law, the standing of the attorney general to enforce a charitable trust is not exclusive. In the words of the Restatement, "[a] person who has a *special interest* in the enforcement of the trust" may be able to enforce a charitable trust.[66] To have special interest standing, a person must show that he is entitled to receive a particular benefit under the trust that is not available to the public at large.[67]

Special interest standing is perhaps best appreciated by way of examples. An elderly, indigent widow living in a charitable home for the aged has been held to have standing to sue the board of trustees who, because of the costs of operating an obsolete facility, proposed to relocate the residents elsewhere.[68] A parishioner can sue to enforce a trust

---

64. Brody, *supra* note 42, at 998-99.

65. Mark Sidel, The Struggle for Hershey: Community Accountability and the Law in Modern American Philanthropy, 65 U. Pitt. L. Rev. 1, 59-60 (2003).

66. Restatement (Third) of Trusts § 94(2) (Am. Law Inst. 2012) (emphasis added); *see also* Restatement (Second) of Trusts § 391 (Am. Law Inst. 1959) (same).

67. *See* Sagtikos Manor Historical Soc'y, Inc. v. Robert David Lion Gardiner Found., Inc., 9 N.Y.S.3d 80 (App. Div. 2015); *see also* Scott and Ascher on Trusts § 37.3.10.

68. *See* Hooker v. Edes Home, 579 A.2d 608 (D.C. 1990).

for the benefit of his church.[69] A minister can sue to enforce a trust to pay the salary of the clergy of his church.[70]

On the other hand, a person who is merely eligible within the trustee's discretion for a benefit from a charitable trust does not have special interest standing.[71] The alumni association of the Hershey School did not have standing to enforce the Hershey Trust.[72] And a charity with a similar purpose to a separate charitable trust did not have standing to enforce that trust on the theory that the charity would have an increased burden if the trust was mismanaged.[73] Nor, in the usual case, does a student have standing to sue college trustees.[74]

Special interest standing extends only so far as the person's special interest. Thus, for example, a senior citizen center has special interest standing to enforce a pledge to contribute funds from a charitable trust, but not to enforce the terms of the trust generally.[75]

5. Federal Supervision

Although there are subtle differences in the definition of charitable purposes under state law versus under federal tax law, in the usual case a trust that is charitable under state trust law will also qualify as charitable under federal tax law. In consequence, through the tax code—and its enforcer, the Internal Revenue Service—the federal government has come to play an increasingly important role in the supervision of charitable trusts and other charitable entities.[76]

Hawaii Journal: The Bishop Estate

The Bishop Estate was established in 1884 as a charitable trust under the will of Princess Bernice Pauahi Bishop, the last descendant of King Kamehameha I, Hawaii's first and most powerful king. The trust assets include an endowment valued in 2015 at $11.1 billion.[77] This figure does not include 350,000 acres of non-income-producing land, characterized by the trustees as "sustainability assets,"[78] consisting of "63 miles of ocean frontage, 100 miles of streams, historic fishponds, forests and lava fields . . . [that] are deeply tied to the Hawaiian culture."[79] The New York Times described this land, which represents nearly 9 percent of Hawaii's total land mass, as "a feudal

---

69. *See* Gray v. St. Matthews Cathedral Endowment Fund, Inc., 544 S.W.2d 488 (Tex. App. 1976).

70. *See* First Congregational Soc'y v. Trustees, 40 Mass. (23 Pick.) 148 (1839).

71. *See* Gene Kauffman Scholarship Found., Inc. v. Payne, 183 S.W.3d 620 (Mo. App. 2006).

72. *See* In re Milton Hershey Sch., 911 A.2d 1258 (Pa. 2006).

73. *See* In re Public Benevolent Trust of Crume, 829 N.E.2d 1039 (Ind. App. 2005).

74. *See* Russell v. Yale Univ., 737 A.2d 941 (Conn. App. 1999).

75. *See* In re Clement Trust, 679 N.W.2d 31 (Iowa 2004).

76. *See* Lloyd Hitoshi Mayer, Fragmented Oversight of Nonprofits in the United States: Does It Work? Can It Work?, 91 Chi.-Kent L. Rev. 937 (2016).

77. Kamehameha Schools, Annual Report: July 1, 2014-June 30, 2015, at 5 (endowment figure as of June 30, 2015).

78. Id.

79. Kamehameha Schools, Annual Report: July 1, 2002-June 30, 2003, at 29.

Princess Bernice Pauahi Bishop
H.L. Chase/Bishop Museum

empire so vast that it could never be assembled in the modern world."[80]

The princess's will directed that there be five trustees, to be appointed by the justices of the Supreme Court of Hawaii, which, in those days, when Hawaii was a monarchy, also served as the probate court. The trustees were to erect two schools, one for boys and one for girls, and to expend the annual income of the trust running the schools. Two schools were built shortly after the princess's death, but many decades later they were combined in a single school for native Hawaiian boys and girls.

A Bishop Estate trusteeship has long been a coveted position in Hawaii. During the 1990s, the trustees paid themselves annual fees of nearly $1 million each and engaged in trust business with friends, relatives, and political associates. Jurisdiction for probate matters had long since passed from the supreme court to the probate court, but the justices continued to select the Bishop Estate trustees, insisting that they were acting "unofficially."

As the twentieth century was nearing its end, the Bishop Estate trustees, supreme court justices, key legislators, and the governor had what might charitably be described as a cozy relationship (others called it corrupt). To be appointed as a justice on the supreme court, a candidate had to be put on an approved list by the judicial selection commission, a majority of whose members were picked by the president of the senate, speaker of the house, chief justice of the supreme court, and the governor. Trustees who served in the 1990s included a president of the senate, speaker of the house, chief justice of the supreme court, and the governor's closest associate.

The trustees' gilt-edged world began to unravel when one of the trustees intervened high-handedly in the day-to-day running of the Schools. Soon she was calling the teachers incompetent and countermanding decisions of the Schools' president and principals. She ordered that no Hawaiian word be taught—or even uttered on campus—unless the word existed in 1884, the year the princess died. She commanded that nothing in writing leave the campus until it had been personally approved by her, creating a long backlog of important communications. When students protested, she summoned the student body president to her downtown office for a two-hour, closed-door interrogation, asking him how he would feel if she wrote a letter to Princeton, where he had been offered a scholarship, denouncing him as a rabble-rouser. Soon thereafter, the Kamehameha Schools ohana (community) revolted. Teachers and students were threatened with sanctions if they participated, but alumni marched, 1,000 strong, through downtown Honolulu, stopping at the supreme court building to ask that the justices do something about the situation.

Then on August 9, 1997, the Honolulu Star Bulletin published "Broken Trust," a 6,500-word essay written by four prominent kupuna (elders) of the native Hawaiian

---

80. Todd S. Purdum, Hawaiians Angrily Turn on a Fabled Empire, N.Y. Times, Oct. 14, 1997, at A1.

community (a senior federal district judge; a retired state judge; a former principal of the Kamehameha Schools; and the head trustee of the Queen Liliuokalani Trust) and Professor Randall Roth of the University of Hawaii Law School.[81] The essay began, "The time has come to say, 'no more.'" Reviewing the basics of trust law and judicial selection, the authors described how Bishop Estate trusteeships had become "political plums" that sullied the process for selecting justices, accused the Bishop Estate trustees of specific breaches of trust, and called for an investigation of trustee selection and performance. The article triggered a public outcry for reform, which prompted the state attorney general, Margery Bronster, to launch an investigation into the trustees' actions.

A few months after the "Broken Trust" article appeared, a court-appointed master found numerous irregularities in the administration of the Bishop Estate. Investment decisions had been "ad hoc," based more on relationships than due diligence and financial analysis. There was no overall plan or apparent effort to diversify investments. The trustees had taken out full-page ads claiming a 17 percent return on investment for the three years under review, but the master determined that the actual return had been 1 percent. The master discovered that the trustees had improperly moved $350 million of income into corpus without noting it in their records or disclosing it in financial statements or annual reports to the court. He was also troubled that trustees created conflicts of interest by investing trust money in private deals in which they had a personal stake.

The trustees and their associates also received private benefits. Most of the trustees accepted free golf memberships from country clubs leasing Bishop Estate land. One pocketed substantial director fees and stock options from a company in which the Estate held a large block of stock. Another used Estate personnel to perform personal services and accepted trips to the Super Bowl and the Olympics in private jets from persons doing business with the Estate. One trustee "recused" himself as trustee in order to negotiate a $40 million deal on behalf of an organization that was buying land from the Estate. A highly placed employee of the Estate, a powerful state senator, charged $28,000 to the Estate's credit card in casinos and sex clubs in Las Vegas and Honolulu. (When this was discovered by the attorney general's investigation, the trustees gave the employee a retroactive bonus in the exact amount he needed to repay the Estate and to cover his taxes on the bonus.) Two trustees were indicted on charges that they received kickbacks in a real estate deal involving the trust and a trustee's brother-in-law.

The trustees hired dozens of big-name lawyers, paying them millions in fees from Estate funds. According to a court-appointed master who later reviewed the legal invoices, "One can easily conclude, as this Master has, that a strategy was adopted to obstruct the legal process, to delay wherever possible, to object wherever possible, to utilize so many lawyers and so many arguments that the opposition would be overwhelmed and would choose to give up. . . . [M]illions of dollars of trust funds were wasted." Through their friends in the legislature, some of whom were on the Estate payroll, the trustees retaliated against Attorney General Bronster. In April 1999, the state senate refused to confirm her to a second term in office.

---

81. Professor Roth later had a hand in getting the Rule Against Perpetuities inserted into the Academy Award winning script for The Descendants (see page 892).

Then the Internal Revenue Service stepped into the breach. On December 31, 1998, the IRS concluded that: the Estate was not being operated primarily for charitable purposes; it had become directly involved in local and national political campaigns; trustee fees were grossly in excess of the value of the trustees' services; and there had been numerous other instances of private benefit from trust assets. The IRS revoked the Estate's charitable tax exemption retroactively and refused to communicate further with the trustees. However, the IRS took the unprecedented additional step of advising the probate court that it would reconsider its position if certain conditions were satisfied, starting with the immediate resignation or removal of all five trustees. Because the immediate cost of a retroactive revocation would have been nearly $1 billion, this was an offer the probate court could not refuse. Within a matter of days the court replaced all five trustees.

The probate court established a new selection process for trustees: a panel of seven committee members, chosen by the probate court, now screens applicants and provides a short list of candidates to the court, which then makes the selection. In addition, the court ordered the trustees to turn over day-to-day control of the Estate's operations to qualified professionals; capped the trustees' fees at $97,500 (now $165,000; $207,000 for the chair); prohibited politicians from serving as a trustee or even serving on the screening committee; and ordered the new trustees to adopt a strict conflicts of interest policy, hire an internal auditor, develop a strategic plan, adopt new investment policies and practices, and spend an average of 4 percent of the Estate's endowment value each year on the charitable mission.

Two separate court-appointed masters recommended that the court impose millions of dollars in surcharges on the former trustees. The attorney general prepared to sue them for nearly $200 million. There was widespread speculation that the justices might also be sued for breach of fiduciary duty in their selection of the Bishop Estate trustees. Although jurists normally enjoy judicial immunity, it applies only to judicial acts like deciding cases, not ministerial and nonjudicial acts — and the justices had long insisted that they had been acting "unofficially" in choosing the trustees.

But then the new attorney general, the current and former trustees, and the many lawyers who had represented the former trustees entered into a "global settlement" that brought an abrupt end to the controversy. The settlement was financed not by the individuals involved, but by a payout on a $25 million insurance policy that the former trustees had acquired years earlier using Estate funds. The former trustees did not return any of their excessive compensation, make good on any of the surcharges that the masters had recommended, or pay any of the damages sought by the attorney general. Their lawyers were allowed to keep all of their fees, including fees charged at the height of the controversy for research into ways to avoid state and federal oversight by moving the trust's situs to an Indian reservation in South Dakota. Numerous records were sealed. Proponents of the settlement and the sealing of records said that it would promote "closure" and "healing." Critics said it would sweep under the rug evidence of corruption and make accountability impossible.

The new trustees, meanwhile, have increased dramatically the amount of money spent each year. The Kamehameha Schools, now with three campuses, is the largest independent school in the country. The trustees have also spent generously on outreach efforts, including support for public charter schools in areas heavily populated by native Hawaiians. There is evidence that these schools and other outreach activities are having a profoundly positive impact on a large number of children.

In 2006, two of the original "Broken Trust" essay authors published an engrossing, page-turner of a book that provides a gripping behind-the-scenes account of the whole Bishop Estate controversy. Samuel P. King & Randall W. Roth, Broken Trust: Greed, Mismanagement and Political Manipulation at America's Largest Charitable Trust (2006). It set local sales records and was named Book of the Year by the Hawaii Book Publishers Association.[82]

NOTES

1. Federal Regulation of Charities.   A charitable trust must comply with complex rules in the federal tax code to be exempt from income taxation and to qualify its donors for an income or estate tax deduction.[83] This was the basis for the IRS's involvement in the Bishop Estate scandal. Some commentators have questioned whether any charity should receive favored tax treatment, arguing that these tax benefits subsidize the whims of donors more than they benefit society.[84]

Much of the federal regulation of charities can be traced to the Tax Reform Act of 1969. Perhaps the most significant is Internal Revenue Code (I.R.C.) § 4942, which imposes substantial tax penalties on private charitable foundations that do not spend at least 5 percent of the value of the endowment each year. Many administrative expenses, however, including board member salaries, count toward this distribution requirement.[85]

Another provision, known as the excess business holdings rule, bars a foundation from holding more than 20 percent of a business's equity. I.R.C. § 4943. This provision put many charities under salutary pressure to diversify. An exception is the Hershey Trust, which qualifies as a "supporting organization" exempt from both the excess business holdings rule and the 5 percent minimum payout rule.[86] Other provisions prohibit private benefits inuring to trustees and other managers and prescribe detailed rules on compensation, effectively a federalization of the duty of loyalty through the tax code.[87]

---

82. For a scholarly review of selected Bishop Estate issues, see Symposium, The Bishop Estate Controversy, 21 U. Haw. L. Rev. 353 (1999). For a comprehensive summary of legal issues and other background materials, see www.BrokenTrustBook.com.

83. *See* Marion R. Fremont-Smith, Governing Nonprofit Organizations: Federal and State Law and Regulation 238-300 (2004).

84. *See, e.g.,* Brian Galle, The Role of Charity in a Federal System, 53 Wm. & Mary L. Rev. 777 (2012); William A. Drennan, Surnamed Charitable Trusts: Immortality at Taxpayer Expense, 61 Ala. L. Rev. 225 (2010); Ray D. Madoff, What Leona Helmsley Can Teach Us About the Charitable Deduction, 85 Chi.-Kent L. Rev. 957 (2010).

85. For a proposal to tax wasteful and lavish spending by charities, see Evelyn A. Lewis, Charitable Waste: Consideration of a "Waste Not, Want Not" Tax, 30 Va. Tax Rev. 39 (2010).

86. *See* Brody, *supra* note 42, at 987-88.

87. *See* Ellen P. Aprill, Reconciling Nonprofit Self-Dealing Rules, 48 Real Prop. Tr. & Est. L.J. 411 (2014); Mark L. Ascher, Federalization of the Law of Charity, 67 Vand. L. Rev. 1581 (2014); Johnny Rex Buckles, The Federalization of the Duty of Loyalty Governing Charity Fiduciaries Under United States Tax Law, 99 Ky. L.J. 645 (2011).

2. IRS Form 990. Probably the most important contribution of federal tax law to the governance of charities is the requirement that tax-exempt organizations with gross receipts or total assets above certain thresholds annually disclose their assets, expenses, and governance structure. This public filing, IRS Form 990, requires information about accomplishments in the prior year, certain governance rules and practices, and compensation for top executives. The Form asks whether the organization has "a written conflict of interest policy," and if so, whether the policy requires "officers, directors, . . . trustees, and key employees . . . to disclose annually interests that could give rise to conflicts." There also are questions about "the process for determining compensation of" the organization's "top management official" and "[o]ther officers or key employees," and about "the process, if any, used by the organization to review [the] Form 990."

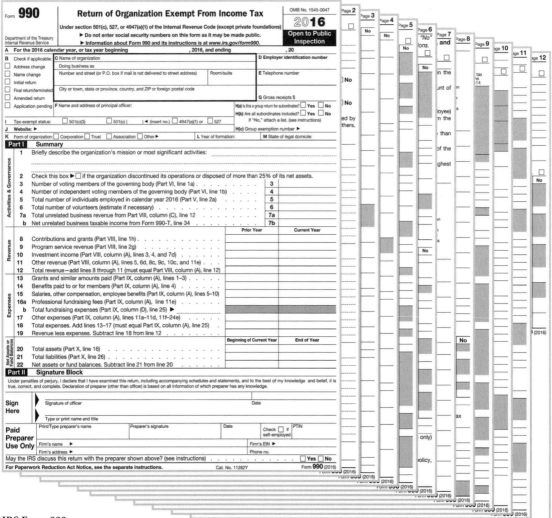

IRS Form 990

3. A Charity Commission? In England and Wales, an independent agency supervises charities. Professor Terri Lynn Helge explains:

> Established by law as the independent regulator and registrar of charities in England and Wales, the Charity Commission for England and Wales (English Charity Commission) has broad regulatory power in addition to quasi-judicial powers over charitable fiduciaries. . . . The English Charity Commission has three main goals: "(1) to ensure that charities can operate for their exempt purposes within an effective legal, accounting and governance framework; (2) to improve charities' governance, accountability, efficiency, and effectiveness; and (3) to identify and address abuses and poor practices." . . .
>
> The English Charity Commission determines charitable status, maintains a registration of charities, monitors the charitable sector to ensure compliance, investigates alleged wrongdoings, publishes outcomes of formal inquiries, and provides a list, for the general public, of charities that are in default. In addition, the commission educates the charitable sector on proper compliance with charitable laws and provides guidance on "best practices."
>
> The English Charity Commission has been the primary regulator of the charitable sector in England and Wales for over a century. . . . [S]everal other countries, including Scotland, have used the English Charity Commission as a model for the oversight of their charitable sector.[88]

Should the English model of an independent agency be emulated in this country? If so, should it be a federal agency? A state agency? How would it be financed? Would a private, for-profit monitoring company be better suited to the task? Might assignable settlor standing rights encourage the development of such companies?[89]

4. A Spend-Down Proposal. Another idea sometimes discussed is to require charities to spend all their resources within a few years. Charities would be disciplined by the need continually to appeal for new donations. Judge Posner explains:

> The incentives to efficient management of foundation assets could be strengthened by a rule requiring charitable foundations to distribute every gift received, principal and interest, including the original endowment, within a short, specified period of years. The foundation would not be required to wind up its operations within the period; it could continue indefinitely. But it would have to receive new gifts in order to avoid exhausting all of its funds. Since donors are unlikely to give money to an enterprise known to be slack, the necessity of returning

---

88. Terri Lynn Helge, Policing the Good Guys: Regulation of the Charitable Sector Through a Federal Charity Oversight Board, 19 Cornell J.L. & Pub. Pol'y 1, 64-65 (2009); *see also* Debra Morris, The Charity Commission for England and Wales: A Fine Example or Another Fine Mess?, 91 Chi.-Kent L. Rev. 965 (2016).

89. *See, e.g.,* Lloyd Hitoshi Mayer & Brendan M. Wilson, Regulating Charities in the Twenty-First Century: An Institutional Choice Analysis, 85 Chi.-Kent L. Rev. 479 (2010); Geoffrey A. Manne, Agency Costs and the Oversight of Charitable Organizations, 1999 Wis. L. Rev. 227.

Bill Gates, Melinda Gates, and Warren Buffett
Spencer Platt/Getty Images

periodically to the market for charitable donations would give trustees and managers of charitable foundations an incentive they now lack to conduct a tight operation. Foundations — mostly religious and educational — that market their services or depend on continuing charitable support, and are therefore already subject to some competitive constraints, could be exempted from the exhaustion rule.[90]

Perhaps the most prominent example of a charity that has voluntarily undertaken to spend its entire endowment within a fixed period of time is the Gates Foundation, a charitable trust created by Microsoft founder Bill Gates and his wife Melinda. In December 2006, six months after Warren Buffett pledged $31 billion to the Foundation — a gift that would roughly double the Foundation's endowment — the Foundation announced that it would terminate 50 years after the death of the survivor of its three principal patrons.

---

90. Posner, *supra* note 17, § 19.3, at 714.

CHAPTER 12

TRUSTS: POWERS
OF APPOINTMENT

*The power of appointment is the most efficient dispositive device that
the ingenuity of Anglo-American lawyers has ever worked out.*

W. BARTON LEACH
24 A.B.A. J. 807, 807 (1938)

T HUS FAR WE HAVE CONSIDERED trusts in which the settlor preserves flexibility by giving the trustee fiduciary discretion over future distributions of trust property (see Chapter 9 at page 611). But the settlor may also provide for a nonfiduciary power to distribute trust property. Such a power is known as a *power of appointment*. The holder of a power of appointment, known as the *donee*, may appoint the property to one or more persons, known as the *objects* of the power, in accordance with the terms of the power.

Consider a typical example: *H* devises property to *X* in trust to distribute the income quarterly to *W* for life, and on *W*'s death to distribute the principal to one or more of *H*'s descendants as *W* shall appoint in her will. *H* is the donor of a power of appointment, *W* is the donee, and *H*'s descendants are the objects. By this power, which *W* holds in a nonfiduciary capacity, *W* may decide who among *H*'s descendants will take the trust property at her death. In this way, *H* empowers *W* to deal flexibly with changing circumstances in the interim between their deaths, which may span years or even decades. *W* can take into account births, deaths, marriages, and divorces; the changing ability of children and more remote descendants to manage property; changes in the economy and investment returns; changes in the law; and other circumstances that *H* could not have foreseen but that *W* will observe firsthand.

Powers of appointment provide benefits beyond building *flexibility* into an estate plan. They are also commonly used for *tax planning* and *asset protection*. In the example given in the prior paragraph, because *W* cannot appoint the trust property for her own benefit, no estate or gift tax will be due upon *W*'s exercise of the power, and no creditor of *W* will have recourse against the property. It would be difficult to overstate the importance of powers of appointment in contemporary estate planning.

We begin in Section A by considering purposes, terminology, and types of powers of appointment. In addition to providing flexibility, we examine the role of powers of appointment in tax planning and in asset protection. In Section B, we consider recurring problems in the exercise of a power of appointment. Finally, in Section C, we consider what happens to the property subject to a power of appointment if the donee fails to exercise the power.

A. PURPOSES, TERMINOLOGY, AND TYPES OF POWERS

The primary reason for using a power of appointment is to build flexibility into an estate plan, but tax planning and asset protection are close seconds.[1] If a power is drafted in accordance with the federal tax code and the state law of creditor rights, the property subject to the power will not be treated as belonging to the donee for tax purposes or for claims of the donee's creditors. No income, estate, or gift tax will be levied on the donee or her estate, and no creditor of the donee will be able to reach the appointive property, by reason of the power or its exercise. Accordingly, the law and practice norms regarding powers of appointment—including the basic terminology—are deeply intertwined with federal tax and local debtor-creditor law.

1. Terminology and Relationships

To understand the law of powers of appointment, you must first learn the terminology and relationships.

a. The Parties

A person who creates a power of appointment is the *donor* of the power. A person who holds a power is the *donee*. Uniform Powers of Appointment Act (UPAA) § 102(14) (Unif. Law Comm'n 2013) refers to a donee as a *powerholder*. The persons in whose favor a power may be exercised are the *objects* of the power, sometimes also called the *permissible appointees*, as under UPAA § 102(11). When a power is exercised in favor of an object, that person becomes an *appointee*. The persons who will receive the property if a donee fails to exercise a power of appointment are the *takers in default of appointment* or, simply, *takers in default*. The property subject to a power of appointment is the *appointive property*.[2] Thus:

> *Case 1.* *T* devises property to *X* in trust to pay the income to *A* for life, or until such time as *A* appoints, and to distribute the principal to such person or persons as *A* shall appoint by deed or by will. If *A* does not exercise the power of appointment, at

---

1. *See, e.g.,* Jonathan G. Blattmachr, Kim Kamin & Jeffrey M. Bergman, Estate Planning's Most Powerful Tool: Powers of Appointment Refreshed, Redefined, and Reexamined, 47 Real Prop. Tr. & Est. L.J. 529 (2013).
2. *See* Restatement (Third) of Property: Wills and Other Donative Transfers § 17.2 (Am. Law Inst. 2011).

A's death *X* is to distribute the principal to *B*. *T* is the donor. *A* is the donee. *B* is the taker in default of appointment. The class of objects is limitless.

Once you understand the relationships, the meaning of a *power of appointment* follows naturally. Under UPAA § 102(13), for example, a power of appointment is "a power that enables a powerholder acting in a nonfiduciary capacity to designate a recipient of an ownership interest in or another power of appointment over the appointive property."[3] In Case 1, *A* (the donee) has a power to appoint the trust property (the appointive property) to anyone he wishes (the objects) during life (by deed) or at death (by will).

b. Creation

To create a power of appointment, the donor must manifest an intent to do so, either expressly or by implication. It is not necessary that the words "power of appointment" or "appoint" be used. All that is necessary, as under UPAA § 201(a)(2), is that "the terms of the instrument creating the power manifest the donor's intent to create in a powerholder a power of appointment over the appointive property exercisable in favor of a permissible appointee."[4]

A power of appointment confers *discretion* on the donee, who may choose whether to exercise the power, and is to be distinguished from a nondiscretionary, direct disposition by the donor. Thus:

> *Case 2.* Aunt Fanny executes a will in 2017 giving her tangible personal property "to my niece Wendy Brown, to dispose of in accordance with a letter addressed to Wendy dated January 4, 2016, which is in my safe-deposit box, and which I incorporate by reference herein." Aunt Fanny has incorporated the letter by reference (see page 245). The tangible personal property must be distributed in accordance with the letter. Wendy is a trustee who has a fiduciary duty to follow Aunt Fanny's instruction. Wendy does not have a power of appointment.

Words that express a mere wish or desire are *precatory* and do not create a power of appointment in the absence of other circumstances indicating such an intent (compare *precatory trusts* at page 403).[5] If, in Case 2, Aunt Fanny had left her tangible personal property to Wendy "with the request but not the legal obligation that she give some of the property to my other relatives," Wendy would take the property free of trust. The precatory words would create neither a trust nor a power of appointment.

c. General and Nongeneral Powers

All powers of appointment can be divided into general powers and nongeneral powers. The distinction is of great significance. The validity of an exercise of a power, the consequences of a failure to exercise a power, the rights of creditors of the donor and

---

3. *See also* id. § 17.1 (similar).
4. *See also* id. § 18.1 cmt. b (similar).
5. *See* id. cmt. e.

the donee to reach the appointive property, and the tax consequences of holding or exercising a power often turn on whether the power is general or nongeneral.

As defined in the Internal Revenue Code, a *general power* is "a power which is exercisable in favor of the [donee], his estate, his creditors, or the creditors of his estate."[6] A power that is not a general power — that is, a power not exercisable in favor of the donee, his estate, his creditors, or the creditors of his estate — is a *nongeneral power*. A nongeneral power is also commonly called a *special power* or a *limited power*, particularly in older sources, but the trend is toward the term nongeneral.

In the past, it was sometimes said that the objects of a general power are necessarily broader or more numerous than the objects of a nongeneral power. Under modern law, this is no longer true. Consider the following two cases:

> *Case 3. General Power with Few Objects. T* devises property to *X* in trust to distribute the income and principal to such of *A*'s creditors as *A* shall appoint by deed.

> *Case 4. Nongeneral Power with Many Objects. T* devises property to *X* in trust to pay the income and principal to any person whom *B* appoints by will except that *B* may not appoint to herself, her estate, her creditors, or the creditors of her estate.

In Case 3, because *A* may appoint to a creditor, the power is general even if *A* has few or no creditors. In Case 4, because *B* cannot appoint to herself, her estate, her creditors, or the creditors of her estate, the power is nongeneral even though the objects of the power number in the billions.[7]

d. Time and Manner of Exercise

A power of appointment may be exercisable by deed during life, as in Case 3; by will at death, as in Case 4; or by deed or by will, as in Case 1, page 808. A power that can be exercised only by will is a *testamentary* power. A power that can be exercised only by deed is an *inter vivos* or *lifetime* power.

A power is said to be *presently exercisable* if it may be exercised at the time in question. A power is said to be a *postponed power* if it is exercisable only upon the

---

6. Internal Revenue Code of 1986 (I.R.C.) § 2041(b)(1) (estate tax). The comparable definition under the federal gift tax is in I.R.C. § 2514(c). The Code includes several exceptions, which we take up below at page 813.

7. The Restatement (First) of Property, published in 1940, is representative of prior law. It took the position that the objects of a nongeneral power could not constitute an "unreasonably large" number. Restatement (First) of Property § 320(2)(a) (Am. Law Inst. 1940). On this view, the power in Case 4 could not be classified as nongeneral for state law purposes, though it is nongeneral for federal tax purposes. Because tax planning is integral to the use of powers of appointment, having one definition for state law and another for federal tax law proved unworkable, and the federal tax definitions prevailed. Today a power is classified within the state law of powers of appointment, as under UPAA § 102(6) and (10) and the subsequent Restatements of Property, as general or nongeneral in accordance with the definitions in the federal tax code. *See* Restatement (Third) of Property: Wills and Other Donative Transfers § 17.3 cmt. b (Am. Law Inst. 2011); Restatement (Second) of Property: Donative Transfers § 11.4 cmt. b (Am. Law Inst. 1986).

occurrence of a specified event, satisfaction of an ascertainable standard, or passage of a specified time.[8] Thus:

> *Case 5.* *T* devises property to *X* in trust to distribute so much of the income and principal to *A* as *A* shall appoint by deed as necessary for *A*'s health, education, support, or maintenance after reaching the age of 30. *A* is the donee of a postponed general power. The power will not be presently exercisable until *A* turns 30 and needs the property for her health, education, support, or maintenance.

e. Ownership Equivalence

Under the *relation-back theory* of the common law, a power of appointment was viewed as merely empowering the donee to do an act for the donor. The appointee was deemed to receive the appointive property directly from the donor, not the donee. Although this theory fairly describes nongeneral powers of appointment, it is no longer descriptive of general powers of appointment.

A general power of appointment may permit the donee to do almost anything with the property that an owner of the fee simple could do. This is clearest in the case of a general power that is presently exercisable. For example, in Case 1, page 808, *T* devises property to *X* in trust to pay the income to *A* for life, or until such time as *A* appoints, and to distribute the principal to such person or persons as *A* shall appoint either by deed during *A*'s lifetime or by will. To acquire title, *A* merely has to write, "I hereby appoint to myself." *A* is therefore very close to being the owner of the appointive property. All that stands between *A* and outright ownership is an act that resembles the writing of a check on *A*'s own bank account. For this reason, in modern practice it is common to speak of a presently exercisable general power as an *ownership-equivalent* power. "Although the donee of such a power is not the technical owner of the appointive property, the donee is the owner in substance."[9]

A nongeneral power, by contrast, is not an ownership-equivalent power. Perhaps the most common example of a nongeneral power is one that limits the objects to members of the donor's or donee's family. Thus:

> *Case 6.* *H* devises property to *X* in trust to pay the income to *W* for life, and on *W*'s death to distribute the principal to such one or more of *H*'s descendants as *W* shall appoint by will. If *W* does not exercise the power, *X* is to distribute the principal to *H*'s then living descendants per stirpes.

There is a profound difference between the general power presently exercisable in Case 1 and the nongeneral power in Case 6. In Case 1, *A* can appoint the property to herself at any time and for any reason. In Case 6, *W* occupies a position similar to that of *H*'s agent, filling in the blanks in *H*'s gift. *W* can exercise the power only to benefit *H*'s descendants.

---

8. *See* Restatement (Third) of Property: Wills and Other Donative Transfers § 17.4 (Am. Law Inst. 2011).

9. Id. cmt. f(1).

As we shall see, the law governing taxation and creditor rights in connection with powers of appointment often distinguishes between general powers and nongeneral powers on the basis of whether the power gives the donee the equivalent of ownership.

f. A Fiduciary Power of Appointment?

Under traditional law, any person who has a power to designate a recipient of a beneficial ownership interest in trust property, even if the person holds the power in a fiduciary capacity, has a power of appointment. Thus, a trustee in a *discretionary trust* was said under traditional law to have a *fiduciary power of appointment*—that is, a power held in a fiduciary capacity to designate a recipient of a beneficial ownership interest in the trust property.

The Restatement (Third) of Property adheres to this traditional terminology, distinguishing between a *fiduciary distributive power* and a *nonfiduciary* or *discretionary power* thus:

> A fiduciary distributive power is a power of appointment (a nongeneral power), but it is not a discretionary power of appointment. In the case of a discretionary power of appointment, . . . the donee may exercise the power arbitrarily as long as the exercise is within the scope of the power. In the case of a fiduciary distributive power, the fiduciary's exercise is subject to fiduciary obligations.[10]

In contrast, UPAA § 102(13) and the Restatement (Third) of Trusts take the position that a power of appointment is a nonfiduciary power, and that a trustee who has discretion over distributions holds a fiduciary distributive power that is distinct from a power of appointment.[11] The comment to UPAA § 102(13) explains:

> In this act, a fiduciary distributive power is not a power of appointment. Fiduciary distributive powers include a trustee's power to distribute principal to or for the benefit of an income beneficiary, or for some other individual, or to pay income or principal to a designated beneficiary, or to distribute income or principal among a defined group of beneficiaries. Unlike the exercise of a power of appointment, the exercise of a fiduciary distributive power is subject to fiduciary standards. Unlike a power of appointment, a fiduciary distributive power does not lapse upon the death of the fiduciary, but survives in a successor fiduciary. Nevertheless, a fiduciary distributive power, like a power of appointment, cannot be validly exercised in favor of or for the benefit of someone who is not a permissible appointee.

In this chapter, we focus on nonfiduciary powers of appointment, primarily in beneficiaries. The defining characteristic of such a power is that it "is not subject to fiduciary obligations and may be exercised arbitrarily within the scope of the power."[12]

---

10. Id. § 17.1 cmt. g.

11. Restatement (Third) of Trusts § 50 cmt. a (Am. Law Inst. 2003).

12. Id.; *see also* In re Estate of Zucker, 122 A.3d 1112 (Pa. Super. 2015) (no duty to exercise a power of appointment in "good faith").

2. Tax Considerations

A key reason that powers of appointment are so important in contemporary estate planning is that they allow for flexibility in a tax-advantaged manner. To understand powers of appointment, therefore, it is necessary to appreciate the basics of the tax rules that apply to them.

a. General and Nongeneral Powers

A donee of a *general power* of appointment has a power that is equivalent to ownership. For tax purposes, therefore, the donee of such a power is treated as the owner of the appointive property. The income from the appointive property is taxable to the donee.[13] If the donee exercises or releases the power during life, the resulting transfer of the appointive property is subject to gift taxation as if the donee had personally made a gift of that property.[14] If the donee dies without exercising the power while alive, the appointive property is subject to estate taxation whether or not the donee exercises the power by will.[15]

The tax code provides for two exceptions that are commonly relied upon in drafting wills and trusts today. The first is for a power of appointment that is subject to an *ascertainable standard*. If the donee is given "[a] power to consume, invade, or appropriate property for the benefit of [himself] which is limited by an ascertainable standard relating to the health, education, support, or maintenance of the [donee, it] shall not be deemed a general power of appointment."[16] So a power in *A*, a beneficiary, to consume the trust property as needed to maintain the standard of living to which *A* is accustomed is treated as a nongeneral power for tax purposes.

The second exception is for a *five-or-five* power of withdrawal. If a donee has a power to appoint property to himself (i.e., to withdraw property from the trust), a lapse of the power, meaning a failure to exercise it, will not be taxed as a general power to the extent of $5,000 or 5 percent of the trust corpus, whichever is greater. So a power in *A*, a beneficiary, to withdraw each year the greater of $5,000 or 5 percent of the corpus, whether or not *A* needs it, will not be treated for tax purposes as a general power in any prior year in which *A* does not exercise the power, allowing it to lapse. Of course, the power may be treated as general in the year of the donee's death. But this is a small price to pay for the flexibility this power allows.

The donee of a *nongeneral power* of appointment does not have an ownership-equivalent power. For tax purposes, therefore, the donee of such a power is not treated

---

13. I.R.C. § 678.
14. Id. § 2514.
15. Id. § 2041.
16. Id. § 2041(b)(1)(A). It is common to speak of a "HEMS standard," meaning a health, education, maintenance, and support standard. A lawyer drafting a power meant to fall within the HEMS exception should track carefully the words of the statute or corresponding regulations. For a cautionary tale, see Estate of Vissering v. Commissioner, page 964, in which the court struggled with the question whether "required for the continued comfort, support, maintenance, or education" was an ascertainable standard. The court held that it was, but this was on appeal after the donee had lost in the tax court below.

Lord Justice Fry

the treatment of nongeneral powers for federal tax purposes, follows from the nature of a nongeneral power. The Restatement (Third) of Property explains: "Because a nongeneral power of appointment is not an ownership-equivalent power, the donee's creditors have no claim to the appointive assets, irrespective of whether or not the donee exercises the power."[18]

For a *general power*, the analysis is more complex. Under traditional law, "the donee's creditors could not reach appointive assets covered by an unexercised general power of appointment if the power had been created by a person other than the donee. The theory was that until the donee exercised the power, the donee had not accepted sufficient control over the appointive assets to give the donee the equivalent of ownership of them."[19] Or in Lord Justice Fry's more colorful words: "The power of a person to appoint an estate to himself is, in my judgment, no more his 'property' than the power to write a book or to sing a song."[20]

Times have changed. Modern law increasingly treats a general power of appointment as an ownership-equivalent power if it is presently exercisable. True, the donee must first exercise the power to become the formal owner of the appointive property. But in substance the donee is already the owner. All that stands between the donee of such a power and formal legal ownership is a piece of paper she can sign at any time.

As we have seen, the federal tax code disregards this formality and treats the donee of a general power of appointment as the owner of the appointive property (page 813). A growing number of states have come to the same conclusion for creditor claims. In these states and under UPAA § 502, the donee of a presently exercisable general power is treated as the owner of the appointive property for purposes of claims by the donee's creditors. These states have brought their law of creditor rights to appointive property into alignment with federal tax and bankruptcy law.[21] The Restatement (Third) of Property summarizes thus:

> A presently exercisable general power of appointment is an ownership-equivalent power. . . . Consequently, property subject to a presently exercisable general power of appointment is subject to the claims of the donee's creditors, to the extent that the property owned by the donee is insufficient to satisfy those claims. Furthermore, upon the donee's death, property subject to a general power of appointment that was exercisable by the donee's will is subject to creditors' claims to the extent that

---

18. Restatement (Third) of Property: Wills and Other Donative Transfers § 22.1 cmt. a (Am. Law Inst. 2011).

19. Id. § 22.3 cmt. c.

20. In re Armstrong, [1886] 17 Q.B. 521, 531 (Eng.).

21. The relevant bankruptcy provision is 11 U.S.C. § 541(b)(1) (2016).

the donee's estate is insufficient to satisfy the claims of creditors of the estate and the expenses of administration of the estate.[22]

Suppose, however, that a donee's presently exercisable power to appoint to himself is subject to an ascertainable standard or is limited to a five-or-five power that the donee released or allowed to lapse. The donee of such a power is not treated as the owner of the appointive property for federal tax purposes. Should the same result obtain under state law for claims by the donee's creditors?

Irwin Union Bank & Trust Co. v. Long
312 N.E.2d 908 (Ind. App. 1974)

LOWDERMILK, J. On February 3, 1957, Victoria Long, appellee herein, obtained a judgment in the amount of $15,000 against Philip W. Long, which judgment emanated from a divorce decree. This action is the result of the filing by appellee of a petition in proceedings supplemental to execution on the prior judgment. Appellee sought satisfaction of that judgment by pursuing funds allegedly owed to Philip W. Long as a result of a trust set up by Laura Long, his mother.

Appellee alleged that the Irwin Union Bank and Trust Company (Union Bank) was indebted to Philip W. Long as the result of its position as trustee of the trust created by Laura Long. On April 24, 1969, the trial court ordered that any income, property, or profits, which were owed to Philip Long and not exempt from execution should be applied to the divorce judgment. Thereafter, on February 13, 1973, the trial court ordered that four percent (4%) of the trust corpus of the trust created by Laura Long which benefited Philip Long was not exempt from execution and could be levied upon by appellee and ordered a writ of execution. . . .

The pertinent portion of the trust created by Laura Long is as follows, to-wit:

ITEM V C

Withdrawal of Principal

When Philip W. Long, Jr. has attained the age of twenty-one (21) years and is not a full-time student at an educational institution as a candidate for a Bachelor of Arts or Bachelor of Sciences degree, Philip W. Long shall have the right to withdraw from principal once in any calendar year upon thirty (30) days written notice to the Trustee up to four percent (4%) of the market value of the entire trust principal on the date of such notice, which right shall not be cumulative. . . .

The primary issue raised on this appeal is whether the trial court erred in allowing execution on the 4% of the trust corpus.

Appellant contends that Philip Long's right to withdraw 4% of the trust corpus is, in fact, a general power of appointment. Union Bank further contends that since Philip Long has never exercised his right of withdrawal, pursuant to the provisions of

---

22. Restatement (Third) of Property: Wills and Other Donative Transfers § 22.3 cmt. a (Am. Law Inst. 2011).

the trust instrument, no creditors of Philip Long can reach the trust corpus. Appellant points out that if the power of appointment is unexercised, the creditors cannot force the exercise of said power and cannot reach the trust corpus in this case. . . .

Appellee . . . argues that Philip has absolute control and use of the 4% of the corpus and that the bank does not have control over that portion of the corpus if Philip decides to exercise his right of withdrawal. Appellee argues that the intention of Laura Long was to give Philip not only an income interest in the trust but a fixed amount of corpus which he could use as he saw fit. Thus, Philip Long would have a right to the present enjoyment of 4% of the trust corpus. A summation of appellee's argument, as stated in her brief, is as follows: "So it is with Philip—he can get it if he desires it, so why cannot Victoria get it even if Philip does not desire it?" . . .

The leading case on this issue is Gilman v. Bell, 99 Ill. 144, 150-151 (1881), wherein the Illinois Supreme Court discussed powers of appointment and vesting as follows:

> No title or interest in the thing vests in the donee of the power until he exercises the power. It is virtually an offer to him of the estate or fund, that he may receive or reject at will, and like any other offer to donate property to a person, no title can vest until he accepts the offer, nor can a court of equity compel him to accept the property or fund against his will, even for the benefit of creditors. If it should, it would be to convert the property of the person offering to make the donation to the payment of the debts of another person. Until accepted, the person to whom the offer is made has not, nor can he have, the slightest interest or title to the property. So the donee of the power only receives the naked power to make the property or fund his own. And when he exercises the power, he thereby consents to receive it, and the title thereby vests in him, although it may pass out of him *eo instanti*, to the appointee. . . .

Contrary to the contention of appellee, it is our opinion that Philip Long has no control over the trust corpus until he exercises his power of appointment and gives notice to the trustee that he wishes to receive his 4% of the trust corpus. Until such an exercise is made, the trustee has the absolute control and benefit of the trust corpus within the terms of the trust instrument. . . .

While not controlling as precedent, we find that the Federal Estate Tax laws are quite analogous to the case at bar. Under . . . the Internal Revenue Code, it is clear that the interest given to Philip Long under Item V C would be considered a power of appointment for estate tax purposes. . . .

For estate tax purposes even the failure to exercise a power of appointment may lead to tax consequences. Under [I.R.C.] § 2041(b)(2) the lapse of a power of appointment will be considered a release of such power during the calendar year to the extent of the value of the power in question. However, the lapsed power will only be considered a release and includable in the gross estate of a decedent if the value of the lapsed power is greater than $5,000 or 5% of the aggregate value of the assets out of which the lapsed power could have been satisfied.

The trust instrument was obviously carefully drawn with the tax consequences bearing an important place in the overall intent of the testator. The trust as a whole is set up to give the grandchildren of Laura Long the substantial portion of the assets involved. We note with interest that the percentage of corpus which Philip Long may receive is carefully limited to a percentage less than that which would be includable in the gross estate of Philip Long should he die within a year in which he had allowed his power of appointment to lapse. . . .

Philip Long has never exercised his power of appointment under the trust. Such a situation is discussed in II Scott on Trusts, § 147.3 as follows:

> Where the power is a special power, a power to appoint only among a group of persons, the power is not beneficial to the donee and cannot, of course, be reached by his creditors. Where the power is a general power, that is, a power to appoint to anyone including the donee himself or his estate, the power is beneficial to the donee. If the donee exercises the power by appointing to a volunteer, the property appointed can be reached by his creditors if his other assets are insufficient for the payment of his debts. But where the donee of a general power created by some person other than himself fails to exercise the power, his creditors cannot acquire the power or compel its exercise, nor can they reach the property covered by the power, unless it is otherwise provided by statute.

Indiana has no statute which would authorize a creditor to reach property covered by a power of appointment which is unexercised.

In Gilman v. Bell, supra, the court analyzed the situation where a general power of appointment was unexercised and discussed the position of creditors of the donee of the power as follows:

> But it is insisted, that, conceding it to be a mere naked power of appointment in favor of himself, in favor of creditors he should be compelled by a court of equity to so appoint, or be treated as the owner, and the property subjected to the payment of his debts. The doctrine has been long established in the English courts, that the courts of equity will not aid creditors in case there is a non-execution of the power.

Appellee concedes that if we find that Philip Long had merely an unexercised power of appointment then creditors are in no position to either force the exercise of the power or to reach the trust corpus. Thus, it is clear that the trial court erred. . . .

Reversed and remanded.

NOTES

1. Traditional Law, Five-or-Five Powers, and Ascertainable Standards. Decided in 1974, *Long* applied the traditional rule that the donee of a general power does not have a property interest in the appointive property that a creditor can attach. The court quoted the then-current Scott treatise for the proposition that if "the donee of a general power created by some person other than himself fails to exercise the power, his creditors cannot acquire the power or compel its exercise, nor can they reach the property covered by the power, unless it is otherwise provided by statute." The trend today is different. The latest edition of the Scott treatise summarizes thus: "Increasingly, . . . statutes now treat property that is subject to a general power of appointment as belonging to the donee, even if the power has never been exercised," including "for purposes of allowing the donee's creditors to reach the trust property."[23]

---

23. Scott and Ascher on Trusts § 14.11.3.

But Philip's power to withdraw was structured to fall within the *five-or-five* exception discussed at page 813. Many of the statutes that treat property subject to a general power as belonging to the donee make an exception for a five-or-five power of withdrawal, as does UPAA § 503(b) and Uniform Trust Code (UTC) § 505(b) (Unif. Law Comm'n 2000), to the extent that the donee released the power or allowed it to lapse. Under these statutes, while the power of withdrawal is in effect, the appointive property is subject to the claims of the donee's creditors. But if the power is released or lapses, a creditor of the donee can no longer make a claim against the property subject to the power. If one of these statutes had applied in *Long*, Victoria would be entitled to enforce her claim against 4 percent of the trust corpus through Philip's current withdrawal power, but not if he released the power nor to the extent the power lapsed in prior years.

Many of the statutes that treat property subject to a general power as belonging to the donee also make an exception for a power subject to an *ascertainable standard*, as does UPAA § 502(b) and UTC § 504(e). These statutes in effect reclassify such a power as nongeneral, aligning their state law treatment with federal tax law.

2. Surviving Spouse of the Donee.   *H* has a general power of appointment over property held in a trust created by his father. When *H* dies, does *W*'s elective share apply to the appointive property? Under traditional law, the elective share applied only to the decedent's probate estate, which does not include appointive property. In most states today, the elective share also applies to many nonprobate transfers. Nonetheless, property subject to a power of appointment—even a general power of appointment—is unavailable to the surviving spouse in most states, as in Bongaards v. Millen, page 532. In a minority of states and under Uniform Probate Code (UPC) § 2-205(1)(A) (Unif. Law Comm'n 1990, rev. 2008), the surviving spouse can reach property over which the decedent had a lifetime general power of appointment.

3. Self-Settled General Power.   Under prevailing law, codified by UPAA § 501 and endorsed by the Restatement (Third) of Property, if the donee of a general power of appointment is also the donor of the power, the appointive property is subject to claims by the donor-donee's creditors as if she owned the property outright.[24] This rule, applied in Phillips v. Moore, 690 S.E.2d 620 (Ga. 2010), is consistent with traditional law governing recourse by a creditor of the settlor against the settlor's interest in a self-settled trust (see Chapter 10 at page 712) and with modern law on the rights of the settlor's creditors to property in a revocable trust (see Chapter 7 at page 461).

B. EXERCISE OF A POWER OF APPOINTMENT

To exercise a power of appointment, (1) a donee must *manifest an intent* to exercise the power; (2) the manner of expression must satisfy any *formal requirements* imposed

___
24. *See* Restatement (Third) of Property: Wills and Other Donative Transfers § 22.2 (Am. Law Inst. 2011).

by the donor; and (3) the appointment must be a *permissible exercise* of the power.[25] In this section, we consider recurring problems under each of these requirements. We also consider (4) *disclaimer* or *release* of a power of appointment and *contracts* to exercise a power.

1. Manifestation of Intent

Whether a donee has *manifested an intent* to exercise a power of appointment is a question of construction resolved under the law governing the kind of instrument at issue.[26] For example, in determining whether a donee's will exercises a testamentary power of appointment, a court will apply the rules for construction of wills (see Chapter 5). If the will is capably drafted, there will be no doubt about the decedent's intention. "Ideally, the donee or the donee's drafting agent will have the instrument creating the power at hand, and will formulate the language intended to express the donee's intent in light of the creating instrument."[27] But not all wills are capably drafted.

Perhaps the most common difficulty involves the question, as in the next case, of whether a residuary clause manifests an intent to exercise a testamentary power. If the clause does not expressly exercise the power, the answer will turn on the applicable jurisdiction's default rule of construction.

Beals v. State Street Bank & Trust Co.
326 N.E.2d 896 (Mass. 1975)

WILKINS, J. The trustees under the will of Arthur Hunnewell filed this petition for instructions, seeking a determination of the proper distribution to be made of a portion of the trust created under the residuary clause of his will. A judge of the Probate Court reserved decision and reported the case to the Appeals Court on the pleadings and a stipulation of facts. We transferred the case here.

Arthur Hunnewell died, a resident of Wellesley, in 1904, leaving his wife and four daughters. His will placed the residue of his property in a trust, the income of which was to be paid to his wife during her life. At the death of his wife the trust was to be divided in portions, one for each then surviving daughter and one for the then surviving issue of any deceased daughter. Mrs. Hunnewell died in 1930. One of the four daughters predeceased her mother, leaving no issue. The trust was divided, therefore, in three portions at the death of Mrs. Hunnewell. The will directed that the income of each portion held for a surviving daughter should be paid to her during her life and on her death the principal of such portion should "be paid and disposed of as she may direct and appoint by her last Will and Testament duly probated." In default of appointment, the will directed that a daughter's share should be distributed to "the

---

25. *See* UPAA § 301(2)-(3); Restatement (Third) of Property: Wills and Other Donative Transfers § 19.1 (Am. Law Inst. 2011).

26. *See* Restatement (Third) of Property: Wills and Other Donative Transfers § 19.2 (Am. Law Inst. 2011).

27. Id. cmt. b.

persons who would be entitled to such estate under the laws then governing the distribution of intestate estates."

This petition concerns the distribution of the trust portion held for the testator's daughter Isabella H. Hunnewell, later Isabella H. Dexter (Isabella). Following the death of her mother, Isabella requested the trustees to exercise their discretionary power to make principal payments by transferring substantially all of her trust share "to the Dexter family office in Boston, there to be managed in the first instance by her husband, Mr. Gordon Dexter." This request was granted, and cash and securities were transferred to her account at the Dexter office. The Hunnewell trustees, however, retained in Isabella's share a relatively small cash balance, an undivided one-third interest in a mortgage and undivided one-third interest in various parcels of real estate in the Commonwealth, which Isabella did not want in kind and which the trustees could not sell at a reasonable price at the time. Thereafter, the trustees received payments on the mortgage and proceeds from occasional sales of portions of the real estate. From her one-third share of these receipts, the trustees made further distributions to her of $1,900 in 1937, $22,000 in 1952, and $5,000 in 1953.

In February, 1944, Isabella, who was then a resident of New York, executed and caused to be filed in the Registry of Probate for Norfolk County an instrument which partially released her general power of appointment under the will of her father. Isabella released her power of appointment "to the extent that such power empowers me to appoint to any one other than one or more of the . . . descendants [surviving me] of Arthur Hunnewell."[28]

On December 14, 1968, Isabella, who survived her husband, died without issue, still a resident of New York, leaving a will dated May 21, 1965. Her share in the trust under her father's will then consisted of an interest in a contract to sell real estate, cash, notes and a certificate of deposit, and was valued at approximately $88,000. Isabella did not expressly exercise her power of appointment under her father's will. The residuary clause of her will provided in effect for the distribution of all "the rest, residue and remainder of my property" to the issue per stirpes of her sister Margaret Blake, who had predeceased Isabella.[29] The Blake issue would take one-half of Isabella's trust share,

---

28. Isabella did this to avoid federal estate taxes. The Internal Revenue Code was changed in 1942 to provide that property subject to a general power created before 1942 was includible in the donee's federal taxable estate if the power was exercised. However, Congress permitted powers created before 1942 to be released partially, converting them into nongeneral powers without adverse tax consequences, if the conversion took place before 1951. —Eds.

29. The significant portion of the residuary clause reads as follows:

> All the rest, residue and remainder of my property of whatever kind and wherever situated (including any property not effectively disposed of by the preceding provisions of this my will and all property over which I have or may have the power of appointment under or by virtue of the last will and testament dated November 27, 1933 and codicils thereto dated January 7, 1935 and January 8, 1935 of my husband, the late Gordon Dexter) . . . I give, devise, bequeath and appoint in equal shares to such of my said nephew GEORGE BATY BLAKE and my said nieces MARGARET CABOT and JULIA O. BEALS as shall survive me and the issue who shall survive me of any of my said nephew or nieces who may predecease me, such issue to take per stirpes.

Isabella and Wellesley, Massachusetts

The town of Wellesley, Massachusetts, and the college located there are both named after Isabella Welles Hunnewell, the mother of the donor, Arthur Hunnewell, and a grandmother of the donee, Isabella H. Hunnewell, later Isabella H. Dexter. Gordon Dexter was the donee's third husband. Her first husband was Herbert M. Harriman.

The beautiful country seat of Mr. and Mrs. Arthur Hunnewell, at Wellesley, was a scene of joy and festivity yesterday, when their daughter, Miss Isabella, was married to Herbert M. Harriman of New-York. The ceremony was performed by the Rev. Leighton Parks, pastor of the Emanuel Church. There were no bridesmaids. The groom's brother, Joseph, was best man.

The ushers were Lawrence Kip of New-York, Belmont Tiffany of New-York, Edgar Scott of Philadelphia, Columbus Baldwin of New-York, Gordon Dexter, and W. S. Patten. Of the bridegroom's kinsfolk there were present: His mother, Mr. and Mrs. Border Harriman, and Mr. and Mrs. Oliver Harriman.

The wedding breakfast was spread beneath the grand old trees which dot the lawn before the mansion. At the expiration of a short wedding trip Mr. and Mrs. Harriman will reside in New-York.*

Isabella and Herbert were divorced 12 years later. Her second marriage, to J. Searlo Barclay, also ended in divorce. Gordon Dexter, "a Boston businessman, clubman and yachtsman,"† was evidently an usher at Isabella's first wedding. She survived him, living to the age of 97.

---

* Harriman—Hunnewell, N.Y. Times, Sept. 28, 1894, at 5.
† Mrs. Gordon Dexter, N.Y. Times, Dec. 16, 1968, at 47.

as takers in default of appointment, in all events. If, however, Isabella's will should be treated as effectively exercising her power of appointment under her father's will, the Blake issue would take the entire trust share, and the executors of the will of Isabella's sister Jane (who survived Isabella and has since died) would not receive that one-half of the trust share which would go to Jane in default of appointment.

In support of their argument that Isabella's will did not exercise the power of appointment under her father's will, the executors of Jane's estate contend that (1) Massachusetts substantive law governs all questions relating to the power of appointment, including the interpretation of Isabella's will; (2) the power should be treated as a special power of appointment because of its partial release by Isabella; and (3) because Isabella's will neither expresses nor implies any intention to exercise the power, the applicable rule of construction in this Commonwealth is that a general residuary clause does not exercise a special power of appointment. The Blake issue, in support of their argument that the power was exercised, contend that (1) Isabella's will manifests an intention to exercise the power and that no rule of construction need be applied; (2) the law of New York should govern the question whether Isabella's will exercised the power and, if it does, by statute New York has adopted a rule that a special power of appointment is exercised by a testamentary disposition of all of the donee's property; and (3) if Massachusetts law does apply, and the will is silent on the subject of the exercise of the power, the principles underlying our rule of construction that a residuary clause exercises a general power of appointment are applicable in these circumstances.

1. We turn first to a consideration of the question whether Isabella's will should be construed according to the law of this Commonwealth or the law of New York.[30] There are strong, logical reasons for turning to the law of the donee's domicil at the time of death to determine whether a donee's will has exercised a testamentary power of appointment over movables. Most courts in this country which have considered the question, however, interpret the donee's will under the law governing the administration of the trust, which is usually the law of the donor's domicil. . . . This has long been the rule in Massachusetts.[31]

If the question were before us now for the first time, we might well adopt a choice of law rule which would turn to the substantive law of the donee's domicil, for the purpose of determining whether the donee's will exercised a power of appointment. However, in a field where much depends on certainty and consistency as to the applicable rules of law, we think that we should adhere to our well established rule. Thus, in interpreting the will of a donee to determine whether a power of appointment was exercised, we apply the substantive law of the jurisdiction whose law governs the administration of the trust.

2. Considering the arguments of the parties, we conclude that there is no indication in Isabella's will of an intention to exercise or not to exercise the power of appointment given to her under her father's will. A detailed analysis of the various competing contentions would not add to our jurisprudence.[32] In the absence of an intention disclosed by her will construed in light of circumstances known to her when she executed it, we must adopt some Massachusetts rule of construction to resolve the issue before us. The question is what rule of construction. We are unaware of any decided case which, in this context, has dealt with a testamentary general power, reduced to a special power by action of the donee.

3. We conclude that the residuary clause of Isabella's will should be presumed to have exercised the power of appointment. We reach this result by a consideration of the reasons underlying the canons of construction applicable to general and special

---

30. The applicable rules of construction where a donee's intention is not clear from his will differ between the two States. In the absence of a requirement by the donor that the donee refer to the power in order to exercise it, New York provides by statute that a residuary clause in a will exercises not only a general power of appointment but also a special power of appointment, unless the will expressly or by necessary implication shows the contrary. "Necessary implication" exists only where the will permits no other construction. In Massachusetts, unless the donor has provided that the donee of the power can exercise it only by explicit reference to the power, a general residuary clause in a will exercises a general power of appointment unless there is a clear indication of a contrary intent. . . . However, in Fiduciary Trust Co. v. First Nat'l Bank, 181 N.E.2d 6 (Mass. 1962), we held that a general residuary clause did not exercise a special testamentary power of appointment in the circumstances of that case.

31. Of course, the law of the donee's domicile would be applied if the donor expressed such an intention. . . .

32. Isabella's residuary clause disposed of her "property." Because the trustees had agreed to distribute her trust portion to her and had largely done so and because, in a sense, she had exercised dominion over the trust assets by executing the partial release, a reasonable argument might be made that she regarded the assets in her portion of the trust as her "property." However, a conclusion that she intended by implication to include assets over which she had a special power of appointment within the word "property" is not justifiable because her residuary clause refers expressly to other property over which she had a special power of appointment under the will of her husband.

testamentary powers of appointment. Considered in this way, we believe that a presumption of exercise is more appropriate in the circumstances of this case than a presumption of nonexercise.

When this court first decided not to extend to a special power of appointment the rule of construction that a general residuary clause executes a general testamentary power (unless a contrary intent is shown by the will), we noted significant distinctions between a general power and a special power. Fiduciary Trust Co. v. First Nat'l Bank, supra, 181 N.E.2d at 9-12 (Mass. 1962). A general power was said to be a close approximation to a property interest, a "virtually unlimited power of disposition," while a special power of appointment lacked this quality. We observed that a layman having a general testamentary power over property might not be expected to distinguish between the appointive property and that which he owns outright, and thus "he can reasonably be presumed to regard this appointive property as his own." On the other hand, the donee of a special power would not reasonably regard such appointive property as his own: "[h]e would more likely consider himself to be, as the donor of the power intended, merely the person chosen by the donor to decide who of the possible appointees should share in the property (if the power is exclusive), and the respective shares of the appointees."

Considering the power of appointment given to Isabella and her treatment of that power during her life, the rationale for the canon of construction applicable to general powers of appointment should be applied in this case. This power was a general testamentary power at its inception. During her life, as a result of her request, Isabella had the use and enjoyment of the major portion of the property initially placed in her trust share. Prior use and enjoyment of the appointive property is a factor properly considered as weighing in favor of the exercise of a power of appointment by a will. Isabella voluntarily limited the power by selecting the possible appointees. In thus relinquishing the right to add the trust assets to her estate, she was treating the property as her own. Moreover, the gift under her residuary clause was consistent with the terms of the reduced power which she retained. In these circumstances, the partial release of a general power does not obviate the application of that rule of construction which presumes that a general residuary clause exercises a general power of appointment.

4. A decree shall be entered determining that Isabella H. Dexter did exercise the power of appointment, partially released by an instrument dated February 25, 1944, given to her by art. Fourth of the will of Arthur Hunnewell and directing that the trustees under the will of Arthur Hunnewell pay over the portion of the trust held under art. Fourth of his will for the benefit of Isabella H. Dexter, as follows: one-third each to George Baty Blake and Julia O. Beals; and one-sixth each to Margaret B. Elwell and to the estate of George B. Cabot. The parties shall be allowed their costs and counsel fees in the discretion of the probate court.

So ordered.

NOTES

1. *Choice of Law.* For a power of appointment over land, the law of the state where the land is located governs the power. If the appointive property is not land, and

the donor and donee live in different jurisdictions, the choice of law is more complex. The argument in favor of applying the law of the donee's domicile to determine the validity of an exercise of the power is that the acts in question are by the donee, who is likely to seek counsel in her own domicile. Despite these "strong, logical reasons" for applying the law of the donee's domicile to an exercise of the power, the court in *Beals* followed the traditional view and applied the law of the donor's domicile on grounds of "certainty and consistency."

A growing body of authority rejects the reasoning in *Beals*. In White v. United States, 680 F.2d 1156 (7th Cir. 1982), the court said: "We recognize the special need for certainty and consistency in laws affecting trusts, but fail to see how that end is promoted by perpetuation of a legal fiction that confuses lawyers and laymen alike." In accord with cases such as *White*, UPAA § 103, the Restatement (Third) of Property, and the Restatement (Second) of Conflict of Laws all take the position that, unless the donor specifies otherwise, the law of the donee's domicile governs the exercise of a power.[33]

2. Residuary Clause.   The main issue in *Beals* was whether a residuary clause presumptively exercises a testamentary power of appointment held by the testator.[34] In a large majority of jurisdictions, a garden-variety residuary clause presumptively does not exercise a power held by the testator, as in Cessac v. Stevens, 127 So. 3d 675 (Fla. App. 2013). States adhering to the majority rule differ on whether a contrary intent may be shown only by reference to the face of the will or whether extrinsic evidence may also be considered. In a minority of jurisdictions, a residuary clause exercises a *general power* of appointment unless a contrary intent affirmatively appears. At the time of the *Beals* case, Massachusetts adhered to the minority rule, but it has since adopted a version of the majority rule based on UPC § 2-608 (1990).[35]

Under UPC § 2-608 and the Restatement (Third) of Property, the presumption is that a residuary clause does not exercise a testamentary power of appointment held by the testator unless the power is general and there is no taker in default of appointment.[36] The theory is that the donor normally expects the gift-in-default clause to control in the absence of "positive evidence of [the donee's] intent to appoint."[37] But if the donor did not provide for takers in default or the gift-in-default clause is ineffective, then it "seems more in accord with the donor's probable intent for the donee's residuary clause to be treated as exercising the power."[38]

---

33. *See* Restatement (Third) of Property: Wills and Other Donative Transfers § 19.1 cmt. e (Am. Law Inst. 2011); Restatement (Second) of Conflict of Laws § 275 (Am. Law Inst. 1971).

34. *See* Susan F. French, Exercise of Powers of Appointment: Should Intent to Exercise Be Inferred from a General Disposition of Property?, 1979 Duke L.J. 747; Sheldon F. Kurtz, Powers of Appointment Under the 1990 Uniform Probate Code: What Was Done — What Remains to Be Done, 55 Alb. L. Rev. 1151, 1162-72 (1992).

35. *See* Mass. Gen. Laws Ann. ch. 190B, § 2-608(a) (2016).

36. Restatement (Third) of Property: Wills and Other Donative Transfers § 19.4 (Am. Law Inst. 2011).

37. Id. cmt. a.

38. Id.

UPAA § 302 is similar. It provides that an ordinary residuary clause does not manifest an intent to exercise a power of appointment unless:

(1) the terms of the instrument containing the residuary clause do not manifest a contrary intent; (2) the power is a general power exercisable in favor of the power-holder's estate; (3) there is no gift-in-default clause or the clause is ineffective; and (4) the powerholder did not release the power.

In a few jurisdictions—New York is the leading example—a residuary clause exercises a *nongeneral power* of appointment if the residuary devisees are objects of the power.[39] In most states and under the UPAA, a residuary clause without more does not exercise a nongeneral power.[40]

3. Blanket-Exercise Clause. To overcome the default rule that a residuary clause does not exercise a power of appointment, some wills include a *blanket-exercise* clause that purports to exercise any power of appointment held by the testator. Such a provision can be folded into a residuary clause, for example by adding language such as "including all property over which I have a power of appointment." A blanket-exercise clause is usually construed as manifesting an intent to exercise all powers of appointment held by the testator, including a power created after execution of the instrument containing the clause but before the donee's death, as under UPAA § 303 and the Restatement (Third) of Property,[41] except for powers for which the donor required a *specific reference* for exercise, an issue we take up below.

2. Formal Requirements Imposed by the Donor

Even if a donee manifests an intent to exercise a power of appointment, the manner of expression must satisfy any *formal requirements* of exercise imposed by the donor. Two categories of issues tend arise under this requirement: (a) the *nature of the instrument* required for exercise, and (b) whether the donee must make a *specific reference* to the power.

a. The Nature of the Instrument

In Beals v. State Street Bank & Trust Co., page 821, because the power held by Isabella H. Hunnewell was exercisable "by her last Will and Testament duly probated," her will had to be admitted to probate for the power to be exercised. If the power had been exercisable "by will" without the additional requirement that the will be probated, the power may have been "exercisable by an instrument that is formally sufficient to be admitted to probate" even if it had not in fact been admitted.[42]

---

39. *See, e.g.,* In re Will of Block, 598 N.Y.S.2d 668 (Sur. 1993).

40. *See, e.g.,* Doggett v. Robinson, 345 S.W.3d 94 (Tex. App. 2011); *accord* UPAA § 302 cmt.; Restatement (Third) of Property: Wills and Other Donative Transfers § 19.4 cmt. d (Am. Law Inst. 2011).

41. *See* Restatement (Third) of Property: Wills and Other Donative Transfers § 19.6 (Am. Law Inst. 2011).

42. Id. § 19.9 cmt. b.

Lumbard v. Farmers State Bank, 812 N.E.2d 196 (Ind. App. 2004), is illustrative. *H* devised property to *X* in trust to pay *W* the income for life, and on *W*'s death to pay the remainder to such persons as *W* named "by will" or, in default of appointment, to *H*'s Daughter, Grandson, and Granddaughter. After *H*'s death, *W* duly executed a will appointing the trust property to Daughter. After *W* died, her will was not offered for probate within the state's three-year limitations period. The court held that the power had been validly exercised by *W*'s will even though the will had not been probated. "[*W*] did all she could do while alive to express her intent to exercise her power of appointment."

Suppose in *Lumbard* that *W* purported to exercise the power in a *revocable trust* rather than in her will. Would this satisfy the donor's formal requirement that the power be exercised "by will"? There is little case law on this question. UPAA § 304 requires only "substantial compliance with a formal requirement of appointment imposed by the donor," and the comment to this section says that "a donor's formal requirement that the power of appointment is exercisable 'by will' may be satisfied by the power-holder's attempted exercise in a nontestamentary instrument that is functionally similar to a will, such as the powerholder's revocable trust that remains revocable until the powerholder's death." The Restatement (Third) of Property likewise takes the position that "[b]ecause a revocable trust operates in substance as a will, a power of appointment exercisable 'by will' can be exercised in a revocable-trust document, as long as the revocable trust remained revocable at the donee's death."[43]

Because revocable trusts have become so common, and because in many well-planned estates there will be no need to probate the decedent's will, some lawyers nowadays draft testamentary powers of appointment so that they may be exercised by a will duly admitted to probate, by a revocable trust agreement signed by the donee, or by a notarized writing signed by the donee and two witnesses. To address the problem of conflicting instruments, the power might provide that the instrument most recently signed by the donee controls, and that a trustee who reasonably relies on a signed instrument without notice of a conflicting instrument is protected against liability.

The prevailing interpretation of a power exercisable "by deed" requires only "an instrument that would be formally sufficient . . . to be legally operative in the donee's lifetime to transfer an interest to the appointee if the donee owned the appointive assets."[44] A power exercisable by deed is therefore exercisable by a revocable trust. A power exercisable "by written instrument" is exercisable by deed or by will.[45]

b. Specific Reference Requirement

To prevent the unintentional exercise of a power of appointment, a donor will sometimes provide that a power can be exercised only by an instrument that is executed after the date of the creating instrument and that refers specifically to the power. UPC § 2-704, which was revised in 2014 to conform with UPAA § 304 (2013) and

---

43. Id.
44. Id. cmt. d.
45. Id. cmt. f.

the Restatement (Third) of Property,[46] codifies this practice but subjects it to a rule of substantial compliance.

Uniform Probate Code (Unif. Law Comm'n 1990, as amended 2014)

§ 2-704. Power of Appointment; Compliance with Specific Reference Requirement

A powerholder's substantial compliance with a formal requirement of appointment imposed in a governing instrument by the donor, including a requirement that the instrument exercising the power of appointment make reference or specific reference to the power, is sufficient if:

(1) the powerholder knows of and intends to exercise the power; and

(2) the powerholder's manner of attempted exercise does not impair a material purpose of the donor in imposing the requirement.

NOTES

1. Strict or Substantial Compliance? Some courts have demanded *strict compliance* with a donor's requirement of specific reference to exercise a power. In In re Estate of Hamilton, 593 N.Y.S.2d 372 (App. Div. 1993), *W* was given a power of appointment by *H*'s will executed in 1982. *W*'s 1967 will specifically exercised a power given to her in a similar will executed by *H* in 1966, since revoked. The court held that *W* had not exercised the power created by *H*'s 1982 will. In Smith v. Brannan, 954 P.2d 1259 (Or. App. 1998), the court reached the same result on similar facts. What result in those cases under UPC § 2-704, excerpted above? Would the wills in *Hamilton* and *Smith* be good candidates for reformation under UPC § 2-805 (2008, rev. 2010), page 341?

2. Blanket-Exercise Clause Revisited. The prevailing rule, as in In re Estate of Shenkman, 737 N.Y.S.2d 39 (App. Div. 2002), is that a blanket-exercise clause is ineffective to exercise a power that requires a specific reference. UPC § 2-704, excerpted above, and UPAA § 304, on which UPC § 2-704 is based, soften that rule by applying a substantial compliance test. The comment to UPC § 2-704 explains:

> The question of whether the powerholder has made a sufficiently specific reference is much litigated. The precise question often is whether a so-called blanket-exercise clause—a clause referring to "any property over which I have a power of appointment"—constitutes a sufficient reference to a particular power to exercise that power. . . . Section 2-704 adopts a substantial-compliance rule. If it could be shown that the powerholder had knowledge of and intended to exercise the power, the blanket-exercise clause would be sufficient to exercise the power, unless it could be shown that the donor had a material purpose in insisting on the specific-reference requirement.

---

46. *See* id. § 19.10.

3. Permissible Exercise of the Power

Even if a donee manifests an intent to exercise a power of appointment and the manner of expression satisfies the formal requirements of exercise imposed by the donor, to be valid the appointment must be a *permissible exercise* of the power in accordance with the substantive requirements of the power.

a. Appointment to an Object

Perhaps the clearest example of an impermissible exercise of a power of appointment is one that purports to benefit someone who is not an object of the power. In the words of UPAA § 307, "an exercise of a power of appointment in favor of an impermissible appointee is ineffective."

Timmons v. Ingrahm
36 So. 3d 861 (Fla. App. 2010)

EVANDER, J. Frank G. Timmons, Jr., and Jacquelyn Timmons Forman (hereinafter jointly referred to as "the Timmons") appeal from a final summary judgment entered in favor of co-trustees Myrtle Timmons Ingrahm and David Carter. We find that the trial court erred in failing to accord the term "lineal descendants" its legal definition in determining the intent of the testator/settlor, Frank Timmons, Sr. ("Frank Sr."). Accordingly, we reverse the summary final judgment entered in favor of the co-trustees and direct that partial summary judgment be entered in favor of the Timmons.

At the time of his death in 1999, Frank Sr. was married to Myrtle Timmons, n/k/a, Myrtle Timmons Ingrahm ("Myrtle"). He had two adopted children, the Timmons, from a previous marriage. Myrtle had four children—none of which was ever adopted by Frank Sr.

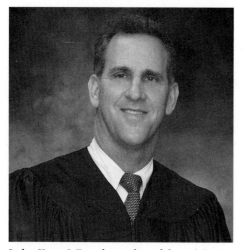

Judge Kerry I. Evander, author of the opinion in *Timmons*, also wrote the opinion in Brown v. Miller, page 835.

In his will, Frank Sr. created two trusts: the Timmons Family Trust ("Family Trust") and the Timmons Marital Trust ("Marital Trust"). The Timmons Family Trust was valued at $650,000. The more substantial portion of Frank Sr.'s estate was placed in the Marital Trust. Myrtle was the sole income beneficiary of the trusts during her lifetime. She was also empowered, in her sole discretion, to annually remove from each trust, up to $5,000 or five percent (5%) of the principal, whichever was greater. The co-trustees were also given authority to encroach on the trusts' principal as necessary for Myrtle's maintenance and support. The Marital Trust provided that upon Myrtle's death, the trust's remaining principal (after payment of estate taxes) would be "poured over" into the Family Trust and distributed in accordance with the terms of the Family Trust. The Family Trust provided that upon Myrtle's death, the trust assets were to be divided "into as many equal shares as there are children of mine then living and deceased children of mine leaving issue then surviving."

Frank Sr.'s will expressly defined "children" to include both his adopted children and Myrtle's children:

> For the purposes of this Will, the term "children" shall include, in addition to my natural and adopted children, the children of my wife, MYRTLE C. TIMMONS.

Thus, if Myrtle had died shortly after Frank Sr., the principal of the Marital Trust would have "poured over" into the Family Trust, and the then-existing principal of the Family Trust would have been equally divided between the six "children"—Frank Sr.'s two children and Myrtle's four children.

The instant dispute arose as the result of Myrtle's attempt, in 2007, to disinherit the Timmons through the purported exercise of a limited power of appointment granted to Myrtle in the Family Trust. The applicable provision reads as follows:

> [M]y said wife shall have the further limited power at any time during her lifetime to appoint by specific reference to this power in an instrument in writing executed and delivered to the Trustee all or any part of the principal of this trust, free and clear of any trust *to and among my then living lineal descendants* in such proportions and subject to such trust and conditions as she may direct. This limited power of appointment may be exercised by said wife even to the point of completely exhausting the entire corpus trust of this trust estate. (Emphasis added.)

```
        D.  In addition to the limited power mentioned above,
my said wife shall have the further limited power at any time
during her lifetime to appoint by specific reference to this
power in an instrument in writing executed and delivered to the
Trustee, all or any part of the principal of this trust, free and
clear of any trust, to and among my then living lineal descend-
ants in such proportions and subject to such trust and conditions
as she may direct.  This limited power of appointment may be
exercised by my said wife even to the point of completely
exhausting the entire trust corpus of this trust estate.
```

The power of appointment at issue in *Timmons*

Specifically, Myrtle executed a document entitled "Exercise of Limited Power of Appointment" that attempted to grant all of the principal and income of the family trust, then in existence or later coming into the trust, to her four (4) natural children:

> Pursuant to the provisions of this limited power of appointment, it is the intent of this writing to exercise said power, which is executed by me and I hereby direct pursuant to the limited power of appointment that all principal and income of said trust now in existence or becoming a part of such trust as the result of my death as a pour over from the Marital Trust C or the Marital Trust A be distributed, per stirpes, among the natural children and their lineal descendants, of Myrtle C. Timmons Ingrahm free from further trust and outright.

The effect of the exercise of this limited power of appointment shall be that the only beneficiaries of the Timmons Family Trust shall be my natural children and their lineal descendants. I understand that this exercise of limited power of appoint [sic] disinherits Frank G. Timmons, Jr., and his lineal descendants, and Jacquelyn Forman and their lineal descendants and that is my intent.

EXERCISE OF LIMITED POWER OF APPOINTMENT

The undersigned, Myrtle C. Timmons Ingrahm, hereby exercises the limited power of appointment given to her pursuant to the last will and testament of Franklin G. Timmons pursuant to Article V, paragraph D, found on page 5 of said will.

Said provision reading as follows:

"In addition to limited power mentioned above, my said wife shall have the further limited power at any time during her lifetime to appoint by specific reference to this power and an instrument in writing executed and delivered to the trustee, all or any part of the principal of this trust, free and clear of any trust, to and among my then living lineal descendants in such proportions and subject to such trust and conditions as she may direct. This limited power of appointment may be exercised by my said wife even to the point of completely exhausting the entire trust corpus of this trust estate."

Pursuant to the provisions of this limited power of appointment, it is the intent of this writing to exercise said power, which is executed by me and I hereby direct pursuant to the limited power of appointment that all principal and income of said trust now in existence or becoming a part of such trust as the result of my death as a pour over from the Marital Trust C or the Marital Trust A be distributed, per stirpes, among the natural children and their lineal descendants, of Myrtle C. Timmons Ingrahm free from further trust and outright.

The effect of the exercise of this limited power of appointment shall be that the only beneficiaries of the Timmons Family Trust shall be my natural children and their lineal descendants. I understand that this exercise of limited power of appoint disinherits Frank G. Timmons, Jr. and his lineal descendants, and Jacquelyn Forman, and their lineal descendants and that is my intent.

IN WITNESS WHEREOF, the above is execute as of the ___14th___ day of ___Febuary___, 2007 by the undersigned, Myrtle C. Timmons Ingrahm.

Witnesses:

_____   _____
                                              MYRTLE INGRAHM
_____

**EXHIBIT
B**

The exercise of the power at issue in *Timmons*

The co-trustees are then alleged to have commenced distributing certain trust assets to Myrtle's children and to have denied the Timmons access to trust records.

The Timmons brought an action against the co-trustees for breach of fiduciary duty and for an accounting. The Timmons asserted that Myrtle's attempt to disinherit them was ineffective because the limited power of appointment could only be executed in favor of Frank Sr.'s "lineal descendants" and Myrtle's natural children did not fall within this definition. In response, the co-trustees contended that Myrtle's exercise of the limited power of appointment was lawful and had the intended effect of disinheriting the Timmons—thereby leaving them without standing to maintain their action.

The parties subsequently filed cross-motions for summary judgment, agreeing that there were no disputed issues of material fact. The trial court denied the Timmons' motion, granted the co-trustees' motion, and entered final summary judgment in favor of the co-trustees. This appeal followed. . . .

In construing a will or testamentary trust, the intent of the testator or settlor should prevail and effect be given to his wishes.

In determining the intent of the settlor, a technical term used in a trust instrument should be accorded its legal definition, unless obviously used by the settlor in a different sense. Knauer v. Barnett, 360 So. 2d 399, 406 (Fla. 1978). "Lineal descendant" or "descendant" is defined to mean "a person in any generational level down the applicable individual's descending line." It includes children, grandchildren, or more remote descendants but excludes collateral heirs. Fla. Stat. § 731.201(9) (2007). Adopted children come within the definition of lineal descendants. Lewis v. Green, 389 So. 2d 235, 241 (Fla. App. 1980).

The co-trustees acknowledge that step-children do not ordinarily fall within the definition of "lineal descendants," but contend that by expressly expanding the definition of "children" to include his step-children for purposes of his will, Frank Sr. similarly intended to expand the definition of "lineal descendants" to include his step-children and their descendants." We reject this argument.

While Frank Sr.'s will expressly provided for a different definition of the term "children" than its common or legal definition, no similar attempt was made to modify the common or legal definition of the term "lineal descendants." The lack of an attempt to redefine "lineal descendant" reflects an intent to have the term interpreted in accordance with its legal definition. Furthermore, Frank Sr. used the term "lineal descendants" on only two other occasions in his will. In one paragraph, Frank Sr. bequeathed his personal property, in the event Myrtle predeceased him, "to my children who survive me, or if none of my children survive me, then to their lineal descendants, per stirpes." In a different paragraph, Frank Sr. bequeathed certain shares of stock "to my son Frank Timmons, Jr., or his lineal descendants per stirpes." Thus, in both of these instances, the term "lineal descendants" was used in a manner consistent with its legal definition. Finally, there is no language elsewhere in the will reflecting an intent on the part of Frank Sr. to grant Myrtle the power to disinherit his children in favor of her own children.

As previously observed, a technical term used in a trust instrument should be accorded its legal definition unless *obviously* used by the settlor in a different sense. *Knauer.* Here, we believe that Frank Sr.'s testamentary document did not reflect an intent (and certainly not an "obvious" one) to expand the definition of lineal descendants to include step-children. Therefore, Myrtle's purported exercise of the limited power of appointment in favor of her natural children was invalid.

Reversed and remanded.

NOTES

1. Blended Families and Lineal Descendants. Why did the court in *Timmons* read the term "lineal descendants" to exclude the donor's stepchildren even though the donor had defined the term "children" to include them? Is it likely that the donor intended to give his widow a power to exclude his children from sharing in his estate after her death?

2. Fraud on a Nongeneral Power.   An appointment to an object for the purpose of circumventing a limitation on a power is a *fraud on the power* and is invalid to the extent of the fraud.[47] Suppose Elsa has a nongeneral testamentary power to appoint among her "kindred." In default of appointment, the property is to pass to Elsa's descendants or, if none, to the donor's heirs. Elsa, who has no descendants, wants to appoint $100,000 to her husband. So she approaches her cousin, Paul, and offers to leave him $250,000 if he will give $100,000 to her husband. Paul agrees, signing a letter prepared by Elsa's lawyer that reads: "I am informed that by your last will and testament you have bequeathed to me $250,000. In the event that you should predecease me and I should receive the bequest, I hereby promise and agree, in consideration of the said bequest, that I will pay to your husband, Foster, $100,000 out of the said bequest." Elsa died leaving a will appointing $250,000 to Paul. Is Paul entitled to $250,000, $150,000, or zero? *See* In re Carroll's Will, 8 N.E.2d 864 (N.Y. 1937); UPAA § 307(b).

3. Lapse—Object Dies Before Donee.   In Beals v. State Street Bank & Trust Co., page 821, the court held that the donee, Isabella, exercised her power in favor of the descendants of her sister, Margaret, who had died before Isabella executed her will. Suppose, however, that Isabella had executed her will during Margaret's lifetime and Isabella had exercised the power by appointing to Margaret. If Margaret then predeceased Isabella, would Margaret's descendants take the appointive property under the antilapse statute? In a handful of states, and in those that have adopted UPC § 2-603 (1990, rev. 2008), the antilapse statute expressly applies to the exercise of a power of appointment, and Margaret's descendants would take in her place.[48] But what result in a state in which the antilapse statute does not expressly apply to a power of appointment? In Thompson v. Pew, 102 N.E. 122 (Mass. 1913), the court held that the antilapse statute would apply.

Suppose that Isabella had a nongeneral power to appoint among her nephews and nieces and that she exercised the power by appointing to the descendants of a niece who had predeceased her. What result? Because Isabella could have appointed to the niece, with the descendants of the niece taking the appointive property under the antilapse statute, why not permit Isabella to appoint directly to the descendants? UPAA § 306(b) and the Restatement (Third) of Property take the position that persons who would be substituted as takers by an antilapse statute may be treated themselves as objects of the power.[49]

Suppose that Isabella had a general testamentary power created by her husband's will and had appointed to her husband's nephew, who predeceased Isabella, leaving descendants. Would the descendants of the deceased nephew take under the antilapse

47. *See* id. § 19.16.

48. *See* Susan F. French, Application of Antilapse Statutes to Appointments Made by Will, 53 Wash. L. Rev. 405 (1978).

49. Restatement (Third) of Property: Wills and Other Donative Transfers § 19.12(c) (Am. Law Inst. 2011).

statute? The question is whether the deceased nephew falls within the protected class under the statute (see page 358), and whether this should be determined in relation to the donor or the donee. The Restatement (Third) of Property takes the position that the statute applies "if the specified relationship exists with respect to either the donor or the donee of the power."[50]

b. Appointment in Further Trust

A recurring question is whether a donee may exercise a power of appointment to appoint in further trust or if instead the appointment must be made outright.

Brown v. Miller
2 So. 3d 321 (Fla. App. 2008)

EVANDER, J. This is an appeal from a partial summary judgment order invalidating a transfer of over seven million dollars from the Elinor Estes Miller Trust to the Thomas W. Miller, Jr., Trust ("Bill Miller Trust") and directing that such monies be held in constructive trust for the benefit of the Elinor Estes Miller Trust and its remainderman, Thomas W. Miller, III, ("Tom"). . . .

Thomas W. Miller, Jr. ("Bill") was the trustee and lifetime beneficiary of a trust established by his wife, Elinor Miller. Upon Elinor's death in 1999, her trust assets were distributed to designated charities and family members with the balance being divided into three separate sub-trusts, designated as Trust A-1, Trust A-2 and Trust B, with each serving a distinct purpose. This appeal relates solely to the Trust A-2 assets. The trust language critical to the resolution of this appeal provides:

V.

Administration of Trust "A"

2. With respect to Trust "A-1" and Trust "A-2", the Trustee shall pay quarterly or oftener, the entire net income derived from the trust estates to my husband, THOMAS W. MILLER, JR., so long as he shall live. In addition thereto, the Trustee shall pay to my husband, THOMAS W. MILLER, JR., such amounts from the principal of Trust "A-2" first and then from "A-1" after the exhaustion of "A-2", as it deems necessary or advisable to provide liberally for his maintenance, health, and support in his accustomed manner of living, taking into account all of his other income and means of support known to the Trustee. *The Trustee shall also pay to my husband such additional amounts of principal from Trust "A-2" as he may from time to time request.* . . .

3. Upon the death of my husband, THOMAS W. MILLER, JR., the Trustee shall pay over and distribute the then remaining balance of Trust "A-2", *if any,* to such person or persons, and in such manner, as he shall appoint by his last Will and Testament, which makes reference to said power of appointment, including in him the power to appoint to his estate. *Any portion of Trust "A-2" not effectively appointed by my husband, THOMAS W. MILLER, JR., shall continue to be held in trust for the lifetime of my son, THOMAS W. MILLER, III.* . . . (Emphasis added.)

---

50. Id. cmt. d.

> 2.   With respect to Trust "A-1" and Trust "A-2", the Trustee shall pay quarterly or oftener, the entire net income derived from the trust estates to my husband, THOMAS W. MILLER, JR., so long as he shall live. In addition thereto, the Trustee shall pay to my husband, THOMAS W. MILLER, JR., such amounts from the principal of Trust "A-2" first and then from "A-1" after the exhaustion of "A-2", as it deems necessary or advisable to provide liberally for his maintenance, health, and support in his accustomed manner of living, taking into account all of his other income and means of support known to the Trustee. The Trustee shall also pay to my husband such additional amounts of principal from Trust "A-2" as he may from time to time request. Upon the death of my husband, any undistributed and/or accrued income of Trust "A-1" and Trust "A-2" shall be distributed to my husband's estate, or to such other party (including any Trust created by my husband during his lifetime) as he may direct in a written statement filed with the Trustee.
>
> 3.   Upon the death of my husband, THOMAS W. MILLER, JR., the Trustee shall pay over and distribute the then remaining balance of Trust "A-2", if any, to such person or persons, and in such manner, as he shall appoint by his Last Will and Testament, which makes reference to said power of appointment, including in him the power to appoint to his estate. Any portion of Trust "A-2" not effectively appointed by my husband, THOMAS W. MILLER, JR., shall continue to be held in trust for the lifetime of my son, THOMAS W. MILLER, III, which shall be administered in accordance with Article VI.

The trust provisions at issue in *Brown*

On February 11, 2000, Bill executed a third codicil to his last will and testament. In this codicil, Bill purported to exercise his power of appointment by directing that, upon his death, the Trust A-2 balance be distributed to The Elinor and T.W. Miller, Jr. Foundation ("the Foundation").

Between the date of his wife's death and January 25, 2002, Bill, as trustee, transferred approximately $420,000 from Trust A-2 to himself and others. On January 25, 2002, Bill, as trustee, then transferred the remaining balance of the Trust A-2 assets (approximately seven million dollars) to the Bill Miller Trust.

Bill died in April 2004. His son, Tom, then brought the underlying action against his estate, the personal representatives of his estate, the trustees of the Bill Miller Trust, and the Foundation (collectively referred to as "Appellants") seeking, *inter alia,* to set aside the seven million dollar transfer to the Bill Miller Trust and to invalidate Bill's purported exercise of his power of appointment. Pursuant to the terms of his mother's trust, the seven million dollars would be held in trust for Tom's benefit if he prevailed on *both* these issues.

In granting Tom's motion for partial summary judgment, the trial court found that the transfer at issue was improper for three reasons: (1) it was contrary to the trust language limiting transfers to Elinor's husband; (2) it was contrary to the trust language limiting transfers from "time to time"; and (3) it violated Bill's duty to act in good faith to protect the interests of the Trust A-2 contingent remaindermen. We respectfully disagree with the trial court's conclusions. . . .

Tom argues that Elinor only authorized transfers from Trust A-2 to "my husband." Based on this argument, Tom contends that the transfer to the Bill Miller Trust was invalid because Elinor was "not married" to the Bill Miller Trust. Appellants respond that the Bill Miller Trust was a revocable trust and, accordingly, a conveyance to the Bill Miller Trust was equivalent to a transfer to Bill Miller. We agree with Appellants. It is undisputed that Bill maintained 100% control over the Bill Miller Trust assets. Furthermore, he had the right to end the trust at any time and thereby regain absolute ownership over the trust property. Florida Nat'l Bank of Palm Beach Co. v. Genova, 460 So. 2d 895, 897 (Fla. 1984). Thus, Bill had complete and unfettered access to the seven million dollars conveyed into his trust. . . . We believe that in authorizing transfers of Trust A-2 assets to her husband, Elinor clearly intended to permit transfers to an entity, such as a revocable trust, over which her husband retained complete control and the right to absolute ownership.

Tom next argues that the trust language "[t]he Trustee shall also pay to my husband such additional amounts of principal from Trust 'A-2' as he may from time to time request" prohibited Bill from depleting the trust in "one fell swoop." This argument is flawed for at least two reasons. First, the parties agree that Bill made transfers from Trust A-2, totaling $420,000, prior to the disputed seven million dollar transfer. Thus, Bill did, in fact, withdraw monies from Trust A-2 "from time to time." Second, we conclude that the "from time to time" language was not intended by Elinor to serve as a limitation on Bill's right to withdraw amounts of principal from Trust A-2. The trust document manifests a clear intent to permit Elinor's husband to withdraw any and all monies from Trust A-2. To accept Tom's argument would mean that it would have been improper for Bill to request payment of all of the Trust A-2 assets at one time, but proper if he had requested payment of all but $10. We are unwilling to assume that Elinor intended such an illogical result. . . .

Pursuant to terms of the trust agreement, Bill had the absolute right to withdraw all of the Trust A-2 assets. He cannot be found to have acted in bad faith by exercising that right. Conn. Bank & Trust Co. v. Lyman, 170 A.2d 130 (Conn. 1961).

Because we find that it was error for the trial court to set aside the seven million dollar transfer, we find it unnecessary to determine whether Bill properly exercised his power of appointment. The trial court's order granting Tom's motion for partial summary judgment is hereby reversed.

Reversed and remanded.

NOTES

1. *The Power of Withdrawal.*   Elinor Miller gave her husband the power to withdraw "such . . . amounts of principal . . . as he may from time to time request." Is this a general or a nongeneral power of appointment? Why would she give him such a power?

2. *Appointment in Further Trust.*   In almost all jurisdictions, a donee of a *general power* of appointment can appoint outright or in further trust, as under UPAA § 305(a)

and the Restatement (Third) of Property.[51] Because the donee could first appoint to herself or to her estate, and then by a second instrument or a second clause in her will appoint in further trust, it would make little sense to forbid the donee to appoint in further trust when she uses only a single instrument or a single clause.

For a *nongeneral power*, under traditional law the donee was not allowed to appoint in further trust unless the governing instrument expressly permitted appointment in trust, as recognized by Loring v. Karri-Davies, 357 N.E.2d 11 (Mass. 1976). Experience has shown, however, that this presumption does not accord with the intent of most donors. Professionally drafted trusts that create a nongeneral power of appointment typically permit appointment in further trust. In modern law, therefore, the default has been reversed, as held prospectively in *Loring* and as provided by UPAA § 305(c)(1) and the Restatement (Third) of Property.[52] Courts nowadays tend to say that the presumption is that the donee of a nongeneral power may appoint in further trust for the benefit of an object.[53]

3. Trust Decanting.   As we have seen, under traditional law a trustee who has discretion to distribute trust property has a fiduciary power of appointment (see page 812). On this view, a *trust decanting*, discussed in Chapter 10 at page 742, involves the exercise of a trustee's power of appointment to appoint the trust property in further trust. In Phipps v. Palm Beach Trust Company, 196 So. 299 (Fla. 1940), page 742, widely credited as the first trust decanting case, the court applied the rule of construction that a power of appointment may be exercised in further trust unless the donor provides otherwise.[54] With the rise of the trust decanting statutes (see page 744), however, decanting has broken off from its roots in the law of powers of appointment to form its own branch of contemporary trust law.

c. Creation of a New Power of Appointment

Another recurring question is whether a donee may create a new power of appointment. In almost all jurisdictions, a donee of a *general power* of appointment can do so. The reasoning is similar to that for appointment in further trust. Because the donee could first appoint to herself or to her estate and then create a power of appointment over the appointed property, it would make little sense to forbid creation of a new power of appointment in the exercise of the initial power.

But what about a *nongeneral power*? Suppose *T* gives a power to *A* to appoint among *A*'s descendants. Can *A* exercise the power by creating in his daughter *B* a life estate plus a nongeneral power to appoint among *B*'s descendants (who are, of course, objects of the original power)? Because *A* could appoint outright to *B*, it seems sensible to

---

51. *See* id. § 19.13.

52. *See* id. § 19.14 cmt. e.

53. *See, e.g.*, In re Chervitz Trust, 198 S.W.3d 658 (Mo. App. 2006); In re Estate of Reisman, 702 N.W.2d 658 (Mich. App. 2005).

54. *See also* Restatement (Third) of Property: Wills and Other Donative Transfers § 19.14 (Am. Law Inst. 2011) ("Subject to fiduciary standards and the terms of the power, a trustee or other fiduciary can exercise a fiduciary distributive power such as a power of invasion to create another trust.").

permit *A* to appoint to *B* something less than absolute ownership. Yet some older cases hold to the contrary.[55]

Following the standard drafting practice of allowing a donee of a nongeneral power to create a new power of appointment, UPAA § 305(c)(2)-(3) and the Restatement (Third) of Property permit a donee of a nongeneral power to create a general power in an object of the original power or a nongeneral power in any person to appoint to an object of the original power.[56]

d. Exclusive and Nonexclusive Powers

A nongeneral power may be exclusive or nonexclusive. If it is *exclusive*, the donee can appoint all of the property to one or more objects, excluding the other objects. If the power is *nonexclusive*, the donee must appoint some amount to each object. Whether a power is exclusive or nonexclusive depends on the intention of the donor as revealed by the governing instrument. Language such as "to any" or "to such of" is usually held to create an exclusive power. Language such as "to all and every one" or "to each and every one" is usually held to create a nonexclusive power. Thus:

> *Case 7.* *T* bequeaths a fund to *X* in trust for *A* for life, remainder as *A* shall appoint by will "to each and every one" of *A*'s children. *A* has three children, *B*, *C*, and *D*. The power is nonexclusive. *A* must give some amount to each of *B*, *C*, and *D* if *A* exercises the power.

> *Case 8.* *T* bequeaths a fund to *X* in trust for *A* for life, remainder as *A* shall appoint by will to "any one or more" of *A*'s children. *A* has three children, *B*, *C*, and *D*. The power is exclusive, as in In re Estate of Zucker, 122 A.3d 1112 (Pa. Super. 2015). *A* can appoint all the property to *C*.

If the donor's intent cannot be determined, whether a power is exclusive or nonexclusive will turn on the presumption in the applicable jurisdiction. UPAA § 203(2) and the Restatement (Third) of Property take the position that a power of appointment is presumptively exclusive, though they change the vocabulary and speak of *exclusionary* and *nonexclusionary* powers.[57]

How much must the donee of a nonexclusive power give each object? Could the donee in Case 7 appoint $1 each to *B* and *C* and the rest to her favored child *D*? Under the *illusory appointment* rule, each object of a nonexclusive power must receive a "reasonable benefit."[58] In Barrett's Executor v. Barrett, 179 S.W. 396 (Ky. 1915), the court upheld a finding below that three appointments of $1,000 each were illusory. The fourth appointee had been given the remaining $147,000. We are aware of no other reported decision in which an American appellate court upheld a finding of an illusory appointment.

---

55. *See* 5 American Law of Property § 23.49 (A. James Casner ed. 1952).
56. *See* Restatement (Third) of Property: Wills and Other Donative Transfers § 19.14 cmt. g (Am. Law Inst. 2011).
57. *See* id. § 17.5.
58. *See* id. cmt. j.

e. Salvage Doctrines: Allocation and Capture

When a donee intends to exercise a power of appointment, but the exercise is ineffective for some reason, it may be possible to carry out the donee's intent through the doctrines of *allocation* or *capture*.

(1) Allocation

If a donee disposes of appointive property and her own property under a common dispositive instrument, under the doctrine of *allocation* the blended property is allocated to the various interests in the manner that best carries out the donee's intent. A typical case involves an ineffective appointment to a nonobject of a power. Thus:

> *Case 9.* A holds a nongeneral testamentary power created by her father to appoint trust property among *A*'s descendants. The trust property is worth $100,000. *A* also owns outright $350,000. *A*'s will provides:
>
>> I give all my property, including any property over which I have a power of appointment under the will of my father, as follows: (1) I give $100,000 to my daughter-in-law, *B*, widow of my deceased son, *S*, and (2) I give all the rest to my daughter, *D*.
>
> None of the trust property can be allocated to *B*, because she is not an object of the power. *A*'s intent can still be carried out, however, by allocating to *B* $100,000 of *A*'s property and to *D* the trust property plus the other $250,000 of *A*'s property.

If *A* had owned assets of only $50,000, *B* would receive only $50,000. To satisfy completely an otherwise ineffective appointment by way of allocation, the donee must have property of her own sufficient to substitute for the appointive property. In a case in which a court allocates assets, the donee could have provided for the same allocation. In applying the allocation doctrine, the court does that which it thinks the donee would have directed if the donee (or the donee's lawyer) had been aware of the problem. The doctrine is a rule of construction.

Suppose in Case 9 there had been no blending — that is, suppose *A* had tried to appoint the trust property to *B* and to give her own property to *D*. Under traditional law, if *A* did not blend the property, the appointment would fail, and none of *A*'s own property could be allocated to *B*. Under UPAA § 308 and the Restatement (Third) of Property, the gifts could still be saved by allocation. Under those authorities, the doctrine may be applied even without a blending.[59]

(2) Capture

The doctrine of *capture* applies if a donee of a general power "manifests an intent to assume control of the appointive property for all purposes and not merely for the limited purpose of giving effect to the expressed appointment."[60] The theory is that, because the donee could appoint to her estate, the appointive property should pass to the donee's estate if the donee would prefer that in the event of an ineffective appoint-

---

59. *See* id. § 19.19.
60. Restatement (Second) of Property: Donative Transfers § 23.2 (Am. Law Inst. 1986).

ment. The doctrine thus applies only to general powers and only if an attempted exercise of such a power is ineffective or incomplete.

The intent of the donee to assume control of the appointive property is typically manifested by a provision in the donee's will that blends the owned property of the donee with the appointive property. As with allocation, the requisite blending can occur in a residuary clause disposing of both the appointive property and the donee's own assets or in an introductory clause stating that the donee intends the appointive property to be treated as her own property. Thus:

> *Case 10.* *A* is the donee of a general power under the will of *X*. *A*'s will provides:
>
> > I give all my property and any property over which I have a power of appointment under the will of *X* as follows: (1) $10,000 to my friend *B* [who predeceases *A*, with no antilapse statute applicable], and (2) all the rest to *C*.
>
> *A* has captured the appointive property by blending it with her own. *C* takes everything, including the appointive property.

On the theory that a valid gift-in-default clause is more likely to represent the donor's intent than capture, UPAA § 309 and the Restatement (Third) of Property modify the doctrine of capture as follows. If the donee of a general power does not effectively exercise the power, the appointive property passes to the takers in default of appointment under the donor's governing instrument. If there is no such provision, or if the provision is ineffective, the appointive property passes to the donee or the donee's estate.[61]

4. Disclaimer, Release, and Contract

A donee may *disclaim* a power of appointment in whole or in part, as under UPAA § 401. If a donee disclaims a power in accordance with the applicable disclaimer statute (see Chapter 2 at page 135), the donee is treated as never having acquired the power in the first place.[62] A disclaimer is therefore to be distinguished from a *release*. A donee who has acquired a power may subsequently release it, causing a lapse of the power to the extent of the release. A release may be in whole or in part, as under UPAA § 402, and in such a manner that reduces or limits the objects, unless the donor intended the power not to be releasable.[63]

A related issue is whether a donee may enter into an enforceable *contract* to exercise a power of appointment. If the power is presently exercisable and the promised appointee is an object of the power, the contract is enforceable, as under UPAA § 405. Because the donee has the authority to make the promised appointment currently, there is no reason not to allow the donee to make an enforceable contract to do so.[64] If, however, the power is not presently exercisable or the promised appointee is not an object of the

---

61. *See* Restatement (Third) of Property: Wills and Other Donative Transfers § 19.21 (Am. Law Inst. 2011).
62. *See* id. § 20.4.
63. *See* id. §§ 20.1-20.2.
64. *See* id. §§ 21.1 cmt. a, 21.2 cmt. a.

power, the contract is not enforceable. Because the donee does not have the authority to make the promised appointment currently, he cannot bind himself to do so by contract, as this would be contrary to the donor's intent. The promisee cannot obtain damages or specific performance, though she may be entitled to restitution to prevent the donee's unjust enrichment.

The rationale for not permitting an enforceable contract to exercise a power that is not presently exercisable is perhaps clearest in the case of a testamentary power. The donor of a testamentary power usually intends to protect the donee from an improvident exercise of the power during life. That the power is testamentary ensures that the donee is free to change his mind up until the moment of death. In Hood v. Haden, 82 Va. 588 (1886), the court put the point thus:

> It doubtless occurred to the testator that by restraining a disposition of his property except by will, which is in its nature revocable, [his widow] would, to the end of her life, retain the influence over, and secure the respect of, the several objects of his bounty, which he intended her to have—a result less likely to be accomplished if power were given her to dispose of the property by deed or other irrevocable act to take effect in her lifetime.

Although a contract to exercise a testamentary power is not enforceable, a similar result can be obtained by releasing the power if the takers in default are the persons in whose favor the donee wants to promise to exercise the power. Thus:

> *Case 11.* *T* devises property in trust for *A* for life, then as *A* by will appoints, and in default of appointment, to *A*'s children equally. By releasing her power of appointment, *A* could effectively grant to her children an indefeasibly vested remainder. Although *A* could not make an enforceable contract to appoint to her children, she achieved her objective by a release.[65]

C. FAILURE TO EXERCISE A POWER OF APPOINTMENT

1. General Power

Under traditional law, if the donee of a *general power* of appointment fails to exercise it, the appointive property passes to the takers in default of appointment. If there is no valid gift in default of appointment, the property reverts to the donor or the donor's estate.

UPAA § 310, excerpted below, and the Restatement (Third) of Property modify this rule so that if there is no valid gift in default of appointment, the property reverts to the donor or the donor's estate only if the donee released or otherwise expressly refrained from exercising the power.[66] In effect, under the UPAA and Restatement every general power of appointment comes with an implied gift in default of appointment to the donee or the donee's estate.

---

65. *See* id. § 20.3 cmt. d.
66. *See* id. § 19.22.

Uniform Powers of Appointment Act (Unif. Law Comm'n 2013)

§ 310. Disposition of Unappointed Property Under Released or Unexercised General Power

To the extent a powerholder releases or fails to exercise a general power of appointment other than a power to withdraw property from, revoke, or amend a trust:

(1) the gift-in-default clause controls the disposition of the unappointed property; or

(2) if there is no gift-in-default clause or to the extent the clause is ineffective:

(A) except as otherwise provided in subparagraph (B), the unappointed property passes to:

(i) the powerholder if the powerholder is a permissible appointee and living; or

(ii) if the powerholder is an impermissible appointee or deceased, the powerholder's estate if the estate is a permissible appointee; or

(B) to the extent the powerholder released the power, or if there is no taker under subparagraph (A), the unappointed property passes under a reversionary interest to the donor or the donor's transferee or successor in interest.

2. Nongeneral Power

If the donee of a *nongeneral power* of appointment fails to exercise it and there is no gift in default of appointment, the appointive property may—if the objects are a defined and limited class—pass to the objects of the power. The theory is one of an *implied gift in default of appointment* to the objects. This theory is adopted by UPAA § 311, excerpted below, and the Restatement (Third) of Property.[67] In the absence of an implied gift in default of appointment, the property reverts to the donor or the donor's estate.

Uniform Powers of Appointment Act (Unif. Law Comm'n 2013)

§ 311. Disposition of Unappointed Property Under Released or Unexercised Nongeneral Powers

To the extent a powerholder releases, ineffectively exercises, or fails to exercise a nongeneral power of appointment:

(1) the gift-in-default clause controls the disposition of the unappointed property; or

(2) if there is no gift-in-default clause or to the extent the clause is ineffective, the unappointed property:

---

67. *See* id. § 19.23.

(A) passes to the permissible appointees if:

(i) the permissible appointees are defined and limited; and

(ii) the terms of the instrument creating the power do not manifest a contrary intent; or

(B) if there is no taker under subparagraph (A), passes under a reversionary interest to the donor or the donor's transferee or successor in interest.

NOTE

Implied Gift in Default of Appointment or Imperative Power?   In some states, courts reach the same result as an implied gift in default by saying that the donee had an *imperative power*. A nongeneral power is imperative if the creating instrument manifests an intent that the objects be benefited even if the donee fails to exercise the power. If the donee of an imperative power fails to exercise it, the court will divide the property equally among the objects.[68]

---

68. *See, e.g.,* Cal. Prob. Code §§ 613, 671 (2016); N.Y. Est. Powers & Trusts Law §§ 10-3.4, 10-6.8 (2016).

CHAPTER 13

TRUSTS: CONSTRUCTION AND FUTURE INTERESTS

> The structure of estates, which was developed over a period of about
> seven centuries, was and is a great achievement. . . . At its heart
> is the abstract concept that present ownership is capable of being
> fragmented in terms of time and in terms of beneficial enjoyment.
> Both types of fragmentation are fundamental to the trust,
> a central device in modern estate planning.
>
> LAWRENCE W. WAGGONER
> 85 Harv. L. Rev. 729, 729 (1972)

THE ANGLO-AMERICAN SYSTEM of *estates and future interests* provides a donor with wide latitude in structuring a transfer of property to be shared by multiple beneficiaries across time. Several generations ago, law schools commonly required a course on the subject. In those days, most future interests were given outright, that is, they were *legal*. Today, future interests almost always arise in trusts, that is, they are *equitable* (see Chapter 6 at page 396).

Consider a simple example: Suppose *O* wants to give certain property to his children and then down the generations. In the past, *O* might have given a life estate in the property to his children, a remainder for life to his grandchildren, and so on, for as long as the Rule Against Perpetuities would allow (see Chapter 14). Today, this transfer is almost always made in trust. Lawyers who deal with trusts must therefore be familiar with the law of future interests, including common constructional and other problems with their use.

The core concept underlying the law of future interests is that a *future interest* is itself a form of property. The owner of a future interest may transfer *it*. Creditors may seize *it*. At the owner's death, *it* passes in probate or by will substitute. What distinguishes a future interest from a *present interest* is that the owner of a future interest does not have a current right to *possession or enjoyment* of the property.

In this chapter, we examine the law of future interests as it relates to the construction of trusts. We consider how to tailor future interests to achieve a settlor's intent and how to avoid intent-defeating technical rules and recurring problems caused by ambiguous language. Although the law of future interests provides tremendous flexibility in structuring a donative transfer, some of the rules in this area are relics of medieval feudalism that can wreck a dispositive plan if the drafter does not take care to avoid them.

The chapter is organized as follows. In Section A, we consider the classification of future interests, both in the transferor (the settlor) and in the transferee (the beneficiary), and we take notice of recent proposals for reform. In Section B, we consider the rules for construing trust instruments and some of the ambiguities lying hidden in common provisions in wills and trusts.

A. FUTURE INTERESTS

1. Classification

All future interests fall into one of two categories: (1) *reversionary* interests retained by the *transferor*, and (2) *nonreversionary* interests given to the *transferee*. There are three kinds of reversionary interests: (a) reversion, (b) possibility of reverter, and (c) right of entry for condition broken (also known as power of termination). There are three kinds of nonreversionary interests: (a) vested remainder, (b) contingent remainder, and (c) executory interest.

Figure 13.1

Future Interests at Common Law

Retained by the Transferor	Given to the Transferee
Reversion	Vested remainder
Possibility of reverter	Contingent remainder
Right of entry	Executory interest

These six interests are called *future interests* because a person who holds one of them is not entitled to current *possession or enjoyment* of the property. Instead, the person may become entitled to possession or enjoyment in the future. A person who is entitled currently to possession or enjoyment is said to have a *present interest*.

Although the holder of a future interest is not yet entitled to possession or enjoyment, she does have present rights and liabilities. Suppose *O* conveys Blackacre "to *A* for life, then to *B*." *B* has a remainder, which *B* can sell or give away. *B*'s creditors can reach it. *B* can enjoin *A* from committing waste or doing other acts that impair the value of *B*'s right to future possession. If *B* dies before *A*, the value of *B*'s remainder passes to *B*'s heirs or devisees and is subject to federal estate taxation. Nonetheless, because *B* does not have the right to present possession of Blackacre, we call *B*'s interest a future interest.

Any estate that may be created in possession, such as a fee simple or a life estate, may also be created as a future interest. *O* may convey "to *A* for life, then to *B* for life, then to *C*." *B* has a remainder for life. *C* has a remainder in fee simple. Each has a future interest in the property. By saying that *B* has a remainder for life, we mean that when *B*'s interest becomes possessory, it will be a life estate. And by saying that *C* has a remainder in fee simple, we mean that when *C*'s interest becomes possessory, it will be a fee simple.

The mandatory categorization of future interests into the six specified categories, and many of the corresponding technical rules of future interests law, are vestigial relics of medieval feudalism (see page 29). Yet these ancient classifications, and their artificial and needless complexity, endure on bar exams and, every once in a while, in real life as well. Let us consider each category more closely.

2. Future Interests in the Transferor

The common law recognizes three types of reversionary interests, that is, future interests that may be retained by the transferor: (a) reversion, (b) possibility of reverter, and (c) right of entry for condition broken (also known as a power of termination).

a. Reversion

The most important of the reversionary interests is the *reversion*:

> A reversion is the interest remaining in the grantor, or in the successor in interest of a testator, who transfers a vested estate of a lesser quantum than that of the vested estate which he has.[1]

A reversion is never created alone; it is a retained interest that arises by operation of law when the transferor has conveyed a lesser estate than the transferor had. If the transfer is inter vivos, the reversion is retained by the grantor. If the transfer is by will, the reversion is retained in the testator's successors, who are substituted by law for the dead transferor.

By definition, a reversion cannot be created in a transferee. A future interest created in a transferee must be a remainder or an executory interest. Thus:

> *Case 1.* *T*'s will devises Blackacre "to *A* for life, then to *B*." *A* has a life estate. *B* has a vested remainder, not a reversion, because *B* is a transferee. We take up remainders below.

Because a reversion is held by a presently ascertained person, and because it is not subject to a condition precedent other than the termination of the preceding estates, all reversions are *vested* interests. This does not mean, however, that all reversions will become possessory. A reversion following a contingent remainder, for instance, might not become possessory. Thus:

> *Case 2.* *O* conveys property in trust "to *A* for life, then to *A*'s children who survive *A*." *A*'s children have a contingent remainder. *O* has a vested reversion, which will be divested if *A* leaves surviving children.

---

1. 1 American Law of Property § 4.16 (A. James Casner ed. 1952).

The reversion in Case 2 may not become possessory, but it is vested in interest. At common law, whether a future interest is vested or not is determined by arbitrary rules that we take up below, not by the certainty or uncertainty of future possession.

b. Possibility of Reverter

A *possibility of reverter* is the future interest that remains in a grantor who conveys a fee simple determinable, that is, a fee estate that will terminate automatically upon the happening of a specified event. Thus:

> *Case 3.* O conveys land "to the School Board so long as the land is used for a school." The School Board has a fee simple determinable. O has a possibility of reverter, which will become possessory automatically upon the expiration of the determinable fee.

c. Right of Entry

A *right of entry* for condition broken, also known as a *power of termination*, is the future interest that is retained by a grantor who conveys a fee simple subject to a condition subsequent. Thus:

> *Case 4.* O conveys land "to the School Board, but if it ceases to be used for school purposes, O has a right to reenter." The School Board has a fee simple subject to condition subsequent; O has a right of entry, which O has the option to exercise or not.

3. Future Interests in Transferees

The common law recognizes three types of nonreversionary interests, that is, future interests in transferees: (a) vested remainders, (b) contingent remainders, and (c) executory interests.

a. Remainders

A *remainder* is a future interest in a transferee that will become possessory, if at all, upon the natural expiration of all prior interests simultaneously created. A remainderperson waits patiently until the preceding estates expire naturally, and then, if the remainder is not contingent, takes possession or enjoyment. A future interest may be a remainder even if it is not certain to become possessory upon the termination of the preceding estates.

(1) Vested and Contingent Remainders

Remainders are either vested or contingent. A remainder is *vested* if it: (a) is given to a presently ascertained person, and (b) is not subject to a condition precedent other than the termination of the preceding estates. A remainder is *contingent* if it: (a) is not given to a presently ascertained person, or (b) is subject to a condition precedent in addition to the termination of the preceding estates. Thus:

Case 5. *O* conveys a fund in trust "for *A* for life, then to *B*." *B* has a remainder that will become possessory upon the expiration of *A*'s life estate. Because *B*'s remainder is certain to become possessory, it is an *indefeasibly vested remainder*. If *B* dies during *A*'s life, *B*'s remainder, like *B*'s other property, passes under *B*'s will or by intestacy.

Case 6. *O* conveys a fund in trust "for *A* for life, then to *B* if *B* survives *A*." *B* has a remainder, for it is possible (but not certain) that *B* will take the property on *A*'s death. If *B* is then alive, *B* will take. If *B* is then dead, the property will revert to *O*. Because *B*'s remainder is subject to a condition precedent (surviving *A*), we call it a *contingent remainder*.

(2) Vested Subject to Partial Divestment

Suppose a remainder is given to a class of persons, some but not all of whom are ascertained, and the remainder is not subject to a condition precedent. This remainder is vested in the present members of the class *subject to partial divestment* or *subject to open* by additional persons coming into the class. Thus:

Case 7. *O* conveys a fund in trust "for *A* for life, then to *A*'s children." If *A* has no children at the time of the conveyance, the remainder is contingent because the takers are unascertained. If *A* has a child, *B*, then *B* will have a *vested remainder subject to partial divestment* or *subject to open*. If *A* has any more children, *B*'s share will be diminished. *B*'s share will depend on how many children, if any, are subsequently born to *A*. If *A* has another child, *C*, *B* will be partially divested, that is, divested of *C*'s share. The class gift will remain subject to partial divestment (or open) until *A*'s death.

A class gift that is subject to a condition precedent is contingent, not vested subject to partial divestment. In Case 7, if the conveyance had been "to *A* for life, then to *A*'s children who survive *A*," the remainder would be contingent even though *A* had one or more children alive. If a remainder is given to a class of persons described as "the heirs of *A* [a living person]," the takers are not ascertained until *A*'s death, and therefore the remainder is contingent.

NOTES

1. A Partial Divestment Problem.   *O* conveys a fund in trust "for *A* for life, and on *A*'s death to *A*'s children in equal shares." At the time of the conveyance, *A* has two children, *B* and *C*. Two years later, *D* is born to *A*. After another year has passed, *B* dies intestate and then *A* dies. To whom should the trust assets be distributed? *See* In re DiBiasio, 705 A.2d 972 (R.I. 1998); Coleman v. Coleman, 500 S.E.2d 507 (Va. 1998).

2. "Heirs" as a Contingency.   In 2010, *O* conveys property in trust "for *A* for life, and on *A*'s death to the heirs of *B*." At the time of the conveyance, *A* and *B* are both alive and *B* has two children, *C* and *D*. If *B* were to die intestate immediately after the conveyance, *C* and *D* would be *B*'s heirs. In 2011, *D* dies, leaving a minor son, *E*, and a will devising all his property to his wife, *W*. In 2013, *B* dies, leaving a will that devises

B's entire estate to the American Red Cross. *A* dies in 2015, survived by *C*, *E*, and *W*. To whom should the trust assets be distributed? What result if *B* had died before *D*?

3. The Restatement (Third) of Property. Under the simplified system of estates and future interests of the Restatement (Third) of Property (see page 854), the future interest of a member of a class that is open to new entrants is labeled "subject to open" and is classified as contingent or vested depending on whether the interest is certain to take effect in possession or enjoyment.[2]

(3) Vested Subject to Divestment or Contingent?

Let us now consider more closely the difference between a *vested remainder subject to divestment* and a *contingent remainder*. A vested remainder subject to divestment is a remainder given to an ascertained person, with a proviso that the remainder will be divested if a *condition subsequent* happens. It is not subject to a *condition precedent*.

Whether a remainder is contingent or vested subject to divestment depends on the language of the instrument. And, with few exceptions, it depends on nothing more than *the sequence of words in the instrument*. If a condition is incorporated into the gift of the remainder—if it comes, so to speak, between the commas setting apart the remainder—it is a condition precedent. But if the remainder is given, and then words of divestment are added, the condition is subsequent. Thus:

> *Case 8. O* conveys a fund in trust "for *A* for life, then to *B* if *B* survives *A*, and if *B* does not survive *A*, to *C*." *B* has a contingent remainder because the words "if *B* survives *A*" are incorporated into *B*'s gift; they come between the commas. (Of course, if the commas were not there, you would have to decide where the court would mentally insert the commas. The essential idea is that the words "if *B* survives *A*" are part of the gift to *B*.) *C* has an alternative contingent remainder because *C*'s interest is contingent on *B* not surviving *A*.

> *Case 9. O* conveys a fund in trust "for *A* for life, then to *B*, but if *B* does not survive *A*, to *C*." *B* has a vested remainder subject to divestment by *C*'s executory interest. There are no words of condition between the commas setting off *B*'s gift. There is a condition subsequent to *B*'s gift introducing the divesting gift over to *C*.

In sum: You must look carefully at the exact language used and classify the interests in sequence. Although *O*'s intent may be identical in both cases, that intent has been expressed in different ways, resulting in the creation of different interests.

NOTES

1. Remainder in Default of Appointment. A power of appointment is viewed as a condition subsequent on the remainder in default of appointment (we consider powers of appointment in Chapter 12). If the donee exercises the power, the remainderperson is divested of his interest.

---

2. Restatement (Third) of Property: Wills and Other Donative Transfers §§ 25.3-25.4 (Am. Law Inst. 2011).

Suppose that *T* devises property in trust "for *A* for life, then to such persons as *A* by will appoints, and if *A* fails to make an appointment, to *A*'s children." Although this language would seem to create a condition precedent, the power is instead treated as a condition subsequent. Thus, this devise is read as if it were "for *A* for life, then to *A*'s children, but if *A* otherwise appoints by will, to such appointees." If *A* has one child, *B*, then *B* has a *vested remainder subject to partial divestment* by the birth of other children and *subject to complete divestment* by *A*'s exercise of the power of appointment. If *A* has no children, the remainder is *contingent* because no taker is ascertained.

2. The Restatement (Third) of Property. The Restatement (Third) of Property abolishes the distinction between contingent and vested subject to divestment. It provides that an interest is contingent or vested depending on whether the interest is certain to take effect in possession or enjoyment. "It is irrelevant whether the interest is subject to a condition that is stated in precedent or subsequent form."[3]

(4) Remainders and Reversions

Let us consider again how reversions interact with remainders. To determine when a transferor has a reversion, you can save yourself much trouble by applying this simple Rule of Reversions:

> *O*, owner of a fee simple, will not have a reversion in fee simple if *O* transfers a possessory fee simple or a vested remainder in fee simple. In all other cases in which *O* transfers a present possessory interest, *O* will have a reversion in fee simple.

If *O* transfers a life estate, not followed by a vested remainder in fee, *O* has a reversion. If *O* transfers a life estate followed by 100 contingent remainders in fee, but no vested remainder in fee, *O* retains a reversion.

NOTES

1. A Remainder or Reversion Problem. *O* conveys property in trust "for *A* for life, then to *B*, but if *B* dies before *A* without descendants surviving *B*, then to *C* at *A*'s death." Does *O* have a reversion? Suppose that *B* dies leaving a surviving child, *D*, and *B*'s will devises all her property to her husband, *H*. Then *D* dies. Then *A* dies. To whom should the trust property be distributed? *Cf.* Jones v. Hill, 594 S.E.2d 913 (Va. 2004).

2. Another Remainder or Reversion Problem. *O* conveys Blackacre in trust "for *A* for life, then to *B* or her heirs." Subsequently *B* dies, devising her property to *C*. *B*'s heir is *D*. On *A*'s death, who owns Blackacre? *See* Rowett v. McFarland, 394 N.W.2d 298 (S.D. 1986).

b. Executory Interests

A remainder never divests a preceding estate prior to its natural expiration; that is the job of an *executory interest*. An executory interest that may divest the *transferor* in the future if a specified event happens is called a *springing* executory interest. If the event

---

3. Id. § 25.3 cmt. f.

happens, the property will spring from the transferor to the transferee. An ancient example is a marriage arrangement in which the father of the bride conveyed land "to my daughter *A* when she marries *B*." In contemporary practice, springing executory interests are rare.

An executory interest that may divest another *transferee* if a specified event happens is called a *shifting* executory interest. If the event happens, the executory interest will shift the property from one transferee to another. In Case 9 above, *C* has a shifting executory interest. Executory interests today are almost always shifting and in one of two basic forms:

> Case 10. *Executory Interest Divesting a Possessory Fee Simple upon an Uncertain Event.* *O* conveys Blackacre "to *A*, but if *A* dies without descendants surviving her, to *B*." *A* has a fee simple subject to divestment by *B*'s shifting executory interest. *B*'s executory interest is subject to a condition precedent (*A*'s death without surviving descendants) and is not certain to become possessory.

> Case 11. *Executory Interest Divesting a Vested Remainder.* *O* conveys a fund in trust "for *A* for life, and on *A*'s death to *B*, but if *B* is not then living, to *C*." *B* has a vested remainder in fee simple subject to divestment by *C*'s shifting executory interest. *C*'s executory interest is subject to a condition precedent (*B* dying before *A* dies) and is not certain to become possessory.

The executory interests in Cases 10 and 11 are analogous to contingent remainders, but they are called executory interests because they are divesting interests. In contemporary law, there is no other difference between a contingent remainder and an executory interest.

NOTES

1. Four Review Problems.   Consider the following problems:

a. *O* conveys a fund in trust "for *A* for life, then to *A*'s children, but if at *A*'s death *A* is not survived by any children, then to *B*." At the time the trust is created, *A* has no children. What interests are created?

b. Consider the same facts as in (a). A few years later, two children, *C* and *D*, are born to *A*. *C* dies, devising his property to his wife, *W*. *A* dies. To whom should the trust assets be distributed?

c. *O* conveys a fund in trust "for *A* for life, then to such of *A*'s children as survive *A*, but if none of *A*'s children survive *A*, then to *B*." At the time the trust is created, *A* has two children, *C* and *D*. Then *C* dies, devising his property to his wife, *W*. *A* dies. To whom should the trust assets be distributed?

d. *T* devises Blackacre to *A* for life, then to *A*'s children who survive her. The residuary clause of *T*'s will devises to *B* "all the rest and residue of my property, including any of the foregoing gifts in this will that for any reason fail to take effect." What is the state of the title to Blackacre?

2. Executory Interests Versus Contingent Remainders.   The repudiation in modern law of the doctrine of destructibility of contingent remainders (see page 855) and the rule in Shelley's Case (see page 881) has rendered irrelevant the distinction between a contingent remainder and an executory interest. More than 50 years ago, Professor Jesse Dukeminier urged that the distinction be abolished:

> A few years ago James Thurber spun a whimsical yarn about a Duke who "limped because his legs were of different lengths. The right one had outgrown the left because, when he was young, he had spent his mornings place kicking pups and punting kittens. He would say to a suitor, 'What is the difference in the length of my legs?' and if the youth replied, 'Why, one is shorter than the other,' the Duke would run him through with the sword he carried in his swordcane and feed him to the geese. The suitor was supposed to say, 'Why, one is longer than the other.' Many a prince had been run through for naming the wrong difference."
>
> Many a student in future interests has been run through by his instructor for an error of equal magnitude: calling a contingent remainder an executory interest (or vice versa). We who pretend to some knowledge of future interests are wont to stress the importance of precise labelling, of carefully classifying the interest by the rigid and artificial criteria of the common law. But if the legal consequences which flow from the label "executory interest" are the same as the consequences which flow from "contingent remainder" then the student is likely to believe he is being impaled by a crotchet. Either label should do. And would, were it not for our professional love of being able to speak well the language of the dead.[4]

The American Law Institute has since agreed, as the Restatement (Third) of Property abolishes the distinction.[5] Might this be a harbinger of coming reform of estates and future interests?

4. Future Interests Reform

Not long after the publication of the Restatement (First) of Property in 1936, which preserved the ancient common law of estates and future interests, Professor Lewis M. Simes, a widely respected authority on the subject at the University of Michigan, predicted that the states were "on the eve of a movement looking toward the improvement and simplification of the law of Future Interests by legislation." Simes reasoned that the new Restatement expressed the "obscure and complicated rules" in such "clear and accurate fashion" that legislation "correcting the difficulties which have been discovered" surely would follow.[6] But it did not.

Professor Lewis M. Simes

---

4. Jesse Dukeminier, Contingent Remainders and Executory Interests: A Requiem for the Distinction, 43 Minn. L. Rev. 13, 13-14 (1958) (quoting James Thurber, The 13 Clocks 20 (1950)).

5. *See* Restatement (Third) of Property: Wills and Other Donative Transfers § 25.2 cmt. c (Am. Law Inst. 2011).

6. Lewis M. Simes, Fifty Years of Future Interests, 50 Harv. L. Rev. 749, 783 (1937).

In 1972, Lawrence W. Waggoner—who would later become the Lewis M. Simes Professor of Law at the University of Michigan—launched a renewed attack on the law of estates and future interests. He identified four core failings:

> The first is its extraordinary complexity, which has proved a barrier to comprehension. . . . This complexity is unnecessary, for the abstract concept of fragmentation of ownership does not require such elaborateness; the same degree of flexibility . . . can be sustained under a vastly simplified system.
>
> Another defect of the present structure is that a considerable proportion of the artificiality with which the law of future interests is riddled is directly attributable to the structure of estates itself. The . . . law frequently makes very little sense. Decisions often turn on the form in which a disposition is stated rather than on its substance. Different legal consequences flow from verbal differences in referring to the same time, the same person, or the same event.
>
> This artificiality leads to a further flaw in the present structure: easy circumvention. . . . Whenever legal consequences turn on differences of form, certain results can be achieved by skillful wording of a disposition or by other maneuvers without otherwise affecting the substance of the transaction. Many rules of law in this area, therefore, serve only to trap those unsophisticated in the available ways of manipulation.
>
> Finally, out of the complexity and artificiality of the present structure has arisen a phenomenon that may be called the classificatory mystique—the notion that classifying the interests created in a transfer solves most problems. The volumes are replete with opinions which discuss at length the distinctions between various types of interests. Often these opinions string together definitions which were meaningless to begin with and are, to boot, irrelevant to the case at hand; lost in verbal mazes, they never come to grips with the real issues.[7]

Today a new generation of scholars has taken aim at the law of future interests,[8] and so has the American Law Institute. The Restatement (Third) of Property, for which Waggoner was the reporter, jettisons the feudal relics of the old law in favor of a rationalized system with intuitive nomenclature reflecting substance rather than form. The executory interest is collapsed into the term remainder;[9] the possibility of reverter and the right of entry are collapsed into the term reversion;[10] and a remainder or a reversion—the only kinds of future interests under the new Restatement—is contingent or vested based solely on whether the interest is certain to take effect in possession or enjoyment.[11] The Restatement also states more straightforward rules of construction.[12]

---

7. Lawrence W. Waggoner, Reformulating the Structure of Estates: A Proposal for Legislative Action, 85 Harv. L. Rev. 729, 729-32 (1972).

8. *See* D. Benjamin Barros, Toward a Model Law of Estates and Future Interests, 66 Wash. & Lee L. Rev. 3 (2009); T.P. Gallanis, The Future of Future Interests, 60 Wash. & Lee L. Rev. 513 (2003).

9. Restatement (Third) of Property: Wills and Other Donative Transfers § 25.2 cmt. c (Am. Law Inst. 2011).

10. Id. cmt. d.

11. Id. § 25.3.

12. Id. §§ 26.1-26.9.

A Restatement, of course, is persuasive authority only, and its authoritativeness is perhaps most precarious when it advances reform. But the Restatements have had considerable influence in the development of the law of trusts and estates. In this chapter, we reference pertinent sections of the new Restatement, which might well provide a roadmap for reform by judges and legislatures. Just before this book went to press in early 2017, the Joint Editorial Board for Uniform Trusts and Estates Acts recommended to the Uniform Law Commission that it prepare a uniform act on future interests based on the new Restatement. For future interests buffs, these are exciting times indeed!

B. CONSTRUCTION OF TRUST INSTRUMENTS

In this section, we examine the rules that courts have developed in construing future interests in trusts.

1. Preference for Vested Interests

The common law had a strong preference for construing an ambiguous instrument as creating a vested rather than a contingent remainder. As Sir Edward Coke said, "the law always delights in vesting of estates, and contingencies are odious in the law, and are the causes of troubles, and vesting and settling of estates, the cause of repose and certainty."[13]

The preference for vested interests arose in feudal England at a time when contingent interests were barely recognized as interests. It continued into the modern era because of the desirable consequences of a vested construction. These consequences were:

Sir Edward Coke

(a) *Acceleration.* A vested remainder *accelerated into possession* upon termination of the preceding life estate, solving vexing problems of possession and undisposed income (see page 856).

(b) *Transferability.* A vested remainder was *transferable* inter vivos, making land more alienable (see page 857).

(c) *Perpetuities.* A vested remainder was not subject to the *Rule Against Perpetuities* (see Chapter 14).

(d) *Destructibility.* A vested remainder was not subject to the doctrine of *destructibility of contingent remainders*, which provides that a legal contingent remainder in land was destroyed if it did not vest at or before the termination of the preceding freehold estate. A feudal relic, this doctrine has been abolished in nearly every state.[14]

---

13. Roberts v. Roberts (1613) 80 Eng. Rep. 1002 (K.B.) 1009; 2 Bulstrode 124, 131.

14. *See* Restatement (Third) of Property: Wills and Other Donative Transfers § 25.5 reporter's note 2 (Am. Law Inst. 2011).

NOTE

Equitable Division on Divorce.   A new problem has emerged in modern times. In many states, upon divorce a court makes an *equitable division* of a couple's "property." Should a future interest in trust be subject to division? The courts appear to agree that an indefeasibly vested remainder is the spouse's property and can be valued in accordance with life expectancy tables. And a vested remainder subject to divestment if the spouse does not survive the life tenant, or a remainder contingent on surviving the life tenant, is not subject to division. But if the divesting event or contingency is something other than surviving the life tenant, the courts have struggled with the vested-contingent dichotomy with varying results.[15]

a. Acceleration into Possession

Under the common law, a vested remainder accelerates into possession whenever and however the preceding estate ends. A contingent remainder, on the other hand, does not accelerate because the remainderpersons are not entitled to possession until they are all ascertained and any condition precedent has occurred. Thus:

> *Case 12. T* devises property in trust for *W* for life, remainder to *T*'s children (who survive *W*). *W* disclaims the life estate. If the language in parentheses is not included, the children of *T* have a vested remainder that accelerates into possession. If the language in parentheses is included, the children of *T* have a contingent remainder that will not accelerate into possession. What is done with the income during *W*'s life?

The rule that a contingent remainder does not accelerate when the life tenant disclaims will sometimes be contrary to the settlor's intent. In Case 12, the settlor probably postponed the gift to his children to give his spouse income during her life. If so, probably the settlor would not want the trust to continue if she rejects the income.

To deal with such situations, some courts decided whether to accelerate the remainder based on the settlor's probable intent rather than the technical classification of the remainder as vested or contingent. But this requires every disclaimer to be litigated. To avoid such litigation, the states enacted disclaimer statutes, such as the Uniform Disclaimer of Property Interests Act (UDPIA) (Unif. Law Comm'n 1999, rev. 2006), which in 2002 was absorbed into the Uniform Probate Code (UPC) as §§ 2-1101 through 2-1117. Under these statutes, the disclaimant is treated as having predeceased the testator (see page 136), and remainders take effect or fail on this assumption.

NOTES

1. Cutting Out Afterborn Descendants.   Older state disclaimer statutes tend to require that a disclaimer be made within nine months of the creation of the interest

---

15. *See* Marc A. Chorney, Interests in Trusts as Property in Dissolution of Marriage: Identification and Valuation, 40 Real Prop. Prob. & Tr. J. 1 (2005). We take up application of equitable division to a present interest in a discretionary trust in Chapter 10 at page 699.

being disclaimed. More recent statutes, including the UDPIA (and so the UPC), do not specify a time limit.[16] Under these statutes, a contingent remainderperson may wait until after the life tenant's death to decide whether to accept the property. Thus:

> *Case 13.* *T* devises property in trust "for my daughter *A* for life, then to my grand-daughter *B* if *B* survives *A*, and if *B* does not survive *A*, to *B*'s descendants." At *A*'s death, *B*, now age 21, can decide whether to disclaim and let the property pass to *B*'s descendants.

> *Case 14.* *T* devises property in trust "for my daughter *A* for life, then to *A*'s descendants." At *T*'s death, *A* can decide whether to disclaim and let the property pass to *A*'s descendants.

In Case 13, *B*'s disclaimer cuts out her afterborn descendants. However, she has a contingent remainder in fee simple. If she does not disclaim, she may receive the property outright, free to dispose of it as she pleases. The structure of this devise strongly implies that the settlor meant to allow *B* to exclude afterborn descendants.

In Case 14, *A*'s disclaimer also cuts out her afterborn descendants. But there is an important distinction: *A* has only a life estate. If she does not disclaim, at her death her surviving descendants—even those born after *T*'s death—will be entitled to a share of the property. *A*'s disclaimer, cutting out her afterborn descendants, may frustrate the intent of *T*, who likely did not mean to allow *A* to exclude afterborn descendants.

2. Strategic Acceleration. Suppose *T*'s will devises property in separate trusts, one "for my son *A* for life, then to the descendants of *A* and *B*," and the other "for my son *B* for life, then to the descendants of *A* and *B*." When *T* dies, *A* has descendants but *B* does not. If *A* disclaims, does this cut off *B*'s afterborn descendants from the first trust, ensuring that its corpus will pass entirely to *A*'s descendants? *See* Pate v. Ford, 376 S.E.2d 775 (S.C. 1989).

b. Transferability

One of the reasons for the ancient preference for vesting was that a vested remainder was transferable inter vivos, making land more alienable, whereas a contingent interest was not. Let us consider now the transferability of future interests, both inter vivos and at death, in modern law.

(1) Inter Vivos Transfer

Although vested remainders, including defeasibly vested ones, have long been transferable inter vivos, at early common law contingent remainders and executory interests were not. The theory, decisively rejected in modern law, was that a contingent interest was a mere chance of ownership. A contingent interest was regarded not as a property interest in which possession was postponed, but rather as an interest that might arise

---

16. A word of caution about taxes: Under Internal Revenue Code § 2518, a disclaimer is treated as a gift by the disclaimant to the persons who take as a result of the disclaimer unless the disclaimer occurs within nine months after the interest is created or nine months after the donee reaches 21, whichever is later (see page 931).

in the future.[17] An overwhelming majority of states have reversed the ancient rule of inalienability for contingent interests, making even contingent future interests alienable during life.[18] A spendthrift clause, however, can render inalienable an interest in trust, whether present or future, for the life of the beneficiary (see Chapter 10 at page 703).

(2) Transfer at Death

Reversions, remainders, and executory interests are descendible and devisable at the death of the owner of the interest unless they are contingent on surviving to the time of possession. Such an interest passes to the heirs or devisees of its owner, and this is true even if the trust has a spendthrift clause:

> *Case 15.* O conveys property in trust "for A for life, then to B," and includes a spendthrift clause that restricts B's right to alienate her interest in the trust. B dies during A's lifetime. B's remainder passes to B's devisees if B leaves a will or to B's heirs if B dies intestate. So held in In re Townley Bypass Unified Credit Trust, 252 S.W.3d 715 (Tex. App. 2008).

A future interest contingent on surviving to the time of possession is not transferable at death. In Case 15, if O had conveyed a remainder "to B if B survives A," B could not transmit the remainder to another person if B died during A's lifetime.

NOTES

1. Taxation of "Transmissible" Interests. The transfer of any property interest at death is potentially subject to estate taxation (see Chapter 15). A future interest, like a possessory estate, is an interest in property, hence it may be subject to estate taxation if *transmissible* at death. Transmissible is a term of art meaning transferable by will or intestacy. Thus, in Case 15, if B dies during A's lifetime, the value of B's remainder is subject to estate taxation because it is transmissible.

If a future interest is subject to estate taxation, the value of the interest depends on the life tenant's life expectancy and the market rate of interest. The federal government publishes life expectancy tables and valuation tables for future interests.

2. Tax Planning. You can give a remainderperson the power to transfer his remainder at death without estate tax exposure by making the remainder contingent on surviving to the time of possession and giving the remainderperson a nongeneral power of appointment. Because such a remainder is not transmissible at death, it is not subject to estate taxation. And as we have seen, property subject to a nongeneral power is not subject to estate taxation either (see Chapter 12 at page 813). Here is an example:

> *Case 16.* T devises his residuary estate in trust "for A for life, then to B if B survives A, and if B does not survive A, then to such of B's spouse or one or more of B's descendants as B appoints by will." B has a contingent remainder that is not transmissible and a nongeneral power of appointment. If B dies during A's life, B's

---

17. *See* Waggoner, *supra* note 7, at 756.
18. *See, e.g.,* In re Will of Keys, 193 P.3d 490, 496 (Kan. App. 2008).

remainder disappears and is not taxable in *B*'s estate. In this event, the property passes on *A*'s death to persons whom *B* appoints or, if *B* fails to appoint, to the takers in default of appointment or *T*'s heirs.[19]

c. Requiring Survival to Time of Possession

Under traditional law, there is no requirement that a remainder beneficiary live to the time of possession. If a remainder beneficiary dies before the life tenant, the remainder passes as part of the beneficiary's estate. This rule of construction yields to the donor's expressed or implied contrary intent. In a handful of recurring circumstances, such as a multigenerational class gift, courts routinely find an implied condition of survival (see page 863).

The default rule of no implied condition of survival is criticized by the Restatement (Third) of Property,[20] and it is reversed by UPC § 2-707 (1990, rev. 2008). Under § 2-707, if a remainder beneficiary does not survive to the distribution date, a substitute gift is created in the remainder beneficiary's surviving descendants unless the governing instrument provides otherwise. In other words, a condition of survival is assumed and the antilapse concept from the law of wills is extended to future interests in trust. UPC § 2-707 or comparable legislation has been adopted in about a third of the states (see page 865).

Let us consider (1) the traditional rule, (2) the traditional exceptions, such as for a multigenerational class gift, and (3) the extension of the antilapse concept to future interests in trust as under UPC § 2-707.

(1) The Traditional No-Survivorship Rule of Construction

Tait v. Community First Trust Co.
425 S.W.3d 684 (Ark. 2012)

GOODSON, J. Appellants Debbie Tait, Kerry Jones, Leanna Lackey, and Lesia Winters appeal the order entered by the Polk County Circuit Court denying their claim to a share in the Fowler Family Trust over which appellee Community First Trust Company (Community First) serves as trustee. For reversal, appellants contend that the circuit court erred in ruling that the interests of beneficiaries who predecease the surviving settlor of an inter vivos trust lapse upon the death of the beneficiaries. . . . We hold that the interests of the beneficiaries did not lapse, and we reverse and remand.

The parties agree on the essential facts. William J. Fowler and his wife Annie R. Fowler resided in Mena in Polk County. William had no offspring, but Annie had six children from a previous marriage. In November 2000, the couple established the Fowler Family Trust. The trust res consisted of the following three classes of property: (1) property that William had owned separately, (2) property that Annie had owned

19. If *T* is *B*'s parent, however, and *B* appoints to *B*'s children, then there would be a taxable termination under the generation-skipping transfer tax when *B* dies (see Chapter 15 at page 976).

20. *See* Restatement (Third) of Property: Wills and Other Donative Transfers § 26.3 cmts. c-d, h (Am. Law Inst. 2011).

Justice Courtney Hudson Goodson

separately, and (3) property that William and Annie had owned jointly. The trust authorized the trustee to dispense to William and Annie the income and principal during their lifetimes as needed for their support. Although initially the trust was revocable, the trust instrument provided that it would become irrevocable when either William or Annie died. At the death of the survivor, the trust was to terminate, and the principal and income of the trust was to be distributed in the following manner. The jointly owned property and William's separate property was to be apportioned equally among William's two stepchildren, Dale Paschal Jones and Billy Ray Jones, and ten of his nieces and nephews, including Tommy Dean Fry. Annie's separate property was to be disbursed in equal shares to three of her children.

Annie died in May 2001. William's stepson Dale Paschal Jones died in November 2004, survived by his daughters, appellants Leanna Lackey and Lesia Winters. William's other stepson, Billy Ray Jones, died in November 2008, survived by his daughters, appellants Debbie Tait and Kerry Jones. William's niece, Tommy Dean Fry, died in June 2009 without issue. After the deaths of these three named beneficiaries, William died in January 2011.

On August 19, 2011, Community First filed a petition to construe the trust. . . . It took the position that the interests of the deceased beneficiaries lapsed because they predeceased William, the surviving settlor, and that appellants, the descendants of William's stepsons, were not entitled to share in the remainder of the trust. As authority for this contention, Community First relied on the anti-lapse provision of Ark. Code Ann. § 28-26-104(2) (2012). Appellants answered the complaint and filed a motion to modify Community First's proposed distribution excluding them from participation in the trust proceeds. They argued that the interests of the deceased beneficiaries did not lapse because their interests vested at the time the trust was created. Citing Kidwell v. Rhew, 268 S.W.3d 309 (Ark. 2007), where this court held that the pretermitted-heir statute of the probate code did not apply to trusts, appellants argued that the anti-lapse statute found in the probate code was not applicable to trusts. . . .

The circuit court found that . . . the anti-lapse statute did not answer the question of whether the interests of the deceased beneficiaries lapsed because they did not survive the settlor. The court rejected appellants' argument that the interests of the beneficiaries vested at the time the property was transferred to the trust. Instead, the court reasoned that vesting occurred upon the death of the settlors. The circuit court noted . . . the "apparent common law rule" that a beneficiary's interest lapses if the beneficiary predeceases the settlor. Applying the "common law rule," the court found that appellants could not share in the trust because their fathers' interests lapsed when they predeceased William. . . .

For reversal, appellants argue that the anti-lapse statute does not apply to trusts and that the circuit court erred by ignoring the intent of the settlors because the trust instrument manifests no intent for the beneficiaries' interests to lapse. . . . Community First responds that the interests of the beneficiaries vested at the death of the surviving settlor and that the circuit court correctly applied the common law of trusts in ruling that the interest of the beneficiaries lapsed.

The question we must decide is whether the interest of a beneficiary to an inter vivos trust lapses when the beneficiary dies before the settlor. . . . As the parties point out, the Arkansas Trust Code, found at Ark. Code Ann. §§ 28-73-101 to 1106 (2012), contains no provision regarding the lapse of interests with respect to inter vivos trusts. . . . Ark. Code Ann. § 28-73-112 (2012) states that "[t]he rules of construction that apply in this state to the interpretation of and disposition of property by will also apply as appropriate to the interpretation of the terms of a trust and the disposition of the trust property." Our probate code contains an anti-lapse provision at Ark. Code Ann. § 28-26-104(2):

> Whenever property is devised to a child, natural or adopted, or other descendant of the testator, either by specific provision or as a member of a class, and the devisee shall die in the lifetime of the testator, leaving a child, natural or adopted, or other descendant who survives the testator, the devise shall not lapse, but the property shall vest in the surviving child or other descendant of the devisee, as if the devisee had survived the testator and died intestate.

Pursuant to this statute, a legacy or devise in a will lapses when the legatee or devisee dies before the testator, except where the legacy or devise is to a child or other descendant of the testator or where there is a gift to a class. In *Kidwell*, we held that "the pretermitted-heir statute, which speaks only in terms of the 'execution of a will,' does not apply in instances in which there is no will." *Kidwell*, 268 S.W.3d at 312.

Here, the circuit court did not rule that the anti-lapse statute worked to divest the deceased beneficiaries and their heirs of their interests in the trust. Instead, the court ruled that the interests of the beneficiaries did not vest until William died, and the court applied what it believed to be the common-law rule with respect to trusts. . . .

The greater weight of authority holds that the interest of a beneficiary to an inter vivos trust does not lapse when the beneficiary predeceases the settlor. This rule is based on the principle that the interests of such beneficiaries vest[] when the trust is created and thus do[] not lapse with the death of the beneficiary. . . .

Perhaps the leading case is the decision of the Ohio Supreme Court in First Nat'l Bank of Cincinnati v. Tenney, 138 N.E.2d 15 (Ohio 1956). The court in *Tenney* held that an inter vivos trust reserving to the settlor the income for life plus the power to revoke, with a remainder over at the death of the settlor, creates a vested interest in the remainderman subject to defeasance by the exercise of the power of revocation. Similarly, the Illinois appellate court in First Galesburg Nat'l Bank & Trust Co. v. Robinson, 500 N.E.2d 995 (Ill. App. 1986), held that a delay in enjoyment of possession does not imply a requirement of survival by the remainderman before the remainder is vested. The court concluded that the words calling for distribution "at death," "after death," or "upon death" do not refer to the time when the remainder vests, but rather to the time when the remainderman becomes entitled to possession. The *Robinson* court thus held that the beneficiaries took a present right to the remainder upon execution of the trust instrument, although enjoyment was postponed until the termination of the life estates of the settlors. . . .

We now hold that the interest of a beneficiary to an inter vivos trust vests at the time the trust is created, and thus the beneficial interest does not lapse when the beneficiary predeceases the settlor. . . . Because we hold that the interests of the deceased beneficiaries did not lapse, we need not address appellants' arguments concerning whether our anti-lapse statute or the provision regarding custodial trusts could apply to an inter vivos trust. We reverse and remand for proceedings consistent with this decision.

Reversed and remanded.

NOTES

1. Remainders and Revocable Trusts. A settlor's exercise of a power of revocation over a revocable trust divests the interests of the remainder beneficiaries, just as a donee's exercise of a power of appointment divests the interest of the takers in default (see page 850). Suppose *O* declares a trust "for *O* for life, then to *O*'s children," reserving a power to revoke the trust. If *O* has one child, *A*, then *A* has a *vested remainder subject to partial divestment* by the birth of other children and *subject to complete divestment* by *O*'s exercise of the power of revocation. If *O* has no children, the remainder is *contingent* because no taker is ascertained.

2. Remainders, Lapse, and the Uniform Trust Code. The traditional rule of construction, followed in *Tait* and in a majority of states, is that a remainder in trust passes as part of the remainder beneficiary's estate if the beneficiary does not survive until the time of possession, unless the instrument provides that the remainder is divested by the beneficiary's death. As in *Tait*, the courts reason that, because there is no lapse, there is no need to bring in the antilapse concept from the law of wills.

A potential complication is Uniform Trust Code § 112 (Unif. Law Comm'n 2000), which provides that the rules of construction applicable to "the interpretation of and disposition of property by will also apply as appropriate to the interpretation of the terms of a trust and the disposition of the trust property." In *Tait*, the court held that enactment of this provision did not override the traditional no-implied-survivorship rule of construction for trusts by drawing in the antilapse rules from the law of wills. So too did the court in Ex parte Byrom, 47 So. 3d 791 (Ala. 2010).

3. Avoiding Drafting Pitfalls. A good lawyer does not rely on presumptions or default rules, but rather provides expressly what is to happen if an intended beneficiary does not survive to the time of distribution. Wagner v. DeSalvio, 860 N.Y.S.2d 146 (App. Div. 2008), is a cautionary tale. In that case, the trust remainder was given to *A*, *B*, and *C*, the settlor's children, "as contingent beneficiaries." *C* predeceased, leaving descendants. The court awarded *C*'s share to *A* and *B* on the basis of a state statute that reallocates ineffective remainders to the surviving remainder beneficiaries. Is this what the settlor likely wanted?

(2) Multigenerational Class Gifts and Other Exceptions

In a handful of recurring circumstances, such as a multigenerational class gift, courts normally find an implied condition of survival.

(a) Multigenerational Class Gift. Courts do not find an implied requirement of survival in gifts to a single-generational class, such as to "children" or "brothers and sisters."[21] They do, however, find an implied requirement of survival in gifts to a multi-generational class, such as to "issue" or "descendants." In such situations, courts apply the concept of *representation* familiar from the law of inheritance.[22]

Suppose that *T*'s will devises property "to *A* for life, then to *A*'s descendants." *A* has a son, *B*, and a daughter, *C*. *B* predeceases *A*, devising all his property to his wife. *B* is also survived by a daughter, *D*. On *A*'s death, *D* takes *B*'s interest by representation; it does not pass to *B*'s wife. Similarly, if there is a gift to the "heirs" of *A*, a survival requirement to the death of *A* is implied.[23]

(b) Condition of Survival Ambiguous Regarding Time. When the testator inserts the word "surviving" in a trust instrument, the word is ambiguous unless additional language specifies *at what time* the donee must be surviving. The requirement of survival may relate to surviving the testator, the life tenant, or a preceding remainder beneficiary.

Suppose *T* devises property in trust "for *A* for life, then to *B*, but if *B* dies before *A*, to *B*'s surviving children." *B* has two children, *C* and *D*. Then *B* dies. Then *D* dies intestate, survived by a child, *E*. *A* dies. Does *E* share? The answer depends on whether "surviving" means "surviving *A*," in which case *E* would not share because *D* did not survive *A*, or "surviving *B*," in which case *E* would share because *D* survived *B*. The prevailing view appears to be that "surviving" means surviving to the time of possession, thus excluding *E*.[24]

Suppose *T* conveys property in trust for *T* for life, and then "upon the death of *T*, the trustee shall pay over whatever remains of the trust estate to *T*'s son *A* if he shall then be living. If *T*'s son *A* shall then be deceased, the remains of the trust estate shall be paid to *T*'s then living descendants." *T* dies. Before the trustee distributes the trust property to *A*, *A* dies. *C* and *D*, the surviving children of *A*'s brother *B*, who predeceased both *A* and *T*, argue that "then living" refers to the time of distribution, not *T*'s death, and that they are entitled to the trust property as *T*'s then living descendants. *E*, the beneficiary of *A*'s will, who is unrelated to *T*, argues that "then living" refers to the time of *T*'s death, and that he is entitled to the trust property. What result? *Compare* Chavin v. PNC Bank, 816 A.2d 781 (Del. 2003), *with* Wilson v. Rhodes, 258 S.W.3d 873 (Mo. App. 2008), *and* Bryan v. Dethlefs, 959 So. 2d 314 (Fla. App. 2007).

(c) Gift Over on Death Without Descendants. Suppose *T* bequeaths a fund in trust "for *A* for life, then to *B*, but if *B* dies without descendants surviving her, to *C*."

---

21. *See* id. § 15.4.
22. *See* id. §§ 14.4, 15.3 cmt. b.
23. *See* id. § 16.1.
24. *See* id. § 26.4.

Does *T* intend *C* to take only if *B* dies *before A* without descendants? Or does *T* intend *C* to take if *B* dies *at any time* without descendants? The prevailing view favors the first construction, which permits the trust to terminate on *A*'s death. If *B* survives *A*, the trust property is distributed to *B* and *C* can never take.[25] If *B* dies before *A*, and then *C* dies during *A*'s life, *C*'s interest passes to *C*'s heirs or devisees.

Clobberie's Case
(1677) 86 Eng. Rep. 476 (Ch.); 2 Ventris 342

In one Clobberie's case it was held, that where one bequeathed a sum of money to a woman, at her age of 21 years, or day of marriage, to be paid unto her with interest, and she died before either, that the money should go to her executor; and was so decreed by my Lord Chancellor Finch.[26]

But he said, if money were bequeathed to one at his age of 21 years; if he dies before that age, the money is lost.

On the other side, if money be given to one, to be paid at the age of 21 years; there, if the party dies before, it shall go to the executors.

NOTES

1. The Three Rules in Clobberie's Case. Each of the three paragraphs in Clobberie's Case sets forth a rule of construction. The first and third are widely followed today. They apply to present interests as well as to remainders, whether to a class or to an individual.

Under the first rule in Clobberie's Case, a gift of the *entire income* to a person or to a class, with principal to be paid at a designated age, indicates that survival to the time of possession is not required. The rationale is that all interests in the property — both income and principal — are given to the same person or persons, with only possession of the principal postponed. If the beneficiary dies before reaching the stated age, there is no point in delaying payment of the principal to the beneficiary's estate.[27]

Under the third rule in Clobberie's Case, a gift *payable* or *to be paid* at a designated age indicates that survival to the time of possession is not required. If the beneficiary dies before reaching that age, the principal will be paid at the beneficiary's death to the beneficiary's estate, unless someone would be harmed by such payment. If the income is payable to another, for example, the principal cannot be paid to the principal beneficiary's estate until the income beneficiary dies.[28]

The American cases are split on the second rule, under which a gift *at* a designated age implies a requirement of survivorship to that age.[29] The distinction between a legacy "at 21" (survivorship to 21 required) and a legacy "to be paid at 21" (survivor-

---

25. *See* id. § 26.8.
26. Lord Chancellor Finch was later titled Lord Nottingham and became famous for launching the Rule Against Perpetuities in the Duke of Norfolk's Case (see Chapter 14 at page 889). — Eds.
27. *See* 5 American Law of Property § 21.20 (A. James Casner ed. 1952).
28. *See* id. § 21.18.
29. *See* id. § 21.17.

ship to 21 is not required) has been criticized as a distinction without a difference. The Restatement (Third) of Property takes the position that, unless the governing instrument provides otherwise, "a future interest that is distributable upon reaching a specified age is conditioned on the beneficiary's living to that age."[30] The Restatement thus rejects the first and third rules in Clobberie's Case, and follows the second.

   2. Three Applications of Clobberie's Case.   Consider the following three problems:
   a. Suppose *T* bequeaths $10,000 "to *A* when *A* attains 21." *A* is age 15 at *T*'s death. Who is entitled to income from the $10,000 before *A* reaches 21? If *A* dies at age 16, does the legacy fail or is *A*'s administrator entitled to demand payment of $10,000 at *A*'s death or when *A* would have reached 21 had *A* lived?
   b. Suppose *T* bequeaths a fund in trust "for *A* for life, then after *A*'s death to *A*'s children, each share payable as each child respectively reaches the age of 30, if he or she has not reached age 30 before *A* dies." A child of *A* dies at age 10 during *A*'s life. What result?
   c. Suppose *T* bequeaths a fund in trust for the benefit of her child Benjamin "until my child attains age 25, at which time the income and principal shall be distributed and paid over to him and the trust shall terminate." *T*'s will did not name a trust beneficiary if Benjamin died under age 25. Benjamin died at 20. Benjamin's heir is his father, who was previously divorced from Ben's mother. What result? *See* Summers v. Summers, 699 N.E.2d 958 (Ohio App. 1997).

(3) The Survivorship-Plus-Antilapse Rule of UPC § 2-707

UPC § 2-707 (1990, rev. 2008) extends the antilapse concept from the law of wills (see Chapter 5 at page 357) to future interests in trust as if the settlor were a testator who died on the distribution date. Although a simple idea in theory, the implementation in § 2-707 is devilishly complex. The statute provides for two or more alternative future interests, for which substitute gifts are created, and also provides for tiebreakers if two groups of substitute takers appear to have equal claims. Even the drafters call the statute "elaborate and intricate."[31]
   Under UPC § 2-707, unless the governing instrument provides otherwise, the following rules apply:
   (a) *Implied Condition of Survival.*   All future interests in trust are contingent on the beneficiary's surviving to the date of distribution.[32]
   (b) *Substitute Gift in Descendants.*   If a remainder beneficiary does not survive to the distribution date, a substitute gift is created in the beneficiary's descendants who survive to the date of distribution.
   (c) *Failed Remainders Revert to Settlor's Devisees or Heirs.*   If a remainder beneficiary dies before distribution and leaves no descendants, the remainder fails.

---

   30. Restatement (Third) of Property: Wills and Other Donative Transfers § 26.6 (Am. Law Inst. 2011).
   31. Edward C. Halbach, Jr. & Lawrence W. Waggoner, The UPC's New Survivorship and Antilapse Provisions, 55 Alb. L. Rev. 1091, 1148 (1992).
   32. In applying to all holders of a future interest, and not just persons who are descendants of the transferor's grandparents, UPC § 2-707 applies more broadly than UPC § 2-603 (see page 358).

If there is no alternative remainder that takes effect, the trust property passes to the settlor's residuary devisees or to the settlor's heirs.[33]

Legislation that extends the antilapse concept to future interests in trust, such as UPC § 2-707, has been adopted in more than a third of the states.[34] The Restatement (Third) of Property preserves the traditional rule, but only because its drafters were concerned that in the absence of authorizing legislation, if a condition of survival was imposed, a court could not effect a substitute gift in the descendants of a remainder beneficiary who did not survive to possession.[35] So it seems fair to say that there is a movement, albeit slowly developing and largely dependent on statutory warrant,[36] toward reversing the common law rule of construction and finding an implied condition of survival with a substitute gift in descendants.

This movement is controversial. Several scholars have risen in fierce opposition to UPC § 2-707.[37] Others, including the statute's drafters, have risen in strong defense.[38] To bring the pros and cons of § 2-707 into clearer focus, consider the following three case studies:

> *Case 17.* *T* devises property in trust "for *W* for life, then to my descendants." *T* has three children, *A*, *B*, and *C*. Under both traditional law and UPC § 2-707, because *T* has made a gift to a multigenerational class, *A*'s remainder is contingent on *A*'s surviving *W*. If *A* dies during *W*'s life, *A*'s descendants take *A*'s share by representation. If *A* is not survived by descendants, *A*'s share is reallocated to *B* and *C*.

> *Case 18.* *T* devises property in trust "for *W* for life, then to my children." *T* has three children, *A*, *B*, and *C*. Under traditional law, because *T* has made a gift to a single-generational class, *A*'s remainder is not contingent on *A*'s surviving *W*. If *A* dies during *W*'s life, *A*'s remainder passes to *A*'s heirs or devisees. Under UPC § 2-707, *A*'s remainder is contingent on *A*'s surviving *W*. If *A* dies during *W*'s life, *A*'s share is

---

33. On the potential tax consequences of this reversion, see F. Philip Manns, Jr., New Reasons to Remember the Estate Taxation of Reversions, 44 Real Prop. Tr. & Est. L.J. 323 (2009).

34. Alaska, Arizona, Colorado, Florida, Hawaii, Illinois, Iowa, Massachusetts, Michigan, Montana, New Mexico, North Dakota, Ohio, Pennsylvania, South Dakota, Tennessee, and Utah.

35. *See* Restatement (Third) of Property: Wills and Other Donative Transfers § 26.3 cmt. h (Am. Law Inst. 2011).

36. In In re Estate of Button, 490 P.2d 731 (Wash. 1971), the court extended the antilapse statute to trusts as a matter of common law interpretation. In an omitted portion of Tait v. Community First Trust Co., page 859, the Arkansas court specifically rejected the reasoning of the Washington court in *Button*.

37. *See* Jesse Dukeminier, The Uniform Probate Code Upends the Law of Remainders, 94 Mich. L. Rev. 148 (1995); Laura E. Cunningham, The Hazards of Tinkering with the Common Law of Future Interests: The California Experience, 48 Hastings L.J. 667 (1997); David M. Becker, Uniform Probate Code Section 2-707 and the Experienced Estate Planner: Unexpected Disasters and How to Avoid Them, 47 UCLA L. Rev. 339 (1999); David M. Becker, Eroding the Common Law Paradigm for Creation of Property Interests and the Hidden Costs of Law Reform, 83 Wash. U. L.Q. 773 (2005).

38. *See* Halbach & Waggoner, *supra* note 31; Lawrence W. Waggoner, The Uniform Probate Code Extends Antilapse-Type Protection to Poorly Drafted Trusts, 94 Mich. L. Rev. 2309 (1996); *see also* Edward C. Halbach, Jr., Uniform Acts, Restatements, and Trends in American Trust Law at Century's End, 88 Cal. L. Rev. 1877, 1902-04 (2000).

Antilapse Rules for Future Interests in Trust (2016)   Figure 13.2

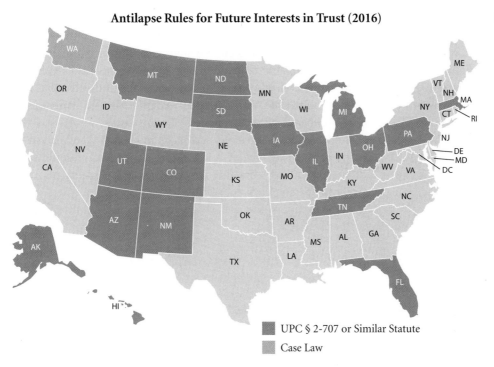

UPC § 2-707 or Similar Statute

Case Law

redirected to *A*'s descendants or, if *A* is not survived by descendants, it is reallocated to *B* and *C*.

Case 19. *T* devises property in trust "for *W* for life, then to my daughter *A*." Under traditional law, *A*'s remainder is not contingent on *A*'s surviving *W*. If *A* dies during *W*'s life, *A*'s remainder passes to *A*'s heirs or devisees. Under UPC § 2-707, *A*'s remainder is contingent on *A*'s surviving *W*. If *A* dies during *W*'s life, *A*'s share is redirected to *A*'s descendants or, if *A* is not survived by descendants, the gift fails and the property reverts to *T*'s heirs or devisees.

Case 17 most resembles what is typical in instruments drafted by skilled estate planners. In a typical estate plan, the first spouse to die will leave his or her property in trust to the surviving spouse for life, with the remainder to such of the settlor's descendants (and perhaps the descendants' spouses) as the surviving spouse names by will. In such a case, the result is the same under traditional law and UPC § 2-707.

The choice between the traditional rule and UPC § 2-707 affects outcomes only in cases in which the remainder is given to a single-generational class, such as to children as in Case 18, or to a specifically identified person, as in Case 19, but a child or the person does not survive to the distribution date. Under traditional law, the remainder passes to the remainder beneficiary's heirs or devisees. Under § 2-707, the remainder passes to the remainder beneficiary's descendants, if any, or otherwise to the settlor's heirs or devisees.

When a remainder is given to children, as in Case 18, one has a nagging suspicion that the drafter carelessly chose the term *children* when the term *descendants*—

incorporating the principle of representation from the law of inheritance—would have better fit the settlor's intent (see page 874). One suspects that the settlor would want a substitute gift to the descendants of a child who does not survive to the distribution date rather than a transmissible remainder that passes to the child's heirs or devisees. UPC § 2-707 implements this intuition, protecting a line of descent that has one or more living members on the distribution date.[39] Whether you are sympathetic or hostile to § 2-707 usually depends on whether you share this intuition.

In the case of a remainder given to a named person, as in Case 19, the analysis is more difficult. If a specific person is named, it is less clear that the settlor would prefer a substitute gift in the person's descendants over the remainder passing to the person's heirs or devisees if the person does not survive to the distribution date. Critics of UPC § 2-707 argue that the traditional rule will yield better outcomes because a transmissible remainder functions like a testamentary power of appointment, enabling the beneficiary to choose a successor taker. This successor taker could be the remainder beneficiary's descendants, as is mandated by § 2-707, or it could be the beneficiary's spouse, a charity, or anyone else, outright or in further trust, as circumstances warrant.

Proponents of § 2-707 counter that the relevant perspective is that of the settlor and that, as evidenced by the frequency in professionally drafted instruments of alternative gifts to the descendants of a predeceasing remainder beneficiary, most settlors would prefer to keep the share of a predeceasing remainder beneficiary in the same line of descent if there is a living descendant on the distribution date. A power of appointment in a remainder beneficiary is rare and may still be provided for expressly if that is what the settlor wants. A substitute gift in the remainder beneficiary's descendants has the further benefit of avoiding taxation of the remainder as it passes through the deceased beneficiary's estate, though a generation-skipping transfer tax may be due on the death of the life tenant if the substituted takers are the settlor's grandchildren or any other persons two or more generations below the settlor (see Chapter 15 at page 975).

A secondary point of controversy concerns whether *words of survivorship* are sufficient, in the absence of additional evidence, to preclude a substitution of descendants for a predeceasing remainder beneficiary. UPC § 2-707 provides that words of survivorship are not sufficient. Under § 2-707, if *T* devises a fund in trust "for *A* for life, then to *B* if *B* survives *A*," the words "if *B* survives *A*" are not enough to indicate that the transferor does not want *B*'s descendants substituted for *B* if *B* predeceases *A*. If *B* predeceases *A*, leaving descendants, those descendants will take despite the express condition of survivorship.

This rule of construction, which appears also in UPC § 2-603, the antilapse statute applicable to wills (see page 360), has been sharply criticized by commentators and has received a chilly reception in state legislatures. As with § 2-603, some states that have enacted § 2-707, such as Massachusetts, have dropped this provision.[40] Others, such as Arizona and Florida, have modified it to state that words of survivorship *are*

---

39. *See* Restatement (Third) of Property: Wills and Other Donative Transfers § 26.3 cmts. e, h (Am. Law Inst. 2011).

40. *See* Mass. Gen. Laws Ann. ch. 190B § 2-707 (2016).

a sufficient indication of an intent contrary to a substitute gift in descendants.[41] One wonders whether § 2-707 would have taken less fire if its drafters had stopped at implying a condition of survival and imposing a substitute gift in a predeceasing remainder beneficiary's descendants without also adding the complexity of disregarding express words of survivorship.

A good lawyer does not rely on presumptions or default rules. These default rules of construction do not come into play if the lawyer makes the client's intent clear by providing expressly what happens if the intended beneficiary does not survive to the time of distribution.

2. Gifts to Classes

As we saw in Chapter 5, a *class gift* arises when the donor is *group minded* (see page 368). A donor is thought to be group minded if she uses a class label in describing the beneficiaries, such as "to *A*'s children" or "to my nephews and nieces." A gift to named beneficiaries who form a natural class may be deemed a class gift if the court decides that the donor would have wanted the survivors to divide the share of a predeceasing beneficiary rather than for it to lapse.

Gifts to classes raise a host of interpretive and constructional problems. We examine here four recurring problems: (a) gifts of income; (b) gifts to children, issue, or descendants; (c) gifts to heirs; and (d) the rule of convenience for determining when a class closes.

a. Gifts of Income

Dewire v. Haveles
534 N.E.2d 782 (Mass. 1989)

WILKINS, J. This petition for a declaration of rights seeks answers to questions arising from an artlessly drafted will that, among its many inadequacies, includes a blatant violation of the rule against perpetuities. . . .

Thomas A. Dewire died in January, 1941, survived by his widow, his son Thomas, Jr., and three grandchildren (Thomas, III, Paula, and Deborah, all children of Thomas, Jr.). His will placed substantially all his estate in a residuary trust. The income of the trust was payable to his widow for life and, on her death, the income was payable to his son Thomas, Jr., the widow of Thomas, Jr., and Thomas Jr.'s children.[42]

---

41. *See* Ariz. Rev. Stat. Ann. § 14-2707(B) (2016); Fla. Stat. Ann. § 736.1106(3)(a) (2016).

42. The language of the will directing this distribution appears in article third of the will and reads as follows:

Third: To my wife, Mabel G. Dewire, I give, devise and bequeath all the rest, residue and remainder of all the estate of which I shall die seized, for and during the term of her natural life, and upon her decease to my son, Thomas A. Dewire, Jr., and his heirs and assigns, but in trust nevertheless upon the following trusts and for the following purposes:

A. To hold, direct, manage and conserve the trust estate, so given, for the benefit of himself, his wife and children in the manner following, that is to say:

To expend out of the net income so much as may be necessary for the proper care, maintenance of himself and wife conformable to their station in life, and for the care, maintenance

After the testator's death, Thomas, Jr., had three more children by a second wife. Thomas, Jr., died on May 28, 1978, a widower, survived by all six of his children. Thomas, III, who had served as trustee since 1978, died on March 19, 1987, leaving a widow and one child, Jennifer. Among the questions presented, and the most important one for present purposes, is to whom the one-sixth share of the trust income, once payable to Thomas, III, is now payable.

In his will, the testator stated: "It is my will, except as hereinabove provided, that my grandchildren, under guidance and discretion of my Trustee, shall share equally in the net income of my said estate." At another point, he referred to the trust income being "divided equally amongst my grandchildren." The rule against perpetuities violation occurred because the will provided for the trust's termination "twenty-one years after the death of the last surviving child of my said son, Thomas A. Dewire, Jr., when the property of the trust shall be equally divided amongst the lineal descendants of my grandchildren."[43]

There is no explicit provision in the will concerning the distribution of income on the death of a grandchild while the gift of income to grandchildren continues, nor is there any statement as to what the trustee should do with trust income between the death of the last grandchild and the date assigned for termination of the trust twenty-one years later.

Our task is to discern the testator's intention concerning the distribution of a grandchild's share of the trust income on his death. As a practical matter, in cases of this sort, where there is no express intention, we must resort to reasonable inferences in the particular circumstances which on occasion shade into rules of construction that are applied when no intention at all can be inferred on the issue. In this case, the reasonable inference as to the testator's intention is that Jennifer should take her father's share in the income.

Certain points are not in serious controversy and are relatively easy to resolve. The gift of net income to the testator's grandchildren, divided equally or to be shared equally, is a class gift. . . . The class includes all six grandchildren, three of whom were born before and three of whom were born after the testator's death. . . . Because there is a gift over at the end of the class gift, the testator intended the class gift to his grandchildren only to be a gift of a life interest in the income of the trust. . . . The general rule is that, in the absence of a contrary intent expressed in the will or a controlling statute stating otherwise, members of a class are joint tenants with rights of survivorship. Old Colony Trust Co. v. Treadwell, 43 N.E.2d 777, 779 (Mass. 1942); Meserve v. Haak, 77 N.E. 377, 379 (Mass. 1906). See G.L. c. 191, § 22 (1986 ed.) (antilapse statute).

This last stated principle becomes important in deciding whether Jennifer, the child of the deceased grandson, takes her deceased father's share in the trust income or whether the remaining class members, the other five grandchildren, take that income

---

and education of his children born to him in his lifetime, in such manner as in his judgment and discretion shall seem proper, and his judgment and discretion shall be final.

43. As we shall explain, the possibility that Thomas, Jr., would have a child born after the testator's death was sufficient to cause the violation of the rule against perpetuities. The fact that Thomas, Jr., had children born after the testator's death makes possible a violation of the rule in actual fact.

share equally by right of survivorship. Jennifer argues, under the general rule, that the will manifests an intent contrary to a class gift with rights of survivorship. We agree with this conclusion. Thus we need not decide, as Jennifer further argues, whether the rule of construction presuming a right of survivorship in class members should be rejected in the circumstances and replaced by a rule based on principles similar to those expressed in the antilapse statute.[44]

Before we explain why the will expresses an intention that, during the term of the class gift, Jennifer, while living, should take her father's share in the income, we discuss the rule against perpetuities problem.[45] The prospect that interests under this will may vest beyond the permissible limit of the rule against perpetuities is not only theoretically possible, it is actuarially likely. The interests of the grandchildren in the trust income vested at their father's death (if not sooner) and, because he was a life in being at the testator's death, those interests vested within the period of the rule. The gift over at the end of the class gift of income to the grandchildren, however, might not vest seasonably because another grandchild could have been born after the testator's death and could be the surviving grandchild. In this case, in fact, the three youngest grandchildren were born after the death of the testator but they are measuring lives for the term of the class gift. The parties agree that the purported gift of the remainder to the lineal descendants of the testator's grandchildren "twenty-one years after the death of the last surviving" grandchild violates the rule against perpetuities in its traditional form and would be void. See Second Bank-State St. Trust Co. v. Second Bank-State St. Trust Co., 140 N.E.2d 201, 205-206 (Mass. 1957). There is no need at this time to decide the question of the proper distribution of trust income or assets at the death of the last grandchild. The question will be acute at the death of the last grandchild, when the class gift of income from the trust will terminate.

---

44. The Massachusetts antilapse statute applies only to testamentary gifts to a child or other relation of a testator who predeceased the testator leaving issue surviving the testator and to class gifts to children or other relations where one or more class member predeceased the testator (even if the class member had died before the will was executed). G.L. c. 191, § 22. The rule of construction of § 22 is that the issue of a deceased relation take his share by right of representation "unless a different disposition is made or required by the will."

In this case, no class member predeceased the testator, and, therefore, § 22 does not explicitly aid Jennifer. The policy underlying § 22 might fairly be seen as supporting, as a rule of construction (absent a contrary intent), the substitution of a class member's surviving issue for a deceased class member if the class is made up of children or other relations of the testator. See Bigelow v. Clap, 43 N.E. 1037, 1038 (Mass. 1896). It has been suggested that "[t]he policy of [antilapse] statutes [dealing with the death of a class member after the testator's death] commends itself to decisional law." Restatement (Second) of Property, Donative Transfers § 27.3 comment i (Tent. Draft No. 9, 1986). If the antilapse statute protects the interests of the issue of a relation who predeceases a testator, there is a good reason why we should adopt, as a rule of construction, the same principle as to a relation of a testator who survives the testator but dies before an interest comes into possession. In the case of a class gift of income from a trust, the interest could be viewed as coming into possession of each income distribution date.

45. In its classic formulation, the rule against perpetuities declares that: "No interest is good unless it must vest, if at all, not later than twenty-one years after some life in being at the creation of the interest." J.C. Gray, The Rule Against Perpetuities § 201, at 191 (4th ed. 1942).

The rule against perpetuities problem need not be resolved at this time. It has some bearing, however, on what should be done during the term of the class gift with the one-sixth share of the trust income that is in dispute. We reject the argument that, because of the violation of the rule against perpetuities, the income interests should be treated as being more than life interests. There is no authority for such a proposition. Although the gift over violates the rule against perpetuities in its traditional form and in time may prove to violate it in actual fact, the language providing for such a distribution may properly be considered in determining a testator's intention with respect to other aspects of his will. . . .

We are now in a position to discuss the question whether the class gift of income to grandchildren calls for the payment of income equally to those grandchildren living from time to time (as joint tenants with rights of survivorship) or whether the issue of any deceased grandchild succeeds by right of representation to his income interest. The latter result better conforms with the testator's intentions.

The testator provided that the trust should terminate twenty-one years after the death of his last grandchild. It is unlikely that the testator intended that trust income should be accumulated for twenty-one years, and we would tend to avoid such a construction. See Meserve v. Haak, 77 N.E. 377, 378-379 (Mass. 1906). Certainly, we should not presume that he intended an intestacy as to that twenty-one year period. See Anderson v. Harris, 67 N.E.2d 670, 672-673 (Mass. 1946). He must have expected that someone would receive distributions of income during those years. The only logical recipients of that income would be the issue (by right of representation) of deceased grandchildren, the same group of people who would take the trust assets on termination of the trust (assuming no violation of the rule against perpetuities).[46] If these people were intended to receive income during the last twenty-one years of the trust as well as the trust assets on its termination, it is logical that they should also receive income during the term of the class gift if their ancestor (one of the grandchildren) should die. Such a pattern treats each grandchild and his issue equally throughout the intended term of the trust. Where, among other things, every other provision in the will concerning the distribution of trust income and principal (after the death of the testator and his wife) points to equal treatment of the testator's issue per stirpes, there is a sufficient contrary intent shown to overcome the rule of construction that the class gift of income to grandchildren is given to them as joint tenants with the right of survivorship.

Judgment shall be entered declaring that (1) Jennifer Ann Dewire in her lifetime is entitled to one-sixth of the net income of the trust during the period of the class gift of income, that is, until the death of the last grandchild (and a proportionate share of the income of any grandchild who dies leaving no issue), [and] (2) no declaration shall be

---

46. "[T]he property of the trust shall be equally divided amongst the lineal descendants of my grandchildren." "Equally," referring to a multigenerational class, normally means per stirpes. New England Trust Co. v. McAleer, 181 N.E.2d 569, 572 (Mass. 1962).

made at this time concerning the disposition of trust income or principal on the death of the last grandchild of Thomas A. Dewire. . . .

So ordered.

NOTES

1. Distribution of Income After the Death of a Class Member. Suppose T bequeaths a fund in trust to pay the income "to each of my children Gertrude, Charlotte, and John in equal amounts during their lives, and upon the death of the last survivor, to distribute the principal to their descendants per stirpes then living." Gertrude dies. What distribution of income is made? If Charlotte and John receive Gertrude's share, Gertrude's spouse and children are cut off from any benefits they have been receiving from Gertrude's share and the surviving children get richer. This does not seem consistent with T's intent, yet this is the traditional construction.[47]

Under the traditional construction, Thomas III's share in *Dewire* would have been paid to the surviving grandchildren, not to his descendants. Although this construction can be overcome by a finding of contrary intent, as in *Dewire*, such findings are rare. To encourage other courts to follow the sensible reasoning in *Dewire,* the Restatement (Third) of Trusts provides that in cases "in which the remainder is to pass to the descendants of the income beneficiaries upon the survivor's death," and one of the income beneficiaries dies, "the normal inference is that the settlor intended the income share to be paid to the issue (if any) of the deceased income beneficiary."[48]

2. Drafting Advice. When you give income to a class of persons, do not dispose of the principal upon the death of the survivor, because that leaves open the question litigated in *Dewire*. Instead, dispose of the principal "upon the death of each life tenant," and specify what is to be done with the individual life tenant's share of the principal upon that life tenant's death.[49]

3. Rule Against Perpetuities. The trust at issue in *Dewire* violated the common law Rule Against Perpetuities. Thomas, Jr. might—and, in fact, did—have a child born after the testator's death. This child might be the last surviving child so that the trust might terminate and the principal vest more than 21 years after the death of the last life in being at the testator's death. The trust was salvaged, however, by applying the *wait-and-see* doctrine (see Chapter 14 at page 903).

---

47. *See* Svenson v. First Nat'l Bank of Boston, 363 N.E.2d 1129 (Mass. App. 1977) (devise of income substantially identical except made to testator's servants rather than her children; court held gift of income was a class gift, to be divided by surviving servants); Westervelt v. First Interstate Bank, 551 N.E.2d 1180 (Ind. App. 1990) (holding income goes to surviving child on theory that each child has an implied cross remainder in the other child's share).

48. Restatement (Third) of Trusts § 49 cmt. c(3) (Am. Law Inst. 2003); *see also* Restatement (Third) of Property: Wills and Other Donative Transfers § 14.1 illus. 5 (Am. Law Inst. 2011) (illustration based on *Dewire*).

49. *See* John L. Garvey, Drafting Wills and Trusts: Anticipating the Birth and Death of Possible Beneficiaries, 71 Or. L. Rev. 47 (1992).

b. Gifts to Children, Issue, or Descendants

(1) Gift to Children

The law presumes that the word *children* means only the immediate offspring of the parent and does not include grandchildren or more remote descendants.[50] The assumption is that the use of the single-generational term was deliberate.

> *Case 20.* *T* bequeaths a fund in trust "for my daughter, *A*, for life, then to *A*'s surviving children." At *T*'s death, *A* has two children, *B* and *C*. Subsequently *C* dies, leaving a child, *D*. Then *A* dies survived by *B* and *D*. If children means what it says, *B* takes the entire trust fund and *D* does not share. So held in Matter of Gustafson, 547 N.E.2d 1152 (N.Y. 1989), denying *A*'s grandchild a share, over a strong dissent.

In a case such as this, one has a nagging suspicion that the term *children* was used carelessly and that the terms *issue* or *descendants*, incorporating the principle of representation familiar from inheritance law, would have better fit *T*'s intent. This suspicion has given rise to numerous cases, often involving homemade wills, litigating the question. Some courts, on the basis of other language in the governing instrument or extrinsic circumstances, have held that a settlor who said children meant descendants.

The Restatement (Third) of Property provides that a gift to children presumptively excludes grandchildren and more remote descendants, but may be read to mean issue or descendants if coupled with language of representation or other reasons for so interpreting it.[51]

(2) Gift to Issue or Descendants

A multigenerational gift to *issue* or *descendants* raises three questions of construction that we consider here: (a) whether distribution should be by representation or per capita; (b) if by representation, by what mode of representation; and (c) the effect of adoption and assisted reproductive technology on the meaning of the terms issue and descendants.

(a) By Representation or Per Capita?   If *T* makes a multigenerational gift in trust, such as "to the descendants of *A*," *A*'s descendants presumptively take *by right of representation* and not *per capita*.[52] Under a per capita distribution, favored by early law but no longer, all of *A*'s descendants alive on the distribution date take an equal share. Under a representational distribution, only the living descendants of nearest degree in each line of descent take. Thus, if *A* has three children, *B*, *C*, and *D*, and *B* predeceases *A* leaving two children, *E* and *F*, who survive *A* (see Figure 13.3), the property is divided into three shares with *E* and *F* splitting *B*'s third.

---

50. *See* Restatement (Third) of Property: Wills and Other Donative Transfers § 14.1(1) (Am. Law Inst. 2011). The same presumption applies to other single-generational gifts, such as to "brothers and sisters" or "nieces and nephews," the latter as in In re Estate of Reistino, 333 S.W.3d 767 (Tex. App. 2010).

51. *See* Restatement (Third) of Property: Wills and Other Donative Transfers § 14.1 cmt. g (Am. Law Inst. 2011).

52. *See* id. § 14.4 cmt. d.

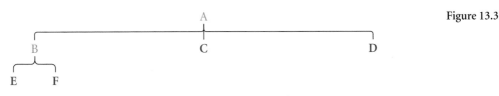

Figure 13.3

Survivors are in **bold**; deceased persons are in regular type.

The courts vary on what language is sufficient to overcome the presumption of distribution by right of representation. Suppose *T* devises property in trust with the remainder to the descendants of *A*, "share and share alike." Should the remainder be distributed per capita, with all living descendants of *A* taking an equal share, including those with a living ancestor in the line of descent? Or should it be distributed by representation, with only the living descendants of *A* of nearest degree in each line of descent entitled to take?[53]

(b) What Form of Representation?   When distribution is by representation, should the court apply English per stirpes, modern per stirpes, or per capita at each generation (see Chapter 2 at page 80)?

The Restatement (First) of Property took the position, still followed by some courts, that the form of representation in the state's intestacy statute should be followed even if the governing instrument used the term *per stirpes*.[54] Modern courts tend to apply the form of representation in the intestacy statute unless the instrument uses the term *per stirpes*, in which case English per stirpes is followed. The theory is that a drafter who uses the term *per stirpes* probably had in mind the traditional English per stirpes system rather than the form of representation provided by the local intestacy statute. The modern rule of construction is codified by UPC §§ 2-708 and 2-709 (1990, rev. 1993), and it is endorsed by the Restatement (Third) of Property.[55]

(c) Adoption and Assisted Reproductive Technology.   Another question that has sometimes vexed the courts is whether a person *adopted* by *A* is included in a gift by *T* to the children, issue, descendants, or heirs of *A*. Today almost all states presumptively include adopted children (and children born out of wedlock) in such gifts, but problems still arise with adult adoptions and with instruments drafted before the presumption of including adopted children took hold (see Chapter 2 at page 95). The new forms of parentage stemming from advances in *assisted reproductive technology*, including *posthumously conceived children*, have likewise raised interpretive difficulties (see page 110).

Under UPC § 2-705 (1990, rev. 2008), terms of relationship in class gifts are construed in accord with the meaning of those terms under the rules of intestate succession subject to certain exceptions such as for an adult adoption.

---

53. *Compare* Estate of Goodwin, 739 N.Y.S.2d 239 (Sur. 2002) (per capita), *with* First Illini Bank v. Pritchard, 595 N.E.2d 728 (Ill. App. 1992) (by representation).

54. Restatement (First) of Property § 303(1) (Am. Law Inst. 1940).

55. Restatement (Third) of Property: Wills and Other Donative Transfers § 14.4 cmt. c (Am. Law Inst. 2011).

(d) Drafting Advice.   The drafting lesson is that you should define terms such as *issue, descendants,* and *per stirpes.* In re Estate of Damon, 128 P.3d 815 (Haw. 2006), is a cautionary tale. Following UPC § 2-709, the court held that the term *per stirpes* referenced English rather than modern per stirpes, changing the amounts payable to two of the competing claimants by about $120 million. The will in *Damon*, by the way, lacked punctuation, except for a single period at the end of its tenth page!

c. Gifts to Heirs

Estate of Woodworth
22 Cal. Rptr. 2d 676 (App. 1993)

DiBiaso, J. The Regents of the University of California (Regents) appeal from an order of the probate court which rejected their claim to the remainder of a testamentary trust. We will reverse. We will apply the common law preference for early vesting and hold that, absent evidence of the testator's intent to the contrary, the identity of "heirs" entitled to trust assets must be determined at the date of death of the named ancestor who predeceased the life tenant, not at the date of death of the life tenant.

STATEMENT OF CASE AND FACTS

Harold Evans Woodworth died testate in 1971. His will was thereafter admitted to probate; in 1974 a decree of distribution was entered. According to this decree,[56] a portion of the estate was distributed outright to the testator's surviving spouse, Mamie Barlow Woodworth. The balance of the estate was distributed to Mamie Barlow Woodworth and the Bank of America, to be held, administered and distributed in accord with the terms of a testamentary trust established by the will of Harold Evans Woodworth. The life tenant of the trust was Mamie Barlow Woodworth. Among the trust provisions was the following:

> This trust shall terminate upon the death of MAMIE BARLOW WOODWORTH. Upon the termination of this trust, my trustee shall pay, deliver and convey all of the trust estate then remaining, including all accrued and/or undistributed income thereunto appertaining, to MRS. RAY B. PLASS, also known as Elizabeth Woodworth Plass [Elizabeth Plass], whose present address is 90 Woodland Way, Piedmont, California, if she then survives, and if not then to her heirs at law.

Elizabeth Plass was the testator's sister; he also had two brothers who predeceased him. One died without issue. The other was survived by two children, Elizabeth Woodworth Holden, a natural daughter, and James V. Woodworth, an adopted son.

Elizabeth Plass died in 1980; she was survived by her husband, Raymond Plass. Raymond Plass died testate in 1988. In relevant part, he left the residue of his estate to the Regents for use on the University's Berkeley campus.

---

56. The decedent's will was not introduced in the probate court proceedings. A decree of distribution is a conclusive determination of the terms of a testamentary trust and the rights of all parties claiming any interest under it. (Estate of Easter, 148 P.2d 601, 602-03 (Cal. 1944).)

Mamie Woodworth, the life tenant, died in 1991. Thereafter, Wells Fargo Bank, as successor trustee of the Woodworth trust, petitioned the probate court pursuant to Probate Code section 17200 to determine those persons entitled to distribution of the trust estate. The petition alleged that "The petitioner [was] uncertain as to whether Elizabeth Plass' 'heirs at law' under [the decree] should be determined as of February 14, 1980, the date of her death, or August 13, 1991, the date of Mamie [Barlow] Woodworth's death."

It is undisputed that (1) as of February 14, 1980, Elizabeth Plass' heirs at law were her husband, Raymond Plass, her niece, Elizabeth Woodworth Holden, and her nephew, James V. Woodworth; and (2) as of August 13, 1991, Elizabeth Plass' heirs at law were Elizabeth Woodworth Holden and James V. Woodworth (the Woodworth heirs). . . .

[T]he probate court concluded that the identity of the heirs entitled to the trust assets must be determined as of the date of death of the life tenant. The probate court therefore ordered the trustee to deliver the remaining trust assets in equal shares to the Woodworth heirs.

DISCUSSION . . .

Issues

The Regents contend the probate court erroneously failed to apply the general rule of construction which requires that the identity of "heirs" entitled to take a remainder interest be determined as of the date of death of the denominated ancestor, in the absence of any contrary intent expressed by the testator. (See Estate of Stanford, 315 P.2d 681, 682-83 (Cal. 1957); Estate of Liddle, 328 P.2d 35 (Cal. App. 1958).) Had the probate court construed the decree in accord with this principle, the Regents would have been entitled to share in the trust assets as a residuary legatee of Raymond Plass, an heir at law of Elizabeth Plass at the time of her death in 1980.

The Woodworth heirs respond by asserting the probate court's decision is consistent with an exception to the general rule which requires that the determination be made at the date of death of the life tenant. (See Wells Fargo Bank v. Title Ins. & Trust Co., 99 Cal. Rptr. 464, 466-67 (App. 1971).) Under this principle, the Regents have no interest in the trust assets, because Raymond Plass predeceased Mamie Barlow Woodworth.[57]

The Early Vesting Rule

Estate of Liddle, supra, 328 P.2d 35, reflects the common law preference for vested rather than contingent remainders. Thus, unless a particular instrument disclosed a different intent on the part of the testator, a remainder to a class of persons, such as children, became vested in the class when one or more of its members came into existence and could be ascertained, even though the class was subject to open for future additional members. (Estate of Stanford, supra, 315 P.2d at 683-84.) Furthermore, the

---

57. It is undisputed that had the testator in this case died on or after January 1, 1985, the Regents would have no claim to the trust assets. Under Probate Code sections 6150 and 6151 which have been in effect since 1985, a devise of a future interest to a class, such as heirs, includes only those who fit the class description at the time the legacy is to take effect in enjoyment.

fact that takers of a postponed gift were described by a class designation did not, under the common law rule, give rise to any implied condition of survival.

The circumstances involved in *Liddle* are substantially indistinguishable from those of the present case. In *Liddle*, the remainder of a testamentary trust was to be distributed to the testatrix's attorney or, in the event of his death, the attorney's heirs-at-law. Although the attorney survived the testatrix, he predeceased the life tenant. [His wife was his heir.] The wife's heirs and the administrator of her estate clashed with certain remote cousins of the attorney over the ownership of the trust assets.

The appellate court ruled in favor of the wife's estate. Relying upon statutes, treatises, and case law expressing common law notions, including Estate of Stanford, supra, 315 P.2d 681, the court construed the phrase "heirs at law" according to its technical meaning, that is, the person or persons who are entitled to succeed to the property of an intestate decedent. The *Liddle* court then held the members of this class must be determined as of the death of the named ancestor. The rule was summarized as follows:

> Normally, when a gift has been made to the "heirs" or "next of kin" of a named individual, the donor has said in effect that he wants the property distributed as the law would distribute it if the named person died intestate. Accordingly, the normal time for applying the statute of descent or distribution is at the death of the named individual. This is, however, merely a rule of construction, and if the testator or grantor manifests an intention that the statute be applied either at an earlier or a later time, such intention will be given effect. (*Liddle*, supra, 328 P.2d at 42-43.)

The designated ancestor in *Liddle* was the attorney. Because his wife was his intestate heir at the time he died, the court found she was the proper recipient of the trust estate.

The Contingent Substitutional Gift Exception

On the other hand, *Wells Fargo Bank*, supra, 99 Cal. Rptr. 464, 466-67, reflects the application of an exception to the early vesting principle. In *Wells Fargo Bank*, a woman had conveyed, by a grant deed, a life estate in certain real property to her daughter, with remainders to the grantor's two other children. If the life tenant died without issue and the two other children died without issue before the grantor's death, the instrument provided that the remainder interest in the property would belong to the grantor's "heirs." The trial court determined the heirs should be ascertained as of the date of the grantor's death. . . .

Application . . .

[The court of appeal reversed, relying on] Simes & Smith, The Law of Future Interests (2nd ed.) § 735, p. 210. . . . [U]nder consideration at the cited portion of this treatise is the situation where "a testator devises a life estate or defeasible fee to *a person who is one of his heirs,* followed by a remainder or executory interest to the testator's heirs." (Simes & Smith, supra, § 735, p. 206; emphasis added.) As Simes and Smith point out, in such circumstances, some courts have rejected the general rule that the members of the class are to be determined at the death of the ancestor (i.e., the testator), and instead have applied an exception which identifies the heirs who will take the remainder as those in being upon the death of the holder of the life estate or defeasible fee. The rationale for these decisions is an assumption the testator did not intend to give both a present and a future interest to the same person.

Wells Fargo Bank involved a bequest of the same type as that which is the subject of section 735 of the Simes and Smith treatise. In *Wells Fargo Bank*, the estate of the life tenant would have been entitled to receive a portion of the remainder if the identity of the grantor's heirs was determined at the time of the grantor's death rather than at the date of the life tenant's death. The *Wells Fargo Bank* court essentially adopted the analysis in section 735 of Simes and Smith that: "[I]f the general rule is applied, an incongruous result would be reached by taking the property away from [the holder of the possessory interest] because he died without issue and giving it back to him because of the same reason." (*Wells Fargo Bank*, supra, 99 Cal. Rptr. at 467.) . . .

By contrast, in the instant case we do not have a contingent, substituted gift to a class of recipients which includes the deceased interim beneficiary. As in *Liddle*, the class of contingent, substituted heirs does not encompass any prior contingent interim beneficiary. . . .

Thus, we believe the exception to the general rule of early vesting, as implemented in *Wells Fargo Bank*, should not be applied to the remainder interest contained in the decree of distribution here.

Other Considerations

For the reasons which follow, we find no other justification for departing from *Liddle*. First, there is nothing in the language of the other provisions of the decree of distribution before us which reveals the testator's intent or desire. Since the record does not include Harold Evans Woodworth's will, we cannot resort to it to attempt to divine his wishes. . . .

It would be pure speculation for us to conclude that Harold Evans Woodworth would not have wanted Raymond Plass to inherit a portion of the trust assets. It appears from the record that Raymond Plass and Elizabeth Plass were married at the time the testator executed his will. It has long been the law in California that a husband is an heir of his deceased wife. Nothing in the decree forecloses the possibility the testator took into account the fact that Elizabeth Plass might predecease, and Raymond Plass might outlive, Mamie Barlow Woodworth, resulting in Raymond Plass' succession to a portion of the trust remainder. . . .

In the absence of any firm indication of testamentary intent, the rules of construction must be implemented in order to insure uniformity and predictability in the law, rather than disregarded in order to carry out a court's ad hoc sense of what is, with perfect hindsight, acceptable in a particular set of circumstances. . . .

DISPOSITION

Accordingly, we must reverse the probate court's ruling that the Regents have no claim to the assets of the testamentary trust.

The judgment (order) appealed from is reversed.

NOTES

1. Future Interests in "Heirs."   Because a transmissible remainder is subject to the federal estate tax, estate planners have successfully urged state legislatures to enact statutes, such as UPC § 2-711 (1990, rev. 1993) and the California statute referenced in footnote 57 of *Woodworth*, providing that if a remainder is given to a person's *heirs*, the heirs will not be ascertained until the remainder becomes possessory. The Restatement (Third) of Property is to similar effect.[58] Under this rule of construction, no remainder beneficiary has a transmissible interest because if he dies before the remainder becomes possessory, he will not be alive when heirs are ascertained and, therefore, cannot be an heir.[59]

2. The Doctrine of Worthier Title.   If a settlor transfers property in trust with a life estate in the settlor or in another, and purports to create a remainder in the *settlor's heirs*, under the *doctrine of worthier title* it was conclusively presumed that the settlor intended to retain a reversion in himself and not create a remainder in his heirs. The rationale for this rule of law is obscure. Probably it was meant to ensure that property passed to descendants by descent (that is, by inheritance) rather than by purchase (that is, other than by inheritance). Property acquired by inheritance was deemed "worthier" and, perhaps more importantly, feudal lords exacted dues on inheritance but not other forms of transfer (see Chapter 1 at page 29).

In England, Parliament abolished this remnant of feudal times in 1833.[60] In the United States, the doctrine was roused from its slumber by then-Judge Benjamin N. Cardozo (see page 595) in Doctor v. Hughes, 122 N.E. 221 (N.Y. 1919), to do justice on the particular facts. As revitalized by Cardozo, the doctrine became a rule of construction that can be avoided by a showing that the settlor intended to create a remainder in his heirs. Thus:

> *Case 21.* *O* transfers property to *X* in trust "to pay the income to *O* for life, then to distribute the principal to *A* if *A* is living, and if *A* is not living, to distribute the principal to *O*'s heirs." The presumption is that *O* has a reversion and *O*'s heirs do not have a remainder. *O* may convey the reversion by will to whomever *O* chooses.

Recasting the doctrine as a rule of construction invites speculative evidence about whether the settlor intended to create a remainder rather than retain a reversion. Today almost every state has abolished the doctrine, both as a rule of law and as a rule of construction, either by statute, such as UPC § 2-710 (1990, rev. 1991), or by judicial decision. Both the Restatement (Third) of Trusts and the Restatement (Third) of Property repudiate the doctrine.[61]

---

58. *See* Restatement (Third) of Property: Wills and Other Donative Transfers § 16.1 (Am. Law Inst. 2011).

59. For a contrary example, determining heirs at the death of the testator, see Stevens v. Radey, 881 N.E.2d 855 (Ohio 2008).

60. Inheritance Act, 3 & 4 Will. 4, c. 106, § 3 (1833).

61. *See* Restatement (Third) of Property: Wills and Other Donative Transfers § 16.3 (Am. Law Inst. 2011); Restatement (Third) of Trusts § 49 cmt. a(1) (Am. Law Inst. 2003); *see also* Katheleen

3. The Rule in Shelley's Case. Under the rule in Shelley's Case, if land was conveyed to a grantee for life, then to the *grantee's heirs*, the attempted creation of a contingent remainder in the heirs was not recognized. Instead, the grantee took the remainder. The life estate then merged into the remainder, giving the grantee a possessory fee simple absolute.[62] The rule arose in feudal England, probably to protect the feudal incidents by ensuring that the grantee's heirs would take by inheritance (see page 29). The rule in Shelley's Case is thus not a rule of construction, but rather is a rule of law that applies regardless of the intent of the transferor.

> *Case 22.* O conveys land in trust "for A for life, and then to A's heirs." Under the rule in Shelley's Case, A (and not A's heirs) has the remainder, which then merges with A's life estate, giving A all the equitable interest in the trust. A may by will dispose of the land as A chooses.

The rule in Shelley's Case has been abolished in nearly all states and in England.[63] In some states, however, abolition is by recent statute and does not apply retroactively. So cases involving the rule may still crop up from time to time. Professor Brian Simpson aptly sums up thus:

> [T]he rule in *Shelley's Case* still enjoys a curious twilight existence. In legal education it flourishes in the American law schools; its archaic nature and sheer incomprehensibility positively attracts some students of property law, who are fascinated by the absurd, whilst utterly repelling others. Those who teach property law can always establish their dominance by teaching the rule, since a high proportion of their class can be relied upon to misunderstand it, and their confusion can always be enhanced by teaching the doctrine of worthier title, another Gothic relic, at the same time. Outside the classroom its status resembles that of the Big Foot, the Yeti, or the Tasmanian Tiger; sightings are still possible.[64]

d. The Rule of Convenience

A central characteristic of a class gift, such as "to the children of *B*," is that the class can increase in number so long as *B* is still alive. The question thus arises, for how long

---

Guzman, Worthier for Whom?, 68 Okla. L. Rev. 779 (2016). Rejection of the doctrine of worthier title leaves us with the problem of securing the consent of the unascertained heirs of a living settlor to modify or terminate a trust. In Case 21, if O and A want to terminate the trust, they must secure the consent of O's unknown heirs. Statutes in some states have dealt with this problem by providing that a trust may be revoked by the settlor and other ascertained beneficiaries if the only other interested persons are the settlor's heirs. *See, e.g.*, N.Y. Est. Powers & Trusts Law § 7-1.9 (2016).

62. Here is a fuller statement: If (a) one instrument (deed, will, or trust) (b) creates a life estate in land in *A*, and (c) purports to create a remainder in *A*'s heirs (or the heirs of *A*'s body), and (d) the estates are both legal or both equitable, then the remainder becomes a remainder in fee simple (or fee tail) in *A*. If there is no intervening estate, the life estate merges into the remainder, giving *A* a fee simple (or fee tail).

63. See Restatement (Third) of Property: Wills and Other Donative Transfers § 16.2 (Am. Law Inst. 2011); Restatement (Third) of Trusts § 49 cmt. a(1) (Am. Law Inst. 2003).

64. A.W. Brian Simpson, Leading Cases in the Common Law 41 (1995); *see also* John V. Orth, The Mystery of the Rule in Shelley's Case, 7 Green Bag 2d 45 (2003).

can the class increase in membership? In a gift "to *B* for life, then to *B*'s children," all of *B*'s children will be alive (or in gestation) when the class is *physiologically closed* at *B*'s death.[65] But suppose the disposition is "to *A* for life, then to *B*'s children." If *A* dies during *B*'s lifetime, what should be done with the property, given that *B* may have more children?

If a class is not closed physiologically when one or more members of the class are entitled to take their shares, as in the example just given, several solutions are possible.[66] Distribution could be postponed until all possible class members are on the scene. Or a partial distribution could be made with a reasonable portion withheld for later-born class members. Or full distribution could be made to the class members now at hand, subject to a requirement that they rebate a portion of each share as new members enter the class. Or the class could close at the time of distribution, to the exclusion of later-born class members.

The practical problems that would be raised by postponing distribution, or by making a partial or defeasible distribution to existing class members, have led the courts to adopt the last alternative, known as the *rule of convenience*. A rule of construction, the rule of convenience yields to an expression of contrary intent.

Under the rule of convenience, *a class will close whenever any member of the class is entitled to possession or enjoyment of his or her share.*[67] The key moment is when one member is *entitled* to demand payment. The fact that actual payment may be delayed because of administrative problems does not keep the class open. The class closes when the right to payment arises.

When a class is open, additional persons can come into the class. When a class is closed, no more persons can be added. All that we mean when we say that a class is closed is that *no person born hereafter can share in the property.*[68] The fact that a class is closed does not, however, mean that all members of the class will share in the property. Present class members can drop out by failing to meet some condition precedent before distribution.

The rule of convenience for closing a class that has not closed physiologically is perhaps best understood by way of illustrative cases. Let us consider: (1) immediate gifts, (2) postponed gifts, and (3) gifts of specific sums.

---

65. On posthumous conception and the class-closing rules, see Chapter 2 at page 118; *see also* Restatement (Third) of Property: Wills and Other Donative Transfers § 15.1 cmt. j (Am. Law Inst. 2011).

66. *See* David M. Becker, A Critical Look at Class Gifts and the Rule of Convenience, 42 Real Prop. Prob. & Tr. J. 491 (2007).

67. *See* Restatement (Third) of Property: Wills and Other Donative Transfers § 15.1 (Am. Law Inst. 2011).

68. More precisely, no person *conceived* after this date can share. Here, as elsewhere in property law, a child is treated as in being from the time of conception if later born alive (see page 107). For an adopted child, the time of adoption, not birth, is controlling. So an adopted child must be adopted into the class before the class closes. A child in being when the class closes, but subsequently adopted, does not share.

(1) Immediate Gifts

If there is an immediate gift to a class, the class closes as soon as any member can demand possession, either at the testator's death or later. Thus:

> *Case 23.* *T* devises $10,000 "to the children of *B*." *B* is alive and has two children, *C* and *D*. When *T* dies, the class closes. *C* and *D* can demand immediate possession of their shares. From *T*'s estate *C* is paid $5,000 and *D* is paid $5,000. If another child is born to *B* a year later, that child does not share in the bequest.

If no members of the class have been born before *T*'s death, the class does not close at that time. Since *T* must have known that there were no class members alive at his death, it is assumed that *T* intended all class members, whenever born, to share. In such circumstances, the class does not close until it is physiologically closed by the death of the designated ancestor of the class. In Case 23, for example, if *B* had no children born before *T*'s death, the class would not close until *B*'s death.[69] Here are two further examples:

> *Case 24.* *T* bequeaths $10,000 "to the children of *B* who reach 21." *B* has children alive, but no child is 21 at *T*'s death. The class will close when a child of *B* reaches 21.

> *Case 25.* *T* bequeaths $10,000 "to the children of *B*, to be paid to them in equal shares as they respectively reach 21." *B* has children alive, but all are under 21. The gift is vested with payment postponed. The class will close when the eldest child of *B* reaches 21 or, if the eldest child dies under that age, when the eldest child would have reached 21 had he lived.[70]

NOTES

1. An Immediate Gift Problem.   *T* bequeaths $15,000 "to the children of *B* who reach 21." At *T*'s death, *B* has two children, *C* (age 7) and *D* (age 4). Three years later, *E* is born to *B*. Thereafter, *C* reaches 21. What distribution is made to *C*? One year thereafter, *F* is born to *B*. *D* dies at age 20. Is any distribution made? *E* then reaches 21. Is any distribution made? *F* then reaches 21. Is any distribution made?

2. The Rule in Wild's Case.   A devise of property "to *B* and her children" is ambiguous. Does *B* take a life estate and the children a remainder? Or do *B* and her children take equal shares as tenants in common? Under the rule in Wild's Case, decided in 1599, if *B* has children at the time of the devise, *B* and her children take as tenants in common. Some states continue to follow this rule. Others construe such a gift as creating a life estate and a remainder. The rule in Wild's Case is repudiated by the Restatement (Third) of Property.[71] In a jurisdiction that still follows the rule in Wild's

---

69. *See* Restatement (Third) of Property: Wills and Other Donative Transfers § 15.1 cmt. k (Am. Law Inst. 2011).

70. *See* id. cmt. m.

71. *See* id. § 14.2 cmt. f.

Case, what effect does the rule of convenience have on *B*'s children conceived after the testator's death?

(2) Postponed Gifts

If a class gift is postponed in possession until a preceding life tenant dies, the class will not close under the rule of convenience until the life tenant is dead and a remainder-person is entitled to possession.

> *Case 26.* *T* bequeaths $10,000 "to *A* for life, then to the children of my daughter *B*." *B* survives *A*. The class will close at *A*'s death if (a) a child of *B* is then alive, (b) a child of *B* predeceased *T* and the remainder was redirected to such child's descendants under an antilapse statute, or (c) a child of *B* was alive at *T*'s death or was born after *T*'s death and this child predeceased *A*. In each of those cases, a child or the child's representative can demand payment at *A*'s death, closing the class under the rule of convenience.

Suppose that at the death of *A*, *B* has not yet had any children. Will the class be left open until the death of *B*, as in the case of an immediate gift to a class into which no one has been born at the time of possession? The Restatement (Third) of Property says the answer is Yes, but there are few cases on the matter. The Restatement also says, however, that "if the circumstances indicate that it is improbable that there will be any after-conceived or after-adopted class members because of the age or physical condition of the prospective parent," the gift should fail.[72]

The foregoing applies only to gifts of principal, not to gifts of income. "An income interest payable to class members from time to time living constitutes a series of successive postponed class gifts. Each of these classes closes on its distribution date."[73] Thus, in a trust to pay income to the children of *B*, the class closes for the payment of income periodically as the income is accrued. "The rule of convenience operates to give the living [children of *B*] absolute ownership in distributed income. It is neither inconvenient nor consistent with donative intent to exclude after-conceived [children of *B*] with regard to future income."[74]

NOTES

1. A Postponed Gift Problem.   *T* bequeaths a fund in trust "to pay the income to *A* for life, then to distribute the principal to the children of *B* who reach 21, and in the meantime the children of *B* who are eligible to receive, but have not yet received, a share of the principal are to receive the income." At *A*'s death, *B* is alive and has one child, *C* (age 5). After *A* dies, the following events occur: *D* is born to *B*; *C* reaches 21; one year later, *E* is born to *B*; *D*, and later *E*, reach 21.

> *a.* After *A*'s death, who is entitled to the income?
>
> *b.* When is the first distribution of principal made, to whom, and how much?
>
> *c.* How is the principal ultimately divided?

---

72. Id. § 15.1 cmt. k.
73. Id. cmt. p.
74. Id. illus. 18.

2. Another Postponed Gift Problem.   T bequeaths a fund in trust "to divide the fund among the children of B, payable to each at age 21, and in the meantime they are to receive the income." At T's death, B is alive and has one child, C (age 5). One year later, C dies. Is C's administrator entitled to demand immediate distribution of C's share? Would your answer be different if B predeceased T?

(3) Gifts of Specific Sums

If a specific sum is given to each member of the class, which is sometimes called a *per capita gift*, the class closes at the death of the testator regardless of whether any members of the class are then alive.[75] Thus:

> *Case 27.* T bequeaths £500 apiece to each child of A. A has no children living at T's death. The class closes at T's death, and no child of A ever takes anything. *See* Rogers v. Mutch, [1878] 10 Ch. 25 (Eng.).

What is the reason for closing the class at the death of the testator when the gift is of a fixed sum to each member of a class?[76]

> Life looked rosy to A as he sat
> By the crepe-draped casket of T.
> Five hundred pounds for each child he begat
> Would soon make him wealthy mused he.
>
> So he married at once, and began procreating
> At five hundred per, he supposed;
> But you know and I know (what hardly needs stating)
> That the class had already closed.
>
> Mistakes of this sort are bound to arise
> When a client takes actions like these
> Without seeing his lawyer as soon as T dies,
> And paying the usual fees.
>
> FRANK L. DEWEY[77]

---

75. *See* id. § 15.1 cmt. l; *see also* id. § 13.1 cmt. l.

76. *See* A. James Casner, Class Gifts to Others Than to "Heirs" or "Next of Kin": Increase in the Class Membership, 51 Harv. L. Rev. 254, 271 (1937).

77. Reproduced from W. Barton Leach, Langdell Lyrics of 1938 11-12 (1938).

CHAPTER 14

THE RULE AGAINST PERPETUITIES AND TRUST DURATION

> A clear, obvious, natural line is drawn for us between those persons
> and events which the Settlor knows and sees, and those which he
> cannot know or see.

> ARTHUR HOBHOUSE
> The Devolution and Transfer of Land, *in* The Dead Hand: Addresses on
> the Subject of Endowments and Settlements of Property 188 (1880)

FREEDOM OF DISPOSITION, the organizing principle of American succession law, is not absolute. Perhaps the most storied limit on freedom of disposition is the *Rule Against Perpetuities*. In this chapter, we consider that rule and two related doctrines that also curb the reach of the dead hand: the *rule against suspension of the power of alienation* and the *rule against accumulations of income*.

The Rule Against Perpetuities requires all interests, whether in trust or otherwise, to vest or fail within the lives of everyone who could possibly have been known to the donor ("lives in being") plus the minority of the next generation ("plus twenty-one years"). Property cannot be subjected to a contingency for longer than the perpetuities period. In this way, the Rule imposes a temporal limit on the reach of the dead hand.

Although there is still strong support for the underlying policy of the Rule Against Perpetuities, its particulars have come under attack. At common law, any interest that *might* not vest or fail within the perpetuities period was void from the outset no matter how implausible the invalidating possibility. The *fertile octogenarian*, *unborn widow*, and other such infamous absurdities that follow from the merciless and unyielding logic of the Rule brought the Rule into disrepute. Today, every state has reformed the Rule in one way or another. Many of these reforms are meant to honor the Rule's purpose, but not all. Most strikingly, in consequence of the competition among the states for trust business, a majority of states have repealed or otherwise modified the Rule to allow for a *perpetual trust*.

We begin in Section A by considering the common law Rule Against Perpetuities: its history, purpose, and structure as a rule of logical proof. In Section B, we consider the debate over reforming the Rule, including the rise of the wait-and-see doctrine and more recently the movement to permit perpetual trusts. In Section C, we consider application of the Rule to class gifts and powers of appointment. Finally, in Section D, we consider the rule against suspension of the power of alienation and the rule against accumulations of income.

A. THE COMMON LAW RULE

1. History[1]

The classic statement of the Rule Against Perpetuities, formulated by Professor John Chipman Gray of Harvard Law School in his magisterial treatise on the Rule, is this:

> No interest is good unless it must vest, if at all, not later than twenty-one years after some life in being at the creation of the interest.[2]

Professor John Chipman Gray

Because of the deference paid to Gray's work by the courts, the Rule has sometimes been treated as if Gray had invented it.[3] In truth, the Rule had a complicated evolution over several centuries.

a. Predicates to the Rule

Following the expansion of freedom of disposition by the Statute of Uses (1535) and Statute of Wills (1540) (see page 30),[4] judges struggled to fashion a rule against perpetuities. The difficulty was in coming up with a definition for what a *perpetuity* was. The prevailing understanding was that a perpetuity was an *entail*—that is, an estate that would pass forever in accordance with a prescribed succession so that the holder of the possessory interest could neither alienate that interest nor alter the subsequent line of succession.

The formal entail originated in the Statute *De Donis Conditionalibus* (1285).[5] Feudal lords, resisting the movement toward free alienation of land, convinced Parliament to authorize in *De Donis* the creation of the fee tail, an estate in land that passes to the original tenant's descendants in a perpetual string of life estates. Courts responded by fashioning the "common recovery," a suit by which

---

1. Portions of this section are adapted from Steven J. Horowitz & Robert H. Sitkoff, Unconstitutional Perpetual Trusts, 67 Vand. L. Rev. 1769 (2014).

2. John Chipman Gray, The Rule Against Perpetuities § 201, at 191 (Roland Gray ed., 4th ed. 1942).

3. *See* Stephen A. Siegel, John Chipman Gray, Legal Formalism, and the Transformation of Perpetuities Law, 36 U. Miami L. Rev. 439 (1982).

4. 27 Hen. 8 c. 10 (Eng.), and 32 Hen. 8 c. 1 (Eng.), respectively.

5. 13 Edw. c. 1 (Eng.).

the possessory tenant could transform his fee tail interest into fee simple, a procedure known as "barring" or "docking" the entail.

The lawyers for England's wealthy families fought back by combining life estates in one generation with contingent remainders in successive generations. In Gray's telling, "it occurred to some ingenious person that it was perhaps possible to keep control over the ownership of property for a time by granting an estate for life with contingent remainders, for, as contingent remainders were not transferable, no alienation of the fee could take place until they vested."[6] In response, the judges developed the law of future interests, which allowed for the destruction of contingent remainders (see Chapter 13 at page 855).

The destructibility doctrines could be avoided, however, by using executory interests, authorized by the Statute of Uses, instead of contingent remainders. By this "ingenuity of conveyancers, aided by the inadvertence of the judges,"[7] wealthy landowners could again implement "an infinite series of future interests that might remove land permanently from commerce."[8] Tellingly, the first cases to use the term "perpetuity," decided in the 1590s, recognized the functional equivalence of this use of indestructible executory interests to the unbarrable entail.[9]

Across the 1600s, the judges developed the law of perpetuities in answer to the indestructible executory interest — that is, to prevent what was in function an entail by way of such interests. Gray summarized the emerging perpetuities law thus: "Any number of life interests could be given in succession to persons in being. Limitations to unborn persons might be good[,] . . . but under what restrictions was far from clear."[10]

b. The Duke of Norfolk's Case

The amorphous body of law governing perpetuities was fashioned into the Rule Against Perpetuities in 1682 in the Duke of Norfolk's Case.[11] Thomas, the eldest son and heir apparent of the Earl of Arundel, was incompetent. The earl therefore assumed that eventually the earldom would descend to his second son, Henry. In that event, the earl wanted the Barony of Grostock, which he planned to give initially to Henry, to shift to his fourth son, Charles.

When the Earl of Arundel died, the earldom descended to Thomas. Henry assumed control of the properties accompanying the title. He also engineered restoration of the title "Duke of Norfolk" to the family. When Thomas died, the dukedom descended to Henry (thus the Duke of Norfolk's Case). But Henry did not want to give up the Barony of Grostock. So Charles brought a bill in chancery to enforce his interest. Henry resisted, arguing that the executory interest in Charles was a perpetuity and thus void.

---

6. Gray, *supra* note 2, § 141.4, at 140.

7. Id. § 141.6, at 141.

8. Jesse Dukeminier & James E. Krier, The Rise of the Perpetual Trust, 50 UCLA L. Rev. 1303, 1320 (2003).

9. *See* Corbet's Case, (1599) 76 Eng. Rep. 187 (K.B.); 1 Co. Rep. 83 b; Chudleigh's Case, (1594) 76 Eng. Rep. 261 (K.B.) 261-325; 1 Co. Rep. 113 b, 113 b-140 b.

10. Gray, *supra* note 2, § 168, at 160 & n.2.

11. (1682) 22 Eng. Rep. 931 (Ch.); 3 Chan. Cas. 1; *see also* Herbert Barry, The Duke of Norfolk's Case, 23 Va. L. Rev. 538 (1937).

The sixth Duke of Norfolk, whose greed brought on the case that originated the Rule Against Perpetuities.

Lord Chancellor Nottingham, one of the greatest of the English Chancellors, was called the "Father of Equity" by Justice Story.

Sympathetic to the rational estate planning of a landowner with an incompetent son, Lord Chancellor Nottingham was of the opinion that Charles's interest would "wear out" in a single lifetime (Thomas's), and, hence, it should not be regarded as a perpetuity. "A perpetuity," said Nottingham, "is the settlement of an estate or an interest in tail, with such remainders expectant upon it, as are in no sort in the power of the tenant in tail in possession to dock by any recovery or assignment." The critical issue was the time at which the contingent interest would vest. Nottingham ruled that, if an interest necessarily would vest or fail during or at the end of a life in being, it is good. The House of Lords agreed.

c. Toward Lives in Being Plus 21 Years

After the Duke of Norfolk's Case, the judges refined the test for a perpetuity in relation to Nottingham's life-in-being holding.[12] Eventually the perpetuities period was settled at any reasonable number of lives in being plus 21 years in gross plus any actual periods of gestation.[13] The judges thus permitted a donor's freedom of disposition to be exercised in a way that included indestructible contingent interests, but only as regards

---

12. In Stanley v. Leigh, (1732) 24 Eng. Rep. 917 (Ch.); 2 P. Wms. 686, the court described the term "perpetuity" as "a legal word or term of art" meaning "the limiting [of] an estate . . . in such manner as would render it unalienble longer than for a life or lives in being at the same time, and some short or reasonable time after." In Stephens v. Stephens, (1736) 25 Eng. Rep. 751 (Ch.); Cases t. Talb. 228, the permissible perpetuities period was clarified as including the minority of a beneficiary, up to 21 years, in addition to lives in being. Thellusson v. Woodford, (1805) 32 Eng. Rep. 1030 (Ch.); 11 Ves. Jr. 112, established that any number of lives in being that could reasonably be traced could be used.

13. *See* Cadell v. Palmer, (1833) 6 Eng. Rep. 956 (H.L.) 974-75; 1 Cl. & Fin. 372.

persons the donor could have known (lives in being) plus the minority of the next generation (21 years). The purpose was to prevent resurrection of the entail by way of a string of successive life estates subject to indestructible contingent interests. Professor Brian Simpson's capsule summary is apt:

> [T]here were many expressions of hostility to perpetuities, and a perpetuity meant an unbarrable entail, in whatever guise it appeared. This hostility found expression in . . . the celebrated "rule against perpetuities." . . . This doctrine . . . prevented the evolution, under some newer guise, of any form of perpetual unbarrable entail, but permitted unbarrable entails of limited duration.[14]

NOTE

Perpetuities in a Nutshell. The classic introduction to the Rule Against Perpetuities for students is Professor W. Barton Leach's famous article, Perpetuities in a Nutshell, 51 Harv. L. Rev. 638 (1938), updated by Leach in Perpetuities: The Nutshell Revisited, 78 Harv. L. Rev. 973 (1965). For a more recent synopsis, see Jesse Dukeminier, A Modern Guide to Perpetuities, 74 Cal. L. Rev. 1867 (1986).

2. The Policy Against Remote Vesting

The Rule Against Perpetuities limits the remote vesting of interests, in trust or otherwise. The basic assumption is that a *contingent interest* is objectionable if the contingency might remain unresolved for longer than "lives in being plus 21 years."

a. The Modern Purposes of the Rule

The Rule Against Perpetuities is said nowadays to have two main purposes: (1) keeping property marketable, and (2) limiting dead hand control. Property cannot be conveyed with clear title unless all persons with an interest in the property agree to the conveyance. By requiring the identity of all persons with a claim on property to be ascertained within the perpetuities period, the Rule ensures that the property will become *marketable* periodically.

The second purpose, *limiting dead hand control,* is perhaps best understood in light of the disagreeable consequences that can arise from property arrangements made obsolete by changes in circumstances. By forbidding contingencies that might remain unresolved beyond lives in being plus 21 years, the Rule puts an outer boundary of roughly 100 years or so on the reach of the dead hand.

Measured against these two purposes, the Rule is both under- and overinclusive. It is *underinclusive* because it applies only to contingent interests. But a vested interest that will not become possessory until long into the future (if ever) might become problematic as circumstances change. The distinction between a vested interest and a contingent interest turns on arbitrary rules of the common law (see Chapter 13 at page 848), not on the certainty that the interest will become possessory. That an interest

---

14. A.W. Brian Simpson, Entails and Perpetuities, 24 Jurid. Rev. 1, 17 (1979).

George Clooney Makes Estate Planning Sexy

By Deborah L. Jacobs

Estate planning doesn't often make it to the Academy Awards. But that's happened this year, when The Descendants was nominated for Oscars in five categories, including best picture, best actor (George Clooney) and best director (Alexander Payne).

Based on the novel by Kaui Hart Hemmings, it's a multi-layered story about Matt King (played by Clooney), a rich trial lawyer in the throes of a midlife crisis and personal tragedy. His wife Elizabeth has been injured in a boat race accident and lies in a coma, leaving him to care for his two daughters—the precocious 10-year-old Scottie (Amara Miller) and rebellious 17-year-old Alexandra (Shailene Woodley). Meanwhile, he discovers that his wife has been having an affair and planning to divorce him.

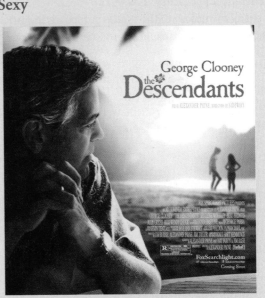

While these plots and sub-plots dominate our attention, the movie title refers to the fact that King is the descendant of a wealthy white banker and a Hawaiian princess. They left valuable real estate on Kauai in a trust. With that trust about to end, King must decide whether to sell the land to a developer, enriching himself and his greedy cousins.

To most viewers, estate planning themes are secondary to the film's other dramas. But it turns out that the legal issues were painstakingly developed and fact-checked. On location in Hawaii in March, 2010 to get the lay of the land and soak up its culture, Alexander Payne, the director, consulted Randall Roth, a professor at the University of Hawaii School of Law and a nationally known trusts and estates expert....

Most movies simplify legal matters. In The Descendants there is one issue that gets much more complicated. In the book, the reader is told that the trust, according to its provisions, was scheduled to end when Matt King's grandfather died—something that wouldn't be unusual. But Roth saw gaps in the facts that he thought would raise questions for people who are knowledgeable about trusts and

estates law. To solve the problem, he recommended an arcane legal principle be added to the script.

Called the rule against perpetuities, it's a law in many states that prevents a trust from lasting indefinitely and sets a maximum term. Traditionally it was measured by "lives in being plus 21 years," which meant that as a practical matter most trusts wound up lasting about 100 years. In the movie,... the descendants anticipate that the trust will end within the next seven years.

In his role as the movie's narrator, Matt King explains the rule against perpetuities in summary fashion. Roth says he "would bet a lot of money" that Clooney hadn't heard of the rule against perpetuities before then. (Clooney was not available for comment.)

Source: Forbes (Feb. 23, 2012). *See also* Randall W. Roth, Deconstructing the Descendants: How George Clooney Ennobled Old Hawaiian Trusts and Made the Rule Against Perpetuities Sexy, 48 Real Prop. Tr. & Est. L.J. 291 (2013).

is vested does not guarantee that it will ever become possessory. If the purpose of limiting the reach of the dead hand is to be implemented fully, the law should curb all future interests, not just contingent ones.[15]

---

15. Statutes in some states impose a time limit on reversionary interests after which the possessory fee becomes absolute. *See* Helene S. Shapo, George Gleason Bogert & George Taylor Bogert, The Law of Trusts and Trustees § 214 (3d ed. 2007).

The Rule is *overinclusive* because it applies whether an interest is *legal* (outright) or *equitable* (in trust). But for an equitable interest, if the trustee has the power to sell the trust property and reinvest the proceeds, as is typical, there is no constraint on the marketability of that property. This is true even if there are numerous beneficiaries with exotic contingent interests that might not vest or fail until long into the future.

In spite of the Rule's loose fit with its purposes, most commentators contend that the Rule does, by and large, prevent the tying up of property for an inordinate length of time. If a legal interest violates the Rule, it is void ab initio. If an interest in trust violates the Rule, the trust is void ab initio to that extent.[16]

b. Why "Lives in Being Plus 21 Years"?

In the era of male primogeniture (see page 29) in which the Rule Against Perpetuities evolved, heads of families—the fathers—were deeply concerned about the possibility of land being inherited by an incompetent son or someone else whom they considered unworthy. In the Duke of Norfolk's Case, Lord Chancellor Nottingham recognized this concern as legitimate. With respect to living persons, the father's judgment would be given effect. But the father could know nothing of unborn persons. So the father's will was permitted to control only as long as the life of anyone possibly known to him ("lives in being") plus the next generation's minority ("21 years") and any actual periods of gestation.[17] Sir Arthur Hobhouse (see page 3) famously put the point thus:

> A clear, obvious, natural line is drawn for us between those persons and events which the Settlor knows and sees, and those which he cannot know or see. Within the former province we may trust his natural affections and his capacity of judgment to make better dispositions than any external Law is likely to make for him. Within the latter, natural affection does not extend, and the wisest judgment is constantly baffled by the course of events.[18]

c. The Rule and Trust Duration

The Rule Against Perpetuities does not impose a direct limit on the duration of trusts. Instead, by requiring that all interests in trust vest or fail within the perpetuities period, the Rule limits trust duration indirectly. The Rule ensures that the identity of all beneficiaries with a claim to the property will be ascertained within the perpetuities period. These ascertained beneficiaries may terminate the trust when the perpetuities period expires. The material purpose rule of the *Claflin* doctrine (see page 728) no

---

16. Subject to the doctrine of *infectious invalidity*, under which a court may invalidate the entire transfer if doing so will better approximate the transferor's intentions than invalidating only the offending interest. *See* Jeffrey A. Schoenblum, Multistate Guide to Estate Planning tbl. 9, q. 25 (2016) (surveying infectious invalidity across the states).

17. The Rule thus follows the general principle of property law that a person is in being from the time of conception, if later born alive (see page 107).

18. Arthur Hobhouse, The Devolution and Transfer of Land, *in* The Dead Hand: Addresses on the Subject of Endowments and Settlements of Property 188 (1880).

longer applies upon expiration of that period.[19] If the beneficiaries do not terminate the trust at that time, the principal will be distributed to the remainder beneficiaries when the preceding life estates expire.

3. A Rule of Logical Proof

The Rule Against Perpetuities is a rule of logical proof. A contingent future interest is void at the outset if it is not certain to *vest or fail*—one or the other *must* happen—within 21 years after the death of "some life in being at the creation of the interest." No matter how implausible the invalidating possibility, an interest that might not vest or fail within the perpetuities period is void. The common law Rule requires absolute certainty at the outset that the interest will vest or fail within the perpetuities period.

a. Some Life in Being

The "life in being" used to determine the period in which an interest must vest or fail can be *any* person. All that matters is whether you can prove that the interest will necessarily vest or fail within that person's life or 21 years after that person's death. This life in being is often called the *measuring life*, but the term *validating life* is more accurate. The life in being does not measure for how long the interest may last, rather it validates (or its absence invalidates) the interest.[20] Case 1 shows how to make the necessary proof that an interest will vest or fail within a validating life.

> *Case 1. O* transfers a fund in trust "to pay the income to *A* for life, then to *A*'s children for their lives, then to pay the principal to *B*." *A* currently has no children. *A*'s life estate is vested in possession upon creation. The remainder to *A*'s children for their lives will vest in possession or, if *A* has no children, fail upon *A*'s death. *B*'s remainder is vested in interest upon creation. All interests created by the transfer are valid.

Under traditional future interests law, in Case 1 all interests in the trust either are vested upon creation or will vest, if at all, within the period allotted by the Rule. The trust is valid in its entirety even though it could possibly endure for longer than the perpetuities period. *B*'s remainder, which is valid because it vests *in interest* upon creation, may not vest *in possession* until well beyond the relevant lives in being plus 21 years—for example, if *A* has one or more children born after the transfer who live for more than 21 years after the death of the last child of *A* born before the transfer.

The crucial inquiry under the Rule is: *When will the interest vest or fail?* An interest that is vested upon creation is not subject to the Rule. A contingent interest satisfies the Rule if it must vest, if at all, *either in possession or in interest* within a life in being plus

---

19. *See* Restatement (Third) of Trusts § 29 cmt. h(1) (Am. Law Inst. 2003).
20. *See* Restatement (Third) of Property: Wills and Other Donative Transfers ch. 27, intro. note (Am. Law Inst. 2011).

21 years. Here are three further illustrations of contingent interests that are valid because they will vest or fail within the perpetuities period:

> *Case 2.* *T* bequeaths $10,000 "to *A*, when she marries" and $5,000 "to *A*'s first child." *A* is unmarried and without children. The bequest to *A* will vest during *A*'s life, if at all; it is valid. The bequest to *A*'s first child also will vest during *A*'s life, if at all; it is valid.

> *Case 3.* *O*, a teacher, declares a trust of her first edition of Charles Dickens's Bleak House "for the first student in my current Trusts and Estates class to be sworn in as a judge." The gift will vest or fail within the lives of the students in the class. The condition precedent will necessarily be met, if ever, before the last surviving student dies.

> *Case 4.* *O* transfers a fund in trust "to pay the income to *A* for life, then to pay the principal to *A*'s children who reach 21." The remainder is valid because it will vest, at the latest, 21 years after *A*'s death, for all *A*'s children must reach 21 within 21 years after *A* dies (plus any period of actual gestation).

NOTES

1. A Perpetuities Problem.   *T* bequeaths a fund in trust "for *A* for life, then to the first child of *A* to be admitted to the bar." Is the latter gift valid? If so, who is the validating life?

2. Another Perpetuities Problem.   Compare the following bequests:
> *a.* To *A* for life, then to *B* if *B* goes to the planet Saturn.
> *b.* To *A* for life, then to *B* if any person goes to the planet Saturn.
> *c.* To *A* for life, then to *B* for life if any person goes to the planet Saturn.

Is *B*'s remainder good in each bequest? Who is the validating life?

b. When the Lives in Being Are Ascertained

Although Gray said the validating life in being must be a person alive "at the creation of the interest," it is more accurate to say that the validating life or lives must be in being *when the perpetuities period starts to run*. If an interest is created by *will*, the validating life or lives must be in being at the testator's death. If the interest is created by *deed* or *irrevocable trust*, the validating life or lives must be persons in being when the deed or trust takes effect.

Different rules for determining validating lives govern revocable trusts and interests created by the exercise of a power of appointment. If the interest is created by a *revocable trust*, the perpetuities period begins when the power to revoke terminates, as this is when the property becomes tied up. The validating life or lives must be persons in being at that time. If the power to revoke terminates at the settlor's death, as is typical, the validating lives must be persons alive at the settlor's death.

We take up interests created by the exercise of *a power of appointment* below in Section C at page 916.

4. What Might Happen and the Fantastical Characters

Under the common law Rule Against Perpetuities, *any* possibility that an interest might vest too remotely invalidates the interest. The test is what *could* happen, not what *actually does* happen or what is *likely* to happen. Professor W. Barton Leach explains:

> A future interest is invalid unless it is absolutely certain that it must vest within the period of perpetuities. Probability of vesting, however great, is not sufficient. Moreover, the certainty of vesting must have existed at the time when the instrument [became irrevocable and] took effect. . . . It is immaterial that the contingencies actually do occur within the permissible period or actually have occurred when the validity of the instrument is first litigated.
>
> It is at this point that the rule becomes a trap to the draftsman. Many perfectly reasonable dispositions are stricken down because on some outside chance not foreseen by the testator or his lawyer it is mathematically possible that the vesting might occur too remotely. Mistakes of this sort are readily classifiable into frequently recurring types.[21]

By giving recurring mistakes under the Rule ludicrous but memorable names — such as the *fertile octogenarian, unborn widow,* and *slothful executor* — Leach drew attention to the Rule's exasperating complexities and absurd assumptions.

Motherhood at 70

By William Saletan

It looks like we have a new record-holder in the ongoing "world's oldest mom" contest. . . .

Your new frontrunner is Rajo Devi of Alewa, India. She just gave birth at 70. Her husband is 72.

It's a heart-warming story of man — or, in this case, woman — overcoming nature's cruelty. Devi and her husband tried for years to have kids. Eventually, menopause claimed her. That was 20 years ago.

Then technology arrived to save the day. No eggs? No problem. We can get you donor eggs. Bad sperm? No problem. We'll fix that, too. "We used the usual intra cytoplasmic sperm injection (ICSI) technique," the couple's fertility doctor, Dr. Anurag Bishnoi, told the Times of India. "The ICSI method enables even poor quality sperms being used creating embryos." In Devi's case, the paper adds, the doctors used "blastocyst culture," transferring the egg after five days in vitro instead of the usual two or three.

The tinkering worked. "Childless for 50 yrs, mother at 70," says the headline in the Hindustan Times.

Rajo Devi, 70, holding her daughter, with her husband Bala Ram, 72
Devendra Uppal/AP photo

Devi exults: "We longed for a child all these years and now we are very happy to have one."

Source: Slate (Dec. 9, 2008).

---

21. W. Barton Leach, Perpetuities in a Nutshell, 51 Harv. L. Rev. 638, 642-43 (1938).

a. The Fertile Octogenarian

The *fertile octogenarian*, perhaps the most famous of the fantastical beings that inhabit the strange world of perpetuities law, usually appears in a two-generation trust such as the following:

> *Case 5. The Fertile Octogenarian. T* bequeaths a fund in trust for her sister "*A* (age 80) for life, then for *A*'s children for their lives, then to distribute the trust assets to *A*'s descendants then living." The law *conclusively presumes* that *A* is capable of having more children. Because of this presumption, the remainder to *A*'s children for their lives may include an after-born child of *A*, and the remainder to *A*'s descendants might vest on the death of this after-born child, which is too remote. The remainder to *A*'s descendants is void.

The conclusive presumption of fertility was laid down in the famous old case of Jee v. Audley, (1787) 29 Eng. Rep. 1186 (Ch.); 1 Cox 324.[22] In that case, the Master of the Rolls, Lord Kenyon, said:

> I am desired to do in this case something which I do not feel myself at liberty to do, namely, to suppose it impossible for persons in so advanced an age as John and Elizabeth Jee [both septuagenarians] to have children; but if this can be done in one case it may in another, and it is a very dangerous experiment, and introductive of the greatest inconvenience to give a latitude to such sort of conjecture.

If you think the conclusive presumption of fertility is absurd, at what age would you presume women could not bear children? Men? Now that adoption has become widely accepted, is it not possible that any living person could have a child at any time? On the other hand, should not perpetuities law be based on probabilities rather than

Lord Kenyon, Master of the Rolls and later Lord Chief Justice

theoretical possibilities? For example, could not the remainder to *A*'s descendants in Case 5 be saved by construing "*A*'s children" to refer to *A*'s children living at *T*'s death? Should a court do this?

A new problem, as in In re Martin B., 841 N.Y.S.2d 207 (Sur. 2007), page 118, is the *fertile decedent*. In that case, the court recognized a future interest in a posthumously conceived child. Should the possibility of posthumous parentage be considered in perpetuities analysis? Perhaps because myriad contingent future interests in children or descendants would be void if courts allowed for the possibility of posthumous parentage (do you see why?), they have not done so. Section 1(d) of the Uniform Statutory

---

22. For a study of the case in historical context, see A.W. Brian Simpson, Leading Cases in the Common Law 76-99 (1995).

Rule Against Perpetuities, which we take up later in this chapter at page 904, disregards the possibility of posthumous parentage.

NOTES

1. A Fertile Octogenarian Problem.   *T* bequeaths a fund in trust "for *A* for life, then to such of *A*'s nephews and nieces as live to attain the age of 21." At the time of *T*'s death, *A* is living and has a sister, *B*, and four nephews and nieces (the children of *B*), all of whom are under age 21. Is the interest given to *A*'s nephews and nieces valid under the Rule Against Perpetuities? (The answer is, "It depends." Do you see why?)

2. Another Fertile Octogenarian Problem.   Keeping in mind the conclusive presumption of fertility, which of the following bequests would be valid? *T* devises Blackacre to Mary Hall, but if the Brooklyn Bridge ever falls—

   a. to the children of Elizabeth Jee now living.
   b. to the children of Elizabeth Jee then living.
   c. to the children of Elizabeth Jee now living who are then living.

3. Sterilizing the Octogenarians.   Statutes in several states, such as Illinois and New York, limit the presumption of fertility to likely childbearing years (say, between 13 and 65) and permit the introduction of evidence of infertility. These statutes also provide that the possibility that a person may adopt a child is disregarded.[23]

4. The Precocious Toddler.   What is the youngest age of procreation? In 1964, the New York Times reported as follows:

> A 10-year-old girl gave birth today to a 5-pound 15-ounce girl, her attending physician reported.
> Dr. Carlo A. Fioretti said the birth was by Caesarean section.
> The mother is a fourth-grade pupil. It was believed she would not see her baby, who was to be sent to St. Vincent's orphanage as soon as possible, hospital administrators said.
> Medical sources said a 9-year-old Arkansas girl was believed to be the youngest mother on record in the United States. She gave birth to a 2 1/2-pound boy in 1957.
> A 5-year-old girl was delivered of a son by Caesarean section in Peru in 1939.
> Authorities refused to reveal the name of the mother, who has named a 16-year-old boy as the father. The boy is undergoing psychiatric tests.[24]

Only one known case has dealt with the issue. In In re Gaite's Will Trusts, [1949] All E.R. 459 (Ch.), at issue was a bequest that would be void only if the court assumed that a person under the age of five could have a child. The court held the gift valid, not on the grounds of physical impossibility, but rather because a child born to so young a person would be born out of wedlock. Under modern law, the constructional escape

---

23. *See* 765 Ill. Comp. Stat. 305/4(c) (2016); N.Y. Est. Powers & Trusts Law § 9-1.3(e) (2016); *see also* Schoenblum, *supra* note 16, tbl. 9, q. 19 (surveying states).
24. Chicago Girl, 10, Gives Birth to a Five-Pound Daughter, N.Y. Times, Feb. 13, 1964, at 12.

from the Rule used by the court in In re Gaite's Will Trusts is no longer available, because in construing wills and trusts today, references to children, descendants, issue, or heirs presumptively includes persons born out of wedlock (see page 108).

b. The Unborn Widow

The next of the fantastical characters in perpetuities land is the *unborn widow*. Thus:

> *Case 6. The Unborn Widow.* T bequeaths a fund in trust to H for life, then to H's widow for life, then the remainder to H's surviving descendants. Even if H is married to W1 at T's death, the marriage might end and then H could marry W2, who might not have been born before T's death. In such a situation, the remainder to H's descendants will not vest until the death of W2, which could happen more than 21 years after the death of all lives in being at the time of T's death.

NOTE

Birthing the Widows.   In Case 6, why not construe the word *widow* to refer to a person in being when the testator died? Such a construction would save the gift and avoid a remote vesting. Statutes in several states do just this.[25] The Illinois statute is representative. It provides that "where the instrument creates an interest in the 'widow,' 'widower,' or 'spouse' of another person, [it is presumed] that the maker of the instrument intended to refer to a person who was living at the date that the period of the rule against perpetuities commences to run."[26]

c. The Slothful Executor

In theory, an estate could be tied up for more than 21 years after the death of everyone alive at the death of the testator.[27] This rather extravagant possibility gives rise to what are known as the *slothful executor* cases.[28] Thus:

> *Case 7. The Slothful Executor.* T devises property "to T's descendants living upon distribution of T's estate." T's purpose is to avoid extra administrative costs and possible taxation in the estates of any of T's descendants who die before T's estate is distributed. However, because T's estate may not be distributed for many years, perhaps after all T's surviving descendants are dead, the gift to T's descendants living at distribution may be held void.[29]

---

25. *See* Schoenblum, *supra* note 16, at tbl. 9, q. 21.

26. 765 Ill. Comp. Stat. 305/4(c)(1)(C) (2016).

27. *Cf.* Jarndyce v. Jarndyce, imagined by Charles Dickens and discussed at page 48.

28. *See* Schoenblum, *supra* note 16, at tbl. 9, q. 22.

29. There are at least two arguments that can be made to save the gift in Case 7. First, it could be argued that distribution of the estate will not be delayed beyond a reasonable time, which necessarily is less than 21 years. *See* Belfield v. Booth, 27 A. 585 (Conn. 1893). Second, it could be argued that, because the testator did not intend the executor to have the power to select recipients by delaying distribution, the class of descendants will close at the time distribution reasonably should be made. *See* In re Estate of Taylor, 428 P.2d 301 (Cal. 1967).

The administrative contingency involved in Case 7 is a true condition precedent: *T*'s descendants must survive to distribution in order to take. Some administrative contingency cases, however, involve language that ought not be construed as creating a condition precedent to vesting. Examples include "to *A* upon distribution of my estate," "to my descendants when my debts are paid," and "to *A* upon probate of this will." Language of this sort, which under traditional law does not require survival, should be construed as merely postponing possession and not imposing a condition precedent, as in Deiss v. Deiss, 536 N.E.2d 120 (Ill. App. 1989).

d. The Magic Gravel Pit and Other Marvels

Here are some other extraordinary occurrences in the fantasy land of perpetuities:

Case 8. The Magic Gravel Pit. *T* devises his gravel pits to his trustees to work them until the pits are exhausted and then to sell them and divide the proceeds among *T*'s descendants then living. Because the gravel pits might produce gravel for hundreds of years, the gift to *T*'s descendants is void. So held in In re Wood, [1894] 3 Ch. 381 (Eng.), even though the pits were in fact exhausted in six years.

Case 9. The War That Never Ends. During World War II, *T*, whose husband was a German immigrant, devised $20,000 to such of her husband's family in Germany who survive the war. The devise was held void in Brownell v. Edmunds, 209 F.2d 349 (4th Cir. 1953), on the grounds that World War II might not have ended within lives in being plus 21 years.

Case 10. The Birthday Present That Blows Up. *T* devises a fund in trust for *A* for life, then to such of *A*'s children as reach their respective twenty-first birthdays. Under the common law, a person reaches 21 at the first moment of the day before his twenty-first birthday. The theory is that a person is in existence on the day of his birth, so on the day before his first birthday he has completed one year. His birthday is the first day of the second year. In effect, then, this remainder is to such of *A*'s children as shall be living one day after they reach the age of 21, which exceeds by one day the period permitted by the Rule.[30]

The foregoing examples do not exhaust the extravagant possibilities that can be dreamed up to invalidate gifts under the Rule Against Perpetuities. But they should suffice to show how, under the what-might-happen possibilities test of the common law Rule, even the most implausible and whimsical possibility can invalidate an interest.

B. PERPETUITIES REFORM

The absurdity of the fantastical characters and the exasperating complexities of the Rule Against Perpetuities have brought the Rule into disrepute. Since the last half of the twentieth century, there has been extensive debate about whether the Rule should be reformed substantially, or even abolished completely. No state today follows the

---

30. *See* W. Barton Leach, The Careful Draftsman: Watch Out!, 47 A.B.A. J. 259 (1961).

pure common law Rule without at least some kind of modification. Reform of the Rule can be sorted into four basic categories: (1) self-help through a saving clause; (2) reformation (or cy pres); (3) wait-and-see; and (4) abolition. In addition, a Restatement provision published in late 2011 proposes a new Rule Against Perpetuities, creating a fifth possibility.

1. Saving Clauses

Because of the ease with which even an experienced lawyer can overlook some possibility of remote vesting, estate planners today normally include in instruments they draft a perpetuities *saving clause*.[31] The purpose of such a clause is to protect against an overlooked violation of the Rule Against Perpetuities. Here is an example:

> Notwithstanding any other provisions in this instrument, any trust created hereunder shall terminate, if it has not previously terminated, 21 years after the death of the survivor of the beneficiaries of the trust living at the date this instrument becomes effective. In case of such termination, the then remaining principal and undistributed income of the trust shall be distributed to the then income beneficiaries in the same proportions as they were, at the time of termination, entitled to receive the income. The term "beneficiaries" includes persons originally named as beneficiaries in this instrument as well as persons, living at the date this instrument becomes effective, subsequently named as beneficiaries by a donee of a power of appointment over the trust assets exercising such power.

Under this clause, the trust will terminate not later than 21 years after the death of all beneficiaries, originally or subsequently named as such, who were in being when the trust became effective. The principal is then distributed as provided in the saving clause. Because the trust will terminate at the end of the perpetuities period (if not sooner), no interest in the trust can violate the Rule.[32]

NOTES

1. Twelve Healthy Babies, Queen Victoria, and Joseph P. Kennedy. The saving clause presented above uses the trust's beneficiaries as validating lives. But the validating lives need not have any connection with the beneficiaries involved. In this famous passage, Professor Leach observed that one could have a saving clause keyed to the lives of *twelve healthy babies*:

> The settled inclusion of twenty-one years in gross and the admission of extraneous lives bring it about that a testator or settlor, when motivated by vanity, is able to tie up his property, regardless of lives and deaths in his family, for an unconscionable period—viz. twenty-one years after the deaths of a dozen or so healthy babies

---

31. Not savings clause, which is grammatically incorrect. As an adjective, saving—without the *s*—has the sense of "rescuing." *See* William Safire, On Language, N.Y. Times Mag., Apr. 2, 1995, at 22 (explaining that savings is the sum of separate acts of saving, as in a savings account).

32. *See, e.g.,* In re Estate of McFadden, 100 A.3d 645 (Pa. Super. 2014).

Joseph P. Kennedy (center) with Joseph P. Kennedy Jr. (left) and John F. Kennedy (right)
AP photo

chosen from families noted for longevity, a term which, in the ordinary course of events, will add up to about a century.[33]

A variant on Leach's twelve-healthy-babies clause is to choose the living members of a large family with a high public profile so that tracking the validating lives is easy. The English solicitors developed a *royal lives* saving clause whereby a trust continues until 21 years after the death of all the descendants of Queen Victoria (or of George V or of some other British monarch) living at the creation of the trust. The American counterpart, occasionally still found in wills and trusts today, is a saving clause that is tied to the descendants of Joseph P. Kennedy, the patriarch of the prominent Kennedy family and father of President John F. Kennedy.

2. Malpractice Liability.   In most states, lawyers are liable to an intended beneficiary of a negligently drafted will or trust (see page 52). On the authority of Lucas v. Hamm, 364 P.2d 685 (Cal. 1961), it is sometimes said that there is no negligence in drafting an instrument that violates the Rule Against Perpetuities. In *Lucas*, the court held that a lawyer who violated the Rule was not negligent on the specific facts of the case. However, given the ease with which satisfying the Rule can be assured by using a saving clause, *Lucas* is a shaky precedent, as a California intermediate appellate court subsequently observed.[34] It is almost certainly malpractice to violate the Rule Against Perpetuities by failing to include a perpetuities saving clause.

---

33. 6 American Law of Property § 24.16, at 52 (A. James Casner ed. 1952).
34. *See* Wright v. Williams, 121 Cal. Rptr. 194, 199 n.2 (App. 1975).

2. Reformation (or Cy Pres)

The *reformation* (or *cy pres*) doctrine is authorized by statute or judicial decision in many states.[35] It allows a court to modify a trust that violates the Rule Against Perpetuities as necessary to carry out the testator's intent within the perpetuities period. In exercising this power, the court might insert a saving clause adapted to the particular possibility that causes the gift to be invalid.[36]

NOTE

Statutory Fixes. As we have seen, statutes in several states address the problem of the *fertile octogenarian* by limiting the presumption of fertility to likely childbearing years (see page 898) and address the problem of the *unborn widow* by providing that the term "widow" should be construed as referring to a person in being when the gift was made (see page 899). Some of these statutes, which in effect provide for per se rules of reformation, also address the possibility of invalidity owing to an *age contingency*, as in In re BNY Mellon, N.A., 2 N.Y.S.3d 757 (Sur. 2014), by reducing the contingency to 21 years.[37]

3. Wait-and-See

In 1947, the Pennsylvania legislature abandoned the what-might-happen possibilities test of the common law Rule:

> Upon the expiration of the period allowed by the common law rule against perpetuities as measured by actual rather than possible events, any interest not then vested and any interest in members of a class the membership of which is then subject to increase shall be void.[38]

Dubbing the Pennsylvania reform "wait-and-see," Professor W. Barton Leach strongly endorsed it in a seminal article, Perpetuities in Perspective: Ending the Rule's Reign of Terror, 65 Harv. L. Rev. 721 (1952). The essence of the *wait-and-see doctrine* is that we wait and see what actually happens; we do not invalidate an interest because of what might happen. The wait-and-see reform replaces the what-*might*-happen test of the common law with a what-*does*-happen test.

When Professor A. James Casner, Leach's younger colleague at Harvard, was appointed reporter for the Restatement (Second) of Property, he proposed adding the wait-and-see doctrine to the new Restatement. This prompted Professor Richard R. Powell of Columbia, who had been the reporter for the prior Restatement and who, by this point, was 88 years old, to come out of retirement to speak against Casner's

---

35. *See* Schoenblum, *supra* note 16, at tbl. 9, q. 5-6.
36. *See* Jesse Dukeminier, A Modern Guide to Perpetuities, 74 Cal. L. Rev. 1867, 1898-1901 (1986).
37. *See, e.g.,* 765 Ill. Comp. Stat. Ann. 305/4(c)(2) (2016); N.Y. Est. Powers & Trusts Law § 9-1.3(d) (2016).
38. 20 Pa. Cons. Stat. § 6104(b) (2016).

Professor W. Barton Leach   Professor A. James Casner

proposal. Casner ultimately prevailed, and wait-and-see was written into the new Restatement.[39] Most states adopted wait-and-see, either by statute or judicial decision.[40]

But for how long should a court wait and see? Leach believed that the common law provided an inherent wait-and-see period — the lives relevant to vesting of the interest plus 21 years. The Restatement (Second) of Property prescribes a fixed list of measuring lives.[41] The Uniform Statutory Rule Against Perpetuities (USRAP) (Unif. Law Comm'n 1986) prescribes a fixed wait-and-see period of 90 years. Under USRAP, all interests are valid for 90 years after creation (§ 1(a)(2)). At the end of 90 years, any interest that has not vested is reformed by the court so as to best carry out the intention of the long-dead settlor (§ 3). A variant of USRAP is in force in roughly half the states.[42]

The theory behind switching from lives in being plus 21 years to a fixed term of years was one of simplification. Professor Lawrence W. Waggoner, the reporter for USRAP, explained that the drafters tried to approximate "the average period of time that would traditionally be allowed by the wait-and-see doctrine."[43] It is true that 90 years is a fair, though probably shorter, approximation of the period that could be obtained with an aggressive perpetuities saving clause.

---

39. Restatement (Second) of Property: Donative Transfers § 1.4 (Am. Law Inst. 1983).

40. *See* Schoenblum, *supra* note 16, at tbl. 9, q. 4.

41. *See* Restatement (Second) of Property: Donative Transfers § 1.3 (Am. Law Inst. 1983).

42. *See* Schoenblum, *supra* note 16, at tbl. 9, q. 1.

43. Lawrence W. Waggoner, The Uniform Statutory Rule Against Perpetuities: The Rationale of the 90-Year Waiting Period, 73 Cornell L. Rev. 157, 162 (1988). Waggoner's article was a response to criticisms of the 90-year rule in Jesse Dukeminier, The Uniform Statutory Rule Against Perpetuities: Ninety Years in Limbo, 34 UCLA L. Rev. 1023 (1987).

Casner, Leach, and Ladies' Day at Harvard Law School

Professors Casner and Leach, both now deceased, remain notorious for calling on female students only on a designated day, which they called "Ladies' Day." Chief Justice Mary J. Mullarkey of the Colorado Supreme Court described her experience in Casner's class thus:

> Our turn at Ladies' Day began when, on a Friday, Professor Casner announced that the following Monday would be "Ladies' Day" and the topic would be marital gifts.... As the one woman seated in the front row, I was called on first. Leaning over, Casner said to me, "Miss Mullarkey, if you were engaged—and I notice you're not"—he paused for laughter—"would you have to return the ring if you broke the engagement?" That was the sole question asked of me in a full-year property class. [Another woman, who would become Chief Justice of the New Mexico Supreme Court,] was asked a question about premarital property settlements, and the other questions were similar.
>
> When it was over, we were angry and felt humiliated by the trivial nature of the questions and Casner's very obvious condescension.... [T]his was no unauthorized student prank done

in secret off-campus. It was a very public silencing of women, carried out by two full professors who held named chairs at the school and acted with at least the tacit approval of the administration. Indeed, within a year, Casner became the acting dean of the law school....

Chief Justice Mary J. Mullarkey

To be fair to the faculty, only Professor Casner and his fellow property law professor, W. Barton Leach, practiced the Ladies' Day tradition. Other professors coped with women students with varying degrees of success; the younger ones seemed to take women students more in stride. But it made me wonder to see so many brilliant legal minds completely undone at the mere prospect of calling on a female student.

Mary J. Mullarkey, Two Harvard Women: 1965 to Today, 27 Harv. Women's L.J. 367, 370-71 (2004).

On similar reasoning, the English Parliament adopted an 80-year period in 1964 and then a 125-year period in 2009.[44] A government report presaging the 2009 legislation concluded plausibly that 125 years "is probably the longest period that can be obtained under the present law."[45]

NOTE

USRAP and the Generation-Skipping Transfer Tax. The generation-skipping transfer (GST) tax is payable on a transfer to a person two or more generations removed from the transferor, such as a grandchild (see Chapter 15 at page 975). However, trusts created before 1986 are excluded from the GST tax by a grandfathering provision, which gives those trusts a tax advantage. Lawyers in USRAP states who deal with grandfathered trusts must take special care not to lose the exemption inadvertently by extending a grandfathered trust in a manner permitted by USRAP but not

---

44. *See* D.J. Hayton, The Law of Trusts 106 (4th ed. 2003); Perpetuities and Accumulations Act, 2009, c. 18, §§ 5, 7 (Eng. & Wales).

45. Eng. Law Comm'n, Report No. 251, The Rules Against Perpetuities and Excessive Accumulations 101 § 8.13 (1998).

the grandfathering rules.[46] In 1990, a provision was added to USRAP to deal with the problem (§ 1(e)), but not all enacting states have adopted this provision. The interaction of USRAP and the GST tax is a complicated matter. Caution is advised.

4. Abolition of the Rule Against Perpetuities

Sparked by a change in the federal tax code in 1986, and coming on the heels of USRAP's move from lives in being plus 21 years to a fixed term of years, a movement to allow *perpetual trusts* took hold in the 1990s. Today, a majority of states, including several in which USRAP remains otherwise in force, have validated perpetual trusts.

Robert H. Sitkoff & Max M. Schanzenbach
Jurisdictional Competition for Trust Funds:
An Empirical Analysis of Perpetuities and Taxes
115 Yale L.J. 356 (2005)

This Article presents the results of the first empirical study of the jurisdictional competition for trust funds. Based on . . . data assembled from annual reports to federal banking authorities by institutional trustees, we find that the interstate competition for trust funds is both real and intense. Our analysis indicates that, on average, through 2003 a state's abolition of the Rule Against Perpetuities increased its reported trust assets by about $6 billion and its average trust account size by roughly $200,000. To put these figures in perspective, in 2003 the average state had roughly $19 billion in reported trust assets and an average account size of about $1 million. In the timeframe of our data, seventeen states abolished the Rule, implying that through 2003 roughly $100 billion in trust assets have moved as a result of the Rule's abolition. This figure represents about 10% of the total trust assets reported to federal banking authorities in 2003. . . .

Prior to 1986, . . . the estate tax could be avoided by using successive life interests. Because a life tenancy terminates at death and the estate tax applies only to the decedent's transferable interests, there is no tax on the death of a life tenant. Thus:

> *Case 2. The Successive Life Estates Loophole.* O creates a trust for the benefit of her daughter A for life, and then to A's daughter B for life (O's grandchild), with the remainder to B's children (O's great-grandchildren). Although O may have to pay a gift or estate tax upon the trust's creation, no estate tax will be levied at the death of A or B. Not until the death of B's children — O's great-grandchildren — will another estate tax be due.

Congress sought to close the successive-life-estates loophole with the [GST] tax under the Tax Reform Act of 1986. In rough terms, a transfer to a grandchild, great-grandchild, or any other person who is two or more generations below the transferor is a generation-skipping transfer; the GST tax is assessed on such transfers. Hence, in *Case 2*, a GST tax would be payable at the death of A and at the death of B. The GST tax rate equals the highest rate of the estate tax [in 2017, 40 percent].

---

46. *See* Treas. Reg. § 26.2601-1(b)(1)(v)(B)(2), (D) (Ex. 6-7).

Under the 1986 Act, however, each transferor has a lifetime exemption from the estate and GST taxes, originally $1 million.... [In 2017, the exemption is $5.49 million.—Eds.] Accordingly, a transferor can fund a trust with the amount of the exemption, free from transfer taxes, which will endure as long as state perpetuities law permits. The federal tax code puts no limit on the duration of the transfer tax exemption. Instead, Congress left it to state perpetuities law to limit the duration of a transfer-tax-exempt trust. Thus:

> *Case 3. The Transfer-Tax-Exempt Trust.* O funds a trust with $1.5 million to pay income to O's daughter A for life. A is given a special [i.e., a nongeneral] power to appoint the trust corpus outright or in further trust to O's descendants or the spouses of such descendants.[47] At A's death, A exercises her power over the trust corpus by appointing it in her will to her children B and C in equal shares and in further trust, giving each a similar special power over the share of each, and so on. Although O may have had to pay some gift or estate tax upon creating the trust, no estate, gift, or GST tax will be due on the exercise of A's, B's, or C's special power or the exercise of any other subsequent special power for as long as state perpetuities law permits.

Accordingly, in 1986 state perpetuities law became a highly salient factor in estate planning. The longer the trust in *Case 3* could be extended, the more generations could benefit from the trust fund free from transfer taxes....

For reasons unrelated to the GST tax, Idaho, South Dakota, and Wisconsin had already abolished the Rule Against Perpetuities before 1986. But ... these states experienced little to no resulting advantage in the jurisdictional competition for trust funds prior to 1986. Then came the Tax Reform Act of 1986. As the practicing bar digested the Act and grasped the nature of the GST tax, it became apparent that making use of the transferor's exemption in a perpetual trust had significant long-term tax advantages. If the trust in *Case 3*, above, were created in Idaho, South Dakota, or Wisconsin, it could continue, free from federal wealth transfer taxation, generation after generation, forever.

As a general matter, prior to 1986 there was little significant variation in trust law across the states. After the GST tax, however, state perpetuities law became a highly salient margin of differentiation. Given prevailing choice-of-law principles and the shift in the nature of wealth from land to financial assets (making trust assets portable), it was only a matter of time until jurisdictional competition sparked a race to abolish the Rule Against Perpetuities.

To ensure that the law of state B will govern the validity and administration of a trust created by a settlor who resides in state A, lawyers usually advise the settlor not only to provide in the trust instrument that the law of state B is to govern, but also to name a trustee located in state B and to give that trustee custody of the trust fund. As a result, an out-of-state settlor who wants to invoke the law of state B typically will appoint as trustee a bank or trust company located in state B. Therein lies the payoff to state B and

---

47. Property subject to a special [i.e., a nongeneral] power, as compared with a general power, is not treated as belonging to the holder of the power for tax purposes [see page 813—Eds.]

The Rule Against Perpetuities: If You Repeal It, The Money Will Come

the political economy of the RAP's demise. Ever since the perpetuities loophole in the GST tax was understood, abolition of the RAP has been "pushed by banking associations . . . [that] wish to remain competitive with banks where perpetual trusts are permitted." Joel Dobris put it more bluntly: "When the bankers want something, they get it." . . .

For a variety of historical reasons, Delaware . . . has long been a trust-friendly jurisdiction and by 1986 had a disproportionate share of the nation's trust funds. Indeed, prior to the GST tax, on several occasions Delaware tweaked its perpetuities law to create tax and other advantages to settling a trust in Delaware. So it was hardly a surprise when in 1995 Delaware became the first state after the enactment of the GST tax to abolish the Rule as applied to interests in trust. The bill's official synopsis makes its purpose plain:

> Several states, including Idaho, Wisconsin and South Dakota, have abolished altogether their rules against perpetuities, which has given those jurisdictions a competitive advantage over Delaware in attracting assets held in trusts created for estate planning purposes. . . .
>
> The multi-million dollar capital commitments to these irrevocable trusts, and the ensuing compound growth over decades, will result in the formation of a substantial capital base in the innovative jurisdictions that have abolished the rule against perpetuities. Several financial institutions have now organized or acquired trust companies, particularly in South Dakota, at least in part to take advantage of their favorable trust law.
>
> Delaware's repeal of the rule against perpetuities for personal property held in trust will demonstrate Delaware's continued vigilance in maintaining its role as a leading jurisdiction for the formation of capital and the conduct of trust business.

The Delaware statute triggered a race to abolish the Rule.

Perpetual Trusts (2016)

Figure 14.1

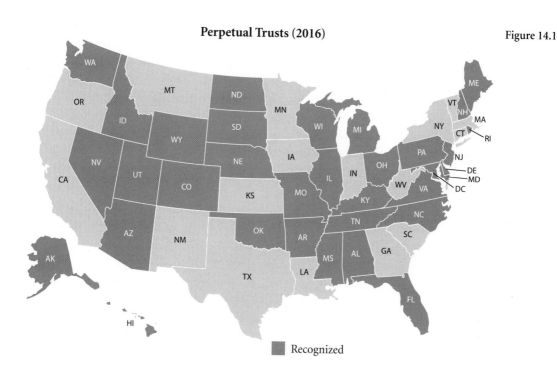

Recognized

NOTES

1. The Perpetual Trust States. As of this writing, perpetual or effectively perpetual trusts appear to be authorized in Alabama (360 years), Alaska (1,000 years), Arizona, Arkansas, Colorado (1,000 years), Delaware, District of Columbia, Florida (360 years), Hawaii, Idaho, Illinois, Kentucky, Maine, Maryland, Michigan, Mississippi (360 years), Missouri, Nebraska, Nevada (365 years), New Hampshire, New Jersey, North Carolina, North Dakota, Ohio, Oklahoma, Pennsylvania, Rhode Island, South Dakota, Tennessee (360 years), Utah (1,000), Virginia, Washington (150 years), Wisconsin, and Wyoming (1,000 years).

Some of these states have abolished the Rule altogether. Others have abolished the Rule as applied to interests in trusts in which the trustee has the power to sell the trust property and then reinvest the proceeds — that is, for trusts that do not render property unmarketable by suspending the power of alienation (see page 922). Still others have abolished the Rule as applied to interests in personal property. Perhaps the oddest change is in the states that have transmogrified the Rule, which had been a mandatory limit on freedom of disposition,[48] into a default rule that applies unless the settlor provides otherwise.

---

48. Gray expressed this view thus:

> The Rule Against Perpetuities is not a rule of construction, but a peremptory command of law. It is not, like a rule of construction, a test, more or less artificial, to determine intention. Its object is to defeat intention. Therefore every provision in a will or settlement is to be construed as if the Rule did not exist, and then to the provision so construed the Rule is to be remorselessly applied.

Gray, *supra* note 2, § 629, at 599.

2. Perpetuities and State Constitutions.   The race to validate perpetual trusts has brought into focus another interesting wrinkle. A ban on perpetuities is enshrined in the constitutions of a handful of states, including a few that allow perpetual (or effectively perpetual) trusts, such as Nevada and North Carolina. In these states, should the courts strike down the statute that authorizes perpetual trusts as a violation of the state constitution? *Compare* Brown Bros. Harriman Trust Co. v. Benson, 688 S.E.2d 752 (N.C. App. 2010) (upholding a perpetual trust statute), *with* Steven J. Horowitz & Robert H. Sitkoff, Unconstitutional Perpetual Trusts, 67 Vand. L. Rev. 1769 (2014) (arguing that "recognition of perpetual trusts is prohibited in states with a constitutional perpetuities ban").

3. The Role of the GST Tax.   To assess the role of the GST tax in sparking the movement to validate perpetual trusts, in a follow-up study Professors Schanzenbach and Sitkoff examined federal banking data on trust accounts prior to the adoption of the GST tax. They concluded that "prior to the GST tax, states that abolished the Rule did not garner more trust business than those that retained the Rule. Taken together, our findings in this and our prior study show that use of the perpetual trust traces to the 1986 GST tax and grew at an increasingly rapid pace thereafter."[49]

Lawrence W. Waggoner

From Here to Eternity: The Folly of Perpetual Trusts
Univ. of Mich. Law Sch. Pub. Law & Legal Theory Research Paper No. 259 (2012)

The perpetual trusts that are now in existence are only in their first or second decade, so experience with them as they continue past the boundary set by traditional perpetuity law is lacking. Nevertheless, some projections can be made, since the prototypical perpetual trust is a discretionary trust for the benefit of the settlor's descendants from time to time living forever (or for several centuries).

GENETIC DILUTION

With each step down the generational ladder, the settlor's genetic relationship with the descendant-beneficiaries will decline rather precipitously. On average, and disregarding nongenetic descendants such as adoptees, a settlor's genetic relationship with his or her descendants is cut in half at each succeeding generation. At the 14th generation (i.e., the generation born about 300 years after the settlor's death), the settlor's genetic relationship is reduced to about 0.0061 per cent, which — due to our common origins — is about the same relationship one has with any randomly selected member of the population.

---

49. Max M. Schanzenbach & Robert H. Sitkoff, Perpetuities or Taxes? Explaining the Rise of the Perpetual Trust, 27 Cardozo L. Rev. 2465, 2496 (2006); *see also* Grayson M.P. McCouch, Who Killed the Rule Against Perpetuities?, 40 Pepp. L. Rev. 1291 (2013) (discussing other reasons for interest in perpetual trusts).

BENEFICIARY PROLIFERATION

As the settlor's genetic relationship with the beneficiaries diminishes, the number of descendant-beneficiaries will proliferate geometrically. One hundred and fifty years after creation, a perpetual trust could have about 450 living beneficiaries; after 250 years, more than 7,000 living beneficiaries; after 350 years, about 114,500 living beneficiaries. This means that 350 years after creation, Michigan Stadium or the Rose Bowl would not be large enough to hold them all. . . .

BENEFITTING STRANGERS

. . . Imagine a perpetual trust in which the more-than-100,000 living beneficiaries include President Barack Obama and his descendants and former President George H.W. Bush and his descendants (including former President George W. Bush). Or, a perpetual trust in which the more-than-100,000 living beneficiaries include President Obama and his descendants, former Vice President Richard Cheney and his descendants, and the living descendants of former President Harry S. Truman. Both trusts would exist and still be operating today if Samuel Hinckley, who died in Massachusetts in 1662, had created a perpetual trust for his descendants and if Mareen Duvall, who died in Maryland in 1694, had created a perpetual trust for his descendants. . . .

TRUST DOCUMENT OBSOLESCENCE

State-of-the-art perpetual-trust documents of today are considered modern, sophisticated, and up-to-date. Will those documents be looked upon as modern, sophisticated, and up-to-date centuries from now? Consider the devices used centuries ago by English landowners to control family estates through subsequent generations. Such devices, which were then considered modern, sophisticated, and up-to-date, first took the form of the unbarrable entail and, after the entail became barrable, the strict settlement. These devices and the terminology associated with them became obsolete long ago. If the past is any guide to the future, an early 21st century perpetual-trust document will seem as obsolete to those in distant centuries as a 17th century document appears to us today.

Jesse Dukeminier & James E. Krier
The Rise of the Perpetual Trust
50 UCLA L. Rev. 1303 (2003)

[In 1955, Professor Lewis Simes described] what we call the problem of first-generation monopoly, meaning by "first generation" the generation of the settlor who sets up a perpetual trust. Simes wrote:

> [I]t is good public policy to allow each person to dispose of his property as he pleases. The policy extends not only to the present generation but to future generations. If we are to permit the present generation to tie up all existing capital for an indefinitely long period of time, then future generations will have nothing to dispose of by will except what they have saved from their own income; and the property which each generation enjoys will already have been disposed of by ancestors

long dead. The rule against perpetuities would appear to strike a balance between the unlimited disposition of property by the members of the present generation and its unlimited disposition by members of future generations.[50]

This is an old and appealing sentiment. . . . [Simes] thought that the force of the argument against first-generation monopoly "can scarcely be denied." And yet it can. . . . Consider, for example, the likely preferences of the mentally incompetent; of minor children; of bad money managers who lack the discipline to lash themselves to the mast; of people (maybe those same people!) hounded by creditors and vulnerable to bankruptcy; of people, supported by the state, who are beneficiaries of discretionary trusts, which the state cannot touch; of people contemplating divorce and interested in having their property out of reach of the other half; of people who reap nice tax advantages from trusts, including spouses who benefit from the marital deduction, and beneficiaries of tax-exempt dynasty trusts, among others. . . .

Beyond that, one should consider goals other than satisfaction of preferences. A goal of equality, for example, might support placing restraints on the ability of one generation to limit the opportunities of the next; a goal of donative freedom, on the other hand, would cut in the opposite direction. . . .

[E]quality of opportunity is not provided by income alone. As Professors Blum and Kalven pointed out years ago, the gravest source of inequality of opportunity is inequality of human capital, the knowledge and education embodied in individuals. Human capital is created by family cultural influence on children, as well as by education. The knowledge and education of parents and more remote ancestors are passed along from generation to generation. . . .

[T]here is an argument that trusts concentrate economic power in the rich or, more accurately, in the trustees for the rich. In the case of trusts, the trustees, not the beneficiaries, have the power of investment. They decide where the trust capital is to be invested. . . . [But] the wealth invested by trustees is only a small fraction of the total amount of risk capital made available by other investors. . . .

Consider finally the argument that the certainty of receiving trust income makes beneficiaries lazy and unproductive. . . . When the Republic was established, England had a "leisure class," composed of nobles and country gentlemen who lived off their land rents and inheritances and refrained from something as low as work. . . . But this country has never had a leisure class like England's. We have no sense of inherited hierarchy. Our work ethic, deeply imbedded from the times of the Puritans, has spared us a class of great drones. . . .

[Our] work ethic is paired with another ethic: The rich should share their wealth with the less fortunate. From the time when great fortunes were accumulated at the end of the nineteenth century to the present, the American rich, to justify their moral instinct, have given great sums to philanthropic enterprises. . . . [C]haritable support has given us in the United States universities and hospitals and cultural institutions that are the envy of the world. The diversity of privately supported philanthropic enterprises is

---

50. Lewis M. Simes, Is the Rule Against Perpetuities Doomed? The "Wait and See" Doctrine, 52 Mich. L. Rev. 179, 191-92 (1953).

enormous, far greater than in Western European countries where the charitable agenda is largely set and supported by the government. . . .

Perhaps the objection is to the creation of family dynasties, which receive trust income generation after generation. The answer is this: The Rule Against Perpetuities has not prevented the creation of family dynasties. Witness the Rockefellers (now in their fifth generation), the Du Ponts of high dynastic numbering (whose fortune dates from the War of 1812), and the Mellons (with a fortune predating the Civil War). . . . If family dynasties are to be prevented, only the federal government, through income and death taxes, can do it. . . .

The short of it is that Congress has come to be in charge of trust duration. The future of perpetual trusts is in its hands, to be dealt with through the tax system. The role of the states is to develop affordable means for modifying and terminating trusts when that is in the best interests of the beneficiaries. We have reached a great turning point in the law of trusts.

NOTES

1. Modification, Termination, and Perpetual Trusts. What legislators give to the dead hand in the form of perpetual trusts, judges can take away in the form of trust modification and termination. As today's perpetual trust instruments become stale with age, courts will be confronted by provisions that are confounded by changed circumstances. Perhaps abrogating the Rule Against Perpetuities will lead to a more liberal law of trust modification and termination (see page 727)? Or more aggressive use of trust decanting (see page 742)?

Model forms for perpetual trusts typically include a provision that gives each generation a nongeneral power to appoint the remainder to the next generation outright or in further trust, as in Case 3 by Professors Schanzenbach and Sitkoff at page 907.[51] Is a trust truly perpetual if each generation can terminate it or appoint the property to a fresh trust with new terms? Professor Bridget Crawford argues that, in view of such provisions, Professor Waggoner's worry about perpetual trusts might be misplaced:

> [W]ith many perpetual trusts, each generation of beneficiaries will have the ability to decide whether to continue the trust or not. Just because a perpetual trust can last forever does not mean that it will. Indeed there is anecdotal evidence to suggest that grantors of perpetual trusts recognize the need for future flexibility and plan for it by granting powers of appointment. By allowing individual beneficiaries to weigh the benefits and burdens of continuing the trust in the future, many perpetual trusts contemplate the control of wealth by the living. This is precisely what Professor Waggoner is after.[52]

---

51. *See, e.g.,* Richard W. Nenno, Delaware Trusts 377 (2013-2014) (model form with such a clause); *see also* John V. Orth, Escaping the Malthusian Trap Dynasty Trusts for Serious Dynasts, 17 Green Bag 2d 29 (2013).

52. Bridget J. Crawford, Commentary, Who Is Afraid of Perpetual Trusts?, 111 Mich. L. Rev. First Impressions 79, 86-87 (2012).

2. Multiplication of Beneficiaries.   The problem of multiplying beneficiaries can be avoided if the trustee is given the power to *divide* the trust into two or more separate trusts. This power is commonly given by statute, such as Uniform Trust Code (UTC) § 417 (2000), and is recognized by the Restatement (Third) of Trusts as a default power under the common law.[53]

If perpetual trusts wind up being divided many times over to keep up with Professor Waggoner's hypothesized geometric expansion in the number of beneficiaries, then the power to *terminate* small trusts might also prove to be important. It seems rather unlikely that any investment program could produce a matching geometric growth in trust corpus, especially if the current beneficiaries make demands on the trust income.[54] UTC § 414 (2000) provides that "the trustee of a trust consisting of trust property having a total value less than [$50,000] may terminate the trust if the trustee concludes that the value of the trust property is insufficient to justify the cost of administration."[55]

3. Reforming the GST Tax?   Should Congress amend the exemption from the GST tax, perhaps levying a tax at the expiration of the common law perpetuities period or the 90-year period of USRAP? The Treasury Department made such a proposal in 2016:

> At the time of the enactment of the GST provisions, the law of most (all but about three) States included the common law Rule Against Perpetuities (RAP) or some statutory version of it. . . .
>
> Many States now either have repealed or limited the application of their RAP statutes, with the effect that trusts created subject to the law of those jurisdictions may continue in perpetuity. . . . As a result, the transfer tax shield provided by the GST exemption effectively has been expanded from trusts funded with $1 million (the exemption at the time of enactment) and a maximum duration limited by the RAP, to trusts funded with $5.45 million [$5.49 million in 2017] and continuing (and growing) in perpetuity. . . .
>
> The proposal would provide that, on the 90th anniversary of the creation of a trust, the GST exclusion allocated to the trust would terminate. . . .
>
> The proposal would apply to trusts created after enactment, and to the portion of a pre-existing trust attributable to additions to such a trust made after that date (subject to rules substantially similar to the grandfather rules currently in effect for additions to trusts created prior to the effective date of the GST tax).[56]

---

53. Restatement (Third) of Trusts § 68 (Am. Law Inst. 2003).

54. *See* Lucy A. Marsh, The Demise of Dynasty Trusts: Returning the Wealth to the Family, 5 Est. Plan. & Community Prop. L.J. 23 (2012); William J. Turnier & Jeffrey L. Harrison, A Malthusian Analysis of the So-Called Dynasty Trust, 28 Va. Tax Rev. 779 (2009).

55. The comment explains that the $50,000 figure is in brackets "to signal to enacting jurisdictions that they may wish to designate a higher or lower figure."

56. *See* U.S. Dep't of the Treasury, General Explanations of the Administration's Fiscal Year 2017 Revenue Proposals 183-84 (2016).

5. The Restatement (Third) of Property

In a Restatement provision drafted by Professor Waggoner and published in 2011, the American Law Institute denounced the perpetual trust movement:

> It is the considered judgment of The American Law Institute that the recent statutory movement allowing the creation of perpetual or near-perpetual trusts is ill advised. The movement to abrogate the Rule Against Perpetuities has not been based on the merits of removing the Rule's curb on excessive dead-hand control. The policy issues associated with allowing perpetual or near-perpetual trusts have not been seriously discussed in the state legislatures. The driving force has been the effort to compete for trust industry (financial services) business from other states.[57]

The Restatement (Third) of Property offers a new perpetuities law, one that is simpler than the common law Rule and more tightly fits the Rule's purposes. But it has yet to be adopted anywhere.

Restatement (Third) of Property:
Wills and Other Donative Transfers (Am. Law Inst. 2011)

§ 27.1 Statement of the Rule Against Perpetuities

(a) A trust or other donative disposition of property is subject to judicial modification . . . to the extent that the trust or other disposition does not terminate on or before the expiration of the perpetuity period. . . .

(b) The perpetuity period expires at the death of the last living measuring life. The measuring lives are as follows:

(1) Except as otherwise provided in paragraph (2), the measuring lives constitute a group composed of the following individuals: the transferor, the beneficiaries of the disposition who are related to the transferor and no more than two generations younger than the transferor, and the beneficiaries of the disposition who are unrelated to the transferor and no more than the equivalent of two generations younger than the transferor.

(2) In the case of a trust or other property arrangement for the sole current benefit of a named individual who is more than two generations younger than the transferor or more than the equivalent of two generations younger than the transferor, the measuring life is the named individual.

NOTE

Two Generations and Reformation. The perpetuities rule of the new Restatement abandons the old "lives in being" period for a two-generations wait-and-see period followed by reformation. The Restatement explains the rationale thus:

> A generations-based perpetuity period is more responsive to the purposes of the Rule than one based on lives in being, because the generational approach produces

---

57. Restatement (Third) of Property: Wills and Other Donative Transfers ch. 27, intro. note (Am. Law Inst. 2011).

a period that self-adjusts to the individual trust and family circumstances and hence imposes a more tailored outer limit on dead-hand control. Trusts commonly confer lifetime benefits on members of one generation before passing benefits to the next generation. Subsection (b)(1) produces a perpetuity period that is tailored to the family, by counting beneficiaries of the same generation as measuring lives whether they were in being at the creation of the interest or not. The traditional lives-in-being period does not self-adjust because it excludes after-born members of the same generation and, as a result, can require judicial modification if an after-born member outlives the in-being members. Subsection (b) allows dead-hand control to go no farther than benefiting children and grandchildren.[58]

Is the new Restatement's approach to perpetuities an improvement over the prior approaches? Is it likely to be adopted? Might it influence Congress in reforming the GST tax?

C. APPLICATION OF THE RULE TO CLASS GIFTS AND POWERS OF APPOINTMENT

1. Class Gifts

a. The All-or-Nothing Rule

Under the common law Rule Against Perpetuities, a class gift must be valid for all members of the class, or it is valid for none.[59] If the interest of any member possibly can vest too remotely, the entire class gift is void. This *all-or-nothing* rule requires that (1) the class must close, and (2) all conditions precedent for every member of the class must be satisfied, if at all, within the perpetuities period.[60] Case 11 illustrates a common class gift that is void under these principles.

> *Case 11.* *T* bequeaths property in trust "for *A* for life, then for *A*'s children for life, and then to distribute the property to *A*'s grandchildren." The remainder to *A*'s grandchildren is void because not every member of the class will be ascertained until the death of *A*'s children, some of whom might not be in being at *T*'s death. If at *T*'s death *A* has a living grandchild, *G*, then *G*'s gift is vested in interest subject to open for after-born grandchildren, but it is not vested for purposes of the Rule, and it is therefore void.

Case 11 illustrates an important proposition: A remainder that is vested subject to open is not vested for purposes of applying the Rule Against Perpetuities. *A class must be closed before a remainder in the class is vested for purposes of the Rule.*

Some gifts to a class may be saved, therefore, by the *rule of convenience* (see Chapter 13 at page 881). Under this rule, a class will close when any member of the class

---

58. Id. § 27.1 cmt. b.
59. *See* Schoenblum, *supra* note 16, at tbl. 9, q. 23 (surveying the states).
60. The all-or-nothing rule originated in Leake v. Robinson, (1817) 35 Eng. Rep. 979 (Ch.); 2 Mer. 363.

is entitled to immediate possession and enjoyment, even if the class would not otherwise close physiologically. Thus:

Case 12. *O* transfers property in an irrevocable trust "for my daughter, *A*, for life, then to distribute the principal to my grandchildren." At the time of the transfer *O* has one living grandchild, *G*. Under the rule of convenience, *G* or her administrator is entitled to demand possession of her share at *A*'s death, closing the class and forcing distribution among the grandchildren then living and the estates of grandchildren then dead. The gift is therefore valid. If *O* had no grandchild alive at the date of the transfer, the gift to grandchildren would be void.

If the instrument in Case 12 were a will or a revocable trust rather than an irrevocable trust, the gift to the transferor's grandchildren would be valid regardless of whether a grandchild were alive when the instrument became effective. Do you see why? (Hint: See page 895.)

It does not follow from the closing of the class within the perpetuities period that the gift is necessarily valid. Even if every member of the class is ascertained, every member must also satisfy any conditions precedent. For a gift of a fee simple to vest, for example, the ultimate number of takers in the class must be fixed so that the class neither increases nor decreases. Thus:

Case 13. *T* bequeaths property in trust "for *A* for life, then to distribute the property to such of *A*'s children as attain the age of 25." The class will close physiologically at *A*'s death (a life in being), but the exact share that each child of *A* will take cannot be determined until all of *A*'s children have passed 25 or have died under that age. Here is what might happen: Suppose, at *T*'s death, *A* has one child, *C*, age 10. After *T*'s death *A* might have another child, *D*. Before *D* reaches age 4, *A* and *C* might die. Since *D* might meet the condition precedent more than 21 years after the expiration of any relevant life in being at *T*'s death, the remainder fails under the Rule Against Perpetuities.

NOTES

1. An All-or-Nothing Problem. *T* devises Blackacre "to such of the grandchildren of *A* as shall attain the age of 25." Unless otherwise stated, assume that no grandchild of *A* has reached age 25. Is the gift valid if at *T*'s death:

    a. *A* is dead?
    b. *A* and all of *A*'s children are dead?
    c. *A* is alive and one grandchild of *A* is 25?
    d. *A* is dead and one grandchild of *A* is 25?
    e. *A* is dead and the eldest grandchild of *A* is 4?

2. Another All-or-Nothing Problem. *T* bequeaths a fund in trust "to pay the income to *A* for life, and then in further trust for the grandchildren of *B*, their shares to be payable at their respective ages of 25."

    a. Suppose that *A* and *B* survive *T* and the eldest grandchild of *B* is 25 at *T*'s death. Is the gift valid?

b. How would your answer to (a) change, if at all, if the eldest grandchild of *B* is 10 at *T*'s death?

c. How would your answer to (b) change, if at all, if the eldest grandchild of *B* is 2 at *T*'s death?

d. Suppose that *B* survives *T*, but *A* predeceases *T*, and the eldest grandchild of *B* is 2 at *T*'s death. Is the gift valid?

e. Suppose that *A* survives *T*, but *B* predeceases *T*, and the eldest grandchild of *B* is 2 at *T*'s death. Is the gift valid?

b. Exceptions to the All-or-Nothing Rule

There are two exceptions to the all-or-nothing rule: (1) gifts to subclasses, and (2) gifts of specific sums to each member of a class.[61]

(1) Gifts to Subclasses

In American Security & Trust Co. v. Cramer, 175 F. Supp. 367 (D.D.C. 1959), the court summarized the exception for *gifts to subclasses* thus:

> [I]f the ultimate takers are not described as a single class but rather as a group of subclasses, and if the share to which each separate subclass is entitled will finally be determined within the period of the rule, the gifts to the different subclasses are separable for the purpose of the rule.[62]

At issue in *Cramer* were remainders in the "heirs" of the testator's four grandchildren. Only two of the grandchildren were born before the testator's death. Because the will gave a remainder to each grandchild's heirs upon the death of *each*, and not a gift to the next generation upon the death of *all* of the grandchildren, the court applied the gifts-to-subclasses exception and upheld the remainders in the heirs of the two grandchildren in being at the testator's death. The remainders in the heirs of the after-born grandchildren, who as such could not be validating lives, were void.

In Estate of Coates, 652 A.2d 331 (Pa. Super. 1994), the court held that if there is a trust for *A* for life, then to *A*'s children for their lives, then "to *A*'s grandchildren per stirpes," the gift-to-subclasses exception could apply even though possession by the grandchildren was postponed until the death of all *A*'s children. The court reasoned that the shares of the grandchildren in each line of descent were fixed at the death of the child who headed the line.

(2) Specific Sum to Each Class Member

The other exception to the all-or-nothing class gift rule applies if there is a gift of a *specific sum to each member of the class*. In Storrs v. Benbow, (1853) 43 Eng. Rep. 153 (Ch.); 3 De G. M. & G. 390, the testator bequeathed £500 apiece to each grandchild of his brothers, to be paid at age 21. The testator had two brothers living at his death. The

---

61. *See* Schoenblum, *supra* note 16, at tbl. 9, q. 24.
62. The exception for gifts to subclasses traces back to Cattlin v. Brown, (1853) 68 Eng. Rep. 1319 (Ch.); 11 Hare 372.

court held that, as a matter of construction, applying the ordinary class closing rule applicable to specific sum gifts (see Chapter 13 at page 885), the gift benefited only grandchildren living at the testator's death. However, in a dictum that has been treated as law ever since, the court also said that if the testator meant to include grandchildren born after his death, the bequest would be valid for all children born to the brothers' children living at the testator's death and invalid for all children of the brothers' after-born children. The amount intended to be received by each member of the class is ascertainable without reference to the number of persons in the class, hence each gift is tested separately under the Rule.

2. Powers of Appointment

In applying the Rule Against Perpetuities to powers of appointment, it is necessary to separate (a) general powers presently exercisable from (b) general testamentary powers and all special powers, and to bear in mind (c) the "Delaware Tax Trap."

a. General Powers Presently Exercisable

(1) Validity of Power

Because the donee of a presently exercisable general power of appointment can reach the appointive property by appointing it to himself, the Rule Against Perpetuities requires only that the power become exercisable, or fail, within the perpetuities period. The Rule does not require that the power necessarily be exercised within the perpetuities period. Suppose *T* devises property "to *A* for life, then to *A*'s children for their lives, with a general power in each child, exercisable by deed, to appoint a proportionate share of the corpus." Each child's power is valid because the power in each child will become exercisable at *A*'s death (or, if a child is then a minor, within 21 years thereafter).

(2) Validity of Exercise

The validity of an interest created by an exercise of a presently exercisable general power of appointment is determined as if the donee—the holder of the power—owned the property in fee. The perpetuities period begins to run when the power is exercised. An unconditional power to revoke a trust is treated as a general power presently exercisable if the holder can exercise the power to revoke for his own benefit. The perpetuities period does not begin to run until the termination of the power.

NOTE

A Presently Exercisable Problem.   *O* creates a revocable trust "to pay the income to *O* for life, then to pay the income to *O*'s children for their lives, then to distribute the principal to *O*'s grandchildren." Does the gift to grandchildren violate the Rule Against Perpetuities? Would it if the trust were irrevocable?

b. General Testamentary Powers and Nongeneral Powers

The holder of a testamentary power or a nongeneral power does not have an absolute present right to alienate the property. Hence, for purposes of the Rule Against

Perpetuities, the donor is treated as still controlling the property through the donee's exercise of the power. The Rule requires that we consider two questions: (1) Is the power itself valid? (2) Are the interests created by the exercise of the power valid?

(1) Validity of Power

For a general testamentary power of appointment or a nongeneral power of appointment to satisfy the Rule Against Perpetuities, it must not be possible for the power to be exercised beyond the perpetuities period. Consequently, neither a general testamentary power nor a nongeneral power can be given to an after-born person unless the exercise of the power is limited to the perpetuities period.

> *Case 14.* *T* bequeaths a fund in trust "to pay the income to *A* for life, then to *A*'s children for their lives, and, as each child of *A* dies, to pay his or her proportionate part of the principal as such child shall appoint by will." At the time of *T*'s death, *A* has one child, *B*. Another child, *C*, is born a year later. The gift to subclasses doctrine applies to the testamentary powers given to *A*'s children because each child has a power exercisable only over the child's portion of the principal at death. The testamentary power given to *B* is valid because *B* was in being at *T*'s death. The testamentary power given to *C*, born after *T*'s death, is void.

For perpetuities purposes, a discretionary power of distribution in a trustee is the equivalent of a nongeneral power of appointment.

> *Case 15.* *T* bequeaths a fund in trust "to pay the income to *A* for life, then in the trustee's discretion to pay the income to *A*'s children during their lives or to accumulate the income and add it to principal." *A* has no children at *T*'s death. The discretionary power in the trustee to pay or accumulate income is either partially or totally void.

Professor Gray took the position that a discretionary trust did not create a single power that was either entirely valid or entirely void, but rather a succession of annual powers that were exercisable with respect to each year's income.[63] On this view, a discretionary power in a trustee exercisable during lives not in being, as during the lives of *A*'s children in Case 15, could be exercised for 21 years after *A*'s death, but no longer. In the few cases in which this issue has been directly before the court, however, the discretionary power has been held void in its entirety if it is capable of being exercised in favor of persons not in being.[64]

(2) Validity of Exercise

In determining the validity of interests created by an exercise of a general testamentary or a nongeneral power, you must keep in mind two principles: (a) the perpetuities period runs from the creation of the power, and (b) the second-look doctrine.

---

63. *See* Gray, *supra* note 2, §§ 410.1-410.5, at 422-27.

64. *See* Arrowsmith v. Mercantile-Safe Deposit & Trust Co., 545 A.2d 674 (Md. 1988); Bundy v. United States Trust Co. of N.Y., 153 N.E. 337 (Mass. 1926).

(a) Perpetuities Period Runs from Creation of Power. Because the donee of a general testamentary power or a nongeneral power is regarded as an agent of the donor, any appointment is read back into the instrument creating the power. The perpetuities period applicable to the appointed interests runs from the creation of the power.

Although in most states a general testamentary power is treated like a nongeneral power under the Rule, in a few states a general testamentary power is treated like a general inter vivos power. The perpetuities period on the appointed interests runs from the exercise of the power.[65]

(b) The Second-Look Doctrine. Although the exercise of a power of appointment is read back into the original instrument, under the *second-look doctrine*, facts existing on the date of exercise are taken into account. Under the second-look doctrine we wait and see how the donee actually appoints the property, and then we determine on the basis of the facts as they exist at the time of the appointment whether the appointive interests will vest or fail within the perpetuities period (computed from the date of creation of the power).

> *Case 16.* T devises property "to A for life, remainder to such persons as A appoints by will, outright or in further trust." A appoints in further trust "to my children for life, remainder to my grandchildren in fee." We now read A's appointment into the will that created the power. The disposition is treated as though T's will read "to A for life, then to A's children for life, then to A's grandchildren in fee." However, under the second-look doctrine we are also allowed to take into account facts existing at the time of A's appointment. If, at A's death, all of A's surviving children were born in T's lifetime, the remainder to the grandchildren is valid because it will vest, if at all, at the death of persons in being at T's death. Otherwise the remainder is void.

c. The Delaware Tax Trap

A Delaware statute provides that all interests created by the exercise of *all* powers, nongeneral as well as general, must vest within 21 years of the death of some life in being at the time the power is *exercised*, not some life in being at the date of creation of the power.[66] Under this statute, a new perpetuities period begins each time a nongeneral power is exercised. T can set up a trust giving her child, A, the income for life and a nongeneral testamentary power to appoint outright or in further trust among A's descendants. A can exercise the power by appointing in further trust for her child, B, for life, giving B a nongeneral testamentary power in favor of B's descendants. B can exercise the power by appointing in further trust for her child—and so on down the generations.

Under the federal estate tax, neither a life estate nor property subject to a nongeneral power of appointment is taxable at the death of the life tenant or donee of the power. Although the property escapes estate taxation at that time, it will become subject to estate taxation within a generation or two thereafter if the Rule Against Perpetuities

---

65. *See* Schoenblum, *supra* note 16, at tbl. 9, q. 13.
66. Del. Code Ann. tit. 25, § 501 (2016).

calls a halt to successive life estates. Under the Delaware statute, however, life estates can be created in indefinite succession through the exercise of successive nongeneral powers of appointment.

Out of concern for estate tax avoidance through the use of Delaware trusts, Congress enacted § 2041(a)(3)(B) of the Internal Revenue Code. As amended, this statute taxes the appointive assets in the donee's estate if the donee exercises a nongeneral power "by creating another power of appointment which under the applicable local law can be validly exercised so as to postpone the vesting of any estate or interest in such property, . . . for a period ascertainable without regard to the date of the creation of the first power."

This provision plugs the tax loophole for Delaware trusts, but it also creates a tax trap for residents of all states. In any jurisdiction, if a donee by will exercises a nongeneral power in such a manner as to create a general inter vivos power, the property subject to the nongeneral power will be includible in the donee's gross estate taxable under the estate tax. Reread the quoted statutory provision, and you will see that this is so.

In 1986, Congress enacted the GST tax, which taxes a transfer to a person two generations below the transferor. In the trust above, in which *T*'s child, *A*, is given a life estate and a nongeneral power of appointment, a GST tax will be levied at *A*'s death if the trust assets pass to the next generation, *unless the trust assets are subject to an estate tax levied on A's estate.* By exercising her nongeneral power to create a general inter vivos power in her child, *B*, *A* can subject the trust assets to the estate tax and, thus, avoid a GST tax. Whether it is better to pay the estate tax or the GST tax depends on the availability of estate and GST exemptions and the applicable current tax rates. The Delaware Tax Trap has therefore turned out to be useful in sophisticated estate planning.[67]

D. OTHER DURATIONAL LIMITS

1. The Rule Against Suspension of the Power of Alienation

The power of alienation is the power to convey title. A suspension of the power of alienation occurs when no living person, or living persons joined together, can convey an absolute fee in the property at issue. The *rule against suspension of the power of alienation* is directed against interests that make the property inalienable. If there is any possibility that the power of alienation will be suspended longer than lives in being plus 21 years, the interests causing such invalid suspension are void ab initio.

Professor Gray insisted that there was no common law rule against suspension of the power of alienation apart from the rule against remote vesting, and his view ultimately prevailed in the cases. However, in 1830, before the question was settled in the cases, New York enacted legislation forbidding suspension of the power of alienation

---

67. *See* Jonathan G. Blattmachr & Jeffrey N. Pennell, Adventures in Generation-Skipping, or How We Learned to Love the "Delaware Tax Trap," 24 Real Prop. Prob. & Tr. J. 75 (1989); *see also* James P. Spica, Means to an End: Electively Forcing Vesting to Suit Tax Rules Against Perpetuities, 40 ACTEC L.J. 347 (2014).

for more than a specified period. Several other states copied or were influenced by the New York statute.[68]

Today there are two views of when the power of alienation is suspended by the creation of a trust. Under the Wisconsin view, the power of alienation is not suspended if the trustee has the power to sell the trust assets, making them alienable, or if a living person has an unlimited power to terminate the trust.[69] In several of the states that have authorized perpetual trusts, the power of alienation must not be suspended in the Wisconsin sense.

Under the New York view, the power of alienation is suspended if *either* the legal fee simple to the property held in trust cannot be transferred *or* the owners of all the equitable interests cannot convey an equitable fee simple. In other words, the creation of a trust suspends the power of alienation *unless* the trustee is given the power to sell the trust property *and* the beneficiaries of the trust can convey their interests. The New York view applies the rule against suspension of the power of alienation to both the underlying trust property and the beneficial interests.[70]

All vested and contingent future interests are today assignable or releasable if the holders are ascertainable and there is no express restraint upon alienation. Accordingly, the only interests that suspend the power of alienation in a New York trust in which the trustee has the power to sell the trust property are (a) those subject to an express restraint upon alienation such as a spendthrift clause, or (b) those given to unborn or unascertained persons. An interesting consequence is this: *The duration of a spendthrift trust in New York is limited to the perpetuities period.* Such a trust is partially or wholly invalid if it can exceed the perpetuities period in duration. Therein lies the most important difference today between the common law Rule Against Perpetuities and the New York version of the rule against suspension of the power of alienation.

> *Case 17.* T, domiciled in New York, dies in 2017. She bequeaths a fund in a spendthrift trust "to pay the income to A for life, then to pay the income to A's children for their lives, and then to pay the principal to New York University." The gift does not violate the Rule Against Perpetuities (for the same reasons as in Case 1 at page 894). However, the income interests in A and A's children are inalienable. Since the power of alienation might be suspended during the lifetime of after-born persons (A's children born after T's death), the life income interests in A's children are void. The remainder in New York University will be accelerated (unless the court determines that the stricken interests are so crucial to T's dispositive scheme that invalidating the entire bequest would better approximate T's intent[71]).

If, in Case 17, T had expressly provided that A's children could alienate their interests, the trust would be wholly valid. The power of alienation would be suspended only during A's lifetime, a life in being. At A's death, all of A's children are in being, and, together with New York University, they can convey a fee simple absolute.

---

68. *See* Shapo et al., *supra* note 15, at § 219; Schoenblum, *supra* note 16, at tbl. 9, q. 26.
69. *See* Wis. Stat. § 700.16 (2016).
70. *See* N.Y. Est. Powers & Trusts Law § 9-1.1(a) (2016).
71. This would be an application of the doctrine of *infectious invalidity* (see page 893, n.16).

2. The Rule Against Accumulations of Income[72]

Originating in Thellusson v. Woodford, (1805) 32 Eng. Rep. 1030 (Ch.); 11 Ves. Jr. 112, there appears to exist a common law doctrine — *the rule against accumulations of income* — that limits the period during which the settlor may direct a trustee to accumulate and retain income in trust.

At issue in *Thellusson* was the will of Peter Thellusson, a wealthy financier who died in 1797. Thellusson's will provided that the bulk of his estate, plus all the income it would earn during the lives of his nine surviving male descendants, should be accumulated for the benefit of the eldest surviving male descendant of each of his three sons at the end of that period. Thellusson thus deviated substantially from the typical practice in which the father left his estate either to the eldest son or to all the sons equally. "This placed the family in an unprecedented and disturbing situation. Like some perverted tontine, it left some of them, who were themselves unable to enjoy any of the money, postponing by their continuing existence its distribution to those golden lads for whom it seemed destined."[73]

Thellusson's family challenged the will. The House of Lords concluded that there was no violation of the Rule Against Perpetuities. The interest in Thellusson's eldest male descendant would vest at the end of the specified measuring lives. It mattered not that none of the measuring lives was a beneficiary.

As for whether the bequest violated a separate rule against accumulations of income, the House of Lords left undisturbed the view of the Lord Chancellor below:

> [A]nother question arises out of this Will; which is a pure question of equity: whether a testator can direct the rents and profits to be accumulated for that period, during which he may direct, that the title shall not vest, and the property shall remain unalienable; and, that he can do so, is most clear law.

On this view, under the common law a direction to accumulate income during the period of the Rule Against Perpetuities is valid.

Thellusson's accumulation plan provoked a public outcry against the possibility of accumulated fortunes. One well-known estimate projected that Thellusson's accumulation would grow from £600,000 to somewhere between £19 and £38.4 million. The family's counsel "came up with the phrase 'posthumous avarice,' which has attached itself to Thellusson's will ever since."[74]

Thellusson's accumulation plan was so unpopular that, two years after the Lord Chancellor upheld it, before the House of Lords rendered its decision on appeal, Parliament enacted the Thellusson Act.[75] The act limited accumulations of income to (1) the life of the settlor; (2) 21 years from the death of the settlor; (3) the minority of any person living (or in gestation) at the time of the settlor's death; or (4) the minority

---

72. Portions of this section are adapted from Robert H. Sitkoff, The Lurking Rule Against Accumulations of Income, 100 Nw. U. L. Rev. 501 (2006).

73. Patrick Polden, Peter Thellusson's Will of 1797 and Its Consequences on Chancery Law 4 (2002).

74. Id. at 144.

75. 1800, 39 & 40 Geo. 3 c. 98 (Eng.).

of any person who, upon majority, would be entitled to the income being accumulated. With minor updating, this statutory rule against accumulations remained good law in England until 2009, when it was repealed. For interests created after April 6, 2010, the effective date of the 2009 law, the common law as stated by the Lord Chancellor in *Thellusson* is again applicable.[76]

Peter Thellusson's "posthumous avarice" was also met with hostility in this country. One Pennsylvania judge expressed a worry that such a trust might "draw into its vortex all the property in the state."[77] Several states adopted statutes similar to the Thellusson Act or, in the case of New York and a few other states, an even more restrictive one.[78]

History has shown the worry over Thellusson's will to have been misplaced. When the trust came to an end with the death of the last grandson in 1856, the predicted vast fortune had not materialized. "[N]early sixty years of accumulation had not produced one million pounds let alone thirty. From being a public menace, Peter Thellusson had become a laughing stock."[79]

Other accumulation plans have also failed. Perhaps the most famous is that of Benjamin Franklin. When Franklin died in 1790, he left two charitable trusts of £1,000 each (about $4,000) that were to accumulate income with no payouts for 100 years, then to spend most of the principal for the benefit of public purposes in Boston and Philadelphia, and then to accumulate again for another 100 years. The Boston trust grew to less than $5 million and the Philadelphia trust to less than half of that.

In the twentieth century, accumulations legislation such as the Thellusson Act fell out of favor. Today, in states with a statutory rule against accumulations of income in private trusts, the accumulation period is typically the same as the period of the Rule Against Perpetuities.[80] Under such a statute Thellusson's will would be upheld.

Benjamin Franklin

In part because the English courts did not develop their accumulations rule before American independence, ambiguity remained in states without an accumulations statute about whether there was an American common law rule against accumulations, and if so, for what duration accumulations would be permitted. This ambiguity was resolved in 1941 by Gertman v. Burdick, 123 F.2d 924 (D.C. Cir. 1941).

At issue in *Gertman* was a bequest in trust to accumulate income during the lives of two named people and then for 21 years after the death of the survivor of them. In a learned opinion by Judge Fred Vinson, who would later become Chief Justice of the United States, the court upheld the bequest, explaining that "a rule permitting

---

76. *See* Perpetuities and Accumulations Act 2009, c. 18, §§ 5, 7 (Eng. & Wales).
77. Hillyard v. Miller, 10 Pa. 326, 336 (1849).
78. *See* Shapo et al., *supra* note 15, at § 216.
79. Polden, *supra* note 73, at 7.
80. *See, e.g.,* Cal. Civ. Code § 724 (2016); N.Y. Est. Powers & Trusts Law § 9-2.1(b) (2016).

Shutting Out the Kids from the Family Fortune

By Robert Frank

Want to avoid raising spoiled kids?

Consider the Wellington Burt School of Wealthy Parenting.

Wellington R. Burt was a rich timber baron from Saginaw, MI. He died in 1919 with a multi-million-dollar fortune—one of America's largest at the time.

Yet rather than risk messing up his kids lives with a huge inheritance, he created an unusual will.

He stated that his fortune would be distributed to the family—but only 21 years after his grandchildren's death.

His children and grandchildren weren't entirely deprived. Burt gave his "favorite son" $30,000 a year but the rest of his children got allowances roughly equal to those he gave his cook and chauffeur, according to the Saginaw News.

"I'm pretty sure he didn't like his family back then," said Christina Cameron, an heir and a great-great-great grandchild of Burt's.

Now that it's 21 years since the death of the last grandchild, the fortune is finally being turned over to Cameron and 11 others, including three great-grandchildren, seven great-great grandchildren and another great-great-great grandchild. The fortune is valued at more than $100 million. (She'll get a little more than $2.6 million, since those further up the family tree get more under a master agreement.)

Saginaw County Chief Probate Judge Patrick McGraw said the estate is "one of the most complicated research projects" he's faced in his 12-year career in Saginaw.

Wellington R. Burt

Of course, skipping a generation is not unusual among rich parents who want to send a message to their kids (but somehow not their grand-kids). Generation-skipping trusts and other estate-planning structures have been around for ages.

But Burt's will takes kid-skipping to a new, almost punitive level. Who knows, maybe his kids and grand-kids were better off for the lack of inheritance, or maybe the money would have allowed them to lead fuller, happier lives. We'll never know. It would be interesting to compare the lives of his new heirs with those who were shut out.

What do you think of Burt's School of Parenting?

Source: Wall St. J. (May 10, 2011).

accumulations for as long as the period of the rule against perpetuities . . . has been the common law of this country." The rule against accumulations was thus recognized as a doctrine independent from the Rule Against Perpetuities, though the accumulations rule's durational limit was that of the applicable perpetuities period.

Because the period under the two rules is the same, compliance with the Rule Against Perpetuities typically ensures compliance with the rule against accumulations—but not always. Here is an example of a transfer that is valid under the Rule Against Perpetuities but offends the rule against accumulations:

> *Case 18.* T bequeaths a fund in trust to X "to pay so much of the income to A during A's life as X may determine, then to pay so much of the income to A's children for their lives as X may determine, then to pay the remainder to B." At T's death, A has no children. A's life estate is vested in possession upon T's death; the life estate in A's children will vest in possession or, if there are no children, fail, upon A's death; and B's remainder is vested in interest upon T's death.

All interests in Case 18 will vest or fail within the perpetuities period (21 years after the death of the survivor of A and B). However, X has discretion to accumulate income in the trust after the perpetuities period expires. This could happen, for example, if after *T*'s death *A* has a child, *C*, who survives *A* and *B* by more than 21 years. In some states, the accumulation is void as to the excess; in others, the accumulation is void in its entirety.[81]

With the rise of the perpetual trust, a new question has arisen: Does a perpetual trust that provides for the accumulation of income violate the rule against accumulations? Some states have dealt with the interaction of the rule against accumulations and perpetual trusts by legislation.[82] In states that have not taken legislative action, the law is less clear. Because the common law rule against accumulations absorbs the period of the applicable Rule Against Perpetuities, it is arguable that statutory perpetuities reform likewise reforms the accumulations rule. In 1999, however, the Supreme Judicial Court of Maine held to the contrary in White v. Fleet Bank of Maine, 739 A.2d 373 (Me. 1999).

At issue in *White* was a holographic will that contained a bequest in trust from which three-fourths of the income would be paid to the testator's lineal descendants and the other one-fourth would be "reinvested annually for the increase of funds in the Trust." The trust was to continue, "following the lines of direct descent, as long as the Trust may be made to endure." The court held that the quoted language was a saving clause such that, under the then-applicable Maine wait-and-see statute, the bequest was not invalid under the Rule Against Perpetuities. It was possible that all future income interests would vest within the perpetuities period.

Regarding the rule against accumulations of income, the trustee argued that Maine's wait-and-see perpetuities reform also applied to the accumulations rule. On this view, which is adopted by the Restatement (Second) of Property,[83] the reinvestment clause would be valid for the duration of the perpetuities period, and invalid thereafter. Applied to the facts in *White*, because the reinvestment clause did not reference any life in being, 21 years of accumulation would be permitted.

The court rejected the trustee's argument. It held that the Maine wait-and-see legislation applied only to the Rule Against Perpetuities. The court thus held the reinvestment clause void from the outset because it was not limited to the applicable perpetuities period of 21 years. Since there was no provision for distribution of the trust corpus or accumulated income, the court ordered the property subject to the reinvestment clause to be disbursed to the testator's heirs on resulting trust.

It remains to be seen whether the reasoning in *White* will be followed in a state that has validated perpetual trusts. *White* involved the application of a wait-and-see statute, not the abolition of the Rule. Wait-and-see does not lengthen the perpetuities period; rather, it modifies the what-might-happen test of the common law. The reasoning in

---

81. *See* Restatement (Second) of Property: Donative Transfers § 2.2 reporter's notes (Am. Law Inst. 1983).

82. *See, e.g.,* Del. Code Ann. tit. 25, § 506 (2016); 765 Ill. Comp. Stat. Ann. 315/1 (2016); 1998 S.D. Sess. Laws 236 § 27.

83. Restatement (Second) of Property: Donative Transfers § 2.2 (Am. Law Inst. 1983).

White was that such a modification does not affect the period of permissible accumulations. In a state that has abolished the Rule Against Perpetuities, the perpetuities period is indefinite. Trusts may be perpetual. Because the accumulations period is tied to the perpetuities period, abolishing the Rule arguably makes the accumulation period infinite as well.

CHAPTER 15

WEALTH TRANSFER
TAXATION

Our new Constitution is now established, and has an appearance
that promises permanency; but in this world nothing can be
said to be certain, except death and taxes.

BENJAMIN FRANKLIN
Letter from Benjamin Franklin to Jean-Baptiste Le Roy (Nov. 13, 1789)
in 12 The Works of Benjamin Franklin 161 (John Bigelow ed., 1904)

PERHAPS THE MOST IMPORTANT limit on freedom of disposition is the federal wealth transfer tax system: the *gift*, *estate*, and *generation-skipping transfer taxes* of the Internal Revenue Code.[1]

Earlier in this book, we surveyed the history of the federal wealth transfer taxes (see Chapter 1 at page 25). To recap, the estate tax, enacted in 1916, was prompted by the need to raise revenue for World War I. When the fighting stopped, the tax was retained in part in response to public hostility toward the enormous family fortunes that had been amassed during the "robber baron" era a generation earlier. In 1932, Congress added the gift tax to prevent avoidance of the estate tax and the income tax through inter vivos transfers to children and others. Finally, in 1986, to ensure a wealth transfer tax at each generation, Congress enacted the generation-skipping transfer tax. In fiscal year 2015, the federal estate tax raised $17 billion, and the gift tax raised $2 billion, for a total of $19 billion—akin to a rounding error in the total $2.9 *trillion* in internal revenue collected by the federal government in that year.[2]

Whatever the policy arguments for and against the federal wealth transfer taxes (see page 28), these taxes have a profound influence on day-to-day estate planning for wealthy clients.[3] In this chapter, we summarize the basic rules of these notoriously

---

1. The editors gratefully acknowledge the assistance of Professor Stephanie J. Willbanks of Vermont Law School in revising this chapter.

2. Internal Revenue Service Data Book 3 (2015).

3. *See, e.g.*, Joseph M. Dodge, Three Whacks at Wealth Transfer Tax Reform: Retained-Interest Transfers, Generation-Skipping Trusts, and FLP Valuation Discounts, 57 B.C. L. Rev. 999 (2016); Wendy C. Gerzog, Toward a Realty-Based Estate Tax, 57 B.C. L. Rev. 1037 (2016).

complicated laws. We also describe some common estate planning techniques for minimizing their impact.[4]

We begin in Section A by considering the federal gift tax. In Section B, we consider the federal estate tax. In Section C, we consider the federal generation-skipping transfer tax. In Section D, we consider state estate and inheritance taxes.[5] Finally, in Section E, we consider related issues in the federal income taxation of trusts, in particular of grantor trusts, which is a tax term of art for trusts over which the settlor (the grantor) retains certain forms of control.

A. THE FEDERAL GIFT TAX

1. Taxable Gifts

a. Inadequate Consideration in Money's Worth

Internal Revenue Code (I.R.C.) § 2501(a) imposes a tax on the transfer of property by *gift*.[6] In general, a transfer of property for *less than adequate and full consideration in money or money's worth* is a taxable gift. If O transfers property to A and receives in return less than full consideration in money or money's worth, O's estate has been diminished, and the gift tax applies. Consistent with this purpose, and to make the gift tax administrable, Treasury Regulations provide a safe harbor for transfers made pursuant to a sale or exchange in the ordinary course of business that is arm's length and free from donative intent.[7] If the owner of a car dealership sells a car to a customer for less than the going market rate, the owner has made a bad deal, not a taxable gift — unless the customer is the owner's daughter or other circumstances suggest donative intent, taking the transfer out of the safe harbor.[8]

b. Completion

A transfer is not subject to gift taxation until it is *complete*, that is, until the donor has relinquished all "dominion and control" over the property. There is no gift tax due upon the funding of a revocable trust, for example, because the settlor retains the power to revoke or amend the trust. The property is treated for tax purposes as still being owned by the settlor. The transfer becomes complete when the trust becomes

---

4. *See, e.g.*, Ray D. Madoff, Cornelia R. Tenney, Martin A. Hall & Lisa N. Mingolla, Practical Guide to Estate Planning (2017); John R. Price & Samuel A. Donaldson, Price on Contemporary Estate Planning (2017); Stephanie J. Willbanks, Federal Taxation of Wealth Transfers (4th ed. 2016).

5. We leave to the side the question of how transfer taxes might apply to the undead. If you are curious, you might look up Adam Chodorow, Death and Taxes and Zombies, 98 Iowa L. Rev. 1207 (2013).

6. *See* Mitchell M. Gans & Jay A. Soled, Reforming the Gift Tax and Making It Enforceable, 87 B.U. L. Rev. 759 (2007) (discussing circumvention of the gift tax and possible reforms).

7. Treas. Reg. § 25.2512-8.

8. *Compare* Estate of Redstone v. Commissioner, 145 T.C. 259 (2015) (arm's length), *with* Redstone v. Commissioner, 110 T.C.M. (CCH) 564 (2015) (not arm's length).

irrevocable. On similar reasoning, there is no gift tax on a transfer to an irrevocable trust if the settlor retains the power to shift beneficial interests among the beneficiaries. A gift that remains incomplete during the donor's lifetime is subject to estate taxation at the donor's death.

A transfer may also be incomplete for gift tax purposes if the property could be used to benefit the donor, as in Estate of Hotz v. Commissioner, 38 T.C. 37 (1962).

NOTES

1. Incomplete Gifts.   Consider the following two problems on whether a gift is complete:

a. O establishes an irrevocable trust funded with $500,000 in securities. The income is to be paid to O for life, "and on O's death the trustee shall distribute the trust property to such of O's descendants as O appoints by will, or in default of appointment, the trustee shall distribute the property to O's descendants then living, per stirpes." Has O made a taxable gift of the remainder? The answer is No, because O retained a power of appointment, which gives him dominion and control over the property, so the gift is not yet complete.[9]

b. Suppose that O releases the power of appointment. Does the release result in a taxable gift of the remainder? The answer is Yes. The value of the remainder interest at the time of the release is subject to gift taxation.

2. Consent of Adverse Party.   A donor is not considered for tax purposes to have dominion and control over property if he retains a power that can be exercised only with the consent of a person who has a "substantial adverse interest in the disposition of the . . . property or the income therefrom."[10] Here are two illustrations of how this rule affects the determination of whether a gift is complete:

a. O transfers property in trust to pay the income to A for life, and on A's death to distribute the principal to B. O retains the power to revoke or amend the trust in whole or in part, but only with the consent of A. Has O made a taxable gift? The answer is Yes. The gift is complete because A is an adverse party whose consent is required for any change.[11]

b. Assume the same facts as in (a), except that O can only revoke or amend with the consent of S, O's spouse, who has no interest in the trust. Has O made a taxable gift? The answer is No, because S does not have an interest that is substantially adverse to any revocation or amendment by O.

3. Disclaimer.   Suppose that a donee, heir, or devisee *disclaims* a donative transfer of property (see page 135). Has the disclaimant made a taxable gift to whoever gets the disclaimed property? I.R.C. § 2518 provides that a disclaimer is not a taxable gift by the disclaimant if each of the following three conditions is met:

---

9. *See* Treas. Reg. § 25.2511-2(b).

10. Id. § 25.2511-2(e).

11. *See* Camp v. Commissioner, 195 F.2d 999 (1st Cir. 1952).

(1) the disclaimer is in writing, irrevocable, and unqualified, and it is made either within nine months after the interest is created or within nine months after the disclaimant reaches 21, whichever is later;

(2) the disclaimant has not accepted an interest in the disclaimed property or any of its benefits; and

(3) as a result of the disclaimer, the property passes without any direction on the part of the disclaimant and passes either to the decedent's spouse or to someone other than the disclaimant.

c. Joint Tenancy

When two people who are not husband and wife own property as joint tenants with right of survivorship, the joint tenancy is generally treated like a tenancy in common for gift tax purposes. The theory is that the donee co-tenant receives the same lifetime rights under a joint tenancy as a tenancy in common, given that the donee co-tenant can petition to convert the joint tenancy into a tenancy in common at any time. If O takes title to property in joint tenancy with A, O has made a taxable gift to A of half of the property. Thus:

Case 1. O pays $40,000 for Blackacre, taking title in the name of O and A. It does not matter whether the title designates O and A as joint tenants or as tenants in common. In either case, O has made a gift of one-half the value of the property, or $20,000, to A.

A joint and survivor bank account is treated differently. Because a joint tenant can withdraw all funds on deposit, whereas a tenant in common is entitled only to her fractional share, there is no completed taxable gift unless the funds are in fact withdrawn by the non-depositing joint tenant.[12] Thus:

Case 2. O deposits $40,000 in a joint and survivor bank account. Because O can withdraw the entire $40,000, the gift is incomplete. If A withdraws funds from the account, a gift from O to A in the amount withdrawn is complete and therefore subject to gift taxation. If O and A each had deposited $20,000 in the joint account, no gift would be made by either until either O or A withdrew more than the $20,000 each deposited.

d. Income Tax Basis

A capital gains income tax is usually levied on a gain from the sale of property. The taxable amount is the difference between the taxpayer's *basis* and the selling price. Generally speaking, if the taxpayer purchased the property, his basis is the purchase price. If O buys Blackacre for $50,000, and then sells it for $75,000, the gain of $25,000 is subject to capital gains income taxation.

---

12. *See* Treas. Reg. § 25.2511-1(h)(4). The rules applicable to a joint bank account also apply to a U.S. government bond registered in the name of "O or A." Under this "or" form of ownership, either O or A can present the bond for payment. There is no completed gift unless A cashes in the bond.

If a donee receives property by *gift* and then sells it, the donee generally must use the donor's basis to compute the donee's taxable gain. For the purpose of computing loss, however, the donee's basis is the lesser of the donor's basis or the value of the property on the date of the gift.[13] If property is acquired from a *decedent*, the basis of the property for computing both gain and loss is usually the value of the asset on the date of the decedent's death, regardless of what was the decedent's basis.[14] For property that has appreciated in value, the basis of the donee will thus be higher than that of the decedent. This *stepped-up basis* at death means that any capital gain on property held until death potentially escapes capital gains income taxation. This point is sometimes raised in justification of the estate tax (see page 28).

e. Liability for Gift and Estate Taxes

The donor has the primary liability for paying the gift tax. If the donor does not pay, the donee is liable for any unpaid amount. The executor or administrator of a decedent's estate has personal liability for payment of the estate tax but is entitled to reimbursement out of the decedent's estate. If there is no administration of the decedent's estate, the persons in possession of the decedent's property are liable for the tax. Which person is liable for a generation-skipping transfer (GST) tax depends on the form of the transfer (we take up GST taxation later in this chapter at page 975).

An executor or administrator who pays the tax is entitled to reimbursement from life insurance beneficiaries for the portion of the tax resulting from the inclusion of the death benefit in the decedent's estate.[15] Similarly, the executor is entitled to proportionate reimbursement from recipients of property over which the decedent had a general power of appointment.[16] Other than these two exceptions, the Code does not generally provide for apportionment of estate taxes to the recipients — instead it leaves the matter to state law.

In most states and under the Uniform Estate Tax Apportionment Act (Unif. Law Comm'n 2003), which has been absorbed into the Uniform Probate Code as §§ 3-9A-101 through 3-9A-115, federal estate taxes must be borne by each beneficiary pro rata unless the testator provides otherwise, as in In re Estate of Shell, 862 N.W.2d 276 (Neb. 2015). A minority of states follow the opposite default rule, as under Estate of Sheppard v. Schleis, 782 N.W.2d 85 (Wis. 2010), whereby the estate tax is paid out of the residuary estate unless the testator provides otherwise.[17]

---

13. I.R.C. § 1015.

14. Id. § 1014. Beginning in 2015, § 1014(f) imposes a consistency standard. The carry-over basis of property may not exceed its value as finally determined for the estate tax or, if no tax was due, as was reported on a statement required under I.R.C. § 6035(a). I.R.C. § 6662 imposes penalties for inconsistent basis reporting.

15. I.R.C. § 2206.

16. Id. § 2207.

17. *See* Mark R. Siegel, Who Should Bear the Bite of Estate Taxes on Non-Probate Property?, 43 Creighton L. Rev. 747 (2010); Douglas A. Kahn, The 2003 Revised Uniform Estate Tax Apportionment Act, 38 Real Prop. Prob. & Tr. J. 613 (2004).

2. The Annual Exclusion

A potentially significant problem with the capacious definition of what is a gift—any transfer of property for less than full consideration in money or money's worth—is that it sweeps into the gift tax system even small gifts made out of affection rather than to avoid estate taxes. It is widely agreed that such gifts do not warrant the administrative costs of applying the gift tax. To deal with this problem, I.R.C. § 2503(b) allows a donor to exclude from gift taxation a certain amount of value given to each donee in the current year. The purpose of this *annual exclusion*, which is $14,000 in 2017 and is indexed for inflation,[18] "is to obviate the necessity of . . . reporting numerous small gifts, and . . . to fix the amount sufficiently large to cover in most cases wedding and Christmas gifts and occasionally gifts of relatively small amounts."[19] Thus:

> *Case 3.* In 2017, *A* gives $20,000 each to *B* and *C*, and $5,000 to *D*. *A* must report $6,000 taxable gifts to *B* and *C*. The gift to *D* need not be reported because it does not exceed the annual exclusion.

Although the annual exclusion deals well with wedding and Christmas gifts and the like, there is a further problem with school tuition payments and medical expenses to the extent that they are not a legal obligation of the donor. If a grandparent pays the school tuition or medical bills of a grandchild, or if a parent makes such payments for a child who is no longer a minor (and so not in satisfaction of a legal obligation of support), then a gift has been made within the meaning of the gift tax. To exclude these kinds of transfers, I.R.C. § 2503(e) allows an unlimited exclusion for *tuition payments* and *medical expenses* paid directly to the provider. Reimbursement of the donee for payments already made by the donee does not qualify.

These two exceptions—the annual exclusion and the exception for tuition and medical expenses—give rise to a substantial planning opportunity. By making full use of these exceptions across one's descendants, doubly so for the annual exclusion for a married couple (see page 942), substantial wealth can be passed down the generations free of gift and estate taxation. Thus:

> *Case 4.* *H* gives $14,000 each per year to both of his children, to their spouses, and to his four grandchildren. In this way, the annual exclusion allows *H* to transfer $112,000 per year out of his estate tax free. *W* makes the same gifts each year, bringing the total to $224,000. In addition to these transfers, *H* and *W* can pay the private school tuition of the four grandchildren. If that tuition is $25,000 each, the total tax-free yearly transfer amount increases to $324,000. In just four years, *H* and *W* can transfer almost $1.3 million to or for the benefit of their children, children-in-law, and grandchildren without incurring any gift or estate tax liability.

---

18. The annual exclusion was $5,000 from 1932 to 1939, $4,000 from 1939 to 1942, and $3,000 from 1943 to 1981. The Economic Recovery Tax Act of 1981 raised the annual exclusion to $10,000 beginning in 1982 and indexed it for inflation, but only in increments of $1,000. As a result, the amount of the annual exclusion did not rise to $11,000 until 2002. It became $12,000 in 2006, $13,000 in 2009, and $14,000 in 2013. It will remain at $14,000 in 2017.

19. H.R. Rep. No. 72-708, at 29 (1932).

A complication in using the annual exclusion for a program of yearly gifting, as in Case 4, is that the exclusion applies only to *present interests*. This limitation follows from the immediate need to determine who is the donee and the value of what was given. As a planning matter, therefore, making an annual exclusion gift in trust is not possible unless the beneficiary receives a present interest. This generally requires that each beneficiary have the right to immediate possession or enjoyment of the property, and that each such beneficial interest be capable of valuation.[20] Thus:

> *Case 5.* O gives property worth $500,000 to A for life, remainder to B. Under the actuarial tables applicable at the time of the gift, the value of A's life estate is $325,000 and B's remainder is worth $175,000. O is entitled to a $14,000 exclusion for the gift to A (a present interest), but not for the gift of the remainder to B (a future interest).

> *Case 6.* O creates a trust that requires the trustee to pay the income annually among O's three children in such shares as the trustee in her uncontrolled discretion deems advisable. Even though all the income must be distributed each year, none of the beneficiaries has a present interest for gift tax purposes, hence O is entitled to no annual exclusions.

The disqualification of future interests from the annual exclusion creates special challenges for gifting to a minor. A sensible donor will not give substantial gifts to a child outright. Instead, the property will be given to a guardian or custodian (see page 125), which qualifies for the annual exclusion, or, even better, to a trustee. To allow donors to make annual exclusion gifts to minors in trust, Congress provided in I.R.C. § 2503(c) that property transferred in trust for a minor will be treated as though it were a present interest if the property and the income it generates:

> (1) may be expended by, or for the benefit of, the donee before his attaining the age of 21 years, and
> (2) will to the extent not so expended —
>> (A) pass to the donee on his attaining the age of 21 years, and
>> (B) in the event the donee dies before attaining the age of 21 years, be payable to the estate of the donee or as he may appoint under a general power of appointment as defined in section 2514(c).

To qualify as a § 2503(c) trust, the donor must give the trustee the power to expend *all* the income and principal on the donee before the donee reaches 21. Unexpended income and principal must pass to the donee at 21 or, if the donee dies before reaching 21, to the donee's estate (or as the donee appoints under a general power of appointment). If the trustee has the power to expend only the income on the donee, the value of the income interest, but not the full value of the property, will qualify as a present

---

20. *See* Treas. Reg. § 25.2503-3(b); *see also* John G. Steinkamp, Common Sense and the Gift Tax Annual Exclusion, 72 Neb. L. Rev. 106 (1993); Jeffrey G. Sherman, 'Tis a Gift to Be Simple: The Need for a New Definition of "Future Interest" for Gift Tax Purposes, 55 U. Cin. L. Rev. 585 (1987); Walter D. Schwidetzky, Estate Planning: Hyperlexis and the Annual Exclusion Rule, 32 Suffolk U. L. Rev. 211 (1998).

interest. In either case, no person other than the minor can have a beneficial interest in the property.

A § 2503(c) trust has two significant planning disadvantages: distributions effectively must be made during the beneficiary's minority, and distribution of the remainder must be made when the beneficiary reaches the age of 21. To get around these disadvantages, imaginative lawyers came up with the idea of giving the beneficiary a power of withdrawal over the property meant to qualify for the annual exclusion. Such a power transforms what would otherwise be a future interest into a present interest. A power of withdrawal, even one limited to use within a few days, is a *general power of appointment*, and the donee of a general power is treated for all tax purposes as the owner of the appointive property (see page 962). Thus:

> *Case 7.* Each year O transfers $14,000 to X in trust to pay so much of the income and principal to B as X determines in X's sole and uncontrolled discretion until B's 35th birthday. When B turns 35, X is to pay the remainder to B or, if B dies prior to the age of 35, then to C. Because these gifts are not present interests and do not satisfy the conditions of § 2503(c), the annual exclusion is not available. However, if O also gives B the power to withdraw $14,000 from the trust within 30 days of each gift, then B has a present interest and the gift qualifies for the annual exclusion even if B does not exercise the power.

> *Case 8.* O transfers $42,000 to X in trust to pay so much of the income and principal to A, B, or C as X determines in X's sole and uncontrolled discretion. So long as O also provides that each beneficiary has a power to withdraw up to $14,000 each, the transfer qualifies for the annual exclusion, even if the power to withdraw is limited to a short period of time.

The use of temporary withdrawal powers to qualify a gift in trust for the annual exclusion, as in Cases 7 and 8, was upheld in Crummey v. Commissioner, 397 F.2d 82 (9th Cir. 1968). Such a power has since come to be known as a *Crummey power*. In contemporary practice, *Crummey* powers are commonly used to transform a transfer in trust into a present interest that qualifies for the annual exclusion, even though the holders of such powers rarely exercise the power of withdrawal.

Estate of Cristofani v. Commissioner
97 T.C. 74 (1991)

RUWE, J. Respondent determined a deficiency in petitioner's Federal estate tax in the amount of $49,486. The sole issue for decision is whether transfers of property to a trust, where the beneficiaries possessed the right to withdraw an amount not in excess of the section 2503(b) exclusion within 15 days of such transfers, constitute gifts of a present interest in property within the meaning of section 2503(b).

FINDINGS OF FACT

Petitioner is the Estate of Maria Cristofani, deceased, Frank Cristofani, executor. Maria Cristofani (decedent) died testate on December 16, 1985. . . .

Decedent has two children, Frank Cristofani and Lillian Dawson. Decedent's children were both born on July 9, 1948. They were in good health during the years 1984 and 1985.

Decedent has five grandchildren. Two of decedent's five grandchildren are Frank Cristofani's children. They are Anthony Cristofani, born July 16, 1975, and Loris Cristofani, born November 30, 1978. Decedent's three remaining grandchildren are Lillian Dawson's children. They are Justin Dawson, born December 1, 1972, Daniel Dawson, born August 9, 1974, and Luke Dawson, born November 14, 1981. During 1984 and 1985, the parents of decedent's grandchildren were the legal guardians of the person of their respective minor children. There were no independently appointed guardians of decedent's grandchildren's property. . . .

On June 12, 1984, decedent executed an irrevocable trust entitled the Maria Cristofani Children's Trust I (Children's Trust). Frank Cristofani and Lillian Dawson were named the trustees of the Children's Trust.

In general, Frank Cristofani and Lillian Dawson possessed the following rights and interests in the Children's Trust corpus and income. Under Article Twelfth, following

Student Life Veers into Armed Robbery Charges

By Eric Bailey

They hardly seem the usual suspects. She was a prestigious National Merit Scholar, a Los Angeles parochial school product and a gifted poet in her freshman year of college. He was a talented dancer and philosophy major on the verge of earning a bachelor's degree.

But now Emma Freeman, 18, and Anthony Cristofani, 23, are accused of two armed robberies in this coastal university town. Some have dubbed the young woman from La Crescenta and her boyfriend a collegiate Bonnie and Clyde.

Their seeming detour—from UC Santa Cruz students with a lifetime of promise to potential convicts—makes for a perplexing story, one that has stunned those who know them well....

Police reports of the brief series of crimes sound like low-grade pulp fiction. Paul Meltzer, Cristofani's attorney in Santa Cruz, called it "a case about extraordinarily bad judgment."

On Jan. 16, Freeman and Cristofani are accused of strolling into the Emerald Iguana hair salon in neighboring Capitola and holding up a lone stylist. Freeman allegedly brandished a handgun in the caper. "Tell her what you want, honey," Cristofani reportedly said. The take was less than $100.

A few days later, the duo is suspected of making off with a boombox and a few other electronic items from a Santa Cruz Costco. At the door, a surveillance camera recorded a confrontation with a staffer who tried to stop the unmasked pair. Authorities said the woman robber, outfitted in a Spice Girls T-shirt, leveled a gun and said, "Don't do anything stupid."

Anthony Cristofani and Emma Freeman
Bill Lovejoy/Santa Cruz Sentinel

Victims in the two crimes, police say, were shaken but not injured.

Officers caught up quickly, nabbing the pair at Cristofani's downtown apartment....

Police say a search of the apartment and Freeman's dorm room yielded some allegedly stolen items, a Spice Girls T-shirt and a .380-caliber Beretta semiautomatic handgun. Police said Freeman told them the gun wasn't loaded during the robberies....

A native of the leafy San Jose suburb of Los Gatos, Cristofani is described by friends as a flamboyant fellow, a philosophical merry prankster. He favored bright clothes, often donning orange shoes and silk shirts, and was known to jump atop a table in the cafeteria and dance, or bellow in Italian.

But friends also say Cristofani was studiously nonviolent, the product of a close, financially secure family.

Source: L.A. Times (Feb. 12, 1999).

a contribution to the Children's Trust, Frank Cristofani and Lillian Dawson could each withdraw an amount not to exceed the amount specified for the gift tax exclusion under section 2503(b). Such withdrawal period would begin on the date of the contribution and end on the 15th day following such contribution. Under Article Third, Frank Cristofani and Lillian Dawson were to receive equally the entire net income of the trust quarter-annually, or at more frequent intervals. After decedent's death, under Article Third, the Trust Estate was to be divided into as many equal shares as there were children of decedent then living or children of decedent then deceased but leaving issue. Both Frank Cristofani and Lillian Dawson survived decedent, and thus the Children's Trust was divided into two equal trusts [and distributed to Frank and Lillian shortly thereafter]. . . .

Under Article Twelfth, during a 15-day period following a contribution to the Children's Trust, each of the grandchildren possessed the same right of withdrawal as described above regarding the withdrawal rights of Frank Cristofani and Lillian Dawson. Under Article Twelfth, the trustee of the Children's Trust was required to notify the beneficiaries of the trust each time a contribution was received. Under Article Third, had either Frank Cristofani or Lillian Dawson predeceased decedent or failed to survive decedent by 120 days, his or her equal portion of decedent's Children's Trust would have passed in trust to his or her children (decedent's grandchildren).

Under Article Third, the trustees, in their discretion, could apply as much of the principal of the Children's Trust as necessary for the proper support, health, maintenance and education of decedent's children. In exercising their discretion, the trustees were to take into account several factors, including "The Settlor's desire to consider the Settlor's children as primary beneficiaries and the other beneficiaries of secondary importance."

Decedent . . . transferred, on December 17, 1984, an undivided 33-percent interest in . . . property to the Children's Trust by a quitclaim deed. Similarly, in 1985, decedent transferred a second undivided 33-percent interest . . . to the Children's Trust. . . . Decedent intended to transfer her remaining undivided interest in the . . . property to the Children's Trust in 1986. However, decedent died prior to making the transfer. . . .

The value of the 33-percent undivided interest in the . . . property that decedent transferred in 1984 was $70,000. The value of the 33-percent undivided interest in the . . . property that decedent transferred in 1985 also was $70,000.

Decedent did not report the two $70,000 transfers on Federal gift tax returns. Rather, decedent claimed seven annual exclusions of $10,000 each under section 2503(b) for each year. . . . These annual exclusions were claimed with respect to decedent's two children and decedent's five grandchildren.

There was no agreement or understanding between decedent, the trustees, and the beneficiaries that decedent's grandchildren would not exercise their withdrawal rights following a contribution to the Children's Trust. None of decedent's five grandchildren exercised their rights to withdraw under Article Twelfth of the Children's Trust during either 1984 or 1985. None of decedent's five grandchildren received a distribution from the Children's Trust during either 1984 or 1985.

Respondent allowed petitioner to claim the annual exclusions with respect to decedent's two children. However, respondent disallowed the $10,000 annual exclusions claimed with respect to each of decedent's grandchildren claimed for the years 1984 and 1985. Respondent determined that the annual exclusions that decedent claimed with respect to her five grandchildren for the 1984 and 1985 transfers ... were not transfers of present interests in property. Accordingly, respondent increased petitioner's adjusted taxable gifts in the amount of $100,000.

OPINION

... The section 2503(b) exclusion applies to gifts of present interests in property and does not apply to gifts of future interests. ... The regulations define a future interest to include "reversions, remainders, and other interests or estates, whether vested or contingent, and whether or not supported by a particular interest or estate, which are limited to commence in use, possession or enjoyment at some future date or time." Sec. 25.2503-3(a), Gift Tax Regs. The regulations further provide that "An unrestricted right to the immediate use, possession, or enjoyment of property or the income from property (such as a life estate or term certain) is a present interest in property. An exclusion is allowable with respect to a gift of such an interest (but not in excess of the value of the interest)." Sec. 25.2503-3(b), Gift Tax Regs.

In the instant case, petitioner argues that the right of decedent's grandchildren to withdraw an amount equal to the annual exclusion within 15 days after decedent's contribution of property to the Children's Trust constitutes a gift of a present interest in property, thus qualifying for a $10,000 annual exclusion for each grandchild for the years 1984 and 1985. Petitioner relies upon Crummey v. Commissioner, 397 F.2d 82 (9th Cir. 1968), revg. on this issue T.C. Memo. 1966-144.

In Crummey v. Commissioner, T.C. Memo. 1966-144, affd. in part and revd. in part 397 F.2d 82 (9th Cir. 1968), the settlors created an irrevocable living trust for the benefit of their four children, some of whom were minors. The trustee was required to hold the property in equal shares for the beneficiaries. Under the terms of the trust, the trustee, in his discretion, could distribute trust income to each beneficiary until that beneficiary obtained the age of 21. ... In addition, each child was given an absolute power to withdraw up to $4,000 in cash of any additions to corpus in the calendar year of the addition, by making a written demand upon the trustee prior to the end of the calendar year.

Relying on these powers, the settlors claimed the section 2503(b) exclusion on transfers of property to the trust for each trust beneficiary.[21] Respondent permitted the settlors to claim the exclusions with respect to the gifts in trust to the beneficiaries who were adults during the years of the additions. However, respondent disallowed exclusions with respect to the gifts in trust to the beneficiaries who were minors during such years. Respondent disallowed the exclusions for the minor beneficiaries on the ground that the minors' powers were not gifts of present interests in property.

In deciding whether the minor beneficiaries received a present interest, the Ninth Circuit specifically rejected any test based upon the likelihood that the minor beneficiaries would actually receive present enjoyment of the property. Instead, the court

---

21. During the years in *Crummey*, 1962 and 1963, the § 2503(b) annual exclusion was $3,000.

focused on the legal right of the minor beneficiaries to demand payment from the trustee. The Ninth Circuit, relying on Perkins v. Commissioner, 27 T.C. 601 (1956), and Gilmore v. Commissioner, 213 F.2d 520 (6th Cir. 1954), stated:

> All exclusions should be allowed under the *Perkins* test. . . . Under *Perkins*, all that is necessary is to find that the demand could not be resisted. We interpret that to mean legally resisted and, going on that basis, we do not think the trustee would have any choice but to have a guardian appointed to take the property demanded.

Crummey v. Commissioner, 397 F.2d at 88.

The court found that the minor beneficiaries had a legal right to make a demand upon the trustee, and allowed the settlors to claim annual exclusions, under section 2503(b), with respect to the minor trust beneficiaries. . . .

Subsequent to the opinion in *Crummey*, respondent's revenue rulings have recognized that when a trust instrument gives a beneficiary the legal power to demand immediate possession of corpus, that power qualifies as a present interest in property. See Rev. Rul. 85-24, 1985-1 C.B. 329, 330 ("When a trust instrument gives a beneficiary the power to demand immediate possession of corpus, the beneficiary has received a present interest. Crummey v. Commissioner, 397 F.2d 82 (9th Cir. 1968)"); Rev. Rul. 81-7, 1981-1 C.B. 474 ("The courts have recognized that if a trust instrument gives a beneficiary the power to demand immediate possession and enjoyment of corpus or income, the beneficiary has a present interest. Crummey v. Commissioner, 397 F.2d 82 (9th Cir. 1968)."). While we recognize that revenue rulings do not constitute authority for deciding a case in this Court, . . . we mention them to show respondent's recognition that a trust beneficiary's legal right to demand immediate possession and enjoyment of trust corpus or income constitutes a present interest in property for purposes of the annual exclusion under section 2503(b). See Tele-Communications, Inc. v. Commissioner, 95 T.C. 495, 510 (1990). . . .

In the instant case, respondent has not argued that decedent's grandchildren did not possess a legal right to withdraw corpus from the Children's Trust within 15 days following any contribution, or that such demand could have been legally resisted by the trustees. In fact, the parties have stipulated that "following a contribution to the Children's Trust, each of the grandchildren possessed the *same right of withdrawal* as . . . the withdrawal rights of Frank Cristofani and Lillian Dawson." (Emphasis added.) . . .

On brief, respondent attempts to distinguish *Crummey* from the instant case. Respondent argues that in *Crummey* the trust beneficiaries not only possessed an immediate right of withdrawal, but also possessed "substantial, future economic benefits" in the trust corpus and income. . . .

In the instant case, the primary beneficiaries of the Children's Trust were decedent's children. Decedent's grandchildren held contingent remainder interests in the Children's Trust. Decedent's grandchildren's interests vested only in the event that their respective parent (decedent's child) predeceased decedent or failed to survive decedent by more than 120 days. We do not believe, however, that *Crummey* requires that the beneficiaries of a trust must have a vested present interest or vested remainder interest in the trust corpus or income, in order to qualify for the section 2503(b) exclusion. . . .

Although decedent's grandchildren never exercised their respective withdrawal rights, this does not vitiate the fact that they had the legal right to do so, within 15 days following a contribution to the Children's Trust. Events might have occurred to prompt decedent's children and grandchildren (through their guardians) to exercise their withdrawal rights. . . . [W]e fail to see how respondent can argue that decedent did not intend to benefit her grandchildren.

Finally, the fact that the trust provisions were intended to obtain the benefit of the annual gift tax exclusion does not change the result. As we stated in Perkins v. Commissioner, supra,

> regardless of the petitioners' motives, or why they did what they in fact did, the legal rights in question were created by the trust instruments and could at any time thereafter be exercised. Petitioners having done what they purported to do, their tax-saving motive is irrelevant. [Perkins v. Commissioner, 27 T.C. at 606.]

Based upon the foregoing, we find that the grandchildren's right to withdraw an amount not to exceed the section 2503(b) exclusion, represents a present interest for purposes of section 2503(b). Accordingly, petitioner is entitled to claim annual exclusions with respect to decedent's grandchildren as a result of decedent's transfers of property to the Children's Trust in 1984 and 1985.

Decision will be entered for the petitioner.

NOTES

1. The IRS Resists. The Internal Revenue Service has not fully accepted the *Cristofani* decision:

> [T]he IRS will deny exclusions for powers held by individuals who either have no property interests in the trust except for *Crummey* powers, or hold only contingent remainder interests. To extend the gift tax benefit of *Crummey* powers to beneficiaries with interests more remote than current income or vested remainders would undermine significantly the unified system of estate and gift taxation which Congress intended, and would invite flagrant abuse in the future.[22]

To reduce the likelihood of a challenge by the IRS, a typical practice is to give each beneficiary written notice of a contribution to the trust and of the beneficiary's power of withdrawal. If the beneficiary is a minor, such notice is given to the parent or other legal guardian. The beneficiary's power of withdrawal must remain open for a reasonable time in which to make a demand, such as 30 days, and the trust should have sufficient liquidity to meet a demand if it is made.[23] Although courts have upheld gifts as

---

22. I.R.S. AOD-1992-09 (Apr. 6, 1992); *see also* I.R.S. Tech. Adv. Mem. 96-28-004 (July 12, 1996); Bradley E.S. Fogel, Back to the Future Interest: The Origin and Questionable Legal Basis of the Use of Crummey Withdrawal Powers to Obtain the Federal Gift Tax Annual Exclusion, 6 Fla. Tax Rev. 189 (2003); Jeffrey S. Kinsler, Has the Internal Revenue Service's Challenge of Semi-Naked Lapsing Powers Become Frivolous?, 15 Widener L.J. 299 (2006).

23. *See* Andrew M. Katzenstein & Lindsay R. Sellers, Giving Crummey Notices: Best Practices, Tr. & Est., Aug. 2011, at 20.

creating a present interest in cases in which not all of these conditions were present,[24] the costs and delay of litigation are more likely to be avoided by following this practice.

2. Lapse of a Crummey Power. The children and grandchildren in *Cristofani* may have made taxable gifts when their *Crummey* powers lapsed. I.R.C. § 2514(e) provides that a lapse of a general power is considered a gift by the donee of the power, but only to the extent that the amount that could have been appointed (i.e., withdrawn from the trust) exceeds the greater of $5,000 or 5 percent of the aggregate value of the assets out of which the exercise of the lapsed power could have been satisfied. So, for example, the holder of a typical $14,000 *Crummey* power will be deemed to have made a taxable gift of $4,000 if the trust estate at the time of the lapse is worth $200,000 (5 percent of $200,000 is $10,000, which is greater than $5,000, but $4,000 less than the lapsed amount). Any such gift by the *Crummey* powerholder will not normally qualify for an annual exclusion. Because of this lapsed-power issue, donors often limit the *Crummey* withdrawal power to the smaller of the following amounts: (a) the powerholder's pro rata share of the value of the gift, (b) the annual exclusion amount, and (c) the greater of $5,000 or 5 percent of the aggregate value of the assets out of which the exercise of the lapsed power could have been satisfied.[25]

3. The Marital Deduction and Gift Splitting

Thanks to the *unlimited marital deduction,* spouses (regardless of whether they are same-sex) are able to make gifts of any size to each other without gift or estate taxation. The theory is that spouses should be able to treat their property as belonging to an integrated economic unit, freely transferable within the unit. A transfer tax is imposed only when property passes outside the marital unit.[26]

When property is transferred by gift from a spouse to a third person, the transfer is subject to gift taxation. However, if the non-donor spouse consents, I.R.C. § 2513 permits the two spouses to report the gift as made one-half by each of them. Thus, if a wife transfers $28,000 to each of her two daughters, this may be treated — with her husband's consent — as transfers by the wife of $14,000 to each daughter, and transfers by the husband of $14,000 to each of his stepdaughters, thereby qualifying for $56,000 of annual exclusion. In this way, a married person can double the size of her annual exclusion, albeit only with the consent of the other spouse and at the cost of the other spouse's exclusion for that recipient. Gift splitting can be quite valuable to married persons of disparate wealth, allowing the wealthier spouse to make use of the poorer spouse's exclusion.

---

24. *See, e.g.,* Mikel v. Commissioner, 109 T.C.M. (CCH) 1355 (2015), analyzed in Phyllis C. Taite, Crummey Delivers Another Knockout Punch to the IRS, 149 Tax Notes 839 (2015).

25. *See* Price & Donaldson, *supra* note 4, at § 7.38.4.

26. *See* Kerry A. Ryan, Marital Sharing of Transfer Tax Exemptions, 57 B.C. L. Rev. 1061 (2016); Bridget J. Crawford, One Flesh, Two Taxpayers: A New Approach to Marriage and Wealth Transfer Taxation, 6 Fla. Tax Rev. 757 (2004).

B. THE FEDERAL ESTATE TAX

1. A Thumbnail Sketch

The first step in calculating an estate tax is to compute the value of the decedent's *gross estate* as that term is defined in I.R.C. §§ 2033-2044. In addition to the decedent's probate estate (§ 2033), the gross estate includes, among other things, lifetime gratuitous transfers over which the decedent retained a possessory interest or control of beneficial enjoyment (§ 2036), or the power to alter, amend, terminate, or revoke the transfer (§ 2038), and also any property over which the decedent had a general power of appointment (§ 2041).

From the gross estate certain *deductions* may be taken, such as for the decedent's debts and other claims against the estate (§ 2053), state death taxes (§ 2058), transfers to the decedent's spouse (the *marital deduction* under § 2056), and transfers to charity (the *charitable deduction* under § 2055). The gross estate minus deductions equals the *taxable estate.*

To compute the estate tax, *adjusted taxable gifts* (a term of art under I.R.C. § 2101 that means taxable gifts made after 1976) are added to the taxable estate. The total of these two amounts is the *estate tax base*, against which the tax rate (40 percent in 2017) is applied to produce a *tentative estate tax*. Then gift taxes that were previously paid on post-1976 taxable gifts are subtracted. Finally, various other credits are subtracted. These may include a credit for taxes on prior transfers that were taxed in the estate of another decedent within the preceding ten years or a credit for foreign death taxes. The most important credit is the *unified credit*. The Code uses the term "applicable exclusion amount" in defining the unified credit, but most lawyers refer to the applicable exclusion amount as the threshold or *exemption amount*. Under current law, the exemption amount is indexed for inflation. In 2017, the exemption is $5.49 million.

Calculation of the Estate Tax   Figure 15.1

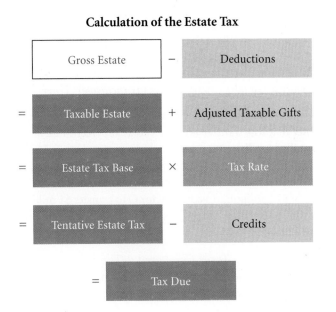

NOTES

1. The Mechanics of the Unified Credit.   The unified credit applies to the estate tax under § 2010 and to the gift tax under § 2505. Section 2505 provides for a credit against the gift tax equal to the amount of tax on the "applicable exemption amount." Assume for the sake of simplicity that the applicable exemption amount is $5 million. *D* gives each of her two children $2.5 million in addition to annual exclusion gifts of $14,000. *D* will not pay any gift tax because her $5 million in taxable gifts are sheltered by the § 2505 credit.

Section 2010 also provides a credit against the estate tax equal to the amount of tax on the "applicable exemption amount." Thus, if *D* dies the following year with a taxable estate of $10 million, then (assuming a tax rate of 40 percent) *D*'s estate will owe $4 million in estate taxes, as *D*'s unified credit was used up during life.

Section 2001 ensures this coordination, that is, it *unifies the credit* across the estate and gift taxes. It requires that the estate tax on *D*'s estate be calculated by adding (1) the amount of adjusted taxable gifts ($5 million) to (2) the amount of the taxable estate ($10 million). A tentative tax (at 40 percent) is imposed on the $15 million total. Any gift tax actually paid (none in this example) is subtracted to ensure that *D*'s transfers are not taxed twice. Then the § 2010 credit is applied. In this example, the tentative tax was $6 million (40 percent times $15 million). The § 2010 credit is $2 million (40 percent times $5 million). So the estate tax due is $4 million; the § 2505 credit is not applied.

2. Tax Advantages of Lifetime Gifts.   Gifts are valued for tax purposes as of the date of the gift. Property included in the gross estate is valued at the time of the decedent's death. By making an inter vivos gift, therefore, the donor can remove from her gross estate any subsequent appreciation in the property's value (plus any income the property generates) between the date of the gift and the date of her death. Such appreciation (and income) is likewise not subject to gift taxation, because it arises subsequent to the gift.

Another advantage of lifetime gifts is that the calculation of gift taxes does not take into account the tax itself (the calculation is *tax exclusive*). Estate taxes, by contrast, are a function of the taxable estate, an amount that includes any estate taxes that will be payable to the government (the calculation is *tax inclusive*). Thus:

> *Case 9.* Suppose *O* wants to transfer $1 million to her daughter, *A*. For simplicity, suppose further that this transfer is subject to a 50 percent rate and that *O* has no exemption (unified credit) remaining. For *A* to receive by gift $1 million, *O* must part with a total of $1.5 million ($1 million to *A* and $500,000 to Uncle Sam). For this transfer, the effective tax rate on the total amount paid by *O* is 33 1/3 percent ($500,000 out of $1.5 million). In contrast, for *O* to transfer $1 million to *A* at death, *O* must part with $2 million. This works out to an effective rate of 50 percent ($1 million out of $2 million).

3. Estate and Inheritance Taxes Compared.   The federal government and some states impose *estate taxes*. The executor or administrator normally pays the tax before making final distributions to the beneficiaries of the estate. So heirs, devisees, and other recipients of estate property do not personally pay estate taxes, at least not directly. A few states instead (or in addition) impose an *inheritance tax* (see Figure 15.2, page 980). An inheritance tax is levied directly on the beneficiaries. The details of state inheritance taxes vary, but in general the amount each beneficiary pays depends not only on the value of the property received, but also on the beneficiary's relationship to the decedent. Bequests to the decedent's children are usually taxed at lower rates than bequests to nephews and nieces. Whether an estate tax is preferable to an inheritance tax is debatable. An estate tax is thought to be easier to administer. But an inheritance tax might be fairer because it is based on the amount each beneficiary receives and it favors close relatives.[27]

J.B. Handelsman/The New Yorker Collection/The Cartoon Bank

2. The Gross Estate

We now consider in more detail the inclusion principles that govern what property and rights to property comprise the gross estate. The difficulty, as with the spousal share (see Chapter 8 at page 528) and creditor rights (see Chapter 7 at page 461), is figuring out which nonprobate assets should be added to the probate estate to have a full picture of the decedent's deathtime transfers.

a. The Probate Estate

I.R.C. § 2033 provides: "The value of the gross estate shall include the value of all property to the extent of the interest therein of the decedent at the time of his death." This section therefore includes in the gross estate any property that under state law is included in the decedent's probate estate.

b. Joint Tenancy

Because a decedent's interest in a joint tenancy vanishes at death, it is not included in the probate estate and is not included in the gross estate under I.R.C. § 2033. However, such an interest may be included under § 2040. The analysis depends on whether the

---

interest was in (1) a joint tenancy between persons other than spouses, or (2) a joint tenancy or tenancy by the entirety between spouses.[28]

(1) Persons Not Married to Each Other.   If the joint tenants are not married to each other, I.R.C. § 2040(a) includes in the gross estate the entire value of the property held in joint tenancy, except any part that is attributable to consideration furnished by the surviving joint tenant. Thus:

> *Case 10.* *O* pays $40,000 for securities, taking title in the name of *O* and *A* as joint tenants. *O* has made a taxable lifetime gift to *A* of one-half the value of the property, or $20,000. When *O* dies several years later, the securities are worth $60,000. Under I.R.C. § 2040, the full value of the securities, or $60,000, is includible in *O*'s gross estate. (There is no double taxation, because as noted at page 943, the tentative estate tax is reduced by the amount of any gift taxes paid on gifts made after 1976.)

If, in Case 10, *O* had contributed three-fourths of the purchase price of the securities ($30,000) and *A* one-fourth ($10,000), three-fourths of the $60,000 date-of-death value of the securities, or $45,000, would be included in *O*'s gross estate. But because the burden of showing the amount contributed by the survivor is on the decedent's personal representative, the value of the entire property will be included in the gross estate if the survivor cannot establish the amount of the survivor's contribution. It is therefore important to keep records showing the source of funds used to acquire or to improve joint tenancy property.

(2) Spouses.   If property is held by the decedent and the decedent's spouse as joint tenants with right of survivorship or as tenants by the entirety, one-half of its date-of-death value is includible in the decedent's gross estate regardless of which spouse furnished the consideration for the property's acquisition or improvement. No estate taxes result from the inclusion of the decedent spouse's one-half interest, however, because it "passes" to the surviving spouse and therefore qualifies for the unlimited marital deduction (see page 967). The price for this deduction is that the surviving spouse receives a stepped-up basis under I.R.C. § 1014 (see page 933) for only one-half of the property. A married couple can sometimes save on capital gains income taxes without increasing estate taxes by transferring sole ownership of joint tenancy property to the spouse who is expected to die first. There is no transfer tax because of the unlimited marital deduction, and the survivor will take a stepped-up basis for the entire property, rather than for only half.

c. Annuities and Employee Death Benefits

Survivor benefits paid under annuity contracts and retirement plans may be includible in the decedent's gross estate. Under I.R.C. § 2039, such benefits are included to the

---

28. *See* Stephanie J. Willbanks, Taxing Once, Taxing Twice, Taxing Joint Tenants (Again) at Death Isn't Nice, 9 Pitt. Tax Rev. 1 (2011).

extent that the decedent had a right to current or future distributions while still living, and another beneficiary will receive distributions by reason of surviving the decedent. However, survivorship benefits that are payable by statute to the decedent's spouse or children are not included because the decedent did not have the power to select the beneficiary. Social Security benefits (see page 560) are therefore not included in the gross estate.

d. Life Insurance

Life insurance is a common mode of nonprobate transfer (see page 471). I.R.C. § 2042 requires inclusion in the gross estate of insurance proceeds on the life of the decedent if (1) the policy proceeds were payable to the decedent's probate estate, or (2) the decedent possessed at death any incident of ownership in the policy. *Incidents of ownership* include the right to change the beneficiary; to surrender, cancel, or assign the policy; or to borrow against the cash surrender value in the policy.[29] With proper planning, therefore, it is often possible to avoid estate taxation on life insurance proceeds.[30]

> *Case 11.* *T* purchases two life insurance policies on his own life, designating his spouse as the beneficiary of one, and his child as the beneficiary of the other. Under the terms of both policies, *T* had the right to change the beneficiary designations at any time. The death benefits payable under both policies are includible in *T*'s gross estate, because *T* held at least one incident of ownership in each policy at the time of his death. (The amount payable to *T*'s wife, however, qualifies for the marital deduction (see page 967).)

> *Case 12.* *T*'s child, *A*, purchases a life insurance policy on *T*'s life and designates himself as the beneficiary at *T*'s death. Because *T* holds no incidents of ownership and the proceeds are not payable to *T*'s probate estate, none of the proceeds are includible in *T*'s gross estate. This is true even if *A* pays the premiums on the policy with funds given to *A* by *T*, for example, in the form of annual exclusion gifts.[31]

Lawyers routinely advise clients to shield life insurance proceeds from estate taxes by having the beneficiary buy and own the policy, or for the policy to be held in an irrevocable trust with someone other than the insured as trustee. Such trusts commonly include *Crummey* powers (see page 936), which allow the insured to make annual exclusion gifts that will fund the paying of the policy premiums.[32]

---

29. If a donee of a nongeneral power of appointment can appoint trust property that includes a life insurance policy on the donee's life, the donee has an incident of ownership, so the value of the insurance will be included in the donee's gross estate. In drafting a nongeneral power of appointment, you should take care to exclude life insurance on the donee from the appointive property.

30. *See* Robert B. Smith, Reconsidering the Taxation of Life Insurance Proceeds Through the Lens of Current Estate Planning, 15 Va. Tax Rev. 283 (1995).

31. If in Case 12 *T* had bought the policy and then given it to *A* within three years of *T*'s death, the proceeds would be includible in *T*'s gross estate under § 2035(a), discussed at page 961.

32. *See* Kelly A. Moore, Rubik's Cube and Tax Policy: Proposed Solutions for Puzzling Components of Estate Planning with Life Insurance, 33 Va. Tax Rev. 429 (2014).

NOTE

Life Insurance Planning.   Consider these two problems:

a. *H* is the insured under a $500,000 whole life insurance policy. The policy was issued in *W*'s name as owner, and *H* has never held any of the incidents of owner-ship. The policy names *W* as the primary beneficiary and the couple's daughter, *D*, as the contingent beneficiary. *H* dies, and the policy proceeds are paid to *W*. *H* leaves a will that devises his entire estate to *W* and *D* in equal shares. The will names *W* as executor. Are the policy proceeds includible in *H*'s gross estate?

b. Consider the same facts as in (a) except that *W* predeceases *H*, leaving a will that devises "all my property" to *H*. On the date of *W*'s death, the cash surrender value of the policy is $100,000. *H* dies a year later, and the $500,000 in policy pro-ceeds are paid to the couple's daughter, *D*, as contingent beneficiary. What are the estate tax consequences in *W*'s estate? In *H*'s estate?

e. Retained Rights or Powers

People sometimes make gifts with strings attached, such as a right to retain possession or enjoyment of the property or to control who will possess or enjoy it. A parent might give a vacation home to a child subject to a right in the parent to continue using the home. In such a case, the value of the vacation home on the donor's date of death will be included in the donor's gross estate under I.R.C. § 2036, which provides:

> The value of the gross estate shall include the value of all property to the extent of any interest therein of which the decedent has at any time made a transfer (except in case of a bona fide sale for an adequate and full consideration in money or money's worth), by trust or otherwise, under which he has retained for his life or for any period which does not in fact end before his death—
>
> (1) The possession or enjoyment of, or the right to the income from, the prop-erty, or
>
> (2) The right, either alone or in conjunction with any person, to designate the persons who shall possess or enjoy the property or the income therefrom.

Although a life estate terminates at death, and therefore is not includible under I.R.C. § 2033, the transfer is subjected to estate taxation under § 2036(a)(1) because the decedent retained the right for life to possess and enjoy the property or to receive its income.

I.R.C. § 2036(a)(2) reaches transfers in which the decedent retains the right to control the beneficial enjoyment of the property. To take an obvious case, if the transferor designates himself as a co-trustee and the trustees have a discretion-ary power to accumulate or distribute trust income to the beneficiary, or a power to distribute the income among several beneficiaries in such shares as the trustees determine, the property's date-of-death value is included in the gross estate. To a con-siderable extent, § 2036(a)(2) overlaps with § 2038, which applies to lifetime transfers in which the transferor possesses the power to alter, amend, or revoke the transfer (see page 960).

NOTE

Two Retained Interest Problems.   Consider these two problems:

a. O transfers property to *X* in trust to pay the income to *O* for life and on *O*'s death to distribute the trust assets to *A*. What are the gift and estate tax consequences of this transfer?

b. O transfers property to *X* in trust. The trustee has unfettered discretion to pay the income to *O* or to accumulate it and to invade the corpus for *O*'s benefit. On *O*'s death, the trustee is to distribute the trust assets to *A*. What are the gift and estate tax consequences?

Estate of Maxwell v. Commissioner
3 F.3d 591 (2d Cir. 1993)

LASKER, J. This appeal presents challenges to the tax court's interpretation of section 2036(a) of the Internal Revenue Code, relating to "Transfers with retained life estate." The petitioner, the Estate of Lydia G. Maxwell, contends that the tax court erred in holding that the transaction at issue (a) was a transfer with retained life estate within the meaning of ... § 2036 and (b) was not a bona fide sale for adequate and full consideration under that statute.

The decision of the tax court is affirmed.

I

On March 14, 1984, Lydia G. Maxwell (the "decedent") conveyed her personal residence, which she had lived in since 1957, to her son Winslow Maxwell, her only heir, and his wife Margaret Jane Maxwell (the "Maxwells"). Following the transfer, the decedent continued to reside in the house until her death on July 30, 1986. At the time of the transfer, she was eighty-two years old and was suffering from cancer.

The transaction was structured as follows:

1) The residence was sold by the decedent to the Maxwells for $270,000;[33]
2) Simultaneously with the sale, the decedent forgave $20,000 of the purchase price (which was equal in amount to the annual gift tax exclusion to which she was entitled);
3) The Maxwells executed a $250,000 mortgage note in favor of decedent;
4) The Maxwells leased the premises to her for five years at the monthly rental of $1,800; and

---

33. The parties have stipulated that the fair market value of the property on the date of the purported sale was $280,000.

5) The Maxwells were obligated to pay and did pay certain expenses associated with the property following the transfer, including property taxes, insurance costs, and unspecified "other expenses."

While the decedent paid the Maxwells rent totalling $16,200 in 1984, $22,183 in 1985 and $12,600 in 1986, the Maxwells paid the decedent interest on the mortgage totalling $16,875 in 1984, $21,150 in 1985, and $11,475 in 1986. As can be observed, the rent paid by the decedent to the Maxwells came remarkably close to matching the mortgage interest which they paid to her. In 1984, she paid the Maxwells only $675 less than they paid her; in 1985, she paid them only $1,033 more than they paid her, and in 1986 she paid the Maxwells only $1,125 more than they paid her.

Not only did the rent functionally cancel out the interest payments made by the Maxwells, but the Maxwells were at no time called upon to pay any of the principal on the $250,000 mortgage debt; it was forgiven in its entirety. As petitioner's counsel admitted at oral argument, although the Maxwells had executed the mortgage note, "there was an intention by and large that it not be paid." Pursuant to this intention, in each of the following years preceding her death, the decedent forgave $20,000 of the mortgage principal, and, by a provision of her will executed on March 16, 1984 (that is, just two days after the transfer), she forgave the remaining indebtedness.

The decedent reported the sale of her residence on her 1984 federal income tax return but did not pay any tax on the sale because she elected to use the once-in-a-lifetime exclusion on the sale or exchange of a principal residence provided for by 26 U.S.C. § 121.

She continued to occupy the house by herself until her death. At no time during her occupancy did the Maxwells attempt to sell the house to anyone else, but, on September 22, 1986, shortly after the decedent's death, they did sell the house for $550,000.

Under I.R.C. § 2036(a), where property is disposed of by a decedent during her lifetime but the decedent retains "possession or enjoyment" of it until her death, that property is taxable as part of the decedent's gross estate, unless the transfer was a bona fide sale for an "adequate and full" consideration. 26 U.S.C. § 2036.

On the decedent's estate tax return, the Estate reported only the $210,000 remaining on the mortgage debt (following the decedent's forgiveness of $20,000 in the two preceding years). The Commissioner found that the 1984 transaction constituted a transfer with retained life estate—rejecting the petitioners' arguments that the decedent did not retain "possession or enjoyment" of the property, and that the transaction was exempt from section 2036(a) because it was a bona fide sale for full and adequate consideration—, and assessed a deficiency against the Estate to adjust for the difference between the fair market value of the property at the time of decedent's death ($550,000) and the reported $210,000.

The Estate appealed to the tax court, which, after a trial on stipulated facts, affirmed the Commissioner's ruling, holding:

> On this record, bearing in mind petitioner's burden of proof, we hold that, notwithstanding its form, the substance of the transaction calls for the conclusion that

decedent made a transfer to her son and daughter-in-law with the understanding, at least implied, that she would continue to reside in her home until her death, that the transfer was not a bona fide sale for an adequate and full consideration in money or money's worth, and that the lease represented nothing more than an attempt to add color to the characterization of the transaction as a bona fide sale.

There are two questions before us: Did the decedent retain possession or enjoyment of the property following the transfer? And if she did, was the transfer a bona fide sale for an adequate and full consideration in money or money's worth?

II

Section 2036(a) provides in pertinent part:

The value of the gross estate shall include the value of all property to the extent of any interest therein of which the decedent has at any time made a transfer (except in case of a bona fide sale for an adequate and full consideration in money or money's worth), by trust or otherwise, under which he has retained for his life or for any period not ascertainable without reference to his death or for any period which does not in fact end before his death—

(1) the possession or enjoyment of, or the right to the income from, the property.

28 U.S.C. § 2036(a). In the case of real property, the terms "possession" and "enjoyment" have been interpreted to mean "the lifetime use of the property." United States v. Byrum, 408 U.S. 125, 147 (1972).

In numerous cases, the tax court has held, where an aged family member transferred her home to a relative and continued to reside there until her death, that the decedent-transferor had retained "possession or enjoyment" of the property within the meaning of § 2036. As stated in Rapelje v. Commissioner, 73 T.C. 82 (1979): "Possession or enjoyment of gifted property is retained [by the transferor] when there is an express or implied understanding to that effect among the parties at the time of transfer." ... In such cases, the burden is on the decedent's estate to disprove the existence of any adverse implied agreement or understanding and that burden is particularly onerous when intrafamily arrangements are involved. ...

As indicated above, the tax court found as a fact that the decedent had transferred her home to the Maxwells "with the understanding, at least implied, that she would continue to reside in her home until her death." This finding was based upon the decedent's advanced age, her medical condition, and the overall result of the sale and lease. The lease was, in the tax court's words, "merely window dressing"—it had no substance. ...

We agree with the tax court's finding that the decedent transferred her home to the Maxwells "with the understanding, at least implied, that she would continue to reside in her home until her death," and certainly do not find it to be clearly erroneous. The decedent did, in fact, live at her residence until she died, and she had sole possession of the residence during the period between the day she sold her home to the Maxwells and the day she died. There is no evidence that the Maxwells ever intended to occupy the house themselves, or to sell or lease it to anyone else during the decedent's lifetime. Moreover, the Maxwells' failure to demand payment by the estate, as they were entitled to do under the lease, of the rent due for the months following decedent's death and preceding their sale of the property, also supports the tax court's finding.

The petitioner argues . . . that the decedent's tenancy alone does not justify inclusion of the residence in her estate, so it argues that the decedent's payment of rent sanctifies the transaction and renders it legitimate. Both arguments ignore the realities of the rent being offset by mortgage interest, the forgiveness of the entire mortgage debt either by gift or testamentary disposition, and the fact that the decedent was eighty-two at the time of the transfer and actually continued to live in the residence until her death which, at the time of the transfer, she had reason to believe would occur soon in view of her poor health.

The Estate relies primarily on Barlow v. Commissioner, 55 T.C. 666 (1971). In that case, the father transferred a farm to his children and simultaneously leased the right to continue to farm the property. The tax court held that the father did not retain "possession or enjoyment," stating that "one of the most valuable incidents of income-producing real estate is the rent which it yields. He who receives the rent in fact enjoys the property." *Barlow*, 55 T.C. at 671 (quoting McNichol's v. Commissioner, 265 F.2d 667, 671 (3d Cir. 1959)). However, *Barlow* is clearly distinguishable on its facts: In that case, there was evidence that the rent paid was fair and customary and, equally importantly, the rent paid was not offset by the decedent's receipt of interest from the family lessor. . . .

Barlow itself recognized that where a transferor "by agreement" "reserves the right of occupancy as an incident to the transfer," § 2036(a) applies. *Barlow*, 55 T.C. at 670. . . .

For the reasons stated above, we conclude that the decedent did retain possession or enjoyment of the property for life and turn to the question of whether the transfer constituted "a bona fide sale for adequate and full consideration in money or money's worth."

III

Section 2036(a) provides that even if possession or enjoyment of transferred property is retained by the decedent until her death, if the transfer was a bona fide sale for adequate and full consideration in money or money's worth, the property is not includible in the estate. Petitioner contends that the Maxwells paid an "adequate and full consideration" for the decedent's residence, $270,000 total, consisting of the $250,000 mortgage note given by the Maxwells to the decedent, and the $20,000 the decedent forgave simultaneously with the conveyance.[34]

---

34. As noted above, the parties have stipulated that the fair market value of the property on the date of the purported sale was $280,000. The Estate contends that $270,000 was full and adequate consideration for the sale, with a broker, for a house appraised at $280,000. We assume this fact to be true for purposes of determining whether the transaction was one for "an adequate and full consideration in money or money's worth."

The tax court held that neither the Maxwells' mortgage note nor the decedent's $20,000 forgiveness constituted consideration within the meaning of the statute. . . .

As to the $250,000 mortgage note, the tax court held that:

Regardless of whether the $250,000 mortgage note might otherwise qualify as "adequate and full consideration in money or money's worth" for a $270,000 or $280,000 house, the mortgage note here had no value at all if there was no intention that it would ever be paid. The conduct of decedent and the Maxwells strongly suggest that neither party intended the Maxwells to pay any part of the principal of either the original note or any successor note.

There is no question that the mortgage note here is a fully secured, legally enforceable obligation on its face. The question is whether it is actually what it purports to be—a bona fide instrument of indebtedness—or whether it is a facade. The petitioner argues not only that an allegedly unenforceable intention to forgive indebtedness does not deprive the indebtedness of its status as "consideration in money or money's worth" but also that "[t]his is true even if there was an implied agreement exactly as found by the Tax Court."

We agree with the tax court that where, as here, there is an implied agreement between the parties that the grantee would never be called upon to make any payment to the grantor, as, in fact, actually occurred, the note given by the grantee had "no value at all." We emphatically disagree with the petitioner's view of the law as it applies to the facts of this case. As the Supreme Court has remarked, the family relationship often makes it possible for one to shift tax incidence by surface changes of ownership without disturbing in the least his dominion and control over the subject of the gift or the purposes for which the income from the property is used. Commissioner v. Culbertson, 337 U.S. 733, 746 (1949). There can be no doubt that intent is a relevant inquiry in determining whether a transaction is "bona fide." As another panel of this Court held recently, construing a parallel provision of the Internal Revenue Code, in a case involving an intrafamily transfer:

when the bona fides of promissory notes is at issue, the taxpayer must demonstrate affirmatively that "there existed at the time of the transaction a real expectation of repayment and an intent to enforce the collection of the indebtedness."

Estate of Van Anda v. Commissioner, 12 T.C. 1158, 1162 (1949), aff'd per curiam, 192 F.2d 391 (2d Cir. 1951).

In language strikingly apposite to the situation here, the court stated:

it is appropriate to look beyond the form of the transactions and to determine, as the tax court did here, that the gifts and loans back to decedent were "component parts of single transactions."

Id. . . .

[T]he tax court found that, at the time the note was executed, there was "an understanding" between the Maxwells and the decedent that the note would be forgiven. In our judgment, the conduct of decedent and the Maxwells with respect to the principal balance of the note, when viewed in connection with the initial "forgiveness" of $20,000 of the purported purchase price, strongly suggests the existence of an understanding between decedent and the Maxwells that decedent would forgive $20,000 each year thereafter until her death, when the balance would be forgiven by decedent's will.

To conclude, we hold that the conveyance was not a bona fide sale for an adequate and full consideration in money or money's worth. The decision of the tax court is affirmed.

NOTES

1. *Retained Interests in Family Residence.*   Subsequent cases have distinguished between transfers of a residence in which the decedent retained exclusive possession and those in which the decedent and the donee jointly occupied the residence. In the latter cases, courts have been reluctant to include the entire value of the residence in the gross estate of the decedent, as in Estate of Stewart v. Commissioner, 617 F.3d 148 (2d Cir. 2010).

2. *The Reciprocal Trust Doctrine.*   Joseph Grace executes a trust instrument providing for the payment of income to his wife, Janet, for her life, and payment to her of any part of the principal that a majority of the trustees think advisable. Janet is given a nongeneral testamentary power of appointment over the remainder. Joseph, his nephew, and a third party are named as trustees. Shortly thereafter, Janet Grace, at Joseph's request, executes a virtually identical trust instrument naming Joseph as life beneficiary. Then Joseph dies. Is the corpus of either trust includible in Joseph's gross estate?

In United States v. Estate of Grace, 395 U.S. 316 (1969), the Court held that, under the *reciprocal trust doctrine*, a substance-over-form rule, the value of the Janet Grace trust must be included in Joseph's estate. "[A]pplication of the reciprocal trust doctrine requires only that the trusts be interrelated, and that the arrangement, to the extent of mutual value, leaves the settlors in approximately the same economic position as they would have been in had they created trusts naming themselves as life beneficiaries." The reciprocal trust doctrine is rather vague, and the IRS has a mixed record in the litigated cases.[35]

Old Colony Trust Co. v. United States
423 F.2d 601 (1st Cir. 1970)

ALDRICH, J. The sole question in this case is whether the estate of a settlor of an inter vivos trust, who was a trustee until the date of his death, is to be charged with the value of the principal he contributed by virtue of reserved powers in the trust. The executor

---

35. *See* Dennis I. Belcher & Kristen Frances Hager, United States v. Estate of Grace: Seeking a More Objective Test for the Application of the Reciprocal Trust Doctrine, 42 ACTEC L.J. 89 (2016); Elena Marty-Nelson, Taxing Reciprocal Trusts: Charting a Doctrine's Fall from Grace, 75 N.C. L. Rev. 1781 (1997).

paid the tax and sued for its recovery in the district court. All facts were stipulated. The court ruled for the government, 300 F. Supp. 1032, and the executor appeals.

The initial life beneficiary of the trust was the settlor's adult son. Eighty percent of the income was normally to be payable to him, and the balance added to principal. Subsequent beneficiaries were the son's widow and his issue. The powers upon which the government relies to cause the corpus to be includable in the settlor-trustee's estate are contained in two articles. . . .

Article 4 permitted the trustees to increase the percentage of income payable to the son beyond the eighty percent, "in their absolute discretion . . . when in their opinion such increase is needed in case of sickness, or desirable in view of changed circumstances." In addition, under Article 4 the trustees were given the discretion to cease paying income to the son, and add it all to principal, "during such period as the Trustees may decide that the stoppage of such payments is for his best interests."

Article 7 gave broad administrative or management powers to the trustees, with discretion to acquire investments not normally held by trustees, and the right to determine what was to be charged or credited to income or principal, including stock dividends or deductions for amortization. It further provided that all divisions and decisions made by the trustees in good faith should be conclusive on all parties, and in summary, stated that the trustees were empowered, "generally to do all things in relation to the Trust Fund which the Donor could do if living and this Trust had not been executed."

The government claims that each of these two articles meant that the settlor-trustee had "the right . . . to designate the persons who shall possess or enjoy the [trust] property or the income therefrom" within the meaning of section 2036(a)(2) of the Internal Revenue Code of 1954, 26 U.S.C. § 2036(a)(2), and that the settlor-trustee at the date of his death possessed a power "to alter, amend, revoke, or terminate" within the meaning of section 2038(a)(1) (26 U.S.C. § 2038(a)(1)).

If State Street Trust Co. v. United States, 1 Cir., 1959, 263 F.2d 635, was correctly decided in this aspect, the government must prevail because of the Article 7 powers. There this court, Chief Judge Magruder dissenting, held against the taxpayer because broad powers similar to those in Article 7 meant that the trustees "could very substantially shift the economic benefits of the trusts between the life tenants and the remaindermen," so that the settlor "as long as he lived, in substance and effect and in a very real sense . . . 'retained for his life . . . the right . . . to designate the persons who shall possess or enjoy the property or the income therefrom. . . .'" 263 F.2d at 639-640, quoting 26 U.S.C. § 2036(a)(2). We accept the taxpayer's invitation to reconsider this ruling.

It is common ground that a settlor will not find the corpus of the trust included in his estate merely because he named himself a trustee. He must have reserved a power to himself[36] that is inconsistent with the full termination of ownership. The government's

---

36. The number of other trustees who must join in the exercise of that power, unless the others have antagonistic interest of a substantial nature, is, of course, immaterial. Treas. Reg. § 20.2036-1(a)(ii), (b)(3)(i) (1958); § 20.2038-1(a) (1958).

brief defines this as "sufficient dominion and control until his death." Trustee powers given for the administration or management of the trust must be equitably exercised, however, for the benefit of the trust as a whole. The court in *State Street* conceded that the powers at issue were all such powers, but reached the conclusion that, cumulatively, they gave the settlor dominion sufficiently unfettered to be in the nature of ownership. With all respect to the majority of the then court, we find it difficult to see how a power can be subject to control by the probate court, and exercisable only in what the trustee fairly concludes is in the interests of the trust and its beneficiaries as a whole, and at the same time be an ownership power.

The government's position, to be sound, must be that the trustee's powers are beyond the court's control. Under Massachusetts law, however, no amount of administrative discretion prevents judicial supervision of the trustee. Thus in Appeal of Davis, 1903, 67 N.E. 604 (Mass.), a trustee was given "full power to make purchases, investments and exchanges . . . in such manner as to them shall seem expedient; it being my intention to give my trustees . . . the same dominion and control over said trust property as I now have." In spite of this language, and in spite of their good faith, the court charged the trustees for failing sufficiently to diversify their investment portfolio. The Massachusetts court has never varied from this broad rule of accountability, and has twice criticized *State Street* for its seeming departure. Boston Safe Deposit & Trust Co. v. Stone, 1965, 348 Mass. 345, 351, n.8, 203 N.E.2d 547; Old Colony Trust Co. v. Silliman, 1967, 352 Mass. 6, 8-9, 223 N.E.2d 504. We make it a further observation, which the court in *State Street* failed to note, that the provision in that trust (as in the case at bar) that the trustees could "do all things in relation to the Trust Fund which I, the Donor, could do if . . . the Trust had not been executed," is almost precisely the provision which did not protect the trustees from accountability in Appeal of Davis, supra.

We do not believe that trustee powers are to be more broadly construed for tax purposes than the probate court would construe them for administrative purposes. More basically, we agree with Judge Magruder's observation that nothing is "gained by lumping them together." State Street Trust Co. v. United States, supra, 263 F.2d at 642. We hold that no aggregation of purely administrative powers can meet the government's amorphous test of "sufficient dominion and control" so as to be equated with ownership.

This does not resolve taxpayer's difficulties under Article 4. Quite different considerations apply to distribution powers. Under them the trustee can, expressly, prefer one beneficiary over another. Furthermore, his freedom of choice may vary greatly, depending upon the terms of the individual trust. If there is an ascertainable standard, the trustee can be compelled to follow it. If there is not, even though he is a fiduciary, it is not unreasonable to say that his retention of an unmeasurable freedom of choice is equivalent to retaining some of the incidents of ownership. Hence, under the cases, if there is an ascertainable standard the settlor-trustee's estate is not taxed, . . . but if there is not, it is taxed. . . .

The trust provision which is uniformly held to provide an ascertainable standard is one which, though variously expressed, authorizes such distributions as may be needed to continue the beneficiary's accustomed way of life. . . . On the other hand, if the trustee may go further, and has power to provide for the beneficiary's "happiness," Merchants Nat'l Bank v. Com'r of Internal Revenue, 1943, 320 U.S. 256, or "pleasure," Industrial Trust Co. v. Com'r of Internal Revenue, 1 Cir., 1945, 151 F.2d 592, or "use and benefit," Newton Trust Co. v. Com'r of Internal Revenue, 1 Cir., 1947, 160 F.2d 175, or "reasonable requirement[s]," State Street Bank & Trust Co. v. United States, 1 Cir., 1963, 313 F.2d 29, the standard is so loose that the trustee is in effect uncontrolled.

In the case at bar the trustees could increase the life tenant's income "in case of sickness, or [if] desirable in view of changed circumstances." Alternatively, they could reduce it "for his best interests." "Sickness" presents no problem. Conceivably, providing for "changed circumstances" is roughly equivalent to maintaining the son's present standard of living. . . . The unavoidable stumbling block is the trustees' right to accumulate income and add it to capital (which the son would never receive) when it is to the "best interests" of the son to do so. Additional payments to a beneficiary whenever in his "best interests" might seem to be too broad a standard in any event. In addition to the previous cases see Estate of Yawkey, 1949, 12 T.C. 1164, where the court said, at p.1170, "We can not regard the language involved ['best interest'] as limiting the usual scope of a trustee's discretion. It must always be anticipated that trustees will act for the best interests of a trust beneficiary, and an exhortation to act 'in the interests and for the welfare' of the beneficiary does not establish an external standard." Power, however, to decrease or cut off a beneficiary's income when in his "best interests," is even more troublesome. When the beneficiary is the son, and the trustee the father, a particular purpose comes to mind, parental control through holding the purse strings. The father decides what conduct is to the "best interests" of the son, and if the son does not agree, he loses his allowance. Such power has the plain indicia of ownership control. The alternative, that the son, because of other means, might not need this income, and would prefer to have it accumulate for his widow and children after his death, is no better. If the trustee has power to confer "happiness" on the son by generosity to someone else, this seems clearly an unascertainable standard.

The case of Hays' Estate v. Com'r of Internal Revenue, 5 Cir., 1950, 181 F.2d 169, is contrary to our decision. The opinion is unsupported by either reasoning or authority, and we will not follow it. With the present settlor-trustee free to determine the standard himself, a finding of ownership control was warranted. To put it another way, the cost of holding onto the strings may prove to be a rope burn. State Street Bank & Trust Co. v. United States, supra.

Affirmed.

NOTE

Powers Held as Trustee or to Replace a Trustee. In *Old Colony Trust*, the court held that "no aggregation of purely administrative powers" held by the decedent as trustee in a trust created by the decedent will result in inclusion of the trust property in the decedent's gross estate. The court reasoned that such powers, held in a fiduciary capacity, were subject to control by the court, and thus they could not be ownership powers for estate tax purposes. The court also held that discretionary powers over distribution, if subject to an ascertainable standard (see page 964), are likewise not subject to inclusion.[37]

Family Limited Partnerships

In a typical *family limited partnership* (FLP), an individual transfers substantial amounts of property, and her children add modest amounts, to the partnership in exchange for limited partnership interests. The general partner is commonly another entity owned by the individual and her children. When the individual's non-controlling partnership interests pass to her children, either by inter vivos gift or at death, the value of those interests are discounted from the underlying prorated value to reflect a lack of control, and the gift or estate tax due is reduced accordingly. If the interest can only be transferred within the family or another limited group, the value is further diminished because of the lack of marketability.[38]

Some people consider it illogical that each of the separate interests in a family-owned entity would qualify for a lack-of-control discount, but *fair market value* is defined for tax purposes as "the price at which the property would change hands between a willing buyer and a willing seller, neither being under any compulsion to buy or to sell and both having reasonable knowledge of relevant facts."[39] In an arm's-length transaction, a business interest that does not afford the buyer control over the business will fetch a lower price than one that does afford such control. The IRS once contended that the separate interests of a family-controlled entity should be aggregated for purposes of determining the fair market value of the interests held by the various family members, but eventually it abandoned that position.[40]

Although a limited partnership or, more recently, a limited liability company is most commonly used in this estate planning technique, other entities can work just as well. Consider a simple example involving a family corporation:

> *Case 13.* Parent transfers $6 million of publicly traded securities to a new corporation in exchange for all its stock, and then gives one-third of that stock to Son and one-third to Daughter. Parent's will devises the final one-third interest to Son and Daughter in equal shares. Because each one-third block of stock is considered separately for valuation purposes, Parent properly reports two gifts of one-third interests, each of which qualifies for non-marketability and lack-of-control discounts. A reputable appraiser opines that, based on the Code's definition of fair market value, each one-third interest is worth 25 percent less than each shareholder's

---

37. These principles apply also to the imputation to the decedent of the powers of a trustee if the decedent could remove and replace the trustee, unless the replacement cannot be related or subordinate to the decedent. *See* Rev. Rul. 95-58, 1995-2 C.B. 191.

38. But note that a limit on transferability may disqualify the interest from the annual exclusion on grounds that it is not a present interest. *See* Fisher v. United States, 2010 WL 935491 (S.D. Ind. Mar. 11, 2010); Price v. Commissioner, T.C.M. (RIA) 2010-002 (2010).

39. Treas. Reg. § 20.2031-1(b).

40. *See* Rev. Rul. 93-12, 1993-1 C.B. 202.

proportionate share of the underlying property, which means that each gift has a value for tax purposes of only $1.5 million (one-third of $6 million, minus 25 percent). When Parent dies a few months later, the same expert applies the same 25 percent discount in valuing the one-third interest that Parent had kept for himself. Assuming for the sake of simplicity that the value of the underlying publicly traded securities did not change during this period of time, Parent managed to transfer $6 million of underlying value to Son and Daughter, but a total of only $4.5 million appeared on Parent's gift and estate tax returns. The other 25 percent, $1.5 million, escaped transfer taxation.

The IRS closely scrutinizes FLPs and similar arrangements and has argued that I.R.C. § 2036 requires inclusion in the gross estate of more than just the discounted value of the decedent's remaining partnership interests. Although much depends on the specific facts, some courts have included in the decedent's gross estate the full value of the property that the decedent had transferred to the FLP. Courts reaching this result do so by finding that there was an implied agreement among the family members to allow the decedent to benefit from or exercise control over the property that she contributed to the FLP, or by finding that the FLP lacked a substantial non-tax or business purpose.

In Turner v. Commissioner, 382 F.3d 367 (3d Cir. 2004), for example, the decedent transferred 95 percent of his assets to two FLPs when he was 95 years old. After the transfers, the decedent did not have sufficient assets to support himself. Neither FLP engaged in any real business or commercial activity, and profits earned by the FLPs passed directly to the original owner of the underlying property. The court found that there was an implicit agreement that the decedent could obtain whatever resources he needed for support from the FLPs. The court concluded that the FLPs had been nothing more than "vehicle[s] for changing the form in which the decedent held his property—a mere recycling of value." The full value of the transferred assets, not the discounted value of the limited partnership interests, was included in the decedent's gross estate. In Kimbell v. United States, 371 F.3d 257 (5th Cir. 2004), by contrast, the court found that there had been substantial non-tax motives for the formation of the FLP, including the decedent's desire to protect her assets from creditors and to retain the assets in a single, well-managed entity rather than separating them through distributions to subsequent generations.

Courts have accepted a wide variety of non-tax motives, including some that appeared to be primarily donative in nature. In Estate of Schutt v. Commissioner, 89 T.C.M. (CCH) 1353 (2005), the court recognized that non-tax motives could be interconnected with estate planning objectives. In Estate of Mirowski v. Commissioner, 95 T.C.M. (CCH) 1277 (2008), the court found that the decedent's interest in providing for each of her daughters equally and having her and her daughters' assets jointly managed was a sufficient non-tax motive. In Estate of Miller v. Commissioner, 97 T.C.M. (CCH) 1602 (2009), the court found the transfer of marketable securities into a FLP had a substantial non-tax business purpose because the decedent had wanted the assets managed according to her husband's irregular investment philosophy. In Estate of Purdue v. Commissioner, 110 T.C.M. (CCH) 627 (2015), the court found consolidation of assets to facilitate management and transfer were sufficient non-tax business purposes.

In 2016, the IRS proposed regulations that would all but eliminate the lack of marketability and minority interest discounts for the transfer of assets in family-controlled entities.[41] Estate planners have objected to the broad reach of the proposed regulations, and legislation has been introduced in Congress to block them.

f. Revocable Transfers

I.R.C. § 2038(a) provides for inclusion in the gross estate of the date-of-death value of interests, usually in inter vivos trusts or other nonprobate transfers, that the decedent had the power to alter, amend, or revoke:

> The value of the gross estate shall include the value of all property . . . [t]o the extent of any interest therein of which the decedent has at any time made a transfer (except in case of a bona fide sale for an adequate and full consideration in money or money's worth), by trust or otherwise, where the enjoyment thereof was subject at the date of his death to any change through the exercise of a power (in whatever capacity exercisable) by the decedent alone or by the decedent in conjunction with any other person (without regard to when or from what source the decedent acquired such power), to alter, amend, revoke or terminate, or when any such power is relinquished during the 3-year period ending on the date of the decedent's death.

In addition to bringing revocable transfers into the gross estate, I.R.C. § 2038 reaches transfers over which the decedent held any one of the enumerated powers, even if the power cannot be exercised to benefit the decedent. Thus, if O creates an irrevocable trust in which O, as co-trustee, has a discretionary power to accumulate or distribute trust income, or a discretionary power to distribute corpus to the income beneficiary, the property is included in O's gross estate under § 2038 because O's discretionary power is a power to alter or amend. O's reserved power would also cause inclusion under § 2036(a)(2).

To a considerable extent, I.R.C. § 2038 overlaps in application with § 2036(a)(2). There are, however, situations covered exclusively by one or the other. While § 2036(a)(2) covers only a retained right to designate the persons who shall enjoy the property, § 2038 applies if the transferor has the power to effect any change to the terms of the gift, including the time of enjoyment. So § 2038 alone applies if the settlor has a power to accelerate enjoyment by a beneficiary. Section 2036(a)(2) applies to powers that are retained by the decedent for her life, while § 2038 applies to powers that the decedent has at the moment of death. Section 2038 thus applies to the decedent's ability to change trust beneficiaries in her will even if she could not do so during life.

---

41. Estate, Gift, and Generation-Skipping Transfer Taxes; Restrictions on Liquidation of an Interest, 81 Fed. Reg. 51,413 (proposed Aug. 4, 2016) (to be codified at 26 C.F.R. pt. 25); *see also* John F. Coverdale, Of Red Bags and Family Limited Partnerships: Reforming the Estate and Gift Tax Valuation Rules to Achieve Horizontal Equity, 51 U. Louisville L. Rev. 239 (2013).

If the power to alter, amend, revoke, or terminate is given to a third person, the transfer is not taxed under I.R.C. § 2038 even if the power is held by a nonadverse party. It is for this reason that a trustee (or trust director, see page 662) who is not the settlor can be given broad discretionary powers, including the power to distribute all or a portion of the trust property, without adverse tax consequences to the settlor. However, if the transferor has the right to remove the trustee and appoint himself as trustee, the transferor is treated as having the power held by the trustee and § 2038 is applicable.[42]

NOTE

Two Revocable Transfer Problems. Consider the following two problems. How would I.R.C. § 2038 apply in each?

a. *O* transfers property to the First National Bank in trust to pay the income to *O*'s daughter, *A*, for life, and on *A*'s death to pay the principal to *O*'s granddaughter, *B*. *O* retains the power to invade principal for the benefit of *B*. On *O*'s death, is the entire value of the trust corpus includible in *O*'s gross estate?

b. What result if *O* has no power to invade principal but retains the power to direct that all or a portion of trust income be accumulated and added to principal each year?

g. Transfers Within Three Years of Death

To prevent deathbed transfers designed to avoid estate taxation, I.R.C. § 2035 includes in the decedent's gross estate the following transfers made within three years of death:

(1) any gift tax paid by the decedent or his estate on gifts made within three years of death; and

(2) any transfer or release of an interest in property that, if such interest had been retained, the property would have been included in the decedent's gross estate under § 2036 (transfers with retained life estate), § 2037 (transfers taking effect at death), § 2038 (revocable transfers), or § 2042 (life insurance).

The first category addresses transfers made in contemplation of death to gain the advantage of the tax-exclusive computation of gift tax liability (see page 944). The second category addresses releases of retained interests that by themselves may have little value, such as a life tenancy held by an elderly person, but that if retained at death would cause inclusion of the entire value of the underlying property at the time of death. This sort of strategy will work only if completed more than three years before the person dies. Thus:

Case 14. In 2013, *O* creates an irrevocable trust of securities worth $300,000, retaining a life estate, with the remainder to *O*'s nephew, *A*. (This results in a taxable gift to *A* of the value of the remainder, which is computed based on *O*'s life

---

42. *See* Treas. Reg. § 20.2038-1(a)(3).

expectancy and the initial value of $300,000.[43]) In 2017, the trust assets are worth $500,000, and *O*, moments before dying, releases her life estate. Without § 2035, *O*'s release would eliminate transfer tax on the value of a remainder in the $200,000 of appreciation in the securities. With § 2035, the entire $500,000 worth of securities is included in *O*'s gross estate (though the gift tax paid in 2013 is credited against the estate taxes payable at *O*'s death).

A similar analysis applies to life insurance. Without I.R.C. § 2035, the owner of a life insurance policy on the owner's life could have a strong tax incentive to give the policy away shortly prior to death, perhaps on her deathbed.

Unless an inter vivos transfer falls into one of these two categories, it is not includible in the decedent's gross estate even if made within three years of death. Thus, if *O* gives Blackacre to *A* two months before *O*'s death, *O* has made a taxable gift at the time of transfer, and the date-of-death value of Blackacre is not included in *O*'s gross estate, though the amount of gift tax paid is included.

NOTES

1. Tax Advantages of a Deathbed Transfer.   In some circumstances, a deathbed gift may save transfer taxes notwithstanding I.R.C. § 2035. The simplest example is a gift that qualifies for the annual gift tax exclusion. However, a gift that reduces *transfer* taxes might be counterproductive for *income* tax purposes. Instead of a *stepped-up basis* at the owner's death (see page 933), the donee might end up with a *carryover basis*, which could be disadvantageous, depending on the circumstances. To advise clients on donative transfers of wealth, lawyers must understand the fundamentals of both transfer and income taxation.

2. Life Insurance Planning Revisited.   Suppose that *A* purchases a life insurance policy and names his daughter, *B*, as the beneficiary. If *A* thereafter assigns the policy to *B*, the insurance proceeds will be included in *A*'s gross estate at death if *A* dies within three years of the transfer. On the other hand, if *B* is the owner of the policy as well as beneficiary from the beginning, the proceeds of the policy are not includible in *A*'s gross estate at his death, even if he dies within three years. The strategy of having *B* buy the policy in the first instance can work even if *A* pays the premiums, provided the amount of the premiums is less than the annual $14,000 exclusion (premiums paid in excess of the annual exclusion would be a taxable gift).

h. Powers of Appointment

As we saw in Chapter 12, a settlor may give to someone other than the trustee a nonfiduciary power to distribute trust property in the future. Such a power is known as a *power of appointment*. The holder of a power of appointment, known as the *donee,*

---

43. If *A* were *O*'s son, then I.R.C. § 2702 would apply, and the remainder would be valued at $300,000, unless *O*'s interest was a grantor retained annuity or unitrust interest. The special valuation rules of § 2702 apply to a transfer to a lineal descendant or sibling but not to a descendant of a sibling, as in Case 14.

may appoint the property to one or more persons, known as the *objects*, in accordance with the terms of the power. By creating a power of appointment, the donor postpones distribution decisions, leaving them to be made by the donee in light of changing circumstances in the future.

All powers of appointment can be divided into two categories: *general* powers and *nongeneral* powers. As defined in I.R.C. § 2041, a general power is "a power which is exercisable in favor of the [donee], his estate, his creditors, or the creditors of his estate."[44] A power that is not a general power — that is, a power not exercisable in favor of the donee, his estate, his creditors, or the creditors of his estate — is a nongeneral power. A nongeneral power is sometimes called a *special* power or a *limited* power, particularly in older sources, but the trend is toward the term nongeneral.

Under I.R.C. § 2041, the gross estate includes the value of property over which the decedent at the time of his death held a general, but not a nongeneral, power of appointment.[45] The theory is that a general power, which by definition allows the donee to appoint for her own benefit, is an ownership-equivalent power. A nongeneral power, which cannot be exercised by the donee for her own benefit, is not an ownership-equivalent power. The tax treatment of each type of power follows accordingly. Thus:

Case 15. *H*'s will creates a testamentary trust providing for the payment of income to *W* for life and on her death "to pay the principal to such person or persons as *W* appoints by will." On *W*'s death, the value of the trust corpus is includible in her gross estate under I.R.C. § 2041 whether or not she exercises the power. Although *W* was restricted to the income from the trust and she could not exercise the power of appointment to benefit herself or her creditors during her lifetime, at death she could exercise the power in favor of her estate or the creditors of her estate, making it a general power.

Case 16. *H*'s will creates a testamentary trust providing for the payment of income to *W* for life and on her death "to pay the principal to such one or more of *H*'s descendants or spouses of *H*'s descendants as *W* shall appoint by will." Because *W*'s power of appointment is nongeneral, the appointive property is not included in her gross estate under I.R.C. § 2041 whether or not she exercises the power. Nor is the trust property included in *W*'s gross estate under § 2033, because her life estate ended at her death, or § 2036, because the life estate was not "retained," it was given to *W* by *H*.

As Case 16 demonstrates, it is possible to give a beneficiary both a life income interest in property and a substantial power to control the ultimate disposition of that property at death without subjecting the property to estate taxation in the beneficiary's estate. The key is that the beneficiary not have the power to appoint the property to herself, her estate, her creditors, or the creditors of her estate. There are two exceptions, however, that make it possible in particular circumstances to give a beneficiary a power

---

44. The comparable definition under the gift tax is in I.R.C. § 2514(c).

45. *See* Treas. Reg. § 20.2041-1(c)(1). There is an important, and sometimes useful, exception to this general rule known as the Delaware Tax Trap (see page 921).

to appoint property to herself during life without the power being treated for tax purposes as ownership equivalent.

The first exception is for a power of appointment that is subject to an *ascertainable standard*. Under I.R.C. § 2041(b)(1)(A), if the donee is given "[a] power to consume, invade, or appropriate property for the benefit of [himself] which is limited by an ascertainable standard relating to the health, education, support, or maintenance of the [donee, it] . . . shall not be deemed a general power of appointment." So a power in *A* to consume the trust property as needed to maintain the standard of living to which *A* is accustomed is treated as a nongeneral power for tax purposes. Lawyers in practice commonly speak of a "HEMS standard," meaning a health, education, maintenance, and support standard.

The second exception is for a so-called *five-or-five* power of withdrawal. If a donee has a power to appoint property to himself (i.e., to withdraw property from the trust), a lapse of the power will not be taxed as the lapse of a general power to the extent of $5,000 or 5 percent of the trust corpus, whichever is greater. So a power in *A*, a beneficiary, to withdraw each year the greater of $5,000 or 5 percent of the corpus, whether or not *A* needs it, will not be treated for tax purposes as a general power in any prior year in which *A* did not exercise the power, allowing it to lapse. Under I.R.C. § 2041(a)(2), when the donee dies, nothing will be in his gross estate if he has in fact exercised the power that year. If he has not exercised the power, only the amount that could be withdrawn in that year is includible in his gross estate, but this is a small price to pay for the flexibility that such a power allows.

Estate of Vissering v. Commissioner
990 F.2d 578 (10th Cir. 1993)

LOGAN, C.J. The estate of decedent Norman H. Vissering appeals from a judgment of the Tax Court determining that he held at his death a general power of appointment as defined by I.R.C. § 2041, and requiring that the assets of a trust of which he was cotrustee be included in his gross estate for federal estate tax purposes. The appeal turns on whether decedent held powers permitting him to invade the principal of the trust for his own benefit unrestrained by an ascertainable standard relating to health, education, support, or maintenance. . . .

The trust at issue was created by decedent's mother, and became irrevocable on her death in 1965. Decedent and a bank served as cotrustees. Under the dispositive provisions decedent received all the income from the trust after his mother's death. On decedent's death . . . , remaining trust assets were to be divided into equal parts and passed to decedent's two children or were held for their benefit. . . .

Under I.R.C. § 2041 a decedent has a general power of appointment includable in his estate if he possesses at the time of his death a power over assets that permits him to benefit himself, his estate, his creditors, or creditors of his estate. A power vested in a trustee, even with a cotrustee who has no interest adverse to the exercise of the power, to invade principal of the trust for his own benefit is sufficient to find the decedent trustee to have a general power of appointment, unless the power to invade is limited by an ascertainable standard relating to health, education, support, or maintenance.

Treas. Reg. § 20.2041-1(c), -3(c)(2). See, e.g., Estate of Sowell v. Commissioner, 708 F.2d 1564, 1568 (10th Cir. 1983) (invasion of trust corpus in case of emergency or illness is an ascertainable standard under § 2041(b)(1)(A)); see also Merchants Nat'l Bank v. Commissioner, 320 U.S. 256, 261 (1943) (invasion of trust corpus for "the comfort, support, maintenance and/or happiness of my wife" is not a fixed standard for purposes of charitable deductions); Ithaca Trust Co. v. United States, 279 U.S. 151, 154 (1929) (invasion of trust corpus for any amount "that may be necessary to suitably maintain [decedent's wife] in as much comfort as she now enjoys" is a fixed standard for purposes of charitable deduction).

The relevant provisions of the instant trust agreement are as follows:

> During the term of [this trust], the Trustees shall further be authorized to pay over or to use or expend for the direct or indirect benefit of any of the aforesaid beneficiaries, whatever amount or amounts of the principal of this Trust as may, in the discretion of the Trustees, be required for the continued comfort, support, maintenance, or education of said beneficiary.

The Internal Revenue Service (IRS) and the Tax Court focused on portions of the invasion provision providing that the trust principal could be expended for the "comfort" of decedent, declaring that this statement rendered the power of invasion incapable of limitation by the courts.

We look to state law (here Florida's) to determine the legal interests and rights created by a trust instrument, but federal law determines the tax consequences of those interests and rights. . . .

Despite the decision in Barritt v. Tomlinson, 129 F. Supp. 642 (S.D. Fla. 1955), which involved a power of invasion broader than the one before us, we believe the Florida Supreme Court would hold that a trust document permitting invasion of principal for "comfort," without further qualifying language, creates a general power of appointment. Treas. Reg. § 20.2041-1(c). See First Virginia Bank v. United States, 490 F.2d 532, 533 (4th Cir. 1974) (under Virginia law, right of invasion for beneficiary's "comfort and care as she may see fit" not limited by an ascertainable standard); Lehman v. United States, 448 F.2d 1318, 1320 (5th Cir. 1971) (under Texas law, power to invade corpus for "support, maintenance, comfort, and welfare" not limited by ascertainable standard); Miller v. United States, 387 F.2d 866, 869 (3d Cir. 1968) (under Pennsylvania law, power to make disbursements from principal in amounts "necessary or expedient for [beneficiary's] proper maintenance, support, medical care, hospitalization, or other expenses incidental to her comfort and well-being" not limited by ascertainable standard); Estate of Schlotterer v. United States, 421 F. Supp. 85, 91 (W.D. Pa. 1976) (power of consumption "to the extent deemed by [beneficiary] to be desirable not only for her support and maintenance but also for her comfort and pleasure" not limited by ascertainable standard); Doyle v. United States, 358 F. Supp. 300, 309-310 (E.D. Pa. 1973) (under Pennsylvania law, trustees' "uncontrolled discretion" to pay beneficiary "such part or parts of the principal of said trust fund as may be necessary for her comfort, maintenance and support" not limited by ascertainable standard); Stafford v. United States, 236 F. Supp. 132, 134 (E.D. Wisc. 1964) (under Wisconsin law, trust permitting husband "for his use, benefit and enjoyment during his lifetime," unlimited power of disposition thereof "without permission of any court, and with the right to use and enjoy the principal, as well as the income, if he shall have need thereof for his care, comfort or enjoyment" not limited by ascertainable standard).

However, there is modifying language in the trust before us that we believe would lead the Florida courts to hold that "comfort," in context, does not permit an unlimited power of invasion. The instant language states that invasion of principal is permitted to the extent "required for the continued comfort" of the decedent, and is part of a clause referencing the support, maintenance and education of the beneficiary. Invasion of the corpus is not permitted to the extent "determined" or "desired" for the beneficiary's comfort but only to the extent that it is "required." Furthermore, the invasion must be for the beneficiary's "continued" comfort, implying, we believe, more than the minimum necessary for survival, but nevertheless reasonably necessary to maintain the beneficiary in his accustomed manner of living. These words in context state a standard essentially no different from the examples in the Treasury Regulation, in which phrases such as "support in reasonable comfort," "maintenance in health and reasonable comfort," and "support in his accustomed manner of living" are deemed to be limited by an ascertainable standard. Treas. Reg. § 20.2041-1(c)(2). See, e.g., United States v. Powell, 307 F.2d 821, 828 (10th Cir. 1962) (under Kansas law, invasion of the corpus if "it is necessary or advisable . . . for the maintenance, welfare, comfort or happiness" of beneficiaries, and only if the need justifies the reduction in principal, is subject to ascertainable standard); Hunter v. United States, 597 F. Supp. 1293, 1295 (W.D. Pa. 1984) (power to invade for "comfortable support and maintenance" of beneficiaries is subject to ascertainable standard).

We believe that had decedent, during his life, sought to use the assets of the trust to increase significantly his standard of living beyond that which he had previously enjoyed, his cotrustee would have been obligated to refuse to consent, and the remainder beneficiaries of the trust could have successfully petitioned the court to disallow such expenditures as inconsistent with the intent of the trust instrument. The Tax Court erred in ruling that this power was a general power of appointment includable in decedent's estate.

Reversed and remanded.

NOTE

An Ascertainable Standard Problem.   Norman Vissering consults you regarding his mother's will, which was prepared by his prior lawyer. You spot the drafting error in the use of the word *comfort*. To avoid litigation and the possible inclusion of his mother's trust in Norman's gross estate, would you recommend that he disclaim the power to use principal for "comfort"?

Treasury Regulations take the position that all interests in the corpus of a trust are treated as a single interest. In order to have a qualified disclaimer of an interest in corpus, the disclaimant must disclaim all such interests, either totally or as to an undivided portion. Thus, if a disclaimant has a testamentary power of appointment over the trust corpus coupled with either an inter vivos power to invade corpus or an

interest as discretionary appointee, a disclaimer by that person can constitute a qualified disclaimer only if both interests are disclaimed.[46]

Perhaps Norman should decline to serve as a co-trustee. In that case, he would not
have a general power of appointment. Does Norman have a good claim for malpractice
against his mother's lawyer? *See* Kinney v. Shinholser, 663 So. 2d 643 (Fla. App. 1995).

3. Deductions

From the gross estate certain deductions may be taken, the most important being
(1) the *marital deduction* and (2) the *charitable deduction*. The gross estate minus these
and other permitted deductions equals the taxable estate.

a. The Marital Deduction

(1) Requirements to Qualify

Since 1981, the marital deduction has been based on the theory that donative transfers between spouses should not be subject to wealth transfer taxation because the
spouses are one economic unit. Under I.R.C. § 2056, unlimited amounts of property,
other than certain "terminable interests," can be transferred between spouses without
gift tax or estate tax liability.

For an interest in property to qualify for the estate tax marital deduction, five
requirements must be met:

(a) The decedent must have been survived by his or her spouse.
(b) The surviving spouse must be a citizen of the United States or the property
    must pass to a *qualified domestic trust* (see page 972).
(c) The value of the interest deducted must be includible in the decedent's gross
    estate.
(d) The interest must pass from the decedent to the surviving spouse.
(e) The interest must not be a "nondeductible terminable interest" within the
    meaning of § 2056(b).

The first, second, and third requirements are straightforward. The term "passing"
in the fourth requirement is defined rather broadly in I.R.C. § 2056(c) to include interests passing by will, by inheritance, by trust, by right of survivorship, by dower or
elective share, by the exercise or nonexercise of a power of appointment held by the
decedent, by designation as a life insurance beneficiary, or by other transfer.

The fifth requirement is the most important and the most productive of litigation.
To qualify for the marital deduction, the interest passing to the surviving spouse must
be subject to taxation in the surviving spouse's estate to the extent not consumed or
disposed of during life. The basic idea is that the marital deduction permits the deferral
of estate taxation only until the surviving spouse's death, when the property that has not
been consumed leaves the marital unit. If the surviving spouse's interest in the property
will automatically terminate prior to the spouse's death, then the property is unlikely to

---

46. *See* Treas. Reg. § 25.2518-3(b), (d) (Ex. 9).

be subject to taxation in the surviving spouse's estate, and the transfer to the surviving spouse is not deductible. The clearest example of an interest that qualifies for the deduction is an outright gift of property to the spouse (in fee simple and free of trust).

(2) The Nondeductible Terminable Interest Rule

That an interest will eventually be taxed in the surviving spouse's estate does not ensure qualification for the marital deduction when the first spouse dies. The interest must also not violate the *nondeductible terminable interest rule* of I.R.C. § 2056(b)(1):

> Where, on the lapse of time, on the occurrence of an event or contingency, or on the failure of an event or contingency to occur, an interest passing to the surviving spouse will terminate or fail, no deduction shall be allowed under this section with respect to such interest—
>
> (A) if an interest in such property passes or has passed (for less than an adequate and full consideration in money or money's worth) from the decedent to any person other than such surviving spouse (or the estate of such spouse); and
>
> (B) if by reason of such passing such person (or his heirs or assigns) may possess or enjoy any part of such property after such termination or failure of the interest so passing to the surviving spouse.

The simplest example of a terminable interest is a legal or equitable life estate given to a surviving spouse, with the remainder given to someone else, perhaps a child of the decedent. Because of the nondeductible terminable interest rule, the transfer of the life estate to the surviving spouse will not qualify for the marital deduction, unless an exception applies.

(3) Exceptions to the Nondeductible Terminable Interest Rule

There are five exceptions to the nondeductible terminable interest rule: (a) estate trust; (b) limited survivorship; (c) life estate plus power of appointment; (d) life insurance with power of appointment; and (e) qualified terminable interest property (QTIP).

(a) Estate Trust. An interest is a nondeductible terminable interest only if, on termination of the spouse's interest, the property passes *to someone other than the surviving spouse or the spouse's estate*. Consequently, a disposition of property "to my husband for life, and on his death to his estate," whether in the form of a legal life estate or in trust, qualifies for the marital deduction. The estate trust is seldom used as a means of qualifying for the marital deduction because of its inflexibility. An estate trust also causes the assets to be subject to creditors' claims and administration expenses in the spouse's estate.[47]

---

47. There is, however, one situation in which an estate trust might be desirable. Under a power of appointment trust or a QTIP trust, which are usually preferred to an estate trust, all trust income must be paid to the surviving spouse for life. If the testator's estate includes unproductive property, a marital deduction power of appointment trust or QTIP trust must include a provision authorizing the surviving spouse to compel the trustee to (a) convert the unproductive assets to income-producing property or (b) pay the spouse a reasonable amount out of other trust assets to compensate for lost income. *See* Treas. Reg. § 20.2056(b)-5(f)(5). This could raise a potentially serious problem if, for example, the

(b) Limited Survivorship Exception. In drafting wills and will substitutes, a common practice is to include a provision requiring that a beneficiary survive the decedent by a stated period, such as 30 or 60 days (see page 79). I.R.C. § 2056(b)(3) provides that a transfer subject to a limited survival requirement is deductible if (i) the condition of survival is for a period not exceeding six months, and (ii) the contingency (the spouse's death within the period) does not in fact occur. What this means is that a requirement of survival for up to six months can be attached to an interest passing to the spouse without disqualifying it for the marital deduction. If the spouse does not survive for the stated period, no marital deduction will be available, because no interest will actually pass from the decedent to the surviving spouse.

A devise to a surviving spouse "if she survives the distribution of my estate," would not qualify for a marital deduction, even if the spouse is alive at that time and receives the decedent's entire estate.[48] Do you see why?

(c) Life Estate Plus Power of Appointment Exception. The transfer of a legal or equitable life estate to the decedent's spouse will qualify for the marital deduction if the spouse also receives a power to appoint the trust corpus to herself or her estate. This exception, provided for in I.R.C. § 2056(b)(5), has four technical requirements:

(1) The surviving spouse must be entitled to all income for life, payable annually or at more frequent intervals. The trust property must be income producing, or the spouse must have the power to compel the trustee to make the property income producing.

(2) The power of appointment must be exercisable in favor of the spouse or her estate, which makes it a general power of appointment. A power in the surviving spouse to appoint only to her creditors or the creditors of her estate is also a general power of appointment, but it would not qualify under § 2056(b)(5).

(3) The power must be exercisable by the spouse "alone and in all events." A testamentary power of appointment satisfies the all events requirement even though it cannot be exercised by the spouse during the spouse's lifetime, but a power exercisable only if a named person fails to survive the spouse does not satisfy the all events requirement.

(4) The spouse's interest must not be subject to a power in another person to divert the property to someone other than the spouse. Thus, a trustee other than the spouse cannot be given a discretionary power to distribute trust corpus to the decedent's children. The spouse can be given the power to appoint to the children, or anyone else, as long as she also has the power to appoint to herself.

This exception to the nondeductible terminable interest rule led to widespread use of the life estate plus general power of appointment trust, commonly referred to as the *marital deduction power of appointment trust.*

---

testator owns closely held stock that does not pay dividends or owns unimproved real estate that is being held for future development. An estate trust might therefore be preferable in this situation.

48. *See* Estate of Heim v. Commissioner, 914 F.2d 1322 (9th Cir. 1990).

(d) Life Insurance with Power of Appointment Exception. Under I.R.C. § 2056(b)(6), rules similar to those for a marital deduction power of appointment trust apply to proceeds of life insurance and annuity contracts.

(e) Qualified Terminable Interest Property (QTIP) Exception. Until 1982, every transfer qualifying for the marital deduction had the effect of giving the surviving spouse an unrestricted power of disposition over the property, either during life or at death. In 1981, Congress noted that this requirement created complications in blended families by making it impossible for the decedent spouse to ensure that the property would eventually pass to the decedent's children, rather than the surviving spouse's children.[49] Congress therefore enacted I.R.C. § 2056(b)(7), which allows a marital deduction for a *qualified terminable interest.* Two conditions must be met:

(1) The surviving spouse must be entitled to all income for life, payable annually or at more frequent intervals, and the trust property must be income producing or the spouse must have the power to compel the trustee to make the property income producing.

(2) No person, including the spouse, can have the power to appoint the property during the spouse's lifetime to any person other than the spouse.

Because the marital deduction permits only the deferral of estate taxes until the death of the surviving spouse, the deduction for qualified terminable interest property (QTIP) is conditioned on an election to have the property included in the surviving spouse's gross estate under I.R.C. § 2044. If the transfer is a lifetime gift, the donor makes the QTIP election. If a transfer is at death, the decedent's executor makes the election. The tax is borne by the beneficiaries who receive the qualified terminable interest property on the surviving spouse's death. Thus, if a trust is involved, the tax attributable to the interest is paid out of the principal of the QTIP trust.

NOTES

1. QTIP and Power of Appointment Trust Compared. A QTIP trust and a marital deduction power of appointment trust both require that all income be payable to the surviving spouse at least annually for life. A provision that terminates the spouse's income interest on remarriage disqualifies both. However, there are two important differences. In a power of appointment trust, the spouse must have the power to appoint the property to herself or her estate. In a QTIP trust, the remainder interest on the spouse's death can pass to any beneficiary designated by the settlor or to persons chosen by the surviving spouse exercising a nongeneral power of appointment (provided that the appointees are permissible objects of the power). Further, in a QTIP trust no one, including the spouse, can have the power to appoint the property to anyone other than the spouse during that spouse's lifetime. Invasions of trust principal by the spouse or by a trustee for the spouse are permitted.

---

49. *See* H.R. Rep. No. 97-201, at 160 (1981) (Conf. Rep.).

A QTIP trust is particularly useful if the spouses have different natural objects of their bounty, such as if one of the spouses has children from a prior marriage or if the surviving spouse is likely to remarry and then favor the new spouse.[50]

2. *Four Nondeductible Interest Problems.*   Consider the following problems:

a. H by will creates a trust providing *W* with "so much of the net income as she may require to maintain her usual and customary standard of living." Does this qualify for the QTIP deduction? *See* Estate of Nicholson v. Commissioner, 94 T.C. 666 (1990) (No, because the surviving spouse was not entitled to *all* trust income).

b. Suppose the trust in (a) gave the trustee the power to accumulate income in excess of the amount necessary for *W*'s "needs, best interests, and welfare." QTIP deduction? *See* Estate of Ellingson v. Commissioner, 964 F.2d 959 (9th Cir. 1992) (Yes, because the wife's "best interests" required that she get all trust income regardless of need).

c. Would it matter in (b) if the testator's will had provided that his intention was to qualify the trust for the marital deduction? *See* Wisely v. United States, 893 F.2d 660 (4th Cir. 1990) (stating that such a provision is influential in establishing intent).

d. W creates a revocable trust for herself to avoid probate. The trust contains a provision that in the event of *W*'s incapacity the trustee may make gifts each year up to the amount of the gift tax annual exclusion to members of *W*'s family. *H* dies, devising property to *W*'s revocable trust. Does *H*'s estate qualify for the marital deduction? (No, because the trustee has the power to appoint trust property to persons other than *W*.)

3. *State Court Decisions and Bosch.*   State courts tend to be receptive to petitions to modify or reform a trust to obtain an income or estate tax advantage (see page 742). A common such petition is to repair a trust so that it could qualify for the marital deduction. Under Commissioner v. Estate of Bosch, 387 U.S. 456 (1967), however, a federal court is not bound in a tax dispute by a decision of a lower state court regarding the meaning or effect of a will or trust instrument.[51] "If there [is] no decision by [the state court of last resort]," said the U.S. Supreme Court, "then federal authorities must apply what they find to be the state law after giving 'proper regard' to relevant rulings of other courts of the State." In some states, such as Massachusetts, it is possible to take an expedited appeal to the state court of last resort, thus binding the federal taxing

---

50. On the other hand, nothing in the Code limits the use of a QTIP trust to such circumstances. Professor Mary Moers Wenig put it crisply: "With QTIP, the new federal law of dower was born." Mary Moers Wenig, Taxing Marriage, 6 S. Cal. Rev. L. & Women's Stud. 561, 572 (1997); *see also* Wendy C. Gerzog, The New Super-Charged PAT (Power of Appointment Trust), 48 Hous. L. Rev. 507 (2011); Donna Litman, The Interrelationship Between the Elective Share and the Marital Deduction, 40 Real Prop. Prob. & Tr. J. 539 (2005); Joseph M. Dodge, A Feminist Perspective on the QTIP Trust and the Unlimited Marital Deduction, 76 N.C. L. Rev. 1729 (1998); Wendy C. Gerzog, The Illogical and Sexist QTIP Provisions: I Just Can't Say It Ain't So, 76 N.C. L. Rev. 1597 (1998); Lawrence Zelenak, Taking Critical Tax Theory Seriously, 76 N.C. L. Rev. 1521 (1998).

51. *See* Jonathan G. Blattmachr & Madeline J. Rivlin, Commissioner v. Estate of Bosch: 50 Years of Relevance, 42 ACTEC L.J. 83 (2016).

authorities to a lower state court's ruling on the meaning or effect of a will or trust, including a modification or reformation of the will or trust.[52]

(4) Qualified Domestic Trusts

In providing for a marital deduction that allows a married couple to avoid estate taxation at the death of the first spouse, Congress intended to defer rather than eliminate the taxation of the first spouse's property. The theory was that property qualifying for the marital deduction at the death of the first spouse would eventually be included in the surviving spouse's gross estate, if not consumed or subjected to gift taxation first. If the surviving spouse is not a citizen of the United States, however, there is a very real possibility that the surviving spouse will not be subject to U.S. estate taxation at death. Accordingly, under § 2056(d)(2), property passing to a noncitizen spouse does not qualify for the marital deduction unless the property passes to a qualified domestic trust (QDOT).

The rules for a QDOT are as follows: At least one trustee must be a citizen of the United States or a domestic corporation; the U.S. trustee must have the right to withhold the deferred estate tax on the QDOT assets; and the trust must otherwise qualify for the marital deduction (i.e., it must also be a marital deduction general power of appointment trust or a QTIP trust). If the decedent did not create a QDOT as part of his or her estate plan, the surviving noncitizen spouse or the decedent's personal representative has the option of creating a QDOT after the decedent's death. A court may also reform a trust to comply with the QDOT requirements. To ensure the collection of the deferred estate tax, the Treasury has issued regulations requiring a bond of an individual trustee and requiring securities to be kept in the United States.[53]

(5) Tax Planning for Spouses: The Credit Shelter Trust and Portability

In a brief treatment of estate taxation such as this, we cannot cover the many complicated tax avoidance devices that practitioners sometimes recommend to their clients. There is one basic tax-saving strategy, however, with which all lawyers should be familiar. It involves taking full advantage of any exemption (unified credit) that is available at the death of the first spouse to die ($5.49 million in 2017).

> *Case 17.* W and H each owns property worth $5.49 million. Neither has made any taxable gifts, and both want their combined wealth to benefit the survivor and then, at the survivor's death, to benefit their children in shares to be determined by the surviving spouse. Each makes a will that devises everything to the surviving spouse, or to their descendants per stirpes if there is no surviving spouse. Under these estate plans, when W dies all her property passes to H. Because of the unlimited marital deduction, no taxes are incurred at that time. But at H's death the next year only $5.49 million of H's $10.98 million estate is sheltered from taxation. H's estate will be taxed on the remaining $5.49 million.

---

52. *See, e.g.,* Pond v. Pond, 678 N.E.2d 1321 (Mass. 1997).
53. *See* Treas. Reg. § 20.2056A-2(d)(1)(B).

In Case 17, *W* wasted her $5.49 million exemption by leaving her entire estate outright to *H*. At a 40 percent rate (as under current law), this could be a $2.196 million mistake.

Avoiding those taxes would have been easy. *H* and *W* could have arranged for their entire $10.98 million in wealth to be available to support the survivor and then have all of it pass to their children without any transfer taxation. All they needed was for the first to die to leave his or her $5.49 million estate in trust for the benefit of the surviving spouse for life, with a nongeneral power of appointment in the surviving spouse to appoint the remainder to such of their descendants as the spouse names by will. In this way, when each spouse dies, his or her $5.49 million in wealth would not be taxed, and the remainder at the death of the survivor could pass tax free to their descendants as directed by the survivor.

Because this trust for the survivor bypasses the survivor's estate for tax purposes, it is sometimes called a *bypass* trust. And because this trust makes full use of the first spouse's unified credit to shelter that spouse's property from estate taxation at the second spouse's death, it is also sometimes called a *credit shelter* trust. Note that at the second spouse's death the *entire* credit shelter trust, including any appreciation in trust property that occurred after the first spouse died, passes to the remainder beneficiaries completely free of estate taxation.

In 2011, Congress enacted a *portability* provision in I.R.C. § 2010(c)(4), which obviates the need for a credit shelter trust for many spouses.[54] Portability means that a surviving spouse's exemption amount is increased by his or her deceased spouse's unused exemption amount (DSUEA). In other words, any exemption amount not used by the first spouse to die is transferred (or "ported," as estate planners are now fond of saying) to the surviving spouse. In the circumstances of Case 17, *H*'s estate will pay no estate tax, as his own applicable exemption amount is increased by *W*'s $5.49 million DSUEA.

There are some important qualifications. First, *W*'s estate in Case 17 must file an estate tax return and elect portability. This requirement means that many more estates, even relatively small estates, will need to file an estate tax return to ensure that the surviving spouse receives the DSUEA. Second, a decedent is only entitled to the unused exemption amount of his "last such deceased spouse." A person cannot amass a huge exemption by way of serial marriages. However, after the death of a prior spouse but before the death of a new spouse, wiping out the prior spouse's unused exemption, the surviving spouse could use the prior spouse's unused exemption to shelter an otherwise taxable lifetime gift.[55] Third, a person is limited to a total of one unused exemption amount, although this can be acquired from more than one prior deceased spouse. What this means is that in 2017 a person can amass a total exemption of $10.98 million, with half of that exemption coming from multiple deceased spouses.[56]

---

54. *See* Austin W. Bramwell & Leah Socash, Preserving Inherited Exclusion Amounts: The New Planning Frontier, 50 Real Prop. Tr. & Est. L.J. 1 (2015).

55. *See* Treas. Reg. § 25.2505-2(a)(3), (b). Here is an example: *A* and *B* are married. *A* dies leaving all his property to *B. B* marries *C. B* can make taxable gifts using *A*'s DSUEA. *C* is not yet dead, so *A* is still *B*'s "last such deceased spouse."

56. *See* id. § 20.2010-3(a)(3), (b).

Although a person cannot accumulate multiple DSUEAs by way of serial marriages, there are other planning opportunities. A DSUEA should be considered in drafting premarital agreements (see page 544). A wealthy person might consider marrying a poorer person who is terminally ill, in order to acquire that person's DSUEA, in return offering to pay the costs of the poorer person's care. Arranging marriage for financial reasons is an ancient custom. The portability provision of I.R.C. § 2010(c)(4) has added another financial consideration to that mix.

b. The Charitable Deduction

Decedents sometimes want to leave property to charity. I.R.C. § 2055 allows an unlimited deduction if the gift is properly structured and the organization that received the property qualifies under the Code.[57] Under § 2055(b), the organization must be

> organized and operated exclusively for religious, charitable, scientific, literary, or educational purposes, including the encouragement of art, or to foster national or international amateur sports competition (but only if no part of its activities involve the provision of athletic facilities or equipment), and the prevention of cruelty to children or animals, no part of the net earnings of which inures to the benefit of any private stockholder or individual, which is not disqualified for tax exemption under § 501(c)(3) by reason of attempting to influence legislation, and which does not participate in, or intervene in (including the publishing or distributing of statements), any political campaign on behalf of . . . any candidate for public office.

If a client wants to make a gift of a remainder interest to charity, special arrangements are required. Except for a remainder interest in a personal residence or in a farm, a charitable deduction is allowed in calculating federal income, gift, and estate taxes only if the remainder is in an *annuity trust* or a *unitrust,* or part of a *pooled income fund.*[58] A bequest in trust "to pay all the income to A for life, remainder to the Y charity" would not generally qualify for the charitable deduction, because such a trust is neither an annuity trust nor a unitrust.

A charitable remainder *annuity trust* provides that a *fixed sum*, which can be no less than 5 percent of the original value of the trust property, must be paid at least annually to the noncharitable beneficiary. The income beneficiary of an annuity trust thus receives the same amount each year. A *unitrust* provides that a *fixed percentage*, which cannot be less than 5 percent of the trust property, valued annually, must be paid to the noncharitable beneficiary. The income beneficiary of a unitrust will thus receive an annual amount that fluctuates as the value of the trust property changes.

---

57. *See, e.g.*, Edward A. Zelinsky, Why the Buffett-Gates Giving Pledge Requires Limitation of the Estate Tax Charitable Deduction, 16 Fla. Tax Rev. 393 (2014); Miranda Perry Fleischer, Equality of Opportunity and the Charitable Tax Subsidies, 91 B.U. L. Rev. 601 (2011); Ray D. Madoff, What Leona Helmsley Can Teach Us About the Charitable Deduction, 85 Chi.-Kent L. Rev. 957 (2010); *see also* Kristine S. Knaplund, Becoming Charitable: Predicting and Encouraging Charitable Bequests in Wills, 77 U. Pitt. L. Rev. 77 (2015).

58. I.R.C. §§ 664(d), 2055(e)(2), and 2522(c)(2); *see also* Wendy C. Gerzog, The Times They Are Not A-Changin': Reforming the Charitable Split-Interest Rules (Again), 85 Chi.-Kent L. Rev. 849 (2010).

A *pooled income fund* is set up by a charitable organization and must meet certain specific requirements of the Code. If the trustee or private beneficiary of an annuity trust, unitrust, or pooled income fund has a discretionary power to invade principal, the trust does not qualify for a charitable deduction.

The objectives of these rules are to reduce the uncertainty involved in valuing the future interest given to charity and to increase the likelihood that an interest will in fact pass to charity on the noncharitable beneficiary's death. But the rules governing the drafting of these trusts are technical and not intuitive. For example, if estate taxes may be paid from a charitable remainder trust, no charitable deduction is allowable; and if taxes are apportioned by state law or by a clause in the decedent's will, a deduction may be denied.

NOTE

A Charitable Deduction Problem. *T*'s will devises his property to Princeton University and Johns Hopkins University. A codicil grants *T*'s executor the discretion "to compensate persons who have contributed to my well-being or who have otherwise been helpful to me during my lifetime," providing that no single bequest should exceed 1 percent of the estate. The executors determined that only two individuals met the definition of eligible persons so that 98 percent of the estate passed to the named universities. Is the estate entitled to a charitable deduction? *See* Estate of Marine v. Commissioner, 990 F.2d 136 (4th Cir. 1993) (No, because the charities did not have an indefeasible right at *T*'s death).

C. THE GENERATION-SKIPPING TRANSFER TAX

1. The Nature of the Tax

Until 1986, it was possible for a wealthy person to put property into a *dynasty trust*, either during life or by will, that would insulate the transferred property from future estate or gift taxation. *O* might transfer property worth $10 million, in trust, income payable to *O*'s children for their lives, then income payable to the children's children for their lives, then income payable to the grandchildren's children for their lives, and so on down the generations until the applicable Rule Against Perpetuities called a halt (see Chapter 14).

Each beneficiary could be given, in addition to a share of the income, a power to consume principal limited by an ascertainable standard, and a nongeneral power of appointment over his or her share of the trust property, all without estate or gift tax cost after the initial creation of the trust. As each beneficiary died, nothing would be taxed in the beneficiary's estate because the beneficiary held only a life estate and nongeneral power of appointment. To achieve even greater flexibility the governing instrument could give an independent trustee a discretionary power to distribute trust principal to the beneficiaries, again incurring no additional gift or estate taxes after the trust's initial creation.

In the Tax Reform Act of 1986, Congress severely limited this tax-avoidance technique by subjecting such arrangements to a *generation-skipping transfer* (GST) tax. The rationale for the GST tax is that wealth should be subject to some kind of transfer tax at least once each generation, though trusts that were irrevocable before 1986 are excluded by a grandfathering provision.

a. A Taxable Generation-Skipping Transfer

A *generation-skipping transfer* is a transfer — whether lifetime or deathtime — to a skip person, a new term invented by Congress in imposing this tax. A *skip person* is a grandchild or any other person assigned to a generation that is two or more generations below the transferor's generation.[59] The transferor's spouse and children (or other persons in the transferor's generation or the generation just below the transferor's) are *non-skip persons*. Hence, a transfer directly from a grandparent to a grandchild, either outright or in trust, is in general subject to the GST tax.

The GST tax is levied on generation-skipping transfers in the form of (1) a *taxable termination*, (2) a *taxable distribution*, or (3) a *direct skip*.

(1) Taxable Termination.   A taxable termination is the

termination (by death, lapse of time, release of power, or otherwise) of an interest in property held in a trust unless —

(A) immediately after such termination, a non-skip person has an interest in such property, or

(B) at no time after such termination may a distribution (including distributions on termination) be made from such trust to a skip person.[60]

Here is an example:

Case 18. *T* bequeaths $5 million in trust to benefit her son *A* for life, remainder to *A*'s children. At *A*'s death, a "taxable termination" takes place. *A*'s life interest terminates and only skip persons (*T*'s grandchildren) have an interest in the property. If the income were payable to *T*'s daughter *B* after *A*'s death, there would be no taxable termination upon *A*'s death. However, there would be a taxable termination upon *B*'s subsequent death, when only skip persons would have an interest in the trust.

The purpose of the exceptions in the definition of a taxable termination ((A) and (B) above) is to limit to one the number of taxable terminations, per dollar of property, that can occur in each generation below the transferor's. If, for example, *T* bequeaths the income from a trust to her children, with principal to be distributed to her grandchildren upon the death of her last surviving child, a taxable termination occurs only at the death of the last surviving child. On the other hand, if at the death of one child that child's share is distributed to that child's children, then a taxable termination of a fractional share of the trust principal has occurred.[61]

---

59. I.R.C. § 2613(a); *see also* Alyssa A. DiRusso, The Generation-Skipping Transfer Tax and Sociological Shifts in Generational Length: Proposing a Generation-Inflation Index for Taxation, 41 ACTEC L.J. 307 (2015-2016).

60. I.R.C. § 2612(a)(1).

61. Id. § 2612(a)(2).

(2) Taxable Distribution.   A taxable distribution occurs whenever a distribution is made from a trust to a skip person (other than a taxable termination or a direct skip). If, in Case 18, *A* had a nongeneral power to distribute income or corpus to *A*'s children, a taxable distribution would take place when such a distribution was actually made.

(3) Direct Skip.   A direct skip is a transfer of property directly to a skip person. Thus:

> *Case 19.* *T* is survived by her son *A* and *A*'s daughter *B*. *T* devises $7.5 million to her granddaughter *B*. This is a direct skip, because it skips the generation of the son. A GST tax (in addition to any estate tax payable on *T*'s death) is due on *T*'s death. This double taxation follows from the principle that a transfer tax must be paid once per generation. Similarly, if *T* had given *B* $7.5 million during life, *T* would have incurred both a gift tax and a GST tax at that time.

There are two important exceptions to the principle that a transfer tax (be it an estate tax, gift tax, or GST tax) must be paid once per generation. First, the GST applies only once in the case of *double* (or even *triple*) *skips*. Thus, a transfer of property directly to a great-grandchild incurs only one GST tax despite skipping two generations.

Second, a *deceased parent exception* applies to transfers to descendants of the predeceased children of the transferor. If a child of the transferor is dead at the time of the initial transfer, the children of that child (the transferor's grandchildren) are treated as the children of the transferor for GST tax purposes.[62] If the transferor has no lineal descendants, this exception applies to transfers to lineal descendants of the parent of the transferor (first line collaterals).

b. When GST Tax Must Be Paid

A direct skip occurs (and is taxable) on the day the transfer is effective. A taxable termination or taxable distribution, by contrast, occurs in the future, sometime after the original transfer in trust. In some cases it will be certain when the trust is established that the trust will produce a GST tax in the future, but in other cases it will not be certain. Thus:

> *Case 20.* *T* devises property in trust to pay the income to *T*'s child *A* until *A* attains the age of 30, at which time the trustee is to distribute the trust principal to *A*. If *A* dies before reaching age 30, the trustee is to distribute the principal to *A*'s children in equal shares. Whether there will be a generation-skipping transfer depends on future events. If *A* lives to age 30 and receives the trust principal, there is no generation-skipping transfer. If *A* dies before age 30, and the trust principal is distributed to *A*'s children, a taxable termination will occur and the tax will be due at that time. The deceased parent exception does not apply.

If a trust turns out to produce a generation-skipping transfer, the tax is payable when that transfer occurs.

---

62. Id. § 2651(a)(2).

All generation-skipping transfers are taxed at a flat rate equal to the highest rate then applicable under the federal estate tax (40 percent in 2017). The amount taxed and the person liable for the tax depend on the type of transfer. If there is a *direct skip*, the transferor must pay the tax on the amount received by the transferee. The taxation of a direct skip therefore resembles the gift tax in that the base excludes the amount of tax levied (that is, it is *tax exclusive*, see page 944).

In the case of a *taxable termination* or *taxable distribution*, the tax is imposed on a *tax-inclusive* basis (that is, the taxable amount includes the tax, see page 944). Upon a taxable termination, the tax base is the entire property with respect to which the termination occurred. The tax is to be paid out of the trust. Upon a taxable distribution, the tax base is the amount received by the beneficiary, who is liable for the tax.

2. Exemption and Exclusions

I.R.C. § 2631 provides a lifetime *exemption* ($5.49 million in 2017) for each transferor, separate from the exemption from the gift and estate tax.[63] For inter vivos transfers by a married person, the transferor and her spouse may elect to treat the transfer as made one-half by each spouse (as under § 2513 for the gift tax, see page 942). So a husband and wife who have not previously used any of their respective GST exemptions can give away $10.98 million in generation-skipping transfers in 2017 without that transfer ever resulting in a GST tax:

> *Case 21.* During life, W transfers $10.98 million to a trustee to pay the income to W's children for their lives, then to distribute the principal to W's grandchildren. H consents to treating this transfer as having been made half by him, thus using his $5.49 million GST exemption. By applying the spouses' total GST tax exemption of $10.98 million to this transfer, the trust property, including subsequent appreciation, will not be subject to GST taxation now or in the future. At the death of W's children, no GST tax is due.

If, in Case 21, W had not made an inter vivos transfer but had devised $10.98 million in a testamentary trust, only $5.49 million would be exempt from GST tax, because the split-gift provision applies only to inter vivos gifts. In case of a testamentary transfer, to take advantage of the spouse's GST tax exemption, it is necessary to make the spouse a "transferor" for estate tax purposes. In Case 21, if the trust had been a testamentary trust and H had been devised a life estate in half of the $10.49 million transferred by W into trust, H's GST tax exemption of $5.49 million could be used.

If the transferor creates more than one generation-skipping trust, or makes generation-skipping transfers in excess of $5.49 million, the transferor or his personal representative can allocate the exemption. If not so allocated, I.R.C. § 2632 provides default rules. Generally, the exemption is first allocated to direct skips and then to taxable terminations and taxable distributions. The exemption is allocated to the "property

---

63. Originally, the exemption amount was $1 million, to be increased by annual cost-of-living adjustments. In 2001, however, Congress amended I.R.C. § 2631 to provide that the GST tax exemption amount would be equal to the estate tax exemption amount.

transferred" and not, in the case of taxable terminations and taxable distributions, to specific generation-skipping transfers that occur in the future. This means that with respect to trusts that might produce taxable terminations or taxable distributions, the entire exemption or a fraction thereof must be allocated to the trust at the time of the transfer into trust. It is important to allocate the exemption so as not to waste it on a trust with property that may decline or fail to appreciate in value, or that is uncertain to produce a generation-skipping transfer, if it could be allocated more effectively elsewhere.

Under I.R.C. § 2653(b)(1), the exempt fraction of the trust property—determined when the trust is created—remains the same for the duration of the trust. If the trust produces successive skips, the transferor's exemption can eliminate or reduce the GST tax generation after generation. If, for example, a GST tax-exempt trust provides for payment of income to T's children for their lives, then to T's grandchildren for their lives, and so on in perpetuity (see page 907), the transferor's exemption will shelter the trust from any GST tax for its entire duration, even if the principal of the trust increases in value far beyond the initial $5.49 million.

I.R.C. § 2642(c) generally *excludes* from GST taxation any transfer not subject to the gift tax because of the annual exclusion (see page 934). So transfers of $14,000 or less annually to grandchildren usually will not produce a GST tax.[64] I.R.C. § 2611(b)(1) excludes any transfers excluded under § 2503(e) of the gift tax for the direct payment of tuition and medical expenses (see page 934). Hence, a grandparent can pay tuition for a grandchild without making a generation-skipping transfer, and a trust can make tuition or medical payments for a skip person without subjecting such distributions to the GST tax.

NOTE

Choosing an Estate or GST Tax. It may be desirable for a non-skip person to be able to decide whether to pay an estate tax or a GST tax on the non-skip person's death. This flexibility may allow the non-skip person to optimize his and his spouse's exemptions. For example, if O transfers property in trust for her son A for life, then to A's children, and O gives A a nongeneral power to appoint the property to A's spouse or to one or more of A's descendants, A can control which type of tax will be applicable at A's death. If A wants the property in his gross estate, thereby avoiding a GST tax, A can by will exercise the power by creating a trust and giving his wife a power of appointment over the trust property. If this power is drafted so that under applicable state law it postpones the vesting of an interest in the trust property without regard to the date that O created the power in A, then the trust property is includible in A's gross estate under I.R.C. § 2041(a)(3) (see the discussion of the Delaware Tax Trap at page 921).

---

64. Gifts in trust that qualify for the gift tax annual exclusion do not automatically avoid the GST tax. To avoid this tax, the trust must be for the benefit of only one individual and must be in that individual's gross estate if that individual dies before the trust terminates. I.R.C. § 2642(c)(2).

D. STATE ESTATE AND INHERITANCE TAXES

Prior to 2001, the federal estate tax included a credit for state death taxes. Congress enacted this credit in the 1920s in response to efforts to repeal the federal estate tax on the grounds that this source of revenue should be reserved to the states. Under former I.R.C. § 2011, every dollar paid in state death taxes reduced the federal estate tax bill by a dollar, up to a specified limit. The states responded by enacting death taxes to take full advantage of the credit, as it permitted diversion of federal revenues to the state without increasing the overall tax burden of that state's residents at death. Most states had only a *pick-up* (or *sponge*) tax that equaled, to the penny, the maximum amount of the § 2011 credit.

In 2001, Congress threw the state death tax systems into turmoil by replacing the I.R.C. § 2011 *credit* (the dollar-for-dollar offset) with a *deduction* against the gross estate, reducing the taxable estate, under § 2058.[65] In the wake of this change, many states repealed their death taxes. Today, as depicted in Figure 15.2, only a handful of states, mostly concentrated in the Northeast and upper Midwest, still impose an estate or inheritance tax.

Figure 15.2

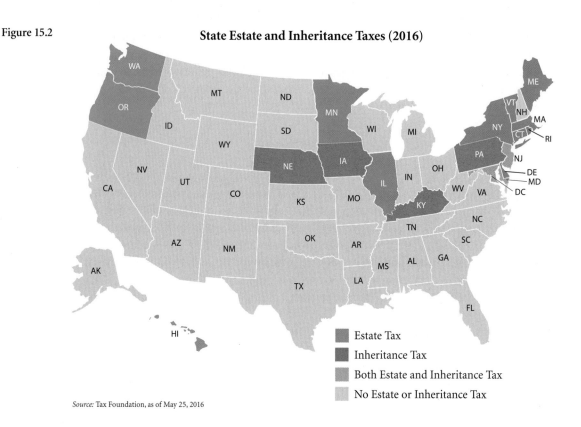

State Estate and Inheritance Taxes (2016)

Estate Tax
Inheritance Tax
Both Estate and Inheritance Tax
No Estate or Inheritance Tax

Source: Tax Foundation, as of May 25, 2016

---

65. *See* Jeffrey A. Cooper, Interstate Competition and State Death Taxes: A Modern Crisis in Historical Perspective, 33 Pepp. L. Rev. 835 (2006).

E. INCOME TAXATION OF GRANTOR TRUSTS

Income taxes on trust income are usually paid by the trustee out of that income or, if the income is distributed, by the beneficiaries, rather than the settlor. An exception is made, however, for certain trusts over which the settlor retains control. In Helvering v. Clifford, 309 U.S. 331 (1940), a taxpayer established a trust of securities with income payable to someone else. The settlor retained complete control over the trust and was entitled to take back the corpus at the end of five years. The Court held that the settlor would be taxable on the trust income on the grounds of retained dominion and control. Subsequently the Treasury issued regulations—the *Clifford* regulations—spelling out the specifics of this rule.

The *Clifford* regulations have since been supplanted by I.R.C. §§ 671-677, applicable to what are now called *grantor trusts*.[66] The income in a grantor trust is taxable to the settlor (grantor), who is deemed still to be the owner of the trust assets for income tax purposes, owing to retained dominion and control. A revocable trust is an obvious example of a grantor trust.[67] If the grantor has a *reversionary interest*, either in the corpus or in the income, and the reversionary interest at the inception of the trust exceeds 5 percent of the value of the corpus or the income, the trust is a grantor trust.[68] There is an exception, however, if the trust is for a minor lineal descendant who has the entire present interest, and the settlor retains a reversionary interest that will take effect only upon the death of the lineal descendant under the age of 21.[69]

A trust is also a grantor trust if the *settlor* or a *nonadverse party* has discretionary power over income or principal exercisable without the consent of an adverse party.[70] There are, however, two major exceptions. The first is that a discretionary power to distribute, apportion, or accumulate income or to pay out principal can be given to an *independent* trustee without adverse tax consequences to the settlor.[71] An independent trustee is one who is not related or subordinate to the settlor nor subservient to her wishes. A nonadverse party is a person who lacks a substantial beneficial interest that would be adversely affected by the exercise or nonexercise of the power.

The other exception permits (a) a power held by the settlor or any trustee to distribute *principal* pursuant to a "reasonably definite standard which is set forth in the trust instrument," or (b) a power held by any trustee other than the settlor or the settlor's spouse to distribute *income* pursuant to a "reasonably definite external standard which is set forth in the trust instrument."[72]

---

66. Although originally intended to prevent abusive tax avoidance, the grantor trust rules have themselves come to be used for tax avoidance. *See* Mark L. Ascher, The Grantor Trust Rules Should Be Repealed, 96 Iowa L. Rev. 885 (2011); *see also* Mark L. Ascher, Helvering v. Clifford: The Supreme Court Spoils the Broth, 42 ACTEC L.J. 29 (2016).
67. I.R.C. § 676.
68. Id. § 673.
69. Id. § 673(b).
70. Id. § 674.
71. Id. § 674(c).
72. Id. § 674(b)(5)(A), (d).

Another type of grantor trust is one in which certain administrative powers can be exercised for the benefit of the settlor. Generally, the settlor will be subject to tax on the income if there is a power exercisable by the settlor or a nonadverse party: (1) to purchase trust property for less than an adequate consideration, (2) to borrow trust property without adequate security, (3) to vote or acquire stock in a corporation in which the settlor has a significant voting interest, or (4) to reacquire the trust principal. Any of these indicia of dominion and control may be sufficient to tax the settlor on the trust income.[73]

The category of grantor trusts also includes a trust in which the settlor, a nonadverse party, or an independent trustee has the power to distribute trust income to the settlor or to the settlor's spouse.[74] Income is not taxable to the settlor merely because the trustee *may* distribute it for the support of a beneficiary (other than the settlor's spouse) whom the settlor is legally obligated to support. If the trust property is in fact used to discharge the settlor's legal obligation, however, the settlor is taxable on the income to the extent income is so used.[75]

A lawyer creating an inter vivos trust should pay close attention to I.R.C. §§ 671-677 and the relevant regulations if the settlor desires to shift taxation on the income to the trust or its beneficiaries. The lawyer should also keep in mind that although the income tax and the estate and gift taxes are not exactly parallel, if the settlor is treated as owner and taxable on trust income, there is a good chance that the trust assets will be subject to estate taxation at the settlor's death under I.R.C. §§ 2036 and 2038. It is possible, however, to create a trust that will be a grantor trust for income tax purposes but not included in the settlor's gross estate. If such a trust includes *Crummey* powers, it may be used to leverage the annual exclusion by removing property from the settlor's estate both through annual gifts and by paying any taxes on the trust's income. Thus:

> *Case 22.* H transfers $42,000 to W in an irrevocable trust to pay so much of the income and principal to their children A, B, or C as W determines in W's sole and uncontrolled discretion. The trust instrument provides that each beneficiary has a power to withdraw up to $14,000 each for 30 days after notice of a contribution, hence the transfer qualifies for the annual exclusion. Any tax on income retained in the trust is a legal obligation of H, hence payment of those taxes is not a further gift. The same process is repeated each year until H dies, whereupon the entire trust corpus, including retained income, is not included in H's gross estate.

---

73. Id. § 675.
74. Id. § 677(a).
75. Id. § 677(b).

TABLE OF CASES

Principal cases are indicated by *italics*.

Author Index

INDEX